Aerial view of open pit boron mine at Boron, CA (courtesy of US Borax and Chemical Corp.).

Industrial Minerals and Rocks

(Nonmetallics other than Fuels)

Fifth Edition
Volume 2

Published by the
Society of Mining Engineers
of the
American Institute of Mining, Metallurgical, and Petroleum Engineers, Inc.
New York, New York ● 1983

THE INSTITUTION OF
MINING
AND METALLURGY

Preface

In 1980, after two printings of the fourth edition of *Industrial Minerals and Rocks,* the members attending a business meeting of the Industrial Minerals Division of the Society of Mining Engineers voted to publish a fifth edition. The original authors of the fourth edition were invited to update or revise their chapters. If the original author was unable to revise his chapter, another author did so. Some chapters were completely rewritten. We added a chapter on Alunite and divided Talc and Pyrophyllite into two chapters. *Industrial Minerals and Rocks* has also become international, with two chapters being written by authors in England and Australia. We hope future editions of *Industrial Minerals and Rocks* will include more chapters by authors from foreign countries.

As in the fourth edition of *Industrial Minerals and Rocks,* this edition is divided into four sections. However, the fifth edition breaks slightly with tradition in that it is printed in two volumes. As with the fourth edition, we made an attempt to be consistent in chapter content. However, we did not edit the papers to the point that they became stylized. Each author was permitted to write what he thought was important and to use his own words. We felt this made for more readable and interesting material. We attempted to incorporate the most recent prices and production data. Due to circumstances beyond our control, this was not possible in some instances.

Sadly, during the preparation of the fifth edition of *Industrial Minerals and Rocks,* we lost two editors of the fourth edition, Robert Grogan and Tom Murphy, and one editor of the fifth edition, Gerry V. Henderson. The fifth edition of *Industrial Minerals and Rocks* is dedicated to them.

The Industrial Minerals Division of SME is grateful to each of the authors and editors who gave so generously of their time and experience. We also appreciate the efforts of the many unknown secretaries who typed and retyped the various manuscripts.

Above all, however, we give our sincerest appreciation to Carmel A. Huestis for her diligence in preparing the various manuscripts for publication and to Marianne Snedeker for her patience in bringing the fifth edition through to publication.

Stanley J. Lefond
Editor-in-Chief

Contents

Volume 1

Fluorspar and Cryolite*

ROBERT B. FULTON †

GILL MONTGOMERY ‡

Fluorspar is the commercial name for fluorite, a mineral that is calcium fluoride, CaF_2. The name, derived from the Latin word *fluere* (to flow), refers to its low melting point and its early use in metallurgy as a flux. It is the principal industrial source of the element fluorine.

Cryolite, sodium aluminum fluoride, Na_3AlF_6, is a rare mineral which has been found in commercial quantities only in Greenland. The natural material has been supplanted by synthetic cryolite for its principal industrial use in the manufacture of aluminum.

History

Fluorspar was used by the early Greeks and Romans for ornamental purposes as vases, drinking cups, and table tops. Various peoples, including the Chinese and the American Indians, carved ornaments and figurines from large crystals. Its usefulness as a flux was known to Agricola in sixteenth century Europe.

Fluorspar mining began in England about 1775 and at various places in the United States between 1820 and 1840. Production grew substantially following the development of basic open-hearth steelmaking, wherein it is used as a flux. Use was stimulated by growth of the steel, aluminum, chemical, and ceramic industries, particularly during World Wars I and II. Fluorocarbons entered the picture in 1931. The use of anhydrous hydrogen fluoride (HF) as a catalyst in the manufacture of alkylate for high octane fuel began in 1942.

Differential flotation for separating fluorspar from galena, sphalerite, and common gangue minerals in the 1930s, and the application of

* Revised from Robert M. Grogan and Gill Montgomery, "Fluorspar and Cryolite," *Industrial Minerals and Rocks*, 4th ed., 1975.

† Basic Materials Planning, Materials and Logistics Dept., E. I. du Pont de Nemours and Co., Inc., Wilmington, DE.

‡ Minerals Consultant, Box 410, Eldorado, IL.

heavy-media concentrating methods to the treatment of low-grade ores in the 1940s were outstanding technological advances that facilitated increased production.

Recently, pelletizing and briquetting of flotation concentrates for use in steel furnaces and the development of flotation schemes for beneficiating ores containing abundant dolomite and barite have been major improvements in the industry.

Uses of Fluorspar

Fluorspar is used to make hydrogen fluoride, also called hydrofluoric acid, an intermediate for fluorocarbons, aluminum fluoride, and synthetic cryolite. It is used as a flux in the steel and ceramic industries, in iron foundry and ferroalloy practice, and has many minor specialized uses.

Hydrogen fluoride (HF) is produced by reacting acid grade (97% CaF_2) fluorspar with sulfuric acid in a heated kiln or retort to produce HF gas and calcium sulfate. After purification by scrubbing, condensing, and distillation, the HF is marketed as anhydrous HF, a colorless fuming liquid, or it may be absorbed in water to form the aqueous acid, usually 70% HF.

Synthetic cryolite, organic and inorganic fluoride chemicals, and elemental fluorine are made from hydrofluoric acid. The acid itself is important in catalysis in the manufacture of alkylate, which is an ingredient in high-octane fuel for aircraft and automobiles, in steel pickling, enamel stripping, glass etching and polishing, and in various electroplating operations. The manufacture of one ton of virgin aluminum requires about 50 to 60 lb of fluorine content in synthetic cryolite and alumnium fluoride. This quantity, through improved technology and recovery practices, is being lowered significantly.

Elemental fluorine is prepared from anhydrous hydrofluoric acid by electrolysis. Gaseous at room temperature and pressure, fluorine is compressed to a liquid for shipment in cylinders or in tank trucks. Elemental fluorine is used to make uranium hexafluoride, sulfur hexafluoride, and halogen fluorides. Gaseous uranium hexafluoride is used in separating U^{235} from U^{238} by the diffusion process. Sulfur hexafluoride is a stable high dielectric gas used in coaxial cables, transformers, and radar wave guides. Halogen fluorides have important applications, mostly as substitutes for elemental fluorine which is more difficult to handle.

Emulsified perfluorochemicals, organic compounds in which all hydrogen atoms have been replaced by fluorine, are undergoing investigation as promising blood substitutes. They transport oxygen and, in conjunction with a simulated blood serum, perform many functions of whole blood. With further development, ultimately they may be useful in saving lives of animals and humans in emergencies during periods of acute shortages of natural blood.

Inorganic fluorides are used as insecticides, preservatives, antiseptics, ceramic additives, in electroplating solutions, as fluxes, antioxidants, and many other ways. Boron trifluoride is an important catalyst.

Organic fluorides are volume leaders in the fluorine chemical industry. Fluorinated chlorocarbons and fluorocarbons are prepared by the interaction of anhydrous HF with chloroform, perchlorethylene and carbon tetrachloride, and are characterized by low toxicity and notable chemical stability. They perform outstandingly as refrigerants, aerosol propellants, solvents, and cleaning agents and as intermediates for polymers such as fluorocarbon resins and elastomers.

Fluorocarbon resins are inert compounds with an unusually low coefficient of friction which have found a number of applications for parts that cannot be oiled, such as the bearings inside of automobile doors, for window raising equipment, in small electronic equipment, and for the manufacture of chemical resistant gaskets and valve parts, pipe and tank linings, flexible tubing and containers, and cookware.

In the steel industry, fluorspar is used as a flux in basic open-hearth, basic oxygen, and electric furnaces where it is added to the heats in amounts ranging from 2 to 20 lb per ton of steel produced. The average in the US is currently about 6 lb per ton. It promotes fluidity of the slag and thus facilitates removal of sulfur and phosphorus from the steel into the slag. It serves the same purpose in iron foundries, where it is added to the cupola charge in the proportion of around 15 to 20 lb per ton of metal melted.

In the ceramic industries, fluorspar is used to make flint glass, white or colored opal glasses, and enamels. Flint glass mixtures commonly contain 3% fluorspar. Opal glasses, containing 10 to 20% fluorspar, are used in containers for foods, drugs and toiletries, and in ornamental glassware and lavatory and restaurant fixtures. Opaque enamels are used to cover steel stoves, refrigerators, cabinets, bathtubs, and cooking ware and for facings on brick and tile, and other structural materials. Fluorspar makes up to 3 to 10% of the weight of the enamel. Many types of welding rod coatings incorporate fluorspar or fluorspar mixtures. Ceramic grade fluorspar is used in the manufacture of magnesium and calcium metals, and in the preparation of some manganese chemicals.

Lower grades of ceramic spar are used in making fiberglass insulation, in zinc smelting, as a clinkering aid in the manufacture of portland cement, as an inhibitor of vanadium green scumming in the manufacture of buff-faced brick, and as an abrasive on certain types of sandpapers. Various grades of fluorspar are used in electric furnace manufacture of calcium carbide, in making electrodes for arc lamps, and as a bonding material for abrasive wheels, among numerous minor uses.

Product Specifications

The three principal market grades of fluorspar are acid, ceramic, and metallurgical. Specifications for these are fairly well defined, although the requirements set by individual consumers may vary in detail.

Acid grade fluorspar is defined as not less than 97% CaF_2 but some manufacturers of hydrofluoric acid both in the US and in Europe can use 96%, or slightly lower if the remaining impurities are acceptable. Since the US tariff structure favors fluorspar of 97% or over, imports of acid grade or imports of material used for ceramic fluorspar purposes must be over 97% CaF_2. Users specify limits for silica, calcium carbonate, arsenic, lead, sulphide sulfur, phosphorous and other deleterious constituents. Moisture content of dried concentrates for acid and ceramic grades is usually specified to be not more than 0.10% H_2O, but in some ceramic uses up to 1 or 2% may be required to relieve dust problems in handling bulk materials.

There are two standard ceramic grades: No. 1 ceramic containing 95 to 96% CaF_2, and No. 2 ceramic which customarily contains 85 to over 90% CaF_2. A medium grade of about 93 to 94% CaF_2 is specified by some users. In some instances buyers of ceramic grades may specify not over 2.5 or 3.0% silica, limited amounts of calcite and ferric oxide, and only traces of lead and zinc sulfides. Practically every ceramic grade user has his own specifications, and producers tailor their products accordingly.

In the United States, metallurgical grade, called "metspar," contains a minimum of 60 "effective" percent of fluorspar and generally not over 0.30% sulfide sulfur and 0.25 to 0.50% lead. The "effective" percentage is calculated by multiplying the silica percentage in the analysis by 2.5 and subtracting this number from the calcium fluoride percentage in the analysis; the result is termed "effective units." Thus, a concentrate with 85% calcium fluoride and 6% silica would be 70% effective grade. To qualify as "lump" or "gravel" spar, it must pass a 1 to 1½ in. screen and contain less than 15% of material passing a ¼₆ in. screen.

In markets outside the United States, metspar may contain a minimum of 80% CaF_2 and a maximum of 15% silica.

In fluorspar's use as a flux in the steel industry, the trend is toward briquets and away from metspar due to growing scarcity of satisfactory gravel fluorspar. Briquets are made from the fines accumulated during metspar preparation and from flotation concentrates. Most of the imported fluorspar concentrates used to make briquettes are acid grade, for tariff reasons. Domestically produced ceramic grade concentrates are also used. Most briquets are made on roll presses, from "peach seed" sizes up to two-inch square briquets. The most popular binders used are molasses and lime, the use of which does not require baking ovens. Pellets have been made on balling machines using sodium silicate binder, and extruded shapes have been made. There is a strong trend toward making diluted briquets containing steel mill wastes, such as mill scale, flue dust, shredded scrap, iron ore fines, and manganese ore fines. Some diluents have fluxing values. Briquets having as little as 25% CaF_2 contained are in common use, but briquets made from acid grade fluorspar grading above 90% are in demand. Users of the diluted briquet

claim fluorspar economy plus a way to make use of steel mill wastes.

Geology

Composition and Properties

Theoretically pure fluorite contains 51.1% calcium and 48.9% fluorine. Substitution of small percentages of cerium and yttrium for calcium has been noted. Inclusions of gases and fluids, such as petroleum and water, and of solid minerals such as pyrite, marcasite, and other sulfides are common. Free fluorine is present in some crystals. The fluorspar of commerce contains attached and admixed mineral impurities, such as calcite, quartz, barite, celestite, various sulfides, or phosphates.

Fluorite tends to occur in well-formed isometric crystals, forming cubes and octahedrons. It also occurs in massive and in earthy forms, and as crusts or globular aggregates with radial fibrous texture. Crystalline fluorspar exhibits a great range of colors, from colorless and water-clear to yellow, blue, purple, green, rose, red, bluish and purplish black, and brown. The colors may occur in alternating bands parallel to cube faces. They may be altered by exposure to X-rays, heat, ultraviolet light, and pressure. Colors are caused by a variety of factors including the presence of trace impurities and displaced ions in the lattice. Long exposure to sunlight, such as occurs on mine dumps, frequently results in the fading of the original coloration.

Some varieties fluoresce blue or violet under ultraviolet light or cathode rays. Some specimens phosphoresce when heated or after exposure to sunlight or ultraviolet light, and some exhibit triboluminescence.

The mineral has a hardness of 4, and is the type-mineral of that hardness on the Mohs' scale. Its specific gravity is 3.18 when crystalline, but ranges from 3.01 to 3.6 in various forms. The luster is vitreous. The mineral has perfect octahedral cleavage, and "diamonds" made by knocking the corners off of cubic crystals are seen in many collections.

When pulverized and treated with sulfuric acid, fluorite decomposes into gaseous hydrogen fluoride and calcium sulfate, which is the fundamental reaction in the production of hydrofluoric acid. When added to metallurgical slags it imparts greater fluidity at lower temperatures making it valuable in steelmaking and ferrous and nonferrous foundry practice. In ceramic mixes it promotes crystallization around individual centers, and thus is useful in making opal glasses. Crystalline fluorite has a very low index of refraction ($n = 1.4339$), low dispersion, is isotropic, and has an unusual ability to transmit ultraviolet light. These are the properties which make it useful in optical systems as prisms and as components of high quality, special-purpose lenses. Synthetic fluorite has replaced the natural mineral for optical uses.

Modes of Occurrence

Fluorite occurs in a wide variety of geological environments, evidencing deposition under an extended range of physical and chemical conditions. At one extreme it is present as an accessory mineral in granites and related igneous rocks; while at the other extreme, it is found as crystals in geodes and as botryoidal linings in limestone caves.

From an economic standpoint, the most important modes of occurrence of the mineral are:

1) Fissure veins in igneous, metamorphic, and sedimentary rocks.

2) Stratiform replacement deposits in carbonate rocks.

3) Replacements in carbonate rocks along contacts with acid igneous intrusives.

4) Stockworks and fillings in shattered zones.

5) Deposits at the margins of carbonatite and alkalic rock complexes.

6) Residual concentrations resulting from the weathering of primary deposits.

7) Occurrences as recoverable gangue in base metal deposits.

Less common modes, in some places commercially important, include:

8) Fillings in breccia pipes.

9) Fillings in open spaces.

10) Pegmatites.

Least common but of potential importance are:

11) Deposits in lake sediments.

Fissure Veins: Fissure veins, usually along faults or shear zones, are the most readily recognized form in which fluorspar deposits occur the world over. Silica, calcite or other carbonates, iron, lead, and zinc sulfides, and barite are the typical associated minerals. In some vein deposits as in the Rosiclare district of southern Illinois, fluorite appears to have replaced a prior vein filling of calcite. Along some veins in carbonate rocks, fluorspar has replaced the wall rock at intersections with favorable beds, providing large minable tonnage mined from some deposits. Although vein structures are remarkably persistent, the fluorspar itself commonly occurs as lenses or ore shoots separated by barren or poorly mineralized portions of vein. Ore shoot widths of 2 to 30 ft and lengths of 200 to 1000 ft are common, but there is great variation from deposit to deposit. Vein systems may be up to several miles in length, and ore may be present to depths of 1000 ft or more below the surface. The CaF_2 content of minable portions of veins normally ranges from 25 to 80%, although grades above 90% occur in limited areas.

Some of the world's great vein deposits include the Osor deposit in northeastern Spain, the Torgola deposit in northern Italy, the Muscadroxiu-Genna Tres Montis vein system in Sardinia, the Longstone Edge-Sallet Hole deposit in England, and the Rosiclare-Goodhope vein system in southern Illinois.

Stratiform Deposits: Stratiform, manto, or bedded deposits occur in carbonate rocks. Certain beds are replaced along or adjacent to structural breaks such as joints or faults. This relationship to structural features is very clear in some deposits, but obscure in others. Frequently there is a sandstone, shale, or clay capping. Typically there is evidence of loss of volume in the replaced zones with attendant development of gentle synclinical structures in overlying strata or of collapse structures, sometimes pipelike in shape. In some districts, as in southern Illinois, no connection is recognized between the mineralization and any igneous activity, whereas in others, such as the Encantada district in northern Coahuila, Mexico, the presence of rhyolite plugs and sills in the general vicinity of the spar deposits, and the association of spar with rhyolite injections along bedding planes, suggests an association. Stratiform deposits are known in many parts of the world and are particularly well developed in the Cave in Rock district of southern Illinois, in the northern part of the State of Coahuila in Mexico, and in the Ottoshoop (Zeerust) District of Transvaal in South Africa. In Illinois the deposits range from a few inches to 20 ft thick, 50 to 500 ft wide, and are up to 4½ miles long. In Coahuila the individual ore bodies are smaller but relatively more numerous and widespread. In the Ottoshoop District bedded deposits occur in an area 10 miles long and 6 miles wide in a dolomite facies underlying a prominent chert bed.

In stratiform deposits, textural features of the parent rock such as sedimentary banding are commonly preserved. Frequently associated with the banded ore is a massive crystalline type which appears to have filled open spaces left from the dissolving of limestone by the ore-bearing solutions or their precursors. Minerals accompanying fluorspar in stratiform deposits are calcite, dolomite, quartz, galena, sphalerite, pyrite, marcasite, barite, and celestite. CaF_2 content in minable deposits ranges from 15% upward. A few ore bodies in Illinois yield direct shipping metallurgical grade fluorspar containing 85% or more CaF_2.

Replacement Deposits: Replacement deposits in carbonate rocks along contacts with intrusive rhyolite bodies are well developed in the Rio Verde, San Luis Potosi, and Aguachile districts in Mexico. They include some of the largest and highest grade fluorspar deposits. The fluorspar is not thought to be contact metamorphic in origin, but introduced later, following the contact zone as a conduit replacing the limestone outward from the contact, either massively or selectively along certain beds. At Aguachile, cross sections show ore shoots resembling one side of a Christmas tree.

Stockworks: Fluorspar often occurs as stockworks and fillings in shear and breccia zones. Many occurrences in the American West are of the stockwork type and, though wide, usually have low overall CaF_2 content. Deposits in the Zuni Mountains of New Mexico and near Jamestown, Colorado are examples. The Zwartkloof deposit in the Transvaal Province of South Africa consists of three vertical breccia zones in an east-west line in felsite containing stockworks of fluorite-carbonate veins. The largest zone is 200 by 600 ft in plan and persists to 3000 ft below the surface. The fluorspar grade is about 14%. The Buffalo deposit, near Naboomspruit in the Transvaal, consists of a network of fluorspar veinlets in sill-like bodies of fine-grained pink granite which are inclusions in coarse red granite of the Bushveld complex.

Carbonatite and Alkalic Rock Complexes: Fluorspar is a common mineral in carbonatite and alkalic rock complexes, rarely in sufficient abundance to be economic. The Okorusu deposit in South-West Africa (Namibia) of this type consists of a number of bodies of fluorspar in limestones, quartzites, and related rocks which have been intruded and metamorphosed by an alkaline igneous rock complex including a nepheline syenite stock. The fluorspar replaces bedded and brecciated limestone, marble, and quartzite, forming large lenticular masses. Apatite and quartz are abundant accessory minerals. At Amba Dongar, India, veins and replacement bodies of fluorspar occur in carbonate rocks bordering ankeritic carbonatite intrusives. Fluorite is also present in the carbonatite itself.

Residual Deposits: Concentrations of fluorspar in clayey and sandy residuum resulting from surficial weathering of fluorspar veins and replacement deposits in some places are sources principally of metallurgical spar. This category includes detrital deposits blanketing the apex of veins, as well as deeply weathered upper portions of the veins themselves extending to depths of 100 ft or more. Such deposits are of major importance in Illinois and Kentucky. Similar deeply weathered ore has been mined in England, Thailand, and the Asturias district of northwestern Spain. Weathered residuum, called *kokoman*, is mined in the Marico district in South Africa, where it is the result of the weathering of gently dipping replacement bodies.

Gangue Mineral: Fluorspar occurs as a major gangue mineral in lead-zinc veins in many parts of the world, and in some, averaging 10 to 20%, is economically recoverable. Acid grade fluorspar is produced on a large scale from lead-zinc mill tailings near Parral in Mexico.

Breccia Pipes: Fluorite occurs in breccia pipes in the Thomas Range, Utah and near Beatty, Nevada. Pipes in the Thomas Range are circular to oval in plan, up to 150 ft in diameter and over 200 ft in depth, and are formed in dolomite by replacement along shattered zones associated with faults and intrusive breccias. Fluorspar occurs as soft friable masses and in boxworks of fine-grained more resistant veinlets, and is nearly unrecognizable. At the Daisy mine near Beatty, fluorspar replaces brecciated dolomite in pipelike bodies bounded by gouge zones along two sets of intersecting faults.

Fillings in Open Spaces: Fluorspar occasionally partially fills open spaces, both in veins and stratiform deposits. Spectacular examples of this type occur in the San Vicente district of northern Coahuila, where fluorspar occurs in veins and mantos as pure massive incrustations of mamillary, stalactitic, and stalagmitic forms. The Fluorspar-Gero-Penber vein system of the Northgate mine in Colorado is a similar occurrence where fluorspar occurs in botryoidal layers on the walls of open fissures and as concretionary coatings surrounding loose fragments of country rock. Lower parts of open areas of these fissures are partly filled with concretionary pebblelike masses, in places cemented into porous, rubbly aggregates.

Pegmatites: Many pegmatites contain minor amounts of fluorspar. Grade was high enough to support a mining operation at the Crystal Mountain occurrence in Montana, where three large tabular bodies of massive fluorspar containing minor amounts of biotite, quartz, feldspar, and other igneous-type accessory minerals, occur in coarse-grained biotite granite.

Lake Sediments: Fluorspar occurs in unconsolidated clayey and sandy pyroclastic sediments in the beds of former lakes near Castel Giuliano, about 25 miles north of Rome, Italy. Fluorine of volcanic origin permeated the lake sediments resulting in deposition of minute disseminated crystals of fluorspar, which make up as much as 50 to 60% of the clayey parts and 15% of the sandy parts of the deposits. It is accompanied by barite, apatite, calcite, dolomite, and opal.

Distribution of Deposits

Fluorspar deposits occur on every continent. Major producers include the United States, Mexico, Spain, England, France, Italy, South Africa, China, Thailand, Mongolia, and the USSR. Lesser producers include Argentina, Brazil, Bulgaria, Czechoslovakia, Kenya, Tunisia, Morocco, West Germany, East Germany, Romania, India, and Korea.

North America: *Canada*—The only large production in Canada was from the St. Lawrence area of the Burin Peninsula in southern Newfoundland, which yielded over 3 million tons of ore from 1940 until operation ceased in 1978. Other deposits occur in Ontario at Madoc and near Wilberforce and Cobden; at Rock Candy and Birch Island near Kamloops and near Quesnel Lake in British Columbia; along the Lower Laird River in northern British Columbia; and at Lake Ainslie on Cape Breton Island in Nova Scotia.

On the Burin Peninsula, fluorspar occurs in veins in granite and rhyolite porphyry along steeply dipping faults. Average thickness of higher grade veins is 3 to 5 ft and of lower grade veins is 15 to 20 ft. Some veins have been traced for more than a mile.

Veins at Madoc are small and have been worked principally in wartime. The veins at Lake Ainslie are low grade fluorspar with associated abundant barite. A deposit at Birch Island remains undeveloped with reserves said to be 1.5 million tons of 29% CaF_2 grade. Bedded deposits on the Lower Laird River near Mile 497 on the Alaska Highway in northern British Columbia have not proved to be of current commercial interest. Two low grade

fluorite deposits near Likely, BC, were reported to be under exploration early in 1981.

Mexico—Mexico is the world's largest producer of fluorspar. In 1981, production was 1 116 332 t, having held at that approximate level steadily since 1975, but sharply declined during 1982, totaling only 605 643 t in the first three quarters compared to 831 687 t in the first three quarters of 1981. Important deposits occur in San Luis Potosi, Coahuila, Chihuahua, and Guanajuato.

Many types of deposits are mined. In the Musquiz district of northern Coahuila, mantos in Cretaceous limestones are most important. Northwestern Coahuila has vein deposits and replacement deposits in limestone associated with rhyolite sills and plugs. Deposits in the Paila district of central Coahuila are veins. In San Luis Potosi and adjoining Guanajuato are several large replacement deposits in limestone associated with rhyolite intrusives. Numerous vein deposits occur in Chihuahua, but its principal production is acid grade concentrate recovered from sulfide mill tailings near Parral.

Eight flotation plants in Mexico have an annual production capacity of approximately 600 kt of acid grade concentrate. A plant just across the border at Eagle Pass, Texas, using Mexican ore, has a nominal capacity of 90 kt/a. Total acid grade production in 1981 was 510 kt; metspar and sub-met production was approximately 501 kt; and ceramic was 108 kt. Total sales in 1981 were 995 kt. While most is exported, Mexican consumption of acid grade has increased substantially with four hydrofluoric acid plants, including two relatively new ones (Quimica Fluor starting in 1975, the Fluorex in 1979), resulting in domestic acid grade sales of 177 kt in 1981.

United States—ALASKA—The Lost River deposit, located in the western portion of the Seward Peninsula 85 miles northwest of Nome, was worked intermittently for tin from 1904 to 1955 and has since been explored for fluorspar, beryllium, and tin. Fluorspar-tin-tungsten-beryllium mineralization occurs in acidic dikes, in skarn deposits along granite-limestone contacts, and brecciated limestone adjacent to thrust faults. Mineralization in one zone was reported to be 27 million tons grading 16.3% CaF_2, 0.15% tin, and 0.03% tungsten. Fluorspar also occurs in six other zones in the district (Anon., 1972), but there has been no production.

ARIZONA.—Although 56 occurrences of fluorspar were listed in one summary (Van Alstine, 1969) and 96 in another (Elevatorski, 1971), to date cumulative production has probably been less than 50,000 tons. Deposits are widely scattered in the southern half of the state, principally as small epithermal veins in fissures and brecciated zones along faults in intrusive, metamorphic, and sedimentary rocks. No large replacement deposits have been found. Fluorite occurs mostly with calcite and quartz in nonmetaliferous veins, although in the Castle Dome district it is a gangue mineral along with barite, quartz, and calcite in veins which were mined on a small scale for their lead-silver content.

The Castle Dome, Duncan, Sierrita Mountain, Tonto Basin, and Whetstone Mountain districts have been producers. The Lone Star mine in the Whetstone Mountain district yielded 10,000 tons of metallurgical spar in 1967, but then closed down.

Vein ore from the Packard and other nearby mines was processed into acid grade fluorspar in a flotation mill at Tonto Basin until these veins were exhausted. Ore from the Turkey mine on McFadden Peak north of Globe was processed at that mill before it was decommissioned in 1979. This mine and other localities in Arizona remain inactive.

CALIFORNIA—Although there are many occurrences of fluorspar in California, only small amounts have been produced for ceramic and metallurgical purposes. Metspar was produced on a small scale from the Clark Mountain area of San Bernardino County in the 1950s and 1960s. California occurrences have been described by Chesterman (1966) and Elevatorski (1968).

COLORADO—Colorado in some years ranked second in annual production, after Illinois. Aggregate production of crude ore to the present is estimated at about 2.5 million tons.

A total of 63 occurrences have been identified in the state (Van Alstine, 1964), including five major districts, all now idle. Northgate and Jamestown districts were the largest and most recently closed. The others are Browns Canyon, Poncha Springs, and Wagon Wheel Gap.

In the Jamestown district, fluorspar occurs in pipelike bodies and breccia zones in granite and granodiorite, and in associated veins. Output of the Burlington mine was treated at the former Valmont Mill near Boulder. Other mines include the Argo, Emmett, and Blue Jay, ore from which was concentrated to acid grade in a mill, located at Jamestown. Neither mill exists now.

At Northgate, fluorspar occurs in veins in shear and breccia zones in granite and schist, and has been mined open cut and underground.

During World War II the district produced metspar. More recently the ore was concentrated to acid grade in a mill built in 1952, now idle. Exploratory drilling continues from time to time and may result in reopening as prices continue to rise.

The Browns Canyon district included a number of mines, developed on veins in rhyolite and in granite. Two flotation mills were operated at various times. In the Poncha Springs district a flotation mill operated for several years in the mid-1950s on low grade ore consisting of fluorspar veinlets in fractured and brecciated zones in granite and granite gneiss. The Wagon Wheel Gap mine was on a vein in a sheeted zone in rhyolite yielding metspar.

IDAHO—The principal deposits of fluorspar in Idaho are in the Bayhorse-Keystone Mt. area of Custer County, southwest of Challis, and in the Meyers Cove, Big Squaw Creek, and Stanley areas (Anderson, 1964).

The Bayhorse dolomite replacement deposits, as outlined by coredrilling and partially developed for mining, may exceed 3.2 million st of 36% CaF_2, with a 25% grade cutoff. Other deposits, both vein and replacement, occur in the Bayhorse district and on adjoining Keystone Mt. The district has potential if production economics can offset freight disadvantages.

A flotation mill operated briefly at Meyers Cove in the fifties, producing about 13,000 tons of acid grade concentrate from fluorspar mined in brecciated volcanics and fissure fillings. Later, a heavy media plant was built to make metallurgical gravel spar, but was unsuccessful due to excessive silica locked in the ore. This mill was moved to the Garden Creek area west of Challis to be used on free-milling vein ores, but is not in operation.

At Big Squaw Creek, a vein is exposed in the northeast canyon wall of the Salmon river west of Shoup. At Stanley, fluorspar occurs in shear zones in granite and volcanics.

ILLINOIS-KENTUCKY—Current production is focused at two flotation mills situated in an area of 700 square miles in southern Illinois and adjacent Kentucky which for a number of years was the world's largest producer (Baxter, et al., 1973) and continues as the major US producing district. Shipments of fluorspar concentrates of all grades during the period 1880 through 1980 are estimated to have totaled 11.5 million st, which is probably equivalent to mine production of approximately 33 million tons of crude ore.

Vein deposits are the most numerous, but since 1950 the bedded deposits near Cave in

Rock, IL, have been the source of most of the district's output, and outrank the vein deposits in terms of total all-time district production. Recently production from vein deposits has resumed importance as some of the older bedded deposits have been depleted.

In addition to the major district, a small production has been recorded from veins southwest of Lexington, in central Kentucky.

Vein deposits of the Illinois-Kentucky district occur along an extensive and intricate system of faults in sedimentary rocks of Mississippian age. Most of these faults are the steeply-dipping normal type, trending northeast, with displacement ranging from a few feet to over 1000 ft. The most important deposits are on faults of 50 to 500-ft displacement. Veins range in width up to 30 ft and to as much as 60 ft in exceptional cases. They have been mined for 900 ft vertically and for two miles in length. Veins pinch and swell horizontally and vertically with the proportion of fluorspar to total vein material ranging from 0 to 100% within short distances. Near the surface and to depths as great as 250 ft, the veins contain much clay owing to the dissolving of vein calcite and limestone wall rock by circulating ground water leaving the argillaceous material in the limestone behind. Strong walls are found at depth in most places. A large inflow of water at high pressure was characteristic of the deeper mines particularly at Rosiclare.

Major replacement deposits occur in Illinois northwest and north of the village of Cave in Rock, others occur in Kentucky south of Carrsville and near Hampton in Livingston County. The Cave in Rock group of mines occupies a zone of minor structural disturbance one mile wide and over six miles long, paralleling a major northeast trending fault which has maximum displacement of about 1000 ft. The deposits lie along one or both sides of minor fractures and small faults and are characteristically long and narrow. Major deposits occur along fracture-fault systems with less than one ft of displacement. Widths of 50 to 150 ft and thicknesses of 3 to 15 ft are typical. Maximum widths of 325 to 350 ft have been found. Lengths are mostly 200 to 1500 ft. One ore body is known to extend continuously for at least 4½ miles. The deposits occur through a vertical range of about 180 ft in four preferred sets of limestone beds and follow these beds down dip from the outcrops (which were discovered originally in a prominent bluff) to depths well over 1000 ft. Mining in the former Minerva mine (now Inverness) currently is below 1300 ft and drill-ing discloses ore at least 120 ft deeper in lower horizons. Three to four bedded horizons often exist superimposed along the same fracture system, and within a vertical interval of 150 ft. Fluorite is the principal mineral, accompanied by sphalerite and galena in many deposits. Quartz, barite, and calcite are common, along with pyrite, marcasite, witherite, and strontianite. Banding, which may be a relic from the replaced limestone or from rhythmic metasomatic deposition, is characteristic of some deposits, known locally as "coontail ore." Crude ores have 15 to 90% calcium fluoride, and some contain up to 3½% zinc and 5% lead.

Residual deposits have been less important producers, but have yielded high quality fluorspar. These "gravel spar" deposits are as much as 60 ft wide and extend to depths of a hundred feet or more. The fluorspar occurs as weathered fragments from the size of boulders down to sand grains dispersed in a clayey matrix.

MONTANA—Most of the fluorspar production has come from the Crystal Mountain deposits near Darby in Ravalli County. The deposits of massive fluorite in granite and metasediments were discovered in 1951 and developed into one of the nation's major metallurgical grade fluorspar mines.

The mine was a side-hill benched open pit, at the 7000 ft elevation on Sapphire Mt. Ore was mined, hand-sorted, and sized at the mine continuously from 1952 to 1973. This roughly concentrated ore was hauled 25 miles by truck to Darby, where finished concentration was accomplished in a 60-ton per hour heavy-media cone plant. The metspar was shipped by rail to steel plant consumers and government stockpiles.

Shipments from the accumulated fines at the heavy-media plant continued from 1973 to 1980 to briquetting plants serving the steel industry. Production from 1952 to 1980 totalled 566,000 tons of which 520,000 was metspar, 2000 tons was metspar-sized jig product (¼ x ½ in.), and 44,000 tons was sub-metgrade fines. Mining and shipment of fines resumed in 1981.

Numerous other fluorspar occurrences have been recorded in Montana but have no production history. Fluorspar occurs as gangue in metalliferous veins in marginal portions of the Boulder batholith in west-central Montana, and is present as veins and replacement seams in intrusive syenite and in limestone in several areas characterized by alkalic intrusives in the north-central part of the state.

The presence of fluorspar has been used as a

guide to gold deposits. In the Old Glory deposit in the Pryor Mountains, fluorspar occurs with the uranium mineral, tyuyamunite, replacing limestone in brecciated and cavernous portions of the Madison limestone.

NEVADA—Fluorspar became commercially important in Nevada in 1919 when the Daisy mine near Beatty began its long productive life. Nevada deposits are described in a recent publication by Papke (1979). Most of the 62 deposits he describes lie in a broad, arcuate band across the southern part of the state, and northward through the central part. Total production has been about 575,000 st, most from the Daisy (Crowell) mine in southern Nye County, the Baxter (Kaiser) mine in northeastern Mineral County, the Goldspar mine near the Daisy, and the Carp (Wells Cargo) mine in southeastern Lincoln County. About 19 other deposits have had some production, but only the Daisy mine is active. More than a fourth of the deposits are in the Quinn Canyon and Adaven district in the southeastern part of the state, but the small size of the deposits and remoteness of this area has hindered their development. Small metspar shipments have been made from Caliente.

Deposits are hydrothermal or pyrometasomatic. They occur as replacement bodies, veins, replacement and/or filling in jasperoid bodies, stockworks, and breccia pipes. The Daisy deposit is mined underground, with total past production of about 225,000 st. It consists of irregular, generally steeply dipping, structurally complex replacement bodies in dolomite. The ore is soft, friable, and relatively low in silica. Most has been used as metspar. Some has been shipped to a southern California cement producer. The Baxter deposit, a vein in andesitic volcanic rocks, developed to a depth of 600 ft, had a total mine production of 182,000 st, of which two-thirds was made into acid-grade concentrate in a mill operated from 1952 to 1957 by Kaiser Aluminum and Chemical Corporation at Fallon, Nevada. The Goldspar and nearby Mary deposits are breccia pipe and replacement bodies in dolomite. All the fluorspar from these open-pit mines was used in making cement. At the Carp mine an estimated 45,000 st of metspar was produced in four open pits. The ore came from nearly flat, manto-like replacement bodies, generally concordant with bedding of the dolomite host rock.

NEW MEXICO—There are numerous occurrences of fluorspar in New Mexico but production has been small. Van Alstine (1965) listed 65 areas in the central, north central, and southwestern parts of the state. The fluorspar map MR-60 of the USGS and accompanying tabulation in 1974, by Worl, Van Alstine, and Heyl, classified some 51 locations as to type, tonnage, and associated minerals.

Eight areas each produced at least 20,000 tons of crude ore and cumulative total statewide production has probably been about 700,000 tons. Production peaked in World War II, when New Mexico was the fourth largest producing state after Illinois, Kentucky, and Colorado.

Most production came from the Zuni Mts., Sierra Caballos Mts., Gila district, Burro Mts., Cooks Peak, and from Fluorite Ridge and Tortugas near Las Cruces. Flotation plants have operated at various times at Chise, Silver City, Gila, Lordsburg, Deming, Los Lunas, San Antonio, and near Hachita. A drum type heavy-media separator making metspar is operating at the Great Eagle Mine north of Lordsburg.

In the Zuni Mts., the "27" vein deposits were the most productive, with the Mirabal deposit contributing. Until closed in 1953, these had produced totally about 224,000 tons of ore which was concentrated to acid grade at the Zuni Milling Co. flotation mill at Los Lunas (Goddard 1966).

In the Cooks Peak district near Deming, White Eagle, Greenleaf and others in the Fluorite Ridge district, and Burro Chief and Shrine deposits in the Burro Mts. were important producers. All are vein deposits in brecciated or fractured zones along faults in igneous rocks. The Lyda K Mine, south of Truth or Consequences, is a siliceous vein in Precambrian granite. The Ruby mine north of Las Cruces contains veins in limestone near an igneous contact. At Chise small manto replacement bodies occur in limestone beds. The Bishops Cap deposit is a vein in limestone, with some adjacent replacement ore. In the Hansonburg district, east of San Antonio, fluorite occurs with lead and barite as vug filling in brecciated limestone.

The Salado deposit, southwest of Truth or Consequences, consists of tabular masses of fractured and brecciated jasperoid with the fluorspar forming a filling and cement. Between 2½ and 3 million tons of low-grade mineralization have been estimated from drilling results. A thickness of over 40 ft in places would permit open-pit mining, with little overburden. Difficult flotation metallurgy, low grade, and remoteness from market have inhibited development.

OREGON—Near Rome in the southeastern part of the state, fluorspar occurs as nearly spherical grains in volcanic tuff, tuffaceous mudstone, and mudstone of Tertiary lake deposits (Sheppard and Gude, 1969). The fluorspar content reaches 16% in some zones, but is generally much lower. The tonnage of contained fluorspar is estimated at 11 Mt. Because of very fine particle size, concentration to acceptable grade has not proved practical.

TENNESSEE—A small amount of metspar was produced from a small fissure vein in limestone in the central part of the state, where it occurs with barite and sulfides (Jewell, 1947).

Fluorite has been noted as a gangue mineral in zinc deposits near Carthage, locally comprising 12 to 15% of the ore but averaging much less.

A drilling program in the Sweetwater area indicated fluorspar-zinc-barite mineralization several hundred feet below the surface in buried karst breccia zones similar to the Mascot district, TN zinc deposits. Exploratory drifting was done from a 600 ft shaft sunk in 1979, now plugged.

TEXAS—Metallurgical grade fluorspar production began in 1971 in the Christmas Mts. south of Alpine from bedded limestone replacement mantos adjacent to intrusive rhyolite bodies. In late 1980, a 900 ft decline was sunk beneath a laccolithic structure where exploration and development work continue.

In the Eagle Mts. southwest of Van Horn, fluorspar occurs as replacement of limestone and as fissure deposits in rhyolite. In the period 1942 to 1950, about 15,000 tons of metallurgical gravel and acid grade were produced.

UTAH—Most of the deposits are located in the west-central part of the state in the Spor Mountain, Indian Peak, Pine Grove, and Star districts. The Spor Mountain district in the Thomas Range northwest of Delta has been the most consistent producer. The deposits are classified as pipes, veins, and disseminated bodies in dolomite and volcanic rocks. Most of the production has come from the pipes. The most productive mines have been the Lost Sheep, Fluorine Queen, and Bell Hill.

In the Indian Peak district veins occur along faults in volcanic rocks. The Cougar Spar and Blue Bell mines were World War II producers of metspar. Small production has also been recorded from the Pine Grove and Star districts, and from the Rain Bow mine in Millard County and the Silver Queen mine in Tooele County.

Cumulative Utah production of crude ore to date is estimated to have been 250,000 tons.

WASHINGTON—A small production of metspar has come from the Mitchem mine near Keller, in Ferry County.

WYOMING—There are reports of fluorspar in Crook and Albany counties.

Central America: Occurrences have been reported in Honduras and Guatemala, but details are not available.

South America: *Argentina*—Vein deposits have been mined intermittently in the Sierra Comechigones, 30 miles northwest of Cordoba and others developed for production in the southern part of Rio Negro province and the adjoining northern part of Chubut. In recent years metspar has been produced from a group of veins in the Sierra Grande district of Rio Negro, including the Delta vein, reportedly with 4.0 million tons of drill-indicated ore of 51% CaF_2 grade. A small flotation mill at Valcheta has produced concentrates for domestic use. In Chubut a number of veins have been discovered in areas west of Puerto Madryn.

Brazil—Principal deposits are in the vicinity of Criciuma in the Santa Catarina province of southern Brazil. Small-scale production has been reported from deposits in the provinces of Rio Grande do Norte, Paraiba, and Bahia.

In the Criciuma district, three flotation mills have an aggregate capacity of about 35 kt/a of acid grade concentrate. Known deposits are not large and continued output will depend on the discovery of new reserves and the resolution of water problems.

Chile—Small tonnage of fluorspar has been produced from veins in granite in the Province of Coquimbo. One deposit, the Mercedes mine, is near the village of Paihwano.

Europe: *France*—Important deposits occur in the Departments of Haute-Loire, Pyrenees-Orientales, Var, Tarn, Saone-et-Loire, and Puy-de-Dome. Details have been described in a series of articles by Chermette (1972–1973 and 1979).

Epithermal vein deposits occur in the Morvan, Auvergne, Limousin, and Albi districts of the Massif Central, the Maures and Esterel districts of the Mediterranean coastal area northeast of Toulon, in the eastern Pyrenees west of Peripignan, and in the Vosges. The vein deposits contain about 50% CaF_2, 20% silica, 5 to 10% barite, and 3 to 5% sulfides. Stratiform deposits with about 35% CaF_2 and 15% barite occur in the Morvan district. Depostis having stratiform characteristics are important producers in the Escaro district in the Pyrenees southwest of Perpignan. Deposits at Le Beix, Chavaniac, and Le Maine in the Massif Central are exhausted. La Charbonniere and

Langeac have also closed. Fonte Sante (near Cannes in Var), Le Burc (near Albi in Tarn), Montroc (near Albi), Escaro and Chaillac continue in operation. Fonte Sante is noteworthy for the economic occurrence of sellaite (MgF_2) which is blended with the fluorspar product and is used at the Lyons hydrofluoric acid plant.

Production of all grades of concentrates in 1979 was about 300 kt, divided 177 kt acid grade and about 116 kt metspar. Exports were 9 kt acid grade and 84 kt metspar.

Germany, East—East Germany is estimated to produce about 100 kt/a of fluorspar. Deposits are in Saxony, Thuringia, and Anhalt, but details are lacking.

Germany, West—Production in 1979 amounted to about 63 kt, derived from vein deposits in the Todtnau, Hesselbach, Oberwolfach, and Pforzheim districts in the Black Forest region in the southwest, and in the Naaburg and Sulzbach districts in Bavaria. Acid-grade concentrate is produced in four flotation plants. As a large consumer of both acid grade and metspar concentrates, West Germany imports a large part of its requirements. Imports in 1979 were from South Africa (53 456 t), Spain (33 910 t), Morocco (16 840 t), UK (13 351 t), and Kenya (10 986 t).

Greece—Fluorspar occurs as a gangue mineral in the silver ores of Laurium, but Greece imports its requirements, having produced only 400 t in 1979.

Italy—Italy produced about 183 kt in 1979. Mines in Sardinia are the principal producers. Smaller outputs have come from Brescia, Trento, Bolzano, and Bergamo in northern Italy. The Genna Tres Montis-Muscadroxiu-S'Acqua Frida vein system in southern Sardinia near the village of Silius is credited with 8 million tons of ore reserve averaging 40 to 45% CaF_2, making it one of the world's largest deposits. Vein widths are 5 to 8 m. Barite and galena are recoverable accessory minerals. Underground workings have demonstrated a strike length of about 3 km. Numerous other vein deposits and a skarn deposit occur in southern Sardinia.

Of two flotation plants at Assemini, near Cagliari, one is active with a nominal capacity of 200 kt/a of acid grade concentrate including metspar briquettes, plus barite and galena concentrates. Actual capacity is said to be about 150 kt/a due to restriction of labor regulations. The other, an older mill with acid grade capacity of 40 kt/a, is idle. In 1979, Sardinia produced 107 kt of acid grade from 320 kt of crude ore.

In northern Italy important deposits include Prestavel and Vallarsa near Bolzano, Torgola near Brescia, and Camerata Cornello near Bergamo. In 1979 Societa Fluormine produced 16 kt of acid grade from 71 kt of ore from Prestavel and Vallersa which also yielded 4.7 kt ceramic grade and 19.7 kt metallurgical grade.

The Pianciano deposit in the Castel Giuliano area 40 km northwest of Rome consists of fluorspar impregnating lake beds of volcanic ash (Spada, 1969). The fluorspar content, ranging from 20 to 55%, was derived from volcanic emanations along with barium, strontium, and phosphorous. The fluorspar is too fine-grained to be recovered by flotation, but tests indicate a possibility of producing metallurgical grade by hydrocyclone separation.

Norway—Veins are reported in the Buskerud, Telemark, Vest Agder, and Drammen regions west and southwest of Oslo. The Lassedal mine near Kongsberg was formerly a producer.

Spain—Spain is estimated to have produced about 200 kt of metgrade and acid grade fluorspar in 1980 mainly for export to Europe with smaller amounts to the US and Canada. In 1979 total production was 191 kt, divided 41 kt metspar and 150 kt acid grade. Principal deposits are in the Asturias region of northern Spain near the ports of Ribadesella and Aviles; in the southeast near the port of Almeria; and in south-central Spain near Seville and Cordoba. Deposits are both veins and replacement bodies. Acid-grade material is derived in the retreatment of old lead mine wastes in the Almeria-Berja area. In 1980, seven companies produced acid grade, four in Asturias, two in the Seville-Cordoba region, and one near Berja. Grades of ore range from 40 to 45% for some of the vein-mines, down to 15 to 20% in the case of old lead mine waste. The large Osor vein in Gerona is exhausted. Weakening market conditions in 1982 led to closure, at least temporarily, of all but three mills: two belonging to Minersa, one of which is in Asturias, the other in Almeria; and one belonging to Minas de Orgiva near Berja.

Sweden—The sole producer in Sweden, the government-owned Yxsjoberg mine near Ludvika, 200 km northwest of Stockholm, where fluorspar occurs with tungsten and copper, closed in 1977. Other deposits have been reported between Branteriks and Onslunda in Skane in southern Sweden. The Osterlen district was formerly a small producer.

Switzerland—Occurrences are known, but none of commercial importance.

United Kingdom—Among numerous fluorite occurrences in the United Kingdom, present operations are located in the Southern Pennine Orefield of north Derbyshire and in the Northern Pennine Orefield of west Durham. Production comes from fissure veins and bedded replacement deposits, together with associated old lead mine waste and tailings dumps. The deposits occur in rocks of the Carboniferous Limestone Series (Mississippian). Ore is mined both underground and open pit. The deposits contain variable amounts of galena, sphalerite, calcite, barite, quartz, and iron sulfides. Some were originally mined for lead, even before written record.

Installed capacity for the production of all grades of fluorspar is now in excess of 300 kt/a of which 245 kt is acid-grade capacity. Two acid-grade mill operations are in the Southern Pennine Orefields, and two in the Northern Pennine Orefield. Problems with ore supply have prevented capacity production.

Imports were 28 102 t in 1979 up from 3 783 t in 1978. South Africa provided 16 580 t followed by Morocco (5 100 t) and Mexico (3 203 t).

USSR and Soviet Bloc—USSR is estimated by the US Bureau of Mines to have produced about 560 kt of fluorspar in 1979, and the same in 1980. Details regarding the sources of this output are not available, but deposits are reported in the Transbaikal, Tashkent, and Yaroslav regions. Czechoslovakia produces about 90 kt/a from deposits in Bohemia. Mongolia produced about 410 kt in 1980, having steadily increased from 80 kt/a in 1972. Deposits are southwest of Ulan Bator in the Dorono Gobi district. Romania produces about 20 kt/a; Bulgaria about 25 kt/a, and Yugoslavia has a small production. The USSR imports about 100 kt/a of acid grade and about 400 kt/a of met grade to supply its requirements of more than 1 Mt/a. Sources include China, Kenya, and Thailand.

Africa: *Angola*—Deposits are reported in Angola, but details are lacking.

Kenya—A 100% government-owned acid grade mill, formerly jointly owned with IMC and Bamburi Portland Cement, produces concentrates relatively high in P_2O_5 from epithermal vein and replacement deposits in the Kerio Valley, about 130 km northwest of Nairobi. Ore ranging from 30 to 45% CaF_2 is mined open pit. The acid grade mill's output capacity is rated at 9,000 tons per month. Concentrates are trucked to rail at Kaptagat, near Eldoret, and loaded on vessel at Mombasa.

Other similar deposits are reported along the Rift structure.

Malawi—Exploration for fluorspar deposits related to carbonatite structures has been reported; five such occurrences are noted by Van Alstine and Schruben (1980).

Morocco—The El Hammam deposit near Meknes is a nearly vertical vein on an east-west fault in sericite schist, grading about 45% CaF_2. A flotation plant with a capacity of 65 kt/a of acid grade concentrate is operated by Samine, owned 55% by Omnium Nord Africain, 10% by Pechiney, and 35% by the Moroccan government (BRPM). Three other deposits are recognized in this region. Other veins occur in the Djebel Tirremi area, 10 km northeast of Taourirt, in eastern Morocco (Van Alstine and Schruben, 1980).

Mozambique—Large vein deposits occur approximately 150 km southeast of Tete. Remote from transportation and from sources of power, this area has been a minor producer of metspar. Further development may result as the area is opened up as a consequence of the construction of the Cabora Bassa dam on the Zambesi River. Six localities are listed by Van Alstine and Schruben (1980).

Nigeria—Deposits containing fluorspar with galena are reported in limestones in the Arufu district of Gongola State near the border with Benue State, in the Benue Trough about 80 km east of Makurdi, and fluorspar in greisens near Jos (Van Alstine and Schruben, 1980).

South Africa—In 1978 the Republic of South Africa achieved its present (1981) rank as third largest fluorspar producing country, surpassed by Mexico and the USSR. Its large reserves indicate it will continue to be prominent in the world picture. Deposits occur in several areas, but production has come principally from mines in the western and northern parts of Transvaal.

Acid grade output of four flotation plants in 1980 was 469 682 t, up from 387 310 t in 1979. Other production consists of metallurgical grade fluorspar, some of which is hand-cobbed *kokoman* residual ore derived from small mines, and small amounts of ceramic grade. Acid grade production is exported to Japan, Europe, Australia, and the United States through the port at Durban. In 1980 total production of all grades was almost 523 kt.

Domestically, AECI consumes acid grade to make hydrofluoric acid and the steel industry consumes essentially all of the metgrade as well as about 20 kt/a of 80% CaF_2 briquettes.

The Buffalo open pit mine of Transvaal Mining & Finance, a subsidiary of General Mining and Finance, near Naboomspruit exploits 14 to 16% grade deposits consisting of a network of fluorspar veinlets in sills in a pink granite which is itself an inclusion in coarse Bushveld granite. Similar deposits occur nearby.

Near Warmbad, the Zwartkloof deposit consists of three breccia zones containing a stockwork of fluorspar veinlets in felsite. Operating difficulties and the low grade of the ore for underground operation, approximately 14% CaF_2, caused operations to close in 1973.

At the open pit Vergenoeg mine of Chrome Chemicals, a subsidiary of Bayer, near Pienaarsrivier, fluorspar ore grading 40% occurs with abundant iron oxides (up to 50%) in a massive deposit in felsite.

In the Marico-Zeerust district, fluorspar occurs as replacements in dolomite and as associated residual deposits. Much of the ore in dolomite is disseminated along intersecting fractures. For many years metspar was produced by screening coarse fragments from residual surface deposits. Exploration has disclosed the existence of large reserves of primary ore probably on the order of 60 million tons containing 15 to 30% CaF_2. Two open pit mines, the Chemspar mine of Phelps Dodge and the Marico mine of Barlow Rand, with capacity of about 120 kt/a, are located here. Armco Bronne, a subsidiary of Armco, Inc., has an active exploration program and expects to develop an underground operation by 1985.

Namibia (South-West Africa)—The Okurusu deposit near Ojiwarongo consists of replacements or segregations in carbonatite and veins in quartzite. After yielding a few thousand tons of metspar, it has been idle. Reserves are indicated to be between 6 and 7 million tons grading 40% CaF_2. Vein ore near Omaruru was mined open pit and concentrated to acid grade in 25 kt/a flotation mill from reserves in excess of 600,000 tons. Vein and replacement deposits are known in other parts of the country. The lack of water and transportation facilities has hindered development.

Sudan—Fluorspar deposits occur at Jebel Semeih and Jebel Dumbeir approximately 200 miles southwest of Khartoum and 830 miles by rail from Port Sudan. At Jebel Semeih a highly siliceous fluorspar vein occurs in a granitic host rock. At Jebel Dumbeir fluorspar occurs in metasediments as replacements of bands of marble, as thin quartz-fluorite veins, and as bodies of fluorite associated with red feldspathic rock. No production is reported.

Tunisia—A flotation mill at the Hamman Zriba deposit near Zaghouan, 54 km south of Tunis, produces about 30 kt/a of acid grade concentrate from a bedded deposit in Jurassic limestone. Proven reserves are said to be 4 million tons of ore containing 35% CaF_2 and considerable barite. In the same general area, replacement vein deposits occur at Djebel Staa, Hammam Djedida, Djebel Oust, and Djebel el Kohol. Other deposits are at Bourchiba, on Cap Bon, and Bou Jaber.

Turkey—Fluorspar deposits in Turkey have been described (Anon., 1965); there is a very small annual production.

Asia: *China*—China is emerging as a major producer with an annual production of about 410,000 t, mainly from deposits in the central and northern parts of Zhejiang Province, northeastern Hebei Province, northern Guangdong Province, northeastern Anhui Province, and eastern Shandong Province. Other production is at Taoling in Hunan Province, Ming Gang in Henan, at Kaiping in Liaoning Province, and at Yulin in Guangxi Province (a new discovery near rail). In all, fluorspar occurrences are reported in 17 provinces. China exported 105 020 t to Japan in 1978 and 205 489 t in 1979, mainly metallurgical grade. Acid grade production is increasing with the conversion of sulfide flotation mills to acid grade, including one in northeastern Hebei and one in eastern Shandong, and the expansion of existing acid grade mills in Henan and Zhejiang.

India—At Amba Dongar, 350 miles north of Bombay in Gujarat State, veins and replacement bodies occur in the carbonate wall rock around ankeritic carbonatite intrusives, similar to the occurrences at Okurusu in Namibia (South-West Africa) (Deans, et al., 1972). A heavy media and flotation concentration plant has been constructed nearby at Kadipani, with a nominal capacity of 37.5 kt/a of product, of which 30% is acid grade and 70% metgrade. Reserves are reported to be 11.6 Mt of 30% fluorite content, of which proved reserves are said to be 4.7 Mt.

Other mineralized areas are reported at Chandri-Dungri in the Drug district of Madhya-Pradesh and at Mando-ki-Pal in the Dungarpur district of Rajasthan.

Japan—Japan formerly produced less than 10 kt/a of fluorspar from the Island of Hokkaido but ceased production in 1972 and imports its requirements.

Korea, North—This country has an annual production of about 40 kt.

Korea, South—Fluorspar deposits occur in the northern, central, and southern parts of the country. Approximately 70 mines have been producers, formerly with annual production of about 50 kt, largely for export (Kim et al.,

1972), but production was down to 8 kt in 1979. Both vein and replacement deposits occur. Minable ore reserves have been estimated at 660 kt (Jee and Kye, 1971). Producers have included the Choonchon Shinpo, Dojon, Kumi, Busang, and Kumbo mines.

Pakistan—Minor production has been reported from the Kalat district 45 to 60 miles south of Quetta in Baluchistan. There are also deposits south of Quetta.

Thailand—After the initiation of commercial fluorspar production in 1960, Thailand advanced to the status of one of the largest producers in the world. In 1979 production was 260 kt, comprising 178 kt metspar and acid grade. Exports totaled 205 kt, largely to Japan (116 kt) and the USSR (50 kt). Acid grade exports were 49.6 kt of that total, of which 39 kt went to Japan; 5 kt to India and 4.5 kt to Australia. In 1980, production reached 306 kt of which 173 kt was metspar and acid grade and 133 kt was low grade. Exports totaled 214 kt, 117 kt to Japan and 47.5 kt to the USSR. Acid grade exports were 60 kt of which Japan received 40 kt; the USSR, 10 kt; India, 5 kt; and Australia 3.5 kt.

Fluorspar deposits occur in a region from the northern border with Burma southward for over 800 miles to a point about 400 miles southwest of Bangkok. Active mines are concentrated in three areas: Chiangmai, Lumphun, and Mai Hongsun Provinces in the north; Kanchanaburi, Petchaburi, and Ratchaburi Provinces southwest of Bangkok; and Krabi Province in the south (Gardner and Smith, 1965; Anon., 1972; and private communication, B. L. Hodge, 1981).

The northern deposits are mainly replacements in Paleozoic limestones which, so far, have been found suitable only for the production of metspar, derived by hand sorting with large resulting waste dumps containing low grade ore. Residual deposits are widespread. A heavy media concentrating plant, with a 60 kt/a production capacity originally installed at Ban Hong in Lamphun Province in the northern area, 320 miles north of Bangkok, has been moved a short distance to Mae Tha. The product is trucked to river barges at Bank Pa In. In the southern area, the deposits are veins in metamorphosed, fine-grained, fractured Paleozoic clastics and in granite. Two flotation plants are operating, one at Ban Lard in Petchburi Province, about 100 miles south of Bangkok, with an annual production of 50 kt of acid grade concentrate and another in Khlong Thom district, Krabi Province, about 60 miles northwest of Trang, with an annual production of about 15 kt of acid grade.

Australia: Deposits of fluorspar have been found in all the Australian states except the Northern Territory (Liddy, 1971), but are undeveloped because they are small and remote. There have been investigations in the Chillagoe-Mungana-Almaden and Forsayth areas of northern Queensland, and in Western Australia in the Pilbara district 135 miles southeast of Port Hedland, the Yinnietharra area 200 miles from Carnarvon, and the Speewah Valley area southwest in Wyndham.

World Activity in Fluorspar

Overall, reported reserves of fluorspar have been increasing for several decades along with increasing annual production as producer interest in fluorspar has grown, either to fill a need for captive raw material or as a marketing opportunity. In the late 1970s, rising prices spurred new mine development and the reopening of some of those previously closed. Growth was particularly noteworthy in South Africa and China and revitalization in Spain, but recession in the early 1980s led to retrenchment with mines being closed, at least temporarily, especially in Spain and Mexico.

Exploration

Because fluorspar resists chemical weathering, it can be traced in the soils overlying weathered veins. Cleavage fragments washed clean by rainwater or exposed in anthills or spoil piles from animal burrows are useful clues. Silicified veins resisting erosion may stand up like a "reef." Bedded deposits are less discernable, but in areas of sufficient topographic relief the outcropping edges of deposits or slumped fragments of ore may be found. Owing to its softness and cleavability, fluorspar does not survive in the beds of streams and ordinarily cannot be traced by panning.

The search for bedded deposits usually involves locating a mineralized horizon and following it with vertical drill holes drilled to intersect the favorable beds.

Geophysical prospecting methods are not applicable. Photogeology can be of assistance in locating and tracing structures and outcrops, as well as the areal distribution of stratigraphic units known to be favorable for veins or replacement deposits.

Geochemical methods have been employed with varying degrees of success. Fluorine anomalies have been found in ground waters and surface streams, in soil samples and in stream sediments, but with little practiced success in discovery of ore deposits. Various non-fluorine elements detectable geochemically can be guides to fluorspar deposits.

Once mineralization has been detected, prospect shafts, drifts, and core or churn drill holes are used to probe the structures.

Preparation for Markets

Mining Methods

In some areas, such as in the Illinois-Kentucky district and the Southern Pennine district of Derbyshire in England, veins may be weathered to depths of as much as 250 ft. Such weathered ore, a mixture of clay and fragments of fluorspar and detached wall rock, may be mined open pit with draglines, scrapers, or power shovels to depths of as much as 150 ft. Below that, underground mining methods are used, involving modified top slicing or overhead shrinkage stoping.

Until the late 1960s, most vein mining in the Illinois-Kentucky district was done by shrinkage stoping and open stoping where strong walls occurred. Closely spaced shrinkage stope bins have given way to widely spaced bins, with electric and air slushers being used in the tops of stopes to transport the overbreak to the ore pass. Air-operated rubber-tired muckhaul units have been adapted to in-stope work. Where shrinkage stoping is used, broken ore is commonly moved to the shaft by track haulage using battery locomotives and one or two-ton side dump cars.

With the development of diesel haul units of less than 5-ft width, one Illinois company changed from shrinkage stope mining to ramp subleveling in veins, serving the loaders which traversed the sublevels and ramps with small diesel trucks carrying three to four tons. Output per manshift improved, with the elimination of labor-intensive timbering, chute building, and track work. Ventilation for the diesel equipment is usually handled by lines of woven plastic tubing. In shafts, bucket hoisting has been supplanted by skips with guides in all instances. In larger mines, crushers are installed over skip loading pockets at the shaft bottom, improving skip loading.

In bedded deposits, room-and-pillar patterns are used, with the widths of rooms governed by roof conditions. Roof bolting has supplanted wooden supports. Most equipment is rubber-tired and diesel-operated, including the muckhaul units which have buckets ranging in size from 1 to 5 yd and rubber-tired diesel trucks ranging in size from 3- to 18-ton capacity. Drilling is done by diesel-propelled jumbos in the bedded ore mines, but the jack-leg drills are still used in narrower working places and drifts. In multileveled ore bodies, haulage ramps on 12 to 15% grades connect the levels. Vertical raises are used to facilitate ventilation requirements. Most drilling uses tungsten carbide bits, or the throwaway type hardened steel bits. In blasting the trend is increasingly toward the use of ammonium nitrate-fuel-oil mixtures. Mine crews, supervisors, and mechanics are usually provided with diesel personnel vehicles to facilitate mobility.

Wherever widths of ore bodies, depths of overburden and the strength of the sidewalls permit, it is common practice to mine by open pit methods, as is the case for all mines now producing in South Africa. This optimizes the advantages to be gained by using lower-cost explosives, rubber-tire earthmoving equipment, and economical quarry bench mining methods.

Beneficiation

Most fluorspar must be upgraded for marketing. It is sold in a range of calcium fluoride contents, and the beneficiation techniques used are tailored to meet the character of the ores and the specifications for particular uses.

Metallurgical spar with a calcium fluoride content in the range of 75 to 85% is often produced by the hand-sorting of high grade lump crude ore, followed by crushing and screening to remove most of the —10-mesh fraction. In the case of ores of lower grade, and/or ores with relatively coarse interlocking of minerals, gravity processes of concentration are used for producing metspar based on the specific gravity of 3.2 for spar and less than 2.80 for most gangue minerals.

Heavy media cone and drum separators are particularly effective in the size range of 1½ x ³⁄₁₆ in., either for producing metallurgical gravel or for preconcentrating the crude ore for flotation feed. For the finer sizes the heavy media cyclone process is frequently used. The high tonnage capacity and low operating costs of heavy media methods give very satisfactory results. The "sink" can be sold as metspar, the "sands" for flotation feed, and the "float" frequently is marketed for road gravel and concrete aggregate. Ores as low as 14% of calcium fluoride are being preconcentrated to yield a flotation feed of 40% CaF_2 or more. Lead and zinc sulfides and barite, by reason of their high gravity, concentrate with the fluorspar to enrich the flotation feed in these valuable minerals. Many ores which would otherwise be too low grade to warrant mining and processing can be preconcentrated to acceptable flotation feed grade with a tailings loss of less than 12% of the CaF_2 in the crude ore. Washing plants are also used ahead of flotation to remove clay or wad (manganese oxides) in some areas.

Barite, a fairly common accessory mineral in fluorspar deposits, in most instances can be effectively separated from the fluorspar by flotation and made into a salable product.

As a consequence of the decreasing supply of natural metspar gravel, the agglomeration of fluorspar products by pelletizing and briquetting has expanded. Feed for agglomeration covers a variety of products such as gravel fines or screenings and various grades of flotation concentrates.

Ceramic and acid grades of fluorspar are produced by the froth flotation process, which has reached a high level of metallurgical efficiency. In many cases ceramic grades with a calcium fluoride content in the range of 90 to 96% can be made with good recovery from ores which otherwise would be difficult to concentrate to 97% CaF_2 acid-grade spar. Ore from the mine is crushed and ground to proper size, care being taken not to overgrind and cause fluorspar to be lost in the slimes. If sulfides are present they are floated off with xanthate collector in separate circuits ahead of the fluorspar, first the lead sulfide and then the zinc sulfide. Then all the easy-floating fluorspar is removed in a quick pass through a rougher flotation circuit and sent on to the cleaner circuit; the rougher tailing is then discarded. The middling product is reground to separate the more finely interlocked grains of fluorspar and gangue, and these are then separated in one or more cleaner circuits. The final products generally comprise an acid-grade concentrate and in some cases one or more concentrates of lower grade which are sold as ceramic grade or pelletized and sold as metallurgical grade. Fatty acids are used as collectors for the fluorspar. Quebracho or tannin is used to depress calcite and dolomite; sodium silicate to depress iron oxides and silica; and chromates, starch, and dextrin to reject barite. Cyanide is used to depress sulfides. Lime, caustic, or soda ash can be used for pH control. Flotation temperatures range from ambient to heating to 25 to 80°C.

A standard method for determination of calcium fluoride in fluorspar is being promulgated by ASTM under Designation E 815–81 wherein the sample is digested with nitric and perchloric acid and the fluorine is expelled by fuming. The residue is dissolved in dilute HCl, the solution made alkaline, and the calcium titrated with standard EDTA solution. Calcium present as carbonate is determined in a separate sample after extracting with dilute acetic acid and a correction for calcium fluoride, solubilized by dilute acetic acid digestion, is applied by determining the fluoride in the acetic acid extract by fluoride ion-selective electrode. The CaF_2 content is then calculated.

Neutron activation is used as an analytical method in determining calcium fluoride in ores and mill products having a content of less than 95%. The method is rapid, and is a particularly useful tool in analyzing ore samples and for mill control. The X-ray fluorescence analyzer is used to determine the abundance of other minerals occurring with the fluorspar such as barite, sphalerite, and galena.

Transportation

Most acid grade fluorspar in world markets is shipped in bulk by boat, rail, or truck in the form of damp filter cake containing about 8 to 10% moisture, because damp spar is easier to load and unload, and dust losses are minimized. This moisture is removed by heating in rotary drying kilns or other types of dryers before treating with sulfuric acid to make hydrofluoric acid because the fluorspar has to be practically bone dry when it goes into the acid reactors. Some acid spar is dried at the point of origin and shipped in covered hopper cars or tank trucks to consumers. A relatively small amount of acid grade spar is dried and bagged for shipment to purchasers of small quantities for specialty uses.

Metallurgical grade fluorspar is shipped as lump or gravel, in barges, ships, or railroad cars. Ceramic grades of fluorspar are usually marketed in bags; larger ceramic users, however, buy dried concentrates shipped in bulk by rail.

Markets, Production, and Consumption

Among market-economy countries, the eight principal producers in 1979 were, in descending order, Mexico, South Africa, France, Thailand, Spain, Italy, United Kingdom, and the US, each of which produced more than 100 kt. Total market-economy production was about 2.8 Mt. World production of all grades approached 4.6 Mt. The principal consuming countries in 1979 were the United States, the USSR, Japan, West Germany, the United Kingdom, Canada, Italy, and France. Because of the disparities in production vs. consumption, the principal importing countries in 1979 were the United States, Japan, the USSR, West Germany, and Canada. Major exporting countries were Mexico, South Africa, Spain, Thailand, Mongolia, France, and China.

The United States relies heavily on imports, especially of acid grade and metspar and does not produce enough ceramic grade to meet full requirements. In 1979, 369 279 t were mined and 322 650 t were treated to produce 96 253 t, compared to reported consumption of 1 030 086 t. Imports in 1979 amounted to 926 kt and declined about 15% to 784 kt in 1980. US consumption in 1980 was 861 kt, about 16% lower than the 1.03 Mt consumed in 1979. Figures of mined, treated, and finished production for 1980 were withheld by the US Bureau of Mines. World production in 1980 reached about 4.7 Mt, a modest increase over 1979.

In 1980, nearly 80% of the domestic US fluorspar production was mined and processed in Hardin and Pope counties, Illinois, in the mills of Ozark-Mahoning Co. and Inverness Company. Ozark's flotation mill, at Rosiclare, IL, is served by the Illinois Central Gulf railroad and by a barge loading facility on the Ohio River. Preconcentration by heavy media is done by Ozark-Mahoning adjacent to several bedded replacement mines northwest of Cave in Rock, IL, and at the new Knight shaft, west of Rosiclare. Metspar and flotation feed are produced at the heavy media separation facilities. In flotation, lead and zinc sulfide concentrates are produced in addition to acid grade fluorspar.

Inverness operates its principal flotation mill 5 miles north of Cave in Rock, adjacent to the No. 1 mine, the largest fluorspar mine in the US. Crude ore is preconcentrated by heavy media separation. The mill produces ceramic spar, lead and zinc sulfide concentrates, and a high grade barite concentrate. The smaller Crystal mill, located northwest of Cave in Rock, is closed. Concentrates are shipped by truck to rail-loading facilities at Rosiclare and Junction, IL, or to Cave in Rock, IL, for barge loading. Ore from Inverness' Spivey vein-mine in northern Hardin County is hauled to the No. 1 mill for treatment.

In Kentucky, Cerro Corp. constructed a heavy media and flotation plant in 1974, with a stated capacity of 60,000 stpy of acid grade flotation concentrate, at the Babb-Barnes prop-

erty north of Salem, KY. It is now owned by Frontier Spar, a subsidiary of Marathon Oil, and is idle. The flotation mill of Pennwalt Corp., near Mexico, KY, with a capacity of about 35,000 stpy of flotation products, was idled in 1973 following mine exhaustion and was subsequently briefly leased to Armco but is now idle. There are several small mines in both Kentucky and Illinois, whose operations are intermittent, that sell ore to the established mills. Drill-indicated ore on several properties in Kentucky is not now being produced.

In Colorado, Ozark-Mahoning Co. operated a flotation mill until late 1973 adjacent to its Northgate mine, one of the nation's largest, near Cowdrey. This mill, with a capacity of 50,000 stpy of acid grade spar, is now idle. At various times, Ozark has operated other vein mines in the area to supplement Northgate production.

Roberts Mining Co. processed ore from its Crystal Mountain mine near Darby, Montana, in a heavy-media plant, producing only metspar. Reynolds Metal Co. operates a flotation plant at Eagle Pass, Texas. For mill feed it uses ores and metallurgical screenings of Mexican origin. Small flotation mills, with short operating histories, have been operated in Arizona, New Mexico, Colorado, Utah, and Nevada. J. Irving Crowell at Beatty, NV produces metspar.

Briquetting presses are operated by Ozark-Mahoning Co. at Rosiclare, IL; Cametco Corp. at Duquesne, PA; Mercier Corp. at Dearborn, MI; and Oglebay-Norton Co., Pennwalt Corp., and Delhi Foundry Sand Co. at Brownsville, TX.

Flux bricks containing varying amounts of fluorspar and other additives, usually patented formulations, are produced by Cleveland Flux Co. in Cleveland, OH, and Allen Park, MI; by Mercier Corp. in Dearborn, MI; and by Glen-Gerry Shale Brick Corp. at Reading, PA.

Most of the metspar screenings used in briquettes and flux brick are imported from Mexico. The imported flotation concentrates used for briquetting are usually filter cake of medium moisture content and are always acid grade because of the lower tariff on imported material assaying over 97% CaF_2. Domestic flotation concentrates used in metspar briquettes are normally below acid grade and contain only enough CaF_2 to achieve acceptable grades.

Binders used in making roll-compacted briquets include molasses-lime mixtures (with self-curing properties), tall oil derivatives and lignin paper mill byproducts, the latter two requiring oven curing. Other binders have practical applications, both in the US and foreign areas. Sodium silicate was used in making disk pellets. Most of the flux bricks use portland cement as a binder.

Future Considerations and Trends

Fluorspar Substitutes in Metallurgical Use

A number of substitutes for the traditional metspar gravel of natural origin have been proposed and investigated from time to time (Buxton and Sandaluk, 1972). From the world-wide viewpoint, high grade sources of natural metspar are declining and most of the crude ores currently available tend to be of lower CaF_2 content and require flotation to separate the fluorspar from the other minerals in the ore. Rising fluorspar prices and shipping costs have stimulated the search for substitutes, as has the need to reduce fluoride air and water pollution at points of consumption. Investigations have taken three general courses: (1) making artificial metallurgical gravel by forming flotation concentrates into pellets and briquettes, with or without the admixture of natural gravel spar screenings; (2) developing substitute nonfluoride fluxes; and (3) making pellets from mixtures of fluorspar and substitute fluxes.

Steel company research groups and governmental agencies have examined various aluminum-bearing materials including bauxite and the "red mud" residue from the manufacture of alumina, dolomite, olivine, serpentine, manganese ores, ferromanganese slags and dusts, titanium ores such as ilmenite and natural ilmenite-hematite mixtures, borates (including borax, colemanite, and rasorite), soda ash, and various iron residues including mill scale and dust.

Mixtures of iron, aluminum, and calcium oxides are used as extenders for fluorspar, to reduce the poundage of fluorspar required per ton of steel produced. In the event that a serious shortage of fluorspar did develop, the work done to date indicates substitutes would be available.

Phosphate-Derived Fluorides

Natural phosphate rock contains approximately 3.5% fluorine as a component of the mineral fluorapatite. In phosphate processing, the fluorine volatilizes as silicon tetrafluoride, which hydrolizes to fluosilicic acid when the gas is passed through water scrubbers. Currently most of this acid is neutralized with lime. However, some fluosilicic acid is converted to alumi-

num fluoride and cyrolite (Steininger, 1972) and several plants in the US are recovering fluorine values in this fashion. Alcoa's plant in Fort Meade, FL, completed in 1970, converts fluosilicic acid to aluminum fluoride, and at Mulberry, FL, Kaiser Aluminum and Chemical Co. converts fluosilicic acid to sodium fluosilicate, which is converted to aluminum fluoride at Kaiser's plant at Chalmette, LA.

The quantity of fluorine present in phosphate rock deposits is enormous (Worl, et al., 1973). Current US identified reserves of phosphate rock are estimated to be 10.5 billion tons, which at 3.5% would contain approximately 370 million tons of fluorine, equivalent to about 740 million tons of fluorspar. In existing operations the quantity of fluorine which is recovered varies widely, but in general may be in the range of 25% to 35% of the amount present in the processed rock. According to Johnson, et al. (1973), if all the recoverable byproduct fluorine from phosphate rock processed in the US in 1968 had been available for domestic consumption, it would have supplied 18% of the total demand. Present high prices for fluorspar which increased 60% in one year's time, January 1979 to January 1980, have accelerated interest in fluosilicic acid.

Depletion and Duties

The depletion allowance is 22% for domestically mined fluorspar and 14% for foreign operations of US companies.

The duty on imported fluorspar, is $2.10 per long ton on fluorspar which assays 97.0% CaF_2 or more (acid grade), and is 13.5% ad valorem for all lower grades and ores, most of which are metallurgical grade.

The Federal Emergency Management Agency, through the General Services Administration (GSA), maintains a strategic stockpile of fluorspar. National defense stockpile objectives as of September 30, 1980 were 1,400,000 st acid grade and 1,700,000 st of metallurgical grade compared to an inventory of 895,983 st acid grade and 411,738 st metallurgical, a shortfall of 504,017 st and 1,288,262 st respectively.

Changes in Patterns of Fluorspar Consumption

In recent years there has been a trend in the aluminum industry toward lower consumption of fluorine salts per ton of metal produced. Aluminum companies are recovering and recycling fluorine values from pot linings and fumes, larger pots are being used which absorb proportionately less fluoride electrolyte, more aluminum fluoride and cryolite are being manufactured from fluorsilicic acid, and greater over-all operating efficiency is being achieved.

Looking ahead, even greater reductions may result from two developments announced by the Aluminum Co. of America. One is a patented process in which up to 99% of the fluoride values in fume and particulate material in the off-gas from the pot lines is recovered by adsorption on a fluidized bed of ordinary alumina which is subsequently used to make aluminum metal. The other is a process for making aluminum which requires no fluorides at all (Anon., 1973). In this system, alumina is reacted with chlorine, and the resulting aluminum chloride is electrolytically processed to yield aluminum metal and chlorine. This process is said to reduce electrical energy requirements by 30%, to be free of undesirable emissions, and if piloting is successful, may be used in new smelters.

Prior to the introduction and widespread adoption of the basic oxygen steel furnace (BOF), there had been a gradual decrease in consumption of fluorspar per ton of steel produced. With the arrival of the BOF, however, fluorspar consumption increased approximately two to three times above the consumption in basic open hearth furnaces. Use is growing of fluorspar concentrates of higher CaF_2 content, which permits closer control of the reactions in the furnace during the short heating cycle characteristic of the BOF process, and the introduction of smaller amounts of possible undesirable contaminants. Current average use is about six pounds of CaF_2 per ton of steel in the US.

Another new development in the steel industry is the bottom oxygen-blowing process which has been applied to both open hearth furnaces and oxygen converters. In both applications, provision is made for injecting hydrocarbon fuel, oxygen, and pulverized fluxes such as fluorspar and lime into the base of the steel-making vessel below the surface of the molten metal. It has been claimed that fluorspar consumption per ton of steel may be reduced by as much as 50% in addition to various other benefits. If this method becomes widely adopted, the requirement for lump metallurgical spar will drop and specifications will call for a finely ground spar, either ceramic or acid grade.

Over the years ahead, increasing industrialization around the world will lead to increased fluorspar production and consumption, but changes can be expected in unit consumption in accordance with new developments, the desire to cut costs, and in response to environmental controls.

Ecology

Environmental restrictions and controls are affecting the fluorspar industry. Meeting official standards will require additional investment and cause significant increases in cost of production.

The disposal of mill tailings creates a problem because even after impounding and clarification the liquid effluents may contain traces of chemicals that are in violation of environmental standards. The trace amount of fluoride ion concentration resulting from the natural solubility of calcium fluoride is itself of concern.

Dust emissions from drying and dry handling equipment can be controlled, and it is desirable from an economic standpoint to reduce the loss of valuable product in the form of dust, as well as for environmental control.

Cryolite

Natural cryolite (Na_3AlF_6) is a colorless mineral containing 54.3% fluorine, 12.8% aluminum, and 32.9% sodium. It has a hardness of 2.5, a specific gravity of 2.96, and crystallizes in the monoclinic system. Its mean index of refraction is about 1.339, which is close to that of water.

Cryolite has been found in commercial quantities only at one place in the world, Ivigtut, West Greenland, although small economically unimportant occurrences have been found in the St. Peter's Dome District near Pike's Peak in Colorado, and in the USSR, Spain, Canada, and Nigeria.

The Greenland deposit is a pegmatite in porphyritic granite in which the cryolite is accompanied by fluorspar, siderite, pyrite, arsenopyrite, galena, topaz, molybdenite, and a number of rare aluminum fluoride minerals. Approximately 90 different minerals have been found in the deposit, several of which have not been found elsewhere. The deposit lies on the shore of the Arsuk Fiord on the southwest coast of Greenland. It was worked by open pit and was mined out in 1962 (Maersk, 1973) after approximately a century of operation. Cryolite was stockpiled at Ivigtut for shipment to a concentrating plant in Copenhagen operated by Kryolitselskabet Oresund, which is partly owned by the Danish government. In this plant the crude ore was concentrated by flotation to a product containing 98 to 99% cryolite. For 100 years crude ore also was shipped to the United States for processing by Pennsalt Chemicals Corp., but this arrangement terminated in 1965.

Originally cryolite was used mainly in the production of soda, alum, and aluminum sulfate, but this eventually became unprofitable, and in 1889 the mineral assumed a new and important role as the molten bath in which alumina was dissolved for electrolytic reduction to aluminum metal by the Hall process. Demand for cryolite in the aluminum industry outstripped the natural supply and the gap was filled by synthetic cryolite manufactured from hydrofluoric acid, sodium carbonate, and aluminum hydrate. In the ceramic industry, cryolite is used as a whitener for enamels and an opacifier in glasses. It is also used in bonding grinding wheels and abrasives, and as an ingredient in welding rod coatings. Very finely ground cryolite is an active agent in some insecticide mixtures.

Acknowledgment

The authors appreciate valuable comments on the manuscript by Dr. B. L. Hodge of B. L. Hodge and Partners.

Bibliography and References

Anon., 1965, "Barytes and Fluorite Deposits of Turkey," Maden Tetkik Arama Enstit. Yayinl, No. 126, Ankara, 11 pp.

Anon., 1972, Annual Report, Lost River Mining Corp.

Anon., 1972a, "Progress in Modernizing Thailand's Fluorspar Industry," Industrial Minerals, No. 56, May, pp. 31–33.

Anon., 1973, "Alcoa Announces Development of Pollution-Free Aluminum Smelting Process," Engineering & Mining Journal, Vol. 174, No. 2, Feb., p. 30.

Anon., 1973a, "Trade and Trends in Fluorspar," Industrial Minerals, No. 64, June, pp. 23–31.

Anon., 1973b, "Thailand Flotation Mill Now," World Mining, Vol. 20, June, pp. 24–25.

Anon., 1978, "Samuk Enters the Major Fluorspar League," Industrial Minerals, No. 135, Dec., pp. 39–43.

Agricola, G., 1546, Bermannus Sive de Re Metallica; De Re Metallica, A. Hoover and H. Hoover, trans., Dover Publications, New York 466 pp.

Anderson, A.L., and Van Alstine, R.E., 1964, "Fluorspar," Mineral and Water Resources of Idaho, 88th Congress, 2nd Session, US Government Printing Office, Washington, DC, pp. 79–84.

Argall, G.O., Jr., 1949, "Fluorspar," in "Industrial Minerals of Colorado," Quarterly of the Colorado School of Mines, Vol. 44, No. 2, pp. 179–208.

Bauxton, F.M., and Sandaluk, P.A., 1972, "Fluorspar Substitutes in Steelmaking," reprint, American Iron and Steel Institute, Regional Technical Meeting, Pittsburgh, Nov. 9.

Baxter, J.W., et al., 1973, "A Geologic Excursion to Fluorspar Mines in Hardin and Pope Counties, Illinois," Guidebook Series II, Illinois State Geological Survey, 28 pp.

Chermette, A., 1950, "L'Exploitation du Spath-Fluor en France de 1938 á 1946," L'Echo des Mines et de la Metallurges, Vol. 427, No. 3, pp. 547–549.

Chermette, A., 1964–65, "Les Ressources du Mexique en Spath-Fluor," Mines et Metallurgie, Oct., pp. 467–469; Nov., pp. 519–521; Dec., pp. 571–574; Jan., pp. 25–27; Feb., pp. 77–79.

Chermette, A., 1972–1973, "Un Demi-Siècle de Spath-Fluor Français (1922–1972)," Mines et Metallurgie, Oct., pp. 179–182; Nov./Dec., pp. 201–204, 213; Jan./Feb., pp. 9–12, 14; Mar., pp. 8, 11; Apr., pp. 10–13; May, pp. 9–16.

Chermette, A., 1979, "Le Spath Fluor est a un Tournant," Mines et Metallurgie, No. 145, pp. 14–19 and No. 146, pp. 20–24.

Chesterman, C.W., 1966, "Fluorspar," Mineral Resources of California, Bulletin 191, California Div. of Mines and Geology, pp. 165–168.

Coope, B., 1978, "Fluorspar—Down But Not Out," Industrial Minerals, No. 125, Feb., pp. 39–66.

Cornwall, H.R., 1972, "Geology and Mineral Resources of Southern Nye County, Nevada," Bulletin 77, Nevada Bureau of Mines and Geology, 49 pp.

Dasch, M.D., 1964, "Fluorine," Mineral and Water Resources of Utah, Bulletin 74, Utah Geological and Mineralogical Survey, pp. 162–168.

Deans, T., et al., 1972, "Metasomatic Feldspar Rocks (Potash Fenites) Associated with the Fluoride Deposits and Carbonatites of Amba Dongar, Gujarat, India," Transactions, Sec. B, Institution of Mining & Metallurgy, Vol. 81, Bulletin 783, p. B6.

Dunham, K.C., 1952, "Fluorspar," Memoir, Special Report on Mineral Research, Geological Survey of Great Britain, Vol. 4, 143 pp.

Elevatorski, E.A., 1968, "California Fluorspar," Mineral Information Service, State of California, Vol. 21, No. 9, pp. 127–130.

Elevatorski, E.A., 1971, "Arizona Fluorspar," Arizona Dept. of Mineral Resources, 51 pp.

Ford, T.D., and Ineson, P.R., 1971, "The Fluorspar Potential of the Derbyshire Ore Field," Transactions, Sec. B, Institution of Mining and Metallurgy, Vol. 80, pp. B185–205.

Funnell, J.E., and Wolff, E.J., 1964, "Fluorspar (Fluorite)," Compendium on Nonmetallic Minerals of Arizona, prepared for Arizona Public Service Co. by Southwest Research Institute, pp. 105–114.

Gardner, L.S., and Smith, R.M., 1965, "Fluorspar Deposits of Thailand," Report of Investigation No. 10, Dept. of Minerals Resources, Bangkok, 42 pp.

Gillerman, E., 1953, "Fluorspar Deposits of the Eagle Mountains, Trans-Pecos Texas," Bulletin 987, US Geological Survey, 98 pp.

Goddard, E.N., 1966, "Geologic Map and Sections of the Zuni Mountains Fluorspar District, Valencia County, New Mexico," Map I-454, Miscellaneous Geologic Investigations, US Geological Survey.

Gossling, H.H., 1972, "A Review of the World's Fluorspar Industry, with Particular Reference to South Africa," Report No. 1424, National Institute of Metallurgy, Johannesburg, 30 pp.

Gossling, H.H., 1978, "Fluorspar, 1973–1980: A Commodity Profile," Report No. 3, Mineral Bureau, Dept. of Mines, Republic of South Africa, p. 36.

Grogan, R.M., and Bradbury, J.C., 1967, "Origin of the Stratiform Fluorite Deposits in Southern Illinois," Genesis of Stratiform Lead-Zinc-Barite-Fluorite Deposits, Monograph 3, The Economic Geology Publishing Co., pp. 40–51.

Grogan, R.M., and Bradbury, J.C., 1968, "Fluorite-Zinc-Lead Deposits of the Illinois-Kentucky Mining District," Ore Deposits of the United States, 1933–1967, Vol. 1, J.D. Ridge, ed., AIME, New York, pp. 370–399.

Guccione, E., 1972, "What's Going on in the Fluorspar Industry," Engineering & Mining Journal, Vol. 173, Dec., pp. 64–72.

Hodge, B.L., 1970, "The U K Fluorspar Industry and Its Basis," Industrial Minerals, No. 31, Apr., pp. 23–37.

Hodge, B.L., 1973, "World Fluorspar Development, Part 1," Industrial Minerals, No. 68, May, pp. 9–25.

Hodge, B.L., 1973a, "World Fluorspar Developments: Part 2," Industrial Minerals, No. 69, June, pp. 9–21.

Hodge, B.L., 1981, "Fluorspar," Mining Annual Review, 1981, pp. 116–117.

Horton, R.C., 1961, "An Inventory of Fluorspar Occurrences in Nevada," Report 1, Nevada Bureau of Mines, 31 pp.

Horton, R.C., 1962, "Fluorspar Occurrences in Nevada," Nevada Bureau of Mines, Map 3.

Horton, R.C., 1964, "Fluorspar," Mineral and Water Resources of Nevada, 88th Congress, 2nd Session, US Government Printing Office, Washington, DC, pp. 198–202.

Jee, J.M., and Kye, J., 1971, "Report on the Fluorite Deposits of Korea," Bulletin No. 13, Geological Survey of Korea, pp. 7–368 (English Abstract).

Jewell, W.B., 1947, "Barite, Fluorite, Galena, Sphalerite Veins of Middle Tennessee," Bulletin 51, Tennessee Div. of Geology, 114 pp.

Johnson, R.C., et al., 1973, "Economic Availability of Byproduct Fluorine in the United States," Information Circular 8566, US Bureau of Mines, 97 pp.

Jones, W.R., and Wolter, F.J., 1973, "Chemical Markets for Hydrofluoric Acid," Preprint No. 73–H–32, Society of Mining Engineers of AIME, SME Fall Meeting, Pittsburgh, Sep.

Kim, H., et al., 1972, "Mineral Requirements for Korea's Industrialization," Korean Institute of Mining, pp. 80–84.

Kostick, D.S., and De Filippo, R.J., 1980, "Fluorspar," Preprint, 1978–1979, US Bureau of Mines, 17 pp.

Liddy, J.C., 1971, "Fluorspar in Australia," Australian Mining, Jan., pp. 34–38.

MacMillan, R.T., 1970, "Fluorine," Mineral Facts and Problems, Bulletin 650, US Bureau of Mines, pp. 989–1000.

Maersk, B., 1973, "Cryolite Concentrator in Copenhagen," World Mining, Vol. 26, No. 3, Mar., pp. 60–63.

McAnulty, W.N., 1970, "Evaluation of Fluorspar Deposits," Preprint 70–S–63, Society of Mining Engineers, AIME Annual Meeting, Denver, Feb.

Northholt, A.J.G., and Highley, D.E., 1971, "Fluorspar," Mineral Dossier No. 1, Mineral Resources Consultative Committee, Institute of Geological Sciences, London, 31 pp.

Ortel, M.K., 1966, "Fluorspar," South African National Resources Development Council, Dept. of Planning, Vol. 5, 31 pp.

Papke, K.G., 1979, "Fluorspar in Nevada," Bulletin 93, Nevada Bureau of Mines and Geology, 77 pp.

Peters, W.C., 1958, "Geologic Characteristics of Fluorspar Deposits in the Western United States," Economic Geology, Vol. 53, pp. 663–688.

Rothrock, H.E., et al., 1946, "Fluorspar Resources of New Mexico," Bulletin 21, New Mexico Bureau of Mines and Mineral Resources, 245 pp.

Sahinen, U.M., 1962, "Fluorspar Deposits in Montana," Bulletin 28, Montana Bureau of Mines and Geology, 38 pp.

Sheppard, R.A., and Gude, A.J., 1970, "Authigenic Fluorite in Pliocene Lacustrine Rocks Near Rome, Malheur County, Oregon," In Geological Survey Research 1969, Professional Paper 650-D, US Geological Survey, pp. D69–D74.

Snyder, K.D., 1978, "Geology of the Bayhorse Fluorite Deposit, Custer County, Idaho," Economic Geology, Vol. 73, No. 2, March-April, pp. 207–214.

Spada, A., 1969, "Il Giacimento de Fluorite e Baritina Esalativo-sedimentario in 'Facies' Lacustre, Intercalato nei Sedimenti Piroclastici della Zona di Castel Giuliano, in Province di Roma," Industria Min., Vol. 20, pp. 501–518.

Staatz, M.H., and Osterwalld, F.W., 1959, "Geology of the Thomas Range Fluorspar District, Juab County, Utah," Bulletin 1069, US Geological Survey, 97 pp.

Steininger, E., 1972, "Making Fluorine Compounds from Waste Fluosilicic Acid," Engineering & Mining Journal, Vol. 173, No. 12, pp. 73–75.

Tabor, J.W., 1953, "Montana's Crystal Mountain Fluorspar Deposit is Big and High Grade," Mining World, Vol. 15, No. 7, pp. 43–46.

Thurston, W.R., et al., 1954, "Fluorspar Deposits of Utah," Bulletin 1005, US Geological Survey, 53 pp.

Van Alstine, R.E., 1964, "Fluorspar," Mineral and Water Resources of Colorado, 88th Congress, 2nd Session, US Government Printing Office, Washington, DC, pp. 159–165.

Van Alstine, R.E., 1965, "Fluorspar," in Mineral and Water Resources of New Mexico, Bulletin 87, New Mexico Bureau of Mines and Mineral Resources, pp. 260–267.

Van Alstine, R.E., 1969, "Fluorspar," in Mineral and Water Resources of Arizona, Bulletin 180, Arizona Bureau of Mines, pp. 348–357.

Van Alstine, R.E., and Schruben, P.G., 1980, "Fluorspar Resources of Africa," Bulletin 1487, US Geological Survey, 25 pp.

Weller, J.M., et al., 1952, "Geology of the Fluorspar Deposits of Illinois," Bulletin 76, Illinois State Geological Survey, 147 pp.

Wood, H.B., 1971, "Fluorspar and Cryolite," *Minerals Yearbook*, US Bureau of Mines, pp. 517–530.

Wood, H.B., 1972, "Fluorspar," *Engineering & Mining Journal,* Vol. 173, Mar., p. 152.

Worl, R.G., et al., 1973, "Fluorine," *United States Mineral Resources,* Professional Paper 820, US Geological Survey, pp. 223–235.

Zijl, P.J. van, 1962, "The Geology, Structure, and Petrology of the Alkaline Intrusions of Kalkfeld and Okorusu and the Invaded Damara Rocks," *Aunale Univ. Stellenbosch,* Ser. A., Vol. 37, No. 4, pp. 237–346.

Zurowski, M., 1972, "Barite-Fluorite Deposits of Lake Ainslie—An Appraisal From an Economic Viewpoint," *Transactions,* Canadian Institute of Mining & Metallurgy, Vol. 75, pp. 318–321.

Glauconite

Original by FRANK J. MARKEWICZ *

and

WILLIAM LODDING †

Revised by JOHN HOWER ‡

Greensand, greensand marl, and green earth are names given to sediments rich in the bluish green to greenish black mineral known as glauconite by the mineralogist. The word glauconite is from the Greek word *glaukos,* meaning bluish green. The term "greensand" as a rock name for a glauconite-bearing sediment is more appropriate than "greensand marl," a term that has been doggedly perpetuated in the literature.

Because of its potash and phosphate content, greensand was dug and marketed as a fertilizer and soil conditioner for more than 100 years. The advent of prepared fertilizers with adjustable nutrient ratios led to the decline of greensand for agricultural application. The material has since been recognized for use in water treatment. Unfortunately, in spite of large reserves and worldwide distribution, the mineral has not been utilized to any significant commercial extent because no major application has been found for a substance with its chemical composition and properties. This lack is probably due to a paucity of research on its potential commercial application.

Extraction of potash received considerable attention during and just after World War I. Because of relatively high extraction costs and generally low potash content (up to 8%), glauconite lost its appeal as a source of this commodity.

Historical Background

Greensand was used as a fertilizer in New Jersey in the latter part of the 1700s. During the early 1800s its use became more common; applications of up to 100 tons per acre were sometimes made, although recommendations for agricultural use suggested 20 to 50 tons per

* Acting State Geologist, New Jersey Geological Survey, Trenton, NJ.

† Formerly of Rutgers University, New Brunswick, NJ; now deceased.

‡ University of Illinois, Urbana, IL.

acre (Tedrow, 1957). Many crops, especially the forage type, were said to improve with greensand application; however, because of slow release of potash, large quantities were required. Certain greensands that contain sulfur and sulfide minerals are harmful to plant growth, and these were classified as "poison," "burning," or "black marls." The availability of higher-grade potash salts from other mineral sources, and the manufacture of prepared fertilizers, displaced the agricultural use of greensand during the later 1800s.

During the mid-1800s the domestic greensand industry, centered in a small section of the eastern United States, grossed more than $500,000 per year. Toward the end of the century, annual production had dwindled to less than $100,000. By 1910 there were only six or eight greensand producers, grossing less than $5000 (Tyler, 1934). There was a small revival in the industry during World War I because of the curtailment of foreign potash, especially from Germany.

During the later 1940s and early 1950s greensand was again recommended as a food nutrient for plants and farm crops. Agronomic studies discussed its potential as a soil additive that gradually releases potash and many trace-element nutrients essential for plant growth (Tedrow, 1957). Greensand was sold with the idea that it would condition soil and absorb and hold water while its base-exchange properties would release trace elements.

For a short time glauconite was utilized in certain parts of New Jersey as a binding additive in the brick industry, and in the 1800s for making green glass (Cook, 1868).

In the early 1900s the base-exchange property of glauconite was recognized for water treatment, and the mineral gained acceptance as a water softener. Mansfield (1922) does not mention base-exchange; however, the base exchange phenomenon was known in 1916 or earlier. From 1916 through 1922, several patents for the use of glauconite as a water-softening agent were granted. A method was also patented for treating greensand to improve it for water softening and ready regeneration with common salt brine (Borrowman, 1920; Spencer, 1924; Kriegsheim and Vaughan, 1930).

Treated glauconite, on contact with water containing magnesia or lime, takes up the magnesium or calcium ions and releases sodium ions. This exchange is limited to the outer surface of glauconite grains, and when all the surfaces have absorbed their capacitive limit, the grains must be regenerated. Regeneration, simply stated, consists of treating or "backwashing" the glauconite charge with a common salt solution, which replaces the hard-water elements with sodium, thus reviving the glauconite. The process has become more sophisticated due to competition by the different companies in the water-softening business.

Greensand products for water softening generally consisted of several different grades, depending on the particular treatment the glauconite was given during processing. The standard greensand water softener was produced from natural glauconite after being washed and classified. Its characteristics for water softening are given in Table 1.

To increase its water-softening capacity, glauconite was treated by a process that made it more porous. Although most of the specifications remained the same as those of the washed greensand shown in Table 1, the porosity changed from 2–3% to 11–13%, and the exchange capacity as $CaCO_3$ from 2800–3000 grains to 3800–4500 grains per cu ft; maximum permissible raw water turbidity dropped from 10 to 5–7 ppm, and the maximum permissible iron in raw water decreased from 2.5 to 1.5 ppm. By increasing the glauconite porosity even more, the exchange capacity was also increased, with a corresponding change in some of the other characteristics shown previously. This special porosity process increased the salt requirement for regeneration from 1.4 to 2.5 lb per cu ft. Another method of processing greensand involved heating glauconite to a temperature of approximately 200° to 400°C to drive off water. After cooling it was treated with a salt brine, which made a more efficient greensand product because the softened water did not become cloudy.

During the later 1940s, greensand was displaced as a water-softening agent by phenol formaldehyde resin, which has twice the softening capacity, is not affected by water temperatures over 105°F, and requires the same amount of salt for regeneration. After 1950, phenol formaldehyde resin was displaced by styrene resins, which have even higher water-softening capacity, yet require no more salt for regeneration.

Current Use

Present-day use of glauconite is limited to two general applications: water treatment and soil conditioning. The industry is localized in the coastal plain of New Jersey, where greensand is extracted from Cretaceous and Tertiary sediments. A small amount of greensand for soil conditioning was dug in Maryland, but this operation was terminated in 1970, leaving New Jersey the sole producer in the United States.

TABLE 1—Greensand in Water Softening

Porosity, %	2 to 3
Effective size, mm	0.30 to 0.33
Uniformity coefficient	1.40 to 1.55
Screen analysis, mesh	18 to 60
Attrition loss per annum, %	2
Weight per cu ft, air-dried, lb	85
Recommended pH operating range	6.6 to 8.3
Maximum permissible temperature of raw water, °F	105
Maximum permissible turbidity in raw water, ppm	10
Maximum permissible iron in raw water as Fe, ppm	2.5
Bed expansion during backwash, %	30 to 35
Exchange capacity as $CaCO_3$, grains per cu ft	2800 to 3000
Salt requirement, lb per cu ft	1.4
Time required for regeneration in water softener, min	40
Recommended maximum softening rate, gpm per sq ft bed area	5
Recommended wash rate, gpm per sq ft bed area	7
Recommended minimum bed depth, ft-in.	2.5
Recommended maximum bed depth, ft	6

Data from New Jersey Geological Survey.

In water treatment, processed greensand is used to remove soluble iron and/or manganese salts. It is called manganese greensand "zeolite" as manufactured by the Inversand Co., Div. of Hungerford & Terry, Inc. The purple to almost black "zeolite" is used in two processes. One, rather old, involves utilizing it as a filter, regenerating it intermittently with a weak solution of potassium permanganate after an exchange cycle in which approximately 750 grains of iron per cu ft or 400 grains of manganese per cu ft has been removed.

A process developed and patented by Hungerford & Terry, Inc. about 1960 has replaced the older intermittent-regeneration process and is called "continuous regeneration" or "CR." Potassium permanganate is injected directly into the water ahead of the manganese oxide glauconite, which does not require an intermittent regeneration, only an intermittent wash. This process utilizes potassium permanganate more efficiently than the older process and has gained favor because of its ability to reduce the iron in water to extremely minute amounts, frequently to less than 10 parts per billion. When a water supply contains very little iron, but significant quantities of manganese, then the old IR, "intermittent regeneration," process is advantageously used.

For home and garden use, greensand is recommended as a mulch; top dressing mixture; and additive to soil for gardens, potted plants, and vegetable starting plots. The usual application is from 1 to 10 lb per 100 sq ft, although larger amounts may be applied depending on the nature of the soil. It is sold in bulk or bagged in 60-lb plastic bags at Sewell, NJ, by the Zeolite Chemical Co., Div. of Hungerford & Terry, Inc.

Geologic Occurrence and Character

Glauconite occurs in rocks ranging from Precambrian to Recent in age; however, when the terms glauconite greensand or greensand are used, a Tertiary or Cretaceous age is generally implied. The term greensand denotes an unconsolidated glauconite-rich sand. Glauconite frequently forms the major constituent in many sandy, silty, or even clayey formations of the Tertiary and Cretaceous. Greensand can occur as a solid massive bed, as disseminated grains, as glauconite-rich masses and clots, or as fillings in fossil worm tubes or in foraminifera. Brown ovoid phosphatic fecal pellets are common as accessory grains in greensand deposits.

Fresh glauconite is typically green to dark

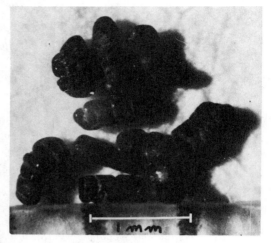

FIG. 1—*Vermiform pellets of glauconite. Note the elongated and segmented shape. X-ray diffraction and thin-section studies indicate that the segments are books of glauconite layers (see Fig. 3). The pellet at the far right has a longitudinal line dividing a more solid, perhaps more recently crystallized, portion from a rougher, perhaps older portion (epitaxial crystal growth?)* (*Tapper and Fanning, 1968*).

green in color and polylobate to rounded or tabular in shape. Irregularly shaped, vermiform to tabular sutured grains are usually authigenic in origin, whereas well-rounded to ovoid, well-polished grains found in some formations are detrital or second-generation (Figs. 1–4). Glau-

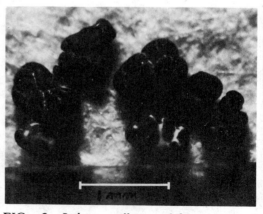

FIG. 2—*Lobate pellets exhibiting typical rounded botryoidal shape. Lobate pellets in the Maryland deposits are more numerous and generally larger than the vermiform and also have a different internal morphology* (*Tapper and Fanning, 1968*).

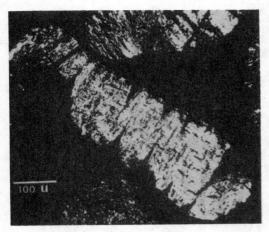

FIG. 3—*Longitudinal section of vermiform pellet showing glauconite layers crossing the pellet. (Thin section viewed with crossed nicols.) Note the appearance of a rectangular "crystal" outline within the pellet just above the center of the photograph. A portion of another pellet with a gross micaceous internal morphology is at the top (Tapper and Fanning, 1968).*

conite imparts a greenish color to the formation in which it occurs, depending on the amount present.

The greensand formations of New Jersey are well known and have long been utilized. So far as known, they are the only commercially productive strata in the United States today. Glauconite occurs as an accessory mineral in many of the New Jersey coastal plain formations, but greensand, as such, is best developed in two

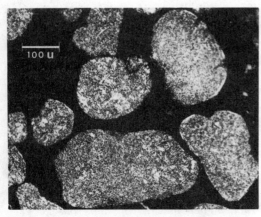

FIG. 4—*Thin section, as viewed under crossed nicols, showing the "grainy" internal morphology that appears to be characteristic of the lobate pellets (Tapper and Fanning, 1968).*

units, the Navesink Formation of Late Cretaceous age and the Hornerstown Formation of Early Tertiary age. Both of these formations are inappropriately termed "marls" on the geologic map of New Jersey, and in Bulletin 50, "The Geology of New Jersey" (Lewis and Kummel, 1940). They crop out in a northeast-trending belt that extends across New Jersey from the vicinity of Sandy Hook to Delaware Bay near Salem. These formations or their equivalents extend into Delaware and beyond, but in general the glauconite content of the strata and the potash content of the glauconite decrease southward. In addition, both formations thin somewhat toward the southwest, and there are local bedding variations along the strike. At the north end in New Jersey, the Hornerstown rests on the Red Bank-Tinton Formation; at the south end, perhaps owing to nondeposition of the Red Bank, it lies directly on the Navesink Formation.

Hornerstown Formation

The Hornerstown Formation is a green medium-grained glauconite sand with a bright green clay cement and a little quartz sand. Locally it contains a few thin brown to reddish brown clayey or indurated limonitic bands. Thickness ranges from 15 to 30 ft. Dip is about 20 ft per mile to the southeast.

Navesink Formation

The Navesink Formation is a massive dark greenish-gray, medium-grained, poorly sorted glauconite sand, with varying amounts of quartz sand. It contains some calcareous clay toward the top, and limonitic bands or masses locally. The thickness ranges from 25 to 50 ft. The formation dips about 20 ft per mile to the southeast.

Table 2 lists some of the major greensand formations in the Coastal Plain of the United States.

Origin of Glauconite

The genesis of glauconite has been a puzzle for a long time, but facts are emerging that permit establishing a workable theory. The process now widely accepted (Hower, 1961; Ehlmann et al., 1963; Triplehorn, 1966; Grim, 1968; Bailey and Atherton, 1969; Zumpe, 1971; Odin, 1971; Odin and Giresse, 1972; Robert; 1972; Shutov et al., 1972) requires the presence of montmorillonite in a shallow marine environment (water depths 100 to 300 m), and very slow rates of sedimentation. Montmorillonite

TABLE 2—Major Greensand Formations of the United States

State	Formation	Age	Thickness, Ft
New Jersey	Hornerstown	Eocene	15 to 30
	Navesink	Cretaceous	25 to 50
Delaware	Aquia	Eocene	
Maryland	Aquia	Eocene	
	Nanjemoy	Eocene	20 to 30
Virginia	Aquia	Eocene	
	Nanjemoy	Eocene	
Alabama	Lisbon	Eocene	
	Eutaw	Cretaceous	
Tennessee	McNairy (?)	Cretaceous	
Mississippi	Winona	Eocene	
	Eutaw	Cretaceous	
Texas	Weches	Eocene	25+
	Reklaw	Eocene	
	Cook Mountain	Eocene	
	Kincaid	Paleocene	

Data from state geological surveys and US Geological Survey.

is converted to glauconite by substitution of Fe^{+3}, Fe^{+2}, and Mg^{+2} for Al^{+3} in the octahedral layer and the consequent fixation of K^+. The resulting mineral is a mixed-layer 10 Å hydrated clay. The 10 Å potassium-rich layers are those which have attained a sufficiently high negative charge (because of the substitution of Mg^{+2} and Fe^{+2} for Al^{+3}) to fix K^+ and dehydrate. Aluminum ions, moving out of the octahedral layer, can form new montmorillonite on the surface of the potassium-iron-enriched globules, continuing the process of accretion. Most of the abundant ferric iron and silicon carried in solution by freshwater are chemically precipitated as hydroxide gels in a brackish environment (Jeans, 1971) and become available for glauconitization.

A suite showing alteration from (1) bleached clear biotite mica containing dark cores and swelled peripheral edges to (2) well expanded light olive-colored altered hydromica grains to (3) light green vermiform peripherally sutured early-stage glauconite has been observed in drill cuttings from several New Jersey coastal plain formations. The mica-glauconite diagenesis reported by Galliher (1939), Takahashi (1939), and Takahashi and Yagi (1929) finds support in these observations. Growth of the globules is limited by currents, which tend to move the newly formed glauconite pellets from areas of formation to those of deposition and burial. Diagenesis continues with the general substitution of hydrated layers by additional potassium, reducing the amount of mixed-layer material, and increasing the 10Å-mica component of mature glauconite.

These processes can adequately explain the formation of iron-potassium-silicate globules in a marine environment, and the accumulation of greensand strata of considerable thickness and extent. Glauconite has been found inside marine microfossils (foraminifera) and, occasionally, derived from fecal pellets (Haven and Morales-Alamo, 1968; Lamboy, 1967, 1968). The time of formation of various glauconites in the New Jersey and Maryland coastal plain was recently determined by K/Ar analysis to be very near 61.1 million years (Owens and Sohl, 1973).

Greensand Composition and Analyses

Most greensand deposits contain, in addition to glauconite, materials such as quartz, mica, pyrite, some heavy minerals, and calcium carbonate in the form of shell material or as a cement derived from marine organisms. Iron oxides, phosphatic nodules, and fecal pellets are common locally. Skeletal remains of marine vertebrates are occasionally found in the greensand deposits of southern New Jersey.

Glauconite grains range in size from 20 to 100 mesh. The largest percentage by weight is in the 20 to 40-mesh size. Grains of authigenic origin are commonly coarse. Many detrital grains are smooth and rounded, and easily pass through a 100-mesh sieve. Clay-size glauconite occasionally fills the interstices of coarse-grained sediments.

Glauconite is a hydrous iron potassium silicate, containing varying amounts of aluminum, magnesium, sodium, and trace elements such as beryllium, cobalt, chromium, nickel, molybdenum, vanadium, titanium, and uranium. Greensand analyses from ten localities in the United States are listed in Table 3.

The composition of glauconites was investi-

TABLE 3—Greensand Analyses (%)

	1	2	3	4	5	6	7	8	9	10
Silica (SiO_2)	51.83	46.28	63.55	77.93	77.80	73.00	35.18	53.61	30.00	36.44
Alumina (Al_2O_3)	6.23	5.42	4.41	7.48	7.86	9.60	5.30	9.56	14.11	29.02
Iron Oxide (Fe_2O_3)	20.08	23.64	15.74	3.54	5.42	7.20	17.35	23.04	25.09	13.36
Lime (CaO)	0.52	1.10	0.48	2.39	2.12	2.88	16.00	1.39	10.80	2.72
Magensia (MgO)	3.66	3.57	2.35	1.01	0.82	1.55	trace	2.87	3.46	1.88
Potash (K_2O)	6.60	7.50	6.24	2.30	3.60	3.30	1.69	3.49	0.80	—
Soda (Na_2O)	0.76	0.83	0.03	0.12	—	—	1.39	0.42	4.41	—
Phosphorus (P_2O_5)	0.31	0.52	0.19	0.22	—	—	3.30	—	0.44	—
Carbonic acid	—	—	—	—	—	—	8.00	—	—	—
Ignition loss	10.34	10.75	6.91	4.83	2.26	2.40	10.10	5.96	—	15.59

[1] Hornerstown greensand, Sewell, NJ (NJ Geological Survey).
[2] Navesink greensand, Sewell, NJ (NJ Geological Survey).
[3] Nanjemoy Formation, Maryland (Grim, 1968).
[4] Aquia Formation, Maryland (Glaser, 1971).
[5] Aquia Formation, Hop Yard, Rappahannock River, VA (Clark, 1912; Gildersleeve, 1942).
[6] Nanjemoy Formation, Woodstock, VA (Clark, 1912; Gildersleeve, 1942).
[7] Lower Eocene greensand, Gas Ridge anticline, Texas (Jones, 1936).
[8] Glauconite, McNairy County, TN.
[9] Weches Formation, Houston County, Texas (Fisher, 1965).
[10] Winona Formation, Montgomery County, MS.

gated by Foster (1969), who computed atomic ratios and layer charges for 32 samples from 12 countries. Table 4 shows the compositional range of these glauconites.

In the mica structure, according to Grim (1968), two silica tetrahedral sheets face one central octahedral sheet. The tips of the tetrahedra point toward the center unit, and the three sheets are combined into a single layer, with a suitable replacement of OH and O. Up to 25% of the silicons are replaced by aluminum, and the resultant charge deficiency is balanced by K-ions. In glauconite, aluminum can substitute 4.2 to 14.3% of silicon in the tetrahedral sheets. Some of the charge deficiency is balanced by Fe^{+2} and Mg^{+2} ions replacing Fe^{+3} and Al^{+3} ions in the octahedral sheet. Most glauconites are not pure dioctahedral micas, but a mixture of 10Å micas and 14Å expandable-lattice clays (Burst, 1958; Cimbalnikova, 1971).

Like other layer minerals, glauconite has the capacity to absorb ions from solutions. The exchangeable sites are on the outside of the silica-alumina-iron framework, and the exchange reaction generally does not affect the glauconite structure. Both cations and anions are exchangeable, but not much information is available on the latter. Ion exchange is important in chemical separations, water softening, and properties of soil (both agricultural and engineering). It is usually expressed in milliequivalents per 100 g; thus a typical cation exchange capacity for glauconite is approximately 20 milliequivalents per 100 g.

The compositional relationship of glauconite with other layer silicates is illustrated in the ternary plot by Yoder and Eugster (1955), Fig. 5. The exterior shapes of typical glauconite grains are shown in Figs. 1 and 2, and the internal morphology in Figs. 3 and 4.

TABLE 4—Compositional Range of Glauconites (%)

SiO_2	46.9-52.9
Al_2O_3	5.8-15.2
Fe_2O_3	9.3-24.1
FeO	1.0-6.3
MgO	2.3-4.6
CaO	Traces-1.9
Na_2O	Traces-1.6
K_2O	5.1-9.3
TiO_2	0 -1.8
H_2O	4.3-7.2

Source: Foster, 1969.

Purification of Greensand

Magnetic Susceptibility

Glauconite has marked magnetic susceptibility; magnetic separation is, therefore, a commonly used method to separate it from impurities. With a Frantz Isodynamic separator the following settings gave a clean separation of glauconite from quartz, coprolites, pyrite, and calcite particles:

side slope	20°
forward slope	15°
current	0.50 amp
mass magnetic susceptibility	$(K_m) = 25 \times 10^{-6} \pm 5$

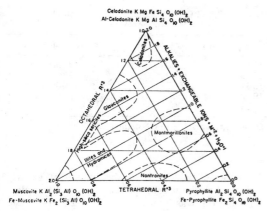

FIG. 5—*The relationships of dioctahedral mica-type phases, with fields indicated in which natural clay-mineral compositions fall (Yoder and Eugster, 1955).*

Three steps of medium-intensity magnetic separation, preceded by washing and removal of the +30, −200-mesh fractions, resulted in a purified glauconite.

Specific Gravity

The specific gravity of glauconites ranges widely, depending on the abundance of mixed-layer minerals and K_2O, the degree of substitutions in the tetrahedral and octahedral layers, and the state of weathering. Shutov et al. (1972) reported the results of careful fractionation of purified glauconites by means of a density column, which permitted separation in heavy liquids in steps of 0.020 ± 0.001 g per cc. The gravity spectra obtained from glauconites of various geologic ages and provenances are summarized in Table 5.

The wide range of specific gravities of glauconites limits heavy-liquid separation as a purification method. It can be used on some greensands with good results to separate glauconite mixtures of different provenances and different stages of diagenesis.

Mining and Treatment

Most greensand beds are unconsolidated sediments. Various adaptations of open-pit extraction have been utilized. These methods have ranged from pick and shovel in the earliest days to crane-operated jaw buckets, draglines, and hydraulicking. At Hungerford & Terry's Inversand operation in Sewell, NJ, which is the only commercially operating greensand company in the United States (perhaps in the free world), the hydraulicking method is used on the Hornerstown and Navesink Formations. The lower Hornerstown Formation, which forms the upper part of the deposit, is approximately 15 to 20 ft thick. Below this are 10 to 15 ft of nearly pure glauconite belonging to the Navesink Formation. After the beds are flushed with a high-pressure water jet, the loosened greensand is suction-pumped to a collecting tank. From this it flows through a complicated piping system containing special classifying and washing apparatus. After a thorough washing, the greensand is treated with chemicals such as aluminum sulfate, sodium silicate, sodium aluminate, and, for some applications, caustic soda and phosphoric acid. This treatment forms a very durable greensand having a high exchange capacity. At the Inversand operation the major application of treated greensand is for the removal of iron, manganese, and sulfide from water. Several grades of greensand are dried and bagged for shipment.

Domestic Production

New Jersey

In the late 1860s almost a million tons of greensand was dug every year for use as fer-

TABLE 5—Localities, Ages, and Specific Gravities of Glauconites

Greensand Locality	Mode, G per Cc	Range
California, Pacific, Recent	2.35	2.32-2.50
Akatosk trench, Pacific, Recent	2.68	2.46-2.78
Russian plateau, Tertiary	2.66	2.54-2.76
Baltic region, Cretaceous	2.68	2.54-2.76
Caucasus, Cretaceous	2.83	2.70-2.86
Basin of Laba, USSR, Jurassic	2.81	2.74-2.84
Baltic region, Ordovician	2.88	2.80-2.92
Pachelma, Precambrian	2.62	2.50-2.70
Ural, Precambrian	2.72	2.58-2.74
Ural, Sinian	2.71	2.66-2.76
Olenek, Sinian	2.70	2.66-2.74

Source: Shutov et al., 1972.

tilizer. In 1855 it brought 7¢ a bushel, and in 1877 it was selling for 60¢ a ton at the pit. Reports indicate that production was principally from New Jersey. By the 1870s it had dropped to less than 100,000 tons. Toward the turn of the century, demand for greensand improved, but in 1908 less than 10,000 tons was produced, at a total value of only $3500. The number of producers dropped from 13 in 1908 to 4 in 1912. The use of greensand for water softening in the early 1920s revived the industry. Table 6 shows tonnage and value, 1922 to 1951.

During 1926 the Inversand Co. started operations near Sewell, NJ. In the late 1940s the National Soil Conservation Co. started operations at Medford, NJ. The company produced greensand at this locality until the early 1960s. Since 1963 greensand production has been about 2000 tpy. Table 7 shows production for water treatment and agricultural uses.

Alabama

The only known commercial utilization of greensand in Alabama was in the production of an elixir made by passing water through the sands of the Lisbon Formation of Choctaw County. This operation was closed by the Pure Food and Drug Administration and no further attempts were made to use greensand commercially.

Delaware

There is no present-day commercial production. Research is being done on the possible economic use of glauconite, especially as a cation-exchange medium for the purification of polluted water.

Maryland

The Kaylorite Corp. mined greensand at Dunkirk, MD, for agricultural purposes and as a soil conditioner until 1970. It is not definitely known whether the operation was shut down

TABLE 6—Greensand Production in New Jersey

Years	Tons	Value, $
1922-23	18,500	188,000
1924-25	27,000	330,000
1926-27	24,000	337,000
1928-29	25,000	460,000
1930	12,700	225,000
1947-51	30,736	—
1967-71, avg	3,437	—

Data from New Jersey Geological Survey and US Bureau of Mines.

TABLE 7—Production of Greensand in New Jersey (Tons)

	Water Treatment	Agricultural Use
1959	2000	4600
1960	1900	3750
1961	1500	2900
1962	1900	2250
1963	2000	n.r.*

Data from New Jersey Geological Survey.

* n.r., not reported.

because of the death of the owner or on account of difficulties in production and/or sales. Production was from the upper 20 ft of the Nanjemoy Formation. Two products were made, a finely ground greensand for use as a soil additive and nonpoisonous dusting agent for plants, and a −30-mesh granular greensand for agricultural application. Production in 1970 totaled 650 tons.

Tennessee

A small amount of greensand in McNairy County was used for direct application on agricultural land. No present-day commercial production is recorded.

Texas

Some limited past production is known from the Eocene horizon in Bexar County and from the Paleocene south of San Antonio. Greensand was mainly used for water purification and soil conditioning (Jones, 1936). No present-day commercial production is recorded.

Virginia

Used in the 1920s as an agricultural supplement because of its potash, phosphoric acid, and lime, greensand was dug from open pits and at some places along the edge of the Pamunkey River from horizontal drifts driven into the Eocene Aquia and Nanjemoy Formations. The potash content ranges from about 1 to 10 (?)% (Clark, 1912). There is no present-day commercial production in Virginia.

Greensand in Other Countries

Belgium

In Belgium the sands of Antwerp contain 40% or more of glauconite. Industrial exploitation has been suggested but there is no current utilization.

Great Britain

During the 19th century greensand was mined as a soil conditioner from pits located in Hampshire, Essex, and Kent. During World War II, the Eocene beds at Knaphill and Chobham Common in Surrey and at Hazeley Heath in Hampshire were explored as potential sources of potash; the beds are 8 to 10 ft thick, and reserves are estimated at 7,000,000 tons, with an average content of 50% glauconite (Oakley, 1943; Bessey, 1949). No greensand is being produced at present.

Netherlands

Glauconite sands occur in the Lower Tertiary and Upper Cretaceous sediments of the southwestern part of South Limburg, and in Lower Cretaceous sediments in the eastern part of Overijssel (Achterhock) (H. M. Harsveldt, 1972, private communication). Between 1940 and 1946 the usability of glauconite was investigated for (1) decalcifying of water, (2) manufacture of soluble potash salts for fertilizer, and (3) manufacture of green paint. Because of the low 2.6 to 6% potash content, its use as a source of potash salts proved uneconomic. Color and coarseness did not fulfill the paint requirements, and attempts to use the greensand to decalcify drinking water were of no avail.

Poland

Several Tertiary and Quaternary sediments have glauconite beds of variable purity. The "glauconite molding sand," from Zielnow near Grudziadz, at Zawichost near Sandomierz, and at Lechowka near Chelm Lubeski contain 13 to 16% glauconite; the remainder is mostly clay and quartz sand with minor muscovite, biotite, manganese, and iron aggregates (R. Osika, 1972, private communication).

USSR

Glauconitic sandstone is widespread in the northwestern region of the European USSR. It occurs in the Ukraine, in the Volga region, on the east slope of the Ural Mountains, in the Kazakhstan (Kazakh Soviet Socialist Republic), in the Uzbekistan (Uzbek Soviet Socialist Republic), and also in the Far East. These glauconitic deposits are mainly in Jurassic, Cretaceous, and Paleocene sands and sandstones. Glauconite content commonly reaches 50 to 80% (P. M. Tatarinov, 1972, private communication).

TABLE 8—Analyses of Glauconite from the USSR (%)

	I	II	III
SiO_2	48.80	44.46	47.92
Al_2O_3	9.25	10.52	5.20
Fe_2O_3	15.24	20.19	22.76
FeO	1.90	1.45	1.08
MgO	3.85	2.31	3.64
CaO	3.78	—	0.56
K_2O	8.20	4.85	5.88
Na_2O	—	11.38	0.18
H_2O	5.32	6.55	12.30
TiO_2	—	—	0.06
P_2O_5	—	—	0.16
Loss on ignition	4.20	—	—
	100.54	101.71	99.74

I. Glauconite, Saratovs deposit.
II. Glauconite sand, Lopatynsky deposit, Moscow region.
III. Glauconite, Changi deposit, Uzbekistan.

Data: Private Communication.

Glauconite is used in limited quantities for producing green mineral pigments and in quantity for softening hard water. It is also used for adsorption in the processing of petroleum products; for cleaning of sewage; and as a fertilizer for cotton, rice, and other agricultural crops. Table 8 gives analyses of glauconites from the USSR.

Australia

At Gingin, 50 miles north of Perth, there are thick greensand beds containing up to 40% glauconite. These beds are extensive and contain up to 3% potash, 1% phosphorus, and 15% calcium carbonate. Glauconite was obtained by electromagnetic separation for use as a water-softening agent, but production ceased in 1965 (McLeod, 1965). Table 9 shows greensand production in Australia.

Pricing

Increasing costs for materials, labor, and taxes have brought about a considerable increase in the cost of production during the past few years. Currently, greensand production for agricultural application is valued at $30 to $35 per ton. Quantities less than a ton are correspondingly higher. Glauconite produced for water purification is valued at $75 to $150 per ton depending on the treatment process it is given. Until more widespread uses are found, the present limited demand for glauconite will govern the price structure.

TABLE 9—Greensand Production in Australia

Year	Tons
1935 to 1950	3300
1950	324
1951	506
1952	230
1953	320
1954	258
1955	197
1956	85
1957	126
1958	112
1959	102
1960	111

Data from McLeod, 1965.

Potential Uses

In the light of declining use of greensand, recent efforts are under way to develop new uses. Its catalytic properties have been investigated in some detail in the United States, the USSR, Japan, Germany, and France (Hartough and Kosak, 1947; Kvirikashvili, 1962, 1964; Gornak, 1963). Acylating reactions, dehydration of cyclohexane to benzene, and condensation of aldehydes have been performed with glauconite catalysts. The relationship between catalytic activity and cation exchange capacity (CEC) has led to efforts to enhance the former by increasing the latter through heat treatment and chemical methods; since CEC increases with the ratio of mixed-layer component of glauconite to 10Å mica component, these efforts also are directed toward replacing more of the potassium in the glauconite structure with hydroxyl ions. Heating of the glauconite in a reducing atmosphere leads to the formation of metaglauconite; its absorbent properties are being studied.

An entirely different approach is the destructive dissolution of glauconite, and the recovery of at least three marketable products: high-purity silica, potash, and iron oxides. This process was first proposed by Turrentine (1925); at present, efforts are under way to prove economic feasibility with the help of up-to-date chemical engineering practice. Some extensive greensand beds are situated near population centers, and their capacity of absorbing waste fluids is being investigated.

A number of other uses have been suggested or locally tried. Finely ground glauconite has been used as a green paint pigment, but its low refractive index and tendency to weather to red iron oxide inhibits its use for this application.

Pure glauconite has been used to a limited extent as a glass-polishing agent. Glauconite from the Weches Formation in Texas contains clayey beds that were formerly cut or sawed and dried to form a tough, reasonably durable building stone (Jones, 1936; Fisher, 1965).

Bibliography and References

Ashley, G.H., 1918, "Notes on the Greensand Deposits of the Eastern United States," Bulletin 660, US Geological Survey, pp. 27–50.

Bailey, R.J., and Atherton, M.P., 1969, "The Petrology of a Glauconitic Sandy Chalk," *Journal of Sedimentary Petrology*, Vol. 39, No. 4, Dec., pp. 1420–1431.

Bessey, G.E., 1949, "Potash from Greensand," Monograph, Mineral Supply, London, pp. 11–105.

Borrowman, G.L., 1920, "Water-Softening Compound and Method of Producing Same," US Patent 1,348,977, Aug. 10.

Bradley, W.F., 1945, "Diagnostic Criteria for Clay Minerals," *American Mineralogist*, Vol. 30, No. 11–12, Nov.-Dec., pp. 704–713.

Burst, J.F., 1958, "'Glauconite' Pellets: Their Mineral Nature and Applications to Stratigraphic Interpretations," *Bulletin of American Association of Petroleum Geologists*, Vol. 42, No. 2, Feb. pp. 310–327.

Cimbálníková, A., 1971, "Chemical Variability and Structural Heterogeneity of Glauconites," *American Mineralogist*, Vol. 56, No. 7–8, July-Aug. pp. 1385–1392.

Cimbálníková, A., 1971a, "Influence of 10 Å/14 Å Interlayering in Glauconites," *American Mineralogist*, Vol. 56, No. 7–8, July-Aug., pp. 1393–1398.

Clark, W.B., 1892, "A Preliminary Report on the Cretaceous and Tertiary Formations of New Jersey," Annual Report for 1892, Pt. 2, Geological Survey of New Jersey, 368 pp.

Clark, W.B., 1912, "The Physiography and Geology of the Coastal Plain Province of Virginia," Bulletin 4, Virginia Geological Survey, 274 pp.

Cook, G.H., 1868, "Geology of New Jersey," State Geological Survey, New Brunswick, 899 pp.

Ehlmann, A.J., et al., 1963, "Stages of Glauconite Formation in Modern Foraminiferal Sediments," *Journal of Sedimentary Petrology*, Vol. 33, No. 1, Mar., pp. 87–96.

Eilertsen, D.E., 1972, "Greensand," *Minerals Yearbook 1972*, US Bureau of Mines, p. 1359.

Fisher, W.L., 1965, "Rock and Mineral Resources of East Texas," Report of Investigations 54, Texas Bureau of Economic Geology, 439 pp.

Foster, M.D., 1969, "Studies of Celadonite and Glauconite," Professional Paper 614-F, US Geological Survey, 15 pp.

Galliher, E.W., 1935, "Geology of Glauconite," *Bulletin of American Association of Petroleum Geologists*, Vol. 19, No. 11, pp. 1569–1601.

Galliher, E.W., 1935a, "Glauconite Genesis," *Bulletin of the Geological Society of America*, Vol. 46, Sep., pp. 1351–1365.

Galliher, E.W., 1939, "Biotite-Glauconite Transformation and Associated Minerals," *Recent Marine Sediments*, P. Trask, ed., pp. 513–515.

Gildersleeve, B., 1942, "Eocene of Virginia," Bulletin 57, Virginia Geological Survey, 43 pp.

Glaser, J.D., 1971, "Geology and Mineral Resources of Southern Maryland," Report of Investigations 15, Maryland Geological Survey, 85 pp.

Goldman, M.I., 1919, "General Character, Mode of Occurrence and Origin of Glauconite," *Washington Academy of Science Journal,* Vol. 9, pp. 501–502.

Gornak, A.I., 1963, "Influence of Preliminary Treatment on the Exchange Capacity of Glauconite from the Loevsk Deposit of White Russia," SSR Ionobmen i Sorbtsiya iz Rastvorov, Akademii Nauk Belorussk, SSR, Inst. Obshch. i Neorgan. Khim.; Chemical Abstracts 61: 67h.

Grim, R.E., 1968, *Clay Mineralogy,* 2nd ed., McGraw-Hill, New York, 596 pp.

Gruner, J.W., 1935, "The Structural Relationship of Glauconite and Mica," *American Mineralogist,* Vol. 20, No. 10, Oct., pp. 699–714.

Hallimond, A.F., 1928, "The Formula of Glauconite," *American Mineralogist,* Vol. 13, No. 12, Dec., pp. 589–590.

Hartough, H.U., and Kosak, S., 1947, "Acylation Studies in the Tiophene and Furan Series, III, Natural and Synthetic Silica-Metal Oxide Catalysts," *Journal of American Chemical Society,* Vol. 69, pp. 1014–1016.

Haven, D.S., and Morales-Alamo, R., 1968, "Occurrence and Transport of Faecal Pellets in Suspension in a Tidal Estuary," *Sedimentary Geology,* Vol. 2, pp. 141–152.

Hendricks, S.B., and Ross, C.S., 1941, "Chemical Composition and Genesis of Glauconite and Celadonite," *American Mineralogist,* Vol. 26, No. 12, Dec., pp. 683–708.

Hower, J., 1961, "Some Factors Concerning the Nature and Origin of Glauconite," *American Mineralogist,* Vol. 46, No. 3–4, Mar.-Apr., pp. 313–334.

Jeans, C.V., 1971, "The Neoformation of Clay Minerals in Brackish and Marine Environments," *Clay Minerals* (London), Vol. 9, pp. 209–217.

Jones, C.A., 1936, "Report on a Mineral Resource Survey of Bexar County, Texas," Mineral Resource Survey Series, Circular 2, Texas Bureau of Economic Geology, 6 pp.

Kriegsheim, H., and Vaughan, W., 1930, "Water-Purifying Material and Process of Making the Same," US Patent 1,757,372, May 6.

Kvirikashvili, V.L., 1961, "Contact Catalytic Conversion of Cyclohexane and Methycylohexane in the Presence of Natural Glauconite Catalyst," Soobschch. Akademii Nauk Gruz. SSSR, Vol. 27, pp. 671–1; Chemical Abstracts 57: 700B.

Kvirikashvili, V.L., 1962, "The Conversion of *n*-Heptane in the Presence of Glauconite," *Transactions,* Inst. Khim. Akademii Nauk Gruz. Vol. 16. pp. 89–98; Chemical Abstracts 60: 9131D.

Kvirikashvili, V.L., 1964, "Contact Conversions of Methylcylopentane in the Presence of a Natural Glauconite Catalyst," *Transactions,* Inst. Khim. Akademii Nauk Gruz. Vol. 17, pp. 201–205; Chemical Abstracts, 62:11697h.

Lamboy, M., 1967, "Répartition de la 'glauconie' sur le plateau continental de la Galice et des Asturies (Espagne)," *Comptes Rendus,* Academy of Sciences, Paris, 266-D, pp. 855–857.

Lamboy, M., 1968, "Sur un processus de formation de la glauconie en grains à partir des débris coquilliers. Rôle des organismes perforants," *Comptes Rendus,* Academy of Sciences, Paris, 266-D, pp. 1937–1940.

Lewis, J.L., and Kummel, H.B., 1940, "The Geology of New Jersey," Bulletin 50, New Jersey Dept. of Conservation & Development, 203 pp.

Light, M.A., 1950, "Glauconite of the New Jersey Coastal Plain," Ph.D. Thesis, Rutgers University, 244 pp.

Manghanani, M.H., and Hower, J., 1964, "Glauconites: Cation Exchange Capacities and Infrared Spectra—Part 1. The Cation Exchange Capacity of Glauconite," *American Mineralogist,* Vol. 49, No. 5–6, May-June, pp. 586–598.

Mansfield, G.R., 1922, "Potash in the Greensands of New Jersey," Bulletin 727, US Geological Survey, 146 pp.

McGrain, P., 1968, "Economic Geology of Calloway County, Kentucky," County Report No. 2, Series X, Kentucky Geological Survey, pp. 32–33.

McLeod, I.R., 1965, "Australian Mineral Industry: The Mineral Deposits," Bulletin 72, Bureau of Mineral Resources, 690 pp.

Nordell, E., 1935, "Zeolites: Mining, Processing, Manufacture, and Uses," Bulletin 61, Michigan State College Engineering Experiment Station, pp. 3–27.

Oakley, K.P., 1943, "Glauconite Sand of Brackesham Beds," Geological Survey of England & Wales, Vol. 33, 28 pp.

Odin, G.S., 1968, "Glauconie, glauconite et phyllosilicate verts," *Bulletin,* Gr. Franc. Argiles, Vol. 20, pp. 11–12.

Odin, G.S., 1971, "Sur la genèse des glauconies et leur signification sédimentologique d'après l'etude détaillée du sondage de Mont Cassel (Nord)," *Comptes Rendus,* Academy of Sciences, Paris, 272-D, pp. 697–699.

Odin, G.S., and Giresse, P., 1972, "Formation des minéraux phylliteux (berthiérine, smectites ferrifères, glauconite ouverte) dans les sédiments du Golfe de Guinée," *Comptes Rendus,* Academy of Sciences, Paris, 275-D, pp. 177–180.

Owens, J.P., and Sohl, N.F., 1973, "Glauconites from the New Jersey-Maryland Coastal Plain: their K/Ar ages and Application in Stratigraphic Studies," *Geological Society of America Bulletin,* Vol. 84, No. 9, Sep., pp. 2811–2838.

Robert, M., 1972, "Transformation experimentale de glauconites et d'illites en smectites," *Comptes Rendus,* Academy of Sciences, Paris, 275-D, pp. 1319–1322.

Ross, C.S., 1926, "The Optical Properties and Chemical Composition of Glauconite," *Proceedings,* US National Museum, Vol. 69, pp. 1–15.

Schneider, H., 1927, "A Study of Glauconite," *Journal of Geology,* Vol. 35, No. 4, May-June, pp. 289–310.

Shreve, R.M., 1921, "Greensand as a Source of Potash," *Chemical & Metallurgical Engineering,* Vol. 35, p. 1056.

Shutov, V.D., et al., 1972, "Crystallochemical Heterogeneity of Glauconite as Depending on the Conditions of its Formation and Post-Sedimentary History," *International Clay Mineral Conference,* Madrid, pp. 327–339.

Smulikowski, K., 1954, "The Problem of Glauconite," *Archiwum Mineralogiczne* (Polska Akademii Nauk, Komitet Geologiezny), Vol. 18, No. 1, 108 pp.

Spencer, A.C., 1924, "Process of Improving Glauconite," US Patent 1,491,561, Apr. 22.

Takahashi, J.I., 1939, "Synopsis of Glauconitization," *Recent Marine Sediments*, P. Trask, ed., pp. 502–512.

Takahashi, J.I., and Yagi, T., 1929, "The Peculiar Mud-Grains in the Recent Littoral and Estuarine Deposits with Special Reference of the Origin of Glauconite," *Economic Geology*, Vol. 24, No. 8, Dec., pp. 838–852.

Tapper, M., and Fanning, D.S., 1968, "Glauconite Pellets: Similar X-Ray Patterns from Individual Pellets of Lobate and Vermiform Morphology," *Clays and Clay Minerals*, Vol. 16, pp. 275–283.

Tedrow, C.F., 1957, "Greensand Soils Subject of Study by Station Scientists," *New Jersey Agriculture*, Nov.-Dec., 3 pp.

Triplehorn, D.M., 1966, "Morphology, Internal Structure, and Origin of Glauconite Pellets," *Sedimentology*, Vol. 6, pp. 247–266.

True, R.H., and Geise, F.W., 1918, "Experiments on the Value of Greensand as Source of Potassium for Plant Culture," *Journal of Agricultural Research*, Vol. 15, pp. 483–492.

Turrentine, J.W., 1925, "Potash from Greensand," *Industrial & Engineering Chemistry*, Vol. 17, Nov., pp. 1177–1181.

Tyler, P.M., 1934, "Greensand," Information Circular 6782, US Bureau of Mines, 8 pp.

Yoder, H.S., and Eugster, H.P., 1955, "Synthetic and Natural Muscovites," *Geochemica et Cosmochimica Acta*, Vol. 8, pp. 225–280.

Zumpe, H.H., 1971, "Microstructure in Cenomanian Glauconite," *Mineral Magazine*, Vol. 38, pp. 215–224.

Graphite*

GEORGE D. GRAFFIN †

The first use of graphite is lost in the mists of time. It was used by primitive man to make drawings on the walls of caves and by the Egyptians to decorate pottery. As early as 1400 A.D. graphite crucibles were being made in the Haffnerzell district of Bavaria.

Through the Middle Ages graphite was confused with other minerals, especially galena and molybdenite. Two common names that are still used for the mineral are "Plumbago," meaning leadlike, and "Black Lead." The latter name implied that graphite is either composed of lead or at least contains a large percentage of it. Gessner is credited with having recognized it as a separate mineral in 1565, but its composition was not determined until 1779, when Scheele demonstrated that graphite oxidized to carbon dioxide, thus proving its carbon constitution. In 1789, Werner named it "graphite" from the Greek word "graphein," meaning to write.

The United States has long relied on foreign countries for its graphite supplies. This reliance has been due more to the lack of suitable domestic graphites than to any particular preference for buying minerals overseas. Ceylon (now Sri Lanka) graphites were imported as early as 1820, and Madagascar graphites have been imported since the properties on that island were opened up about a hundred years later. Mexico has long supplied the United States with most of its requirements for amorphous graphite.

Physical Properties and Classification

Graphite is found in laminated, flaky aggregates disseminated in schistose rocks. It also occurs in veins and exhibits a foliated or fibrous structure.

* The author has drawn heavily from the chapter on Graphite by Eugene N. Cameron in the third edition of *Industrial Minerals and Rocks.*

† Vice President, The Asbury Graphite Mills, Inc., Asbury, Warren County, NJ.

Graphite is a black lustrous mineral that crystallizes in the hexagonal system, with rhombohedral symmetry. The crystals have tabular form and are six-sided; the faces are commonly striated. The flakes have perfect basal cleavage and are opaque. When well crystallized, the flakes have a black metallic luster while the amorphous material is black and earthy, with a microcrystalline compactness. The flakes feel greasy. Graphite is an excellent conductor of heat and electricity. It melts at approximately 3550°C at a triple point under 1250 psi. It sublimes between 3300–3500°C at 14.7 psi. At 3726°C a second triple point occurs at approximately 100,000 atmospheres. Thermal oxidation in the presence of oxygen begins at 300°C and the rate increases with temperature.

The three forms of carbon (charcoal, graphite, and diamond) are distinguished by chemical and physical tests. The specific gravity of charcoal is 1.3 to 1.9, of graphite 2.266 g/cm³ (crystal density), and of diamond 3.5. Graphite has a hardness of 1 to 2 (Mohs' scale).

Natural graphite can be divided into three classes: disseminated flake, crystalline vein (fibrous or columnar), and amorphous. Flake graphite is a lamellar form found in metamorphic rocks, such as marble, gneiss, and schist. Each flake is separate, having crystallized as such in the rock. Crystalline vein graphite is found in the form of well defined veins or as pocket accumulations along the intrusive contacts of pegmatites with limestones. The graphite of such deposits is of two types, foliated and columnar. The important Sri Lanka (Ceylon) deposits are vein type.

Amorphous graphite is commonly found as minute microcrystalline particles more or less uniformly distributed in feebly metamorphic rocks, such as slates and shales, or in beds consisting practically entirely of graphite. The latter usually are metamorphosed coal seams and carry as much as 80–85% graphitic carbon, while the former, being altered carbonaceous sediments, commonly range from 25 to 60%

carbon. The graphite content of such amorphous deposits is dependent on the amount of carbon originally present in the sediments. There is no evidence of enrichment by the intrusive rocks. Certain amorphous graphite deposits have undoubtedly been formed by contact (thermal) metamorphism, while others are probably the result of dynamic (regional) metamorphism.

Manufactured (artificial) graphite is produced in electric furnaces from petroleum coke.

Definition of Terms, Grades, and Specifications

Through its long history of use graphite has been marketed as "graphite," "plumbago," or "black lead." Furthermore, industrial usage of terms may be confusing to one not intimately associated with the industry. For example, even though natural and manufactured (artificial) graphite are used extensively by industry, commercially the two main categories are *crystalline* and *amorphous.* Inasmuch as all graphite is truly crystalline and the distinction is only one of the size of the crystals themselves, the term "amorphous" is actually a misnomer.

"Amorphous," as applied to graphite, has been further complicated by long-standing industrial application of the term to very fine particles of crystalline flake graphite that can be sold only for low-value uses, such as foundry facings. Also, fine grained varieties of lump graphite that can be reduced easily to fine particle size by grinding are called *amorphous lump* to distinguish them from tough, platy, and acicular varieties, known as *crystalline lump,* that can be reduced in particle size with difficulty.

Crystalline flake graphite is well defined in paragraph 213 of the Tariff Act of 1930 as follows:

The term "crystalline flake" means graphite or plumbago which occurs disseminated as a relatively thin flake throughout its containing rock, decomposed or not, and which may be or has been separated therefrom by ordinary crushing, pulverizing, screening, or mechanical concentration process, such as flake being made up of a number of parallel laminae, which may be separated by mechanical means.

Under the foregoing definition finely divided particles of crystalline flake graphite would be classified as crystalline graphite.

However, the Court of Customs Appeals has repeatedly held that commercial designations and not scientific terms must govern classification and that when a commercial meaning differs from the technical meaning the commercial designation must govern. Thus, large quantities of fine crystalline flake graphite are imported under the *amorphous* classification.

Sri Lanka lump graphite, one of the most important, is classified either as amorphous or crystalline. Each type is divided into a number of grades, depending upon the particle size (lump, ranging from the size of walnuts to that of peas; chip, from the size of peas to about that of wheat grains; dust, finer than 60 mesh), graphite carbon content, and degree of consolidation.

Amorphous graphite is graded primarily on graphitic carbon content. Commercial ores contain about 50 to 94% carbon, depending on their source.

Crystalline flake graphite from the Malagasy Republic is divided into two main grades, "flake" (coarse flake) and "fines" (fine flake). Malagasy crucible flake must have a minimum of 85% carbon and be essentially all −8 to +60 mesh. Other crystalline flake graphite is graded according to graphitic carbon content and particle size.

The terms "manufactured," "secondary artificial," "primary artificial," "electric-furnace," and "synthetic" are used to describe graphite produced from petroleum coke in electric furnaces.

The synthetic graphites generally are classified as electrodes, anodes, molded shapes, "secondary," and "primary" graphites. The term "secondary" artificial graphite mostly is used to describe the lathe and machine cuttings from formed shapes of artificial graphite. The term "primary" artificial graphite generally is used to describe granular particles of carbon which have been thermally converted to a graphitized state. Secondary artificial graphite generally is manufactured from calcined petroleum coke, coal tar pitch, iron oxide, and other minor ingredients. The ingredients are homogeneously blended and then extruded or molded into the desired shape. The shapes are commonly called "green" carbons. The "green" carbon shapes are then baked to a temperature of 810°C which usually requires two to three weeks, depending on the size and the mix composition. Small sizes may be baked in a matter of hours. "Green" carbons that have been heat treated are known as "baked" carbons. After the carbon shapes are heat treated, they are then processed in an electric furnace to a temperature of between 2,200°C and 2,800°C+. This may range from a few hours to several days, again depending upon the size and shape, base material, and mix formulation. These carbons are commonly known as "synthetic," "graphitized products," "electro-graphite" or graphite. The lathe and machine cuttings and turnings will generally range between 1.5 to 1.76 g/cm³; special mix formulations may have a density of from 1.0 to 2.1 g/cm³.

Primary artificial graphite is produced by heat treating carbon granulars in an electric furnace to a temperature of 2,200°C along with a catalyst in order to obtain higher purities and to lower the temperature of graphitization. The base material is generally calcined petroleum coke. The apparent density will range from 1.35 to 1.55 g/cm³. The major difference between secondary and primary artificial graphite is the base raw material and purity.

The choice of graphites used is primarily dependent upon the application. In general, artificial graphite will have a lower density than natural graphite. It will have a higher electrical resistance and a higher porosity than natural graphite.

The one characteristic in natural graphite which has not been matched by artificial graphite is its excellent molding properties and high densities.

Mode of Occurrence

Graphite is widely distributed throughout the world. It occurs in many types of igneous, sedimentary, and metamorphic rocks. Many occurrences are, however, of little economic importance. The more important are those found in metasomatic-hydrothermal deposits and in sedimentary rocks that have been subjected to regional or thermal metamorphism.

Most, if not all, of the world's deposits of flake and crystalline graphite occur in metamorphic rocks of Precambrian age. Marble, gneiss, and schists are the most common types of rock in which the economic deposits of flake graphite occur. In many cases, the rocks have been intruded by pegmatitic veins. Vein graphite is normally found in rocks similar to these, but the enclosing wall rock is not necessarily graphitic. This type of deposit assumes the character of a true lode.

Economic deposits of graphite include five main geological types:

1) Flake graphite disseminated in metamorphosed, silica-rich sedimentary rocks.

2) Flake graphite disseminated in marble.

3) Deposits formed by metamorphism of coal or carbon-rich sediments (amorphous).

4) Veins filling fractures, fissures, and cavities in country rock.

5) Contact metasomatic or hydrothermal deposits in metamorphosed, calcareous sedimentary rocks.

Natural graphite in these deposits varies widely in physical appearance. Klar (1958) classified graphite occurrences on the basis of crystal characteristics into microcrystalline dense graphites and macrocrystalline silvery-bright graphites.

Microcrystalline graphites occur in deposits of high carbon content as exceptionally small crystals discernible only by high-powered microscopes, while the macrocrystalline types generally occur in lower concentrations and in a larger crystal form.

Following are descriptions of the five main geological types.

Flake Graphite Disseminated in Metamorphosed Silica-Rich Sedimentary Rocks

A large part of the world's total production of graphite is derived from rocks such as quartz-mica schists, feldspathic or micaceous quartzites, and gneisses. The graphite flakes in these rocks are oriented so that they lie parallel to the plane of foliation. The graphite varies widely in physical appearance and characteristics. The flakes may range in size from a fraction of a millimeter to an average of 16 in., and may vary from one deposit to another in thickness, toughness, density, and shape.

The principal deposits of flake graphite occur in lenses or layers that may reach as much as 100 ft in thickness and extend for many thousands of feet. The lenses have a variable graphite content both within themselves and from one lens to another. The content of an average deposit is about 25%. Some deposits containing as little as 2% graphite have been worked. In Madagascar one rich lens contains 60% graphite. Crystals in each deposit vary in size, usually reflecting the grain size in the parent rock. In a moderately good deposit crystals ranging up to ¼ in. are common.

Description of Deposits: *Alabama*—The deposits of northeastern Alabama, in Chilton, Coosa, and Clay counties, occur in two northeast-trending belts that are 1 to 2 miles in width and that have a combined length of about 55 miles. Worked intermittently since the late 1800s, the mines reached their peak production during World War I. The deposits, called "leads," are groups of parallel layers and lenses in the Ashland quartz-mica schist that contain

1 to 5% disseminated flake graphite. The leads mined range from 20 to more than 100 ft in thickness, dip gently to steeply, and have been traced up to 4000 ft along strike. Some are essentially constant in strike and dip over long distances; others are folded, faulted, or both. The deposits are weathered to depths as great as 100 ft. Weathered "ore" has furnished most of the graphite produced but unweathered ore has been worked at some mines. In general, the flake ranges from less than 0.05–0.20 in. in diameter, but most of it is less than 0.05 in. in diameter. Assays of samples from 32 properties in the northeastern belt by the US Bureau of Mines gave the following results:

Size	Lb of Flake per Ton of Ore
+50 mesh	6 to 14
−50 +100 mesh	7 to 38
−100 mesh	8 to 70
Total flake	35 to about 130

Reserves of flake graphite in unweathered rock (measured, indicated. and inferred) are estimated by the US Bureau of Mines at 14,410,-000 tons. How much of each of the commercial grades that could be produced from the deposits, however, is uncertain. Most of the graphite produced in Alabama during and since World War II has been stockpiled, but Alabama graphite has been marketed at one time or another for most of the uses to which graphite is put.

Texas—The flake graphite deposits of Texas occur in the Precambrian Packsaddle schist in Llano and Burnet Counties. The deposits show a wide range of graphite content and flake size. The most important deposit is one in Burnet County operated in recent years by the Southwestern Graphite Co. The deposit consists of flake graphite disseminated in mica schist and micaceous quartzite. These rocks are cut by dikes of granite and granite pegmatite and contain abundant lenses and knots of similar material. Reserves of graphitic rock are substantial. The flake recovered is mostly small and has been marketed chiefly for foundry facings and for lubricants, packing materials, and pencils.

Norway—In Europe the principal productive graphite deposits of Norway, West Germany (Bavaria), and Czechoslovakia, and the graphite deposits in lower Austria, all consist of flake graphite disseminated in mica schist or mica gneiss, or are closely associated with these rocks. The productive deposits of Norway (A/S Skaland Grafitverk) are on Senja Island, North Norway (latitude 60°39′N; longitude,

17°E) and are lenses of graphitic rock enclosed in mica schists. The richest ore contains 25 to 30% graphite. The ore is hard and must be crushed to recover the graphite. The refined products are crystalline battery-grade concentrates and fine-ground graphite concentrates. Exploration has reportedly shown reserves amounting to one million tons of rock averaging 25% carbon. Reserves of 500,000 tons are also reported at Jennestad in the Lofoten Islands, a little southwest of Senja Island, but half the graphite is said to be amorphous and difficult to concentrate.

West Germany—Deposits east of Passau, Bavaria (West Germany, on the Austrian border), were known to prehistoric man and have been worked since the Middle Ages. They consist of crystalline graphite in seams, lenses, and disseminated flakes in gneiss and schist. Individual seams and lenses up to several tens of feet in thickness are mined for hundreds of feet. At Kropfmuhl, the only mine now operated, some 20 folded seams of graphite are interbedded with marble and micaceous gneiss in a zone that is 450 ft in stratigraphic thickness. Seams 1 to 5 ft thick are mined. Graphite forms 10 to 30% of the lenses and averages 20 to 25% after hand sorting. Associated minerals are mainly feldspar and calcite, with less quartz, pyrrhotite, pyrite, biotite, hornblende, sphalerite, and galena. Both weathered and unweathered rock have been mined. Two grades of crucible flake (92 to 95%), three of pencil flake (96 to 98%), and five of fines are produced. There is some question whether the deposits are epigenetic or due to metamorphism of carbonaceous sediments followed by hydrothermal alteration.

Madagascar—Probably the largest resources of high-grade, crystalline flake graphite in the world are on the Island of Madagascar. The deposits occur in belts of micaceous gneiss and schist over a distance of more than 500 miles in the eastern half of the island, from the latitude of Tamatave to the southern end. The principal producing area extends about 70 miles along the east coast, from Tamatave to Marovintsy. There are ten principal producers. Individual deposits are graphite-rich layers that range from 10 ft to more than 100 ft in thickness; some can be followed for thousands of feet. The graphite content reportedly ranges up to 60%, but ore averaging 4 to 11% disseminated graphite has been worked in recent years. Operations are confined to the weathered upper parts of the deposits, and reserves of weathered ore are considered ample for many years at current rates of production. Flake graphite from Madagascar is noted for its high proportion of coarse flake, for its uniform thickness, toughness, and cleanness, and for the care with which it is graded for export. It sets the world standard for high quality flake.

Brazil—In the area of Itapecerica, Minas Gerais, Brazil, graphite deposits with 20 to 25% carbon are mined in an open cut. Flotation and final cleaning yield flake and amorphous products with carbon contents up to 99%.

China—The deposits in China yield carbons 80 to 99% and have a flake up to ¼ in. in size, but the majority of the production is confined to −30 +80 mesh and −100 mesh.

India—The deposits in India yield carbons 70 to 88% and have flakes in the primary range of −30 +80 mesh and −100 mesh.

Flake Graphite Disseminated in Marble

Flake graphite disseminated in marble probably derives from carbonaceous impurities. It is commonly less than 1% of the rock, although in some localities it is as much as 5%. Deposits of this type exhibit much variation in grade and kind of accessory minerals over short distances and are structurally complex. Their contribution to world production is consequently much less than that from deposits in schists and gneisses.

Deposits Formed by Metamorphism of Coal or Carbon-Rich Sediments (Amorphous)

The graphite in deposits formed by the metamorphism of coal or carbon-rich sediments is almost invariably of the microcrystalline variety known to the graphite trade as amorphous graphite. A substantial part of the world production of amorphous graphite is from such deposits. The graphite occurs in seams, often distorted by folding and faulting, and is frequently intimately mixed with ungraphitized material. The ratio of graphite to ungraphitized material can vary widely. For example, some high-grade Mexican varieties contain as much as 95% graphite, while low grade Korean graphites are frequently burned for fuel because of the high nongraphitic carbon content.

Description of Deposits: *United States*—In the United States, coals in the Narragansett Basin of Rhode Island have locally been metamorphosed to graphitic anthracite. The material has been mined intermittently for many years as a source of low grade amorphous graphite for such uses as paint pigment. Amorphous graphite also occurs southwest of Raton, New Mexico, where Cretaceous coal beds have been converted to graphite adjacent to dikes.

Mexico—The most important deposits of amorphous graphite in the western hemisphere occur in the State of Sonora, Mexico, in an area 20 miles long by 10 miles wide, approximately 40 miles southeast of Hermosillo. The deposits were discovered in 1867. They were early described as beds of coal interlayered with sandstone, folded, and then intruded by granite, thereby being converted to graphite. Six beds of graphite are reported, the thickest averaging 9 to 10 ft but locally swelling to 24 ft because of folding. As the result of recent detailed examinations, however, the deposits at the Moradillas mine are now believed to be hydrothermal veins; no evidence has been found to indicate that they are metamorphosed coal beds. The veins are said to occupy fissures that cross the bedding of the country rocks at low angles. In the district as a whole, the graphite deposits are reported to be steeply dipping and are said to range from mere stringers to seams that are locally 12 to 15 ft wide. High grade Mexican graphite averages 80% carbon, but some contains as much as 95% carbon.

Italy—The principal Italian deposits, near Turin (Pinerolo) consist of material rich in finely crystalline graphite. The deposits are as much as 19 ft thick, consisting of layers or lenses enclosed in micaceous gneiss, phyllite, and schist. The graphite seams locally enclose masses of anthracite. The graphite content is 60 to 80%. The material is used chiefly for foundry facings and paint.

Austria—In southeastern Austria, large resources of graphite are present in a 30 mile-long belt of folded metasediments extending from Leoben to Rottenmann, in the Styrian Alps. There are two producing mines. At Kaiserberg, the principal mine, a series of graphitic beds with an aggregate thickness of 40 ft are enclosed in graphitic schists and quartzites. Crude ore contains 30 to 80% carbon and averages 50 to 60%. Refined graphites ranging from 66 to 95% carbon are produced by grinding and flotation. A new chemical process that will yield graphite with 99% carbon is reported to have been developed. The products are all amorphous graphite and are used for foundry facings, pencils, paint, and lacquer pigments and lubricants.

South Korea—The important amorphous graphite deposits of southern Korea, which have yielded about 1 million tons, occur as irregular lenses parallel to the structure of enclosing schists and phyllites of sedimentary origin. In the Kyeng-Sang district three seams having mineable widths of 78, 18, and 48 ft, respectively, have been reported. Neither the nature of the source rocks of these seams nor the origin of the seams is clear from published data. Deposits formed by dynamic and contact metamorphism of coal beds occur in southern Korea, but Overstreet (1947) reports that these are impure. Korean graphite is low in carbon content and is mostly exported to Japan for foundry facings and pigment; much of it is burned for fuel. Reserves of graphite in southern Korea are said to be large.

Other Areas—Elsewhere, deposits formed by the metamorphism of coal are worked in northern Italy, in the Styrian Alps of Austria, and at Undercliff in New South Wales, Australia. At Mt. Bopple, Collinsville, Cape Upstart, and Killarney, and in the Gympie goldfield, all in Queensland, igneous intrusions have locally altered Permian or Jurassic coals to amorphous graphite.

Vein Deposits Filling Fractures and Cavities

Vein deposits of graphite are typically fillings of fractures or cavities in country rocks. The veins are commonly sharply defined, and the graphite filling is typically banded and zoned. In the thinner veins, graphite occurs as crusts or layers of closely packed, coarse, elongate plates (needle lump) oriented perpendicular to the vein walls. Plates vary in length with vein thickness and may be as much as 4 in. long. Central portions of thicker veins may consist of platy layers parallel to the vein walls. Masses of coarse graphite and rosettes of radiating plates also occur. Gangue minerals are present in some deposits, totally absent in others.

The origin of vein deposits of graphite is uncertain. Winchell (1911), discussed various hypotheses and has concluded that the most probable mode of origin involved deoxidation of oxides of carbon.

Description of Deposits: *United States*—Deposits of this type at Sturbridge, MA, were worked in the 1640s and were the basis of the first graphite mining in the United States. Other deposits are known near Ticonderoga, NY. The only sizable domestic vein deposits, however, are those of the Crystal Graphite mine near Dillon, MT. There graphite fills networks of fractures in gneiss and pegmatite around the northwesterly plunging nose of an isoclinal fold, a structure that involves granite gneiss, schists, marbles, and quartzites of the Precambrian Cherry Creek series. The veins are fractions of an inch to 2 ft thick and range from a few feet to 50 ft in length. They pinch and swell rapidly both along strike and dip. No gangue minerals are present in the veins. The formation of the veins has been linked with the development of the pegmatites, but Ford (1954) has shown that fracturing and vein formation took place after formation of these rocks. He favors an origin from carbon originally present in the country rocks and introduced by gaseous emanations. Textural and structural features of the veins suggest deposition from fluids at no great depth.

Sri Lanka—The vein graphite deposits of Sri Lanka (Ceylon) have been worked systematically for more than 140 years, yielding more than 1.3 million tons of graphite since 1880. The main deposits are in Southern, Western, and Sabaragamuwa provinces. During some years more than 2000 pits have been active concurrently, and mining has reached depths as great as 1600 ft. The deposits occur in a complex series of Archean granulites, quartzites, garnet-sillimanite gneisses, and marbles in narrow, structurally controlled belts that persist for many miles along strike. The productive deposits range from simple fissure veins to branching veins or stockworks. Veins commonly range from fractions of an inch to several feet in thickness. Some of the larger deposits are tabular bodies parallel to foliation of enclosing rocks. Graphite filled "vugs" up to 80 ft in length and 6 x 5 ft in cross section are reported. The highest grades of Sri Lanka graphite carry 97 to 98% carbon. Lumps of pure, coarsely crystalline, platy graphite as much as a foot or more in diameter are found, and both needle and platy crystalline lump graphite are produced. A variety of minerals, chiefly quartz, pyrite, calcite, apatite, and pyroxene, with rutile, allanite, magnetite, and various lime-magnesia silicates, has been reported to be associated with graphite in the veins, but it is not clear whether these minerals were deposited with the graphite or are merely minerals of the wall rocks accidentally enclosed in the veins. Reserves of graphite in Sri Lanka are regarded as very large.

Mexico—The most important deposits of amorphous graphite in the western hemisphere occur in the state of Sonora, Mexico. Deposits of amorphous graphite occur in the area southeast of Navajoa approximately 25 miles from Empalme, but they are low grade and are not of economic importance at the present time.

The five companies that produce amorphous Mexican graphite are, in order of magnitude: Grafitos Mexicanos, S.A.; Compania Minera

Moraguirre; Grafitera de Sonora S.A. de C.V.; Grafito Superior S.A.; and Explotadora Sonorense.

Substantially more than half of the total production comes from the Lourdes Mine at Moradillas, owned and operated by Grafitos Mexicanos, S.A. These deposits, interlayered with sandstone, consist of steeply dipping N-S striking graphite veins ranging from small stringers to seams that at depth average 10 to 12 ft wide. Some veins more than 20 ft wide are being mined. The graphite content averages 95%. One mine, now defunct, averaged 90% carbon with pockets in excess of 95% carbon.

Other deposits were mined in the late 1940s in the Tonichi area, approximately 50 miles northeast of Guaymas. The graphite in this area was high grade, containing 85% carbon, and some veins as much as 5% carbon. However, the extraction process and the location of the mine, plus the long haulage to the railroad station at LaDura made it difficult to produce economically. After 1950, a dam was built in the Tonichi-Onavas-LaDura area, thereby causing all mining operations to cease.

Other—Vein deposits have also been reported from southern India (e.g., in the Madras province), from Madagascar, and from Brazil. Vein deposits also appear to be represented at the Sennotani mine, Toyama prefecture, Japan, and in certain deposits in Manchuria.

Contact Metasomatic or Hydrothermal Deposits in Marble

Concentrations of graphite occur in various parts of the world in silicified carbonate rocks. Some are clearly contact metasomatic; others show gradations to typical hydrothermal deposits. As a group, they are characterized by variable but generally small size, variability in flake size and content, and irregularity of form. The average grade of most deposits is low, and, consequently, they have accounted for only a minor part of total world production.

In the United States and Canada, deposits of this type occur at a number of places in the Grenville series of northern New York, southwestern Quebec, and southeastern Ontario. Small deposits west and northwest of Ticonderoga, NY were worked between 1850 and 1900. They consist of fine-to-coarse flake graphite irregularly concentrated in silicified marble adjacent to bodies of pegmatite. Some deposits in Quebec and Ontario are similar, but others appear to have been formed by metasomatic replacement of marble subsequent to silication. The most important Canadian graphite deposit,

the Black Donald mine at Calabogie, Ont., which was worked until 1954, is an example. It is described as a thickened, northwesterly plunging lens of drag-folded ore more than 1000 ft long, 15 to 70 ft thick in one direction and 50 to 80 ft in another. The ore contained up to 55 to 65% graphite, but averaged 25%. The flake produced was mostly fine-grained, and 80% was sold to the foundry industry. Several grades of lubricant flake, two averaging 97 to 98% carbon were also produced.

Contact metamorphic deposits in silicified marbles also occur in Sosangun, Korea.

Regional Occurrence, Production, and Use

Asia

Republic of Korea: The Republic of Korea is the world's largest producer of natural graphite and produces both amorphous and flake. In 1961, the ratio was about seven of amorphous to one of flake.

Fifteen amorphous-graphite mines yielded 719,400 st in the seven-year period 1955 through 1961. Principal mining areas are in the provinces of Shung Chong Puk Do, Kiong Sang Puk Co, and Kang Won Do. Almost all the deposits are in the vicinity of anthracite coal mines, which lends support to the idea that amorphous graphite is derived from coal.

The refined amorphous graphite is 80% carbon or higher. One sample of amorphous lump was 87.86% carbon.

Flake graphite mines yielded 3400 st in the seven-year period 1955 through 1961. Of four mines, two are in the Seoul area. Material with 90% carbon remaining on a 60-mesh sieve has been mined.

The nongraphitic portion of Korean graphite is mainly silico-aluminous material. The iron content of associated minerals is the lowest of all known natural graphites; the ash is a distinctive white.

Exports were 131 kt of amorphous and 1.9 kt of flake for the period 1959 to 1961; 80% of exports were to Japan. The Korean government restricts the exportation of anthracite coal, and it is often shipped as graphite. Therefore, the actual tonnage of graphite exported is probably less than the reported figure.

Estimated reserves are 3.3 million st of amorphous graphite averaging 75% carbon and 1.8 million st of flake averaging 80% carbon.

Sri Lanka (Ceylon): Sri Lanka contains the largest known deposits of vein graphite. Very large deposits are located in the western and southwestern sections of the island. The Dutch government first reported graphite deposits in Sri Lanka in 1675.

The extent of the deposits has inspired much study, but, although the resulting literature is extensive, little is known about the origin of this vein graphite. According to Wadia (1943):

> Graphite occurs in a large area in the southwestern part of Ceylon in the extremely metamorphosed series of Archean sediments known as the Khondalite system. Disseminated graphite in granitic gneisses and in sillimanite-garnet rocks was probably formed by metamorphism of carbonaceous impurities, but vein graphite is secondary and fills cracks, fissures and foliation and joint planes. The vein graphite deposits are believed (by some) to have been formed by reduction, at high temperatures and pressures, of carbon dioxide liberated during the assimilation of limestones and dolomites by charnockitic and related igneous magmas. Pyrite, quartz, calcite and augite are the minerals most commonly associated with graphite; others include scapolite, wollastonite, forsterite, tremolite and phlogopite. Reserves of mineable graphite are believed to be large.

The structures contrast markedly with other forms of graphite and are typical of ores deposited as vein, dike, pegmatitic, or pneumatolytic occurrences. One feature is that the crystals grow inward from both margins of the vein toward the center. Changing conditions during the formation have also resulted in many parallel bands of columnar structure. These bands may vary considerably in width, texture, hardness, and purity. Many variations from the regular crystalline structure are seen. Often a jumbled maze of interlocking fibers is produced, or the fibers may radiate from centers, forming rosettes of graphite. Large flexible folia occur and bear the typical twinning striations so often seen on flake graphites. In places slippage has taken place, drawing out the fibers to form the so-called needle variety of graphite, or an amorphous dust may be formed.

The great bulk of high-quality vein graphite still comes from Sri Lanka. Despite rising labor costs, a considerable proportion of the production is still prepared by hand cobbing and hand sorting in order to satisfy those buyers who still retain a preference for lump grades. On the other hand, one of the larger operators has found it expedient to install complete mechanical beneficiation equipment for handling particle sizes below 6μ. Beneficiation in this case is based largely on the use of pneumatic tables, from which it is possible to obtain a wide range

of carbon contents. Since most graphites are eventually utilized in industry in the form of powder, present operators anticipate a trend toward the direct supply of the powder from the mine to the importer. The requirements for hand sorting would be reduced progressively.

Sri Lanka graphite is highly graphitized; the best grades are completely graphitized. It is favored for lubrication purposes, pencils, electromotive brushes, and other uses requiring quality graphite.

The State Graphite Corp. of Sri Lanka is in charge of the mining operations and the sale of the Sri Lanka graphite.

Other Asian Sources: In 1847, Jean Pierre Alibert, a French merchant residing in Tawasthus, Asiatic Siberia, brought to Europe the knowledge of graphite in Siberia. He had discovered graphite in one of the mountain gorges near Irkutsk and traced the source to the summit of Mount Batougal (later renamed Mount Alibert) in the Saian Mountain range. In 1856, Alibert made an agreement with the German pencil company, A. W. Faber, that only Siberian graphite would be used in the production of Faber's pencils. The graphite is said to have been carried from the mountains to the ocean on the backs of reindeer.

One graphite deposit was worked on West Brother Island, off Hong Kong. The product is similar to Korean amorphous graphite.

The best graphite in India is found near Begumpet in Hyderabad. Deposits also occur near Bihar and Orissa. The Indian deposits are incompletely explored.

Europe

Austria: Two distinct mineralogical regions, Styria and Lower Austria, combine to make Austria the world's second largest known producer of natural graphite. As in all other European deposits, the graphite is thought to have originated by the metamorphism of carboniferous and bituminous substances under high pressure, temperature, and rock deformation. The deposits, therefore, occur in comparatively small lenses and, with one exception, must be mined underground.

Styria contains the more important deposits. A lode of graphitic phyllite extends from the Semmering over Aflenz and Bruck/Leoben into the Palten Valley. The major mines, some of them two centuries old, occur near Kaiserberg and Triben. Reserves are estimated at several million tons. Geologically, these Alpine deposits are embedded in a zone of fine grained, scaly schists and occur as lenses and individual beds up to 35 ft thick. The ore is black, soft, fine grained, and dense, with carbon content of 40–88%. It is low in sulfur (0.2–0.3%) and iron and practically free of carbonate and phosphate. The sorted ore is ground to 200 mesh and used in foundries and steel mills.

The first and only flotation plant for amorphous graphite is in Kaiserberg. The process was developed in the laboratories of Franz Mayr-Melnhof & Co.'s Grafitbergbau Kaisersberg, where fine (2μ average particle size) graphite of 92% carbon is produced, suitable for lubrication, pencils, pigment, and mud drilling. Work is under way to produce purities suitable for nuclear use.

Lower Austrian graphite is harder and more crystalline than that of Styria; moreover, it contains sulfides, carbonates, lime, and pyrrhotite. It is mostly used in foundries and in blast furnaces. It occurs in an area from Spitz, on the Danube, northward to the Bohemian massif in a belt of highly metamorphosed and coarse grained schists, partly of sedimentary origin and always accompanied by marble. Modern earthmoving equipment used in open pit mining has made these deposits economical to exploit. About 60,000 tons of graphite 40–45% carbon is produced annually for use in blast furnaces.

West Germany: The Passau district (Bavaria) has long produced flake graphite suitable for crucibles. Old documents frequently refer to this graphite, which probably furnished the graphite in the Middle Ages for alchemists' crucibles. Mines at Gruben (near Taxberg) are mentioned. By law the inhabitants of Pfaffenreuth in 1250 had to deliver graphite worth one-tenth of their income as a tax. In 1496, Deggendorf levied a tax of four Regensburger pfennigs on each 100 crucibles from the Passau district.

Today, Graphitewerk Kropfmuhl A.G. produces flake graphite exceeding 95% graphitic carbon suitable for crucibles, pencil leads, and lubricants. This company also chemically purifies graphite to 99.9+% carbon in several grades of fineness. The country rock is a part of the "kristallines Grundgebirge," the old gneissic and schistose rocks of the Bohemian massif; the gneissic rocks are considered to have been metamorphosed during the Carboniferous period.

Typically four or five graphitic beds averaging 5 ft thick are mined. Thicker layers occur where there is folding. Some mines have as many as eight layers. The ore runs 20–25% graphitic carbon. It is beneficiated and processed by flotation, grinding, and screening.

Other European Sources: Europe is more self-sufficient in natural graphite than the United States. In 1962, Austria, West Germany, and Norway were able to supply the full complement of kinds and purities of graphites required by all European industry.

Norway—A/S Skaland Grafitverk is the only operating mine in Norway. The deposit, on Senja Island, northern Norway, is of the vein type. One million tons of 25% carbon graphite is the estimated ore reserve. Flotation brings the carbon content up to 80–93%.

Italy—The principal Italian deposits are amorphous graphite associated with gneiss, slate, chalk, and marble. Several mines are located in the Germanasca and Chisone valleys in northern Italy near the French-Italian border. Another deposit is at Bormida, near Genoa. The main workings are southwest of San Germano, about 6600 ft above sea level; the graphite is brought down into the valley for processing.

Spain—Although Spain produces little graphite, there are large deposits in the province of Jaen and near Toledo. A graphite mine operates in Los Cotos de Guadamur.

North America

United States: Graphite production in the United States is inadequate to supply the demand. The one flake producer, Southwestern Graphite Co., of Burnet, TX, closed its mine operation in 1980. However, other mines could be reopened in an emergency. Some 20 to 25 states have deposits that were worked in the past. Most of the deposits are of either fine flake or low grade ores. A deposit of lump graphite is near Dillon, MT. The graphite plants in the United States process imported graphites that are beneficiated, ground, and blended as required to maintain the individual company grades.

Flake graphite deposits in both Alabama and Pennsylvania have been worked intermittently. The latest closing in Alabama was 1953 and in Pennsylvania, 1961. The only domestic production of amorphous graphite ceased in Rhode Island in 1959.

Canada: Canada is endowed with many deposits of commercially important flake graphite. It seems probable that many deposits are yet to be discovered because flake graphite is a common constituent of the Grenville-type Precambrian marble and gneiss of Ontario and Quebec.

Mining started in 1846 in Grenville, Que., and many small properties in the vicinity of

Buckingham were producers between then and 1936.

The only sizable Canadian operation was the Black Donald mine, about 65 miles west of Ottawa. It produced high quality flake graphite between 1897 and 1954, when it closed. The principal country rock is the Grenville marble, associated with which are bands of hornblende schist and pegmatite dikes.

In 1981, Asbury Carbons began production at its Canadian mine operation. It has the capability of producing −30 +80 mesh flake graphite ranging in carbon content from 75 to 95%. With the present know-how, it can be upgraded to a purity of 99.5% in carbon should demand increase.

Mexico: The state of Sonora contains extensive deposits of amorphous graphite and here are located Mexico's graphite mines and mills.

The Sonora deposits are homogeneous, contain about 80% graphitic carbon, and are an important source of amorphous graphite. They were discovered in 1867 and exploitation began in 1891. There are said to be as many as seven distinct beds of graphite within alternating layers of metamorphosed andalusite-bearing Triassic rocks.

The mines under active exploitation are located about 250 miles southeast of the US border in the region of Moradillas. This region is arid, and water for the operations is scarce. Trucking of graphite to the railroad during the brief rainy reason is sometimes interrupted for several days at a time.

Other amorphous graphite deposits are reported in the states of Baja California, and Coahuila in Northern Mexico, and in Hidalgo, Guerrero, and Oaxaca in central and southern Mexico.

The mineral suite for amorphous ore includes mica, clay minerals, tourmaline, and hematite with occasional pyrite and gypsum. The ore is prepared for shipment by hand sorting the admixed rock that comes from the hanging walls; then it is crushed, screened, and dried.

Africa

Malagasy Republic (Madagascar): The island of Madagascar is one of the most important producers of graphite because of the size and quality of its flake. Occurrences are widespread along the eastern coast near Tamatave, in the central section near Tananarive, and in a southern section between Betroka and Bekily. Reserves are undetermined, but considered to be exceptionally large. The first commercial interests were started by French settlers. Present production comes from the deposits along the eastern coast. The main producers are Société Minière de la Grande Ile (also manages the interests of Société Lyonnaise Agriole, Minière et Industrielle, SLAMI), Establissments Gallois, Establissments Izouard, Société Louys, and Establissments Rostaing (Pettifer, 1980). Each company markets its own graphite; graphites from different deposits are not blended.

The deposits are in a region where lateritic deposits of iron and bauxite also are found. The graphite, being resistant to weathering, is found among the weathered residue. Thus, quartz granules from the original crystalline rocks are common, the feldspathic constituents having been completely converted to clay. Some of the mica has survived in partly altered form and is usually found interlaminated between lamellae. The graphite occurs in highly metamorphosed schists and gneisses that have weathered deeply to soft, ferruginous clays. The graphitic content of the original rock has been raised through the natural leaching process.

The crude ore runs from 3 to 10% graphite, of which about two-thirds is large flake, and one-third fine flake. Commercial interest is primarily in the large flake.

The flake is large, strong, and flexible and is the best graphite for refractories. It is also favored for crucibles. The pyrometric cone equivalent (PCE) of the ash runs from cone 16 to cone 20 and is higher than the ash of other flake graphites.

The nongraphitic portion of the flake is uniform and consists (after oxidizing) chiefly of a clayey residue with some quartz. There exists a sprinkling of accessory minerals such as mica, zircon, rutile, and epidote. Sulfur compounds are absent and iron is low. Manganese may run higher than in most graphites. Potassium predominates in the alkali metal content. Carbonates are absent. Volatile matter, including water, is about 1.5%.

Other African Sources: South-West Africa (Namibia) produces an 85% carbon graphite in the district of Bethanien.

Deposits exist in the Transvaal at Carolina and Mopani.

Kenya graphite was mined in open pits near Kanziku. The ore runs about 10% graphitic carbon.

Two mines operate in the Republic of South Africa, at Cumbu and at Mutali. The ore is high in flake graphite, on the order of 20%, but the final product runs about 80% carbon.

Other Sources of Graphite

South America: Itapecerica in Minas Gerais, Brazil, is estimated to produce yearly some 1500 tons of a medium quality vein graphite and is the one commercially important source of Brazilian graphite. Some of this graphite is reportedly refined by flotation to 99% carbon.

Limited production in Argentina is reported. Some deposits are found in the mountains of Pie de Palo; the graphite mined there is shipped to Rosario for beneficiation. The final product is reported to be on the order of 65% carbon.

Australia and New Zealand: There has been small production from Mountain Bopple, Queensland; from Sleaford Bay, Eyre's Peninsula, South Australia; and from Undercliffe, New South Wales. There are also small deposits in West Australia. A deposit about 30 miles from Cloncurry, Queensland, is reported to have large reserves. Several occurrences are also reported in New Zealand.

USSR: Information on Russian deposits is still fragmentary. Resources of graphite, chiefly in Asiatic Russia, have repeatedly been stated to be large. Most of the principal types of deposits are probably represented. For example, thermally metamorphosed coal seams in the Tungusk coal basin west of Irkutsk yield amorphous graphite containing 87 to 94% carbon. Flake graphite deposits are present in the Ukraine, contact-metasomatic deposits have been reported from western Uzbekistan, and small vein deposits are reported from the Alibert mine and from the Krasnaya Polyana region, North Caucasus. The main Alibert deposits are unusual in that the graphite occurs as disseminated flakes and masses in nepheline syenite and in lenses along contacts of nepheline syenite and marble.

Exploration and Development

Prospecting has consisted primarily of outcrop examination, trenching, and sampling. This more-or-less standard procedure has from time to time been augmented by either churn drilling or diamond core drilling. However, the nature of disseminated deposits in particular makes accurate evaluation of grade and tonnage difficult to achieve by only drilling. The successful program of churn drilling near Burnet, Texas, by the Southwestern Graphite Co. in 1928 may have been one of the first to employ the drill as part of an exploration and development program. A diamond drilling program at Notre Dame du Laus in Canada in 1956 was abandoned when the test results showed widely varying percentages.

During World War II several more integrated programs involved geological mapping of specific areas both in Alabama and Pennsylvania in addition to trenching, pitting, and sampling. In 1942 there was some small production at one of these, the Benjamin Franklin Mine, Chester County, PA; the ore was of low grade (3%), however, and mining ceased in 1943.

Because of the high electrical conductivity of graphite, geophysical methods such as resistivity and self-potential have been employed in the search for deposits in Japan, Australia, India, and, to a limited extent, North America.

In the past it appears that the small economic return from graphite mining, at least in North America, has discouraged the launching of any large, integrated, or very sophisticated exploration programs.

Mining Methods

During the period 1890 to 1920, underground mining of graphite was practiced in New York and Pennsylvania. From 1942 until the end of World War II, open pit operation was the only method used, primarily because of the comparative ease of working in weathered rock. Graphite was mined underground at Dillon, MT during World War II and shortly thereafter until extraction of the ore became too costly to compete with Sri Lanka graphite and all operations ceased.

Madagascar operations are entirely open pit, but in Sri Lanka, Korea, Mexico, Bavaria, and Italy, underground mining is essential due to the depth and physical characteristics of the deposits.

Mexican underground mining operations range from a depth of 300 to 1100 ft below the surface, measured on the angle of the vein. Some of the older mines in Sri Lanka reached depths in excess of 1500 ft on a vertical plane.

For many years mining operations in Sri Lanka were primitive and ore extraction slow and cumbersome. The mines were fully mechanized after World War II.

Madagascar operations also were primitive because of the low labor cost. After 1938 the mines began to use mechanical equipment to remove the overburden, and the graphite-bearing schists were easily removed by bulldozers and tractors.

Preparation for Market

In Sri Lanka, the graphite ore is extracted in lumps and hand cobbed on a sorting patio to remove any quartz inclusions. The finished product is graded as follows large lump, 97 to 99% carbon; ordinary lump, 94 to 96% carbon; ordinary lump, 90% carbon; chips, 85 to 90% carbon; and chippy dust, 80% carbon. However, the chippy dust and flying dust are not produced in any quantity today.

In Madagascar the crude ore averages 10 to 12% carbon. It is crushed by a primary crusher and then conveyed to a series of roll crushers and classifiers to remove the oversizes and gangue. The -¼-in. product is then passed to rougher cells, which separate the graphite flakes from the clay and sand. The product of the rougher cells passes to the finishing cells where each particle of graphite is recovered by means of a pine oil frothing process. This yields an 80 to 84% carbon concentrate, which is dried; any residual pine oil is volatized. The run-of-mill product is upgraded by mechanical means, such as rod-mill grinding, to a 50 mesh US Standard sieve with 85 to 90% carbon. Higher carbon concentrates (up to 95%) are obtained by regrinding and flotation.

At the mill of Graphitwerk Kropfmuhl, S.A., in Bavaria, crude ores carrying 10 to 12% carbon are crushed, passed through a series of rolls, and finally a rod mill, which reduces the ore to 40 mesh. This product is fed to a series of flotation cells, and the graphite concentrate is filtered and kiln dried until the final product averages 90 to 93% carbon. For further refinement this product is milled and screened, producing grades with 95 to 96% carbon.

At Skaland, Norway, the crude ore averages 25 to 30% carbon. The crushing and flotation process used at this mine is similar to those already described. Grades of 80, 85, and 90% carbon are produced. The mill had a capacity of 12,000 tons in 1971.

Uses

Foundry Facings: The largest single use for natural graphite is foundry facings, which account for more than one-third of the tonnage and about one-fifth of the value of the total. This use, combined with graphite used in steelmaking (such as carbon raiser, hot topping, and ingot wash), accounts for about one-half of the total consumption of graphite and about one-third of the total value of all natural graphite used in the US.

Batteries: Natural graphite is suitable for batteries that are required to furnish small currents over long periods of time. However, it is not particularly efficient for use in the type of battery currently used in flashlights and has been replaced by a form of carbon black. With rural electrification and the declining use of large dry batteries, graphite consumption has declined. Since carbon black is satisfactory and cheap, there seems to be little opportunity for natural graphite to reverse this downward trend through product improvement.

Bearings: Graphite is used extensively in bearings but the reactions both of producers and consumers to the potential for increased use varies with respect to the type of bearings being produced. One bearing producer thinks the use of graphite will increase because of the increased sales of fully molded, self-lubricating, phenolic bearings. Graphite use might also be stimulated if graphite could be included in high-speed, high-load bearings.

Another producer of powder-metal bronze bearings uses graphite only when special formulations are specified by its customers. Despite this specialized use, graphite consumption has increased, particularly in ferrous-base formulations. This producer has found natural graphite better suited to his purpose than artificial.

The use of graphite in bearings subjected to extreme heat or low humidity causes problems. For example, if the humidity is low, graphite will act as an abrasive, scoring the surface with which it comes in contact.

Use of natural graphite in bearings should continue to increase, but the rate of increase might be accelerated if the problems of using it under conditions of high load, high speed, high temperature, and low humidity could be solved.

Brake Linings: As long as organic friction materials impregnated with graphite are used and accepted as satisfactory, the consumption of graphite should increase gradually in accordance with the increased number of vehicles on the road. Graphite is particularly useful in brake linings for heavy-duty vehicles as opposed to passenger vehicles.

Molybdenum disulfide is the only potential competitor, but it has been tried with only limited success in some applications and has a decided cost disadvantage.

The appearance of new, iron-based, sintered, friction materials containing up to 30% graphite may be significant. If these are utilized, the use of graphite in friction materials could increase more rapidly in the future. One consumer has suggested the desirability of a reduced content of abrasive alumina and silica in graphite but has emphasized that cost is more important than minor improvements along this line.

Crucibles: Consumers vary in their opinion as to the future trend of clay-graphite vs. carbon-bonded crucibles and the relative importance of fine vs. flake graphites. The disagreement centers primarily around how important the use of more oxidation-resistant, clay-graphite compositions with molten aluminum will become. The introduction of the clay-graphite bell in the immersion-bell technique for converting cast iron to ductile iron may create a new market.

The recent gradual decline in the use of graphite in crucibles may halt and a slight recovery is possible. On the negative side, the increase in ladle sizes will cause less use of stoppers and the consequent reduction in continuous casting might eliminate the need for stoppers. However, these negative trends might be balanced by the greater use of clay graphite for nozzles and perhaps for the well block.

One consumer has suggested the need for greater uniformity in graphite shipments, especially with respect to carbon content and particle size distribution, and a need for the reduction of impurities in graphite for stopper use.

Carbon Brushes and Other Electrical Uses: Natural graphite encounters considerable competition from artificial graphite for this use. Despite this competition, the tremendous growth of the electrical industry is expected to result in increased consumption of natural graphite. It seems that where artificial graphite has advantages it has already captured the market. For example, in the production of sliding contacts the variation in the ash content of natural graphite has proved unacceptable; now artificial graphite in which the abrasive materials can be controlled is being used.

Lubricants: This market is tremendously complex because of the variety of lubricating jobs that must be done and the imposing array of types of lubricants that are available. Graphite has been an important lubricant and will probably continue to be, but competition is stiff.

Graphite added to a soapy lubricant is considered to be a good die lubricant, particularly for galvanized wire, though the discoloration it produces is not a desirable feature. Natural graphite is a good antiseize agent in steel mill and railroad applications because it creates a solid lubricant film that retains its properties under pressure and high temperature. In this particular use the graphite content is specified by the customer; hence its use may not be based on strictly technical grounds. Natural graphite is used in greases where the grease application is such that the siliceous portion of the natural graphite is overshadowed by the indigenous contamination of dirt and sand, i.e., gear lubrication for mining machinery.

Graphite of colloidal size dispersed in kerosene, oil, or some other carrier can be used when a high-temperature film with a quick-drying characteristic is desired in high-temperature lubricating jobs, i.e., conveyors passing through ovens.

Packings: Fine flake graphite used with oils or greases is very satisfactory because of its resistance to heat up to 600°F. Closely controlled particle size is not too important for packing use. Use of graphite will tend to remain steady, but it may decline because equipment being manufactured today doesn't utilize old style packings. One consumer has mentioned that very small quantities of molybdenum offer excellent lubricating qualities.

Pencils: The use of pencils is increasing and, with it, the total market for graphite will increase. There is some shift from Sri Lanka graphite to Mexican and domestic amorphous graphite because of the grayish cast of the Sri Lanka variety. The pencil industry seeks to make improvements that would lead to greater jetness, higher carbon content, smaller particle sizes, and more unctuousness (opacity) in the graphite. However, such improvements must not add to the cost of graphite to the pencil manufacturer.

Refractories: The demand for graphite in linings that will impart non-wetting characteristics when in contact with molten metals should remain constant. Any improvement in oxidation resistance would be desirable. Though the quantity involved is small, the use of graphite should increase gradually in graphite magnesite refractories, plastic refractories, and patching materials.

Prices

The *Chemical Marketing Reporter,* formerly the *Oil, Paint and Drug Reporter,* quotes prices on an ex-warehouse basis. June 13, 1983 quotations:

	$ per Lb
No. 1 flake graphite, 90 to 95% carbon	0.45–0.75
No. 2 flake graphite, 90 to 95% carbon	0.45–0.75

$ per Lb

Powdered crystalline graphite:
  88 to 90% carbon   0.25–0.60
  90 to 92% carbon   0.35–0.65
  95 to 96% carbon   0.45–0.75
Powdered amorphous graphite   0.14–0.38
Powdered amorphous or crystalline
  graphite, minimum of 97% carbon   0.60–1.00

April, 1983 prices, f.o.b. sources, were
quoted in *Engineering & Mining Journal* for
two major classifications of graphite imported
by the United States:

$ per Mt, 1983

Flake and crystalline graphite, bags:
  Sri Lanka   600–1700
  Germany, West   350–3500
  Malagasy Republic   250–700
  Norway   300–900
  China   250–1700
Amorphous, nonflake, cryptocrystal-
line graphite (80 to 85% carbon)
  Mexico (bulk)   70–100
  South Korea (bags)   90–120

TABLE 1—Tonnage and Value of Graphite Imports, Exports, and Consumption in the US, and World Production, 1976-1980

		1976	1977	1978	1979	1980
United States:						
Apparent consumption*	short tons	†66,862	†73,773	90,396	77,562	52,438
Exports	do	12,236	13,783	9,595	8,623	8,880
Value	thousands	$2,388	$2,662	$2,304	$3,741	$3,695
Imports for consumption‡	short tons	79,098	87,556	99,991	86,185	61,318
Value	thousands	$6,753	$8,058	$11,700	$13,035	$15,765
World: Production	short tons	ʳ495,481	ʳ546,022	ʳ583,030	ʳ590,774	597,429

Source: Taylor, 1981.
ʳRevised.
*Excludes domestic production.
†Revised to include some manufactured graphite imported for consumption.
‡Includes some manufactured graphite.

TABLE 2—Consumption* of Natural Graphite in the United States, 1980, by Use

Use	Crystalline		Amorphous†		Total	
	Quantity (short tons)	Value	Quantity (short tons)	Value	Quantity (short tons)	Value
Batteries	W	W	W	W	1,737	2,178,963
Brake linings	933	959,438	2,013	1,534,062	2,946	2,493,500
Carbon products‡	182	243,258	408	360,378	590	603,636
Crucibles, retorts, stoppers, sleeves, nozzles	W	W	W	W	2,340	2,063,869
Foundries	1,366	1,092,086	6,466	2,411,549	7,832	3,503,635
Lubricants§	867	1,176,091	5,521	1,983,113	6,388	3,159,204
Pencils	977	1,502,433	340	337,236	1,317	1,839,669
Powdered metals	288	360,528	112	182,287	400	542,815
Refractories	1,062	224,887	11,577	2,161,400	12,639	2,386,287
Rubber	31	24,894	241	167,931	272	192,825
Steelmaking	386	164,875	9,373	4,732,611	9,759	4,897,486
Other††	6,928	5,471,546	805	693,470	3,656	1,922,184
Total	13,020	11,220,036	36,856	14,564,037	49,876	25,784,073

Source: Taylor, 1981.
ʳRevised. W Withheld to avoid disclosing company proprietary data; included with "Other."
*Consumption data incomplete. Small consumers excluded.
†Includes mixtures of natural and manufactured graphite.
‡Includes bearings and carbon brushes.
§Includes ammunition, packings, and seed coating.
†† Includes paints and polishes, antiknock and other compounds, drilling mud, electrical and electronic products, insulation, magnetic tape, small packages, and miscellaneous and proprietary uses.

TABLE 3—Graphite: World Production, by Country

(Short tons)

Country *	1976	1977	1978	1979ᴾ	1980ᵉ
Argentina	160	94	28	11	†13
Austria	36,439	38,898	44,645	44,664	44,000
Brazil (marketable)	6,634	10,127	11,417	11,979	13,200
Burma‡	177	106	309	295	300
China mainlandᵉ	55,000	66,000	88,000	110,000	110,000
Czechoslovakiaᵉ	49,600	49,600	49,600	49,600	49,600
Germany, Federal Republic ofᵉ§	ʳ10,528	ʳ9,178	7,034	4,047	4,000
India	42,189	53,412	70,310	56,141	†53,787
Italy	4,242	4,210	4,528	4,522	4,500
Korea, Northᵉ	ʳ22,000	ʳ22,000	ʳ22,000	28,000	28,000
Korea, Republic of:					
Amorphous	42,193	68,904	59,288	59,789	†65,209
Crystalline flake	3,762	3,799	2,793	2,704	†1,575
Madagascar	19,193	17,336	18,326	15,699	16,000
Mexico:					
Amorphous	66,510	64,410	57,611	56,086	61,000
Crystalline flake	—	—	—	—	200
Norway	9,999	10,028	12,292	13,226	12,200
Romaniaᵉ	6,600	6,600	6,600	6,600	6,600
Sri Lanka	ʳ9,138	9,783	11,581	10,397	10,600
South Africa, Republic of	584	1,004	643	434	—
Thailand	33	33	25	25	25
Turkey	NA	NA	NA	231	220
USSRᵉ	105,000	105,000	110,000	110,000	110,000
United States	W	W	W	W	—
Zimbabwe	ᵉ5,500	ᵉ5,500	ᵉ6,000	6,324	6,400
Total	ʳ495,481	ʳ546,022	583,030	590,774	597,429

Source: Taylor, 1981.

ᵉEstimated. ᴾPreliminary. ʳRevised. NA, Not available. W, Withheld to avoid disclosing company proprietary data.

In addition to the countries listed, Namibia may have produced graphite during the period covered by this table, but output is unreported and available general information is inadequate for formulation of reliable estimates of output levels.

†Reported figure.

‡Data are for fiscal year beginning Apr. 1 of that stated.

§Series revised; data now presented represents estimated marketable product derived from raw graphite mined indigenously, assuming that marketable output equals one-half of officially reported raw graphite production.

Graphite is granted a depletion allowance of 22%. Prices of imported graphite were generally higher, which indicated that importers were, for the time being, absorbing the cost increases and not passing them on to their customers.

Nevertheless, published prices for natural graphite merely represent the range of prices. Actual prices are negotiated between buyer and seller on the basis of a wide range of specifications.

Recent Production

Tables 1, 2, and 3 present basic data on the production, consumption, imports, and exports of graphite in the United States and on world production.

Manufactured graphite was produced at 28 plants in 1981 with additional production for in-house use likely. Table 4 lists US producers of manufactured graphite. Manufactured graphite was produced at other plants in the United States, but their output could not be included in this tabulation. Most of these plants produced specialty products, which were small in total tonnage, although their unit values were relatively high.

TABLE 4—US Producers of Manufactured Graphite

Company	Plant location	Product*
Airco Carbon, Div. of Airco, Inc.	Niagara Falls, NY	Anodes, electrodes, crucibles, motor
Do	Punxsutawney, PA	brushes, refractories, unmachined
Do	St. Marys, PA	shapes, powder.
Avco Corp., Avco Specialty Materials Div.	Lowell, MA	High-modulus fibers.
The Carborundum Co., Graphite Products Div.	Hickman, KY †	Electrodes, motor brushes, unmachined shapes, cloth.
Do	Niagara Falls, NY	
Do	Sanborn, NY	
Celanese Corp., Celanese Research Lab.	Summit, NJ	High-modulus fibers.
Fiber Materials, Inc.	Biddeford, Maine	Do.
BF Goodrich Co., Engineered Systems Div., Super Temp Operation.	Santa Fe Springs, CA	Other.
Great Lakes Carbon Corp.	Morganton, NC	Anodes, electrodes, powder.
Do	Niagara Falls, NY	
Do	Rosamond, CA	
Hercules Inc.	Salt Lake City, Utah	High-modulus fibers.
HITCO Materials Group ARMCO Co.	Gardena, CA	Cloth and high-modulus fibers.
Pfizer Minerals, Pigments & Metals Div.	Easton, PA	Other.
Poco Graphite, Inc.	Decatur, TX	Unspecified.
Polycarbon, Inc.	North Hollywood, CA	Cloth.
Sigri Carbon Corp.	Hickman, KY	Electrodes, other.
The Stackpole Corp., Carbon Div.	Lowell, MA	High-modulus fibers, anodes, motor brushes, unmachined shapes, powder.
Do	St. Marys, PA	
Superior Graphite Co.	Chicago, IL	Powder and other.
Do	Hopkinsville, KY	
Union Carbide Corp., Carbon Products Div.	Clarksburg, WV	Anodes, electrodes, unmachined shapes, motor brushes, powder, cloth, high-modulus fibers.
Do	Columbia, TN	
Do	Fostoria, Ohio	
Do	Greenville, SC	
Do	Niagara Falls, NY	
Do	Yabucoa, PR	

Source: Taylor, 1981.

*Cloth includes low-modulus fibers; electric motor brushes includes machined shapes; crucibles includes vessels.

†Plant sold to Sigri Carbon Corp., May 31, 1980.

Bibliography and References

Alling, H.L., 1917, "The Adirondack Graphite Deposits," Bulletin 199, New York State Museum, 150 pp.

Bascom, F., and Beach, L.M., 1922, "Graphite" and "History of Graphite Mining in Pennsylvania," *Mineral Resources of the United States, 1919*, Pt. 2, *Nonmetals*, US Geological Survey, pp. 309–324.

Bastin, E.S., 1912, "The Graphite Deposits of Ceylon, with a Description of a Similar Graphite Deposit near Dillon, Montana," *Economic Geology*, Vol. 7, No. 5, Aug., pp. 419–443.

Cameron, E.N., 1960, "Graphite," *Industrial Minerals and Rocks*," 3rd ed., J.L. Gillson, ed., AIME, New York, pp. 455–468.

Cameron, E.N., and Weis, P.L., 1960, "Strategic Graphite, a Survey," Bulletin 1082–E, US Geological Survey, pp. 250–252.

Chelf, C., 1943, "Graphite in Llano County, Texas," Mineral Resources Circular 57, Bureau of Economic Geology, Texas University, 10 pp.

Clark, T.H., 1921, "The Origin of Graphite," *Economic Geology*, Vol. 16, No. 3, Apr.-May, pp. 167–183.

Cole, J.W., 1965, "Graphite," *Mineral Facts and Problems*, Bulletin 630, US Bureau of Mines, pp. 399–409.

Ford, R.B., 1954, "Occurrence and Origin of the Graphite Deposits near Dillon, Montana," *Economic Geology*, Vol. 49, No. 1, Jan.-Feb., pp. 31–43.

Gupta, B.C., 1949, "Graphite," *Indian Minerals*, Vol. 3, No. 1, p. 17–31.

Jones, W.B., 1929, "Summary Report on Graphite in Alabama," Circular 9, Alabama Geological Survey, 29 pp.

Kemberling, S.M., and Walker, P.L., Jr., 1961, "Progress Report on Natural Graphite Studies," Fuel Technology Dept., The Pennsylvania State University, University Park, pp. 1–6.

Klar, G., 1958, "The Important Graphite Deposits of the World," *Mining Magazine*, pp. 98, 137–142.

Lewis, R.W., 1970, "Graphite (Natural)," *Mineral Facts and Problems*, Bulletin 650, US Bureau of Mines, pp. 1025–1038.

Miller, B.L., 1912, "Graphite Deposits of Pennsylvania," Report 6, Pennsylvania Topographical and Geological Survey, 147 pp.

Murdock, T.M., 1963, "Mineral Resources of the Malagasy Republic," Information Circular 8196, US Bureau of Mines, pp. 112–121.

Needham, A.B., 1946, "Mining and Milling Operations of Southwestern Graphite Co., Burnet County, Texas," Information Circular 7339, US Bureau of Mines, 3 pp.

Overstreet, W.C., 1947, "Graphite Deposits of Southern Korea," *Economic Geology*, Vol. 42, No. 4, June-July, pp. 424–425.

Paige, S., 1911, "Mineral Resources of the Llano-Burnet Region, Texas," Geological Atlas, Folio 183, US Geological Survey, 16 pp.

Pallister, H.D., and Thoenin, J.R., 1948, "Flake Graphite and Vanadium Investigations in Clay, Coosa, and Chilton Counties, Alabama," Report of Investigation 4366, US Bureau of Mines, 84 pp.

Pettifer, L., 1980, "Natural Graphite—The Dawn of Tight Markets," *Industrial Minerals*, No. 156, Sept., pp. 19–39.

Pettifer, L., 1980a, "Synthetic Graphite—Electrodes Continue to Lead," *Industrial Minerals*, No. 158, Nov., pp. 19–31.

Piper, E.L., 1973, "Manufactured Graphites," SME Preprint 73H14, AIME Annual Meeting, Chicago, IL, Feb., 15 pp.

Rauch, H.W., Sr., 1971, "Graphite Fiber: Another Wonder Material," *Ceramic Age*, Vol. 87, No. 5, May, p. 24.

Schanz, J.J., Jr., 1960, "Natural Graphite Market Research," Progress Reports Nos. 1, 2, Jan. 1-Nov. 30, College of Mineral Industries, The Pennsylvania State University, University Park.

Shobert, E.I., II, 1964, "Natural and Synthetic Graphites," SME Preprint 64H56, AIME Annual Meeting, New York, Feb., 14 pp.

Seeley, S.B., 1963, "Natural Graphite," *Encyclo-pedia of Chemical Technology*, Vol. 4, 2nd ed., Kirk-Othmer, ed., Interscience Publishers, New York, pp. 304–335.

Spence, H.S., 1920, "Graphite," Canada Dept. of Mines, pp. 1–9.

Taylor, H.A., Jr., 1978–1979, "Graphite," Preprint, US Bureau of Mines, p. 9.

Taylor, H.A., Jr., 1981, "Graphite," *Minerals Yearbook, 1980*, US Bureau of Mines, pp. 375–384.

Tron, A.R., 1964, *The Production and Uses of Natural Graphite*, Her Majesty's Stationery Office, London, Feb., pp. 1–83.

Wadia, D.N., 1943, "Origin of the Graphite Deposits of Ceylon," Professional Paper 1, Records, Dept. of Mineralogy, Ceylon, Pt. 2, pp. 15–24.

Weis, P.L., 1973, "Graphite," *United States Mineral Resources*, Professional Paper 820, US Geological Survey, pp. 277–283.

Weis, P.L., and Salas, G.A., 1978, "Estimating Reserves of Amorphous Graphite in Sonora, Mexico," *Engineering and Mining Journal*, Vol. 174, No. 10, Oct., pp. 123–128.

Willard, D.G., 1971, "Graphite," *Minerals Yearbook 1971*, US Bureau of Mines, pp. 561–567.

Willard, D.G., 1971, "Graphite," *Minerals Yearbook 1972*, US Bureau of Mines, pp. 589–595.

Winchell, A.N., 1916, "A Theory for the Origin of Graphite as Exemplified in the Graphite Deposits near Dillon, Montana," *Economic Geology*, Vol. 6, pp. 218–230.

Gypsum and Anhydrite

FRANK C. APPLEYARD *

The two calcium sulfate minerals—gypsum and anhydrite—occur in many parts of the world, and gypsum has long been of economic importance in the family of industrial minerals. Gypsum, the dihydrate form of calcium sulfate ($CaSO_4 \cdot 2H_2O$) and anhydrite, the anhydrous form ($CaSO_4$) are frequently found in close association, and it is seldom that a calcium sulfate deposit will consist exclusively of one mineral or the other.

Although known gypsum deposits are extensive, anhydrite makes up the largest part of total calcium sulfate reserves. However, it has very minor economic use, and most of the following discussion will be devoted to gypsum.

Calcium sulfate is one of the principal constituents of evaporite deposits, and when pure, has the following composition:

	Lime (CaO)	Sulfur Trioxide (SO_3)	Combined Water (H_2O)
Gypsum	32.6%	46.5%	20.9%
Anhydrite	41.2%	58.8%	—

Deposits of pure gypsum or of pure anhydrite which are large enough to be considered commercial have never been found because of both the metastable relationship between the two minerals, and the presence of impurities such as calcium or magnesium carbonates, chlorides, other sulfate minerals, clay minerals, or silica. As a result most mine production of gypsum will range between 85 and 95% pure. Often it is used as mined, although in certain cases, one or more forms of mineral beneficiation are employed to upgrade the product.

End Uses

The largest use for gypsum is based upon the unique property which calcium sulfate has of readily giving up, or taking on, water of crystal-

* Formerly Vice President, Raw Material Resources, US Gypsum Co., Chicago, IL. Now retired, Tubac, AZ.

lization. With the application of a moderate amount of heat in a process known as calcining, gypsum is converted to plaster of paris (the hemihydrate of calcium sulfate, $CaSO_4 \cdot \frac{1}{2} H_2O$) which when mixed with water will set or harden as the calcium sulfate returns to the dihydrate form. This semifinished product, usually called stucco, is then manufactured into a large variety of plasters, wallboard, and block for construction use, or into plasters for industrial applications. About 75% of the gypsum used in the United States is calcined for these purposes.

Uncalcined uses of gypsum are principally as a retarder for portland cement, as a soil conditioner, as a mineral filler, and other minor industrial applications. About 25% of the gypsum mined in the United States goes into these markets; however, in less developed countries where construction and other industrial uses may be quite limited, the use of uncalcined gypsum for portland cement retarder may well be the dominant—if not the only—market for the mineral.

It has often been noted that calcium sulfate constitutes the world's largest reserve of sulfur, and minor use of both anhydrite and gypsum has been made to produce sulfuric acid or other sulfur compounds such as ammonium sulfate. However, because sulfur is readily available at lower cost from other sources, use of calcium sulfate has been limited to only a few locations where it could compete economically. No such use is reported in the United States at this time.

Mineralogy

Anhydrite, $CaSO_4$, because of its geologically rapid conversion to gypsum, and relatively high solubility (about 0.2 g per 100 g H_2O) is not often found outcropping in climates wet enough to support abundant vegetation except on steeply dipping slopes or other places where hydrated material is continuously removed. Anhydrite rock is most often light to bluish gray in color, and under the microscope, varies from granoblastic (ver Planck, 1952) to felty-lath crystal aggregates. Fig. 1 shows felty-lath anhydrite crystals from Shoals, IN.

Bassanite, $CaSO_4 \cdot \frac{1}{2} H_2O$, is a distinct phase intermediate between anhydrite and gypsum, but is identifiable only by X-ray diffraction or petrographic techniques using very carefully prepared samples. Bassanite is metastable under ordinary conditions (Wood and Wolfe, 1969); however, its occurrence in amounts under 1% is suspected to be widespread in calcium sulfate mineral deposits.

Gypsum, $CaSO_4 \cdot 2H_2O$, is the commonly observed calcium sulfate mineral in rock outcrops because of its diverse origins. It is easily distinguished from anhydrite by its inferior hardness (2.0 vs. 3 to 3.5) and lower specific gravity (2.2 to 2.4 vs. 2.7 to 3.0). Most gypsum is white to grayish white although the impurities in any given deposit frequently determine the color of the rock and resulting products. Petrographically, most rock gypsum is granoblastic (Goodman et al., 1957). Commercial deposits show a great variety of crystal sizes and textures, both from deposit to deposit and within a single deposit. Relatively undisturbed deposits often contain texturally consistent stratigraphic units, but in deposits that have been deformed the gypsum is often recrystallized and shows a variety of textures. Many deposits exhibit porphyroblastic textures wherein two distinct sizes and ages of crystals occur (Holiday, 1970), and in some deposits fibrous gypsum similar to felty-lath anhydrite makes up the mass (Van't Hoff et al., 1903).

Alabaster is a compact, very fine grained variety of rock gypsum prized by sculptors for its uniform workability under the chisel, and occasionally is found within commercial deposits. Fibrous gypsum composed of needle-shaped crystals in orientation parallel to the C-axis (Schmidt, 1914), is known as **satin spar** and is a type of stress mineral indicative of deformation. It is universally a secondary mineral and occurs widely as a fracture filling wherein the needle lengths are perpendicular to the fracture walls, and less commonly in shear zones wherein the needles are parallel to the direction of movement. Large euhedral gypsum crystals and large cleavages commonly known as **selenite** form in fluid-filled spaces or in an easily deformable host material, and are sometimes mistakenly identified as mica by the uninitiated. Both satin spar and selenite are of little or no economic importance other than being accessories in rock gypsum, although one deposit consisting primarily of coarse selenite crystals is being worked near Apex, NV (Bergstrom, 1961). Fig. 2 shows selenite from Sperry, Iowa.

Origin and Occurrence

The calcium sulfate minerals are deposited by precipitation from aqueous solution when the concentration of the components and the physical conditions are suitable, with the majority of the deposits originating from evaporation and concentration of marine brines in a dry climate, i.e., evaporite conditions. That this is the basic mechanism of formation of economic calcium sulfate deposits is unquestioned; however, there is considerable discussion in the literature as to the physical environment in which precipitation takes place, and as to whether the originally precipitated mineral is gypsum or anhydrite.

The older, well established concept of de-

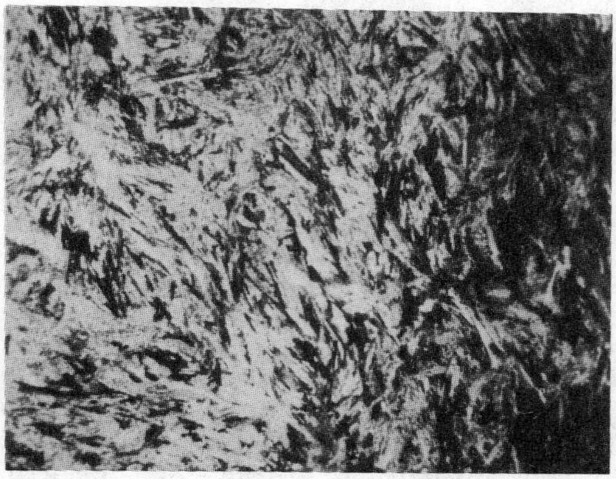

FIG. 1—*Felty-lath anhydrite from Shoals, IN. X39, polarized light.*

FIG. 2—*Selenite crystal from Sperry, Iowa.*

posit formation idealizes a brine-filled basin having restricted circulation (Branson, 1915; King, 1971) which permits limited replenishment of the brine as it evaporates. The resulting concentration causes precipitation of the contained salts in the inverse order of their solubility, and substantial thickness of essentially monomineralic deposits (e.g., calcium sulfate) are visualized as being derived from this type regime, an example of which is the A subzone of the Mississippian Windsor series of southeastern Canada.

A more recent concept of evaporite deposition has resulted from considerable work done in the Trucial Coast of Arabia (Butler, 1970; Kinsman, 1966, 1969) which describes the sabkha supratidal environment wherein calcium sulfate minerals are currently being deposited (*sabkha*, an Arabic word denoting salt-flat— Kinsman, 1966). These deposits are characterized by a distinctive sequence of sediments including lagoonal limestones, intertidal algal mat limestones, and precipitation of gypsum crystals and nodular anhydrite in the preexisting host sediments, which if originally calcium carbonate, become dolomitized. Clastic sediments, if present, are unaffected chemically, but are contorted and displaced as the gypsum crystals and nodular anhydrite grow in them. In the sabkha regime a basin is not required for deposition, although some concentration of the original seawater brine does take place in alongshore lagoons. Thick chloride accumulations would not be expected (Schroeder, 1970). The Mississippian evaporites of southwestern Indiana illustrate this type of deposit (Jorgensen and Carr, 1972).

The classical in-basin accumulations of sulfates and chlorides might be expected to have sabkha deposits along the margin of the basin, and the Silurian gypsum of Ohio, Ontario, and New York is possibly of this origin. The individual sulfate beds in sabkhas do not commonly exceed 20 to 40 ft in thickness, although 200-ft accumulations have been described in Jamaica, W.I. (Holliday, 1971).

Gypsum may also precipitate along fractures, bedding planes or in other available spaces where ground water carrying sulfate ions from the oxidation of sulfides comes into contact with carbonate rocks. Such deposits, however, are of limited extent, and rarely—if ever— could be expected to have economic importance.

Because gypsum will precipitate wherever brine concentration is appropriate, and recrystallizes or dissolves readily as the metastable or temporary environments change, interpretation of geologic evidence to determine exact depositional environments is difficult at best. Several recent works (Dean and Schreiber, 1978; Kendall, 1978; and others) are helpful in determining depositional environments.

Gypsite deposits usually occur in semiarid and arid climates, and result from the solution of existing gypsum deposits by ground water, which in turn is drawn toward the surface by capillary action where it evaporates to deposit the dissolved sulfate as a porous aggregate of gypsum containing considerable impurities. Also, in a few cases, reworking of existing deposits by wind erosion has concentrated gypsum in sand deposits, as at White Sands, NM or Cuatrocienegas, Coahuila, Mexico.

Of totally different origin are those calcium sulfate deposits which constitute part of the cap rock of salt domes in the Gulf Coast basin. The exact origin of these domes is not fully understood but most prevailing views involve flowage and upward movement of plastically deformed salt in response to overburden pressure from the overlying sediments (Martinez, 1974). Once the upward movement is initiated, it is possible for the top of the lighter salt mass to be injected into and through the overlying sediments.

The theory most widely accepted as to the origin of the cap rock is that it represents a residue of anhydrite and other relatively insoluble minerals which accumulate at the upper surface of the salt dome as it rises through water-bearing sediments and the salt is dissolved. The anhydrite crystals, which make up about 99% of the water insoluble residue (Walker, 1974), are then recrystallized and compacted to form a massive rock which may be locally hydrated to form gypsum.

The total height of a salt dome can exceed 10,000 ft, with the cap rock being well over 1000 ft. Most domes are roughly circular in plan view, and range in diameter from about 3280 ft to more than 4 miles, although there is great diversity in dome geometry and dome-to-cap-rock relationships. Most domes do not reach the present surface, although occasionally cap rock is found at or near the surface and might be of economic significance.

Distribution of Deposits

Calcium sulfate minerals have been found within every geologic system from Silurian through Quaternary. The largest production in North America is from Mississippian rocks in southeastern Canada, Michigan, Indiana, and Virginia, followed by that from Permian rocks in Texas, Oklahoma, Kansas, Colorado, Wyoming, Nevada, and Arizona. Production from Tertiary rocks is obtained in California, Jamaica, and Arizona, from Jurassic rocks in Iowa, New Mexico, Colorado, Utah, Wyoming, and Montana, and from Silurian rocks in New York, Ontario, and Ohio. Elsewhere, Tertiary rocks in Australia, France, and Italy, Permian and Jurassic rocks in England, and the Triassic in France, Germany, and England contain large commercial deposits. Commercial deposits range in thickness from 40 in. to over 100 ft, and reserves of individual deposits are usually measured in millions of tons. Production rates commonly average 200,000 to 300,000 tpy from each operation, but range from a few thousand tons up to about two million tons.

Although gypsum is produced from rocks of many ages, many deposits are Quaternary in age due to the recent and continuing conversion of anhydrite to gypsum that occurs under certain conditions. This conversion of anhydrite to gypsum, as well as the reverse reaction, has been extensively studied because of its importance in the original sequence of deposition from brines, as well as in metamorphism that occurs in calcium sulfate deposits after deposition. Several reviews have been made (Braitsch, 1971; Hardie, 1967; Mac Donald, 1953; Wood and Wolfe, 1969) of such variables as brine composition, temperature, water pressure, and overburden pressure. From these it is evident that no one set of conditions applies to all deposits. On the contrary, all these variables, plus structural, lithological, and topographical considerations which might affect water migration, must be examined in order to understand the degree of hydration of any given calcium sulfate deposit. To date, however, only limited attempts have been carried out in an effort to integrate theoretical models with field evidence of rock textures and structures.

Most commercial gypsum deposits are believed to have resulted from the action of surface and ground waters upon anhydrite, and hydration has been found at depths ranging from zero to more than 2000 ft below the surface. In many deposits, the degree of hydration is readily predictable once the variables controlling it are understood; however, in others the degree of hydration can vary widely, with corresponding reduction in the amount of available reserves, and increase in the cost of mining. In all cases, the operator is well advised to thoroughly explore and understand the anhydrite-gypsum relationship prior to development of a mine.

Impurities in Calcium Sulfate Deposits

The number of minerals which can occur in evaporite deposits is quite large (Braitsch, 1971), and many can be found as impurities in calcium sulfate deposits. Their occurrence is often dependent upon the mode of formation of the deposit. In varying degrees, most gypsum and anhydrite deposits contain clastic sediments, commonly clay minerals and fine sands, as well as chemical sediments such as limestones and dolomites. In sabkha-type deposits, these preexisting sediments will fill intermodular spaces of the gypsum and anhydrite, or form crude layers, and often appear to be replaced when they actually are displaced. Relatively insoluble evaporite minerals such as celestite, certain borates, some carbonate minerals, and silica may occur in calcium sulfate deposits as discrete crystals, crystal aggregates or nodules, and probably are in many cases original depositional features. However, strontium or boron, which may be present in only trace amounts in anhydrite, may migrate during gypsification to result in strontium and boron mineral accumulations.

Soluble evaporite minerals, e.g., halite, sylvite, mirabilite, epsomite, and others are also frequently found in calcium sulfate deposits. These too are expelled from anhydrite during gypsification, and most commonly, become associated with the clay minerals that may be present, probably being adsorbed on the clay mineral surfaces. They also are associated with the carbonate impurities where they may be absorbed into mineral surfaces, held as fluid inclusions, or included in a disordered lattice. In addition, these soluble minerals can occur as microfracture filling. The hydration halo of mixed gypsum-anhydrite commonly contains many times the soluble salt content of either unhydrated anhydrite or hydrated gypsum. Individual deposits show great variation in the quantity and type of soluble salts present, i.e., sulfates or chlorides, and it has been noted that, in general, chloride salts predominate in gypsum deposits of eastern North America, whereas sulfate salts exceed chlorides in western North American deposits.

In addition to the foregoing evaporite mineral impurities whose origin is generally a feature of original calcium sulfate deposition, impurities in any given mining operation may also be encountered as a result of structural features such as tight folding or faulting, or from recent erosional activity. These usually take the form of clays, sands, or gravels and occur most often in near surface deposits, although structural deformation can result in severe impurity problems at considerable depth. More often than not, the greatest quantity of impurity in a gypsum deposit is anhydrite (and vice versa), a result of the metastable relationship of these two minerals as previously discussed.

As utilized, most gypsum contains from 10 to 15% of impurities, although some deposits may be exceptionally pure (i.e., plus 95%) or somewhat impure (i.e., 80%). In general, the amount of impurity which can be tolerated depends upon: (1) the type of impurity, (2) the product being manufactured, and (3) the competitive situation.

Based upon the effect impurities may have upon the manufacturing process and finished products, impurities may be separated into three categories:

1) Insoluble or relatively insoluble minerals such as limestone, dolomite, anhydrite, anhydrous clays, silica minerals, etc.

2) Soluble chloride minerals such as halite, sylvite, etc.

3) Hydrous minerals such as the sulfate salts mirabilite and epsomite, and the montmorillonite group of clays.

The first category, to the extent that the minerals replace gypsum, reduce the strength of rehydrated stucco and increase weights of the finished plaster or wallboard, i.e., more pounds of an impure stucco are required to obtain a given strength. Nevertheless many commercial gypsum deposits contain as much as 10 to 15% of these insoluble impurities. The presence of the second category, chloride salts, affects calcining temperature, and stucco slurry consistency and set time. These impurities are usually limited to no more than 0.02 to 0.03%. The principal impact of the third category is in moisture pickup of the finished product and on bonding characteristics of the gypsum stucco core of wallboard to its paper covering. Hydrous sulfate salts must be limited to 0.02 to 0.03%; however, hydrous clays up to 1.0 to 2.0% may be tolerated.

Major North American Producing Areas

The principal gypsum producing areas in North America are shown on Fig. 3. Table 1 lists the North American gypsum production. In addition, there are many more known, but undeveloped gypsum deposits, especially in the midwestern and western states, southeastern Canada, and Mexico. Domestic reserves are geographically distributed in 23 states and have

been estimated to contain 20 billion tons, or approximately 2000 years' supply at current production rates (Schroeder, 1970). Quantitative information is lacking on gypsum reserves in the rest of the world, but deposits are widespread, and inferred reserves are considered to be unlimited in relationship to requirements.

A brief description of the major North American producing districts follows.

Southeastern Canada

Marine evaporites of Mississippian (Visean) age underlie much of southern New Brunswick, northern Nova Scotia, and southwestern Newfoundland. The first production of gypsum in North America was recorded in Nova Scotia about 1735, and has grown to make this the largest gypsum mining region in the world, with an annual production exceeding 6 million tons.

Calcium sulfate is found in, or is correlative with, the Windsor Group which has been divided into five subzones: A, B, C, D, and E in ascending order. Although calcium sulfate is present in each of these subzones, the economic deposits of gypsum and anhydrite are confined to the Lower Windsor, i.e., subzones A and B. The most extensive is the A subzone, consisting of up to 1000 ft of anhydrite with occasional thin dolomite beds. Where topographic conditions are favorable, surface hydration, which rarely exceeds 30 to 40 ft, has produced several deposits of dense, white, high purity gypsum. Fig. 4 shows the operations in the Windsor B subzone of the Little Narrows Gypsum Co., Nova Scotia.

The B subzone, which varies in thickness from 250 to 500 ft, consists of interbedded calcium sulfate, limestones, and siltstones. The calcium sulfate, representing about 80% of the section, has been hydrated to depths varying from 150 to 700 ft, although occasional remnant anhydrite lenses with associated soluble salts are encountered. Unlike most gypsum deposits which have only minor structural features, if any, the rocks of the B subzone are frequently deformed by complex plastic folding and by occasional faults of substantial displacement, which make for difficult mining conditions. Nevertheless, the B subzone accounts for approximately 75% of the region's total production.

The southeastern Canada gypsum deposits are usually covered by glacial till which may be as thick as 200 ft, but averages 40 to 50 ft. All mining is by open pit methods, and in 1979 eight different companies operated in the region.

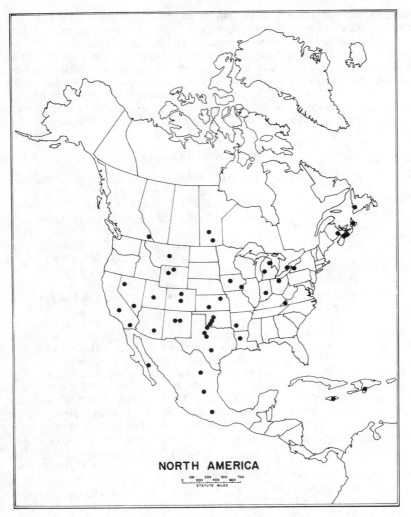

FIG. 3—*Location of North American gypsum-producing districts.*

NORTH AMERICA

0 100 200 300 400 500 600 700
STATUTE MILES

Iowa

The largest single gypsum producing district in the United States is at Fort Dodge, Iowa, where mining began in 1872. Long considered to be an outlier of the Permian Basin, this deposit is now thought to be Jurassic in age (Cross, 1966). It consists of a single bed of gypsum up to a maximum of 30 ft in thickness, but which probably averages nearer 12 to 14 ft. Its areal extent of some 15 square miles appears to be limited by post-depositional erosion, particularly during the period between Late Cretaceous and the Pleistocene. Its continuity is interrupted by wide channels apparently formed prior to and/or during the glacial period, chan-

nels which cut through the gypsum into the underlying shales.

Overburden consisting of glacial till, varies from 20 to 60 ft, and the rock surface is commonly cut with mud-filled erosion crevices which must be cleaned out, thereby posing a mining problem; however, gypsum purity as used is usually plus 90%. Mining is by open pit methods, with four companies operating in the district. Total production in 1979 was approximately 1,250,000 tons.

Another gypsum operation at Sperry in southeastern Iowa went into production in 1961, and at 600 ft below the surface, is the deepest currently operating gypsum mine in North America. It is reached through a 15-ft-

TABLE 1—Gypsum Production, North America

Country	Thousand Short Tons		
	1978	1979 ᵖ	1980
Canada:			
Nova Scotia	6,117	6,216	5,435
Newfoundland	892	884	733
New Brunswick	55	57	47
Ontario	817	845	946
Manitoba	201	141	150
British Columbia	819	790	825
Subtotal	8,901	8,933	8,136
United States:			
Arizona	184	231	209
California	1,578	1,624	1,640
Colorado	235	275	227
Iowa	1,602	1,695	1,468
Michigan	2,765	2,526	1,382
Nevada	1,335	1,075	852
New Mexico	263	251	182
Ohio	171	151	136
Oklahoma	1,398	999	1,326
Texas	1,864	1,903	1,681
Utah	316	772	287
Wyoming	370	366	312
Other States	2,812	2,762	2,674
Subtotal	14,893	14,630	12,376
Mexico	1,928	2,100	1,884
Dominican Republic	190	100	190
Jamaica	144	64	66
Total	26,056	25,827	22,652

Source: Pressler, 1979; Stonehouse, 1978, 1979, 1980.
ᵖPreliminary.
*Included with Other States.

diam concrete lined shaft, uses a room-and-pillar system in an average 9 to 10 ft of mining height, and is located in the Wapsipinicon formation of Devonian age. This calcium sulfate was apparently originally deposited as anhydrite, with hydration apparently confined to a zone paralleling the edge of the subcrop. Although the areal extent of the calcium sulfate is probably quite large, commercial gypsum reserves are restricted to this hydrated zone.

Michigan

Another important gypsum source in the midwest is the Michigan Basin, with two pro-ducing districts: Grand Rapids in the southwestern portion of the basin, and Alabaster-National City near the northeasterly edge on Lake Huron. These deposits are in the Michigan formation of Mississippian age, and consist of multiple units of gypsum 5 to 40 ft thick, separated by beds of shale varying from a few feet to 40 or 50 ft thick.

Three operations are active in the Alabaster-National City area, using open pit mining methods to recover three gypsum beds (separated by 5 ft of shale) at Alabaster, and a single bed at National City and Turner. This production serves seven manufacturing plants: one at National City, and after water shipment via the Great Lakes, plants at Waukegan, IL; East Chicago, IN; Detroit, MI; Lorain and Gypsum, Ohio; and Clarence Center, New York; as well as numerous cement plants. Overburden is glacial till ranging in thickness from 40 to 70 ft, and at Alabaster, where the gypsum grades into anhydrite as the overburden thickness increases, a minor amount of anhydrite is also produced.

Two operations are also active in the Grand Rapids district, both being shallow (less than 100 ft deep) underground mines employing the room-and-pillar system. Two different beds, 8 to 12 ft thick, are being mined with the production utilized by manufacturing plants at the mine sites.

New York—Ontario

Gypsum is found in a belt of Upper Silurian rocks which extends eastward from the Niagara Peninsula in Ontario across New York to the vicinity of Utica. The first recorded mining of gypsum in the United States took place in this belt in 1808 near Syracuse. In recent years, however, all production has come from the Oakfield area near Buffalo in the western part of the state, where one operation currently is active. The economic gypsum here consists of a 36- to 48-in. thick bed in the Salina Group of Upper Silurian age, overlain by 10 to 40 ft of thinly bedded shales and dolomites, covered by glacial till ranging up to 50 ft in thickness. Mining is by underground methods using the room-and-pillar system, and the gypsum averages about 88% purity.

In the westerly end of this belt, two underground mines in the Caledonia-Hagersville area of Ontario are important producers. The Hagersville mine also operates in a 36 to 48-in. bed which is correlative with the gypsum being mined in the Oakfield-Clarence Center district

FIG. 4—*Operation of Little Narrows Gypsum Co., Cape Breton Island, Nova Scotia.*

of New York, giving these operations the dubious distinction of having the lowest mining heights in the gypsum industry of North America. However, the Caledonia mine is in a bed 8 to 10 ft thick that stratigraphically is approximately 200 ft below the Hagersville seam.

In addition to the Caledonia-Hagersville mines, a new operation came into production approximately 30 miles northwest of this area in 1978 near the town of Drumbo, mining a bed averaging 5.5 ft thick, about 380 ft below the surface.

Ohio

On the shores of Sandusky Bay of northern Ohio, gypsum has been continuously mined since 1849, with one open-pit mine being currently active. Several beds of calcium sulfate are found in the Tymochtee formation of Upper Silurian age, all of which are relatively impure due principally to inclusion of dolomite stringers and nodules, and to a lesser degree, anhydrite. As mined, this gypsum is probably the lowest grade of any commercial deposit in the United States (with the exception of gypsite in California) being in the 65 to 70% range; however, mine production is beneficiated by heavy media sink-float to produce an approximately 80 to 81% gypsum product.

Indiana

In 1952, gypsum was discovered in southern Indiana near the town of Shoals, and this has become one of the most important commercial gypsum producing districts in the United States. In part of the Illinois Basin, gypsum occurs in the St. Louis formation of Mississippian age, and lies 350 to 550 ft below the surface of this rather hilly area. The bed averages 14 to 16 ft thick, with room-and-pillar mining methods being employed by the two mines operating in the district.

The St. Louis limestones overlying the gypsum have been subjected to solution along bedding and joint planes to create a network of water-filled cavities of undetermined extent and location. This results in the creation of a flooding hazard to the mine workings, and one of the mines has been flooded on two different occasions. However, careful study of all the factors affecting the hydrology of the area, plus the adoption of precautionary operating measures has enabled mining to proceed with an acceptable level of safety.

Virginia

In the western tip of Virginia near Saltville, gypsum has been produced continuously since 1835, first from shallow pits or quarries and currently from one underground mine. Another mine located at the small community of Plasterco has the distinction of being the world's deepest gypsum mine, having reached a depth of 1300 ft below the surface. However, operations ceased in 1979 due to depletion of reserves and high operating costs. Fig. 5 shows a load-haul unit on the 1300-ft level, Plasterco, VA.

The calcium sulfate originated in the McCready formation of Mississippian age, but the deposits are structurally very complex as a result of Appalachian mountain building, and in particular, the Saltville fault, a major northeast-southwest trending thrust fault which in the Plasterco area has a vertical displacement of over 14,000 ft. As mined, the calcium sulfate is found in part as a more or less continuous bed, approximately vertical and varying in width from 8 to 10 ft up to 20 ft; and in part as remnants or fragments of an originally horizontal bed (or beds) known locally as "boulders." The host rocks are shales and limestones, and mining is done by developing horizontal levels at 100-ft intervals from which continuous prospecting is carried out to locate and provide access to either "boulders" or the vertical bed. A combination of sublevel and cut-and-fill mining methods are used to extract the mineral, which is then brought to the surface by conveyor belt (after underground crushing) up a 1330-ft 18° incline (Appleyard, 1965).

Hydration of the calcium sulfate is highly irregular, and as with most deposits, is a function of the availability of ground waters. As a general trend, there is less hydration at depth than near the surface; however, the ultimate limit of sufficient hydration to support a viable operation is as yet unknown.

The Permian Basin

One of the major geological features of the United States is the Permian Basin extending over parts of Texas, New Mexico, Oklahoma, and Kansas, and calcium sulfate is found extensively over this area. Where hydration has occurred, the resulting gypsum is usually of high (plus 92%) purity, and in fact most of the specialty gypsum products which require high quality raw material are made from deposits of Permian age. The best purity and whitest color gypsum being commercially exploited in the United States is found in the Blaine formation of the Permian at Medicine Lodge, KS and Southard, OK, and in the Easly Creek formation of the Permian at Blue Rapids, KS.

FIG. 5—*Load-haul-dump unit on 1300-ft level, Plasterco, VA.*

At the present time, there are seven operating mines in Texas, six in Oklahoma, and two in Kansas. All of the Texas and Oklahoma deposits are worked by open pit methods, but the two Kansas mines are underground and employ room-and-pillar mining methods.

Although considerable Permian calcium sulfate is found in southeastern New Mexico, none currently is being mined. There are, however, two operating mines (open pit) in the north central part of the state working gypsum of the Todilto formation of Jurassic age.

Rocky Mountain and Inter-Mountain States

This general area is particularly rich in calcium sulfate deposits, most of which are at, or just below, the surface and lend themselves to low cost open pit mining. As might be expected in this region, structural features play an important part in limiting the size of the deposits, and in mine design. In general, purity is good, but the extent of hydration is frequently difficult to predict. A major deterrent to development is the cost of transportation due in part to the distance to roads and railroads, and also, the long hauls to major markets.

Gypsum is currently produced in the Powder River Basin area of Wyoming from rocks of Upper Permian to Middle Jurassic age, and from the Front Range of Colorado in Larimer and Fremont Counties. Production has also been developed in Fergus County, MT (Piper formation, Jurassic age) and Sevier County, Utah (Arapien shale, Jurassic age).

In Nevada, two deposits are mined in Clark County and one in Pershing County, with most of the product from these operations being shipped to California markets. In Arizona, a deposit at Winkleman provides gypsum for a calcining and manufacturing operation in Phoenix, and three smaller operations in the state supply portland cement retarder and agricultural markets. All of these western operations are open pit mines with the exception of Montana where an underground mine using the room-and-pillar system operates with approximately 7 ft of mining height.

California

Gypsum rock for five of the seven calcining and manufacturing plants in California is shipped into the state from Mexico (four plants) and Nevada (one plant). The other two utilize gypsum from a deposit in Imperial County, which in 1979 produced approximately 900,000 tons, making it the largest operating gypsum mine in the United States. This deposit, of Miocene age, occurs as a remnant of a calcium sulfate bed well over 100 ft thick whose present extent is limited by structure and erosion. Nevertheless, it contains large reserves, in part because hydration has taken place to a greater degree than in many other cases. Little or no overburden is present, and mining is carried out by multi-bench open pit methods (ver Plank, 1952).

For many years, several low grade gypsite deposits have been worked in San Joaquin Valley to produce a 50 to 75% gypsum content material for use as a soil conditioner. These deposits are Holocene in occurrence and are of limited extent. Although of too low a purity for portland cement retarder or plaster products, they are important in treating the alkaline soils which predominate in the great agricultural valleys of the state.

Western Canada

Gypsum is produced from two open-pit mines, one in Manitoba, the other in British Columbia. These operations provide rock for eight calcining and manufacturing plants in the western provinces. Also, one plant in Vancouver is supplied with rock imported from Mexico.

Production from these deposits is used almost entirely in the manufacture of building products and as a portland cement retarder. In both cases, only mining and primary crushing operations are carried on at the mine site, with the crushed gypsum rock being shipped to plants located in or near the major cities of Winnipeg, Saskatoon, Calgary, Edmonton, and Vancouver.

Mexico

The primary use for gypsum in Mexico is as a retarder for portland cement and for building plaster, although in 1971 two small wallboard plants began operation in the city of Puebla in an attempt to introduce wallboard to the construction markets. Considerable gypsum is also exported to the West and Gulf Coasts of the United States, and on occasion, to the Far East.

Many large deposits are known to exist; however, at the present time the major producers are located on San Marcos Island in the Gulf of Baja California, and in the states of Puebla, San Luis Potosí, and Nuevo Leon. In general, the gypsum is found in rocks of Mesozoic and Tertiary age.

The largest volume of production in Mexico is from San Marcos Island where an open pit mine and deep water ship loading facilities are operated to produce and ship a crushed gypsum rock. Another large highly mechanized open pit mine is operated at Estación La Borreguita in the state of San Luis Potosí to produce a crushed gypsum which is shipped by rail to local cement companies and to the port of Tampico for export.

In the state of Puebla, from the town of Izucar de Matamoros on the east to the village of Axochiapan on the west, a zone of gypsum bearing rocks of Miocene-Pliocene age occurs in which several small quarries are operated. These provide gypsum for some eight or nine cement plants in the Mexico City-Puebla area, for two new gypsum board plants at Puebla, and for several small calcining operations making gypsum plaster. The highest purity gypsum presently mined in Mexico comes from near Monterrey, Nuevo Leon, where at least two calcining plants operate to produce plaster for both construction and industrial uses.

Caribbean Area

Two deposits are being worked in the Caribbean Area: one at Bull Bay, Jamaica, about 10 miles east of the capital of Kingston; and the other near Barahona, Dominican Republic, some 130 miles west of the capital city of Santo Domingo. In both countries only small domestic gypsum markets have been developed primarily for portland cement retarder, and the major part of the production serves the export trade.

In Jamaica calcium sulfate is of Lower Eocene age, and occurs as several separate bodies of relatively small size in a northwest-southeast trending basin known as the Wagwater Trough (Holliday, 1971). Perhaps 60 to 70% of the calcium sulfate mass has been hydrated, and gypsum is currently being mined from three different deposits, utilizing multi-bench open pit methods.

The Dominican Republic gypsum is of probable Upper Miocene age, and the largest outcrop is found in the Cerro de Sal, a 12-mile-long hogback trending northwest-southeast. Calcium sulfate is interbedded with limestones, claystones, sandstones, and salt of the Cerro de Sal formation with a total thickness of some 2000 to 2500 ft. Bentonite clays and soluble salts are a potential problem associated with some stratigraphic members. The geological structure has been complicated due to several repetitions of the stratigraphic column caused by faulting; however, large deposits of economic gypsum may exist. Mining is by open pit methods. At least three other gypsum outcrops are known in this general area, but to date have not been developed for production.

Gypsum Resources Outside North America

Reflecting its wide geologic occurrence and its basic use in the construction industry, gypsum is produced in some 72 countries around the world, as shown in Table 2. In 1980, with a total world production of 78,290,000 tons being reported, the US consumed 21,106,000 tons, or 27%. No statistics are available as to the potential world reserves of calcium sulfate, but it can be safely predicted that they are enormous both in terms of total tons and of years at the present rates of consumption.

In many of the countries reporting production, gypsum was used only for portland cement retarder, this being by far the most common use of the mineral on a worldwide basis. As a general rule, the calcining of gypsum for use as plaster and wallboard building materials, or for industrial plasters, is limited to the United States, Canada, Europe (including Russia), and Japan, although a few wallboard plants have recently been built or are being considered in certain South American and Asian countries. In these countries, the general practice of open structural frames, usually made of wood, to form a building has historically required the use of some type of covering material for walls and ceilings, and gypsum products have gained wide acceptance for this use. That is, gypsum in the form of either plaster or precast wallboad is a versatile, fireproof covering material, and these products account

for over two-thirds of the gypsum used in the United States and Canada.

Conversely, in those countries where the usual methods of construction rely heavily on masonry products, such as concrete, concrete block, stone, and brick (including adobe), the need for fireproof covering materials is much less, and the use of gypsum for the manufacture of building materials will be very small, or even nonexistent. The production and use of gypsum in a given country, therefore, is usually a result of its mode of use rather than the availability of gypsum deposits.

Exploration Methods

As for most minerals, a thorough understanding of the origin and occurrence of gypsum is essential before undertaking an exploration program. This may be obtained by a review of published literature, and a basic reference would be "Selected Annotated Bibliography of Gypsum and Anhydrite in the United States and Puerto Rico" by C. F. Withington and M. C. Jaster (1960).

By studying the stratigraphic column in regions where sedimentary rocks occur, an indication can usually be obtained from the lithology whether or not an evaporite environment may have existed, this being, of course, a requisite for the deposition of calcium sulfate. If evaporite rocks are indicated, further details can be obtained from examination of outcrops of the particular formations, or if outcrops are not available, from logs of oil or gas wells, or from water wells which may have been drilled in the vicinity. Perhaps drill cuttings, or even core, might be available for inspection. As stratigraphic and lithologic details of an area are thus developed, structure should also be mapped so as to provide as detailed a picture of the area as the basic data will permit. From this, the possibility of calcium sulfate occurrence usually can be predicted, and also, it may be possible to judge the potential for hydration of the sulfate zones.

Sources of this type of information are published literature, unpublished university theses, geological surveys, geological departments of colleges and universities, oil companies, and water well drillers.

Geophysical work is only partially applicable to the search for calcium sulfate. The right combination of logs may indicate gypsum or anhydrite, but no log has yet been devised that will replace accurately a laboratory chemical or purity analysis. Geophysical logs are useful

TABLE 2—Gypsum: World Production, by Country

(Thousand Short Tons)

Country	1976	1977	1978	1979ᵖ	1980ᵉ
North America:					
Canada*	6,616	7,974	8,901	8,927	†7,947
Cubaᵉ	94	100	105	100	100
Dominican Republic	243	249	190	193	190
El Salvador	ᵉ7	8	8	8	10
Guatemala	15	35	42	28	†37
Honduras	ᵉ11	20	ᵉ25	ᵉ25	25
Jamaica	279	237	148	64	66
Mexico	1,559	1,649	1,938	2,228	†1,884
Nicaraguaᵉ	33	40	40	40	44
United States‡	11,980	13,390	14,891	14,630	†12,296
South America:					
Argentina	559	603	674	648	†656
Bolivia	ᵉ1	—	1	1	†1
Brazil§	ʳ568	ʳ608	512	515	550
Chile	134	ʳ224	246	240	242
Colombia	226	231	281	283	285
Ecuador	48	ʳ46	38	39	39
Paraguay	18	15	10	12	11
Peru	189	237	263	239	242
Venezuela	122	172	404	464	485
Europe:					
Austria*	849	ʳ892	844	880	†919
Belgium*	242	185	202	212	210
Bulgaria	ʳ256	ʳ325	375	341	†343
Czechoslovakia	728	752	768	809	834
France*	7,308	6,649	6,654	6,503	6,600
German Democratic Republic	ʳ375	ʳ375	385	400	410
Germany, Federal Republic of (marketable)*	2,315	2,445	2,467	2,481	2,480
Greece	490	452	474	496	510
Ireland	391	377	432	460	463
Italy	1,652	ʳ1,674	1,624	1,630	1,810
Luxembourg	2	3	1	1	1
Polandᵉ§	1,380	ʳ1,480	1,490	1,500	1,430
Portugal	176	194	222	ʳᵉ220	220
Spain	ᵉ4,600	ʳ6,042	5,918	5,815	6,060
Switzerlandᵉ	80	80	80	80	80
USSRᵉ††	5,500	5,700	5,800	6,000	6,500
United Kingdom*	3,693	3,648	3,662	ᵉ3,600	3,600
Yugoslavia	ʳ465	ʳ532	554	626	635
Africa:					
Algeriaᵉ	190	190	190	210	220
Angolaᵉ	22	ʳ22	ʳ28	ʳ28	28
Egypt	ʳ819	ʳ923	875	877	†761
Ethiopia	—	7	1	1	1
Kenya*	86	29	ᵉ33	ᵉ33	33
Libya	66	320	198	200	200
Mauritania	12	11	15	18	19
Niger	3	ᵉ3	3	ᵉ3	2
South Africa, Republic of	532	485	429	416	†478
Sudan*	20	17	22	33	33
Tanzania	ʳ9	9	24	12	12
Tunisia	43	ᵉ44	ᵉ44	ᵉ44	44
Zambia	5	5	2	—	—

TABLE 2—Gypsum: World Production, by Country

(Thousand Short Tons)

Country	1976	1977	1978	1979ᵖ	1980ᵉ
Asia:					
Afghanistan	NA	NA	7	NA	NA
Burma	50	37	39	42	†40
China:					
Mainlandᵉ	1,100	1,100	ʳ1,700	ʳ2,200	2,200
Taiwan #	3	8	4	3	9
Cyprus	71	92	76	68	61
India	801	858	974	949	†943
Iran	7,165	7,600	8,800	ᵉ7,000	3,900
Iraqᵉ	180	180	180	180	180
Israel	220	ᵉ220	ᵉ220	72	65
Japan #	5,581	ʳ6,118	6,387	6,915	7,165
Jordan	23	24	40	40	†77
Korea, Republic ofᵉ #	550	660	680	680	700
Lebanon	ᵉ14	17	12	11	11
Mongoliaᵉ	28	ʳ31	ʳ31	ʳ31	33
Pakistan	493	312	279	378	375
Philippines‖	130	123	123	121	121
Saudi Arabia	19	22	231	331	331
Syrian Arab Republic	69	94	ᵉ95	ᵉ70	72
Thailand	295	419	310	388	†454
Turkey	36	72	67	ᵉ70	70
Vietnamᵉ	11	13	15	15	17
Oceania: Australia	1,038	1,010	1,036	1,278	†1,420
Total	ʳ72,888	ʳ78,718	83,839	83,455	78,290

Source: Pressler, 1981.

  ᵉEstimated.   ᵖPreliminary.   ʳRevised.   NA, Not available.

 *Includes anhydrite.

 †Reported figure.

 ‡Excludes byproduct gypsum.

 §Series revised to represent sum of (1) mine product sold without beneficiation and (2) output of concentrates.

 # Includes byproduct gypsum. (In the case of Japan, byproduct gypsum was virtually all gypsum consumed during 1976-1980.)

 ‖Series revised to include byproduct gypsum, which constitutes total output in 1979-1980 and virtually all output in 1976-1978.

for determining structural details and can be used, in conjunction with other tests, to help determine mining environment conditions. Geochemical methods are rarely applicable to calcium sulfate, although heavy concentrations of sulfate in ground waters might serve as a useful clue, and in a few instances differences in plant species may indicate changes in rock types that can aid in surface mapping.

Even though the extent of gypsum can be mapped from surface outcrops, drilling is necessary to predict the amount and regularity of hydration, i.e., how much of the calcium sulfate is gypsum, and how much is either only partially hydrated or is anhydrite. For deeper deposits, additional drilling data is almost al-

ways required to map projections of lithologies and/or structures. Core drilling is usually preferred, taking BX (or larger) size core to provide adequate material for sampling and to permit good core recovery. In some cases where it is only necessary to determine the depth of overburden, or to locate the contact between gypsum and anhydrite, rotary drilling is sufficient and is much less expensive. Also geophysical methods can be successfully used under some conditions to determine the depth of overburden.

Although calcium sulfate beds may sometimes be continuous over tens—or even hundreds—of miles, the exploration geologist should keep in mind that they may also occur as discontinuous lenses. Also, the extent of hydration is even less predictable, as is the occurrence of minor, but detrimental, amounts of impurities. Hence, a successful exploration program requires knowledgeable consideration and interpretation of all the factors involved, and sums of money which can run into six figures.

Evaluation of Deposits

The single most important factor in the evaluation of a gypsum deposit is its location with respect to markets, i.e., the logistical realities of the industry. The term "place value" is often used to describe this characteristic, which results because a local market demand will make nearby deposits more valuable even though they may not be as pure nor as easily mined as more remote deposits. Thus, the factor which more often than any other determines the value of one deposit as against another is the cost of transportation from the mine to the major market areas.

Also basic to the exploitation of gypsum is the fact that it is a relatively low priced commodity. This is due in part to the low cost inherent to extraction of the mineral from the ground and its preparation for market, and in part to the fact that in its major product areas, it must compete with relatively low priced materials. With this highly competitive pattern, which as a practical matter results in differing price structures from one country to another, or in the United States and Canada, from one section of the country to another, there is no set "market price" to measure against, and each deposit must be evaluated within the market area it might logically serve. Hence, early in the evaluation of any gypsum deposit, an investigation of marketing factors is essential.

The geologist and mining engineer should carefully study the geological environment of a deposit, looking at such features as overburden ratio (if a shallow deposit) or roof conditions if an underground mine is indicated. Also, thickness of the bed, structural features, and the possibility of unusual water conditions are important, as these translate into capital investment and operating costs. There is no simple rule as to how much overburden one can afford to strip for an open pit, or how much depth one might consider for underground mining. In general, the economics of the industry are such that mining costs must be relatively low, and many operating deposits today mine and deliver

rock to the mill (on site) for a cost between $1.50 and $4.50 per ton (not including depreciation) although some others are in the $5.00 to $8.00 per ton range.

The grade of the deposit must also be assessed, particularly the type and amounts of impurities. As a rule of thumb, the higher the gypsum content the better, but in no case should the gypsum content be more than a percent or two lower than that of other deposits serving the same market. Impurities should be carefully analyzed, and if they are outside the limits, steps to eliminate or reduce them by beneficiation should be investigated. In such a case, the penalty may well eliminate the deposit from further consideration.

A separate chapter on utilization, discussing processing methods, markets, and price trends, provides further background for the evaluation of gypsum deposits.

Mining Methods

Gypsum is mined both from open pit and underground. Open pit mining of gypsum employs conventional methods and equipment, such as draglines and scrapers to remove overburden, and shovels or front end loaders to load rock. Rotary and/or auger drilling is almost universally used because of the relative softness of the rock, and penetration rates of 5 to 10 fpm are common. Drill holes are usually from 2 to 3.5 in. in diameter, and spaced relatively close together in order to distribute the explosive throughout the rock mass in a somewhat dense pattern. This is because gypsum tends to absorb explosive force without readily fracturing, and a hole pattern in excess of perhaps 12×12 ft may result in unsatisfactory fragmentation. Ammonium nitrate-fuel oil explosive is used where water conditions permit, and a ratio of three tons of rock broken per pound of explosive is about average.

Because little or no beneficiation is usually performed in the processing steps following mining, extra effort is required to remove all overburden, or to selectively mine a face in order to eliminate impurities or to blend varying grades of rock. Quality control is most important in the mining step, and may often result in somewhat higher per ton costs.

Underground mining commonly employs room-and-pillar methods with pillar design based upon the conditions of each mine; however, recovery of total rock is in the 65 to 80%

range. Auger drilling is standard practice, and loading is done with gathering arm type loaders, front end loaders or load-haul-dump units. Underground haulage may be by rail, or by diesel-powered trucks. In a few cases, conveyor belts are used. The use of diesel power has become quite common in gypsum mines, in part because explosive gas conditions do not exist, and in part because mine design usually can readily incorporate good ventilating conditions.

In general, gypsum mining operations are highly mechanized, although the limited volume of production, usually 500 to 1500 tpd, does restrict the size of equipment which can be utilized economically. The physical environment of most gypsum deposits favors good working and safety conditions, a major factor in contributing to low cost.

Future Considerations

As indicated throughout this discussion, there is no foreseeable shortage of either gypsum or anhydrite in the United States or in the world. Paradoxically, however, there are instances where it may be difficult to find gypsum which can be considered economic at a given time and location, a problem which has its roots in "place value." The best evidence of this situation is that the United States historically has imported 33 to 36% of its needs from Canada, Mexico, Jamaica, Dominican Republic, and Spain, as shown in Table 3.

All of this gypsum (with the exception of a few thousand tons of special grade rock) is used by plants on the Atlantic, Pacific, and Gulf Coasts of the United States. The basic

reasons for this situation are: (1) large markets for gypsum products are concentrated in and around the coastal cities, (2) there are no known gypsum deposits along any of the three United States coastlines, and (3) large gypsum deposits exist on or near deep water of the exporting countries from which rock can be shipped to these major markets at lower cost than from inland United States deposits.

It is likely that these conditions will persist into the future, and the industry is built upon this premise, having made investments in offshore deposits, shipping facilities, and domestic port locations with appropriate marine rock handling equipment. There is no import duty on crude gypsum rock, but duties are placed upon processed gypsum.

Because of its widespread occurrence and huge potential reserves and also because its uses are such that it is not basic to survival in the event of a national emergency, gypsum is not considered to be a "strategic" mineral. This has permitted natural economic factors to prevail in the development of the mineral, literally on a worldwide basis, which overall is a healthy situation that hopefully will continue to prevail.

Future Trends and Problems

Competition between manufacturers of gypsum building products, as well as from manufacturers of substitute materials, has resulted in a continuing pressure to improve the quality of gypsum products. In turn, mine operators are being asked to reduce the average quantity of impurities, i.e., upgrade the gypsum purity, and maintain a uniform ton-to-ton level of impurities. To date, these objectives are being accomplished by selective mining techniques and screening during primary and secondary crushing stages to reject a size fraction in which impurities tend to concentrate. Other beneficiation techniques can be and are considered, but are slow to be adopted because of adverse economic impact.

Environmental concern in the mining of gypsum is limited almost exclusively to open pit operations, although in a few cases, shallow mines (less than 100 ft deep) may have an occasional subsidence problem that requires attention. Land reclamation of open pits has become a requirement as new laws and regulations take effect, and considerable ingenuity is needed to do a satisfactory job at a reasonable cost. It is believed that gypsum miners have as good, and in some cases, a better opportunity of

TABLE 3—US Imports of Crude Gypsum (Including Anhydrite)

(Thousand St)

Country	1977	1978	1979	1980
Canada	5,307	6,610	5,700	5,463
Mexico	1,448	1,610	1,815	1,565
Jamaica	238	167	5	11
Dominican Republic	70	144	80	69
Spain	—	198	125	250
Other countries	11	29	12	8
Total imports	7,074	8,308	7,773	7,366
Domestic production *	14,187	15,560	15,458	13,039
Total	21,261	23,868	23,231	20,405
% Imports	33	35	33	36

Source: Pressler, 1979; 1981.
*Includes byproduct gypsum.

doing satisfactory reclamation than miners of many other types of minerals, because there seldom are associated minerals which lead to such problems as acid waters. Also, the configuration of many gypsum open pits is such that surface restoration is readily feasible. In general, the water pumped from either open pit or underground gypsum mines is of a quality not considered as a pollutant; however, it is necessary to sample and analyze the pump discharge from time to time to develop adequate background data, and to assure that requirements are being met.

Processing of gypsum is energy-intensive; energy requirements represent the largest single cost in the production of gypsum wallboard. Future increases in energy cost will require innovation in conservation techniques and process technology to offset at least partially this adverse trend. For further discussion, see the section on Energy Considerations in the chapter "Gypsum and Anhydrite" under Construction Materials, Volume 1.

Synthetic or Byproduct Gypsum

Synthetic gypsum as a byproduct of various chemical operations has been available for some time in various parts of the world. Whether or not it might be substituted for natural gypsum requires analysis of the same factors that one would investigate in evaluating a calcium sulfate deposit, the most important being logistics, quality, and cost. In many cases, byproduct gypsum is of unacceptable quality for the majority of gypsum uses because of the type and amounts of impurities, or crystal size and shape. In all cases, it is a relatively fine, wet material which comes out of the chemical process as a filter cake or after settling in ponds or tanks.

Both the chemical and physical characteristics of byproduct gypsum are such that further treatment is necessary to make it into a useful product. The cost of such treatment varies widely with the type of byproduct and the use for which it is intended. By far the major source of byproduct gypsum at present is the manufacture of phosphoric acid. As pollution regulations are tightened, much additional byproduct material will also be developed by neutralization of the sulfur dioxide in stack gas and/or from waste sulfuric acid.

In the United States, use of synthetic gypsum is very small. It is not economical to go through the treatment required to make it suitable for major uses such as plasters or wallboard. On the other hand, minor quantities (828,000 tons in 1979) of synthetic gypsum, primarily "phosphogypsum," are being sold as a soil conditioner in California and the southeastern states, a use which tolerates the type and amount of impurities present and requires relatively low-cost processing to put the material in a useful form. Synthetic gypsum is being used in Japan for both portland cement retarder and wallboard. However, this is a unique situation; Japan's gypsum industry is well developed but there is a shortage of natural gypsum. The high cost of importing gypsum rock results in a condition where it is economical to upgrade the synthetic material. Additional use of synthetic gypsum to manufacture wallboard has recently been started in Australia and in Europe in situations where economics favor this use.

Bibliography and References

Adams, J.E., 1971, "Upper Permian Ochoa Series of Delaware Basin, West Texas and Southeastern New Mexico," *Origin of Evaporites*, American Association of Petroleum Geologists, Tulsa, OK, Reprint Series No. 2, pp. 60–89.

Appleyard, F.C., 1965, "The Locust Cove Mine," *Mining Engineering*, March, pp. 59–62.

Bergstrom, J.H., 1961 "Pabco's Gypsum Crystals Sparkle," *Rock Products*, April, pp. 90–95.

Borchert, H., and Muir, R.O., 1964, *Salt Deposits, The Origin, Metamorphism, and Deformation of Evaporites*, D. Van Nostrand, London, 338 pp.

Braitsch, O., 1971, *Salt Deposits, Their Origin and Composition*, Springer-Verlag, New York, 297 pp.

Branson, E.B., 1915, "Origin of Thick Gypsum and Salt Deposits," *Geological Society of America Bulletin*, Vol. 26, pp. 231–242.

Briggs, L.I., 1970, "Geology of Gypsum in the Lower Peninsula, Michigan," *Proceedings, Sixth Forum on Geology of Industrial Minerals*, Michigan Geological Survey, Misc. 1, pp. 66–76.

Butler, G.P., 1970, "Holocene Gypsum and Anhydrite of the Abu Dhabi Sabkha, Trucial Coast: An Alternative Explanation of Origin," *Proceedings, Third Symposium on Salt*, Northern Ohio Geological Society, Cleveland, Vol. 1, pp. 120–152.

Buzzalini, A.D., et al., 1969, ed. "Evaporites and Petroleum," American Association of Petroleum Geologists Bulletin, Vol. 53, No. 4, April, pp. 775–1011.

Cole, L.H., 1930, *The Gypsum Industry of Canada*, Canadian Dept. of Mines, Publication 714, pp. 1–164.

Conley, R.F., and Bundy, W.M., 1958, "Mechanism of Gypsification," *Geochimica et Cosmochimica Acta*, Vol. 15, pp. 57–72.

Cross, A.I., 1966, "Palynologic Evidence of Mid-Mesozoic Age of Fort Dodge (Iowa) Gypsum," Abstract, San Francisco Meeting, Geological Society of America, Nov. 14–16.

Dean, W.E., and Schreiber, B.C., eds., 1978, "Marine Evaporites," Mineral Short Course, Notes, No. 4, Society of Economic Paleontologists, 188 pp.

Friedman, G.M., and Sanders, J.E., 1978, Principles of Sedimentation, John E. Wiley & Sons, Inc., New York.

Gay, P., 1965, "Some Crystallographic Studies in the System CaSO₄—CaSO₄·2H₂O, The Hydrous Forms," Mineralogical Magazine, Vol. 25, pp. 354–362.

Goodman, N.R., et al., 1957, "Gypsum." The Geology of Canadian Industrial Mineral Deposits, 6th Commonwealth Mining and Metallurgical Congress, pp. 111–137.

Ham, W.E., 1962, "Economic Geology and Petrology of Gypsum and Anhydrite in Blaine County," Oklahoma Geological Survey Bulletin, Vol. 89, pp. 100–151.

Ham, W.E., et al., 1961, "Borate Minerals in Permian Gypsum of West-Central Oklahoma," Oklahoma Geological Survey Bulletin, Vol. 92, 77 pp.

Hardie, L.A., 1967, "The Gypsum-Anhydrite Equilibrium at One Atmosphere Pressure," American Mineralogist, Vol. 52, Jan.-Feb., pp. 171–200.

Holliday, D.W., 1970, "The Petrology of Secondary Gypsum Rocks: A Review," Journal of Sedimentary Petrology, Vol. 40, No. 2, June, pp. 734–744.

Holliday, D.W., 1971, "Origin of Lower Eocene Gypsum-Anhydrite Rocks, Southeast St. Andrew, Jamaica," Transaction Sec. B, Institution of Mining and Metallurgy, Vol. 80, pp. B305–B315.

Jorgensen, D.B., and Carr, D.D., 1972, "Influence of Cyclic Deposition, Structural Features, and Hydrologic Controls on Evaporite Deposits in the St. Louis Limestone in Southwestern Indiana," Proceedings, Eighth Forum on Geology of Industrial Minerals, Iowa Geological Survey, 195 pp.

Keith, S.B., 1969, "Gypsum and Anhydrite," Arizona Bureau of Mines Bulletin 180, pp. 371–382.

Kelly, K.K., et al., 1941, "Thermodynamic Properties of Gypsum and Its Dehydration Products," Technical Paper 625, US Bureau of Mines, 73 pp.

Kendall, A.C., 1978, "Calcium Sulfate Diagenesis, Mississippean of Eastern Williston Basin," Abstract, American Association of Petroleum Geologists Bulletin, Vol. 62, No. 3, p. 530.

Kerr, S.D., and Thompson, A., 1963, "Origin of Nodular and Bedded Anhydrite in Permian Shelf Sediments, Texas and New Mexico," American Association of Petroleum Geologists Bulletin, Vol. 47, pp. 1726–1732.

King, R.H., 1971, "Sedimentation in Permian Castile Sea," Origin of Evaporites, American Association of Petroleum Geologists, Tulsa, OK, Reprint Series No. 2, pp. 90–97.

Kinsman, D.J.J., 1966, "Gypsum and Anhydrite of Recent Age, Trucial Coast, Persian Gulf," Second Symposium on Salt, Northern Ohio Geological Society, Cleveland, Vol. 1, pp. 302–326.

Kinsman, D.J.J., 1969, "Modes of Formation, Sedimentary Associations, and Diagenetic Features of Shallow Water and Supratidal Evaporites," American Association of Petroleum Geologists Bulletin, Vol. 53, No. 4, April, pp. 830–840.

MacDonald, G.F.J., 1953, "Anhydrite-Gypsum Equilibrium Relations," American Journal of Science, Vol. 251, pp. 883–898.

Martinez, J.D., 1974, "Tectonic Behavior of Evaporites." Proceedings, 4th Symposium on Salt, Northern Ohio Geological Society, Cleveland, Vol. 1, pp. 155–168.

McAide, H.G., 1964, "The Effect of Water Vapor Upon the Dehydration of CaSO₄·2H₂O," Canadian Journal of Chemistry, Vol. 42, pp. 792–801.

Murray, R.C., 1964, "Origin and Diagenesis of Gypsum and Anhydrite," Journal of Sedimentary Petrology, Vol. 34, No. 3, Sep., pp. 512–523.

Newland, D.H., and Leighton, H., 1910, "Gypsum Deposits of New York," New York State Museum Bulletin 143, 94 pp.

Posnjak, E., 1938, "The System, CaSO₄·H₂O," American Journal of Science, Vol. 235A, pp. 247–272.

Posnjak, E., 1940, "Deposition of Calcium Sulfate From Sea Water," American Journal of Science, Vol. 238, pp. 559–568.

Pressler, J.W., 1979, Annual Advance Summary, "Gypsum in 1979," US Bureau of Mines, 17 pp.

Pressler, J.W., 1981, "Gypsum," Minerals Yearbook 1980, US Bureau of Mines, pp. 385–396.

Riley, C.M., and Byrne, J.V., 1961, "Genesis of Primary Structures in Anhydrite," Journal of Sedimentary Petrology, Vol. 31, pp. 553–559.

Schenk, P.E., 1969, "Carbonate-Sulfate-Redbed Facies and Cyclic Sedimentation of the Windsorian Stage (Middle Carboniferous), Maritime Provinces," Canadian Journal of Earth Sciences, Vol. 6, pp. 1037–1066.

Schmidt, R., 1914, "Uber die Beschaffenheit und Entstehung parallelfaseriger Aggregate von Steinsalz und Gips," Kali, 8, pp. 161, 218, 239.

Schroeder, Harold J., 1970, "Gypsum," Mineral Facts and Problems, Bulletin 650, US Bureau of Mines, pp. 1039–1048.

Shearman, D.J., 1966, "Origin of Marine Evaporites by Diagenesis," Transactions Sec. B, Institution of Mining and Metallurgy, Vol. 75, pp. B208 to B215.

Stone, R.W. et al., 1920, "Gypsum Deposits of the United States," Bulletin 697, US Geological Survey, 326 pp.

Stonehouse, D.H., 1970, "Gypsum and Anhydrite," Canadian Minerals Yearbook, Mineral Resources Branch, Dept. of Energy, Mines, and Resources, Ottawa, pp. 775–1011.

Stonehouse, D.H., 1972, "Gypsum and Anhydrite," Canadian Minerals Yearbook, Mineral Resources Branch, Dept. of Energy, Mines, and Resources, Ottawa, preprint, 7 pp.

Stonehouse, D.H., 1978, "Gypsum in Canadian Mineral Industry," Dept. of Energy, Mines and Resources, Ottawa, pp. 211–216.

Stonehouse, D.H., 1979, "Gypsum in Canadian Mineral Industry," Dept. of Energy, Mines and Resources, Ottawa, pp. 221–228.

Stonehouse, D.H., 1980, "Gypsum in Canadian Mineral Industry," Dept. of Energy, Mines and Resources, Ottawa, preprint, 8 pp.

Van't Hoff, J.H., et al., 1903, "Gips und Anhydrit,"
    Zeitschrift fuer Physik Chem., Vol. 45, pp. 257–
    306.
ver Planck, W.E., 1952, "Gypsum in California,"
    Bulletin 163, California Div. of Mines, 151 pp.
Walker, C.W., 1974, "Nature and Origin of Cap
    Rock Overlying Gulf Coast Salt Domes," *Pro-
    ceedings,* 4th Symposium on Salt, Northern Ohio
    Geological Society, Cleveland, Vol. 1, pp. 169–
    175.
Withington, C.F., 1962, "Gypsum and Anhydrite in
    the U.S.," Min. Inv. Res., Map MR-33 and text,
    US Geological Survey, 18 pp.

Withington, C.F., and Jaster, M.C., 1960, "Se-
    lected Annotated Bibliography of Gypsum and
    Anhydrite in the United States and Puerto
    Rico," Bulletin 1105, US Geological Survey,
    126 pp.
Wood, G.V., and Wolfe, M.J., 1969, "Sabkha Cy-
    cles in the Arab-Darb Formation of Trucial
    Coast of Arabia," *Sedimentology,* Vol. 12, pp.
    165–191.
Zen, E-An, 1965, "Solubility Measurements in the
    System $CaSO_4$-NaCl-H_2O at 35°, 50°, and 70° C
    and One Atmosphere Pressure," *Journal of
    Petrology,* Vol. 6, pp. 124–164.

Iodine

JOHN JAN *
Revised by L. A. ROE †

Iodine is a soft, lustrous, grayish-black non-metallic element with a density of 4.9. It is the least active of the four members of the halogen family. The other members are, in order of increasing activity, bromine, chlorine, and fluorine. Iodine is a solid at ordinary temperatures, while bromine is a liquid and chlorine and fluorine are gases. Iodine melts at 113°C and volatilizes at 184.4°C to a blue-violet gas with an irritating odor. It occurs in nature only as iodates and iodides or other combined forms.

It was discovered by Bernard Courtois in France in 1811, who noticed its presence as an unknown substance in crude soda ash obtained from burning seaweed. Gay-Lussac recognized it as a new element and named it iode, from the Greek word "ioeides or iodes" for violet color (MacMillan, 1970).

The world production is not known with any great certainty, but it is probably between 25 and 35 million lb per year, of which about 30% is consumed in the United States.

Geology and Mineralogy

Iodine compounds occur as a minor constituent as a mineral in the Chilean nitrate deposits and in solution in brines and seawater. According to the US Geological Survey, it is the 47th most abundant element in the earth's crust. The minerals lautarite, Ca$(IO_3)_2$ (calcium iodate), and dietzeite, Ca$_2$$(IO_3)_2$ (CrO_4), (calcium iodate-chromate) are found in Chilean nitrate deposits which are located in Antofagasta and Tarapacá provinces on the eastern slope of the coast range in a desert area.

Various brines contain iodine compounds. Seawater contains about 0.05 ppm of iodine and some seaweeds will extract and accumulate it up to 0.45% on a dry basis. Some coals in

West Germany also contain iodine compounds.

The known and potential sources of iodine reported in 1968 are given in Table 1. Table 2 lists estimated world iodine reserves.

Iodine has been recovered from brines in Java, Indonesia, France, England, and the USSR. Iodine has also been recovered from seaweed in Ireland, Scotland, France, Japan, Norway, and the USSR. The indicated reserves and future resources of iodine are large but have never been adequately measured.

Analysis

Iodine as the free element can be detected by the characteristic blue color it gives to a starch solution. Quantitatively it is determined as the free element by titration with standard thiosulfate solutions using starch as an indicator. Colorimetric methods are also applicable.

Markets and Prices

Iodine and its compounds are generally marketed in the form of: iodine, crude; iodine, resublimed; calcium iodates; calcium iodide; potassium iodide, sodium iodide, and numerous organic compounds.

Product Specifications

Crude iodine, World market: 99–99.5% I_2.

Crude iodine, US produced, average: 99.8% I_2.

Crude iodine, USP XVII Specs: not less than 99.8% percent I_2.

Resublimed iodine is usually 99.9% and ACS specifications call for not over 0.005% total bromine and 0.020% nonvolatile materials (Anon., 1971).

Prices, c.i.f. United States, for iodine have been steadily increasing from $1.18 per lb of crude in 1967 to $6.37–7.27 in January 1981 (Anon., 1981). In 1980 the price of iodine increased by 50%.

* Western Knapp Engineering Div., Arthur G. McKee Co., San Francisco, CA.

† Consultant, Downers Grove, IL.

TABLE 1—Known and Potential Sources of Iodine Reported in 1968

Location	Source	Estimated Iodine Content, % or Ppm	Estimated Reserves, Tons
Chile	Caliche nitrate deposits	Avg. 0.04%	400,000
Producer			
Sociedad Quimica y Minera de Chile			
Plants			
Maria Elena, 800 t/a			
Pedro de Valdivia, 2700 t/a			
Officina Victoria, 200 t/a			
Japan			
Producers			
AiOi Industrial Co.	Natural gas	0.01%	500,000-
Nippon Development Co.	well brines		1,500,000
Nippon Natural Gas Co.			
Daiichi Pharmaceutical Co.			
Ise Chemical Co.			
Chiba Iodine Co.			
US			
Anadarko Basin, OK	Oil field brine	Some contain over 500 ppm	
Los Angeles Basin, CA	Seal Beach		
Midland, MI,	Oil field brine	60-70 ppm	
Dow Chemical Co.	Well brine	38 ppm	
Shreveport, LA	Oil field brine	35 ppm	

Source: MacMillan, 1970.

End Uses

US consumption by principal end uses in the year 1980 is given in Table 3.

Other uses include iodine or its compounds used in lubricants for titanium and stainless steel, catalysts for producing such compounds as polybutadiene rubber, stabilized rosin, and tall oil products.

As of early 1981, extensive use was predicted for iodine or iodine derivatives as catalysts in plants using coal feedstock in the production of synthetic fuels and downstream products.

Iodine is also used in the modification of selenium to make semiconductors; manufacture of high-purity metals such as titanium, zirconium, boron, and hafnium; additives in rechargeable dry cells; smog inhibitors; cloud seeders to induce rainfall; and in certain dyes and food colorings.

An artificially prepared radioactive isotope I-131, with a half-life of eight days, is finding extensive use as a radioactive tracer (Anon., 1971; MacMillan, 1970).

Croft (1972) describes research efforts in Australia which point out advantages of cyclic iodination in upgrading ilmenite. Enriched titanium dioxide products were made by iodina-

TABLE 2—Estimated World Iodine Reserves

(Million pounds)

	Reserves *
North America: United States:	
Michigan	30
Oklahoma, California, and Louisiana	500
Total	530
South America: Chile	800
Europe:	
Federal Republic of Germany	10
Other †	400
Total	410
Asia:	
China, Mainland	NA
Japan	4,000
Indonesia	10
Total	4,010
World total	5,750

Source: Absalom, 1980.
NA, Not available.
*Except for Chile and Japan, figures denote only an order of magnitude.
†Includes the USSR, France, the United Kingdom, Norway, Italy, and Ireland.

tion of prereduced ilmenite to produce vapor phase iron iodide which can be treated for recovery of iodine which is recycled to the process. The upgraded titanium product consists of titanium oxide pseudomorphs of ilmenite grains.

The advantages of iodine in Croft's process over chlorine or bromine are numerous. Iodine is easily stored as a solid phase under normal conditions and it offers other advantages relating to vapor leakages, spillage, and corrosion.

New methods for the production of potassium iodide, potassium iodate, and ethylenediamine dihydriodide were reviewed by Garrison (1980) and their energy-saving features emphasized.

The US Bureau of Mines (1980) reported laboratory scale testing of a technique for recovery of silver from pregnant solutions generated in hydrometallurgical treatment of complex base-metal sulfide concentrates with oxidizing chloride media. The silver was precipitated as an iodide and then regeneration of the iodide salt recovered the iodide for reuse. Sodium or potassium iodide was used to precipitate silver iodide, which was then contacted with sodium sulfide to produce silver sulfide, with resulting regeneration of the iodide solution.

Principal Producing Countries

The production of iodine usually depends on production of other materials. In Chile, it is a byproduct of nitrate production. In Japan, it comes from natural gas well brines. Dow Chemical Co., recovers iodine along with salt, potassium, bromine, magnesium, and calcium

TABLE 3—US Consumption of Iodine in 1980

	Estimated Million lb	Quantities, %
Photographic chemicals, photolithographic supplies	1.71	19
Food supplements:		
animal & fowl	1.12	13
human (iodized salt)	0.13	1
Pharmaceutical	0.95	11
Disinfectants, industrial and household	1.75	20
Other (includes catalysts)	3.24	36
Total	8.90	100

Source: Absalom, 1980.

chlorides from natural brines at Midland, MI. A plant at Woodward, Oklahoma is under the control of PPG Industries and has a capacity of 2 million lb per year. In 1980, this plant was being expanded to an unstated capacity (Anon., 1980).

Chile was long the principal world producer of iodine from its nitrate fertilizer. In recent years, however, Japan has produced more iodine than Chile, as brines production has increased. In 1981, production in Chile was 5,800,000 lb and in Japan, it was 15,000,000 lb.

Aside from Chile and Japan, production in all other countries is considered minor. Available data for 1970 shows that West Germany produced 125 st of crude iodine. Other countries that are or may be iodine producers are: England, France, Indonesia, Java, Ireland, Norway, Scotland, and the USSR.

The two US producers are Dow Chemical Co. and PPG Industries. The US imports most of its requirements in the form of crude iodine. About 10,720 lb of resublimed iodine were also imported in 1969, of which Japan supplied 10,500 lb, Sweden 220 lb. Chile supplied about 40% of total imports. Kelp beds or brines continue as the best potential sources for iodine production (Anon., 1971; MacMillan, 1970). US demand for iodine is expected to double in this decade (Anon., 1980, 1980a).

Preparation for Market

Chilean Nitrate Deposits—The iodine-bearing nitrate ore is leached with an alkaline solution, with the iodine going into solution as sodium iodate (Anon., 1965). Sodium bisulfite is introduced to convert the iodate to iodide. Fresh leach solution with iodate is mixed with the iodide solution to precipitate iodine according to the equation:

$$5 \ NaI + NaIO_3 + 3H_2SO_4 \rightarrow 3I_2 + 3Na_2SO_4 + 3H_2O.$$

The iodine is filtered, washed, and dried as crude iodine and sublimated to produce the purified grade. Only about 50 to 75% of the iodine in the ore is recovered. The recovery method for seaweed ash is similar to that used with Chilean nitrates.

Michigan Natural Brines—The natural brine is acidified, chlorinated, and passed downward through a packed tower, countercurrent to a stream of air. Iodine, displaced from the brine by chlorine, is blown to an absorption tower in which the iodine is absorbed in a solution of sulfuric and hydriodic acids. The solution is then treated with sulfur dioxide, after which iodine is precipitated with chlorine, filtered, and melted under a layer of sulfuric acid.

Japanese Gas Well Brines—In Japan iodine compounds are recovered from natural brine found in gas wells on the Chiba peninsula. The brines are first clarified to remove oil and suspended matter and then treated by one of the following processes:

1) Sulfuric acid, chlorine, and sodium nitrate are mixed with brine and the liberated iodine absorbed by activated carbon. The crude iodine is then dissolved in hot caustic solution and reprecipitated with chlorine to yield a refined iodine.

2) Iron sulfate and copper sulfate are added to the clarified brine, precipitating copper iodide which is oxidized to yield crude iodine.

3) Electrolysis of brines containing sulfuric acid, with absorption of the iodine on activated charcoal.

4) Brine containing iodine which has been liberated with chlorine is passed over copper wire to form insoluble cuprous iodide. The cuprous iodide is periodically washed off the copper wire, dried, and shipped as finished product.

Other Techniques—Although little used today, the recovery method from seaweed ash is similar to that used for Chilean nitrates. Silver nitrate was also used at one time in brine treatment. The brine was treated with silver nitrate solution to produce the highly insoluble silver iodide which was recovered by filtration. A suspension of silver iodide in water will react with iron to displace the silver. The resulting solution can be treated with chlorine to displace the iodine product.

Transportation

Crude iodine is shipped in double polyethylene plastic-lined fiber drums holding 100 to 200 lb each. Resublimed iodine is also shipped in the same type of container as well as in 25-lb glass jars and ¼-, 1-, and 5-lb bottles. Freight classification is "chemicals, not otherwise indexed by name" (NOIBN) and requires no special label.

Subsidies, Depletion, and Tariffs

On Nov. 30, 1981, the US government strategic stockpile contained 8,010,000 lb of iodine. The stockpile also contained 3,238 pounds of nonstockpile grade material. The stockpile objective established by the Office of Emergency Preparedness is 5 million lb.

Depletion allowances for domestic iodine producers were changed under terms of the Tax Reform Act of 1969. Effective after October 1969, the depletion allowance for iodine from both domestic and foreign production is 14%.

Tariffs on iodine and potassium iodide are as follows:

	Most Favored Nation (MFN)		Non-MFN
	1/1/82	1/1/87	1/1/82
Iodine, crude	Free	Free	Free
Iodine, resublimed	7.2¢/lb	6¢/lb	10¢/lb
Potassium iodide	3.2% ad val.	2.8% ad val.	7.5% ad val.

Bibliography and References

Anon., 1951, "Iodine—Its Properties and Technical Applications," Chilean Iodine Educational Bureau, Inc., New York, 74 pp.

Anon., 1965, "Iodine Into the Pool," *Chemical Week,* Vol. 97, No. 9, Aug. 28, pp. 127–128.

Anon., 1965a, "Iodine Lubricants Smooth the Way for Broader Use of Titanium," *Iron Age,* Vol. 196, No. 22, Nov. 25, pp. 68–69.

Anon., 1966, "Iodine Additives Reduce Friction," *Production Engineering,* Vol. 37, No. 20, Sep. 26, p. 40.

Anon., 1971, "Iodine in 1971," *Mineral Industry Surveys,* US Bureau of Mines, annual preliminary survey.

Anon., 1971a, "Minor Nonmetals in 1971," *Mineral Industry Surveys,* US Bureau of Mines, advance summary.

Anon., 1973, "Iodine 1972," *Commodity Data Summaries,* Division of Nonmetallic Minerals Bureau of Mines, January.

Anon., 1980, "Iodine Production is Planned for U.S. by Calabrian, With Start-Up in 1982," *Chemical Marketing Reporter,* Vol. 218, No. 18, Nov. 3, pp. 7, 23.

Anon., 1980a, "Growing Iodine Markets Spark Plant Expansions," *Chemical Week,* Vol. 127, No. 20, Nov. 12, p. 44.

Anon., 1981, "Iodine Price is Boosted Again, While Tight Market Eases Briefly," *Chemical Marketing Reporter,* Vol. 219, No. 4, Jan. 26, p. 24.

Absalom, S.T., 1980, "Iodine," Bulletin 671, Preprint, US Bureau of Mines, 9 pp.

Carnahan, T.G., et al., 1980, "Recovery of Silver from Chloride Leach Solutions by Iodide Precipitation," Report of Investigations 8428, US Bureau of Mines, 9 pp.

Collins, A.G., 1966, "Here's How Producers Can

Turn Brine Disposal into Profit," *Oil and Gas Journal,* Vol. 64, No. 27, July 4, pp. 112–113.

Collins, A.G., 1967, "Geochemistry of Some Tertiary and Cretaceous Age Oil-Bearing Formation Waters," *Environmental Science and Technology,* Vol. 1, No. 9, pp. 725–730.

Collins, A.G., and Eggleston, G.C., 1967, "Iodine Abundance in Oilfield Brines in Oklahoma," *Science,* Vol. 156, No. 377, May 19, pp. 934–935.

Collins, A.G., et al., 1967, "Bromide and Iodide in Oilfield Brines in Some Tertiary and Cretaceous Formations in Mississippi and Alabama," Report of Investigations 6959, US Bureau of Mines, 27 pp.

Croft, R.C., 1972, "Removal of Iron From Ilmenite by Cyclic Iodination," *International Symposium on Hydrometallurgy,* D.J.I. Evans and R.S. Shoemaker, eds., AIME, New York, pp. 920–942.

Dickson, T., 1979, "Iodine Ups and Downs," *Industrial Minerals,* No. 147, Dec., pp. 54–55.

Garrison, J., and Robe, K., 1980, "Hydrazine Reduction of KIO_3 Saves $5600/year, Ups Yield 5%," *Chemical Processing,* Vol. 43, No. 14, Dec., p. 154.

Hart, A.W., 1963, "Iodine and Iodine Compounds," *Encyclopedia of Chemical Technology,* Vol. 2, 2nd ed., Kirk-Othmer, ed., Interscience Publishers, New York, pp. 847–870.

Lyday, P.A., 1982, "Iodine," *Mineral Commodity Summaries 1982,* US Bureau of Mines, pp. 74–75.

MacMillan, R.T., 1970, "Iodine," *Mineral Facts and Problems,* Bulletin 650, US Bureau of Mines, pp. 1049–1058.

Palache, C., et al., 1951, "Iodates," *Dana's System of Mineralogy,* 7th ed., Vol. 2, pp. 312–319.

Park, F., 1967, "The Printed Word," *International Science and Technology,* Jan., pp. 24–26.

Park, W.G., 1969, "Iodine," *Minerals Yearbook,* US Bureau of Mines, pp. 1187–1191.

Shelton, R.A.J., 1968, "Thermodynamic Analysis of the Van Arkel Iodide Process," *Transactions,* Institution of Mining & Metallurgy, Vol. 77, No. 736, Sec. C., Mar., pp. C32–35.

Wang, K.P., 1972, "Iodine," *Minerals Yearbook 1972,* US Bureau of Mines, pp. 1359–1362.

Kyanite and Related Minerals

PAUL J. BENNETT *

JAMES E. CASTLE †

The sillimanite family of minerals, including kyanite, sillimanite, and andalusite, are anhydrous aluminum silicates with the formula $Al_2O_3 \cdot SiO_2$. Dumortierite and topaz are also included in this group because they are closely allied in composition and thermal behavior. However, neither are mined commercially today. They are typical metamorphic minerals which are found in metamorphic rocks on every continent. Sillimanite minerals are prized chiefly for their refractoriness and are important components in a broad range of acid refractory products, especially in mortars and castables. World production of sillimanite minerals is currently about 400,000 tpy and has been increasing at the rate of 3 to 8% a year for many years (Anon., 1972). While these minerals have widespread occurrence, the consumption of sillimanite minerals is concentrated in the relatively few highly industrialized areas where refractories are manufactured, and which in turn are typically close to the major iron and steel producing regions of the world. Thus northern Europe, England, the United States, and Japan are the principal consumers of refractories and sillimanite minerals. Of these countries only the US is a significant producer.

Uses of Kyanite

The following specifications are typical for the domestic kyanite industry:

Raw Kyanite Concentrates
Chemical Analysis

56% Al_2O_3 min	0.1% CaO max
42% SiO_2	0.1% MgO max
1% Acid soluble	0.3% combined
Fe_2O_3	alkali max
1.2% TiO_2 max	

Available Sizes

35, 48, 100, 200, and 325 mesh

* Bennett Mineral Co., Washington, GA.
† Consulting Mining Engineer, York, SC.

The largest use for domestic kyanite, both raw and calcined, is in the manufacture of refractory mortars, cements, castables, and plastic ramming mixes. In these applications kyanite constitutes from 10 to 40% of the mixture, the balance being refractory clays and coarser grog materials. A certain proportion of raw kyanite is used to offset the shrinking of the clay binder, whereas the calcined kyanite is used in the coarser sizes for body.

Certain high grade refractory shapes and kiln furniture are composed chiefly of graded sizes of calcined kyanite bonded with a little ball clay. In most applications, however, kyanite is used only to fortify the mix or as a minor ingredient. Some manufacturers of mullite brick use domestic calcined kyanite for the fine-grained portion of the brick, but seldom in quantities exceeding 10% by weight. Kyanite is used by ceramic manufacturers of wall tile and sanitary ware to offset shrinkage and cracking after firing.

Indian kyanite has traditionally been used to make the coarse grog sizes needed for the manufacture of mullite brick, and for the grog portions of mortar, cement, and castable mixes. It has been largely replaced, however, by synthetic mullite, high fired flint, and diaspore clay or calcined bauxite for other applications.

Indian kyanite has been available in lump as well as in granules and concentrates, as are sillimanite materials from India and South Africa. Andalusite is available as 8 mesh granules and as fines with chemical analyses not unlike those of domestic kyanites. From time to time and from place to place minor amounts of other aluminum silicate minerals such as dumortierite, topaz, and pyrophyllite have been made available at various prices and specifications, but have not been significant factors in the refractory industry. A mixture of kyanite and sillimanite of relatively fine grain-size and of low iron content was at one time offered to the molding sand industry by the Du Pont Co. as a byproduct from their deposits of heavy mineral sands in Florida. This product, "Kya-sill," has been withdrawn from the market.

Sillimanite—Granular and massive forms of sillimanite are used in much the same way as granular and massive kyanite. Massive sillimanite from India and South Africa has been used for sawed block refractories principally in the glass industry in Europe. The massive varieties of kyanite and sillimanite have not enjoyed much use in the United States in recent years, but have been widely used by European refractory producers. Conversely, until recently, little granular domestic kyanite had found much application outside of North America. The use pattern is changing as a result of the depletion of the high grade massive deposits of the world, and of the increasing production of kyanite, andalusite, and sillimanite concentrates in India and Africa from deposits formerly thought to be unworkable. Andalusite concentrations are now being produced in France and are displacing or augmenting aluminum silicate sources from abroad.

The potential use of kyanite, sillimanite, and andalusite for the production of aluminum-silicon alloys has been investigated. To be an economic possibility, however, it appears that it would be necessary to produce aluminum silicate concentrates considerably purer than those currently produced and at a cost about half what the present market will bear. Short of some unforeseen and dire circumstances cutting off the free world trading and marketing of bauxite and silica, the likelihood of such production seems remote.

Other potential nonrefractory uses such as in wall and floor tile seem unlikely due to the high price of aluminum silicates compared to wollastonite, talc, and clays which are the raw materials currently used.

Prices

The average price for kyanite in the United States in 1981 ranged from $85 to $137 (depending upon grain size) per ton f.o.b. Georgia

and Virginia. Aluminum silicate minerals of like specification are generally priced competitively throughout the world after freight considerations have been accounted for.

Geology

Mineralogy

The properties of the kyanite group of minerals are given in Table 1.

Classification of Deposits

Kyanite: *Kyanite Quartzite*—The kyanite produced in the United States comes from kyanite quartzites. Kyanite quartzites are rocks containing 15% to 40% kyanite and usually about 5% of other minerals such as pyrite, lazulite, rutile, and mica. The rock is characterized by an anomalously low content of potash and soda and the virtual absence of calcium and magnesium. The alumina content of kyanite quartzite ranges between 10% and 25% and averages about 18% Al_2O_3, which is generally similar to that of the schistose rocks which enclose the kyanite-bearing strata.

Kyanite quartzite deposits occur in the Piedmont region of the Appalachian Mountain system in a relatively narrow zone extending from northeastern Georgia through central South and North Carolina to southeastern Virginia. They are enclosed within a wider band of mildly metamorphosed acid metavolcanics and sediments known as the Volcanic Slate Belt in Virginia and the Little River Series in Georgia. The age of the rocks is uncertain, but several workers have suggested that they are lower Cambrian in age (Bennett, 1961).

More recent studies by Carpenter and Allard (1980) expand the mineralization and alteration theories of kyanite in the Georgia-South Carolina-McCormick district.

There are at least 13 distinct deposits of kyanite quartzite within this zone. All of them are known as "mountains" owing to their soli-

TABLE 1—Properties of Kyanite Group Minerals

	Andalusite	Kyanite	Sillimanite	Mullite
Formula	$Al_2O_3 \cdot SiO_2$	$Al_2O_3 \cdot SiO_2$	$Al_2O_3 \cdot SiO_2$	$3Al_2O_3 \cdot 2SiO_2$
Crystal system	Orthorhombic	Triclinic	Orthorhombic	Orthorhombic
Cleavage	{110} good	{100} perf.	{010} good	{010} perf.
	{100} poor	{010} good		
		{001} parting		
Hardness	6 − 5 − 7	5.5 − 7*	6.5 − 7.5	6 − 7

* Varies with direction.

tary prominence rather than their relatively modest height. Graves Mountain in Georgia, and Willis Mountain, Baker Mountain, and East Ridge all in Virginia are being mined at the present time. Until 1970 the Henry's Knob deposit in South Carolina was also mined (Espenshade and Potter, 1960).

In southeastern California and extending into southwestern Arizona there is a zone of meta-volcanics whose composition and lithology resembles that of the Carolina Slate Belt in which kyanite quartzite deposits are also found. However, the kyanite in these deposits, while averaging 25 to 35% of the rock in apparently large and recoverable crystals, has proven to be contaminated with extremely fine inclusions of quartz. To date, it has not been possible to produce a competitive kyanite product from these western kyanite quartzite deposits.

Kyanite quartzite has been described in several places in the world, and usually seems to occur within a geologic framework similar to that of the deposits of the southeastern United States. Such deposits have been described and explored in Surinam, Norway, Kenya, and Austria (Varley, 1968).

Kyanite Schist and Gneisses—Kyanite is very common in the highly metamorphosed schists and gneisses of the metamorphic regions of the world. Typically, the kyanite occurs in quantities ranging from a percent or two to as much as 25% in a gangue of biotite, feldspar, muscovite, garnet, and occasionally hornblende and other common rock forming minerals. Rocks containing a few percent of kyanite are extremely abundant and widespread. They are exposed over hundreds of square miles in the eastern and western metamorphic areas of North America and in the metamorphic rocks of other continents.

Repeated attempts to recover the kyanite from such rocks have been made and have been described in earlier editions of this volume. The most recent attempt was in the Timiskaming district in western Quebec by North American Refractories Co. of Cleveland, Ohio. An earlier effort was made in the late 1930s near Burnsville, NC. At the present time no kyanite schists are being mined for kyanite.

In order for such kyanite to be economic it is necessary that the region be deeply weathered and of gentle relief so that a mantle or segregation of resistant kyanite nodules, cobbles, and boulders can be accumulated at the surface. It is further necessary for labor to be abundant and cheap.

A great deal of literature has been published by the US Bureau of Mines, the US Geological Survey, and agencies of other governments describing investigations of kyanite-bearing schists. A recent exhaustive study was conducted by the USBM in Idaho on the huge deposits of kyanite, sillimanite, and andalusite at Goat Mountain and the kyanite deposit on Woodrat Mountain near Kemiah (Van Noy, 1970). Hundreds of millions of tons of 25% aluminum silicate ore available for open cast mining has been postulated. However, remoteness from the major markets and the difficulty of beneficiation have stalled development at this locality.

Massive Kyanite—Kyanite is found locally as nodules, knots, and huge boulder-sized segregations in very highly metamorphosed areas of aluminous sediments. This had been the principal source of kyanite from India for the past 40 years. Similar segregations were the basis for the kyanite production in Kenya which has been discontinued.

In several counties in Georgia, similar lumps of massive kyanite are found (Furcron and Teague, 1945). While the abundance and purity of the Georgia massive kyanite meet the requirements for commercial exploitation, high labor cost makes economic production by hand-sorting and gathering unfeasible and production has been limited to a few carloads during World War II.

Kyanite mineral segregations are probably the result of local pneumatolytic migration of silica and alumina during the late stages of regional metamorphism. Introduction of alumina does not seem to have been a factor since the overall composition of the segregations are similar to that of the country rock if the sample area considered is large enough to include the barren quartz segregations which invariably accompany the kyanite-corundum segregations. Aside from the size and abundance of the segregations in the Lapsa Bura deposits of India, they do not seem mineralogically dissimilar from kyanite segregations found occasionally in all kyanite schists.

Massive kyanite typically contains corundum and minor amounts of rutile. The kyanite is often felty and acicular and occurs in tightly interlocking aggregates. Kyanites from India are usually produced in lumps large enough to be hand-sorted according to kyanite and corundum content, and three grades are offered. Massive Indian kyanite has properties quite unlike that of large coarse kyanite crystals. Massive Indian kyanite is essentially volume-stable and calcines to a dense white aggregate that is much prized by European refractory manufacturers. On the other hand, the coarse kyanite produced from Georgia placer deposits in the 1940s, and more recently in Kenya, crumbles and loses much of its density and physical strength upon calcining. Apparently the interlocking acicular crystal mode of "Indian" kyanite prevents such expansion and consequent breakdown.

Sillimanite: *Sillimanite Schists*—Sillimanite is a very common rock-forming mineral in metamorphic rocks of relatively high rank. It is common in a series of metamorphosed rocks to find sillimanite, kyanite, and andalusite interchanging occurrences in given strata as the local conditions of temperature vary, as in the proximity to intrusives. For this reason the aluminum silicate minerals are often used to identify parameters of metamorphic intensity. Sillimanite, while common, seldom occurs as potentially exploitable crystals. The typical mode is what is often called "fibrolite" which is a felty aggregate of extremely fine "whiskers" of acicular sillimanite interlaced and interlocked with quartz, mica, and other minerals. Beneficiation is usually impossible. In some areas the sillimanite occurs as nodules and buttons which are marginally potential as in the Peltzer area of South Carolina (Espenshade and Potter, 1960).

In Hart County, Georgia, there is a northeasterly trending zone about ten miles long in which "matchstick" sillimanite occurs. Beneficiation tests have been conducted, from which it appears that a limited production of sillimanite in the 35 mesh range could be accomplished. However, the deposits are narrow and limited, and there is presently no existing market or incentive for production of sillimanite concentrates in the United States (Furcron and Teague, 1945).

Massive Sillimanite—Massive sillimanite has been produced for many years from the state of Assam, India. Production has been falling off in recent years as the cost of production has risen and as other materials are substituted for the sawed blocks which were formerly an important use of sillimanite. The deposits of Assam consist of huge segregations of sillimanite and corundum, often in intimate association, and weighing several tons. Considerable hand effort is employed to recover the boulders in a form suitable for sawing to refractory shapes, particularly for the English glass industry.

In the vicinity of Adelaide, South Australia, late-stage metasomatism resulted in a mixture of kaolin and included boulders and nodules of sillimanite. The sillimanite is recovered as a byproduct in the process of manufacturing refractory clays. Other deposits of residual boulders of massive sillimanite have been exploited in this region. Beneficiation has been tried with some success on the sillimanite itself and on the byproducts too low in grade to use directly. The Australian domestic market for such concentrates is limited, however, and thus far no large scale production has been reported.

The most important deposits of massive sillimanite-corundum occurs in the Republic of South Africa, in the Pella District near Pofadder, Namaqualand. Production reached a high of 56,000 tons in 1963, but has dropped steadily in recent years to an estimated 18,000 tons in 1971 (Anon., 1972).

Andalusite: *Andalusite*—Andalusite is a frequent constituent of metamorphic rocks, although it is not as abundant or common as sillimanite or kyanite. It is found in argillaceous and micaceous slates, and in schists and gneisses resulting from the contact metamorphism of intrusive rocks. Andalusite readily incorporates foreign matter in its crystals, and frequently grows around preexisting materials, including carbon. One variety, chiastolite, is so named for the crosslike inclusions of carbon oriented normal to the axis of the crystal.

In France, near Glomel in Brittany, an extensive, deeply weathered body of andalusite schist is being mined at the present time. Here the andalusite occurs as matchstick-sized crystals embedded in a fine-grained black groundmass composed of biotite, hornblende, muscovite, and feldspar. The andalusite is evenly disseminated and constitutes about 20% of the rock. The rocks in the area are very poorly exposed, and the geology of this occurrence is not well understood.

Near Canso, Nova Scotia, there is an extensive deposit of andalusite schist. Here the andalusite makes up about 15% of the rock and is evenly disseminated as large porphyroblasts averaging about 1 × ½ in. in cross section. The groundmass is principally muscovite, garnet, and feldspar. The crystals of black andalusite incorporate about 10% of finely disseminated magnetite and muscovite, however, and effective beneficiation is not practical.

Near Hillsboro, NC, a monadnock of andalusite-pyrophyllite-sericite rock is being mined by the Piedmont Minerals Co. The ore consists principally of pyrophyllite and quartz and contains 15 to 20% of disseminated pink andalusite. The andalusite is mined along with the pyrophyllite, and the resulting mixture is almost entirely consumed by the parent company in the manufacture of refractory products.

In the Goat Mountain deposit in Idaho, andalusite coexists with kyanite and sillimanite. No attempt has been made to separate it from the other aluminum silicate minerals in the tests made so far. The andalusite in this deposit typically incorporates a great many deleterious impurities. The Goat Mountain deposit is extremely large, but to date no commercial exploitation of the deposit seems feasible owing to beneficiation difficulties (Abbott and Prater, 1954).

Residual Andalusite—Alluvial deposits of andalusite sand occur in South Africa. These deposits have been worked on a very large scale, and current production is in the vicinity of 45,000 tpy. The source of the andalusite are shales of the Pretoria Series that have been intruded and metamorphosed by the Bushveld Complex. The andalusite has been weathered free from the parent rock and subsequently concentrated by the action of wind and water. Apparently concentration is still going on. The andalusite sand commonly contains 50% of recoverable andalusite. The reserves are estimated to be in the neighborhood of 800,000 tons of +50% andalusite. In 1964 a heavy media separation plant was installed, and since then the production of high grade concentrates has increased markedly.

Reserves

Domestic: The potential supply of kyanite minerals vastly exceeds the potential market. Therefore, what constitutes a reserve can not be defined without considering the probability of production. The two producing domestic kyanite deposits have enormous proven reserves. At least 65 million tons of kyanite quartzite containing at least 25% kyanite and amenable to open pit mining were indicated by an extensive US Bureau of Mines drilling program undertaken in 1949 at Willis Mountain in Virginia (Jones and Eiletsen, 1954). The potential reserves in this locality are probably twice the indicated reserves. At Graves Mountain, geologic mapping and diamond drilling has indicated a reserve of 25% ore in excess of 30 million tons. From these figures, which translate into many decades of production at current rates, it is readily apparent that the existing producers have little interest in acquiring new reserves unless a considerable

economic advantage would result. If the +10% kyanite-bearing schists and gneisses are included, the reserves in the United States and Canada are truly vast. At current prices these reserves are obviously submarginal.

World: Most of the comments made about the reserves of kyanite minerals in the United States apply to other areas of the world as well. However, the massive kyanite reserves of India, being relatively rare and unique in occurrence, are more susceptible to reserve considerations. The Lapsa Buru area is credited with 700,000 tons of massive kyanite to a depth of 10 ft, and the Madhya Predesh area with 250,000 tons of massive sillimanite.

In the Republic of South Africa 800,000 tons of +50% andalusite sand are reported for the Transvaal and millions of tons of sillimanite reserves have been credited to Namaqualand in the Cape Province.

No figures have been reported from the Province of Brittany, France, where andalusite production recently began. However, the body of andalusite schist is reported to be at least 1 km wide and about 10 km long, and to contain an average of about 15 to 25% andalusite. This translates into many tens of millions of tons of potential reserves.

It is apparent that the existing producers of aluminum silicate minerals have adequate reserves, with the possible exception of the unique and relatively rare deposits of massive kyanite-corundum and massive sillimanite-corundum. It should be noted, however, that the primary use for the massive varieties is being increasingly challenged by the more consistent synthetic mullite materials which are produced from more available high alumina clays and bauxite.

The heavy mineral beach sand deposits of the world generally contain a significant proportion of andalusite, sillimanite, or kyanite. The US Bureau of Mines has described a method of producing a kyanite coproduct from the ilmenite sand treatment plants in Florida. The potential production from heavy mineral deposits throughout the world is large.

Exploration and Evaluation

Kyanite and sillimanite are fairly common minerals, and are found in the metamorphosed rocks on every continent. Andalusite is less abundant but still common. However, kyanite is consumed principally by the highly developed industrialized nations and its consumption is therefore restricted to certain areas. For example, the bulk of the American production of kyanite is consumed in a relatively small region extending from the northeastern part of the United States to central Missouri. A similar pattern exists in Europe, where consumption is concentrated in those parts of England, France, and Germany where the producers of refractories are concentrated. Kyanite and related minerals must be delivered to the consuming areas at competitive prices. Therefore, a very important preliminary consideration in any exploration project is the prospective cost of delivering the kyanite to the market. In the United States, typical freight costs for delivering kyanite concentrates from traditional sources to consumers ranges between $30 and $40 per ton. A relatively small market exists on the west coast of the United States where the freight is as high as $90 per ton.

The second problem to be considered is the probability of producing a salable product. Kyanite consumers are notoriously finicky about the specifications of materials used by them in the manufacture of refractory products. Thus any deviation from the commonly accepted specifications imposes a considerable burden on products attempting to enter the market. Probably the most important consideration in this regard when evaluating a raw prospect is the liberation size of the kyanite crystals. In the western United States there are several otherwise attractive kyanite-quartzite deposits which cannot be beneficiated to the required specifications without grinding the ore to about −200 mesh, which is quite fine considering that most existing kyanite deposits can produce concentrates in a size range of at least −35 to 28 mesh.

If the initial investigation indicates that both freight and quality of product can be competitive, then the normal exploration techniques apply. These consist of surface sampling, trenching, geologic mapping, and some limited diamond drilling to test the material in depth. Kyanite deposits are in reality kyanite-bearing rocks produced by regional metamorphism. They have inherently consistent compositions, unlike the hydrothermal deposits which are typical of the precious and base metals. Geochemical and geophysical exploration techniques are generally not useful for evaluating kyanite and other aluminum silicate deposits.

After a deposit has been explored, the potential markets determined, and studies indicate that a competitive product could be produced and delivered to the market, the next step should be a pilot plant production of the material intended to be marketed. Bench scale and laboratory testing are not sufficient in this regard. As an example, in recent years a major attempt was made to produce kyanite from schists and kyanite-bearing gneisses in Canada. After the construction of a plant and the expenditure of a great deal of money it was found that a salable concentrate could not be produced economically. Similar failures have occurred in the United States and in other countries. Therefore, it is most important to produce, by reproducible pilot plant techniques, a quantity of concentrates from a representative selection of ores sufficient to permit prospective consumers to test the new material extensively in their plants. There is no laboratory substitute for this kind of field testing in the plants of the intended consumers. Quoted physical and chemical specifications are to be used only as approximations of the suitability of a given kyanite or aluminum silicate material. New producers of aluminum silicates have found to their sorrow that kyanite conforming to specifications supplied by the prospective consumers may not in fact be what those consumers are really willing to use when confronted with the decision to utilize a new material from a new area. Competitive testing and specific approval is the only sure way that the marketability of a given kyanite concentrate can be assured.

Preparation for Markets

In the United States for the past 30 years kyanite concentrates have been produced by flotation and magnetic separation. The four kyanite-quartzite deposits currently being exploited, Willis Mountain, Baker Mountain, and East Ridge all in Virginia, and Graves Mountain in Georgia, are monadanock-type features which were created by differential weathering of the softer schists and phyllites surrounding the more resistant hard kyanite-quartzite ore bodies. As a result, the ore is exposed with little or no overburden.

The ore is drilled and blasted with ammonium nitrate. Secondary breaking is typically accomplished with a drop ball. The ore is picked up with diesel-powered shovels, loaded into trucks, and carried to the crushing plant, where it is reduced to approximately −1½ in. in size and stockpiled. The ore is withdrawn from the stockpile by conveyor belt controlled by an automatic feeder and fed into a rod mill in closed circuit with a rake classifier set to grind the ore to −28 mesh. The resulting slurry is carefully deslimed. This is an important prerequisite for successful flotation, but one which results in a considerable loss of fine-grained kyanite. The deslimed slurry is conditioned with pine oil and xanthate and an amine collector and passed through a series of flotation cells which remove the pyrite and micaceous contaminants from the slurry. The tailings from the pyrite circuit are again deslimed and conditioned with sulfuric acid and petroleum sulfonate and passed through a section of rougher flotation cells. The rougher concentrate goes to a two-stage recleaning circuit. The tails of the rougher circuit go to waste.

Flotation concentrate consists of about 91% kyanite, 2–5% iron oxides, and the balance quartz. The concentrates are dewatered by draining in open stockpiles or in drainage silos and are subsequently conveyed to a dryer where the moisture is reduced from 6–8% to essentially 0%. One American producer utilizes a reducing roast technique, elevating the temperature during the drying process to 900° F, followed by cooling in an oxygen-deficient atmosphere to render the iron oxide highly magnetic and to oxidize any residual pyrite. The other producer does not find this to be necessary. The dried concentrates are passed over high-intensity three-to-five-roll magnetic separators which reduce the acid-soluble iron in the concentrate to less than 1%. The resultant material is known as a raw 35 mesh kyanite and is ready for use. However, about 75% of the kyanite sold in the United States is further reduced in granite-lined pebble mills to —48, 100, and 200 mesh sizes. Until recently, about 30% of the kyanite was calcined in rotary kilns at a temperature of approximately 2900° F and sold as mullite or calcined kyanite. However, in the past year or two the demand for calcined kyanite leveled off and began to decline as cheaper calcined kaolin and bauxite became available. Approximately one-half of the kyanite sales made in the United States are shipped in bulk hopper cars, and the balance is packaged in 100-lb multiwall paper bags. Of the kyanite produced, 96% is shipped by rail to consumer's sidings.

Kyanite exports have increased over the past several years with an estimated tonnage of 25,000 exported in 1980 to Europe, Australia, Japan, South America, Mexico, and Canada.

Andalusite concentrates are produced near Gommel, in Brittany, France, by LaFerriere Aux E. Tangs. The ore is a black andalusite schist containing about 20% coarse euhedral andalusite porphyroblasts. The andalusite crystals are about the diameter of matchsticks and range from ¾ to 1 in. in length. The andalusite schist is deeply weathered and friable to at least a depth of 30 ft. The ore is drilled with a wagon drill, blasted, and transported with a rubber-tired Hough front-end loader with a 2½ to 3-yd bucket. It is fed into a surge hopper through an 8 x 8-in. grizzly and discharged onto a 24-in. conveyor belt by a reciprocating feeder. Oversized material is reduced with a sledge hammer to pass the 8-in. grizzly.

The conveyor belt carries the broken ore about 150 ft to an autogenous mill, which consists of a drum 15 ft in diameter revolving on eight truck tires, and which reduces the ore to 100% —⅛ in. The furnace is air-swept with heated air in closed circuit with two air classifiers. The sized ore is fed into a hopper, from which it is passed over a four-roll, high-intensity magnetic separator. The nonmagnetic fraction is conveyed to the heavy media separator and the magnetics are discarded.

The heavy media separator circuit consists of a hopper in which the andalusite ore is blended with a ferrosilicon slurry and then pumped through a hydrocyclone. The specific gravity of the slurry is controlled automatically by a water-metering device ahead of the blending hopper. The first stage of the two-stage heavy media separator circuit is controlled at about 2.3 specific gravity. The final effective specific gravity is adjusted by regulating the velocity of the slurry through the cyclone. The second stage is controlled in similar fashion. The sink product from the heavy media separator is screened at about 35 mesh to recover the media. About one-half of the andalusite is lost in the fine sizes at present. In the future, it is intended to install flotation cells to recover these fines.

The andalusite now being produced consists of dark brown to black, roughly equidimensional grains ranging in size from —8 mesh to +35 mesh, and containing about 59.2% Al_2O_3 and 1.0% Fe_2O_3. The plant is capable of producing 15 to 20,000 tpy.

The kyanite deposits of India have traditionally been exploited by labor-intensive techniques. In the beginning it was sufficient to simply gather the cobbles and boulders of kyanite which had been released and exposed by weathering. Later, primitive mining methods were initiated and the large segregations were drilled and blasted and hand-cobbed in preparation for shipment. Dozens of these small operations employed numerous men and women. As time passed and the availability of readily hand-picked material decreased, the beneficiation methods became more sophisticated. The picking belt is still an important beneficiation technique, however. High-grade kyanite nodules, and segregations too low in grade to be shipped directly, are now crushed and subjected to more sophisticated beneficiation techniques including flotation and magnetic separation. At the present time there are no large-scale integrated beneficiation plants in India of the kind employed in America.

In South Africa andalusite sands of the Marico district of the Transvaal are beneficiated with heavy media separators and high-intensity magnetic separators. A typical analysis of the product is as follows:

Al_2O_3	52-57%
SiO_2	35-44%
Fe_2O_3	1-4.5%
TiO_2	0.04-4%

Segregations of sillimanite-corundum rock in the Pellar District in the northwestern part of the Cape Province have been produced for many years by labor-intensive techniques similar to those employed in India.

In general, the large disseminated deposits containing 20 to 30% recoverable aluminum silicates are treated by modern beneficiation techniques, while the segregation-type deposits including the massive kyanites of India and the sillimanite-corundum segregations of South Africa are mined by more primitive labor-intensive techniques. As time passes the African and Indian deposits are increasingly subjected to the more sophisticated ore dressing techniques, and more aluminum silicate concentrates are being offered to the market from those areas which previously yielded only hand-selected products.

Future Considerations and Trends

The sillimanite family of minerals will be increasingly challenged in the future by synthetic mullite, calcined bauxite, and especially by the calcined kaolin which has only recently been produced and promoted on a large scale. The unique thermal expansion characteristics of kyanite at elevated temperatures should ensure its continued use in acid refractories designed for service in temperatures up to 3200° F. The increased use of castable and monolithic refractories also should dictate a correspondingly increased consumption of kyanite. The growth rate of the kyanite industry in the United States has been at a rate of 8 to 10% a year.

Although there is a likelihood that this rate of growth will not be maintained indefinitely, a decline in absolute consumption is not anticipated.

Kyanite mining in the United States is subject to a depletion allowance of 22%. There is no tariff on imports of kyanite. There are no specific programs sponsored by the US government directed to the development or production of kyanite deposits, although the US Bureau of Mines has from time to time conducted research and development on particular aspects of production, and from time to time the US Geological Survey publishes exploration reports on promising deposits.

Recent reports by Coope (1980) indicate that kyanite production is on the rise in Brazil with a capacity of 40,000 tons per year from two operating mines. With this increase in world supply from Brazil, there is a decline in available material from India due to a governmental ban on export of high grade material and strict ceilings placed on allowable export tonnages of low grade product. In 1980 it was reported that 1,000 t/a were exported as compared to 70,000 t/a in 1970.

The major kyanite and kyanite-group mineral deposits of the world are located in relatively remote areas. The industry is relatively small in scope, and at the present and for the foreseeable future no special environmental problems are foreseen.

Bibliography and References

Anon., 1972, "Refractory Raw Materials," *Industrial Minerals*, No. 59, Aug., pp. 13–17.

Abbott, A.T., and Prater, L.S., 1954, "The Geology of Kyanite-Andallusite Deposits, Goat Mountain, Idaho, and Preliminary Beneficiation Tests on the Ore," Pamphlet 100, Idaho Bureau of Mines and Geology, 27 pp.

Bennett, P. J., 1961, "The Economic Geology of Some Virginia Kyanite Deposits," unpublished Ph.D. Thesis, University of Arizona, Tucson.

Browning, J.S., and McVay, T.L., 1963, "Flotation of Kyanite Quartzite Rock, Graves Mountain, Lincoln County, Georgia," Report of Investigations No. 6268, US Bureau of Mines, 9 pp.

Carpenter, R.H., and Allard, G.O., 1980, "Mineralization, Alteration and Volcanism in the Lincolnton-McCormick District, Georgia and South Carolina," Abstract, Bulletin of Geological Society of America, Nov., pp. 398–399.

Coope, B., 1980, "Patterns of Raw Material Supply to the Refractories Industry," Paper presented at ILAFA Conference, Lima, Peru.

Espenshade, G.H., and Potter, D.B., 1960, "Kyanite, Sillimanite and Andalusite Deposits of the Southeastern States," Professional Paper 336, US Geological Survey, 121 pp.

Furcron, A.S., and Teague, K.H., 1945, "Sillimanite and Massive Kyanite Deposits in Georgia," Bulletin 51, Georgia Dept. of Natural Resources, 76 pp.

Grametbaur, A.B., 1959, "Selected Bibliography of Andalusite, Kyanite, Sillimanite, Dumortierite, Topaz, and Pyrophyllite in the United States," Bulletin 1019–N, US Geological Survey, pp. 973–1046.

Jones, J.O., and Eiletsen, N.A., 1954, "Investigation of the Willis Mountain Kyanite Deposit, Buckingham County, Virginia," Report of Investigations No. 5075, U.S. Bureau of Mines, 41 pp.

Klinefelter, T.A., and Cooper, J.D., 1961, "Kyanite—A Materials Survey," Information Circular 8040, US Bureau of Mines, 54 pp.

Potter, M.J., 1982, "Kyanite and Related Minerals," *Mineral Commodity Summaries 1982*, US Bureau of Mines, pp. 82–83.

Van Noy, R.M., 1970, "Kyanite Resources in the Northwestern United States," Report of Investigations 7426, US Bureau of Mines, 81 pp.

Varley, E.R., 1965, *Sillimanite, Andalusite, Kyanite,* Overseas Geological Surveys, Mineral Resources Div., London, 165 pp.

Varley, E.R., 1968, *Sillimanite,* Chemical Publishing Co., New York, 165 pp.

Wells, J.R., 1972, "Kyanite and Related Minerals," *Minerals Yearbook*, US Bureau of Mines, pp. 689–693.

Williamson, D.R., 1960, "The Sillimanite Group," *Mineral Industries Bulletin,* Colorado School of Mines, Vol. 3, No. 4, July, 12 pp.

Lime

ROBERT S. BOYNTON *
KENNETH A. GUTSCHICK *
Revised by ROBERT C. FREAS †
and JEFFREY L. THOMPSON ‡

Lime, the "versatile chemical," is, generally speaking, a calcined or burned form of limestone commonly known as quicklime, calcium oxide or calcia, or, when water is added, calcium hydroxide or slaked lime. Almost 40 different lime products are available, a fact which has contributed to the rather loose use of the term *lime* as well as to much confusion and misunderstanding. The term is frequently, albeit erroneously, used to denote almost any kind of calcareous material or finely ground form of limestone or dolomite.

Lime is usually made from high-calcium or high-magnesium limestone, generally having a minimum of 97% combined carbonate content. Normally, high-calcium limes contain less than 5% MgO. When the lime is produced from a high-magnesium limestone, the product is referred to as dolomitic lime.

Calcination, or the production of lime, has its origins in the earliest days of alchemy, with the general reaction class having been identified in an Arabic text printed in 1000 A.D. It was much later, however, in the mid-1700s to the mid-1800s before this basic reaction became understood from a scientific perspective. The production of lime has been so basic and simple that its underlying scientific principles have over the years received only intermittent investigation. Rather, much of the thought and inquiry has been directed toward the development of kilns. Thus, it has only been in the last 15 to 20 years that lime has received any concentrated scientific investigation relative to the thermodynamics and kinetics of the calcination and hydration reactions.

* Article for 4th edition prepared by Robert S. Boynton, retired, formerly Executive Director, National Lime Assn., and Kenneth A. Gutschick, Technical Director, National Lime Association, Washington, DC.
† Limestone Products Corp., Sparta, NJ.
‡ Dravo Lime Co., Pittsburgh, PA.

Calcination refers to a broad class of reactions, of which the lime/limestone reaction is just one, wherein a substance is heated to less than its melting point, resulting in a weight gain or weight loss. In the calcination of limestone to produce lime, the basic chemical reaction is as follows:

$$CaCO_3 \text{ (limestone)} + \text{heat (1000° to 1300°C)} \rightleftharpoons$$
$$100$$
$$CaO \text{ (quicklime)} + CO_2 \uparrow$$
$$56 \qquad 44$$

or

$$CaCO_3 \cdot MgCO_3 \text{ (limestone)}$$
$$100 \qquad 84$$
$$+ \text{heat (900°C to 1200°C)} \rightleftharpoons$$
$$CaO \cdot MgO \text{ (quicklime)} + 2CO_2 \uparrow$$
$$56 \quad 40 \qquad\qquad 88$$

While there is nearly universal agreement about the equilibrium conditions related to the limestone/lime reaction above, there have been numerous and varied calcination models developed for the reaction. Recent investigations have resulted in the development of the model shown in Fig. 1. From this model it can be seen that calcination is a function of both temperature and CO_2 pressure. It does not, however, provide any indication of the rate at which the reaction takes place.

Calcination is strongly time variant with different limestones. In a very broad sense this relates to the fact that the calcination reaction starts on the exterior surface of the limestone and then proceeds toward the center. As the calcination reaction takes place, the CO_2 released at the reaction interface must make its way through the lime to the exterior surface. Therefore, because calcination is limited by gas diffusion to the surface of the partially calcined limestone, natural impurities in the stone, differences in crystallinity, grain boundary chemistry, density variations, and imperfections in the atomic lattice all play a significant role in

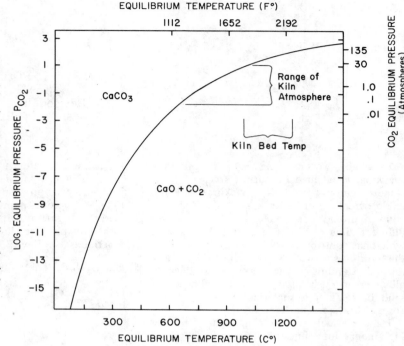

FIG. 1—*Equilibrium graph for $CaCO_3 \rightleftharpoons CaO + CO_2$ as a function of temperature and CO_2 pressure in atmospheres. Conditions below the curve cause the reaction to go toward lime (CaO), while above the curve the reaction proceeds toward calcite. Only on the curve is the equilibrium maintained and the reaction out does not proceed in either direction. Most like kilns have production bed temperatures of 1000 to 1150°C.*

calcination rate. The suitability of a given limestone as a source material for lime production can be determined only after completion of adequate burn tests designed to evaluate the various limiting factors. When a coal-fired kiln system is considered, the entire process of calcination is made even more complex. The reader is referred to the references for a more detailed description of the complete calcination reaction.

In the foregoing discussion it was noted that CO_2 is released during the reaction. This release results in a 44% weight loss during the complete calcination of a high calcium limestone, or a 48% weight loss for a highly dolomitic limestone. The trade term for this weight percent loss is *loss on ignition*, or LOI.

Because the calcination reaction is chemically reversible, *quicklime* or *burned lime* is frequently referred to as being highly reactive, or unstable. The more stable form of lime, *hydrated lime*, is commonly preferred and specified by the user. Hydrated lime is obtained by adding water to quicklime to produce a dry, fine powder. Quicklime's affinity for moisture is then satisfied, although it still retains a strong affinity for CO_2.

Hydration is the combining of calcium oxide with water in a reversible reaction to form calcium hydroxide:

$$CaO + H_2O \rightarrow Ca(OH)_2.$$

As a standard condition the reaction is exothermic for the formation of hydrate, with the accepted value for the heat of hydration being 15.456 kcal/g mol of CaO. This is a three-step reaction, with the first being the dissociation of CaO into a Ca++ ion and an O= ion:

$$CaO \rightarrow Ca^{++} + O^=.$$

Next, the water ionizes into two hydroxyl ions due to the strong attraction that an oxygen anion exerts on a water molecule:

$$H_2O + O^= \rightarrow 2(OH)^-.$$

Finally, the calcium and hydroxyl ions combine to form calcium hydroxide:

$$Ca^{++} + 2(OH)^- \rightleftharpoons Ca(OH)_2 + heat.$$

As noted this is a reversible reaction, and hydrated lime therefore can, when heated, revert to the original oxide form.

Analysis and Properties

The value of lime for most purposes is dependent upon its available lime content (CaO), or in the case of dolomitic lime its total oxide content. The purity of lime is influenced primarily by the purity of the limestone, and secondarily by its manufacture. The major impurities are silica, iron, alumina, and sulfur. During calcination these impurities react with some of the calcium oxide, yielding mineral forms (silicates, aluminates, ferrites, etc.) that reduce the available CaO by 3 to 5% or more. Even the purest calcium limes assay less than 95% in available CaO, several percentage points less than the total oxide content. In addition, uncalcined limestone particles may remain as core in the individual lime pieces. Typical chemical analyses of commercial quicklimes are presented in Table 1.

Impurities and core also affect the hydration reaction. As an example, sulfur in the form of calcium sulfate inhibits the hydration reaction out of all proportion to its actual weight percent concentration (perhaps more than 100 times). If the parent stone contains dolomite, this will also inhibit the reaction as its hydration may be nearly three orders of magnitude slower than that of calcium oxide. Early in the hydration reaction dolomite appears practically inert, but given sufficient time it will hydrate. The heat of reaction is nearly the same as for calcium oxide, but the time necessary for complete hydration may be hours, whereas for calcium oxide it is only seconds.

Important physical properties of lime are listed in Table 2. Lime is white in color of varying intensities, but some limes have a light cream, buff, or gray cast, depending upon the impurities present. The severity of calcination (time and temperature) determines the degree of porosity and chemical reactivity of the lime. When a lime is soft-burned, very little or no shrinkage occurs and a porous, softer, very reactive lime is produced.

When a lime is hard-burned, a denser, physically stronger, less reactive lime results. In either case the lime will readily hydrate in water except the rapidity of hydration is much greater with the former type than with the latter. In any event the heat of hydration is appreciable: 1134 and 886 kJ/kg of quicklime for high calcium and dolomitic types, respectively. This strong exothermic reaction will boil water easily and, under certain hydration conditions, temperatures of 290 to 315°C have been reached, causing dehydration of the freshly

TABLE 1—Typical Analyses of Commercial Quicklimes

Component	High Calcium Quicklimes, Range,* %	Dolomitic Quicklimes, Range,* %
CaO	93.25-98.00	55.50-57.50
MgO	0.30-2.50	37.60-40.80
SiO_2	0.20-1.50	0.10-1.50
Fe_2O_3	0.10-0.40	0.05-0.40
Al_2O_3	0.10-0.50	0.05-0.50
H_2O	0.10-0.90	0.10-0.90
CO_2	0.40-1.50	0.40-1.50

Source: Anon, 1981.
*The values given in this range do not necessarily represent minima and maxima percentages.

slaked lime. Quicklime can be made so reactive that it will literally explode on contact with water.

Although limestone is almost totally insoluble, lime is slightly soluble in water in the range of 1.4 to 0.54 mg/L, depending on temperature. As water temperature rises, lime's solubility diminishes. The addition of sugar will increase these solubilities manyfold.

On slaking into a slurry or milk-of-lime, the saturated solution ionizes immediately into Ca^{++}, Mg^{++}, and OH^- ions, one of the strongest bases. Even a trace of lime will yield a pH of 11.2 and on up to nearly pH 13 at saturated solution and low temperature.

As an alkali, unlike other strong bases, (NaOH, KOH), $Ca(OH)_2$, and $Mg(OH)_2$ are diacid bases. Therefore, one molecule of lime will neutralize two molecules of acid (sulfuric, hydrochloric, etc.). For example, at equal weights CaO has 30% more neutralizing power than caustic soda (sodium hydroxide). However, dolomitic quicklime, because of its MgO content, has 16% greater neutralizing power than pure CaO.

Lime Manufacture

Production of lime involves three main processes—stone preparation, calcination, and hydration—although the latter is not necessary for several lime uses. The simplified flowsheet (Fig. 2) outlines the various production steps. Details of stone preparation, which comprises quarrying or mining, crushing, and screening to produce kiln-size stone, are covered in other chapters. However, because lime must meet existing chemical specifications, the various steps in stone production are carefully con-

TABLE 2—Properties of Typical Commercial Lime Products

Quicklimes

	High Calcium	Dolomitic
Primary constituents	CaO	CaO and MgO
Specific gravity	3.2-3.4	3.2-3.4
Bulk density (pebble lime), g/cm³	0.88-0.96	0.88-0.96
	(55-60 lb per cu ft)	(55-60 lb per cu ft)
Specific heat at 38°C (100°F), kJ/kg	0.4	9.94
Angle of repose	55° *	55° *

Hydrates

	High Calcium	Normal Dolomitic	Pressure Dolomitic
Primary constituents	$Ca(OH)_2$	$Ca(OH)_2 + MgO$	$Ca(OH)_2 + Mg(OH)_2$
Specific gravity	2.3-2.4	2.7-2.9	2.4-2.6
Bulk density, g/cm³	0.40-0.56	0.40-0.56	0.48-0.64
	(25-35 lb per cu ft) †	(25-35 lb per cu ft) †	(30-40 lb per cu ft) †
Specific heat at 38°C (100°F), kJ/kg	0.62	0.62	0.62
Angle of repose	70° *	70° *	70° *

Source: Anon., 1981.

* The angle of repose for both types of lime (hydrate in particular) varies considerably with mesh, moisture content, degree of aeration, and physical characteristics of the lime; e.g., for quicklime it generally varies from 50° to 55° and for hydrated lime it may range as much as 15° to 80°.

† In some instances these values may be extended. The Scott method is used for determining the bulk density values. In calculating bin volumes the lower figure should be used.

trolled to prevent contamination with undesirable impurities, particularly silica, alumina, and iron oxide. Accordingly, at several lime plants practices such as selective quarrying and washing are carried out.

Calcining

Although lime calcining (or burning) is a relatively simple operation chemically, a wide variety of kiln systems are used today. These include vertical, rotary, rotary with preheaters, multiple-shaft regenerative, and a variety of other types of kilns, in striking contrast to the portland cement industry which utilizes rotary kilns and rotary kilns with preheaters almost exclusively.

Lime kiln selection depends upon several factors, the most important ones being burning characteristics of the stone, fuel consumption, and capital equipment costs. Other factors include market requirements, fuel availability and air pollution regulations. Traditionally, vertical kilns have been considered to have the following advantages over rotaries: lower capital investment, more efficient fuel utilization, less attrition loss of stone and less refractory wear, and lower pollution control costs. Rotary kilns, on the other hand, have the advantages of being

able to burn small stone readily, greater versatility (capable of producing a wide range of burn, from soft to hard, even dead-burned, and using all types of fuels, singly or in combination), more uniform product quality, greater capacity, and less manpower requirements. In addition, fuel efficiencies now being achieved with rotary kilns having preheaters and the adaptability of rotaries to the large size units (1000 tons or more per day) have had the effect of offsetting some of the advantages of vertical kilns. Today over 85% of the commercial lime produced in the US and Canada is from rotary kilns. However, current developments in calcining technology and the tremendous fuel cost increases experienced in the late 1970s and early 1980s have generated renewed interest in the US in the multiple-shaft regenerative kilns, as they are particularly fuel efficient.

Vertical Kilns: A revolution has taken place in recent years in vertical kiln design. These design changes have been largely the result of increasing fuel and capital costs, and are supplanting more traditional designs as new and replacement capacity is being brought on line. Among the newer vertical kilns are the European multiple-shaft parallel flow regenerative kilns (Fig. 3), the center burner gas-fired

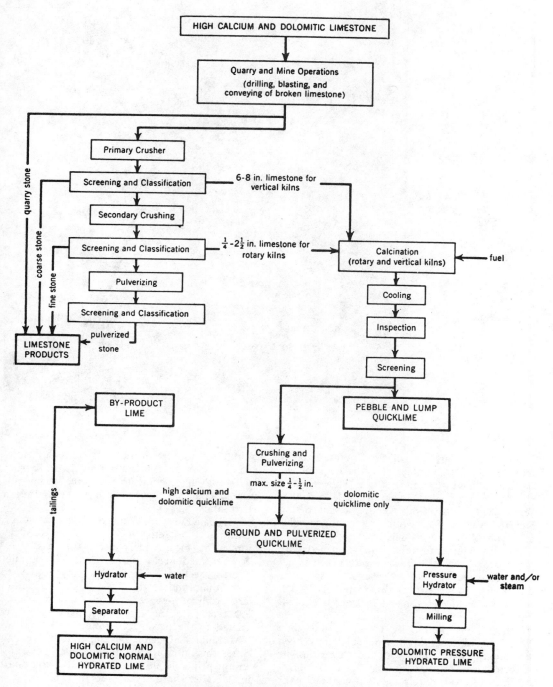

FIG. 2—*Simplified flowsheet for lime and limestone products.*

FIG. 3—*Multiple shaft parallel flow regenerative kiln.*

(Azbe, Union Carbide), oil-fired (West Catagas and Beckenback) annular, and the Beckenback double-inclined (cascade) kilns. The multiple shaft kilns are now available in the US through Warwick Furnace Co., Kennedy Van Saun, and the Fuller Co., while the annular kilns are available through Allis-Chalmers.

Vertical kilns traditionally have burned only larger stone (75 to 300 mm) with a size range of approximately 1:2. However, the newer designs can handle stone sizes as small as 20 mm and a widened size range to as much as 1:4. Fuel consumption has been a major advantage of shaft kilns, nominally requiring less than 5.2 GJ/t of lime produced. This has been further improved upon with the newer designs reportedly operating as low as 3.3 to 3.9 GJ/t of lime. Power requirements for these kilns will vary with stone size, but at nominal capacity will be in the range of 54 to 90 MJ/t. A disadvantage of traditional vertical kilns in today's energy environment is their fuel re-

quirement of oil, natural gas, or coke. However, several recent developments in burner technology have come to the point where pulverized coal can now be utilized in a modern shaft kiln.

Vertical kilns may be of stone masonry, reinforced concrete, or boiler plate construction. The most widely used kiln has a refractory-lined steel shell and is usually circular in cross section. These kilns may be 2.7 to 7.3 m diam and 15 to 48.5 m high. Capacities vary from as low as 9.5 t/d to in excess of 700 t/d, with the larger tonnages being restricted to the newer generation of kilns.

Multiple Shaft Kiln: Developed to burn small stone, this kiln utilizes the parallel flow calcining principle in double- and triple-shaft units. The shafts are interconnected in the burning zone, and while one shaft is being fired (Fig. 4), the other is preheated. Fuel and combustion air are supplied to the burning shaft from above, ignite at the upper end of

FIG. 4—*Installation of fuel lances for natural gas and fuel oil in a multple shaft kiln.*

the burning zone, and calcine the lime in uniflow. The exhaust gases then pass into the second shaft, preheating the stone in counterflow. After a 10- to 15-min interval the shaft firing is reversed. Cooling air is blown into both shafts simultaneously. Because of the novel heat regeneration system, fuel consumption is 5.4 to 5.7 GJ/t of lime produced. Kilns vary in capacity from 90 to 550 t/d, and while nominally gas- or oil-fired, recent developments in burner technology have led to several installations now being equipped to fire pulverized coal. Kilns of this type have found worldwide acceptance. The recent installation of new multiple-shaft kilns in Japan and the United States brings their total number to over 185.

Annular Shaft Kiln: The burning process in this kiln is based upon counterflow for preheating and calcining and uniflow for residual calcination. Partitions provided by an inner cylinder and by staggered bridges in the burning zone permit even distribution of heat and uniform flow of material down the kiln. Stone as small as 25 x 75 mm can be calcined to produce a soft-burned lime, using either oil or gas firing. Capacities vary from 90 to 270 t/d, with fuel consumption reported under 6.2 GJ/t.

Rotary Kilns: Unlike vertical kilns, which operate fully charged, the rotary kiln has about 90% of its volume filled with flame and hot gases. As the kiln slowly rotates, new surfaces of stone are exposed to the hot gases, but there is little passage of the gases through the solids; hence radiation interchange between gas, solids, and refractory wall plays an important part in the overall heat transfer. Because the area of solids exposed is relatively small, a rotary kiln is less efficient than a shaft kiln. However, the rotary has the advantage of burning stone from as small as 6.5 mm to as large as 57 mm.

Generally, though, the size ratio is 1:3 in order to minimize segregation, wherein the finer particles would sift to the bottom of the kiln and remain largely uncalcined.

Rotary kilns vary greatly in size, ranging from 2 x 25 m to 5.5 x 190 m, with capacities of 45 to 945 t/d. Because of the relatively high length to diameter ratios these kilns have come to be termed *long kilns*. In North America these long kilns are typically 2.5 to 4.0 m diam by 45 to 105 m long, producing 181 to 410 t/d of lime. While rotary kilns can burn a wide range of fuels, a major drawback of these long kilns has been their lack of fuel efficiency. Many of the earlier rotaries require in excess of 18.6 GJ/t of lime. This high fuel requirement has led to the development of more fuel efficient equipment such as external preheaters, internal heat exchangers and dams, recuperative-type coolers, more sophisticated and complex instrumentation, and improved refractories.

Preheaters: Of the several advances which have been made in improving the heat efficiency of rotary kilns, probably the most pronounced has been the trend away from long kilns to medium length kilns with external preheaters. Shaft-type preheaters (Fig. 5), available through Kennedy Van Saun, Fuller Co., and others, are the most widely employed. This preheater. a refractory-lined chamber located below the raw feed bin and ahead of the kiln. Exhaust gases from the kiln are drawn countercurrent through the stone, preheating it to 650 to 900°C. Retention time within the preheater is 1.0 to 1.5 hr, depending upon the system design, burning characteristics of the stone, etc. During preheating approximately 30% calcination is achieved before the stone is discharged to the kiln. Following preheating, the partially calcined stone is fed to the kiln at a predetermined rate by means of hydraulically actuated plungers. This type preheater has been adapted to the new large volume kilns which typically may be 5.2 m diam by 62.5 m long and have a capacity of 900 to 1000 t/d.

A second type preheater is the grate-type, developed by Allis-Chalmers as part of its grate-kiln system. This is a single pass, downdraft, enclosed traveling grate on which the finer stone sizes, placed on top of the coarser sizes are virtually calcined while the coarser sizes are preheated. Then, in the rotary kiln which follows, the coarse sizes are calcined, while the finer sizes are protected from overburning because they sink into the kiln load through a sifting action. Grate-kiln systems

FIG. 5—*Modern preheater rotary kiln system.*

of 272 to 545 t/d capacity are in operation in North America.

Heat exchangers and coolers which recuperate waste heat are also utilized to effect improved fuel efficiency. The heat exchangers, principally trefoil or quadrant sections, are mounted at the feed end. Their purpose is to turn over the stone more effectively and increase the turbulence of the hot gases. Dams and lifters may also be used to turn over the stone, create gas turbulence, or retard the passage of the stone. Coolers, on the other hand, are located at the discharge end of the kiln and serve to return hot gases to the kiln as secondary air. Three types of coolers are generally used with rotary kilns—the shaft or contact, the planetary, and the rotary. The most prevalent type is the Niem's contact (counterflow), which is refractory lined and mounted below the kiln hood. Cooling air is provided by a fan of sufficient size to reduce the lime temperature to 65°C or less. The planetary cooler consists of eight or more tubes approximately 4.2 x 6.2 m in size, mounted at the kiln discharge end. The lime is moved in each tube by conveyor flights counterflow to the cooling air. The rotary cooler is generally not as effective as the other two, and has the additional disadvantage of attrition loss during rotation.

The net effect of the use of both shaft and grate preheaters, and improved heat exchange and recovery within the kiln, has been the reduction of fuel ratios in rotary kilns to 6.9 to 8.5 GJ/t of lime produced. In addition, advances in instrumentation and monitoring (Fig. 6) have reduced manpower requirements and increased product quality and uniformity. Taken together, these changes have helped the large-capacity rotary kiln with preheater become the most commonly selected system today for new or expanded lime production facilities.

Other Kilns: The rotary hearth calciner, or Calcimatic kiln, consists of a preheater, circular hearth, and cooler, all refractory lined. Like the rotary, this kiln burns small stone which is typically sized in a 1:3 ratio. The stone is carried on the hearth in a thin layer, and one revolution of the hearth constitutes the calcining cycle. Numerous burners located inside and outside the hearth are used for firing, utilizing gas, fuel oil, coke-oven gas, and, most recently, pulverized coal. Fuel requirements approximate 7.7 GJ/t, with a wide range of burns possible because of the ease of operator control in calcining. One of the primary advantages of this kiln is the fact that attrition loss is negligible. Stone rests virtually motionless on the hearth, therefore permitting the utilization of soft limestones which would otherwise be subject to high mechanical breakage. A number of 90- to 273-t/d-capacity kilns of this design are in use in North America and Europe.

FluoSolids Kiln: For limestone that is friable or decrepitates during calcining, the Dorr-Oliver FluoSolids has been used to produce highly reactive lime. In this fluid bed process the material is maintained in a suspension in a rising current of hot gases until calcined. Kiln feed is normally 6 x 65 mesh. The system,

FIG. 6—*Modern control panel and instrumentation for a multiple kiln facility.*

which can be fired with gas or oil, incorporates a FluoDry unit (preheater) and FluoSolids reactor (calciner), the latter resembling a vertical kiln. Fuel consumption is approximately 7.8 GJ/t. Fluid bed calciners are available in sizes ranging from 45 to 226 t/d.

Flash Calciners: The flash calciner is one of the most recent developments in calcination, and in reality is not a kiln (Fig. 7). This system, developed by Fuller Co., is designed to calcine the undersized material, or fines, remaining after the primary kiln feed has been sized. The system includes preheater, flash calciner, and cooler. Preheating is achieved in a series of cyclones in which the heat of rising hot gases is absorbed in the counterflowing material which is fed from the top (Fig. 8) and heated to 980°C. As the preheated feed drops into the furnace or calciner, a forced air vortex flow patern pulls the particles into the center of the furnace and then up the sides before discharge. Within the furnace the temperature is 1200°C, but retention time is only a few seconds. A suspension-type cooler recovers heat from the calcined product before it is conveyed to the product bin. The system is designed in two modes depending upon what size feed is to be used. Where stone fines are to be calcined, 60 to 80% of the calcination occurs in the furnace. The final calcination takes place in a fluid bed located between the furnace and the cooler. In those systems where —28 mesh material is fed to the calciner no fluid bed reactor is necessary. This system can utilize gas, oil, or coal, and will normally require 6.2 to 8.5 GJ/t of product.

Milling and Hydrating

Following cooling, quicklime is carefully inspected to avoid *core*, or pieces of uncalcined rock. This is particularly true for shaft kilns burning large stone. The quicklime is then crushed and sized for shipment. Generally, the fines are converted to hydrated lime.

Hydrated lime, shipped in 23-kg bags or in bulk, is available in two principal forms: standard, where 85% passes a No. 200 sieve; and superfine or spray hydrate, where 98% or more passes a No. 325 sieve. These in turn are manufactured in two types, N (normal) and S (special) (see ASTM Designation C207–80), each including high calcium or dolomitic hydrates.

Type S limes are highly hydrated, generally by processes involving pressure hydration. They contain less than 8% unhydrated oxides and

develop high and quick (15 min) plasticity and high water retentivity. Since World War II, the demand for type S lime has grown rapidly until currently it is the chief lime for structural uses. Some lime manufacturers now add entraining catalysts to lime to increase plasticity and durability (called S.A. and N.A. lime).

Mechanical hydrators used for type N lime are made in various designs, including batch hydrators like the Clyde and continuous hydrators like the Kritzer, Schaffer, Knibbs, Hardinge, and Kennedy Van Saun. The hydration process consists of adding water slowly to quicklime (usually in crushed or ground form), followed by agitation to produce intimate contact of lime with water. Accurate proportioning is essential, and this is accomplished by using flowmeters for water and weighing feeders for lime. More than the theoretical amount of water required should be used for hydration in order to allow for the water that is lost as steam caused by heat of hydration. Following hydration, the product is generally fed to a pulverizing or tube mill equipped with an air separator. The core, together with most of the silica and alumina, is rejected by the air separator. By adjusting the separator, hydrates of varying degrees of fineness can be made.

Type S hydrates are manufactured by various processes, the principal one being the Corson explosion method of continuous pressure hydration. In this process ground dolomitic quicklime and water are automatically fed in constant proportions to a high-speed slurry mixer. Hydration then takes place in an insulated autoclave operating at about 5.3 kg/cm² and 150°C. After about 30 min retention time, the product is discharged continuously (or exploded) through a small pipe at the rate of 3,050 m/s into a special cyclone collector at atmospheric pressure. There the hydrate and water are separated by the spray-drying principle. The product is then ground in a tube mill to increase the plasticity. Several US plants use the Corson process, marketing their product under the registered trade name Miracle Lime®.

Consumption

Chemical-Industrial Uses

Although lime to the average layman still connotes a mortar, plaster, or agricultural material and although it still enjoys these formerly predominant traditional uses, most lime today— over 90%—is utilized by the chemical and

uses of any chemical or mineral commodity. However, by far its greatest tonnage lies in the metallurgical industries. Metallurgical uses, including MgO and Al_2O_3, account for 49% of total chemical-industrial usage, and of this amount, 83% is used for steel manufacture (nearly 50% of commercial noncaptive lime is for steel flux).

Steel: Commencing during World War II, steel became lime's foremost market; however, it was not until the early 1960s that this use of lime surged ahead as a direct result of the basic oxygen furnace (BOF). Previously, lime was used as a flux in the open hearth steel furnace in varying amounts, usually with limestones as a coflux. But the factor of lime in a ton of open hearth steel averaged only 12.5 kg. With the BOF, only lime is used as the flux because the keynote of this process is speed. As a result, the lime factor in BOF steel markedly increased to 40 to 85 kg/t (64 kg/t average). Electric steel furnaces require an average of 30 kg of lime per ton of steel. As the BOF replaced the open-hearth and as overall steel production increased during the 1960s lime flux soared—from about 1.4 Mt in 1961 to 8.1 Mt in 1979.

Lime acts as a scavenger in purifying steel by fluxing out, into the molten slag, acid oxide impurities such as silica, alumina, phosphorus, and sulfur.

At first only a reactive high calcium quicklime of 90 to 93% available lime, with low core content and meeting strict tolerances on sulfur (0.03 to 0.06%), was used. Later it was discovered that if a pure dolomitic quicklime was substituted for a portion of the high calcium flux, greater refractory life was obtained, reducing the cost of BOF steel. As a result, most US steel plants use dolomitic lime as a 10 to 30% replacement of high-calcium lime— but this is not true in Europe or Japan.

Most steel companies use pebble or pelletized lime as flux, although the former type is preferred. Some European steel mills use pulverized quicklime, introducing it through their oxygen lances into the furnace. U.S. Steel Corp. developed a modification of the BOF, called the Q-BOP process, which also requires pulverized lime. There is also experimental usage of premixed fluxes in Europe, Japan, and jointly by Republic Steel Co. and Alabaster Lime Co. This involves blending and mixing by grinding high-calcium quicklime, ferrous flue dust from steel plants, alumina-bearing wastes such as red mud from alumina plants, with and without fluorspar, and then pelletizing

FIG. 7—*Flash calciner.*

metallurgical process industries as a flux, acid-neutralizer, causticizing agent, flocculant aid, hydrolyzer, bonding agent, absorbent, and raw material. An allied product, dead-burned dolomite, is used as a refractory material. Lime has possibly the greatest number of diverse

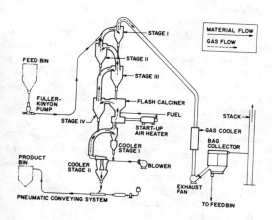

FIG.8—*Flash calcining system with suspension preheater and suspension deheater.*

the mixture into 25.4-mm pellets for charging into the BOF.

Minor lime uses in steel and steel fabricating plants are for wire drawing, neutralization of sulfuric pickle liquor wastes, water softening, and coating molds for "pig" casting. There has been experimental use of hydrated lime in place of pulverized limestone in making self-fluxing ferrous sinters.

Refractory lime, known as dead-burned dolomite, is universally used to line the bottom of open hearth steel furnaces, thereby extending the life of the costly refractory brick linings. With the growth of the BOF at the expense of the open hearth, this use has steadily declined from 2.2 Mt at its peak in 1956 to 0.7 Mt in 1979. This loss has been muted by the development of tar-bonded refractory brick made from dead-burned dolomite.

Nonferrous Metallurgy: *Copper*—Most domestic copper mining companies use lime as the principal reagent in beneficiating copper ores in flotation processes. Lime is used to neutralize the acidic effects of pyrites and maintain the proper pH. There is limited use of lime as a flux in smelting concentrated copper ores and to adsorb SO_2 from the stack gases of copper smelters.

Alumina—In the manufacture of alumina by the Bayer process, large quantities of lime are used in a few plants to causticize sodium carbonate solutions to regenerate sodium hydroxide for recyclical use. Nearly all plants will use some lime for secondary desilification in refining alumina. Some of the experimental processes developed by the US Bureau of Mines (USBM) for making alumina from clay or kaolin, instead of bauxite ore, require lime.

Magnesia—Most processes for the manufacture of magnesia and magnesium metal, such as the Dow seawater and natural brine processes, ferrosilicon process, and seawater magnesium process, require lime. Dolomitic lime, because of its magnesium content, is generally preferred, but high calcium lime has been successfully used. Two processes are diagrammed as follows:

$$CaCl_2 \cdot MgCl_2 + MgO \cdot CaO +$$
$$2CO_2 \rightarrow 2CaCO_3 + 2MgCl_2$$
$$MgCl_2 + electrolysis \rightarrow Mg + Cl_2 \quad (1)$$
$$Ca(OH)_2 + MgCl_2 \rightarrow Mg(OH)_2 +$$
$$CaCl_2$$
$$Mg(OH)_2 + heat \rightarrow MgO + H_2O \quad (2)$$

Miscellaneous—In South Africa huge amounts of lime are used to recover uranium from the gangue (called gold slimes) of gold mining in flotation processes. In the US and Canada lime is employed to neutralize sulfuric acid waste liquors in acid uranium ore extraction plants. In the recovery of gold and silver by flotation processes, lime is used to curtail the loss of cyanides and for pH control. It is employed as a flux in the sintering of low-carbon chrome and in the recovery of nickel by precipitation.

Sanitation: *Water Treatment*—Over 1.5 Mt of lime are used annually in the treatment of municipal potable water and industrial process water. The former use exceeds the latter in tonnage.

Lime is used along or with soda ash to soften water in competition with ion exchange processes (zeolite, etc.). Lime is required to remove the temporary bicarbonate hardness from the water. The high pH of 11.5 induced by the lime is of value as a secondary sterilization agent to chlorine because retention for 3 to 10 hr at this pH will kill 99+% of the bacteria and most viruses. By introducing CO_2 into the lime-treated water, the pH is lowered to acceptable levels and most of the lime in solution is precipitated as a carbonate sludge.

An important application is in coagulation, where lime is employed with such coagulants as alum or iron salts to remove turbidity from river waters used for potable purposes or suspended solids from industrial water. Lime is used for pH control to negate the acid effect of the coagulants and to achieve optimum coagulating efficiency.

Subsidiary to its role in water softening, sterilization, and coagulation is its absorption of iron, manganese, and organic tannins from untreated water.

Sewage—For several decades many sewage disposal plants have used lime for a variety of functions: for chemical precipitation of sewage practiced by a small minority of plants; for pH control in the sludge digester in biological treatment plants; and for conditioning sludge when dewatering, usually with ferric chloride.

As a result of the growing problem of eutrophication of surface waters caused to some extent by sewage plant effluents, more lime will be used in the future. Sewage effluents will require much more treatment to remove dissolved and suspended solids which contain plant nutrients—phosphates and nitrogen compounds. Lime is useful in precipitating phosphates directly. When alum or iron salts are used as the coagulant, lime is generally required for pH control. It appears that a high pH of

10 to 11, inherent in lime treatment, is necessary for efficient removal of nitrogen. Therefore, the future of sewage treatment processes is swinging more from biological to chemical treatment processes that include lime, although there will be no standard treatment method because of the many divergent sewage conditions.

Pollution Abatement: Lime has been used for many years in treating liquid trade wastes and to a lesser extent industrial gaseous effluents to abate pollution of surface waters and air.

Lime is used to neutralize acid mine drainage and to precipitate iron; in coal washing plants, the acidic waste wash water is neutralized by lime. Wastes from sulfuric acid steel pickling plants and plating wastes are neutralized with lime in which heavy metal contaminants are also precipitated. Neutralization of chemical and pharmaceutical plant wastes is also achieved with lime. Clarification and color removal of paper mill wastes is obtained with lime alone or with supporting chemicals as well as other specialized applications.

A major new market for lime is air pollution control. Lime originally was envisioned as the primary reagent material for removing acidic gases from the stack gases of metallurgical and chemical plants. However, during the late 1970s it became apparent that the most significant tonnages of lime would be used by coal-fired electric utility generating stations for the removal of sulfur dioxide from flue gases (Fig. 9). Flue gas desulfurization, or scrubbing, currently requires nearly 1.8 Mt/a of lime, with this amount projected to double by 1990. The development of this market has been greatly enhanced by advances in scrubber hardware, including both wet and dry processes, and by the success achieved by Dravo Corp.'s Thiosorbic® lime. Lime scrubbing has been proven to be both an effective and viable means of meeting the US Environmental Protection Agency's air pollution control requirements.

Chemicals Manufacture: *Alkalies*—In the manufacture of soda ash and bicarbonate of soda by the Solvay process, lime is employed in large quantities to recover ammonia for recyclical use in the process; 635 kg of quicklime are required per ton of soda ash produced. In the process the lime reacts with the chloride ion to form calcium chloride, much of which is recovered and sold commercially. Another recovered byproduct is precipitated calcium carbonate. Additional lime is used to causticize sodium carbonate solutions to produce sodium

FIG. 9—*Sulfur dioxide scrubbers at a modern electric generating station.*

hydroxide (caustic soda). All alkali manufacturers make their own lime because they require an abundance of CO_2 in these as a coproduct. However, Solvay process ash is losing ground to natural soda ash (trona) and electrolytic caustic soda. Stringent pollution control regulations are imposing still greater economic pressure on this process. The future of the Solvay process is bleak, though undoubtedly its use will continue to some extent.

Carbide—Calcium carbide, formerly the main source of acetylene, is made in electric furnaces through the fusion of quicklime and coke in the presence of nitrogen at very high temperatures. About 1 t of quicklime is required to make 1 t of carbide. When water is added to carbide, acetylene gas is evolved, leaving a waste calcium hydroxide residue. The future of this product is poor because less costly processes for making acetylene from natural gas have been perfected. Furthermore, acetylene is losing ground to ethylene as a basic organic chemical building block. However, with increasing costs for natural gas this process may make a mild comeback.

Bleaches—High-test calcium hypochlorite (70% available chlorine) and chloride of lime, both dry sources of bleach, are made through the interaction of chlorine and hydrated lime.

Liquid calcium hypochlorite is made by paper plants for bleaching pulp.

Inorganics—Other inorganic chemicals made from lime include caustic magnesia by the brine and seawater processes (previously referred to); mono-, di-, and tricalcium phosphates; chrome chemicals; purifying salt brines to produce USP food grade salt; pesticides such as lime-sulfur sprays and powders; Bordeaux mixtures (copper sulfate and lime) and calcium arsenate; and paint pigments.

Organics—Lime is required in the manufacture of ethylene and propylene glycols in the chlorohydrin process; in calcium-based organic salts, such as calcium stearate, acetate, lactate, lignosulfonate, etc.; in the refinement and concentration of citric acid and glucose; and for dyes and dyestuff intermediates.

Pulp and Paper: In the manufacture of sulfate (kraft) paper pulp, lime is universally used to causticize the waste sodium carbonate (black liquor) to regenerate sodium hydroxide for reuse in this continuous chemical process. In spite of the fact that pulp mills in turn recover 90 to 96% of the lime employed by recalcining the dewatered calcium carbonate sludge precipitate, a substantial quantity of lime (over 680 kt) is required as makeup. Counting the regenerated lime, technically over 5.4 Mt/a of lime is actually consumed in the sulfate paper industry.

Secondary uses of lime by the paper industry include making calcium hypochlorite bleach; clarification of process water, including recyclical water; clarification and color removal of waste water effluents.

Building Products and Ceramics: Lime is used to make calcium silicate building products, such as dense sand-lime brick and block, cellular concrete block and insulation panels, and microporite; however, most of this is made in European and other foreign countries and very little in the US. West Germany alone consumes about 2.2 Mt/a of lime for these products. Lime is reacted with sand and fine forms of available silica under steam pressure in an autoclave to form stable, durable, and very strong cementing compounds (calcium silicates). To produce lightweight masonry units and insulation materials, aluminum powder is added to the mix which is attacked by the lime, producing a cellular effect of varying degrees of porosity.

Glass—In the manufacture of glass, dolomitic quicklime granules of Nos. 10 to 100 mesh are used interchangeably with limestone or dolomite of similar sizes as a flux raw material in the glass batch. Next to sand and soda ash, glass plants use far more lime and/or limestone than any other material in glassmaking. Most of the lime is used in bottle glass plants rather than plate glass.

Refractory Products—Silica refractory brick is made with hydrated lime, another calcium silicate reaction. Periclase (dead-burned MgO) is made from the aforementioned seawater magnesia processes as a raw material for basic refractory brick, and refractory brick is made from tar-bonded dead-burned dolomite.

Miscellaneous: *Sugar*—Lime is essential for sugar making in both beet and cane sugar refining processes. Large amounts of lime are required for beet sugar, averaging 0.2 t of quicklime per ton of sugar; with cane sugar only 1.9 to 4.9 kg/t of lime is required. Lime helps purify the sucrose juices by removing phosphatic and organic acid compounds as insoluble calcium compounds which are removed by filtration. Beet sugar plants invariably make their own lime in on-site kilns because they need a massive quantity of CO_2, which is obtained from the lime kiln stack gases. Cane sugar refiners purchase their much smaller requirements.

Produce Storage—Lime is used as a CO_2 adsorbant in controlled atmospheric storages for fresh fruit and certain vegetables to extend the freshness of the produce. This prevents CO_2 from building to abnormally high levels, which would accelerate rotting of produce. It is used to recover glue and gelatin from packinghouse byproducts. In citrus fruit processing, lime is used to treat the waste pulp, which after grinding and drying is sold as cattle feed. There are several other small isolated uses in the food industry.

Petroleum—Lime has limited use for neutralizing organic sulfur compounds (mercaptans) and SO_2 emissions in petroleum refineries. A common type of lubricating grease is made with lime acting as a saponifying agent of the petroleum oil. An ingredient of "red lime" drilling muds for oil drilling is hydrated lime. In a proprietary process, lime and pozzolans such as fly ash are used instead of cement in sealing producing offshore oil wells in the Gulf of Mexico.

Paints and Pigments—In addition to lime whitewash, proprietary water paints for masonry are made with hydrated lime, white portland cement, and pigments. Lime has minor uses in varnish manufacture, casein paints, and certain types of pigments.

Leather—Since biblical times, lime suspensions have been used for dehairing and plumping hides preparatory to leather tanning.

Construction

Stabilization: The total use of lime for soils stabilization for highways and off-highway uses now exceeds total structural lime consumption. In the construction of pavements for highways, city streets, airport runways, and parking lots, lime may be used to stabilize the clay subgrade, subbase, and/or base course. Clay must be present for lime to react with the available silica and alumina in the soil to form complex cementing compounds which bind the soil into a hard, stable mass that is not sensitive to water saturation. The plasticity of the soil, as well as shrinkage and swell, are markedly reduced. The amount of lime used generally ranges between 3 to 5% of the weight of the dry soil. Over 80% is hydrated lime, with the balance being pebble or ground quicklime. Lime is recognized by all federal agencies and most state highway departments, and has been used in at least 3200 km of interstate construction in 26 states. In the construction of the largest airport in the world in 1971–1974—The Dallas/Ft. Worth Airport—about 272 kt of hydrated lime was used in pavement and building areas, including access roads.

Lime also is used with pozzolan fly ash and varied aggregates in the preparation of base material at central-mix plants, which competes with crushed stone and soil-cement base courses. This process was introduced by the Corson Co. in a proprietary process called Poz-O-Pac. The Newark, NJ airport used lime-fly ash mixtures throughout its pavement system, with hydrated lime consumption of about 68 kt.

Use of lime continues to grow as its applications multiply into such diverse areas as building foundation construction, reinforcement of earth levees and dams, irrigation channels, railroad beds, race tracks, and even clay tennis courts. Contractors use it to expedite construction by drying up muddy subgrades and to construct temporary all-weather haul roads.

Asphalt: Increasingly, 1 to 2% of hydrated lime is added to asphalt hot mix in central-mix plants as paving material. The lime acts as an antistripping agent preventing the aggregate from raveling from the bituminous binder. In remote areas it permits use of marginal, unwashed aggregates and where needed serves as a filler. Based on the immersion compression test with some asphalts and aggregates, it markedly increases the wet/dry strength ratio and reduces volume change.

Mortar: For thousands of years lime has been employed as a mortar material—and it is still used today. Before the advent of portland cement in the latter part of the 19th century, mortars were composed only of lime and sand. Now, lime-cement mortars of varying proportions are used, ranging from 3 to 1/4 parts of lime by volume to 1 part cement. Lime is still the most dependable plasticizer for mortar, making it workable and more trowelable. Cement provides the rapid set.

In the US most hydrated lime is mixed at the job site. Rarely is quicklime slaked and used at the job site anymore, and what little is used is in pulverized form. Lime putty and ready-mixed lime-based mortars, with sand and even with cement, both in dry and wet form are also mixed at central plants and delivered in bulk. Additional lime is also mixed with cement or cement-blast furnace slag mixtures or with pozzolans such as fly ash, which is packaged for mortar mixing with sand at the job site. These proprietary compounds are known as mortar mixes or masonry cements. The biggest proportion of building lime used in the US is type S or S.A. dolomitic.

Lime encounters severe competition from masonry cements made by cement companies. Most masonry cements do not contain lime; instead they usually consist of a 50:50 mixture of pulverized limestone and portland cement, plus organic air entraining agents, the latter providing plasticity.

Plaster: In interior plastering today, lime is used only in the finish or white coat, usually gaged with gypsum or Keene's cement. Formerly it was used along with sand in the base coat, but it has been replaced by gypsum-aggregate plasters. Lime suffered a second loss as gypsum drywall construction replaced much conventional interior plaster. Some lime is also used in exterior plaster or stucco, particularly in California and Florida, again with mixtures of portland cement and sand in varying proportions. It is also purchased by stucco compounders for their proprietary stucco finishes of widely varying textures, white or pigmented.

Agriculture

Although most agricultural liming today is achieved with pulverized limestone, many farmers still use ground quicklime and hydrated lime, particularly in the middle Atlantic states. Many Amish farmers, in fact, are proponents of burned lime. Although lime costs more than limestone on an equivalent calcium oxide basis, it reacts faster, neutralizing soil acidity rapidly so crop yields do not suffer. In truck farming, use of burned lime for maintaining the optimum pH enables three crops to be grown per year. The added cost for lime is easy to justify in higher-value crops. In some sandy soil areas dolomitic lime only is used, due to persistent magnesium deficiencies. County agents who make pH tests recommend the amount of liming material to apply and the desired pH for a given crop. Most of these agents and state agronomists, however, promote the use of limestone, making it difficult for the lime industry to promote its product. Furthermore, the federal subsidies for liming markedly favor limestone over lime.

Some secondary farm uses of lime are for whitewashing dairy barns as a sanitation aid, for composting, in chicken litters, etc.

Hydraulic Lime

At one time there was a small production of hydraulic lime in the US. Currently, however, only one plant, located in Virginia, manufactures hydraulic lime, all of which is consumed internally. This product still flourishes in some foreign countries, notably Italy, Germany, and France. Chemically this product, which is high in silicates, aluminates, and ferrites, could be defined as an impure lime; its chemical composition is intermediate between portland cement and lime. It is solely a structural lime, developing greater strength than pure lime and sand but much less than portland cement. It possesses limited hydraulic qualities, though much less pronounced than portland cement, in being able to harden under water.

A detailed statistical summary of lime uses for 1979 and 1980 is contained in Table 3. Note that refractory dolomite is included with lime, and that commercial and captive limes are differentiated.

Economics

Fig. 10 shows the trends in lime consumption since 1904, when the USBM first began compiling statistics; as in Table 3, four major end use categories are depicted. Three periods of growth are evident as well as the possible early phases of a fourth period. The three prominent growth periods include the late 1930s following the Great Depression, the decade following World War II, and the late 1960s and early 1970s, including the 1974 record consumption of slightly over 20 Mt of lime. The statistics for the late 1970s and early 1980s suggest that a fourth period may be starting, one which is underpinned with a strong new environmental applications demand including scrubbing, or flue gas desulfurization.

Further inspection of the trends depicted in Fig. 11 clearly shows that nearly all of the growth in lime since 1960 has been accounted for by chemical and industrial uses, particularly fluxing lime for steel. Assuming that environmental applications such as flue gas desulfurization are counted as chemical applications, this increasing tonnage trend for chemical and industrial uses would be expected to continue. Other growth areas for lime include water treatment, sewage treatment, and soil stabilization, while refractory dolomite and building lime continue to show little or no growth.

Competition

Traditionally the lime industry has been intensely competitive, on both an intra- and interindustry basis. As evidence of this, the number of lime plants has declined from about 1200 in 1910 to 154 commercial lime plants in 1980. This competitive pressure was further reflected in the average f.o.b. price of lime which only doubled from the 1920s to the early 1970s. In fact, only since the oil embargo of 1974 have truly significant increases in lime prices been effected. At one time lime was one of the commodities least affected by inflation. This is no longer the case; prices nearly tripled from 1972 to 1980.

Although cement, gypsum, caustic soda, and other chemical coagulants and neutralizers have provided serious competition in vying for common markets, limestone is still lime's most formidable competitor. This competition obviously has been fostered by the price differential between these two commodities as well as their many interchangeable applications such as open-hearth furnaces, alumina, glass, and a variety of environmental uses. As the price difference between lime and limestone continues to increase, the competitive pressure from limestone will be even more keenly felt by the lime industry.

Also of great importance in terms of competition and lime prices is the fact that there has always been a sizable percentage of captive lime produced, ranging between 26 and 40% of the total lime consumed. Traditionally much of this captive lime was produced in conjunction with alkali and beet sugar plants whose processes demand cheap CO_2 in order to be economically viable. However, large lime con-

TABLE 3—Lime (Quicklime, Hydrated Lime, and Refractory Dolomite), By Uses*, 1979 and 1980 (1000 st)

Use	1979			1980		
	Sold	Captive	Total	Sold	Captive	Total
Agriculture	71	—	71	79	—	79
Construction:						
Soil stabilization	695	—	695	170	—	170
Mason's lime	350	41	391	288	40	328
Finishing lime	195	—	195	99	—	99
Other uses	34	35	69	16	27	44
Total Construction	1,274	76	1,350	652	67	720
Chemical and Industrial:						
Steel, BOF	5,611	1,706	7,317	4,409	1,441	5,850
Steel, electric	964	28	992	755	34	789
Steel, open-hearth	603	49	652	564	38	602
Copper flotation	427	344	771	340	318	658
Aluminum and bauxite	162	111	273	160	114	275
Magnesium	W	W	177	W	W	187
Other metallurgy	55	3	58	31	4	35
Magnesia from seawater	W	W	682	W	W	648
Alkalies	6	1,252	1,258	6	1,167	1,173
Pulp and paper	1,149	109	1,258	1,039	116	1,156
Sugar refining	47	727	774	58	909	967
Calcium carbide	146	72	218	121	63	185
Glass	191	—	191	180	—	180
Other chemical	425	83	508	—	—	—
Other uses†	411	296	707	645	714	523
Total Chemical & Industrial	10,268	5,228	15,496	8,308	4,918	13,226
Environmental:						
Water treatment	1,846	79	1,925	1,487	9	1,496
Sewage	799	16	815	848	12	860
SO$_2$ removal	604	—	604	743	—	743
Total Environmental	3,249	95	3,344	3,078	21	3,099
Refractory dolomite	670	123	793	420	75	494
Total, All Uses‡	15,461	5,522	20,983	12,537	5,081	17,618

Source: Pressler, 1981.
*Excludes regenerated lime. Includes Puerto Rico.
†Includes petrochemicals, whiting, adhesives, plastics, explosives, and uses indicated by symbol W.
‡Data may not add to totals shown because of independent rounding.

sumers in steel, copper, alumina, and other chemical industries—and potentially even major utility companies—have turned to captive plants for a portion of their lime requirements. With the larger capacity kilns now coming on line this frequently leads to surplus capacity from captive plants finding its way into the open market. Consequently, the large percentage of captive lime produced has tended to have a depressant effect on lime prices.

Calcining Plants

Several decades ago nearly every lime plant operated its own adjacent or nearby limestone quarry. In the last few decades, particularly in the 1960s, there has been a marked increase in the number of plants that purchase their limestone kiln feed, usually transported by water, to their calcining plants. Fifteen such plants are located on the Great Lakes from Minnesota to Ohio, including seven captive operations that obtain limestone by boat from northern Michigan. Two calcining plants in Louisiana burn water-transported oyster and clamshell, dredged from the Gulf of Mexico and Lake Pontchartrain, respectively. Economically these plants are usually justified, in spite of much higher kiln feed costs, because they are located

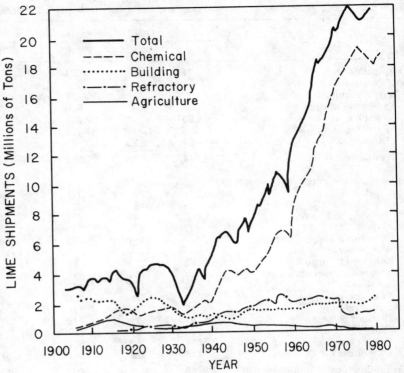

FIG. 10—*Trends in major uses of lime, 1904–1980. Sizable increase in 1959 was due largely to increased coverage of captive lime, with an additional 1.9 Mt added (based on US Bureau of Mines data).*

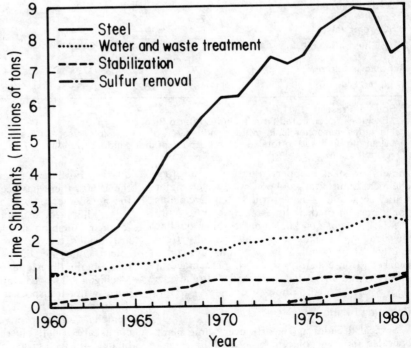

FIG. 11—*Trends in selected major uses of lime, 1960–1981.*

near large consuming markets. Similarly, two lime hydration plants have been built 200 or more miles from their company's calcining plant—in the Los Angeles and San Francisco bay areas. These plants also serve as distribution terminals for quicklime products, and are only the forerunners of other remote hydration and distribution facilities being considered by other lime producers.

Transportation

For many years railroads were the primary carrier of bulk lime. However, as rail service declined and the interstate highway system came into use, truck shipments became increasingly popular, to the point that in the late 1960s and early 1970s over 50% of lime shipped was moved by truck. While truck and rail shipments continue to predominate, an increasing tonnage of lime is moved by barge on the nation's inland waterways. Today over 15% of the lime produced in the US is moved via barge. The importance of this mode of transportation is seen in the fact that in addition to Mississippi Lime located at Ste. Genevieve, MO, two large new plants have been built on the Ohio River in northern Kentucky.

Distribution

Lime is produced in 40 states and consumed in all states. Table 4 lists the major consuming and producing states, including both commercial and captive lime as well as refractory dolomite. As would be expected, the two lists are similar but not identical.

Considering commercial lime only, the largest producing states in order of volume are Ohio, Missouri, Pennsylvania, Texas, Illinois, Alabama, Kentucky, Virginia, Michigan, and Arizona. Interestingly, as recently as 1977 neither Kentucky or Arizona were counted among the top producing states. Other locations which have experienced significant additions to their commercial production since 1978 include Tennessee, Utah, Texas, Michigan, and Illinois. Added to this are several plant modifications which have served to increase the capacity of existing facilities without the addition of new kilns.

On the consumption side, the leading quicklime-consuming states in 1979 were Pennsylvania, Ohio, Indiana, Michigan, and New York, each of which consumed more than 0.9 Mt. These five states accounted for 51% of the total quicklime consumed. Leading hydrate-consuming states were Texas, Pennsylvania, Illinois, Ohio, and Louisiana, each of which consumed more than 900 kt. These five states accounted for 52% of the total hydrate consumed.

Taxes and Prices

Since 1951 those lime companies which extract their own stone have had the benefit of percentage depletion, as applied to the federal income tax, on their kiln feed used to make lime. Until 1971 the percentage depletion rate was 15%, but then it was reduced to 14% along with similar reductions on most other minerals. The value of the kiln feed upon which percentage depletion is based has been subject to controversy and is often negotiated in accordance with various IRS interpretations on what to allow. Field market prices covering the quality and gradation of the stone and costs of producing the kiln feed (proportionate profits) are methods that have been applied.

The only statistics on prices are compiled by the USBM. The average mill price (bulk) for all types of lime is given in Table 5.

During the 1960s lime prices advanced very little, in spite of a moderate inflation rate. However, beginning in 1969 lime prices increased steadily due to fuel costs, air pollution and other government-mandated controls, escalating labor costs, inflation, etc. Then in 1974 the oil embargo initiated substantial increases in energy costs which have been clearly reflected in the cost of production and the cost of lime. These cost increases have been further exacerbated for the lime consumer by substantial increases in the cost of transportation. In addition to the cost of energy, the 1970s were a period of increased interest rates, which in 1980 reached and exceeded 20% for the first time in history. While these interest rates did not directly affect several producers, a large segment of the producers experienced major capital outlays in the period 1975 through 1980. Therefore, with the continuing impact of fuel costs, inflation, and high interest rates, annual price increases can be expected for the next several years.

Foreign Trade

Historically there has been relatively little foreign trade in lime in most countries, including the United States, because of the occurrence in most industrialized countries of limestone suitable for the production of lime, its

TABLE 4—Leading Lime Consuming and Producing States, 1979 and 1980* (1000 st)

Consuming	1979	1980	Producing	1979	1980
Pennsylvania	2662	2306	Ohio	3392	2786
Ohio	2380	1959	Pennsylvania	2153	1768
Indiana	2097	1699	Missouri	1790	1667
Michigan	1603	1355	Texas	1507	1515
Texas	1537	1535	Alabama	1273	1128
New York	1153	1077	Kentucky	1162	—
Illinois	1068	893	Michigan	1057	836
California	898	819	Illinois	W	—
Alabama	612	530	Virginia	872	824
Arizona	520	389	Arizona	673	514
Maryland	473	396	California	564	554
Florida	441	439	Indiana	W	—

Source: Pressler, 1981.
*Includes commercial lime, refractory dolomite, and captive lime.
W, Information withheld.

low cost, and the relative perishability of quicklime (and to a lesser extent, hydrate). US foreign trade in lime has included both exports and imports with Canada accounting for over 90% of this trade.

Exports of lime in recent years have generally been in the range of 36.2 to 45.3 kt and are normally measured against the record year of 1968 when nearly 63.5 kt of lime were exported. Of the total exports in recent years, Canada has received 60 to 65%, followed by Surinam, Guyana, and Mexico, each of which normally receives less than 10%. The remaining export tonnage is received by 30 to 40 other nations around the world, the exact number varying from year to year.

Imports of lime to the US have grown at an average rate of over 14% during the last 10 years. From 1976 to 1979 total imports, quicklime plus hydrate, have increased from 331 kt/a to 580 kt/a. The vast majority of this tonnage is imported from Canada, with the remainder coming from Mexico. In light of expanded production capacity in the northern half of the US and new lime production in Mexico, it is anticipated that the Mexican share of the import market will show modest gains.

The only worldwide foreign trade of consequence involves exports from Belgium and Germany into the Netherlands, where limestone production is virtually nil. Each of these countries exports 500 to 600 kt into the Netherlands annually. Belgium is also the main lime supplier for the Luxembourg steel industry and exports to France.

Tests and Specifications

Because of the number of limes available, their many uses, and their wide variation in physical and chemical characteristics, there is no overall lime specification. Numerous specifications and buyer requirements for lime exists, not only for most of the major uses, but even among individual companies or plants.

The National Lime Assn., with its member lime companies, and a majority of the lime consumers, subscribe to the ASTM specifications on lime, which are promulgated by Committee C–7 on Lime. These specifications,

TABLE 5—Average Mill Price (Bulk), All Types of Lime

Year	Price Per Net st, $
1965	$13.87
1966	13.27
1967	13.42
1968	13.39
1969	13.94
1970	14.53
1971	15.78
1972	16.78
1973	17.42
1974	22.02
1975	27.45
1976	30.19
1977	33.42
1978	36.76
1979	41.18
1980	44.34
1981	46.20

which cover many uses and testing procedures, are:

ASTM Specifications

C25–79	Chemical Analysis of Limestone, Quicklime, and Hydrated Lime
C50–78	Sampling, Inspection, Packing, and Marking of Quicklime and Lime Products
C51–76	Terms Relating to Lime
C110–76	Physical Testing of Quicklime, Hydrated Lime, and Limestone
C400–76	Testing Quicklime and Hydrated Lime for Neutralization of Waste Acid
C593–76	Fly Ash and Other Pozzolans for Use with Lime
C602–75	Agricultural Liming Materials
C706–76	Limestone for Animal Feed Use
C737–78	Limestone for Dusting of Coal Mines
C821–78	Lime for Use with Pozzolans
C911–79	Quicklime, Hydrated Lime, and Limestone for Chemical Uses

Among the tests included in the C110–76 standard are residue (particle size), plasticity as determined by the Emley plasticimeter, soundness, water retention, settling rate, slaking rate, and air entrainment. The plasticity, water retention, soundness, and air entrainment tests apply especially to the mortar and finishing lime specifications. Slaking rate determination is of prime importance to many chemical lime uses, especially water and chemical treatment.

The C25–79 standard covers wet chemical tests for determining calcium and magnesium oxides, available lime content, CO_2 (loss on ignition or LOI), silica and other insolubles, sulfur, phosphorus, and various trace elements. In view of the many chemical uses for lime, the C25–79 standard is widely used in industry.

Another important lime specification is the AWWA Standard for Quicklime and Hydrated Lime (B202–77), which was promulgated by the American Water Works Assn. This specification includes a bonus and penalty arrangement based on available lime content, slaking rate, and slaking residue. It is also applicable to sewage and industrial waste treatment plants.

Bibliography and References

Because lime is one of mankind's oldest materials and its end-use pattern is diverse, the literature on lime is so extensive it would be impossible to give a complete bibliography. The following list of sources presents the more general references on lime, with emphasis on manufacture and major uses.

Among the principal sources of information are R. S. Boynton's textbook, *Chemistry and Technology of Lime and Limestones*, (2nd edition); publications of the National Lime Assn.; articles from *Pit and Quarry, Rock Products*, and *Zement-Kalk Gips* magazines; and publications of the US Bureau of Mines (particularly statistics) and the various state geological surveys (particularly Illinois, Indiana, Virginia, Pennsylvania, Ohio, and Missouri).

A selected bibliography follows.

Anon., 1920, "Lime—Its Properties and Uses," Circular 30, National Bureau of Standards, 25 pp.

Anon., 1927, "Manufacture of Lime," Circular 337, National Bureau of Standards, 104 pp.

Anon., 1940, *Symposium on Lime*, American Society for Testing and Materials, Philadelphia, 118 pp.

Anon., 1965, "Standard for Quicklime and Hydrated Lime," Standard B 202–65, American Water Works Assoc., 12 pp.

Anon., 1967, "Lime for Steelmaking: Tailored to Fit New Demands," *Metals Producing Magazine*, Vol. 33, Jan., 18 pp.

Anon., 1968, "Phosphate Extraction Process," Dorr-Oliver, Inc., 22 pp.

Anon., 1969, "Lime for Water and Wastewater Treatment," Reference No. I.22–24, B.I.F., 24 pp.

Anon., 1969a, *Reaction Parameters of Lime*, American Society for Testing and Materials, Symposium, Atlantic City, NJ.

Anon., 1969b, *Water Treatment Plant Design*, American Water Works Association, AWWA Inc., 359 pp.

Anon., 1970, "Lime," Bulletin T60.350–1, Wallace and Tiernan.

Anon., 1971, *Process Design Manual for Phosphorus Removal*, Black & Veatch, EPA Tech. Transfer, Oct.

Anon., 1981, *Chemical Lime Facts*, 4th ed., Bulletin 214, National Lime Assoc., Washington, DC, 44 pp.

Ahlberg, H.L., and Barenberg, E.J., 1965, "Pozzolanic Pavements," Engineering Equipment Station Bulletin 473, University of Illinois, 130 pp.

Azbe, V.J., 1946, *Theory and Practice of Lime Manufacture*, St. Louis, MO, 423 pp.

Azbe, V.J., 1954, "Rotary Kiln Performance, Evaluation and Development," National Lime Assn., pp. 89; also *Rock Products*, series, Feb. 1953-Oct. 1955.

Bishop, D.L., 1939, "Particle Size and Plasticity of Lime," *Journal of Research*, Vol. 23, No. 2, pp. 285–292.

Boynton, R.S., 1980, *Chemistry and Technology of Lime and Limestone*, John Wiley, New York, 578 pp.

Boynton, R.S., and Gutschick, K.A., 1968, *Building*

Lime, Its Properties, Uses, and Manufacture, United Nations Ind. Dev. Organization, New York, July, 104 pp.

Boynton, R.S., and Jander, F.K., 1952, "Lime and Limestone," *Encyclopedia of Chemical Technology,* R.E. Kirk, et al., eds., Interscience, New York.

Bowles, O., 1952, "The Lime Industry," Information Circular 7651, US Bureau of Mines, 43 pp.

Bowles, O., and Jensen, N.C., 1947, "Industrial Uses of Limestone and Dolomite," Information Circular 7402, US Bureau of Mines, 19 pp.

Burchard, E.F., 1912–1913, "Stone," *Mineral Resources of the U.S.,* US Geological Survey, Pt. 2, 1911, pp. 782–831; 1912, pp. 754–815; 1913, pp. 1335–1408. These contain a series of maps showing the location of every limestone quarry and lime-kiln in the United States.

Burchard, E.F., and Emley, W.E., 1913, "Source, Manufacture, and Use of Lime," *Mineral Resources of the United States,* US Geological Survey, Pt. 2, pp. 1509–1593.

Davison, J.L., 1969, "Curing of Lime Cement Mortars," STP 472, American Society for Testing & Materials, pp. 193–208.

Derge, G., and Shegog, J.R., 1969, "Observations on the Solution of Calcium Oxide in Slag Systems," STP 472, American Society for Testing & Materials, pp. 132–142.

Dickson, T., 1982, "North American Lime," *Industrial Minerals,* No. 177, June, pp. 51-63.

Eades, J.L., and Sandbert, P.A., 1969, "Characterization of the Properties of Commercial Limes by Surface Area Measurements and Scanning Electron Microscopy," STP 472, American Society for Testing & Materials, pp. 3–24.

Eckel, E.C., 1928, *Cements, Limes, and Plasters,* John Wiley, New York, 699 pp.

Emley, W.E., 1913, "Manufacture of Lime," Technical Paper 16, National Bureau of Standards, 130 pp.

Emley, W.E., 1920, "Measurement of Plasticity of Mortars and Plasters," Technical Paper 169, National Bureau of Standards, 27 pp.

Emley, W.E., 1927, "Manufacture of Lime," Circular 337, National Bureau of Standards, 104 pp.

Goudge, M.F., *Limestones of Canada, Their Occurrence and Characteristics,* Canada Dept. of Mines, published in five volumes, 1927 to 1938; Vol. 1, Introductory, 19; Vol. 2, Maritimes, 19; Vol. 3, Quebec, 19; Vol. 4 No. 781, Ontario, 362 pp.; Vol. 5, Western Canada, 19 pp.

Grancher, R.A., 1970, "Lime Marches On . . . Maybe," *Rock Products,* Mar., pp. 64–67.

Grancher, R.A., 1970a, "Past, Present and Future of Lime in the United States," International Lime Conference, Salzberg, Austria, May, 34 pp.

Hatmaker, P., 1931, "Utilization of Dolomite and High-Magnesium Limestone," Information Circular 6524, US Bureau of Mines, 18 pp.

Hatmaker, P., 1937, "Lime," *Industrial Minerals and Rocks,* 1st ed., AIME, New York, pp. 395–426.

Hedin, R., 1961, "Structural Processes in the Dissociation of Calcium Carbonate," Azbe Award No. 2, National Lime Assn., 12 pp.

Hedin, R., 1962, "Plasticity of Lime Mortars," Azbe Award No. 3, National Lime Assn., 11 pp.

Hirsch, A.A., 1962, "Dry Feed of Quicklime Without a Slaker," *AWWA Journal,* Dec., pp. 1531–1542.

Hoak, R.D., 1953, "How to Buy and Use Lime as a Neutralizing Agent," *Water and Sewage Works,* Dec., 6 pp.

Knibbs, N.V.S., 1924, *Lime and Magnesia,* Ernest Benn, Ltd., London, 306 pp.

Knibbs, N.V.S., and Gee, B.J., *Lime and Magnesia,* Pt. 1, H.I. Hall Corp., Ltd., 113 pp.

Lamar, J.E., 1961, "Uses of Limestone and Dolomite," Circular 321, Illinois Geological Survey.

Lamar, J.E., 1967, "Handbook on Limestone and Dolomite for Illinois Quarry Operators," Bulletin 91, Illinois Geological Survey, 119 pp.

Landes, K.K., 1953, *Metallurgical Limestone Reserves in the U.S.,* 2nd ed., National Lime Assn., July, 31 pp.

Lazell, E.W., 1915, *Hydrated Lime,* Jackson-Remlinger Ptg. Co., 95 pp.

Lewis, C.J., and Crocker, B.B., 1969, "The Lime Industry's Problem of Airborne Dust," *Journal of Air Pollution Control Assn.,* TI-2 Report No. 10, Jan.

Limes, R., and Russell, R.O., 1969, "Crucible Test for Lime Reactivity in Slags," STP 462, American Society for Testing and Materials, pp. 161–172.

Mayer, R.P., and Stowe, R.A., 1964, "Physical Characterization of Limestone and Lime," Azbe Award No. 4, National Lime Assn., Aug., p. 26.

McClellan, G.H., and Eades, J.L., 1969, "Textural Evolution of Limestone Calcines," STP 462, American Society for Testing and Materials, pp. 209–227.

McDonald, E.B., 1971, *Lime Stabilization Training Manual,* South Dakota Dept. of Highways, 79 pp.

McDowell, C., 1972, "Flexible Pavement Design Guide," Bulletin 327, National Lime Assn., 43 pp.

Miller, T.C., 1960, "A Study of the Reaction Between Calcium Oxide and Water," Azbe Award No. 1, National Lime Assn., p. 50.

Minnick, L.J., 1971, "Control of Particulate Emissions from Lime Plants—A Survey," *Journal of Air Pollution Control Assn.,* Apr., pp. 195–200.

Mullins, R.C., and Hatfield, J.D., 1969, "Effects of Calcination Conditions on Properties of Lime," STP 462, American Society for Testing and Materials, pp. 117–131.

Moyer, F.T., 1941, *Lime-fuel Ratios of Commercial Lime Plants in 1939,* Information Circular 7174, US Bureau of Mines, 9 pp.

Murray, J.A., 1956, *Summary of Fundamental Research at M.I.T. on Lime and Application of Results to Commercial Problems,* National Lime Assn., 19 pp.

Obst, K., et al., 1969, "Present Status and Technical Advances in Steelworks Lime for Basic Oxygen Furnaces in Germany," STP 462, American Society for Testing and Materials, pp. 173–192.

Parsons, W.A., 1965, "Chemical Treatment of Sewage and Industrial Wastes," Bulletin 215, National Lime Assn., 139 pp.

Philbrook, W.O., and Natesan, K., 1966, "Mixed-Control Kinetics in the Thermal Decomposition of Calcium Carbonate," Azbe Award No. 6, National Lime Assn., pp. 55.

Pressler, J.W., 1981, "Lime," *Minerals Yearbook, 1978–1979;* US Bureau of Mines, pp. 539–549; and 1980, pp. 507–518.

Pressler, J.W., 1982, "Lime," *Mineral Commodity Summaries 1982,* US Bureau of Mines, pp. 86–87.

Reed, A.H., 1971, "Lime," *Minerals Yearbook 1971*, US Bureau of Mines, pp. 695–702.

Riehl, M.L., 1970, *Water Supply and Treatment*, 10th ed., National Lime Assn., 220 pp.

Ritchie, T., 1969, "Influence of Lime in Mortar on the Expansion of Brick Masonry," STP 462, American Society for Testing and Materials, pp. 67–81.

Rockwood, N.C., 1922, "Lime and Tuberculosis," *Rock Products*, Jan., pp. 56–61.

Rockwood, N.C., 1949, "Lime," *Industrial Minerals and Rocks*, 2nd ed., AIME, New York.

Rooney, L.F., and Carr, D.D., 1971, "Applied Geology of Industrial Limestone and Dolomite," Geological Survey Bulletin 46, Indiana Dept. of Natural Resources, 59 pp.

Schlitt, W.J., and Healy, G.W., 1969, "A Comparison and Scaling Down of Coarse Grain Titration and ASTM Slaking Rate Test," STP 462, American Society for Testing and Materials, pp. 143–160.

Schwarzkopf, F., 1970, "A Comparison of Modern Lime Calcining Systems," *Rock Products*, July, pp. 68–71.

Searle, A.B., 1935, *Limestone and Its Products*, London, Ernest Benn, Ltd., 709 pp.

Staley, H.R., and Greenfeld, S.H., 1947, "Surface Areas of High Calcium Quicklimes and Hydrates," *Proceedings*, American Society for Testing and Materials.

Thompson, J.L., 1979, "Pebble Lime From Preheater Kilns," *Trans. SME-AIME*, Vol. 266, pp. 2041–2044.

Thompson, M.R., 1968, "Lime Stabilization of Soils for Highway Purposes," Series No. 25, Illinois Highway Engineering, Dec.

Timucin, M., and Morris, A.E., 1969, "Phase Equilibria and Thermodynamic Properties of Lime-Iron Oxide Melts," STP 462, American Society for Testing and Materials, pp. 25–31.

Voss, W.C., 1960, "Exterior Masonry Construction," Bulletin 324, National Lime Assn., 70 pp.

Wells, L.S., et al., 1936, "Differences in Limes as Reflected in Certain Properties of Masonry Mortars," Research Paper RP 952, National Bureau of Standards, 14 pp.

Wuhrer, J., 1965, "On the Reactivity of Lime from Different Kiln Systems," Azbe Award No. 5, National Lime Assn., p. 44.

The following are also good sources of information on lime:

Highway Research Board, National Academy of Sciences, Washington, DC, various bulletins on lime stabilization.

"Lime," *Minerals Yearbook*. These chapters contain statistical and general information, published each year by the US Bureau of Mines.

National Lime Association, Washington, DC:

Bull. 192, *100 Questions and Answers on Liming Lawns*, 1955, 32 pp.

Bull. 211, *Water Supply & Treatment*, 11th ed., 1976, 220 pp.

Bull. 213, *Lime Handling, Application, and Storage in Treatment Processes*, 1976, 73 pp.

Bull. 214, *Chemical Lime Facts*, 4th ed., revised, 1981, 42 pp.

Bull. 215, *Chemical Treatment of Sewage & Industrial Wastes*, 1965, 139 pp.

Bull. 216, *Acid Neutralization With Lime*, 1976.

Bull. 217, *Lime in Municipal Sludge Processing*, 1980.

Bull. 304-G, *Whitewash and Cold Water Paints*, 1955, 15 pp.

Bull. 322, *Specifications for Lime and Its Uses in Building*, 1966, 16 pp.

Bull. 324, *Exterior Masonry Construction*, 2nd ed., 1960, 70 pp.

Bull. 325, *Hydrated Lime in Asphalt Paving*, 1962, 15 pp.

Bull. 326, *Lime Stabilization Construction Manual*, 5th ed., 1972, 47 pp.

Bull. 327, *Flexible Pavement Design Guide*, 1972, 43 pp.

Bull. 328, *A Long Range Durability Study of Lime Stabilized Bases*, 1977.

Bull. 400, *Lime Industry Safety Manual*, 2nd ed., 1970, 43 pp.

Pamphlet, *Lime Dries Up Mud*, 1970, 4 pp.

Pamphlet, *Masons Lime*, 1969, 12 pp.

Map, *Commercial Plants in U.S. and Canada*, 1981.

Lime Brochure (1980).

Pit and Quarry magazine, Chicago, IL, numerous articles on lime manufacturing, with May issue each year devoted to lime.

Pit and Quarry Handbook, Chicago, IL, annual handbook on production, including sections on lime plant equipment.

Rock Products magazine, Chicago, IL, numerous articles on lime manufacturing, with July issue each year devoted to lime.

Zement-Kalk-Gips, Wiesbaden, West Germany, numerous articles on lime manufacturing, in German.

Limestone and Dolomite*

DONALD D. CARR †

LAWRENCE F. ROONEY ‡

Perhaps no other mineral commodity in this volume has as many uses as limestone and dolomite. These carbonate rocks are the basic building blocks of the construction industry, the material from which aggregate, cement, lime, and building stone are made. Carbonate rocks, and their derived products, are used as fluxes, glass raw material, refractories, fillers, abrasives, soil conditioners, ingredients in a host of chemical processes, and much more. Although the use of limestone and dolomite goes back before recorded history, new uses and products are continually being found.

Carbonate rocks form about 15% of the earth's sedimentary crust and are widely available for exploitation. Found extensively on all continents, they are quarried and mined from formations that range in age from Precambrian to Recent. Reserves of carbonate rock are large and will last indefinitely, although high-purity deposits may be absent or have limited availability in certain areas.

Limestone and dolomite are so useful and so abundant that in 1981 about 644 million tons were produced in the United States. In fact, about 75% of all stone quarried or mined in the United States was carbonate rock. Sand and gravel was the only mineral commodity produced in greater quantity.

* In addition to acknowledging the valued support of the Indiana Geological Survey and Flathead Valley Community College, we thank the many members of the Survey who provided assistance on particular problems. We extend special thanks to H. W. Allen, Chief Staff Geologist, Martin Marietta Cement Co., J. B. Patton, State Geologist, Indiana Geological Survey, and J. W. Baxter, Illinois Geological Survey, for their critical review of the manuscript.
† Indiana Geological Survey, Bloomington, IN.
‡ Formerly Flathead Valley Community College, Kalispell, MT; now US Geological Survey, Jeddah, Saudi Arabia.

In this chapter we have sought to provide the general reader an overview of carbonate rocks, their composition, distribution, production, and uses, with emphasis on developments since 1960. In doing so we borrowed extensively from our report on the applied geology of limestone and dolomite (Rooney and Carr, 1971). The literature on the limestone and dolomite resources of the United States and Canada is so vast and diverse that one can easily become mired down in print. We tried to list those references that are easily accessible and that provide the economic geologist with a starting point for more intensive study. The table listing selected references on limestone and dolomite resources in Canada and the United States reflects our attempt to be selective rather than exhaustive and to direct the reader to the best sources of detailed information.

Geology

Mineralogy

The principal carbonate rocks used by industry are limestone and dolomite. Limestones are sedimentary rocks composed mostly of the mineral calcite ($CaCO_3$) and dolomites are sedimentary rocks composed mostly of the mineral dolomite ($CaCO_3 \cdot MgCO_3$). Aragonite ($CaCO_3$), which has the same chemical composition as calcite but a different crystal structure, is economically important only in modern deposits, such as oyster shells and oolites. Aragonite is metastable and alters to calcite in time. Some other carbonate minerals, notably siderite ($FeCO_3$), ankerite ($Ca_2MgFe(CO_3)_4$), and magnesite ($MgCO_3$), are commonly found associated with limestones and dolomites but generally in minor amounts.

Because of their similar physical properties, the carbonate minerals are not easily distinguished one from the other. Specific gravity,

TABLE 1—Physical Properties of Some Common Carbonate Minerals

Calcite: $CaCO_3$, hexagonal crystal system, commonly good rhombohedral cleavage. Mohs' hardness, 3. Specific gravity, 2.72. Commonly colorless or white but may be other colors due to impurities.
Dolomite: $CaCO_3 \cdot MgCO_3$, hexagonal crystal system, commonly good rhombohedral crystals with curved faces. Mohs' hardness, 3.5 to 4. Specific gravity, 2.87. Commonly white or pink.
Aragonite: $CaCO_3$, orthorhombic crystal system. Mohs' hardness 3.5 to 4. Specific gravity, 2.93-2.95. Commonly colorless, white, or yellow, but may be other colors due to impurities.
Siderite: $FeCO_3$, hexagonal crystal system, commonly distorted rhombohedral crystals. Mohs' hardness, 3.5 to 4. Specific gravity, 3.7 to 3.9. Commonly brown or black.
Ankerite: $Ca_2MgFe(CO_3)_4$, hexagonal system, commonly rhombohedral crystals. Mohs' hardness, 3.5 to 4. Specific gravity, 2.9. Commonly white, pink, or gray.
Magnesite: $MgCO_3$, hexagonal, usually in granular or earthy masses. Mohs' hardness, 3.5 to 4.5. Specific gravity, 2.96 to 3.1. Commonly white or yellowish but may be other colors due to impurities.

color, crystal form, and other physical properties (Table 1) are aids to mineral identification if the rock is relatively monomineralic and compact. The interested geologist can find further information on the chemical and physical properties of the carbonate minerals in Graf and Lamar's (1955) comprehensive review.

The rate of solubility of the different minerals in dilute hydrochloric acid is perhaps the most useful technique to identify them in the field. Calcite is much more soluble in dilute acid than dolomite; hence, if a fresh rock surface is etched, the amount of dolomite left standing in relief can be estimated by the use of a hand lens. Some staining techniques are based on differences in solubility of the carbonate minerals (in decreasing order of solubility: aragonite, calcite, and dolomite). These techniques are useful in the laboratory and have limited application in the field (Friedman, 1959; Högberg, 1971; Warne, 1962). Staining of thin sections is particularly effective in the laboratory (Dickson, 1965, 1966).

The X-ray diffractometer is commonly used in the laboratory for determining carbonate mineralogy of bulk samples. Techniques of determining calcite and dolomite ratios or the percentage of these minerals based on comparison of their diffraction intensities with those of known standards can be found in Azároff and Buerger (1958), Cullity (1956), Graf and Goldsmith (1963), Gulbrandsen (1960), Müller (1967), and Runnells (1970).

Thin section analysis may be a helpful adjunct to binocular examination of carbonate rocks. Although it is difficult to distinguish between calcite, dolomite, and ankerite in thin section unless staining techniques are used, identification of some other minerals, types of carbonate grains, fabrics, textures, and structures are sometimes facilitated by this method (see also "Physical Properties," p. 842). Appropriate parts of "Microscopic Sedimentary Petrography" (Carozzi, 1960) and "Petrology of Sedimentary Rocks" (Hatch and Rastall, 1971) provide introductions to microscopic investigation of carbonate rocks, as does the review on that subject by Gubler, et al. (1967). Good places for assistance in the identification of fossils and fossil fragments in thin section are "Introductory Petrography of Fossils" Horowitz and Potter (1971) and Scholle (1978).

Color, an important property of carbonate rocks, can be a rough guide to purity, but it can also be misleading. Only a small amount of noncarbonate material is necessary to produce a marked change in color. The famous building stone called Indiana Limestone, for example, with its distinct gray and buff colors, commonly contains less than 0.2% Fe_2O_3; "Carthage Marble," a fossiliferous dimension limestone from Missouri in shades of gray, generally has a total iron and aluminum oxide content less than 0.2%. Most high-purity limestones are shades of light brown and gray to white. Limestones in shades of gray or green generally indicate the presence of minerals containing ferrous iron oxides and (or) carbonaceous matter. As the state of oxidation increases, the colors change to yellows, browns, or reds. A color reference chart is useful in maintaining uniformity of rock descriptions. One of the most useful has been made available by the Geological Society of America (Goddard, 1963).

Impurities in carbonate rock vary considerably in type and amount but are important from an economic standpoint only if they affect the usefulness of the rock. Generally the two most important considerations of each impurity are how much is present and how it is distributed. A considerable amount of some impurities is tolerable in carbonate rock for some uses if the impurity is disseminated throughout the rock. On the other hand, if the impurity is concentrated in laminae, it may form planes of weakness that seriously affect the performance of the rock.

Perhaps the most common impurity in carbonate rocks is clay. The clay minerals—mainly kaolinite, illite, chlorite, smectite, and mixed-lattice types—may be either disseminated throughout the rock or concentrated in laminae or thin partings. The basic molecular building blocks of clay minerals are silica tetrahedra (a silicon atom and four oxygen atoms) and alumina and (or) magnesium octahedra (an aluminum or magnesium atom and six hydroxyl ions). Other chemical elements are incorporated into the structure, however, so that it is difficult to determine the type of clay mineral by chemical analysis alone. If clay mineral identification is important, other analysis techniques, such as X-ray diffraction, differential thermal analysis, and electron microscopy, may be employed. A comprehensive review of clay minerals can be found in the chapter of that title in this volume.

Chert is another common impurity in carbonate rocks and may be disseminated as grains throughout the rock or concentrated in nodules, lenses, or beds. It is composed mainly of very fine grained quartz (SiO_2) that may appear under the microscope as minute subequant crystals, usually 1 to 10 μ in diameter (microcrystalline quartz), or as radiating fibers (chalcedonic quartz). Chert easily incorporates impurities, including water, into its structure so that it may be found in almost all colors; its surface texture may range from dense or porcelaneous to porous or earthy. Dense cherts have a Mohs hardness of 7 and high impact toughness (greater than 6 in. per sq in.), which make them particularly abrasive to crushers and other processing equipment. Porous cherts, mainly because of their large surface area available for chemical reaction and moderate solubility in alkalies, are considered as deleterious components in aggregates used in concrete. Comprehensive coverage of the deleterious properties of cherts can be found in Dunn and Ozol (1962) and Kneller, et al. (1968), the latter of which contains a useful bibliography with 600 entries. A good place to start for further information on the texture and composition of chert is a paper by Folk and Weaver (1952).

Silica is also found in carbonate rocks as discrete silt- or sand-size grains of the mineral quartz. These grains may be disseminated throughout the rock or concentrated in laminae and beds. Detrital limestone especially may contain a considerable percentage of quartz silt and sand. These grains may act as the nuclei for coated carbonate grains, such as some ooliths and pisoliths.

Finely disseminated organic matter is a common constituent of limestones and dolomites and may give the rock a pronounced brown or black color. Bituminous material, an organic derivative of petroleum and residue of former pore fluids, may be present in sufficient quantity to make the rock undesirable for some uses.

Thin-section and insoluble-residue studies reveal trace amounts of a wide variety of other minerals in most carbonate rocks. Although these trace minerals may affect the economic usefulness of rocks used for chemical purposes, such as glass manufacture, they have little effect on rocks used principally for physical properties, such as construction materials.

Origin

Most limestones of economic importance were partly or wholly biologically derived from seawater and accumulated in a relatively shallow marine environment. The obvious skeletal material in limestones speaks of a biologic origin, but even nondescript, fine-grained material may derive from the life of organisms. Pellets in many instances are fecal material, and silt- and clay-size particles may be aragonitic-sheath crystals released upon the death of algae. Ooliths, which in the past have largely been thought to be the inorganic accumulation of calcium carbonate around a nucleus, may also depend in part on algal activity.

In some places, lime-secreting organisms, such as corals, calcareous algae, and mollusks, are able to erect large, wave-resistant structures called reefs. The biologically active parts of these structures are generally near the edge of shallow marine shelves where upwelling currents supply nutrients for the growth of the organisms. In other places along such shelves, small skeletal particles or other material may become coated by concentric layers of calcium carbonate to form ooliths. Oolites develop best in the high-energy zone of shelves where water currents agitate the grains, and as the oolites build up they form elongate lenticular bars that nearly reach the water surface. Very fine-grained carbonate muds (micritic limestone) derived from the comminution of coarser skeletal material or precipitated directly from seawater accumulate in low-energy environments, such as lagoons or deep water.

Environment of deposition is significant to the economic geologist because it determines the size, shape, purity, and other economically significant characteristics of the carbonate rock deposit. Limestones that form in high-energy zones generally contain little noncarbonate material and hence may be the source of high-purity carbonate material. Micrite, which accumulates in zones of low energy, is more likely to be diluted by clay and silt-size noncarbonate material.

Carbonate sediments are highly susceptible to postdepositional alteration and modification. The origin of dolomite is especially significant to the economic geologist. Although some dolomite may be precipitated directly from seawater, most dolomite is a result of the alteration of calcium carbonate sediments or rocks by hypersaline brines. Good examples are the almost-pure dolomite Silurian reefs in northern Illinois, Indiana, and Ohio, and in southern Michigan.

To understand the depositional environment and postdepositional history of carbonate rocks, economic geologists are well advised to study modern carbonate deposition. Good places to start for this information are the general reviews by Baars (1963), Ginsburg, et al. (1963), and Milliman (1974). For further information on locations and distributions of modern carbonate sediments, the summaries by Graf (1960a) and Taft (1967) are useful; the comprehensive discussions of the origin and occurrence of carbonate rock in the papers compiled by Jordan (1978), in the book by Wilson (1975), and the reviews of limestone by Sanders and Friedman (1967) and of dolomites by Friedman and Sanders (1967) fill the gaps of the other coverages. A good guide to the literature of both modern and ancient carbonate rock deposits is Potter's (1968) annotated bibliography of 202 references.

Classification

The explosive growth in the study of modern carbonate sedimentation from the late 1950s to the present has had a notable effect on carbonate-rock classification. Numerous classification schemes have emerged based on this new-found information with the result that carbonate rock descriptions are now more explicit and more conducive to genetic interpretation than before. It is unlikely that the ultimate objective of the industrial geologist is the origin of the rock; still a classification is useful in providing a written record that can be used to interpret the rock's physical and chemical properties.

Many aspects of carbonate rocks can be used as the basis of a classification scheme, but

perhaps the most useful are composition and texture. Composition can be thought of in terms of mineralogy, types of fossils or grains, or chemical constituents. Texture refers to both depositional and post-depositional features, such as relative proportions of framework grains and lime mud, grain size, cement, and pores.

Carbonate rocks are rarely monomineralic in nature; thus, a mineralogical classification of these rocks needs to take into consideration the variation in amounts of calcite, dolomite, and noncarbonate materials (Fig. 1). Such a classification is useful in rock descriptions, especially when combined with textural parameters, but it commonly is not sufficient for industrial purposes. Although limestone and dolomite can be used equally well for a large number of uses, certain uses have special chemical requirements. These special requirements are stated in terms of chemical composition rather than mineralogical composition and specify the quantity of $CaCO_3$ (or CaO) and $MgCO_3$ (or MgO) or both in the rock along with the maximum percentage of impurities that can be tolerated. A practical chemical classification considers that ultrahigh calcium limestone is more than 97% $CaCO_3$, high-calcium limestone is more than 95% $CaCO_3$, high-purity carbonate rock is more than 95% combined $CaCO_3$ and $MgCO_3$, and high-magnesium dolomite is more than 43% $MgCO_3$ (theoretically pure dolomite is 45.7% $MgCO_3$).

A textural classification, along with a mineralogical classification, is fundamental to geologic studies aimed at determining the origin

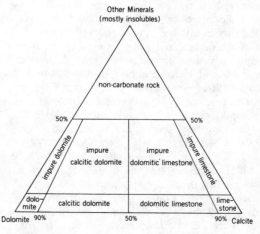

FIG. 1—*Mineralogical classification of carbonate rocks.*

of carbonate rocks. One such classification by Leighton and Pendexter (1962) considered that most limestones can be characterized by the types and relative amounts of four textural components: grains, lime mud (micrite), cement, and pores. The ratio of the relative proportions of grains to micritic material, which is the basis of their nomenclatural system (Fig. 2), gives some indication of water turbulence because muds cannot be deposited in areas of high bottom currents. Other classifications, such as the ones by Folk (1959, 1962), Dunham (1962), and Bissell and Chilingar (1967), make use of framework grains to mud ratios and have practical applications.

Dolomite presents a special problem in classification and may require separate handling from limestone. The textural classification can be used for secondary dolomite if the original depositional texture is preserved. Some dolomites, however, show only faint traces of original texture, called "ghosts" or "relics," and others may have had their original texture completely obliterated. For these cases, and for dolomite of primary origin, a classification based on crystal size may be required.

Distribution of Deposits

Carbonate rocks have been deposited from Precambrian to Recent time, and although they compose only about 0.25% of the volume of the crust of the earth (Parker, 1967), they comprise about 15% of the sedimentary rocks. In 1980, limestone and (or) dolomite were quarried or mined in all of the 50 states except Delaware, Louisiana, New Hampshire, and North Dakota; they were mined in all Canadian provinces except Saskatchewan.

Because carbonate rocks are widely distributed and differ in their geologic characteristics, each deposit must be considered on its own attributes. The best source of information for carbonate rock deposits is the state geological surveys, or their equivalents. Most state publications are oriented toward areal geology, commodities, or the two combined, rather than uses or methods. The US Bureau of Mines (USBM) and the US Geological Survey (USGS) also publish information on limestone and dolomite. The USGS's 7½-min geologic quadrangle maps are especially useful, as are the Bureau's circulars that contain cost analyses of limestone production (Eilertsen, 1964; Evans and Eilertsen, 1957; Kline, 1962; Kusler and Corre, 1968; Marshall, 1963; Riley and Schroeder, 1963). Table 2 lists the most useful publications on the limestone and dolomite resources of the different states and provinces. The annotated bibliographies of Gazdik and Tagg (1957) on high-calcium limestone deposits and of Davis (1957) on some high-magnesium dolomite deposits are helpful guides to the older literature, as is the report on high-grade dolomite deposits by Weitz (1942).

Although high-purity carbonate rock deposits are not overly abundant, they are by no means rare. Virtually all of the states except Delaware, Louisiana, New Hampshire, and Rhode Island, and all of the Canadian provinces have

Grain/ Micrite Ratio	% Grains	Grain Type					Organic Framebuilders	No Organic Frame- builders
		Detrital Grains	Skeletal Grains	Pellets	Lumps	Coated Grains		
9:1	~90%	Detrital Ls.	Skeletal Ls.	Pellet Ls.	Lump Ls.	Oolitic Ls. Pisolitic Ls. Algal Encrusted Ls.	Coralline Ls. Algal Ls. Etc.	Caliche Travertine Tufa
1:1	~50%	Detrital-Micritic Ls.	Skeletal-Micritic Ls.	Pellet-Micritic Ls.	Lump-Micritic Ls.	Oolitic-(Pisolitic-Etc.) Micritic Ls.	Coralline-Micritic Ls. Algal-Micritic Ls. Etc.	
1.9	~10%	Micritic-Detrital Ls.	Micritic-Skeletal Ls.	Micritic-Pellet Ls.	Micritic-Lump Ls.	Micritic-Oolitic (Pisolitic Etc.) Ls.	Micritic-Coralline Ls. Micritic-Algal Ls. Etc.	
		← Micritic Limestone →						

FIG. 2—*Textural classification of limestone. From Leighton and Pendexter, 1962.*

	Limestone and Dolomite Currently Being Produced	High-Calcium Limestone and/or High-Magnesium Dolomite Currently Being Produced	Potentially Commercial Deposits of High-Calcium Limestone and/or High-Magnesium Dolomite are Present	Selected References (Numbers Keyed to Bibliography) on Limestone and Dolomite Resources
CANADA				
Alberta	x	x	x	133,134,140,151,180,181,344,345
British Columbia	x	x	x	87,140,245
Manitoba	x	x	x	20,135,140
N. Bruns. and Nova Scotia	x	x	x	136,268,327
Nfld. and Labrador	x	x	x	56,91
Ontario	x	x	x	135,139,169,170
Quebec	x	x	x	135,137
Saskatchewan			x	123,140,214
UNITED STATES				
Alabama	x	x	x	3,225,358
Alaska	x		x	53,191,288,304,315
Arizona	x	x	x	202
Arkansas	x	x	x	46,178
California	x	x	x	40,41,42,154
Colorado	x	x	x	13,14,260,359,381
Connecticut	x	x	x	74,179,263
Delaware				
Florida	x	x	x	57,182,294,295,300,321,325,361,362,363,389,390
Georgia	x	x	x	47,250,287,290
Hawaii	x	x	x	374
Idaho	x	x	x	318,319
Illinois	x	x	x	186,216,218,219,220,221,382
Indiana	x	x	x	60,63,64,118,187,248,249,283,285,305,306,307,370
Iowa	x	x	x	100
Kansas	x		x	124,146,190,201,302,311,312,313,314,368
Kentucky	x	x	x	92,93,94,95,203,204,247,341,342,343
Louisiana				
Maine	x	x	x	4
Maryland	x	x	x	7,240,244
Massachusetts	x	x	x	12,67,112,284,297
Michigan	x	x	x	196,225,226,333
Minnesota	x		x	108,231,291,322,334,352,353
Mississippi	x	x	x	33,34,232,251,266
Missouri	x	x	x	9,49,50,175,176,185,238,239,377
Montana	x	x	x	66,81,227,228
Nebraska	x	x	x	54,73
Nevada	x	x	x	275,280,281
New Hampshire				
New Jersey	x	x	x	212,213,378,387
New Mexico	x	x	x	193,209,210,211
New York	x	x	x	19,155,194,195,274,292,356,366,391,392
North Carolina	x	x	x	2,29,32,75
North Dakota			x	10,55,58,152
Ohio	x	x	x	223,224,265,338,339,340,346
Oklahoma	x	x	x	8,28,30,109,149,150,197,309,348,369
Oregon	x	x	x	5,230,241,286,298,365
Pennsylvania	x	x	x	90,257,276,277,278,349
Rhode Island	x			284,296,297,379
South Carolina	x	x	x	71,167
South Dakota	x		x	145
Tennessee	x	x	x	168,351
Texas	x	x	x	21,69,106,126,234,270,303,323,337
Utah	x	x	x	51,264
Vermont	x	x	x	82,83,110,117,360,373
Virginia	x	x	x	22,23,76,77,104,105
Washington	x		x	31,86,259,261
West Virginia	x	x	x	215,246,376
Wisconsin	x		x	48,184,336
Wyoming	x	x	x	153,161,162,163,279

potentially commercial deposits of high-calcium limestone and (or) high-magnesium dolomite (Table 2). Twenty-one Mexican states had production of high-calcium limestone or high-magnesium dolomite in 1982 (Fig. 3). Because these deposits are present, however, does not necessarily mean that they can be exploited. In many areas competition is intense for potential mineral lands for construction sites, recreation areas, and highways; even nature has her own requirements for flowing streams and soil development. Society has also imposed environmental controls, now firmly ensconced in state and federal statutes, which prohibit or restrict mineral production in areas where it might significantly affect the quality of man's environment.

Exploration

Exploration for limestone and dolomite in North America is largely the detailed examination of known deposits. Because most limestone is a sedimentary rock, it occurs in strata generally of considerable extent. Some data as to chemical composition and physical character are available for most such strata in the published reports or files of state, provincial, and national geological surveys. Exploration for a new limestone deposit, therefore, in most instances begins with a search of these records to find the locations of deposits that satisfy the various economic factors and proceeds to a sampling program of favorable deposits. Geophysical techniques, if used at all, are used to determine the thickness of overburden. Geochemical techniques are not used.

All aspects of exploration are important, but the one most likely to be slighted is sampling. Yet it determines the validity of further study and may become the basis for hundreds of thousands and sometimes millions of dollars-worth of development work. Its goal must be the accurate representation of the limestone deposit. Coring, rock bitting, and surface (ledge) sampling are the most common sampling methods, and the choice among these depends on such matters as the geology of the deposit, the proposed use of the material, and the availability of equipment.

Special care should be taken when sampling weathered outcrops. In humid regions, the surface layer of a carbonate rock may be leached of calcite and dolomite and hence be less pure than the rest of the unit. On the other hand, in arid and semiarid regions, where evaporation exceeds precipitation for long periods of time, the surface layer may be enriched in calcite and dolomite. Thus if surface samples must be taken under these conditions, the geologist should be aware of a potential bias.

Coring

Coring is generally the best method of exploring a new deposit. A single core may not always be more representative than a section sampled in a quarry or in a natural exposure, where some judgment may be used as to what is representative, but cores taken on a grid pattern constitute a more representative and unbiased sample of a deposit than an equal number of surface sections. Coring avoids contamination by soil and weathered material and disproportionate sampling of different parts of a single unit, yet retains the surface material that may have worked down in solution cavities.

Initial drilling is generally widely spaced both to locate a potential deposit and to determine its potential size. Once an apparently large and suitable deposit is discovered it should be drilled in a more or less regular pattern. The core grid and type of drilling depends largely on the proposed use of the limestone, although other factors, such as the homogeneity of the deposit, geologic complexity, topography, and cost of drilling, are significant. In areas of steeply dipping strata, the grid spacing must take into account whether vertical or inclined drilling will be used. If stone is to be used as cement raw material and the magnesium content of the rocks is believed to be marginal and unpredictable, no greater than 100-ft centers would be required. If the deposit is relatively homogeneous in one direction and not in another, a rectangular rather than a square grid might be used. If the stone is to be used as aggregate and has proved relatively uniform in other deposits, generally only a few cores need to be taken in several hundred acres. We recommend that for most deposits of flat-lying strata in which the chemical composition of the rocks is important, cores be spaced on 100-ft centers until a pattern of uniformity indicates that the spacing can be increased safely. We know of one lime company, quarrying in a structurally complex area of Pennsylvania, that found coring on 50-ft centers was necessary for adequate quality control.

For most limestone exploration a BX core (1⅝ in. in diam.) suffices, but if physical tests are required, a core of larger diameter must be used. NX core (2⅛ in. in diam.) is adequate

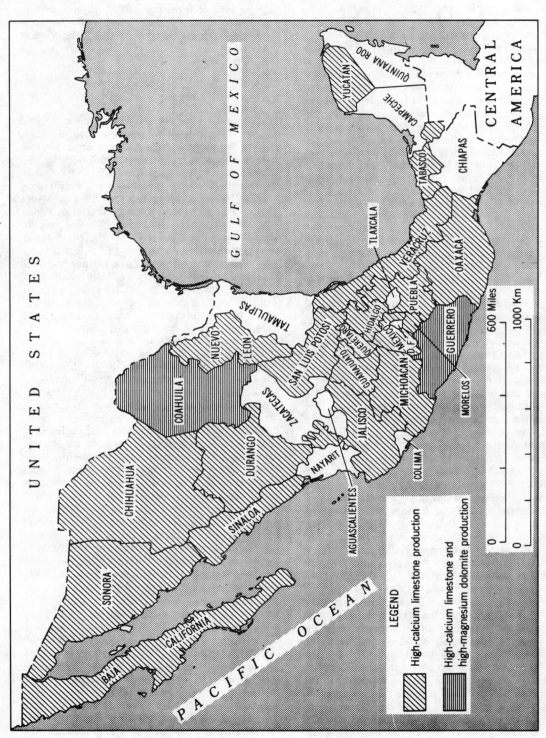

FIG. 3—Map showing states in Mexico producing high-calcium limestone and high-magnesium dolomite in 1982. Data from the Consejo de Recursos Naturales No Renovables.

for chemical analyses and limited physical testing, but too small for some physical tests.

Each common physical test of rock used for aggregate requires about 5 kg (11 lb) of rock. If tests for absorption, abrasion, and soundness are performed, more than 30 lb of rock is required. (Some useful data concerning weight and volume of limestone are given in Table 3.) If stone is to be tested for use as highway materials (ASTM D75–59 and AASHO T2–60), a minimum of 50 lb of rock is required. Highway commissions in some states do not perform physical testing of cores and accept only ledge samples. Testing agencies in other states will run physical tests on cores. For example, in prospecting for a quarry site near Skaneateles, NY, the General Crushed Stone Co. took a core 12 in. in diam and had the stone tested for quality by the New York State Dept. of Public Works before opening the quarry (Moore, et al., 1968).

Rock Bitting

If used alone, drill cuttings are probably the least reliable samples in exploration, but if used to supplement cores or information obtained from nearby quarries or outcrops, they are a cheap, rapid method of acquiring much information. If the drilling is done in a carefully cased hole so as to prevent contamination by overburden, if the cuttings are collected carefully, and if the geologist is experienced in interpreting well cuttings, these samples may be as reliable as core and surface sampling for some purposes. In fact, the percussion air drill is probably the fastest and least expensive method for preliminary sampling.

Because of the large amount of drilling for oil and gas during the past few decades, cuttings of thousands of wells are on file in government and other sample libraries. Although not intentionally so, these cuttings constitute the largest exploration program for industrial minerals that has ever been undertaken. Cuttings cannot be interpreted properly unless the interpreter understands drilling techniques, and the best interpretation of the well cuttings requires considerable well-site experience.

Surface Sampling

Chip samples taken carefully on a quarry face can provide a good representation of the limestone deposit. The geologist should first inspect the quarry face and divide the face into units of uniform lithology. He should mark tops of units by paint or flagging. He should subdivide thick homogeneous beds arbitrarily, so that no sample is more than about 5 ft thick. Starting at the base of the unit, he should take chips of uniform size as nearly as possible along a selected vertical line to the top of each unit. (He might start at the top and work down, but it is easier to work up than down.) This method of sampling is sometimes called "channel sampling." Chip samples should be taken from unweathered surfaces even if the weathered rind must be chipped away. Samples should be washed to remove some contaminants, such as lichens or soil, from the samples, but care should be taken not to wash out thin, interbedded shales.

Many channel or core samples weigh 10 to 20 lb, and this amount must be crushed, thoroughly mixed, and quartered several times to reduce the sample to the few ounces needed for chemical determination.

Evaluation and Testing

If given sufficient cores or exposures of rock, an experienced industrial minerals geologist

TABLE 3—Approximate Density of Limestone, Dolomite, Shale, and Cement

Material	Weight Lb, per Cu Ft	Weight Lb, per Cu Yd	Weight Tons, per Acre-Ft
Limestone, broken or crushed	95	2,570	
Limestone solid	160*	4,320	3,500
Dolomite, broken or crushed	105	2,840	
Dolomite solid	170	4,590	3,700
Shale, broken or crushed	100	2,700	
Shale solid	167	4,500	3,600
Portland cement	100	2,700	

* 1 ft of 2 1/8-in. limestone core weighs about 3.7 lb.

can evaluate a limestone deposit largely just by looking at it, using a hand lens, hammer, and weak hydrochloric acid as his only tools. He can generally appraise whether a stone will make class A aggregate and (or) cement raw material. He may not be able to determine whether it is of sufficient purity for some other uses, but he can eliminate much stone that is not of sufficient purity for those uses. Final evaluation of rocks suitable for aggregate, dimension stone, and similar uses requires physical testing. Rocks used for making lime, cement, or other products that depend on chemical purity should be chemically analyzed.

A list of laboratories capable of making chemical and physical determinations of rocks can be found in "Directory of Testing Laboratories, Commercial-Institutional," which is available from the American Society for Testing and Materials, 1916 Race St., Philadelphia, PA 19103.

Physical Properties

Procedures for physical testing can be obtained from two main sources: the American Society for Testing & Materials (ASTM) and the American Association of State Highway and Transportation Officials (AASHTO). Both organizations describe explicit procedures, in cookbook fashion, for testing limestone and dolomite. State highway commissions may specify slightly different procedures and should be consulted if stone is to be used as aggregate. In earlier years, several federal organizations developed physical tests for building stone, such as reported by the US Census Office (1884) and the US Bureau of Standards (Kessler and Sligh, 1927), but now building-stone testing generally follows procedure outlines by ASTM. Testing methods and procedures developed by USBM for testing diamond drill cores of mine rock are described in a report by Obert, et al., (1946).

Physical tests are designed to test how well a rock will perform for a particular use. As might be expected, a great number of tests have been developed in response to the many uses to which rock is put. The selected physical properties of carbonate rock shown in Table 4 are from reports of a lengthy study of the physical properties of mine rock by USBM. In addition to the physical properties listed in Table 4, many other properties have been reported in this same study, which include tensile strength, abrasive hardness, scleroscope hardness,

Young's modulus, modulus of rigidity, Poisson's ratio, specific damping capacity, and longitudinal bar velocity. A large number of physical properties of limestones and other rocks have been collected and published in *Handbook of Physical Constants* (Birch, et al., 1950). This handbook contains data on bulk density, compressive strength, compressibility at high and low temperature, dielectric constant, electrical resistivity, porosity, thermal conductivity, thermal expansion, and other properties that are especially useful to the geophysicist. Considerable research on the properties of rock that have application to blasting and mining have been undertaken by USBM (Atchison, et al., 1964; Atchison and Pugliese, 1964; Bur, et al., 1969; Dick, et al., 1973; Merrill, 1956; Pugliese, 1972; Thill, et al., 1969; Willard and McWilliams, 1969). A tabulation of porosity and bulk density determinations of carbonate rock, as reported in the more accessible American, British, German, and Swiss literature, was published by Manger (1963).

A great many physical tests of carbonate rock used for aggregate have been performed in connection with state and federal road building programs, but much of this information is unpublished. In 1953, Woolf (1953) compiled results of physical testing of road-building aggregate as performed by the US Bureau of Public Roads up to 1951. Table 5 shows average values of physical properties for selected rock types from this compilation. Unfortunately data from later testing of aggregate in the federal highway program have not been tabulated. The Highway Research Board of the National Research Council has sponsored much research dealing with the relationships of the physical properties of carbonate rock to its serviceability as an aggregate. A report by Renninger and Nichols (1970) reviewed some of this work and gave the current status of aggregate research.

Through the years, the US Army Corps of Engineers has tested carbonate rock from many quarries in the continental United States in order to evaluate its potential use in constructing locks, dams, and other structures. A summary of this testing, which includes the standard tests for sulfate soundness, abrasion resistance, specific gravity, and absorption, can be found in Technical Memorandum No. 6–370, "Test Data—Concrete Aggregates in Continental United States" of the US Army Corps of Engineers, Waterways Experiment Station. This compilation, which occupies more than 2 ft of shelf space, cannot be purchased,

TABLE 4—Physical Properties of Some Carbonate Rocks

Age	Formation	Location	Rock Type	Apparent Specific Gravity	Apparent Porosity, %	Compressive Strength, Psi × 10³	Modulus of Rupture, Psi × 10³	Impact Toughness, In. per Sq. In.	Reference
Miocene	Unspecified	Eniwetok	Ls. (fossil.)	2.39	4.0	14.1	2.4	1.0	Blair (1956)
Eocene	Unspecified	Eniwetok	Ls. (dense)	2.53		17.7	3.2	2.9	Blair (1956)
Cretaceous	Niobrara	S. Dakota	Ls. (chalky)	1.81	8.3	3.7	0.6	1.2	Blair (1955)
Mississippian	St. Louis	Missouri	Ls. (oolitic, fossil.)	2.56		16.8	2.3	2.9	Blair (1956)
Mississippian	Maxville	Ohio	Ls. (fn.-grained)	2.41		15.8	2.5	3.1	Blair (1956)
Mississippian	Salem(Spergen)	Indiana	Ls. (fossil.)	2.37	11	10.9	1.6	1.9	Windes (1949)
Devonian	Columbus	Ohio	Ls. (v. fn.-grained)	2.60	5.4	17.9		3.6	Blair (1956)
Devonian	Columbus	Ohio	Ls. (fn.-grained)	2.69	0.7	28.5	2.9	8.6	Windes (1949)
Silurian	Brassfield	Ohio	Ls. (dolomitic)	2.8	1.3	26.	28	4.0	Windes (1950)
Silurian	Niagara	Ohio	Dol. (fn.-grained)	2.4	8.6	13.	11	1.8	Windes (1950)
Silurian	Clinton	Alabama	Ls. (cs-grained)	2.83	0.9	24.0		6.6	Windes (1949)
Ordovician	Chickamauga	Tennessee	Ls.	2.73	3.4	>25.1	0.8	5.7	Blair (1956)
Ordovician	Lenoir	W. Virginia	Ls. (siliceous)	2.68	6.	23.0	1.9	2.5	Windes (1950)
Ordovician	Knox	Tennessee	Dol. (fn.-grained)	2.84	0.7	46.7	3.8	5.9	Windes (1949)
Cambrian	Bonne Terre	Missouri	Ls. (dolomitic)	2.66	3.3	25.4	1.8	4.8	Blair (1955)
Cambrian	Oro Grande	California	Marble	2.72	0.2	24.0	2.4	1.9	Blair (1955)
Precambrian	Cockeysville	Maryland	Marble (dolomitic)	2.87	0.6	30.8	2.8	2.7	Windes (1949)

TABLE 5—Average Values for the Physical Properties of Rocks Used for Aggregate*

Rock Type	Bulk Specific Gravity		Absorption, %		Loss of Abrasion				Toughness[†]	
					Deval Test, %		Los Angeles Test, %			
Basalt	(229)	2.86	(228)	0.5	(203)	3.1	(24)	14	(203)	19
Chert	(74)	2.50	(74)	1.6	(78)	8.5	(6)	26	(29)	12
Diabase	(332)	2.96	(309)	0.3	(340)	2.6	(63)	18	(285)	20
Dolomite	(668)	2.70	(667)	1.1	(708)	5.5	(134)	25	(612)	9
Gneiss	(419)	2.74	(424)	0.3	(602)	5.9	(293)	45	(386)	9
Granite	(662)	2.65	(666)	0.3	(718)	4.3	(174)	38	(703)	9
Limestone	(1695)	2.66	(1673)	0.9	(1677)	5.7	(350)	26	(1315)	8
Marble	(184)	2.63	(162)	0.2	(175)	6.3	(41)	47	(188)	6
Quartzite	(208)	2.69	(204)	0.3	(233)	3.3	(119)	28	(161)	16
Sandstone	(716)	2.54	(707)	1.8	(699)	7.0	(95)	38	(681)	11
Schist	(297)	2.85	(296)	0.4	(314)	5.5	(136)	38	(212)	12

* Number of samples tested in parenthesis.
† Height in cm for a 2 kg steel plunger to cause a rock core about 1 in. in diameter and 1 in. high to fail.

Source: Woolf, 1953.

but it is available for inspection at the Corps of Engineers' libraries. Other more accessible publications that give physical test values and results of the Corps' extensive research relating to the use of carbonate rock as aggregates in portland cement concrete are those by Curry and Buck (1966) and Stowe (1969).

Some manufacturers of pulverized limestone, defined as limestone or dolomite having a minimum fineness of 97% passing a 325 mesh sieve, have established standards and test methods through the Pulverized Limestone Association. Test methods that are recommended include particle size, pH, dry brightness, water demand, and calcium and magnesium carbonate content.

A petrographic examination of carbonate rock can often foretell its physical properties and subsequent suitability for certain uses, but unfortunately too few people make use of this method. The definitive reference for this type of applied petrography is ASTM Standard C 295–65, "Petrographic Examination of Aggregates for Concrete," which is based on the work of Mather and Mather (1950). Techniques of petrographic examination and some applications of this kind of work can be found in Mather (1953), Mielenz (1954, 1955), and Newlon, et al., (1972).

Rippability is a physical property of rock that concerns mainly the construction industry. Limestones that are thinly bedded, low in compressive strength, or sufficiently inhomogeneous so as to contain horizontal planes of weakness can generally be ripped easily. Empirical testing by the Caterpillar Tractor Co. (1972) found a relationship between seismic wave velocities and rock rippability: the higher the wave velocity, the more difficult it is to rip the rock.

Various research workers have examined the relationships between different physical as well as chemical properties of carbonate rocks. These attempts have not met with much success because of the inhomogeneity of the rocks. Further information can be found in Judd and Huber (1961), D'Andrea, et al., (1964, 1965), West and Johnson (1965), Mutmansky and Singh (1968), Baxter and Harvey (1969), and Carr, et al., (1970).

Further information on physical requirements of carbonate rock can be found in the chapters of this book on "Crushed Stone," "Dimension and Cut Stone," and "Cement and Cement Raw Materials."

Chemical Properties

The techniques for making chemical analyses are beyond the scope of this chapter. Instrumental methods of analysis have become popular in recent years, and as a result a wide selection of instructional material is available on theory and techniques. Some of the most useful are those on atomic absorption spectroscopy by Angino and Billings (1967), Galle and Angino (1967), and Slavin (1968); and one on rapid chemical methods by Shapiro and Brannock (1962). Details of standard gravimetric and complexometric (EDTA titration) methods can be found in Hillebrand and Lundell (1953) and Diehl (1964), respectively.

The chemical and physical properties of carbonate rocks are interdependent. Pure calcite in the form of poorly cemented chalk is not only unique in its low strength and high absorption among the carbonate rocks, but it is also highly reactive chemically due to the large surface area of the component grains. Pure calcitic marble of the same chemical composition as the chalk is relatively strong, unabsorptive, and unreactive. Dolomite that contains quartz sand grains may have the same overall composition as dolomite that contains chert, but their suitability as aggregate differs widely due to the difference in reactivity of the two forms of silica. Processing also affects the degree of fracturing of stone and thus the surface area and chemical reactivity. Therefore, physical and mineralogic descriptions of carbonate rocks are of considerable use in predicting the chemical properties of the product from a deposit.

For some uses of carbonate rocks, chemical analysis may be of little or no help in estimating the suitability of a rock unit; for other uses various chemical determinations must be available to compare with specific optimum compositions. For example, in .stone used for chemical purposes, such as glass raw material, flux, or cement, the percent of certain elements must fall within specified limits or ranges. On the other hand, the chemical content may or may not be important for stone that is used because of its physical properties, such as aggregate, building stone, or riprap. A thick section of rock that is almost pure dolomite is likely to be well-cemented reefal dolomite, and it can be predicted generally to make good aggregate. Rock that is pure calcite, however, may be a skeletal or oolitic limestone that is either well cemented or poorly cemented and thus might make excellent or only fair aggregate.

The proportion of alumina (Al_2O_3) and silica (SiO_2) in the rock may be helpful in determining the value of a carbonate rock for a use in which physical properties are important. Most of the silica in a carbonate rock is likely to be present as clay, silt- and sand-size quartz, or chert. For the common clay minerals found in limestones and dolomites, as much as 2% silica may be present for each 1% of alumina. The higher the alumina content, the more argillaceous the sample is likely to be. The alumina content can be multiplied by two to obtain an estimate of the amount of silica tied up in the clay. The way the remaining silica occurs can be determined only by reference to the sample description or by examining the sample itself.

The chemical analysis of a carbonate rock is essential for estimating the neutralizing value of agricultural limestone, which is usually expressed in terms of calcium carbonate equivalent (CCE). Pure calcite ($CaCO_3$) is assigned a CCE value of 100. Pure dolomite ($CaCO_3 \cdot MgCO_3$) has a theoretical CCE value of 108.6; that is, it is 8.6% more effective than pure limestone as a neutralizer. Such interpretation assumes that a molecule of $MgCO_3$, with a molecular weight of 84.32, is as effective a neutralizer as 1 molecule of $CaCO_3$, with a molecular weight of 100.09. Thus, a given weight of $MgCO_3$ is 1.19 times as effective as the same weight of $CaCO_3$. Because of differences in solubility, however, a dolomitic liming material will take longer to neutralize a given amount of acid than a limestone one, even though the CCE of the two is the same. A useful guide to selecting agricultural limestone materials has been prepared by Goodwin (1979).

Numerous chemical analyses of carbonate rocks have been published to show the varied compositions of limestones and dolomites (Clarke, 1924; Gillson, et al., 1960; Graf. 1960b; Siegel, 1967; Wedepohl, 1970), but these may not always be typical of the formation from which they were taken. Most sedimentary carbonate rocks vary in their impurities—including clay minerals, resistant minerals such as quartz, and organic material—because they were deposited in different environments. In addition, the rocks have evolved chemically as well as physically during compaction, dehydration, and lithification. Subsequent processes, including burial and exposure to percolation of water, provide for synthesis of authigenic minerals and alteration, such as oxidation of organic matter. Because of the limited extent of identical environments of deposition and subsequent postdepositional conditions, composition of any given rock unit is likely to be variable. Analyses of many samples taken at different sites are required to reveal the approximate composition of a particular unit of rock.

Good sources of chemical data on carbonate rocks are the state geological surveys or their equivalents. Many state surveys have files of chemical data obtained from quarry sampling and coring programs. Many of the references listed in Table 2 contain extensive lists of chemical analyses. The USGS published 1131 analyses of carbonate rocks from Montana, Wyoming, North Dakota, South Dakota, Nebraska, Colorado, and Kansas (Hill, et al., 1972) and 3585 analyses of carbonate rocks from Alaska, Idaho, Oregon, and Washington (Hill and Werner, 1972).

Specifications and Uses

The uses of limestone and dolomite depend largely on physical properties, chemical properties, or both. Physical properties are more important if stone is used "as is," such as for aggregate or building stone. Chemical properties are more important if stone undergoes changes from one form of matter to another, such as the manufacture of cement or lime. Chemical and physical properties are often interrelated; in whiteness, for example, the physical property of color is largely determined by the purity and chemical composition of the rock.

Specifications for carbonate rock should be considered generally as guidelines. For some limestones, minimum and maximum percentages of certain constituents are based on rea physical or chemical characteristics, but the precise figure may have been determined by custom, composition of the limestone being used, or "what the market will bear."

Published specifications may be based on a survey of manufacturers, but some are based on a survey of literature. For example, Bingham's (1916) recommended specifications for limestone used in manufacturing calcium carbide have been repeated often (Table 6). These repeated specifications are based on physical and chemical reactions during the manufacture and use of calcium carbide, but they have more latitude than the figures quoted from Bingham indicate or than Bingham himself suggested in his text. One should not interpret agreement in published specifications as corroboration so much as repetition of other published specifications.

As an example of "what the market will bear," a steel manufacturer in the midwest specified a maximum of 3% $MgCO_3$ and 0.04% sulfur in flux limestone obtained from a contract supplier in Indiana. When the magnesium and sulfur content of the initial material proved to be much lower, the steel company revised its specifications to 1.5% $MgCO_3$ and 0.025% sulfur.

Specifications for a particular limestone may be based on the average composition of the limestone being used regardless of the fact that limestone of a different composition might be cheaper and better. The cost of manufacturing is generally greater than the cost of the raw material, and a change in raw material might prove a costly mistake. Inadequate or unreliable supply could also be costly, and therefore a manufacturer is likely to be loyal to a dependable supplier.

Some specifications are primarily economic rather than physical or chemical. For example, a low silica content in limestone and dolomite used for flux stone is desirable, but the cost is an equally important factor. Generally a silica content lower than 2% is desired, but if only stone of much higher silica content (say, 8%) is available within an economical distance, it can be used. The drawback is that more high-silica stone than low-silica stone is required to flux the same amount of iron ore.

Some specifications may be in terms of tolerances from one shipment to the next rather than specific amounts. This is particularly true in glass manufacture where it is desirable to have uniform composition of raw materials from batch to batch. For example, one large US glass producer specifies that for glass-grade limestone and dolomite, the composition, except for iron content, must remain within specified tolerances (Kephart, 1972). Thus, a limestone containing 1% silica could be used by making adjustments for silica in the other batch components. The Fe_2O_3 content, however, must be less than 0.1% because of its colorant effect on glass.

Virtually hundreds of uses for limestone and dolomite exist, but for simplicity these can be grouped into about 30 uses that include more than 99% of the total crushed and dimension stone production (Table 7). Extensive lists of

TABLE 6—Some Published Specifications of Limestone Used for Manufacturing Calcium Carbide

$CaCO_3$, %	MgO, %	SiO_2, %	$Al_2O_3 + Fe_2O_3$, %	S	P, %	Reference
>97	<0.5	<1.2	<0.5	Tr*	<0.004	Bingham (1916)
>97	<0.5	<1.2	<0.5	Tr	<0.004	Mantell (1931)
>97	<0.5	<1.2	<0.5	Tr	<0.004†	Bowen (1957)
Very high	<0.5	<1.2	<0.5	Tr	<0.004	Gillson, et al. (1960)
>97	<0.5	<1.2	<0.5	Tr	<0.004	McGregor (1963)
Very high	<0.5-2.0	<1.5-3.0	Low	Tr	<0.05	Searle (1935)
>97	<0.5-2.0	<1.0-3.0	<0.05-0.75	Tr	<0.004-0.01	Lamar (1965)

* Tr—trace.
† The figure given in Bowen's publication is 1.2, a typographical error.

TABLE 7—Limestone and Dolomite Shipped or Used by Producers in the United States by Use in 1979

Crushed and Broken

Use	Quantity, 1000 St	Value, $1000
Agricultural limestone	32,902	116,457
Agricultural marl and other soil conditioners	436	2,136
Poultry grit and mineral food	2,442	19,567
Concrete aggregate	113,407	342,599
Bituminous aggregate	66,788	212,707
Macadam aggregate	22,646	59,884
Dense-graded roadbase stone	169,281	422,723
Surface treatment aggregate	38,517	122,515
Other construction aggregate and roadstone	134,839	371,024
Riprap and jetty stone	16,229	43,028
Railroad ballast	14,035	37,635
Filter stone	2,689	7,911
Manufactured fine aggregate (stone sand)	15,609	51,371
Terrazzo and exposed aggregate	624	7,531
Cement manufacture	104,908	223,603
Lime manufacture	34,054	98,042
Dead-burned dolomite	1,779	4,903
Flux stone	21,271	64,945
Refractory stone	20	64
Chemical stone for alkali works	1,966	6,409
Abrasives	141	656
Mine dusting	1,267	10,379
Asphalt filler	1,007	5,425
Whiting or whiting substitute	1,085	29,970
Other fillers or extenders	2,792	31,691
Acid neutralization	W	W
Building products	129	350
Other chemicals	41	152
Bedding materials	—	—
Dam construction	22	44
Drain fields	W	W
Fill	2,127	4,090
Glass manufacture	2,146	14,507
Paper manufacture	128	446
Roofing granules	376	2,307
Sugar refining	1,367	5,968
Waste material	39	76
Sulfur removal from stack gases	967	2,942
Other uses*	3,977	11,033
Total	812,054	2,335,089

Dimension Stone

Use	Quantity St	1000 Cu ft	Value, $1000
Rough Stone:			
Rough blocks	207,843	2,672	$6,276
Irregular-shaped stone	5,785	74	172
Rubble	43,939	573	647
Flagging	26,645	357	414
Other rough stone	45	1	1
Dressed stone:			
Cut stone	55,884	754	10,866
Sawed stone	55,860	766	3,932
House stone veneer	64,569	853	3,063
Construction	5,823	69	223
Curbing	311	4	15
Flagging	2,679	35	117
Other uses	280	4	118
Total	469,663	6,161	25,845

Source: US Bureau of Mines *Minerals Yearbook.*
*Includes ferrosilicon, disinfectant and animal sanitation, magnesium metal manufacture, porcelain, and other uses.

uses can be found in Hatmaker (1931), Goudge (1937), Lamar and Willman (1938), Colby (1941), Bowles and Jensen (1941, 1947), Bowles (1956), Johnstone and Johnstone (1961), Lamar (1965), and Siegel (1967). Comstock (1963) listed many uses for magnesium compounds, some of which are derived from dolomite.

Preparation for Markets

Mining Methods and Costs

Open-Pit Mining: Most limestone is mined by open-pit methods, and most limestone producers will choose that method even where underground mining might be equally or slightly more economical.

Mining Methods—Limestone mining as compared to other mining does not require any special equipment. Overburden must be removed, whether by bulldozer, dragline, or shovel. The rock must be drilled and blasted. Oversized rock must be redrilled and blasted, broken by a drop ball, or otherwise disposed of. The broken stone must be loaded into a dump truck and hauled to the primary crusher (or it may be loaded onto a conveyor and carried directly to a portable or permanent crusher). And finally, for most uses of limestone, it must travel through a secondary crusher and be sized. For some uses limestone is ground or heated. For description of mining equipment and processing techniques the reader is referred to such trade publications as *Rock Products* and *Pit and Quarry,* the latter of which is published by a company that also publishes a useful handbook (Herod, 1980–81). For further information on mining and quarrying of stone, the reader may want to consult the proceedings of a symposium organized by the Institution of Mining and Metallurgy (1965) on "Opencast Mining, Quarrying and Alluvial Mining" or a compendium by John Sinclair (1969).

Overburden—Open-pit mining is less costly than underground mining if the overburden can be removed cheaply. We do not know the practical limit in thickness of overburden that can be removed. One large aggregate producer in Indiana has adopted a rule of thumb that overburden can be removed economically if the rock to overburden ratio is greater than three to one. In Indiana, that rule assumes that the overburden is unconsolidated material, such as till or residual clay. Where the overburden is extremely thick, however, this rule apparently

does not apply. In some parts of Indiana the market could support a large quarry, but rock is not quarried even though the quarryable section is 300 ft thick and the drift thickness is about 100 ft. Where the drift is so thick, the length of a boom on a dragline, disposal of overburden and water, sloping of drift walls, and necessity to quarry high faces for volume production become limiting factors. On the other hand, in areas where thick limestone is not part of the stratigraphic succession, such as southwestern Indiana, overburden equalling or even exceeding the thickness of the limestone is removed.

At Marquette Cement Manufacturing Co.'s quarry near Superior, Ohio, as much as 90 ft of overburden, part of it bedrock, was removed to quarry an average 6 ft of limestone. The quarry was closed in 1965 (Bates, 1966).

In the 1960s, the Allegheny Minerals Corp. was mining 16 to 18 ft of limestone under 60 ft of overburden in two quarries in Pennsylvania (Herod, 1969). Moreover, the overburden consisted of 10 to 15 ft of clay and soil underlain by 12 ft of highly abrasive sandstone, 10 to 12 ft of soft shale, and 25 ft of hard shale. The hard shale and sandstone were blasted at the same time and the entire overburden stripped. In some areas the limestone is also immediately overlain by 2 ft of "ironstone" that had to be blasted separately and stripped. Even then, some clay had to be removed from solution channels in the limestone. Although the limestone was sold as portland cement raw material, bituminous concrete aggregates, road base, and aglime, clearly its market location and isolation from other sources of low-magnesium limestone must be the major factors in making the operation economical.

In Indiana about 40 or 50 ft is the maximum thickness of glacial drift that is removed consistently in any limestone quarry. In some quarries where the thickness of the drift averages less than 30 ft, more than 50 ft of drift has been removed in small areas. A few feet of rock overburden can be removed economically, especially if it is platy and weathered. Under exceptional circumstances—such as a small area of rock overburden, an exceptionally good market location, or a high-value product like dimension stone—a greater thickness of rock can be removed.

In most instances overburden is used as fill or is wasted, but sometimes it may have economic importance. Quarries that have sand and gravel overburden may use it for aggregate or other purposes (Bates, 1972; Rooney and Carr, 1971). In Indiana, one limestone aggregate quarry sells its shale overburden for cement raw material. In Ohio one cement company permits a brick company to remove and use the clay overburden from its limestone operation.

Underground Mining: The most important fact about underground mining of limestone is that it is done. In fact, 87 underground limestone mines were operating in the United States in 1979. In 1900, total production of limestone from all underground mines was 105,000 tons, or 0.37% of the total limestone production (Thoenen, 1926). In 1924, production was 5.8 million tons, or 4.5% of the total production. In 1965, it was 34.7 million tons (US Bureau of Mines, written communication, 1966), or about 6% of the total limestone production. In 1979, it was 36.1 million tons or about 4% of the total production. Many of the mines are in the midwest (Fig. 4), but their concentration reflects the abundance of high-quality limestone in horizontal beds in that part of the country as much as a concentration of population. We believe that this distribution pattern will change gradually as more mines are built to serve urban centers.

Mining Methods—Most limestone mines consist of horizontal drifts into the sides of hills (sometimes called tunnel mines) or into the walls of open-pit mines, but some consist of vertical or inclined shafts. Few limestone mines are more than 1000 ft deep, and most are only a few hundred feet deep. The deepest limestone mine known to us was the Pittsburgh Plate Glass Co.'s mine near Barberton, Ohio, in which the floor of the mined level was 2250 ft below the surface.

Most limestone mines are of the room-and-pillar type and, like salt mines, are characterized by cathedral-like dimensions. The rooms in the Mississippi Lime Co.'s tunnel mines near Ste. Genevieve, MO, are 90 ft high. The rooms in the Pittsburgh Plate Glass Co.'s mine near Barberton, Ohio, were 46 ft high. The inclined shaft that gives access to the Thomasville Stone and Lime Co.'s quarry near Thomasville, PA, is so large that a transcontinental bus can be driven down it.

Underground mining is generally more expensive than open-pit mining, but no single cost ratio applies. It is misleading to compare the relative cost of underground mining of one deposit in one part of the country with open-pit mining of another deposit in another part of the country. Some open-pit mining might prove more expensive than some underground

mining. Perhaps the best comparison is of costs of simultaneous underground and surface mining in the same formation at the same general location. We know of no published costs of this type, but one operator reported that stone mined by the room-and-pillar method, at about 400-ft depth, in a 40-ft face, and hauled out by truck via an inclined shaft cost $1.05 per ton to produce, 57% more than the $0.67 per ton for the same company to produce stone in its adjoining quarry in 1969. Conversations with other mine superintendents have led us to believe that these costs were fairly representative.

Pros and Cons of Underground Mining— Assuming then that limestone costs about 50% more to produce underground, why is it economical to do so, even in conjunction with open-pit operations? Some of the reasons are:

1) Lack of surface deposits near the market. This is probably the most important reason. If no deposits of limestone suitable for a specific purpose are found at the surface, the additional cost of underground mining must be weighed against the cost of transporting stone into the area.

In some places the lack of surface deposits may be caused by urbanization of the area near a quarry, and thus the operator is prevented from acquiring new land or even from expanding the open pit on land already owned.

2) Unfavorable geologic structure. In some areas limestone may be found at the surface near markets, yet not be suitable for quarrying. Beds that dip steeply but are not vertical can be quarried, but the development of the quarry in two directions is limited to the thickness of the beds. In such places open-pit mines must become shaft mines so that the deposit can be worked downdip.

3) Efficient utilization of reserves. Many tunnel mines are simply the extension of surface quarries into adjoining hills where the overburden is too thick to remove. Thus, when the rock that can be quarried has been exhausted, the plant need not be moved to a new location. In some places tunneling and quarrying are carried on side by side to extend the life of the quarry or for the reasons given under 5 or 6 below.

4) Lowered cost by mining more than one commodity. In some places commodities other than limestone might be mined at different levels but serviced by a single shaft. Such mining would appreciably lower costs. In northern Indiana, both limestone suitable for cement raw material or aggregate and gypsum

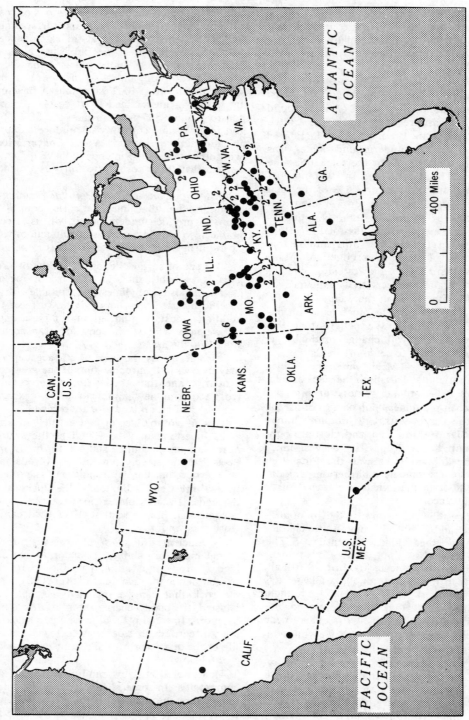

FIG. 4—Map showing locations of active underground limestone mines in the United States. The figure beside a location symbol indicates the number of mines represented by the symbol. Information supplied by the US Bureau of Mines in 1972.

could be produced by mining at different levels (Rooney and Ault, 1970).

5) Selective mining. Underground mining permits the selective removal of particular beds without removal of, or contamination by, the overlying materials or clay seams. Room-and-pillar mining of low-dipping beds also permits some horizontal selection of materials. Many underground operations in the United States selectively mine premium-grade material for chemical flux stone, portland cement raw material, or other purposes. The mines near Barberton, Ohio (now abandoned), Carntown, KY, and Riverside, CA are examples.

6) All-weather mining and uniform production. Underground mining is generally not affected by inclement weather. The operator of a shallow underground mine in Indiana reported that the temperature in the mine remains about 55° F summer and winter. The superintendent of a midwestern mine 350 ft deep reported a constant temperature of 59° F away from the air shafts. The superintendent of a mine 600 ft deep reported a temperature of 65° F. Deeper mines might be somewhat warmer, but few limestone mines are deep enough for the temperature to be above 70° F. The rock temperature in the Barberton mine, about 2250 ft deep, was 85° F, but the air was cooled to 80° by forced-air ventilation. A rule of thumb for increase in temperature with depth is 1° F for each 60 ft.

Some economies are thus possible through year-around operation. The workers have stable employment, stockpiles do not need to be large, rock does not freeze, and responses to unexpected demands of material are possible at any time. Some of the advantages of year-around operation, however, are lost in production of construction and agricultural materials because the maximum use of these materials is seasonal.

(7) Environmental problems. Underground mining is less conspicuous than open-pit mining and consumes less land. Most dust and noise are confined below ground, neighbors are not endangered by thrown rocks, and the choice of mining site depends less on surface topography and cultural features. If the roof is competent and sufficient limestone is left as pillars, say 30%, collapse of the roof causing subsidence at ground level should pose little threat. Underground mining, therefore, is favored where the surface is expensive or pre-empted, as near cities.

(8) Underground storage and waste disposal. Some operators have reported that the space created by mining can prove more profitable than the rock removed. Under some conditions the open space can be used for waste disposal or storage of gas or liquids. Mines above the water table with large rooms, solid roof, and level floor can be used for warehouses, frozen-food storage facilities, factories, office space, and fallout shelters (Dean, et al., 1969; Herod, 1972; Jewett, et al., 1967; Stearn, 1965). An abandoned mine in Indiana was even used commercially for raising poultry and one in Missouri is now used for a marina (Vineyard, 1969). Such facilities are less expensive than surface structures to build, and a constant temperature is easily maintained. Limestone mines are generally large enough to permit truck traffic and even railway spurs.

Inasmuch as most limestone is mined by the open-pit method, we feel that the disadvantages of underground mining compared with open-pit mining are well known and need to be cited only briefly:

1) A shaft mine requires a large initial investment before the first ton of rock is produced.

2) The size of equipment is controlled by the dimensions of the entrance and rooms, and less rock can be shot down at one time. Thus, an underground mine is not so adaptable to large-volume production.

3) About 30% of the reserves are left in the ground.

4) Equipment cannot be moved so easily in and out of the mine.

5) Water is more likely to be a threat, and its removal more costly. In areas of karst topography and subsurface drainage, rain storms may cause sudden flooding of the mine.

6) Safety precautions must be greater. Roof fall is a major threat.

7) Fresh air must be circulated through shaft mines.

8) State and federal regulations are more stringent for underground mines than for open-pit mines.

Only a few of the more than a hundred articles written on the underground mining of limestone are included in our bibliography. The US Bureau of Mines report on the underground mining of limestone (Thoenen, 1926) is out of date and has never been revised, but it probably remains the best single reference on this specific subject. More recently Loofbourow (1966) has written on underground mining of industrial minerals in general. The handbook by Lamar (1967) compiled for quarry operators gives a good account of the physical characteristics of limestone and dolomite deposits and their importance to open-pit mining.

Transportation

If a number of independent characteristics are essential to the value of a product, it is difficult to say which characteristic is most important. For most purposes to which limestone is put, however, location with regard to market is probably the prime variable. Cost of mining, except for thickness of overburden (discussed previously), and cost of exploration are much the same within any given region. Costs imposed by zoning restrictions are so arbitrary that it is not possible to generalize on them. Quality of stone is important; in fact, it is essential. (Dolomitic siltstone will not be used as concrete aggregate or the major cement raw material no matter how close to the market it may be.) But limestone and dolomite are so plentiful and their transportation relatively so costly that an inferior stone locally available is likely to be used rather than a superior stone shipped in by rail or barge.

Of course use is an important factor in determining how far limestone can be shipped economically. Ground white limestone used as a filler, say in putty, could probably be transported thousands of miles without adding appreciably to the cost of the finished product. High-calcium limestone used as a flux in open-hearth steel furnaces can bear transport more than 100 miles if none is available near the steel mill. Cement and lime plants are constructed generally, but not necessarily, at the raw material site.

Aggregate cannot be transported long distances economically, except under most unusual circumstances. Aggregate is carried as ballast in some ships and thus might travel thousands of miles. Limestone quarried on the fringe of a market area without limestone might bear long transportation, especially by water or rail. Limestone quarried on a waterway can be transported past producing areas that are not on a waterway but that are much closer to the market. Most limestone used as aggregate, however, is transported short distances and by truck.

In 1979, more than 80% of the crushed stone produced in the United States was transported by truck. The amount shipped by the next most important methods of transportation, rail and waterway, was about equally divided (Table 8). Trucks are generally used

TABLE 8—Crushed Stone Shipped or Used in the United States in 1979, by Methods of Transportation

Method of Transportation	Thousand St	% of Total
Truck	900,707	82
Rail	86,201	8
Waterway	62,818	6
Other	47,381	4
Total	1,097,107	100

Source: US Bureau of Mines *Minerals Yearbook*.

for transporting distances less than 50 miles, whereas rail and water are used for longer distances.

Because so many factors influence the cost of transporting stone, it is difficult to determine average costs. A study of transportation of aggregate in Indiana was made by French (1969), and his generalizations probably hold true for the rest of the United States. He found that once trucks had replaced horse-drawn wagons and most rail gondola cars, most aggregate was hauled in trucks owned by the producing companies, later in trucks owned by the drivers, and now in trucks owned mostly by large contract haulers. Because these contract haulers are required in Indiana to file their rates with the Public Service Commission, he was able to estimate trucking costs, although actual rates may depart from the published rates. French found that one hauler charged ". . . approximately 5¢ per ton-mile for the first 6 miles, 3¢ per ton-mile for the next 18 miles, and 2½¢ per ton-mile thereafter." He also found that a haul of about 30 miles in rural areas would about double the cost of crushed rock, and that a haul of only about 9 or 10 miles might be required to double the cost in urban areas.

O'Donnell and Sliger (1972) conducted a more regional study than did French and obtained information from various limestone producers. They found that truck rates ranged from 5 to 10¢ per ton-mile for 10-mile shipments and 2 to 5¢ per ton-mile for hauls of 100 miles. In recent years, transportation costs have risen rapidly because of fuel prices. These costs vary so much, month by month and area by area, that average figures have little value. Nevertheless as a point of reference, in 1980 a trucking firm in a rural area of southern Indiana reported a price to ship aggregate of 15¢ per ton-mile for the first 10 miles and 5¢ per ton-mile for each additional mile. Costs in urban areas are generally higher.

Cost of transportation by rail is more difficult to determine. Because of the cost of loading and unloading, most stone shipped by rail is shipped long distances, and the rail cars are likely to be switched from one line to another, a practice which results in additional costs. But if a quarry is on a railway line and stone is shipped directly to the market on that one line, the only additional cost is the rehandling at the market end. In addition, if a large amount of stone is shipped, say on a unit train, the cost can be low. If the stone is shipped in cars owned by the aggregate company, the cost may be even lower. French (1969) found that the average charge for rail transport of aggregate in southern Indiana was 0.61¢ per ton-mile with a 99¢-per-ton minimum, but in northern Indiana the charge was an average 0.92¢ per ton-mile with a $1.84-per-ton minimum. These rates are similar to those rates published by the Interstate Commerce Commission in its 1% sampling of terminations in 1966 (Fig. 5).

Water transportation of crushed stone is the cheapest method, although for distances less than 300 miles railroads may be competitive (Fig. 5). Barging, which in 1965 accounted for 7.2% of the nation's freight movement exclusive of the Great Lakes (Fulkerson, 1969)

is expected to increase in the future. Limestone shipments on the Great Lakes, which in 1966 ranked in tonnage only behind iron ore and bituminous coal, are expected to about double by 1995 (Aase, 1970). Fulkerson (1969) reported that the average revenue per ton-mile for carriers on the Mississippi River and its tributaries was 0.328¢. French (1969) reported one rate for transporting aggregate on the Ohio River to be 0.4 to 0.65¢ per ton-mile for minimum barge loads of 1200 tons (plus 50¢ to $1 per ton for loading and $1 to $2 per ton for unloading).

US Production

The best source for statistics on limestone and dolomite production is the US Bureau of Mines *Minerals Yearbook*, which is published annually. The *Yearbook's* chapter on "Stone" gives national and state production figures for limestone, dolomite, marble, shell, and calcareous marl, as well as the amount and value of limestone and dolomite produced for different uses. The chapters on the mineral industry of the various states give data on

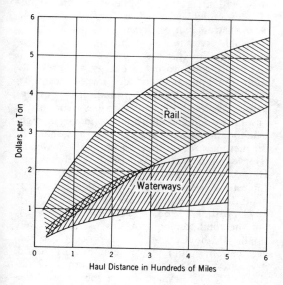

FIG. 5—*Graph showing range in rail and waterway transportation rates for shipments of crushed stone in the United States. Rail data from the Interstate Commerce Commission,* Carload Waybill Statistics, *1966 (1968). Waterway data from O'Donnell and Sliger (1972).*

TABLE 9—Crushed and Broken Limestone and Dolomite Shipped or Used by Producers in the States That Account for About 90% of the Total United States Production in 1979

State	Quantity, 1000 St
1. Texas	70,661
2. Florida	63,609
3. Illinois	63,551
4. Pennsylvania	56,122
5. Missouri	54,246
6. Ohio	49,703
7. Tennessee	45,714
8. Michigan	39,721
9. Kentucky	39,298
10. Indiana	34,121
11. New York	32,578
12. Iowa	32,471
13. Oklahoma	27,649
14. Alabama	24,597
15. Virginia	22,689
16. Wisconsin	20,625
17. California	19,156
18. Kansas	18,853
19. Maryland	13,889
20. West Virginia	10,684
Total	739,937
Others	72,117
Total US	812,054

Source: US Bureau of Mines *Minerals Yearbook*.

production and uses of the rock in those individual states.

In 1979, twenty states accounted for about 90% of the total United States production of crushed limestone and dolomite (Table 9); seven states accounted for about 90% of the total United States production of dimension stone (Table 10); and one state, Louisiana, accounted for 71% of the total United States production of shell (Singleton, 1980). Nine states produced most of the calcareous marl (Table 11).

Between 1950 and 1979, the total production of carbonate rock in the United States increased a total of 357% (Table 12). In 1979, the tonnage of carbonate rock produced exceeded that of any other single mineral commodity except sand and gravel.

Future Trends

According to the US Bureau of Mines (Singleton, 1980) the demand for dimension stone in the year 2000 will probably be between 1,000,000 and 2,500,000 st corresponding to an average annual growth rate of 1.4%; the demand for crushed stone in the year 2000 will probably be between 1,200,000,000 and 2,400,000,000 st corresponding to an average annual growth rate of 2.2%. The actual demand for limestone and dolomite—the nation's chief raw materials for dimension stone and crushed stone—could differ greatly from the predicted demand because of changes in population growth and in the gross national product.

These predictions take into consideration long-range economic forecasts and various

TABLE 11—Calcareous Marl Shipped or Used by Producers in the United States in 1979, by States

State	Quantity, 1000 St	Value $ 1000
1. North Carolina	260	957
2. Michigan	23	50
3. Indiana	13	19
Other States Florida, Maine, Mississippi, South Carolina, Texas, Virginia	2,354	3,507
Total	2,650	4,533

Source: US Bureau of Mines *Minerals Yearbook.*

contingencies such as technologic changes, competition from alternate raw materials, increasing labor costs, and new construction methods. But who can say how great these changes will be? As the frame house disappears from the construction scene, will concrete dwellings as well as mobile homes largely replace it? Will concrete poles replace the millions of wooden utility poles across the nation? As buildings and streets are demolished in the cities, will the aggregate be recycled? How will mass transit systems affect the demand for highway construction materials? No clear answers can be given.

Social pressures to clean up the environment and the imminent conversion from oil and gas to other forms of energy will probably affect the limestone and dolomite industry in ways that cannot now be predicted. For example, removal of sulfur oxides from stack gases may demand enormous tonnages of high-calcium limestone as either the absorbant or regenerant for other absorbant materials (Harvey and Steinmetz, 1971; Drehmel and Harvey, 1974; Harvey, et al., 1974, 1976). Limestone and dolomite are being used to neutralize acid mine waters (Ford, 1974; Hill, 1974; Mihok, 1968, 1970; Wilmoth, 1973), but the total tonnage for this use is relatively small. If the CO_2 Acceptor process for coal gasification should prove economically sound, it would create a new use for dolomite (Goodridge, 1973). Perhaps far in the future limestone may be used as raw material to produce hydrocarbon fuels and protein food supplements (Salotti, et al., 1970).

Whatever the new uses of limestone and dolomite, high purity deposits must be conserved through improved mineral extraction

TABLE 10—Dimension Limestone and Dolomite Shipped or Used by Producers in the States That Account for About 90% of the Total United States Production in 1979

State	Quantity, St
1. Indiana	337,502
2. Wisconsin	47,757
3. Iowa	10,197
4. Minnesota	9,832
5. Alabama	7,880
6. California	5,443
7. Texas	5,201
Total	423,812
Others	45,851
Total US	469,663

Source: US Bureau of Mines *Minerals Yearbook.*

TABLE 12—Carbonate Rock Shipped or Used by Producers in the United States, 1950 to 1979

Year	Crushed and Broken Limestone and Dolomite, St	Crushed and Broken Marble, St	Crushed and Broken Shell, St	Crushed and Broken Marl, St	Dimension Limestone and Dolomite, St	Dimension Marble, St	Total, St
1950	180,111,000	178,000	*	*	807,590	89,290	181,185,880
1951	204,673,000	169,000	*	*	806,842	87,191	205,736,033
1952	216,469,000	149,000	*	*	786,757	89,051	217,493,808
1953	223,915,000	378,000	*	*	798,911	76,255	225,168,166
1954	323,800,000	454,000	11,428,000	*	1,174,389	84,626	336,941,015
1955	362,196,000	976,000	15,130,000	*	1,182,459	116,029	379,600,488
1956	379,342,000	842,000	19,852,000	*	1,028,759	105,431	401,170,190
1957	384,295,000	1,274,000	18,510,000	1,917,000	1,131,376	149,000	407,276,376
1958	390,468,000	1,269,000	18,916,000	1,803,000	979,000	136,000	413,571,000
1959	433,003,000	1,758,000	20,180,000	2,043,000	952,000	137,000	458,073,000
1960	450,393,000	1,515,000	18,934,000	1,283,000	860,000	129,000	473,114,000
1961	437,398,000	1,435,000	20,973,000	1,099,000	855,000	157,000	461,917,000
1962	460,953,000	1,623,000	20,054,000	1,182,000	896,000	146,000	484,854,000
1963	488,348,000	1,752,000	19,019,000	1,164,000	895,000	150,000	511,328,000
1964	510,247,000	1,963,000	19,493,000	1,043,000	779,000	130,000	533,655,000
1965	554,034,000	2,046,000	21,560,000	1,291,000	732,000	126,000	579,789,000
1966	568,849,000	2,161,000	21,662,000	1,358,000	728,000	83,000	594,841,000
1967	568,902,000	2,158,000	22,026,000	1,227,000	561,000	74,000	594,948,000
1968	603,136,000	2,470,000	20,268,000	1,211,000	602,000	89,000	627,776,000
1969	628,362,000	2,271,000	19,731,000	2,490,000	574,000	77,000	653,505,000
1970	625,313,000	1,722,000	21,713,000	1,739,000	482,000	63,000	651,032,000
1971	628,035,000	1,641,000	18,537,000	3,459,000	468,000	75,000	652,215,000
1972	671,496,000	2,247,000	16,610,000	2,650,000	411,000	71,000	693,485,000
1973	774,397,000	2,023,000	19,896,000	2,327,000	370,000	48,000	799,061,000
1974	751,515,000	1,679,000	18,235,000	3,889,000	517,000	73,000	775,908,000
1975	664,820,000	1,461,000	15,453,000	3,504,000	420,000	50,000	685,708,000
1976	662,880,000	1,456,000	13,753,000	3,371,000	414,000	56,000	681,930,000
1977	706,521,000	1,540,000	13,492,000	2,517,000	443,000	97,000	724,610,000
1978	785,734,000	1,417,000	12,436,000	2,585,000	370,000	115,000	802,657,000
1979	812,054,000	1,461,000	12,177,000	2,650,000	470,000	80,000	828,892,000

Source: US Bureau of Mines *Minerals Yearbook.*
* Included with crushed and broken limestone and dolomite.

and processing techniques. Selective quarrying of specific lithologies is not new but neither is it widely practiced. The custom of "drill the blasthole to the bottom and shoot" should be replaced by benching based on composition of different strata. The use of selective recovery, such as described by Ames (1966) for portland cement raw materials, applies equally well to limestones for other uses and may allow a deposit of marginal quality to be utilized. High-purity deposits are uncommon and should not be wasted for uses not demanding such material. For example, impure limestone with a low-magnesium content can be used to manufacture portland cement. Thus some current practice of using high-calcium limestone and then adding clay, sand, and other materials to it in processing is comparable to flaring gas in an oil field. It may be desirable from the standpoint of present-day technology, but it is a waste of a valuable resource.

If future demands for limestone and dolomite are to be met at somewhat near the low costs that have prevailed, people must compromise their life styles. The desirability of sprawling urban areas and mini-farms, which cover potentially valuable deposits, will have to be placed in perspective against the need for building and construction materials. Underground mining must gain favor as a means of providing minerals while still allowing the land surface to be used for man's activities (Baxter, 1980; Carr and Ault, 1980). City and county planning must take into account the nature of mineral resources: economic deposits are rare, they are essential, and they should be produced before the land is urbanized.

Bibliography and References

1. Aase, J.H., 1970, "Transportation of Iron Ore, Limestone, and Bituminous Coal on the Great Lakes Waterway System, With Projections to 1995," Information Circular 8461, US Bureau of Mines, 61 pp.
2. Adair, R.B., et al., 1947, "Evaluation of North Carolina Raw Materials for the Production of Portland Cement, Part 1, Preliminary Laboratory Investigation," Bulletin 35, North Carolina State College, Dept. Eng. Research, 31 pp.
3. Alabama Geological Survey, see Publications List of County Reports and Maps.
4. Allen, H.W., 1953, "Progress Report of Limestone Survey, Knox County," Report of the State Geologist for 1951–1952, Maine Development Commission, pp. 11–30.
5. Allen, J.E., 1946, "Reconnaissance Geology of Limestone Deposits in the Williamette Valley, Oregon," Short Paper 15, Oregon Dept. of Geology and Mineral Industries, 15 pp.
6. Ames, J.A., 1966, "Limestone Deposits Vs. Beneficiation," Ohio Journal of Science, Vol. 66, No. 2, pp. 131–136.
7. Amsden, T.W., 1954, "Geology of Garrett County," Geology and Water Resources of Garrett County, Bulletin 13, Maryland Dept. of Geology, Mines and Water Resources, pp. 1–95.
8. Amsden, T.W., and Rowland, T.L., 1965, "Silurian Stratigraphy of Northeastern Oklahoma," Bulletin 105, Oklahoma Geological Survey, 174 pp.
9. Anderson, K.H., et al., 1979, "Geologic Map of Missouri," Scale: 1 in. = 8 miles, Missouri Geological Survey and Water Resources.
10. Anderson, S.B., and Haraldson, H.C., 1969, "Cement Rock Possibilities in Paleozoic Rocks of Eastern North Dakota," Report of Investigation 48, North Dakota Geological Survey, 62 pp.
11. Angino, E.E., and Billings, G.K., 1967, Atomic Absorption Spectrometry in Geology, Elsevier, New York, 144 pp.
12. Apfel, E.T., 1944, "Dolomite Marble in the Vicinity of Lee, Massachusetts, as an Available Source of Metallic Magnesium," Open File Report, US Geological Survey, 34 pp.
13. Argall, G.O., Jr., 1949, "Dolomite," in "Industrial Minerals of Colorado," Colorado School Mines Quarterly, Vol. 44, No. 2, pp. 144–149.
14. Argall, G.O., Jr., 1949, "Limestone," in "Industrial Minerals of Colorado," Colorado School of Mines Quarterly, Vol. 44, No. 2, pp. 254–274.
15. Atchison, T.C., et al., 1964, "Effect of Decoupling on Explosion-Generated Strain Pulses in Rock," Report of Investigations 6333, US Bureau of Mines, 49 pp.
16. Atchison, T.C., and Pugliese, J.M., 1964, "Comparative Studies of Explosives in Limestone," Report of Investigations 6395, US Bureau of Mines, 25 pp.
17. Azároff, L.V., and Buerger, M.J., 1958, The Powder Method in X-Ray Crystallography, McGraw-Hill, New York, 342 pp.
18. Baars, D.L., 1963, "Petrology of Carbonate Rocks," Shelf Carbonates of the Paradox Basin, Four Corners Geological Society 4th Field Conference, pp. 101–129.
19. Baird, G.C., 1979, "Sedimentary Relationships of Portland Point and Associated Middle Devonian Rocks in Central and Western New York," New York State Museum & Science Service Bulletin 433, 24 pp.
20. Bannatyne, B.B., 1975, "High-Calcium Limestone Deposits of Manitoba," Man. Mines Br., Pub. 75–1, Manitoba Mines Branch, 103 pp.
21. Barnes, V.E., and Bell, W.C., 1977, "The Moore Hollow Group of Central Texas," Report of Investigations 88, Bureau of Economic Geology, University of Texas, Austin, 169 pp.
22. Bartlett, C.S., Jr., and Biggs, T.H., 1980,

"Geology of the Abingdon, Wyndale, Holston Valley and Shady Valley Quadrangles, Virginia," Publication 16, Virginia Division of Mineral Resources, 39 pp.

23. Bassler, R.S., 1905, "Cement Materials of the Valley of Virginia," Bulletin 260, US Geological Survey, pp. 531–544.

24. Bates, R.L., 1966, "Geology of Cement Raw Materials in Ohio: A Summary," *Proceedings of 2nd Forum on Geology Industrial Minerals,* Indiana Univ., Indiana Geological Survey, pp. 23–29.

25. Bates, R.L., 1972, "Limestone Quarry in a Gravel Pit," *Proceedings Eighth Forum on Geology of Industrial Minerals,* Pub. Info. Series 5, Iowa Geological Survey, pp. 5–10.

26. Baxter, J.W., 1980, "Factors Favoring Expanded Underground Mining of Limestone in Illinois," *Mining Engineering,* Vol. 32, No. 4, pp. 1497–1504.

27. Baxter, J.W., and Harvey, R.D., 1969, "Alumina Content of Carbonate Rocks as an Index to Sodium Sulfate Soundness," Industrial Minerals Notes 39, Illinois Geological Survey, pp. 5–10.

28. Beach, J.O., and English, S.G., 1940, "Dolomite and Magnesium Limestone," Mineral Report 6, Oklahoma Geological Survey, 19 pp.

29. Beatly, K.O., and Adair, R.B., 1948, "Evaluation of North Carolina Raw Materials for the Production of Portland Cement, Part 2, Small-Scale Production of Portland Cement," Bulletin 42, North Carolina State College Engineering School, 51 pp.

30. Bellis, W.H., and Rowland, T.L., 1976, "Shale and Carbonate-Rock Resources of Osage County, Oklahoma," Circular 76, Oklahoma Geological Survey, 50 pp.

31. Bennett, W.A.G., 1944, "Dolomite Resources of Washington, Part 1," Report of Investigations 13, Washington Div. of Mines and Geology, 35 pp.

32. Berry, E.W., 1947, "Marls and Limestones of Eastern North Carolina," Bulletin 54, North Carolina Div. of Mineral Resources, 16 pp.

33. Bicker, A.R., Jr., 1970, "Economic Minerals of Mississippi," Bulletin 112, Mississippi Geological Survey, 80 pp.

34. Bicker, A.R., Jr., and May, J.H., 1976, "Agricultural Lime in Central Mississippi," Information Series MGS–77–1, Mississippi Geological Survey, 55 pp.

35. Bingham, C., 1916, *The Manufacture of Carbide of Calcium,* Raggett & Co., London, 219 pp.

36. Birch, F., et al., 1942 (reprinted 1950), "Handbook of Physical Constants," Special Paper 36, Geological Society of America, 325 pp.

37. Bissell, H.J., and Chilingar, G.V., 1967, "Classification of Sedimentary Carbonate Rocks," *Developments in Sedimentology, Carbonate Rocks,* Vol. 9A, G.V. Chilingar, H.J. Bissell, R.W. Fairbridge, eds., Elsevier, New York, pp. 87–168.

38. Blair, B.E., 1955, "Physical Properties of Mine Rock, Part III," Report of Investiga-

tions 5130, US Bureau of Mines, 69 pp.

39. Blair, B.E., 1956, "Physical Properties of Mine Rock, Part IV," Report of Investigations 5244, US Bureau of Mines, 69 pp.

40. Bowen, O.E., Jr., 1957, "Limestone, Dolomite, and Lime Products," *Mineral Commodities of California,* Bulletin 176, California Div. of Mines and Geology, pp. 293–306.

41. Bowen, O.E., Jr., 1966, "Limestone, Dolomite, and Lime Products," *Mineral Resources of California,* Bulletin 191, California Div. of Mines and Geology, pp. 221–233.

42. Bowen, O.E., et al., 1973, "The Mineral Economics of the Carbonate Rocks," *Limestone and Dolomite Resources of California,* O.E. Bowen, ed., Bulletin 194, California Div. of Mines and Geology, 60 pp.

43. Bowles, O., 1956, "Limestone and Dolomite," Information Circular 7738, US Bureau of Mines, 29 pp.

44. Bowles, O., and Jensen, M.S., 1941, "Limestone and Dolomite in the Chemical Processing Industries," Information Circular 7169, US Bureau of Mines, 15 pp.

45. Bowles, O., and Jensen, M.S., 1947, "Industrial Uses of Limestone and Dolomite," Information Circular 7402, US Bureau of Mines, 19 pp.

46. Branner, G.C., 1941, "Limestones of Northern Arkansas," Miscellaneous Publication, Arkansas Geological Commission, 24 pp.

47. Brantley, J.E., 1916, "Limestones and Marls of the Coastal Plain of Georgia," Bulletin 21, Georgia Geological Survey, 300 pp.

48. Buckley, E.R., 1898, "On the Building and Ornamental Stones of Wisconsin," Bulletin 4, Wisconsin Geological Survey, 544 pp.

49. Buckley, E.R., and Buehler, H.A., 1904, "The Quarrying Industry of Missouri," Missouri Geological Survey, Vol. 2, Series 2, 371 pp.

50. Buehler, H.A., 1907, "The Lime and Cement Resources of Missouri," Missouri Geological Survey, Vol. 6, Series 2, 255 pp.

51. Bullock, K.C., 1966, "Minerals of Utah," Bulletin 76, Utah Geological and Mineral Survey, 237 pp.

52. Bur, T.R., et al., 1969, "An Ultrasonic Method for Determining The Elastic Symmetry of Materials," Report of Investigations 7333, US Bureau of Mines, 23 pp.

53. Burchard, E.F., and Chapin, T., 1920, "Marble Resources of Southeastern Alaska," Bulletin 682, US Geological Survey, 118 pp.

54. Burchett, R.R., 1980, "Mineral Resource Map of Nebraska," Scale, 1:1,000,000, Nebraska Geological Survey.

55. Burr, A.C., et al., 1950, "Raw Materials for the Manufacture of Portland Cement in North Dakota," *1949 Proceedings,* North Dakota Academy of Science, Vol. 3, pp. 15–18.

56. Butler, J., and Bartlette, G., 1969, "Bibliography of the Geology of Newfoundland

and Labrador, 1814 through 1968," Bulletin 38, Newfoundland and Labrador Mineral Resources Div., 273 pp.

57. Calver, J.L., 1957, "Mining and Mineral Resources," Bulletin 39, Florida Geological Survey, 132 pp.

58. Carlson, C.G., 1964, "The Niobrara Formation of Eastern North Dakota; Its Possibilities for Use as a Cement Rock," Report of Investigation 41, North Dakota Geological Survey, 56 pp.

59. Carozzi, A.V., 1960, *Microscopic Sedimentary Petrography,* John Wiley, New York, 485 pp.

60. Carr, D.D., 1973, "Geometry and Origin of Oolite Bodies in the Ste. Genevieve Limestone (Mississippian) in the Illinois Basin," Bulletin 48, Indiana Geological Survey, 81 pp.

61. Carr, D.D., and Ault, C.H., 1980, "Potential for Deep Underground Limestone Mining in Indiana," Preprint 80–334, SME-AIME Fall Meeting, Minneapolis, Oct., 11 pp.

62. Carr, D.D., et al., 1970, "Relationships Between Physical and Chemical Properties of the Brassfield Limestone (Silurian) in Indiana, Ohio, and Kentucky," *Proceedings, 6th Forum on Geology of Industrial Minerals,* Miscellany 1, Michigan Geological Survey, pp. 127–137.

63. Carr, D.D., et al., 1971, "Crushed Stone Aggregate Resources of Indiana," Bulletin 42-H, Indiana Geological Survey, 38 pp.

64. Carr, D.D., et al., 1978, "Crushed Stone Resources of the Blue River Group (Mississippian) in Indiana," Bulletin 52, Indiana Geological Survey, 225 pp.

65. Caterpillar Tractor Co., 1972, "Handbook of Ripping, A Guide to Greater Profits," 4th ed., Caterpillar Tractor Co., Peoria, IL, 44 pp.

66. Chelini, J.M., 1965, "Limestone, Dolomite, and Travertine in Montana," Bulletin 44, Montana Bureau of Mines and Geology, 53 pp.

67. Chute, N.E., 1967, "Structural and Mineralogical Features of the Stockbridge Marble and Berkshire Schist Near Adams, Massachusetts," *Economic Geology in Massachusetts,* O.C. Farquhar, ed., Univ. of Massachusetts Graduate School, Amherst, pp. 169–180.

68. Clarke, F.W., 1924, "The Data of Geochemistry," Bulletin 770, US Geological Survey, 841 pp.

69. Cloud, P.E., Jr., and Barnes, V.E., 1946, "The Ellenburger Group of Central Texas," Publication 4621, University of Texas, Austin, 473 pp.

70. Colby, S.F., 1941, "Occurrences and Uses of Dolomite in the United States," Information Circular 7192, US Bureau of Mines, 21 pp.

71. Colquourn, D.J., and Duncan, D., 1966, "Geology of the Eutawville Quadrangle, South Carolina," MS-12, Map with Text, South Carolina Div. of Geology.

72. Comstock, H.B., 1963, "Magnesium and Magnesium Compounds," Information Circular 8201, US Bureau of Mines, 128 pp.

73. Condra, G.E., and Reed, E.C., 1959, "The Geological Section of Nebraska," Bulletin 14A, Nebraska Geological Survey, 82 pp.

74. Connecticut Geological and Natural History Survey, see Publications List of Geologic Quadrangle Maps and Quadrangle Reports.

75. Conrad, S.G., 1960, "Crystalline Limestones of the Piedmont and Mountain Regions of North Carolina," Bulletin 74, North Carolina Div. of Mineral Resources, 56 pp.

76. Cooper, B.N., 1944, "Industrial Limestones and Dolomites in Virginia: New River-Roanoke River District," Bulletin 62, Virginia Div. of Mineral Resources, 98 pp.

77. Cooper, B.N., 1945, "Industrial Limestones and Dolomites in Virginia: Clinch Valley District," Bulletin 66, Virginia Div. of Mineral Resources, 259 pp.

78. Cooper, J.D., 1970, "Stone," *Mineral Facts and Problems,* Bulletin 650, US Bureau of Mines, pp. 1219–1235.

79. Cullity, B.D., 1956, *Elements of X-Ray Diffraction,* Addison-Wesley, Reading, MA, 514 pp.

80. Curry, R.L., and Buck, A.D., 1966, "Development of Methods of Testing Aggregates Larger than 1½ Inch," Technical Report 6–747, US Army Engineer Waterways Experiment Station, 44 pp.

81. Czehura, S.J., and Berg, R.B., 1977, "Index of Graduate Theses on Montana Geology," Special Publication 77, Montana Bureau of Mines and Geology, 104 pp.

82. Dale, T.N., 1914, "The Commercial Marbles of Western Vermont," Report of the State Geologist on the Mineral Industries and Geology of Vermont, 1913–1914, Vermont Geological Survey, pp. 1–160.

83. Dale, T.N., 1914, "The Calcite Marble and Dolomite of Eastern Vermont," Report of the State Geologist on the Mineral Industries and Geology of Vermont, 1913–1914, Vermont Geological Survey, pp. 224–276.

84. D'Andrea, D.V., et al., 1964, "Prediction of Compressive Strength from Other Rock Properties," *Colorado School Mines Quarterly,* Vol. 59, No. 4B, pp. 623–640.

85. D'Andrea, D.V., et al., 1965, "Prediction of Compressive Strength from Other Rock Properties," Report of Investigations 6702, US Bureau of Mines, 23 pp.

86. Danner, W.R., 1966, "Limestone Resources of Western Washington," Bulletin 52, Washington Div. of Mines and Geology, 474 pp.

87. Danner, W.R., 1976, "Limestone Resources of Southwestern British Columbia," *Proceedings, 11th Forum on Geology of Industrial Minerals,* Special Publication 74, Montana Bureau of Mines and Geology, pp. 171–186.

88. Davis, R.E., 1957, "Magnesium Resources of the United States—A Geologic Summary and Annotated Bibliography to 1953," Bulletin 1019-E, US Geological Survey, pp. 373–515.

89. Dean, T.J., et al., 1969, "Underground Mining in the Kansas City Area," *Missouri*

Mineral Industry News, Vol. 9, Apr., Missouri Geological Survey, pp. 37–56.

90. Deasy, G., et al., 1967, "Supplement, Limestones and Dolomites of Pennsylvania," *Atlas of Pennsylvania's Mineral Resource, Pt. 1,* Mineral Resource Report M 50, Pennsylvania Geological Survey, 83 pp.

91. Degrace, J.R., 1974, "Limestone Resources of Newfoundland and Labrador," Report 74–2, Newfoundland Department Mines Energy, 117 pp.

92. Dever, G.R., Jr., 1973, "Stratigraphic Relationships in the Lower and Middle Newman Limestone (Mississippian), East-Central and Northeastern Kentucky," M.S. Thesis, University of Kentucky, Lexington, 121 pp; 1980, Thesis Series 1, Ser. 11, Kentucky Geological Survey, 49 pp.

93. Dever, G.R., Jr., 1974, "High-Carbonate Rock in the High Bridge Group (Middle Ordovician), Boone County, Kentucky," Information Circular 22, Ser. 10, Kentucky Geological Survey, 35 pp.

94. Dever, G.R., Jr., and McGrain, P., 1969, "High-Calcium and Low-Magnesium Limestone Resources in the Region of the Lower Cumberland, Tennessee, and Ohio Valleys, Western Kentucky," Bulletin 5, Ser. 10, Kentucky Geological Survey, 192 pp.

95. Dever, G.R., Jr., et al., 1978, "Industrial Limestone Resources along the Ohio River Valley of Kentucky," *Mining Engineering,* Vol. 30, No. 4, pp. 396–401.

96. Dick, R.A., et al., 1973, "A Study of Fragmentation from Bench Blasting in Limestone at a Reduced Scale," Report of Investigations 7704, US Bureau of Mines, 24 pp.

97. Dickson, J.A.D., 1965, "A Modified Staining Technique for Carbonates in Thin Section," *Nature,* No. 4971, Feb. 6, pp. 587.

98. Dickson, J.A.D., 1966, "Carbonate Identification and Genesis as Revealed by Staining," *Journal of Sedimentary Petrology,* Vol. 36, pp. 491–505.

99. Diehl, H., 1964, "Calcein, Calmagite, and o,o'-Dihydroxyazobenzene Titrimetric, Colorimetric and Fluorometric Reagents for Calcium and Magnesium," G. Frederick Smith Chemical Co., Columbus, Ohio, 124 pp.

100. Dorheim, F.H., 1970, "Mineral Resources of Iowa," Map with Text, Iowa Geological Survey.

101. Drehmel, D.C., and Harvey, R.D., 1974, "Carbonate Rock Properties Required by Desulfurization Processes," *Proceedings, 10th Forum on Geology of Industrial Minerals,* Miscellaneous Report 1, Ohio Geological Survey, pp. 59–66.

102. Dunham, R.J., 1962, "Classification of Carbonate Rocks According to Depositional Texture," *Classification of Carbonate Rocks,* W.E. Hamm, ed., American Association of Petroleum Geologists, Mem. 1, pp. 108–121.

103. Dunn, J.R., and Ozol, M.A., 1962, "Deleterious Properties of Chert," *Physical Research Report No. 12,* New York Dept. of Public Works, 121 pp.

104. Edmundson, R.S., 1945, "Industrial Limestones and Dolomites in Virginia: Northern and Central Parts of Shenandoah Valley," Bulletin 65, Virginia Div. of Mineral Resources, 195 pp.

105. Edmundson, R.S., 1958, "Industrial Limestones and Dolomites in Virginia: James River District West of the Blue Ridge," Bulletin 73, Virginia Div. of Mineral Resources, 137 pp.

106. Eifler, G.K., Jr., 1968, "Industrial Carbonates of the Texas Gulf Coastal Plain," *Proceedings, 4th Forum on Geology of Industrial Minerals,* Texas Bureau of Economic Geology, pp. 45–56.

107. Eilertsen, N.A., 1964, "Mining Methods and Costs, Kimballton Limestone Mine, Standard Lime, and Cement Co., Gile County, Va.," Information Circular 8214, US Bureau of Mines, 50 pp.

108. Emmons, W.H., and Grout, F.F., 1943, "Mineral Resources of Minnesota," Bulletin 30, Minnesota Geological Survey, 149 pp.

109. English, S.G., et al., 1940, "Limestone Analyses," Mineral Report 5, Oklahoma Geological Survey, 28 pp.

110. Erwin, R.B., 1957, "The Geology of the Limestone of Isle LaMotte and South Hero Island, Vermont," Bulletin 9, Vermont Geological Survey, 94 pp.

111. Evans, T.B., and Eilertsen, N.A., 1957, "Mining Methods and Costs at the Sunbright Limestone Mine, Foote Mineral Co., Sunbright, Virginia," Information Circular 7793, US Bureau of Mines, 44 pp.

112. Farquhar, O.C., 1967, "Drill Records of stone and Basalt in Western Massachusetts," *Economic Geology in Massachusetts,* O.C. Farquhar, ed., Univ. of Massachusetts Graduate School, Amherst, pp. 75–82.

113. Folk, R.L., 1959, "Practical Petrographic Classification of Limestones," *Bulletin,* American Association of Petroleum Geologists, Vol. 43, pp. 1–38.

114. Folk, R.L., 1962, "Spectral Subdivision of Limestone Types," *Classification of Carbonate Rocks,* W.E. Hamm, ed., American Association of Petroleum Geologists, Mem. 1, pp. 62–84.

115. Folk, R.L., and Weaver, C.E., 1952, "A Study of the Texture and Composition of Chert," *American Journal of Science,* Vol. 250, pp. 498–510.

116. Ford, C.T., 1974, "Selection of Limestones as Neutralizing Agents for Coal-Mine Water," *Proceedings, 10th Forum on Geology of Industrial Minerals,* Miscellaneous Report 1, Ohio Geological Survey, pp. 30–42.

117. Fowler, P., 1950, "Stratigraphy and Structure of the Castleton Area, Vermont," Bulletin 2, Vermont Geological Survey, 83 pp.

118. French, R.R., 1967, "Crushed Stone Resources of the Devonian and Silurian Carbonate Rocks of Indiana," Bulletin 37, Indiana Geological Survey, 127 pp.

119. French, R.R., 1969, "Transportation of Mineral Aggregates in Indiana," *Proceedings for 1968,* Indiana Academy of Science, Vol. 78, pp. 348–354.

120. Friedman, G.M., 1959, "Identification of Carbonate Minerals by Staining Methods," *Journal of Sedimentary Petrology*, Vol. 29, pp. 87–97.

121. Friedman, G.M., and Sanders, J.E., 1967, "Origin and Occurrence of Dolostones," *Developments in Sedimentology, Carbonate Rocks*, Vol. 9A, G.V. Chilingar, H.J. Bissell, R.W. Fairbridge, eds., Elsevier, New York, pp. 267–348.

122. Fulkerson, F.B., 1969, "Transportation of Mineral Commodities on the Inland Waterways of the South-Central States," Information Circular 8431, US Bureau of Mines, 88 pp.

123. Fuzesy, L.M., 1980, "Geology of the Deadwood (Cambrian), Meadow Lake and Winnepegosis (Devonian) Formations in West-Central Saskatchewan," Department Mineral Resources Report 210, Saskatchewan Geological Survey, 64 pp.

124. Galle, O.K., 1967, "The Geochemistry of the Oread Limestone," *Proceedings 3rd Forum on Geology of Industrial Minerals*, Special Distribution Publication 34, Kansas Geological Survey, pp. 97–109.

125. Galle, O.K., and Angino, E.E., 1967, "Determination of Calcium and Magnesium in Carbonate and Silicate Rocks by Atomic Absorption," Bulletin 187, Pt. 1, Kansas Geological Survey, pp. 9–11.

126. Garner, L.E., et al. (compilers), 1979, "The Mineral Resources of Texas," Map, Scale, 1:1,000,000, Bureau of Economic Geology, University of Texas, Austin.

127. Gazdik, G.C., and Tagg, K.M., 1957, "Annotated Bibliography of High-Calcium Limestone Deposits in the United States Including Alaska, to April 1956," Bulletin 1019-I, US Geological Survey, pp. 675–713.

128. Gillson, J.L., et al., 1960, "The Carbonate Rocks," *Industrial Minerals and Rocks*, 3rd ed., J.L. Gillson, ed., AIME, New York, 1960, pp. 123–201.

129. Ginsburg, R.N., et al., 1963, "Shallow-Water Carbonate Sediments," *The Sea*, Vol. 3, John Wiley, New York, pp. 554–582.

130. Goddard, E.N., et al., 1963, *Rock-Color Chart*, Geological Society of America, 16 pp.

131. Goodridge, E., 1973, "Status Report: the AGA/OCR Coal Gasification Program," *Coal Age*, Vol. 78, No. 1, pp. 54–59.

132. Goodwin, J.H., 1979, "A Guide to Selecting Agricultural Limestone Products," Illinois Mineral Note 73, Illinois Geological Survey, 7 pp.

133. Gotts, R.J., 1966, "The Cadomin Limestone Quarry," *Eighth Field-Trip Guidebook*, Edmonton Geological Society, pp. 17–18.

134. Gotts, R.J., 1980, "Minerals," *Industry and Resources 1980*, Alberta Department Economic Development, Edmonton, pp. 49–57.

135. Goudge, M.F., 1933, "Canadian Limestones for Building Purposes," Report 733, Canadian Bureau of Mines, 196 pp.

136. Goudge, M.F., 1934, "Limestones of Canada, Their Occurrence and Characteristics; Part 2, Maritime Provinces," Report 742, Canadian Bureau of Mines, 186 pp.

137. Goudge, M.F., 1935, "Limestones of Canada, Their Occurrence and Characteristics; Part 3, Quebec," Report 755, Canadian Bureau of Mines, 274 pp.

138. Goudge, M.F., 1937, "Limestone and Lime—Their Industrial Uses," *Mining and Metallurgy*, Vol. 18, No. 368, pp. 371–374.

139. Goudge, M.F., 1938, "Limestones of Canada, Their Occurrence and Characteristics; Part 4, Ontario," Report 781, Canadian Bureau of Mines, 362 pp.

140. Goudge, M.F., 1944, "Limestones of Canada, Their Occurrence and Characteristics; Part 5, Western Canada," Report 811, Canada Bureau of Mines, 233 pp.

141. Graf, D.L., 1960a, "Geochemistry of Carbonate Sediments and Sedimentary Carbonate Rocks, Part I, Carbonate Mineralogy, Carbonate Sediments," Circular 297, Illinois Geological Survey, 39 pp.

142. Graf, D.L., 1960b, "Geochemistry of Carbonate Sediments and Sedimentary Carbonate Rocks, Part IV-A, Isotopic Composition, Chemical Analyses," Circular 308, Illinois Geological Survey, 42 pp.

143. Graf, D.L., and Goldsmith, J.R., 1963, "Carbonate Mineralogy," *Subsurface Geology of Eniwetok Atoll*, by S.O. Schlanger, Professional Paper 260 BB, US Geological Survey, pp. 1048–1053.

144. Graf, D.L., and Lamar, J.E., 1955, "Properties of Calcium and Magnesium Carbonates and Their Bearing on Some Uses of Carbonate Rocks," *Economic Geology*, 50th Anniversary Vol., pp. 639–713.

145. Gries, J.P., 1964, "Limestone," *Mineral and Water Resources of South Dakota*, Bulletin 16, South Dakota Geological Survey, pp. 96–102.

146. Grisafe, D.A., 1977, "Kansas Building Limestones," Mineral Resource Series 4, Kansas Geological Survey, 42 pp.

147. Gubler, Y., et al., 1967, "Petrology and Petrography of Carbonate Rocks," *Developments in Sedimentology, Carbonate Rocks*, Vol. 9A, G.V. Chilingar, H.J. Bissell, R.W. Fairbridge, eds., Elsevier, New York, pp. 51–86.

148. Gulbrandsen, R.A., 1960, "A Method of X-Ray Analyses for Determining the Ratio of Calcite to Dolomite in Mineral Mixtures," Bulletin 1111-D, US Geological Survey, pp. 147–152.

149. Ham, W.E., 1949, "Geology and Dolomite Resources, Mill Creek-Ravina Area, Johnson County, Oklahoma," Circular 24, Oklahoma Geological Survey, 104 pp.

150. Ham, W.E., et al., 1943, "Geology and Chemical Composition of St. Clair Limestone near Marble City, Oklahoma," Mineral Report 16, Oklahoma Geological Survey, 24 pp.

151. Hamilton, W.N., 1973, "Economic Minerals," *Industry and Resources 1973*, Alberta Bureau of Statistics, Alberta Dept. of Industry & Commerce, pp. 39–60.

152. Hansen, M., 1953, "Geologic Report on Limestone Deposits in Stark County and Hettinger County, North Dakota," Report of Investigation 8, North Dakota Geological Survey, 71 pp.

153. Harrier, C.M., 1966, "Wyoming Iron-Ore Deposits," Information Circular 8315, US Bureau of Mines, 114 pp.

154. Hart, E.W., 1978, "Limestone, Dolomite, and Shell Resources of the Coast Ranges Province, California," Bulletin 197, California Div. of Mines and Geology, 103 pp.

155. Hartnagel, C.A., and Broughton, J.G., 1951, "The Mining and Quarry Industries of New York State, 1937 to 1948," New York State Museum & Science Service Bulletin 343, 130 pp.

156. Harvey, R.D., and Steinmetz, J.C., 1971, "Petrographic Properties of Carbonate Rocks Related to Their Sorption of Sulfur Dioxide," Environmental Geology Notes 50, Illinois Geological Survey, 37 pp.

157. Harvey, R.D., et al., 1974, "Lake Marls, Chalks, and Other Carbonate Rocks with High Dissolution Rates in SO_2-Scrubbing Liquors," Proceedings, 10th Forum on Geology of Industrial Minerals, Miscellaneous Report 1, Ohio Geological Survey, pp. 67–80.

158. Harvey, R.D., et al., 1976, "Behavior of Dolomite in Absorption of H_2S from Fuel Gas," World Mining and Metals Technology, AIME, New York, pp. 163–188.

159. Hatch, F.H., and Rastall, R.H. (rev. by J.T. Greensmith), 1971, Petrology of the Sedimentary Rocks, Vol. 2, Hafner, New York, 502 pp.

160. Hatmaker, P., 1931, "Utilization of Dolomite and High Magnesium Limestone," Information Circular 6524, US Bureau of Mines, 18 pp.

161. Hausel, W.D., and Glass, G.B., 1980, "Minerals and Coal Plate, Natrona County," Ser. 6, Wyoming Geological Survey.

162. Hausel, W.D., and Lageson, D.R., 1978, "Minerals Plate, Sheridan County," Ser. 5, Wyoming Geological Survey.

163. Hausel, W.D., et al., 1979, "Wyoming Mines and Minerals Map," Map MS-5, Scale, 1:500,000, Wyoming Geological Survey.

164. Herod, B.C., 1969, "Pennsylvania Producer Handles Tough Recovery Problem," Pit & Quarry, Vol. 62, No. 4, Oct., pp. 125–127, 129.

165. Herod, B.C., editor-in-chief, 1980–81, Pit and Quarry Handbook, 73rd ed., Pit and Quarry Publications, Chicago, 686 pp.

166. Herod, B.C., 1972, "Rock Removed = Valuable Space," Pit & Quarry, Vol. 64, No. 11, May, pp. 72–75, 82.

167. Heron, S.D., Jr., 1962, "Limestone Resources of the Coastal Plain of South Carolina," Bulletin 28, South Carolina Div. of Geology, 128 pp.

168. Hershey, R.E., and Maher, S.W., 1963, "Limestone and Dolomite Resources of Tennessee," Bulletin 65, Tennessee Div. of Geology, 231 pp.

169. Hewitt, D.F., 1960, "The Limestone Industries of Ontario," Industrial Mineral Circular 5, Ontario Div. of Mines, 177 pp.

170. Hewitt, D.F., and Vos, M.A., 1972, "Limestone Industries of Ontario," Industrial Mineral Report 39, Ontario Div. of Mines, 79 pp.

171. Hill, R.D., 1974, "Overview of Use of Carbonate Rocks for Controlling Acid Mine Drainage," Proceedings, 10th Forum on Geology of Industrial Minerals, Miscellaneous Report 1, Ohio Geological Survey, pp. 25–29.

172. Hill, T.P., and Werner, M.A., 1972, "Chemical Composition of Sedimentary Rocks in Alaska, Idaho, Oregon, and Washington," Professional Paper 771, US Geological Survey, 319 pp.

173. Hill, T.P., et al., 1967, "Chemical Composition of Sedimentary Rocks in Colorado, Kansas, Montana, Nebraska, North Dakota, South Dakota, and Wyoming," Professional Paper 561, US Geological Survey, 241 pp.

174. Hillebrand, W.F., and Lundell, G.E.F., 1953, (rev. by G.E.F. Lundell, H.A. Bright, J.I. Hoffman), Applied Inorganic Analysis, with Special Reference to the Analysis of Metals, Minerals, and Rocks, 2nd ed., John Wiley, New York, 1034 pp.

175. Hinchey, N.S., 1946, "Missouri Marble," Report of Investigation 3, Missouri Geological Survey, 47 pp.

176. Hinchey, N.S., et al., 1947, "Limestones and Dolomites in the St. Louis Area," Report of Investigation 5, Missouri Geological Survey, 80 pp.

177. Högberg, E., 1971, "Staining Method for Examination of Siliceous, Cretaceous Limestone II," Geol. Fören. Stockholm Förh., Vol. 93, Pt. 4, pp. 707–713.

178. Holbrook, D.F., 1965, "High-Calcium Limestones in Independence and Izard Counties, Arkansas," Miscellaneous Publication, Arkansas Geological Commission, 21 pp.

179. Holmsley, F., 1935, "Marbles and Limestones of Connecticut," Bulletin 56, Connecticut Geological and Natural History Survey, 56 pp.

180. Holter, M.E., 1976, "Limestone Resources of Alberta," Alberta Research Council Economic Geology Report 4, Edmonton, 91 pp.

181. Holter, M.E., 1976, "Limestone Resources of Alberta," Proceedings, 11th Forum on Geology of Industrial Minerals, Special Publication 74, Montana Bureau of Mines and Geology, pp. 37–50.

182. Hopkins, R.H., 1942, "The Dolomitic Limestones of Florida," Report of Investigation 3, Florida Geological Survey, 105 pp.

183. Horowitz, A.S., and Potter, P.E., 1971, Introductory Petrography of Fossils, Springer-Verlag, New York, 302 pp.

184. Hotchkiss, W.O., and Steidtmann, E., 1914, "Limestone Road Materials of Wisconsin," Bulletin 34, Wisconsin Geological Survey, 137 pp.

185. Howe, W.B., et al., 1961, "The Stratigraphic Succession in Missouri," Missouri Geological Survey and Water Resources, Ser. 2, Vol. 40, 185 pp.

186. Illinois Geological Survey, see Publications List of Road Materials Resources Maps,

Regional and County Resource Reports, and Research Reports on Various Uses of Limestone.

187. Indiana Geological Survey, see Publications List of Regional Geologic Maps.

188. Institution of Mining & Metallurgy, 1965, *Opencast Mining, Quarrying and Alluvial Mining*, American Elsevier, New York, 772 pp.

189. Interstate Commerce Commission, 1968, "Carload Waybill Statistics, 1966, State-to-State Distribution, No. 32, Stone, Clay, and Glass Products," Interstate Commerce Commission, Washington, D.C., 58 pp.

190. Ives, W., and Runnels, R.T., 1960, "Lime Raw Materials in Kansas," Bulletin 142, *Pt. 3*, Kansas Geological Survey, pp. 123–148.

191. Jasper, M.W., and Mihelich, M., 1961, "Kings River Limestone Deposits, Anchorage Quadrangle," Report for the Year 1961, Alaska Div. of Mines and Minerals, pp. 40–48.

192. Jewett, J.M., et al., 1967, "Inland Underground Facilities," *Guidebook for Third National Forum on the Geology of Industrial Minerals*, Kansas Geological Survey, University of Kansas, April, 13 pp.

193. Jicha, H.L., Jr., 1956, "A Deposit of High-Calcium Lime Rock in Valencia County, New Mexico," Circular 36, New Mexico Bureau of Mines & Mineral Resources, 5 pp.

194. Johnsen, J.H., 1958, "Preliminary Report on the Limestones of Albany County, New York," Special Publication, New York State Museum & Science Service, 43 pp.

195. Johnsen, J.H., 1971, "Limestones (Middle Ordovician) of Jefferson County," Map and Chart Series 13, New York State Museum & Science Service, 88 pp.

196. Johnson, A.M., and Sorensen, H.O., 1978, "Drill Core Investigation of the Fiborn Limestone Member in Schoolcraft, Mackinac, and Chippewa Counties, Michigan," Report of Investigation 18, Michigan Geological Survey, 51 pp.

197. Johnson, K.S., 1969, "Mineral Map of Oklahoma (Exclusive of Oil and Gas Fields)," Map GM-15, Scale, 1:750,000, Oklahoma Geological Survey.

198. Johnstone, S.J., and Johnstone, M.G., 1961, "Limestone, Chalk and Whiting" in *Minerals for the Chemical and Allied Industries*, 2nd ed., John Wiley and Son, New York, pp. 293–326.

199. Jordan, C., (compiler), 1978, "Sedimentology Processes: Carbonate Sedimentology," Reprint Series 5, Society of Economic Paleontologists and Mineralogists, 235 pp.

200. Judd, W.R., and Huber, C., 1961, "Correlation of Rock Properties by Statistical Methods," *Proceedings, Symposium on Mining Research*, Vol. 2, Pergamon Press, New York, pp. 621–648.

201. Kansas Geological Survey, see Publications List of Regional and County Reports.

202. Keith, S.B., 1969, "Limestone, Dolomite, and Marble," *Mineral and Water Re-* *sources of Arizona*, Bulletin 180, Arizona Bureau of Mines, pp. 385–398.

203. Kentucky Dept. of Commerce and Kentucky Geological Survey, 1962, "Mineral Resources and Mineral Industry Map of Kentucky."

204. Kentucky Geological Survey, see Publications List of Geologic Quadrangle Maps.

205. Kephart, W.W., 1972, "Limestone and Dolomite Requirements for Glass Containers," *Proceedings of Eighth Forum on Geology of Industrial Minerals*, Public Information Series 5, Iowa Geological Survey, pp. 11–15.

206. Kessler, D.W., and Sligh, W.H., 1927, "Physical Properties of the Principal Commercial Limestones Used for Building Construction in the United States," Technical Paper 349, Part of Vol. 21, National Bureau of Standards, pp. 497–590.

207. Kline, H.D., 1962, "Methods and Costs of Mining and Crushing Limestone at Three Quarries, Anderson-Oxandale Rock Co., Kansas," Information Circular 8084, US Bureau of Mines, 15 pp.

208. Kneller, W.A., et al., 1968, "The Properties and Recognition of Deleterious Cherts which Occur in Aggregate Used by Ohio Concrete Producers," Final Report No. 1014, University of Toledo Research Foundation, 201 pp.

209. Kottlowski, F.E., 1957, "High-Purity Dolomite Deposits of South-Central New Mexico," Circular 47, New Mexico Bureau of Mines & Mineral Resources, 43 pp.

210. Kottlowski, F.E., 1962, "Reconnaissance of Commercial High-Calcium Limestones in New Mexico," Circular 60, New Mexico Bureau of Mines & Mineral Resources, 77 pp.

211. Kottlowski, F.E., 1965, "Limestone and Dolomite," *Mineral and Water Resources of New Mexico*, Bulletin 87, New Mexico Bureau of Mines & Mineral Resources, pp. 345–353.

212. Kümmel, H.B., 1901, "Report on Portland Cement Industry," Annual Report of the State Geologist for the Year 1900, New Jersey Geological Survey, pp. 9–101.

213. Kümmel, H.B., 1940, "The Geology of New Jersey," Bulletin 50, New Jersey Geological Survey, 203 pp.

214. Kupsch, W.O., 1953, "Ordovician and Silurian Stratigraphy of East Central Saskatchewan," Report 10, Saskatchewan Geological Survey, Dept. of Natural Resources, 62 pp.

215. Kusler, D.J., and Corre, H.A., 1968, "Limestone Resources in Western West Virginia," Information Circular 8369, US Bureau of Mines, 15 pp.

216. Lamar, J.E., 1957, "Chemical Analyses of Illinois Limestones and Dolomites," Report of Investigations 200, Illinois Geological Survey, 33 pp.

217. Lamar, J.E., 1961, reprinted 1965, "Uses of Limestone and Dolomite," Circular 321, Illinois Geological Survey, 44 pp.

218. Lamar, J.E., 1966, "High-Purity Limestones

in Illinois," Industrial Minerals Notes 27, Illinois Geological Survey, 20 pp.

219. Lamar, J.E., 1967, "Handbook on Limestone and Dolomite for Illinois Quarry Operators," Bulletin 91, Illinois Geological Survey, 119 pp.

220. Lamar, J.E., 1979, "Selected and Annotated List of Industrial Minerals Publications of the Illinois State Geological Survey," Industrial Minerals Notes 69, Illinois Geological Survey, 13 pp.

221. Lamar, J.E., et al., 1956, "Preliminary Report on Portland Cement Materials in Illinois," Report of Investigations 195, Illinois Geological Survey, 34 pp.

222. Lamar, J.E., and Willman, H.B., 1938, "A Summary of the Uses of Limestone and Dolomite," Report of Investigations 49, Illinois Geological Survey, 48 pp.

223. Lamborn, R.E., 1945, "Recent Information on the Maxville Limestone," Information Circular 3, Ohio Geological Survey, 18 pp.

224. Lamborn, R.E., 1951, "Limestones of Eastern Ohio," Bulletin 49, Series 4, Ohio Geological Survey, 377 pp.

225. Landes, K.K., 1963, "Metallurgical Limestone Reserves in the United States," 2nd ed., National Lime Assn., Washington, DC, 31 pp.

226. Landes, K.K., et al., 1945, "Geology of the Mackinac Straits Region," Publication 44, Michigan Geological Survey, 204 pp.

227. Landreth, J.O., 1968, "High Calcium Limestone Deposit in the Rattler Gulch Area, Granite County, Montana," Special Publication 44, Montana Bureau of Mines & Geology, 10 pp.

228. Lawson, D.C., 1980, "Directory of Mining Enterprises for 1979," Bulletin 111, Montana Bureau of Mines and Geology, 52 pp.

229. Leighton, M.W., and Pendexter, C., 1962, "Carbonate Rock Types," Classification of Carbonate Rocks, W.E. Hamm, ed., American Association of Petroleum Geologists Memoir 1, pp. 62–84.

230. Libby, F.W., 1957, "Limestone Resources of the Pacific Northwest," Resource Report 9, Raw Materials Survey, Inc., Portland, OR, 92 pp.

231. Lipp, R.J., 1979, "Minnesota Industrial Minerals Directory," Mineral Resources Research Center, University of Minnesota, Minneapolis, 41 pp.

232. Logan, W.N., 1916, "Preliminary Report on the Marls and Limestones of Mississippi," Bulletin 13, Mississippi Geological Survey, 82 pp.

233. Loofbourow, R.L., 1966, "Will Aggregate Shortages Drive Stone Producers Underground?" Rock Products, Vol. 69, No. 10, Oct., pp. 67–75.

234. Lozo, F.E., 1959, "Stratigraphic Relations of the Edwards Limestone and Associated Formations in North-Central Texas," Symposium on Edwards Limestone in Central Texas, Publication 5905, University of Texas, Austin, pp. 1–20.

235. Manger, G.E., 1963, "Porosity and Bulk Density of Sedimentary Rocks," Bulletin 1144-E, US Geological Survey, 55 pp.

236. Mantell, C.L., 1931, Industrial Electrochemistry, 1st ed., McGraw-Hill, New York, 528 pp.

237. Marshall, L.G., 1963, "Mining and Beneficiating Costs at Two Crushed Limestone Operations, Madison County, Iowa," Information Circular 8199, US Bureau of Mines, 18 pp.

238. Martin, J.A., 1967, "Limestone and Dolomite," Mineral and Water Resources of Missouri, Missouri Geological Survey & Water Resources, Vol. 43, Series 2, pp. 126–133.

239. Martin, J.A., 1967, "Cement and Cement Raw Materials," Mineral and Water Resources of Missouri, Missouri Geological Survey & Water Resources, Vol. 43, Series 2, pp. 172–183.

240. Maryland Geological Survey, see Publications List of County Reports.

241. Mason, R.S., 1969, "Stone," Mineral and Water Resources of Oregon, A.E. Weissenborn, ed., Bulletin 64, Oregon Dept. of Geology & Mineral Industries, pp. 246–268.

242. Mather, K., 1953, "Crushed Limestone Aggregates for Concrete," Mining Engineering, Vol. 5, No. 10, Oct., pp. 1022–1028; Trans. AIME, 1953, Vol. 196, 1954.

243. Mather, K., and Mather, B., 1950, "Method of Petrographic Examination of Aggregates for Concrete," Proceedings, American Society for Testing & Materials, Vol. 50, pp. 1288–1312.

244. Mathews, E.B., and Grasty, J.S., 1909, "The Limestones of Maryland," Vol. 8, Pt. 3, Maryland Geological Survey, pp. 227–484.

245. Mathews, W.H., and McCammon, J.W., 1957, "Calcareous Deposits of Southwestern British Columbia," Bulletin 40, British Columbia Dept. of Mines, 105 pp.

246. McCue, J.B., et al., 1939, "Limestones of West Virginia," West Virginia Geological Survey, Vol. 12, 560 pp.

247. McGrain, P., and Dever, G.R., Jr., 1967, "Limestone Resources in the Appalachian Region of Kentucky," Bulletin 4, Series 10, Kentucky Geological Survey, 12 pp.

248. McGregor, D.J., 1958, "Cement Raw Materials in Indiana," Bulletin 15, Indiana Geological Survey, 88 pp.

249. McGregor, D.J., 1963, "High-Calcium Limestone and Dolomite in Indiana," Bulletin 27, Indiana Geological Survey, 76 pp.

250. McLemore, W.H., and Hurst, V.J., 1970, "The Carbonate Rocks in the Coosa Valley Area, Georgia," Geology Dept., University of Georgia, Athens, 170 pp.

251. Mellen, F.F., 1942, "Mississippi Agricultural Limestone," Bulletin 46, Mississippi Geological Survey, 20 pp.

252. Merrill, R.H., 1956, "Roof-Span Studies in Limestone," Report of Investigations 5348, US Bureau of Mines, 38 pp.

253. Mielenz, R.C., 1954, "Petrographic Examination of Concrete Aggregate," Proceedings, American Society for Testing & Materials, Vol. 54, pp. 1188–1218.

254. Mielenz, R.C., 1955, "Petrographic Examination," *Significance of Tests and Properties of Concrete and Concrete Aggregates,* American Society for Testing & Materials, Special Technical Publication 169, pp. 253–273.

255. Mihok, E.A., 1968, "Mine Water Research-The Limestone Neutralization Process," Report of Investigations 7191, US Bureau of Mines, 20 pp.

256. Mihok, E.A., 1970, "Mine Water Research-Plant Design and Cost Estimates for Limestone Treatment," Report of Investigations 7368, US Bureau of Mines, 13 pp.

257. Miller, B.L., 1934, "Limestones of Pennsylvania," Mineral Resource Report M20, Pennsylvania Geological Survey, 729 pp.

258. Milliman, J.D., 1974, "Marine Carbonates," Part 1, Springer-Verlag, New York, 375 pp.

259. Mills, J.W., 1962, "High-Calcium Limestones of Eastern Washington," Bulletin 48, Washington Div. of Mines & Geology, 268 pp.

260. Mineral and Water Resources of Colorado, 1964, *Report of the US Geological Survey,* US Government Printing Office, Washington, DC, 302 pp.

261. Moen, W.S., 1966, "Stone, Including Limestone and Dolomite," *Mineral and Water Resources of Washington,* Reprint 9, Washington Div. of Mines & Geology, pp. 265–273.

262. Moore, F.C., et al., 1968, "Problems Encountered in the Design and Construction of a New Aggregate Plant," SME Preprint 68–H–324, 24 pp.

263. Moore, F.H., 1935, "Marbles and Limestones of Connecticut," Bulletin 56, Connecticut State Geological & Natural History Survey, 56 pp.

264. Morris, H.T., 1969, "Limestone and Dolomite," *Mineral and Water Resources of Utah,* Bulletin 73, Utah Geological and Mineral Survey, pp. 188–194.

265. Morse, W.C., 1910, "The Maxville Limestone," Bulletin 13, Ohio Geological Survey, 128 pp.

266. Morse, W.C., 1930, "Paleozoic Rocks," Bulletin 23, Mississippi Geological Survey, 212 pp.

267. Müller, G., 1967, *Methods in Sedimentary Petrology,* Pt. 1 (English trans. by Hans-Ulrich Schmincke), Hafner, New York, 283 pp.

268. Murray, D.A., 1975, "Limestones and Dolomites of Nova Scotia, Part II, Antigonish, Guysborough, Picton and Cumberland Counties," Bulletin 2, Nova Scotia Department of Mines, 155 pp.

269. Mutmansky, J.M., and Singh, M.M., 1968, "A Statistical Study of Relationships Between Rock Properties," *Status of Practical Rock Mechanics,* AIME, New York, pp. 161–177.

270. Nelson, H.F., 1959, "Deposition and Alteration of the Edwards Limestone, Central Texas," *Symposium on Edwards Limestone in Central Texas,* Publication 5905, University of Texas, Austin, pp. 21–95.

271. Newlon, H.H., Jr., et al., 1972, "An Evaluation of Several Methods for Detecting Alkali-Carbonate Reaction," Progress Report 5, Virginia Highway Research Council, 73 pp.

272. Obert, L., et al., 1946, "Standardized Tests for Determining the Physical Properties of Mine Rock," Report of Investigations 3891, US Bureau of Mines, 67 pp.

273. O'Donnell, J.J., and Sliger, A.G., 1972, "Availability of Limestones and Dolomites," Task 1 Final Report, M. W. Kellogg Co., National Technical Information Service PB–206–963, Feb. 1, 191 pp.

274. Oliver, W.A., Jr., 1956, "Biostromes and Bioherms of the Onondaga Limestone in Eastern New York," New York State Museum & Science Service Circular 45, 23 pp.

275. Olson, R.H., 1964, "Limestone," *Mineral and Water Resources of Nevada,* Bulletin 65, Nevada Bureau of Mines, pp. 217–220.

276. O'Neill, B.J., Jr., 1964, "Limestones and Dolomites of Pennsylvania," *Atlas of Pennsylvania's Mineral Resources,* Pt. 1, Mineral Resource Report M50, Pennsylvania Geological Survey, 40 pp.

277. O'Neill, B.J., Jr., 1975, "Potential High-Calcium Limestone Resources in the Mount Joy Area, Lancaster County," Information Circular 76, Pennsylvania Geological Survey, 18 pp.

278. O'Neill, B.J., Jr., 1976, "The Distribution of Limestones Containing At Least 90 Percent $CaCO_3$ in Pennsylvania," *Atlas of Mineral Resources,* Part 4, Mineral Resources Report M50, Scale, 1:500,000, Pennsylvania Geological Survey.

279. Osterwald, F.W., et al., 1966, "Mineral Resources of Wyoming," Bulletin 50, Wyoming Geological Survey, pp. 180–184.

280. Papke, K.G., 1973, "Industrial Mineral Deposits of Nevada," Map 46, Nevada Bureau Mines and Geology.

281. Papke, K.G., 1979, "List of Nevada Industrial Mineral Producers," Special Publication L-1, Nevada Bureau Mines and Geology, 3 pp.

282. Parker, R.L., 1967, "Composition of the Earth's Crust," *Data of Geochemistry,* 6th ed., M. Fleischer, ed., Professional Paper 440–D, US Geological Survey, 19 pp.

283. Patton, J.B., 1951, "Industrial Limestone in Indiana," *Scientific Monthly,* Vol. 72, No. 4, pp. 259–265.

284. Pearre, N.C., 1956, "Mineral Deposits and Occurrences in Massachusetts and Rhode Island, Exclusive of Clay, Sand and Gravel, and Peat," Mineral Investigations Resources Map MR 4, US Geological Survey.

285. Perry, T.G., and Smith, N.M., 1958, "The Meramec-Chester and Intra-Chester Boundaries and Associated Strata in Indiana," Bulletin 12, Indiana Geological Survey, 110 pp.

286. Peterson, N.V., and Mason, R.S., 1958, "Limestone Occurrences in Western Oregon," *The Ore Bin,* Vol. 20, No. 4, pp. 33–39.

287. Pickering, S.M., Jr., 1970, "Stratigraphy, Paleontology, and Economic Geology of Portions of Perry and Cochran Quad-

rangles, Georgia," Bulletin 81, Georgia Geological Survey, 67 pp.

288. Plafker, G., and Berg, H.C., 1964, "Limestone and Marble," *Mineral and Water Resources of Alaska*, US Geological Survey Report, pp. 135–138.

289. Potter, P.E., 1968, "A Selective, Annotated Bibliography on Carbonate Rocks," *Bulletin of Canadian Petroleum Geology*, Vol. 16, No. 1, pp. 87–103.

290. Power, W.R., 1978, "Economic Geology of the Georgia Marble District," *Proceedings, 12th Forum on Geology of Industrial Minerals*, Information Circular 49, Georgia Geological Survey, pp. 59–68.

291. Prokopovich, N., and Schwartz. G.M., 1956, "Minnesota Limestone Suitable for Portland Cement," Summary Report 8, Minnesota Geological Survey, 39 pp.

292. Prucha, J.J., 1953, "The White Crystal Dolomite Deposit near Gouverneur, New York," Report of Investigations 9, New York State Museum & Science Service, 13 pp.

293. Pugliese, J.M., 1972, "Designing Blast Patterns Using Empirical Formulas, A Comparison of Calculated Patterns with Plans Used in Quarrying Limestone and Dolomite, with Geologic Considerations," Information Circular 8550, US Bureau of Mines, 33 pp.

294. Puri, H.S., and Vernon, R.O., 1959, "Summary of the Geology of Florida and a Guidebook to the Classic Exposures," Special Publication 5, Florida Geological Survey, 255 pp.

295. Puri, H.S., et al., 1967, "Geology of Dixie and Gilchrist Counties, Florida," Bulletin 49, Florida Geological Survey, 155 pp.

296. Quinn, A.W., 1971, "Bedrock Geology of Rhode Island," Bulletin 1295, US Geological Survey, 68 pp.

297. Quinn, A.W., et al., 1949, "Bedrock Geology of the Pawtucket Quadrangle, Rhode Island-Massachusetts," Geological Quadrangle Map 1, Scale 1:31,680, US Geological Survey.

298. Ramp, L., and Peterson, N.V., 1979, "Limestone," *Geology and Mineral Resources of Josephine County, Oregon*, Bulletin 100, Oregon Dept. Geology and Mineral Industries, pp. 37–38.

299. Renninger, F.A., and Nichols, F.P., Jr., 1970, "Aggregate Technology—Wider Horizons Through Research," *Trans. SME/AIME*, Vol. 247, pp. 38–42.

300. Reves, W.D., 1961, "The Limestone Resources of Washington, Holmes, and Jackson Counties, Florida," Bulletin 42, Florida Geological Survey, 121 pp.

301. Riley, H.C., and Schroeder, H.J., 1963, "Crushed Limestone Operations, Watauga Quarry, Watauga Stone Co., Carter County, Tenn." Information Circular 8198, US Bureau of Mines, 21 pp.

302. Risser, H.T., 1960, "Kansas Building Stone," Bulletin 142, *Pt. 2*, Kansas Geological Survey, pp. 53–122.

303. Rodda, P.V., et al., 1966, "Limestone and Dolomite Resources, Lower Cretaceous Rocks, Texas," Report of Investigations 56, Texas Bureau of Economic Geology, 286 pp.

304. Roehm, J.C., 1946, "Some High Calcium Limestone Deposits in Southeastern Alaska," Pamphlet 6, Alaska Div. of Mines & Geology, 85 pp.

305. Rooney, L.F., 1970, "High-Calcium Limestone and High-Magnesium Dolomite Resources of Indiana," Bulletin 42–B, Indiana Geological Survey, 20 pp.

306. Rooney, L.F., 1970, "Dimension Limestone Resources of Indiana," Bulletin 42–C, Indiana Geological Survey, 29 pp.

307. Rooney, L.F., and Ault, C.H., 1970, "Potential Limestone and Dolomite Resources of Northern Indiana," *Proceedings Fifth Forum on Geology of Industrial Minerals*, Mineral Resources Report M64, Pennsylvania Geological Survey, pp. 179–224.

308. Rooney, L.F., and Carr, D.D., 1971, "Applied Geology of Industrial Limestone and Dolomite," Bulletin 46, Indiana Geological Survey, 59 pp.

309. Rowland, T.L., 1972, "General Survey of Carbonate Mineral Deposits in Oklahoma," *Oklahoma Geology Notes*, Vol. 32, No. 3, pp. 73–89.

310. Runnells, D.D., 1970, "Errors in X-Ray Analysis of Carbonates Due to Solid-Solution Variation in Composition of Component Minerals," *Journal of Sedimentary Petrology*, Vol. 40, pp. 1158–1166.

311. Runnels, R.T., 1951, "Some High-Calcium Limestones in Kansas," Bulletin 90, *Pt. 5*, Kansas Geological Survey, pp. 77–104.

312. Runnels, R.T., 1959, "Cement Raw Materials in Kansas," *1959 Reports of Studies*, *Pt. 2*, Bulletin 134, Kansas Geological Survey, pp. 105–124.

313. Runnels, R.T., and Dubins, I.M., 1949, "Chemical and Petrographic Studies of the Fort Hays Chalk in Kansas," Bulletin 82, *Pt. 1*, Kansas Geological Survey, 36 pp.

314. Runnels, R.T., and Schleicher, J.A., 1956, "Chemical Composition of Eastern Kansas Limestone," Bulletin 119, *Pt. 3*, Kansas Geological Survey, pp. 81–103.

315. Rutledge, F.A., et al., 1953, "Preliminary Report—Nonmetallic Deposits Accessible to the Alaska Railroad as Possible Sources of Raw Materials for the Construction Industry," Report of Investigations 4932, US Bureau of Mines, 129 pp.

316. Salotti, C.A., et al., 1970, "Limestone as a Raw Material for Hydrocarbon Fuels," *Proceedings, 6th Forum on Geology of Industrial Minerals*, Miscellany 1, Michigan Geological Survey, pp. 48–55.

317. Sanders, J.E., and Friedman, G.M., 1967, "Origin and Occurrence of Limestone," *Developments in Sedimentology, Carbonate Rocks*, Vol. 9A, G.V. Chilingar, H.J. Bissell, and R.W. Fairbridge, eds., Elsevier, New York, pp. 169–265.

318. Savage, C.N., 1965, "Economic Geology of Carbonate Rocks Adjacent to the Snake River South of Lewiston, Idaho," Mineral Resources Report 10, Idaho Bureau of Mines & Geology, 26 pp.

319. Savage, C.N., 1969, "Distribution and Economic Potential of Idaho Carbonate

Rocks," Bulletin 23, Idaho Bureau of Mines & Geology, 93 pp.

320. Scholle, P.A., 1978, "A Color Illustrated Guide to Carbonate Rock Constituents, Textures, Cements, and Porosities," American Association of Petroleum Geologists Memoir 27, 241 pp.

321. Schmidt, W., et al., 1979, "The Limestone Dolomite and Coquina Resources of Florida," Report of Investigation 88, Florida Bureau of Geology, 54 pp.

322. Schwartz, G.M., et al., 1959, "Investigation of the Commercial Possibilities of Marl in Minnesota," Office of Iron Range Resources and Rehabilitation, 190 pp.

323. Scott, A.J., 1968, "Environmental Factors Controlling Oyster Shell Deposits, Texas Coasts," *Proceedings, 4th Forum on Geology of Industrial Minerals,* Texas Bureau of Economic Geology, pp. 129–150.

324. Searle, A.B., 1935, *Limestone and Its Products; Their Nature, Production, and Uses,* Ernest Benn, London, 709 pp.

325. Sellards, E.H., et al., 1911, "Roads and Road Materials of Florida," Bulletin 2, Florida Geological Survey, 31 pp.

326. Shapiro, L., and Brannock, W.W., 1962, "Rapid Analysis of Silicate, Carbonate and Phosphate Rocks," Bulletin 1144–A, US Geological Survey, 56 pp.

327. Shea, F.S., and Murray, D.A., 1967, "Limestones and Dolomites of Nova Scotia, Part 1, Cape Breton Island," Bulletin 2, Nova Scotia Department of Mines, 300 pp.

328. Siegel, F.R., 1967, "Properties and Uses of the Carbonates," *Developments in Sedimentology, Carbonate Rocks,* Vol. 9B, G.V. Chilingar, H.J. Bissell, R.W. Fairbridge, eds., Elsevier, New York, pp. 343–393.

329. Sinclair, J., 1969, *Quarrying, Opencast and Alluvial Mining,* Elsevier, New York, 375 pp.

330. Singleton, R.H., 1980, "Stone," Preprint, Bulletin 671, *Mineral Facts and Problems,* US Bureau of Mines, 16 pp.

331. Slack, A.V., 1973, "Removing SO_2 from Stack Gases," *Environmental Science & Technology,* Vol. 7, No. 2, pp. 110–119.

332. Slavin, W., 1968, *Atomic Absorption Spectroscopy,* Interscience Publishers, New York, 307 pp.

333. Smith, R.A., 1915, "Limestones in Michigan," Publication 21, Pt. 2, Michigan Geological & Biological Survey, pp. 103–402.

334. Stauffer, C.R., 1950, "The High Magnesium Dolomites and Dolomitic Limestones of Minnesota," Summary Report 4, Minnesota Geological Survey, 29 pp.

335. Stearn, E.W., 1965, "Underground Storage: How Does It Look Today?" *Rock Products,* Vol. 68, No. 12, Dec., pp. 86–87, 96.

336. Steidtmann, E., 1924, "Limestones and Marls of Wisconsin," Bulletin 66, Wisconsin Geological Survey, 208 pp.

337. Stenzel, H.B., et al., 1948, "Geological Resources of the Trinity River Tributary Area in Oklahoma and Texas," Publication 4824, University of Texas, Austin, 252 pp.

338. Stith, D.A., 1969, "Potential Use of Ohio Limestones and Dolomites for Architectural Aggregate," Report of Investigations 73, Ohio Geological Survey, 14 pp.

339. Stith, D.A., 1972, "High-Calcium Limestone Facies of the Devonian Dundee Limestone," Report of Investigations 86, Ohio Geological Survey, 14 pp.

340. Stith, D.A., 1979, "Chemical Composition, Stratigraphy, and Depositional Environments of the Black River Group (Middle Ordovician), Southwestern Ohio," Report of Investigations 113, Ohio Geological Survey, 36 pp.

341. Stokley, J.A., 1949, "Industrial Limestones of Kentucky," Report of Investigations 2, Series 9, Kentucky Geological Survey, 51 pp.

342. Stokley, J.A., and McFarlan, A.C., 1952, "Industrial Limestones of Kentucky No. 2," Report of Investigations 4, Series 9, Kentucky Geological Survey, 95 pp.

343. Stokley, J.A., and Walker, F.H., 1953, "Industrial Limestones of Kentucky No. 3," Report of Investigations 8, Series 9, Kentucky Geological Survey, 62 pp.

344. Stonehouse, D.H., 1979, "Construction Materials and Other Industrial Minerals," *Canadian Minerals Survey 1979,* Energy, Mines and Resources Canada, Ottawa, pp. 63–67.

345. Stonehouse, D.H., 1979, "Lime—Report 26," Annual Review of the Canadian Mineral Industry 1979, Mineral Policy Sector of Energy, Mines and Resources Canada, Ottawa, 4 pp.

346. Stout, W., 1941, "Dolomites and Limestones of Western Ohio," Bulletin 42, Ohio Geological Survey, 468 pp.

347. Stowe, R.L., 1969, "Strength and Deformation Properties of Granite, Basalt, Limestone and Tuff at Various Loading Rates," Miscellaneous Paper C-69-1, US Army Engineer Waterways Experiment Station, 168 pp.

348. Suffel, G.G., 1930, "Dolomites of Western Oklahoma," Bulletin 49, Oklahoma Geological Survey, 155 pp.

349. Swain, F.M., et al., 1966, "High-Calcium Limestone Deposits of Cumberland Valley, Pennsylvania," *Ohio Journal of Science,* Vol. 66, No. 2, pp. 116–123.

350. Taft, W.H., 1967, "Modern Carbonate Sediments," *Developments in Sedimentology, Carbonate Rocks,* Vol. 9A, G.V. Chilingar, H.J. Bissell, R.W. Fairbridge, eds., Elsevier, New York, pp. 29–50.

351. Tennessee Division of Geology, see Publications List of Geologic Quadrangle Maps.

352. Thiel, G.A., and Dutton, C.E., 1935, "The Architectural, Structural and Monumental Stones of Minnesota," Bulletin 25, Minnesota Geological Survey, 160 pp.

353. Thiel, G.A., and Stauffer, C.R., 1947, "The High Calcium Limestones of Minnesota," Summary Report 1, Minnesota Geological Survey, 13 pp.

354. Thill, R.E., et al., 1969, "Correlation of Longitudinal Velocity Variation with Rock Fabric," *Journal of Geophysical Research,* Vol. 74, No. 20, pp. 4897–4909.

355. Thoenen, J.R., 1926, "Underground Limestone Mining," Bulletin 262, US Bureau of Mines, 100 pp.

356. Trainer, D.W., Jr., 1932, "The Tully Limestone of Central New York," New York State Museum & Science Service Bulletin 291, 23 pp.

357. US Census Office, 1884, "Report on the Building Stones of the United States and Statistics of the Quarry Industry for 1880," *10th Census,* Government Printing Office, Washington, DC, 410 pp.

358. US Geological Survey and US Bureau of Mines, 1968, "Mineral Resources of the Appalachian Region," Professional Paper 580, US Geological Survey, 492 pp.

359. Vanderwilt, J.W., 1947, "Mineral Resources of Colorado," Colorado State Mineral Resources Board, Denver, 547 pp.

360. Vermont Geological Survey, see Publications List of Quadrangle Reports.

361. Vernon, R.O., 1942, "Geology of Holmes and Washington Counties, Florida," Bulletin 21, Florida Geological Survey, 161 pp.

362. Vernon, R.O., 1943, "Florida Mineral Industry," Bulletin 24, Florida Geological Survey, 207 pp.

363. Vernon, R.O., 1951, "Geology of Citrus and Levy Counties, Florida," Bulletin 33, Florida Geological Survey, 256 pp.

364. Vineyard, J.T., ed., 1969, *Missouri Mineral Industry News,* Missouri Geological Survey, Vol. 9, July, pp. 102.

365. Wagner, N.S., 1958, "Limestone Occurrences in Eastern Oregon," *The Ore Bin,* Vol. 20, No. 5, pp. 43-47.

366. Walker, K.R., 1973, "Stratigraphy and Environmental Sedimentology of Middle Ordovician Black River Group in the Type Area—New York State," New York State Museum & Science Service Bulletin 419, 43 pp.

367. Warne, S.S.J., 1962, "A Quick Field or Laboratory Staining Scheme for the Differentiation of the Major Carbonate Minerals," *Journal of Sedimentary Petrology,* Vol. 32, pp. 29–38.

368. Waugh, T.C., 1966, "Analyses of High Calcium Chert-Free Beds in the Keokuk Limestone, Cherokee County, Kansas," Bulletin 180, *Pt. 2,* Kansas Geological Survey, 7 pp.

369. Wayland, J.R., and Ham, W.E., 1955, "General and Economic Geology of the Baum Limestone, Ravia-Mannsville Area, Oklahoma," Circular 33, Oklahoma Geological Survey, 44 pp.

370. Wayne, W.J., 1971, "Marl Resources of Indiana," Bulletin 42-G, Indiana Geological Survey, 16 pp.

371. Wedepohl, K.H., 1970, "Geochemische Daten von Sedimentären Karbonaten und Karbonatgesteinen in Ihrem Faziellen und Petrogenetischen Aussagewert," *Verhandl. Geol. Bundesanst,* (Austria), Vol. 4, pp. 692–705.

372. Weitz, J.H., 1942, "High-Grade Dolomite Deposits in the United States," Information Circular 7226, US Bureau of Mines, 86 pp.

373. Welby, C.W., 1961, "Bedrock Geology of the Central Champlain Valley of Vermont," Bulletin 14, Vermont Geological Survey, 296 pp.

374. Wentworth, C.K., 1939, "Physical Geography and Geology [of the Hawaiian Islands]," Hawaii Territorial Planning Board, 1st Progress Report, Honolulu, pp. 13–20.

375. West, T.R., and Johnson, R.B., 1965, "Analysis of Textural and Physical Factors Contributing to the Abrasion Resistance of Some Indiana Carbonate Aggregates," *Indiana Academy of Science Proceedings for 1964,* Vol. 75, pp. 153–162.

376. West Virginia Geological and Economic Survey, see Publications List of County Reports.

377. Wharton, H.M., et al., 1969, "Missouri Minerals—Resources Production and Forecasts," Special Publication 1, Missouri Geological Survey, 303 pp.

378. Widmer, K., 1964, *The Geology and Geography of New Jersey,* Van Nostrand, Princeton, NJ, 193 pp.

379. Willard, B., 1931, "Commercial Limestones of Rhode Island," *Pan-American Geologist,* Vol. 56, No. 2, pp. 116–122.

380. Willard, R.J., and McWilliams, J.R., 1969, "Microstructural Techniques in the Study of Physical Properties of Rock," *International Journal of Rock Mechanics and Mining Sciences,* Vol. 6, No. 1, pp. 1–12.

381. Williamson, D.R., and Burgin, L., 1960, "Limestone Occurrences in Colorado," Colorado School of Mines *Mineral Industries Bulletin,* Vol. 3, No. 1, 12 pp.

382. Willman, H.B., 1943, "High-Purity Dolomite in Illinois," Report of Investigations 90, Illinois Geological Survey, 89 pp.

383. Wilmoth, R.C., and Hill, R.D., 1973, "Mine Drainage Pollution Control Via Reverse Osmosis," *Mining Engineering,* Vol. 25, No. 3, pp. 45–47.

384. Wilson, J.L., 1975, *Carbonate Facies in Geologic History,* Springer-Verlag, New York, 471 pp.

385. Windes, S.L., 1949, "Physical Properties of Mine Rock, Part I," Report of Investigations 4459, US Bureau of Mines, 79 pp.

386. Windes, S.L., 1950, "Physical Properties of Mine Rock, Part II," Report of Investigations 4727, US Bureau of Mines, 37 pp.

387. Wolfe, P.E., 1948, "Agricultural Mineral Resources of New Jersey," Bulletin 2, Rutgers University, Bureau of Mineral Research, pp. 18–50.

388. Woolf, D.O., 1953, "Results of Physical Tests of Road-Building Aggregate," US Dept. of Commerce, Bureau of Public Roads, Washington, DC, 225 pp.

389. Yon, J.W., Jr., and Hendry, C.W., Jr., 1969, "Mineral Resource Study of Holmes, Walton and Washington Counties," Bulletin 50, Florida Geological Survey, 161 pp.

390. Yon, J.W., Jr., and Hendry, C.W., Jr., 1972, "Suwannee Limestone in Hernando and Pasco Counties, Florida," Bulletin 54, Pt. 1, Florida Geological Survey, pp. 1–42.

391. Zenger, D.H., 1965, "Stratigraphy of the Lockport Formation (Middle Silurian) in

New York State," New York State Museum & Science Service Bulletin 419, 210 pp.

392. Zenger, D.H., "Stratigraphy and Petrology of the Little Falls Dolostone (Upper Cambrian), East-Central New York," New York State Museum & Science Service Map and Chart Series 34, in press.

Lithium Raw Materials

IHOR A. KUNASZ *

Introduction

Lithium minerals occur predominantly in pegmatites which contain mineral assemblages derived from the crystallization of postmagmatic fluids or from the metasomatic action by residual pegmatitic fluids. They have been the traditional sources of raw materials for ceramic and chemical industries. With the discovery of Searles Lake, brines became new sources of lithium.

Indeed, the 1960s may well be referred to as the "brine decade" because several brine bodies of significant economic importance were discovered. In the United States, the brines of Clayton Valley, Nevada, are presently exploited by Foote Mineral Co. The brines of the Great Salt Lake of Utah, the Smackover formation, and the Imperial Valley geothermal field, have been defined as important resources of lithium. In South America, new occurrences have been identified in Bolivia and Argentina. At the Salar de Atacama, Chile, new production capacity is scheduled for 1984.

Following the termination of the AEC purchase program in 1959, several companies such as Maywood Chemical Co., American Lithium Chemicals, and Quebec Lithium Corp. were forced to close their operations. Nevertheless, with the development of new applications in glass ceramics, air conditioning systems, synthetic rubber, and metallurgy (aluminum potlines), the lithium industry grew steadily, and with the potential application of lithium metal in batteries and nuclear reactors, a healthy growth can be foreseen. New products and new applications are likely to stimulate exploration for expanded reserves as well as the search for new sources from which lithium could be extracted economically.

* Chief Geologist, Foote Mineral Co., Exton, PA.

Geochemistry of Lithium

Lithium is the third element in the periodic table. It is the lightest of all the metals, having an atomic weight of 6.938, an ionic radius of 0.68Å and a charge of +1.

The geochemistry of lithium has been extensively studied and has been summarized by Rankama and Sahama (1950), Goldschmidt (1937), and Hortsman (1957).

The distribution of lithium in igneous rocks is controlled by its size and its charge, and by the $(MgO+FeO)/Li_2O$ ratio. In the early stages of crystallization of a magma, that ratio is very large. Consequently, both magnesium and iron are removed by ferromagnesian minerals in preference to lithium which is then concentrated in the residual magma. This results in an enrichment of lithium in silicic rocks and pegmatites (Strock, 1936).

Pegmatites are coarse-grained igneous rocks formed by the crystallization of postmagmatic fluids. Minerals within pegmatites may also form by metasomatism (Jahns, 1955). Genetically, the pegmatites are associated with neighboring intrusives. Mineralogically, granitic pegmatites contain feldspar, quartz, and mica as the main constituents and a variety of exotic elements such as lithium, beryllium, tantalum, tin, and cesium, which may or may not occur in economically significant concentrations.

Detailed studies by numerous investigators (Cameron et al., 1949, 1954; Hanley et al., 1950; Jahns, 1953, 1955; Page et al., 1953) indicate that pegmatites often exhibit an internal zonal arrangement, with each zone containing a specific suite of minerals. The lithium minerals are usually found in the intermediate zones, and although as many as 13 zones have been recognized by Cameron, et al. (1949), a complete zonal arrangement is rarely found. Zoning of pegmatite bodies has also been observed on a regional basis. The regionally zoned pegmatite sequences exhibit mineral assemblages and complexity according to their respective distance from the granitic bodies to which they are genetically related.

Lithium is also found in small proportions in a variety of rocks. The average lithium content of igneous rocks is estimated at about 28 ppm Li. Sedimentary rocks contain an average of 53 ppm Li, the highest being recorded in shales (Hortsman, 1957).

Unusual amounts of lithium are found in the clay mineral, hectorite, which is expandable and belongs to the magnesian end member of the smectite group. Recent work by the US Geological Survey suggests that lithium-rich clays are ubiquitous in a number of clay environments.

Lithium is also present in significant amounts in waters associated with geothermal areas (White, 1957), in oil well brines (Mayhew and Heylmun, 1966), and certain brines of California (Searles Lake), Nevada (Clayton Valley), Utah (Great Salt Lake), and Chile (Salar de Atacama), Bolivia (Salar de Uyuni), and Argentina.

Lithium Minerals

Although lithium occurs in some 145 minerals, only spodumene, lepidolite, petalite, amblygonite, and eucryptite have been commercial sources of lithium.

Spodumene, a lithium aluminum silicate ($LiAlSi_2O_6$), is a monoclinic member of the pyroxene group. It has a very pronounced cleavage plane (110) which results in typically lath-shaped particles upon breaking. The color of spodumene is variable, being nearly white in low iron variety and dark green in iron-rich crystals.

When clear, spodumene is considered a gemstone. Three varieties are known: *hiddenite,* the green variety from Alexander County, North Carolina, first discovered in Brazil; *triphane,* the yellow variety also from Alexander County; and the lilac-colored *kunzite* from the Pala district, California, Brazil, and Afghanistan.

Spodumene undergoes pseudomorphic alteration to a variety of minerals. Norton and Schlegel (1955) have described spodumene replacement by quartz, albite, perthite, muscovite, beryl, amblygonite, apatite, and tourmaline. Weathering commonly alters spodumene to kaolinite and to montmorillonite.

Spodumene constitutes the most abundant commercial source of lithium. Theoretically, it may contain up to 3.7% Li, but the actual lithium concentrations vary from 1.35% to

3.56%, probably as a result of sodium and potassium substitution for lithium. Spodumene concentrates typically contain 1.9% to 3.3% Li.

Lepidolite is a phyllosilicate with the general formula $K_2(Li,Al)_{5-6}\{Si_{6-7}Al_{2-1}O_{20}\}(OH,F)_4$. The chemical variability expressed in the formula stems from a structural complexity attributed to a mixture of different polymorphs which include muscovite, lithium muscovite, and polylithionite (Winchell, 1942). On the other hand, Foster (1960) and Deer, et al. (1962) suggest that there is a continuous series between muscovite with a $2M_1$ structure to lepidolite, with 1M, $2M_2$, and 3T structures. The structural transition takes place when the lithia content in the mica reaches 1.53%.

The lithium concentration in lepidolite varies between 1.53% to a possible theoretical maximum of 3.6%. In commercial deposits, the concentrations are more normally 1.4% to 1.9% Li. In addition to lithium, lepidolites also carry substantial concentrations of rubidium and cesium (Deer, et al., 1962).

The major commercial occurrences of lepidolite are located in Zimbabwe (Bikita), Namibia (Karibib), Canada (Bernic Lake, Manitoba), and Brazil.

Petalite, $LiAlSi_4O_{10}$, is a monoclinic mineral with a framework silicate structure. Its color is grayish white and more rarely pinkish. It has two cleavage directions which form an angle of 38.5°. The basal cleavage is perfect.

The theoretical lithium content of petalite is 2.27%. In actual commercial deposits, the concentration varies from 1.6% to 2.1% Li. Sizable deposits of petalite occur with lepidolite in Zimbabwe (Bikita), Namibia (Karibib), Brazil (Araçuai), Australia (Londonderry), in the USSR (eastern Transbaikalia), and Sweden (Utö).

In certain pegmatites, there is evidence that petalite alters to a mixture of spodumene and quartz. In the Bernic Lake pegmatites of Manitoba, Cerny, et al. (1971) have described pseudomorphs of spodumene and quartz after petalite.

Eucryptite is also a lithium aluminum silicate which is deficient in silica. It has a formula $LiAlSiO_4$ and may contain 5.53% Li. The only large deposit of eucryptite is found in Zimbabwe (Bikita) where its occurrence with quartz suggests a spodumene origin (Westenberger, 1963). The grade of the eucryptite is 2.34% Li.

Amblygonite, with the generalized formula $LiAl(PO_4)(F,OH)$, is the fluorine-rich end member of a phosphate series, while montebrasite represents the hydroxyl-rich end member. It occurs in white to gray masses. Basal cleavage planes are pearly, others are vitreous. Amblygonite weathers to earthy apatite, wavellite, and other lithium deficient phosphates. Although amblygonite may contain as much as 4.74% Li, commercial ores usually carry 3.5% to 4.2% Li. Amblygonite has been mined in Canada, Brazil, Surinam, Zimbabwe, Ruanda, Mozambique, Namibia, and the Republic of South Africa.

Brines. Lithium is found in commercial quantities in certain brine deposits. The brines are present in desert areas and occur in playas and saline lakes where solutions have been concentrated by solar evaporation. In Searles Lake where production of dilithium phosphate began in 1938, the lithium concentration is 70 ppm Li. In Clayton Valley, Nevada, lithium-bearing brines contain 200 ppm Li. Smaller concentrations of lithium (28 to 60 ppm Li) are found in the Great Salt Lake. Rich concentrations of lithium have been identified at the Salar de Uyuni in Bolivia (100–700 ppm) and the Salar de Atacama in Chile (1000–5000 ppm).

Reserves

Projections of lithium metal requirements to satisfy the needs of the automotive and storage battery system as well as the potential use in thermal nuclear fusion energy generation resulted in concern regarding the availability of sufficient lithium. The US Geological Survey created the Lithium Exploration Group, which subsequently sponsored two symposia, one held in Denver, CO and another in Corning, NY. Concurrently, the Energy Research and Development Administration requested the National Academies of Sciences and Engineering to form a National Research Council Committee on Nuclear and Alternative Energy Systems (CONAES). One of the groups was the Lithium Subpanel consisting of experts from the industry and the government, formed to evaluate the lithium availability in the western world. The results of the Subpanel study were presented at the second lithium symposium held at Corning, NY in 1977. This document is considered the best reference regarding reserves and resources and the serious student of lithium should have this particular publication on hand (Penner, 1978). Many of the figures quoted in this review have been taken from the Subpanel study.

Major Producing Districts

At the present time, the United States and Zimbabwe supply the bulk of the free world's demand for lithium raw materials (Fig. 1), and the United States is the leading producer. Within the communist bloc, the Soviet Union probably represents an important producer; production figures, however, are not available. The People's Republic of China is reported to produce lithium compounds from ores mined in the northwestern part of the country.

United States

Lithium ores and lithium chemicals in the United States are supplied by three producing areas. Two of the areas are in the tin-spodumene belt of North Carolina, while brines are exploited in Clayton Valley (Silver Peak), Nevada.

The tin-spodumene belt of North Carolina constitutes the largest developed reserve of lithium in the free world. The area is characterized by numerous pegmatites that intrude amphibolites and schists along the eastern margin of the Devonian Cherryville quartz monzonite (Kesler, 1961).

The pegmatites are typically unzoned, and spodumene is distributed throughout the bodies. The contact zones and aplitic layers contain substantially lower percentages of spodumene. On the average, the pegmatites consist of 20% spodumene, 32% quartz, 6% muscovite, 41% feldspar (including albite and microcline), and about 1% trace minerals, such as beryl, lithiophilite, columbite, tantalite, pyrite, sphalerite, apatite, and rhodochrosite (Kesler, 1961).

Two companies exploit the spodumene-bearing pegmatites: Foote Mineral Co. and Lithium Corp. of America.

Foote Mineral Co., 83% owned by Newmont Mining Corp., mines spodumene from a pegmatite cluster located about one mile southwest of the town of Kings Mountain. Extensive drilling has outlined ore reserves of 29 million tons averaging 0.7% Li. At the present time, only the northern pegmatites are included in this estimate. Approximately one-half of the property where surface outcrops of spodumene-bearing pegmatites exist has not been evaluated by drilling. Geological inference permits an estimate of some additional 14 million tons of spodumene-bearing pegmatites for the unexplored portion of the property.

Lithium Corp. of America, a wholly-owned subsidiary of Gulf Resources and Chemicals Corp., has developed an open pit in the Long

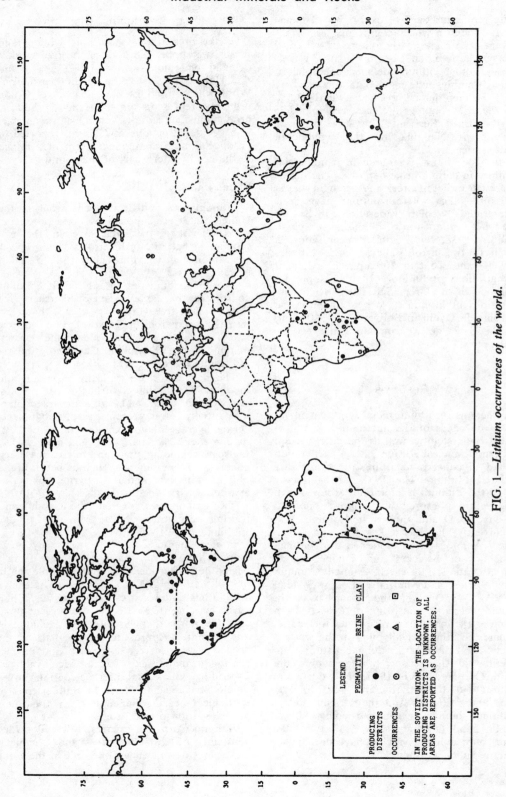

FIG. 1—*Lithium occurrences of the world.*

Creek area in western Gaston County. Proven and probable reserves on the Hallman-Beam property are reported at 25,700,000 tons of spodumene-bearing pegmatite grading 0.64% Li.

The tin-spodumene belt has a length of about 30 miles and the exploration activity has been restricted to the upper 984 ft. The geological setting and distribution of pegmatites suggest that pegmatites may well occur at greater depth. Kesler, in a study of the potential lithium contained in the total belt down to a 4921-ft level, has suggested the potential existence of a resource of 754 million tons at a grade typical for the area.

Other known pegmatite sources in the United States are not of great significance. These include the Black Hills of South Dakota, the Pala district of southwestern California, the White Picacho District of Arizona, the Harding and Pidlite mines in New Mexico, and several smaller areas in Colorado, Wyoming, Utah, and New England.

In addition to pegmatitic sources, significant amounts of lithium are produced from a brine deposit located in Clayton Valley (Silver Peak), Nevada. Lithium was also produced for a number of years from the brines of Searles Lake, where brines are presently beneficiated only for potash, sodium carbonate, and borate salts.

In Clayton Valley, located in Esmeralda County, NV, lithium-bearing brines occur in an undrained structural depression filled with Quaternary sediments composed mainly of clay minerals, including hectorite, volcanic sands, alluvial gravels, and saline minerals consisting of gypsum and halite (Kunasz, 1970).

The brine which saturates the sediments is chemically simple. It occurs as a concentrated sodium chloride solution containing subordinate amounts of potassium and minor amounts of magnesium and calcium. The lithium concentration is variable; the composite average pumped into the ponds is 200 ppm Li.

Foote Mineral Co. is presently operating a series of wells ranging from 500 to 1000 ft in depth. The brine is pumped through transite pipelines into evaporating ponds where it is concentrated by solar evaporation. The lithium resources, to a depth of 1000 ft, are estimated at 775,000 tons Li. The total recoverable reserves are estimated at 49,450 tons Li.

Zimbabwe

The largest lithium-bearing area in Zimbabwe is that of the Bikita tinfields, located about 45 miles east of Fort Victoria. Exploration has indicated the presence of an important mineralized zone within the Al Hayat, Bikita, and Southern sectors. The pegmatite is about 5100 ft long and its width varies from 95 to 210 ft. It strikes north-northeast and dips from 14° to 45° east. The property is operated by Bikita Minerals (Pvt.) Ltd., controlled by B.P. Minerals.

The pegmatite is asymmetrically zoned and contains a variety of commercially important lithium minerals as well as beryl and pollucite.

Drilling and development work have proved a reserve of 12 million tons of quarry ore grading 1.4% Li. Mining is presently done in the Al Hayat sector. The plant produces about 2,200 tons per month of petalite, 800 tons per month of lepidolite and 800 tons per month of spodumene. In the reduction plant, feldspar is separated from petalite and ground for sale (Wegener, 1980).

Other minor lithium-bearing occurrences are known in the Wankie, Salisbury, Umtali, Mtoko, Insizia, Matobo, and Mazoe districts (Toombs, 1962).

Minor Producing Districts

South America

Only two countries produce small amounts of lithium minerals in South America: Brazil and Argentina. The amblygonite deposit in Surinam has been essentially depleted.

In Brazil, lithium-bearing pegmatites are known in the districts of Minas Gerais and in the northeastern portion of the country which includes the states of Paraiba, Rio Grande do Norte, and Ceará (Heinrich, 1964).

The pegmatites which carry spodumene and amblygonite usually have been mined for cassiterite, tantalite, and beryl, while the lithium minerals have been sporadically recovered as byproducts.

An important occurrence of petalite has been reported in the tin-producing district near Araçuai, Brazil, located about 250 miles northeast of Belo Horizonte in the state of Minas Gerais. The pegmatite is reported to contain about 100,000 tons of petalite grading 2.0% Li.

Spodumene reserves have been estimated at 300,000 tons, while lepidolite reserves are considered to be nearly exhausted.

In 1976, production of spodumene was estimated at 900 tons and petalite at 2,500 tons (Afghouni, 1978).

In Argentina, lithium-bearing pegmatites occur in the western portion of the state in the Sierras Pampaneas, which include the productive districts of San Luis, Cordoba, and Catamarca. The pegmatites are zoned and contain spodumene. The reserves, considered to be small, total about 18,000 tons as spodumene (Angelleli and Rinaldi, 1963, 1965). Recently, the occurrence of brine has been reported in the salares of northwestern Argentina.

Namibia

Following a low production period, mining in the Karibib district was stimulated by the trade sanctions imposed on Southern Rhodesia (now Zimbabwe) in 1964. The district, located approximately 120 miles from Walvis Bay on the Atlantic Ocean, contains several strongly zoned pegmatites which contain lepidolite, petalite, and small amounts of amblygonite. In 1968, Klockner & Co. A.G. acquired the Rubicon and Helicon mines previously operated by S.W.A. Lithium Mines (Pty.) Ltd. Production has been expanded by the installation of a lepidolite flotation plant. Lepidolite reserves suitable as flotation feed material have been estimated at 1,000,000 tons (Anon., 1968a). Petalite reserves consist of some 200,000 tons of crude ore (Gevers, 1953).

Other African Deposits

In Africa, smaller productive areas occur in Mozambique, Uganda, and Ruanda.

In the Alto Ligonha area of Mozambique, lepidolite, amblygonite, and spodumene occur in zoned pegmatite bodies. Only lepidolite is exploited commercially. Amblygonite is rare, and spodumene is completely altered to kaolinite (Hutchinson and Claus, 1956).

Large amblygonite masses are found in pegmatite districts located west of the capital city of Kigal, in Ruanda (Valarmoff, 1954), and north of Kampala in Uganda (Roberts, 1948).

Other occurrences of lithium minerals include the Sudan, the Malagasy Republic, the Ivory Coast, and the Republic of South Africa (Nel, 1968).

Australia

The most important lithium-bearing districts occur in western Australia. Mining is active only in the Coolgardie district where small quantities of petalite and minor amounts of spodumene and amblygonite are produced at Londonderry. In the same area near Mt. Marion, the Western Mining Corp. has discovered a spodumene deposit. Drilling has indicated reserves in excess of 1,000,000 tons of ore (Anon., 1968).

Other lithium mineral occurrences include spodumene near Ravensthrope, lepidolite near Wodgina and Londonderry, and minor amblygonite near Euriowie, New South Wales (McLeod, 1965).

In addition to the producing areas described above, lithium minerals are known to occur in many European countries and in Ireland, India, Korea, and Japan. Sizable deposits exist in the Soviet Union but actual reserves data are not available.

Potential Producing Districts

Probably the largest lithium resources in the world are contained in the Manono and Kittolo pegmatites located in the Belgian Congo (Zaire). At the present time, only cassiterite and columbite are mined by Congo-Etain from the Manono pegmatite which has a length of 3 miles and a width ranging from 325 to 1300 ft. The adjoining Kittolo pegmatite has similar dimensions. Although the pegmatites are apparently zoned, their dimensions imply spodumene reserves which dwarf the presently known world reserves. However, the deposit may not have an economic value for years because of the very poor transportation facilities. The deposit is located about 1,360 miles from the Angolan port of Lobito.

Although many pegmatite districts have been described in Canada, only two are known to contain commercial quantities of lithium minerals: the Preissac-Lacorne district of western Quebec and the Bernic Lake area of Manitoba.

In the Preissac-Lacorne district, spodumene-bearing pegmatites intrude Precambrian metamorphic rocks. In addition to spodumene, they contain a variety of other minerals such as lepidolite, beryl, pollucite, molybdenite, and minor amounts of columbite and tantalite. The largest reserves occur on the property of the Quebec Lithium Corp. where drilling has indicated 15,000,000 tons of ore grading 0.56% (Mulligan, 1965). Although the company produced spodumene concentrates for a few years, the operation is presently inactive. Several other companies control spodumene-bearing properties in the district.

In the Bernic Lake area of southeastern Manitoba, the lithium-bearing pegmatites are part of a zoned complex, presently exploited for tantalum by the Tantalum Mining Corp. The property is located in the Cat Lake-Winnipeg River district which lies some 80 miles northeast of Winnipeg. The pegmatite is complexly zoned and contains several lithium-bearing units. It is a lenticular body about 3600 ft long, 1500 ft wide with a maximum thickness of 280 ft (Cerny and Turnock, 1971).

The spodumene reserves have been measured at 7,400,000 tons grading 1.34% Li. In addition to spodumene, three lepidolite zones averaging from 0.87% to 1.31% Li provide an additional 107,000 tons of ore (private communication).

The pegmatite also contains 300,000 tons of pollucite averaging 23% Cs_2O. 1,128,766 tons of tantalite grading 0.16% Ta_2O_5, and 1,000,-000 tons of beryl ore averaging 0.22% BeO.

Lithium-bearing pegmatites are also known in the Herb Lake and East Braintree-West Hawk districts of Manitoba; the Yellowknife-Beaulieu district of the Northwest Territory; and the Nipigon, Dryden, Lac La Croix, Root Lake, Falcon Lake, and O'Sullivan Lake districts of Ontario (Mulligan, 1965).

Among the recently discovered brine deposits, the Salar de Atacama constitutes a very important future source of lithium. The salar is located in northern Chile, where it straddles the Tropic of Capricorn. The basin proper has a surface area of approximately 1200 square miles and the salt nucleus proper covers approximately 540 square miles. The salar, which lies at an elevation of 7500 ft, is bounded on the eastern side by the Andean Cordillera and on the western side by the Cordillera Domeyko. The salt nucleus consists almost exclusively of halite facies with a development of very narrow marginal facies of sulfate and carbonate.

The interstitial brine contains an average lithium concentration of 1500 ppm. Lithium resources are reported at 4.3 million tons.

In 1975, Foote Mineral Co. entered into an agreement to evaluate the feasibility of producing lithium carbonate.

Future Raw Materials

Several areas of the world carry potential lithium raw materials in the form of brines, geothermal brines, oil well brines, and clays.

Among the existing brine deposits, the Great Salt Lake of Utah constitutes an important potential source of lithium chemicals. The lake holds a brine formed as a result of concentration by solar evaporation of waters contained in a much larger and more dilute Pleistocene lake—Lake Bonneville. In the Bear River Basin, the Great Salt Lake Minerals and Chemicals Corp. has constructed 14,000 acres of ponds and is producing potassium and sodium sulfates. The recoverable lithium resources are estimated at 286,000 tons (Evans, 1978).

A potential geothermal area lies within the Imperial Valley of southern California. The chemically complex brine contains large concentrations of sodium, calcium, and potassium. It also carries about 0.020% Li. Koenig (1970) indicates that the brine volume which exists under an area of 12 to 24 sq miles is in excess of 1 cu mile. This suggests a potential reserve exceeding 840,000 tons Li. Exploitation of lithium will depend upon whether or not some complex chemical engineering problems are solved.

Other geothermal areas include the Reykanes Field of Iceland where the visible active area covers an area of about 2 sq miles. Feasibility studies (Ludviksson and Hermannsson, 1970) indicate that a yearly production of 500 tons of lithium compounds is possible. The brine contains 8 ppm Li. Additional thermal areas are known at Reykir, Hveragardi, and Krysuvik (Karlsson, 1961; Prast, 1972).

A similar potential source of lithium exists in the geothermal waters at Wairakei, New Zealand. Potential production from bore waters containing 13 ppm Li are estimated at 2400 tpy as Li_2CO_3, assuming a discharge rate of 1,000,000 gal per hr (Kennedy, 1964).

Lithium-bearing clays are known to occur in several localities in the United States. The highest lithium value of 0.53% has been recorded at Hector, CA, where the Baroid Division of National Lead Co. mines hectorite for its swelling characteristics (Ames, et al., 1958). Hectorite has been identified in Clayton Valley where it occurs as an alteration product of volcanic ash along a fault zone and is one of the clay minerals in Tertiary and Quaternary lake sediments (Kunasz, 1970). The hectorite contains 0.24% to 0.35% Li. At Spor Mountain, Utah, 0.11% Li has been reported in beryllium-bearing tuffs (Shawe, 1968, Shawe, et al., 1964), where lithium probably also occurs in hectorite. The occurrence of lithium-bearing clays is also reported (Norton, 1965) in Yavapai County, AZ (0.10% Li), in Tertiary clays at Kramer, CA (0.19% Li) (Muessig, 1966), and in the Turilari playa (0.14% Li) in Argentina (Muessig, 1966). An extensive survey by the Lithium Exploration Group of the US Geological Survey has indicated that vast resources of lithium lie in a great number of sedimentary clays (Vine, 1976).

Although the clays contain lithium concentrations of the same order of magnitude as commercial pegmatites, they are not likely to become lithium sources in the near future because of technological problems associated with the extraction of lithium from the crystal lattice.

Production

The bulk of the world's lithium is manufactured in the United States by two companies: Foote Mineral Co., at Silver Peak, NV, Kings Mountain, NC, Sunbright, VA, and at Frazer, PA; and Lithium Corp. of America at Bessemer City, NC, and in the United Kingdom. In Europe, an important chemical producer is Metallgesellschaft A.G. in Germany. In addition, lithium chemicals are produced in Japan and Brazil. Significant quantities of lithium ores are produced in Zimbabwe by Bikita Minerals (Pvt.) Ltd. The USSR produces sizable quantities of chemicals. Lithium chemicals also have been supplied recently by the People's Republic of China.

Mining of lithium ores can be divided into three categories: underground, open-pit, and "mining" of brines.

Where practical, such as at Kings Mountain, NC, the open pit is the most economical method. Higher cost underground methods are used in Brazil and Namibia.

Although hand cobbing and screening are still used in Brazil and Africa, flotation is the main beneficiation method of lithium ores. In the production of spodumene concentrates, the mined ore undergoes several stages of crushing, grinding, and classification, followed by flotation with organic reagents. At Foote Mineral Co., the spodumene concentrate collected from the flotation cells is further processed into a chemical grade used in the manufacture of lithium chemicals. A low iron spodumene variety produced by the chlorination of β-spodumene (Fishwick, 1967; Richardson and Fishwick, 1968) is used as a substitute for petalite in glass-ceramic applications.

In addition to spodumene concentrates, the beneficiation of pegmatite ore includes several byproducts such as quartz, feldspar, and mica. Other potential byproducts are beryl, columbite, tantalite, cassiterite, and wolframite.

The extraction of lithium from spodumene can be achieved by several methods. Presently, the process used by Foote Mineral Co. and Lithium Corp. of America involves calcination to β-spodumene, which is then reacted with sulfuric acid to produce lithium sulfate. Conversion to lithium carbonate is accomplished by soda ash addition (Ellestad and Leute, 1950). Other processes have included the calcination of a spodumene-calcium carbonate mixture, followed by hot water leaching, evaporation-crystallization to produce lithium hydroxide as a final product. Another process, used in the past by the Quebec Lithium Corp., involved the calcination of spodumene and its reaction with an aqueous solution of sodium carbonate. Purification involved reaction with carbon dioxide, and then heating to produce a final lithium carbonate product (Archambault, 1963).

Lithium is produced from brines at only one location in the world—Clayton Valley, Nevada. Foote Mineral Co. "mines" by pumping saline solutions contained in sediments into large solar evaporation ponds (Barrett and O'Neil, 1970). Following a 20- to 30-fold concentration, the final lithium chloride solution is converted to lithium carbonate by addition of soda ash. Small impurities are removed within the pond system by the addition of lime (Shay, 1967).

At the Salar de Atacama, lithium rich brines will also be concentrated in solar evaporation ponds. Following the removal of calcium, magnesium, and sulfate impurities, the concentrated lithium chloride solution will be reacted with soda ash to produce a final lithium carbonate product. Production of lithium carbonate by the Sociedad Chilena de Lithio—a joint venture between Foote Mineral Co. (55%) and CORFO (45%)—is scheduled for 1984.

Uses

Lithium is marketed and used in three basic forms: as an ore and concentrate, as a metal, and as chemical compounds. As shown in Table 1, there are numerous applications.

Ores and concentrates are consumed by the glass, ceramic, and porcelain enamel industries. Petalite, lepidolite, and amblygonite can be used without prior beneficiation, except hand-cobbing, while spodumene must be concentrated and treated for removal of iron. Lithium is useful because it creates favorable internal nucleation conditions. By comparison, sodium favors external crystallization. Because of its small ionic radius and high field strength,

TABLE 1—Applications

		Ores		
Spodumene	Petalite	Lepidolite	Amblygonite	Metal
Ceramics	Ceramics	Glasses	Li-Chemicals	Deoxidation
Glass ceramics	Glasses			Degasification
Enamels	Glazes			Alloys
Glasses	Enamels			Organic compounds
Li-Salts				Synthetic rubber
				Vitamins
				Nuclear energy
				Battery

			Chemicals			
Lithium Carbonate	Lithium Hydroxide	Lithium Chloride	Lithium Fluoride	Lithium Bromide	Butyllithium	Other Lithium Compounds
Ceramics	Greases	Li-Metal	Porcelains	Absorption refrigeration	Polymerization	Electrolytes
Li-Chemicals	Li-Salts	Fluxing	Enamels		Pharmaceuticals	Catalysis
Fluxing	CO_2 absorption	Dehumidification	Glazes		Organic synthesis	
Pharmaceuticals		Synthetic fibers	Welding			
Aluminum electrolysis cells		Tracer	Brazing			
			Optics			

lithium imparts high mechanical strength, thermal shock resistance, as well as good chemical resistance to the product (Fishwick, 1966). In these applications, lithium is also introduced in the form of lithium carbonate.

In metal form, lithium is the lightest solid element, having an atomic weight of 6.94 and a specific gravity of 0.534 (20°C). It is manufactured by the electrolysis of a molten salt mixture of lithium and potassium chlorides. Lithium metal is used in the synthesis of butyllithium. In nonferrous metallurgy, the high reactivity of lithium with gases is used for scavenging oxygen and sulfur, converting them into stable compounds. Lithium is also used in lithium-aluminum and lithium-magnesium alloys where it imparts high temperature strength, improves elasticity, and increases the tensile strength (Bach, et al., 1967). An important development has been the production of lithium batteries used in pacemakers, electric calculators, and watches (Grady, 1980).

Among the various chemicals produced, the most important are: lithium carbonate, lithium hydroxide, lithium chloride, lithium bromide, and butyllithium. The remaining compounds constitute only a small proportion of the lithium market.

Lithium carbonate, in addition to its consumption by the ceramic industry, is being used at an increasing rate in the aluminum industry. When added to aluminum reduction cells, it increases the conductivity of the molten bath, reduces operating temperature, and results in higher production. It is also very effective in reducing fluorine emissions by retaining the fluorine as lithium fluoride in the bath. In purified form, lithium carbonate is being used in the chemotherapeutic treatment of manic depression.

Lithium hydroxide was first employed as an ingredient in alkaline storage batteries where its presence increased the life of the cells (Bach, et al., 1967). In the 1940s, a new application was discovered by Clarence Earl who developed a new grease by reacting lithium hydroxide with fatty acids. The resulting grease was found to retain its viscosity over a wide temperature range and remain stable in the presence of water. Today, lithium-based greases have become a standard product in military, industrial, and automotive lubrication fields. Anhydrous lithium hydroxide is capable of absorbing large quantities of carbon dioxide, a property that has been utilized in the air regeneration system of the Apollo command and lunar modules, as well as new applications in the mining industry for rescue-breathing apparatus.

Lithium chloride and lithium bromide brines have low vapor pressures and are used in absorption refrigeration systems. Lithium chloride also constitutes the feed material for the production of lithium metal. Lithium fluoride is used mainly as a flux in enamels, glasses, glazes, and in welding and brazing.

The most important organic compound is butyllithium. It serves as a catalyst in the polymerization of butadiene, isoprene, and styrene to produce polymers with special properties.

Numerous miscellaneous applications of lithium chemicals include sanitation and bleaching, hydrogen generation, oxygen generation, catalysis, and vitamin synthesis.

Prices

In the United States, the price of chemical spodumene is approximately $180 per net ton f.o.b. Freight rates for lithium ores vary from $25 to $35, according to the distance from the producing plants.

In other parts of the world, the 1983 prices of various ores (in dollars per long ton, c.i.f.) are as follows:

Spodumene—4 to 7% Li_2O: 315–485
Petalite   —3.5 to 4.5% Li_2O: $315

Prices for lithium chemicals in 1983 are shown in Table 2.

Future Trends

Lithium is still a developing commodity. Its applications in various phases of the metallurgical and chemical industries have been rapidly diversifying and expanding in the past few years. In 1980, the estimated world consumption of lithium metal and chemicals was reported at 54.5 million pounds of lithium carbonate equivalents (Alexander, 1981). In addition, it was also estimated that the USSR consumes probably about 10 million pounds of lithium carbonate equivalents. At the present time, the industry has sufficient production capacity to supply the existing market,

TABLE 2—Typical Prices of Lithium Compounds in 1983

	$ per Lb
Lithium carbonate, powder	1.48
Lithium hydroxide, monohydrate, bulk	1.93
Lithium chloride, anhydrous, bulk	3.15
Lithium fluoride, bulk	4.50
Lithium metal, 1,000-lb lots	21.70
n-Butyllithium, 15% solution, bulk	13.39
Lithium bromide, anhydrous, bulk	6.51
Lithium bromide, brine, bulk	3.00
Lithium chloride, brine, bulk	2.67

and the announced increases for new capacity appear to be sufficient to meet future growth.

A potential application for lithium is in nuclear power as an absorption blanket in fusion generation. In thermonuclear reactions, the most likely fuel will be a deuterium-tritium mixture because of its very large reaction rate (Bogart, 1980). Although tritium is naturally scarce, it can be artificially generated within the reactor itself by bombarding the lithium-6 isotope in the blanket with the neutrons created by the fusion reaction.

A promising application for lithium metal is in batteries. In the past decade, large efforts have been made to find a battery with a high energy-weight ratio. Because of its low weight and high electrochemical potential, lithium is a prime candidate (Grady, 1980). Primary lithium batteries have moved from the development laboratory into pilot plant production. Commercial utilization could require many thousands of pounds of lithium metal.

Singleton (1979) estimates that the world demand for lithium will quadruple by the end of the century. If the potential applications in nuclear power and batteries are considered, the growth rate may be considerably greater.

Presently known reserves exceed the cumulative conventional demands by about two orders of magnitude. Thus the amount of exploration has been justifiably limited. Should increasing demands be imposed on the lithium industry, vast resources can be tapped within a short period of time (Kunasz, 1980).

Bibliography and References

Anon., 1967, "Batteries," *Metals Week*, Sep. 25, pp. 11–27.

Anon., 1967a, "Lithium and the Electric Car," *Foote Prints*, Vol. 36, pp. 96–97.

Anon., 1968, "Lithium Find for Western Mining," *Mining Journal*, Mar. 8.

Anon., 1968a, "Klockner Buys SWA Lithium," *Metal Bulletin*, No. 5288, Apr. 5, p. 26.

Anon., 1976, "Lithium By the Year 2000," *Industrial Minerals*, No. 108, Sep., pp. 45–46.

Anon., 1977, "Lithium Chemical Expansion Insures Supply," *Industrial Minerals*, No. 122, Nov., pp. 67–73.

Afghouni, K., 1978, "Lithium Ores in Brazil," *Energy*, S.S. Penner, ed., Vol. 3, No. 3, pp. 247–253.

Alexander, J.H., 1981, Lithium Annual Review, *Engineering and Mining Journal*, pp. 111–113.

Ames, L.L., et al., 1958, "A Contribution on the Hector, California Bentonite Deposit," *Economic Geology*, Vol. 53, No. 1, Jan.–Feb. pp. 22–37.

Angelleli, V., and Rinaldi, C.A., 1963, "Yacimientos de Minerales de Litio de las Provincias de San Luis y Cordoba," Info. No. 91, Argentina, Com. Nac. Energia Atomica, 79 pp.

Angelleli, V., and Rinaldi, C.A., 1965, "Resena Acerca de la Estructura, Mineralizacion, y Aprovechamento de Nuestras Pegmatita Portadoras de Minerales de Litio," *Acta Geologica Lilloana*, Vol. 5, pp. 1–18.

Archambault, M., 1963, US Patent 3,112,171, Nov. 26.

Bach, R. O., et al., 1967, "Lithium and Lithium Compounds," *Encyclopedia of Chemical Technology*, A. Standen, ed., Vol. 12, 2nd ed., Interscience, New York.

Barrett, W.T., and O'Neill, B.J., Jr., 1970, "Recovery of Lithium from Saline Brines Using Solar Evaporation," *Third Salt Symposium*, J.L. Rau, and L.F. Dellwig, eds., Vol. 2, The Northern Ohio Geological Society, Inc., Cleveland, pp. 47–50.

Bogart, L.S., 1980, "Potential Lithium Requirement for Fusion Electric Power," *Foote Prints*, Vol. 43, No. 1, pp. 2–11.

Buckley, S., 1983, "Lithium—Recession Delays Market Lift Off," *Industrial Minerals*, No. 185, Feb., pp. 25–35.

Caldwell, H.C., et al., 1971, "A Pharmaco-Kinetic Analysis of Lithium Carbonate Absorption from Several Formulations in Man," *Journal of Clinical Pharmacology*, Vol. 11, No. 5, pp. 349–356.

Cameron, E.N., et al., 1949, *Internal Structure of Granitic Pegmatites*, Monograph 2, Economic Geology Publishing Co., Urbana, IL.

Cameron, E.N., et al., 1954, "Pegmatite Investigations, 1942–1945, New England," Professional Paper 255, US Geological Survey, 352 pp.

Cerny, P., and Turnock, A.C., 1971, "Pegmatites of Southeastern Manitoba," Special Paper No. 9, Geological Association of Canada, pp. 119–127.

Deer, W.A., et al., 1962, "Lepidolite," *Rock-Forming Minerals*, Vol. 3, J. Wiley and Sons, New York, pp. 85–91.

Eardley, A.J., 1970, "Salt Economy of the Great Salt Lake," *Third Symposium on Salt*, J.L. Rau and L.F. Dellwig, eds., Vol. 1, The Northern Ohio Geological Society, Inc., Cleveland, pp. 78–105.

Ellestad, R.B., and Leute, K.M., 1950, US Patent 2,516,109, July 25.

Fishwick, J.H., 1966, "Glass Ceramics," *Foote Prints*, Vol. 35, No. 1, pp. 20–23.

Fishwick, J.H., 1967, US Patent 3,394,988, Oct. 31.

Foster, M.D., 1960, "Interpretation of the Composition of Lithium Micas," Professional Paper 354–B, US Geological Survey, 146 pp.

Goldschmidt, V.M., 1937, "The Principles of Distribution of Chemical Elements in Minerals and Rocks," *Journal of the Chemical Society*, pp. 655–673.

Hanley, J.B., et al., 1950, "Pegmatite Investigations in Colorado, Wyoming, and Utah, 1942–1944," Professional Paper 227, US Geological Survey, 125 pp.

Hegelson, H.C., 1968, "Geological and Thermodynamic Characteristics of the Salton Sea Geothermal System," *American Journal of Science*, Vol. 266, March, pp. 129–166.

Heinrich, E.W., 1964, "The Tin-Tantalum-Lithium Pegmatites of Sao Joao Del Rei District, Minas Gerais, Brazil," *Economic Geology*, Vol. 59, No. 6, Sep.–Oct., pp. 982–1002.

Holdren, J.P., 1971, "Adequacy of Lithium Supplies as Fusion Energy Source," Hearing Before the Joint Committee on Atomic Energy, Congress of the United States, Nov. 10 and 11.

Hortsman, E.L., 1957, "The Distribution of Lithium, Rubidium, and Cesium in Igneous and Sedimentary Rocks," *Geochimica et Cosmochimica Acta*, Vol. 12, pp. 1–28.

Hutchinson, R.W., and Claus, R.J., 1956, "Pegmatite Deposits, Alto Ligonha, Portuguese East Africa," *Economic Geology*, Vol. 51, pp. 757–779.

Jahns, R.H., 1952, "Pegmatite Deposits of the White Picacho District, Maricopa and Yavapai Counties, Arizona," University of Arizona *Bulletin*, Vol. 23, No. 5, 105 pp.

Jahns, R.H., 1955, "The Study of Pegmatites, *Economic Geology*, 50th Anniversary Volume, Part II, pp. 1025–1130.

Karlsson, T., 1961, "Drilling for Natural Steam and Hot Water in Iceland," *Proceedings of the United Nations Conference on New Sources of Energy*, Rome, Vol. 3, pp. 215–221.

Kennedy, A.M., 1964, "Recovery of Lithium and Other Minerals from Geothermal Water at Wairakei," *Proceedings of the United Nations Conference on New Sources of Energy*, Rome, Vol. 3, pp. 502–511.

Kesler, T.L., 1961, "Exploration of the Kings Mountain Pegmatites," *Mining Engineering*, Vol. 13, No. 9, Sep., pp. 1062–1068.

Koenig, J.B., 1970, "Geological Setting of the Imperial Valley and its Geothermal Resources," Compendium of Papers Presented at the Imperial Valley—Salton Sea Area Geothermal Hearing, Oct. 22–23, Sacramento, CA, pp. E1–E5.

Kunasz, I.A., 1970, "Geology and Geochemistry of the Lithium Deposit in Clayton Valley, Esmeralda County, Nevada," Ph.D. Thesis, The Pennsylvania State University, 114 pp.

Kunasz, I.A., 1975, "Lithium Raw Materials," *Industrial Minerals and Rocks*, 4th ed., S.J. Lefond, ed., AIME, New York, pp. 791–803.

Kunasz, I.A., 1980, "Lithium, How Much?" *Foote Prints*, Vol. 48, No. 1, pp. 23–27.

Ludviksson, V., and Hermannsson, S., 1970, "Some Possibilities for Major New Industries in Iceland," National Research Council, Reykjavik, 26 pp.

Mayhew, E.J., and Heylmun, E.B., 1966, "Complex Salt and Brines of the Paradox Basin," *Second Symposium on Salt,* J.L. Rau, ed., The Northern Ohio Geological Society, Inc., Cleveland, pp. 221–235.

McLeod, I.R., 1965, *Atlas of Australian Resources Mineral Deposits,* 2nd ed., Department of National Development, Canberra.

Muessig, S., 1966. "Recent South American Borate Deposits," *Second Symposium on Salt,* J.L. Rau, ed., The Northern Ohio Geological Society, Inc., Cleveland, pp. 151–159.

Mulligan, R., 1965, "The Geology of Canadian Lithium Pegmatites," Economic Report No. 21, Geological Survey of Canada, 131 pp.

Nel, L.T., 1968, "Ore Deposits of Lithium in the Republic of South Africa," Atomic Energy Board, Republic of South Africa, PEL 23, 23 pp.

Norton, J.J., and Schlegel, D.M., 1955, "Lithium Resources of North America," Bulletin 1027–G, US Geological Survey, pp. 325–350.

Norton, J.J., 1965, "Lithium-Bearing Bentonite Deposit, Yavapai County, Arizona," Professional Paper 525–D, US Geological Survey, pp. D163–D166.

Page, L.R., et al., 1953, "Pegmatite Investigations, 1942–1945, Black Hills, South Dakota," Professional Paper 247, US Geological Survey, 228 pp.

Penner, S.S., 1978, "The Lithium Symposium 1977," *Energy,* Vol. 3, No. 3, 413 pp.

Prast, W.G., 1972, "Scope for Expanded Use of Iceland's Resources," *Mining Magazine,* Nov., pp. 465–468.

Rankama, K., and Sahama, T.G., 1950, "The Alkali Metals: Lithium, Sodium, Potassium, Rubidium, Cesium," *Geochemistry,* University of Chicago Press, Chicago, pp. 422–442.

Richardson, L.S., and Fishwick, J.H., 1968, "Removal of Iron from Spodumene Concentrates by Chlorination," *Glass Industry,* July, pp. 377–81.

Roberts, R.O., 1948, "Amblygonite and Associated Minerals from the Mbale Mine, Uganda," *Imperial Institute Bulletin,* Vol. 46, pp. 342–347.

Shawe, R.D., 1968, "Geology of the Spor Mountain Beryllium District, Utah," *Ore Deposits in the U.S., 1933/1967,* J. Ridge, ed., Vol. 2, AIME, New York, pp. 1143–1161.

Shawe, R.D., et al., 1964, "Lithium Associated with Beryllium in Rhyolitic Tuff at Spor Mountain, Western Juab County, Utah," Professional Paper 501–C, US Geological Survey, pp. 86–87.

Shay, F.B., 1967, "Low Cost Lithium from Brine at Silver Peak, Nevada," paper presented at AIME Annual Meeting, Los Angeles, Feb. 21.

Singleton, R.H., 1979, "Lithium," *Mineral Commodity Profiles,* US Bureau of Mines, 25 pp.

Strock, L.W., 1936, "Zur Geochemie des Lithiums," Nachrichten von der Gesellschaft der Wissenschaften zu Goeltingen, Mathematisch-Physikalische Klasse, IV, N.F. 1, No. 15, 171 pp.

Toombs, R.B., 1962, "A Survey of the Mineral Industry of Southern Africa," Mineral Information Bulletin MR 58, Department of Mines and Technical Survey, Ottawa, 275 pp.

Valarmoff, N., 1954, "Matériaux pour l'Etude des Pegmatites du Congo Belge et du Ruanda-Urundi," *Annales de la Société Géologique Belgique,* Vol. 78, pp. 1–25.

Vine, J.D., 1976, "Lithium Resources and Requirements by the Year 2000," Professional Paper 1005, US Geological Survey, 162 pp.

Wegener, J.E., 1980, "Lithium Minerals in Zimbabwe with Special Reference to the Operations at Bikita Minerals (Pvt) Ltd.," International Conference on Zimabwe, Sep. 1–5, Salisbury.

Wegener, J.E., 1981, "Profile on Bikita—Processed Petalite, The New Priority," *Industrial Minerals,* No. 165, June, pp. 51-53.

Westenberger, H., 1963, "The Lithium Minerals, Their Formation and Occurrence," *Review of Activities,* No. 6, Metallgesellschaft A.G., Frankfurt/Main.

White, D.E., 1957, "Thermal Waters of Volcanic Origin," *Geological Society of America Bulletin,* Vol. 68, pp. 1637–1658.

Winchell, A.N., 1942, "Further Studies of the Lepidolite System," *American Mineralogist,* Vol. 27, pp. 114–130.

Magnesite and Related Minerals

O. M. WICKEN *

L. R. DUNCAN †

Magnesium, the eighth most abundant element in the earth's crust, is found widely distributed in a variety of minerals. Among the more commercially important ones are magnesite ($MgCO_3$), brucite ($Mg[OH]_2$), dolomite ($CaMg[CO_3]_2$), and the salts magnesium sulfate and chloride often found in natural brines. Among other commercially important magnesium-containing minerals are olivine ($[MgFe]_2$-SiO_4), talc ($H_2Mg_3[SiO_3]_4$), and serpentine ($H_4Mg_3Si_2O_9$). These are valuable because of desirable characteristics given them by the magnesium content and its placement in the particular crystal structure.

These minerals are the raw materials for a host of products including magnesium metal and several grades of magnesia or magnesia-containing materials for refractories, fluxes, fillers, insulation, cements, decolorants, fertilizers, and chemicals.

Considering only those minerals valued for their magnesia or magnesium content, over 85% of the material tonnages are processed to be used as refractories. Dolomite, which is used in enormous tonnages for its physical properties in construction, has an important use as a refractory raw material in its own right and, after calcination, as a precipitant for magnesium hydroxide, which is an intermediate for the production of magnesia or magnesium metal. Magnesia from the reaction of calcined dolomite (or limestone) with seawater or magnesium-containing brines has supplanted much of the production of magnesia from mined magnesite, particularly in the United States.

* CEO, SRM Associates, Pittsburgh, PA.

† Vice President, Technical and Manufacturing Services, Harbison-Walker Refractories International, Div. of Dresser Industries Inc., Pittsburgh, PA.

The best known of the minerals directly and widely exploited for magnesia content is magnesite, one of the calcite group of rhombohedral carbonates which includes calcite ($CaCO_3$), siderite ($FeCO_3$), and rhodochrosite ($MnCO_3$) among others. The members of this group enter into a wide range of substitutional solid solutions when the positive ions have similar radii. The radii of magnesium and iron ions are within 6% of each other; hence, magnesite and siderite form a complete series of which breunnerite (ferroan magnesite) is a well-known end member. However, the radius of calcium ion is 36% larger than that of magnesium ion, and only limited substitution exists at each end of the $MgCO_3$-$CaCO_3$ series. Dolomite is not a member of the calcite group, but results when calcium and magnesium ions alternate in equal number in an ordered structure among carbonate ions. The result of these relationships is that calcite and dolomite, often found intermixed with magnesite, occur commonly as identifiable crystal entities which can often be separated to a varying degree from the magnesite by various beneficiation techniques.

Magnesite, when pure, contains 47.8% MgO and 52.2% CO_2. The pure mineral is sometimes, but rarely, found as transparent crystals resembling calcite, but, preponderantly, magnesite contains variable amounts of the carbonates, oxides, and silicates of iron, calcium, manganese, and aluminum. Magnesite may be either crystalline or amorphous (cryptocrystalline). The crystalline form has a hardness of 3.5 to 4.0. The color may range from white to black with shades of yellow, blue, red, or gray. The color is not a fundamentally significant indicator of purity, but in a given deposit, an experienced person can often roughly grade magnesite by assessing color and crystallinity.

The crystalline form of magnesite occurs in

relatively few but large deposits whereas the cryptocrystalline variety tends to occur in many but small deposits. Cryptocrystalline magnesite is massive with no cleavage and is sometimes descriptively called *bone magnesite*. The fracture is usually conchoidal, and hardness is 3.5 to 5.0. The color is normally white, but it can be tints of yellow, orange, or buff. Accessory siliceous minerals such as serpentine, quartz, or chalcedony are usually present. Calcium minerals are usually absent or in low concentration in cryptocrystalline magnesite as contrasted to their almost invariable presence and higher concentration in the crystalline variety.

The specific gravity of cryptocrystalline magnesite runs between 2.90 and 3.00, while that of pure, crystalline form is 3.02. In actuality, the crystalline form is often higher than 3.02 because of the presence of iron carbonate.

Magnesite dissociates upon heating to form magnesia (MgO) and carbon dioxide. When heated sufficiently, magnesia develops a crystal structure identical with that of the natural mineral periclase. The mineral periclase occurs only rarely in nature and not in any known, commercially workable deposits.

Brucite (Mg[OH]$_2$) is another mineral which can be directly reduced to periclase through the application of heat (Comstock, 1963). Brucite has been mined for the production of magnesia, but is no longer an important source. Theoretically it contains 69.1% MgO and 20.9% H$_2$O. The mineral is often associated with limestone, but most commonly with magnesite. The mineral has a translucent appearance and is relatively soft and lightweight with hardness of 2.5 and specific gravity of about 2.4. The color may be white, but blue or green with a gray cast is a more common coloration.

Nomenclature of Products

The word *magnesite* literally refers only to the natural mineral, but common usage has applied the name plus a prefatory word to two other types of materials. These are *dead-burned magnesite* and *caustic-calcined magnesite*. For the most part, these materials are essentially magnesia differing mainly in density and crystal development as the result of different levels of heat application. When magnesia produced from seawater or brines made its appearance, the products also received the appellations "dead-burned" or "caustic-calcined" magnesite, but of late years, the technical literature, particularly in the United States,

increasingly refers to the materials as "refractory magnesia" or "refractory grade magnesia," and "caustic-calcined magnesia," as appropriate. These terms are now also increasingly applied to magnesias derived from the mineral magnesite, particularly for those materials with high MgO content. Nevertheless, the older terms are still widely used in the trade, particularly abroad.

The term *dead-burned magnesite* (refractory magnesia) refers to the granular product produced by firing magnesite, magnesium hydroxide, or other material reducible to magnesia at temperatures in excess of 1450°C and for enough time to produce a dense, weather-stable granule suitable for use in the manufacture of refractory materials.

The use of terms in describing magnesia products is somewhat confusing to those not closely connected with the industry. The vagueness of terminology may lead to misreading of statistics to a degree that simultaneous shortage and surplus of magnesia products can be indicated. Confusion has been further amplified by use of such undefined terms as "high-purity" or "super-high-purity" magnesias. In most cases, these terms have been used for magnesia being supplied to the refractory industry and refer to content and relationship of the accessory oxides rather than a specific amount of MgO.

The loose term, "high-grade," refers to refractory magnesia containing roughly over 96% MgO and having a density greater than 3.20 as a result of processing at high temperatures. The mineral name *periclase* is sometimes used in the trade as a catchall term for any refractory magnesia having high MgO content and density. The term *standard grade*, as distinguished from *high-grade*, applies to material of relatively lower purity.

Caustic-calcined magnesia is the product produced when magnesite, or material reducible to magnesia by heat, is heated to such degree that less than 10% ignition loss remains and the product displays adsorptive capacity or activity. The degree of sintering is much less than in the case of refractory magnesia, and commonly the firing temperature is lower than 900°C.

Origin and Occurrence of Magnesite

Crystalline Magnesite

Deposits of crystalline magnesite are usually found associated with dolomite, but some major deposits such as found in Brazil are in limestone measures. But even in these cases, the magnesite is not in direct contact with limestone, but is separated by a dolomitized zone. The major deposits of crystalline magnesite of the world are those in Austria, USSR, Korea, Manchuria, Brazil, Canada, Australia, Nepal, and the United States. All are in dolomite host measures or zones. Further, all are in regions which have had orogenic activity. Commonly, such areas also show igneous activity, and an early and strongly supported theory postulated that magnesite resulted from action of igneous intrusions and associated solutions on the dolomite.

The dolomite measures are widely viewed as being sedimentary (Dunbar and Rogers, 1957), and a few investigations have suggested a sedimentary origin for both the magnesite and the enclosing dolomite (Paone, 1970; Schroeder, 1948), but consensus favors secondary placement of magnesite in preexisting dolomite by hydrothermal action on a volume for volume basis (Bain, 1924; Bennett, 1943; Campbell and Loofbourow, 1962).

In the rather unique deposit of magnesite near Kilmar, Que., Canada, the intermixed rock of magnesite-dolomite is thought to be the product of hydrothermal dolomization of the limestone (Bray and Hilchey, 1957).

Magnesite is often closely associated both spatially and in time with intrusive activity (Bain, 1924; Bodenlos, 1954; Siegfus, 1927; Spencer, 1972). Igneous rocks associated with magnesite vary widely in composition. Bodenlos (1954) compiled a list which includes amphibolite, pyroxenite, diabase, peridotite, rhyolite, quartz, basalt, granite, and others.

The minerals associated with several crystalline magnesite deposits suggest relatively high temperature of formation (Niiomy, 1925). These associated minerals include dolomite, talc, serpentine, diopside, hematite, and enstatite. Olivine, pyrrhotite, and magnetite have been recognized in the Chewelah (Washington) deposits, while scapolite has been found in the Manchurian deposits. On the basis of associated minerals, Bodenlos (1954) has suggested a temperature of formation of 300°C or higher, and Schroeder (1948), a temperature within the hypothermal range of 300–500°C. It is reasonable to conclude on the basis of associated minerals that these magnesite deposits formed at a temperature in excess of 300°C.

Although the field evidence is clear and consistent, the nature of the hydrothermal solutions and the mechanism of replacement remains a problem. Mechanisms suggested for the hydrothermal emplacement of magnesite in dolomite involve reaction with Mg-rich, CO_2-bearing solutions. Although CO_2-bearing solutions may be conveniently derived from nearby intrusive bodies, it is not easy to account for the required Mg-enrichment of such solutions. An experimental investigation (Rosenberg and Holland, 1964; Rosenberg and Mills, 1966), throws new light on this problem. The investigation was carried out to conform with observed field relations and under conditions that obviated the necessity for Mg-rich solutions; the results were consistent with the presence of high-temperature mineral assemblages associated with magnesite. The proposed mechanism may be summarized as follows:

1) Attack on preexisting dolomite by CO_2-bearing solutions at temperatures below 200°C resulting in solutions with Ca:Mg ratio of unity.

2) Heating of these solutions to temperatures in excess of 200°C, resulting in the replacement of host rock dolomite by magnesite with the production of Ca-rich solutions.

In the discussion on the origin of the magnesite deposits occurring in the Kumaun Himalaya, India, the role of algae was presented (Valdiya, 1968). A chain of lentiform deposits of coarsely crystalline magnesite extends for 130 km northwest from the Kali Valley to the Alaknanda Valley. The Almora mining district immediately west of Nepal is within the mineralized zone. The deposits are of uniform thickness and chemical and mineralogical composition. The reported average chemical composition is $MgCO_3$, 90.2%; $CaCO_3$, 2.9%; and $SiO_2 + R_2O_3$, 6.9%. The magnesite is restricted to a narrow stratigraphic interval in the upper part of the Gangolihat Dolomites and is almost invariably associated with the stromatolite-bearing dolomite. Barred embayments, attributed to barrier building by algae, were formed in the back reef shelf of the ancient Gangolihat Sea. The Mg:Ca ratio of the basin waters progressively increased with the passage of time as a cumulative result of biogenic and organic precipitation of $CaCO_3$ during the aqueous stages of the sedimentary process. Accumulation of algoid debris further increased the concentration of magnesium. The Mg:Ca ratio became so high that during periods of high pH attributable to prolific growth of the algae, the carbonates formed earlier were converted into carbonate assemblages of higher magnesium content, including magnesite. Coarse granularity of magnesite is attributed to later recrystallization during regional metamorphism. The Sinian magnesite of Malyghingen of Manchuria and of northern China form irregular, though concordant, bedded deposits of a similar nature (Nishihara, 1956).

Cryptocrystalline Magnesite

Cryptocrystalline or "amorphous" magnesite is an alteration product of serpentine or allied magnesium rocks which have been subjected to the action of carbonate waters. The serpentine which lies near or surrounds the magnesite is itself an alteration product of the ultrabasic rocks. The mode of formation of the magnesite usually limits the amount of impurities to small amounts of iron, lime, and silica.

Occurrences of this type of magnesite are fairly common throughout the world, but because of their usually limited size, few—with the notable exceptions of those in Greece, Turkey, and Australia—are worked commercially. The action of surface water containing carbon dioxide percolating down through serpentinized fissures can convert serpentine to magnesite and other minerals. Also, waters rising through fissures could produce magnesite. In both cases, the relationship between temperature and carbon dioxide pressure is very critical to the formation of magnesite. The zones closer to the earth's surface are more favorably situated for the reaction. Therefore, most of the deposits of this type of magnesite are found near the surface and have limited extent in depth.

Distribution of Deposits

From the natural mineral magnesite, total world production (1980) of all grades of deadburned and calcined magnesite was about 4.3 million st, representing about 10 million st of crude magnesite. The production came from many countries, with those of central Europe and Asia contributing more than 80%.

Prior to 1938 when the first large-scale seawater magnesia plant was started, these areas were the principal suppliers of refractory magnesia to the industrial nations of the world, including the United States. Even today, there is no major competition from seawater magnesia plants for markets in areas such as USSR, China, North Korea, and Czechoslovakia. The largest deposits of crystalline magnesite in the United States are those near Chewelah, WA (Bennett, 1941; Siegfus, 1927) and near Gabbs, NV (Vitaliano and Callaghan, 1956; 1957). Only the deposit at Gabbs is being worked commercially at the present time following the closure of the Chewelah operation of Northwest Magnesite Co. in 1969.

In Canada (Goudge, 1942) a deposit of crystalline magnesite near Kilmar, Que., is being mined commercially. Other Canadian deposits are in northern Ontario and in British Columbia. Three types of magnesite are found in British Columbia (McCammon, 1968). In the East Kootenays, beds of crystalline magnesite occur interlayered with sedimentary rocks. Pods of cryptocrystalline magnesite are common in the serpentine of the Clinton and Bridge River areas of central British Columbia. Veins of white magnesite are present in fault zones along the Yalakom River and Pinchi Mountain. A processing plant for commercial exploitation of the crystalline magnesite was being erected for possible operation by 1981.

The major producing countries of natural magnesite are USSR, North Korea, China, Czechoslovakia, Yugoslavia, Austria, and Greece. Brazil, Spain, Turkey, India, and South Africa produce important but lesser amounts.

The identified reserves of crystalline magnesite in the USSR are on the order of 400 million tons in the southern Ural Mountains and 2000 million tons in the Savan Mountains area of eastern Siberia. Most of the USSR production comes from the area of the Ural Mountains, particularly from the deposits near Satka in Ufa Province. The Satka deposits alone have more than 250 million tons of reserves. The ore has an average MgO content of 46%, and it is similar to Austrian magnesite in appearance and quality except for lower iron content. Production of crude magnesite—at one time as high as 3 million st—was estimated in 1980 to be approximately 1.8 million stpy. The deposits in the Savan Mountains have not been exploited to the same degree as those in the Ural Mountains; the deposits are remote from industrial centers and of relatively lower grade than those of the Urals.

North Korea has about 3000 million st of magnesite reserves. The main deposits are located in Kankyo Province and average about 45% MgO on a crude basis. Annual production of crude magnesite is in excess of 1.5 million st. The producers are beneficiating some of the crude ore to make a more acceptable product. Most of the dead-burned and caustic-calcined magnesite is exported.

China has 5000 million tons of reserves largely centered at the famous Manchurian deposits located near Ta-shin-chiao in the Province of Shengking. There are also 21 known deposits in Szechuan in an area of 500 sq km. Total production figures for China are difficult to verify, but from trading information, they have been placed at 1 million stpy of crude magnesite.

Czechoslovakia reserves are on the order of 100 million st. Dead-burned magnesite was produced at an annual rate of 0.6 million tons in 1979 from the extensive deposits of breunnerite in Slovakia. Large deposits are in the region of Kosice, Jelsava, and Lobinobana.

Yugoslavia has deposits of magnesite located in Serbia and Bosnia; these are operated as underground mines and open-pit quarries producing about 500,000 stpy. The magnesite deposits can be subdivided into hydrothermal-sedimentary and hydrothermal-vein types. Mines are located in the Kraljevo area at Bela Stena and Ilinjaca. Similar sedimentary deposits are located at Beli Kamen and Evati. Vein-type deposits are located at Sumadija, Goles, Dubovac, and Ibar. Recently deposits have been mined at Zlatibor, which run northwest from Kraljevo in Serbia. All the ore requires some beneficiation, such as heavy-media separation, to make it suitable for commercial purposes.

Austria, the oldest producer in western Europe, has a narrow belt of breunnerite magnesite extending westward from Semmering, Austria. The most important deposits are located at Semmering, Veitsch, Breitenau Trieben, Radentheim, and Dientin. These are important commercial deposits from which magnesia containing about 6% Fe_2O_3 is obtained. Austria produced 1.6 million st of crude magnesite in 1970 which was converted to 540,000 st of dead-burned magnesite and 180,000 st of caustic-calcined magnesite (Anon., 1971). By 1979, the output of crude magnesite had decreased to approximately 1 million stpy.

Greece has large deposits of cryptocrystalline magnesite which are being mined. A deposit located at Vavdos in the Khalkidiki region in southwest Thessaloniki was originally worked in 1957. Several other deposits have now been worked especially on the island of Euboea and in Ormylia in Khalkidiki. Greek production of crude magnesite increased from approximately 0.7 million st in 1970 to 1.3 million st in 1976. Since then it decreased, to under 0.8 million st in 1979. The magnesite in the deposits is of high purity, but the close intermixture with gangue makes beneficiation of all ore necessary before sintering.

Brazil has crystalline magnesite deposits which are among the largest in the world. Total known reserves are on the order of 500 million st. The two major deposits are located in the Alencar area of Ceará Province and in the Eguas range near the town of Brumado in southwestern Bahiá. Production of crude magnesite increased from approximately 0.3 million st in 1972 to over 0.7 million st in 1980.

Spain has magnesite deposits in Navarra Province, near the French border. Other deposits are located in northwest Spain. Total production for Spain is about 300,000 stpy of crude magnesite.

Turkey has several deposits of cryptocrystalline magnesite mainly located in the Eskisehir and Kutaya regions. Production of crude magnesite from 1977 through 1980 averaged 0.5 million stpy.

India, until recently, supplied crude, caustic-calcined and dead-burned magnesite from the white cryptocrystalline magnesites of the Salem district in Madras. Those deposits are essentially exhausted, and most of the mining is now centered in the Almora district in Uttar Pradesh. The Almora magnesite is coarsely crystalline and of white to yellowish color. Most is converted to dead-burned magnesite. Total crude magnesite production in India was about 0.4 million stpy from 1977 to 1979. The dead-burned product is standard grade material.

South Africa has been a producer of magnesite for more than 30 years, but the output rate has been irregular and generally declining. From the level of 100,000 st in 1966, output decreased to 40,000 st in 1979. The deposits exploited are in the eastern Transvaal near Olifantsfontein and Burgersfort. The cryptocrystalline magnesite often occurs in pockets at irregular intervals, making mine planning difficult.

Zimbabwe has become a moderately important producer during the past five years, and in 1979 produced as much as South Africa.

Australia has a deposit of cryptocrystalline magnesite that is being mined near Fifield in New South Wales. The magnesite occurs as small boulders rarely over 18 in. diam and randomly distributed in a layer of loose soil a few meters thick. Reserves are unknown, but are thought to be small. Another deposit is located near Ravensthorpe in Western Australia. The cryptocrystalline magnesite occurs in veins and stockwork in mineralized zones up to several meters thick. The only commercial production has been from the Fifield deposits; in 1980, output was approximately 30,000 st of crude magnesite.

Magnesite is found in many other countries of the world and some, such as Nepal, have large reserves awaiting development. Nepal's reserves are on the order of 300 million st of coarsely crystalline magnesite. Cryptocrystalline magnesite occurs in Baja California and in many countries of Central America. Guatemala has a deposit which may become commercially important.

A magnesite deposit in Saudi Arabia at Jabal Ar Rokhan, north of Jiddah, is a hydrothermal replacement of dolomite by magnesite, and inferred reserves are 40 million st. Other deposits are located at Zarghat and Jabal Wask in the Hijaz Mountains.

Prospecting and Exploration

The search for deposits of any type of magnesite should be guided by considerations of the probable origin of magnesite. In the case of crystalline magnesite, possible locations of deposits are areas of limestone or dolomite terrane that have been subjected to folding or igneous activity. In the case of cryptocrystalline magnesite, possible locations are areas of ultrabasic rocks which show extensive alteration to serpentine. Thus, in either case, the search can be confined within the boundaries of areas that show evidence of dynamic geologic activity. Areas such as midwestern United States would not be fruitful in spite of large deposits of limestone and dolomite.

Magnesite formations are generally more resistant to weathering than associated formations; consequently, bold outcrops characterize magnesite deposits. Outcrops are sampled by surface chipping and shallow trenching. Field differentiation between commercial and noncommercial magnesite can be aided by the use of cold, dilute hydrochloric acid; limestone will effervesce when treated with hydrochloric acid whereas magnesite will not. Sometimes the Jolly balance is used for the determination on the basis of specific gravity of the minerals (magnesite, 3.0+; dolomite, 2.85).

Following the preliminary investigation, a diamond drilling program may be carried out to assess the commercial potential of the deposit. The evaluation is based on the size and location of the deposit and on the quantity and distribution of undesired minerals containing silica, lime, iron-oxide, and alumina. Tests to determine whether the impurities can be removed by ore dressing aids the evaluation. Magnesite, to be commercially acceptable, should contain at least 95% magnesium carbonate, an amount which, depending on the accessory oxides, would result in a dead-burned product containing 90 to 94% MgO. Refrac-

tory magnesia of that quality would have some demand, but the present and growing demand is for a product with even higher MgO content. This demand places increasing emphasis on beneficiation of the ore.

Mining and Processing

The type of the deposit dictates the method of mining. Large, massive deposits are usually worked by open-pit methods; narrow and deep deposits by underground drifts and stopes or surface openings.

The mined ore is rarely shipped or used in crude form, but is processed to yield refractory magnesia or caustic-calcined magnesia. Invariably, some degree of sorting or beneficiation is given the ore prior to dead-burning or calcining.

Examples of mining and processing practices of varying degrees and complexity are found in many places around the world.

North America

United States: *Nevada*—The discovery of magnesite in the Gabbs area in 1927 followed the finding of deposits of brucite in terrane originally prospected for tungsten. Exploration delineated total magnesite reserves in excess of 25 million st. The ore bodies occur in Upper Triassic dolomites. The beds are folded, faulted, and intruded by a variety of dikes and granodiorite stocks.

The deposits are being worked by Basic Refractories Division of CE Minerals. The plant is located at 5000 ft and the open pit at 6000 ft in the foothills of the Paradise Range in Nye County.

All mining is by the open pit method, with 10- to 15-ft benches. From 6000 to 8000 stpd of ore and waste are selectively mined. The indicated bench height was found necessary to maintain proper ore control. Blast holes 2¾ in. in diameter are drilled 16 to 20 ft deep on an 8-ft diamond pattern to give good pit floor for the benches and good fragmentation. Blasting is done with fertilizer grade ammonium nitrate premixed with fuel oil, and charges are primed with ¾ lb booster and primadet attached to the trunk line. From 800 to 1500 holes are shot at a time, each hole giving approximately 61 st of rock. Secondary blasting is seldom necessary. The broken ore is trucked approximately two miles to the crushing plant (Jepsen, 1980).

The different grades of ore cannot be readily distinguished visually and sorting into grades is controlled by chemical analysis. All cuttings from drill holes are analyzed for lime and silica, and values are plotted on maps of the deposit. Contour lines are drawn through points of equal lime content on one map and of equal silica on another. Contour intervals are chosen to correspond to various grade limits. Super-imposition of one map on the other allows selection of any particular grade of ore by following the colored area representing the lime limits around to where it is bounded by contours representing the desired silica limits. A grid is staked on the broken ore, which has not shifted appreciably during blasting, to show the shovel operator which portion of the rock to load. Loading is by two 4.5-yd power shovels and by two 5-yd front-end rubber-tired loaders. Haulage is by 35-ton trucks to the crushing plant, which has a capacity of 380 stph. Depending on the grade of the ore, the crushed material is placed on one of three stockpiles which respectively feed the kiln, flotation, and heavy media plants. Concentrates from the beneficiation plants also feed the kiln plant. The flotation plant has a capacity of approximately 42 stph; the heavy media plant, 125 stph.

The kiln plant feed goes into two separate circuits. One, for the production of dead-burned magnesite, uses two rotary kilns; the other, for caustic-calcined magnesite, uses two Herreshoff furnaces and a small rotary kiln. Some of the raw feed is mixed with flue dust and briquetted prior to being dead-burned in the rotary kiln.

Washington—Washington magnesite occurs as massive lenses in dolomite. Distributed throughout the magnesite are stringers of siliceous and calcareous impurities. The magnesite deposits are found within the Stensgar dolomite formation. While the magnesite outcroppings are numerous, only a few of the deposits have been worked, and with the discontinuance of the Red Marble Quarry operation in 1968, production in Washington ceased. However, the mining methods were typical of those used for similar magnesite deposits.

At this mine, the magnesite was removed in a series of 40-ft benches. Primary rock breakage was obtained by drilling 6 in.-diam holes with a rotary drill and blasting (Fisk, 1953). This was followed by some secondary breakage. The broken ore was put through a 42 in. gyratory crusher, loaded into aerial tramway buckets and transported to the mill, a distance of eight miles.

The rock from the quarry was crushed, scrubbed, and screened into two major fractions. The coarse fraction, 1½ × ⅛ in., was sent to the heavy media separation plant (Utley, 1954). The −⅛-in. material was stockpiled for further treatment by flotation. Separation of magnesite from the lighter impurities, consisting largely of dolomite and siliceous minerals, was carried out in ferrosilicon medium in a 20-ft-diam cone. The magnesite "sinks" were crushed, screened, and stored in bins, from which they were either transported 5 miles by aerial tramway to the calcining plant, or sent to the flotation mill for further treatment. Most of the magnesite was sent directly to the calcining plant where it was blended with a small amount of iron ore and fired in a rotary kiln at 2900°F to produce dead-burned magnesite of standard quality.

The magnesite which was conveyed to the flotation mill was reduced to minus 65-mesh (Tyler) by a ball mill in closed circuit with a classifier. In the two-stage flotation process, siliceous minerals were floated first, followed by flotation of magnesite from the calcareous minerals. The magnesite concentrate was thickened, filtered, dried in a rotary dryer, and transported to the calcining plant. Here it was fired in a rotary kiln to produce a high grade dead-burned magnesite.

Canada: *Quebec*—A deposit of high-lime magnesite is being mined at Kilmar, Que. (Bray and Hilchey, 1957). The magnesite ore body consists of a series of veins which dip about 85°. The footwall is quartz monzonite, and the hanging wall consists of serpentine, diopside, and quartzite.

The mine, from 1915 to 1936, was operated in narrow, deep opencuts, but since 1936 the mine has been operated by underground methods. Shafts are sunk to the desired level, and drifts and crosscuts are driven into the veins. The ore is removed from shrinkage stopes, hoisted to the surface in cars in a cage.

The ore is crushed, washed, and screened to separate it into two fractions. The coarse fraction, 1½ to ³⁄₁₆-in., is fed to the heavy-media separation plant, and the −³⁄₁₆-in. material is sent to a holding bin prior to transportation to the calcination plant for use as a blending material. The waste material, "floats," is discarded; the heavier "sinks" containing the magnesite goes to storage. The sinks are transported by truck to the calcination plant and placed in different piles according to chemical analysis. The ore is reclaimed from piles by a front-end loader which feeds a series of bins. Materials from the bins are reclaimed and proportioned through feeders onto a belt to give the required compositional blend. Blended ore goes to a ball mill where it is crushed and transported to blending silos for final compositional adjustments. The blended, fine feed is transported to a rotary kiln and calcined to dead-burned products. After dead-burning, the magnesia is crushed, loaded into railway hopper cars, and shipped either to the company's refractory brick plant or to customers.

Europe

Greece: The northern part of the island of Euboea consists of schists-hornstones and serpentines of the "oriental Greece" zone and is well known for important magnesite deposits. The magnesite is of the cryptocrystalline variety located in ruptures and stratified zones. Three types of magnesite deposits are present:

1) Vein type which may be from ¼ in. to 14 ft in width and of varying length.

2) The stockwork type which is a dense network of veins varying from a few inches to several feet in thickness.

3) Mass type, forming lenticular concentrations of magnesite with volumes of a few to several thousand cubic feet. This type is a local anomaly of the vein or stockwork magnesite types.

Among the operations of companies in Euboea, those of Financial Mining-Industrial and Shipping Corp. are the largest. The magnesite is exposed by extensive stripping of the overburden and then mined by open-pit methods. Benches are established at heights of 35 to 65 ft. Broken ore is loaded by shovel or front-end loaders into 35-ton capacity trucks and transported to the ore dressing plants. For one ton of dressed ore, more than 20 tons of crude ore and overburden must be moved.

At the dressing plants, the ore is washed, crushed, and beneficiated by a combination of optical, magnetic, and heavy-media separations. The beneficiated ore is stored in bins until transported to the calcining plant. An extensive program of sampling and chemical analysis facilitates separate storage of different grades of material at the calcining plant. The ore is reclaimed from the storage piles by a front-end loader and fed to six rotary kilns, which in total can produce 320 t/a of dead-burned magnesite (Manos, 1979). The dead-burned magnesite is cooled and transferred to the nearby port.

Output of raw magnesite by all producers was approximately 760,000 st in 1979, marking a steady decrease from 1,270,000 st in 1976.

Asia

Turkey: Magnesite is found in several places in Turkey. The main mining operations are near Eskisehir and Kutaya in the west-central part of the country. The magnesite is cryptocrystalline and is usually mined in narrow opencuts. The veins are more or less vertical, and in at least one operation near Kutaya, underground mining is practiced to some extent. The mined ore in all cases is sorted by hand and shipped to nearby calcining plants. The lump ore is calcined in shaft or rotary kilns.

Other Magnesium Minerals

Brucite is sometimes found associated with commercial deposits of magnesite as in Nevada and Washington. In those cases, it would be processed along with the magnesite to produce refractory magnesia.

By itself, as an exploitable mineral, there are no known operations for brucite. There was one at Wakefield, Que., but it closed down several years ago. At Wakefield, the brucite occurs as ricelike grains ¹⁄₁₆- to ⅛-in.-diam disseminated through a limestone matrix (Goudge, 1944). The process of winning the magnesia was based on controlled slaking of carefully sized and calcined ore. The system was controlled so that the discharge from the slaker consisted of an impalpable dust of hydrated lime mixed with magnesia granules. The granules were air separated, washed, and wet classified. The lime was sold directly, and the magnesia granules were further processed to refractory magnesia.

Olivine is composed of forsterite ($2MgO \cdot SiO_2$) and fayalite ($2FeO \cdot SiO_2$) in solid solution; in common olivine the latter is the minor constituent present to about 15%. Olivine is a common constituent of igneous rocks, but deposits of sufficient purity to be commercially attractive are not numerous.

North Carolina and Georgia reserves of olivine are estimated at 230 million tons averaging 48% magnesia (Hunter, 1941). In Washington, olivine occurs as dunite rock, a peridotite in which olivine is the dominant mineral. Reserves are estimated at 50 million st on Cypress Island and several million tons in the Twin Sister Region.

Small quantities of olivine were mined in the United States and Norway from 1930 to 1940, but it was not until the 1950s that world production reached 20,000 stpy. By 1974 world production was approximately 350,000 stpy, and in 1980 it was almost 1.5 million st. In addition, 400,000 st of dunite were produced. By far the largest producer of olivine is Norway; over 1 million st in 1980 (Watson). Other producing countries in order of rank are the US, Austria, and Italy. Dunite is produced mainly in Spain.

The largest Norwegian operation belongs to A/S Oliven, which operates a quarry at Aaheim. The ore is crushed, some is washed, and sized into various grain and flour categories. The other producer is K/S Norddal Olivin A/S & Co., one of the H. Björum group.

The Austrian production comes from a quarry at St. Lorenzen in Styria. Here Magnolithe GmbH, a subsidiary of Continental Ore Corp., produces forsterite brick, ramming mixtures, mortars, and foundry sand.

The only currently producing areas in the US are Washington State and North Carolina. Together they produce about 170,000 stpy, of which one company, International Minerals and Chemicals, accounts for more than 60%. In Washington, the company mines a talus accumulation at the base of the Twin Sister deposit. This material is washed, crushed, and transported to the processing plant at Hamilton. IMC has operations in North Carolina at Eddie and Burnsville. The ore varies in impurities content and must be beneficiated.

The second largest producer is National Olivine Co., which operates a wet processing facility at Dillsboro, near Asheville, North Carolina. Plant capacity is 100,000 stpy.

Synthetic Magnesite

Prior to 1938, natural magnesite was the source of essentially all grades of refractory magnesia. Since that time, the manufacture of refractory magnesia and caustic-calcined magnesia from other than natural magnesite has increased in importance until today over 85% of refractory magnesia produced in the US and suitable for brickmaking comes from nonmagnesite sources. Several basically different methods for production of magnesia from nonmagnesite sources have been studied, and at least four have been operated commercially. All center on the production and calcination of either magnesium hydroxide or magnesium chloride. The magnesium hydroxide may be obtained as a precipitate from a magnesium salt solution or as a residue remaining after the lime fraction of calcined dolomite is removed as a soluble compound by reaction with solutions of ammonium chloride or hydrogen sulfide. Magnesium chloride may be obtained as an end liquor after solar concentration of solutions of natural brines for production of salt or potash, or from well brines.

There are now 25 plants around the world producing refractory and caustic-calcined magnesia from magnesium hydroxide. In these plants, magnesium hydroxide is obtained by precipitation from liquids such as seawater, seawater bitterns, inland well brines, or end liquors from other chemical processes. One plant in Israel produces refractory magnesia by pyrolytic decomposition of magnesium chloride.

The commercial production of magnesia from seawater dates back to around 1885 when a small operation existed for a short time on the Mediterranean coast of France (Egleston, 1886). In that operation, milk of lime and seawater were combined in large masonry tanks which overflowed continuously into two similar tanks in series. From the last tank, the mixture of spent seawater and precipitated magnesium hydroxide was discharged into shallow troughs about 16 ft wide and 1000 ft long excavated in the beach sand. The sand acted as a filter for removal of the liquid. When the troughs became full of magnesium hydroxide mud, the inflow was stopped and after a few weeks in the sun, the material became sufficiently dry to allow excavation and handling. The broken lumps were then calcined. The plant shut down, presumably because it could not compete with mineral magnesite operations, but the principles of operation were similar to those now practiced by seawater-magnesia plants.

All the presently operating plants which make chemical magnesia by calcining magnesium hydroxide follow a basically similar process (Wicken, 1949). In all, the soluble magnesium salts are converted to insoluble magnesium hydroxide by treating with calcium hydroxide, which may come from oyster shells, limestone, or dolomite. Any of the common magnesium-bearing solutions such as seawater or brines may be used provided they can be treated to reduce carbonate and sulfate levels sufficiently so insoluble calcium compounds do not precipitate with magnesium hydroxide. The main considerations in selecting reactants are their purity and economic availability. After the reactants are established for any given plant, the limitations of pumping and thickening equipment will prevent that plant from changing to more dilute reactants without loss of capacity. A plant using seawater bitterns cannot change to using raw seawater, nor can one using dolomite change to using limestone without sacrifice of production. However, the reverse changes are feasible.

The stoichiometric requirements for production of one ton of magnesia are 2.3 st of dolomite or 2.5 st of limestone. Half of the magnesia comes from dolomite when it is used, but when limestone is used, all the magnesia comes from the seawater. Thus, when limestone is used, as compared to dolomite, twice the volume of seawater must be processed to obtain the same amount of magnesia.

In 1938 a commercial plant for refractory magnesia was built at Hartlepool, Durham, England (Gilbert and Gilpin, 1951). Calcined dolomite is used to treat the seawater to obtain magnesia. Dolomite is quarried, crushed, and sized and, then, calcined in a rotary kiln. The calcined dolomite is slaked to a fine, dry powder in hydrators. The hydrated product is made into a slurry to facilitate handling and mixing with seawater. The slurry is classified to remove impurities before being mixed with the seawater.

Incoming seawater is treated with sulfuric acid to remove carbon dioxide. The decarbonated water is pumped to reaction vessels and mixed with the slurry of calcined dolomite. Magnesium hydroxide is formed and the dilute suspension is delivered to large-diameter primary thickeners. The underflow of thickened magnesium hydroxide is repulped with treated seawater or, alternatively, freshwater and is then rethickened. The underflow from the secondary thickener is fed to a filter press operating at 2000 psi. The cake, containing about 70% solids, is fed directly into a rotary kiln for dead-burning.

The first commercial producer of magnesium compounds from seawater in the US was Marine Magnesium Products Corp., now part of the Merck & Co. group. In addition to the Merck & Co. operation, in south San Francisco, other plants in the US using seawater as a source of magnesium hydroxide are those of Harbison-Walker Refractories at Cape May, NJ; Kaiser Aluminum and Chemical Co. at Moss Landing, CA; Dow Chemical Co. at Freeport, Texas; Basic Refractories Div. of CE Minerals Co. at Port St. Joe, FL; and Corhart Refractories at Pascagoula, MS.

In all these operations, the processes are fundamentally alike. Seawater is treated with a small amount of slaked lime to precipitate the soluble bicarbonates as calcium carbonate or with acid to liberate carbon dioxide. The softened seawater is combined with either dry or slaked lime (or dolime). The resulting mag-

nesium hydroxide is thickened and washed in a countercurrent system with freshwater in order to remove the calcium chloride reaction product and most of the seawater, and to concentrate the slurry. The washed and thickened magnesium hydroxide is then filtered, and the cake is either directly burned to produce refractory or caustic-calcined magnesia, or it may be calcined and pelletized prior to dead-burning to give the product desirable size and density characteristics.

In the Dow Chemical plant, the magnesium hydroxide is not dead-burned, but is converted to magnesium chloride for use in electrolytic cells to produce magnesium metal.

In Japan, seawater plants for magnesia production are at five locations. They are those of Ube Chemical Industries Ltd. at Ube, Yamaguchi; Shin Nihon Chemical Ind. Co. at Minamata, Kyushu; Nihon Kaisui Kako Co. Ltd. at Naoetsu; Asahi Glass Co. Ltd. at Iho; and the salt brine plant of Hokuriku Sein Kogyo KK at Hotsu. All these plants use calcined limestone as precipitant.

Two chemical magnesia plants owned by Industrias Peñoles are located in Mexico. Combined annual production in 1979 was 100,000 st. One, based on seawater, is that of Quimica del Mar, Ciudad Madero, Tampico; the other, based on end-liquor from a sodium sulfate operation, is that of Quimica del Rey, Laguna del Rey, Coahuila.

Sardamag SpA has a plant located at Sant'-Antico in Sardinia; the plant produces refractory magnesia from seawater using calcined limestone as the precipitant. The production in 1973 was over 100,000 st of refractory magnesia. By 1978, production capacity had been increased to 180,000 st. Another Italian plant, Co.GE.MA SpA, with capacity of 60,000 stpy, is located in Sicily.

The Pfizer plant at Dungarvan, County Waterford, Eire manufactures refractory magnesia from magnesium hydroxide precipitated from seawater by calcined dolomite.

A plant reported at Sevash, Crimea (USSR), is said to be able to produce 100,000 stpy of magnesia from seawater.

A plant to produce magnesium hydroxide from seawater is operated by Norsk Hydro AS near Porsgrun, Norway. The magnesium hydroxide is used for the production of magnesium oxide for the pulp and paper industry.

The most recent entrants to the ranks of those producing magnesia from seawater or well brines are Premier Periclase, Ltd. and Magnesia International, BV. Premier Periclase at Drogheda in Ireland is owned by Cement Roadstone Ltd. Production of dead-burned magnesite from seawater and limestone commenced mid-1980 in a 100,000-stpy plant. Magnesia International, a subsidiary of Billiton International, which in turn is part of the Royal Dutch Shell group, has completed a 100,000-stpy plant at Veendam in the Netherlands. Imported calcined dolomite and the plant's own well brines are the raw materials for production, which began in early 1982.

Three US companies produce magnesium hydroxide from deep well brines. They are Dow Chemical Co. at Ludington and Midland, MI; Martin Marietta Chemicals at Manistee, MI; and Morton Chemical Co., a small operation also located in Manistee. The thickened product from Dow at Ludington is pumped to Harbison-Walker Refractories Div. of Dresser Industries, Inc., where the material is filtered and processed to refractory magnesia. The two other companies process their own material to yield caustic-calcined or refractory magnesia. A typical analysis of the Michigan brine is NaCl, 5.8%; $CaCl_2$, 17%; $MgCl_2$, 9.9%; KCl, 2.5%; Br_2, 0.1%; sp gr 1.29; and pH, 5 ± 0.5. The brine does not contain carbonate or sulfate; thus pretreatment ahead of magnesium hydroxide precipitation is not needed.

The brine is pumped to the surface from depths of 2500 to 3500 ft. The processes for recovery of magnesium hydroxide are based on the reaction between soluble magnesium salt and calcium hydroxide to produce magnesium hydroxide.

In 1937, Westvaco Chemical Co., a division of Food Machinery Co., started production of refractory magnesia at Newark, CA. Their process was based upon seawater bittern which was an end-liquor from a nearby solar salt-making operation. Seawater was concentrated by solar evaporation until most of the sodium chloride was crystallized leaving a bittern with nominal composition: NaCl, 12 to 16%; $MgCl_2$, 6 to 9%; $MgSO_4$, 4 to 5%; KCl, 1 to 2%; and $MgBr_2$, 0.16%. During the early years of the operation, calcined oyster shell was used as precipitant, but after 1943, calcined dolomite was used because it contained less sulfate than the oyster shell, thus resulting in less CaO in the final magnesia.

The bitterns were treated with calcium chloride solution to remove the sulfate ions as calcium sulfate before the magnesium hydroxide precipitation. The sulfate-free bittern was then reacted with finely ground, calcined dolomite to form magnesium hydroxide. The pre-

cipitate was washed, thickened, filtered, and fed into a rotary kiln for dead-burning.

The foregoing processes based on seawater or brines lead simply and directly to production of magnesium hydroxide and magnesia with no flowsheet interlocks for production of other products except that magnesium metal may be made from the magnesia. Other processes exist in which the production of magnesium hydroxide is less direct. These processes are of two general types: one in which relatively low-grade magnesium compounds or minerals are upgraded by insertion into a flowsheet primarily designed to produce something else; the other in which production of magnesia is locked in with the simultaneous production of a useful byproduct. Examples of these follow:

A process at one time but no longer used for the production of magnesia, is based on the substitution of calcined dolomite for calcined limestone in the Solvay process for making soda ash. The spent material from the ammonia stills consists of a slurry of dissolved calcium chloride and insoluble magnesium hydroxide rather than only a solution of calcium chloride as is characteristic of standard Solvay system. The slurry was thickened and filtered to recover the magnesium hydroxide which was converted to refractory magnesia.

The Dead Sea Works, a subsidiary of Israel Chemicals Ltd., has a plant at Arad to recover magnesium chloride from the Dead Sea brines. The magnesium chloride is converted to magnesia and hydrochloric acid by pyrolytic decomposition. The plant has an annual production of 60,000 st of refractory magnesia.

The world total annual capacity for chemical production of magnesia is about 2.5 million st. While there are many seawater magnesia plants, the choice of suitable sites is more limited than one would suspect. Large land masses can cause the seawater to be diluted because of freshwater runoff and tide action so it becomes merely brackish. The more dilute the seawater becomes, the less magnesia a given plant can produce. Normal seawater contains about 34 g of dissolved salts per kg; of this, 23 g reports as sodium chloride and the rest mainly as magnesium and potassium compounds. The amount of magnesium ion is equivalent to about 2.1 g of magnesia (MgO) per kg of seawater or over 17 lb per 1000 gal. The importance of seawater concentration as related to size of process equipment is evident. Other factors such as coastal topography, availability of high purity limestone or dolomite, fuel sources, and market locations must be closely studied before a site is selected.

Political and Commercial Control

The use of magnesia as a refractory material has a relatively short history when compared to that of other heat-resisting materials used in connection with metallurgy since antiquity.

The use of magnesite for metallurgical operations was first mentioned in 1866, and the first brick were manufactured in 1868 (Caron, 1868). Prior to World War I, magnesia was not produced regularly in the United States; industrial needs were largely met by imports from Central Europe. A small quantity of magnesite was mined in California as early as 1886, but output did not reach 10,000 st until 1910. Under the impetus of World War I, production of ore increased until in 1917, production reached 21,000 st. The state of Washington recorded its first production in 1916 and soon became the leading producer in the United States reaching a level of over 200,000 stpy. This rate was continued for many years until the increasing needs of the refractory industry for product of higher purity coupled with exhaustion of high grade ore forced the closure in 1968.

Depletion, Taxes, and Tariffs

Depletion allowance for magnesite, dolomite, and brucite mined from deposits in the United States is 14% and for olivine, 22%.

Soon after World War I, the infant magnesite industry in the United States needed protection to survive attack from low-cost imports. As a result, an import tariff of $11.50 per st of dead-burned magnesite was established (US Tariff Act, 1922, parg. 204). This rate held until October 1951 when it was decreased to

$7.67 per st (Torquay). Subsequent differentiations as to types of refractory magnesia and inclusion of other refractory materials has resulted in the US tariff structure shown in Table 1 as it applies to countries in the "Most Favored Nation" category. The rates applied against imports from other countries are fixed at the higher rates of $15 per st and 30% ad valorem for the under- and over-4% lime types, respectively (Petkof, 1980). Other major countries around the world have followed a similar pattern of decreasing tariff for refractory magnesia.

Production and Consumption

About 75% of all refractory magnesia is used in one form or another by the steel industry, and any changes in technology or rate of production in that industry result in a change in the market for magnesite. Hence, trends in the total industrial use of magnesite can conveniently be expressed in terms relating to steel production. On that basis, the total apparent consumption of refractory magnesia by all industries in 1930 was equivalent to 4.1 lb per ton of steel produced. By 1958, the rate reached 11.5 lb as magnesia refractories supplanted other materials in steel and other industries. The advent of the basic oxygen process in 1954 began a new era in steelmaking technology (Price, 1969). The process was not fully exploited in the United States until the early 1960s, but it is now fully established as the major steel production method. The process changed the magnesia consumption pattern in that the new technology, as compared with open-hearth practice, requires much less magnesia per ton of steel produced. Some shops are now reporting under 5 lb of magnesia refractories consumed per ton of steel.

Development of the new steelmaking technology has resulted in heavy demand for sev-

TABLE 1—US Import Duties

Commodity	Most Favored Nation (MFN)		Non-MFN
	Jan. 1, 1982	Jan. 1, 1987	Jan. 1, 1982
Crude magnesite Refractory magnesia (including dead-burned and fused magnesite)	$1.64/lt	Free	$10.50/lt
4% or less lime	.18¢/lb	.16¢/lb	.75¢/lb
Over 4% lime	6% ad valorem	6% ad valorem	30% ad valorem
Caustic-calcined magnesite	$2.10/lt	$2.10/lt	$21/lt

eral grades and types of magnesia of high purity, controlled composition, and specific physical properties (Laming, 1971). The result of this proliferation of product requirement has been an emphasis on the production of chemical magnesia which is more amenable to compositional control than is that obtained from the mineral magnesite.

The net consumption of refractory magnesia in the US in 1979 was approximately 907,000 st, against a raw steel production of 139 million st. Domestic sources accounted for 814,000 st and imports the balance.

The US has long been an importer of refractory magnesia. The trade divides refractory magnesia into that containing over and under 4% lime. In 1972 the importation of the under-4% grade material was 128,000 st; of the over-4% grade material, 6,000 st (Chin, 1972). In 1979 the respective amounts were 65,000 and 28,000 st. The figures reveal that US producers have concentrated on producing more high-grade material but have left the less profitable standard-grade for foreign supply.

The market for caustic-calcined and technical grades of magnesia in the United States has grown from 100,000 to 130,000 stpy (1968–1972) to approximately 170,000 stpy in 1979. The country essentially is self-sufficient in these magnesias.

Marketing, Uses, and Prices

Crude Magnesite: Crude magnesite has been used in negligible quantities for the preparation of such chemicals as Epsom salts. Consumption for these purposes is extremely variable and probably has never exceeded a few tons per year in the United States. Crude magnesite has limited sale in Europe and the Middle East by producers who do not have their own processing facilities for conversion of the crude material to calcined products or chemicals. At present, in the United States, there is no known market for crude magnesite because manufacturers of chemicals prefer to use natural brines or caustic-calcined magnesia as starting material. The selling price for crude magnesite outside the United States ranges between $30 and $60 per short ton.

Dead-Burned Magnesite: Dead-burned magnesite is used almost entirely as a refractory material. It can be used directly as a grain product or as a constituent of brick, ramming mixes, gunning mixes, or castables. The refractories made from magnesia have a wide variety of uses but find their main use in the cement, glass, steel, and copper industries (Mc-

Dowell and Howe, 1920). The great merit of magnesia-based refractories is their ability to resist basic slags at high temperatures (Spencer, 1972) and to lower the refractory cost per ton of product (Rigby, 1971).

Refractory magnesia is freely sold on the market, but many refractory producers have their own source of supply. The total production of refractory magnesia is generally adequate to meet market demands although shortages in certain special grades of high purity occur periodically.

The price of refractory magnesia is determined, in part, by the physical and chemical properties of the product. The magnesia content alone is not the sole control in establishing the price; the amounts and proportions of accessory oxides and the physical characteristics of the product are equally influential. Thus, different kinds of refractory magnesia, even though they contain the same amount of MgO, may be priced at different levels. The prices of refractory magnesias have increased greatly since 1973. In that year the range was $90 to $150 per st for the high-purity grades. In 1980 prices on the world market ranged up to over $500 per st. Similarly, prices for standard or maintenance grades have escalated from a range of $35 to $80 per st to more than $150 per st.

Caustic-Calcined Magnesia: Caustic-calcined magnesite has many uses, among which an important one is for the production of magnesium oxychloride and oxysulfate cements. The cement is prepared by mixing a solution of magnesium chloride or sulfate with ground caustic-calcined magnesite. The main use of the cement is as a resilient, fireproof, sparkproof, and vermin-proof flooring in industrial and institutional buildings. Additional large amounts of the cement are used for wall board, moldings, and acoustical tile (Anon., 1956).

Other major uses are found in the pulp and paper (Hull, et al., 1951), rayon, fertilizer, insulation, and chemical industries (Anon., 1977). It is used in stack gas scrubbing applications to remove sulfur dioxide and as an additive to decrease corrosion in furnaces burning high-vanadium oil.

The price of caustic-calcined magnesia varies widely with different grades. The grade used most widely in bulk for the paper, fertilizer, and chemical industries costs on the order of $300 per st.

Olivine: The patterns of use in Europe and the US are widely different in both markets

and tonnages. In Europe about 70%, or about 1.2 million tons, of the total olivine and dunite produced is used as slag conditioner in blast furnaces. In the US, the blast furnace market in 1980 consumed about 50%, or 85,000 st of olivine produced. The second and third largest uses in Europe are as aggregates and as heat-storage blocks. The amounts used in the US for those purposes is essentially nil. The second largest use in the US is as a foundry sand (Watson, 1980).

The first commercial use of olivine was as a raw material for refractory brick in the early 1930s. Forsterite ($2 MgO \cdot SiO_2$) is the constituent in olivine that gives the material value as a refractory. However, after a period of slowly growing demand, largely for use in open-hearth steel operations through the 1950s, the use declined. In 1980 use as a refractory was around 15,000 stpy in the US. Olivine is also used in limited amounts for sandblasting, chemical manufacturing, and as an ingredient in fertilizer. Olivine is a relatively inexpensive material; prices in 1980 ranged from $25 to $90 per st depending on quality and size specifications.

Tests and Specifications

Crude Magnesite: Crude magnesite is used largely to produce dead-burned or caustic-calcined magnesite. The only characteristics of the raw magnesite that survive the calcining operation are those related to chemical composition; thus, the only tests regularly made on raw magnesite are for determining composition.

Refractory Magnesia: Refractory magnesia (dead-burned magnesite) is subjected to both physical and chemical tests. The nature of the tests and the product specifications are somewhat dependent upon the use to which the material is put. If the material is to be used for the manufacture of monoliths, certain characteristics are needed to assist sintering in service; these characteristics would not be necessarily needed nor desired in brick making mixes. Both services, however, would require dense, well-burned grain with a predominance of large grains.

Resistance to hydration is an important determination often made. The presence of free lime in dead-burned magnesite is deleterious and can result in shattered refractories as hydration takes place. In most dead-burned magnesites, lime is not free but is combined with other oxides in stable mineral combinations which are resistant to hydration. However, some combinations and magnesia itself can hydrate unless stabilization has been achieved during manufacture.

In synthetic and high purity magnesites, the size of the periclase crystal is considered important and is checked under the microscope. The presence and relationship of trace elements are important, as is the density of the grain of the final product.

Caustic-Calcined Magnesia: Most caustic-calcined magnesia is a commercial product sold on a tonnage basis in relatively large lots to chemical, paper, and fertilizer manufacturers.

The specifications for magnesia of this type are as varied as the uses. In general, specific requirements as to particle size, color, ignition loss, chemical analyses, bulk density, and activity may have to be met.

Magnesia for oxychloride cements is tested by making test slabs. Standards of setting time, dimensional change, and strength have been published by the American Society for Testing & Materials. The other requisites are that the magnesia have little or no free lime, have insufficient iron to color the magnesia, and be ground substantially through 200 mesh.

A class of magnesia products differing from commercial grades of caustic-calcined magnesia is that sold to specific technical and USP standards. These grades of magnesia are distinguished from others by being specially processed to meet rigorous physical and chemical standards. The products are used for medicinal purposes, specialized fillers, and various chemical needs. They may be referred to as "light" or "heavy" calcined magnesia.

When calcined at extremely high temperatures, the product finds use in refractory and electrical applications. These products are usually sold by the pound.

Environmental Considerations

Magnesite mining operations, being largely in mountainous regions, have little interface with urban society. Contestation as to land use is not a problem.

Mine drainage from underground or open-pit operations does not contribute significantly to pollution of streams because the drained area contains no significant amounts of soluble or oxidizable minerals.

Calcining plants, at one time, emitted substantial amounts of stack dust, but modern dust collectors and precipitators have removed most of these emissions and allowed the recovery of valuable products.

The greatest and most evident impact of magnesia operations on the environment has centered around seawater magnesia plants. Here, seawater, after having magnesia removed, is returned to the ocean. Recent innovations leading to greater control of the characteristics of the effluent have decreased the amount of turbid effluent.

Seawater magnesia plants calcine dolomite or limestone for use as a precipitant. The stack gas from the kilns is, in modern plants, controlled by suitable dust collecting devices.

During the calcination and dead-burning of magnesium hydroxide, substantial quantities of steam and some soluble salts are discharged. Wet scrubbers and electrical precipitants are used to control these discharges.

None of the discharges from either natural or synthetic magnesia plants has a noxious quality, and with modern remedial measures, even the cosmetic quality of the discharges is acceptable.

Bibliography and References

Anon., 1956, "Magnesium Chemicals," *Chemical Engineering*, Vol. 63, Aug., pp. 346–349.

Anon., 1960, "Basic Inc. Increases Magnesite," *Mining World*, Vol. 12, Nov., pp. 30–32.

Anon., 1971, "Magnesite," *Mining Annual Review*, 1971 ed., Mining Journal, London, pp. 115–117.

Anon., 1972, "Refractory Raw Materials—The Producers Reviewed," *Industrial Minerals*, No. 59, Aug., pp. 9–30.

Anon., 1977, "Magnesia—From Shortage to Surplus," *Industrial Minerals*, Sept., pp. 31–35.

Bain, G.W., 1924, "Types of Magnesite Deposits and Their Origin," *Economic Geology*, Vol. 19, No. 5, Aug., pp. 412–433.

Bennett, W.A.G., 1941, "Preliminary Report on Magnesite Deposits of Stevens County, Washington," Report of Investigation No. 5, Washington State Div. of Geology, 25 pp.

Bennett, W.A.G., 1943, "Character and Tonnage of the Turk Magnesite Deposit," Report of Investigation No. 7, Washington State Div. of Geology, 22 pp.

Bodenlos, A.J., 1954, "Magnesite Deposits in Serra Das Equas, Brumado, Bahiá, Brazil," Bulletin 975-C, US Geological Survey, pp. 87–170.

Bray, W.T., and Hilchey, G.R., 1957, "Magnesite Deposits of Kilmar, Quebec," *Geology of Canadian Industrial Mineral Deposits*, Canadian Institute of Mining & Metallurgy, Montreal, pp. 164–166.

Campbell, I., and Loofbourow, J.S., 1962, "Geology of Magnesite Belt of Stevens County," Bulletin 1142-F, US Geological Survey, pp. F1–F53.

Caron, M.H., 1868, "Preparation de La Magnesie Employee Comme Mature Refractaire," *Comptes Rendus*, Academie Science, Paris, Vol. 62, p. 839.

Chin, E.L., 1972, "Magnesium Compounds," *1972 Minerals Yearbook*, Vol. 1, US Bureau of Mines, pp. 747–755.

Comstock, H.B., 1963, "Magnesium and Magnesium Compounds," Information Circular 8201, US Bureau of Mines, 128 pp.

Coope, B., 1981, "Caustic Magnesia Markets—Agricultural Oversupply and Industrial Underdemand," *Industrial Minerals*, No. 161, Feb., pp. 43–51.

Dunbar, C.O., and Rogers, J., 1957, *Principles of Stratigraphy*, John Wiley and Sons, New York, 356 pp.

Egleston, T., 1886, "Basic Refractory Materials," *Trans. AIME*, Vol. 14, pp. 460–492.

Fisk, R.L., 1953, "Changes in Primary Drilling at Northwest Magnesite," *Mining Congress Journal*, Vol. 39, Feb., pp. 48–54.

Gilbert, F.C., and Gilpin, W.C., 1951, "Production of Magnesite from Seawater and Dolomite," *Research*, No. 8, pp. 348–353.

Goudge, M.F., 1942, "Sources of Magnesite and Magnesia in Canada," *Transactions*, Canadian Institute Mining & Metallurgy, Vol. 45, pp. 191–207.

Goudge, M.F., 1944, "Brucite Magnesia," *Journal of the American Ceramic Society*, Vol. 27, No. 1, pp. 8–10.

Hull, W.Q., et al., 1951, "Magnesia-Base Sulphite Pulping," *Industrial Engineering Chemistry*, Vol. 43, Nov., pp. 2424–2435.

Hunter, C.E., 1941, "Forsterite Olivine Deposits of North Carolina," Bulletin 41, Dept. of Conservation and Development, Div. of Minerals Research, 114 pp.

Krimball, H.M., 1972, "Magnesia Compounds," *Mining Engineering*, Vol. 24, Jan., pp. 46–47.

Ladoo, B., and Myers, W.M., 1951, *Nonmetallic Minerals*, 2nd ed., McGraw-Hill, New York, pp. 296–311; 431–436.

Laming, J., 1971, "Raw Materials and Refractories Performance," The Frank Scott Memorial Lecture, The Refractories Assn. of Great Britain, Mar. 24.

Lindgren, W., 1933, *Mineral Deposits*, 4th ed., McGraw-Hill, New York, pp. 388–390.

McCammon, J.W., 1968, "Magnesite, Hydromagnesite, and Brucite Occurrences in British Columbia," Information Circular, British Columbia Dept. of Mines and Petroleum Resources, Jan., 7 pp.

McDowell, J.S., and Howe, R.M., 1920, "Magnesite Refractories," *Journal of the American Ceramic Society*, Vol. 3, Mar., pp. 185–246.

Manos, A., 1979, "Greek Minerals—Development Through the 1970s," *Industrial Minerals*, Dec., pp. 37–53.

Niinomy, K., 1925, "The Magnesite Deposits of Manchuria," *Economic Geology*, Vol. 20, No. 1, Jan.-Feb., pp. 25–53.

Nishihara, H., 1956, "Origin of the Bedded Magnesite Deposits of Manchuria," *Economic Geology*, Vol. 51, No. 7, pp. 698–711.

Paone, J.O., 1970, "Magnesium," *Mineral Facts and Problems*, Bulletin No. 650, US Bureau of Mines, pp. 621–638.

Petkof, B., 1980, "Magnesium," *Mineral Facts and Problems*, Bulletin No. 671, US Bureau of Mines.

Petkof, B., 1982, "Magnesium Compounds," *Mineral Commodity Summaries 1982*, US Bureau of Mines, pp. 92–93.

Price, F.C., 1969, "An Industry in Transition: Iron and Steel Today," *Chemical Engineering,* Vol. 76, Aug., pp. 76–88.

Rigby, G.R., 1971, "Future Trends in Refractory Materials for Steel Production," *The Refractories Journal,* Vol. 46A, May, pp. 27–30.

Rosenberg, P.E., and Holland, H.D., 1964, "Calcite-Dolomite-Magnesite Stability Relations in Solutions at Elevated Temperatures," *Science,* Vol. 145, pp. 700–701.

Rosenberg, P.E., and Mills, J.W., 1966, "A Mechanism for the Replacement of Magnesite in Dolomite," *Economic Geology,* Vol. 61, No. 3, May, pp. 582–586.

Schroeder, N.C., 1948, "The Genesis of the Turk Magnesite Deposits, Stevens County Washington," *Compass,* Vol. 26, No. 1, Nov., pp. 37–46.

Siegfus, S.S., 1927, "Some Geological Features of the Washington Magnesite Deposits," *Engineering & Mining Journal,* Vol. 124, No. 22, Nov. 26, pp. 853–856.

Spencer, D.R.F., 1972, "Basic Refractory Raw Materials," *Transactions and Journal of British Ceramic Society,* Vol. 71, No. 5, pp. 123–134.

Utley, H.F., 1954, "Heavy-Media Separation Supplements Flotation in Magnesite Plant," *Pit and Quarry,* Vol. 46, June, pp. 90–92.

Valdiya, K.S., 1968, "Origin of the Magnesite Deposits of South Pithoragarh, Kumaun Himalaya, India," *Economic Geology,* Vol. 63, No. 8, Dec., pp. 924–934.

Vitaliano, C.J., and Callaghan, E., 1956, "Geologic Map of the Gabbs Magnesite and Brucite Deposits," Mineral Investigations Field Studies Map, MF 35, US Geological Survey.

Vitaliano, C.J., et al., 1957, "Geology of Gabbs and Vicinity, Nye County, Nevada," Mineral Investigations Field Studies Map, MF 52, US Geological Survey.

Watson, I., 1980, "Olivine and Dunite Slag Uses Foster Right Market," *Industrial Minerals,* Dec., pp. 57–63.

Wicken, O.M., 1949, "Production of Seawater Magnesite," *Electrical Furnace Steel Conference Proceedings,* Vol. 7, AIME, New York, pp. 212–217.

Willard, H.P., and Gates, R.W., 1963, "Selective Open Pit Mining Featured at Gabbs," *Mining Engineering,* Vol. 15, No. 10, Oct., pp. 44–46.

Manganese

CHARLES H. JACOBY *

In 1774 a Swedish chemist, C. W. Schule, first recognized manganese as an element. That same year Schule's associate, J. G. Gahn, isolated the element manganese for the first time. In 1856 the Bessemer process of steelmaking gave birth to the economic importance of manganese. Later, in 1882, Robert Hadfield discovered high manganese steels.

Although the primary use of manganese is in the ferroalloy industry, two additional important uses for manganese are making chemicals and dry cell batteries. Manganese is also vital to plant and animal life. Various chemical compounds of manganese are used in fertilizers, feeds, glass manufacture, paints, varnishes, and for numerous medicinal and chemical purposes.

For the study of industrial minerals and rocks, only the chemical and battery grade material is of concern, but for the sake of comparison, metallurgical aspects are included in this presentation. Although currently the world's largest consumer of manganese, the United States is producing only minor amounts of ore at the present time. This is due primarily to the fact that although huge deposits of manganese occur within our borders, all are of such low grade as to be economically unfeasible to mine.

For many years various government agencies and segments of private industry have devoted sizable sums of money and time in an attempt to upgrade ores from the various deposits, and also in an attempt to recover manganese from blast furnace slags. In view of current world prices, and the quantity of high grade material available, there is little likelihood that any of these approaches will be found to be economically feasible in the near future.

Geology and Mineralogy

Mineralogy

There are over one hundred minerals that contain manganese. These minerals vary from those with compositions that are predominantly manganese to those having only minor percentages.

Mineral	Chemical Composition	% Mn
Hausmannite	Mn_3O_4	72
Polianite	MnO_2	63.1
Pyrolusite	MnO_2 .	60–63
Cryptomelane	$KR_8O_{16}R$ (R=Mn)	Variable
Psilomelane	Ba Mn Mn_8O_{16} (OH)$_4$	45–60
Coronadite	Pb $R_8O_{16}R$ (R=Mn)	Variable
Hollandite	Ba $R_8O_{16}R$ (R=Mn)	Variable
Manganite	$Mn_2O_3 \cdot H_2O$	62
Braunite	3 $Mn_2O_3 \cdot MnSiO_3$	62
Tephroite	2 $MnO \cdot SiO_2$	54.3
Rhodochrosite	$MnCO_3$	47
Rhodonite	$MnSiO_3$	42
Spessartite	3 $MnO \cdot Al_2O_3 \cdot 3SiO_2$	33.3
Wad	Hydrous Mn Oxides	Variable
Franklinite	(Fe Mn Zn)O(Fe Mn)$_2O_3$	Variable
Asbolan	Cobaltiferous wad	Variable
Alabandite	MnS	63.14

Geology

From a geological standpoint most manganese deposits are complex. In general, it can be said that all primary deposits of manganese are carbonates or silicates. The most productive and profitable have been those of sedimentary origin and residual concentrations. Examples of these residual types of deposits are associated with the metamorphosed lodes of Madhya, Pradesh, India, and the lateritic deposits of Orissa and Bihar, India; nodules in the residual clays of the Philippine Islands, US southern Appalachians and Arkansas, Ghana, and Brazil.

Sedimentary manganese deposits are best exemplified by the Nikopol district of Russia and the Tchiatouri area of Georgia, USSR.

Hydrothermal replacements are characterized by the rhodochrosite deposits of Butte and Phillipsburg, MT. In general, the hydrothermal type deposit has not resulted in any large tonnages being produced, but may have given

* Jacoby & Co., Earth Science Consultants, Tempe, AZ.

rise to the formation of sedimentary deposits throughout geological history.

Some sedimentary and residual-type deposits have been metamorphosed, giving rise to small high-grade ore bodies. These deposits are regionally metamorphosed, occurring in marbles, slates, quartzites, schists, and gneisses. Some of these metamorphosed deposits, such as the Franklin, NJ, deposit, are rich enough to be commercial without secondary enrichment. However, most of the exploitable deposits have been secondarily enriched.

Manganese is widely distributed and, to a greater or lesser degree, replaces two sets of elements; first, alkaline earths, calcium, barium, and magnesium and, secondly, aluminum and iron. Due to the diversity and complexity of manganese deposits, both with respect to deposition and chemistry, a wide range of impurities is almost invariably present in the ores.

Distribution of Deposits

Distribution of manganese deposits can best be described by the term "scattered." They vary from occurrences such as the nodules on the bottom of Lake Michigan at Green Bay to the bog ores of Wickes, MT; the rhodochrosite of Phillipsburg, MT; the franklinite of Franklin, NJ, to the residual pyrolusite deposits of Cartersville, GA. More than 2100 manganese deposits are listed in 35 states. Currently the free world's largest deposits of manganese ore are in Gabon, Brazil, Republic of South Africa, Ghana, and India.

Principal reserves in foreign countries are as follows:

	Million Tons of Mn
USSR	Unknown-in excess of 200
Republic of South Africa	300
Gabon	96
Brazil	46
Australia	44
India	22
World reserves, total	700

Russia possesses what are probably the world's two largest manganese deposits. The largest of these is the flat-lying Eocene deposit at Tchiatouri in Georgia, south of the Caucasus Mountains. These are beds of oolitic pyrolusite interbedded with layers of clays, sandstones, and marls. Upon beneficiation, primarily washing, these ores produce concentrates containing 50% MnO_2, and from 1 to 2% iron. The second great deposit of Russia lies in the

Nikopol District on the Dnieper River in the Ukraine. Again, these are flat-lying beds close to the surface and easily accessible to strip mining. The beds of pyrolusite are interbedded with sand and glauconitic clays. These beds of Oligocene age rest on crystalline rocks covering approximately 160 square miles.

The largest deposit, or at least one of the largest, in the United States is located at Chamberlain, SD. This deposit is sedimentary in origin and consists of manganiferous concretions in the Pierre shale which is Upper Carboniferous in age. This formation varies in thickness from a few feet to 38 ft at Chamberlain.

The Batesville, AR, deposit contains a sporadic scattering of pyrolusite and wad-type residual materials in clay. Also buttons and thin layers of oxides are found in the Cason Shale. This deposit rests on a fine grained weathered limestone which gives rise to pinnacles precluding the use of normal strip mining operations.

The Cuyuna iron range in Minnesota contains iron ore carrying varying quantities of manganese. The manganese content ranges from less than 1% to more than 17%. The manganese was originally sedimentary in origin but has undergone some secondary deposition in the filling of fractures and crevices.

Southern Appalachian deposits begin in the area of the Shenandoah Valley and extend south to the area of Cartersville, GA, and on into Alabama. While a wide variety of manganese minerals occur in lenses, beds, and residual pockets, only the oxides in residual pockets have been of any economic importance. In Virginia these occur as a series of small deposits extending for 80 miles along the foot of the Blue Ridge Mountains. In general, most of the mines which have produced in excess of one million tons of manganese concentrates have been small operations conducted by local operators. Exceptions to this are the Crimora mine, working residual layers and pockets in the Erwin sandstone and the Kendall and Flick mines. These deposits, which have proven of economic importance, are the result of deep weathering. While the geological features of the primary deposits are undoubtedly dissimilar, the secondary residual deposits have many similarities.

The deposit at Artillery Mountains in Arizona has been operated from time to time during national emergencies. It has been estimated that the deposit contains approximately 175 million tons of ore averaging from 3 to 4%

manganese, with zones of material carrying values as high as 20% manganese. Beneficiation studies have made concentrates from which ferromanganese has been produced. The average iron content of these stratified oxides is 3% with 0.08% phosphorous.

The Three Kids property near Henderson, NV, was operated by Manganese, Inc. during World War II. At that time it was the largest producer of manganese in the United States. The primary ore, containing about 18% manganese, was beneficiated to produce a concentrate averaging 45% manganese.

Numerous other districts supply varying quantities of manganese during times of national emergency and stockpiling. The Anaconda Co. has produced approximately four million pounds of manganese from the Butte District in Montana. Manganese, zinc, and silver have been deposited in the peripheral zone as rhodochrosite and manganosiderite. Almost all of the production has come from the mining of rhodochrosite. The Emma mine, located in the southernmost Anaconda vein, mined the "great bulge" at the east end. The Phillipsburg District gave rise to manganese, silver, lead, and zinc as replacement veins in limestones and shales. In part, the rhodochrosite of these deposits has been altered with the formation of high grade oxides. The primary source of the manganese was the Granite-Bimetallic vein, which produced silver and gold. Aroostook County, Maine, contains large reserves of manganese mixed with iron in a 1 to 2 ratio. The ore is a mixture of fine grained minerals including silicates and carbonates. These bedded deposits are steeply dipping slates which have been folded and faulted. Over 40 deposits are known to exist in an area 90 miles long by 30 miles wide.

Manganese Nodules on the Ocean Floors: The occurrence of large tonnages of manganese nodules in the three major oceans has been well established. Cardwell (1973) gives detailed chemical analyses for nodules taken from 54 different Pacific Ocean locations. The two major elements are manganese and iron. The minimal manganese analyses averaged 8.2% Mn, the maximum 50.1% Mn, and a median value of 24.2% Mn was determined. The percent nickel values on the same samples were 0.16%, 2.0%, and 0.99%, respectively.

The three manganese minerals found were todorokite, birnesite, and delta manganese dioxide. Todorokite varies in its chemical composition and can contain significant amounts of other elements substituted for manganese in the crystal lattice. It is basically a calcium, sodium, manganese, potassium, and magnesium oxide with three molecules of water. Birnesite contains less lattice substituted elements and has the typical formula:

$$(Na_7Ca_3) \ Mn_{70} \ O_{140} \ 28H_2O.$$

These three forms of manganese show the degrees of oxidation increasing from todorokite, through birnesite, to delta manganese dioxide. The only iron mineral which has been recognized in the nodules is goethite.

Archer (1973) in reviewing the progress and prospects of marine mining estimates that a commercial manganese nodule mining operation would operate at a rate between 1 and 3 million stpy (dry weights). Allowing for processing losses, a 1 million-stpy operation is likely to be capable of providing about 13,000 tons of nickel, 11,000 tons of copper, 2500 tons of cobalt, and 270,000 tons of manganese. It is highly probable that manganese and cobalt will be considered byproducts with the scale of mining depending mostly on the world demand for nickel.

Sources of Manganese: Table 1 (DeHuff and Jones, 1981) gives production statistics and sources of manganese for the years 1976–1980.

Exploration and Evaluation

Manganese deposits are one of the more difficult ores to evaluate. In general, the deposits are small and scattered and expensive geophysical means are not usually economically feasible. Also the geophysical exploration costs are often beyond the financial capacity of the small operator. However, since manganese has relatively high solubility, geochemical techniques can be an effective tool in an exploration program.

One of the main difficulties is securing representative samples of an ore body for proper evaluation and analysis. In the past, a large percentage of the holes drilled for samples were by cable or churn drill methods. These methods require extreme care in order to secure valid data. In most cases the data have been inaccurate.

Rotary drilling techniques are somewhat better, but again, extreme care must be exercised in order to secure representative samples. Where the deposit contains wad or soft oxides in clay, soil sampling methods can be used. Generally, where residual or detritus has occurred in a clay, the particle size of the manganese mineralization ranges from large boul-

TABLE 1—Manganese Ore: World Production, by Country

(Short tons)

Country*	% Mn[e]	1976	1977	1978	1979[p]	1980[e]
North America: Mexico[†]	35+	499,579	[r]536,409	576,692	543,108	[‡]492,874
South America:						
Bolivia[†§]	28-54	[r]13,520	9,464	1,364	11,574	4,960
Brazil[#]	38-50	1,869,738	1,670,741	2,113,239	2,490,483	2,400,000
Chile	36-40	26,058	19,843	25,621	27,524	24,900
Peru	26	676	—	—	—	—
Europe:						
Bulgaria	30-	44,100	44,100	44,100	46,300	44,100
Greece	48-50	9,075	8,631	7,727	6,338	6,600
Hungary	30-33	138,000	132,000	126,000	91,000	97,000
Italy	22+	4,917	10,267	10,738	9,921	[‡]10,103
USSR[‖]	35	9,520,000	9,470,000	9,984,000	11,292,000	[‡]11,300,000
Yugoslavia	30+	20,944	27,282	30,203	33,235	33,000
Africa:						
Egypt	28+	4,691	4,225	191	—	—
Gabon	50-53	2,443,556	2,039,857	1,830,959	2,535,417	[‡]2,366,386
Ghana	30-50	343,780	321,417	347,864	298,481	[‡]278,279
Morocco	53-50	129,305	125,164	139,112	149,017	165,000
South Africa, Republic of	30-48+	[r]6,010,079	5,564,411	4,758,721	5,712,615	[‡]6,278,125
Sudan	48	505	504	496	[e]500	400
Zaire	30-57	200,824	42,216	—	—	—
Asia:						
China, mainland[e]	20+	1,100,000	[r]1,200,000	1,400,000	1,650,000	1,750,000
India[¶]	10-54	[r]2,022,405	2,055,865	1,784,503	1,934,641	[‡]1,813,692
Indonesia	47-56	10,839	6,593	6,492	6,514	7,700
Iran**	33+	44,100	44,100	33,100	[e]25,000	22,000
Japan	26-28	156,244	[r]139,063	114,802	96,925	85,900
Korea, Republic of	23-40	1,524	732	823	39	[‡]89
Pakistan	35-	71	58	317	121	110
Philippines	35-45	11,658	22,706	4,311	5,508	5,500
Thailand	46-50	55,364	[r]84,836	79,599	38,984	[‡]54,299
Turkey	35-46	18,696	21,275	[e]22,000	[re]26,000	26,000
Oceania:						
Australia	37-53	2,374,560	1,531,113	1,376,699	1,836,752	[‡]2,161,511
Vanuatu (formerly New Hebrides)	40-44	[††]38,664	[#]25,397	[#]22,853	[#]11,663	—
Total	NA	[r]27,113,472	[r]25,158,269	24,842,526	28,879,660	29,428,528

Source: DeHuff and Jones, 1981.

[e]Estimated.   [p]Preliminary.   [r]Revised.   NA Not available.

    * In addition to the countries listed, Colombia, Cuba, and the Territory of South-West Africa (Namibia) may have produced manganese ore and/or manganiferous ore, but available information is inadequate to make reliable estimates of output levels. Low-grade ore not included in this table has been reported as follows in short tons: Argentina (16% to 22% Mn) 1976—58,517, 1977—90,814, 1978—20,389, 1979—11,233, 1980—10,692; Czechoslovakia (about 17% Mn) 1976—1,211, 1977—1,003, 1978—[e]1,000, 1979—[e]1,000; 1980— [e]1,000; Malaysia (grade unspecified but apparently a manganiferous ferruginous ore) 1976—103,741, 1977—50,040, 1978—47,092, 1979—34,839, 1980—4,413; Romania (about 22% Mn) an estimated 90,000 in each year; the Republic of South Africa (15% to 30% Mn, in addition to material listed in table) 1976—56,178, 1977—266,930, 1978—105,490, 1979—1980—nil.

    [†] Estimated on the basis of reported contained manganese.

    [‡] Reported figure.

    [§] Exports.

    [#] Figures are the sum of (1) sales of direct shipping manganese ore and (2) production of beneficiated ore, both as reported in the 1977 through 1980 editions of Annuario Mineral Brasileiro.

    [‖] Source: 1976-79, The National Economy of the USSR, Central Statistical Administration, Moscow; 1980, Pravda, Moscow. Grade represents the annual averages obtained from reported metal contents of the gross weights shown in the table for 1976-1979.

    [¶] Much of India's production grades below 35% Mn; recent details on output by grade are not available, but in 1976, 65% of total exports of 787,533 short tons were below 35% Mn.

    ** Reported as if data are for calendar years, but may actually represent output for Iranian calendar years beginning March 21 of the year stated.

    [††] Japanese imports.

    [#] Figures revised from Japanese imports to reported production.

ders to −200 mesh material. This makes soil sampling procedures difficult to employ.

In general the hard and deeper deposits are easier to sample with some degree of accuracy.

Although a great many manganese occurrences are known, the limited size of many of these deposits make them marginal to submarginal. Other large deposits are not economically exploitable due to the low concentration of manganese. The third consideration, and of prime importance, are the impurities associated with the manganese mineralization.

Due to the diversity and complexity of manganese formations, the impurities are many in number and complex in nature. Following is a broad generalization of the types of impurities:

1) Metallic impurities: iron, lead, zinc, copper, arsenic, and silver minerals.

2) Nonmetallic impurities: sulfur and phosphorous minerals.

3) Gangue: silica, alumina, lime, magnesia, and barium.

4) Volatiles: water, carbon dioxide, and organic matters.

Primary factors in the evaluation of deposits within the United States are the amenability of the material to beneficiation, and the price projection over the life of the necessary capital investment. Considerable effort has gone into the upgrading of ores from the various larger deposits within the continental limits of the United States.

Prior to World War II, few manganese operations had milling plants which were more complicated than washing, screening, jigs, tables, and, in a few instances, flotation. Now it is not only necessary to increase the manganese content, but also to decrease the percentage of impurities. Because each deposit is distinctly different from most other deposits, no single process is applicable to all.

End Use Specifications

The manganese industry in the US is confined to the processing of foreign ores having manganese content of 35% or greater. Low-grade ores containing from 5 to 35% manganese are produced and shipped in South Carolina, New Mexico, and Minnesota. South Carolina ore is used primarily as a pigment in the manufacture of brick in both North and South Carolina. Most of the ore produced in New Mexico and Minnesota is used for the production of pig iron. As of May 2, 1980, the Federal Emergency Management Agency (FEMA) established new stockpile goals: natural battery ore, 62,000 st; synthetic manganese dioxide, 25,000 st; chemical ore, 170,000 st; metallurgical ore, 2,700,000 st; and 439,000 st of high carbon ferromanganese.

The present processing plants in the US consist of 16 facilities owned by ten companies. Basically the plants may be expected to continue to diminish in number and capacity. Union Carbide has signed an agreement in principle to divest itself of all its ferromanganese alloy and metal plants to a group of investors. This group of Norwegians is relating to cheap hydroelectric power for processing. The most recent plant to begin production of ferromanganese is the plant at Theodore, Alabama. Tinsley (1974) reported on the close ties between manganese consumption and steel production. In 1977 the steel industry accounted for 80.2% of manganese consumption (DeHuff, 1977). Approximately 13 to 14 lb of manganese are used per ton of steel for deoxidation and control of sulfur.

Manganese dioxide (pyrolusite) is used in the manufacture of dry cell batteries. This market has been challenged in recent years by mercury, alkali, and lithium batteries. Additional inroads on the market can be expected with further technical advances.

Due to the complex nature of the geology of many manganese deposits, chemistry of the ores varies widely. Some analyses of ores from major areas of production are given in Table 2. In general, manganese ores can be classified as follows:

	% Mn
Manganese ore	+35
Ferruginous manganese ore	10 to 35
Manganiferous iron ore	5 to 10

The most promising segment of the industrial manganese picture is the heavy demand for synthetic manganese dioxide, which has prompted expansion of facilities in both Japan and South Africa. In most cases this expansion constitutes a doubling of capacity; in the case of Mitsui Mining & Smelting, however, capacity will be quadrupled.

The National Stockpiling Specifications of the General Services Administration are given in Table 3.

Only rich manganese ores can produce the standard 70 to 90% manganiferous alloys used in the manufacture of steel in the most industrially oriented countries. Standard grades of ferromanganese used in the United States are given in Table 4.

TABLE 2—Analyses of Manganese Ores

Country	Mining Area	Composition, %			
		Mn	Fe	SiO	P
Brazil	Miguel Burnier	50	—	1.0	0.03-0.05
Congo	Kisanga	50	—	—	1.5
Ghana	Nsuta	46-52	1.6-7.7	2.4-5.5	0.11-0.14
India	Balaghat	48-53	4.2-10.3	3.5-10.7	0.03-0.19
	Shivrajpur	46-50	4.7-5.5	6.0-9.3	0.24-0.25
	Bhandra*	52-58	1.5-5.1	0.6-2.6	0.23-0.38
Morocco	Imini	50-54	—	3-4	
Republic of South Africa	Postmasburg	43-52	8.7-15.3	2.8-3.9	0.03-0.05
USSR	Chiatury	48-49	0-1.8	6-10	0.15-0.18
	Nikopol	48-51	0.7-1.2	7.5-10.5	0.16-0.33
United States	Montana	48-50	1-2.5	10-12	
	Nevada	45-57	1.1	13-14	0.06

Source: Cole, 1960.

* Battery grade.

Chemicals and Glass Products

Manganese is used in the manufacture of numerous chemicals, disinfectants, glass, fertilizers, colored brick, tile, paints, and as a flux in the melting of gold and silver ore. As a chemical raw material manganese is used in both organic and inorganic chemicals as oxidizers, catalysts, and chemical intermediates. Small percentages of manganese dioxide are used to take the color out of glass which contains iron.

Manganese, as a base forming element, forms two series of salts. One series is bivalent and the other is tetravalent. Manganese also forms a series of compounds in which it acts as an acid radical. These compounds include the permanganates which are strong oxidants.

In the ceramic industry manganese gives a variation of colors from a bright reddish purple to a purplish brown or black.

Solution Mining.

Because of its position in the electromotive series, it will displace arsenic, antimony, bismuth, tin, lead, copper, iron, nickel, cobalt, cadmium, and zinc. It plays a role in the forming of cement metals in the solution mining of certain metalliferous deposits.

Fertilizers

With respect to fertilizers, manganese, because of its high solubility has often been depleted from the soil. Generally, this is replenished to the soil in the form of manganese sulfate either in its pure form or as an admix.

Paint

The paint industry uses manganese to promote the absorption of oxygen in the drying of paints and varnishes.

Batteries

The manufacture of batteries is the most important nonmetallurgical use of manganese. Its use as a solid cathodic material was a point of progress in battery development. Either the naturally occurring pyrolusite or synthetic MnO_2 may be used. Other systems, including the newly commercialized lithium batteries, may be expected to somewhat reduce the consumption of manganese for this purpose.

Preparation for Markets

Beneficiation

Both the Anaconda Co. at Butte, MT, and Manganese, Inc. at Three Kids, NV, have employed flotation techniques with either oil emulsions or conventional soap flotation.

In the case of Anaconda's treatment of manganese carbonates, rotary kilns were used to produce oxide nodules from the flotation concentrates. Some ores have been treated by heavy media separation, while others have been subjected to electromagnetic separation. Slime losses in the treating of soft ores such as pyrolusite and wads are always high, and recovery of the manganese from these slimes has been attempted with Humphreys spirals and various classifiers.

The Dean-Leute ammonium carbonate process is one of the methods which has been de-

TABLE 3—General Services Administration National Stockpiling Specifications

	% Wt
Metallurgical Grade*	
Manganese (Mn)	40.0
Iron (Fe)	16.0
Silica plus alumina ($Si_2O_3 + Al_2O_3$)†	
Phosphorus (P)	0.30 max
Copper plus lead plus zinc‡	1.00 max
Battery Grade	
Grade A (Military)	
Manganese dioxide in synthetic, ore, or concentrate form, suitable for use in the manufacture of dry cell batteries. This must conform to Signal Corp. Specifications SCL-3175.	
Grade A (Commercial)	
Manganese MnO_2	75 min.
Arsenic	— max
Copper	— max
Lead	0.5 max
Iron	3.0 max
Total heavy metals other than Fe & Pb	0.5
Total Insolubles	10.0
Total Mn	48.0 min.
pH	4 to 7.0
Chemical Grade	
Type A	
Manganese dioxide	80 min.
Iron	3 max

Type B	P81		P-81-R	
Manganese dioxide	85.0	min.	82.0	min.
Manganese	—	min.	53.0	min.
Iron	3.0	max	3.0	max
Silica	3.0	max	5.0	max
Alumina	3.0	max	3.0	max
Phosphorus	0.10	max	0.20	max
Arsenic	0.05	max	0.10	max

Ferromanganese	
Manganese	75.00 min.
Carbon	7.50 max
Silicon	1.25 max
Phosphorus	0.35 max
Sulfur	0.05 max
Iron	Balance

* In a separate category from the metallurgical grade ore is a National Stockpiling Specification P-30a-R of 3/4/58.

† No limit specified, but if over 15% purchased in exceptional cases only.

‡ Of which not more than 25% may be copper.

veloped for the processing of low grade manganese concentrates. This process has experienced some success in producing manganese dioxide from Cuyuna iron range ore. The process involves the roasting of the Cuyuna ore, leaching with ammonium carbonate solution to obtain a high grade carbonate, and the reduction of the carbonate to the oxide.

High manganese slags have been developed by the selective oxidization-reduction process using open hearth slags as feed stock. Manganiferous materials from Aroostook County, Maine, have been treated by chloride volatilization processes without economic success. The Sylvester process, in which limestone has been used to form a manganese clinker, has been tested on the siliceous ores of Aroostook as well as on open hearth slags. The material was treated in a ball mill and then fed to a magnetic separator to separate the high Mn-Fe material. Another process for treating siliceous ores was the Udy electric furnace process, in which two or three stages of reduction were employed to produce the desired quality of ferromanganese.

Fine-sized manganese ore particles have been successfully agglomerated into balls or pellets with an organic binder, and then introduced into a short stack blast furnace. In the presence of a high quality coke, which produces a reducing environment, 77% of the manganese is recovered in metal form having a composition: manganese, 92.0%; carbon, 6.8%; iron, 1.0%; and silicon, 0.2%.

In the Daugherty process of the Republic Steel Corp., low grade ores are ground, subjected to water and sulfur dioxide gas to produce $MnSO_3$ and $MnSO_4$, boiled by live steam injection into the solution, then filtered, and roasted in a kiln to produce manganese oxides. Similarly, the Welch process of Manganese Chemicals Corp. dissolves the manganese from low grade ores with sulfuric acid to form $MnSO_4$. This is introduced into an electrolytic cell to form MnO_2 of excellent battery grade.

The Bruce Williams process involves the roasting of a low grade manganese feed with ammonium salts to produce a manganese carbonate. The Sheer Korman process of Vitro Corp. treats siliceous ores with a high intensity arc.

The Nossen process recommends a regenerative nitric acid system to produce manganese dioxide from low grade manganous oxides.

In the evaluation of the economic feasibility of any low grade deposit, its amenability to processing, and the efficiency and cost of upgrading the ore will often be the deciding factor in commercial exploitation.

Transportation

The major centers of manganese consumption in the United States are east of the Mississippi River. During times of national emergency we are faced with long rail hauls from the low grade western sources.

Most of the foreign ore is transported by ocean freighters with the exception of imports

TABLE 4—Standard Grades of Ferromanganese Used in Steel Manufacture

	(1)	(2)	(3)	(4)	(5)	(6)
High-Carbon						
Manganese, %	78 to 82					
Iron, %	12 to 16					
Carbon, %	6 to 8					
Silicon, %	1.00 max					
Phosphorous, %	0.30 max					
Sulfur, %	0.05 max					
Low-Carbon						
Manganese, %	90.00	80 to 85	80 to 85	80 to 85	80 to 85	80 to 85
Carbon, %	0.07 max	0.10 max	0.15 max	0.30 max	0.50 max	0.75 max
Silicon, %	1.00 max	1.00 max	1.00 max	1.00 max	1.00 max	7.00 max
Phosphorus, %	0.06 max	0.20 max	0.20 max	0.20 max	0.20 max	0.25 max
Medium-Carbon						
Manganese, %	80 to 85					
Carbon, %	1.50 max					
Silicon, %	1.50 max					
Spiegeleisen or Spiegel						
Manganese, %	16 to 19	19 to 21	26 to 28			
Carbon, %	6.50 max	6.50 max	6.50 max			
Silicon, %	3.00 max	3.00 max	1.00 max			

from Canada and Mexico. In wartime our sea lanes are subject to severance, but with the value and strategic importance of manganese, it might be air-lifted from sources such as Brazil.

Markets and Consumption

By far the largest consumption of manganese is in the manufacture of manganiferous alloys used in the production of steel.

The sources of manganese in the production of ferromanganese, silicomanganese, spiegeleisen, and manganese metal are listed in Table 5. The quantities of ferromanganese produced in the US and the quantities of manganese ores consumed in manufacturing from 1973 to 1980 are listed in Table 6.

Table 7 shows consumption, and stocks of manganese ore in the US in 1980. Manganese consumption from 1960 to 1979 is given in Table 8.

Future Consideration and Trends

Substitutes and Synthetics

The substitution of other materials for manganese is very limited. In special cases, titanium, zirconium, and rare earth metals can replace manganese, but such substitutions are confronted with technological problems, adverse cost factors, and the availability of the material being used as a substitute. It might be said that because of its low cost, manganese is

a substitute for several other alloying elements, including nickel.

Several substitutes exist for manganese in dry cells. Perhaps the substitute with the greatest future potential and the least strategic significance is lithium.

Synthetic manganese dioxide can be produced by electrolytic and chemical methods. Some of this material is of battery grade.

TABLE 5—Manganese Ore Used in Producing Ferromanganese, Silicomanganese, and Manganese Metal in the United States in 1980, by Source of Ore

Source	Gross weight (short tons)	Mn content, natural (%)
Domestic*	34,877	45
Foreign:		
Africa	288,991	46
Australia	49,021	52
Brazil	204,580	46
Chile*	18,754	45
India	39,676	48
Mexico	32,957	39
USSR*	7,452	48
Unidentified	49,819	—
Total or average	726,127	46

Source: DeHuff and Jones, 1981.
*Most, if not all, from US Government excess stockpile disposals.

TABLE 6—Ferromanganese Produced in the United States and Manganese Ore Consumed in Its Manufacture (+35%Mn)

Year	Ferromanganese Produced			Manganese Ore* Consumed (Short Tons)		
	Gross Weight, St	Manganese Content		Gross Weight+		Gross Weight+ per Ton of Ferroman-ganese+ Made
		%	St	Foreign	Domestic	
1973	683,075	78.8	538,119	1,648,806	25,912	2.4
1974	544,361	78.0	424,405	1,348,425	55,822	2.5
1975	575,809	78.9	454,309	1,389,300	48,011	2.4
1976	482,662	79.0	381,328	1,208,336	53,632	2.5
1977	334,134	78.8	362,136	889,296	35,769	2.6
1978	272,530	80.6	219,707	740,906	90,660	2.7
1979	317,102	80.2	254,398	785,664	125,130	2.5
1980	189,472	79.7	150,982	691,250	34,877	1.9

Source: DeHuff, 1978-1979; DeHuff and Jones, 1981.
* Containing 35% or more manganese (natural).
+ Includes ore used in producing silicomanganese and metal.

Subsidies

Where a national emergency exists or it is determined that it is in the nation's best interest to build stockpiles of strategic minerals, the United States Government has entered into extensive and effective subsidy programs for manganese ores. These programs have in the past varied widely in prices paid the operators as well as being realistic in the quality of ore that the districts could produce, keeping in mind the end use to which the material was needed. No such purchase program is currently active.

The US Geological Survey's Office of Mineral Exploration is encouraging the exploration for manganese with financial assistance. Since all manganese consumed in the United States at the present moment is of foreign import, the strategic importance is obvious.

Taxes and Depletion Allowance

Even though manganese bears a 22% depletion allowance, it has been insufficient tax incentive to encourage operators to mine even the best of the low grade properties in America. The 14% depletion allowance on foreign de-

TABLE 7—Consumption and Stocks of Manganese Ore* in the United States (Short Tons, +35% Mn)

	Consumption					Stocks 12/31/80
	1976	1977	1978	1979	1980	
By Use:						
Manganese alloys & metal	1,263,531	926,635	832,179	913,491	727,530	546,840
Pig iron & steel	143,761	200,803	219,663	230,742	131,516	158,422
Dry cells, chemicals & misc.	193,581	231,373	229,637	227,957	211,729	325,225
Total	1,600,873	1,358,811	1,281,479	1,372,190	1,070,775	1,030,487
By Origin						
Domestic	81,607	61,152	106,900	144,404	60,701	52,332
Foreign	1,519,266	1,297,659	1,174,579	1,227,786	1,010,074	978,155
Total	1,600,873	1,358,811	1,281,479	1,372,190	1,070,775	1,030,487

Source: DeHuff, 1978-1979; DeHuff and Jones, 1981.
* Containing 35% or more manganese (natural).

TABLE 8—US Manganese Consumption
(Thousand short tons)*

Year	Consumption	Mine[†] Production	Imports	Exports	Inventories Private	Inventories Government	Price[‡]
1960	1,077	177	1,318	6	1,447	4,241	0.94
1961	842	78	1,172	7	1,278	4,811	0.94
1962	978	73	1,078	9	1,114	5,139	0.91
1963	1,096	94	1,125	6	1,043	5,327	0.81
1964	1,216	79	1,154	13	948	5,426	0.69
1965	1,373	83	1,432	12	977	5,527	0.73
1966	1,353	88	1,444	10	1,093	5,580	0.76
1967	1,207	73	1,171	11	1,171	5,528	0.67
1968	1,150	48	1,053	15	1,180	5,455	0.60
1969	1,317	93	1,249	14	1,241	5,405	0.50
1970	1,327	66	1,085	30	1,175	5,265	0.54
1971	1,170	38	1,150	30	1,281	5,147	0.60
1972	1,366	29	1,098	19	1,241	4,929	0.60
1973	1,554	31	1,058	40	978	4,687	0.65
1974	1,492	35	969	114	1,183	3,880	0.90
1975	1,133	19	1,112	131	1,359	3,571	1.38
1976	1,364	31	1,127	74	1,373	3,277	1.45
1977	1,523	27	935	78	1,092	2,919	1.48
1978	1,415	38	882	120	756	2,640	1.40
1979[e]	1,463	30	896	73	866	2,490	1.40

[e] Estimated.
* After DeHuff.
[†] Includes manganese in manganiferous ores.
[‡] Average price for metallurgical ore containing 46% to 48% Mn in $ per 22.4 lb.

posits owned by US investors has been a factor in stimulating the development of deposits in developing nations. This incentive, plus the reduction in tariff from the 1967 level of 25¢ per lb of contained manganese, to 22¢ under the "General Agreement on Tariffs on Trade" of Jan. 1, 1968, undoubtedly helped to build the US supply from foreign sources.

Under this agreement the tariff has been steadily reduced so that on Jan. 1, 1972 the amount was 12¢ per lb. In June of 1964 the tax was completely suspended for three years. This suspension of duty was again initiated in 1967 for three years with no levy since that time.

Ecology

Since deposits are small and production is low even during times of national emergency, little or no damage is suffered even though the major portion of our ore is mined by the open pit method. Tailings ponds have effectively handled washing and milling rejects. A good example of such a tailings pond exists near Cushman, AR, in the Batesville District.

Bibliography and References

Anon, 1943, "Concentrating and Nodulizing 'Pink' Manganese at Anaconda," Mining World, Vol. 5, No. 1, Jan., pp. 3–8.

Archer, A.A., 1973, "Progress and Prospects of Marine Mining," Mining Engineering, Vol. 25, No. 12, Dec., pp. 31–32.

Barnard, P.G., et al., 1962, "Problems in Substituting Titanium for Manganese in Steel," Report of Investigations 6030, US Bureau of Mines, 27 pp.

Boardman, L.G., 1961, "Manganese in the Union of South Africa," Paper presented at the 7th Commonwealth Mining and Metallurgical Congress Johannesburg, Republic of South Africa, Preprint, 12 pp.

Brooke, D.B., 1966, Low-Grade and Nonconventional Sources of Manganese, Resources for the Future, Johns Hopkins Press, Baltimore, MD, 123 pp.

Caldwell, A.B., 1971, "Deepsea Ventures Readying Its Attack on Pacific Nodules," Mining Engineering, Vol. 23, No. 10, Oct., pp. 54–55.

Cardwell, P.H., 1973, "Extractive Metallurgy of Ocean Nodules," Preprint, American Mining Congress Meeting, Denver, Sep., 27 pp.

Chilton, C.H., 1958, "High Purity Manganese Via Electrolysis," Chemical Engineering, May 19, pp. 136–139.

Coetzee, J.J., 1961, "The Production of Ferro-Alloys," Paper presented at the 7th Commonwealth Mining and Metallurgical Congress, Johannesburg, Republic of South Africa, Preprint, 11 pp.

Cochran, A.A., and Falke, W.L., 1967, "A One-Step Operation for Recovery of Manganese as Chloride from Ores and Slags," Report of Investigations 6859, US Bureau of Mines, 22 pp.

Cole, S.S., 1960, "Manganese Ore," *Industrial Minerals and Rocks,* 3rd ed., J.L. Gillson, ed. AIME, New York, pp. 545–549.

DeHuff, G.L., 1960, "Manganese," *Mineral Facts and Problems,* Bulletin 585, US Bureau of Mines, pp. 493–510.

DeHuff, G.L., 1965, "Manganese," *Mineral Facts and Problems,* Bulletin 630, US Bureau of Mines, pp. 553–571.

DeHuff, G.L., 1971, "Manganese," *Minerals Yearbook—1971,* Vol. 1, US Bureau of Mines, pp. 717–729.

DeHuff, G.L., 1972, "Manganese," *1972 Minerals Yearbook,* Vol. 1, US Bureau of Mines, pp. 757–769.

DeHuff, G.L., 1977, "Manganese," *Minerals Yearbook 1977,* US Bureau of Mines.

DeHuff, G.L., 1978, "Manganese," Preprint, 1978–1979, *Minerals Yearbook,* US Bureau of Mines, 15 pp.

DeHuff, G.L., 1980, "Manganese in 1980," *Mineral Industry Surveys,* US Bureau of Mines.

DeHuff, G.L., and Jones, T.S., 1981, "Manganese," *Minerals Yearbook 1980,* US Bureau of Mines, pp. 543–553.

Dickson, T., 1980, "Manganese, Non-Metallic Market Development," *Industrial Minerals,* No. 155, Aug., pp. 21–29.

Douglas, W.S., et al., 1963, "The Production of Ferromanganese from Low-Grade Manganiferous Ores Using a Rotary Kiln and an Electric Smelting Furnace," *Canadian Mining & Metallurgical Bulletin,* Vol. 56, No. 5, May, pp. 387–389.

Dykstra, F.R., 1979, "Manganese—Its Strategic Implications," *Industrial Minerals,* No. 145, Oct., pp. 55–61.

Elkins, D.A., 1964, "Estimated Cost of Exploiting Enriched, Hard Manganese Ore from the Maggie Canyon Deposit, Artillery Mountains Region, Mohave County, Arizona," Report of Investigations 6438, US Bureau of Mines, 78 pp.

Falke, W.L., and Cochran, A.A., 1966, "Reduction-Volatilization Processes for Recovery of Manganese from Ores," Report of Investigations 6738, US Bureau of Mines, 19 pp.

Farnham, L.L., and Stewart, L.A., 1958, "Manganese Deposits of Western Arizona," Information Circular 7843, US Bureau of Mines, 87 pp.

Fillo, P.V., 1963, "Manganese Mining and Milling Methods and Costs, Mohave Mining Company, Maricopa County, Arizona," Information Circular 8144, US Bureau of Mines, 29 pp.

Huttl, J.B., 1955, "How Manganese, Inc. Upgrades Complex Three Kids Ore," *Engineering & Mining Journal,* Vol. 156, No. 11, Nov., pp. 88–93, 116.

Jacoby, C.H., 1975, "Manganese," *Industrial Minerals and Rocks,* 4th ed., S.J. Lefond, ed., AIME, New York, pp. 821–836.

Joyce, F.E., Jr. and Prasky, C., 1973, "Sulfatization-Reduction of Manganiferous Iron Ore," Report of Investigations No. 7749, US Bureau of Mines, 17 pp.

Johnson, A.C., and Trengove, R.R., 1956, "The Three Kids Manganese Deposit, Clark County Nevada: Exploration, Mining and Processing," Report of Investigations 5209, US Bureau of Mines, Apr., 31 pp.

Kline, H.D., 1958, "Methods and Costs of Mining and Washing Manganese Ore, Batesville District," Report of Investigations 5411, US Bureau of Mines, 46 pp.

Kline, H.D., 1962, "Methods and Costs of Mining and Washing Manganese Ore, Batesville District, Arkansas," Information Circular 8095, US Bureau of Mines, 22 pp.

Kraus, E.H., et al., 1959, *Mineralogy,* 5th ed., McGraw-Hill, New York, 686 pp.

LeVan, H.P., et al., 1965, "Extraction of Manganese from Georgia Umber Ore by a Sulfuric Acid-Ferrous Sulfate Process, Part One, Countercurrent Decantation Extraction and Agglomeration of Leached Residue," Report of Investigations 6692, US Bureau of Mines, 21 pp.

Lewis, W.E., et al., 1958, "Investigation of Cuyuna Iron Range Manganese Deposits, Crow Wing County, Minn., Progress Report One," Report of Investigations 5400, US Bureau of Mines, 49 pp.

Mero, J.L., 1961, "Economics of Deep-Sea Mining," *Mining Congress Journal,* Vol. 47, No. 9, Sep., pp. 52–56, 68.

Mero, J.L., 1968, "Seafloor Minerals: A Chemical Engineering Challenge," *Chemical Engineering,* July 1, pp. 73–80.

Nossen, E.S., 1951, "Manganese Concentration from Low-Grade Domestic Ore," *Industrial & Engineering Chemistry,* Vol. 43, No. 7, July, pp. 1695–1700.

Perkins, E.C., 1957, "Caustic Leaching of Manganese Flotation Concentrate from Artillery Peak, Arizona," Report of Investigations 5341, US Bureau of Mines, 16 pp.

Perkins, E.C., and Novielli, F., 1962, "Bacterial Leaching of Manganese Ores," Report of Investigations 6102, US Bureau of Mines, 11 pp.

Prasky, C., et al., 1961, "Evaluating Cuyuna Manganese Resources by Sulfatizing," Report of Investigations 5887, US Bureau of Mines, 27 pp.

Sears, C.E., 1957, "Manganese Deposits of the Appalachian Area of Virginia," *Mineral Industries Journal,* Virginia Polytechnic Institute, Vol. 4, No. 1, Mar., pp. 1–4.

Sheridan, E.T., 1970, "Manganese," *Mineral Facts and Problems,* Bulletin 650, US Bureau of Mines, pp. 315–331.

Sidwell, K.O.J., 1957, "The Woodstock, N.B. Iron-Manganese Deposits," *Canadian Mining & Metallurgical Bulletin,* Vol. 50, No. 7, July, pp. 411–416.

Sittig, M., 1968, *Inorganic Chemical and Metallurgical Process Encyclopedia,* Noyes Development Co., Park Ridge, NJ, pp. 437–444.

Sullivan, G.V., et al., 1962, "Extraction of Manganese from Low-Grade Dolomitic Materials by a Roast-Leach Process," Report of Investigations 6121, US Bureau of Mines, 24 pp.

Tinsley, C.R., 1973, "In Search for Commercial Nodules, Odds Look Best in Miocene-age Pacific Tertiary System," *Engineering & Mining Journal,* Vol. 174, No. 6, June, pp. 114–116.

Tinsley, C.R., 1973, "Mining of Manganese Nodules: An Intriguing Legal Problem," *Engineering & Mining Journal,* Vol. 174, No. 10, Oct., pp. 84–87.

Tinsley, C.R., 1974, "Manganese-Prices Boosted
    by Record Steel Output in 1973," *Engineering
    & Mining Journal*, Vol. 175, No. 3, Mar., pp.
    81–84.
Weiss, S.A., 1980, "Manganese, the Other Uses,"
    Metals Bulletin Book, London, 360 pp.
Williamson, D.R., et al., 1959, "Future United
    States Manganese Sources," *Colorado School of*

Mines & Mineral Industries Bulletin, Vol. 2,
    No. 4, July, 12 pp.
Young, W.E., 1966, "Manganese Occurrences in
    the Eureka-Animas Forks Area of the San Juan
    Mountains, San Juan County, Colorado," In-
    formation Circular 8303, US Bureau of Mines,
    52 pp.

Meerschaum

B. F. BUIE *

For over 200 years meerschaum has been a significant item of trade between the Near East and countries to the west. Best-known for its use in making smoking pipes and cigar and cigarette holders, it is also used in making a variety of decorative and ornamental items. It is easily carved, and is given an attractive, lustrous finish by rubbing. No published specifications are known, but compact form, purity, uniform whiteness or light color, and uniform, porous texture appear to be requisites. Fig. 1a shows the appearance of a piece of crude meerschaum from Turkey; Fig. 1b a carved item; and Fig. 1c, d, and e show the fibrous and porous texture as revealed by the scanning electron microscope.

Neither a major industrial mineral nor a precious stone, meerschaum nevertheless holds a record of long—and continuing—association with art and personal affairs of man. It is also a mineral to which modern methods of exploration and production probably could be profitably applied. An interesting account of the preparation and use of meerschaum in the early part of this century is given by Sterrett (1907).

Geology and Mining

Mineralogy

Meerschaum is recognized now to be the compact variety of sepiolite, the claylike variety of which is one of the minerals included in the chapter on clays. The word *meerschaum*, from the German meaning "sea foam," was in earlier times used synonymously with *sepiolite*, a word of Greek origin suggestive of the resemblance of the compact variety—then the only variety known—to cuttlefish bone. At one time *meerschaum* was used as the commercial name, and *sepiolite* for the scientific name. However, to think of meerschaum as the name by which sepiolite is known commercially is no

longer valid, in view of the recent emergence of the earthy variety as a competitor of bentonite and other clay materials. Present tendency is to restrict the term *meerschaum* to the compact variety, and to use the term *sepiolite* as a more general name to include both the compact and earthy varieties. This is the terminology followed in this publication.

Meerschaum typically is white to light gray, has a hardness of 2 to 2½, conchoidal to irregular fracture, and specific gravity varying with porosity from about 2 to less than 1. The composition is somewhat variable, but is near that determined by Schaller (1936) for sepiolite as $2MgO \cdot 3SiO_2 \cdot 4H_2O$. A more modern formula based on X-ray determination of the crystal structure is given by Caillère and Hénin (1961) as $(Si_{12})(Mg_9)O_{30}(OH)_6(OH_2)_4 6H_2O$. The reason for the firm, compact nature of meerschaum, in contrast with the earthy variety of sepiolite, is not fully understood. It may be due to the presence of a very minor amount of some bonding material such as silica. Scanning electron microscope (SEM) photographs of a specimen from Turkey (Figs. 1c-1e) indicate that the meerschaum is composed predominantly, if not entirely, of crystalline fibers which merge into sheetlike forms in a complex, intertwined mass.

Detailed X-ray and crystal structure data, as well as some data on thermal stability range, are given by Caillère and Hénin (1961) for the sepiolite family of minerals.

Mode of Occurrence and Origin

Most authors have attributed the origin of meerschaum to alteration of serpentine or other magnesian minerals. The occurrence in alluvium and other surficial deposits does not necessarily indicate that the alteration was supergene. In fact, hydrothermal origin appears more likely for some deposits, though not for all.

* Professor of Geology, Dept. of Geology, Florida State University, Tallahassee, FL.

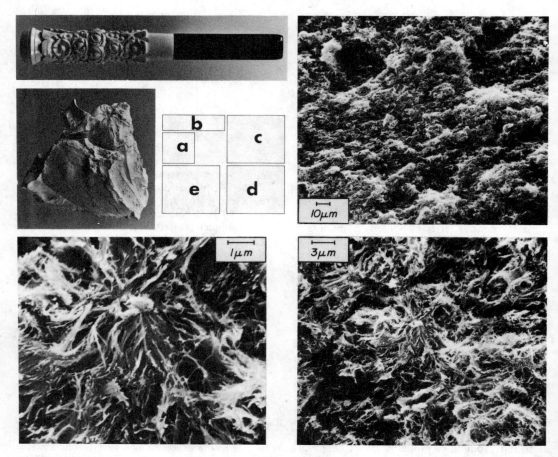

FIG. 1—*Meerschaum from Turkey. a—Broken piece of crude meerschaum showing characteristic fracture. b—Carved cigarette holder. c-e—Scanning electron microscope photographs at different magnifications showing porous texture and fibrous form.*

According to Bateman (1950) the Turkish meerschaum occurs as scattered nodules, from the size of an egg to that of a football, in a cemented valley fill that presumably came from the adjacent mountain sides. Oelsner and Krüger (1957) mention its occurrence in Eskishehir, Turkey, as bedded deposits very closely associated with serpentine, being an alteration product of olivine-rich rocks.

Sterrett (1907) describes the New Mexico meerschaum as occurring in veins, lenses, seams, and balls in limestone, in both nodular and massive form. Although he states that the deposits were not sufficiently studied to permit the expression of an opinion as to their origin, his description indicates hydrothermal action.

Sampson (1966) provides an excellent description of the meerschaum deposits in Tanzania and contributes much toward an under-standing of their origin. The meerschaum occurs as irregular masses and as veins and films along bedding planes, faults, and fracture zones in dolomitic limestone, and to a lesser extent in an overlying unit of sepiolitic mudstone. The author believes that the sepiolitic mudstones and clays constitute the local source of the meerschaum. He states that the mode of emplacement of much of the meerschaum appears to have been simple deposition under wet conditions, by water percolating downward from the surface, and by pressure forcing the plastic meerschaum into cavities of the limestone. The lacustrine beds of limestone and mudstone have been subjected to folding, and the distribution of the meerschaum is partly attributed to structural control.

Concerning the origin of the highly magnesian sepiolitic mudstones and clays, Sampson notes that their color and fine grain, the absence of bedding, and their geographical position in relation to Kilimanjaro would allow for them to be volcanic ash. Lacking direct petrologic evidence, however, he declines to express an opinion as to the method of deposition.

Distribution and Description of Deposits

Meerschaum has been reported from many countries, including Turkey, Iran, India, Somali Republic, Kenya, Tanzania, France, Greece, Spain, Austria, Morocco, Republic of South Africa, and the United States. Only a few of these have been consistent producers.

Turkey: Turkey has been the major producing and exporting country for many years. Most production has been from the province of Eskishehir, in the vicinity of the town having the same name located about 200 km west of Ankara. All of the workings appear to be small; 31 separate localities are named in Eskishehir province. One deposit is in the province of Bilecik, near the town Inonu about 30 km northwest of Eskishehir. One is at the town of Kutahya in the province of the same name, adjacent to and west of Eskishehir province. Another deposit is reported near the town of Sharki-Karaagac, about 200 km south-southeast of Eskishehir. The deposit is in the Sultan Mountains, in the eastern part of Isparta province. Report No. 113 (Anon., 1963) of the Institute of Mineral Research and Exploration includes detailed information, in Turkish, on the location of each deposit. A less detailed summary in English is given by Ryan (1957).

New high-grade deposits of meerschaum were discovered 100 m below ground in Eskishehir in 1973.

Somali Republic: The deposits of meerschaum in Somali Republic first became recognized in international trade in 1965 (Woodmansee, 1967). The deposits are in the Mudugh region near El Bur, which is about 350 km north-northeast of Mogadiscio, and about 130 km from the coast. The Somali meerschaum is reported to be of good quality, with low density and high porosity, but little specific information is available. An early statement indicated that reserves were believed to total several million tons. It seems likely, however, that this included the earthy variety of sepiolite as well as meerschaum.

Tanzania: Little information has been found on the Tanzanian deposits other than the article by Sampson (1966). The deposits are located at Sinya, northwest of Kilimanjaro, near the northeastern boundary of Tanzania; they extend northward into Kenya. The Sinya meerschaum is light-colored, either white, light gray, light brown, or light green. It darkens quickly when wetted. Quality is variable. Sampson's data show that the bulk density ranges from 0.38 to 0.92 g per cc. Material below the water table is generally better quality than that above. Downward mining and exploration have been hindered by large amounts of ground water in the limestone, and reserves are not well-known. The average content of meerschaum in the rock mined is about ½ to ¾ lb per ton of rock.

United States: In the literature meerschaum is mentioned as occurring in several states, including Arizona, California, Pennsylvania, New Mexico, and Utah, but some of the reported occurrences are the earthy variety of sepiolite rather than meerschaum. Deposits in Arizona and New Mexico are the only ones which appear to be worthy of consideration for possible commercial development.

Arizona—Fibrous sepiolite, which from its description appears to be meerschaum, is the subject of a study by Kaufmann (1943). The material occurs in a contact zone in southwestern Yavapai County. According to Kaufmann the deposit was prospected thoroughly and found to be too limited in extent for commercial development.

New Mexico—The two known deposits in New Mexico are located in Grant County. In addition to the discussion by Sterrett (1907), the following is a summary given by Talmage and Wootten (1937):

> Two deposits of meerschaum from the same general locality in New Mexico have been described [by Sterrett], one about 12 miles northwest and the other about 24 miles north of Silver City. The meerschaum is described as occurring in veins in Tertiary igneous rocks. The veins carried the meerschaum in nodules or in blocks, some of them several feet across, but few if any of these nodules or blocks were clear and free from impurity. Nearly everywhere the meerschaum was shot through with crystals of quartz or calcite, so that grinding and washing were necessary to eliminate these crystals. Several shipments were reported to have been made some years ago, part of the material being used for pressing into tobacco pipes and part used as an absorbent for nitroglycerine.
>
> No detailed information is available as to the extent or success of the use of New Mexico ground meerschaum for these purposes, nor as to costs and prices at the time the deposits were worked. Either the quality of the material was too low, or more probably the cost of extraction and shipment

TABLE 1—Turkish Production of Meerschaum, 1969-1979

	1969	1970	1971	1972	1973	1974	1975	1976	1977	1978	1979
Kg	41,250	20,250	18,300	19,350	22,150	20,850	30,900	12,600	4,150	3,050	3,000
Lb	90,750	44,550	40,260	42,570	48,730	45,970	60,130	27,800	9,150	6,730	6,610

Source: *Minerals Yearbooks,* US Bureau of Mines.

was too high, to justify the continued production of this material, as the properties have been idle for many years.

Ford (1932), mentions meerschaum or sepiolite as occurring near Sapella, San Miguel County, New Mexico, but no other reference to this occurrence has been seen.

Production and Trade

Combined world production figures for meerschaum are not available, but some indication of their magnitude is given by the figures on production from Turkey, long the major producer. Data for production in Turkey for the years 1969 through 1979 are given in Table 1. No consistent trend is evident and production has dropped off considerably. For approximately the past decade, the Turkish government has discouraged, or prohibited, the export of crude meerschaum. The objective is to stimulate the manufacture of the finished products in Turkey.

Mining of meerschaum in what is now Tanzania began in 1954, with four tons reported for that year. Production increased to 110 tons in 1965, but subsequently declined. The indicated total through 1971 is over 320 tons; all apparently had gone to the pipe factory of the operating company, Tanganyika Meerschaum Corp., originally located in Nairobi but moved to Arusha in 1960. Pieces of meerschaum too small for whole pipes are used for making bowl inserts, or are ground and reconstituted into blocks. The reconstituted material is known as *Arcon.*

Other producing countries include Somali Republic, Kenya, France, India, and Iran. In 1965 about 2000 lb of meerschaum, 5% of the total imports, came into the United States from Somali Republic. This percentage increased, somewhat erratically, in subsequent years; in both 1970 and 1971 over 90% of US imports were from Somali Republic.

Total imports of meerschaum into the United States in 1971 amounted to 17,482 lb valued at $25,825; the quantity was 28% less (and the value 13% less) than in 1970. In 1972 US imports declined sharply for the second straight year, to a total of 11,137 lb, valued

at $22,791. Sources of imports in 1972 were Belgium, Luxembourg, Japan, and Turkey.

No crude meerschaum was imported into the US during 1973 or 1974. In 1975 meerschaum imported for domestic consumption totaled 11,263 lb, valued at $20,337. The principal source of imports in 1975 was the Somali Republic (99.8%). In 1976 imports of crude meerschaum totaled 1200 lb, valued at $310 or $0.26 per lb; all from the Federal Republic of Germany (West Germany). In 1977 imports decreased to 485 lb, 68% from Spain and 32% from the Federal Republic of Germany. Customs value of the imported meerschaum was declared at $2.62 per lb. US imports of crude meerschaum in 1978 amounted to 14,055 lb, 78% from Somalia and 22% from the Federal Republic of Germany. Value of all imported meerschaum in that year was $35,405, or $2.52 per lb. The material was used by companies in New York and Ohio for the manufacture of smokers' pipes. No imports of meerschaum into the US were recorded for 1979. In 1980, imports of crude meerschaum totaled 3,793 lb, all from the United Kingdom. Customs declared value was $17,720, or $4.67 per lb (*Minerals Yearbook, 1971* through *1980*, US Bureau of Mines).

No domestic production has been reported by the Bureau of Mines since 1914. Bateman (1950) states that about 1000 tons has come from New Mexico.

Acknowledgments

The kind assistance of Yoldoray and Carolyn Buie Erdener, in supplying the specimens of meerschaum shown in Fig. 1 and in translating Turkish articles, is greatly appreciated. Credit and appreciation are due William Miller and Thomas Fellers for taking the SEM photographs, and to Dennis Cassidy for preparing Fig. 1.

Bibliography and References

Anon., 1963, Bilinen Maden Zuhurlari (No. 113), Maden Tetkik ve Arama Enstitüsünce, [Mineral Research and Exploration Institute of Turkey, Publication No. 113; in Turkish], Ankara.

Anon., 1973, "A New Meerschaum Deposit," *Industrial Minerals*, No. 66, Mar., p. 32.

Anon., 1981, "Meerschaum," *Minerals Yearbook, 1980*, US Bureau of Mines, p. 941.

Bateman, A.M., 1950, *Economic Mineral Deposits*, 2nd ed., John Wiley & Sons, New York, pp. 774–775.

Caillère, S., and Hénin, S., 1961, "Sepiolite," *The X-ray Identification and Crystal Structures of Clay Minerals*, Mineralogical Society, Clay Minerals Group, London, pp. 325–342.

Ford, W.E., 1932, *Dana's Textbook of Mineralogy*, 4th ed., John Wiley & Sons, New York, p. 679.

Kaufmann, A.J., Jr., 1943, "Fibrous Sepiolite from Yavapai County, Arizona," *American Mineralogist*, Vol. 28, Nos. 9–10, Sep.-Oct., pp. 512–520.

Nahai, L., 1958, "The Mineral Industry of Turkey," Information Circular 7855, US Bureau of Mines, p. 124.

Oelsner, O., and Krüger, E., 1957, *Lagerstätten der Stein und Erden*, Bergakademie Freiberg, p. 100.

Ryan, C.W., 1957, reprint 1960, "A Guide to the Known Minerals of Turkey," Mineral Research and Exploration Institute of Turkey, Ankara, 196 pp.

Sampson, D.N., 1966, "Sinya Meerschaum Mine, Northern Tanzania," *Transactions*, Institution of Mining & Metallurgy, Sec. B, pp. B23–B34.

Schaller, W.T., 1936, "Chemical Composition of Sepiolite (Meerschaum)," *American Mineralogist*, Vol. 21, No. 3, p. 202.

Sterrett, D.B., 1907, "Meerschaum in New Mexico," Bulletin 340, US Geological Survey, pp. 466–473.

Talmage, S.B., and Wootten, T.P., 1937, "Nonmetallic Mineral Resources of New Mexico," Bulletin 12, New Mexico School of Mines, State Bureau of Mines and Mineral Resources, p. 8.

Woodmansee, W.C., 1967, "The Mineral Industry of Other Areas of Africa," *Minerals Yearbook, 1965*, Vol. 4, US Bureau of Mines, p. 973.

Mica

GEORGE P. CHAPMAN *

Mica is a platy mineral occurring in a variety of complex hydrous aluminosilicate forms with differing chemical composition and physical properties. Principal minerals in the mica group include:

Muscovite—potassium mica (colorless or pale green/ruby)

Phlogopite—magnesium mica (dark brown or amber)

Biotite—magnesium-iron mica (black or dark green)

Lepidolite—lithium mica (lilac)

Selected properties are given in Table 1. Muscovite is most important commercially with phlogopite of lesser use. The laminated structure of mica enables it to be split into very thin films which are transparent and tough as well as having outstanding dielectric and insulating properties.

Commercially, mica is used in a number of forms (Chowdbury, 1941; Rajgarhia, 1951; Skow, 1962). *Sheet mica* consists of flat sheets mined from naturally occurring books of mica, free from defects and capable of being punched or stamped into required shapes. Sheet mica is separately classified into *blocks*, *films*, or *splittings* according to thickness.

Built-up mica, or *micanite*, is made by arranging overlapping splittings in layers cemented with a binder and pressed together at high temperature.

Reconstituted mica, or *mica paper*, is made by depositing fine flakes of high-quality scrap mica in a continuous film impregnated with binder.

Scrap and *flake mica* are normally unsuitable in quality or size for making sheet mica. Originally the term *scrap mica* referred to the waste byproduct of mining and fabricating sheet mica, and distinct uses were developed for this material. Subsequently it became economically feasible to mine lower quality mica

for these uses, and the term *flake mica* was introduced. Although the two terms are still used somewhat synonymously, it is considered better, at least in the United States, to use the term *flake mica* in referring to mica mined for uses other than as sheet mica; and to restrict the term *scrap mica* to mica mined for or with sheet mica, but which will not meet the specifications.

Synthetic mica, such as fluorophlogopite, is produced by slow crystallization of a melted blend of pure raw materials.

Mineralogy

In the true sense the term *mica* does not relate to a particular mineral, but to a group or family of minerals of similar chemical composition and to some extent similar physical properties. These minerals are predominantly potassium aluminum silicates with varying amounts of magnesium, iron, and lithium. The precise formulas and isomorphic relationships of the various group members have been studied, but general agreement has not been reached (Grimshaw, 1971; Hurlbut, 1952; Skow, 1962). The general formula describing the chemical composition of micas is

$$X_2Y_{4-6}Z_8O_{20}(OH, F)_4,$$

where

X is mainly K, Na, or Ca;

Y is mainly Al, Mg, or Fe;

Z is mainly Si or Al

(Deer, et al., 1962).

These minerals have an internal structure of the layered lattice type where the silicon atoms are in the center of a tetrahedral grouping of oxygen atoms. The groups are linked together in a single plane by three oxygen atoms that lie within the common plane. Each of these oxygen atoms is shared by two tetrahedra. These linked tetrahedral groups, when continually extended, produce a hexagonal network within the plane. This internal structure of the mica has been used to explain the ex-

* Managing Director, Microfine Minerals and Chemicals Ltd., Derby, England.

TABLE 1—Selected Properties of Various Micas

Chemical Constituent	Muscovite	Phlogopite	Biotite
SiO_2	46	40	37
Al_2O_3	35	17	18
K_2O	10.5	10	9
MgO	0.5	26	8
Fe_2O_3	1	0.2	2
FeO	1	2.8	21
Na_2O	1	0.5	1
Minor	0.5	0.5	1
H_2O	4.5	3	3
Total	100	100	100
Specific gravity	2.77-2.88	2.76-2.90	2.70-3.30
Mohs' hardness	2½-3	2-2½	2½-4
Optic axial angle	30°-47°	0-15°	0-25°
Temp. of Decomposition	400-500°C	850-1000°C	
Dielectric constant	6.5-9.0	5.0-6.0	
Specific heat (25°C)	0.206-0.209	0.206-0.209	

ternal pseudohexagonal structure of a mica crystal. When a pair of silicon-oxygen sheets that have had about one-fourth of the silicon atoms replaced by aluminum to form a mica are oriented with the tetrahedra vertices pointing at each other, a firm double-layered structure is formed with hydroxyl groups and metallic atoms such as aluminum, magnesium, and lithium between them. These double-layered structures are joined together by potassium atoms. The cleavage plane of the mica is found between these double-layered structures.

In addition to the better known members of the mica group—muscovite, phlogopite, biotite, lepidolite—there are zinnwaldite, a lithium-iron mica, fuchsite, a chromium mica, and roscoelite, a vanadium mica. The mineral vermiculite, related to the mica group, is treated elsewhere in this volume. Of the known micas, only muscovite and phlogopite exhibit any large commercial demand.

These micas crystallize in the monoclinic system with crystals that usually form in hexagonal or rhomb-shaped scales, prisms, or plates, with plane angles on the base of about 60° or 120°. The crystal faces are rarely smooth or well defined except for the basal plane. When a mica cleavage plate is struck sharply by a blunt needle, a six-rayed percussion figure is formed. The figure's most prominent line is parallel to the crystal's plane of symmetry; the remaining two lines are almost parallel to the crystal's prismatic edges. The percussion figure, in conjunction with the position of the optic axes as seen in an interference figure under the polarizing microscope, is useful in making a quick distinction between muscovite and phlogopite, which may closely resemble each other visually. Phlogopite, like biotite, has the plane of the optic axes parallel with the plane of symmetry of the crystal; muscovite has the plane of the optic axes perpendicular to the plane of symmetry. (When a blunt punch is pressed on a mica cleavage plate, a pressure figure is produced. The lines of the pressure figure are perpendicular to those of the percussion figure, but the pressure figure generally develops only partially.)

Minerals of the mica group have the distinctive physical property of being both flexible and elastic. On this basis they are readily distinguished from chlorite, talc, and vermiculite, flakes of which will readily bend but will not snap back to their original position when released.

Muscovite has excellent basal cleavage that allows it to be split into very thin sheets exhibiting a high degree of flexibility, elasticity, and toughness. Very thin sheets of clear muscovite are transparent and colorless or almost colorless. In thicker sheets, it can be translucent and exhibit light shades of yellow, brown, green, or red. The mineral is strongly birefringent and exhibits a feeble pleochroism unless it is dark colored. The material is optically negative. The axial angle varies from 30° to 47° and is dependent on variation in the material's composition. The optic axes lie in a plane that is normal to the crystal's plane of symmetry. Upon heating, muscovite commences to lose water at about 500°C. Muscovite is decomposed only by hydrofluoric acid.

The utility and value of sheet mica depends on the freedom from certain physical defects that occur as a result of the environment and events that occurred during and after crystallization of the mica. These defects are structural imperfections of the cleavage surfaces due to mineral inclusions.

Some of the structural imperfections associated with mica are reeves or cross grains which are lines, striations, or sharp folds in the plane of cleavage; "A" structure, which usually consists of two sets of reeves intersecting on a cleavage surface at about 60°; herringbone structure formed by two sets of reeves intersecting at about 120° along a central line of reeves; wedge mica which consists of mica runs that are thicker at one end than the other; warping which causes a mica characterized by shallow waves or ridges; ruled mica which has regular, sharply defined parting planes that intersect the basal cleavage plane at about a 67° angle; and tangle-sheet mica which is formed by an intergrowth of parts of one mica crystal with another. Most of these defects preclude use of the mica as sheet mica but do not interfere with its use as flake mica.

Mineral inclusions in mica can also limit the utility of sheet mica. These inclusions and intergrowths of other minerals are broadly classed as stains. Some mineral stains appear parallel with the cleavage, but others can penetrate the cleavage plane and cause pinholes. Examples of staining are those formed during mica crystallization and include mottling, inorganic stains, mineral inclusions, and intergrowths. Additional staining can be caused by the circulation of ground water. Mica deposits that have been stained will yield little usable sheet mica.

Phlogopite has a pearly to submetallic luster and varies from translucent to transparent in thin sheets. Phlogopite has been identified in colors ranging from brownish red through yellowish brown, greenish brown, and dark pearl gray to an almost colorless pale green. The color intensifies as the iron content of the mineral increases. Darker colored samples of this mineral exhibit greater hardness than those of lighter color. Phlogopite can contain fluorine which is usually most prominent in reddish brown samples and least in greenish specimens. Phlogopite generally exhibits a distinct pleochroism.

The mineral is optically negative and its optic axial angle varies from 0° to 15°, apparently increasing directly as a function of the iron content. The plane of the optic axes is parallel to the crystal's plane of symmetry. When heated, phlogopite will not dehydrate greatly until about 1000°C. The reaction to acids is variable. Hydrochloric acid will attack the mineral mildly. Hot concentrated sulfuric acid decomposes phlogopite completely.

Historical Background

Sheet Mica

Evidence exists of the use of mica as far back as the earliest civilizations, especially in the Nile Valley and India prior to 2000 B.C.

One of the earliest uses of mica was as a medicine, and even today Hindu physicians use fused biotite. The lustre, iridescence and transparency of the larger sheets led to applications as windows, mirrors, adornments, and plates for painting mythological scenes and the like. The American Indians of the southern Appalachians are known to have used mica in ornamentation at grave sites in the 14th century.

The Romans were probably responsible for the name, from the Latin word *micare* meaning to shine or glitter. Pliny mentioned material scattered over the Circus Maximus to impart a shining whiteness, and window coverings of transparent stones; these may have been in reference to mica.

Muscovite probably derives from the Russian district of Moscovia where de Boodt found and identified potash mica in 1609. The Russians also used mica for medicine. Their men-of-war had mica portholes. Thin sheets of mica were used to protect the surface of icons from being kissed by worshippers.

Commercial mica mining was started in the United States in 1803 at the Ruggles Mines in Grafton County, NH. Primary uses of mica in the 1800s were for stove windows, shades for open-flame lights, and for furnace viewing glass. Although the United States originally was self-sufficient in its mica production, by 1885 India had become a major supplier of muscovite sheet.

The appearance of Thomas Edison's bipolar generator in 1878, his incandescent lamp in 1879, and his system of central-station power production in 1882 stimulated commercial development of electric power-generation.

Growth of the US electrical industry opened up many uses for sheet mica. Mica has proved to be the best insulation for use in commutator segments of large electric generators and motors. The US electrical industry grew so fast that the domestic reserves of large sheets were rapidly depleted.

A patent was issued in 1892 for the first built-up mica that maintained the dielectric and mechanical properties of natural mica. The use of splittings for built-up mica further depleted US reserves and led to increased imports of Indian mica.

Mica was used as spacers and insulators in the diode vacuum tube developed in 1904, and in the triode which followed in 1906. The vacuum tube industry grew in importance with the outbreak of World War I, and large quantities of mica were required to support the war effort. Mica retained its importance in the interwar period through use in the radio industry as well as in the growing electrical industry.

During World War II mica demand was heightened by the great increase in sophisticated electronic gear. The United States worked with the United Kingdom to stimulate production in India and other mica-producing countries. After the war, sheet mica production dropped off dramatically and the decline continues in the 1980s, caused by the rapid advancement of solid-state electronics.

Ground Mica

In 1890 J.S. Williams of the Richmond Mica Co. in Virginia produced ground mica as an ingredient for axle greases. Soon afterward the Vance brothers installed the first chaser mill in North Carolina producing wet ground mica for pigments, to be followed by wet-grinding by Williams.

From there the American industry grew. In 1908 Thomas English formed the English Mica Company in Spruce Pine, North Carolina. In the 1920s J.B. Preston Co. bought English Mica and merged it with the Biotite Mica Co. and Roofing Mica Co. Franklin Mica Products was started by John Davenport in Franklin, NC. In New Hampshire, what is now Concord Mica Co. was formed by Earl Moore. Diamond Mica Co. and Hayden Mica Co. were formed after World War II.

In the 1930s wet ground mica production started in Derby, England, and some dry grinding production began in Europe and India. Micronized mica emerged in Norway and England in the 1960s with further wet grinding plants in Norway, France, and South Africa.

The large growth in mica grinding came in dry ground mica from the 1940s onward, first with the uses in roofing felts and shingles in the US and, as that declined, with the emergence of drywall joint cements and oil-well lost circulation additives.

The 1970s saw the decline of water-grinding as rising energy costs made the products uneconomic and several plants in the US and Europe closed.

Countries of Origin

The most important countries producing mica are listed in Table 2, together with an estimate of their mica-scrap output. An attempt has been made to show how the total supply is distributed around the world for use in the manufacture of ground mica.

It will be seen that approximately 50% of the mica arises in the United States with four other countries—USSR, India, China, and Canada—making up the next 35%.

United States

Approximately 60% of US scrap is from North Carolina and consists of byproduct mica from the feldspar, kaolin, and lithium producers. Virtually all is ground in mills located near the mines. The remaining mica comes mainly from Alabama, Connecticut, Georgia, New Mexico, and South Carolina.

USSR

The pegmatite deposits of Karelia and Maura River regions appear to dominate production, but little information is published regarding mica-grinding. Apparently no exports are made outside Eastern Bloc countries.

India

High quality mica is mined in the States of Bihar, Rajasthan, and Andhra Pradesh for sheet mica production, and the consequent scrap is exported for mica-paper manufacture or ground in India for home and overseas consumption.

China

Mica is produced in a number of regions from pegmatite or as a feldspar byproduct. The most important area is Tientsin province.

Canada

Output consists of flake phlogopite mined in Quebec province and ground at a plant near Montreal. This is the only significant production of ground phlogopite on a world basis.

TABLE 2—Countries of Origin and Consumption of Mica, t/a

Country of Origin as Raw Material	Eventual Consumption as Mica Powder or Flakes							
	US and Canada	USSR and Eastern Bloc	Europe	Far East and Australia	Middle East	Africa	South America and West Indies	Total
USA	105,000	500	2,500	1,000	200	300	500	110,000
USSR		35,000						35,000
India	1,000	7,000	3,000	5,000	4,000	1,000		21,000
China			8,000	4,000				12,000
Canada	12,000		1,500	1,500				15,000
Brazil	1,000		5,000				1,000	7,000
France			6,000					6,000
Spain			4,000					4,000
South Africa			1,500	500		1,000		3,000
Korea				3,000				3,000
Norway			2,000					2,000
Argentina			1,000				1,000	2,000
Italy			1,000					1,000
Others		1,000	1,000	1,000				3,000
European Re-exports	500	1,000	(4,000)	500	800	700	500	
Total	119,500	44,500	32,500	16,500	5,000	3,000	3,000	224,000

Madagascar

High quality phlogopite is mined for use as sheet mica to satisfy the electrical and mica paper markets of Europe and America.

Geologic Features of Mica Deposits

Sheet Mica

Large crystals or books of muscovite and phlogopite mica are generally found in regionally metamorphosed rocks. Granitic pegmatites are the source of muscovite sheet. Phlogopite sheet is found in areas of metamorphosed sedimentary rocks into which pegmatite-rich granite rocks have intruded.

Pegmatites are generally the only source of usable quality sheet mica. Although there are many mica-bearing deposits throughout the world, only a few localities have deposits that are of economic importance. These pegmatites are light-colored, coarsely crystalline igneous rocks. They can be found as dikes or sills in metamorphic rocks and large granite intrusions. The mica crystals found in these deposits range from less than one inch to many feet in length. Variation of size within an individual deposit is not uncommon. Mica-bearing pegmatites have been known to exceed 200 ft in thickness and 1000 ft in length and have been worked to depths ranging from 200 to 500 ft. However, mica also has been produced from shallow surface deposits.

Pegmatites are composed primarily of feldspar, quartz, and mica. In many geologic situations accessory minerals such as garnet, tourmaline, and beryl occur with the primary pegmatite constituents. The distribution of minerals in pegmatites may be even, zoned, or segregated into layers.

Deposits of large books of phlogopite mica that can economically provide large quantities of sheet mica are available in only a few places. Skow (1962) has classified phlogopite deposits into vein, pocket, and contact deposits. Vein deposits, which are generally narrow and are enclosed in fine to medium grained pyroxenite, are the major source of phlogopite sheet mica. Pocket deposits have been found to be irregular in shape, size, course, and persistence. The surrounding pyroxenite of this type of deposit is usually more coarsely crystalline and open textured than that found with vein deposits. The phlogopite crystals may be irregularly distributed throughout the pocket along with crystals of other minerals such as pyroxene and calcite or may occur as very large solid masses of phlogopite.

Scrap and Flake Mica

Originally scrap mica was derived from the mining and processing of sheet mica and included poor quality sheet mica that did not meet the specifications for size, color, and quality. However, the industrial demand for scrap mica began to increase greatly in the 20th century, and mica deposits were mined specifically for the smaller size mica crystals or flake mica found in coarse-grained, weathered, granitic rocks such as alaskite and pegmatite, and in some schists. Flake mica is also recovered as a coproduct from the production of clay, feldspar, and spodumene.

Technology has been developed that permits the recovery of small particle size flake mica from various mica-bearing sources such as mica schist, graphitic mica schist, granite, silt, and recovery plant tailings. Good recovery rates for mica have been reported by the use of grinding and flotation techniques.

Exploration

Sheet Mica

Exploration for sheet mica is not amenable to most of the methodology used to search for other minerals. The sporadic occurrence of large runs of books of mica crystals in the host rock makes it uneconomic to drill a deposit to any great extent to determine the mica content. Any drilling that is done can only delineate the existence of pegmatite and may reveal very little information about the mica content.

Prospecting for sheet mica has failed to advance beyond the trial and error method. Geological evidence is generally insufficient to supply enough information for the evaluation of a deposit. The most practical prospecting method for sheet mica is to sink a test pit in an effort to determine the percentage, size, and quality of trimmed sheet that might be obtained from a deposit. A potential deposit may be stripped or trenched by mechanical or hand methods to outline the size, shape, and attitude of the pegmatite vein for the purpose of selecting the sites for test pits or to supplement the information obtained from test pits. A common method of further exploration for sheet mica consists of sinking a shaft either downdip in the pegmatite body or vertically to cut the pegmatite at the desired depth. Drifts can then be driven along the strike of the deposit in both directions. Any large mica crystals that are found are visually examined by experienced mica workers who determine their freedom from structural imperfection and their suitability for sale. Steeply dipping pegmatites can be explored by the construction of adits. As yet, geophysical and geochemical techniques have not been applied to prospect and evaluate deposits containing sheet mica. The search for

mica sheet remains basically a pick and shovel operation with some limited usage of mechanized equipment.

Flake Mica

Small particle size flake mica that is distributed in deposits of pegmatite, schist, and clay can be evaluated by conventional methods. The location of a deposit can be determined from surface geology. If the surface outcrops are of sufficient size, surface sampling may be justified, but it is more likely that the deposit would be augered or drilled to a shallow depth to furnish samples for testing and delineation of the deposit.

Ore samples obtained in this manner are crushed to a range of sizes to determine the optimum crushing size at which the ore will release the maximum quantity of mica. Chemical analysis is not effective for mica determination because of the wide variation of the chemical composition of the various micas. Petrographic analysis is not completely satisfactory to evaluate the mica content of a sample. The mica industry has not established a standard method of analysis to determine the mica content of an ore sample.

Sink-float techniques can be applied to the crushed samples of pegmatites and schists to assess the capability of separating mica from its accessory minerals by the use of a heavy liquid such as tetrabromoethane or mixtures of tetrabromoethane and kerosene or trichloroethylene. Experiments can be carried out to determine if mica can be extracted from the ore sample by some method of flotation.

As a result of preliminary studies a flowsheet for the recovery of mica can be developed and a small pilot plant operation erected to determine the feasibility of the method of recovery.

The final test of any flake mica is reached when it is ground and/or classified to a particular particle size and accepted for an industrial end use.

Mining and Milling

Mining

Hydraulic mining methods are used where practical because screening and washing operations for the recovery of the mica require large quantities of water. One or more high-pressure streams of water are directed against the quarry face. The ore is broken up by the force of the water, washed from the working face into a sump, and then flumed or pumped to a processing plant. If necessary in partially weathered strata the quarry face is fractured by blasting prior to hydraulic mining.

Most flake mica ore is mined by the use of power-driven mechanical equipment. The exposed mica-bearing ore can be mined by power shovels, bulldozers, or tractor-drawn drag pans and moved to the processing plant by suitable means. Mining with power-driven equipment requires more equipment and labor than hydraulic methods but allows greater flexibility for mining deposits that are not suited for hydraulic methods. Power equipment allows the concentrating plant to be located favorably to a water supply, ore deposit, and transportation facilities. In addition, more small deposits can be worked economically.

Sheet Mica Mining: The recovery of sheet mica in all countries is dependent on the operation of a relatively large number of small mica mining operations that generally use little or no basic mechanical equipment such as compressors, air drills, and hoists. Mine workings are irregular in an effort to follow mica runs or books along rich shoots or from pocket to pocket in a pegmatite deposit. The methodology utilized must allow for the sporadic distribution of the mineral, recovery of undamaged crystals, and any other special condition of the deposit.

Where feasible, open pit, open cut, and stripping are the least expensive methods for the recovery of mica. These methods are used where the mica-bearing pegmatite lies in relatively flat or gently rolling country and appears as a surface outcrop or is covered by easily removed overburden.

In underground mining a main shaft is driven through the pegmatite deposit at suitable angles to the dip and strike of the deposit. Crosscuts and raises are developed to follow promising exposures of mica. Underground mining of pegmatites requires some use of drilling and explosives because the deeper pegmatites are harder than weathered surface pegmatites. Great care is taken to avoid drilling through mica crystals. Explosives are used only in small charges, consisting of low-velocity 40 to 60% strength dynamite, around pockets of mica. After mining, mica crystals are hand-picked from the broken waste rock, boxed or bagged, and raised to the surface. In some operations where difficulties are encountered in hoisting, waste material is left in the mine for fill.

No current data relating to the cost of mining sheet mica are available because only small quantities of low-grade punch and circle mica have been domestically produced in recent years. However, if any significant quantity of good quality sheet mica were produced in the United States, its production cost would be much greater than that of imported foreign mica because of the higher cost of domestic labor.

Flake Mica Mining: Small particle size mica suitable for industrial use is recovered in the United States primarily from pegmatite and residual deposits formed by the weathering of mica-bearing rocks. Because of the regular distribution of the mica particles in the host rock, the mining of flake mica is amenable to conventional mining and beneficiation techniques. Most operations are open pit using conventional equipment to remove any overburden overlying a working face. The exposed mica ore is mined by hydraulic methods, power-driven equipment, or a combination of both methods.

Milling

Mica can be recovered from the mined ore by several general methods. The simplest method separates the mica from its host rock by differential crushing and screening in washer plants. Another method utilizes screens, classifiers, and Humphrey's spirals to concentrate differentially ground ore. The mica is also recovered by the use of screens, classifiers, and flotation techniques. Small particle size material such as sericite mica in clays can be concentrated by grinding, air classification, and drying.

Washer Plant Methods: Standard washer plants used to recover mica are low-cost units that are simple in design and can effectively recover +¼-in. or +³⁄₁₆-in. mica. This type of plant cannot economically recover small-size mica, which is generally discarded. A washer plant generally has a series of roll crushers, trommel screens, and storage facilities through which material is moved by gravity flow or bucket elevators. The flake mica recovery process requires large quantities of water.

When entering the plant, mine-run ore is initially disintegrated by high-pressure water streams. The ore is then crushed in a jaw crusher and washed through a series of trommel screens and roll crushers. The process has little effect on the mica because of its platy and flexible characteristics. However, minerals such as the associated quartz and feldspar are reduced to fine grain sizes. The fine-sized gangue is removed by use of a trommel screen. The undersized gangue material consists of quartz, feldspar, clay, and fine mica. The coarse material is retained on the screen for the next operation. The crushing and screening operation is repeated as many times as necessary to remove the maximum quantity of gangue minerals. The wet, relatively clean coarse mica remaining from this process is then placed in a storage bin. Loss of mica from the original ore can be as high as 50% by this beneficiation process. The undersize discharge from this process can be stored for future recovery of the fine mica by other methods.

Humphrey's Spiral: The addition of Humphrey's spiral technique to a processing plant permits the recovery of a finer size mica than can be recovered from a roll and trommel washer plant. A spiral plant has a low initial and operating cost and minimal skilled labor requirements. Basic plant equipment consists of grinding, classification, and screening equipment, spirals, and storage facilities. In this type of plant, mine-run ore is washed by high-pressure hose into a bowl-rake classifier for initial desliming. Sand from the classifier is fed to a rod mill that discharges to a trommel screen. Any oversize material is returned to the rod mill for additional grinding. Undersize material from the trommel screen is directed to another bowl-rake classifier for additional desliming. The classifier sand is sent to a bank of Humphrey's spirals for initial concentration. The spiral rougher concentration is fed to the cleaner spirals, which produce a middling and a cleaner concentrate. The middling output is returned through the rougher spirals. The cleaner concentrate is passed over a series of screens to remove clay and fine-size gangue minerals. The screen oversize is fed to a hammer mill to delaminate the mica and remove fine-size quartz adhering to the mica. The concentrate is screened, centrifuged, and stored.

Flotation: Flotation methods for the recovery of mica from schists, pegmatites, and sediments have been developed by the Bureau of Mines during the past several years. This work led to the development of the acid cationic and alkaline anionic-cationic flotation methods for the recovery of mica from various types of ore.

The acid cationic flotation method allows the recovery of mica as coarse as 14 mesh. However, the ore must be completely deslimed at 150 to 200 mesh, allowing the loss of a significant quantity of fine mica. The ground ore pulp must be conditioned with sulfuric acid at 40 to 45% solids. Sulfuric acid is used for pH control and quartz depression. Optimum mica flotation was obtained in a pulp with a pH of 4.0. Cationic reagents, such as long-carbon-chain amine acetates, were the most effective collecting agents for floating mica.

The cationic method has been applied to the recovery of mica from pegmatite ores, and a flowsheet for the recovery of mica by this method is shown in Fig. 1.

The alkaline anionic-cationic method of mica flotation is effective for the recovery of mica when slimes are present. The ore is usually deslimed sufficiently to remove clay slimes, fine particle size mica, and any other granular material. This process allows the flotation of material as coarse as 20 mesh. The process requires conditioning the finely ground ore pulps at 40 to 45% solids with sodium carbonate and calcium lignin sulfonate and floating the mica with a combination of anionic and cationic collectors. Excellent recoveries were obtained in a pH range of 8.0 to 10.5. Separation was not greatly sensitive to pulp pH.

Continuous treatment of ore using the alkaline anionic-cationic method requires grinding, trommel screening, preconcentration, classification, conditioning, and flotation. A process flowsheet is shown in Fig. 1.

Recovery of mica is amenable to continuous flotation methods requiring relatively low capital investment in processing equipment and limited requirements for labor to operate the processing plant.

Pneumatic Processes: More recently, the US Bureau of Mines has concluded research on the recovery of flake mica using a dry pneumatic process. A system of crushers, screens, and zig-zag classifiers has been developed to concentrate mica particles. A generalized flowsheet is shown in Fig. 2. An alternative to the zig-zag classifier is the air-table or air jig. Such processes are in operation on pegmatite micas and mica schists in Europe and on phlogopite in Canada.

Preparation of Finished Products

Sheet Mica

The preparation of sheet mica for market relies entirely on hand labor that requires great expertise and experience to recover the maximum usable crystal area while developing minimal waste or scrap mica. Large quantities of scrap are produced during the preparation of

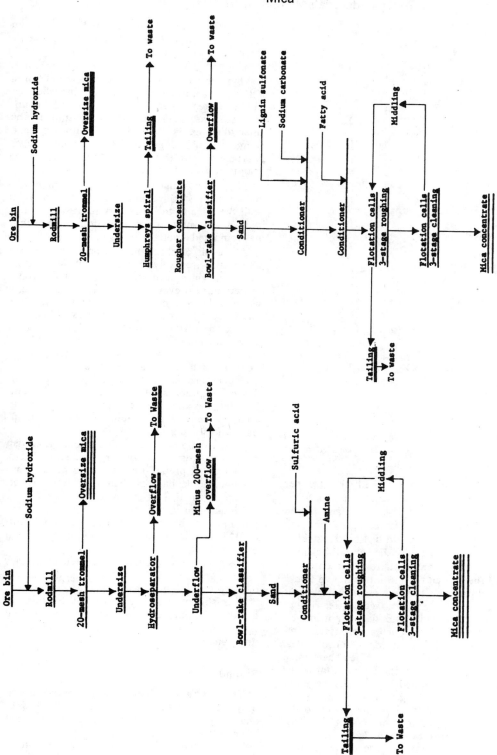

FIG. 1—Flowsheet for recovery of mica; acid cationic method at left and alkaline anionic-cationic method at right.

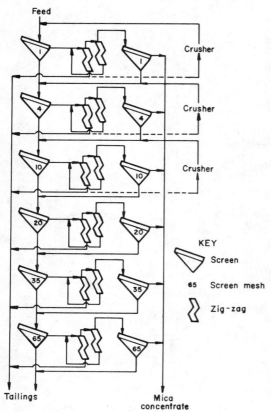

FIG. 2—*Generalized flow diagram of US Bureau of Mines pneumatic concentration method.*

the mica despite the use of skilled labor, proper preparation methods, and suitable precautions. The raw crystal is hand-cobbed and rifted using hammers, knives, and fingers. Trimming of the crystal is done with knives, sickles, shears, or fingers. Initially the rough books are cobbed to remove any dirt, rock, or defective mica and then rifted or split into suitable thicknesses. During these operations any obvious flaws in the crystals are removed. After rifting, the mica can be broadly classified as untrimmed sheet and scrap mica. Further processing removes broken and ragged edges, loose scales, and any other imperfections. When sheet mica was actively produced in the United States, the mica crystal was trimmed to a beveled-edge cut with a knife. The rifting and trimming operations required great care and judgment to determine what part of the mica should be removed to minimize waste and maximize the usable area of the crystal. The trimmed mica is classified according to grade (size), quality,

and clarity. A visual determination, that can vary from one observer to another, is made of the quality of the natural sheet mica.

Additional splitting operations are required for the production of mica films and splittings. Films and splittings are not ordinarily produced in the United States. In other producing countries such as India and Brazil, splitting to the finer thickness is done by hand with a special, pointed double-edged knife with both edges sharpened near the point. A high degree of manual dexterity is necessary to split mica.

The fabrication of film and splittings demands highly skilled and experienced labor to split the mica to the necessary narrow thickness ranges. In India the preparation of splittings has remained a cottage industry.

All forms of sheet mica, especially in Brazil and India, are likely to move from the production area via a succession of mica buyers and traders until it eventually reaches a coastal city where sales are negotiated between exporters and importers from other countries. Most producing countries export their sheet mica to other consuming industrial countries. India does consume some of its own sheet production, but detailed data are not available.

Sheet mica is classified according to color, degree of preparation, thickness, visual examination, size and electrical quality according to a comprehensive and detailed series of descriptions and standards.

Color definitions include green, yellowish green, yellowish olive, brown, pinkish buff, etc.

Degree of preparation refers to crude, run-of-mine, book, hand-cobbed, untrimmed sheet, thumb-trimmed, half-trimmed, etc.

Block mica is not less than 0.007 in. thick; film mica in specified thickness from 0.0012 to 0.004 in.; "thick-thins" from 0.004 to 0.007 in., etc.

Visual quality is described in ten categories including clear, fair stained, good stained, densely stained, and black dotted.

Size is identified by the area of the minimum enclosed rectangle in square inches ranging from 8 x 12 in. down to 1½ x 2 in. plus circle and punch.

Ground Mica

Three different methods of grinding are employed each leading to products with distinct characteristics: water-ground mica, micronized mica, and dry-ground mica.

Water-Ground Mica: About half the total tonnage of mica is still made by traditional

Mica

methods using equipment 20 to 30 years old. The process consists of grinding good quality scrap with up to 20% of moisture, in edge-runner mills followed by drying and classification to 100, 200, 325 mesh sizes. The resulting products have very thin and smooth particles providing sheen and good slip for use in wallpaper, tire manufacture, and paint.

Two manufacturers have introduced more up-to-date and economic proprietary processes. Their output, while not having the sheen required for the declining wallpaper industry, has the necessary properties for the bulk of the market, i.e., tires and paint.

Micronized Mica: First introduced in Europe to retain the paint markets previously held by water-ground mica, micronized mica involves grinding fine-grained byproduct scrap to sizes smaller than 40 microns. The method consists of accelerating the mica particles to very high speeds in a confined space so that they collide and disintegrate. A variety of such fluid energy micronizers exists, operating with superheated steam or compressed air. Particle size is controlled by adjusting the residence time in the mill and removing oversize by air classification.

Dry-Ground Mica: In general, US dry grinding practice differs from elsewhere as a consequence of the uniquely dominant requirement for mica in plasterboard joint-cements. Using minus 6-mesh scrap, the major production is by means of air micronizers; oversize (plus 60 or 100 mesh) is removed on dry screens.

Oil-well flakes, the second largest demand, are extracted from feldspar/kaolin byproducts by flotation or water classification. After drying, the various grades are sieved on multi-

deck screens, any oversize (plus ¼ in.) being reduced by impact milling. Some oil-well flakes are extracted during the production of mica scrap of the mines by winnowing the output from the primary crusher through air boxes and cyclones. Other markets are satisfied by screening products from drilling flakes or joint-cement mica.

Dry-ground mica elsewhere in the world is made predominantly from prime scrap (plus 1 in.) fed through high-speed hammer-type mills, then topped and tailed through vibrating screens. The products generally are more highly delaminated and are therefore referred to as *high-aspect* ratio mica flakes and powders.

A wide variety of product specifications is necessary to meet user requirements. Examples of some of these are given in Table 3.

Mica Markets and Production Data

In production and marketing, as well as in usage, sheet mica and scrap and flake mica constitute almost entirely separate commodities. An exception is that scrap mica, recovered from block and film sheets from which fabricated shapes have been punched or stamped, is sold to the manufacturers of mica paper (reconstituted mica).

Sheet Mica

World production of sheet mica is principally from India, with lesser amounts from Brazil and Madagascar. US annual production for the past several years has been estimated at not more than 1000 lb, hand-picked from blast

TABLE 3—Particle Size Distribution of Ground Mica Products

Sieve Analysis Mesh	% Finer than Micron	Water-Ground Mica Rubber Grade	Micronized Mica Paint Grades	Dry Ground Mica				Plastics
				Oil Wells		Joint-Cement	Welding Electrodes	
¼-inch	6400			100				
7	2800			80	100		100	
14	1200			30	98		98	
30	500			10	50		60	
44	355				10		40	100
60	250					100	10	99
100	150	100				99		70
150	105	99.9				95		50
200	75	85				85		35
300	53	80	100			75		20
325	44	75	99.9			70		5
Bulk Density (kg/L)		0.18	0.22	0.30		0.29	0.26	0.24

TABLE 4—US Sheet Mica Production and Consumption

	Sheet Mica Production		Block and Film Consumption		Splitting	
	1000 lb	Value, $1000	1000 lb	Value, $1000	1000 lb	Value, $1000
1975	5	3	623	1608	4746	2634
1976	5	3	534	1413	5025	3226
1977	1	—	448	990	4144	2718
1978	—	—	247	1362	5537	3031
1979	1	—	282	1866	4877	3248
1980	NA	NA	147	1829	4383	3101

NA = Not available.
Source: Zlobik, 1980; Tepordei, 1981.

rubble at feldspar and mica quarries. Although world production of sheet mica has shown a moderate increase in the last five years, production declined from over 25 million lb in 1969 to 17 million lb in 1979. US demand during this period has remained fairly stable at approximately 5 to 7 million lb annually (Zlobik, 1980). The contrast between production and consumption of sheet mica in the US for 1975–1980 is shown in Table 4.

It is expected that growth in the use of substitutes will further reduce demand for sheet mica in the US and possibly elsewhere.

Most block and film mica is fabricated into mica parts by highly specialized mica fabricators for electrical, electronic, and other industrial users. Mica splittings are processed into built-up mica products such as molding plates, segment plates, heater plates and tape through the use of binders, adhesives, and backing materials.

Consumption of sheet mica products is divided into four categories: electrical, vacuum tubes, capacitors, and other uses. Demand pattern for these products is shown in Table 5.

Flake and Ground Mica

In comparison with the rest of the world, the United States has a disproportionate demand for plasterboard joint-cements resulting from building methods not normally found in other countries. In this context, it is interesting to note that the largest mica producer is also the largest gypsum and plasterboard producer. Apart from that, a higher-than-average proportion of water-ground mica goes to the American paint industry; elsewhere more micronized mica is used. The geographic demand for oil-well drilling flakes reflects the activity of exploration and development of the world's oilfields.

Quality and value of scrap and flake mica produced in the United States are shown in Table 6. An estimate of the world supplies of each type of ground mica is given in Table 7. The consumption of various types of ground mica produced outside the USSR is shown in Table 8.

TABLE 5—Sheet Mica Supply-Demand Relationships, 1975-1979
(1000 lb)

	1975	1976	1977	1978	1979
World Production	13,400	14,300	15,200	17,600	17,000
US Demand					
Electrical	4746	5025	4144	5537	4877
Vacuum tubes	375	318	241	152	170
Capacitors	7	8	7	8	5
Others	241	207	200	86	107
Total	5369	5558	4592	5783	5159

Source: Zlobik, 1980.

TABLE 6—US Production and Value of Scrap and Flake Mica and Ground Mica, 1975-1980 *

Year	Scrap and Flake		Ground Mica	
	Quantity (1000 st)	Value ($1000)	Quantity (1000 st)	Value ($1000)
1975	132	5,205	112	9,366
1976	123	5,667	115	10,027
1977	129	7,039	122	11,906
1978	139	7,916	124	12,979
1979	134	7,708	122	14,555
1980	117	5,296	109	12,992

* Excluding low-quality sericite.
Source: Zlobik, 1980; Tepordei, 1981.

The uses of the various types of mica are summarized as follows:

1) Water-ground mica:
   a) wallpaper — to provide sheen; significant but diminishing market;
   b) rubber tires — for mould lubrication and dusting; heavily dependent on automotive markets;
   c) paint — several uses including anti-corrosion and anti-settling; largely being replaced by micronized mica because of cost-saving.

2) Micronized mica:
   used almost entirely in paints with a small quantity in phenolic moulding powders and adhesives;

prices are highly competitive since production is from cheap mica byproducts from kaolin and feldspar.

3) Dry-ground mica:
   a) Oil-well drilling — flakes used to seal well walls when drilling mud seeps into fractured strata; market follows pattern of oil development; prices normally very cheap and qualities variable;
   b) Joint-cements — imparts crack resistance and assists smooth finishing; very large US market but less significant elsewhere; normally above-average bulk density;
   c) Surface-coatings — medium and fine flakes used in house facade and interior textured plasters, textured stone paints, and roof paints;

TABLE 7—Estimated World Production of Ground Mica, Excluding USSR
t/a

Country	Water-Ground Mica	Micronized Mica	Dry-Ground Mica	Total
US	13,000	10,000	87,000	110,000
India	—	1,000	14,000	15,000
UK	1,000	3,000	11,000	15,000
Canada	—	—	15,000	15,000
France	1,500	3,000	3,000	7,500
W. Germany	—	—	5,000	5,000
Japan	500?	1,000?	4,000?	5,500
Norway	—	3,000	2,000	5,000
Italy	—	1,000?	2,000?	3,000
China	—	—	3,000	3,000
South Africa	1,500	—	—	1,500
Brazil	—	—	1,000	1,000
Spain	—	500	500	1,000
Zimbabwe	500	—	500	1,000
Australia	—	—	1,000	1,000
Total	18,000	22,500	149,000	189,500

TABLE 8—Analysis of World Ground Mica Markets, Excluding USSR Products
1000 t/a

Consuming Nations	Water-Ground Mica	Micronized Mica	Dry-Ground Mica			
			Oil Wells	Joint Cements	Other	Total
US/Canada	13.3	9.0	25.2	66.0	11.0	123.5
USSR/Eastern Bloc	0.5	2.0	1.0	1.0	5.0	9.5
Europe	3.5	8.0	3.0	4.0	15.0	33.5
Far East/Australia	3.0	2.0	3.0	1.5	7.0	16.5
Middle East	0.5	0.5	3.5	—	0.5	5.0
Africa	0.5	0.5	1.0	—	1.0	3.0
South America/West Indies	0.2	0.5	1.3	—	1.0	3.0
	21.5	22.5	38.0	66.5	40.5	189.0
Total				155.0		

d) Insulation boards   a number of isolated uses in asbestos-free applications in low-density fire-resistant boards;

e) Welding electrodes   an essential ingredient in certain electrodes for control of flux and slag characteristics;

f) Plastics   growing use as reinforcement in rigidized plastics for automotive, electrical, and construction industries;

g) Miscellaneous   including roofing, rubber, foundry coatings, fire extinguishers, acoustic products, adhesives and lubricants.

Satisfying the market requirements creates a complexity of problems for the producer, arising from conflicts of specification between industries and even within the same industry. The examples in Table 3 do not reveal that a standard product list might well comprise three water-ground grades, three micronized grades, and over twenty dry-ground grades. Even within the dry-ground range, three or four products would be needed for oil-wells and six or seven for welding electrodes. In the latter case two or three different raw materials could be needed to satisfy the specified chemical analyses.

Health and Safety Requirements

Insufficient knowledge exists to state categorically whether dust from mica production is hazardous. It is accepted that if any danger exists it is confined to the inhalation of respirable dust. Various authorities have therefore fixed limits on the levels of such dust permitted in the workplace.

The American Conference of Government Industrial Hygienists has adopted the following Threshold Limited Values (TLV) for mica dust:

Total dust	—	6 mg/m^3
Respirable dust	—	3 mg/m^3

(TLV refers to airborne concentration of dust)

The Health and Safety Executive of Great Britain applies a standard of 10 mg/m^3 of total airborne dust for all grades of mica with an additional limit of 1 mg/m^3 for the respirable portion. Measurements are based on sampling carried out using a C.F. Casella size-selective cone sampler, and the "respirable" portion is that passing the cyclone and collected on the filter membrane.

Where TLV's are exceeded, the workers should wear approved masks to cover the nose and mouth.

Acknowledgments

This chapter has relied heavily on extracts from available published information included in the bibliography and references listed below.

The author particularly wishes to thank Mr. Benjamin Petkof for permission to reproduce significant portions of his chapter on Mica in the 4th edition of *Industrial Minerals and Rocks*, and the US Bureau of Mines for assistance in making data and publications available.

Bibliography and References

Adair, R.B., and Browning, J.S., 1969, "Flotation of Mica from Pegmatites of Randolph County, Ala.," Report of Investigation 7159, US Bureau of Mines, 9 pp.

Adair, R.B., and Browning, J.S., 1969a, "Flotation of Muscovite from Alabama Graphitic-Mica Schist Ore," Report of Investigation 7263, US Bureau of Mines, 7 pp.

Adair, R.B., and Crabtree, J.O., 1971, "Recovery of Mica from Silt Deposits in the Nolichucky Reservoir, Tenn.," Report of Investigation 7488, US Bureau of Mines, 9 pp.

Browning, J.S., 1973, "Mica Beneficiation," Bulletin 662, US Bureau of Mines, 21 pp.

Browning, J.S., and Adair, R.B., 1966, "Selective Flotation of Mica from Georgia Pegmatites," Report of Investigation 6830, US Bureau of Mines, 9 pp.

Browning, J.S., and Bennett, P.E., 1965, "Flotation of California Mica Ore," Report of Investigation 6668, US Bureau of Mines, 7 pp.

Browning, J.S., and McVay, T.L., 1963, "Concentration of Fine Mica," Report of Investigation 6223, US Bureau of Mines, 7 pp.

Browning, J.S., et al., 1965, "Anionic-Cationic Flotation of Mica from Alabama and North Carolina," Report of Investigation 6589, US Bureau of Mines, 9 pp.

Chapman, G.P., 1980, "The World Mica Grinding Industry and Its Markets," Proceedings, 4th Industrial Minerals International Congress, Atlanta, 7 pp.

Chowdhury, R.R., 1941, Handbook of Mica, Chemical Publishing Co., Brooklyn, NY, 340 pp.

Deer, W.A., et al., 1962, "Sheet Silicates," Rock-forming Minerals, Vol. 3, Longmans, London, 270 pp.

Eddy, W.H., et al., 1969, "Selective Flotation of Minerals from North Carolina Mica Tailing," Report of Investigation 7319, US Bureau of Mines, 10 pp.

Grimshaw, R.W., 1971, The Chemistry and Physics of Clays and Allied Related Ceramic Materials, Wiley-Interscience, New York, 1024 pp.

Hawley, G.C., 1981, "Expanding Markets and Technologies for Mica from Suzor Township, Quebec," Preprint 81–121, SME-AIME Annual Meeting, Chicago, 10 pp.

Hill, T.E., Jr., et al., "Separation of Feldspar, Quartz and Mica from Granite," Report of Investigation 7245, US Bureau of Mines, 25 pp.

Hurlbut, C.S., Jr., 1952, Dana's Manual of Mineralogy, 16th ed., John Wiley, New York, 530 pp.

Ivey, K.N., and Haskiel, R.S., 1969, "Fluorine Micas," Bulletin 647, US Bureau of Mines, 291 pp.

Jordan, C.E., Sullivan, G.V., and Davis, B.E., 1980, "Pneumatic Concentration of Mica," Report of Investigation 8457, US Bureau of Mines, 23 pp.

Lesure, F.G., 1973, "Mica," "United States Mineral Resources," Professional Paper 820, US Geological Survey, pp. 415–425.

Lusis, I., 1980, "Review of the Health Effects of Micas," Industrial Minerals, London, Oct., pp. 45–55.

Petkof, B., 1975, "Mica," Industrial Minerals and Rocks, S.J. Lefond, ed., 4th ed., AIME, New York, pp. 837–850.

Preston, J.B., 1973, "Aluminum Potassium Silicate—Mica," Pigment Handbook, Vol. 1, Properties and Economics, John Wiley & Sons, pp. 249–263.

Rajgarhia, C.M., 1951, Mining, Processing and Uses of Indian Mica, McGraw-Hill, New York, 388 pp.

Skow, M.L., 1962, "Mica: a Material Survey," Information Circular 8125, US Bureau of Mines, 240 pp.

Stanczyk, M.H., and Feld, I.L., 1972, "Ultrafine Grinding of Several Industrial Minerals by Attrition Grinding Process," Report of Investigation 7641, US Bureau of Mines, pp. 6–10.

Tepordei, V.V., 1981, "Mica," Minerals Yearbook, US Bureau of Mines, pp. 563–572.

Zlobik, A.B., 1980, "Mica," Mineral Facts and Problems, Bulletin 671, US Bureau of Mines, 16 pp.

Nepheline Syenite

D. GEOFFRY MINNES * †
Revised by STANLEY J. LEFOND ‡
and RAY BLAIR §

Nepheline syenite is a silica deficient crystalline rock consisting of albite and microcline feldspars and nepheline, together with varying but small amounts of mafic silicates and other accessory minerals. Nepheline-bearing rocks are widely distributed around the world but only in Canada, Norway, the Union of Soviet Socialist Republics, and the United States are deposits worked commercially.

Because of its low melting point and fluxing ability, nepheline syenite was investigated in the early 1900s by many students of glass and ceramics. Although the nepheline syenite deposits in Methuen Township, Ont., Canada, were discovered as early as 1897 it wasn't until 1935 that the first mill was erected to produce nepheline syenite products.

In Canada, nepheline syenite deposits are worked by Indusmin Ltd. and International Minerals and Chemical Corp. (Canada) Ltd. who have combined production capacity in excess of 1800 stpd. Between 1935 and 1972 seven million tons valued at $78 million were produced from the Methuen Township deposits. In Norway, the Norsk Nefelin Div. of Elkem Spigerverket has produced nepheline syenite from a deposit on Stjernöy Island in western Finland since early 1960. Production has increased from 8 kt in 1961 to over 200 kt in 1980.

Nepheline syenite has been under investigation in the Union of Soviet Socialist Republics (USSR) since at least 1928. In 1951 the first commercial alumina works was brought on stream at Volkhov, near Leningrad, utilizing nepheline concentrates from the Kola peninsula as mill feed. Since then two others have been completed and more are planned. Large quantities of portland cement, sodium carbonate, and potassium carbonate are produced in conjunction with the alumina.

A material called nepheline syenite, but actually a pulaskite, is produced in Pulaski County, Arkansas, by the McGeorge Construction Co. for construction aggregates and by the 3M Co. for roofing granules. The Dome Fill Co. purchases the fines and uses them in the preparation of enclosed construction fill. Production is over 2,000,000 stpy.

Chap. 16 on "Feldspar, Nepheline Syenite, and Aplite" in the 3rd ed. of *Industrial Minerals and Rocks* (Castle and Gillson, 1960) and *Nepheline Syenite Deposits of Southern Ontario* (Hewitt, 1960) contain excellent accounts of earlier commercial development of nepheline syenite as a glass and ceramic material. As in the 4th ed., this chapter deals mostly with the period since 1960 and with matters not previously reported in detail. An English monograph on *Nepheline-Syenite and Phonolite* (Allen et al., 1968) is a complete survey, at the time, of nepheline syenite which, with its very complete list of references, is an excellent source book.

End Uses

Nepheline syenite from the Canadian and Norwegian producers finds use primarily in the manufacture of glass and ceramics. One producer also makes several grades of nepheline syenite that are useful as extender pigments and fillers in paint, plastics, and rubber. In the Soviet Union nepheline is used in increasing quantities in the manufacture of alumina, alkali carbonates, and portland cement and to a lesser degree it is used in the manufacture of colored container glass.

*Geologist, Ontario Ministry of Natural Resources, Industrial Minerals Sec., Toronto, Ont., Canada.

†Acknowledgments: The writer is indebted to Hans-Peter Geis, D. F. Hewitt, and K. H. Teague for invaluable advice and assistance in the preparation of this chapter.

‡Consultant, Evergreen, CO.

§Consultant, Arvada, CO.

931

Glass

By far the largest use of nepheline syenite is in the manufacture of glass products including container glass, fiber glass, opal glass, plate glass, sheet glass, and tableware glass. Nepheline syenite provides necessary additions of alumina and alkalis in the glass batch; it is low in silica and contains no free quartz; it has a favorable ratio of sodium oxide to potassium oxide of 2/1. Nepheline syenite bearing glass batches have lower viscosity and easier workability compared with those containing potash feldspar.

The lower fusion point of nepheline syenite lowers the melting temperature of the glass batch with attendant faster melting, high productivity, and fuel savings.

In Canada about 70% of nepheline syenite is used for glass manufacture; over 75% of Canadian nepheline syenite is exported to the United States and much of this is used in glass manufacture. 85% of Norwegian production is believed to be used in the glass industry and 15% for ceramics.

Ceramic Ware

Nepheline syenite is being used for the manufacture of a wide variety of whiteware products including dinnerware, sanitaryware, floor and wall tile, electrical porcelain, art pottery, chemical porcelain, dental porcelain, porcelain balls, and mill liners. In ceramics, nepheline syenite serves as a vitrifying agent, contributing to the glassy phase which binds other constituents together and gives strength to the ware. The ready fusibility and abundant fluxing capacity of nepheline syenite benefits manufacturers by permitting reduced body flux content, lower firing temperatures, or faster firing schedules than could be attained with other raw material combinations.

Canadian consumption of nepheline syenite for ceramic applications in 1971 represented 12% of total consumption. Twelve percent of Norwegian production of nepheline syenite in 1971 was "ceramic grade." There is no direct statistical data to indicate the level of Canadian exports of ceramic grades of nepheline syenite but analysis of export data suggest the amount is not large, relative to total exports.

Extender Pigment and Fillers

Applications for nepheline syenite as extender pigments and inert fillers have been found and developed. These include exterior and interior latex and alkyd paint systems, traffic paints, metal primers, exterior wood stains, sealers, undercoats, and hardboard ground coats. Nepheline syenite for these products has desirable high dry brightness, high bulking value, low vehicle demand, extreme ease of wetting and dispersion, and a stabilizing pH value. In paint formulations nepheline syenite has exceptionally good tint retention characteristics.

In plastics nepheline syenite has found increasing use in rigid, flexible, and plastisol-type polyvinyl chloride, and in epoxy and polyester resin systems. It exhibits extremely low resin demand thus making high loadings possible. In PVC resins it exhibits extremely low tinting strength, has a refractive index close to that of vinyl resin, and has a very low optical dispersion. It has a specific gravity lower than calcium carbonate and talc and the properties described for paint applications are beneficial in plastics applications as well.

Nepheline syenite is also used as an inert filler in the manufacture of foam carpet backing.

Alumina

In the USSR nepheline syenite and nepheline are used to manufacture alumina for aluminum production, sodium and potassium carbonates, and portland cement. USSR production comes from Kola peninsula and Kiya Shaltyrsk deposits. The USBM (Anon., 1961–71) estimates that the present level of consumption of nepheline concentrates in the Soviet Union is 1 million ltpy. More recent data on nepheline syenite production in the USSR are not available. In addition, the Volkhov, Pikalevo, and Achinsk alumina plants require at least 3 million lt of nepheline syenite annually. Nowhere at this time outside the Soviet Union is nepheline or nepheline syenite used as the basis for such industries.

Product Specifications

Nepheline syenite used by the glass industry is characteristically a —30 mesh +200 mesh product having an alumina content in excess of 23%, alkali content in excess of 14%, and iron oxide content less than 0.1%. Other metallic contaminants must be very low. For the ceramic industry nepheline syenite is ground to typically —200 mesh and is characterized by its high fluxing and low level of iron and other impurities. For extender pigment and filler industries, nepheline syenite offers high dry brightness, uniformity, chemical inertness, and specific index of refraction and is supplied in various finenesses.

Market requirements vary and while the European markets accept a 0.1% Fe_2O_3 content, North American markets require 0.08% Fe_2O_3 or less. Norwegian nepheline syenite products are higher in alumina and alkalis than Canadian ones. Other contaminating metallic ions must be at acceptably low levels and refractory minerals must be absent.

Complete product specifications for Canadian and Norwegian glass, ceramic, and filler grades of nepheline syenite are shown in Tables 1, 2, and 3, respectively.

Geology

Mineralogy

Nepheline syenite is a coarse to medium-grained crystalline *rock* generally considered of igneous origin in which the essential mineral constituents are microcline, orthoclase or albite feldspars, the feldspathoid nepheline, and ferromagnesium minerals of which the principal are hornblende, pyroxene, and biotite. The most frequently occurring accessory minerals include magnetite, ilmenite, calcite, garnet, zircon, and corundum. Nepheline syenites are quartz-free.

Commercial deposits of nepheline syenite contain at least 20% nepheline, at least 60% feldspar, and seldom more than 5% accessory minerals. For a deposit to be of interest, refractory minerals such as corundum and zircon must be absent or easily removed along with other accessory minerals and characterizing mafic silicates during processing.

Nepheline—Nepheline is the most common of the feldspathoid *minerals*. Its formula is $Na_3K Al_4 Si_4 O_{16}$. Potassium is always present in natural nepheline, most frequently in ratio amounts of Na/K: 3/1, although ratios of 4/1 and 6/1 are known. It crystallizes in the hexagonal system and frequently forms 6 or 12-sided prisms. It has a distinct and an imperfect cleavage and a subconchoidal fracture. It is brittle; the hardness is 5½ to 6 on Mohs' scale, the specific gravity is 2.5 to 2.7; the luster is vitreous to greasy, occasionally opalescent. It is colorless, white, or yellowish but when massive may be dark green, greenish, bluish-gray, brownish-red, and brick-red. It is also known as elaeolite. It gelatinizes readily in acid and because it is more soluble than associated minerals can be readily spotted in outcrops by the pitted appearance of the rock surfaces. Nepheline alters to various zeolites, analcite, sodalite or cancrinite, and the gieseckite micaceous materials.

TABLE 1—Nepheline Syenite—Typical Product Specifications, Glass Grades

Product Designation Typical Chemical Analysis	Indusmin		IMC		Norsk Nefelin
	330, %	333, %	Summit, %	Ridge, %	North Cape, %
Silica	59.9	60.0	60.2	60.1	55.9
Alumina	23.5	23.4	23.5	23.4	24.2
Ferric Oxide	0.08	0.35	0.07	0.5	0.1
Calcia	0.6	0.7	0.3	0.3	0.1
Magnesia	0.1	0.1	trace	trace	1.3
Soda	10.2	9.9	10.6	10.5	trace
Potash	5.0	4.8	5.1	4.9	7.9
BaO	—	—	—	—	9.0
SrO	—	—	—	—	0.3
P_2O_5	—	—	—	—	0.3
L.O.I.	0.6	0.7	0.4	0.3	0.1
					1.0

Typical Sieve Analysis

US Sieve No.						Tyler Sieve No.	
On 25 mesh %	0.0	0.0	(−30) (−40)	(−30) (−40)		On 28 mesh %	0.0
30	0.1	0.1	0.2	1.3		32	0.1
40	14.5	14.0	15.7 1.0	19.5 0.3		35	4.9
50	48.0	46.0	— —	— —		48	30.0
60	—	—	50.8 32.1	43.3 40.1		65	52.0
100	86.0	84.0	20.1 31.9	13.0 38.7			
140	—	—	6.3 16.5	10.2 13.4			
200	98.0	97.2	3.9 7.9	5.4 3.5		200	89.0
pan	2.0	3.0	2.0 10.6	7.3 4.0		pan	11.0

TABLE 2—Nepheline Syenite—Typical Product Specifications, Ceramic Grades

	Indusmin			IMC			Norsk Nefelin
Product Designation	A-200	A-270	A-400	Crest	Peak	Apex	North Cape
Typical Chemical Analysis	%	%	%	%	%	%	%
SiO_2	60.7	60.7	60.7	60.2	60.2	60.2	56.0
Al_2O_3	23.3	23.3	23.3	23.5	23.5	23.5	24.2
Fe_2O_3	0.07	0.07	0.07	0.07	0.07	0.07	0.1
CaO	0.7	0.7	0.7	0.3	0.3	0.3	1.2
MgO	0.1	0.1	0.1	trace	trace	trace	trace
Na_2O	9.8	9.8	9.8	15.3-0.4	15.3-0.4	15.3-0.4	7.8
K_2O	4.6	4.6	4.6	15.3-0.4	15.3-0.4	15.3-0.4	9.1
L.O.I.	0.7	0.7	0.7	0.4	0.4	0.4	1.0

Sieve Analysis
US Sieve No.

US Sieve No.	A-200	A-270		Crest	Peak		Tyler Sieve No.	
On 70 mesh %	0.01	0.0		—	—		On 32 mesh %	—
100	0.05	0.01					35	—
140	0.20	0.05					48	—
170	—	—					65	—
200	0.70	0.15		0.3	0.3		200	0.1
270	2.00	0.40		—	—		270	—
325	5.25	1.75		4.7	2.9		325	0.5
pan	94.75	98.25		95.0	96.8		pan	99.4

Microns

	A-200	A-270	A-400	Apex 400	Apex 700		Tyler % Finer than	
% Finer than 30	70.0	78.0	98.0	98.0			30	—
20	55.0	65.0	90.0	90.0	98.0		20	—
10	33.5	42.0	65.0	60.0	90.0		10	50
5	19.0	23.0	33.5	35.0	60.0		5	—
2.5	10.0	12.5	16.0	18.0			2.5	—

TABLE 3—Typical Properties of Nepheline Syenite for Extender Pigment and Filler Applications

Product Designation	Apex 400	Apex 700	Minex 2	Minex 3	Minex 4	Minex 7	Minex 10
Appearance				bright white powder			
Density, g per cc				2.61			
lb per US gal				21.7			
Bulking value, US gal per lb				0.046			
Hardness, Mohs' scale				5.5–6.0			
Refractive index, composite				1.53			
pH value, ASTM D-1208				9.9			
Particle shape				nodular			
Dry brightness, %, CIE Tristimulus	96	98	94	95	96	98	98
Oil Absorption,* ASTM D-281	22+	28+	21+	21+	22+	28+	28+
Particle size, μ							
mean	7.5	4.5	16	14	7.5	4.5	2.3
maximum	49	17	105	74	44	17	10
Specific surface area, sq m per g (Fisher Sub-Sieve Sizer)	0.95	1.45					
Specific resistance, ohm-cm, ASTM D-2448	3600	3300		4000	3600	3300	
Hegman grind	3.5–4.0	5.5–6.0		1.0	3.5–4.0	5.5–6.0	6.5–7.0
Screen Fineness							
thru 200 mesh, %	100	100	99.3	99.9	100	100	
thru 325 mesh, %	98.9	100	95.8	98.3	99.9	100	
thru 400 mesh, %							100

* Nepheline syenite tends to have a lower vehicle demand than indicated by its oil absorption value.

Feldspar—The major feldspars present are microcline and orthoclase with a theoretical composition SiO_2 64.7%, Al_2O_3 18.4%, and K_2O 16.9%; and albite with a theoretical composition SiO_2 68.7%, Al_2O_3 19.5%, and Na_2O 11.8%.

Pyroxene—The aegerine member of this series of minerals is customarily present in feldspathoid rocks but the theoretical composition ranges from aegerine SiO_2 52.0%, Fe_2O_3 34.6%, and Na_2O 13.4%; to that of diopside SiO_2 55.6%, CaO 25.9%, and MgO 18.5%.

Amphibole—A wide variety of amphiboles are present in nepheline syenites including hornblende, hastingsite, barkevikite, arfvedsonite, and riebeckite. These are calcium, magnesium, sodium, and iron aluminosilicates of various compositions.

Biotite—Two types of biotite are found in feldspathoidal rocks; the golden-brown variety, but more frequently the high-iron variety lepidomelane. It is a hydrated aluminosilicate of potassium, iron, and magnesium.

Accessory Minerals—Among the more frequently found accessory minerals are sodalite, noselite, hauynite, scapolite, cancrinite, calcite, apatite, magnetite, ilmenite, hematite, pyrite, zircon, sphene, pyrochlore, garnet, and corundum.

Nepheline syenites have a wide variety of textures which can be generally classified according to the origin of the rock; plutonic and hypabyssal nepheline syenites; nepheline syenite pegmatites, and the migmatic nepheline rocks or "nephelinized gneisses."

Classification of Deposits

Several methods can be used to classify nepheline syenite deposits—by the percentage of principal minerals present in the deposit, by their origin, and also by their color. Nepheline syenites have been studied intensively and works by Deer et al. (1963) and Eitel (1965) provide an introduction to complete studies of nepheline and nepheline syenite. Little information about worldwide nepheline syenite occurrences and their commercial potential was available in concise form until publication of *Nepheline-Syenite and Phonolite* by Allen and Charsley in 1968. The book is an excellent summary of the present state of commercial interest in this and allied rocks.

Although a wide variety of names have been given to nepheline-bearing rocks and the term nepheline syenite is often given to any such

rock containing 5% or more nepheline, it is unlikely that a rock would be of commercial interest unless the nepheline content is at least 20%.

Nepheline Syenite Rocks: Some of the more common varieties of nepheline syenite are:

Congressite: mostly nepheline with minor orthoclase and albite.

Craigmontite: nepheline predominates, oligoclase, and minor corundum.

Ditroite: nepheline, microcline or microcline perthite, biotite, aegerine, and soda amphibole.

Fenite: nepheline, 70 to 90% perthite and 5 to 25% aegerine.

Foyaite: nepheline, orthoclase, biotite, hornblende, and augite-aegerine.

Ijolite: aegerine and from 50 to 70% nepheline.

Laurdalite: nepheline, cryptoperthite, pyroxene, biotite, and hornblende.

Litchfieldite: nepheline, albite, orthoclase, lepidomelane, and sodalite.

Melteigite: aegerine and less than 50% nepheline.

Miascite: nepheline, microperthite, biotite, and minor oligoclase.

Monmouthite: nepheline, hastingsite, and minor oligoclase.

Raglanite: nepheline with predominant oligoclase and minor corundum.

Rouvillite: nepheline, gabbro-nepheline, hornblende, augite, and labradorite.

Urtite: aegerine and more than 70% nepheline.

Feldspar-free feldspathoidal rocks are also classified on the basis of color index number with rocks of lower index number being of possible economic interest.

Nepheline Syenite Deposits: Deposits are rarely of great areal extent, the largest being those in the Kola peninsula of the Soviet Union (450 and 250 square miles), Brazil (300 and 100 square miles), and Greenland (80 square miles). Most others are typically much smaller, less than 20 square miles, and those in Blue Mountain, Ont. (3 square miles), and Stjernöy, Norway (0.2 square miles) are even smaller. Classification may also be made based on the mode of occurrence and origin of the nepheline syenite. Moorhouse (1959) for one has divided them into five groups:

1) Feldspathoidal rocks associated with undersaturated volcanics.

2) Differentiated ring complexes, often associated with carbonatite and usually characterized by metasomatism around their borders.

3) Layered intrusives, possibly related to the ring complexes.

4) Borders or satellitic stocks associated with syenites or granites.

5) Nephelinized gneisses, usually associated with nepheline pegmatites.

The first type has no economic significance. Examples of the others would be: group 2, Nemegos, Ont.; Mont St. Hilaire, Que.; and Kola peninsula, Karelian ASSR; group 3, Ice River, B. C.; Julienhaab, Greenland; group 4, Blue Mountain, Ont.; group 5, Stjernöy, Norway.

A variety of origins are possible (Turner and Verhoogen, 1951): from low temperature residual magmas which have been conditioned by volatile components; by fractional crystallization of undersaturated olivine-basalt magma; by desilication of granitic magmas, that might have invaded the limestone with evolution of a CO_2-rich gas phase which may be important; nepheline syenite magmas, and metasomatic alteration of various preexisting rocks, i.e., "nephelinization."

Distribution of Deposits

Nepheline-bearing rocks are widespread throughout the world and deposits of nepheline syenite are common. Those in Canada, the

United States, Norway, and the Union of Soviet Socialist Republics have been well described and much is known about those in other countries of Asia, Africa, and the South Pacific. Two of the largest known are the Khibiny (450 square miles) and Lovozero (250 square miles) intrusives in the Karelian ASSR (Vlasov et al., 1966) of the USSR. Other large ones are located in Siberia. In Brazil, nepheline syenites occur in several extensive intrusive areas, the largest of which cover some 300 square miles in Minas Gerais and São Paulo, and 100 square miles in São Paulo. Other deposits are rarely large, seldom covering more than a few square miles or a few tens of square miles in area. Fig. 1 shows the location of many nepheline syenite occurrences in the world.

However size is not an overly important criterion in commercial considerations; more important are the purity and location of the deposits.

There are now seven known mining ventures in different parts of the world producing nepheline or nepheline syenite products; two in Canada, one in Norway, two in the USSR, and two in the United States.

In Canada, nepheline syenite deposits are common in several provinces. Occurrences in the vicinity of Lake Albanel, Gouin, Labelle, Mont St. Hilaire, and Oka, Que. are well known. In Ontario, Hewitt (1960) has de-

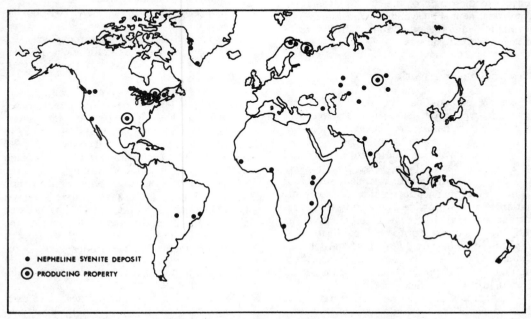

- ● NEPHELINE SYENITE DEPOSIT
- ◉ PRODUCING PROPERTY

FIG. 1—*Location of principal nepheline syenite occurrences of the world.*

scribed deposits in the vicinity of Blue Mountain, Haliburton-Bancroft, French River, Callander Bay, Nemegos, and Port Caldwell as well as other minor occurrences. In British Columbia, the Ice River and Kruger Mountain complexes are well known. Much of the interest in Canadian deposits has stemmed from the successful development of the Blue Mountain intrusive in Methuen Township but none other has proven pure enough to warrant exploitation.

In Norway, nepheline syenite is known in the vicinity of Oslo and on several islands in western Finland, although only that on the southwest side of Stjernöy Island has the necessary characteristics for commercial development.

Reserves: The only known deposits of nepheline syenite suitable for low-iron products are being mined at existing operations in Norway and Canada. Reserves are considered limitless. In Norway at Norsk Nefelin, the volume of proven nepheline syenite exceeds 135 million cu m representing nearly 400 million tons of rock of a nature the company considers suitable for mining. In Canada, Indusmin has published a reserve figure of 14 million tons of proven ore, sufficient for 35 years at present mining rates. The company owns 85% of the Blue Mountain intrusive and believes potential reserves of minable rock are satisfactory for an indefinite period.

International Minerals and Chemical Corp. (Canada) Ltd. owns 500 acres of nepheline syenite at Blue Mountain, Ont. Since 1956 less than 50 acres of ground have been mined and reserves are considered to exceed 30 million tons, ample for any production requirements.

In the Soviet Union, there are no firm indications of reserves of nepheline-bearing rocks suitable for chemical conversion. The estimated production of apatite from the Kola peninsula mines exceeds 27 Mt/a and consequently the operation generates more than 35 Mt of nepheline-bearing tailings annually from which an estimated 15 Mt of nepheline concentrate could be recovered. In addition many square kilometers of nepheline syenite are present so reserves can be considered adequate for projected chemical needs. Nepheline syenite reserves at Goryachegorsk in central Siberia have been estimated at over 100 Gt. The planned production rate of 900 kt of alumina per year at Achinsk would require at least 3½ million tons of nepheline syenite rock from the Goryachegorsk deposit.

Principal Producing Countries: The principal producing countries of glass and ceramic grades of nepheline syenite are Canada and Norway. In the years between 1972 and 1981 combined production of the two countries has grown from 597 to 826 kt. Most of the Norwegian nepheline syenite was of glass grade destined for countries of western Europe, mainly the United Kingdom, West Germany, and the Netherlands. There is widespread acceptance of nepheline syenite in Europe as a feldspathic source. Canadian production of nepheline syenite has grown steadily from 438.4 kt in 1972 to 606 kt in 1981. Seventy percent of the total production was exported to the United States.

Canada—Indusmin Ltd. and International Minerals and Chemical Corp. (Canada) Ltd. operate the only two nepheline syenite mines in Canada. Although numerous nepheline syenite bodies have been examined in Ontario, Quebec, and British Columbia, only the Blue Mountain intrusive in Methuen Township, Ont., about 120 miles northeast of Toronto has the proven quality to produce uniform low-iron products.

The Blue Mountain intrusive is of Precambrian age having been emplaced, according to determinations, 1.3 billion years ago and was subsequently folded to its present attitudes some 300 million years later during the Grenville orogeny. Indicated temperature of the magma was 700° C and that of the country rock 400° C to 500° C.

The nepheline syenite intrusive consists of an elongate, irregular stock, having a length of 2½ miles in a north-south direction, and a width of 1¼ miles in an east-west direction. A long sill-like arm up to ¼ mile wide extends southwest from the main mass for 4 miles. The nepheline syenite intrudes and partially replaces para-amphibolite, paragneiss, and marble of the Blue Mountain metasedimentary band and is itself intruded and replaced by pink syenite and syenite pegmatite. The deposit appears to occupy the trough of a syncline plunging 20° southwest. Near the contacts the nepheline syenite is well foliated and within the main mass metamorphic lineation is readily observed. On vertical surfaces the usual plunge of the lineation is 10° to 30° SW. The accompanying map, Fig. 2, together with the table of formations, Table 4, shows the distribution of rocks and the relationship of the Blue Mountain intrusive with adjacent rocks.

The Blue Mountain nepheline syenite is a uniform, foliated, fine to medium-grained rock, composed essentially of: nepheline, 20 to 25%; albite, 48 to 54%; and microcline 18 to 23%.

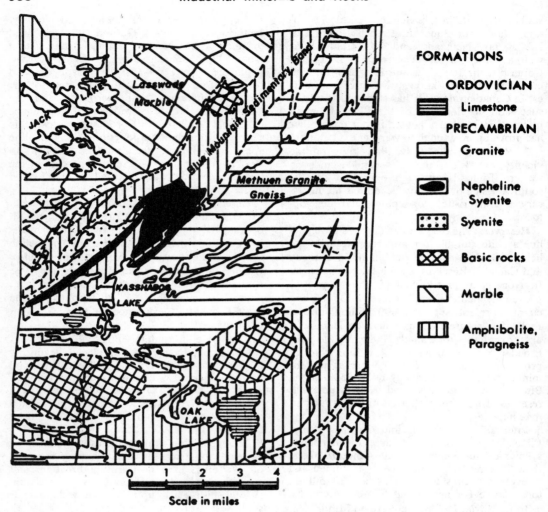

FIG. 2—*Geology of Methuen Township, Ont., Canada (after Hewitt, 1961; Payne, 1966).*

Characteristic accessory minerals are magnetite, 0.2 to 0.6%; biotite, 0 to 4%; hastingsite, 0 to 3%; muscovite, 0 to 2%; and aegerine; these in total seldom amount to more than 6%. Minor accessories encountered are: garnet, corundum, zircon, calcite, apatite, and titanite. Secondary hydrothermal and pegmatite minerals include epidote, riebeckite, natrolite, prehnite, analcite, hydronepheline, cancrinite, sodalite, and tourmaline. Recent studies (Guillet, 1962; Payne, 1966) indicate that a nepheline syenite magma intruded metasediments and hybrid syenite gneiss as a sill. The sill was fractioned during emplacement into five distinguishable zones: muscovite, muscovite-magnetite, biotite-muscovite, biotite, hornblende

and pink syenite. Late-stage fluids of the magma were the source of pegmatites that intrude the sill as well as surrounding country rock. Lens, sheets, and pods of country rock that sloughed into magma are found in the nepheline syenite aligned parallel with the direction of flow. Some metasomatic and metamorphic effects of the intrusion developed above and to a minor extent below the sill. Analyses of typical nepheline syenites are shown in Table 5 and analyses of typical products derived therefrom are shown in Tables 1, 2, and 3.

Norway—By HANS-PETER GEIS, · Elkem Spigerverket—The nepheline syenite deposit which is mined by Norsk Nefelin is situated within a Caledonian province of basic and

TABLE 4—Table of Formations, Methuen Township, Peterborough County*

ozic
eistocene
  Recent   Sand, gravel, clay, silt, till
                                          Great Unconformity

eozoic
rdovician   Limestone, dolomitic limestone
                            Red argillaceous limestone and shale
                            Basal grit and arkose
                                          Great Unconformity

cambrian
lutonic Rocks   Granitic rocks: granite, granite gneiss, granite pegmatite
                                          Intrusive Contact
                            Syenite rocks: syenite gneiss, hybrid syenite gneiss, syenite pegmatite
                                          Intrusive Contact
                            Nepheline syenite
                                          Intrusive Contact
                            Basic intrusives: diorite, gabbro, norite, pyroxenite, amphibolite
                                          Intrusive Contact

                            Southeast Methuen   Northwest Methuen
                            (stratigraphic succession)
                                                                       Blue Mountain
                            Vansickle formation (approximate   sedimentary band
                              thickness, 4500 ft + (1370 m +)]   Casswade marble
                              Upper schist   Apsley formation
                              Upper marble
                              Middle schist
                              Vansickle conglomerate
                              Middle marble
edimentary and   Lower schist
olcanic Rocks   Lower marble
                              Lower conglomerate

                            Oak Lake Formation [approximate thickness, 5000 ft (1525 m)]
                              Pink arkose, quartzite, amphibolite schist, feldspar schist, some volcanic amphibolite

                            Big Island Beds:
                              Interbedded marble and schist [approximate thickness, 2000 ft + (610 m +)].

                            Kosh Lake Beds:
                              Epidotized amphibolite, paragneiss.

                            Troutling Bay Volcanics.

ource: Hewitt, 1960.

ultrabasic rocks near the northern tip of Norway. This province has an areal extension of 30 sq km.

The deposit itself lies near the southern shore of the island of Stjernöy, cropping out at a height of 250 to 700 m above sea level. The outcrop is a lens-shaped form with a length of 1800 m and a maximum width of 300 m giving a total area of about 270,000 sq m.

The deposit has been mapped and sampled in great detail, both at the surface and underground. The wall rock on the northeastern side is an alternation of carbonatite and hornblendite; on the southwestern side it is gabbro gneiss. The accompanying map, Fig. 3, shows the different petrological types within the main

nepheline syenite. It also shows a few minor bodies parallel to the main body which have not been studied in detail or mined.

There are two major types of nepheline syenite, viz., biotite type and hornblende type. Both types consist essentially of perthite feldspar (average 56%) and nepheline (average 34%), together with some minor minerals like plagioclase, calcite, clinopyroxene, hornblende, biotite, sphene, and magnetite. In the biotite type, the dominating dark mineral is biotite (2.5 to 6.0%), and in the hornblende type, common hornblende (0.3 to 2.5%) and aegerine (1.3 to 3.8%) together with small amounts of biotite. There is more sphene in the hornblende type than in the biotite type (0.2 to

TABLE 5—Typical Chemical and Mineralogical Composition of Some Nepheline Syenites, %

Chemical Composition	Canada,* Methuen Township Hornblende	Biotite	Norway,† Stjernoy Pyroxene	Biotite	Krasnoyarsk‡	United States,§ Litchfield, Maine	USSR,# Khibiny	Greenland,¶ Ilimaussaq	Congo**	Portugal††	Malawi‡‡	Brazil,§§ Cannon Mine
SiO_2	58.8	59.4	52.73	52.37	54.57	60.39	54.01	49.46	55.44	55.22	55.77	57.8
Al_2O_3	23.0	23.0	23.71	23.22	22.56	22.51	21.50	23.53	23.59	22.59	22.26	23.5
Fe_2O_3	0.8	0.7	1.9	1.1	3.44	0.42	2.60	3.04	0.44	1.14	1.33	0.1
FeO	1.4	1.5	1.89	1.14	—	2.26	1.80	1.02	1.42	1.17	2.50	—
TiO_2	0.004	0.004	0.51	0.61	0.15	—	1.20	0.16	0.20	0.59	0.50	—
Na_2O	9.4	9.5	7.78	6.87	9.69	8.44	9.50	14.71	10.20	8.76	8.05	10.9
K_2O	5.2	4.9	8.08	8.30	5.51	4.77	5.30	4.34	6.26	5.59	6.66	6.2
CaO	0.82	0.64	2.54	3.11	1.61	0.32	1.80	0.80	1.56	2.12	1.25	0.5
MgO	0.04	0.03	0.24	0.25	0.19	0.13	0.77	trace	0.14	0.28	0.58	0.05
MnO	0.049	0.045	0.06	0.09	—	0.08	0.17	0.17	0.15	0.13	0.19	—
P_2O_5	0.01	0.01	0.05	0.09	0.02	—	0.09	n.a.	0.18	—	0.21	—
CO_2	0.05	0.15	0.77	1.88	—	trace	—	—	—	nil	0.07	—
H_2O	0.3	0.4	0.26	0.26	—	0.57	1.14	1.38	1.07	2.16	0.50	—
BaO	—	—	0.40	0.47	—	—	0.12	—	—	—	—	—
Ignition Loss	—	—	—	—	—	—	—	—	1.62	—	—	0.9
Mineralogical Composition												
Albite	48.4	52.0	trace	6.0	20.3	47.8						
Microcline	22.7	18.9	—	—	37.8	16.5						
Microperthite	minor	minor	57.0	55.5	—	—						
Perthite	24.9	24.1	37.0	29.0	26.9	23.7						
Nepheline	0.1	2.2	trace	3.5	0.1	5.5						
Biotite	—	—	1.0	—	—	—						
Hornblende	3.0	—	1.0	—	6.1	—						
Pyroxene	0.2	—	1.0	1.5	—	—						
Magnetite	0.4	0.5	2.0	5.0	—	—						
Calcite	—	0.1	—	—	—	—						
Muscovite	—	0.7	—	—	—	—						
Zeolite	—	—	—	—	8.7	6.5						

Sources:
* Payne, 1966, p. 140.
† Heier, 1966.
‡ Leucocratic nepheline syenite; Central Tartar Massif, 1968, Krasnoyarsk Territory, Siberia. Allen and Charsley, 1968, p. 109.
§ Allen and Charsley, 1968, p. 134.
# Gerasimovskii, 1956; Allen and Charsley, 1968, p. 101.
¶ Greenland—Ilimaussaq. Allen and Charsley, 1968, p. 127.
** Nepheline syenite Kirumba, Democratic Republic of The Congo. Allen and Charsley, 1968, p. 114.
†† Algarve Province. Allen and Charsley, 1968, p. 95.
‡‡ Biotite and hastingsite nepheline syenite, Lulwe Hill, Malawi. Allen and Charsley, 1968, p. 54.
§§ Harben, 1981.

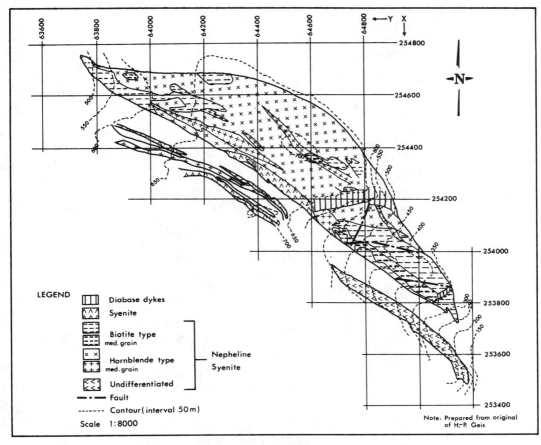

FIG. 3—*Surface geology of Stjernöy nepheline syenite deposit.*

1.2% as compared to trace). Traces of corundum and zircon have been observed but their content in the finished product are subject to routine control within the mine.

Under the microscope one can see that the rock consists of a network of feldspars in which there are veins containing the other minerals. The nepheline crystals contain more or less resorbed remainders of feldspar. The microscopic picture might, by these reasons, be interpreted as indicating a metasomatic origin of the nepheline syenite in its present form.

Geochemical studies have shown that the contents of Fe_2O_3 and CaO are lowest in the central part of the deposit near the southwestern contact and that they increase toward the northeast and toward both ends. Mining has been started in these central parts because the recovery here is highest. In the same direction as above, SiO_2 and Na_2O contents decrease.

A marked foliation has been observed in the nepheline syenite, caused by an elongated appearance of all minerals along strike and dip of the whole body. From the center of the body to the southeast end, foliation dips 70° SW. From the center toward the northwest, it dips steeper and at the northwest end it dips 70° NE. This foliation is so regular that by measurements at the surface it was possible to predict the contacts 500 m below with only very small deviation.

A number of diabase dykes from a few centimeters to tens of centimeters thick cross through the body. Their amount is estimated to represent from 6 to 7% of the whole nepheline syenite mass. A few fault zones intersect the nepheline syenite. Along them the rock is partly altered to zeolite, prehnite, and kaolin. For further reading one is referred to Barth (Barth, 1963) and Heier (Heier, 1961, 1964, 1965, 1966).

Union of Soviet Socialist Republics—The nepheline rock *urtite* is waste from the production of apatite at mines on the Kola peninsula. Production of apatite in 1970 was 27 Mt which would require mining an average of 62 Mt of ore and would make available over 15 Mt of nepheline concentrate. Production of nepheline concentrate was estimated by the US Bureau of Mines (Anon., 1961–71) to have grown from 350 kt in 1961 to 1 Mt by 1970.

Production is derived presently from the Khibiny pluton of probable Devonian Age at the west side of Lake Umpjaur in the central Kola peninsula. Seven phases of intrusion have been identified, and are listed in order of decreasing age (Polkanov, 1937):

1) Syenites and nepheline syenite. Adjoining Archean gneisses show evidence of both injection and metasomatism by the syenite magmas.

2) Coarse aegerine-nepheline syenites injected as a peripheral ring dyke.

3) Trachytoid aegerine-nepheline syenites forming an imperfect ring within and adjoining the coarse rocks of phase two.

4) An imperfect ring dyke of poikilitic micaceous nepheline syenites of variable composition. The assemblage of alkali feldspar, nepheline, mica, aegerine, astrophyllite is typical.

5) A massive cone sheet of silica-poor nepheline-rich rocks of the ijolite family.

6) Foyaites (alkali feldspars, nepheline, biotite, and hornblende or aegerine-augite), making the central core of the pluton.

7) Dikes of tinguaite, monchiquite, shonkinite, theralite, nepheline basalt, and leucite basalt.

The pluton is characterized by abundance of phosphorus, fluorine, titanium, zirconium, columbium, strontium, and rare earths, especially the cerium group. High grade deposits of apatite, sphene, and aegerine pegmatites rich in rare earths, are known. One apatite rock deposit is a flat lens 1½ miles long and 500 ft thick. Chemical analyses and mineral composition of some Soviet nepheline rocks are shown in Table 5.

Numerous other nepheline deposits in the Soviet Union have been described and at least one in central Siberia near Achinsk is mined to provide feed for alumina plants. Production of nepheline rocks is expected to continue to grow and eventually provide half the country's alumina requirements.

Minor Producing Countries:

United States—The nepheline syenite deposits of Pulaski, Saline, and Hot Spring counties in central Arkansas are well known. Attempts to produce ceramic and glass grade products from them have not been successful because the impurities are too finely divided within the feldspars for appropriate removal. Analyses of typical crude and treated rock, from Fourche Mountain in Pulaski County, are shown in Table 6.

The McGeorge Construction Co. operates a large construction aggregate quarry in the Fourche Mountain nepheline syenite intrusive near Little Rock. Nearby the 3M Co. has operated a roofing granule manufacturing plant since 1947. Its annual capacity is understood to exceed 1,000,000 st. Because the activities of these two companies are more properly dealt with in chapters dealing with construction materials and granules, they will not be considered further here.

Mexico—In Mexico, Industrias Peñoles, S.A. de C.V. is said to be developing reserves of alumina contained in 3 billion st of nepheline syenite near Cuidad Victoria, in the state of Tamaulipas.

Brazil—In 1981, Austral Ltd. (Austral Mineração Serviços Ltda.) of Brazil started a pilot plant with an annual capacity of 5,000 stpy to produce a glass-grade material from a nepheline syenite deposit near Rio de Janeiro.

Other Occurrences: Allen and Charsley (1968) in their monograph have assembled an impressive list of occurrences of nepheline syenite in many countries of the world together with initial information on the character of the rocks and the results of test work. In addition to the producing properties described herein they number deposits in 20 African countries, 5 Asian countries, Australia and New Zealand, 7 European countries, Mexico, 3 South American countries, and Greenland. The distribution of some occurrences is shown in Fig. 1. While few, if any described, could be used to prepare low-iron products, some might well be suited for the manufacture of colored glass and certain types of ceramic ware.

Exploration

As with most industrial minerals the "place value" of a nepheline syenite deposit is critical. In addition to the following comments on field examination, the exploration geologist should consider the overriding importance of costs of

TABLE 6—Analyses of Pulaski County, Arkansas, Nepheline Syenite*

	Crude Ore		Treated Ore	
	Hornblende Type Blue Syenite, %	Biotite Type Gray Syenite, %	Hornblende Type Blue Syenite, %	Biotite Type Gray Syenite, %
SiO_2	60.3	60.8	61.2	61.9
Al_2O_3	19.9	19.6	21.5	21.1
Fe_2O_3	4.7	4.3	0.9	1.1
TiO_2	1.1	1.2	0.3	0.2
CaO	1.3	0.8		
MgO	1.2	0.9		
Na_2O	6.3	6.7		
K_2O	5.3	5.9		
Ignition loss	0.1	1.3		

* Smothers et al., 1952.

production and the costs of transporting products to market.

Only by examining the interrelationship of all factors bearing on exploitation of a given nepheline deposit can one determine if development is warranted.

Field Techniques

The field geologist needs to search for a deposit that consists of a coarse to medium-grained rock. Crushing to minus US Standard 30 mesh should liberate all the impurities that need to be removed before a product is salable. Careful mapping of the deposit in detail will reveal textural, structural, and mineralogical changes that might affect mining. Samples need to be selected carefully to provide a representative suite on which initial microscopic, physical, chemical, and ceramic tests can be made.

If examination reveals that impurities are scattered through the feldspar crystals in a finely divided state, such a deposit would be unsuited for glass and ceramic uses. Only if impurities can be readily liberated by crushing should a deposit receive more detailed evaluation. One would normally expect to mine feldspathic materials by open-pit methods and due consideration needs to be given to bench heights, berms, and mining regulations when determining if a given deposit would be satisfactory. Ore reserves should be large enough to sustain an operation for a long time because customers demand assurance of ample supply and, in industrial mineral ventures, ten or more years may be needed to repay the invested capital. Normally one would not consider a deposit having ore reserves for less than 20 years operation.

Consideration must be given to possible methods that might be used to beneficiate nepheline syenite from a deposit. Present feldspar and nepheline syenite benefication plants have relatively simple schemes for flotation and electromagnetic removal of impurities, and flotation separation of quartz and feldspar. Flotation, electrostatic, electromagnetic, and other techniques can all be successfully used on different mineral assemblages but if the mineral suite in a given deposit is too complex, the combination of techniques needed to remove impurities could well be too expensive and involve too many operating variables to permit economical operation.

In areas where chemical weathering is a factor one must have fresh specimens with which to work. Nepheline dissolves from rock surfaces relatively easily, feldspars are altered to kaolin, iron oxides and sulfides may be leached away, all of which tends to distort results obtained when surface samples are examined.

Complex nepheline syenite deposits such as the ring-complex type and carbonatite type intrusives show little promise for utilization in glass and ceramics. They are too variable in normal feldspar and mafic constituents and furthermore may contain rare earths, halides, and numerous other trace elements that detract from the intended applications for the rock.

Nepheline syenite deposits of the sheet, gneissic, and border phase of granite and syenite intrusive types seem to offer the greatest chance of uniformity and quality needed.

Drilling

Deposits of merit need to be drilled to confirm the nature of the rocks and to provide samples for laboratory work. Depending on circumstances AX, BX, and NX diameter core may be recovered. In laying out a drill program, care must be taken that holes intersect all rock types at appropriate angles of inclination. **Bands** of biotite gneiss, for instance, might be erratic in distribution and unless drilling is adequate, erroneous conclusions might be drawn about the amount of such impurities present. A deposit may be zoned and although mapping indicates rock of one type, the core of the deposit may be another. There are always variations to be encountered in nepheline syenite deposits, as may be guessed from their mode of origin, and drilling a deposit provides assurance that surprises will be minimal.

Spacing of drill holes is determined by the uniformity of the rock and the stage of the investigation. Initial drilling is widespread, followed by grid drilling at perhaps 400-ft spacing, followed by spacing of 100 ft or less if conditions demand.

Geophysical and geochemical techniques are not a normal part of exploration for nepheline syenite although seismic surveys may be useful for helping to determine the depth of overburden.

Other Considerations

Consideration should be given to matters such as the size and character of the market, the mode and cost of transportation, availability of auxiliary services, labor supply, and laws that might be restrictive. Due concern for them at an early stage in exploration could provide a basis for judging which deposits have the greatest worth and save much time and wasted expense on further laboratory evaluation permit one to study the rock for signs of product warrants.

Evaluation of Deposits

Specifications—General

Deposits should lend themselves to preparation of products comparable to those in Tables 1, 2, and 3. Total waste should be as low as possible, preferably not more than 25%, with product in the −30 mesh +200 mesh range using US standard testing sieves. Impurities such as refractory minerals, sulfides, other oxides or ferromagnesian minerals, silicates other than feldspars and feldspathoids, should be absent or readily removed from material during processing. For filler products, whiteness is as important as the chemical composition. For production of chemicals from nepheline rocks, alumina levels should be 30% or higher but other elements are not as deleterious

as in glass grade products. For all applications, a deposit must be consistently uniform in mineral content and character.

Testing and Evaluation

The first requirement is to characterize the nepheline syenite by describing as many of its properties as possible, then subject selected samples to laboratory-scale processing that attempts to reproduce techniques that would be used in an operating plant. Throughout the test work it is important to follow accepted mineral dressing practice.

Microscopic Examination: Much wasted time and expense can be avoided in studying nepheline syenites if thin sections and polished sections of the rock are made and the microscopic and macroscopic characteristics of the rock are determined. It is important to find out if the feldspars and feldspathoids can be liberated from mafic and other mineral impurities because, if not, the deposit cannot be considered further for most commercial uses.

Thin sections, polished sections, or appropriately sized fractions of nepheline syenite immersed in oils of specific indices of refraction permit one to study the rock for signs of impurities within the feldspar and nepheline grains. They also permit one to estimate the degree of liberation of impurities from the desired minerals in the grain sizes to which the rock was crushed.

Sample Preparation and Analysis: Samples collected from a deposit are crushed and screened to provide −30 mesh +200 mesh material. Care should be taken to not overcrush material. While test work is carried out on this screen fraction some nepheline syenite is screened at intermediate size fractions. The −200 mesh fraction is kept for study if warranted. It is important to record the weight of all fractions so that material balances can be calculated. Specimens should be cut from the sample prior to any particular test so that their chemical and physical properties can be determined.

Physical Tests: The objectives of any sample testing program are, first, to determine if a commercially acceptable product can be made from the rock, and second, to establish if practical methods of treatment can be used to prepare those products.

Liberation of usable feldspathoid and feldspar minerals from coexisting contaminants is required. Because so much nepheline syenite is sold to glass manufacturers who purchase a coarsely granular product, commercial practice dictates that effective liberation should be achieved in size fractions coarser than 200 mesh.

It is customary to commence work on a sample that has been reduced in size to −30 mesh and from which the −200 mesh fraction has been removed. From this material any tramp iron introduced during crushing is removed completely either with a hand magnet, drum magnet, or low intensity electromagnet of adequate field strength. Carpco, Dings, Exolon, Jones, Rapid, and Stearnes type induced-roll, high-intensity, electromagnetic separators are available in models convenient for laboratory use. Samples are passed through such a unit one or more times to reduce the level of those impurities having medium to low magnetic susceptibility. Models of the Carpco and Jones separators are available that treat samples in a water medium which may be more successful than dry methods as dust will not coat the mineral grains in it. Minerals such as magnetite, hornblende, tourmaline, garnet, and biotite are readily removed by this magnetic method.

If the sample responds inadequately to magnetic treatment it may be subjected to flotation techniques. Sulfides, heavy minerals and non-magnetic iron minerals can often be removed by flotation. Detailed procedures for treating samples can be developed from study of Taggart's *Handbook of Mineral Dressing* (1956) and AIME's *Froth Flotation* (Baarson et al., 1962).

Other methods of treatment could involve roasting, calcination, and various leaching media as well as combinations of methods. If impurities are present within the feldspar crystals then it is unlikely that suitable products can be prepared by normal mill practices.

Of course it is important during testing of nepheline syenite samples to perform some chemical tests on the crude sample, screen fractions of the sample as it is subjected to physical and chemical processing procedures, and on the derived products. Testing different screen fractions may provide a hint respecting any tendency of impurities to be present in disproportionate amounts in certain grain sizes and thus provide a basis for separation in a production flowsheet.

It is customary to analyse samples for SiO_2, Al_2O_3, Fe_2O_3, FeO, MgO, CaO, Na_2O, K_2O, and loss on ignition. One should check for chromium, manganese, titanium, copper, or other suspected metallic ions which, if present,

would make the nepheline syenite unsuitable for glass or ceramic purposes.

It is useful to perform a heavy-media test on the nepheline syenite samples to detect the presence of minerals such as zircon, chromite, rutile, corundum, ilmenite, and sphene. This procedure is especially helpful in isolating non-magnetic refractory minerals that may be present in small quantities but which adversely affect the value of a nepheline syenite deposit. Sufficient samples must be processed to detect their presence or absence. Acetylene tetrabromide (tetrabromethane) with a specific gravity of 2.96 is the commonly used separating medium. It can be diluted with carbon tetrachloride with a specific gravity of 1.59 to provide solutions of lower specific gravity if desired.

One may wish to prepare a small quantity of a typical glass composition in which the sample nepheline syenite is substituted for commercially available feldspathic materials, melt it, and compare the color and appearance with a regular glass melt. This test has the advantage that the effect of any previously undetected impurities will be readily apparent.

The foregoing tests are sufficient where a nepheline syenite is being considered for glass manufacturing applications. When applications for the ceramic, paint, and plastics industries are contemplated, further test work is needed.

Tests for Ceramic Applications: A sample of beneficiated nepheline syenite is ground to correspond in grain size to commercially available nepheline syenite or feldspar. The characteristics of nepheline syenite materials used in ceramic applications are shown in Table 2.

The fluxing character of nepheline syenites is important for ceramic applications. Typical Canadian ceramic grades have pyrometric cone equivalents ranging from three to six, depending on the fineness of the product. They start sintering at cone 08 and have a sintering range of 13 cones. This is attributed to the fact that the product consists of a mixture of the three minerals, albite, nepheline, and microcline, listed in order of abundance. Norwegian nepheline syenite consists essentially of perthite and nepheline. Standard cone fusion tests under controlled conditions of time and temperature are used to establish the fusion characteristics of samples. These are a function of the particle size, particle size distribution, and chemical composition of finely ground nepheline syenite products. A specially shaped cone of nepheline syenite is fired at a set rate with pyrometric cones 6, 7, and 8, and changes in the height and diameter of the fired cone are compared with established standards. Another test of fluxing ability is the "inclined plane" viscosity test wherein a given weight of nepheline syenite is packed in a specially designed wedge and fused under controlled conditions. The relative flows of the sample and standards are noted.

In addition to the cone fusion test, the +200 mesh residue from a wet sieve analysis of the specimen may be fused to provide a useful indication of the fired color and number of speck-producing impurities in the sample.

Of great importance in any test program are the grain size characteristics of the sample. Detailed description of test methods for determining these and discussion of the importance of grain size can be found in Grimshaw's (1971) text.

For screening of coarse fractions one can refer to the American Society for Testing & Materials (ASTM) specifications for sieves for testing purposes, ASTM designation E.11; sieve analysis of raw materials for glass manufacture, ASTM designation C-429; and wire cloth sieve analysis of nonplastic pulverized ceramic materials, ASTM designation 371.

For determining the size of subsieve particles the Andreasen method is used frequently. This is a refinement of the ordinary pipette method for the determination of subsieve grain sizes. For substances of common specific gravities, when water is used as a sedimentation liquid, the apparatus allows determination of fineness of substances, the grains of which range from 30 to 0.5 μ. The method is based on Stoke's law relating to the rate of fall of particles in a liquid medium. The procedure is described in detail in Grimshaw (1971). For rapid size determination the Bahco method is often employed. It involves the use of a Bahco Micro-Particle Classifier which is a combination air centrifuge elutriator in which various size fractions may be obtained by controlled air velocities. The classifier has been calibrated against the Andreasen Pipette Sedimentation method to determine the grain size of the various fractions. The method is described in a paper by Taylor and Wilson (1962).

Determination of the pH of a given nepheline syenite and water mixture provides an indication of the presence and solubility of impurities.

In addition, the following are typical tests that may be carried out on ceramic bodies made from nepheline syenite and in combination with other raw materials to determine its relative usefulness.

1) Deflocculation and flocculation curves.
2) Casting or extrusion properties.
3) Body preparation.
4) Thermal gradient analysis.
5) Dry properties—shrinkage, ASTM designation C326; modulus of rupture, ASTM designation C369; bulk density, ASTM designation C373; linear thermal expansion, ASTM designation C372.
6) Fired properties—shrinkage, ASTM designation C326; modulus of rupture, ASTM designation C369; adsorption, ASTM designation C373; bulk density, ASTM designation C373; linear thermal expansion, ASTM designation C372.

Body compositions and test methods are discussed in both Grimshaw (1971) and *Industrial Ceramics* (Singer and Singer, 1963).

When consideration is being given to nepheline syenite for extender pigment or filler applications, useful and important tests of samples include determination of dry brightness, refractive index, and oil absorption as well as grain size distribution, pH, and chemical composition. Samples should be compared with commercially available products to provide a basis for judgment of their value.

Evaluation of Results

The test results must indicate that nepheline syenite products can be prepared that are as good as or better than those being offered to consuming glass, ceramic, and other industries. From the test data, engineering analyses will show if a plant could be designed to produce products at competitive prices.

Other Important Considerations

An undeveloped nepheline syenite deposit must be assessed for its "place value." Transportation costs to carry products to market, the nature of markets, the specific product demands of individual companies, the capital and operating costs, and the effect of jurisdictional regulations imposed by government must all be considered in a deposit evaluation. It goes without saying that the field and laboratory evaluation of samples are only two of the many aspects of the overall feasibility study that must be made to assess the merit of a given nepheline syenite deposit. The overwhelming interdependency of the information developed in a study is evident only when favorable facts spur, or unfavorable ones hinder, a project.

Preparation for Markets

Canada

Indusmin Ltd.: Indusmin operates a mine at Nephton, Ont., some 120 miles northeast of Toronto (Fig. 4). Canadian Nepheline Ltd., the predecessor of Indusmin, was the first company in the world to produce commercial grades of nepheline syenite for the glass and ceramic markets. Production began in 1935 and has been continuous to the present. Credit must be given to Ernest Craig, Harold Deeth, C. J. Koenig, and C. L. Cruickshank for their enormous pioneering effort during the first 30 years of nepheline syenite utilization for they were the first to realize its potential and guide nepheline syenite to full industrial acceptance.

Mining—Indusmin mines rocks from two quarries, situated three miles apart on the Blue Mountain ridge, at the rate of 1800 stpd, a single shift. The ore to waste ratio is approximately 4/1. There is practically no overburden on the deposit because of the scouring effect of numerous continental ice masses that passed over the area. What little dirt there is can be readily removed by bulldozer and Grade-All equipment. Typical rock waste consists of biotite gneiss bands that parallel the lineation of ore bands and are scattered through it.

A Joy Air-Trac crawler-mounted drill, powered by a Gardner Denver 600 rotary compressor is used in rough terrain and to develop new benches. Drilling pattern in new areas is 7 x 7 ft and hole diameter is 3 in. Developed benches are drilled on an 11 x 13-ft pattern by a Joy Challenger rubber-mounted, self-propelled drill, powered by a 1200-cfm stationary compressor located at the mill. Holes are 4½ in. in diameter drilled to a depth of up to 41 ft. Bench heights may be 30 to 40 ft. Amex II ammonium nitrite primed with 60% Forcite is detonated with short-period electric caps; 2½ x 8 in. sticks of 60% Forcite are spaced through the Amex II to ensure complete detonation. A 5500-lb drop ball is used for secondary breaking.

Two front-end loaders place the pit-run ore into four 35-ton capacity off-the-highway rear-dumping trucks.

Milling and Processing—Pit-run ore is discharged into a surface bin feeding a 42 x 48 in. Allis-Chalmers jaw crusher set to reduce rock to —7 in. This is further reduced in a 4½-ft Symons standard cone crusher to —2 in. and transferred to a 60 x 96-ft 4500-st-capacity crude ore storage building. The primary and

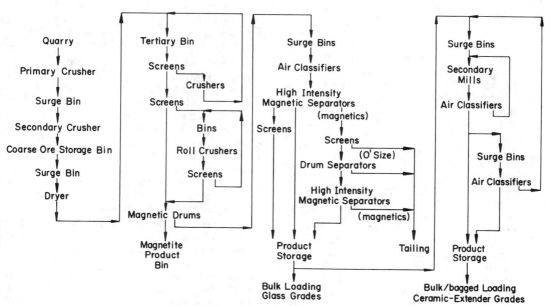

FIG. 4—*Production flow chart of Indusmin Ltd. plant, Nephton, Ont. Canada.*

secondary crushing is carried out on one shift-per-day.

Minus 2-in. ore is dried in 70-in. by 50 ft parallel flow oil-fired rotary dryers and conveyed to a 300-st-capacity bin. Ore then passes over double-deck mechanical screens, the first of many different screens in the plant. Plus $3/16$ in. material goes to two 3-ft Symons short-head cone crushers or one impact crusher and the discharge is returned to the mechanical screens. Minus $3/16$ in. material is fed to six 4 x 10 ft Tyler Hummer double-deck screens. Minus $3/16$ in. + 30 mesh sand is fed to roll crushers for further reduction. Minus 30 mesh sand is fed to low intensity magnetic drums and other screens prior to being directed to banks of Exolon and Lurgi type high-intensity electromagnetic separators. Discharge from the separators constitutes the glass-grade nepheline syenite having an Fe_2O_3 content of 0.07%. There are four mill units consisting of feed bins, roll crushers, screens, magnetic drums, high intensity electromagnetic separators, and scalping screens together with necessary materials handling equipment. Rejects from the magnetic circuits are mixed with water and **pumped to a tailings pond. Magnetite is collected from the magnetic drums and sold as iron ore. Total mill and mine recovery ranges from 75 to 80%.**

Ceramic and extender grades of nepheline syenite are ground in pebble mills operating in closed circuit with air classifiers.

Finished product storage consists of concrete bulk silos—four of 800-st capacity, four of 600-st capacity, and three of 150-st capacity each. In addition, warehousing is provided for several hundred tons of bagged products.

Throughout the entire mill particular attention is paid to dust collection. In the dryer building 30,000 cfm of air are provided and in the main mill building 400,000 cfm.

Quality Control—The quality control program starts with the mine development drilling and carries through to sampling drill cuttings, mining faces, numerous checkpoints in the mill, and as products are loaded into conveyances for delivery to customers. Routine chemical analyses include determination of Al_2O_3, Na_2O, K_2O, CaO, MgO, Fe_2O_3; determinations of heavy mineral content, screen analyses, and subsieve particle size distribution; cone fusion tests and dry brightness. The company maintains a technical and research center in Toronto, Ont., responsible for new product development, customer service, and quality control.

The mine is served by rail and all-weather highway. Products are shipped from the mine to more than 21 countries around the world.

International Minerals and Chemical Corp. (Canada) Ltd.: Although the Blue Mountain property was explored as early as 1912 by Norman B. Davis and staked by him in 1936 it was developed in 1956 by International Minerals and Chemical Corp. (Canada) Ltd. (IMC) who erected a mill to produce glass and ceramic grades of nepheline syenite. The mine and plant are four miles northeast of Nephton, Ont., at the northeast end of the Blue Mountain Intrusive.

Mining—Mining conditions are similar to those elsewhere on the Blue Mountain ridge. Maximum relief of the nepheline syenite deposit controlled by IMC is approximately 300 ft above local lake level. Three benches are under development at the 25, 70, and 100-ft levels. To date less than 10% of the IMC property has been opened for mining. Quarry faces are generally advanced either parallel or normal to the strike of the gneissic rock, taking advantage where possible of the joint patterns. Normal quarry methods are employed with the drill pattern being usually 6 x 6 ft. Individual shots range up to 20,000 tons of rock. Broken rock is reduced in size, drop-balling where necessary, loaded with a front-end loader, and moved to the primary jaw-crusher at the plant by truck. Quality control in the quarry is practiced by close sampling of drill cuttings. Grade of rock to be broken is known prior to shooting; thus it is possible to blend for optimum mill feed and ultimate product control.

Milling and Processing—Dry processing involves various methods of size reduction, including rod mills, to —30 and —40 mesh, followed by iron mineral removal with various types of magnetic-type separators, further sizing, fine grinding of ceramic grades, and preparation for either bagged or bulk shipment. Frequent sampling throughout the plant of in-process material and of finished products is practiced to permit size and chemical control. Fig. 5 provides a detailed listing of equipment and the sequence of operations.

IMC produces eight main products; low iron "Summit" glass-grade nepheline syenite and "Crest" and "Peak" ceramic grades. "Ridge" grade in two screen sizes is produced for colored glass. *Apex* 400 and 700 are produced for the filler, extender, and ceramic markets. The present plant capacity is in the 350,000 stpy range of product.

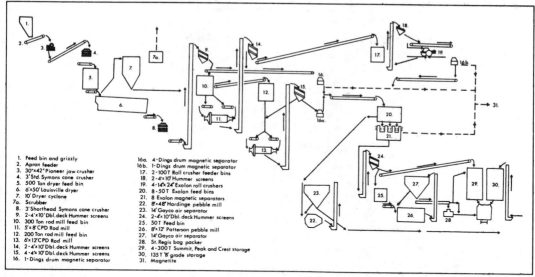

1. Feed bin and grizzly
2. Apron feeder
3. 30"x42" Pioneer jaw crusher
4. 3'Std. Symons cone crusher
5. 500 Ton dryer feed bin
6. 6'x50'Louisville dryer
7. 10' Dryer cyclone
7a. Scrubber
8. 3'Shorthead Symons cone crusher
9. 2-4'x10'Dbl.deck Hummer screens
10. 300 Ton rod mill feed bin
11. 5'x8'CPD Rod mill
12. 200 Ton rod mill feed bin
13. 6'x12'CPD Rod mill
14. 2-4'x10'Dbl.deck Hummer screens
15. 4-4'x10'Dbl.deck Hummer screens
16. 1-Dings drum magnetic separator
16a. 4-Dings drum magnetic separator
16b. 1-Dings drum magnetic separator
17. 2-100T Roll crusher feeder bins
18. 2-4'x10'Hummer screens
19. 4-14'x24'Exolon roll crushers
20. 8-50T Exolon feed bins
21. 8 Exolon magnetic separators
22. 8'x48'Hardinge pebble mill
23. 14'Gayco air separator
24. 2-4'x10'Dbl.deck Hummer screens
25. 50T Feed bin
26. 8'x12' Patterson pebble mill
27. 14'Gayco air separator
28. St. Regis bag packer
29. 4-300T Summit, Peak and Crest storage
30. 135 T 'B' grade storage
31. Magnetite

FIG. 5—*Production flow chart of International Minerals & Chemical Corp. (Canada) Ltd. plant, Blue Mountain, Ont., Canada (Source: Anon., 1973).*

Rail and an all-weather highway serve the IMC mine. More than 90% of shipments are in bulk.

Norway

Norsk Nefelin Division of Elkem S/A: Evaluation of the nepheline syenite deposits in northern Norway was started in 1951 by the Norwegian Geological Survey. Christiania Spigerverk undertook, in 1959, to build a 45-kt-capacity plant at Stjernøy at a reported cost of $1.1 million to exploit the deposit its geologists had defined. Commercial samples were available in early 1960 and production has increased annually since then.

In 1972 the Norsk Nefelin Division of Christiania Spigerverk became part of the enlarged corporation, Elkem Spigerverket, now Elkem S/A.

Mining—The mine and plant are situated on the southwest coast of the island of Stjernøy. The island is 250 miles north of the Arctic Circle some 25 miles northwest of Alta. The deposit lends itself to underground mining methods. Additionally, the arctic climate, heavy snowfall, prevalence of avalanches, and rugged topography all helped to dictate the mining method chosen by Norsk Nefelin. Fig. 6 shows schematically the mine layout in relation to the

Nabbaren Mountain and the plant on Lillebukt Inlet. Mining is by room-and-pillar method. Ore is loaded on Kiruna 25- and 33-ton-capacity trucks by Caterpillar 966 front-end loader. Cutler-Sater filters are fitted to the trucks to reduce the amount of gases emitted within the mine. The excellent natural ventilation helps keep the mine air fresh also. Ore is trucked to the 28 x 40 in. Blake-type jaw-crusher where it is reduced to —4 in., thence transported 1600 yd by truck to the 4-ft Symons standard cone crusher for reduction to —1½ in. Ore may be stored in a 2500-t underground bin or a 250-t steel bin on the hill slope above the mill.

Milling and Processing—Ore is drawn into the plant by conveyor and passes over a 6 x 20-ft single deck screen. Oversize passes through a 5½-ft Symons shorthead cone crusher and the —⅜ in. stone passes to a 7½ x 45 ft oil-fired rotary dryer where moisture is reduced from 1.5% to 0.04%. The ore then is distributed to one of five 200-ton-capacity steel bins. Further size reduction is handled in circuits consisting of four 4 x 10-ft double-deck Hummer screens, 16 double-deck Rotex screens, 18 rolls crushers with 14 x 24 in. rolls, two 24 x 80 in. drum magnets, and one 2 x 20 ft screen at which point 90% of the nepheline syenite has been reduced to 30 mesh (Fig. 7).

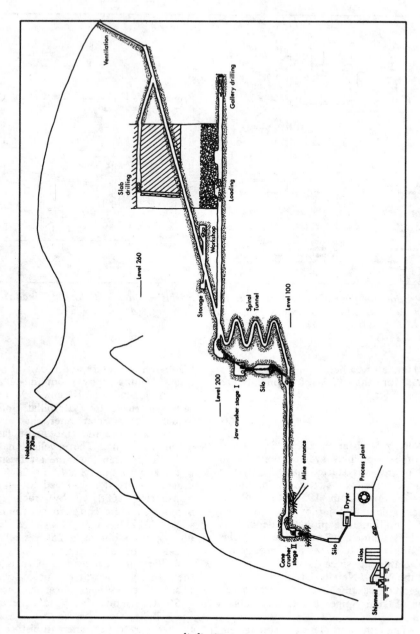

FIG. 6—*Schematic diagram of mine workings, Stjernöy, Norway.*

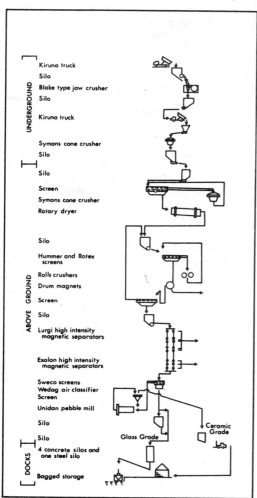

FIG. 7—*Flowsheet for production of nepheline syenite, Stjernöy, Norway.*

The sand is passed through high intensity magnetic separator circuits consisting of 3 single roll Lurgi separators followed by double roll Lurgi separators followed by 14 three-roll Exolon separators during which the iron oxide level is reduced from 1.5% to 0.1%.

The sand then passes over 12 Sweco 48-in. screening units where the remaining +30 mesh material is removed. Oversize provides mill feed to the Unidan 7 x 39 ft pebble mill. Undersize passes through an 8-ft-diam Wedag air classifier from which the oversize passes to the glass grade finished product bins and the undersize is fed to the pebble mill for grinding into ceramic grade nepheline syenite.

The original plant capacity in 1961 was 45 kt of glass-grade nepheline syenite annually but this has been increased several times to the present 200 kt of glass grade and about 25 kt of ceramic grade. The company has the capacity to increase production further, if market conditions warrant it.

Quality control consists of complete analyses of ore faces in the mine, drill cuttings, and preproduction diamond drill samples and mill samples. Size analysis and Fe_2O_3 determinations are carried out on plant samples. Regular particle size determinations of the ceramic grades of nepheline syenite are made to ensure the consistency that is so important in this material. Other chemical analyses are carried out as requested on a Perkin-Elmer atomic absorption spectrophotometer.

Between the mine and Alta, Norsk Nefelin operates a fast ferry service for its employees that makes at least four round trips each day throughout the year.

The ocean-side location and remoteness dictates the need for water transport of products to markets in 17 countries, principally those in western Europe. Glass-grade North Cape nepheline syenite is shipped in bulk loads of about 850, 4000, and 6000 tons. Norsk Nefelin has built or leased modern storage silos at several ports (Anon., 1968)—5000-ton-capacity silos at Birkenhead, near Liverpool in England; a 6000-ton silo at Terneuzen in the Netherlands; and a 5000-ton silo at Duisburg in West Germany. Stockpiles are also maintained in France and Spain.

Ceramic-grade North Cape nepheline syenite is packed in 50-kg bags and shipped in loads of 700 to 850 tons to stockpiles in western Europe. Distribution of both grades to customers from the stockpiles is by truck or covered hopper car. Large consignments may be discharged from the freighters onto barges for direct delivery to customers with plants on European waterways.

Union of Soviet Socialist Republics

As early as 1931 a process was advanced by Vladavits for the preparation of alumina from nepheline concentrates. Prior to that various workers had tested its value in glass, ceramics, and agriculture. A cement plant was built in

1938 at Volkhov near Leningrad to use nepheline slurry and in 1941 a plant to produce alumina utilizing the same material. Actual commercial production began at Volkhov in 1951 utilizing nepheline concentrate from the Kola peninsula as mill feed. A second and larger plant was completed at Pikalevo, also near Leningrad, in 1959. The third and largest alumina works built to date was operational in 1970 and is situated at Achinsk in central Siberia. Plant feed is nepheline syenite from Goryachegorsk about 90 miles southwest of Achinsk.

Mining: The processes of conversion of nepheline concentrates and nepheline syenite to alumina, portland cement, and alkali carbonates (Fig. 8) have been well described by a number of authors, among whom are Allen and Charsley (1968); Bozhenov and Kavalerova (1966); Dudkin, Kozyreva, and Pomerantseva (1964); Smirnov (1971); and Talmud (1957, 1961). Brief outlines also appeared in *Engineering and Mining Journal* (Baer, 1959) and in *Phosphorus and Potassium* (Anon., 1971). The following account was prepared largely from these sources.

Preliminary Treatment: The urtite rock tailings, from the production plants at Kirovsk and Apatity in the Kola peninsula, consist largely of nepheline (65 to 75%), apatite (6 to 10%), and titanite (1 to 3%), having a chemical analysis of 23.8% alumina, 6.8% Fe_2O_3, and 4.5% P_2O_5. This is concentrated by flotation and 44% of the mill feed is recovered as nepheline concentrate, 12.9% as apatite concentrate, and the remainder is waste. The nepheline concentrate is 90 to 93% nepheline and has an approximate composition of 29.3% alumina and 7% other compounds including iron oxide.

The dry concentrate is transported by rail to Volkhov and Pikalevo near Leningrad where it constitutes the feed for complex plants that convert it.

Processing: RAW MATERIALS—The nepheline concentrate is about 50% −170 mesh and is mixed with appropriate portions of preground limestone which are then pulped and reground in a wet state. Suitably pure limestone is available in the area of the alumina works, and it must be less than 1% in MgO and low in SiO_2, otherwise treatment costs rise.

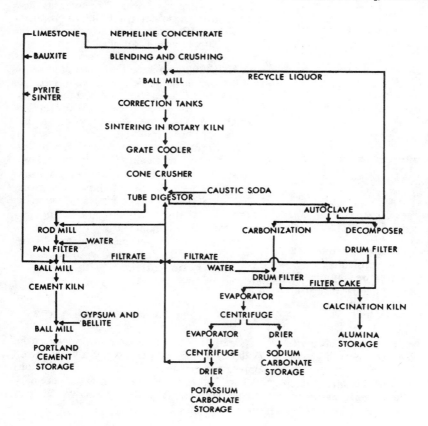

FIG. 8—*Simplified flowsheet for production of alumina, a l k a l i carbonates, and portland cement from nepheline syenite.*

The nepheline-limestone mixture is ground to less than 5% on 170 mesh.

PRODUCTION OF ALUMINA—The pulp passes through a coal-fired sinter kiln where the intake temperature ranges from 1500°C to 1600°C. Reaction between the limestone and nepheline takes place at 1300°C and the product is a sinter cake of essentially beta dicalcium silicate and sodium and potassium aluminate together with any impurities present. The chemical reaction is:

$$4CaCO_3 + (Na,K)_2O \cdot Al_2O_3 \cdot 2SiO_2 \rightarrow$$
$$(Na,K)_2O \cdot Al_2O_3 + 2Ca_2SiO_4 + 4CO_2.$$

The cake is cooled, then crushed in a cone crusher, and wet ground in a ball mill to a specific grain size and distribution being about 3% +10 mesh, 30% −200 mesh, and the balance as much as possible within the size range −10 +40 or +50 mesh. The pulp is leached in a tube digestor with a solution of caustic soda and mother liquor derived from other circuits in the plant, and passes continuously to a special vacuum filter-condenser to remove the alkali aluminates. The dicalcium silicate slurry is washed and thickened and is available for manufacture into portland cement.

Contaminating silica is removed from the aluminate in pressurized autoclaves and the solution filtered. The indicated reactions are:

$$6NaAlO_2 + 5Na_2SiO_3 + Ag \rightarrow$$
$$(3-4)Na_2O \cdot 3Al_2O_3 \cdot 5SiO_2 \cdot nH_2O +$$
$$(8-10)NaOH + Ag.$$

Filtrate from the desilication circuit is returned to the primary nepheline-limestone wet grinding circuit. The potassium reaction is similar. The solutions then pass to the carbonization towers where the alkalis remain as soluble carbonates in solution and the alumina is precipitated as aluminum hydroxide. The hydroxide is calcined to form alumina and the carbonates are separated by a process of selective crystallization.

The reactions are $2(Na_2K)AlO_2 + CO_2 + 3H_2O \rightarrow 2Al(OH)_3 + (Na,K)_2CO_3$.

The indicated product characteristics in 1972 were:

Alumina

Al₂O₃	99.39%
Fe₂O₃	0.001%
Na₂O	0.37%
SiO₂	0.062%
Ignition loss	0.22%
Alpha alumina content	0.35%

Soda (Approx.)

Na₂CO₃	97.1%
K₂CO₃	2.1%
K₂SO₄	0.6%
KCl	0.07%
Fe₂O₃	0.01%

Potash

K₂CO₃	98.0% (min.)
Na₂CO₃	0.9% (max)
KCl	0.15% (max)
K₂SO₄	0.73% (max)
Fe₂O₃	0.005% (max)
Residue	0.1% (max)

PRODUCTION OF PORTLAND CEMENT—The dicalcium silicate from the alumina plant is known as "bellite." The typical chemical composition of bellite used in the Volkhov works in 1961 was SiO₂, 29.85%; Al₂O₃, 3.57%; Fe₂O₃, 2.7%; CaO, 56.58%; Na₂O, 2.21%; MgO, 1.27%; SO₃, 0.34%; ignition loss, 3.61%. Since then improved recoveries in the alumina circuits have resulted in bellite in 1972 of typical composition: SiO₂, 31.5%; Al₂O₃, 1.8%; Na₂O, 0.9%; K₂O, 0.3%; ignition loss 3.0%. This material constitutes about 40% of the cement mix. It is combined in slurry form with additional limestone, low-grade bauxite, and pyrite clinker in appropriate amounts for the manufacture of normal type-one portland cement and ground in a ball mill.

The ground mixture is fired in a rotary kiln at about 1600°C, then cooled. Coal is the customary heat source. The clinker is mixed with about 15% of dry bellite and 5% gypsum and ground to the required fineness to make finished portland cement.

COSTS AND EFFICIENCY (ANON., 1969)—In the USSR, the raw materials required for, and products obtained from, the lime-sinter process are:

Raw Materials:

1) Nepheline concentrate or rock	3.9	to	4.3	t
2) Limestone for alumina	6.0	to	7.8	t
for cement	5.0	to	6.0	t
3) Fuel (min. 7000 kcal/kg)				
for alumina	1.67	to	1.70	t
for cement	1.3	to	1.6	t
4) Steam heat	4.68	to	4.12	g-cal
5) Electric power				
for alumina	1050	to	1190	kw-hr
for cement	700	to	860	kw-hr

Products:

1) Alumina		1.0		t
2) Sodium carbonate	0.62	to	0.76	t
3) Potassium carbonate	0.18	to	0.28	t
4) Portland cement	9.0	to	11.0	t

Studies indicate that the operating costs for the manufacture of alumina, portland cement, soda, and potash in an integrated plant are from 10 to 15% lower than costs of producing these in separate plants where alumina is made by the Bayer process, soda by the ammoniated method, potash from other raw materials, and cement from limestone and clay. The capital cost of the necessary plant however is somewhat higher than indicated for other methods of manufacturing these products.

Production Costs: No cost information has been published by the producers of nepheline syenite and one is left to estimate costs on the basis of the published flowsheets of each company.

Markets

Consumption—There are no complete data on world consumption of nepheline syenite. Between 1961 and 1982 world production of high quality nepheline syenite (excluding the USSR) rose from 250,000 to 911,000 st. Major expansion of markets in Europe and the United States were responsible for much of the growth in demand. In 1981, nearly 70% of the Canadian nepheline syenite production was exported to the United States.

Of the 240,000 tons of nepheline syenite produced by Norsk Nefelin, about 85% is used in the glass industry and 15% in ceramics. Only about 1000 tons per year are used internally, with the balance being exported to France, the U.K., West Germany, Belgium, the Netherlands, Italy, and Greece. In addition, some material is exported as far away as Thailand and Singapore.

The principal use of nepheline syenite is in the manufacture of glass of all types, but especially for glass containers. Glass containers typically contain 1 to 3% alumina, and feldspathic materials are the chief source of this important oxide. Statistical information on the quantities of nepheline syenite sold to individual industries in the United States is not available. Table 7 shows the consumption of feldspar in the United States and the consumption of nepheline syenite by industry in Canada.

It is apparent that nepheline syenite markets are heavily weighted in favor of glass, whereas feldspar markets are more evenly distributed between glass, whitewares, and other markets. Table 8 shows the amount of feldspar or nepheline syenite that may be used by segments of the ceramic manufacturing industry in typical product compositions.

Only small quantities of nepheline syenite are used in extender pigment and filler applications by paint, plastics, and rubber manufacturers. In 1970 in Canada, the latest year for which figures are available, 5000 st, representing 6% of nepheline syenite consumption, were sold for all nonglass and nonceramic applications including the aforementioned. No comparable figures are available for consumption of nepheline syenite in the United States for these purposes although the figure for feldspar was 7%.

Prices—The prices for nepheline syenite have been very low since 1955 when glass grade was sold for US $15 per st f.o.b. plant. The comparable price for feldspar was nearly US $14 per ton. Because of the intense competition between producers of feldspathic materials the price of glass-grade feldspar reached a low of US $8 per ton in 1961 while that of nepheline syenite dropped to US $9 per ton. By 1970 prices had recovered to US $11 for feldspar and Canadian $12 for nepheline syenite. The United States average import value of nepheline syenite was US $10 in 1966, and rose to US $11.60 in 1970, and US $11.88 in 1971. Today's

TABLE 7—Percentage Consumption of Feldspar and Nepheline Syenite By Industry

	Feldspar Consumption			Nepheline Syenite Consumption
	1968 US, %	1970 US, %	1980 US, %	1970 Canada, %
Flat glass	11	—		—
Container glass	44	—	57	—
All glass	—	55		70
Whiteware	33	36	39	12
Mineral wool	—	—	—	12
Porcelain enamel	3	2		0.3
Paint	—	—	4	2
Other	9	7		3.7
Total	100	100	100	100

feldspar costs vary between $27.50 to $64 per st, f.o.b. plant.

Norwegian nepheline syenite is exported mainly to the United Kingdom, West Germany, and the Netherlands. The average import value of Norwegian nepheline syenite in the United Kingdom remained constant between 1966 and 1970 at $22.70 per st. Most is used in the manufacture of glass although some glass grade material is ground by customers for ceramic applications. Prices of nepheline syenite in 1982 varied from $22 to $47 (Canadian) for Canadian nepheline syenite to $76 to $116 c.i.f. for Norwegian products.

Competition—Nepheline syenite competes with feldspar, aplite, certain slag derivatives, and silica-feldspar sand mixtures in glass applications.

Several methods are used to determine the relative value of these feldspathic materials to container and other glass manufacturers. In Tooley (1953) and Feitler (1967) are to be found complete descriptions of various procedures. Using that described by Feitler (1967) to calculate raw material batch compositions for desired glass composition, 90 lb of feldspar, 79 lb of aplite, and 73 lb of Canadian nepheline syenite would be required in a given container glass batch. In Table 9 is shown a comparison of the chemical values of the three principal feldspathic materials used in eastern North America and the basis whereby glass container companies can calculate the relative values of each.

The total weight of the oxides is not identical with the indicated weight of raw material needed to contain unit weight of alumina due to minor constituents not reported in the chemical composition, i.e.; loss on ignition. With the data in Table 9, and knowing the delivered cost of silica, feldspathic materials, soda ash, limestone, and alumina, and by crediting each raw material with its SiO_2, $Na_2O + K_2O$, and CaO content, a glass company can calculate which of the available feldspathic materials provides the lowest net cost of alumina and is consequently a best buy. The same methods can be helpful in estimating if a nepheline syenite deposit has potential merit. The value of higher alumina and alkali in nepheline syenite is apparent in calculations such as the foregoing and indicates why nepheline syenite has successfully competed with other comparable raw materials.

Since 1970 several large United States feldspar producers have completed major plant expansions allowing them to meet growth in domestic demand close to their plants. Canadian nepheline syenite producers will find competition keen in traditional market areas.

Future Considerations and Trends

It is expected that the glass and ceramic industries will continue to be the principal users of nepheline syenite. New types of better, stronger, and cheaper glass containers and ceramic ware will undoubtedly be available from manufacturers and a healthy demand for feldspathic materials should continue.

Nepheline syenite competes directly with feldspar, aplite, feldspar-silica sand mixtures, and slag as a source of alumina and alkalis for the glass and ceramic industries. Because they are the cheapest available forms of the needed compounds, nepheline syenite, feldspar, and similar materials are not threatened by mineral substitutes or synthetics. Suppliers are well situated to satisfy market needs and competition between them will remain strong.

TABLE 8—Weight of Feldspathic Material Used in Ceramic Ware

	Feldspar or Nepheline Syenite, %
Sanitary ware	25 to 35
Hotel ware	15 to 35
Chemical porcelain	15 to 30
Semi-vitreous chinaware	15 to 30
Floor and wall tiles	15 to 55

TABLE 9—Calculation of Chemical Values

Raw Material Chemical Composition

Oxides	Aplite	Feldspar	Nepheline Syenite
SiO_2	63.5%	67.9%	60.0%
Al_2O_3	22.4	19.2	23.7
$Na_2O + K_2O$	8.58	11.2	15.4
CaO	5.2	0.01	0.03
Fe_2O_3	0.1	0.07	0.07

Raw Material Needed for Unit Alumina Weight

	Aplite	Feldspar	Nepheline Syenite
Weight of Raw Material	4.46	5.21	4.22

Weight of Contained Oxides		

	Aplite	Feldspar	Nepheline Syenite
Al_2O_3	1.00	1.00	1.00
SiO_2	2.84	3.54	2.53
$Na_2O + K_2O$	0.38	0.58	0.65
CaO	0.23	—	—
Total weight	4.45	5.12	4.18

Nepheline syenite sold as an inert filler or extender pigment competes to a limited degree with other materials having similar properties, and even dissimilar materials. Demand for all types of fillers is strong but increased sales of nepheline syenite will depend on more widespread acceptance of the advantages it offers over less inert materials.

Trends

North America: United States glass container production grew at an average rate of 8% during the period 1966 to 1971. The US Bureau of Mines (Cooper and Wells, 1970) report suggests a median growth rate for glass containers of 4% per year through to the year 2000. The same report suggests median annual growth rates for feldspar demand of from 3.6 to 5.1%. Using this same method of calculation for nepheline syenite, the demand in the year 2000 would be between 1.3 million and 2.1 million st for Canadian products.

The consumption of nepheline syenite depends to a significant degree on transportation rates' to the principal consuming industries in Canada and the United States. In the 1950s and 1960s new glass manufacturing plants were built in the northeastern mid-Atlantic states and midwestern states which could be supplied equally well by most feldspathic material producers. In the 1970s there was an apparent trend toward erection of glass plants away from the northeast which favors feldspathic materials other than nepheline syenite.

The glass container industry needs a lightweight, unbreakable bottle that will compete with other containers of similar use. One move in this direction is the bulb-shaped glass container enclosed in plastic which serves to reinforce and keep the bulb upright. These can be manufactured at the rate of 600 to 800 units per min.

New machinery for filling glass containers at the rate of 2000 bottles per min, more than three times the conventional rate, is available. Nepheline syenite helps impart greater strength to such containers and will certainly be needed for these and other improved containers.

For the ceramic industry the US Bureau of Mines report (Cooper and Wells, 1970) projected a growth in demand for feldspar of 4% and 1.75% per year for use in whiteware and porcelain enamel, respectively, to the year 2000. For other uses, such as extender pigments and fillers, a rate of 4% was used also.

Similar rates should apply to demand for nepheline syenite in these applications, although actual performance of nepheline syenite will depend on developments in its traditional marketing areas.

Europe: Using growth rates of 3.6 to 5.1% demand for Norwegian nepheline syenite would amount to between 245 kt and 390 kt by the year 2000. The rate of growth of Norsk Nefelin since 1961 has been much higher than this.

Norwegian nepheline syenite is readily available at moderate cost to consuming industries in Europe and other parts of the world. It competes with feldspars from other European countries, with Cornish Stone in the United Kingdom (Johnstone and Johnstone, 1961), and with North American nepheline syenite in certain of the glass and ceramic producing areas. Norwegian nepheline syenite can be shipped in almost any quantity, bagged or bulk from the ocean-side plant at Stjernöy, and stocks of bulk syenite are maintained at major European ports for truck delivery to customers.

Although the Norwegian plant has been expanded several times, expansion of other European feldspar producers and the entry of new Finnish and Norwegian feldspar producers make the markets highly competitive. If all the planned expansions are completed European producers face a serious state of overcapacity.

Substitutes: Nepheline syenite and other feldspathic materials are the cheapest sources of necessary alkalis and alumina for many glass and ceramic manufacturers and consequently are not vulnerable to competition from higher priced and purer alternatives such as alkali carbonates and alumina, in most applications.

Trends to thin-walled, stronger, and lighter bottles as well as changes in the percentage of returnable and nonreturnable bottles produced will certainly affect nepheline syenite requirements in years to come. How, is not clear. Plastic and metal containers emerged during the 1960s to capture many traditional glass markets and can be expected to continue the challenge in the 1980s. The changing character of the container industry certainly adversely affects demand for nepheline syenite.

One reason why nepheline syenite has not been used more for extender pigment and filler applications is the ready availability of excellent alternative materials such as calcium carbonate, feldspar, kaolin, silica, and talc. Increased utilization of nepheline syenite will depend wholly on increased demand for its special properties.

Transportation: Any inequality in the application of freight rate increases tends to work to the detriment of users of Canadian nepheline syenite. Rail and truck rates for international movements are generally higher than rates for comparable domestic movements and for comparable movements of feldspar within the United States. Consequently the numerous freight rate increases by United States and Canadian carriers in the 1970s and 1980s tend to hurt producers of nepheline syenite. Similar trends apply in Europe. However, because Norwegian nepheline syenite is waterborne for most of the journey to customers, the effect of increased rail and truck rates will be less on users of nepheline syenite than users of feldspar in Europe. Increases in freight rates the world over are bound to affect traditional supply patterns and cause reorientation in favor of local producers.

Government Control, Zonal Restrictions

There are no specially inhibiting government controls affecting producers of nepheline syenite. In the case of Norsk Nefelin, its efforts are accorded full government encouragement because of the expressed desire to develop industry in the Norwegian far north. Canadian producers of nepheline syenite are subject to normal business regulations. Various acts are of particular significance to IMC and Indusmin, among which are The Mining Act, The Act to Protect the Natural Environment, The Municipal Act, and the Planning Act. These acts bear on land use in Ontario and directly affect the way nepheline syenite producers operate.

Taxes, Depletion and Tariffs

Taxes and Depletion—Since 1970 Canadian federal taxes on mining companies have tended to increase and much of the encouragement granted mine developers is in the process of being withdrawn. These changes affect nepheline syenite producers and inhibit development of many mining properties. Effective Jan. 1, 1972, depletion allowances granted shareholders of mining companies were withdrawn. Depletion allowances granted operators of mines in the past were progressively reduced until 1976 when they ceased and were replaced by new allowances based on profits and eligible capital expenditures. The three-year exemption

from federal income taxes of new mines terminated on Dec. 31, 1973, and purchases and sale of mining properties after Dec. 31, 1971 are treated as income transactions and taxable as such. After 1976 a 15% abatement of federal tax was allowed in respect to mining profits.

The maximum federal tax rate to which Canadian nepheline syenite producers would be subject is 48%. Mineral rights in Canadian provinces are normally owned by the province and licenses to explore for and develop minerals are granted by them for fixed periods. Nepheline syenite is subject to provincial regulations and provincial taxes. Currently there is a trend in Canada, generated by provincial authorities, encouraging companies to develop mining properties held under license or else to abandon the license. There is an equally strong trend to increased taxation of mining companies.

The Norwegian government has indirectly encouraged development in its northern regions by granting tax incentives and quick write-offs for capital investments.

Tariffs—Nepheline syenite, whether processed or unprocessed, enters the United States duty-free from all countries. The United Kingdom levies no duty on nepheline syenite from Commonwealth and European Free Trade Area countries. Nepheline syenite enters European Economic Community countries free of duty but EEC members may levy value added taxes. Exports of Canadian nepheline syenite are permitted to all countries but export permits are required for shipments to Communist countries.

Recycling

Public interest and concern in glass containers as sources of waste quickened in the latter part of the 1960s and will be of significant importance to raw material producers in the 1980s. Although glass represents only about 6.5% of municipal waste, it is highly visible and consequently is the focus of legislative reaction against the growing quantities of waste generated by society.

Throughout the United States and Canada, glass container manufacturers have established depots in major traffic areas where people may return clean glass containers for recycling. In 1970 the Glass Container Manufacturers Institute (Anon, 1972a) sponsored a pilot program for bottle reclamation at the plants of eight member companies in the Los Angeles area. Subsequently the project was expanded to nearly 100 collection centers at bottle factories in 25 states. Glass container manufacturers pay an average of 1¢ per lb for used glass containers brought to collection centers, the only stipulation being that the glass be free of metal contamination and sorted as to color. Properly prepared waste glass (cullet) can constitute up to 50% of the glass batch. In many glass plants 10 to 15% waste glass is being used, up from 2 to 3% only a few years ago.

Throughout the United States and Canada, governments are considering ways to encourage the reuse and recycling of all types of materials including plastic, metal, and glass beverage containers.

The glass recycling program is too recent for significant effects to be felt by producers of raw materials but manifestly the recycling of glass into new containers, fiber glass, and other products will affect the markets for nepheline syenite and other feldspathic materials.

Ecology

The direct impact of current international interest in ecology on nepheline syenite producers is minimal. All three operating nepheline syenite plants prepare products by "dry" methods with attendant need for large and efficient dust collection systems to keep plants clean and to prevent atmospheric emissions. Between 1966 and 1972 Norsk Nefelin spent over $1 million at Stjernöy on improved dust control equipment and between 1966 and 1972 Indusmin spent $750,000 at Nephton to improve dust control and tailings disposal systems.

All industry, including mining, can expect to spend significant sums in the 1980s to make their activities correspond to the realities of environmental protection. Reports by the American Chemical Society (Reese, 1969, 1971) attempt to catalog the environmental conditions in North America and indicate the magnitude of the task ahead. *Chemical Engineering* (Anon., 1972) in 1972 summarized international activity in the field of pollution control.

More and more public and governmental interest and intervention in the affairs of nepheline syenite producers can be expected. While the results will mean cleaner, better, and more efficient operations, the cost will be high and will to some degree tend to affect the competitive position of producers in world markets.

Nepheline Syenite in Other Countries

There is little likelihood that nepheline syenite from the Soviet Union will be a competitive factor in world glass and ceramic markets in the near future. The emphasis has been on the internal utilization of nepheline syenite for the manufacture of alumina, alkali carbonates, and portland cement, and only small quantities have been used for the production of drainage tile, floor tile, and green glass. Indications are that Soviet deposits are not suited for economic production of products comparable to those from Canadian and Norwegian sources.

Soviet technology for the chemical conversion of nepheline-bearing rocks may well be of interest to other nations in the near future. While similar technology has been developed in the United States (Lundquist and Singleton, 1962; Johnson and Peters, 1968; Archibald and Nicholson, 1948) and Canada (Archibald, 1942), the only commercial operations based on nepheline and feldspar minerals are located in the Soviet Union. The trend in Soviet plants is to larger and larger units to take advantage of any economies that result from such scale-up. The annual production capacity of nepheline-based alumina plants has grown from the original Volkhov plant (estimated 50 kt/a) to the Pikalevo plant (estimated 200 kt) to the Achinsk plant (800 kt) to the currently planned 1.5 Mt plant near the Sayano-Shushenskaya dam. Present methods of production of alumina and cement in non-Soviet countries are low cost and nepheline syenite will not be used for such production until comparable costs are attained. Many such deposits would be satisfactory for applications requiring good fluxing character where iron impurities are not detrimental such as colored glass, drainage and sewer pipe, brick, floor tile, and backup wall tile.

Elsewhere in the world no nepheline syenites have been found that lend themselves to production of low-iron products. Some nations in Africa, Europe, and South America may satisfy local industrial needs for feldspathic raw materials by mining domestic nepheline-bearing deposits.

Bibliography and References

Anon., 1967, "Mining and Milling Nepheline Syenite," *Canadian Clay and Ceramics,* Vol. 40, No. 5, p. 12.
Anon., 1968, "Nepheline Syenite 30 Years Rapid Growth," *Industrial Minerals,* Metal Bulletin Ltd. London, England, No. 7, Apr., pp. 9–19.
Anon., 1969, *Alumina from Nepheline,* V. O. Licensintorg, Moscow, 8 pp.
Anon., 1971, "Potash: A By-Product of Soviet Alumina from Nepheline," *Phosphorus and Potassium,* May/June, pp. 40–41.

Anon., 1972, "Environmental Engineering," *Chemical Engineering*, Vol. 79, No. 10, May 8, p. 259.

Anon., 1972a, *Glass Containers*, 1972 ed., Glass Container Manufacturers Institute, Inc., New York, 20 pp.

Anon., 1973, "Ceramic Manufacturing Sales Estimates," *Ceramic Age*, Jan. p. 12.

Anon., 1961–1971, "Nepheline Syenite," *Canadian Minerals Yearbook*, Mineral Resources Div., Dept. of Energy, Mines and Resources, annual publication.

Anon., 1961–1971a, "Feldspar, Nepheline Syenite and Aplite," *Minerals Yearbook*, US Bureau of Mines, annual publication.

Allen, J.B., and Charsley, T.J., 1968, *Nepheline-Syenite and Phonolite*, Institute of Geological Sciences, Minerals Resources Div., London, England, 169 pp.

Archibald, F.R., and Nicholson, C.M., 1948, "Alumina from Clay by the Lime-Sinter Method II," AIME, Tech. Pub. 2390, 25 pp.

Archibald, F.R., 1942, "Report of Investigation on Production of Alumina and Alkalis from Nepheline Syenite," unpublished report to Bureau of Mines, Ottawa, 40 pp.

Baarson, R.E., et al., 1962, "Plant Practice in Non-Metallic Mineral Flotation," Chap. 17, *Froth Flotation*, D.W. Fuerstenau, ed., AIME, New York, pp. 427–453.

Baer, F.H., 1959, "Soviets Push Ambitious Aluminum Plans," *Engineering and Mining Journal*, Vol. 160, No. 5, May, 1959, pp. 102–105.

Barth, T.F.W., 1963, "The Composition of Nepheline," *Schweiz, Min. Petr. Mitt.* 43/1, pp. 153–164.

Bozhenov, P.I., and Kavalerova, V.I., 1966, *Nepheline Slurries*, Editor of Literature for the Building Industry, Moscow-Leningrad, (in Russian), 243 pp.

Castle, J.E., and Gillson, J.L., 1960, "Feldspar, Nepheline Syenite and Aplite," *Industrial Minerals and Rocks*, J.L. Gillson, ed., 3rd ed., AIME, New York, pp. 339–362.

Cooper, J.D., and Wells, J.R., 1970, "Feldspar," *Mineral Facts and Problems*, Bulletin 650, US Bureau of Mines, pp. 977–988.

Deer, W.A., et al., 1963, *Rock-Forming Minerals*, Vol. 4, Longmans Green and Co. Ltd., London, England, pp. 231–269.

Dudkin, O.B., Kozyreva, L.V., and Pomerantseva, N.G., 1964, *Mineralogy of Apatite Occurrences of the Khibinsk Tundra*, Academy of Sciences, Moscow-Leningrad.

Eitel, W., 1965, *Silicate Science*, Vol. 3, Academic Press, New York, pp. 236–264.

Feitler, S.A., 1967, "Feldspar Resources and Marketing in Eastern United States," Information Circular 8310, US Bureau of Mines, 41 pp.

Gerasimovskii, V.I., 1956, "Geochemistry and Mineralogy of Nepheline Syenite Intrusions," *Geochemistry*, No. 5, pp. 494–510.

Grimshaw, R.W., 1971, *The Chemistry and Physics of Clays and Allied Ceramic Materials*, 4th ed., John Wiley and Sons Inc., New York, pp. 372–442.

Guillet, G.R., 1962, "A Chemical and Inclusion Study of Nepheline Syenite for Petrogenetic Criteria," unpublished M.A. Thesis, University of Toronto, Canada, 75 pp.

Harben, P.W., 1977, "Raw Materials for the Glass Industry," *Industrial Minerals*, Metal Bulletin, Ltd., London, pp. 6–14.

Heier, K.S., 1961, "Layered Gabbro, Hornblende, Carbonatite and Nepheline Syenite on Stjernöy, North Norway," *Norsk Geol. Tidsskr 41*, pp. 109–155.

Heier, K.S., 1964, "Geochemistry of the Nepheline Syenite on Stjernöy, North Norway," *Norsk Geol. Tidsskr 45*, pp. 205–215.

Heier, K.S., 1965, "A Geochemical Comparison of the Blue Mountain (Ontario, Canada) and Stjernöy (Finnmark, North Norway) Nepheline Syenites," *Norsk Geol. Tidsskr 45*, pp. 41–52.

Heier, K.S., 1966, "Some Crystallo-Chemical Relations of Nepheline and Feldspars on Stjernöy, North Norway," *Journal of Petrology*, Vol. 7, Pt. 1, pp. 95–113.

Hewitt, D.F., 1960, "Nepheline Syenite Deposits of Southern Ontario," Ontario Dept. of Mines, Vol. 69, Pt. 8, 194 pp.

Huvos, J.B., 1980, "The Mineral Industry of Norway," Preprint, US Bureau of Mines, 14 pp.

Johnson, P.W., and Peters, F.A., 1968, "Methods for Producing Alumina from Anorthosite, and Evaluation of a Lime-Soda Sinter Process," Report of Investigation 7068, US Bureau of Mines, 42 pp.

Johnstone, S.J., and Johnstone, M.G., 1961, *Minerals for the Chemical and Allied Industries*, Chapman and Hall, London, England, pp. 188–194.

Lundquist, R.V., and Singleton, E.L., 1962, "Some Characteristics of Iron in the Lime-Soda Sinter Process for Recovering Alumina from Anorthosite," Report of Investigation 6090, US Bureau of Mines, 13 pp.

Merrett, A.J., and Sykes, A., 1963, *The Finance and Analysis of Capital Projects*, Longmans Green and Co. Ltd. London, England, 539 pp.

Minnes, D.G., 1975, "Nepheline Syenite," *Industrial Minerals and Rocks*, S.J. Lefond, ed., 4th ed., AIME, New York, pp. 861–894.

Moorhouse, W.W., 1959, *The Study of Rocks in Thin Section*, Harper and Brothers, New York, pp. 302–312.

Payne, J.G., 1966, "Geology and Geochemistry of the Blue Mountain Nepheline Syenite Body," Ph.D. Thesis, McMaster University, Canada, 183 pp.

Polkanov, A.A., ed., 1937, *The Northern Excursion, Kola Peninsula*, 17th International Geological Congress, Moscow, 119 pp.

Reese, K.M., ed., 1969, "Cleaning Our Environment, the Chemical Basis for Action," report by the Sub-Committee on Environmental Improvements, Committee on Chemistry and Public Affairs, American Chemical Society, Washington, DC, 249 pp.; 1971 Supplement, 20 pp.

Robie, E. H., ed., 1959, *Economics of the Mineral Industries*, AIME, New York, 755 pp.

Singer, F., and Singer, S.S., 1963, *Industrial Ceramics*, Chemical Publishing Co. Inc., New York, 1455 pp.

Smirnov, M.N., 1971, *Physical-Chemical Fundamentals of Alumina Production from Nepheline*, Vol. 3, Proceedings, 2nd International Symposium of ICSOBA, pp. 337–345.

Smothers, W.J., et al., 1952, "Ceramic Evaluation of Arkansas Nepheline Syenite," Arkansas Resources and Development Commission, Research Series No. 24, pp. 21.

Taggart, A.F., 1956, "Electrical Concentration," Sec. 13, *Handbook of Mineral Dressing*, John Wiley and Sons Inc., New York, pp. 13–01—13–47.

Talmud, I.L., 1957, "Aluminum from Nepheline," *Science and Life*, No. 4, Moscow, April (in Russian).

Talmud, I.L., 1961, "Complex Treatment of Nepheline Ore," *Chemical Industry*, No. 4, April, (in Russian), pp. 226–232.

Taylor, G.H., and Wilson, R.C., 1962, "Particle Size Control of Nepheline Syenite for Whitewares," *Bulletin*, American Ceramic Society, Vol. 41, No. 1, pp. 12–13.

Tooley, F.V., 1953, *Handbook of Glass Manufacture*, Vol. 1, Ogden Publishing Co., New York, pp. 75–79.

Turner, F.J., and Verhoogen, J., 1951, *Igneous and Metamorphic Petrology*, McGraw Hill, New York, pp. 338–342.

Vlasov, K. A., et al., 1966, *The Lovozero Alkali Massif*, Oliver and Boyd, Edinburgh and London, 627 pp.

Watson, I., 1981, "Feldspathic Fluxes—The Rivalry Reviewed," *Industrial Minerals*, No. 163, Apr., pp. 21–45.

Watson, I., 1981a, "The Industrial Minerals of Scandinavia—Norway," *Industrial Minerals*, No. 171, Dec., pp. 34–45.

Nitrogen Compounds

E.A. HARRE and R.D. YOUNG *

Nitrogen exists in two broad categories commonly designated as elemental nitrogen and fixed nitrogen. Elemental nitrogen is found in nature as a diatomic molecule and constitutes about 78%, by volume, of the earth's atmosphere. Fixed nitrogen is a common term used for nitrogen that is chemically bound to other elements. Although elemental nitrogen is very abundant, nonleguminous plants cannot utilize nitrogen unless it is in the chemically combined form. The content of this chapter is confined to fixed nitrogen since the uses and properties of elemental nitrogen and the fixed nitrogen compounds are different.

Certain bacteria associated with legumes are able to fix atmospheric nitrogen, but not to the extent required by succeeding nonleguminous crops. The need to use fertilizers containing fixed nitrogen compounds to grow food crops has been recognized for hundreds of years, and from antiquity farmers have used organic wastes such as animal manures, vegetable wastes, sewage sludge, fish scraps, etc., containing these compounds for fertilizers. These organic materials have a low nitrogen content, however, and cannot support large-scale food production.

Known commercial-size deposits of natural nitrates containing much higher nitrogen content exist only in Chile, and the possibility of the discovery of other significant deposits is remote. The Chilean deposits were the major source of nitrogenous fertilizers until the Haber-Bosch process for the production of synthetic ammonia was developed. In the Haber-Bosch process, nitrogen reacts with hydrogen at high temperatures and pressures and in the presence of a catalyst to form ammonia. Modern plants use air, water, and natural gas or other hydrogen sources to produce the ammonia that is now the key building block of the fixed nitrogen industry.

Several major problems that developed in the 1970s continue with the nitrogen industry into the 1980s. These are (1) the continuing sharp escalation in the cost of feedstocks for ammonia production as well as all energy sources, and (2) the very steep increase in the investment cost of production facilities.

More than 75% of the fixed nitrogen produced domestically is consumed as fertilizers. The types of materials used as fertilizers have changed significantly during the past years. There has been a trend from the use of low-analysis fertilizers to types which contain high percentages of plant nutrients. The average plant nutrient content $(N + P_2O_5 + K_2O)$ of fertilizers used in the United States has increased from 18% in 1930 to 32% in 1960 and today approaches an average of 44%.

In the case of nitrogen fertilizers, the low analysis natural nitrates (16% N) gave way to ammonium sulfate (20% N) after about 1920. After World War II, ammonium nitrate (33.5% N) previously used in munitions, became established as the leading nitrogen fertilizer. Urea use as a fertilizer (46% N) began in the 1960s, and in the past 10 years has become the world's leading solid nitrogen fertilizer.

Nitrogen Materials

Anhydrous Ammonia—Anhydrous ammonia is a colorless gas at ambient temperatures and pressures and has a sharp pungent odor. Anhydrous ammonia is stored and transported as a liquid in high-pressure cylinders and tanks at ambient temperature, and in low-pressure tanks, barges, and ships at −28°F. Anhydrous ammonia is applied directly at 4 to 7-in. depths in the soil as a high-pressure liquid by special applicators, after which it expands to a gas that dissolves in the soil moisture or is absorbed on soil colloids. In other systems ammonia is metered into irrigation water and is thereby introduced into the soil.

* Office of Agricultural and Chemical Development, Tennessee Valley Authority, Muscle Shoals, AL.

Aqua Ammonia—Aqua ammonia is obtained by reacting anhydrous ammonia with water. Commercial aqua ammonia solutions usually contain between 22 and 25% nitrogen and are strongly alkaline. Aqua ammonia has a significant vapor pressure and must be contained in pressure vessels to prevent loss of ammonia. Equipment for the direct application of aqua ammonia is similar to that used for the application of anhydrous ammonia.

Ammonium Nitrate—Fertilizer ammonium nitrate is sold as a solid, normally in small round pellets called prills or granules, or dissolved in water as a component of nitrogen solutions. Solid ammonium nitrate is hygroscopic and it is usually treated with a conditioning agent, such as kaolin clay, to prevent caking. In addition to its use as fertilizer, large amounts of ammonium nitrate are used as blasting agents when sensitized with fuel oil.

Ammonium Nitrate-Limestone—This product is a mixture of ammonium nitrate and limestone, and is marketed as a solid in prilled or pellet form. Its soil reaction is alkaline or neutral. Used quite widely in Europe, Asia, and Latin America, where it is usually called calcium-ammonium nitrate (CAN), it is of little importance in the United States.

Urea—Prilled urea is marketed as products containing 45 and 46% nitrogen. Urea is popular as a direct application fertilizer because of its high nitrogen content, and it is also used extensively in nitrogen solutions. Urea is used as a reactant in many industrial chemical applications, including the production of plastics and synthetic foams.

The rapid growth of urea to its place as the world's leading nitrogen fertilizer resulted to a large extent from its being a "natural" for production from ammonia and carbon dioxide, the coproduct from ammonia synthesis.

Nitrogen Solutions—The nutrient content of nitrogen solutions can vary from 19 to 59%. Nitrogen fertilizer solutions are prepared, for the most part, from various mixtures of ammonium nitrate, urea, ammonia, and water. There are, of course, an infinite number of possible combinations. The vapor pressure ranges from nearly zero for the low-analysis solutions to high vapor pressures for the high-analysis materials. Vapor pressure increases with increasing ammonia content. The nonpressure mixtures are easy to handle, store, ship, and apply. The grade of the very popular urea-ammonium nitrate solutions (UAN) ranges from 28 to 32% N, depending on ambient temperature.

Ammonium Sulfate—The nitrogen content of ammonium sulfate averages about 20.5%. Ammonium sulfate also contains a large percentage of sulfur which is of value for sulfur-deficient soils. Ammonium sulfate is marketed as a white crystalline salt and is often an ingredient of mixed fertilizers. It is a byproduct of coke oven and steel industries, the fibers industry, and is also manufactured synthetically. Its importance as a fertilizer in the United States and the world continues to decline in comparison with higher analysis nitrogen materials.

Calcium Nitrate—Calcium nitrate (15.5% N) is extremely hygroscopic and, if exposed to sufficiently humid air, may liquefy. Its main source is as a byproduct from some nitric phosphate fertilizer plants located in Europe. A paraffin coating is used to provide moisture protection.

Sodium Nitrate—Only about 550,000 tons of this once important fertilizer was produced worldwide in 1980. Sodium nitrate contains 16% nitrogen, is produced synthetically in small amounts, but is obtained primarily from natural nitrate deposits in Chile. Sodium nitrate has a residual alkaline effect on the soil. It is also used as a food preservative.

Calcium Cyanamide—Calcium cyanamide for fertilizer use contains about 21% nitrogen, which means that it has a low purity, since pure calcium cyanamide contains about 35% nitrogen. Calcium cyanamide has a high liming effect and is equivalent to about 2 lb of calcium carbonate per pound of nitrogen applied.

Nonfertilizer Uses of Nitrogen

Other significant end uses for fixed nitrogen compounds are for plastics, textiles, and elastomers, some of which are described in the following (Billmeyer, 1971).

Nitrile Rubbers—Nitrile rubbers are polymers of butadiene and acrylonitrile and are used in applications which require resistance to oil, such as in gasoline hoses and fuel tanks. Also, nitrile rubbers are used in adhesives.

Acrylic Fibers—Acrylic fibers are polymers containing 85% or more of acrylonitrile along with copolymers such as vinyl acetate, acrylic esters, and vinyl pyrrolidone. Acrylic fibers exhibit high strength, abrasion resistance, resilience, and have good moisture and chemical resistance.

Nylon—Nylon is a generic term used for synthetic polyamides. The nylons are perhaps the most familiar of the plastics and synthetics.

Nylon 6/6 is the polymer of hexamethylene-diamine and adipic acid. About half of the nylon fiber produced is consumed as tire cord, but other end uses include rope, thread, cloth, and garments. Nylon plastics are used as metal substitutes in bearings, gears, rollers, slides, etc.

Other nylon polymers are made from dimerized vegetable oil acids and diamines such as ethylene diamine. These materials are used in paints, for paper coatings, and as curing agents for epoxy resins.

Polyurethanes—Polyurethanes are typically formed through the reaction of a diisocyanate and a glycol. The urethane polymers are used to produce foams, fibers, elastomers, and coatings. Polyurethane elastomers are noted for their abrasion resistance and hardness combined with a resistance to oils and solvents. The materials are used in tire treads, heel lifts, and small industrial wheels.

Urethane foams can be made in either flexible or rigid foams. Flexible urethane foams are used for furniture and automobile cushions, while rigid foams are used for thermal insulations and for imparting buoyancy to boats.

Amino Resins—The two important classes of amino thermosetting resins are the condensation products of urea and of melamine with formaldehyde. Melamine is a trimer of cyanamide. Almost all urea molding compounds are cellulose-filled while the melamine molding resins are filled with cellulose, asbestos, glass, or cotton fabric. The resins are used, among other things, for appliance housings, hardware, and dinnerware. Also, amino resins are used widely for adhesives such as the adhesives used in the lamination of plywood and the fabrication of furniture. Melamine resins are often used for the production of laminates for counter, cabinet, and table tops. Urea-based enamels are used for refrigerator and kitchen appliances, and melamine enamels are used in automobile finishes.

Ammonium Nitrate-Fuel Oil—In recent years ammonium nitrate sensitized with fuel oil has dominated the industrial explosives market. The primary reason for this is the relatively low cost of the ammonium nitrate explosives.

Black Blasting Powder—Black blasting powder is perhaps the oldest of the blasting agents and consists of a mixture of sodium nitrate, sulfur, and charcoal.

Dynamite—Dynamite is a combination of nitroglycerine absorbed in kieselguhr and ammonium nitrate in various proportions.

Other Nitrogen-Containing Explosives—Other industrial or military explosives include nitrocellulose, nitroglycerine, nitrostarch, trinitrotoluene (TNT), pentraerythritol tetranitrane, cyclonite, trinitrobenzene, ammonium picrate, and picric acid. Nitrogen-containing detonators include lead azide and mercury fulminate.

Animal Feed—Urea is used as a supplement in the feed of ruminant animals, and in 1980 about 250,000 tons of urea was produced for use in feed compounds.

There are also other uses of fixed nitrogen compounds. Weak solutions of ammonia in water are used in industrial and home cleaning agents, usually in combination with detergents. Ammonia is used as a curing agent in leather-making, and ammonia and certain amines are used as depilatories in the leather industry. Many pharmaceuticals are chemicals containing fixed nitrogen. Ammonia is used in commercial and industrial refrigeration units. Nitrogen tetroxide and hydrazine are sometimes used as rocket propellants. Nitric acid has a wide range of industrial applications, but is usually an intermediate chemical for some other end use.

Synthetic Nitrogen Fixation Processes

Production of Anhydrous Ammonia

The fixed nitrogen industry of today is largely based upon the production of synthetic anhydrous ammonia. Although the process for producing ammonia has been known for 70 years, the technology has continued to improve through the years, with major changes occurring in the technology since the early sixties. One of the most significant changes was the development of high-pressure centrifugal compressors that paved the way for single-train plants of much higher production capacity.

Engineering firms completely redesigned the ammonia plant to utilize the new compressors and to achieve efficient utilization of plant energy. These changes resulted in a capacity of 1000 tpd becoming the standard and a few plants of 1500 tpd were built by 1980.

Two chemical elements, nitrogen and hydrogen, are combined to synthesize ammonia (NH_3). Nitrogen is readily available from the air but providing hydrogen is more difficult and expensive. About 94% of the ammonia plants in the United States use natural gas to obtain the process hydrogen, while in other parts of the world, naphtha has been used in a number of plants instead of natural gas. Some ammonia plants have used coke-oven gas, a wide range of hydrocarbons, or pulverized coal to produce hydrogen. By 1980 the interest in use of coal had increased because of increased cost and uncertainty of resources of natural gas in many areas. A demonstration plant (135 tpd NH_3) was in test operation in the United States in 1980 (Anon., 1980c).

In a typical new ammonia plant, a feed gas such as methane is compressed, if necessary, to 550–600 psi and desulfurized before it enters the primary reformer. Steam is added and the mixture of steam and hydrocarbon is passed through a series of tubes containing a nickel catalyst. In the primary reformer tubes, which are heated externally, the hydrocarbon and steam react to form hydrogen, carbon monoxide, and carbon dioxide. The gas exit temperature from the primary reformer ranges from 1400° to 1600°F.

Next, the gas mixture enters a secondary reformer, which also contains a nickel catalyst. Compressed air enters the secondary reformer and the oxygen in the air is completely consumed in exothermic reactions with hydrogen, carbon monoxide, and residual methane from the primary reformer. Exit gas temperature in the secondary reformer is from 1700° to 1900°F. The temperature of the outlet stream from the secondary reformer is reduced in a tubular waste heat boiler in which high pressure steam is generated for use in the plant.

From the secondary reformer, the process stream enters a two-stage shift converter where most of the carbon monoxide is converted to carbon dioxide. Steam and/or water are added to a catalyst bed in the shift converter to effect the conversion of carbon monoxide to carbon dioxide. In the first stage, shift conversion is carried out over a chromium-promoted iron catalyst at temperatures of 600° to 800°F. The second-stage shift conversion is carried out over a copper-zinc-alumina catalyst at temperatures of 400° to 500°F.

The next step in the process is the removal of carbon dioxide from the gas stream. A number of processes have been used, all based on the scrubbing of the gas with various solvents. One of the popular processes uses ethanolamines which have a high solubility for carbon dioxide. The process is relatively simple, consisting of countercurrent extraction in the absorber and subsequent regeneration of the ethanolamines in a reactivator by steam stripping and heating.

Before the synthesis gas is sent to the ammonia converter, the carbon dioxide and carbon monoxide content must be reduced to very low levels. In the widely used methanation process, carbon dioxide and carbon monoxide are reacted with hydrogen over a nickel catalyst to form methane and water.

After the previous steps, the gas mixture consists of the proper ratio of hydrogen and nitrogen and is ready for the ammonia-synthesis process. The synthesis gas must be compressed for the ammonia reaction, and the newer plants use centrifugal compressors. The more economical centrifugal compressors can be driven by electric motors, gas turbines, or steam turbines. Pressure of 600 psig is used in the modern 1000- to 1500-tpd plants.

In the new plants of 600 tpd and larger, all of the compressors are centrifugal including both the process air and ammonia refrigerant compressors. Pressures in the ammonia converter have historically covered a wide range from 100 to 1000 atm. The ammonia synthesis is generally carried out at a temperature of about 950°F over an iron oxide catalyst promoted by aluminum oxide, potassium oxide, calcium oxide, and/or magnesium oxide.

The size of the ammonia converters has increased dramatically in recent years and 1000 tpd single-train units are now common with a few 1500 tpd plants now onstream. At the other extreme, small skid-mounted converters with a capacity of 30 tpd are also available.

The reaction of hydrogen and nitrogen in the presence of a catalyst to form ammonia is highly exothermic and means must be provided in the converter for dissipating the excess heat generated in the system. Starting in the mid-1970s, the pressure toward, and incentives for, increased energy efficiency have resulted in design innovations that will be beneficial in conservation of energy. These generally consist of improved heat transfer for steam generation and a series of small improvements in the efficiency of various components in the system.

Liquid ammonia is withdrawn from a separator at about 20°F. The ammonia stream is passed to a flash drum where the pressure is reduced to about 14 atm. In the flash drum, dissolved inerts are flashed and vented. Product ammonia from the flash drum is passed into a weighing tank and then into storage or transportation lines or vessels for shipment (McVickar, 1966; Noyes, 1967; Sittig, 1965; Slack and James, 1979; Anon., 1979). Fig 1 is a diagram of the Kellogg ammonia process.

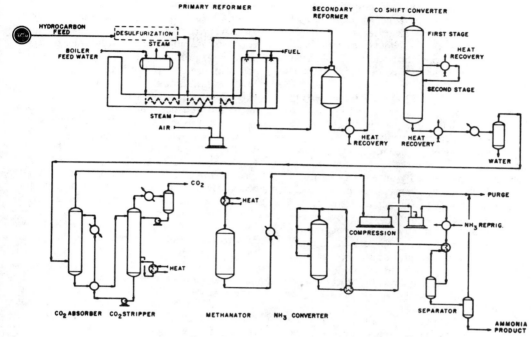

FIG. 1—*The Kellogg ammonia process (courtesy of the M.W. Kellogg Co.).*

Production of Nitric Acid

Ammonia and air are the raw materials in all modern plants for the manufacture of nitric acid. Gaseous ammonia is mixed with air and converted to nitric oxide in a high-temperature reaction which is usually catalyzed by a noble metal catalyst. The conversion reaction is rapid and essentially complete with about 96% conversion of ammonia to nitric oxide.

Next, the nitric oxide is further oxidized with air to form nitrogen dioxide which is then dissolved in water in a specially designed absorption tower to produce nitric acid of 52 to 64% concentration. There is an increasing demand for concentrated, about 98%, nitric acid. Early methods to produce concentrated acid used dehydrating agents such as sulfuric acid or magnesium. Some newer methods produce high-concentration nitric acid directly by oxidation of ammonia with oxygen or air. In the new methods used to produce high-concentration acid, the option of producing dilute acid also can be included.

Although the basic chemistry of the nitric acid processes is the same, there are several different processes which are used and there is a constant effort within the industry to lower capital and production cost and to improve energy efficiency. Nearly all nitric acid plants in the US are of the high-pressure (7 atm) type for conversion and absorption. In Europe and some other areas most nitric acid plants are of the low-pressure type or operate at low pressure for oxidation and high or medium pressure for absorption. The high-pressure (7 atm) design saves considerably on investment because of the smaller equipment. Conversion is more efficient in a larger catalyst bed at atmospheric pressure.

One widely used process is the Chemical Construction (Chemico) process. In the past Chemico has designed and installed low and medium-pressure nitric acid plants, but the more recent plants operate at what is called high pressure, 7 atm. Air is compressed in the oxidation section and about 80% of the hot compressed air is filtered and mixed with superheated and filtered ammonia vapor. The ammonia and air mixture flows to the ammonia burner where it passes through a series of platinum-rhodium catalyst gauzes which convert the ammonia to nitric oxide. Hot gases leave the burner at 1650°F and pass through a number of heat exchangers before entering the absorption tower. Nitrogen dioxide, which is formed on cooling, is absorbed in the water and weak acid of the absorption tower. Pure steam condensate ordinarily is used as feed water. The nitric acid produced is then contacted with compressed air to remove dissolved oxides before going to storage. Tail gas leaving the tower is under pressure and can be used to provide most of the energy for the air compressor and to generate additional steam.

The major power consumer in a high-pressure nitric acid plant is the air compressor, which can be operated by an electric motor, a steam turbine, or by a gas turbine. If a gas turbine is used and the tail gas utilized, there is a saving in power but an increase in investment. There is also a reduction in steam consumption that can be used in other processes. Several options in energy utilization and recovery systems for nitric acid plants are available.

The nitric acid industry was hit hard in meeting environmental standards for emissions of oxides of nitrogen (NO_x). After experimentation and limited experience with catalytic combustion and ion exchange, the predominant effective control by the late 1970s was "extended absorption," essentially a smaller second stage of absorption.

The relative importance of nitric acid worldwide as an intermediate for production of ammonium nitrate fertilizer continues to decrease as urea dominates in new facilities. It is used in substantial amounts in the production of ammonium nitrate for use in blasting agents, and for explosives and a variety of industrial chemicals (Anon., 1979).

Production of Urea

Urea is synthesized when ammonia and carbon dioxide combine in an exothermic reaction to form ammonium carbamate and in a subsequent reaction, which is endothermic, the ammonium carbamate is dehydrated to form urea and water. The urea process is credited as being the first industrial application of organic synthesis from inorganic chemicals.

In a typical plant the reaction takes place at about 4000 to 5000 psi and 400°F. Reactor effluent containing excess ammonia and a portion of the unconverted carbamate is reduced to a pressure of about 250 psi and flashed in a primary decomposer. The residual liquid is then heated to decompose most of the remaining carbamate to ammonia and carbon dioxide for recycling to the process. Gases from the flash stage and the carbamate decomposition are combined and sent to a primary absorber for recovery of the reactants. To minimize the formation of biuret, an undesirable urea decomposition product, the residence time at elevated temperature in the primary decomposer is held to a minimum.

The aqueous urea solution is further depressurized and heated in a secondary decomposer at atmospheric pressure to achieve the optimum recovery of ammonia and carbon dioxide. The vacuum flash reduces the temperature of the urea solution to further inhibit biuret formation. The off-gas from the primary decomposer is contacted in countercurrent flow with an aqueous ammonia solution in the primary absorber to recover all of the carbon dioxide and a portion of the ammonia for recycle to the reactor. After all of the carbon dioxide is removed, the bulk of the ammonia is condensed with cooling tower water without additional compression or refrigeration.

Inert gases introduced with the carbon dioxide feed stream leave the top of the absorber and pass through the wash tower where they are scrubbed with the process water used in the primary absorber for final recovery of a small amount of ammonia. The overhead vapors from the secondary decomposer and flash tower are sent to the secondary absorber where they are absorbed in a water solution.

The aqueous urea solution from the synthesis unit has a concentration of about 75%. It can be used at that concentration for preparation of urea-ammonium nitrate solution, but for most uses is concentrated, by evaporation, to about 99.5% urea melt. The steam-heated evaporators operate under vacuum to lower the operating temperature and are designed for a short retention of urea to minimize the formation of undesirable biuret. Stainless steel or similar alloys are used for construction of the falling-film or forced-circulation types of evaporators. A flow diagram of a typical urea synthesis process is shown in Fig. 2.

The 99+% concentrated urea solution or melt is formed into small round pellets called prills in most facilities. The concentrated melt is sprayed downward from a spinning perforated basket or from shower-head sprays at the top of towers 60 to 100 ft tall. The droplets of urea-melt cool and solidify as they fall through upward moving air from large fans. The product is cooled and the small proportion of offsize prills is removed by screening and redissolved or remelted. Since urea is hygroscopic, the product is treated with a surface

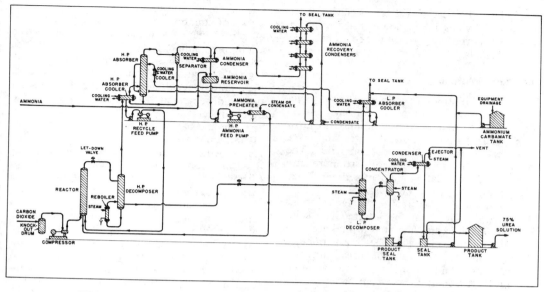

FIG. 2—*Typical total-recycle urea process* (*TVA plant*) (*Anon., 1979*).

coating or a chemical additive to minimize caking.

During the 1970s processes were commercialized for the production of urea in granular form by spray-drum granulation (*spherodizing*) and by inclined-pan granulation. Granules have the advantages of greater crushing strength (hardness) as compared with prills and the granulation processes can be readily controlled to produce granules that are much larger than prills. The larger granules are desired for aerial application on forests and for other uses.

There were no major improvements in the basic urea synthesis process in most of the 1970s, but engineering firms and process designers developed innovations late in the decade to decrease energy consumption and in some cases to increase production capability. These innovations are mainly related to designs for improved heat transfer and for more efficient pumps, motors, etc. (Anon., 1979; Young, 1974; McCamy and Norton, 1977; Anon., 1980c).

Production of Ammonium Nitrate

Nitric acid (HNO_3) and ammonia (NH_3) are the intermediates needed for the production of ammonium nitrate. It has been produced industrially since before World War I; its main use then was in munitions. The importance of ammonium nitrate and its production increased sharply after its use as a good high-analysis fertilizer was demonstrated in the United States and Europe in the early 1950s.

Production of ammonium nitrate is not particularly difficult. It consists of (1) neutralization of nitric acid with anhydrous ammonia, (2) concentration of the solution to either 96% or 99+% by evaporation, and (3) forming the product into prills or granules.

There are a number of designs of systems for neutralization and concentration. They all take into account the potential explosive hazard of ammonium nitrate, so temperatures and retention of material at high temperature are minimized. Care also is exercised to prevent contamination with oils and other organic materials that can sensitize ammonium nitrate to detonation.

Concentrators are operated under vacuum like those described earlier for urea. Prilling also is by far the main method used for forming ammonium nitrate, and design and operation are about the same as described earlier for urea. Spherodizing and pan granulation of ammonium nitrate came into the commercial picture during the 1970s (Young and McCamy, 1967; Young, 1980).

Ammonium nitrate is produced in two prilled forms: (1) *high-density prills* made from 99+% melt in a short prill tower (60 ft) for fertilizer and other industrial uses, and (2) *low-density prills* made from 95–96% solution in a tall (100–110 ft) prill tower. Porosity is provided by voids in the low-density prills to facilitate incorporation of oil added to produce blasting agents.

Nitrogen Solutions

Nitrogen solutions containing various combinations of urea, ammonium nitrate, and in some cases ammonia, have continued to grow in popularity in the United States and to a lesser extent in a few other countries. The greatest use of these solutions (nonpressure type) is in formulating fluid mixed fertilizers and for direct application.

Urea-ammonium nitrate (UAN) solutions are usually made from the intermediate solutions produced as the first step in making urea and ammonium nitrate. The most popular combination is a mixture of urea and ammonium nitrate in proportion to give maximum solubility. It contains by weight about 45% ammonium nitrate, 35% urea, and 20% water. Its crystallization (salting-out) temperature is 32°F and it contains 32% nitrogen. Solutions of 30 and 28% nitrogen content can be handled at temperatures below freezing (Hignett, 1971; Anon., 1979).

Ammonium Sulfate

Ammonium sulfate continues as an important industrial chemical product and in some countries remains important as a fertilizer for direct application. The main source of ammonium sulfate is byproduct material from the coke oven gas and steel industries. It also is produced from ammonia and sulfuric acid, although the cost usually is higher than for byproduct ammonium sulfate. When ammonium sulfate is produced directly, ammonia and sulfuric acid react to form the product which is crystallized from solution. The ammonium sulfate crystals can be recovered by recycling a side stream of the reaction solution through centrifuges, or the ammonium sulfate crystals can be collected batchwise for centrifuging. The crystals are usually washed with ammonia or water and dried in a rotary drum dryer and then screened before being put in bulk storage or bagged.

More refined types of crystallizers are used to grow large "grains of rice" crystals that are preferred for bulk blending with other fertilizer materials and for direct application.

Another major source of byproduct ammonium sulfate since the 1960s is from the process for production of caprolactam, an in-

termediate used in production of nylon. About 4 tons of ammonium sulfate is obtained per ton of caprolactam produced. In some cases the ammonium sulfate is fed directly to a fertilizer process as a 40% solution rather than preparing solid product. When produced as a solid, the ammonium sulfate is crystallized from solution and separated by centrifuging as in the other processes.

A method has been used for the manufacture of ammonium sulfate from gypsum ($CaSO_4 \cdot 2H_2O$) which, in the finely divided state, is agitated in a concentrated solution of ammonium carbonate formed by introducing ammonia and carbon dioxide into the aqueous medium. Calcium carbonate precipitates and ammonium sulfate remains in solution. Ammonium sulfate can then be obtained by the standard procedures. This process is not economically suitable for operation in the United States. It has found limited use in other countries where sulfur is not readily available or is very expensive.

Ammonium sulfate is a particularly good fertilizer for paddy rice. It is superior to ammonium nitrate and sometimes measurably better than urea, depending on application methods and water management practices. Another substantial use for ammonium sulfate is as an additive to supply nitrogen in fermentation processes. Much smaller amounts are used in medicinal and industrial chemical applications (Anon., 1979).

Ammonium Phosphates

Ammonium phosphates are generally classified as phosphates rather than nitrogen compounds. However, since these compounds contain 11 to 18% nitrogen (46–54% P_2O_5) and are so important in the world as fertilizers, they are covered here.

The ammonium phosphates are in two main forms, monoammonium phosphate (MAP) and diammonium phosphate (DAP). They were of comparatively minor importance until the simple and dependable process for their production for use as fertilizers from economical materials was developed and introduced to industry by the Tennessee Valley Authority (TVA) in 1961. By 1970, ammonium phosphate production had grown rapidly to become the leading phosphate fertilizer in the United States and reached this status in the world by the mid-1970s.

The first industrial production of ammonium phosphates was as compounds made in crystalline form from high purity phosphoric acid and ammonia. Later, there was some production of crystalline ammonium phosphates as by-products from the coke-oven gas and steel industries that were used mainly as fertilizers. The TVA process, which is easily adaptable to production of either DAP or MAP, utilizes much lower cost and more readily available "wet-process" phosphoric acid. The wet-process acid is made by acidulating pulverized phosphate rock with sulfuric acid followed by filtration and concentration. It is the major phosphate intermediate for fertilizer production. Partial neutralization of the acid with ammonia in a single reactor is a simple operation. The remaining ammonia is fed during granulation in a conventional rotary drum of the type widely used in industry. Product drying, cooling, and sizing are conventional steps. The granules do not require conditioning and have excellent bulk and bagged storage and transporting properties. Diammonium phosphate (18% N and 46% P_2O_5) is most popular, but production and use of monoammonium phosphate (12% N and 53% P_2O_5) is growing (Young, 1962; Young and Hicks, 1967; Anon., 1979).

As is the case with most fertilizer and other chemical processes, the main improvements in granular ammonium phosphate production starting in the mid-1970s were directed toward energy conservation and lower capital investment. A main innovation in ammonium phosphate and NPK fertilizer granulation units is the comparatively simple pipe reactor for acid(s) and ammonia. Effective use of the heat of reaction evaporates most of the water in the acid and drying of the product is eliminated or decreased substantially. Total investment is lower for new plants with pipe reactors and environmental controls are simpler. At the end of 1980, there were about 35 pipe-reactor installations in operation or nearing completion. Seven are in countries other than the United States (Achorn and Salladay, 1976; Shields, 1975).

Nonsynthetic Sources of Nitrogen

Biological Nitrogen Fixation

It has been known for many years that certain types of bacteria are capable of producing fixed nitrogen directly from elemental nitrogen. Total world biological nitrogen fixation was estimated at 100 million tpy (Postgate, 1971). The mechanisms of bacterial fixation have intrigued scientists for years, and for good reason. The biological nitrogen fixation takes place at atmospheric pressure and ambient temperature while the present synthetic processes take place at high temperatures and pressures and require large amounts of energy. If scientists are able to understand and duplicate the process of bacterial nitrogen fixation, major changes possibly could result in the fixed nitrogen industry.

There is a symbiotic relationship between members of the bacterial genus Rhizobium and leguminous plants. Some of the most familiar of the legumes include alfalfas, clovers, peas, beans, lupines, soybeans, and cowpeas; and nitrogen-fixing bacteria are found, for the most part, in nodules on the roots of the leguminous plants. Botanists estimate that there are from 10,000 to 12,000 species of leguminous plants, most of which are found in the tropics. About 200 species are cultivated by man and about 50 species are grown commercially in the United States. The planting and plowing under of legumes was recommended in the United States in many areas until about 1950 as a major practice in nitrogen fertilization.

In addition to the rhizobia, some types of free-living bacteria are capable of nitrogen fixation. Most of these bacteria occur in shallow muddy ponds or estuarine muds, or in environments with a relatively high content of organic matter. Estimates indicate that no more than 6 lb of nitrogen per acre is added to the soil each year through the combined activities of free-living nitrogen-fixing microorganisms.

There is evidence that more than a dozen species of blue-green algae are capable of direct nitrogen fixation. The algae occur in almost every environmental situation where sufficient sunlight is available for photosynthesis, including barren rock surfaces and frozen wastelands. They form symbiotic relationships with a variety of organisms, the most important being the lichen fungi. The blue-green algae may play an important role in the nitrogen economy of rice soils in India and in the Peoples Republic of China; for example, the ability to produce at least a modest yield of rice on the same land for many years without applying nitrogen fertilizer is believed to be due to nitrogen fixation by algae.

There are other bacteria which cause denitrification, a process just the opposite of nitrogen fixation, and the gaseous loss of nitrogen from soil. Biological denitrification is of considerable importance in well-drained and actively nitrifying soils which become partially anaerobic during wet periods, or through additions of large quantities of decomposable organic matter. The ability to reduce nitrates and nitrites to gaseous products fortunately appears to be limited to a relatively few bacteria (Postgate, 1971; Sauchelli, 1964).

Production of Nitrogen Compounds from Coke-Oven Gases

Coal carbonized at high temperature releases fixed nitrogen in the form of ammonia, which coke-oven operators recover as anhydrous ammonia, aqua ammonia, ammonium sulfate, or diammonium phosphate. The ammonia must be removed from the gas prior to further processing; otherwise it would form corrosive salts which would damage equipment or, if released as a waste material, would create pollution problems.

The ammonia formed during coking exists in both the water and gas that form part of the volatile products. The recovery of this ammonia can be accomplished by several methods. The most widely used method is called the semidirect process in which the ammonia in the liquor produced during coal carbonization is removed by distillation and alkali treatment and added to the gas stream. Then the gas containing all of the ammonia is passed through an absorber containing dilute sulfuric acid that reacts with the ammonia.

In an Otto-type ammonia absorber, coke-oven gas enters near the bottom and is sprayed with a dilute solution of sulfuric acid as it rises to the top. Ammonia in the gas reacts with the acid to form ammonium sulfate. The resulting solution drains into a crystallizer from which it is recirculated to the absorber, and a constant flow of sulfuric acid is added to the ammonia absorber to replace the acid neutralized by the ammonia in the coke-oven gas. After the solution becomes supersaturated, crystals of ammonium sulfate are precipitated in the crystallizer and accumulate as a slurry in the bottom. A portion of this slurry is removed and pumped to the slurry tank where the salt settles and the liquid overflows and returns to the ammonia absorber. The concentrated slurry is withdrawn from the bottom of the tank and is fed continuously or in batches to centrifuges that spin at high speed to separate and dewater the crystals. The partially dried ammonium sulfate is conveyed to heated rotary-drum dryers for final drying to a moisture content of about 0.1%.

Another process used for the recovery of ammonia is the Wilputte process for producing ammonium sulfate. Coke-oven gas is passed through a spray-type absorber over which is circulated a 6% solution of sulfuric acid nearly saturated with ammonium sulfate. Leaving the absorber, the solution is delivered to the solution-circulating system of a crystallizer in which crystallization takes place by the combined cooling and concentration effects of vacuum evaporation. By variation of the circulating rate and the degree of concentration, the size range of the ammonium sulfate crystals can be controlled within narrow limits. As the crystals grow in size, they settle to the bottom of the suspension tank and are delivered to a continuous centrifuge or filter, followed in either case by a dryer, as in the other processes. Essentially all of the byproduct ammonium sulfate produced is sold for use as fertilizer (McGannon, 1971; Sauchelli, 1964).

In the US Steel "Phosam" process, coke-oven gas is treated to recover anhydrous ammonia as the product. After the gas has passed through coolers and conventional gas cleaning equipment which removes entrained solids, water, and tar, ammonia is scrubbed from the gas by countercurrent contact with low-pH ammonium phosphate solution. Gas leaves the top of the absorber with 98 to 99% of the ammonia removed.

The ammonia-rich solution from the absorber is pumped through heat exchangers and into the stripper, recovering heat enroute. In the stripper the solution is contacted with steam at elevated pressure, stripping out the absorbed ammonia and regenerating the lean solution. The lean solution (low pH) is cooled and returned to the absorber. The overhead vapor from the stripper is condensed to form an aqueous ammonia feed to the fractionator where anhydrous ammonia is produced by steam fractionization. All the ammonia recovered is normally produced as liquid anhydrous ammonia, although gaseous ammonia can be produced if desired.

Deposits of Natural Nitrates

Deposits of natural nitrates, primarily the sodium and potassium salts, occur in the United States, Mexico, South Africa, Egypt, and Chile. The Chilean deposits of natural nitrates are the only deposits of commercial significance with estimated reserves of 200 million tons. The Chilean deposits and mining operations have been described in several publications (Anon., 1964; Graham, 1949; Sauchelli, 1964).

These naturally occurring inorganic nitrates were an important source of nitrate for fertilizers and explosives in the western hemisphere until about 1930. Their history of use goes back about 150 years. At one time the Chilean nitrates accounted for 40% of world nitrogen production. As production of synthetic nitrogen grew, their importance has waned. Total world production of Chilean nitrates in 1980 was only about 90,000 tons of nitrogen, a very small fraction of total world nitrogen production of 60 million tons. Although quite unimportant in the total fertilizer picture, these naturally occurring nitrates still are preferred for specific crops in some locations.

The nitrate fields in Chile are situated in the northern desert regions of the country in an area covering approximately 20,000 km^2. Several theories have been put forward to explain the origin of these deposits, and it seems likely that the nitrate content was derived from several sources including electrical discharge, atmospheric oxidation, and the action of nitrifying bacteria. After the formation of the nitrate, a secondary process peculiar to the area was probably responsible for concentrating the salts into economically workable deposits.

The nitrate-bearing ore is known as caliche. It is a hard rock-like layer varying from 0.5 to 5 m in thickness and occurring 1 to 3 m below the surface of the soil. In addition to a sodium nitrate content of from 5 to over 20%, caliche also contains chlorides, sulfates, borates, and iodates, as well as other salts. Certain of the deposits also contain potassium in workable amounts.

The mining and processing of the deposits is by the state-owned Sociedad Quimica y Minera de Chile SA (SQM), which operates two major plants having a combined capacity of up to 800,000 tons of product per year. The two production sites, Pedro de Valdivia and Maria Elena, are near the port of Tocopilla.

Open cast mining methods are used to remove the crude ore from the ground. The overburden is stripped away and the caliche is then blasted free and transported by electric railway to the processing plant. Here crushing and sieving are the primary operations and the screened caliche is then conveyed to extracting tanks, using water. The extraction process depends on the differing water solubilities of the salts present in the ore. By dissolving them as far as possible, the insoluble or slightly soluble substances such as clay or gypsum can be separated, and sodium chloride also can be largely eliminated. Fractional crystallization leads to the various salts being separated by centrifuges. A fine crystalline powder is the end result, and since this had a tendency to cake during storage, the product is melted and prilled in large towers similar to those used for ammonium nitrate and urea.

Various methods of processing the Chilean nitrate have evolved over the years, with the object of increasing the yield and decreasing the cost of operation. Solar energy makes a very real contribution to fuel requirements. Huge evaporation ponds are used to concentrate the weaker nitrate solutions. By this means economies can be made, since thousands of tons of fuel oil would otherwise be needed. Further work along these lines is continuing, with the objective of further use of solar energy and more efficient overall heat utilization.

Chilean nitrate is used primarily as a fertilizer for particular crops and in particular agronomic situations. Sugar beets, for example, have a definite sodium demand if maximum yields are to be obtained, and in European countries the sugarbeet crop is a major user of Chilean nitrate. Use in the United States is primarily limited to tobacco and cotton fertilization in the south Atlantic states.

Sodium nitrate is widely used in the explosives industry, especially in the manufacture of slurry and gel explosives and also in the production of SANFO, a mixture of sodium nitrate, ammonium nitrate, and fuel oil (Anon., 1980).

Although world production of Chilean nitrate was only about 90,000 tons of nitrogen in 1980 with 13,000 tons consumed in the United States, this naturally occurring material continues to be of some world significance and its export is important to the economy of Chile.

Ecology

Some controversy has developed concerning the possible accumulation of nitrate in soil, water, and plants. Some environmentalists and ecologists claim that we are faced with a crisis from the use of commercial nitrogen fertilizers and the release of nitrogen oxides by high temperature combustion in power plants and internal combustion engines.

The US Dept. of Agriculture published a report in 1971, giving an appraisal on the accumulation of nitrate (Viets and Hageman, 1971). The authors concluded that, on the basis of available information, the potential for nitrate accumulation does not pose a threat of an environmental crisis, and there is no indication of widespread upward trends of nitrate concentrations in foods, feeds, surface or ground water. The report concluded that the levels of nitrate currently found in foods pose no major health hazard to human adults, but, in isolated instances, the nitrate content of water and foods has been toxic to infants. In some of the cases, the toxicity resulted from microbial contamination that converted nitrate to nitrite. Future cases can be eliminated by more extensive testing for nitrate in water and foods consumed by humans. These findings generally have been substantiated in later studies.

A comprehensive research program is underway at the Tennessee Valley Authority (TVA) National Fertilizer Development Center at Muscle Shoals, Alabama, to study the fate of nitrogen fertilizers applied to the soil. Fertilizer nitrogen-soil interactions are being studied in cooperation with land-grant universities to determine effects on the environment and efficiency of nitrogen use for crop production.

To isolate the fertilizer nitrogen from that already present in nature, the scientists *tag* the fertilizer nitrogen by changing its isotope composition. In nature, nitrogen is composed of one Nitrogen-15 atom for every 273 Nitrogen-14 atoms.

TVA makes fertilizers with "depleted" material, in which the proportion of Nitrogen-14 and Nitrogen-15 is very different from that in the soils, plants, waters, and other natural substances. When this nonradioactive tagged fertilizer is added to the soil and taken up by the plant, the isotope composition of the plant changes. Then the amount of nitrogen in the plant that came from the fertilizer can be measured by instrumental analysis (mass spectrometry). Or the amount of fertilizer nitrogen in the drainage water can be determined. How much of the fertilizer remains in the soil, how far it moves in the soil, or whether some of it is available for plant use the next growing season can be determined.

TVA research scientists point out that "tracer" technology has not identified all the problems, nor has it helped develop many solutions as yet. But nitrogen tracers have given more accurate information about nitrogen in the biosphere and have proven to be valuable tools in tracing the movement of nitrogen. This in turn will help in the long-range search for ways to improve efficiency of plants in their use of nitrogen and, as a consequence, will help protect the quality of the environment (Anon., 1976).

Besides making tagged nitrogen fertilizers available to university scientists, the TVA program helps graduate students and senior researchers gain experience in using the nitrogen isotopes. University students and professors work in the nitrogen isotope laboratories at Muscle Shoals for periods of a few days to several months for training and experience.

Much work remains to be done to better determine the fate of soluble nitrogen in fertilizers and to assess any effect on our environment. But work underway at several locations is beginning to provide some answers.

Recent Changes in Design and Production Capacity of Manufacturing Processes

Since about 1975 there have been no major breakthroughs in basic process designs for ammonia, urea, nitric acid, and ammonium nitrate. There have been a number of improvements related mainly to conservation of energy and emphasis will continue in this area well into the 1980s. Some innovations have resulted in decreases of 15 to 30% in energy consumption for various processes without major changes in the basic processes. A large nitrogen fertilizer complex due to come onstream in Canada in 1985 will have several energy saving innovations. The total natural gas consumption per ton of NH_3 will be 25 to 26 million Btu's as compared with an average of 33 million Btu's in existing plants. Together with other features, this will cut total energy requirements by 16% (Anon., 1981e). Use of a physical solvent in CO_2 removal and recovery greatly decreases the heat required for regeneration.

Changes in various facilities include a series of minor modifications that allow greater recovery and use of process heat. Also, changes in pumps and compressors to combine some duties have decreased utility requirements. Engineering rationalization of the use of process-generated steam drivers in a complete production complex concept rather than piecemeal has also lowered energy requirements. Efforts in this direction will continue as energy costs increase.

There also have been important developments in the control of atmospheric emissions and aqueous effluents within required limits. In a number of cases this has been accomplished without massive expenditures by the application of sound engineering and practical judgment. One of the main problem areas is keeping the emission of brown oxides of nitrogen fumes from nitric acid plants within required limits. After trial of costlier and more difficult schemes, the technique of "extended absorption" has generally proved best. This involves use of a second, shorter absorption stage operating with cooled, dilute-process liquid.

Impoundment and reuse of process and cooling water has necessitated soundly engineered systems and tight operating controls for meeting essentially "zero discharge" of pollutants and limited heat in effluent water. In production units for prilled or granular urea and ammonium nitrate, dust collection is now required. A major step has been the successful use of bag filter units for dust collection. Good design and rigid operating discipline are keys to the use of these very effective collectors.

Product quality has been improved substantially by development of new or modified process schemes for preparation of finished solid urea and ammonium nitrate products. Pan granulation allows a wider range of particle sizes and better quality of products. This system is used in a few commercial plants. "Spray-drum" granulation (spherodizing) is used in several plants. A recent development is TVA's new "curtain-granulation" process that was demonstrated in a 2-tph pilot plant in late 1980. A decrease of about 40% in energy requirements for cooling is realized and very hard spherical product with an unlimited selection of particle size range is produced (Anon., 1980c).

By the mid-1970s the move to larger production units had leveled off, and the more-or-less standard size for large units now is 1000 tpd for ammonia, with a companion 1520-tpd plant for urea. Ammonium nitrate units had already leveled off at 900 to 1100 tpd. A few ammonia plants have been built for capacity of 1500 tpd, but most engineering firms are not venturing into this area. A major factor is the continuing sharp escalation in the investments required for production units. Units of 1500-tpd capacity put even greater pressure on the operation at a high percentage of the time (90% or more) to control the investment-related costs per ton of product. Depending on feedstock costs, investment costs can represent more than half of the total production cost.

World Review

There have been dramatic changes in nitrogen fertilizer production and trade patterns. A much greater interdependence among regions has developed with countries no longer isolated from world market trends as they were 20 years ago. These changes are indicated by the production, consumption, and trade statistics for the major regions presented in Table 1. In 1980, for the fertilizer year ending June 30, Asia and East Europe were the leading consumers of nitrogen fertilizers. Both of these regions have increased nitrogen consumption at a faster rate than North America and West Europe—the leading nitrogen use areas in

1967. Table 1 also indicates production and use statistics for developed, developing, and the Central Planned Economies of East Europe, USSR, and the Peoples Republic of China (PRC). The developed countries remain net exporters of nitrogen fertilizers. The developing countries, while increasing fertilizer use at a rapid rate, have done so by increasing their dependence on imported materials. The Central Planned Economies remain largely self-sufficient, with the exception of large nitrogen imports by the PRC.

Total world nitrogen use was estimated to be about 57 Mt of N in 1980. From 1967 to 1980, world nitrogen use increased at an average rate of more than 7% per year. By 1985, world use is expected to exceed 70 Mt of N—an average growth of about 4% per year. This lower average annual increase reflects the maturing of the nitrogen market as application rates on major agricultural and cash crops come closer to optimum rates given today's crop varieties, management levels, and commodity prices.

In 1967, world ammonia plant capacity was just under 37 Mt of nitrogen. By 1980 total world ammonia capacity had increased to more than 92 million tons and indications are that capacity will exceed 110 million tons by 1985 (Table 2).

World nitrogen fertilizer production is dominated by urea and ammonium nitrate. The remainder consists of ammonium sulfate, and other lower analysis materials such as calcium and sodium nitrate, along with ammonia for direct application and in combination with phosphate and potash materials. Urea has emerged as the leading nitrogen fertilizer material in many parts of the world. Capacity is about 34 million tons of nitrogen—an increase of more than 27 million tons since 1967. Ammonium nitrate capacity doubled during the same period but should increase very little as compared to the continued expansion in urea capacity over the next five years.

Most nitrogen production has been located in the developed regions: North America, West Europe, and Japan. However, the rapidly changing world energy supply situation and rising energy costs are shifting the location of nitrogen supplies. As indicated in Table 3, natural gas is the most common feedstock for ammonia production. Developed regions, however, account for less than 20% of total world reserves while the developing regions are estimated to control almost half of all natural gas reserves. The share of world ammonia capacity in the developing regions is less than

**TABLE 1—World Nitrogen Fertilizer Production, Trade, and Consumption
by Region
Mt, N**

Region		1966-1967	1972-1973	1977-1978	1979-1980	Forecast 1984-1985 [#]
North America	Production	6.02	9.20	11.07	12.86	—
	Export*	0.87	1.16	2.55	3.32	—
	Import	0.63	0.64	1.79	2.48	—
	Consumption	5.74	7.92	9.74	11.15	13.07
Latin America	Production	0.50	0.84	1.33	1.50	—
	Export	0.21	0.27	0.18	0.20	—
	Import	0.53	1.07	1.41	0.14	—
	Consumption	0.81	1.63	2.52	2.67	4.07
Western Europe	Production	7.03	8.95	9.73	11.25	—
	Export	2.65	2.83	3.36	3.96	—
	Import	0.83	1.44	2.15	2.65	—
	Consumption	5.02	6.99	8.36	9.54	10.05
East Europe-USSR	Production	5.07	10.68	15.09	15.51	—
	Export	0.24	1.27	2.35	2.37	—
	Import	0.33	0.45	0.30	0.33	—
	Consumption	4.76	9.29	12.11	12.45	15.00
Africa	Production	0.24	0.55	0.77	0.84	—
	Export	—	0.03	0.06	0.04	—
	Import	0.32	0.65	0.64	0.71	—
	Consumption	0.55	1.06	1.33	1.52	2.27
Asia	Production	4.03	8.16	13.20	17.46	—
	Export	0.97	2.16	1.76	2.12	—
	Import	2.34	3.26	3.87	4.78	—
	Consumption	5.30	9.31	15.54	19.56	25.60
Oceania	Production	0.04	0.18	0.22	0.21	—
	Export	—	0.02	—	—	—
	Import	0.06	0.05	0.06	0.07	—
	Consumption	0.12	0.21	0.26	0.27	0.34
Developed Countries[†]	Production	15.09	21.17	3.33	26.73	—
	Export	4.45	5.72	6.85	8.16	—
	Import	1.62	2.20	4.07	5.34	—
	Consumption	12.06	16.47	19.85	22.60	25.60
Developing Countries[‡]	Production	1.29	3.86	6.23	8.12	—
	Export	0.23	0.75	1.09	1.51	—
	Import	2.01	3.50	4.27	5.24	—
	Consumption	2.98	6.39	9.59	11.33	15.90
Central Planned Economies[§]	Production	6.56	13.56	21.83	24.78	—
	Export	0.26	1.27	2.33	2.35	—
	Import	1.41	1.87	1.89	1.83	—
	Consumption	7.25	13.54	20.43	23.22	28.90
World	Production	22.95	38.58	51.39	59.64	—
	Trade	4.94	7.74	10.27	12.03	—
	Consumption	22.29	36.40	49.86	57.16	70.40

Source: Anon., 1968, 1974, 1980b, 1981c.
 * Export and import data for finished nitrogen products only and does not include anhydrous ammonia used for production of other fertilizer materials.
 † North America, West Europe, Oceania, Japan, Israel, and Republic of South Africa.
 ‡ Latin America, Africa excluding Republic of South Africa, and Asia excluding Japan, Israel, and Central Planned Economies.
 § East Europe, USSR, Peoples Republic of China, Vietnam, North Korea, and Mongolia.
 # Forecasts from Harris and Harre (1979) revised to reflect historical data revisions for USSR and China.

TABLE 2—World Nitrogen Fertilizer Product Capacity, By Region
Mt, N

Region	Product	1966-1967	1972-1973	1977-1978	1979-1980	Forecast 1984-1985
North America	Ammonia	11.08	14.03	18.47	17.66	18.88
	Ammonium Nitrate	2.88	3.00	3.47	3.70	3.70
	Urea	1.34	1.96	3.49	3.78	4.38
Latin America	Ammonia	1.02	1.76	3.54	4.03	6.84
	Ammonium Nitrate	0.23	0.26	0.44	0.44	0.54
	Urea	0.18	0.38	1.21	1.29	2.74
Western Europe	Ammonia	9.22	14.15	14.85	15.62	15.30
	Ammonium Nitrate	2.69	4.15	4.70	5.08	5.41
	Urea	1.36	3.45	4.52	5.00	5.41
East Europe-USSR	Ammonia	8.01	15.61	22.80	29.75	37.48
	Ammonium Nitrate	3.32	6.11	8.27	8.53	8.78
	Urea	1.96	4.78	7.83	9.83	12.91
Africa	Ammonia	0.35	0.93	1.21	1.83	3.14
	Ammonium Nitrate	0.04	0.21	0.34	0.66	0.79
	Urea	0.09	0.28	0.57	0.88	1.37
Asia	Ammonia	7.01	13.62	18.81	23.26	28.31
	Ammonium Nitrate	0.62	0.96	0.97	1.13	1.09
	Urea	2.33	5.43	10.02	13.78	17.34
Oceania	Ammonia	0.13	0.45	0.45	0.45	0.52
	Ammonium Nitrate	0.03	0.11	0.11	0.11	0.11
	Urea	0.12	0.10	0.10	0.10	0.18
Developed Countries	Ammonia	23.07	33.53	38.11	38.00	39.57
	Ammonium Nitrate	5.81	7.76	8.86	9.56	10.04
	Urea	3.80	7.58	9.99	10.26	11.57
Developing Countries	Ammonia	2.71	6.99	12.21	15.77	23.66
	Ammonium Nitrate	0.26	0.57	0.81	1.18	1.39
	Urea	1.01	3.27	7.36	10.29	14.61
Central Planned Economies	Ammonia	11.03	20.03	29.80	38.82	47.24
	Ammonium Nitrate	3.74	6.48	8.64	8.89	9.01
	Urea	2.58	5.54	10.38	14.10	18.15
World	Ammonia	36.82	60.55	80.12	92.59	110.46
	Ammonium Nitrate	9.81	14.80	18.31	19.63	20.43
	Urea	7.39	16.39	27.73	34.65	44.33

Source: Capacity data from the records of Marketing and Distribution Economics Section, Tennessee Valley Authority, National Fertilizer Development Center, Muscle Shoals, AL, May 1981.

20% of total world capacity, but will gain in the share of total capacity, as the developed nations continue to decline in relative importance.

This shift in nitrogen capacity to areas having large reserves of natural gas will mean an increasing level of nitrogen trade as greater amounts of ammonia are shipped to developed regions.

Transportation

Nearly all forms of transportation are used to move nitrogen fertilizer materials from production points to the market. Anhydrous ammonia is transported by barges, railroad tank cars, pipelines, transport trucks, and nurse tanks (Table 4). Large tonnages of anhydrous ammonia move by barge up the Mississippi River and along other inland waterways. Barge transportation is relatively low-cost for those areas having access to waterways. Barges for anhydrous ammonia are of two types: high-pressure (250 psig), capable of transporting anhydrous ammonia at ambient temperatures and a fairly high vapor pressure; and low-pressure (10 to 55 psig), with insulated storage tanks and mechanical refrigeration units to

TABLE 3—Estimated Proved Reserves of Natural Gas

Region	Natural Gas	Share of World Natural Gas Reserves	Share of Ammonia Capacity 1980	1985	Ammonia Capacity Based on Natural Gas (1980)
	(10^9 cu ft)	(%)	(%)	(%)	(%)
North America	278,300	11	19	18	96
Latin America	159,811	6	4	6	87
West Europe	157,815	6	17	14	67
East Europe	930,900	35	32	35	85
Africa	208,470	8	2	3	45
Asia	867,105	33	25	27	35
Oceania	36,100	1	—	—	42
Developed Countries	472,815	18	41	36	75
Developing Countries	1,210,286	46	17	21	58
Central Planned Economies	955,400	36	42	43	72
World	2,638,501	—	—	—	71

Source: Auldridge, 1980; and capacity data from the records of Marketing and Distribution Economics Section, Tennessee Valley Authority, National Fertilizer Development Center, Muscle Shoals, AL, April 1981.

keep the vapor pressure of the anhydrous ammonia below the maximum allowable design pressure.

Two types of rail tank cars are used in ammonia transport. Standard tank cars are of 11,000-gal capacty and transport 25 to 26 tons of liquid ammonia. These cars have an inner high-pressure (300 psig) tank covered by a layer of insulating material with an outer light steel shell. Jumbo tank cars of 30,000-gal, 70-ton capacity now move most of the rail-shipped ammonia. The jumbo tank cars have noninsulated tanks designed for 400 psig test pressure.

Anhydrous ammonia is also delivered through long-distance pipelines from major producing areas to major consuming areas. In the early 1970s Gulf Central placed in operation a 1700-mile-long pipeline system that carries liquid anhydrous ammonia from Louisiana to Iowa, Nebraska, Illinois, Indiana, Missouri, and other midwest consuming areas. The Gulf Central pipeline cost about $59,000 per mile and has a capacity of 3 million st per year. Gulf Central offers shippers the option of contract storage and has constructed refrigerated storage tanks at strategic points along the line.

A second long-distance anhydrous ammonia pipeline has been operating since 1967. Built by MidAmerica Pipeline Co. (MAPCO), it stretches 720 miles from Borger, Texas, to distribution points in Kansas, Nebraska, and Iowa. The MAPCO pipeline has a design capacity of 3,000 to 3,500 tpd.

A third ammonia pipeline in Florida with a capacity of 600,000 tpy began operation in December 1979. The capacity of the pipeline is leased by two phosphate fertilizer producers and extends from the partners' respective anhydrous ammonia terminals on Tampa Bay to their phosphate manufacturing complexes, as well as other manufacturing facilities in central Florida.

Nitrogen solutions containing 29% N are being transported by pipeline by the Williams Pipe Line Company of Tulsa, Oklahoma. The line extends from Tulsa into the midwest and north through Iowa, Minnesota, Nebraska, and North and South Dakota. Material can be accepted at three locations and unloading facilities are available at nine other locations. The minimum shipment is 6,000 tons and the carrier does not provide storage at either point of origin or destination. As petroleum products are shipped in the same line, shipments of nitro-

TABLE 4—Fertilizer Transportation by Mode, 1978, Percentage

Product	Rail	Truck	Water	Pipe-line
Anhydrous ammonia	27.2	42.8	11.7	18.3
Nitrogen solutions	19.8	45.4	23.8	11.0
Urea	46.2	25.6	28.2	—
Ammonium nitrate	66.6	33.4	—	—

Source: Anon., 1980a.

gen solutions in the winter months are scheduled only when temperatures and operating conditions are satisfactory and no damage will occur to the pipeline or the other products being transported. The route of the long-distance ammonia and nitrogen solutions pipelines in relation to US ammonia plant locations is shown in Fig. 3.

Highway transport trucks are still another means used for transporting anhydrous ammonia. These trucks are usually semitractor trailer rigs with high-pressure, 265 psig, tanks varying in size from 6000 to 9000 gal and which haul from 12 to 19 tons of anhydrous ammonia per trip. Some transport trucks are equipped with vapor compressors or liquid pumps for unloading. Other trucks have no pumping equipment and must be unloaded by pumps or compressors located at the receiving plant.

Barges, rail cars, and transport trucks are often used for both liquefied petroleum gas and ammonia service. For dual service, however, all fittings must be of steel and approved for ammonia service. For direct farm fertilizer applications, anhydrous ammonia is moved from the bulk plant or storage to the farmer's fields in high-pressure (up to 265 psig) tanks, usually 1000-gal capacity, mounted on heavy duty, two- or four-wheel wagons. Tanks are generally not filled to more than 85% of capacity as a safety precaution. A 1000-gal tank contains about 2.2 tons of ammonia.

In international trade, modern ships are designed to handle both liquefied petroleum gas and anhydrous ammonia. A typical vessel is designed for refrigeration down to −45° C to keep the vapor pressure of the cargo at a low level. World ammonia trade has increased from 1.7 Mt N in 1972 to an estimated 5.3 Mt N in 1980. Leading exporters include the United States, Mexico, Trinidad, Venezuela, the Middle East, and the USSR, which represents one-third of all ammonia exports.

United States: Production, Consumption, and Trade

Nitrogen Fertilizer Consumption

Total nitrogen fertilizer consumption in the United States has increased from 2.7 million st in 1960 to 11.4 million st in 1980—or four times the level of 20 years ago. The rate of increase in nitrogen use has been declining from an average of about 10% per year between 1960 and 1970 to slightly more than 4% from 1970 to 1980.

Marketing patterns for nitrogen fertilizers have changed dramatically since 1960 when mixed fertilizers accounted for 37% of total nitrogen use. In 1980, mixtures were down to 22% of total consumption. Direct application of ammonia increased from less than 600,000 tons N in 1960 to 4.5 million tons in 1980. Similar gains also have been made by nitrogen solutions and urea while lower analysis materials have either declined in tonnage or shown little gain. Ammonium nitrate use increased from 415,000 tons N in 1960 to a peak of 1.1 million tons in 1973. Since then use has slowly declined to just under 900,000 tons N in 1980. Consumption of nitrogen fertilizers as mixtures and materials over the past 20 years is shown in Table 5.

While consumption of most nitrogen fertilizers has increased or remained relatively stable over the past 20 years, there have been some dramatic changes in the share of the market for the major nitrogen materials. Anhydrous ammonia has moved from 20% of total nitrogen use in 1960 to almost 40% of today's market. Urea has increased from only 3% in 1970 to about 9% in 1980 and nitrogen solutions have expanded from 7% to more than 16% since 1960. The nitrogen in diammonium phosphate for direct application today represents more than 5% of total use compared to less than 1% in 1960. Losers in market share include ammonium nitrate, ammonium sulfate, and the dry mixed fertilizers containing nitrogen.

Nitrogen fertilizer consumption is centered primarily in two regions of the United States—the East and West North Central states. In 1980 almost 57% of all nitrogen use was in this area, which has 59% of the harvested acreage and 43% of the nation's total crop and livestock receipts. Nitrogen use in these two regions has increased at more than 10% per year for the past 20 years and still leads the country with a 5% average gain per year since 1970. The West South Central states and the Pacific Coast states are also large consumers of nitrogen fertilizers, followed by the South Atlantic and East South Central area. Regional use patterns for nitrogen fertilizers in the United States during the past 20 years are shown in Table 6.

Industrial Explosives

Consumption of explosives and blasting agents in the United States totaled 4.55 billion lb in 1980. In the past 20 years the use of explosives has increased at about the same annual

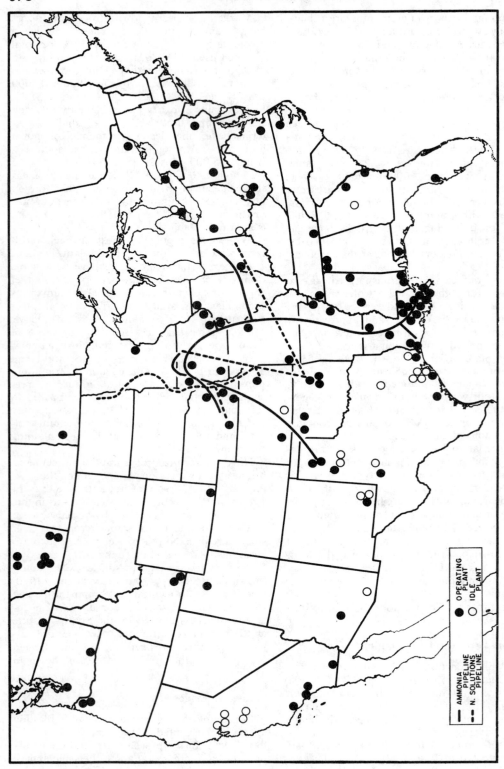

FIG. 3—*North American ammonia plants and pipeline systems, 1981.*

TABLE 5—Nitrogen Fertilizer Consumption in the US

| Year[†] | Nitrogen in Mixtures | Anhydrous Ammonia | Nitrogen Solutions | Direct Application Materials* St, N | | | Total | Total Nitrogen Consumption |
				Ammonium Nitrate	Urea	Ammonium Sulfate		
1960	1,017,415	581,924	194,740	415,855	64,596	106,959	1,720,632	2,738,047
1961	1,071,224	666,234	292,566	446,585	92,448	115,715	1,959,564	3,030,788
1962	1,147,266	767,425	371,379	468,523	132,804	116,687	2,222,714	3,369,980
1963	1,263,641	1,006,762	471,392	499,378	165,198	147,121	2,665,448	3,929,089
1964	1,377,033	1,148,071	526,755	555,320	184,327	148,865	2,975,776	4,352,809
1965	1,452,084	1,281,968	595,859	547,488	193,713	161,848	3,186,454	4,638,538
1966	1,591,927	1,606,872	712,445	610,705	211,615	165,797	3,734,376	5,326,303
1967	1,764,372	1,973,596	784,392	710,503	227,952	174,834	4,262,625	6,026,997
1968	1,867,091	2,457,261	803,092	786,346	243,359	167,306	4,920,474	6,787,565
1969	1,901,393	2,576,431	839,925	863,792	264,755	157,042	5,056,207	6,957,600
1970	1,939,077	2,844,058	969,882	952,861	242,758	160,911	5,519,927	7,459,004
1971	2,062,782	3,254,160	1,036,498	969,091	273,607	185,386	6,070,824	8,133,606
1972	2,131,639	2,982,274	1,009,119	1,015,548	357,386	192,205	5,890,627	8,022,266
1973	2,391,300	2,700,704	1,144,407	1,095,651	432,420	197,088	5,903,805	8,295,105
1974	2,431,387	3,427,672	1,184,507	1,061,743	467,934	193,025	6,725,821	9,157,208
1975	2,098,763	3,294,794	1,191,691	941,881	524,183	170,614	6,502,056	8,600,819
1976	2,417,282	4,025,258	1,620,308	985,555	729,250	219,760	7,994,302	10,411,584
1977	2,551,338	4,040,328	1,685,028	936,863	855,344	220,226	8,096,065	10,647,403
1978	2,374,999	3,721,289	1,591,935	820,356	880,753	188,208	7,589,620	9,964,619
1979	2,573,382	4,003,845	1,723,860	841,272	967,040	157,846	8,141,337	10,714,719
1980	2,501,355	4,499,947	1,908,917	884,718	946,359	175,566	8,898,153	11,399,508

Source: Anon., 1981a.

*Includes some materials reported prior to blending with phosphate and potash materials for delivery to farm.

[†]Fiscal year ending June 30.

growth rate as nitrogen fertilizers—7.0% per year vs. 7.4% for fertilizer. Unlike fertilizer use, the rate of increase has been maintained throughout the period and has averaged 6.6% from 1970 to 1980 and 7.4% per year from 1960 to 1970.

Coal mining remained the single largest consumer of industrial explosives accounting for 56% of total use in 1980. Use in other mining and construction declined in 1980 reflecting economic and market conditions. Consumption by major use category is shown in Table 7.

In 1979 seven states accounted for 59% of all explosives used in the United States. Kentucky was the leading market followed by Pennsylvania, Alabama, Arizona, Ohio, West Virginia, and Indiana.

Of the 4.55 billion lb of explosives used in 1980, half was unprocessed ammonium nitrate, while 36% was mixed ammonium nitrate-fuel blasting agents. The principal distinction between explosives and blasting agents is sensitivity to initiation. Explosives are cap-sensitive while blasting agents are not and require a primer.

Fertilizer Trade

Since 1960 US foreign trade in nitrogen fertilizer materials has grown in importance as world events have had an ever-increasing impact on the domestic nitrogen market. In the early 1960s the United States was a net importer of nitrogen; the trade balance however, seldom exceeded 200,000 tons of nitrogen in any given year. In 1966, the nation became a net exporter with annual trade balances reaching as high as 860,000 tons of nitrogen in 1969. This rapid rise in nitrogen exports was brought about by large surpluses in the United States and a worldwide program to increase food supplies in developing countries.

Between 1975 and 1979 the nation once again was a net importer of nitrogen materials. Since then import and export tonnages have been expanding rapidly but the nation's nitrogen fertilizer trade has remained in balance.

As energy costs have increased sharply, ammonia plants have been forced to close, little capacity has been added, and ammonia imports have increased from 400,000 tpy in 1970 to

TABLE 6—Nitrogen Fertilizer Consumption in the US, by Region
1000 St, N

Year*	Northeast	South Atlantic	East North Central	West North Central	East South Central	West South Central	Mountain	Pacific
1960	166.2	462.9	423.2	494.8	315.0	314.7	126.7	382.1
1961	167.7	476.8	484.0	645.0	317.1	340.3	149.7	392.7
1962	179.3	496.3	558.7	700.0	344.2	442.4	160.6	421.9
1963	201.9	539.8	674.0	882.9	364.5	539.4	172.3	466.3
1964	217.0	582.2	848.3	973.3	385.4	588.0	193.0	504.1
1965	228.3	581.8	951.4	1,075.5	385.2	612.7	207.4	537.1
1966	249.8	628.6	1,174.4	1,345.2	417.3	667.6	240.5	549.3
1967	261.4	687.6	1,308.0	1,655.4	452.5	725.1	275.3	609.3
1968	270.4	722.6	1,319.7	2,139.8	442.4	880.4	323.9	637.2
1969	265.9	772.7	1,354.8	2,074.8	486.7	986.3	366.7	601.8
1970	277.5	806.1	1,419.0	2,337.5	487.0	1,059.9	374.7	645.9
1971	310.1	833.0	1,692.1	2,567.1	532.7	1,080.9	386.8	678.2
1972	280.7	834.8	1,415.1	2,545.4	577.3	1,167.0	412.3	738.2
1973	330.7	882.3	1,396.8	2,646.5	593.8	1,154.9	457.4	784.0
1974	321.2	901.6	1,676.5	2,906.5	644.8	1,317.2	488.8	848.8
1975	310.0	853.2	1,696.0	2,784.7	562.4	1,053.7	458.2	836.4
1976	326.2	1,008.8	2,063.6	3,620.7	641.1	1,258.7	539.2	911.0
1977	354.7	1,090.6	2,258.1	3,490.3	692.6	1,302.5	514.9	898.4
1978	333.6	937.0	2,074.2	3,364.2	616.8	1,179.9	534.9	878.5
1979	351.4	963.1	2,247.3	3,743.2	569.5	1,285.8	559.7	951.6
1980	356.8	944.3	2,437.6	4,032.0	595.9	1,347.8	605.1	1,036.4

Source: Hargett and Berry, 1981.
*Fiscal year ending June 30.

almost 2 million tons in 1980. Imports of other nitrogen products have generally been on the decline from their peaks of 1977 and 1978.

While the nation has been importing more ammonia in the past few years, it has been able to maintain a favorable trade balance by rapidly increasing trade in ammonium phosphates and urea. In 1980 the nitrogen content of ammonium phosphates accounted for 35% of total nitrogen exports. Urea and ammonia each accounted for an additional 25% while ammonium sulfate and nitrogen solutions made up most of the remainder. Total nitrogen exports represented about 17% of total nitrogen production in 1980. Exports of nitrogen products for 1960 to 1980 are shown in Table 8 and imports for the same period in Table 9.

Nitrogen Production

In 1980, the US ammonia industry operated at more than 90% of total capacity, producing just over 19 million tons of material. Ammonia production has increased steadily at an annual growth rate of about 7% per year. Only twice in the past 20 years has production declined from the previous year, once in 1968 in

response to oversupply, and again in 1978 primarily because of feedstock shortages (Table 10). Nitrogen production is expected to continue to expand but the rate of increase will be relatively slow.

Anhydrous ammonia is produced primarily in areas having large reserves of natural gas, and where water transport is available for both domestic shipments and export of nitrogen products to world markets. This represents a shift from the concept of establishing production units in market areas that prevailed through the early years of the US nitrogen industry. In 1980, Louisiana accounted for 33% of US ammonia capacity followed by Oklahoma with 11% and Texas with 9%. Other major-producing states are Mississippi, Iowa, Alaska, and Arkansas. These seven states make up about 70% of the total US ammonia capacity. North American ammonia capacity for the years 1967, 1973, 1978, and 1980 is shown in Table 11. Anticipated additions and expansions of ammonia capacity by 1985 are also indicated.

In the past 10 years urea production has increased faster than any of the other nitrogen fertilizer materials. Total urea production in

1980 exceeded 7.2 million tons of primary solution, of which 3.15 million tons was solid (prilled or granular) urea. Production of solid urea has been expanding at more than 10% per year over the past decade. In 1980 total US urea capacity was estimated to be 7.8 million tons of material yielding a 90% operating rate for the year.

Ammonium nitrate, the other leading solid nitrogen fertilizer, has experienced declining production levels in the past few years. From a high of almost 4 million tons of material in 1973, production reached a low of 3 million tons in 1978 and in 1980 was about 3.2 million tons. Production of ammonium nitrate solution has continued to increase for use as an intermediate for nitrogen solutions and in nonfertilizer materials. During the 1970s production levels averaged a 3% annual growth rate. In 1980, total ammonium nitrate capacity was estimated to be 10.9 million tons of material, with a total production of almost 8.6 million tons.

Nitric acid production, primarily as an intermediate for producing ammonium nitrate, has been steadily increasing from 3.3 million tons of material in 1960 to almost 9 million tons in 1980. About 75% of the nitric acid produced is used in producing ammonium nitrate.

Since 1964, ammonium sulfate production has remained relatively constant, ranging between a high of 2.8 million tons in 1966 and 1978 to a low of 2.3 to 2.4 million tons in the early 1970s and in 1980. Of the total production in 1980, byproduct ammonium sulfate production from coke ovens amounted to 400,000 tons, while the remainder consisted of 640,000 tons of synthetic material and 1.45 million tons of byproduct—58% of total production—from the fiber industry. While much of the production is involuntary, the total estimated capacity for ammonium sulfate production in the United States was more than 3.1 million tons in 1980.

Nitrogen solutions have gained in importance in the nitrogen fertilizer market in recent years. Production has increased from 800,000 tons of nitrogen equivalent in 1960 to more than 3 million tons in 1980. During the 1970s, production increased at an average rate of almost

TABLE 7—US Consumption of Industrial Explosives by Use
1000 lb, Gross Wt.

Year	Coal Mining	Metal Mining	Quarrying and Nonmetal Mining	Railway and Other Construction Work	All Other Purposes	Total
1960	414,667	221,186	262,749	209,739	64,657	1,172,998
1961	414,697	234,155	268,479	209,796	76,497	1,203,624
1962	437,895	245,187	287,609	273,412	68,304	1,312,407
1963	506,045	252,800	320,632	305,837	70,608	1,455,922
1964	549,286	318,299	361,246	332,120	104,602	1,665,553
1965	594,964	356,715	371,034	411,384	150,803	1,884,900
1966	618,158	353,331	396,283	437,020	165,364	1,970,156
1967	661,581	327,596	409,525	412,447	93,564	1,904,713
1968	684,166	403,444	397,998	411,664	50,466	1,947,738
1969	820,114	470,791	438,789	411,784	55,000	2,196,478
1970	962,331	479,508	455,424	446,568	49,660	2,393,491
1971	1,071,309	457,286	489,572	478,317	57,534	2,554,018
1972	1,212,585	430,686	493,677	467,273	65,568	2,669,789
1973	1,177,062	495,879	643,292	393,821	44,892	2,754,946
1974	1,186,614	465,490	551,380	362,617	196,189	2,762,290
1975	1,652,251	449,271	493,125	328,337	196,043	3,119,027
1976	1,798,873	488,653	493,656	339,237	208,110	3,328,529
1977	2,093,312	446,406	522,678	350,222	297,132	3,709,750
1978	2,168,630	574,213	604,955	416,609	164,782	3,929,189
1979	2,237,393	612,820	653,033	474,122	113,090	4,090,458
1980*	2,559,142	552,944	576,086	412,038	451,961	4,552,171

Source: Anon., 1976, 1981.
*Preliminary.

TABLE 8—US Exports of Nitrogen Fertilizer Materials
1000 St, N

Year*	Ammonia	Ammonium Nitrate	Ammonium Sulfate	Urea	Nitrogen Solutions	Ammonium Phosphates	Other	Total
1960	66.0	21.0	51.0	16.0	—	8.0	26.0	188.0
1961	72.0	11.1	43.9	43.5	—	21.4	23.4	215.3
1962	66.0	12.4	90.4	41.7	—	13.6	10.5	234.6
1963	41.2	8.8	102.0	11.1	—	22.0	11.9	197.0
1964	66.9	12.9	86.8	20.0	—	49.4	30.5	266.5
1965	101.7	38.6	135.3	18.8	—	66.4	35.8	396.6
1966	107.8	28.1	296.5	17.2	—	83.1	18.2	550.9
1967	211.7	24.7	271.1	30.6	—	172.0	25.6	735.7
1968	382.0	16.2	257.6	67.1	—	273.0	31.4	1,027.3
1969	818.3	36.3	248.9	254.3	—	174.7	34.0	1,566.5
1970	627.0	26.8	111.0	301.9	—	177.5	50.2	1,294.4
1971	490.7	19.3	126.1	168.4	—	204.3	46.3	1,055.1
1972	345.1	11.1	117.1	209.0	—	277.5	53.9	1,013.7
1973	569.0	7.1	102.0	235.3	—	370.9	46.6	1,330.9
1974	436.3	12.2	117.1	145.1	—	387.7	52.6	1,151.0
1975	211.4	7.4	117.7	202.5	—	403.8	60.4	1,003.2
1976	276.3	20.3	157.9	261.2	—	489.8	28.6	1,234.1
1977	365.6	3.7	103.1	165.6	—	570.2	29.8	1,238.0
1978	468.5	10.5	136.9	412.7	2.5	730.6	29.2	1,790.9
1979	455.5	27.7	231.6	697.3	101.9	900.2	48.4	2,462.6
1980	638.8	24.8	176.6	660.3	164.3	924.2	41.0	2,630.0

Source: Anon., 1981d.
* Fiscal year ending June 30.

6% a year, exceeded only by the urea products. Total nitrogen solution capacity in the United States in 1980 was more than 3.1 million tons of nitrogen as 32% solution.

Challenges for the Industry

During the 1980s and beyond, the nitrogen industry will continue to face the severe challenges that arose or became much more severe during the 1970s.

There are four general areas of concern:

1. Meeting and maintaining environmental standards and continuing to improve the industrial work environment.

2. Continuing the substantial work already accomplished in energy conservation in existing and new production facilities.

3. Adapting processes and developing new schemes for conservation of key natural resources, including natural gas and petroleum derivatives.

4. Coping with the continuing sharp escalation in the investment for new facilities and plant modifications.

The US fertilizer industry, and in particular the important nitrogen segment, made great strides in meeting rather rigid environmental standards during the 1970s. Considerable work remains to be done, and much effort and money will be needed to maintain established environmental standards.

Energy conservation quickly became a major endeavor of industry in the early 1970s as the cost of natural gas, fuel oil, and electric power increased sharply. Major improvements were made by repairing steam leaks, operating equipment only when needed, and enforcing other good housekeeping practices. Tight surveillance on the nonprocess use of fuels such as natural gas became essential as its cost rose from 30¢ per million Btu's in the 1950s to $3 and higher in the late 1970s. Higher costs led to innovations in process design that allow greater heat recovery and consume less total energy. A large part of the improvements so far involve redesign of systems and components to better use and conserve heat energy from chemical reactions. These efforts must continue and will become even more important as the cost of natural gas, fuel oil, and electricity continues to increase. Unless proven reserves of natural gas are extended well past the turn of the century, the situation will become critical.

Considerable effort is underway in adapting processes to the use of coal instead of natural gas or petroleum fuels as the process feedstock for preparation of hydrogen. The United States and other countries have abundant coal reserves that will last for hundreds of years. Use of coal for producing hydrogen, however, is untested in most countries. The technology is difficult and investment in process systems is much higher. The experience gained in using coal as process feedstock in Germany and South Africa, and in the past few years in India, can be drawn on. The Tennessee Valley Authority began testing a demonstration plant in late 1980 using coal gasification to provide hydrogen equivalent for 135 tpd of ammonia to an existing plant. This is the first large facility of this type in the western hemisphere.

The sharp escalation in the investment required for new and modified production facilities throughout the 1970s had an immense effect on the production cost of nitrogen products. The cost of materials, process equipment, and total construction doubled between 1970 and 1980. The increase in construction cost indices showed no tendency to slow down in 1981.

Investment related costs comprise a large percentage of the total production costs for primary nitrogen compounds such as ammonia and urea. Estimates (1981 basis) indicated that $87 of the total production cost of $154 for urea was related directly to investments. This is about 57% of the total manufactured cost of urea in a facility with a 1000-tpd ammonia plant and a 1520-tpd urea plant. A high rate of capacity utilization for those large facilities is important because investment related costs continue whether the facilities are operating or standing idle.

Since a large part of the sharp escalation in investment costs throughout the 1970s was tied to general inflation in the economy, there is not much that can be done unless inflation is brought under control. However, the trend to larger production units has leveled off, raising the question of a new trend toward smaller facilities with lower capital outlay.

Not all opportunities for effective use of resources and controlling costs are on the supply

TABLE 9—US Imports of Nitrogen Fertilizer Materials
1000 St, N

Year*	Ammonia	Ammonium Nitrate	Ammonium Sulfate	Urea	Nitrogen Solutions	Ammonium Phosphates	Other	Total
1960	—‡	78.0	54.0	12.0	6.0	22.0	126.0	298.0
1961	—‡	80.0	40.7	40.6	19.3	18.4	128.3	327.3
1962	—‡	90.6	56.7	61.5	23.9	26.1	144.3	403.1
1963	—‡	101.1	47.4	96.2	23.5	27.7	114.4	410.3
1964	74.5	84.7	47.8	126.2	26.3	19.2	102.9	481.6
1965	145.8	59.4	40.5	110.9	23.6	20.1	93.2	493.5
1966	211.7	59.3	32.2	90.7	25.7	32.8	96.1	548.5
1967	321.9	57.9	35.8	123.8	26.4	34.9	86.8	687.5
1968	344.5	74.2	30.1	108.5	22.3	40.4	67.1	687.1
1969	348.6	77.7	28.3	113.0	25.9	49.9	62.7	706.1
1970	391.3	101.0	37.7	190.6	31.2	71.2	63.0	886.0
1971	411.2	120.8	45.9	148.3	62.2	84.9	74.5	947.8
1972	322.2	128.8	55.3	164.3	38.3	88.0	67.9	864.8
1973	281.3	108.7	58.0	302.3	46.3	78.1	60.1	934.8
1974	358.9	153.7	57.3	300.7	53.2	71.4	140.4	1,135.6
1975	490.6	153.7	52.1	365.3	29.3	44.5	130.3	1,265.8
1976	628.7	103.2	88.3	237.4	60.1	61.1	92.5	1,271.3
1977	793.4	130.3	95.4	659.7	142.2	69.7	88.4	1,979.1
1978	864.3	103.0	69.2	643.6	172.1	61.7	92.9	2,006.8
1979	1,429.4	90.5	54.0	490.5	59.9	54.0	83.2	2,261.5
1980	1,819.4	87.2	58.1	511.2	44.0	57.2	89.9	2,667.0

Source: Anon., 1981d.

*Fiscal year ending June 30.

†Includes materials for nonfertilizer use.

‡Included in other nitrogen materials.

TABLE 10—Production of Nitrogen Fertilizer Materials in the US
1000 St

Year	Ammonia	Nitric Acid	Ammonium Nitrate Total	Solid*	Urea Total	Solid*	Nitrogen Solutions[†]	Ammonium Sulfate
1960	4,817.7	3,315.0	3,121.7	1,572.0	746.8	301.9	804.0	1,491.7
1961	5,206.7	3,379.7	3,235.3	1,653.4	914.7	421.3	812.6	1,545.4
1962	5,809.7	3,669.6	3,405.5	1,668.2	1,029.4	466.0	891.2	1,697.5
1963	6,693.0	4,242.4	3,989.9	1,926.8	1,105.8	478.5	1,107.3	1,823.1
1964	7,634.2	4,732.5	4,543.0	2,161.5	1,243.6	546.1	1,156.1	2,306.1
1965	8.869.4	4,898.0	4,663.1	2,287.6	1,399.5	546.4	1,111.5	2,656.1
1966	10,604.7	5,513.8	5,116.8	2,516.8	1,768.4	693.5	1,198.5	2,859.5
1967	12,194.1	6,462.7	6,005.0	2,851.8	2,179.8	875.6	1,517.0	2,824.3
1968	12,119.9	6,992.0	5,737.1	2,951.7	2,436.4	985.1	1,149.8	2,723.3
1969	12,768.8	7,223.4	5,891.2	3,213.5	2,976.1	1,351.8	1,359.2	2,563.7
1970	13,824.0	7,602.8	6,456.0	3,314.6	3,250.0	1,201.6	1,720.6	2,489.4
1971	14,537.6	7,638.2	6,635.3	3,566.0	3,181.1	1,050.2	1,499.5	2,359.8
1972	15,169.3	7,981.2	6,863.2	3,813.5	3,424.2	1,317.0	1,464.9	2,419.1
1973	15,208.1	8,397.7	7,235.2	3,995.0	3,486.9	1,456.2	1,882.9	2,587.8
1974	15,732.5	8,119.7	7,541.9	3,858.5	3,664.5	1,435.1	2,101.8	2,658.0
1975	16,419.0	7,527.4	7,087.6	3,320.6	3,564.5	1,497.5	2,067.8	2,595.3
1976	16,716.1	7,791.1	7,185.5	3,574.2	3,928.2	2,433.1	2,117.1	2,507.2
1977	17,764.6	7,987.1	7,177.3	3,148.3	4,445.5	2,684.1	2,468.1	2,733.9
1978	17,119.3	7,933.7	7,210.1	3,000.7	6,272.6	3,161.6	2,286.2	2,877.1
1979	18,523.3	8,464.6	7,542.8	3,280.5	7,027.1	3,673.0	2,244.9	2,818.3
1980[‡]	19,035.9	8,932.5	8,589.5	3,249.6	7,218.2	3,150.7	3,031.4	2,493.8

Source: Anon., 1981b; Bridges, 1979.
* Fertilizer material only.
[†] Tons of nitrogen.
[‡] Preliminary.

TABLE 11—North American Ammonia Plant Capacity
1000 St

Company	Location	1967	1973	1978	1980	1985
Agrico Chemical Co.—Williams	Blytheville, AR	340	390	407	407	407
	Donaldsonville, LA	—	400	468	468	468
	Verdigris, OK	—	—	840	840	840
Air Products & Chemicals, Inc.	New Orleans, LA	210	210	210	210	210
	Pace Jct, FL	100	100	100	100	100
Allied Corp.	Laplatte, NE	200	200	172	172	172
	Hopewell, VA	400	340	340	340	425
	Geismar, LA	—	340	340	340	340
	South Point, OH	240	240	160	—	—
	Helena, AR	—	—	210	210	210
American Cyanamid	Fortier, LA	394	340	340	580	580
Amoco Oil Co.	Texas City, TX	198	720	522	522	—
Apache Powder Co.	Benson, AZ	15	15	15	—	—
Apple River Chemical	East Dubuque, IL	230	230	—	—	—
Arkla Chemical Corp.	Helena, AR	210	210	—	—	—
Atlas Chemical (Tyler)	Joplin, MO	136	136	136	136	136
Beker Industries	Conda, ID	—	—	100	100	100
Borden Chemical Co.	Geismar, LA	—	340	340	340	400
	San Jacinto, TX	40	—	—	—	—
Calumet Nitrogen	Hammond, IN	140	—	—	—	—
Car-Ren, Inc.	Columbus, MS	—	—	68	68	68
CF Industries, Inc.	Donaldsonville, LA	—	750	1,590	1,590	1,590
	Fremont, NE	48	48	48	48	48
	Terra Haute, IN	150	150	150	150	150
	Tunis-Ahoskie, NC	—	210	210	210	210
	Tyner, TN	170	170	170	170	170

TABLE 11—North American Ammonia Plant Capacity (Continued)

Company	Location	1967	1973	1978	1980	1985
Chemical Distributors	Chandler, AZ	—	—	—	33	33
Chemicals, Inc.—IMCC	Bartow, FL	105	—	—	—	—
Chevron Chemical Co.	Pascagoula, MS	—	530	530	530	530
	Richmond, CA	130	130	130	—	—
	Fort Madison, IA	95	95	95	95	95
	El Segundo, CA	—	4	20	20	20
Cities Service	Lake Charles, LA	140	—	—	—	—
	Tampa, FL	120	120	—	—	—
Columbia Nitrogen	Augusta, GA	122	122	122	510	510
Cominco-American	Borger, TX	—	400	400	400	400
Diamond Shamrock	Deer Park, TX	35	—	—	—	—
	Dumas, TX	160	160	160	160	160
Dow Chemical Co.	Freeport, TX	115	115	115	115	115
	Midland, MI	34	—	—	—	—
	Plaquemine, LA	60	—	—	—	—
	Pittsburg, CA	12	—	—	—	—
E. I. du Pont de Nemours & Co.	Beaumont, TX	—	340	340	340	340
	Belle, WV	275	340	340	—	—
	Gibbstown, NJ	75	—	—	—	—
	Victoria, TX	100	100	100	100	100
Duval Corp. (Oxy)	Hanford, CA	—	21	42	—	—
El Paso Products	Odessa, TX	135	115	115	115	115
Estech General Chemical	Beaumont, TX	—	—	300	—	—
Farmland Industries	Fort Dodge, IA	210	210	210	210	210
	Dodge City, KS	—	210	210	210	210
	Hastings, NE	140	140	140	140	140
	Enid, OK	—	—	840	840	840
	Lawrence, KS	190	340	340	340	340
	Plainview, TX	26	—	—	—	—
	Pollock, LA	—	—	420	420	420
Felmont Oil Corp.	Olean, NY	85	85	85	85	85
First Mississippi Corp.	Fort Madison, IA	—	340	365	365	365
First Mississippi Corp. (Ampro)	Donaldsonville, LA	—	—	—	400	400
FMC Corp.	S. Charleston, WV	24	24	24	24	24
Gardinier	Tampa, FL	—	—	120	120	120
Georgia Pacific	Plaquemine, LA	—	—	—	196	196
Goodpasture, Inc.	Dimmitt, TX	31	31	71	40	40
Grace-Oklahoma Nitrogen	Woodward, OK	—	—	400	400	400
W. R. Grace & Co.	Woodstock, TN	275	340	340	340	340
	Big Springs, TX	100	100	—	—	—
Green Valley Chemical	Creston, IA	35	35	35	35	35
Gulf Oil Corp.	Pittsburg, KS	189	—	—	—	—
	Henderson, KY	107	—	—	—	—
	Vicksburg, MS	81	—	—	—	—
Hawkeye Chemical Co. (Getty)	Clinton, IA	138	138	138	138	220
Hercules, Inc.	Hercules, CA	70	70	—	—	—
	Louisiana, MO	70	70	70	70	70
Hooker Chemical Co.	Tacoma, WA	28	28	28	—	28
International Minerals	Sterlington, LA	140	340	770	400	770
Jupiter Chemical	Lake Charles, LA	—	—	78	78	78
Kaiser Agricultural Chemicals Co.	Savannah, GA	150	150	150	100	100
	Pryor, OK	—	—	—	105	105
Ketona Chemical Corp.	Ketona, AL	51	—	—	—	—
Mississippi Chemical Corp.	Yazoo City, MS	453	340	393	393	393
	Pascagoula, MS	175	175	175	175	175
Mobil Chemical Co.	Beaumont, TX	300	300	—	—	—
Monsanto Co.	El Dorado, AR	280	—	—	—	—
	Luling, LA	450	450	850	850	850
	Muscatine, IA	100	—	—	—	—
New Jersey Zinc-Gulf & Western	Palmerton, PA	35	35	35	35	35
Nipak, Inc. (Enserch)	Pryor, OK	105	105	105	—	—
	Kerens, TX	96	96	115	—	—

TABLE 11—North American Ammonia Plant Capacity (Continued)

Company	Location	1967	1973	1978	1980	1985
Nitrin, Inc.	Cordova, IL	140	—	—	—	—
Northern Chemical Industries	Searsport, ME	40	—	—	—	—
N-Ren Corp.	East Dubuque, IL	—	—	238	238	238
	Pine Bend, MN	90	—	—	—	30
	Carlsbad (Hobbs) NM	—	—	68	68	68
	Pryor, OK	55	55	94	94	94
Occidental Agricultural Chemical Co.	Taft, LA	—	—	90	90	90
	Lathrop, CA	120	120	160	—	—
	Plainview, TX	52	52	52	—	—
Olin Corp.	Lake Charles, LA	588	490	490	490	490
Pennwalt Chemicals	Wyandotte, MI	34	—	—	—	—
	Portland, OR	8	8	8	8	8
Phillips Pacific Chemical Co.	Kennewick, WA	155	155	155	155	155
Phillips Petroleum	Beatrice, NE	210	210	210	210	210
	Etter, TX	210	210	—	—	—
	Pasadena, TX	230	230	—	—	—
PPG Industries	Natrium, WV	50	50	50	50	50
Reichhold Chemicals	St. Helens, OR	—	90	90	90	90
Reserve Oil & Gas	Hanford, CA	21	—	—	—	—
Rohm & Haas	Deer Park, TX	45	45	45	—	—
Shell Chemical Co.	St. Helens, OR	90	—	—	—	—
	Pittsburg, CA	110	—	—	—	—
	Ventura, CA	165	—	—	—	—
J. R. Simplot	Pocatello, ID	54	54	108	108	108
	El Centro, CA	—	—	—	—	210
Southwest Nitrochem	Chandler, AZ	40	—	—	—	—
Sun Oil Co.	Marcus Hook, PA	133	133	—	—	—
Tenneco Chemical	Houston, TX	210	210	210	—	—
Tennessee Valley Authority	Muscle Shoals, AL	45	74	74	74	74
Terra Chemicals	Port Neal, IA	—	210	210	210	210
Texaco, Inc.	Lockport, IN	77	—	—	—	—
Triad Chemical	Donaldsonville, LA	—	340	340	340	340
Union Carbide Co.	Texas City, TX	88	—	—	—	—
Union Chemical Co.	Kenai, AK	—	510	1,020	1,020	1,020
	Brea, CA	380	260	280	280	280
U.S. Industrial Chemicals	Tuscola, IL	80	—	—	—	—
USA Petrochem Corp.	Ventura, CA	—	—	60	60	60
U.S.S. Agri-Chemicals	Clairton, PA	—	325	325	325	325
	Crystal City, MO	98	—	—	—	—
	Cherokee, AL	175	175	175	175	175
	Geneva, UT	70	70	70	70	70
Valley Nitrogen Producers	El Centro, CA	—	210	210	210	—
	Helm, CA	164	164	164	—	—
	Chandler, AZ	—	—	33	—	—
	Hercules, CA	—	—	70	—	—
Vistron Corp.	Lima, OH	136	450	475	475	475
Vulcan Materials	Wichita, KS	23	23	35	—	—
Wycon Chemical Co.	Cheyenne, WY	33	167	167	167	167
Total US		**13,287**	**17,373**	**22,028**	**20,935**	**21,068**
Canada						
Canadian Ind., Ltd.	Courtright, Ont.	340	340	400	400	810
	Millhaven, Ont.	66	—	—	—	—
Canadian Fert., Ltd.	Medicine Hat, Alta.	—	—	800	800	800
Cominco, Ltd.	Calgary, Alta.	125	125	125	125	125
	Trail, B.C.	155	70	70	70	70
	Carseland, Alta.	—	—	400	400	400
Cyanamid of Canada	Welland, Ont.	250	250	250	250	250
Dow Chemical of Canada	Sarnia, Ont.	140	—	—	—	—
Esso Chemicals	Redwater, Alta.	—	210	260	260	860

Compnay	Location	1967	1973	1978	1980	1985
Genstar Chemical	Maitland, Ont.	125	88	88	88	88
N. W. Nitro Chemicals	Medicine Hat, Alta.	66	—	—	—	—
Sherritt-Gordon Mine	Ft Saskatch, Alta.	160	160	160	160	572
J. R. Simplot Co.	Brandon, Manitoba	110	110	110	110	195
Western Coop Fertilizer	Calgary, Alta.	70	70	70	70	70
	Medicine Hat, Alta.	—	66	66	66	66
Total Canada		1,607	1,489	2,799	2,799	4,306
Total North America		14,894	18,862	24,827	23,734	25,374

Source: Capacity data from the records of Marketing and Distribution Economics Section, TVA-NFDC, Muscle Shoals, AL, May 1981.

side of the equation. It is estimated that as much as 50% of the nitrogen applied to the soil is unused by the crop and is eventually lost to the atmosphere or in surface and subsurface water runoff. Potential savings with increases in efficiency of as little as 10% has brought about a renewed research effort to find ways of reducing losses and developing new products that effectively control nitrogen release.

The demand for nitrogen fertilizers, essential to the future world food supply, will continue to expand as population and the demand for improved living standards continue to pressure the world's food supply. The challenge facing the nitrogen industry, both in the public and private sector, is to continue to meet these growing needs using the limited resources available as effectively as possible.

With an expanding market for its products and a sound technology base to work from, the world nitrogen market is in a good position to meet the challenge that it will face in the 1980s. Since the alternative is world famine and economic chaos, the nitrogen industry must continue the research and development programs that have been so important to agriculture.

Bibliography and References

Anon., 1964, "Chilean Nitrate Modernizes to Stay," *World Mining*, Vol. 17, No. 10, Sep., pp. 32–36, 89.

Anon., 1968, *Fertilizers: An Annual Review of World Production, Consumption, and Trade 1967*, Food and Agriculture Organization, United Nations, Rome, Italy, 211 pp.

Anon., 1974, *Annual Fertilizer Review 1973*, Food and Agriculture Organization, United Nations, Rome, Italy, 190 pp.

Anon., 1976, "Apparent Consumption of Industrial Explosives and Blasting Agents in the United States, 1912–1975," *Mineral Industry Surveys*, Aug. 21, US Bureau of Mines, 15 pp.

Anon., 1976a, "Nitrogen Fertilizer—A Potential Polluter," *Tennessee Valley Perspective*, Vol. 6, No. 4, Summer, pp. 15–19.

Anon., 1979, *Fertilizer Manual*, Ref. Manual IFDC–R–1, IFDC/UNIDO, International Fertilizer Development Center, Muscle Shoals, AL, 353 pp.

Anon., 1980, "Chilean Nitrate in the 1980s," *Nitrogen*, No. 28, Nov./Dec., pp. 25–28.

Anon., 1980a, *Fertilizer Reference Manual*, June, The Fertilizer Institute, Washington, DC, p. 86.

Anon., 1980b, *FAO Fertilizer Yearbook 1979*, Food and Agriculture Organization, United Nations, Rome, Italy, 143 pp.

Anon., 1980c, "New Developments in Fertilizer Technology," 13th Demonstration, Bulletin Y–158, National Fertilizer Development Center, Tennessee Valley Authority, Muscle Shoals, AL, 93 pp.

Anon., 1981, "Apparent Consumption of Industrial Explosives and Blasting Agents in the United States," *Mineral Industry Surveys*, annual reports, 1976–1981, US Bureau of Mines.

Anon., 1981a, *Commercial Fertilizers*, annual reports, 1969–1980, US Department of Agriculture Statistical Reporting Service, Washington, DC.

Anon., 1981b, "Inorganic Fertilizer Materials and Related Products," *Current Industrial Reports*, monthly, 1979–1980, Bureau of the Census, US Department of Commerce, Washington, DC.

Anon., 1981c, "Fertilizers: Production, Trade, and Consumption of Nitrogen, Phosphate, and Potash," *Monthly Bulletin of Statistics*, Vol. 4, No. 3, Mar., Food and Agriculture Organization, United Nations, Rome, Italy, pp. 13–20.

Anon., 1981d, *The Fertilizer Supply*, annual reports, 1960–1980, US Department of Agriculture, Agriculture Stabilization and Conservation Service, Washington, DC.

Anon., 1981e, "New Ammonia Technology Saves Energy," *Farm Chem.*, Vol. 144, No. 2, Feb., pp. 48, 50.

Achorn, F.P., and Salladay, D.G., 1976, "Pipe-Cross Reactor Eliminates the Dryer," *Farm Chem.*, Vol. 139, No. 7, July, pp. 34, 36, 38.

Auldridge, L., 1980, "World Oil Flow Slumps, Reserves Up," *Oil and Gas Journal*, Vol. 78, No. 52, Dec. 29, pp. 75–82.

Billmeyer, F.W., Jr., 1971, *Textbook of Polymer Science*, 2nd ed., Wiley-Interscience, New York, 598 pp.

Bridges, J.D., 1980, "Fertilizer Trends 1979," Bulletin Y–150, Jan., Tennessee Valley Authority, Muscle Shoals, AL, 48 pp.

Briggs, T.C., 1975, "Nitrogen Compounds," *Industrial Minerals and Rocks,* 4th ed., S.J. Lefond, ed., AIME, New York, pp. 895–920.

Graham, H.R., 1949, "Nitrates and Nitrogenous Compounds," *Industrial Minerals and Rocks,* 2nd ed., AIME, New York, pp. 643–660.

Hargett, N.L., and Berry, J.T., 1981, "1980 Fertilizer Summary Data," 12th ed., Bulletin Y–165, Apr., Tennessee Valley Authority, Muscle Shoals, AL, 136 pp.

Harris, G.T., and Harre, E.A., 1979, "World Fertilizer Situation and Outlook—1978–85," Technical Bulletin IFDC–T–13, Mar., International Fertilizer Development Center, Muscle Shoals, AL, 27 pp.

Hignett, 1971, "Liquid Fertilizer Production and Distribution," TVA Circular Z–27, National Fertilizer Development Center, Tennessee Valley Authority, Muscle Shoals, AL, 38 pp.

McCamy, I.W., and Norton, M.M., 1977, "Have You Considered Pan Granulation of Urea?" *Farm Chem.,* Vol. 140, No. 2, Feb., pp. 61, 64–65, 68.

McGannon, H.E., 1971, *The Making, Shaping and Treating of Steel.* 9th ed., US Steel Corp., Pittsburgh, PA, pp. 168–170.

McVickar, M.H., et al., 1966, "Agricultural Anhydrous Ammonia Technology and Use," Agricultural Ammonia Institute, Memphis, TN, 314 pp.

Noyes, R., 1967, "Ammonia and Synthesis Gas," Chemical Process Monograph No. 26, Noyes Development Corp., Park Ridge, NJ, 177 pp.

Postgate, J.R., 1971, *The Chemistry and Biochemistry of Nitrogen Fixation,* Plenum Press, New York, 326 pp.

Sauchelli, V., 1964, *Fertilizer Nitrogen—Its Chemistry and Technology,* Reinhold, New York, 424 pp.

Shields, J.T., et al., 1975, "An Appraisal of the Fertilizer Market and Trends in Asia," Bulletin Y–95, National Fertilizer Development Center, Muscle Shoals, AL, 141 pp.

Sittig, M., 1965, *Nitrogen In Industry,* Van Nostrand, Princeton, NJ, 278 pp.

Slack, A.V., and James, G.R., 1979, *Ammonia* (four parts) Fertilizer Science and Technology Series, Part IV, Marcel Dekker, Inc., New York, pp. 16–17.

Viets, F.G., Jr., and Hageman, R.H., 1971, "Factors Affecting the Accumulation of Nitrate in Soil, Water, and Plants," *Agriculture Handbook* No. 413, US Dept. of Agriculture, Washington, DC, Nov. 63 pp.

Young, R.D., et al., 1962, "TVA Process for Production of Granular Diammonium Phosphate," *Journal of Agriculture Food Chemistry,* Vol. 10, Nov./Dec., pp. 442–447.

Young, R.D., and Hicks, G.C., 1967, "Production of Monoammonium Phosphate in a TVA-Type Ammonium Phosphate Granulation System," *Commercial Fertilizer,* Vol. 114, No. 2, Feb., pp. 26–27.

Young, R.D., and McCamy, I.W., 1967, "TVA Development Work and Experience with Pan Granulation of Fertilizers," *The Canadian Journal of Chemical Engineering,* Vol. 45, Feb., pp. 50–56.

Young, R.D., 1980, "TVA Development of Pan Granulation Processes for Nitrogen Fertilizers," Bulletin Y-160, Dec., National Fertilizer Development Center, Tennessee Valley Authority, Muscle Shoals, AL, 16 pp.

Olivine

KEFTON H. TEAGUE *

Olivine is a mineral containing a mixture of forsterite (Mg_2SiO_4) and fayalite (Fe_2SiO_4) in solid solution. The name *olivine* was first applied by Werner in 1790 (Hunter, 1941) because of the olive-green color of the mineral.

Olivine is the principal component of the rock dunite, which itself is a member of the peridotite group of ultrabasic igneous rocks. European uses of the terms *olivine* and *dunite* are somewhat different than US usage. In commerce European usage defines *dunite* as containing 36 to 42% MgO, 36 to 39% SiO_2, and loss on ignition of approximately 10%. The term *olivine* is used to designate a material containing approximately 85% forsterite, with a chemical composition of approximately 45 to 50% MgO, 40 to 43% SiO_2, 5 to 8% Fe_2O_3, and ignition loss of 1 to 2%.

Uses

The principal use of olivine is in various applications involving hot metal. Table 1 shows the best estimate available as to the amount of olivine consumed by various industries worldwide. In excess of 90% of world uses involve hot metal, with approximately 75% as a slag conditioner in the blast furnace production of pig iron. Approximately 15% of total olivine usage is as a special foundry sand in mold making for the brass, aluminum, magnesium, and manganese steel foundries (Schaller, 1957, 1958; Snyder, 1957; Anon., 1977).

Olivine was first used as an industrial mineral in the early 1930s for a refractory material (Anon., 1970; Hunter, 1941). As a refractory raw material, olivine was first introduced in the United States as hand-cobbed, selected, shaped blocks of crude olivine. This use met with limited success. More recently, finely ground olivine blended with MgO and pressed

into bricks, which are then fired, has found use in glass tank furnaces and open-hearth furnaces. Ramming or gunning mixes for basic furnace linings also utilize olivine. Olivine has been used in ladle linings with varied success. In Europe, substantial tonnages of olivine are utilized in refractory brick for night storage heaters (Anon., 1970).

A limited amount of olivine has been used in the past as a fertilizer (magnesium source) and has been fused with rock phosphate to produce a magnesium phosphate as a plant food. The relatively high magnesia (MgO) content of olivine also attracted attention to it as a potential source of both magnesium compounds and as a source of metallic magnesium (Bengston, 1956; Hunter, 1941). The use of olivine as an additive in the blast furnace is relatively new, having been developed during the last decade. J.W. Currier (Private communication, 1978) describes the behavior of olivine in the blast furnace as follows:

Olivine (Mg, Fe_2, SiO_4) represents a unique lime-free source of magnesia and silica as a blast furnace charge component. Only recently has the magnesia-rich mineral been recognized as beneficial cleaner for blast furnace experiencing the problems associated with excessive alkali inputs and/or low coke stabilities.

For some time it has been known that alkalis tend to recycle and accumulate in blast furnaces. In the high temperature region of volatilization the elemental alkalis formed attack the integrity of the graphite structure. This alkali attachment is enhanced when poor coke is used. Higher in the furnace stack volatile alkali cyanides condense and oxidize. This accumulation of alkalis tends to agglomerate the burden materials, producing scabs and scaffolds. These structures not only inhibit the downward movement of burden materials and the upward passage of wind, but also lead to erratic furnace performance

* Senior Geologist, Industry Group, International Minerals & Chemical Corp., Mundelein, IL.

TABLE 1—World Olivine Usage, 1978

Use	Short Tons
Blast furnace	3,000,000
Foundry sand	600,000
Heat storage blocks	75,000
Refractories	75,000
Abrasives	50,000
Miscellaneous	100,000
Total	3,900,000

such as irregular cast temperatures, off-quality hot metal, burden slips, broken tuyeres, coke messes, and excessive coke consumption and restricted production. In short, under an alkali problem a furnace fails to function and respond to control predictably.

Since alkali problems can occur at alkali inputs as low as 4 lb total alkali oxides per net ton of hot metal, the restriction of alkali inputs is not always practical. Indeed, the reduction in the quality of ores and coals available mandates higher alkali inputs. In order to handle these larger inputs special cleaning practices have been developed to cope with the problem. Calcium chloride has been found to be slightly effective in alleviating some of the symptoms associated with high alkali loadings. The charging of calcium chloride does not alleviate the problem; however, more effective in coping with the alkali problems is a reduction of the slag base/acid ratio in order to allow the slag to carry and purge more of the basic alkali components. This has several limitations, however. The acidic slags usually cannot produce the appropriate quality hot metal. Therefore, most operators resort to the intermittent charging of quartzite to purge the alkalis on an intermittent basis. While this can be shown to have some effect on the quantities of alkali purged, it serves to accentuate the nonsteady rate of the furnace operation and performance.

Comparatively recently it has been found that continuous charging of olivine can have a marked effect on a blast furnace alkali problem. An appropriate charging of olivine in the region of 20 to 25 lb/NTHM has been shown to be effective even at alkali oxide loadings as high as 30 lb/NTHM. This charge rate corresponds to 25 tons of olivine per day for an average sized furnace. The olivine is charged as continuously as practicable for the particular charge sequence and system. For the most part the olivine should be toward the outside of the furnace and segregated from all lime components as much as possible. The tendency toward higher MgO contents in the slag can be compensated for by reduced additions of dolomite without diminishing the beneficial effect.

Under the above continuous charging conditions smoother alkali purging results and the tendency for alkali accumulation is markedly reduced. As a result, erratic furnace performance, slips, peels, coke messes, and the like are dramatically reduced. It becomes possible to achieve a steady state furnace performance in which the normal controls predictably influence the independent variables of temperature, hot metal quality, permissible wind rates, and burden movement.

The blast furnace tests with olivine to date have been reasonably consistent. Production increases of as much as 10% have been documented. Coke savings of the order of 4% are common and provide an adequate economic incentive to use this practice. In addition, uniform hot metal quality within the limits that can be expected of this slag operating practice are attained without exception.

As a foundry sand olivine is used in mold making for the brass, aluminum, magnesium, and manganese steel foundries. It has a fusion point of approximately 1816°C (3300°F) and lower thermal expansion than silica; thus, it exhibits less defects in the castings such as "rat tails," "scabs," and "buckles." Little or no free silica occurs with olivine, so the silicosis hazard is reduced as compared to the use of normal silica sand in foundry applications.

Normally, coarse sand is used in manganese steel foundries and the finer sands in aluminum, magnesium, and brass foundries. Fine sand is used in the manufacture of "hot tops" where quartz sand is not permitted because of health hazards.

Industries using olivine have not standardized specifications. Normally, producers supply a product which meets individual customer requirements. Such requirements involve type and amount of impurities, grain size of product, refractory characteristics, chemical analysis, etc.

Geology

Olivine occurs commonly as accessories in basic igneous and basic metamorphic rocks. Economic deposits are of magmatic origin and are restricted to essentially the dunite variety of peridotite. Dunites are medium to coarse-grained crystalline rocks, generally reddish brown on weathered outcrop, and are composed primarily of olivine.

Mineralogy

The name *olivine* is a generic term used to indicate a group of orthosilicate minerals in isomorphous series, with magnesium-rich forsterite (Mg_2SiO_4) and iron-rich fayalite (Fe_2SiO_4) as end points (Ramberg and DeVore, 1951; Reed, 1959). In commercial practice, use of the term olivine applies to deposits containing a mixture of forsterite and fayalite in solid solution with fayalite content usually restricted to less than 15%. Accessory constituents may include the primary minerals: ilmenite, magnetite, chromite and garnet; and various secondary minerals as alteration products.

The chemical composition of typical olivine may be expressed either as $(Mg,Fe)_2SiO_4$ or as $2(Mg,Fe)O.SiO_2$. The ratio of Mg:Fe varies from 16:1 to 2:1, passing from forsterite on the one hand to fayalite on the other. Chemical analyses of some commercial olivines are noted in Table 2.

Mode of Occurrence and Origin

Commercial olivine occurs as alpine-type and zoned dunite bodies. Controversy exists among various researchers concerning the origin and mode of emplacement (Astwood et al., 1972; Bennett, 1940; Bowen and Schairer, 1935, 1936; Gaudette, 1963; Mossman, 1972; Ragan, 1959, 1961; Ross et al., 1954; Yudin, 1959). There is general agreement, however, that most olivines have been emplaced in a partially crystallized condition (mush) and that in part, at least, foliation present in many unmetamorphosed dunites results from flowage during emplacement prior to complete crystallization.

All commercial bodies are of igneous origin and may be in part magmatic segregates from basic magmas. Domestic olivine bodies, of present or potential economic importance, range in age from pre-Ordovician for the North Carolina deposits, to post early-Tertiary age for the Washington dunites.

TABLE 2—Chemical Analyses of
Some Commercial Olivines, %

	1	2	3	4	5	6
MgO	47.5	43-44	49.0	47.7	46.4	46.9
SiO$_2$	40.4	24-35	42.6	40.8	42.5	40.8
Fe$_2$O$_3$	9.0	7.6-7.7	6.0	7.5	8.0	9.4
Other oxides	2.5	0.7-0.8	1.8	1.9	2.4	3.2
LOI	0.8	?	0.6	2.0	0.5	0.6

1 Ste. Anne des Monts, P. Q., Canada
2 Leoben, Austria
3 Aaheim, Norway
4 Norddal, Norway
5 Burnsville, NC
6 Hamilton, WA

Source: Anon., 1970.

Distribution of Deposits

Large deposits of olivine-bearing dunites crop out in Norway, Sweden, USSR, Austria, Japan, New Zealand, Zimbabwe, South Africa, United States, New Caledonia, Italy, Greece, Spain, India, Brazil, and Canada (Anon., 1970; Bennett, 1940; Brothers, 1960; Du Rietz, 1935; Francis, 1956; Gwinn, 1943; Hunter, 1941; Ragan, 1961; Roberts, 1930; Yudin, 1959).

In the United States numerous lenslike bodies extend in a belt from northeastern Georgia, northeastward across western North Carolina. Some 25 of these deposits are relatively fresh, with each containing up to five million tons of recoverable olivine.

Many small to large dunite bodies occur in northwestern Washington, with the Twin Sisters deposit being the largest.

Taylor (1967) describes eight zoned ultramafic complexes in southeastern Alaska containing cores of dunite. Some of these olivine cores are as great as one mile in diameter.

Reserves

The largest body of olivine in the United States is the Twin Sisters deposit in Whatcom and Skagit Counties, Washington. This dunite has an outcrop area of approximately 36 square miles and has a relief of about 5000 ft.

Other countries containing large reserves of olivine include Norway, where the Aaheim deposit is reported to contain two billion tons. Several other Norwegian deposits contain up to five million tons. In Sweden the largest deposit is at Arutats and is reported to be comparable in size to the Twin Sisters deposit. In Austria large deposits of serpentinized-olivine occur in the Province of Styria. Scotland, Spain, and Italy contain large deposits of serpentinized olivine. In New Zealand the Dun Mountain dunite is reported to be approximately 1½ miles in diameter. This deposit is located near Nelson, New Zealand (Gwinn, 1943). A dunite deposit in the coastal area of southern New Zealand has been described by Mossman (1972) "as exceeding 600 meters in thickness." This occurrence apparently is a magmatic differentiate in the Greenhills Ultramafic Complex.

Unaltered dunite crops out as a lenslike body approximately 25 miles south of Ste. Anne des Monts on the Gaspé Peninsula of Quebec, Canada. Dunite is also reported in Newfoundland.

Exploration

Most of the dunites containing economic olivine outcrop as prominent ridges or domes. Soils developed from the weathering of dunites support limited vegetation, thus many deposits crop out as "balds."

As a first step in exploration, an olivine deposit should be thoroughly investigated by reconnaissance techniques followed by detailed topographic and geologic mapping. Grab samples, representing various varieties of dunite which occur in the deposit, should be collected for petrographic and chemical evaluation. Grain size, alteration products, and distribution of impurities should be noted, both in samples and throughout the deposit. Portions of the deposit covered with soil should be trenched to determine whether or not the bedrock is olivine. For example, some of the North Carolina olivines, originally regarded as being relatively continuous, have shown by trenching and drilling that areas covered by soil are underlain by non-olivine material that has resulted from alteration of the olivine.

After the surface extent of the olivine deposit is established, details of vertical variation should be determined. As most olivine bodies in the Southeastern deposits are rather closely fractured and jointed and may contain alteration products considerably softer than olivine, core drilling is not recommended for determining vertical continuity. Some variety of percussion drilling, such as Air-Trac drilling or down-the-hole drilling is normally superior to core drilling in olivine deposits. The driller can note variations in drilling rates as well as character of cuttings. If the drill is equipped with a vacuum pump, continuous samples of cuttings can be collected and evaluated.

Evaluation of Deposit

A commercial olivine should contain in excess of 40% MgO, before any beneficiation. Many olivine deposits, such as Twin Sisters in Washington, and those in Norway and Sweden, are relatively pure and are amenable to evaluation by dry crushing, followed by screen analysis of the crushed product and chemical and petrographic analysis of the various size fractions. Refractory characteristics also should be determined on the various screen sizes.

Olivine samples which contain objectionable impurities can be evaluated by crushing to a size that will permit removing these impurities and evaluating the clean olivine. Perhaps the most efficient laboratory method to accomplish removal of impurities from crushed or broken samples is to use heavy liquids. Most objectionable impurities which occur with olivine "float" on a liquid of specific gravity of about 3.0. Accessory chromite and olivine report as "sinks." If complete liberation is obtained prior to separation with heavy liquid, the resultant olivine product can be evaluated as outlined previously. Olivine deposits, which require beneficiation in order to produce a usable olivine concentrate, should yield at least 65% product to be considered commercial.

Most accessory minerals associated with olivine lower its refractory characteristics. For example, serpentine, chlorite, and vermiculite contain 12 to 17% water of crystallization, and unless these materials are removed from the olivine, they will contribute to a high loss-on-ignition of the product. Also, the platy minerals, chlorite and vermiculite, react explosively when heat shocked. Olivine sands which are to be coated should contain a minimum amount of platy minerals because of the surface area-weight ratio.

Preparation for Market

Mining Methods

Methods employed in the United States and in Europe in mining olivine are similar. Where possible, open cut methods are used with bench heights ranging from 12 to 20 ft .

North Carolina: There is considerable variation in accessory and alteration minerals in the North Carolina deposits; therefore, prior to mining, rather detailed quality data is needed for mine planning. Percussion drill holes, up to 70 ft deep, spaced on centers up to 50 ft, are drilled in advance of mining. Samples of the drill cuttings are collected and are evaluated for olivine and impurity content. Data developed from this exploration are used in mine planning.

Face heights range up to 20 ft and blasting charges are relatively small, generally yielding less than 10,000 tons of crude olivine. Holes are drilled on a 4 to 6-ft grid pattern which normally results in reasonably good breakage. Some secondary drop-ball work is required at times.

Washington: One of the Twin Sisters olivine deposits presently being worked is a talus accumulation along the south side of the Twin Sisters body. Olivine fragments have accumulated at the base of the slope. It is loaded by shovel and trucked to a portable crushing-washing plant. This plant consists of a jaw crusher, which reduces the olivine to approximately —4 in., screening facilities where the —1/8-in. material is removed, and a picking belt from which the non-olivine material is removed. The olivine is trucked approximately 25 miles to the processing plant at Hamilton, WA.

At one time underground mining methods were attempted on the Twin Sisters deposit. A high quality product was produced; however, the nature of the rock, especially its closely spaced fractures and joints, resulted in heavy, unsafe ground. Ore costs from underground mining were substantially greater than presently experienced utilizing the talus material.

In the near contact zone of the Twin Sisters deposit, relief is severe. It would be possible to mine this rock by open cut methods, but mining cost again would exceed present cost experienced by mining talus accumulation of olivine. One producer active on the Twin Sisters deposit is currently producing material from bedrock in an area on the northwestern side, where relief is relatively moderate.

In the production of olivine for use as a slag conditioner, processing involves crushing and sizing to normal sizes of —1¼ +¼ in. Depending on the amount of impurities in the —¼ in., this may or may not be used as a sand source. In production of fine sizes (sand), again crushing and sizing are involved. Dry processing is utilized where possible, such as for the Washington, Norway, and Sweden operations.

Mining cost of the ore ranges between $3 and $7 per ton. The uniformity and purity of the ore and topography of the deposit are major factors in mining cost.

Milling and Processing Techniques

Olivine is reduced by jaw crushers, cone crusher, and impact or roll crushers to the desired size. In addition to a dry operation, the A/S Olivine operation at Aaheim, Norway, is reported to process the sand through a washing procedure. This process is described as follows (Anon., 1970):

> Part of the material fed through the primary crusher is damp. This is passed through a washing plant, which comprises the second line at Aaheim. Before being washed, the olivine is crushed in the Prall-Mühle impact mill to give a suitable grain size. Washing takes place in two Callow cones placed in line. From the washing plant the olivine—which is now mainly free from particles less than 0.02 mm in size, is conveyed to a screw classifier for primary dewatering. Simultaneously, with the removal of water, some of the remaining fine particles (fines) are eliminated. In the next stage the water content of the sand is reduced to 8% by passing it through a centrifuge. The moisture content is finally reduced to maximum 0.5% in a vertical dryer.

Because of the relatively high content of undesirable impurities in the North Carolina olivine, it is necessary to beneficiate it in order to produce a high quality foundry sand. Flotation was used when beneficiation was first commenced in the 1940s. Later gravity methods, using Humphrey's spiral or tables, replaced flotation. Processing in North Carolina is essentially as follows:

Quarry rock in the —2 ft range is loaded, using either shovels or front-end loaders, trucked from quarry to the primary crusher, reduced to —4 in., and stage crushed by jaw or shorthead crushers to —1 in. Fines (—20 mesh) are removed, slurried, deslimed at 200 mesh, sized, and sent to either concentrating tables or flotation. The plus 20 mesh material is wet rod milled, deslimed, sized, and moved either to concentrating tables or flotation.

Concentrate is recombined and dewatered, dried, and sized. Foundry sand may be shipped either in bulk or bagged.

Milling cost in the production of olivine relates closely to the purity of the olivine ore and beneficiation requirements. In general, cost of milling ranges between $12 and $20 per ton.

Normally, the finer sands have a f.o.b. price approximately $10 greater per ton than does the coarser sands. Price ranges for sand are generally between $40 and $60 per ton (bagged) and somewhat less per ton for bulk. Special sands with special size distribution command higher prices.

Transportation

In the United States olivine is transported from plant to market by either truck or rail. Transportation cost to the main consuming markets are substantial, frequently equaling the f.o.b. plant cost of the olivine.

In Europe truck, rail, and water transportation is used for moving the olivine to market. These transportation costs are thought to be substantially less than those experienced by US producers.

Consumption

Industries utilizing olivine generally are located in those countries which have major production or have access to this production. Industries in Japan utilizing olivine represent the largest market.

Table 3 represents the best available data of current production figures for the principal producing countries.

In Europe major consuming industries are located in Norway, Sweden, West Germany, France, Spain, Italy, and England. In these countries substantially larger tonnages of olivine enter the foundry sand application than in the United States. This situation is brought about, in part, by the higher cost of good silica foundry sand and the desire to avoid all risks of silicosis.

TABLE 3—World Olivine Production, 1978

Country	Short Tons
Japan	2,100,000
Spain	700,000
Norway	400,000
United States	240,000
Italy	100,000
Sweden	50,000
Austria	30,000
Other	300,000
Total	3,900,000

Future Considerations and Trends

As mentioned under uses, perhaps 90% of olivine is used in conjunction with the production and utilization of hot metal. Therefore, demand for olivine is closely related to the activity in this industry. When blast furnaces are operating at a high level, a correspondingly high demand for slag conditioner is to be expected. The requirements for foundry sand fluctuate with the activity in the nonferrous and manganese steel foundries.

Palmour, et al. (1979) indicates the demand for high heat capacity refractory ceramics utilizing olivine for use in heat storage furnaces in the United States may offer a substantial market for olivine.

TABLE 4—Comparison of Applications, Olivine vs. Other Refractory Materials

Advantages	Disadvantages
Resistance to most basic slags.	Resin-bonded foundry cores cannot be made with olivine sand unless calcined.
No silicosis hazard.	Attacked by acid slags.
Price advantage over similar materials (chromite & zircon) for use in applications requiring low expansion, high cooling, and penetrating resistance.	Melting point is lowered in a reducing atmosphere (ferric to ferrous iron).
Requires smaller amounts of bentonite as binder (disperse grain-size distribution).	Hydrated contaminant causes high loss on ignition.
Can be recycled, owing to its long life and grain-size durability.	Requires larger amounts of liquid binders such as self-curing oil; also, cold-setting resins must be neutral, hardened by an isocyanate and a catalyst to equal the characteristics attained with silica sands.
Washed sand product is more concentrated and has lower content of fines (suitable for fluid binders used in core production and in resin-coated sand for shell moldings).	High chilling capacity of olivine linings and limited resistance to thermal shocks.
Grain surfaces are more angular than silica sands.	Relatively low durability of forsterite bricks compared to chromite bricks, because of spalling.
Improved finish of foundry castings (no scabs or metal penetration).	Not as plentiful or readily available as silica sand.
High mechanical strength from the texture and fabric of dunite (irregular intergrowth of olivine crystals).	
Very accurate dimensions of castings (free from microporosity) produced in nonferrous foundries (aluminum, bronze, etc.).	

Source: Beckius, 1970.

For foundry sand uses olivine competes with quartz, chromite, and zircon. The price of quartz sand is less than that of olivine; however, chromite and zircon sands command substantially higher prices than olivine. There is general concern in foundries where silica sand is used because of the silicosis hazard; in those applications where olivine is substituted for silica sand, the silicosis hazard is removed. Future increased uses of olivine as a foundry sand may be at the expense of silica sand because of the silicosis problem.

Table 4 summarizes the advantages and disadvantages of olivine as a foundry sand with competitive materials.

Olivine is permitted a 22% depletion allowance for tax purposes. It may enter either the United States or Canada duty free.

As has been mentioned previously, almost all of the United States production of olivine is by open cut methods. State or federal regulations now require that all disturbed areas in the course of open cut mining of olivine be reclaimed. Also all dissolved and suspended solids must be removed from process water before it is returned to streams. These and possible other regulations pertaining to environmental protection and land use must be considered concerning their effect on the economics and hence market position of olivine. On the positive side is the health and safety factor of elimination of silicosis when olivine is substituted for silica sand.

Bibliography and References

Anon., 1970, "Opportunities for Increasing Olivine Output," *Industrial Minerals,* No. 29, Feb., pp. 11–21.

Anon., 1976, "The Industrial Minerals of Spain," *Industrial Minerals,* Apr., pp. 15–51.

Anon., 1977, "Olivine and Dunite—Blast Furnace Usage Adds New Dimension," *Industrial Minerals,* May, pp. 39–50.

Ashby, G., 1976, "Minerals in the Foundry Industry," Second Industrial Minerals International Congress, Munich.

Astwood, P.M., et al., 1972, "A Petrofabric Study of the Dark Ridge and Balsam Gap Dunites, Jackson County, North Carolina," *Southeastern Geology,* Vol. 14, No. 3, Sep., pp. 183–194.

Beckius, K., 1970, "Olivine: Its Properties and Uses," *Industrial Minerals,* No. 29, Feb., pp. 22–26.

Bengston, K.B., 1956, "Magnesium from Olivine *via* Chlorination: A Possibility, Trend in England," University of Washington, Vol. 8, Jan., pp. 21–26, 35–36.

Bennett, W.A.G., 1940, "Ultrabasic Rocks of the Twin Sisters Mountains, Washington," *Bulletin,* Geological Society of America, Vol. 51, p. 2019.

Bowen, N.L., and Schairer, J.F., 1935, "The System MgO, FeO, SiO₂," *American Journal of Science,* 5th Ser., Vol. 29, pp. 151–217.

Bowen, N.L., and Schairer, J.F., 1936, "The Problem of the Intrusion of Dunite in the Light of the Olivine Diagram," *Proceedings,* 16th International Geological Congress, Vol. 1, pp. 391–396.

Brothers, R.N., 1960, "Olivine Nodules from New Zealand," *Proceedings,* 21st International Geological Congress, Pt. 13, pp. 68–81.

Dana, E.S., and Ford, W.E., 1940, *Textbook of Mineralogy,* John Wiley, New York, 851 pp.

Du Rietz, T., 1935, "Peridotites, Serpentines, and Soapstones of Northern Sweden," *Geologiska Foreningen i Stockholm,* Forh. 401, Vol. 57, pp. 133–260.

Francis, G.H., 1956, "The Serpentine Mass of Glen Urquahart, Iverness-Shire, Scotland," *American Journal of Science,* Vol. 254, pp. 201–226.

Gaudette, H.E., 1963, "Geochemistry of the Twin Sisters Ultramafic Body, Washington," unpub. Ph.D. Thesis, University of Illinois, Urbana, 104 pp.

Goldschmidt, V.M., 1938, "Olivine and Forsterite Refractories in Europe," *Industrial & Engineering Chemistry,* Vol. 30, pp. 32–33.

Gwinn, G.R., 1943, "Olivine," Information Circular 7239, US Bureau of Mines, 11 pp.

Hunter, C.E., 1941, "Forsterite Olivine Deposits of North Carolina and Georgia," Bulletin 41, North Carolina Dept. of Conservation & Development, Div. of Mineral Resources, 117 pp.

Kaufman, A.J., 1952, "Industrial Minerals of the Pacific Northwest," Information Circular 7641, US Bureau of Mines, p. 37.

Lamont, W.E., et al., 1977, "Olivine Foundry Sand from North Carolina Dunite by Differential Grinding," Preprint 77–H–369, SME-AIME Fall Meeting, St. Louis, 22 pp.

Misra, K.C., and Keller, F.B., 1978, "Ultramafic Bodies in the Southern Appalachians: A Review," *American Journal of Science,* Vol. 278, pp. 389–418.

Mossman, D.J., 1972, "The Geology of the Greenhills Ultramafic Complex, Bluff Peninsula, Southern New Zealand," *Abstracts with Programs,* Vol. 4, No. 7, Oct., p. 605.

Palmour, H., III, et al., 1979, "Ceramics for Energy Storage Units: Bricks from North Carolina Olivine for Heat Storage Furnaces," North Carolina Minerals Research Laboratory Report No. 79–16–P.

Ragan, D.M., 1959, "The Mode of Emplacement of the Twin Sisters Dunite, Washington," *Bulletin,* Geological Society of America, Vol. 70, pp. 1742–1743.

Ragan, D.M., 1961, "Geology of the Twin Sisters Dunite in the Northern Cascades, Washington," unpub. Ph.D. Thesis, University of Washington, 88 pp.

Ralston, O.C., 1937, "Annual Report of the Non-metals Division, Fiscal Year 1937," Information Circular 6974, US Bureau of Mines, p. 9.

Ralston, O.C., et al., 1938, "Annual Report of the Nonmetals Division, Fiscal Year 1938," RI 3427, US Bureau of Mines, pp. 5–9.

Ralston, O.C., et al., 1939, "Annual Report of the Nonmetals Division, Fiscal Year 1939," Report of Investigations, 3473, US Bureau of Mines, pp. 27–28.

Ramberg, H., and DeVore, G.W., 1951, "The Distribution of Fe and Mg in Coexisting Olivines and Pyroxenes," *Journal of Geology,* Vol. 59, pp. 193–210.

Reed, J.J., 1959, "Chemical and Modal Composition of Dunite from Dun Mountain, Nelson," *New Zealand Journal of Geology and Geography,* Vol. 2, No. 5, pp. 916–919.

Roberts, M., 1947, "Washington's Vast Olivine Deposit," *Mining Congress Journal,* Vol. 33, No. 6, pp. 29–32.

Ross, C.S., et al., 1954, "Origin of Dunites and of Olivine-rich Inclusions in Basaltic Rocks," *American Mining,* Vol. 39, pp. 693–737.

Schaller, G.S., 1957, "New Foundry Sand," *Modern Metals,* Vol. 13, No. 9, Oct., pp. 82–86.

Schaller, G.S., and Snyder, W.A., "Industrial Applications of Olivine Aggregate," *Modern Castings,* Vol. 33, No. 6, June, pp. 99–104.

Snyder, W.A., 1957, "How to Use Olivine Sand," *Foundry,* Vol. 85, No. 9, pp. 100–105.

Taylor, H.P., Jr., 1967, "The Zones Ultramafic Complexes of Southeastern Alaska," *Ultramafic and Related Rocks.*

Yudin, M.I., 1959, "Dunite of the Boris Mountain Range and Their Origin," *Academy of Science Bulletin,* USSR, Geol. Ser. 2., pp. 47–62.

Perlite

FREDERIC L. KADEY, JR.*

Perlite, as a volcanic glass, has been recognized since the Third Century, B.C. (Langford, 1978). The precise details of discovery often become lost in antiquity, and the variations among the stories pertaining to the more recent discovery of perlite as a material of commerce are no exception. Credit in the United States is given to a dentist who, while experimenting with tooth enamels about 1941, discovered that perlite—the rock—intumesced when subjected to heat. At about the same time it is reported that the chief geologist of Silver and Barytes Ores Mining Co. attempted to put out a picnic bonfire on the shores of Milos Island, Greece by throwing beach sand on it. The ensuing pyrotechnic display immediately conjured up in that man's mind the possibility of a new use for the volcanic rock that constituted most of the island. Very little was done with this discovery either here or abroad until after World War II.

Today the name perlite is applied to both the hydrated volcanic glass, generally of rhyolitic composition, and to the lightweight aggregate that is produced from the expansion of the glass after it has been crushed and sized. Petrologically, it is defined as a glassy rhyolite that has a pearly luster and concentric, onionskin parting. Occurrences of perlite are restricted to several Tertiary to Quaternary age rhyolitic belts that trend in a generally north-south direction around the world. Commercially suitable deposits generally occur as domes of several hundred feet in height, although glassy zones in welded ash-flow tuffs and others associated with dikes and sills also have been reported. Mining is by ripping and blasting from open pits. Because of weight considerations, perlite usually is shipped to the local market area for subsequent expanding. In the United States, New Mexico leads in production with Arizona, California, Nevada, Idaho, and Colorado following in approximately that order. The prin-

cipal use for expanded perlite is as a lightweight insulating aggregate in cryogenics, in plaster, concrete, and in loose fill insulation. Expanded perlite is also used in horticultural applications, and after subsequent milling and classification, as a filter aid.

The United States is the world's largest producer and consumer of perlite. Table 1 shows the world production of perlite and Table 2 shows the perlite mined, processed, expanded, and sold or used by producers in the United States.

Geology

Composition and Morphology

Any discussion of perlite must take into consideration its dual nomenclature, for it is known by the same name as both the naturally occurring rock and, after processing and expansion, as the lightweight aggregate of commercial significance.

In its naturally occurring form, perlite is a rhyolitic glass that contains from 2 to 5% combined water. While perlite also can occur as andesitic or dacitic glass, these latter types are of negligible commercial significance. Table 3 lists the chemical composition of a few typical perlites (Anderson, et al., 1956; Langford, 1979).

What sets perlite of commercial significance apart from other volcanic glasses is the fact that under the proper conditions of preparation—crushing and sizing—it will, when rapidly introduced into a flame of sufficient temperature, expand or "pop." All of the elements of composition contribute to the expansibility of the rock. The role of the combined water, however, is the most significant because it is believed not only to produce a fluxing effect in the softening of the highly siliceous glass prior to expansion, but it is also responsible for the explosive force of expansion through volatilization during heating. The current theory of the origin of the water in perlite is now less con-

---

* Retired. Formerly Exploration Manager, Manville Products Corp., Denver, CO.

TABLE 1—World Production of Perlite*, 1969-1979
(Thousand short tons)

Country	1969	1970	1971	1972	1973	1974	1975	1976	1977	1978	1979[e]
North America:											
United States[t]	471	456	432	545	544	555	512	553	597	641	660
Mexico	12	14	12	14	15	13	21	16	5	27	28
Total	483	470	444	559	559	568	533	569	622	668	668
Europe:											
Greece[‡]	108	118	105	120	139	126	125	[r]140	163	148	150
Hungary[§]	67	66	67	94	106	103	79	106	114	102	103
Italy[e]	80	90	90	95	105	110	100	105	100	100	100
USSR[e]	125	150	200	250	300	320	340	360	380	400	400
Others[e]	26	31	38	45	52	55	60	62	62	60	60
Total	406	455	500	604	702	714	704	[r]773	819	810	813
Asia:											
Japan[‡e]	40	45	50	55	60	63	68	72	77	80	83
Philippines	—	13	1	1	1	1	1	2	2	2	2
Turkey	3	4	16	32	16	19	13	27	33	30	30
Others[e]	—	—	33	33	35	30	28	28	28	30	30
Total	43	62	100	121	112	113	110	129	140	142	145
Africa: Total[e]	#	#	1	1	#	#	#	#	1	1	1
Oceania:											
Australia	1	1	2	2	3	2	[e]2	4	2	2	3
New Zealand	[e]1	2	2	3	3	3	[e]2	2	1	[e]1	1
Total	[e]2	3	4	5	6	5	[e]4	6	3	[e]3	4
World total[‖]	934	990	1,049	1,290	1,379	1,400	1,351	[r]1,477	1,585	1,624	1,651

Source: Meisinger, 1980.
[e] Estimated. [r] Revised.
* Perlite mined and/or processed.
[t] Processed ore sold or used by producers.
[‡] Processed ore.
[§] Mined ore.
Less than ½ unit.
‖ Does not include minor quantities of perlite mined from several deposit areas in South America.

TABLE 2—Perlite Mined, Processed, Expanded, and Sold and Used by Producers in the United States
(Thousand short tons and thousand dollars)

		Processed perlite					Expanded perlite		
		Sold to expanders		Used at own plant to make expanded material		Total quantity sold and used		Sold and used	
Year	Perlite mined* Quantity	Quantity	Value	Quantity	Value		Quantity produced	Quantity	Value
1977	871	298	5,514	299	5,239	597	504	498	53,600
1978	939	320	6,813	321	6,927	641	553	546	64,300
1979	847	322	7,996	338	8,439	660	[r]551	[r]543	[r]61,200
1980	824	334	9,053	304	7,447	638	544	537	69,200
1981	710	324	9,888	267	7,530	591	484	475	65,900

Source: Meisinger, 1982.
* Crude ore mined and stockpiled for processing.
[r] Revised.

TABLE 3—Some Typical Perlite Chemical Compositions
(Percent)

	No Agua, NM	Superior, AZ	Pioche, NV	Big Pine, CA	Milos, Greece	Akita, Japan	Bulgaria	Argentina	Hungary
SiO_2	72.1	73.6	73.1	73.6	74.2	74.2	73.8	72.3	73.5
Al_2O_3	13.5	12.7	12.8	13.2	12.3	12.9	12.8	13.4	13.0
Fe_2O_3	0.8	0.7	0.7	0.8	0.95	0.68	0.56	1.0	1.8
TiO_2	0.06	0.1	0.08	0.07	0.08	0.06	0.07	0.08	—
CaO	0.89	0.6	0.9	0.6	0.85	0.45	0.50	0.59	1.5
MgO	0.50	0.2	0.2	0.1	0.13	0.05	0.03	0.3	0.4
Na_2O	4.6	3.2	3.0	4.1	4.0	4.1	3.0	3.4	3.5
K_2O	4.4	5.0	4.7	4.1	4.4	4.0	4.9	4.7	3.8
H_2O+	3.0	3.8	3.9	3.3	2.8	3.3	4.0	3.7	3.0

troversial than it was a decade earlier. The 2 to 5% range for total combined water in perlite was originally thought to have been chilled or frozen into the glass as it was injected under an ice sheet or into a lake (Huntting, 1949). Now, there is universal acceptance of the theory that perlite was formed by the secondary hydration of obsidian after its emplacement (Ross and Smith, 1955; Friedman, et al., 1966; Jesek and Noble, 1978). Studies have shown that the combined water in perlite exists in at least two forms (Lehmann and Knauf, 1973; Lehmann and Rossler, 1974): one as molecular water and the rest as hydroxyl water. The ratio of one kind of water to the other is different for perlites of different origins. The composition of the perlite, particularly the amount of MgO and CaO, is believed to influence the rate of hydration of the obsidian.

Perlite of commercial significance occurs in a variety of textures that appear to be related to the depth of emplacement. An emplacement model for perlitic domes suggests that the outermost material will be pumiceous, grading inward into increasingly more compact textures and finally into a felsitic core. The following textures that fit the above model have been observed at No Agua Mountain, New Mexico and elsewhere (Whitson, 1981). While these textures also may be known by other names, the following seems to be a convenient and logical nomenclature.

Pumiceous: Near surface, this is a lightweight and frothy perlite where vesiculation is less confined by lithostatic and hydrostatic pressures. The vesicularity and the degree of distortion of the vesicles is a function of local confining pressures and of the amount of viscous flow during vesiculation of the super-cooled liquid. Flattening of vesicle walls increases with depth while elongation occurs during flow.

Hence, at depth, the vesicles of pumiceous perlite when viewed with a 10 X hand lens appear elongated and taffy-like. At No Agua Mountain, this taffy-like texture is referred to as "shardy." Pumiceous perlite is usually light grey but may be buff. ·

Although the expansibility of pumiceous perlite may be quite satisfactory, its usefulness as a commercial grade is limited by its pronounced friability during milling and subsequent handling. Not only are excessive quantities of undersize material produced but suitably sized material is less likely than other textures to survive handling during transit to the expanding location and may arrive out of specification by virtue of excessive fines content. During exploration, near surface pumiceous perlite is difficult to core drill. In the field, the more compacted pumiceous varieties of perlite—shardy—are characteristically difficult to sample because they tend to powder when struck by a geologist's pick and much of the energy is absorbed rather than expended in breaking a chip off the outcrop.

Granular: This texture is found adjacent to and deeper than pumiceous perlite in the emplacement model. It is more dense than the overlying textures, has a "sugary" or saccharoidal appearance and commercially is highly satisfactory from the milling, classification, and expansibility standpoints. It cores well during drilling and blasts easily during mining. Color usually is buff but varies from grey to brown. It often displays flow banding (see Fig. 1).

Classical: This is the typical pearl grey material with "onionskin" concentric parting. Classical texture also may be dark grey to black. The name is derived from the classical description of perlite in the literature (Johannsen, 1939). Classical perlite is found stratigraphically below the granular perlite in the

FIG. 1—*Hand specimen of granular perlite showing flow banding.*

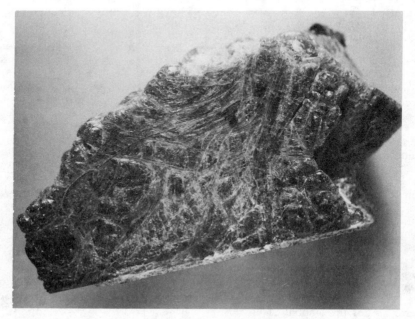

FIG. 2—*Hand specimen of classical perlite. Concentric onionskin-like cracks are evident. The name is derived from the classical description of perlite rock.*

FIG. 3—*Hand specimen of perlite breccia consisting of granular perlite in felsitic matrix. Granular fragments may vary from microscopic to several centimeters in cross-section.*

dome. Obsidian, whenever present, is always encased in classical perlite lending substance to the theory that perlite is formed from the hydration of obsidian. The concentric rings around each obsidian nodule were probably formed as the result of volume increase due to the hydration which advanced only as far as the perlite-obsidian interface (see Fig. 2). Toward the interior of the flow, the amount of obsidian in classical perlite tends to increase. Also found in perlite deposits are a rhyolitic or felsitic core, flow breccia (Fig. 3), and other materials and structures associated with volcanic flows and domes.

In addition to obsidian which may contain what have been identified as tridymite inclusions, often such nonexpansibles as quartz, feldspar, biotite, magnetite, and other accessory minerals, as well as products of devitrification, may be present.

Thin section studies of expanded perlite particles reveal the internal structure to be cellular and quite variable depending on the source (Bailey and Kadey, 1962). A comparison of Figs. 4, 5, and 6 explains why some perlites are considered *hard* and have high compaction resistance while others have low compaction resistance and are known as *soft* perlites. Hard perlites are particularly suited for plaster and concrete aggregate. Soft perlites which are not suited for these applications will mill readily to produce good filter aids. The size of the internal cell compartments and the thickness of the individual cell walls all depend on the expansibility of the particle. These in turn are thought to be a function of the composition and in particular the amount and distribution of the combined water.

Obsidian which contains less than one percent water can also be made to expand, but at a higher temperature (see Fig. 7).

Distribution of Deposits

Perlite deposits are restricted to Tertiary or younger volcanics of rhyolitic composition. Because rhyolitic glasses are unstable, they devitrify with age. Very young acidic volcanics have not had sufficient time to hydrate, hence they are still essentially obsidian and not expansible within the temperature range of perlite. There is a belt of Tertiary and Quaternary rhyolites that begins in Iceland, extends south into Ireland, Scotland, through the Massif Central of France into some of the Aegean Islands, through Sardinia and mainland Italy and farther south into Morocco, Algeria, and into South Africa. A Pacific belt splits, with a western limb extending through Japan, the Philippines, China, New Zealand, and Aus-

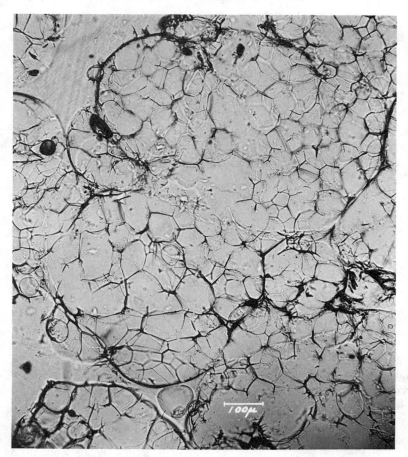

FIG. 4—*Thin section micrograph through perlite aggregate expanded to low density (less than 2 lb per cu ft). The thin fragile walls will break under pressure. This material, while not having sufficient compaction resistance for plaster or concrete aggregate, is quite suitable for milling into a filter aid.*

tralia. The eastern part of the circum-Pacific belt extends from Alaska (Plafker, 1963) through western Canada, down through the western United States into Mexico, and emerges in parts of the Andes in Chile and Argentina. Fig. 8 shows the perlite resources of the United States.

North America: While perlitic occurrences have been noted in Alaska and western Canada, the continental United States has the largest known reserves and commercial production in the world (Jaster, 1956; Meisinger, 1980).

There are 12 operations in six of the western states. In 1982, New Mexico accounted for approximately 83% of US production. No Agua Mountain in Taos County mined by both Manville Products Corp. and Grefco, Inc. is considered to be the largest commercial deposit in the world and accounts for most of this production. Fig. 9 shows the perlite operations at No Agua, New Mexico. Other producing locations in the state are Brushy Mountain about 20 miles northeast of No Agua, mined by Silbrico Corp., a deposit in Socorro County operated by Grefco (Weber, 1963), and one near Grants that is mined by U.S. Gypsum Co. for use in plaster (Bassett, et al., 1963). Elsewhere in the southwestern part of the state are smaller and lower quality occurrences.

Main production in Arizona, which centers

around the area near Superior and the southern half of the state, is accounted for by Filters International Corp. and by Harborlite Corp. Much of the perlite from the Superior area displays classical texture. Commercial grade perlite produced by Delamar-Mackie and U.S. Gypsum comes from Nevada. Perlite is also produced from deposits in California by American Perlite Corp., in Idaho by Oneida Perlite Corp. (Staley, 1962), and in Colorado by Persolite Products, Inc. Utah, Oregon, and Washington report lesser occurrences with negligible current production (Huntting, 1949; Jaster, 1956).

Mexican production is centered in the state of Sonora by Aislantes del Pacifico, S.A., in Pueblo by Cia. Minera Oriental, S. A., in Durango by Termolita, S.A., and in Pueblo by Dicalite de Mexico, S.A. (a Grefco, Inc. affiliate).

South America: Argentina is the major producer of South American perlite. Perfiltra S.A. and Minaclar, S.A. mine perlite from deposits in Salta Province near Salar de Pocitos (Quartino, 1975). The only other significant source of perlite in South America is in Chile where Cia Perlite Ltda. mine from a deposit in the Lagana de Maula area.

Europe: Greece is the largest western European producer of perlite. Major production comes from the Island of Milos where Silver and Barytes Ores Mining Co., General Enterprises Sarides, S.A., Mycobar Mining Co. S.A. (a subsidiary of Dresser Industries), and N. Bouras and Co. are the principal producers. The Greek Islands of Kos and Lesbos in the

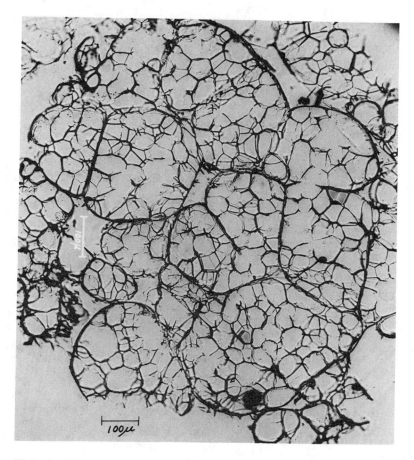

FIG. 5—*Thin section micrograph through perlite aggregate expanded to intermediate density (approximately 4½ lb per cu ft). Note the relatively coarse cell wall structure compared with Fig. 4.*

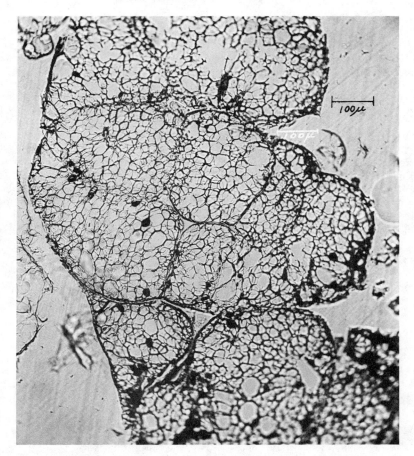

FIG. 6—*Thin section micrograph through perlite aggregate expanded to relatively high density (approximately 8 lb per cu ft). Note the small cells and coarse wall structure. This perlite would produce excessive floaters content if milled into a filter aid. The apparent strength of the aggregate would be ideal for plaster and concrete aggregate.*

Aegean Sea also have commercial grades of perlite from which there has been some production. Numerous other Greek islands contain perlite (Anastopoulos, 1963). Turkey has substantial reserves of high quality perlite in the western part of the country. There are also occurrences in central and eastern Turkey as well. Etibank, the government controlled mineral producing company, has substantial reserves near Cumoavasi in western Turkey and is the only source to date with processing facilities (Anon., 1977). Turkey could become a major producer of high quality perlite for both filter aid and aggregate use if the owners of the various deposits could attract the neces-sary capital to construct crushing and screening facilities. Some of these producers are shipping mined crude elsewhere for processing.

Italy is an important source of perlite with the most important deposits located on the island of Sardinia near the town of Uras (Carta, 1976). Perlite SpA is jointly owned by British Gypsum Ltd. CECA (Carbonisation et Charbons Actifs.), also mines from a deposit on Sardinia. Perlite is mined on the island of Ponza by Vic Italiana SpA. In Eastern Europe, Hungary (Perlaki and Szoor, 1973) and the Soviet Union are significant producers of perlite (Rudnyanszky, 1978). Bulgaria, Czechoslovakia, and Yugoslavia have smaller but growing industries (Vladimirov, 1975). Iceland has a commercially challenging but as yet unproductive perlite deposit at Priest Mountain (Prestahnukur) located about 100 km northeast of Reykjavik. The remoteness of the deposit, the relatively high concentrations of obsidian, and the short four-month mining season offset the otherwise good quality of perlite in many parts of the mountain. A smaller occurrence at Lodmundarfjordur has been investigated, but the location and quality do not justify commercial consideration. Northern Ireland did at one time have limited production from deposits in the Sandy Braes area of County Antrim.

Small deposits in France and Germany are devitrified or have not been economical to mine.

Africa: The only known commercial production of perlite is in southern Africa by Pratley Perlite Mining Co. (Pty.) at the Nxwala Estate, Zululand and by Perlite Industries (Pty.) Ltd. from a deposit in the Lebombo Mts. area both in northern Natal, South Africa (Coetzee, 1976; Anon., 1977a).

Asia: Japan is the most significant producer of perlite in Asia, which because of the volcanic nature of the islands has numerous perlite deposits. Mitsui Mining and Smelting Co. Ltd., the dominant Japanese perlite producer, operates mines at Kitakata, Ippongisita, and at Arita, Tomioka. Other deposits are located at the Kushiro prefecture of Hokkaido; at Akita; in Yamagata; in Nagano; in Chiba prefecture; in Kawasaki and Osaka; in Yamaguchi; in Kumamoto and in Fukuoka.

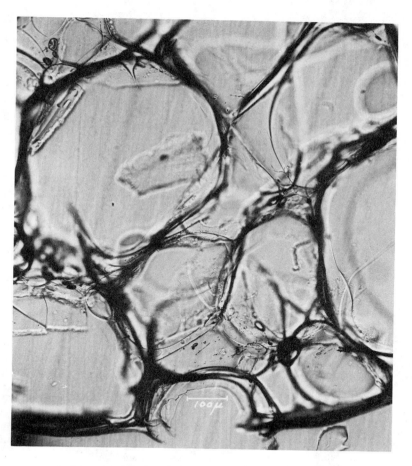

FIG. 7—*Thin section micrograph through expanded particle of obsidian. Note coarse size of walls and large size of cells compared with those aggregates in Figs. 4, 5, and 6.*

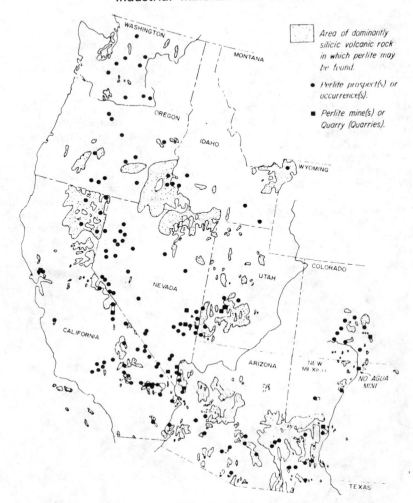

FIG. 8—*Perlite resources of the United States (after Jaster, 1956; updated, 1977, by A. L. Bush, US Geological Survey).*

New Zealand has a deposit at Kenlieth which is mined by New Zealand Perlite, Ltd. A substantial deposit occurs on Great Barrier Island, located a few miles off the east coast northeast of Auckland. Several other deposits in New Zealand have been described (Thompson and Reed, 1954). Perlite in Queensland, Australia, is mined and processed by Australian Gypsum Industries, Ltd.

The Philippines have perlite on Luzon Island. A deposit near Pagaspi is operated by Perlite Industries and Minerals Corp. Grefco, Inc. mines from a deposit in the Albay area of Luzon and Trinity Lodge Mining Corp. also mines ore from the Albay area.

Reserves

There does not appear to be any accurate or complete estimate of total world ore reserves. The US Bureau of Mines has estimated US reserves to be approximately 700,000,000 tons (Meisinger, 1979). Depending on the quality for specific applications and on the growth of the industry, this is enough to supply domestic needs for approximately 500 to 1,000 years. Although foreign reserves are even less known, it is reasonable to assume that on a worldwide basis, there is enough perlite for the foreseeable future.

Exploration

Exploration for perlite is restricted to those areas of rhyolitic volcanism between Tertiary and Quaternary age. Any glassy rhyolites of earlier than the Tertiary age have long since devitrified and are not of commercial interest. Younger acidic volcanics will not as yet have hydrated from obsidian. Perlite is recognized in the field by its characteristic appearance, whether it be a rather light grey pumiceous to classical onionskin or the grey to buff granular texture. The presence of marekanite or obsidian nodules (*Apache teardrops*), while detrimental in commercial perlite, are a good field indicator that the prospector may not be far from "pay dirt." Once grab samples have been taken from outcrops or shallow trenches, and upon receipt of encouraging test results, the next step includes the careful mapping of the dome or flow. Careful field work should ascertain the nature and distribution of rock textures and identify other such features as flow banding, joint systems, faults, etc.

The next step, diamond core drilling, is one in which considerable difficulty may be encountered. The friable nature of some perlitic textures, together with fracturing and jointing, may result in poor core recovery. Often only sludge samples can be obtained. In many cases such mechanical difficulties as hung bits, lost drill steel, and loss of circulation of drilling fluid may be encountered. Such problems can be minimized with the use of a triple tube wire line core barrel and NQ size core. On some occasions and in less accessible terrain, portable drilling equipment will produce adequate results and often can furnish information not otherwise attainable. The spacing between drill holes and the intervals into which the core is to be split for testing depends on the variability of quality. In many occurrences, variability is so great that the economics of the matter determines the closeness of the drilling and sampling

FIG. 9—*Aerial view of No Agua Mountain, New Mexico. The Manville Products Corp. North Hill Quarries may be seen in the center foreground with the crushing and screening plant in the lower right foreground. Manville is also mining the southern flank of the south hill (rear left peak). The east peak is out of view, to the left. Grefco, Inc. is mining a flow that is hidden in this photo by the west hill (rear right peak).*

pattern. In general multistage drilling programs, in which drilling is begun on wide spacings, then tightened up in subsequent stages, are most economical in time and costs.

Evaluation of Deposits

As is the case with so many industrial minerals, laboratory evaluation is based on tests designed to simulate commercial conditions of processing and application. Foremost among such tests is one that measures the expansibility of the sample. This can be accomplished in its simplest form by dropping dry crushed perlite into a bunsen flame and observing the resulting popping. A more refined apparatus is required to obtain some degree of control. One of the best laboratory expanders is the test furnace manufactured by the Perlite Corporation of Chester, PA. The basic design consists of a 48 in. long (40 in. effective length from feed port to flame) vertical tube, about 4 in. in diameter. It has a cyclone type collecting device fitted to the upper end, with a burner at the lower end. The crushed and sized test sample can be fed into the tube at any one of three side ports, whereupon it drops into the flame and upon expansion rises in the hot draft and passes over into the cyclone collecting system. The furnace can be modified and the design embellished so that either liquid propane or natural gas can be used, and the feed rate, draft, and other parameters monitored. One of the restrictions of laboratory expansion, however, is that the short tube length requires the furnace feed to have a very narrow size gradation. The relative expansibility of an unknown sample can be judged against that of a reference standard that is run at the same time. A 50/100 mesh gradation works moderately well, although narrow distributions of coarser gradations can be expanded with careful control of temperature and draft. There is no known suitable scale-down to laboratory size to simulate the expansibility of perlite in a horizontal furnace. Whether a crude perlite sample is worth laboratory testing can be ascertained by a petrographic examination for percent contamination, refractive index of the glass, and other criteria (Kadey, 1963).

The properties of the laboratory expanded sample can be measured in the same way as are properties of perlite expanded in a commercial size furnace. Loose density and compacted density in pounds per cubic foot, percent yield, percent nonexpansibles, compaction resistance, etc., are all standard tests that have been described in the Perlite Institute handbook of tests (Perlite Institute, 1977). For filter aid evaluation, further treatment beyond the expansion of the granule must be performed. Laboratory milling and filter aid testing that simulates commercial filter aid performance is required. Evaluation of the data depends on comparison of test properties against those of the reference standard and/or against the specifications required by the marketplace.

Preparation for Markets

Mining Methods: Open pit mining is the only method of ore removal that is economically feasible and practical for the extraction of perlite. With pumiceous textures, the ore is friable enough that rippers on the back of bulldozers are used to loosen the rock which is then pushed into hoppers or bins (traps), under which trucks are loaded for transit to the stockpile or mill. With harder ore, blasting is necessary and the ore is mined from benches. It is then loaded into trucks by front-end loaders. The variable nature of perlite deposits often necessitates selective mining techniques to avoid clay seams, obsidian, or other non-perlitic areas. The nature of some ore is such that it doesn't even have to be ripped. The Priest Mountain, Iceland deposit and parts of the Sardinian deposits are fractured enough in place that front-end loaders can break and load what otherwise appears to be solid rock. Rock of this type, however, is difficult to core drill and has some of the same commercial drawbacks as pumiceous textured perlite.

Assuming satisfactory quality, the part of the flow that is overlain by the least amount of overburden and in which maximum advantage can be taken of topography in the development of the mine plan is usually selected as the first mine site.

Milling Techniques: Perlite is usually used in the expanded form and the applications for which it is intended dictate the particle range into which it must be crushed and sized prior to expansion. Theoretically, equidimensional particles, which when expanded, fall between a maximum of ⅜ in. for horticultural grades and a minimum of 200 mesh for most other applications, are ideal. Axiomatically, the coarser the required product, the coarser the corresponding furnace feed must be. The size range of the expanded perlite dictates the size range of the furnace feed. This relationship, however, is not necessarily the same for all perlites and must be determined for each source since no two deposits are alike.

The crushing and sizing of crude perlite is designed with this objective in mind. The first step is to reduce the stockpile to lumps of less than 3 in. because much of the mine run ore is of boulder size. This is done by a jaw crusher. Further reduction to less than ⅝ in. is done by cone crusher, whereupon reduction to minus 8 mesh is accomplished by impact milling. Vibratory screening and air classification separates the milled perlite into basic grades for storage in silos, whereupon it is blended to meet specifications or to meet the customer's requirements. Undersize material is wasted, but research in recent years has been directed toward finding uses for undersize material.

Processing Techniques: The processing of crushed and sized perlite consists essentially of its expansion or "popping" into a lightweight, cellular aggregate. This is accomplished at temperatures ranging between 1400°F and 2100°F depending on the composition of the perlite (Sharps, 1961). As has been previously noted, the name perlite is also used for the expanded material. The largest volume of perlite is used in this form; however, the application of perlite as a filter aid requires a subsequent milling and classifying stage.

Although there have been many styles of furnaces patented for the expansion of perlite, two basic types have survived—the vertical (Fig. 10) and the horizontal furnace (Fig. 11). Both types depend on the relatively rapid introduction of the crushed and sized perlite into a hot zone during which the particle reaches its softening range, coincident with the volatilization of combined water. In the case of the vertical furnace, perlite is gravity fed through a side port into the hot zone (see Fig. 10).

Upon expansion, the density of the expanding particle decreases to a point where the downward force of gravity on its mass is exceeded by the updraft which carries it over into the cyclone. Large particles, therefore, fall further down into the hot zone than do finer particles before expanding and rising in the draft. Nonexpansible particles like obsidian, felsite, and other contaminants continue to drop out the bottom whereas the shattered fines, etc., are carried upward and trapped in the bag house.

In the case of a horizontal furnace, the furnace feed is introduced at the hot end through an arrangement of baffles which cause the perlite to cascade into the hot zone. It travels down the length of the rotating furnace during which it is expanded and is then drawn up the stack by the draft and over into the collecting system. The expansibility of some perlites can be enhanced by preheating below 800°F (Sharps, 1961). In vertical furnacing, this is accomplished by passing the furnace feed through a separate heater at about 700°F. Horizontal furnaces preheat the feed by passage between an inner and outer shell of the furnace before it cascades into the hot zone (see Fig. 11).

There must be a good balance between the softening of the glass and the volatilization of the combined water. Excessive combined water will cause some perlites to explode or shatter with the subsequent production of excessive fines. Insufficient water or an overly viscous glass, on the other hand, will result in partially expanded, heavy density perlite. The former is often termed *lively* and the latter *dead*. Lively perlites can be modified by preheating to reduce some of the combined water. Some dead perlites may be helped by preheating. Otherwise, they are less suitable commercially and must be relegated to applications where a low density thin-walled product is not needed.

Expansion for the various aggregate uses requires that the perlite be expanded to a specific size range and density. Processing into a filter aid, in addition to expansion to a specified size and density, requires a subsequent milling

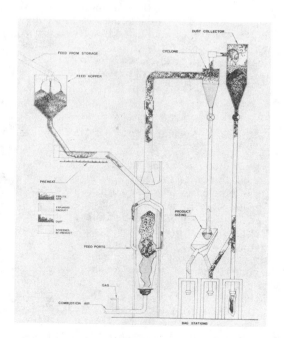

FIG. 10—*Vertical expander and handling system.*

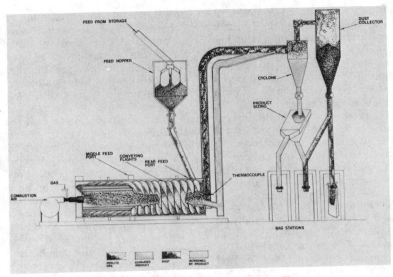

FIG. 11—*Horizontal expander and handling system.*

and classifying operation. The perlite bubble aggregates must be broken into curved glass plates and bubble junctions. A filter aid requires the right proportion of these with a minimum of unmilled cells. Residual unmilled cells, or "floaters," are undesirable in a filter aid. There are, of course, additional requisites and specifications for both aggregates and filter aids. These will be discussed later.

Table 4 shows typical size distributions for a range of perlite ores.

Testing and Specifications

Guidance for the maintenance of production and performance standards for expanded perlite is handled through the auspices of the Perlite Institute with offices at 45 West 45th Street, New York. The Perlite Institute publishes a *Manual of Test Methods* and related standards that control every phase of perlite quality and performance from the shipment of the unexpanded material in box and hopper cars to its ultimate incorporation into such applications as plaster and concrete. Many of these test methods are the creation of the Technical Committee of the Perlite Institute whereas others are selected specifications of the American Society for Testing & Materials (ASTM) applicable to the perlite industry. Following is a list of current Perlite Institute tests:

PI 108–77 Method for Bulk Box Car Sampling of Sized Perlite Ore
PI 109–77 Method for Sampling Sized Perlite Ore from Hopper Cars
PI 110–77 Sampling of Perlite
PI 111–77 Preparation of Perlite Sample for Testing by Coning and Quartering Method
PI 112–77 Preparation of Perlite Sample for Testing by Splitter or Riffle Method
PI 113–77 Sieve Analysis of Fine Materials
PI 114–77 Sieve Analysis of Expanded Perlite, Volume Basis
PI 115–77 Sieve Analysis of Expanded Perlite, Weight Basis
PI 116–77 Fractional Density of Expanded Perlite
PI 117–77 Wet Screen Analysis
PI 118–77 Determination of Free and Combined Moisture in Perlite
PI 200–77 Loose Weight Determination of Expanded Perlite
PI 201–77 Compacted Density
PI 202–77 Test for pH Value of Expanded Perlite
PI 300–77 Determination of *Floats* and *Sinks* in Expanded Perlite
PI 303–77 Water Repellency Test
PI 305–77 Yield Test for Perlite Aggregate
PI 306–77 Compaction Resistance Test
PI 307–77 Perlite Ore Expansibility Test
PI 400–77 Setting Time of Gypsum Plaster
PI 401–77 Plaster Coverage Test

The following specifications of the ASTM are applicable to the perlite industry:

C 28–76 Specification for Gypsum Plasters
C 29–76 Test Method for Unit Weight of Aggregate
C 35–76 Specification for Inorganic Aggregates for Use in Gypsum Plaster
C 136–76 Test Method for Sieve or Screen Analysis of Fine and Coarse Aggregates
C 331–77 Specification for Lightweight Aggregates for Concrete Masonry Units
C 332–77 Specification for Lightweight Aggregates for Insulating Concrete
C 472–73 Physical Testing of Gypsum Plasters and Gypsum Concrete
C 495–77 Test Method for Compressive Strength of Lightweight Insulating Concrete
C 513–69 Method for Securing, Preparing, and Testing Specimens from Hardened Lightweight Insulating Concrete for Compressive Strength
C 520–65 Test Method for Density of Granular Loose Fill Insulations
C 549–73 Specification for Perlite Loose Fill Insulation
E 11–70 Specification for Wire-Cloth Sieves for Testing Purposes
E 380–76 Standard for Metric Practice

Marketing

Because of its low bulk density, perlite is generally shipped in the unexpanded form to the local marketing area, and expanded at that point. Perlite mined from twelve operations in six western states is shipped to 73 expanding locations in 32 states (Table 5). Foreign producers likewise ship crushed and sized perlite all over their marketing areas to the local expanding points for redistribution. The foreign distances are considerably greater. For example, Greek perlite is shipped throughout Europe. There was considerable interest in the early 1960s in importing Greek and Icelandic perlite to the East Coast of the United States. The attempt failed for a number of reasons, one of which was the lack of sufficient warehousing space for boatloads of crude perlite. The United States, therefore, continues to supply all its own needs.

Because of its unique internal cellular structure, perlite offers many advantages as an insulating material for the construction industry. Perlite aggregate combined with portland cement and water produces a lightweight concrete that is used for lightweight floor and roof fill, lightweight structural roof decks, precast components, and numerous other insulating applications. In roof deck construction, in

TABLE 4—Typical Size Distribution for Some Perlite Ores

	Manville Grade				
	PA-1000	PA-115	PA-220	PA-420	PA-610
	Application				
Sieve Size	Plastic and Resin Filler	Cryogenics, Acoustical Tile, Filter Aid	Plaster Aggregate	Concrete Aggregate, Masonry, Loose Fill	Horticulture, Foundry Slag
+8					
8-16				0-2	10-25
8-12				22-30	
12-16					40-60
+20					25-42
16-20			7-16		
+30		0-2			0-8
16-30					
20-30				53-65	
-20			26-35		
30-50		4-12	40-52		0-4
50-100		30-55	6-13	10-21	
-50				0-4	
-100			0-4		
+100	0-8				
100-200	20-47	25-45			
-200	50-75	0-20			

Source: Manville Bulletin FF 391, January, 1980.

TABLE 5—Producers of Expanded Perlite in the United States, 1979

Company	Address
Airlite Processing Corp. of Florida	Vero Beach, FL
American Perlite Products, Inc.	Gilliam, LA
Armstrong Cork Co.	Lancaster, PA
Aztec Perlite Co.	Escondido, CA
Brouk Company	St. Louis, MO
Buffalo Perlite Div. of Pine Hill Concrete Mix Corp.	Buffalo, NY
Carolina Perlite Co.	Gold Hill, NC
C-E Refractories	Port Kennedy, PA
Chemrock Corp.	Nashville, TN
Cleveland Gypsum Co.	Cleveland, OH
Conwed Corp.	St. Paul, MN
Filter Media, Inc.	Houston, TX
Filter Products Corp.	Lake Zurich, IL
Georgia-Pacific Corp.	Portland, OR
Grefco, Inc.	Los Angeles, CA
Harborlite Corp.	Escondido, CA
Manville Products Corp.	Denver, CO
Lite Weight Products, Inc.	Kansas City, KS
Mica Pellets, Inc.	DeKalb, IL
Midwest Perlite Co.	Appleton, WI
National Gypsum Co.	Buffalo, NY
Oneida Perlite Corp.	Malad City, ID
Pacific Coast Products	Sebastopol, CA
Pamrod Products	McQueeney, TX
Paramount Perlite Co., Inc.	Paramount, CA
Pennsylvania Perlite Corp.	Lehigh Valley, PA
Perlite Manufacturing Co.	Carnegie, PA
Perlite of Houston, Inc.	Houston, TX
Perlite Popped Products	Santa Fe Springs, CA
Perlite Processing Co.	Santa Fe Springs, CA
Persolite Products, Inc.	Florence, CO
Redco, Inc.	North Hollywood, CA
Schundler Co.	Metuchen, NJ
Scolite International Corp.	Troy, NY
Silbrico Corp.	Hodgkins, IL
Sil-Flo, Inc.	Port Jefferson, NY
South Texas Perlite	San Antonio, TX
Strong-Lite Products	Pine Bluff, AR
Supreme Perlite Co.	Portland, OR
The Celotex Corp.	Tampa, FL
The Pax Co.	Salt Lake City, UT
Thermo-O-Rock Div. of Allied Block Chemical Co.	New Eagle, PA
United States Gypsum Co.	Chicago, IL
Whittemore Perlite Co., Inc.	Andover, MA
W. R. Grace & Co.	Cambridge, MA

Source: Meisinger, 1980.

addition to its insulating capacity, it is stronger, more rigid, and more fire safe than other roof insulations. On flat roofs, it can be applied to provide the proper drainage slopes and it makes an excellent base for conventional built-up roofing. It is also nailable. Perlite plaster consists of a blend of expanded perlite aggregate and neat gypsum (or portland cement) properly mixed with water for application to wall and ceiling surfaces or for fireproofing structural steel. Perlite plaster walls have low sound transmission. Silicone treated loose fill insulation is used for cavity wall and concrete or cinder block wall construction. Its use will minimize winter heat loss and summer heat gain. The silicone treatment renders it water repellent to improve its insulating capacity. Perlite is rot-proof, nonsettling, and non-combustible. Its insulating capacity is used in cryogenic insulations. It fills the space between double shelled tanks for liquid oxygen and similar chemicals. In this and other loose fill applications, it is easy to apply. It has horticultural use as a soil conditioner—an application that is more apparent to the general public, particularly to the home gardener, than is its more commercial uses.

As a filter aid for the separation of suspended solids from fluids, in addition to use with pressure leaf filters, it has particular application in rotary precoat filtration. The criteria for a good filter aid are as follows:

1) Inert in the liquid to be filtered
2) Unaffected by temperature
3) High permeability
4) Low wet density
5) Ability to remove nonsettleable solids
6) Easily kept in suspension
7) Precoatability
8) Neutral

A properly processed perlite filter aid will meet all these criteria. It has established itself particularly in the filtration of sugar, of alginates, and of pharmaceuticals. Unexpanded perlite has demonstrated suitability in certain specialty uses such as scouring compounds, blasting sands, and some filler applications. Table 6 shows the amount of expanded perlite sold or used in the United States by producers.

Pricing

The US Bureau of Mines reported (Meisinger, 1982) that the total value of processed perlite sold or used by producers in 1981 was $17.4 million compared with $13.7 million in 1978. The average price, f.o.b. plant for raw, crushed grades in 1980 was $25.86 per ton, and for 1981, was $29.47 per ton. Transportation costs can more than double the delivered price to the East Coast. The trend for previous years is shown in Table 7. The price of expanded perlite is variable depending on use, grade, and competitive market location.

The range for expanded perlite in 1979 was $75 to $275 (loose fill) with the average price $127.79.

Health and Ecology

Perlite per se is not known to present a health hazard either in the mining, milling, or processing of the material. As a glass, it is amorphous and regarded as innocuous. Most environmentally conscious companies, however,

TABLE 6—Expanded Perlite Sold and Used by Producers in the United States, by Use
(Short tons)

Use	1979	1980	1981
Concrete aggregate	37,000	29,800	21,800
Fillers	9,000	10,000	6,200
Filter aid	96,500	102,300	94,400
Formed products*	291,000	289,900	256,000
Horticultural aggregate[†]	41,400	40,900	40,200
Low-temperature insulation	6,200	7,700	5,900
Masonry and cavity fill insulation	21,800	20,900	20,000
Plaster aggregate	23,200	24,000	16,700
Other[‡]	16,900	11,200	14,100
Total [§]	543,000	537,000	475,000

Source: Meisinger, 1982.

* Includes acoustic ceiling tile, pipe insulation, roof insulation board, and unspecified formed products.

[†] Includes fertilizer carriers.

[‡] Includes fines, high-temperature insulation, paint texturizer, refractories, and various nonspecified industrial uses.

[§] Data may not add to total shown because of independent rounding.

consider all dusts to be a nuisance, and in this regard, protect their workers with dust masks and practice dust control at considerable cost. Furthermore, as an abrasive and glassy material, crude and expanded perlite dust can be a serious irritant to the eyes and safety glasses are a necessity in the mine and in the plant.

With the recent emphasis on pollution of the environment, any operation that emits dust is suspect. Blasting, crushing, screening, and expansion of perlite are all dusty operations. Most perlite deposits are located in remote places and are not likely to cause complaints. The expansion of perlite is usually carried out in populated and industrial locations so dust collection and waste disposal problems must be recognized and dealt with effectively.

Further Considerations and Trends

Substitutes

Just as the advent of perlite produced a competitive threat to other industrial minerals, some of these have in turn replaced perlite in the marketplace or have joined perlite to share the market. Vermiculite probably ranks highest on the list of perlite competitors. Both are used in plaster and in loose fill insulation. In loose fill application, vermiculite is less amenable to beneficiation because it cannot be rendered water repellent with a monomolecular silicone coating. This treatment is preferable to asphalt treatment which can be applied to vermiculite. Vermiculite is also used for soil conditioning. From an aesthetic viewpoint, the white color of perlite which is so much of an advantage

otherwise is less preferable than the color of the vermiculite, which does not stand out as white aggregates in the darker soil. Dark coatings can be applied to the perlite but at added cost. While perlite invaded the realm of filtra-

TABLE 7—Time-Price Relationships for Crude Perlite

Average annual price, dollars per ton*

Year	Actual prices	Based on constant 1978 dollars
1958	8.44	19.42
1959	8.43	18.98
1960	8.54	18.91
1961	8.59	18.85
1962	8.31	17.91
1963	8.39	17.82
1964	8.78	18.36
1965	8.55	17.49
1966	9.67	19.16
1967	9.62	18.51
1968	9.87	18.18
1969	10.82	18.97
1970	10.75	17.89
1971	11.44	18.12
1972	11.44	17.39
1973	10.28	14.77
1974	12.66	16.59
1975	14.22	17.01
1976	16.99	19.32
1977	18.01	19.33
1978	21.44	21.44
1979	24.90	22.88

Source: Meisinger, 1980.
* F.o.b. processing plant.

tion long held by diatomite and considered to be superior in this application, each of these filter aids appears to have its own area of influence. The particulate structure of some diatomite filter aids is such that perlite performs better in rotary precoat filtration. On the other hand, where high clarity is required, the ratio of clarity to flow rate is higher for diatomite. Since most filter aids are sold on a weight basis and used on a volume basis, the lower density of perlite can be considered a competitive advantage.

Tariffs and Taxes

There is no tariff imposed on the importation of perlite into the country. The depletion allowance for perlite is 10%.

Acknowledgments

The author gratefully acknowledges the assistance of J. M. Sharratt, D. N. Whitson, R. O. Y. Breese, and J. A. Sarles of the Manville Exploration Department for their review and comments on the manuscript; and of Ann B. Michael, Kathy Hodges, and Judith Neale of the Manville Corporate Information Center in the compilation of the bibliographical references. The patience and expertise of S. J. Lefond, editor-in-chief, in the final draft is also greatly appreciated.

Bibliography and References

With some exceptions, the references listed herein are dated 1970 and later. The reader is referred to the Perlite chapter in the 4th edition of *Industrial Minerals and Rocks* for additional bibliographic information prior to 1970.

Anon., 1972, "Perlite: New Sources to Meet Growing Demand but Consumption Undergoing Change," *Industrial Minerals*, June, pp. 9–26.

Anon., 1977, "Perlite—Market Patterns and Future Potential," *Industrial Minerals*, May, pp. 17–37.

Anon., 1977a, "Perlite in North America," *Industrial Minerals*, July, pp. 31–35.

Anderson, F.G., et al., 1956, "Composition of Perlite," Report of Investigations 5199, US Bureau of Mines, 13 pp.

Austin, G.S., and Weber, R.H., 1976, "Perlite Operations in New Mexico," *Geological Society of America*, Vol. 8, No. 5, pp. 564–565.

Bailey, D.A., and Kadey, F.L., 1962, "Petrographic Thin-Section Study of the Structure of Expanded Perlite," *Trans. SME-AIME*, Vol. 223, pp. 37–40.

Bassett, W.A., et al., 1963, "Potassium-Argon Ages of Volcanic Rocks Near Grants, New Mexico," *Geological Society of America Bulletin*, Vol. 74, pp. 221–226.

Bush, A.L., 1974, "National Self Sufficiency in Lightweight Aggregate Resources," address given at the Perlite Institute Annual Meeting in Colorado Springs, CO, Apr. 22, pp. 94–99.

Carmichael, I.S.E., 1979, "Glass and the Glassy Rocks," Chap. 8, *The Evolution of the Igneous Rocks*, Princeton University Press, pp. 233–244.

Carta, M., et al., 1976, "The Industrial Minerals of Sardinia: Present Situation and Future Prospects," Second Industrial Minerals International Congress, Munich, pp. 41–55.

Chesterman, C.W., 1954, "Genesis of Perlite" (abstract), *Geological Society of America Bulletin*, Vol. 65, No. 12, p. 1336.

Chesterman, C.W., 1975, "Perlite," *Industrial Minerals and Rocks*, 4th ed., S.J. Lefond, ed., AIME, New York, pp. 927–934.

Christiansen, R.L., and Lipman, P.W., 1966, "Emplacement and Thermal History of a Rhyolitic Lava Flow Near Fortymile Canyon, Southern Nevada," *Geological Society of America Bulletin*, Vol. 77, pp. 671–684.

Coetzee, C.B., 1976, "Perlite in Lenses and Intermittent Layers," *Perlite—South Africa Geological Survey Handbook*, pp. 397–398.

Dunn, L.R.L., and Billinghurst, W.M., 1954, "Perlite Deposits in New Zealand," Part II, Evaluation, *New Zealand Journal of Science and Technology*, Nov., pp. 218–226.

Elevatorski, E.A., 1975, "Perlite in Pinal County near Superior," *Arizona Industrial Minerals*, Minobras, 73 pp.

Friedman, I., et al., 1966, "Hydration of Natural Glass and Formation of Perlite," *Geological Society of America Bulletin*, Vol. 77, Mar., pp. 323–328.

Huntting, M.T., 1949, "Perlite and Other Volcanic Glass Occurrences in Washington," Report of Investigation No. 17, Division of Mines and Geology, State of Washington, 77 pp.

Jaster, M.C., 1956, "Perlite Resources of the United States," Bulletin 1027–1, US Geological Survey, pp. 375–403.

Jesek, P.A., and Noble, D.C., 1978, "Natural Hydration and Ion Exchange of Obsidian: An Electron Microprobe Study," *American Mineralogist*, Vol. 63, pp. 266–273.

Johannsen, A., 1939, "A Descriptive Petrography of Igneous Rocks," University of Chicago Press, 318 pp.

Kadey, F.L., 1963, "Petrographic Techniques in Perlite Evaluation," *Trans. SME-AIME*, Vol. 229, pp. 332–336.

King, C.R., 1948, "Pumice and Perlite as Industrial Materials in California," *California Journal of Mines and Geology*, Vol. 44, No. 3, July, pp. 293–319.

Lacroix, A., 1916, "Volcanic Glasses of the Central Massif," *Comptes Rendus Hebdomadaires des Seances; Memoires de l'Academie de Sciences de l'Institut de France*, Vol. 163, No. 12, pp. 406–411.

Langford, R.L., 1979, "Mineral Dossier No. 21," Institute of Geological Sciences, London.

Lehmann, H., and Knauf, A., 1973, "Entwicklung Einer Pruemethode 2UR Beuteilung Der Blahfahigkeit Von Perlitgestein," *Tomind-Ztg.*, Vol. 97, No. 3, pp. 65–66.

Lehmann, H., Rossler, M., 1974, "A Contribution to the Nature of Water-Binding in Perlites,"

Thermal Analysis, Vol. 2, Proceedings, Fourth ICTA, Budapest, pp. 619–628.

Lehmann, H., and Rossler, M., 1976, "Thermoanalytische Untersuchungen An Perliten Und Perlitartigen Gestein," *Tomind-Ztg.,* Vol. 100, No. 7, pp. 271–274.

Lipman, P.W., and Mehnert, H.H., 1979, "The Taos Plateau Volcanic Field, Northern Rio Grande Rift, New Mexico," *Rio Grande Rift: Tectonics and Magmatism,* R. E. Riecker, ed., American Geophysical Union, Washington, DC, pp. 289–309.

Loney, R.A., 1969, "Flow Structure and Composition of the Southern Coulee, Mono Craters, California, A Pumiceous Rhyolite Flow," Memoir 116, Geological Society of America, pp. 415–440.

Meisinger, A.C., 1979, "Perlite," *Mineral Commodity Profiles,* US Bureau of Mines, 14 pp.

Meisinger, A.C., 1980, "Perlite," *Mineral Facts and Problems,* Bulletin 671, US Bureau of Mines, pp. 1–12.

Meisinger, A.C., 1982, "Perlite in 1981," *Mineral Industry Surveys,* US Bureau of Mines.

Meisinger, A.C., 1982a, "Perlite," *Mineral Commodity Summaries, 1982,* US Bureau of Mines, pp. 110–111.

Perlaki, E.I., and Szoor, Gy., 1973, "The Perlites of the Tokaj Mountains," *Acta Geologica Academiae Scientiorum Hungaricae,* Vol. 17 (1–3), pp. 85–106.

The Perlite Institute, *Perlite Design Manual.*

The Perlite Institute, 1977, *Manual of Test Methods.*

Plafker, G., et al., 1963, "Investigations for Perlite in the Alaska Range," Bulletin 1155, US Geological Survey, pp. 49–66.

Quartino, B.J., Zardini, R.A., and Llorente, R.A., 1975, "Estudio Geologico Economico de los Yacimientos de Perlita Taurus Y Anfitrite Salar De Pocitos, Prov. de Salta," *Ed. Cientificas Arg Librart* (ECAL), pp. 337–351.

Ricker, K., 1960, "Perlite with Special Reference to Icelandic Occurrences," *Zeitschrift der Deutschen Geologischen Gesellschaft,* Vol. 112, pp. 197–207.

Ross, C.S., and Smith, R.L., 1955, "Water and Other Volatiles in Volcanic Glasses," *American Mineralogist,* Vol. 40, Nos. 11, 12, Nov.-Dec., pp. 1076–1089.

Rudnyanszky, P., 1978, "Development and Uses of Perlite in Hungary," Perlite Institute Annual Meeting, Dubrovnik, Yugoslavia, May, pp. 135–138.

Sharps, T.I., 1961, "Perlite in Colorado and Other Western States," *Mineral Industries Bulletin,* Vol. 4, No. 6, Nov., Colorado School of Mines, pp. 1–15.

Staley, W.W., 1962, "The Oneida Perlite Deposit," Idaho Bureau of Mines and Geology Resources Report 9, 6 pp.

Stamboliev, H.T., and Sapunov, P., 1973, "Perlite-Vorkommen in Mazedonien/Jugoslawien," *Tomind-Ztg.,* Vol. 97, No. 3, pp. 63–64.

Stein, H.A., and Murdock, J.B., 1955, "The Processing of Perlite," *California Journal of Mines and Geology,* Vol. 51, No. 2, Apr., California Div. of Mines, pp. 105–116.

Stewart, D.B., 1979, "The Formation of Siliceous Potassic Glassy Rocks," Chap. 11, *The Evolution of the Igneous Rocks,* Princeton University Press, pp. 339–350.

Szep, E., 1976, "Die Forderung und Aufbereitung Des Perlits in Ungarn," *Tomind-Ztg.,* Vol. 100, No. 8, pp. 297–299.

Thompson, B.N., and Reed, J.J., 1954, "Perlite Deposits in New Zealand," *New Zealand Journal of Science and Technology,* Series B., Vol. 36, No. 3, pp. 208–218.

Toth, K., 1972, "Untersuchungen Zur Bestimmung Des Blahuermogens Von Perlitgestein," *Tomind-Ztg.,* Vol. 96, No. 6, pp. 137–142.

Toth, K., 1973, "Ein Mikrover Fahren Zur Bestimmung Der Eigenfestigkeit Von Perlithauewerken," 67 pp.

Varju, G., 1976, "Perlitrohstoffe und Einege Problem Ihrer Genese," *Tonindustrie Zeitung,* 100 Jahrg, Nr. 8, pp. 285–312.

Vassiliou, B.E., 1975, "Perlite in Greece," address given at Perlite Institute Annual Meeting, Athens, Greece, pp. 33–37.

Vassiliou, B.E., 1975, "The Market Outlook for Perlite Today," Industrial Minerals International Congress, *Proceedings,* No. 1, pp. 190–195.

Vgenopoulos, A., 1977, "Der Chemismus Einiger Sauren Vulkaniten Aus Dem Evros Gebiet Westthrakiens/Griechenland," Inst. Geol. Min. Res., Athens, Greece, *Proceedings,* 6th Colloquium on the Geology of the Agean Region, Vol. 3, pp. 945–954.

Vlaointirov, I., 1975, "The Perlite Industry in Bulgaria," Address given at the Perlite Institute Annual Meeting, Athens, Greece, pp. 39–46.

Weber, R.H., 1955, "Processing Perlite, the Technologic Problems," *Mining Engineering,* Vol. 7, No. 2, pp. 174–176.

Weber, R.H., 1957, "Geology and Petrography of the Stendel Perlite Deposit, Socorro County, New Mexico," Circular 44, New Mexico Institute of Mining and Technology, 22 pp.

Weber, R.H., 1963, "Geologic Features of the Socorro Perlite Deposit," New Mexico Bureau of Mines and Mineral Resources, New Mexico Institute of Mining and Technology, New Mexico Geological Society, 14th Field Conference, pp. 144–145.

Whitson, D.N., 1981, "Geology of the No Agua Peaks, New Mexico Perlite Deposit," *Proceedings,* 17th Forum on Geology of Industrial Minerals (Paper Presented May 15).

Williams, H., 1932, "The History and Character of Volcanic Domes," Bulletin of the Dept. of Geological Sciences, Vol. 21, No. 5, University of California, pp. 51–146.

Williams, H., 1941, "Calderas and Their Origin," Bulletin of the Dept. of Geological Sciences, Vol. 25, No. 6, University of California, pp. 239–346.

Phosphate Rock

G. DONALD EMIGH *

Nothing is more important to life—plant and animal—than phosphate. Its compounds are essential to the energy functions of all living systems and for the formation of bones and teeth. Animals get their phosphate from eating plants and other animals, or domestically from feed supplements. Plants get their phosphates from the soil.

Man's most important use of phosphate is for fertilizer; approximately 95% of the world's phosphate rock production is consumed by fertilizers. Most of the balance is processed in electric furnaces into elemental phosphorus, the important raw material for making industrial phosphates. Recovery of uranium from phosphates has been possible but not widely used. However, recent significant developments have generated interest in such recovery in the US and elsewhere.

Phosphate occurs in all igneous and sedimentary rocks, and in all fresh and salt water. However, economical recovery is limited to deposits where natural concentration of the phosphate mineral has occurred. Occasionally natural concentration is great enough that the material can be used as mined; generally, however, the ore is low grade and must be concentrated.

Phosphate rock is produced in 31 countries. Fig. 1 shows the location of major phosphate rock producers as well as some of the known phosphate deposits not yet in production.

In the last decade the world phosphate industry has experienced steady growth. World production rose from 98 Mt of phosphate rock in 1973 to 140 Mt in 1982. Fig. 2 shows the growth curve of rock production and graphically illustrates the almost straight-line rise since 1945 in both US and world production. Table 1 gives the breakdown, by countries, of world rock production, 1974 through 1979. Table 2 shows US rock production by producing areas.

Definitions of Terms Used in the Phosphate Industry

Phosphate Rock: Commonly called *rock* in sedimentary deposits and *apatite* in igneous deposits. Those expressions generally include any mined, or mined and beneficiated, fluorine-containing calcium phosphate used as the raw material for the next stage of manufacturing. The average phosphate content in rocks is 0.1 to 0.2% P_2O_5, as documented by McKelvey (1973). About 200 minerals contain more than 1% P_2O_5. However, the important mineral in igneous rocks is fluorapatite, [$Ca_5(PO_4)_3 F$], containing about 42% P_2O_5 and 3.8% F_2; in sedimentary rocks the important mineral is francolite, a carbonate fluorapatite containing up to 2% molecular CO_2. Both are in the apatite family of minerals.

Most phosphate rock, whether beneficiated or not, is a fine-grained material. The expression *phosphate rock* has no relation to its phosphate content. For example, phosphate rock from Idaho used in the production of phosphorus may contain about 24% P_2O_5, whereas rock from Morocco may contain 36.6% P_2O_5.

Phosphorite: A deposit of phosphate directly or indirectly of sedimentary origin, which is of economic interest.

Grade of Phosphate Rock: The calcium phosphate content of phosphate rock is expressed in different world areas by one of the following terms:

BPL (bone phosphate of lime)
TPL (triphosphate of lime)
P_2O_5 (phosphorus pentoxide)
P (phosphorus—not commonly used)

An illustration of relationship is:
   80% BPL = 80% TPL = 36.6% P_5O_2 = 16% P

* Consultant, Burley, ID.

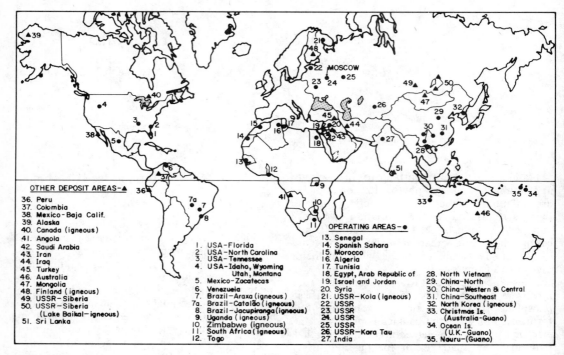

FIG. 1—*Location of the major phosphate rock-producing areas of the world and some of the known deposits not now in operation. All deposits are pellet phosphates except where indicated in legends to be igneous.*

Units of Weight:

metric ton (t) = 2205 lb
long ton (lt) = 2240 lb
short ton (st) = 2000 lb

Ore or Matrix: Used to denote naturally occurring phosphatic material to be upgraded into phosphate rock.

Wet-Process Acid: Phosphoric acid produced by treating phosphate rock with acid. It is sometimes called *green acid*.

Food Grade Acid: A very pure phosphoric acid produced from elemental phosphorus.

Processing of Phosphate Rock

Phosphate rock is commercially processed in three ways:

Acidification Treatment

1) With sulphuric acid to make:
Normal superphosphate—a fertilizer.
Concentrated superphosphate—a fertilizer.
Phosphoric acid—a fertilizer or the base for making ammonium phosphate fertilizers or calcium phosphate for animal feed supplements.

Phosphoric acid to be purified for production of industrial chemicals.

2) With nitric acid to make nitric phosphate fertilizers.

3) With hydrochloric acid to make phosphoric acid. Hydrochloric acid treatment has had only limited use.

Electric Furnace Treatment

The electric furnace treatment of rock produces elemental phosphorus which is converted largely to very pure phosphoric acid used in the production of such industrial chemicals as phosphates of sodium, calcium, potassium, and ammonia. The phosphoric acid is also called food-grade phosphoric acid when further purified.

Simple Physical Treatment

1) Fine grinding for use as a fertilizer by direct application to acid soils.

2) Removal of fluorine by heat to produce calcium phosphate for animal feed supplement.

3) Heat treatment of wavellite (aluminum

TABLE 1—World Phosphate Rock Production, 1000 t

Country	1974	1975	1976	1977	1978	1979	% Change, 1974-1979 (Selected)
Western Europe	104	125	138	150	100	60	−42
France	19	20	28	19	20	0	
West Germany	85	75	85	81	0	0	
Sweden	—	30	25	50	80	58	
Finland	—	—	—	—	—	2	
Eastern Europe							
USSR	22 500	24 155	24 230	24 375	24 000	25 000	+11
North America							
United States	41 445	44 450	44 670	47 256	50 037	50 996	+21
Central America	179	153	147	150	150	171	
Curacao	107	83	77	80	80	47	
Mexico	72	70	70	70	70	124	
South America	432	471	555	661	1 164	1 699	
Brazil	281	345	465	608	1 094	1 694	+503
Colombia	10	10	10	10	10	5	
Venezuela	141	116	80	43	60	0	
Africa	33 089	25 555	25 545	29 661	32 637	33 829	+2
Algeria	802	669	820	1 001	1 136	1 073	
Egypt	550	536	550	580	642	645	
Morocco	19 326	13 548	15 285	17 285	19 278	20 175	
Morocco (Sahara)	2 385	2 682	172	232	400	—	
Zimbabwe (Rhodesia)	130	140	140	140	100	140	
Senegal	1 878	1 677	1 580	1 802	1 843	1 619†	
South Africa	1 550	1 651	1 631	2 403	2 699	3 221	+108
Toga	2 553	1 161	2 068	2 857	2 827	2 916	
Tunisia	3 903	3 481	3 294	3 614	3 712	4 040	
Uganda	11	10	5	5	0	0	
Asia	9 906	9 515	10 317	11 401	13 217	15 643	+58
China	3 000	3 400	3 750	4 000	4 300	5 500	+83
Christmas Island	1 809	1 343	1 037	1 260	1 386	1 367	
India	431	429	613	635	690	514	
Indonesia	6	5	5	4	5	—	
Israel	1 000	660	741	1 232	1 759	2 216	+122
Jordan	1 600	1 353	1 702	1 782	2 223	2 826	+77
North Korea	400	420	450	450	450	550	
Philippines	11	6	9	13	4	—	
Syria	500	500	511	425	800	1 170	+134
North Vietnam	1 150	1 400	1 500	1 600	1 600	1 500	
Oceania	2 838	2 178	1 446	2 054	2 677	2 248	
Australia	1	124	254	496	210	0	
Nauru	2 288	1 534	757	1 146	1 999	1 828	
Banaba (Ocean Island)	549	520	438	419	468	420	
Total World	110 498	106 602	107 049	115 959	123 982	128 157	+16

Source: The British Sulphur Corp., London.
* Compiled largely from *Phosphate Rock Statistics*, ISMA, 1979.
† Excluding aluminum phosphates.

TABLE 2—US Production of Phosphate Rock, Mt

State	1974	1975	1976	1977	1978	1979	1979-1980*
Florida and North Carolina	40.0	40.7	41.5	40.6	43.3	44.3	47.1
Tennessee	2.4	2.3	1.8	1.7	1.7	1.9	2.1
Western states	6.3	5.8	5.9	4.9	5.1	5.5	5.3

Source: US Bureau of Mines.
*Fertilizer year July 1979 through June 1980.

phosphate in Senegal) to produce fertilizer and animal food supplement.

4) Heat treatment with alkaline rocks, or other alkaline materials, to produce fused phosphate fertilizer. The process has only limited use.

Geology of Phosphate Deposits

Phosphate of economic importance occurs in two types of rocks—igneous and sedimentary. A comprehensive and detailed report on the world's phosphate deposits by the British Sulphur Corp. (Anon., 1971) covers nearly all the known phosphate occurrences and describes their geology, mining, and beneficiation. Among other information are maps and chemical analyses of the phosphate rock. Barr (1960) gives a good short description of the world's major phosphate areas. Emigh (1973) describes phosphate deposits in the United States and some in other parts of the world.

Igneous Phosphate Deposits

About 20% of the world's phosphate rock now comes from the mining and beneficiation of igneous deposits, but this percentage will drop as production from sedimentary deposits increases.

Igneous apatite in relatively small quantities has been recovered from veins and from magnetite ore bodies where it occurs in minor amounts.

The important igneous apatite deposits of commercial interest are found in certain intrusive complexes of alkalic rocks. They generally occur as ringlike structures with limited areal extent (generally 1 to 20 square miles). Commonly near the center are veins and larger bodies rich in carbonates (calcite, dolomite, siderite, and ankerite) emplaced either in a molten condition or by metasomatic processes. These carbonate deposits are called carbonatites.

Apatite of economic interest can be in the carbonatites or in the alkalic rocks located outward from the central carbonatite. In carbonatites, it may be in a weather-enriched surface mantle, or in the unweathered rock. Carbonatites are well described by Heinrich (1966) and by Tuttle and Gittins (1966).

The following description of igneous apatite deposits associated with alkalic rocks are excerpts from Deans (1968).

> The most outstanding apatite deposit in the world occurs in the Khibina nepheline syenite massif near Kirovsk, in the Kola Peninsula, USSR. . . . The Khibina massif is a circular pluton about 25 miles in diameter, consisting of foyaite surrounded by concentric inward-dipping sheets of other varieties of nepheline syenites characterized by eudialite, aegirine, arfvedsonite or mica. The apatite deposits are restricted to a phase of layered ijolitic (nepheline-aegirine-apatite-sphene) rocks which occupy only four percent of the area of the complex, mainly in an arcuate zone parallel to, and about two to four miles within, the southwestern boundary. . . .

> Carbonatitic alkaline igneous complexes, once regarded as rare and isolated phenomena, are now known to be widely scattered over all the continents, except (as yet) Australasia and Antarctica. They constitute a distinctive subvolcanic and volcanic rock association, characteristic of deeply faulted regions in continental shield and platform areas, but not strictly confined to these areas. Eruptions of this type are believed to originate at deep subcrustal levels, and have occurred at many periods extending back from the present to the Precambrian of about 2000 million years ago. The carbonatites, low-temperature magmatic and in part metasomatic in origin, are typically associated with feldspathoidal or alkaline ultrabasic rocks, and the surrounding country rocks display a characteristic form of metasomatic alteration termed fenitization, often accompanied by widespread breccia-

tion. Commonly they form rather small intrusive ring complexes, about one to five miles in diameter, although the pattern and suites of rocks exposed varies considerably, depending partly on the depth to which they have been uncovered by erosion, and probably partly on conditions at the deeper point and time of origin. The surface volcanic manifestations of this activity are gas-drilled explosion craters of the Laacher See (Germany) type, or nephelinitic volcanoes, such as Oldoinyo Lengai in Tanzania, whose eruptive cycle includes nephelinite lavas and tuffs, sodic carbonatite lavas and mixed carbonatitic and nephelinitic ashes. The older eroded complexes may reveal a core of calcitic or dolomitic carbonatites surrounded by syenitic rocks, usually nepheline syenites (ijolites and/or foyaites), often forming ring dykes or cone sheets, or in other cases by ultrabasic suites comprising dunites, pyroxenites or biotite or vermiculite-rich rocks. In other cases the carbonatites are emplaced along major rift faults, forming long dykes or zones of metasomatism. The petrology of these complexes is highly varied, often including extremely calcic, sodic or potassic suites, but a general characteristic is enrichment in minor elements such as fluorine, phosphorus, strontium, barium, niobium and the cerium-group of the rare earths. In association with the carbonatites there are several examples of workable deposits of these elements. Among the latter some nine apatite deposits have been worked successfully in South Africa, Rhodesia [Zimbabwe], Uganda, and Brazil, and several others appear to be of potential economic importance.

Carbonatites have been found in Australia in 1968, New Zealand in 1970, and recently in Paraguay.

World production of apatite (igneous) concentrates in 1980 was about 25 Mt. Table 3 lists the operating apatite mines in the world in 1980. Brazil is actively developing new apatite mines; by the mid-1980s its production of phosphate rock, largely igneous apatite, should be 5.8 Mt, compared to 1.7 Mt currently. The USSR continues to develop new operations in the Kola area and soon will have a new mine operating on apatite in the Lake Baikal region in Siberia. Foskor in South Africa is planning another large mine-beneficiation operation on the Phalaborwa carbonatite complex.

Some of the USSR's apatite mines in the Kola Peninsula are underground, but the majority of its mines, as well as all other apatite mines in the world, are surface operations (Anon., 1979, 1979a).

Sedimentary Phosphate Deposits

Sedimentary phosphorites are of two types: guano and pelletal. A suggested classification is shown in Table 4.

Guano deposits result from the accumulation of animal excrement, principally that of large sea birds. They are of historical importance and, although they still contribute significant tonnage, now account for only a small percentage of total production. Guano deposits are mined on two islands—Nauru and Christmas—where combined production is about 3 Mt/a. Christmas Island contains the largest deposit of guano-type rock known, with reserves of over 200 Mt. More detailed information on origin and geology, which can be complex, may be found in the works of Hutchinson (1950), Warin (1968), and Barrie (1967).

TABLE 3—World Apatite Mines (1980)

Country	No. Mines	No. Beneficiation Plants	Conc., 1000 t/a	Grade % P_2O_5	Type Deposit
USSR (Kola)	6	2	20	17	Nepheline syenite (unweathered)
South Africa	2	1	3.5	7	Pyroxenite and foskorite (unweathered)
Brazil	5	3	1.7	13.5-15	1 carbonatite (unweathered) 4 carbonatite weathered residual

TABLE 4—Classification of Sedimentary Phosphatic Formations as Proposed by Emigh

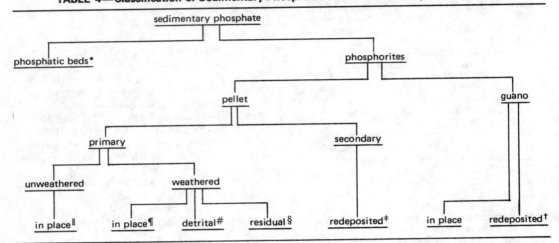

* Marine sediments in which the phosphate is believed present always as pellets—examples, Hawthorne formation, Florida, and Bigby limestone, Tennessee.

† Phosphate from guano—examples, Curacao, Nauru, and Christmas Island.

‡ Phosphate from pellet phosphorites—examples, white rock of Tennessee, hard rock of Florida, nonpelletal rock of Queensland, Australia.

§ Derived from phosphatic beds—example, brown rock of Tennessee.

Examples, pebble field of Florida and other similar fields in the southeastern United States.

¶ Surface and near surface weathered parts of all marine phosphorites—examples, Phosphoria formation of western USA, presently worked beds of North Africa (one exception is Kalaa-Djerda, Tunisia), Beetle Creek formation in Queensland, Bu-Craa phosphorite of Spanish Sahara.

‖ Unweathered parts of all marine phosphorites—examples, Phosphoria formation, La Caja formation of Mexico, lower unworked beds in Morocco, the "black" rock found at lower levels at Youssoufia, Morocco, and the bed at Kalaa-Djerda, Tunisia.

The greatest phosphate deposits are pelletal phosphorites. These are in marine formations—commonly associated with dolomite or limestone. They furnish over 80% of the world phosphate rock requirements and this proportion will increase in the future. As previously noted, the phosphate is present as the mineral francolite—a carbonate fluorapatite. In 1870, this mineral was named collophane, and it was believed to be isotropic. Subsequently, it was found to be anisotropic, conforming to the mineral francolite. Unfortunately, the word collophane still appears occasionally in modern literature.

The francolite of pelletal phosphorites was originally emplaced as small pellets, and most of it is still in this form. These are commonly ovoid in shape although some skeletal pellets, such as broken shells, can be elongate. Emigh (1967) describes six pellet types. In any one bed pellets are about the same size, but in differing beds they can be of different size. The sizes of pellets in some phosphorites are shown in Emigh (1967); an average is in the range of 0.25 to 0.35 mm. Practically all pellets represent original aragonite pellets of diverse origin, later phosphatized by phosphate ions in seawater.

Under certain weathering conditions, the phosphate of pellets can move and be emplaced elsewhere. Examples include the white rock of Tennessee, the hard rock of northern Florida, and the nonpelletal parts of the phosphorites of Queensland, Australia, as pointed out for the latter by Cook (1972).

Highly phosphatized marine formations can be very large in areal extent. For example, the Phosphoria formation of Montana, Idaho, Wyoming, Utah, and Nevada originally covered 135,000 square miles and is being mined in several places along a 450-mile belt across this area.

The thickness of a bed of phosphorite may vary from a few inches up to tens of feet. Beds may extend several miles laterally, maintaining fairly equal thickness and phosphate content.

The phosphate content of a phosphorite bed ranges from a few percent P_2O_5 up to practically solid francolite pellets—about 35% P_2O_5. Dark brown to black hydrocarbons commonly are in the phosphorite beds together with varying amounts of detrital materials—largely quartz. Such beds may even be referred to as black shales. Chert is commonly associated with phosphorites, sometimes in the matrix containing the phosphate pellets, but more commonly as either thin or thick marine beds located stratigraphically close to the phosphorite—either above or below. In the famous Rex chert of the Phosphoria formation of the western United States, the chert appears to be derived from siliceous sponge spicules (skeletons). This is also true of thin chert beds associated with the phosphorites of middle Tennessee.

Sheldon et al. (1967) describes, for the Phosphoria formation, the theory of deep upwelling ocean currents depositing phosphate on and near outer continental shelves. This theory has been applied elsewhere in the world. Not everyone believes this condition is necessary for the deposition of phosphatic marine formations of economic interest, but there is generally common agreement that moving seawater is necessary for providing the phosphate.

Phosphorites occur widely scattered throughout geological history. Table 5 shows the ages of various phosphorites.

Among the many descriptions of pellet phosphorites, the following excerpts are taken from an article by Notholt (1968):

> Most marine phosphorites appear to have been formed in somewhat restricted basins of deposition, occupying arms or

TABLE 5—Age of Phosphate in Some Pellet Phosphorites*

Location	Formation or Group	Age
Canada, Alberta	Rocky Mountain	Permian
Western USA, MT, ID, UT, WY, NV	Phosphoria	Permian
Western USA, Utah	Brazer	Mississippian
California	Monterey	Miocene
Arkansas, Searcy Co.	Morrow	Upper Pennsylvanian
Iowa	Maquoketa Shale	Upper Ordovician
Tennessee, Brown Rock	Bigby	Ordovician
Tennessee, Blue Rock	Chattanooga Shale	Lower Mississippian
North Carolina	Pungo River	Lower Miocene
Florida, Pelletal Type	Hawthorne	Middle Miocene
Mexico, Zacatecas and Coahuila	La Caja	Upper Jurassic
Venezuela, Western		Upper Cretaceous
Venezuela, Falcon State	Riecito	Lower Miocene
Colombia	Guadalupe	Upper Cretaceous
Peru, Sechura Desert	Zapayal	Upper Miocene
Brazil, Pernambuco	Gramamme	Upper Cretaceous
Angola, Cabinda Enclave		Upper Cretaceous
Togo		Middle Eocene
Senegal, Taiba		Eocene
Spanish Sahara, Bu-Craa		Upper Cretaceous/Lower Tertiary
Morocco		Upper Cretaceous/Lower Tertiary
Algeria		Upper Cretaceous/Lower Tertiary
Tunisia	Metlaoui	Upper Cretaceous/Lower Tertiary
Egypt		Upper Cretaceous
Israel		Upper Cretaceous
Jordan	Belqa	Upper Cretaceous/Lower Tertiary
Saudi Arabia	Hibr	Lower Tertiary
	Aruma	Upper Cretaceous
Iran	Pabdeh	Lower Tertiary
	Geirud	Upper Devonian
Iraq		Upper Cretaceous/Lower Tertiary
Lebanon		Upper Cretaceous
Syria		Upper Cretaceous/Lower Tertiary
Turkey	Germav	Upper Cretaceous
	Karabogaz	
	Karababa	
USSR		Upper Precambrian, Cambrian, Ordovician Jurassic, Lower Cretaceous
India		Precambrian, Jurassic, Upper Cretaceous
North Vietnam	Coc Xan	Lower Cambrian
Australia	Beetle Creek	Middle Cambrian

* Source: Anon., 1971b.

gulfs of preexisting seas and developed either on the neritic shelf areas of geosynclines or as subsiding areas on relatively stable continental platforms. Marine phosphate deposits have thus been classified into geosynclinal and platform varieties, each being recognizable in a very general way by the differences in petrography of the phosphorite beds themselves and of the associated sediments and in various structural relationships. The classification is unsatisfactory in many ways, however, and at best the two groups, where typically developed, can only be regarded as representing end members of a continuous series. Most phosphate deposits show features characteristic of both geosynclinal and platform-type deposits. Nevertheless, in the absence of a much-needed classification based on precise stratigraphical and structural criteria, it seems that a separation into the two groups of deposits can usefully be made for preliminary exploration purposes, the distinction being modified subsequently where their gross geological characteristics are known.

The phosphorite lithofacies was first recognized as such by Russian geologists during the early 1930s, the frequent association of phosphorite with black, carbonaceous or bituminous shales or mudstones, cherts (or other siliceous sediments), as well as various carbonate rocks probably providing to date one of the most effective aids to phosphate exploration. Although some important variations exist, the black shale-phosphorite-chert-carbonate rock assemblage characterizes geosynclinal phosphate deposits in many parts of the world. Its recognition in some cases after examining samples obtained in the course of oil-drilling operations, has led in recent years to the successful discovery of promising deposits.

The Permian Phosphoria Formation of the western United States, embracing one of the largest phosphate fields in the world, contains a classic example of what may be termed the *geosynclinal phosphorite lithofacies*. This facies occurs in the western part of the phosphate field where the Phosphoria and its partial equivalents form part of a thick sedimentary pile deposited in the Cordilleran miogeosyncline. It is characterized by black, high-grade phosphorite, phosphatic and carbonaceous mudstone, cherty mudstone and chert. Calcareous rocks, as well as sandy beds, are generally absent. Accordingly, McKelvey has concluded that almost any marine black bituminous shale or bedded chert (except for those occurring with volcanic rocks or other thick eugeosynclinal sediments) may be suspected of being associated with phosphorite or phosphatic shale, although the latter rocks may not necessarily contain sufficient amounts of phosphate to be of commercial interest. The close association of bedded chert and phosphorite was not recorded by Kazakov although radiolarian and diatomaceous cherts had been known for many years previously from the North African phosphate fields and elsewhere. Of interest is the association of Miocene phosphorites with diatomite in the Monterey formation of California and the Zapallal formation underlying large areas of the Sechura Desert, northwestern Peru.

The British Sulphur Corp., in "World Survey of Phosphate Deposits" (Anon., 1971b), includes phosphate reserves; however, it issues a word of caution in the following statement:

> Quantitative information on reserves of phosphorus-containing minerals is most unsatisfactory. Published data are seldom given in sufficient detail that their significance can be evaluated, and even where this detail is available it may only serve to reflect the widely different methods of assessment used to calculate and classify reserves throughout the world.

Some phosphate reserves are given in Table 6, although this list does not represent total reserves. Reserves of phosphate rock are for all practical purposes unlimited (Emigh, 1972).

Weathering

The wide range of geologic time over which phosphorite deposits have been deposited has been noted. Over this long period of time tectonic movements have moved the original flat-lying phosphorite beds into all attitudes—from gently dipping to vertical and to overturned, all further complicated by faulting. Such rearrangement of beds, with its attendant faulting, complicates exploration and mining, but it does aid substantially that all important factor—surface and near-surface weathering.

With a few notable exceptions, such as the unconsolidated phosphorite deposits along the coast of North Carolina and the Sechura Desert of Peru, all phosphate deposits were originally hard rock. Certainly this is true of igneous deposits. The originally unconsolidated pellet phosphorite beds became dense hard rocks as they were subjected to lithification. In these phosphorites, the hard cementing matrix is commonly dolomite, but sometimes calcite. Less commonly the cementing matrix can be cryptocrystalline quartz, or chert, derived from

TABLE 6—Summary of Uraniferous Phosphate Resources of the Free World

Area	Phosphate Resource (millions of st)	Typical P$_2$O$_5$ Content of Phosphate Resource	Average Uranium Content of Phosphorite (ppm U)	Potentially Mineable Phosphate Product (~30% P$_2$O$_5$)* (millions of st)	Estimated Recoverable Phosphate Product (~30% P$_2$O$_5$)† (millions of st)	Average Uranium Concentration of Phosphate Product (ppm U) e = estimated	Uranium Contained in Potentially Mineable Phosphate Product (thousands of st)	Estimated Recoverable Uranium‡ (thousands of st)
United States								
Southeastern								
Central Florida	9,760	15-18%	65	1,737	1,129	110	191	124
Southern Extension	25,854	10-15%	36	5,084	3,050	110	560	336
North Florida-South Georgia	19,110	8-10%	64	3,230	1,764	70	225	123
East Florida	25,590	8-16%	51	4,437	2,662	102	453	272
East Georgia-South Carolina	18,179	4-15%	30-60	3,469	1,787	60-90	276	142
North Carolina	71,761	8-18%	30	15,086	9,429	60	906	566
Others	272	16-23%	20-33	144	69	25	3	2
Subtotal	170,526			33,187	19,890		2,614	1,565
Western Phosphate Field								
Idaho	324,904§	24-26%	96	203,065[‖]	84,072	124	25,180	10,425
Utah	154,479§	24-26%	76	96,204[‖]	35,171	98	9,428	3,447
Wyoming	287,573§	24-26%	64	178,778[‖]	67,397	83	14,839	5,594
Montana	58,306§	22-24%	65	35,861[‖]	15,684	84	3,012	1,317
Subtotal	825,262			513,908	202,324		52,459	20,783
Other¶	9,412	12-28%	30-76	2,257[‖]	1,128	98	221	111
Total United States	1,005,200			549,352	223,342		55,294	22,459
Rest of Free World								
Algeria	1,100	25%		700	525	100	70	52
Australia	4,000	17%		1,600	1,200	68	110	82
Brazil	2,200	5-15%		422	316	e 65	30	22
Egypt	1,645	20-26%		1,000	750	100	100	75
Iraq	2,360	18%		770	579	130	100	75
Jordan	16,000	15-33%		4,000	3,000	120	480	360
Mexico	51,190	3-27%		5,534	4,150	e100	553	415
Morocco	88,000	25-34%		60,000	45,000	110	6,600	4,950
Peru	10,000	8-12%		3,000	2,250	e100	300	225
South Africa	105,300	7-16%		50,770	3,600**	12	3,147	43
Syria	900	19-28%		540	405	130	70	52
Tunisia	1,300	26-30%		910	682	60	55	41
Western Sahara	11,000	31-33%		7,400	5,550	100	740	555
Others	4,941	13-30%		1,834	1,378	30-160	167	126
Total, Rest of Free World	299,936			138,480	69,385		12,522	7,073
Total, All of Free World	1,305,136			687,832	292,727		67,816	29,532

Source: Anon., 1979b.

* Includes the phosphate product (of approximate 30% P$_2$O$_5$ content) that could be producible from the total phosphate resource, without accounting for a mining recovery factor, but accounting for an unavailability factor. In the United States, resources unavailable for mining development because of federal land classifications, cultural features, or other environmental factors are included in the total phosphate resource column but are excluded from the potentially mineable phosphate product column. Only the portion of RARE II lands recommended for wilderness designation are considered unavailable for purposes of this table.

† Average mining recovery factors generally of 50 to 75% for surface mineable resources, depending on the district, 50% for underground resources to a depth of 5,000 feet and subocean resources, and 35% for deep underground (greater than 5,000 foot depth) resources have been applied to the "Potentially Mineable Phosphate Product" to determine this "Estimated Recoverable Phosphate Product."

‡ The total uranium contained in the estimated recoverable phosphate product.

§ Includes ore-grade (≥18.0% P$_2$O$_5$) resources in all resource depth categories.

‖ A beneficiation recovery factor of 1.6:1, the operating experience in the Western Phosphate Field, has been applied to the phosphate resources in order to obtain the potentially mineable phosphate product. In other words, 1.6 tons of phosphate resource must be mined and beneficiated to produce 1.0 ton of approximately 32% P$_2$O$_5$ product.

¶ Includes all other marine phosphorites of the United States, but not any of the monazite placer or igneous apatite deposits, because of their clear lack of economic viability.

** The offshore phosphorites off South Africa, which are lithified to a great extent, are considered to be not mineable with current technology.

Note: tons are short tons (2,000 pounds)

siliceous skeletons of tiny marine animals and plant life. Commonly also dark brown-black hydrocarbon is present.

Surface weathering, with its solubilizing and leaching away of cementing carbonates, is a most important factor in the development of economic phosphate deposits. The removal of carbonates in phosphorites and carbonatites softens the formation, upgrades the phosphate content, removes carbonate material which is deleterious to the treatment of the final concentrate, and makes mining and beneficiation easier. In pellet phosphorites, weathering also changes the originally finely dispersed pyrite into iron oxide and reduces the quantity of hydrocarbons, changing the original black color to gray or brown.

Hale (1967) describes the effects of weathering on the Phosphoria formation of the western United States, and Emigh (1973) describes the effects on pellet phosphorites in general.

Exploration and Development

Phosphate deposits of economic interest, both igneous and sedimentary, are difficult to recognize in the field. Commonly, even the discrete apatite crystal, or the small phosphorite pellet, cannot be positively identified. But a simple field test is possible by placing a drop of acid (sulfuric, nitric, or hydrochloric, not weaker than approximately 20% concentrated acid in water by volume) on the questionable area with a medicine dropper and then adding a small crystal, or. a small amount of powder, of ammonium molybdate off the end of a knife blade. The rapid development of a bright yellow color indicates phosphate. This field test is very sensitive but positive results, however, do not mean a commercial deposit has been found.

Exploration is generally directed toward: (1) finding new deposit areas and (2) searching for new deposits associated with known fields. In the case of (2) exploration will, of course, be guided by the practical knowledge acquired in that field before the new exploration begins.

The report of the United Nations (Anon., 1968d) contains over 50 articles by authoritative authors on the geology and exploration of world phosphate deposits as well as the use of rock.

Igneous Deposits

Although the world's great phosphate deposits are of the pellet phosphorite type, igneous deposits are also important as they yield about 20% of the present world production of phosphate rock.

Deans (1968) states the number of known alkalic complexes favorable for apatite has grown from 20 in 1945 to about 200 in 1967. At least 20 of these probably contain apatite deposits. The following are excerpts from Deans' chapter:

It may be useful to outline practical steps which can be taken to initiate a wider search for carbonatites in the Economic Commission for Asia and the Far East (ECAFE) region. The new books on carbonatites should be studied to provide a factual background. Then, before field work begins, there must be a critical search for possible clues in the regional literature, maps, files and rocks and mineral collections of all the geological departments in each country so that specific areas may be selected for reconnaissance inspection. The clues may be sought under three headings: petrological, mineral records, and geological and geophysical information.

Petrological information: Occurrences of alkaline rocks obviously deserve consideration since carbonatites are genetically linked with these rocks, but it should be noted that many occurrences have no carbonatites associated with them. . . .

Having selected localities or small districts for examination on the basis of the more promising clues found in this search, a round of geological field inspections can begin. The objective is now to locate carbonatites, 'promising' alkaline or ultrabasic rocks, or fenites etc. for further study, and to eliminate fruitless clues and if possible explain them so that similar mistakes are not repeated unnecessarily. The methods and intensity of search are matters for the geologist to decide in the particular circumstances, but collecting material for identification or confirmation in the laboratory is the major task, and in addition to rock specimens, samples of residual soils are most important. This is because they are often more representative of the chemistry and mineralogy of the bedrock as a whole than are the resistant and often heterogeneous rocks which form outcrops. Normally they will be enriched relative to bedrock in some of the diagnostic elements of carbonatites, notably in phosphorus, barium, rare-earths and niobium (strontium is leached out). . . .

In the field it is useful to carry a strong hand-magnet, conveniently shielded in a thin aluminum cup, for detecting magnetite-rich soils, as magnetite and apatite are commonly associated in carbonatites and phosphorites, and both are enriched in the residual soils overlying them. . . .

Having located carbonatitic alkaline or ultrabasic complexes, the chances of apatite discoveries may still be uncertain, and finding them may not be easy. Apatite-rich material may be quite nondescript and variable in appearance, especially when fine-grained or weathered, and chemical or microscopic checks should be applied to all doubtful or suspect rocks, coupled with soil sampling. In general the most deeply eroded complexes appear to be most favourable for apatite deposits of the phosphorite or pyroxenite type. In these, carbonatites may be relatively minor constituents of the complex (at Palabora they form only about 2 percent of the outcrop area), so a complex should not be underrated just because the area of carbonatite is small. The maximum development of carbonatites appears at a somewhat higher level of intrusion in the form of large carbonatite plugs, and these may yield important residual deposits of apatite, provided climatic and erosional factors are favourable. In the less eroded volcanic complexes one may find apatite associated with the highly potassic feldspathic breccias and trachytic rock, as exemplified by the Tundulu deposits and several minor occurrences. The grade of deposit which may be regarded as of possible practical interest depends on many factors, but present practice suggests that a recoverable apatite content of about 15 percent (6 percent P_2O_5) may prove economic, provided there are adequate reserves, and location and working costs are favourable.

A brief description of prospecting for igneous phosphate deposits in the USSR is given by the USSR Delegation (Anon., 1968b), both for those associated with carbonatites and those associated with alkaline rocks such as the nepheline syenites of the Kola Peninsula. The following is an excerpt from the article:

In the first stage of prospecting, on the basis of data of the Complex Geological Survey and other sources, general small-scale forecast maps are compiled for the areas of possible occurrence of these deposits. For carbonatites, they are the regions of ancient platforms and areas of completed folding; while for magmatic deposits associated with basic rock, they are the areas of a wide development of ancient basic gabbro-anorthosite and gabbrodiorite complexes.

At the initial stage of search for carbonatites, the usual aeromagnetic and aeroradiometric surveys are particularly useful, as they reveal anomalies that are distinctly outlined in the regions of development of normal sediments. At the ground control of these anomalies, the areas of possible apatite occurrence are selected where reconnaissance prospecting is carried out in order to reveal their possible commercial importance.

The USSR article refers to the use of boreholes (presumably diamond drill holes). The article states in the reconnaissance survey that the exploration network of holes is roughly 500×200 m for simple deposits and 250×150 m for complex deposits. The maximum depth of drilling during the preliminary survey is about 700 m. In the following detailed survey, category A reserves are those drilled out on grids of about 125×100 m and category B on grids of about 250×200 m. Cores are sectionally sampled in lengths of 2.5 to 3 m and analyzed for P_2O_5 and Al_2O_3. Other chemical analyses are performed on groupings of eight or ten of the individual samples.

Pellet Phosphorites

Only in the last 25 years has there been concerted worldwide search for pellet phosphorites with the greatest emphasis occurring in only the last 15 years.

Fig. 2 shows the rapid increase in demand for phosphate rock since the mid-1940s. Prior to that time, the relatively modest world rock requirements came from deposits that had been long known and worked. These deposits had been found largely by chance.

The surge in world demand for rock sparked a rapid buildup in capacity in the producing fields and attendant exploration worldwide.

Especially for areas beyond known fields, planned exploration applies new ideas about the origin and emplacement of pellet phosphorite. Of special value was the recognition of the importance of the movement of phosphate-containing seawater in large basins.

The exploration and development of pellet phosphorites in new areas might be separated into four phases as follows:

Phase 1: The search for areas of marine sedimentation.

Phase 2: Within areas of marine sedimentation, search for beds of chert, or marine diatomite and/or black shales.

Phase 3: Search for beds of phosphorite in or near the black shales or cherts. Also search for residual phosphatic soil areas associated with beds of phosphatic dolomite or limestone.

Phase 4: Determine thickness, grade and extent of weathering by trenching and drilling.

The thickness of chert beds, so commonly associated with pellet phosphorites, may be from a few inches to over 200 ft. Pellet phosphorite commonly contains from 0.001% to 0.02% U_3O_8. Where the higher percentage is present in exposed beds, airborne scintillator equipment can also be employed.

Commonly, an outcrop of phosphorite will have patches of a thin skin of "phosphate bloom" where exposed at the surface. Its characteristic light gray-blue color is readily visible up to distances of several feet. A 10 to 20-power

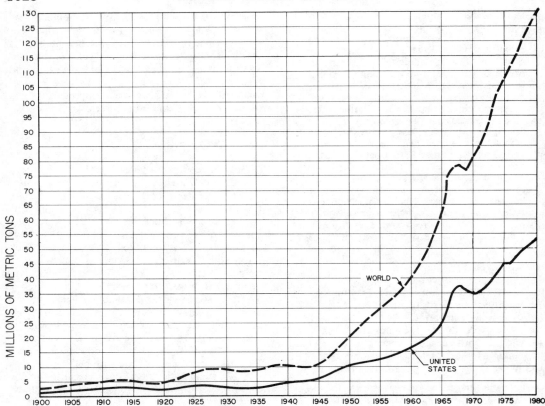

FIG. 2—*Production of phosphate rock in metric tons for the world and the United States, 1900–1980. Through 1965 curves are drawn on five-year averages; after 1965 they are drawn on a yearly basis.*

hand lens is indispensable to aid in identifying the small ovoid-shaped phosphate pellets.

In areas of marine sedimentation which appear to be a favorable locale for phosphorite, but where no outcrops are present, previously drilled holes, if present, can prove a valuable aid. For example, in the mid-1950s water wells in North Carolina when flushed out revealed phosphate pellets. Later, preliminary and successful exploration of the field was conducted by gamma-ray testing of about 100 existing holes drilled for water.

The important pellet phosphorites of the Georgina Basin in the Queensland-Northern Territory of northeastern Australia were found in 1966. This discovery resulted from a study of cores of holes drilled in a search for oil. It was then established that phosphate beds could be identified on the gamma-ray logs of the holes. The phosphate beds so identified were then found in outcrops some distance away (Howard, 1971, 1972).

Early in 1962, chemical testing of sludge obtained from many holes drilled for oil in Turkey showed a few holes with enough phosphate to merit interest. Later gamma-ray logs of such holes were examined for phosphate. The results obtained from the drill holes led to the discovery of pellet phosphorite outcrops.

Other than gamma-ray measuring techniques, there has been to date very little application of geophysical methods in the exploration of pellet phosphorites. Cooksley (1967) describes some work on the Phosphoria formation in southeastern Idaho made in connection with obtaining additional information on previously discovered phosphorite deposits. Limited seismic work in northern Florida and Tennessee has been unproductive. Except for the possibilities outlined by Cooksley, and the use of gamma-ray measurements, it appears probable that the geophysical approach to phosphorite exploration has only a minor role to play.

To the writer's knowledge, geochemical prospecting has not been used in the exploration for phosphate deposits. Presumably it might have some value, especially in exploration for residual phosphorites of the Tennessee type.

Under Phase 3 of exploration mention was made of residual phosphorites represented by deposits in Tennessee. The brown-rock pellet phosphorites of Tennessee are residual deposits formed by weathering of the underlying phosphatic limestone. The brown-colored phosphorite is covered with up to several feet of brown-colored soil. The soil mantle, coupled with the low uranium content of the phosphorite (less than 0.001% U_3O_8), makes airborne scintillator prospecting useless. Road cuts and an occasional gully will reveal the underlying phosphorite. Even at such places the inexperienced eye probably would not distinguish between the soil and the phosphorite. Prospecting for isolated phosphate deposits is simply by blind drilling at the proper horizon, i.e., on top of the phosphatic limestone. Individual economic deposits may contain from 20 kt to over 1 Mt of matrix (ore). It seems probable that throughout the world there are many areas of residual phosphorites of the Tennessee type. They are difficult to recognize and, in all likelihood, generally have not been looked for.

Phosphorite beds vary laterally in thickness and phosphate content. In some places, as in western United States' Phosphoria formation, this lateral variation is small for long distances —several tens of miles—but in other places, and other formations, more extreme variations do occur. In exploration therefore, extensive lateral exploration should be made even though preliminary exploration may detect only low grade ore. The economically important detrital (reworked residual) phosphorites of the Bone Valley formation in middle and northern Florida occur as unevenly distributed beds over large areas. Their lateral variation in thickness and grade requires extensive drilling to ascertain the sometimes tortuous outlines of minable material.

After a bedded primary pellet phosphorite has been found, it is commonly difficult to follow the bed in outcrop because weathering has softened the formation releasing loose soil-like material that masks the beds. Even when the exact location is known, pellets or small pieces of phosphorite are difficult to find or recognize. Therefore, harder "marker" beds stratigraphically above or below the phosphorite often can be better used to map for location of a phosphorite bed than the phosphate bed itself.

Utilization of existing holes drilled for oil in exploration for pellet phosphorite has been mentioned. However, to date, present economic conditions would not justify extensive drilling for the primary purpose of finding phosphate. But in certain areas, shallow drilling has proven itself where the objectives are near-surface deposits. Residual phosphate deposits of Florida-Georgia-South Carolina-North Carolina and Tennessee are representative. Drilling in those areas is generally limited to depths that could be open pit mined. For the past several years, exploration drilling for phosphate deposits in selected areas of Florida and North Carolina has reached depths of 300 ft or greater. Present exploration drilling for both shallow and deep deposits is done with a truck mounted rotary rig collecting a 4 to 5 in. core with a 10 ft single tube core barrel.

In wet places, tests can be made by washing cuttings from the hole. Cuttings are caught in tubs on the surface. This type drilling commonly results in loss of slimes and, consequently, under-reporting of the quantity of slimes in the final laboratory tests.

In Tennessee exploratory drilling is most economical by using powered 4-in. augers. One type is a two-wheel trailer with weight of the drill only being applied to the drill stem. But a preferred type is mounted on the back of a truck and the drill stems are forced downward hydraulically. Again, field inspection suffices to determine whether phosphate of interest has been found. Even until recently, hand drilling was done in Tennessee and Florida using a cup auger drilling head mounted on a 1-in. pipe. Diameter of the hole was 4 in., and the head was pulled out and cleaned every 8 in. Some hand-drilled holes require casing through the soil overburden. Here the casing is forced ahead of the drill.

The discovery of the economically important Bu-Craa phosphate in Spanish Sahara in the early 1960s is an example of drilling being used in the exploration phase. As described by ENMINSA (Anon., 1967), geological reconnaissance work started at the already known low-grade phosphate horizon in the Izic district. These studies, in a flat desert terrain with poor rock exposures, indicated a richer phosphate concentration 60 miles away. Drilling in this area on a 1-km grid found the important Bu-Craa deposit. This drilling was done with a rotary rig using a tricone bit. Diameter was 11.34 cm (4.5 in.) with cuttings air-blown to the surface where they were collected as samples.

Phase 4 in the exploration and development of pellet phosphorites involves the determination of the thickness, grade, and extent of weathering by surface work which may include one or more of the following: trenching, shafts, or drilling. Trenching can be by hand or with mechanical equipment—dozers or backhoes. Its purpose is to expose the phosphatic beds for measurement and sampling. Depths of 15 ft or more may be necessary to get through loose overburden and minimize the effects of surface creep. Down-slope surface creep can significantly string out and thin the phosphatic beds and change the apparent dips of the beds. Surface slopes as low as 5° can result in significant creep. Where the material moved is dry and relatively incoherent, deep trenches pose a real danger to men and equipment from sudden slumping of the vertical walls.

A brief description has already been given of the kinds of drills used for exploration of residual pellet phosphorites in Florida and Tennessee. The same Phase 3 equipment is used for the additional holes required for Phase 4. In the western US Phosphoria field, diamond drilling (commonly NX) is used as well as rotary drilling with air return of cuttings. When the rotary drilled hole has reached the phosphate zones (and this is determined visually), the cuttings are collected as samples. Coring can, of course, also be done with a rotary drill rig, but this is not common nor is drilling with water common with these rigs. Air return of cuttings works very well, and without casing, up to depths of several hundred feet; however, encountering wet material usually prevents recovery of cuttings.

Rotary rigs may average 400 ft per 8-hr shift vs. perhaps 30 to 40 ft for the diamond drill. Nevertheless, diamond drilling has certain advantages, i.e., ability to make deeper holes needed to determine the limits of alteration, wet ground does not stop drilling, holes can be angled to better intersect dipping beds, and a core is a more accurate sample for geological study. A common criticism of coring in soft shales is that core recovery is not good. Proper drilling, however, results in good core recovery—largely due to not forcing the bit.

In Phase 4 exploration for a pellet phosphorite bed such as present in the Phosphoria formation of western United States there is no established rule for the lateral spacing of holes, but trenches and drilled holes about 1000 ft apart are generally sufficient to establish thicknesses and grades. As the time approaches for mining, however, additional information is required, but this is more for the purpose of better defining local structures such as faulting and change of dip of the beds. These local structural features dictate the amount of additional drilling; however, different operators have different approaches. One may be satisfied with holes before mining being spaced several hundred feet apart, where another, in a similar situation, may want 50-ft spacing.

In the Florida fields, the matrix (phosphate ore) is commonly separated every 5 ft into an individual sample. Each sample is processed in laboratories by bench tests to simulate plant operations, i.e., a weighed sample is pulped with water and deslimed; slime is any material less than 150 mesh. The deslimed material is then screened at 14 mesh to obtain coarse phosphate aggregate called pebble, and the undersize $-14 +150$ mesh portion is floated to recover a phosphate concentrate (rock). The pebble and flotation feed portions furnish the sample for assaying and not the original matrix.

In Tennessee, the matrix obtained by drilling is separated into 4-ft sections, sacked, and sent to a laboratory. The sample is split and analysis made for P_2O_5. The other split is saved until a minable deposit has been drilled. Then one composite is made, proportioning weights by feet of core in each sample. This composite sample is split down to a working sample of about 6000 g. One half is analyzed for P_2O_5, SiO_2, Al_2O_3, Fe_2O_3, and CaO. The other half is wet screened. There may be one screen size used (325 mesh) or three, i.e., 200, 325, 400. All products, including undersize, are weighed and analyzed for P_2O_5, SiO_2, Al_2O_3, Fe_2O_3 and CaO. As in Florida, Tennessee samples are handled to simulate plant beneficiation practices.

In the western Phosphoria field, about half of the phosphorite is utilized without beneficiation into the elemental phosphorus industry. Samples from trenches and drilling are taken at about 5-ft intervals, dried, and analyzed for P_2O_5, SiO_2, Al_2O_3, Fe_2O_3, and CaO.

In the United States, analyses on samples are performed by the old established wet chemical procedures or by X-ray fluorescence. The X-ray process, however, is not always accurate. It depends on the establishment of standard curves but between deposits or even within one deposit variations frequently do not fit these curves. For exploration and development, therefore, the X-ray procedure should not be used. A titration process is used for P_2O_5, Fe_2O_3 and CaO, but SiO_2 and Al_2O_3 analyses are determined gravimetrically.

Evaluation of Deposits

Even before exploration begins, a search for phosphate deposits has an end-use objective. Objectives include export of rock, export of fertilizer, export of phosphorus, or satisfying domestic markets for fertilizer or industrial chemicals.

With the exception of an occasional unusual deposit such as the wavellite (aluminum phosphate) of Senegal, and guano, the world's phosphate deposits contain the mineral fluorapatite. Deposits containing this mineral, whether of igneous or sedimentary origin, can be processed to make both phosphorus and fertilizer.

Where igneous apatite is contained in unweathered alkalic rocks, such as in the Kola Peninsula area of the USSR and in South Africa, the absence of carbonates permits flotation of apatite after fine grinding. Where the igneous apatite is in a carbonatite, the presence of the large quantities of carbonates in the unweathered rock heretofore has prevented the recovery of rock by flotation because flotation reagents work on the calcium end of the mineral molecule and calcium carbonate will float along with calcium phosphate. This condition has been overcome in Brazil and will be commented on later.

With pelletal phosphorites, impurities contained in the phosphate ore may influence end use of the rock. Such impurities include detrital silica grains, cryptocrystalline silica derived from siliceous skeletons of small organisms, clay, iron oxide, calcite, dolomite, iron sulfide (pyrite), and hydrocarbons. Most of these impurities occur in the ore as discrete particles separate from the phosphate; however, a certain amount is present in the individual phosphate pellet or particle.

Impurities present as discrete particles in weathered phosphorites can be partially, or nearly wholly, removed by simple washing or by washing followed by flotation. However the small particles of impurities present in a phosphate pellet generally cannot be economically removed, except that calcining, generally in the range of 900° to 950°C, removes the CO_2 of carbonates and the hydrocarbons. The remaining CaO can be removed by slaking and screening. This is done at Oron in Israel.

Because under normal conditions phosphate rock for any use has a relatively low sales value, the evaluation of phosphate deposits from the start is involved with limiting cost factors. Among these are the need for low-cost open pit mining, large volume operations with their cost benefits, low-cost large supplies of water for beneficiation, and low-cost transportation to markets. If a large, high-grade phosphate deposit were found in the middle of the Sahara Desert it would have no value for the foreseeable future because of transportation costs to say nothing of the possible lack of water.

The mining and milling techniques for the preparation of rock are essentially the same whether the rock is used to make phosphorus or fertilizer. Rock for phosphorus production can be as low-grade as 24% P_2O_5; therefore, it may require no beneficiation, or, if beneficiated, a low-grade concentrate is acceptable. On the other hand, for fertilizer use, the rock (concentrate) should be as high-grade as economically possible.

Mining

About 15% of the world's phosphate rock production in 1981 was mined underground, coming largely from the USSR, Morocco, and Tunisia, and minor quantities from the Arab Republic of Egypt and the state of Montana, USA. China also produces a significant amount of phosphate ore from underground operations. In Morocco and Tunisia underground mining employs room-and-pillar methods. The relatively soft ore does not require drilling and blasting but large quantities of timber posts are used to prevent roof slabs from falling. Underground mining of the USSR Kola ore is done by sublevel open stoping. (Anon., 1968a, 1979, 1979a; Woodrooffe, 1972).

The bulk of the world's phosphate rock is mined open-pit for the simple reason that it is the least expensive way to move large volumes of material—both overburden and ore. Unit costs are largely affected by the thickness, and hardness, of the overburden. Thus larger equipment with its lower unit cost of operation permits removal of greater thicknesses of overburden. Both overburden and phosphate ore are moved by (1) shovels and trucks, (2) draglines and trucks, (3) rubber-tired scrapers, (4) draglines and slurry pipelines, (5) bucket wheel excavators, and (6) grabbing cranes (guano).

Where the overburden is hard, such as the thin-bedded carbonate formations in Morocco and Utah and the chert bed in Idaho, drilling with rotary rigs and shooting with ANFO (ammonium nitrate fuel oil) may be required. Rippers on heavy-duty dozers are also useful.

Generally, more efficient use of equipment, and therefore lower overall costs, results from using the same equipment to both strip and mine. This is the practice in Florida where the mining operations use 30- to 65-cu-yd walking draglines. The same machine strips the sandy overburden, then picks up the matrix (ore) and dumps it into a pump-sump from where it is pumped to beneficiation plants. Stripping and mining of the residual brown-rock deposits of Tennessee is done with the same dragline equipment with the matrix loaded into trucks. These trucks either deliver directly to the phosphorus furnace plants or they dump into open gondola railroad cars for final delivery to the plants. Small crawler draglines with 1.5 to 3.5-cu-yd buckets are used because the small buckets are needed to dig matrix out of frequent narrow and deep troughs called cutters. One operator in Idaho uses rubber-tired scrapers both for removing overburden and picking up and delivering the ore to a truck-loading tipple. The scrapers are assisted in loading by pusher dozers. These dozers are equipped with ripper teeth used to loosen both overburden and ore. Another operator in Idaho in moving overburden uses both scrapers and 4½-cu-yd shovels loading 35-ton end-dump trucks.

Because of the nature of the deposits, other operators find it best to use different size equipment in their operations. The North Carolina operation uses two hydraulic dredges to remove the overburden. The area is drained, and a 50- and a 72-cu-yd dragline remove the remaining 50 ft of overburden to expose 40 ft of sandy phosphorite. The draglines remove the ore and place it on the surface where a 20-cu-yd dragline feeds the ore into sumps from which slurried ore is pumped to the beneficiation plant.

At some open-pit operations in Morocco larger draglines are used on the overburden and smaller ones on the matrix. Belts deliver matrix to beneficiation plants. The overburden consisting of thin-bedded carbonate rocks is drilled and blasted, then removed with draglines up to 65 cu yd in size. The matrix draglines are about 10-cu-yd size. In Togo, overburden is stripped with crawler-mounted bucket wheel excavators, each with a capacity of 2600 cu yd per hr. Matrix is mined with a 600-tph bucket wheel excavator.

At the Fosfago mine in Catalão, Brazil, mining is conducted by open pit techniques using rippers, loaders, and trucks on an altered carbonatite with ore grading from 13 to 15% P_2O_5. Beneficiation is similar to Jacupiranga

except the major contaminate, magnetite, is removed by magnetic separation prior to fine grinding and flotation. Current production is 500 kt/a of 36 to 38% P_2O_5 apatite concentrate.

The examples given here of equipment used in surface mining of phosphate rock do not, of course, cover all world phosphate mining. They do indicate types and sizes commonly used. In soft material the large draglines move material at the lowest cost—several cents a cubic yard. With harder material and smaller machines, of whatever type used, costs are much greater.

For details on earth-moving equipment, refer to Pfleider (1968). This excellent volume covers not only equipment, but other matters relevant to surface mining, including mine design, drilling, blasting, excavation, transportation, and maintenance. The importance of maintenance cannot be overemphasized. For those contemplating a new operation, and without previous experience in maintenance of heavy equipment, use of an experienced contractor can be well worthwhile. The manufacturers of earth-moving equipment have a wealth of accumulated information on the performance of their equipment. They are glad to make this information available to a potential client.

Brief summaries of mining methods and equipment for most of the world's phosphate mining operations are given in Anon., 1971b.

Beneficiation

Igneous Deposits

At present, there are four areas producing substantial quantities of apatite—USSR, South Africa, Brazil, and Zimbabwe.

USSR: In 1972 production of Kola concentrates was about 12 Mt, containing 39% P_2O_5 (Woodrooffe, 1972). By 1980 this had increased to about 20 Mt. In the Kola area the unweathered nepheline syenite ore containing about 17% P_2O_5 is crushed, ground, and floated.

South Africa: In South Africa the unweathered apatite-bearing ore of the Phalaborwa alkalic igneous complex (pyroxenite and foskorite) is crushed, ground, and floated. The flotation concentrate contains about 36% P_2O_5. The ore contains about 7% P_2O_5. Production in 1980 was about 3.5 Mt.

Brazil: At the Jacupiranga mine in Brazil, mining operations are on an unweathered carbonatite containing 5% P_2O_5. Beneficiation consists of crushing, grinding, and floating an apatite concentrate containing 36 to 38% P_2O_5.

The operations are described by Silvia and Andery (1972).

In addition to Brazil's long established apatite mines and plants at Jacupiranga and Aráxa, several other apatite-bearing carbonatites have been developed in recent years. These are all in southwestern Brazil in the adjoining states of Sao Paulo, Minas Gerais, and Goias. By 1979 Brazil's yearly production of apatite rock (concentrates) had increased to 1.7 Mt. In 1980 production was from four mines on three carbonatites (Jacupiranga, Aráxa, and Catalão). By 1985 five more mining and beneficiating operations will raise Brazil's yearly production of rock to 5.8 Mt. Four of these will be on carbonatites (Tapira, Ipanema, and Santa Catarina). The fifth will be on a pellet phosphorite at Patos de Minas. With the exception of Jacupiranga all apatite is on soft residual ore resulting from weathering. Grade of ore is 7 to 15% P_2O_5 and beneficiation is crushing, grinding, magnetic separation, desliming, and flotation. Brazil's rapidly developing phosphate industry is described in Anon., 1978 and Breathitt and Finch, 1977.

Zimbabwe: At the Dorowa alkalic complex in Zimbabwe, weathered surface material is mined at about 7% P_2O_5. The beneficiation plant grinds, washes, and floats the ore to produce about 90 kt/a of apatite concentrate.

Pellet Phosphorite Deposits

Table 7 shows the chemical composition of beneficiated pellet rock for some of the grades of many of the world's phosphorites.

United States: Florida, with some 20-odd beneficiation plants, is the largest phosphate rock producing area of the world. One operation is in northern Florida, but the others are in the vicinity of the city of Bartow in central Florida. The rock-producing capacity, all

TABLE 7—Chemical Analyses of Some Pellet Phosphorites*†

Location Code	P_2O_5	CaO	Fe_2O_3	Al_2O_3	MgO	Na_2O	K_2O	MnO	Cr_2O_3	TiO_2	V_2O_5	SiO_2	CO_2	SO_3	F_2	Cl_2	Org. C	Insol.
1	30.31	45.52	1.54	1.31	0.52	0.24	0.16	0.05	0.02	0.07	0.01	10.25	4.02	0.91	3.62	0.01	0.30	
2	34.42	49.34	1.20	0.95	0.17	0.22	0.12	0.02	0.01	0.15	0.01	4.21	3.12	0.68	3.84	0.01	0.18	
3	32.95	46.45	0.55	1.50	0.25	0.50	0.15					4.25	3.40	0.90	3.60		0.15	4.50
4	30.08	49.00	0.45	0.40	0.50										3.53		1.20	2.28
5	33.10	52.10	0.75	0.45	0.60										3.90		0.04	2.00
6	34.26	52.78	0.26	0.37	0.48	0.84	0.09					1.36	3.59	1.59	3.05	0.03		
7	37.21	54.24	0.13	0.39	0.10	0.27	0.06					0.97	2.64	0.62	4.17	tr		
8	33.05	51.95	0.21	0.43	0.40	0.80	0.07					2.46	4.48	1.22	2.49	0.03		
9‡	36.60	51.90	0.14	0.35	0.06	0.24	0.14					4.52	1.83	0.44	3.93	0.036	tr	
10	37.68	51.08	1.02	1.15	0.04	0.17	0.03					2.95	1.45	0.25	3.32	0.03		
11	36.85	51.69	1.30	1.00	0.03	0.27	0.05					2.99			3.75	0.12		
12	30.23	48.92	0.37	0.77	0.76	1.50	0.08					3.12	5.18	3.42	3.26	0.09		
13	34.58	54.25	0.45	0.46	0.77	0.60	0.02					2.35	1.25	1.60	4.00	tr		
14	29.86	48.96		1.50	0.98							4.98	6.09	2.51	2.95	0.40		
15	35.10	55.60	0.10	0.30	0.20	0.40	0.03					1.60	1.40	1.80	4.00	0.07		
16	31.20	47.70	0.35	0.27	0.35	0.58	0.06					3.00		1.16	3.00	0.23		
17	34.60	53.60										0.83			4.05	0.10		
18	34.50	42.50	1.75	3.50	0.40			0.40				9.50	0.95		3.05			
19‡	29.00	46.14	2.15	1.96	0.77	0.73	0.32	0.03				6.78	5.33	1.51	2.95		0.33	
20‡	30.10	54.04	0.37	0.65	0.16				0.006		0.07	8.68	2.95		3.25		0.04	
21‡	31.30	43.86	2.10	3.05	0.10	0.34	0.46	0.11				12.66	1.76	0.52	4.06		0.07	
22‡	29.90	47.04	3.56	1.31	0.91	1.46	0.35	0.01	0.06			3.70	5.41	2.22	3.49		1.04	
23‡	32.30	45.85	0.95	2.13	0.17	0.46	0.61	0.01	0.09	0.05	0.25	9.87	2.10	0.84	2.99		2.50	
24‡	33.12	47.70	0.51	1.26	0.30													
25‡	25.20	37.33	1.63	4.36	0.25	0.52	1.48	0.02	0.14	0.09	0.20	20.56	0.45	2.62				
26‡	33.00	47.86	0.75	1.28	0.36	0.81	0.77		0.25		0.39	5.06	2.15	1.68	3.28	2.53		

KEY TO LOCATION CODES

1. Central Florida (66% BPL grade from one producer)
2. Central Florida (75% BPL grade from one producer)
3. North Florida
4. North Carolina (Texasgulf Inc.)
5. North Carolina (Texasgulf Inc., calcined)
6. Morocco (Khouribga area, 75% TPL grade)
7. Morocco (Khouribga area, 80-82% TPL grade)
8. Morocco (Youssoufia)
9. Spanish Sahara (80% TPL grade)
10. Senegal (Taiba)
11. Togo
12. Tunisia (65-68% TPL grade)
13. Algeria (Djebel-Onk)

14. Arab Republic of Egypt (Kosseir area)
15. Israel (Oron)
16. Syria (Kneifess area)
17. Jordan (El Hassa)
18. North Vietnam (Lao-Kay)
19. Baja California, Mexico (beach sands, beneficiated, not calcined)
20. Mexico (Saltillo area, La Caja formation, calcined, washed)
21. Tennessee, Maury Co. (washed brown rock)
22. 40-mile bank off coast of Southern Calif. (sea floor nodule)
23. Idaho, Caribou Co. (Phosphoria Frm., main bed—high grade, 6-ft thick)
24. Idaho, Caribou Co. (washed, calcined)
25. Idaho, Caribou Co. (electric furnace shale rock—not beneficiated)
26. Tennessee, Maury Co. (washed electric furnace brown rock)

* Selected from Anon., 1971b.
† All are beneficiated concentrates except where otherwise indicated.
‡ Obtained from various sources other than *.

grades, of these plants is about 47 Mt/a.

Basically the beneficiation flowsheets are about the same. The matrix is pumped several miles as water slurry containing about 35% solids from the mines to the plants in steel pipes. At the plants the slurry passes over coarse screens to remove trash and waste rock, then over about 14 mesh screens to remove pebble rock. The −14 mesh material is deslimed at 150 mesh. The −14 +150 mesh material is called flotation feed, and its grade is 6.4 to 11.4 P_2O_5. It is separated into two sizes and each is floated to recover the concentrate (rock). References for more details on beneficiation practices are: Beall and Merritt (1966), Aparo (1969), Anon. (1971b), and Lawver et al. (1978). Beall and Merritt not only describe beneficiation operations in Florida, but mining as well. Additionally, they describe mining and beneficiation in North Carolina. Beneficiation of the North Carolina pellet phosphorite is described also by Wright (1971) and Breathitt and Finch (1977).

Rock production in the western United States was 5.5 Mt in 1979. About 50% goes to electric furnaces without beneficiation except screening to remove unweathered carbonate rock and unweathered phosphorite. Of the 2.75 Mt going to fertilizer plants, about 2.5 Mt is beneficiated in four plants—a calcining plant and a washing-flotation plant in Utah, and a washing-calcining plant and a washing plant in Idaho. For description of past and present beneficiation plants, refer to Clitheroe and Mele (1967).

Morocco: In 1979 Morocco's phosphate rock capacity (phosphate pellets) was 24 Mt. Capacity will be over 37 Mt by 1985, and planned rock capacity by the year 2000 is 100 Mt/a.

The major part of the known phosphate reserves are located in marine pelletal phosphorite districts. The three northern deposits are 50 miles inland from the Atlantic Ocean along a northeast-southwest trend 150 miles long. Within this district are the two established (1920s) rock-producing districts of Khouribga and Youssoufia. At the southern end is the newly established Meskala area. Still further south in former Spanish Sahara (now Western Sahara) is the Bu-Craa mine complex built by the Spanish government, which was taken over by Morocco in 1976.

The three northern phosphate areas contain four to seven phosphate beds of economic importance with thicknesses of 3 to 6 ft and grades of 24 to 34% P_2O_5. In the fourth area, the Bu-Craa mine in western Sahara, the phosphate beds total 18 ft thick and contain 31 to 33% P_2O_5. The Bu-Craa complex operated at near capacity for one year, 1975, then was transferred to Morocco. Thereafter, Polisario guerrilla activity disrupted operations by sabotaging the 60-mile belt transportation system connecting the mine to the plant and living quarters complex on the coast at El Aaium.

Morocco's past rock production has been from the two northern areas of Oulad Abdoun (Khouribga) and Ganntour (Youssoufia) from both underground and surface mines. The main producing area is Khouribga, where for many years the soft, flat upper bed was high grade enough (about 33% P_2O_5) that beneficiation was not required. Where beneficiation is now required the ore is crushed, ground, and separated by elutriation practices. Over the years the ore has become less weathered and therefore is harder and lower grade, due to cementing calcium carbonate. This ore will require new beneficiation techniques.

The ore at Bu-Craa is weathered and soft and is crushed, washed with seawater, then finally washed with fresh water to remove chlorides.

The Meskala area has not been developed but tentative plans provide for the USSR to develop a 10 Mt/a rock operation for a period of 30 years.

Morocco's energetic program to develop its export rock and finished fertilizer industry has been well described in Anon. (1975), Anon. (1980), and Anon. (1980a).

Tunisia: Tunisia produced 4 Mt in 1979 from about seven underground mines and one surface mine. The ore was beneficiated (in 1977) in four mills using both wet and dry elutriation methods to concentrate the pellet phosphate. Expansions are planned, including a second open-pit mine. Part of the rock is processed in fertilizer plants in the cities of Sfax and Gabes and part is exported by ship.

Israel: In 1980 there were four operating plants in Israel—Oron, Arad, Makhtesh Qatan, and Nahal Zin. 1980 production at Oron was about 450 kt. At the Oron phosphate deposit in Israel the phosphate pellets are associated with soft carbonate rock; grade of the ore is about 24% P_2O_5. Shortage of water originally led to beneficiation by air separation. Later flotation was tried, but both processes still yielded relatively low-grade concentrates, i.e., about 30% P_2O_5 concentrate. The process consists of calcining at 950°C, slaking with controlled amounts of water to convert CaO to $Ca(OH)_2$, and air separation at 325 mesh to remove part of the $Ca(OH)_2$. Finally the coarse product is washed in hydrocyclones. The beneficiation process is described in Anon. (1968c).

The production of the newest mine in Israel, Nahal Zin, was about 1.7 Mt of concentrates in 1980. The surface-mined ore is crushed and wet-screened to remove +1 mm waste. Hydrocycloning removes −0.1 mm slimes. The pulp is washed with fresh water to reduce chlorides, then dried. A description of Israel's deposits and mining/beneficiation operations is given in Anon. (1980b).

Jordan: Phosphates, one of Jordan's few valuable mineral resources, were discovered in 1934. The most important deposits are found in an area about 25 miles wide which extends from north of Amman south along the Hegas railroad to El Hasa, about 80 miles. Deposits include Ruseija, El Hasa, Naki Musa, Es Salt, and Qatrana. The phosphate occurs in the Upper Cretaceous to Eocene sequence that is about 1300 ft thick. Today Jordan produces about 4.5 Mt of phosphate rock. Most of this is exported as internal requirements are small.

As an additional beneficiation process, calcining of pellet phosphate rock, is being increasingly used. When the objective is elimination of hydrocarbons, temperature on the order of 800°C is adequate, but removal of CO_2 from carbonates requires higher temperatures, from 900 to 950°C.

There are a number of advantages in using calcined rock in the production of wet process phosphoric acid. Among them is the ability to produce clear acid (light green to amber in color), which is a more acceptable component of liquid fertilizers.

Worldwide, phosphate calcining capacity in 1981 is about 14 Mt/a. About 75% of world calcining is treated in Dorr-Oliver FluoSolids systems (Table 8). Allowing 85% equipment availability, the yearly design capacity is 8.9 Mt/a. Actual production is probably 120% of design capacity, or 10.70 Mt/a for Dorr-Oliver equipment and 14.3 Mt/a for all calcining installations. These installations are designed to reduce the organic content of phosphate rock. However, in Algeria, the calciners, which are operated at higher temperatures, are used to drive off CO_2 from carbonates.

Phosphate Rock Use

Fertilizer Industry

Fertilizers consume 95% of the world's rock production. The future of the phosphate rock industry is, therefore, directly related to the future of phosphate fertilizer; accordingly, it is pertinent that any description of the rock industry be tied in with comments on the fertilizer industry. Table 9 shows world phosphate consumption by region.

The United States is the world's largest producer and user of fertilizer and is the leader in developing new types of fertilizers and their uses. Particularly in the last 15 years there has been a rapid switch to mixed and higher grade fertilizers, both granular and liquid types. The world trend is also in this direction.

Most world fertilizer manufacturing processes use sulfuric acid, although some, mostly in Europe, use nitric acid. Where acid soil conditions favor its use, some finely ground rock is applied directly to the soil, but the quantity used is minor and in the United States continues to decline.

A continuing trend is to produce phosphoric acid (52 to 54% P_2O_5) which is then used in the formulation of final fertilizers. A more recent trend is to use superphosphoric acid (67 to 76% P_2O_5) for the same purpose.

Export of phosphoric acid continues to grow. Most involves ocean shipment from countries with indigenous rock resources. These include the United States, Morocco, Tunisia, and South Africa. Other exporters, based on imported rock, include Spain, Mexico, France, The Netherlands, and Belgium (Anon., 1978a).

The grade of a fertilizer is denoted by the use of three numbers such as (18–46–0). The first number defines the percent elemental nitrogen (N), the second, P_2O_5, and the last is K_2O. In recent years there has been a trend to using numbers referring to the element only as (N-P-K). Chief among the types of phosphate fertilizers are the following:

Normal superphosphate (0–18–0) to (0–20–0) (solid).

Concentrated superphosphate (0–42–0) to (0–50–0) (solid).

Diammonium phosphate (18–46–0) (solid).

Monoammonium phosphate (16–48–0) and (11–48–0) (solid).

Granular mixed fertilizers (combination of foregoing types and K_2O where needed).

Liquid mixed fertilizers (phosphoric acid

TABLE 8—World Phosphate Calcining Capacity, 1981

Installation	Location	Units	Design Capacity, t/d
Djebel Onk	Algeria	3	3 000
OCP	Morocco	2	3 700
Beker	Idaho	4	5 830
Simplot	Idaho	4	5 000
Stauffer	Wyoming	3	2 000
Texas Gulf	North Carolina	6	9 000
Total		22	28 530

neutralized with ammonia and nitrogen solution and potash added where needed).

As pointed out earlier, any phosphate rock, igneous or sedimentary, can be used to meet any of man's required end products; however, economics help govern the selection. Grindability and reactivity in acid influence costs. For example, the fluorapatite crystals in igneous apatite are denser than the francolite crystals of pellet phosphorites. Igneous apatite is, therefore, not as easy to grind nor is it as reactive to acid. Conversely, igneous apatite does not have the hydrocarbon content which generally occurs in all pellet phosphorites and which may impose a penalty during acidification. Robinson (1972), Hill (1960), Everhart (1971), and Pacl et al. (1978) describe the physical and chemical characteristics of phosphate rock which influence its reaction to acidulation.

The following is quoted from Everhart:

In the acidulation of phosphate rock, the presence of too much combined iron and aluminum oxide (known as "I and A" in the industry) is a serious trouble-maker in chemical plants and is the factor in ruling out many deposits as ore. A combined iron and aluminum oxide content of greater than 2.5% to 4.0% (depending on the end use) is generally considered prohibitive. Another critical factor is the weight ratio of CaO to P_2O_5 content in the rock. If this ratio is above 1.6 to 1, the cost of sulphuric acid consumption is generally so prohibitive as to eliminate the candidate rock. Inasmuch as the origin of phosphorite is marine, many such formations in the world have a substantial chloride content, if the geologic history of the marine sediments under consideration has involved the subsequent formation of evaporites in the area. Acidulation of phosphate rock in wet acid plants commonly can tolerate no more than 0.13% of chlorine in chlorides, because of the resulting severe corrosion problems in processing equipment.

Still another deleterious element in the chemical processing of phosphate is magnesium oxide. No more than 0.25% is desirable if fluid fertilizers produced from superphosphoric acid are the principal end products. Even small quantities of MgO in the raw phosphate rock will result in an intolerable viscosity index in superphosphoric acid produced by the wet acid process.

Fluorapatite is the principal phosphate mineral in marine phosphorites, and so deposits of this origin characteristically have a constant P_2O_5 to F_2 ratio. The range is 8 to 11:1 and tends to be about the same within an individual deposit but differs from district to district. A P_2O_5 to F_2 ratio of less than 8:1 would indicate possible troublesome fluorine problems in processing. Even organic matter in phosphate is undesirable since it leads to discolored acid that is very difficult to sell. Pyrite in the phosphate rock can lead to danger in a wet acid plant because of the generation of lethal H_2S during acidulation.

Phosphorus (Industrial Chemicals) Industry

Phosphorus is produced in electric furnaces charged with calcined phosphate rock, silica, and coke. It is used to produce high purity compounds—mostly sodium, calcium, potassium, and ammonium phosphates. The manufacturing steps begin with burning the phosphorus in air and dissolving the resultant oxide in water to make a relatively pure phosphoric acid suitable for the manufacture of industrial phosphates. They include detergents, industrial cleaners, and forest fire retardants. Further purification with hydrogen sulfide to remove traces of arsenic yields a very pure "food grade" acid which is used extensively in the manufacture of toothpaste and food additives. Phosphorus is also used in the manufacture of organophosphorus compounds for such uses as flame-retardant additives for fabrics and plastics, and insecticides.

Until about 30 years ago the United States produced the majority of the world's phosphorus with lesser amounts largely from England, France, Canada, and Germany. Since 'n, however, production capacity has increased in many countries so that by 1972 the United States accounted for about half the world production.

A rough estimate of the yearly world production of elemental phosphorus in 1979 was 3,400 million pounds. Of this, 1,500 million pounds was attributed to Russia (for fertilizer), 1,300 million pounds to North America, and 600 million pounds to Western Europe. Except for Russia, the world's phosphorus is used largely in the production of detergents.

Based on the foregoing statistics, in 1979 about 11% of the world's rock production was used to make elemental phosphorus and 6% went into detergents. In the US about 12% of the rock consumed went into elemental phosphorus.

Phosphorus electric furnaces (enclosed) operate in a reducing atmosphere so that the vaporized phosphorus can be pulled off in the gases without contacting oxygen in the air. The gases are mainly CO and vaporized phosphorus. They are first cleaned of entrained particulate matter, then sprayed with water which cools them, causing condensation of the phosphorus into droplets which settle and are collected underwater.

In the phosphorus furnace coke is the reducing agent. Silica in the melt reacts with the calcium end of the phosphate mineral to produce a calcium silicate slag. Any other calcium, magnesium, or aluminum mineral, such as calcite, dolomite, or clay also reacts with silica and adds to the slag. Part of any iron oxide present in the phosphate rock is reduced to molten iron which settles to the bottom of the furnace under the silicate melt. As the iron is formed it reacts with phosphorus at a ratio of about three parts iron to one part phosphorus to make an alloy called ferrophosphorus. It is tapped separately from tapholes located below the silicate-melt tapholes.

Calcium, magnesium, and clay minerals, therefore, are undesirable in the phosphate rock, as they consume electricity. Iron is undesirable for the same reason, but, even worse, it ties up phosphorus in a low-value end product—ferrophosphorus.

The calcined phosphate rock charged to the furnace cannot be fine-grained because a porous bed must be maintained in the furnace to permit circulation of gases. The rock is charged as prepared material about an inch in size. This prepared material is made by one of two routes—nodulizing and calcining at about 1350°C in nearly horizontal kilns or calcining rolled flakes, or round pellets, in grate kilns.

Phosphate rock used to produce phosphorus can be as low grade as 24% P_2O_5. The CaO/P ratio should be in the range of 3.30 to 3.60—preferably the lower figure. An acceptable

TABLE 9—Summary of P_2O_5 Consumption, Mt, World and Five Regions

Year	North America	Western Europe	East Europe & USSR	Asia	Remainder	Total
1962*	2.71	3.68	1.75	1.07	1.38	10.58
1963	2.97	3.84	1.82	1.24	1.44	11.31
1964	3.29	4.12	2.12	1.52	1.63	12.67
1965	3.44	4.33	2.61	1.60	1.98	13.95
1966	3.86	4.38	2.95	1.66	2.11	14.95
1967	4.28	4.51	3.21	1.91	2.20	16.11
1968	4.44	4.78	3.48	2.01	2.24	16.96
1969	4.54	4.92	3.85	2.43	2.43	18.17
1970	4.43	5.19	4.05	2.68	2.47	18.82
1971	4.68	5.49	4.41	2.68	2.53	19.79
1972	4.76	5.72	4.80	3.09	2.73	21.10
1973	5.02	5.84	5.04	3.41	3.13	22.44
1974	5.11	5.99	5.51	3.90	3.65	24.16
1975	4.59	5.04	6.09	3.81	3.15	22.69
1976	5.25	4.91	6.89	3.84	3.24	24.13
1977	5.64	5.29	7.19	4.45	3.93	26.49
1978	5.15	5.60	7.50	4.75	4.25	27.25
1980	5.80	6.00	8.50	5.15	4.80	30.25
1985	6.50	6.50	10.50	6.50	6.00	36.00

Source: Douglas, 1979 and F.A.O. Fertilizer Statistics.
* 1962-1977 actual, 1978 estimated, 1980 and 1985 projected.

CaO/P ratio is, however, directly related to the cost of power. About 6 kw-hr is required in a phosphorus plant for each pound of phosphorus produced. The iron content of phosphate rock should not exceed a few percent Fe_2O_3.

In the early 1930s while planning for the new phosphorus industry in the US, pilot plant furnace plants of up to 1500-kw capacity were built and operated. Since that time, however, with the experience gained in operating large commercial plants, pilot plants have not been considered necessary.

Cost calculations for the production of phosphorus are based on chemical analyses. Pilot plant work is required, however, in determining the manner of preparing the calcined rock product to be added to the furnace.

In the United States phosphorus produced at an electric furnace plant is shipped in closed and insulated railroad tank cars to manufacturing plants located near markets for the end product. These tank cars, with capacities of 8,000 to 22,000 gal (holding 117,000 to 317,000 lb of phosphorus), are jacketed so that if the temperature of the phosphorus drops to 44°C (when the liquid phosphorus becomes a solid), the contents can be remelted by steam at destination for pumping to the burning towers. In the burning tower oxygen in air reacts with the phosphorus to make P_2O_5 powder, which is mixed with water to make a very pure phosphoric acid containing 54% P_2O_5.

Outside the US, most phosphorus plants are located near markets for end products and the phosphorus therefore is converted to industrial chemicals at the plant site. However, a phosphorus plant built in Newfoundland to take advantage of low-priced electricity, ships phosphorus overseas in two specially designed 5000-st vessels. The USSR is reported to have six phosphorus plant installations. Rail transportation of some of the phosphorus may be involved, but there is no readily available information on such movements.

Phosphorus is not inexpensive. The principal production cost factors are electricity, coke, and rock coupled with heavy capital investment. Its production is justified by its high purity which is required to meet strict specifications of end products.

Very little has been published, at least in English, on the production of phosphorus. A detailed description was compiled by Burt and Barber (1952) and reprinted in 1967. This TVA report mentions furnaces of 20,000 to 25,000-kw size; however, since 1952, many of the more modern furnaces are over double these sizes. In Waggaman (1952), there is a chapter on the manufacturing of phosphorus and other chapters on the use and manufacturing of industrial phosphates produced from phosphorus. Other publications by TVA personnel are Barber and Marks (1962) and Hignett and Stripling (1967). Several articles on phosphorus production including a description of world furnace plant installations in 1968 can be found in Anon., 1966, 1966a, and 1968.

Phosphate Fertilizer Industry *

The world supply-demand situation has rapidly come back toward a balanced position since 1975. This was accomplished as a result of many changes. Demand has increased; many older plants closed as the chaotic financial situation led to economic obsolescence. Planned plants were postponed indefinitely, and some were scrapped altogether. The result has been a rapid recovery of the remaining wet phosphoric (W-P) acid and nitric phosphates (N-P) segments of the industry. In 1978 they were able to operate at almost 90% of the rate at which they operated during the shortage of 1972–1974—a real recovery from the 81% level in 1975.

Further improvement is expected through 1980. If we accept the statistics projected for new plants, by 1980 the relative operating rate will be about 94%—possibly even higher, because some of the new plants announced are in regions that historically have time slippages on construction schedules. Regardless, the phosphate supply-demand situation should become progressively better through 1980.

Many new plants are proposed for 1981 and 1982. The new plants planned and announced are sufficient to lead to another serious downswing if all plants are completed as planned. Based on history, this seems unlikely.

On the other hand, only one new W-P acid plant has been announced for North America, though there have been recurring rumors of four or five other major expansions which could lead to another 2 million st capacity by 1982–1983. If these plans are completed, in conjunction with other plants already announced, the industry by 1983 could well re-

---

* Summarized from J.R. Douglas, 1979, "World Phosphate Supply Plagued by Questions," Tennessee Valley Authority National Fertilizer Development Center, presented at the 7th Phosphate-Sulphur Symposium, Innsbruch, FL, Jan. 18–19.

vert to a position comparable to 1968 and 1975.

Western Europe: The recovery of the phosphate industry in Europe has been remarkably rapid but at great sacrifices on the part of much of the industry. Many plants have been closed altogether. Less basic slag is being sold—and less NSP. Imports of finished phosphates or intermediate wet-process acids have increased. The net result has been a rapid recovery of the remnants of the industry, but no new plants are operating or scheduled. Further progress in attaining a balanced supply-demand situation can be expected unless imports are increased.

Eastern Europe and the USSR: A casual glance at the supply-demand situation for the phosphate industry at first appears to indicate that this region is planning on building sufficient N-P and W-P acid capacity to remain, as in the past, relatively self-sufficient. At the same time, the region is embarking on long-range trade which will result in annual importation of about 700,000 st of P_2O_5. We don't know if this will be a net import or if the area will in turn begin exporting finished phosphate fertilizers to the world market. If the importation of the wet-process acid works out satisfactorily, the USSR could delay some of its proposed high-cost construction and divert funds to other uses. Or it might decide to substitute finished phosphate fertilizer for some of the million tons or so of P_2O_5 it now uses in the form of ground rock phosphate or the large amounts of NSP now used.

Asia: We know too little of the fertilizer industry—past, present, and future—in communist Asia to attempt a prediction. In the past, the Asian industry has been relatively self-sufficient. There is some conjecture that, at least temporarily, Asia will begin importing relatively large amounts of finished phosphate fertilizers while building its own industry. Such an approach would not be abnormal in a planned development program, and would only tend to improve the world demand situation.

A quick glance at the figures might lead one to believe that noncommunist Asia is rapidly building toward self-sufficiency by the early 1980s. However, most of the new capacity planned is to be in the Near East. Much of the subcontinent will remain major importers. Some few nations who now import P_2O_5 may become self-sufficient. Others will need to import more. The major question here is: Who will furnish this material.

Central and South America: Although there are many new P_2O_5 plants proposed for Central and South America between now and 1985, it appears certain that this region will remain a major net importer—even if all plants now planned are built, which is doubtful. The region could become an even larger net importer over the next five to seven years.

Africa: A plethora of plants were announced and built in Africa in the past ten years. Many more are planned. Many of these will be delayed; some, however, will be built, and Africa can well be expected to become an increasingly strong competitor for sales of world traded finished phosphate materials.

Oceania: This region has always been relatively self-sufficient with a major reliance on NSP. No changes are foreseen.

North America: The North American phosphate industry has pulled out of the doldrums of 1975 almost entirely by rapid increases in exports. Net exports have increased from less than 1 million st P_2O_5 in the 1960s to more than 1.5 st in 1975 and an estimated 2.75 million st in 1978. In 1979, exports were considerably above those of previous years. A new major export has been developed to the USSR which is to reach a reported 700 kt annually by 1980. Domestic use has increased about as expected—with some annual decreases offset by a continuing upward trend in use—but exports have skyrocketed. As a result, the operational rates of North American W-P acid plants have increased and last year approached the relative rates of the shortage period of 1972–1974. If the total demand for domestic use and exports is to be met, plant operations will have to exceed the highest rates of any past date. Inventories could be pulled down to very low levels. Even then we could very easily run into a shortage of material during the middle of the spring rush reason.

If we assume exports will continue in the future and will be expanded by the new trade with the USSR, this North American industry as presently configured will not be able to meet domestic and export demand for long, if at all. More plants will be needed, or considerable debottlenecking of existing plants. We will need more production capacity—again—if the export demand holds up.

There have been rumors of four or five new expansions for the 1980–1981 period. These, if accomplished, could add 2 million st capacity or more, almost overnight. Even this 2 million st capacity would not throw the North American industry into a large oversupply position if domestic demand increases as expected and exports continue at the current projected levels.

If, as historically often happens, this capacity becomes available all at once, and if at the same time there should be a reduction of exports of 1.5 million tons from projected levels, then our industry would face the same degree of problems it faced in 1968 and 1975. With rising fertilizer prices offsetting relatively stable world prices in grain and farm products, at some point exports will drop. It is hoped that the industry can more adequately judge what this price level is and thus avoid a recurrence of the chaos of past cycles.

The future of the North American industry is as bright as we make it. We have a natural competitive advantage in producing finished phosphate fertilizer. We are the only region of the world with ample supplies of phosphate rock in close conjunction economically with ample supplies of sulfur—and both close to the world's sea lanes. In addition, we have leading technology. With such a combination, we have a real competitive advantage over other areas of the world and should, if proper decisions are made, remain the world's major trader in finished phosphates.

World Phosphate Fertilizer Production *

The phosphate market differs from the nitrogen market in that there are two basic sources of finished phosphate materials: products produced with phosphoric acid including TSP, most nitric phosphates, ammonium phosphates, and other complex fertilizer materials, and products produced without phosphoric acid. Normal superphosphate, made by treating phosphate rock with sulfuric acid, is the major product. Others include basic slag (a byproduct of steel production) available for fertilizer use in Europe and the portions of concentrated superphosphate and nitric phosphate that come directly from phosphate rock. This second group of products is declining in importance and, as the scheduled expansion in phosphoric acid comes into production, the decline should accelerate.

Total phosphate fertilizer capacity is not very meaningful because capacity of NSP and TSP usually is well above actual production levels. Thus fertilizer capacity is considerably

* Excerpted from G.E. Harris and E.A. Harre, "World Fertilizer Situation and Outlook," International Fertilizer Development Center, and National Fertilizer Development Center, TVA, Muscle Shoals, AL, March, 1979.

larger than most estimates if market conditions become very favorable.

One of the most important changes taking place in the phosphate industry is the trend toward phosphoric acid-based fertilizers with the phosphate rock-producing countries producing and exporting greater amounts of phosphate fertilizers and phosphoric acid. Normal superphosphate will continue to face increased competition from higher analysis products. Its usage, primarily in the production of low-analysis mixed fertilizers, is expected to remain at about today's levels through 1985; however, its market share will decline. Normal superphosphate still comprises a large portion of the phosphate market in all regions except North America. Also, NSP contains sulfur, which is needed in some soils. Future production will be concentrated in only a few areas. An increase is expected in the total world production of TSP by 1985 with the largest increase in Asia. The ammonium phosphates and other high-analysis complex fertilizers are fast becoming the most popular way of providing phosphates to the farmer.

Basic slag production is centered in Western Europe. Usage of this product as a source of phosphate has been declining with changes in the steelmaking process. Because this product is directly related to the region's steel industry, it appears that a shift to new steelmaking processes or use of different ores would be necessary to bring about any significant changes from the current production pattern.

The future of the world phosphate industry will depend on developments in phosphoric acid and to a lesser extent in nitric phosphates. World nitric phosphate capacity is expected to climb from the 1978 level of about 3.2 Mt of P_2O_5 to almost 4.5 Mt of P_2O_5 by 1985. Production will center in Eastern and Western Europe, which together will have 3.7 Mt of capacity by 1985. Nitric phosphates will be of minor importance in other regions of the world.

Phosphoric acid is sometimes used in the manufacture of complex fertilizers by the nitric phosphate process. Only that portion of the P_2O_5 from the nitric acid acidulation of phosphate rock was considered to avoid double counting.

Phosphoric Acid Capacity: World phosphoric acid capacity in 1977 was 26.4 Mt, a 92% increase over eight years ago (Table 10). Capacity is expected to increase 30% during the next eight years and reach 34.2 Mt by 1985. The largest percentage increase will occur in

TABLE 10—World Phosphoric Acid Capacity, Mt, P_2O_5, by Region

Region	1976	1977	1980*	1985*	Rate of Change, % 1969-1977	Rate of Change, % 1977-1985
North America	9.1	9.3	9.4	9.4	48	1
Latin America	0.9	1.0	1.4	2.2	54	122
Western Europe	4.7	4.7	4.7	4.7	54	1
Eastern Europe	1.5	1.6	2.1	2.5	166	56
USSR	4.0	4.5	5.4	6.8	276	51
Asia	2.4	3.1	3.5	5.3	154	73
Africa	1.4	2.0	2.5	3.2	290	60
Oceania	0.3	0.3	0.3	0.3	14	0
World	24.2	26.4	29.3	34.2	92	30

Source: Harris and Harre, 1979.
*Numbers after 1977 are estimates.

Latin America, but the largest absolute increase will be in Asia and the USSR, where capacity in both areas will increase by over 2 Mt. These two regions will have 35% of the world's phosphoric acid capacity by 1985, compared to 29% currently. All regions except North America, Western Europe, and Oceania are projected to increase their phosphoric acid capacity by 50% or more between 1977 and 1985. North America, which now has 35% of the world's capacity, will have only 27% by 1985.

In order to analyze the future supply capability of the phosphate industry, it is necessary to look at the raw materials important in the manufacture of phosphate fertilizers. World production of phosphate fertilizers is given in Table 11.

Byproducts from the Use of Phosphate Rock

Gypsum: Gypsum, $CaSO_4 \cdot 2H_2O$, is produced as a byproduct in making wet-process phosphoric acid. Above five tons of gypsum results from the production of a ton of P_2O_5—equivalent to roughly 1.5 tons of gypsum for each ton of rock used. Commonly, the gypsum is stockpiled near the fertilizer plant. Because of the increasing use of rock, with the trend to wet-process phosphoric acid production, together with the trend to larger plants, the quantity of gypsum accumulating in stockpiles is becoming large.

Much attention has been given to putting this byproduct gypsum into the main market—plasterboard. For a number of reasons, efforts to use any significant quantity of byproduct gypsum have not been successful.

Appleyard, in the chapter "Gypsum and Anhydrite," in Part 4, comments on byproduct gypsum resulting from production of phosphoric acid.

Uranium: Uranium occurs in minor quantities in the mineral apatite [$3Ca_3(PO_4)_2CaF_2$], which is the source of phosphorous in phos-

TABLE 11—World Phosphate Fertilizer Production, Mt, P_2O_5, by Region

Region	1969	1977	1980*	1985*	Rate of Change, % 1969-1977	Rate of Change, % 1977-1985
North America	5.1	7.8	7.8	7.9	53	1
Latin America	0.3	1.2	1.3	2.1	319	84
Western Europe	5.6	5.5	6.1	6.0	-2	9
Eastern Europe	1.8	2.9	4.0	4.4	65	52
USSR	1.9	4.4	5.9	7.5	127	70
Asia	2.0	3.6	4.7	6.8	83	92
Africa	0.7	0.9	2.2	2.8	26	205
Oceania	1.2	1.1	1.4	1.4	-8	30
World	18.5	27.3	33.3	38.9	47	42

Source: Harris and Harre, 1979.
*Based on 90% operating rates in developed countries and 70% rate in developing countries. Numbers after 1979 are estimates.

phate ore. After mining, phosphate ore is crushed and ground, leaving an apatite concentration with a grade of 30 to 34% P_2O_5. If the apatite is derived from a marine deposit, as most are, this concentrate generally carries 50 to 200 ppm U_3O_8; and lower if the apatite is derived from an igneous deposit.

During the last ten years, there has been much interest in the United States in the recovery of uranium from wet-acid by solvent extraction methods. Several plants are now recovering uranium from Florida wet acid; more are planned both in the US and elsewhere. A good summary of the worldwide status of uranium recovery from pellet phosphate rock is given in Anon., 1980c.

Because uranium is recovered as a byproduct from existing operations, the environmental difficulties are significantly less troublesome than those associated with new mining and milling facilities. Given the environmental attractiveness and competitive position with conventional ore deposits, it is likely that more extraction facilities will be constructed in the US and other countries, and that henceforth these facilities may supply about 10% of the world's uranium requirements.

Vanadium: Pellet phosphorites commonly contain significant quantities of other metals besides uranium. Those of the Phosphoria formation of the western US in places contain considerable vanadium. In the 1930s and 1940s, rock mined in Idaho was processed into wet-process acid at a plant in Montana and red cake, sodium vanadate, recovered. The ferrophosphorus from an electric furnace operation in Idaho is processed in a separate plant for recovery of vanadium.

Fluorides: The world's phosphate rock deposits represent the largest known resources of the all-important element fluorine. Much of the fluorine in rock is evolved in gaseous form in the production of fertilizer. Plants in Florida have long recovered H_2SiF_6, used by municipalities to fluorinate water. In recent years, fluorides recovered from Florida fertilizer plants have been converted to synthetic cryolite and aluminum fluoride in two plants, one in Florida and one in Louisiana. The products are used by the aluminum industry. Other plants around the world either in production or planned to recover fluorides from rock are located in Canada, Mexico, USSR, India, Japan, West Germany, China, and Austria. In all likelihood the future will see a growing recovery of fluorine from this source.

Other Byproducts: Nepheline syenite tailings from the Kola apatite operation in the USSR are utilized in the production of aluminum and ceramics.

In Brazil, a plant makes cement from calcite tailings resulting from the flotation of apatite (igneous) from a carbonatite phosphate deposit.

The calcium silicate slag resulting from production of electric furnace phosphorus is used for road metal, railroad ballast, and for concrete aggregate. It has a ready market in Florida, where there is a shortage of natural stone. Where natural stone is readily available as in Tennessee and the western United States, the slag has limited markets.

Over the past few years governmental agencies have expressed concern that the small amount of uranium in the slags might be harmful to humans.

Governmental and Environmental Influences

In the United States, federal and state laws and regulations affect the mining of rock. The phosphorite beds of the Phosphoria formation occur largely in Montana, Idaho, Wyoming, and Utah. In the early 1900s, the federal government withdrew nearly all the phosphate land from the location of mining claims for phosphate. In 1920, Congress passed a law, commonly referred to as the Mineral Leasing Act of 1920, retaining all federal ownership of phosphate and certain other minerals. The great majority of the Phosphoria formation is, therefore, owned by the federal government with lesser amounts on Indian, state, and private lands. Federal and Indian phosphate deposits can be leased. Federal lands are leased by the Department of the Interior for an indefinite time period; however, the government retains the right to make reasonable changes in lease terms and conditions every 20 years. Indian lands are leased by the tribes involved and are for 10 years. Leases are administered by the US Department of the Interior. The Mineral Leasing Act of 1920 is administered under regulations of the Department of the Interior. Numerous changes in regulations have been made, particularly since 1966, designed for protection of the environment, so that as of 1972, prior to surface mining operations, mining and reclamation plans would have to be approved by the Dept. of the Interior. Environmental impact statements may be required. Beginning in 1969, the western phosphate states of Monna, Idaho, and Wyoming have enacted surface mining laws. These require that operations have state permits, approval of reclamation plans, and bonding for reclamation.

In the late 1960s, a company obtained federal phosphate prospecting permits in the Los Padres National Forest of California. Test drilling proved the presence of phosphate, and a preference right phosphate lease application was made to the Department of the Interior. All of this was prior to Congress passing the National Environmental Policy Act of 1969. Environmental groups protested issuance of the federal leases, and public hearings were held in July 1971. As of July 1983, The Department of Interior had not issued a preference right lease to the holders of phosphate prospecting permits.

A somewhat similar situation exists for phosphate lease applications on the Osceola National Forest of northern Florida. There the issuance of phosphate leases after phosphate was found under federal permits also has been held up by a law suit filed in a federal court by the State of Florida through the Attorney General in 1971. The suit requests that the Secretaries of the Interior and of Agriculture be enjoined from approving federal leases for various alleged causes including threatening the existence of endangered species of wildlife, possibly destroying the freshwater aquifer, etc. The courts have held that the holders of federal permits in the Osceola National Forest have the right to convert to federal leases. Early in 1983, the Dept. of the Interior denied the lease applications on the Osceola National Forest, stating that the lands, if mined, could not be properly reclaimed. One of the parties applying for leases has filed suit in federal court, and others may do the same.

Nearly all of the phosphate-bearing lands of Florida, North Carolina, and Tennessee are in private ownership. Much of that in Tennessee is in areas of rapid housing developments and has for years been subjected to city and county zoning ordinances. Starting July 1, 1971, the phosphate rock industry in Florida was subjected to a 3% severance tax on the value of the rock which in 1975 was raised to 5% with certain credits for other taxes and cost of land reclamation. The tax was increased to 10% of value of wet rock in 1981. By 1982, the severance tax on Florida rock had increased from $0.16 per ton in 1973 to $2.03.

Tennessee passed surface mining legislation in 1967 requiring, among other things, yearly permits, publishing of plans to mine, and bonding for reclamation.

The generation of large quantities of by-product gypsum from phosphoric acid production has been mentioned. Sweeney and Timmons (1972) list existing stockpiles of this gypsum in Florida in 1972 at 153 million tons covering 1800 acres with a yearly addition rate of 21 million tons. They point out that it is not an environmental threat, but does present a potential aesthetic problem.

Beginning in the late 1960s concern developed, especially in the United States, over the possibility that phosphate in freshwater was the cause of excessive growth of algae—particularly in some lakes. Phosphate enters freshwater through many sources, predominately natural leaching of phosphate from rocks and soils, animal excrement (largely human waste through sewage systems), phosphate detergents used for cleaning, and runoff from fields fertilized with phosphate. It quickly became popular to believe that elimination of phosphate detergents was desirable and, by the early 1970s, hastily devised laws were enacted by several states, counties, and cities. Some of these laws set lower phosphate content in detergents, some eliminated it entirely. By 1980 public emotionalism over phosphates in detergents had subsided from that of the early 1970s; however, damage has been done to the detergent industry markets. By the late 1970s detergent markets were holding steady. Similar public emotionalism about phosphate fertilizers had also subsided by that time.

Tests by researchers from Purdue University revealed that the Indiana ban on phosphate detergents made no difference in the water quality of 15 Indiana lakes (Anon., 1978b). Another group from Cornell University has preliminary results from ten lakes in New York which confirm the findings of the Purdue team.

Phosphate fertilizer plants, rock defluorination plants, and electric furnace plants emit gaseous fluorides in the rock treatment process. By early 1970s a number of states had passed laws setting maximum allowable limitations on fluorine emission. The principal purpose of such laws is to limit excess buildup of fluorine in forage plants, thereby preventing fluorosis primarily in cattle, although there has been concern, also, over certain flower and orchard crops.

Various state laws establish limits in any, or all, of the following: accumulation of fluorine in animal forage, the quantity of HF in ambient air around industrial plants, and the quantity of fluorine emitted by the plant operation. Allowable maximums differ from state to state but that for fluorine in forage is generally about 40 ppm, ambient air fluorine is generally 1 to 4 ppb. Plant emissions are stated in parts per billion over certain periods of time or by fraction of a pound of fluorine per ton of P_2O_5 equivalent produced.

In complying with laws on fluorine emission, the phosphate industry is faced with substantial capital costs for control equipment and the continuing costs to operate such equipment.

Phosphate rock is a large commodity in world export markets. World rock production in 1982 was 140 Mt. Of this, about 60 Mt were exported, largely by ship. The balance was processed domestically into individual uses or exported.

With a few minor exceptions, the movement of rock is not hampered by tariffs or other restrictions. There are some tariffs on the international movement of phosphate fertilizer, although the United States has none. An example of such tariffs is the European Economic Community (EEC), which imposes a duty of 13.2% c.i.f. (cost, insurance, and freight) on phosphoric acid and 8% c.i.f. on diammonium phosphate (DAP). These EEC duties do not apply to Tunisia and Morocco, as they are Common Market associates.

Costs, Prices and Taxes

In this chapter there has been no reference to the cost of producing phosphate rock. Producers consider such costs confidential, and the same is true for the production of phosphate fertilizer.

Until 1974, finished phosphate rock was a low-value material. In 1971, for example, the rate price of 72% BPL Florida rock f.o.b. Tampa was only $6 per long ton. This quickly changed in October, 1973, when Morocco announced export prices effective January 1, 1974 which nearly tripled existing prices. Shortly thereafter, the other ex-US rock exporters went along with the Morocco increase. In November 1973, the Phosphate Rock Export Association (Phosrock), made up of most of the Florida rock producers, announced increased prices of export rock from the United States effective Jan. 1, 1974.

Domestic and export prices fluctuate. The US Bureau of Mines periodically publishes rock prices. One of these reports on "Marketable Phosphate Rock," February 1983, gives the following information on 1982 prices per metric ton for rock from Florida and North Carolina, f.o.b. mines: domestic rock prices for grades of 60 to 74% BPL were $23.22 and $30.93; export rock prices for grades of 60 to 74% BPL were $26.63 and $29.08. The shipping cost from mines to ports averaged $5.24/t.

For federal income tax purposes a phosphate rock producer in the United States can take either cost depletion or percentage depletion. If percentage depletion is used, the producer is allowed a depletion deduction of 14% of gross income from the mining property, but limited to 50% of net income (gross income less costs). The dollar amount of the allowable deduction is subtracted from income, thereby reducing the taxable profit. Put another way, the allowable deduction can be considered as an expense and, added to other expenses, establishes the profit subject to federal income tax.

Future of the Phosphate Rock Industry

The future of the industry is largely tied to the future of the fertilizer industry. Phosphate rock, used in fertilizer, is necessary to the life of modern man. There is no substitute. In today's economics only a minor quantity is recovered, from municipal sewage, but it appears likely the future will see more phosphate recovered from this source.

The rapid growth of the world rock industry since 1945 is shown in Fig. 2, but whether future growth can be projected from this past growth is questionable.

Harre et al. (1972) states: ". . . In many areas of the world, developed and developing, the fertilizer market is maturing to a point where increased productivity will depend more heavily on an optimum combination of farm inputs—fertilizer, water, pesticides and herbicides, varieties, etc.—rather than just the result of increased use of one input factor only. Fertilizer has been the key to acceptance of these new management techniques; thus, its major impact in some areas may have already been achieved, and a slowing in demand growth can be expected in the next decade."

As Fig. 2 graphically shows, US and world rock production since 1945 has grown rapidly almost along a straight line. The 1980s will see expansion of existing rock-producing capacity as well as production from new areas. A straight-line projection of the growth curves in Fig. 2 indicates a world production of 180 Mt in the year 2000, with a US production of 72 Mt.

In mid-1980, the producers of rock and fertilizer in Florida began reducing operating rates to correct imbalances between supply and demand in the United States. Such reductions continued through 1981 and by the end of 1982 had resulted in a number of mines and plants stopping operations as well as others curtailing production. Phosphate rock production in the US was 37.414 Mt in 1982, 30% less than 1981. By early 1983, it appeared rock and fertilizer production for 1983 may exceed 1982 by 5%. Complete recovery to normal will be a slow process, but should take place between 1985 and 1987.

The rock production for Florida and North Carolina accounts for over 85% of US production. This large production raises questions about life of the phosphate rock reserves, especially for the main producer—Florida.

Government and other surveys go back over many years; since 1978, there have been a number of new estimates published. Four of these are: Zellar-Williams, Inc., 1978, done for the US Bureau of Mines; Anon., 1979b, done for the US Dept. of Energy; Sandvick, 1979; and Mayberry, 1981.

The US Bureau of Mines in using its report by Zellar-Williams tends to tie reserves into past historically low costs and prices for rock. This limits life of reserves, especially for Florida.

The other three estimates take the approach that continually improving methods of producing and using marketable rock will allow for developing more reserves as well as recognizing that costs and prices will adjust for production as long as there is a market for the rock. These three estimates paint a brighter picture for a long reserve life.

Table 6 (Anon., 1979b) shows known estimated phosphate rock reserves in the noncommunist world.

Bibliography and References

Anon., 1965, "Phosphate Rock Mining and Treatment Plant at Phalaborwa," *Phosphorus & Potassium*, No. 19, The British Sulphur Corp., London, October, pp. 12–18.

Anon., 1966, "Elemental Phosphorus in the United States," *Phosphorus & Potassium*, No. 24, The British Sulphur Corp., London, August–September, pp. 12–24.

Anon., 1966a, "World Elemental Phosphorus—Part II," *Phosphorus & Potassium*, No. 25, The British Sulphur Corp., London, October–November, pp. 10–16.

Anon., 1967, *A Study of the Bu-Craa Phosphate Deposit,* Empresa Nacional Minera del Sahara, S.A. (ENMINSA), Madrid, 28 pp. (English translation).

Anon., 1968, "Elemental Phosphorus Developments," *Phosphorus & Potassium*, No. 36, The British Sulphur Corp., London, July–August, pp. 16–25, 33.

Anon., 1968a, "Kola," *Phosphorus & Potassium*, No. 37, The British Sulphur Corp., London, September–October, pp. 13–20.

Anon., 1968b, "Methods for Prediction, Search and Prospecting of Agrochemical Raw Materials in the USSR," *Proceedings on Sources of Mineral Raw Materials for the Fertilizer Industry in Asia and the Far East,* United Nations Mineral Resources Development Series, No. 32, pp. 119–124.

Anon., 1968c, "Phosphate Rock Calcination in Israel," *Phosphorus & Potassium*, No. 35, The British Sulphur Corp., London, May–June, pp. 12–15, 21.

Anon., 1968d, *Proceedings of the Seminar on Sources of Mineral Raw Materials for the Fertilizer Industry in Asia and the Far East,* United Nations Mineral Resources Development Series, United Nations, No. 32, 392 pp.

Anon., 1969, "Calcined Phosphate Rock," *Phosphorus & Potassium*, No. 41, British Sulphur Corp., London, May–June, pp. 13–17, 19.

Anon., 1971, *Fluorides,* Committee on Biologic Effects of Atmospheric Pollutants, National Academy of Sciences, Washington, 295 pp.

Anon., 1971a, "The Phosphate Fertilizer Industry of the U.S.," *Phosphorus & Potassium*, No. 55, The British Sulphur Corp., London, September–October, pp. 21–28.

Anon., 1972, "Developments in Morocco's Calcined Rock Capacity," *Phosphorus & Potassium*, No. 62, The British Sulphur Corp., London, November–December, pp. 24–26.

Anon., 1975, "Morocco Plans for the Future," *Phosphorus & Potassium*, The British Sulphur Corp., Ltd., London, March-April, pp. 25–36.

Anon., 1978, "Brazil's Phosphate Rock Industry," *Phosphorus & Potassium*, The British Sulphur Corp., Ltd., London, January-February, pp. 21–24.

Anon., 1978a, "Phosphorus Acid Trend in 1977," *Phosphorus & Potassium*, The British Sulphur Corp., Ltd., London, July-August, pp. 17-21.

Anon., 1978b, "Does Banning Detergent Phosphate Make Any Significant Difference?" *Phosphorus & Potassium*, The British Sulphur Corp., Ltd., London, January-February, p. 42.

Anon., 1979, "Soviet Phosphates in the Tenth FYP-I (Five-Year Plan)" *Phosphorus & Potassium*, The British Sulphur Corp., Ltd., London, July-August, pp. 16–20.

Anon., 1979a, "Soviet Phosphates in the Tenth FYP-II (Five-Year Plan)" *Phosphorus & Potassium*, The British Sulphur Corp., Ltd., London, September-October, pp. 21–23, 43.

Anon., 1979b, "Uraniferous Phosphate Resources and Technology and Economics of Uranium Recovery from Phosphate Resources, United States and Free World," Open File Report GJBX–110 (79), Earth Sciences, Inc., US Dept. of Energy, Grand Junction, CO.

Anon., 1980, "OCP Unveils Its Plans for the Future, Part I," *Phosphorus & Potassium,* The British Sulphur Corp., Ltd., London, January-February, pp. 20–26.

Anon., 1980a, "OCP Unveils Its Plans for the 1980s, Part II," *Phosphorus & Potassium,* The British Sulphur Corp., Ltd., London, March-April, pp. 34–39.

Anon., 1980b, "Negev Phosphates Comes of Age," *Phosphorus & Potassium,* The British Sulphur Corp., Ltd., May-June, pp. 27–32.

Anon., 1980c, "Uranium Extraction from H_3PO_4— A Review," *Phosphorus & Potassium,* The British Sulphur Corp., Ltd., London, July-August, pp. 20–23.

Altschuler, Z.S., 1973, "The Weathering of Phosphate Deposits, Geochemical and Environmental Aspects," *Environmental Phosphorus Handbook,* John Wiley—Interscience, New York, pp. 33–96.

Aparo, S.J., 1969, "Current Flotation Practices in the Beneficiation of Florida Phosphate," Preprint 69-H-319, Society of Mining Engineers of AIME, New York, 13 pp.

Barber, J.C., and Marks, E.C., 1962, "Phosphorus Furnace Operations," *Journal of Metals,* December, pp. 1–5.

Barr, J.A., 1960, "Phosphate Rock," *Industrial Minerals and Rocks,* 3rd ed., J.L. Gillson, ed., AIME, New York, pp. 649–668.

Barrie, J., 1967, "The Geology of Christmas Island," Australia Department of National Development, Bureau of Mineral Resources, Geology and Geophysics, Canberra, 46 pp.

Beall, J.V., and Merritt, P.C., 1966, "Phosphate and Potash," *Mining Engineering,* Vol. 18, No. 10, October, pp. 83–89.

Breathitt, H.W., and Finch, E.P., 1977, "Phosphate Rock Beneficiation," Preprint 77-H-134, SME-AIME Annual Meeting, Atlanta, 31 pp.

Burt, R.B., and Barber, J.C., 1952, *Production of Elemental Phosphorus by the Electric-Furnace Method,* Chemical Engineering Report No. 3, Tennessee Valley Authority, Muscle Shoals, AL, (republished 1967), 312 pp.

Clitheroe, J.B., and Mele, S., 1967, "Beneficiation Techniques for Western Phosphate Rock," *Anatomy of the Western Phosphate Field,* L.A. Hale, ed., Intermountain Association of Geologists, Salt Lake City, Utah, pp. 225–235.

Cook, P.J., 1972, "Petrology and Geochemistry of the Phosphate Deposits of Northwest Queensland, Australia," *Economic Geology,* Vol. 67, No. 8, pp. 1193–1213.

Cooksley, J.W., Jr., 1967, "Application of Geophysical Methods in Phosphate Exploration Southeastern Idaho," *Anatomy of the Western Phosphate Field,* L.A. Hale, ed., Intermountain Association of Geologists, Salt Lake City, Utah, pp. 161–166.

Deans, T., 1968, "Exploration for Apatite Deposits Associated with Carbonatites and Pyroxenites," *Proceedings of the Seminar on Sources of Mineral Raw Materials for the Fertilizer Industry in Asia and the Far East,* United Nations Mineral Resources Development Series, No. 32, pp. 109–119.

Douglas, J.R., 1979, "World Phosphate Supply Plagued with Questions," prepared for presentation at the 7th Phosphate-Sulphur Symposium, Innisbrook, FL, January 18–19, TVA National Fertilizer Development Center, Muscle Shoals, AL, 10 pp.

Emigh, G.D., 1967, "Petrology and Origin of Phosphorites," *Anatomy of the Western Phosphate Field,* L.A. Hale, ed., Intermountain Association of Geologists, Salt Lake City, Utah, pp. 103–114.

Emigh, G.D., 1972, "World Phosphate Reserves— are there really enough," *Engineering and Mining Journal,* Vol. 173, No. 4, April, pp. 90–95.

Emigh, G.D., 1973, "Economic Phosphate Deposits," *Environmental Phosphorus Handbook,* John Wiley—Interscience, New York, pp. 97–116.

Emigh, G.D., 1975, "Phosphate Rock," *Industrial Minerals and Rocks,* 4th ed., S.J. Lefond, ed., AIME, New York, pp. 935–962.

Everhart, D.L., 1971, "Evaluation of Phosphate Rock Deposits," Preprint No. 71-H-52, Society of Mining Engineers of AIME, New York, 7 pp.

Hale, L.A., 1967 "Phosphate Exploration Using Gamma-Radiation Logs, Dry Valley, Idaho," *Anatomy of the Western Phosphate Field,* L.A. Hale, ed., Intermountain Association of Geologists, Salt Lake City, Utah, pp. 147–159.

Harben, P., 1980, "Where Is Florida's Phosphate Industry Going?" *Industrial Minerals,* No. 148, London, January, pp. 48–55.

Harre, E.A., et al., 1972, *Estimated World Fertilizer as Related to Future Demand,* Tennessee Valley Authority, Muscle Shoals, AL, August, 25 pp.

Harris, G.E., and Harre, E.A., 1979, "World Fertilizer Situation and Outlook," International Fertilizer Development Center and National Fertilizer Development Center, TVA, Muscle Shoals, AL, March, 27 pp.

Heinrich, E.W., 1966, *The Geology of Carbonatites,* Rand McNally & Co., Chicago, 607 pp.

Hignett, T.P., and Striplin, M.M., Jr., 1967, "Elemental Phosphorus in Fertilizer Manufacture," *Chemical Engineering Progress,* Vol. 63, No. 5, May, pp. 85–92.

Hill, W.L., 1960, "Phosphate Rock: Reactivity Scales for Ground Rock," *Chemistry and Technology of Fertilizers,* V. Sauchelli, ed., Reinhold Publishing Corp., New York, pp. 116–138.

Howard, P.F., 1971, "The Discovery of Phosphorites in Australia—A Case History," Preprint 71-H-97, SME-AIME Annual Meeting, 11 pp.

Howard, P.F., 1972, "Exploration for Phosphorite in Australia—A Case History," *Economic Geology,* Vol. 67, No. 8, pp. 1180–1192.

Hutchinson, G.E., 1950, "Survey of Contemporary Knowledge of Biogeochemistry: 3. The Biogeochemistry of Vertebrate Excretion," *Bulletin,* American Museum of Natural History, Vol. 96, 554 pp.

Jayawardena, D., 1979, "The Occurrence of Rock Phosphate Deposits in Sri Lanka in Relation to the Precambrian Basement," Paper presented at I.G.C.P. Project 156, East-West Center, Hawaii, August 9.

Lawver, J.E., et al., 1978, "New Techniques in Beneficiation of Phosphate Rock," Preprint 78–B–331, SME-AIME Fall Meeting, Orlando, FL, 36 pp.

Mayberry, R.C., 1981, "Phosphate Reserves, Supply and Demand—Southeastern Atlantic Coastal States, 1980–2000 A.D.," Preprint 81–409, SME-AIME Fall Meeting, Denver, Nov., 39 pp.

McKelvey, V.E., 1973, "Abundance and Distribution of Phosphorus in the Lithosphere," *Environmental Phosphorus Handbook,* John Wiley —Interscience, New York, pp. 13–31.

Merriman, G.M., and Hobbs, C.S., 1962, "Bovine Fluorosis from Soil and Water Sources," *Tennessee Agricultural Experiment Station Bull. 347,* University of Tennessee, Knoxville, 46 pp.

Notholt, A.J.G., 1968, "Phosphate Exploration Techniques," *Proceedings of the Seminar on Sources of Mineral Raw Materials for the Fertilizer Industry in Asia and the Far East,* United Nations Mineral Resources Development Series, No. 32, pp. 214–228.

Pacl et al., 1978, "The Reactivity of Natural Phosphates," *Phosphorus & Potassium,* The British Sulphur Corp., Ltd., London, November–December, pp. 20–25.

Pfleider, E.P., ed., 1968, *Surface Mining,* AIME, New York, 1061 pp.

Robinson, N., 1972, "The Assessment of Phosphate Rocks for Phosphoric Acid Ammonium Phosphate Manufacture," *Phosphorus & Potassium,* No. 57, The British Sulphur Corp., London, January–February, pp. 31–36.

Sandvik, P.O., 1979, "US Phosphates—Abundant Resources Will Last for Hundreds of Years," *Engineering & Mining Journal,* October, pp. 99–101.

Sheldon, R.P., et al., 1967, "Sedimentation of Rocks of Leonard (Permian) Age in Wyoming and Adjacent States," *Anatomy of the Western Phosphate Field,* L.A. Hale, ed., Intermountain Association of Geologists, Salt Lake City, Utah, pp. 1–13.

Silvia, A.F., and Andery, P.A., 1972, "Mining and Beneficiation of Apatite Rock at the Jacupiranga Mine, Brazil," *Phosphorus & Potassium,* No. 57, The British Sulphur Corp., London, January–February, pp. 37–40.

Sweeney, J.W., and Timmons, B.J., 1972, "Availability and Potential Utilization of Byproduct Gypsum in Florida Phosphate Operations," Eighth Forum on Geology of Industrial Minerals, Iowa City, Iowa, April 13, pp. 89–97.

Stowasser, W.F., 1980, "Phosphate Rock," Preprint, *Mineral Facts and Problems, 1980,* Bulletin 671, US Bureau of Mines, 20 pp.

Stowasser, W.F., 1980a, "Phosphate Rock," Preprint, *Minerals Yearbook, 1978–1979,* US Bureau of Mines, 21 pp.

Stowasser, W.F., 1982, "Phosphate Rock," *Mineral Commodity Summaries 1982,* US Bureau of Mines, pp. 112–113.

Tuttle, O.F., and Gittins, J., eds., 1966, *Carbonatites,* John Wiley—Interscience, New York, 610 pp.

Waggaman, W.H., 1952, *Phosphoric Acid, Phosphates and Phosphoric Acid,* 2nd Ed., Reinhold Publishing Corp., New York, 683 pp.

Warin, O.N., 1968, "Deposits of Phosphate Rocks in Oceania," *Proceedings of the Seminar on Sources of Mineral Raw Materials for the Fertilizer Industry in Asia and the Far East,* United Nations Mineral Resources Development Series, No. 32, pp. 124–132.

Woodrooffe, H.M., 1972, "Phosphate in the Kola Peninsula, USSR," *Mining Engineering,* Vol. 24, No. 12, December, pp. 54–56.

Wright, T.J., 1971, "Texas Gulf Sulphur Beneficiation of North Carolina Phosphate," Preprint No. 71-H-116, Society of Mining Engineers of AIME, New York.

Zellar-Williams, Inc., 1978, "Evaluation of the Phosphate Deposits of Florida Using the Minerals Availability System," Open File Report 112–78, US Bureau of Mines, 199 pp. Available from NTIS PB 286 648/AS.

Potash

SAMUEL S. ADAMS *†
Revised by ROBERT J. HITE ‡

Potash, the generic term for a variety of potassium-bearing minerals, ores, and refined products (Table 1), owes its importance as an industrial mineral to the potassium requirement of growing plants. The term *potash* originally referred to potassium carbonate produced by the leaching of wood ashes. This process, for which the first US patent was issued in 1790, was the basis for the largest United States chemical industry in the early nineteenth century. The agricultural use of potash soon eclipsed the chemical applications following the German discovery in 1840 that potassium is essential to plant growth. The initial discoveries of large deposits of soluble potassium minerals, essential for agriculture applications, were made in 1857 in Germany and in 1914 in the United States. More than 90% of the 27.5 Mt K_2O produced in the world in 1980 (Searls, 1981) was derived from marine evaporite deposits and approximately 90% was used in fertilizers. The potassium content of an ore, mineral, or product is customarily expressed as % K_2O, a unit of measure which is neither a natural nor synthetic compound of potassium (1.0% K is equivalent to 1.2046% K_2O).

Geology

Potassium, the seventh most abundant element in the earth's crust, is present in silicate minerals in igneous, sedimentary and metamorphic rocks. Potassium is also a major constituent of many surface and subsurface brines (Table 2). Economic potash deposits are es-

sentially restricted, however, to widespread, thick accumulations of marine chloride evaporite deposits. These deposits yield high grade, large tonnage ore bodies, many of which are amenable to low cost mining and beneficiation. The products from these deposits are, moreover, ideal for use in fertilizer because of the high relative solubility of the potassium chloride and sulfate evaporite minerals. World potash production and reserves for such deposits so vastly overshadow other sources of potassium that the following discussion will be limited largely to potash deposits in marine evaporites with brief reference to certain potash-rich brines. Approximately 85% of current domestic production is from bedded salt deposits and much of the balance is from brines.

Marine evaporite deposits are accumulations of salt minerals deposited in structural sedimentary basins through the evaporation of seawater or mixtures of seawater and other brines. The salt minerals are precipitated in assemblages and sequences of assemblages as determined by the compositions of the brines and the solubility relations in the salt systems (D'Ans, 1933). The evaporation of seawater normally yields carbonate minerals as the first precipitates (Table 3). Further evaporation and concentration of the brine leads to the precipitation, in succession, of sulfate, chloride, and supersaline mineral assemblages including the salts of potassium and magnesium. The common minerals, ores, and products of potassium deposits are listed in Table 1. Many potash deposits contain accessory evaporite minerals together with a variety of detrital and authigenic silicates (Braitsch, 1971).

The structural basins within which marine evaporites occur are of two main types: (a) cratonic basins formed by broad epirogenic movements (for example, the Michigan Basin of the midwestern United States and the Permian Zechstein Basin of eastern Europe), and (b) grabens, commonly related to continental

* Retired, formerly Chief Geologist-Uranium and Aluminum, The Anaconda Co., Salt Lake City, Utah.

† The author gratefully acknowledges the assistance of T. L. Britt, D. L. Everhart, H. A. Gorrell, R. J. Hite, K. O. Linn, E. C. Pendery, G. P. Salas, and A. T. Wells in preparing this manuscript. The staff of International Minerals and Chemical Corp. provided considerable data. The Anaconda Co. kindly granted the author permission to prepare the manuscript.

‡ US Geological Survey, Denver, CO.

TABLE 1—Some Minerals, Ores, and Products of Potash Deposits*

Name	Formula	K_2O, Equivalent Wt %	Remarks
Marine Evaporite Deposits			
MINERALS			
Chlorides			
Sylvite	KCl	63.17	Principal ore mineral
Carnallite	$KCl \cdot MgCl_2 \cdot 6H_2O$	16.95	Ore mineral and contaminant
Kainite	$4KCl \cdot 4MgSO_4 \cdot 11H_2O$	19.26	Important ore mineral
Bischofite	$2MgCl_2 \cdot 12H_2O$	0	Accessory contaminant
Halite	NaCl	0	Principal ore contaminant
Sulfates			
Polyhalite	$K_2SO_4 \cdot MgSO_4 \cdot 2CaSO_4 \cdot 2H_2O$	15.62	Ore contaminant
Langbeinite	$K_2SO_4 \cdot 2MgSO_4$	22.69	Important ore mineral
Leonite	$K_2SO_4 \cdot MgSO_4 \cdot 4H_2O$	25.68	Ore contaminant
Schoenite (Picromerite)	$K_2SO_4 \cdot MgSO_4 \cdot 6H_2O$	23.39	Accessory
Glaserite (Aphthitalite)	$3K_2SO_4 \cdot Na_2SO_4$	42.51	Accessory
Syngenite	$K_2SO_4 \cdot CaSO_4 \cdot H_2O$	28.68	Accessory
Bloedite	$Na_2SO_4 \cdot MgSO_4 \cdot 4H_2O$	0	Accessory
Loeweite	$6Na_2SO_4 \cdot 7MgSO_4 \cdot 15H_2O$	0	Accessory
Vanthoffite	$3Na_2SO_4 \cdot MgSO_4$	0	Accessory
Kieserite	$MgSO_4 \cdot H_2O$	0	Common ore contaminant
Hexahydrite	$MgSO_4 \cdot 6H_2O$	0	Accessory
Epsomite	$MgSO_4 \cdot 7H_2O$	0	Accessory
Anhydrite	$CaSO_4$	0	Common ore contaminant
ORES			
Sylvinite[†]	KCl + NaCl	10-35	Canada, USA, USSR, Brazil, Congo, Thailand
Hartsalz	$KCl + NaCl + CaSO_4 + (MgSO_4 \cdot H_2O)$	10-20	Germany
Carnallitite[‡]	$KCl \cdot MgCl_2 \cdot 6H_2O + NaCl$	10-16	Germany, Spain, Thailand
Langbeinite[§]	$K_2SO_4 \cdot 2MgSO_4 + NaCl$	7-12	USA, USSR
Mischsalz	Hartsalz + Carnallite	8-20	Germany
Kainite	$4KCl \cdot 4MgSO_4 \cdot 11H_2O + NaCl$	13-18	Italy, Ethiopia
PRODUCTS			
Potassium chloride	KCl	63.17	Principal potassium product
Potassium sulfate	K_2SO_4	54.05	Artificial product
Potassium-magnesium-sulfate (langbeinite)	$K_2SO_4 \cdot 2MgSO_4$	22.69	Natural product (New Mexico)
Manure salts	KCl + NaCl	40-60	USSR and East Germany
Other Sources			
Alunite	$K_2Al_6(SO_4)_4(OH)_{12}$	11.4	
Niter (caliche)	$KNO_3 + NaNO_3 + Na_2SO_4 + NaCl$	0.6-1.9	Chile
Potassium nitrate	$KNO_3 + NaNO_3$	10-14	

* Source: Modified after Adams, 1968.
† May contain one or more sulfate minerals or carnallite.
‡ May contain sylvite.
§ May contain sylvite and leonite, kainite or other sulfate minerals.

TABLE 2—Potassium Content of Selected Rocks and Waters

	K_2O, Equivalent Wt %
Rocks*	
Average for earth's crust	3.01-3.13
Continental crust	2.10-3.00
Average for igneous rocks	3.12-3.13
Basalts	1.00
Granites	3.02-5.07
Average for sediments	1.90
Clays and shales	2.74-3.20
Sandstones	1.29
Carbonate rocks	0.35
Marine evaporites[†]	0.0029-63.17
Waters	
Oceans[†]	0.0458
Rivers (world average)[‡]	0.0003
Searles Lake, CA[§]	1.86-3.17
Great Salt Lake, UT[#]	0.506-0.846
Salton Sea, CA[‡]	0.0135
Mono Lake, CA[‡]	0.135
Dead Sea, Israel[‡]	0.45-0.758
Sechura Desert, Peru[¶]	0.35-0.65
Lake Eyre, Australia[**]	0.18
Lake McLeod, Australia[¶]	0.41
Lake bed, Wendover, UT[††]	0.63
Subsurface thermal waters[‡‡]	0.0012-0.2310
Salton Sea geothermal water, CA[§§]	3.0
Subsurface brines associated with salt deposits[‡‡]	0.25-3.12
Subsurface oil field brines[‡‡]	0.0005-0.475
Subsurface brine, Dariala, West Pakistan[¶¶]	4.100

   * Source: Parker, 1967, except as noted
   [†] Source: Stewart, 1963
   [‡] Source: Livingstone, 1963
   [§] Source: Ryan, 1951
   [#] Source: Hahl and Handy, 1969
   [¶] Source: W. A. Seedorff, personal communication, 1972
   [**] Source: Johns and Ludbrook, 1963
   [††] Source: M. W. Lallman, personal communication, 1973
   [‡‡] Source: White et al., 1963
   [§§] Source: White, 1965
   [¶¶] Source: Anon., 1966

margin rift systems (for example, the deposits of the Danakil Depression, Ethiopia, and Sergipe, Brazil). Significant concentrations of potassium minerals are commonly restricted to certain parts of those halite deposits of greatest thickness and areal extent. The potash deposits of the cratonic basins are generally of Paleozoic age and are characterized by assemblages containing sylvite and potassium sulfate-bearing phases, commonly of a diagenetic or metasomatic origin. The deposits of the continental margin rift systems are related to the early stages of crustal rifting and are of Triassic or younger age. These deposits commonly have experienced less post-depositional metasomatism, hence primary carnallite-bearing assemblages are more commonly preserved.

Marine evaporite deposits of one age or another are present on all continents with the possible exception of Antarctica (Table 4). Evaporite deposits of various ages are, however, unevenly distributed between continents and within the individual continents. Proterozoic and Paleozoic deposits of the cratonic basins (Fig. 1), for example, are widely distributed within the continental masses with the notable exception of Africa. It may be inferred that Africa did not experience this type of Paleozoic tectonism and sedimentation. Mesozoic, Cenozoic and Recent marine evaporites (Fig. 2), on the other hand, occur at the edges of continents or in linear zones such as that extending from England and Spain through Turkey to Thailand. These distributions apparently reflect a different tectonic pattern related, in part at least, to rifts associated with crustal separations.

Marine evaporite deposits are composed of sequences of tabular beds which are characterized by the proportions of the minerals they contain as well as by color, texture, and grain size. Mappable beds may be a few inches to several feet in thickness and may be present over hundreds of square miles. These strati-

TABLE 3—Natural Evaporite Salt Sequences Compared with Sequences for the Theoretical, Static Evaporation of Seawater*

Rock Type (in order of precipitation)	Approximate Thickness Normalized to 100 M of Halite			
	Zechstein Evaporites, Germany	Average of Other Evaporites	Theoretical From Seawater	Equivalent Layer in Table 5
Carbonate	4	10	0.5	—
Sulfate	20	40	5	—
Halite	100	100	100	100 (A)
Na-Mg sulfates	1	0.3	7	10.8 (B)
Potash salts	3	2	15	17.3 (C, D)

* Source: Adapted from Borchert and Muir (1964) and Braitsch, (1971).

TABLE 4—World Occurrences of Halite-Bearing, Marine Evaporite Deposits.*

Country	Geological Age	Geographical Region	Geological Designation	Potash Occurrences	Remarks
NORTH AMERICA					
Canada	Cambrian (?)	Great Bear Lake, N.T.	MacDougal Fm.	None reported	3000-5000 ft deep
	Ordovician (?)	Great Slave Lake, N.T.		None reported	1000-3000 ft deep
	Cambrian ?-Ordovician?	Arctic Islands	Cornwallis	None reported	Salt structures
	Devonian	Saskatchewan, Manitoba, Alberta	Elk Point group	Sylvite, carnallite	10 potash mines
	Mississippian	Maritime Provinces	Windsor group	Sylvite, carnallite	Salt deformed, new mine development
Cuba	Jurassic-Triassic (?)	Cunagua	Punta Alegre Fm.	None reported	Salt domes
Dominican Republic	Miocene (?)	Las Salinas		None reported	
Mexico	Permian (?)	Chihuahua	Cuchillo Parado	None reported	Possible Salado equivalent
	Jurassic	Monterrey	Minas Viejas group	None reported	
	Jurassic	Isthmus of Tehuantepec	Salina Fm., Isthmian salt	Carnallite, sylvite	
	Jurassic-Cretaceous	Tehuantepec-Guatemala	Chiapas salt	None reported	Chiapas Basin
United States	Silurian	Michigan, New York, Pennsylvania, Ohio, W. Virginia, (Ontario, Canada)	Salina Fm.	Sylvite, carnallite polyhalite	Potash beds below 8300 ft in Michigan Basin
	Devonian	Michigan	Detroit River	None reported	Michigan Basin
	Devonian	North Dakota, Montana	Prairie evaporite	Sylvite, carnallite	Williston Basin
	Mississippian	Michigan	Michigan	None reported	
	Mississippian	Virginia	McCrady Fm.	None reported	Salt deformed
	Mississippian	North Dakota, Montana	Charles Fm., Mission Canyon Fm.	None reported	Williston Basin
	Pennsylvanian	SE Utah, SW Colorado	Hermosa Fm.	Sylvite, carnallite	Salt deformed, 1 mine Paradox Basin
	Pennsylvanian	Colorado	Eagle Evaporite	Sylvite, langbeinite	
	Permian	SE New Mexico, West Texas	Castile, Salado, and Rustler Fms.	Sylvite, carnallite langbeinite, polyhalite	7 potash mines
	Permian	Western Oklahoma	Blaine Fm., Clear Fork group, Flower Pot shale	None reported	
	Permian	Western Kansas	Wellington Fm., Salt Plain Fm. (?)	Polyhalite	
	Permian	Nebraska, Wyoming	Goose Egg Fm.	None reported	
	Permian	North Dakota, Montana	Opechi Fm.	None reported	Williston Basin
	Permian	Arizona	Supai Fm.	Sylvite	
	Permian-Jurassic (?)	North Dakota, Montana	Pine salt	None reported	
	Jurassic	North Dakota, Montana	Dunham salt	None reported	

TABLE 4—(Continued)

Country	Geological Age	Geographical Region	Geological Designation	Potash Occurrences	Remarks
	Jurassic	Idaho, Utah, Wyoming	Preuss sandstone	None reported	
	Jurassic	Gulf Coast	Louann salt, Werner Fm.	Sylvite	Salt domes
	Jurassic	Texas, Alabama	Buckner	None reported	Salt domes
	Jurassic	Utah	Arapien shale	None reported	
	Cretaceous	Florida	Comanchean, Trinity	None reported	
	Cretaceous	Texas	Fredericksburg	None reported	
SOUTH AMERICA					
Argentina	Cretaceous	Neuquen	Salina Fm.	None reported	
Bolivia	Cretaceous	Chiquisaca	Margas-Multicolors	None reported	
Brazil	Pennsylvanian	Amazon Basin	Novo Olinda	Sylvite	
	Cretaceous	Sergipe	Muribeca	Carnallite, sylvite, new mine development	
Chile	Cretaceous	Salinas de Purilactis	Purilactis	None reported	
Colombia	Cretaceous	Cordillera Oriental	Caqueza, Villeta groups	None reported	
Peru	Permian	Eastern Cordillera	Mintu group	None reported	
	Triassic	Eastern Cordillera	Pucara	None reported	
	Jurassic	Utcumbamba	Saraxaquillo	None reported	
	Miocene-Pliocene	Cerros de la Sol	San Pedro	None reported	
EUROPE					
Austria	Permian(?)-Triassic(?)	Nordliche Kalkalpen		None reported	
Bulgaria	Permian(?)-Triassic(?)	Provadiar		None reported	
Cyprus	Miocene(?)	Xeri		None reported	
England, Ireland	Triassic	Cheshire, Carrickfergus Yorkshire, Cleveland	Keuper	None reported	
	Permian		Zechstein	Sylvite	1 mine
East Germany, West Germany, Netherlands, Denmark, Poland, England	Permian	Western Europe	Zechstein Fm.	Sylvite, carnallite, kainite, polyhalite	Mines in East and West Germany
East Germany, West Germany	Triassic		Bundsandstein, Rot Salz	Polyhalite	
France	Triassic	Lorraine, Franche-Compte	Keuper-Muschelkalk	None reported	
	Triassic	Dax	Keuper	Sylvite	Salt domes
Italy	Miocene	Sicily	Tortorian	Kainite, carnallite sylvite	Mines

TABLE 4—(Continued)

Country	Geological Age	Geographical Region	Geological Designation	Potash Occurrences	Remarks
	Miocene	Lungro		None reported	
	Miocene	Volteranno		None reported	
Netherlands	Triassic	Hengalo	Rot Salz	None reported	
Portugal	Triassic	Coastal Provinces		None reported	
	Miocene		Tortorian	None reported	Several salt basins
Rumania, West Ukraine, Poland, Czechoslovakia		Bachnia-Wieliczka		Sylvite, langbeinite	
		Presov-Trebisov		None reported	
				None reported	
Russia	Cambrian	Angara-Lena	Ussolskaja Series	Sylvite	
	Devonian	Byelorussia, Latvia	Fammenian	Sylvite, carnallite	Several basins; salt domes
	Permian	Embya, Manych, Dneiper, Donetz	Kungurian	None reported	
	Permian	Urals, Upper Kama, Kugitang, Gaurdak	Kungurian (?)	Sylvite, carnallite	Several mines
	Jurassic	Nakhichevan		None reported	
	Oligocene-Miocene	West Ukraine		Sylvite, kainite, langbeinite	
	Miocene	Yakutsk, Krasnoyarsk		Sylvite, kainite langbeinite	
Spain	Triassic-Jurassic	Eastern Province	Keuper	None reported	
	Eocene-Oligocene	Catalonia and Navarra	Ludian	Sylvite, carnallite	Several potash mines
Switzerland	Triassic	Zurgach-Bex	Muschelkalk	None reported	
West Germany	Permian	Hamburg	Rotliegendes	None reported	
	Triassic	Southern Area	Keuper	None reported	
	Triassic		Werfener	Polyhalite, sylvite, langbeinite, kainite	
	Triassic	Southern Area	Muschelkalk	None reported	
West Germany, France	Triassic / Jurassic		Munder	None reported	
	Oligocene	Buggingen, Alsace		Sylvite, carnallite	Several potash mines
Yugoslavia	Eocene-Miocene(?)	Tuzla		None reported	
AFRICA					
Algeria,	Triassic	Constantine-Laghourt, Jeffara Plains	Bu Sceba	None reported	Salt domes

TABLE 4—(Continued)

Country	Geological Age	Geographical Region	Geological Designation	Potash Occurrences	Remarks
Algeria	Miocene	Ouled Kebbeb		None reported	
Cabinda				None reported	
Egypt	Miocene	Gulf of Suez	South Gharib Fm.	Polyhalite	
Ethiopia	Quaternary	Danakil Depression	Houston Fm.	Sylvite, kainite, carnallite	
Gabon, Congo, Angola	Cretaceous(?)	Atlantic Coast		Carnallite and sylvite	Abandoned mine
				None reported	
Libya	Tertiary	Edri, Pisida, Marada		Carnallite and brine	Shallow marsh deposits
Morocco	Triassic	Mogador	(?)	None reported	Salt domes
Morocco	Triassic	(?)	(?)	Carnallite, sylvite	Salt domes
Tanzania	Pre-Jurassic	Mandawa	(?)	None reported	
Tunisia	Triassic	Djebel Hadifa	(?)	None reported	
ASIA					
Afghanistan		Northern Provinces		None reported	Salt domes
China				No information	No information
India		Mandi District	Krol Series or Subathu group	None reported	
Iran, Saudi Arabia	Cambrian(?)	Persian Gulf	Hormuz	None reported	Salt domes
Iran, Saudi Arabia, Kuwait	Jurassic	Persian Gulf	Riyadh group	None reported	Salt domes
Iran	Oligocene	Tehran	Lower Red Fm.	None reported	Salt domes
Iran	Miocene	Tehran	Asmari	None reported	Salt domes
Iran, Iraq	Miocene	Persian Gulf	Fars Fm.	None reported	
Israel, Jordan	Tertiary-Pleistocene	Dead Sea Graben	Dead Sea group	None reported	
Saudi Arabia	Miocene	Red Sea Coast		None reported	Salt structures
Syria	Miocene	Eastern Syria	Fars Fm.	None reported	
Thailand, Laos	Cretaceous	Khorat Plateau	Maha Sarakham Fm.	Sylvite and carnallite	

TABLE 4—(Continued)

Country	Geological Age	Geographical Region	Geological Designation	Potash Occurrences	Remarks
Turkey	Oligocene-Miocene	Anatolia		None reported	
West Pakistan	Eocene (Cambrian ?)	Punjab Ranges		Sylvite, kainite carnallite, langbeinite	
	Tertiary(?)	Kohat		None reported	
Yemen	Miocene	Red Sea Coast		None reported	Salt structures
OCEANIA					
Australia	Precambrian	Amadeus Basin	Bitter Springs Fm.	None reported	
	Precambrian-Lower Paleozoic(?)	Officer Basin	Browne Beds(?)	None reported	Salt domes
	Cambrian	Amadeus Basin	Chandler Limestone	None reported	
	Ordovician(?)-Devonian(?)	Bonaparte Gulf	Not known	None reported	Salt dome offshore
	Ordovician(?)-Devonian(?)	Canning Basin	Carribuddy Fm.	None reported	
	Silurian	Carnarvon Basin	Dirk Hartog Fm.	None reported	
	Devonian	Adavale Basin	Etonvale Fm.	Minor occurrences	

* (Compiled from references in bibliography, in particular; Benavides, 1968; Lefond, 1969; Liechti, 1968; Pierce and Rich, 1962; Rios, 1968; Stocklin, 1968; Tortochaux, 1968; A. T. Wells, personal communication, 1972; H. A. Gorrell, personal communication, 1972; R. J. Hite, personal communication, 1973.

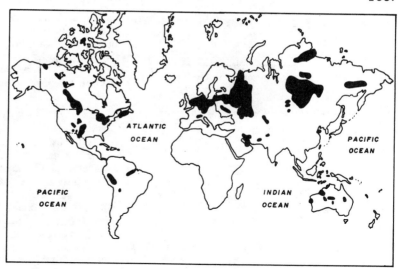

FIG. 1—*Approximate distribution of Proterozoic and Paleozoic halite-bearing marine evaporite deposits (adapted from Lefond, 1969; Pendery, 1970; Kozary et al., 1968; and Lotze, 1957).*

graphic features reflect relatively rapid precipitation in comparatively stable structural settings.

Theoretical and experimental salt assemblages bear sufficient resemblance to natural assemblages that they are useful in the study of marine potash deposits. Study of the origin of these deposits is aided by a knowledge of the original composition of the ore forming fluid (seawater) and the duplication of most salt assemblages in the laboratory. As an example, Table 5 lists the sequence of chloride-bearing salt assemblages which precipitate from seawater under conditions of static evaporation at 25°C. Fig. 3 traces the changes in brine composition which accompany the precipita-

tion of the assemblages in Table 5. Similar data for a variety of temperatures and initial brine compositions may be prepared from the data of D'Ans (1933). The proper interpretations of field relations in the context of these chemical data improve the evaluation of known potash deposits and the exploration for new ones. However, most salt deposits were not formed from the isothermal, static evaporation of seawater and are, therefore, more complex than the sequence in Table 5. Whereas precipitation generally results from evaporation at the brine-air interface, it may also occur with temperature changes, the mixing of brines of different compositions, and the reaction of brines with previously precipitated salt. Repeated brine in-

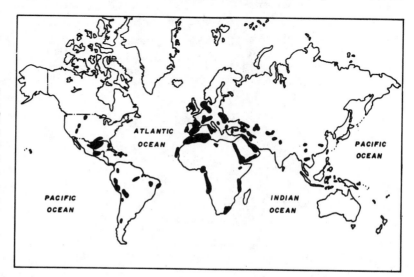

FIG. 2—*Approximate distribution of Mesozoic, Cenozoic, and Recent halite-bearing marine evaporite deposits (adapted from Lefond, 1969; Pendery, 1970; Kozary et al., 1968; and Lotze, 1957).*

TABLE 5—Theoretical Primary Precipitation of Stable
Chloride Assemblages from Normal Seawater + Static
Evaporation at 25°C (without
Reaction at Transition Points)*

| Layer | Mineral Assemblages | | | Thickness of Layer, M |
	Mineral	%	
A	Halite	100	100.0
B₁	Halite	72	6.3
	Bloedite	28	
B₂	Halite	20	4.5
	Epsomite	80	
C₁	Halite	29	6.3
	Epsomite	30	
	Kainite	41	
C₂	Halite	21	5.7
	Hexahydrite	3	
	Kainite	76	
C₃	Halite	11	1.7
	Kieserite	4	
	Kainite	85	
D₁	Halite	12	3.6
	Kieserite	40	
	Carnallite	48	
E	Halite	0.5	38.0
	Kieserite	1	
	Carnallite	0.5	
	Bischofite	98	

* Source: Adapted from Braitsch, 1971.

fluxes of differing composition and incomplete evaporation lead to random and/or cyclic repetition of assemblages. Post-depositional metamorphism and metasomatism may substantially alter the mineral assemblages. The study and exploration of an evaporite deposit should be based, therefore, on (1) the thorough study of its stratigraphy and mineralogy, and then (2) on the interpretation of these features in the context of the chemistry of the salt systems.

Exploration

The search for new evaporite deposits requires the use of subsurface and indirect surficial evidence because the soluble chloride minerals rarely crop out at the surface. Evaporites of cratonic basins are commonly associated with extensive chemical, biochemical, and clastic sediments such as shelf carbonates, fringing reefs, and red beds. Evaporite deposits at the continental margins occur where crustal extensions developed during the Mesozoic and Cenozoic periods. The proximity of buried evaporites may be inferred from saline waters in springs and wells, thick outcrops of gypsum or anhydrite, and domal or collapse structures or geophysical anomalies such as those associated with the piercement salt structures under and around the Gulf of Mexico (Halbouty, 1967). Surface geophysical techniques, particularly gravity and seismic methods (Sawatzky et al., 1960), may be useful in determining the distribution and shape of evaporite bodies.

Initial exploration of an evaporite deposit may require the evaluation of geophysical logs from oil and gas exploration drill holes. Gamma-ray, neutron, sonic, caliper, density,

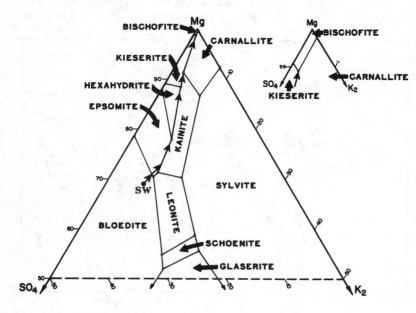

FIG. 3—*Magnesium-rich portion of six component (Na-K-Mg-Cl-SO₄-H₂O) system at 25°C and NaCl saturation (from Braitsch, 1971, Table 6, Fig. 16). Diagram calculated for solution composition where Mg+K₂+SO₄= 100. Transition boundaries for minerals shown in fine lines; crystallization path for static evaporation of seawater (SW) without reaction at transition points shown in heavy lines with arrows.*

and resistance logs are useful in the interpretation of evaporite lithology, stratigraphy, and mineralogy (Alger and Crain, 1968). The gamma-ray log is particularly useful as it detects the gamma radiation from the natural potassium isotope K^{40}, hence it provides a continuous measure of the potassium content of the salt section. Initial exploration core holes are drilled on several mile centers using a sodium chloride saturated brine. If a natural brine is not available, rock salt can be added to the drilling fluid. Where potash salts are present, the brine must be saturated with respect to all the readily soluble minerals with due allowance for possible higher temperatures (hence greater solubilities of all evaporite minerals) in deep holes. If the composition of the brine cannot be rigorously controlled, a petroleum-based drilling fluid is used.

The ratio of sodium to potassium in seawater is 27.7 to 1. Minable potash beds, therefore, are generally accompanied by considerably thicker halite deposits. Furthermore, the potassium mineral assemblages commonly occur in the younger, upper portions of the thick halite deposits because the potash salts are precipitated late in the evaporation sequence.

Multiple potash horizons may occur in the upper one-quarter to one-third of major halite deposits reflecting the cyclic nature of precipitation (Fig. 4).

The principal potash deposits of a district may be associated with areas of greatest halite thickness, peripheral to them or in nearby sub-basins, depending on the tectonic history of the area. Figs. 5 and 6 are simplified maps for the Carlsbad, New Mexico, and Saskatchewan, Canada, potash districts showing the gross salt thickness, the areas of significant potash deposits, and the location of mining operations. Thick halite deposits in some basins do not have associated potash deposits, the potash-rich brines having been lost by reflux before potash precipitation or the precipitated salts having been subsequently dissolved by refreshened brines.

The exploration for potash deposits in known evaporite basins is based on studies of the chemical and physical characteristics of the salt beds. Stratigraphic criteria favorable to the occurrence of economic potash deposits include: (a) halite sequences in excess of 200 to 300 ft in thickness, (b) the presence of potassium in sulfate beds (possibly as polyhalite) or as disseminated grains of potassium chloride or sulfate minerals in halite beds, and (c) the presence of clastic zones of mixed

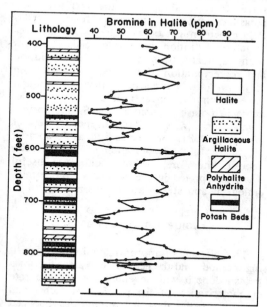

FIG. 4—*Stratigraphy and bromine content of halite in potash-bearing upper Salado Formation, core test IMC 115, Carlsbad potash district, New Mexico. Bromine curve smoothed by averaging successive groups of three analyses (modified after Adams, 1968).*

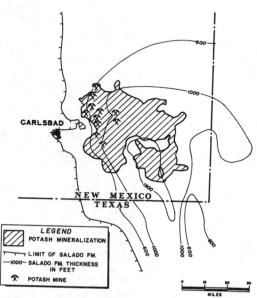

FIG. 5—*Mines, evaporite thickness, and potash deposits exclusive of polyhalite beds, Carlsbad potash district, New Mexico (modified after Pierce and Rich, 1962; and Adams, 1970).*

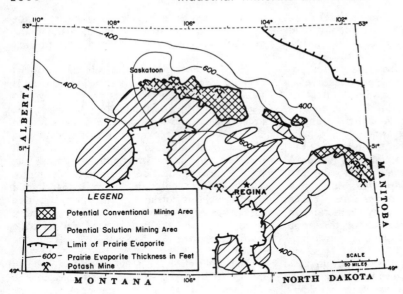

FIG. 6—*Potash deposits, mines, and evaporite thickness, Saskatchewan potash district, Canada (modified after Holter, 1969).*

layer clays, particularly in the upper part of the evaporite section. Bedded or disseminated potassium chloride and sulfate minerals are clearly the product of more concentrated brines. The presence of clays interbedded with, and disseminated within, the salt beds, on the other hand, indicates a closer source for detrital material and a decreasing rate of chemical relative to clastic sedimentation. The clastic source may be closer because the size of the basin has been reduced through evaporation. The rate of chemical sedimentation may have decreased due to the lower vapor pressure of the residual concentrated brines. Both conditions infer higher brine concentration, hence the possibility of potash deposition. In the Prairie Evaporite formation of Saskatchewan, not only do the insolubles increase toward the top of the formation but the concentration of insolubles within the three potash-bearing members increases from the lowest to the highest (Fig. 7). The insolubles of the potash beds in the Yorkton area of Saskatchewan include anhydrite, gypsum, dolomite, quartz, hematite, and micas or illite (Streeton, 1967). In the Salado formation of New Mexico, both insoluble-rich beds and polyhalite beds are more common with the potash deposits in the upper portion of the formation (Fig. 4).

The bromine content of halite may be used to infer the favorability of a salt deposit for potash horizons. The substitution of bromine for chlorine in the halite crystal lattice increases as the concentration of the brine increases, hence

halite in and near potash beds contains more bromine. In deposits formed from the simple evaporation from seawater the absolute bromine content of halite is an indication of the stage of evaporation, hence the likelihood of a potash deposit being present (Holser, 1968). Potash beds might be expected when the bromine concentration in halite exceeds 150 ppm bromine. Halite beds formed by the dissolution and reprecipitation of salt beds or the mixing of marine and nonmarine brines will contain lower bromine concentration. For example, halite in potash deposits in the Salado formation, largely a secondary evaporite deposit (Adams, 1968), contains as little as 70 ppm Br (Fig. 4). In the exploration of an evaporite deposit, therefore, bromine data are useful when interpreted in the context of other mineralogical and stratigraphic information.

Evaluation of Deposits

The selection of appropriate mining and milling methods and the economic exploitation of a potash deposit will depend upon the accurate characterization of the physical and chemical features of the deposit. Similarities between deposits render much of this evaluation routine. The recognition and evaluation of features peculiar to a deposit may, however, determine the success of the mining operation. Some general guidelines are listed in Table 6.

NX or NC cored drill holes are the basis for

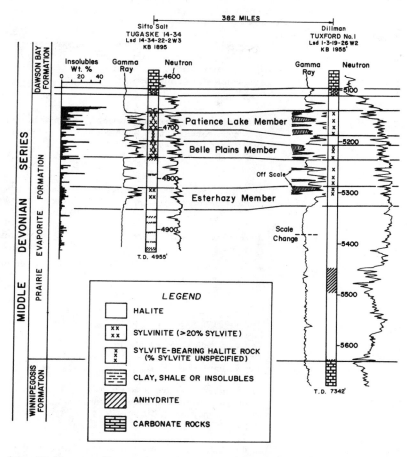

FIG. 7—*A section from the Prairie Evaporite Formation, Saskatchewan. Geophysical logs not necessarily at same scale (modified after Holter, 1969).*

the initial appraisal of a deposit. Due to the coarse grain size of salt assemblages, smaller core is generally unrepresentative. Development drill holes are spaced on ¼ to 1 mile centers, depending on the depth and complexity of the deposit. The salt cores are logged with attention to all mappable stratigraphic, lithologic, and mineralogic features (a logging scale of 1 in. = 10 ft is appropriate for the halite section; 1 in. = 1 ft for potash horizons). The potash horizons should be sampled by individual geological units for chemical analysis and determinative mineralogy without compositing dissimilar mineral assemblages. It is generally sufficient to analyze for K, Na, Ca, Mg, Cl_2, SO_4, and H_2O after drying to constant weight at 90°C. The accuracy of the sampling and analytical procedures may be confirmed if the megascopic mineralogy of the sample, estimated from hand specimen and thin section, can be calculated from the chemical analyses within the accuracy of the estimates and the analytical methods. The geological interpreta-

tion of these data in terms of the factors listed in Table 6 should indicate the potential for a minable deposit or the need for additional drilling or metallurgical tests.

World Potash Resources

The reserves of potash recoverable with existing technology from known deposits are estimated to be approximately 135 billion short tons K_2O. Russia and Canada have, respectively, 40 and 37% of the total. The United States' share is 4%. The resource estimates compiled in Table 7 are based largely on an evaluation of published information. For the most part, the reserves may best be referred to as "probable ore," that is to say, "ore whose occurrence is to all essential purposes reasonably assured but not absolutely certain." There is some question, for example, as to the reliability of the reserves reported for Russia as well as the portion of the Canadian solution mining reserve that will actually be recoverable.

TABLE 6—Guides to the Evaluation of Potash Deposits

Factor to be Considered	Potential Problem	Observation to be Made
Structure of ore horizon	Faulting, folding, or flowage of ore horizon complicating or precluding room-and-pillar mining method	a) Correlation of stratigraphy between drill holes b) Examination of core for evidence of deformation and recrystallization
Stratigraphy	Incorrect correlation of ore horizons; salt thickness above ore insufficient to protect deposit from water; slabbing and ore dilution from clay beds above ore horizon	Detailed core logging and correlation of beds between drill holes
Ore depth	Low mine extraction or excessive development and mining costs.	Mining method and size of mine openings designed on basis of rock mechanics and geology
Ore thickness	Local systematic or random thinning of ore zone	a) Isopach maps of stratigraphic units and mineralization in ore zone b) Inspection of core for evidence of metasomatism and potash leaching, i.e., recrystalized halite, clay in intergranular clots, and horizontal mineral zoning
Ore mineralogy	Assemblages incompatible with proposed mill circuit; certain assemblages reduce stability of mine openings; high insoluble content requires extra desliming capacity.	Determinative mineralogy of core
Ore grade	Grade may be too low or erratic to maintain acceptable mill feed; recoverable K_2O may be significantly less than total K_2O	Correlation and interpretation of drill hole data; comparison of chemical analyses with determinative mineralogy
Ore continuity	Erratic barren or thin areas in ore zone	Correlation of stratigraphic units and mineralization in ore zone; inspect core for evidence of recrystallization and horizontal mineral zoning
Ore crystallinity	Inclusion of contaminants within potash minerals; fine-grained assemblages requiring finer grind	Correlation of microscopic examination of ore samples with chemical analyses of mineral separates
Ore reserves	Insufficient reserves or excessive mining and milling costs	Accurate geological description of deposit for mining and metallurgical studies

A more conservative estimate of world reserves, perhaps more closely approaching "proven ore," yields about 50 billion tons K_2O (Adams, 1968).

The distribution of potash reserves and production by continent and the geological age of the host rock is presented in Table 8. Paleozoic evaporites account for 98% of the potash production plus reserves. This is particularly striking when one notes that the principal Paleozoic deposits occur on the continents of North America and Europe which represent only 23% of the earth's crustal area. Despite their widespread occurrence, Mesozoic and younger evaporites (see Fig. 2) account for only 2% of potash production plus reserves.

North America

Canada has the largest reserves of high grade sylvinite ore in the world. Reserves recoverable by underground mining are now placed at

TABLE 7—Estimated World Potash Resources*

Country	Potash Mineralogy	Grade, % K₂O	Depth, Ft	K₂O Equivalents, Millions St		Remarks
				Subtotal	Breakdown	
NORTH AMERICA						
Canada				55,000		
Saskatchewan and Manitoba	Sylvite and carnallite	14-32	3000 – 8000		5,000	Conventional mining ore
	Sylvite and carnallite	5-25	800 – 4000		50,000	Solution mining ore
Maritime Provinces					Potential	Salt deformed
United States				500		
Arizona	Sylvite	14-16	1800		Potential	Holbrook Basin
California	Brine	3.0	Lake bed		20	Searles Lake
Michigan	Sylvite	4.0	8300		Potential	Michigan Basin
New Mexico	Sylvite and langbeinite	10-22 7-12	600 – 2000		90	Additional potential
North Dakota	Sylvite and carnallite	NA	5500 – 12,500		Potential	Williston Basin
Utah	Sylvite and carnallite	20-25	1000 – 10,000		280	Paradox Basin, Deformed and undeformed
	Brine	0.5	Surface		100	Great Salt Lake
	Brine	0.7	Lake bed		10	Wendover
Mexico	Carnallite and sylvite	NA	200 – 2000		Potential	Tehuantepec and Yucatan
SOUTH AMERICA				58		
Brazil	Carnallite and sylvite	0-25	1500 – 2000		30	Sergipe
Chile	Nitrates	1.0	Surface		15	
Peru	Brine	0.35-0.65	Shallow		13	Sechura Desert
EUROPE (WEST)				12,420		
Denmark	Sylvite and carnallite	10-20	700 – 3000		Potential	
England	Sylvite	15-30	3200 – 4500		340	
France	Sylvite and carnallite	15-25	1400 – 3400		400	Alsace
West Germany	Sylvite Hartsalz Carnallite	15-20 9-15 9-15	1300 – 3500		11,000	
Italy	Kainite Carnallite Sylvite	12-18 11-13 18-29	1000 – 2600		170	Sicily

TABLE 7–(Continued)

Country	Potash Mineralogy	Grade, % K$_2$O	Depth, Ft	K$_2$O Equivalents, Millions St Subtotal	Breakdown	Remarks
Netherlands		15	3200		10	Zechstein salt
Spain	Sylvite	15-25	1000 – 4000		500	Catalonia and Navarra
	Carnallite	14				
EUROPE (EAST)				65,180		
East Germany	Sylvite	13-17	1000 – 3200		10,000	
	Carnallite	12				
Poland	Carnallite	8	600 – 900		180	Zechstein Salt
Russia						
West Ukraine	Hartsalz	16	250 – 2200		55,000	Stebnik-Kalush
	Sylvite	8-30				
	Kainite	10				
	Langbeinite	NA				
Byelorussia	Sylvite	9-30	1000 – 3100			Starobin-Soligorsk
Urals	Sylvite	15-30	200 – 1300			Solikamsk-Brezhniki
Siberia						
Irkutsk	Sylvite	NA	2300 – 3400			
Krasnoyarsk	Sylvite, kainite, langbeinite	NA	4000 – 4600			
AFRICA				134		
Congo	Sylvite	15-20	850 – 1300		44	Holle
	Carnallite	15				
Ethiopia	Sylvite	20-30	80 – 400		50	Danakil Depression
	Kainite	NA				
Libya	Brine and carnallite	1-4	Shallow		10	Marada
Morocco	Sylvite	10-11	1600 – 2600		4	Khemisset Basin
	Carnallite	11-13			26	

TABLE 7—(Continued)

Country	Potash Mineralogy	Grade, % K$_2$O	Depth, Ft	K$_2$O Equivalents, Millions St — Subtotal	K$_2$O Equivalents, Millions St — Breakdown	Remarks
ASIA				2,000		
Israel and Jordan	Brine	0.7	Surface			Dead Sea
Pakistan	Brine	4.2	4000 – 8000		2,000 Potential	Punjab Range
Thailand and Laos	Sylvite, carnallite, and langbeinite	NA	NA		Potential	Khorat Plateau
OCEANIA	Carnallite and sylvite					
Australia	Brine	0.41	Surface		Potential	Lake McLeod, W.A.
				Total 135,292		

* Source: Anon., 1968; Adams, 1968; Koepke, 1971.

TABLE 8—Potassium Production and Reserves for Marine Evaporites by Continent and Geological Age of Host Rock*

	Cumulative Area of Continents — Square Miles, Millions	Cumulative Area of Continents — % of Total	Paleozoic Potash Deposits — Cumulative Production† Millions St K$_2$O	Paleozoic Potash Deposits — Reserves, Millions St K$_2$O	Paleozoic Potash Deposits — % of Production Plus Reserves	Mesozoic and Younger Potash Deposits — Cumulative Production† Millions St K$_2$O$_3$	Mesozoic and Younger Potash Deposits — Reserves, Millions St K$_2$O	Mesozoic and Younger Potash Deposits — % of Production Plus Reserves
North America‡	9.4	16	77	55,370	42			
Europe‡	3.8	7	197	75,530	58	67	2,070	90
Subtotal	13.2	23	274	130,900	100%	67	2,070	93%
South America	6.9	12						
Asia	17.1	30					30	2
Africa	11.7	20					124	5
Oceania	3.3	6						
Antarctica	5.1	9						
Subtotal	44.1	77					154	7
Grand Total	57.3	100%	274	130,900	100%	67	2,224	100%

* Source: Adapted from US Bureau of Mines Mineral Yearbooks, Anon., 1966, and Table 7 of this paper.
† Figures are approximations only and may include some production from sources other than marine evaporites.
‡ Includes portion of Russia west of Ural Mts.

5 billion tons K_2O (Holter, 1969; reserve calculations based on minimum 20% K_2O ore grade, minimum ore thickness 8 ft, 3500 ft maximum depth, minimum 20 ft of salt above ore, 40% mine extraction, and 90% mill recovery). In-place solution mining reserves are estimated to be 65 billion tons K_2O, 50 billion tons of which may be recoverable (Holter, 1969; calculation of in-place reserves based on minimum depth of 3500 ft, minimum of 20 ft of salt above ore, and minimum ore thickness of 30 ft).

Nine mines and one solution operation currently produce from the Prairie Evaporite of the Mid-Devonian Elk Point cratonic basin (Fig. 6). Three potash horizons, the Esterhazy, Belle Plains, and Patience Lake members, occur in the upper part of the evaporite sequence (Fig. 7). The thickness and continuity of the ore permit the use of continuous mining machinery, which minimizes rock stability and ventilation problems, in a room-and-pillar mining method. Canada will play a major role in world potash production and marketing, a fact apparent since 1970 when the Saskatchewan Provincial Government imposed production limitations in an effort to stabilize prices and bring potash supply and demand into closer balance.

Exploration continues (1981) in the Mississippian evaporite basin of the Maritime Provinces. Scattered, low grade sylvite and carnallite mineralization has been encountered in the deformed evaporites of Nova Scotia. Recent drilling by the government of New Brunswick, however, has encountered high grade (21 to 25% K_2O) mineralization in zones 9 to 32 ft thick at depths of 850 to 1000 ft. If minable reserves are developed, they will enjoy a significant transportation advantage in world trade. Potash Corp. of America has completed sinking a 2,000-ft shaft and currently is exploring this deposit with expectations of production sometime in early 1983. Shaft sinking at a second mine is underway by Denison Mines Ltd. (Denison/Potacan), with first production scheduled for 1984.

United States potash production since 1931 has come principally from the Permian evaporites of the Carlsbad District, southeast New Mexico. By 1961 gross revenue for the district had exceeded one billion dollars. The current reserves of 90 million tons K_2O include sylvinite, argillaceous sylvinite (more than 3% insoluble material) and mixed ores containing sylvite, langbeinite and lesser amounts of other sulfate minerals. Substantial additional reserves are available in thin and lower grade beds. The average grade of sylvinite mined in 1981 was about 16% K_2O.

The thick evaporite deposits of the Carlsbad district occur in the basin and shelf provinces of the cratonic Permian Delaware Basin. The potash salts occur at 12 horizons irregularly over an area of approximately 2000 square miles. Post-depositional metasomatism has locally reconstituted the ore mineralogy and produced barren areas within the ore zones. These barren areas, referred to as salt horses, complicate mining operations (Linn and Adams, 1966). Seven companies currently operate seven mines which produce from 5 of the 12 potash horizons.

Domestic potash production from brines is increasing. In 1972, the Texasgulf potash mine at Moab, Utah, then the only underground potash mine outside the Carlsbad district, was converted to a solution mining operation. Deformation of the ore zone precluded successful underground mining. Potash brines are being pumped from the flooded mine workings, concentrated through solar evaporation, and processed in the existing plant. Recently Buttes Oil and Gas Co. has been exploring a deep solution-mining prospect 30 miles north of Moab. Several other potential solution-mining prospects are known in this region.

In 1971, potassium sulfate production began from the Great Salt Lake, Utah. Initial production was less than anticipated due reportedly to a poor evaporation year and harvesting problems. Potash production from other brines continues at Searles Lake, California; Bonneville, Utah; and in Michigan.

Argillaceous sylvinite has been delineated in the Permian Supai formation of northeastern Arizona and the Dow Chemical Co. has discovered potash minerals at depths of 8000 ft in the Michigan Basin (Matthews, 1970). These deposits are not likely to be mined in the foreseeable future.

South America

Significant proven potash reserves in South America occur only in the marine evaporite deposits of Sergipe, Brazil, the nitrates of Chile, and the brines of the Sechura Desert, Peru. The continent has but few marine evaporites and thus far no known large, epicontinental basin with extensive, high grade potash deposits, such as occur in North America and Europe, have been discovered. The very large Amazonas

Basin of *Brazil* contains sylvite-bearing evaporite deposits of Permian age (Szatmari et al., 1979). Reportedly, these deposits are now being explored by Petrobras Mineracão.

The sylvite and carnallite deposits of Sergipe, Brazil, occur in subbasins of a coastal Cretaceous evaporite basin. Sylvinite reserves, estimated at 30 million tons K_2O, could be substantially increased by mining multiple horizons. The mining of these reserves, however, may be complicated by the occurrence of tachyhydrite ($CaMg_2Cl_6 \cdot 12H_2O$), an extremely hygroscopic mineral, and by faulting. A Brazilian company, Kalium Mineracão S.A., is undertaking the development of the potash and tachyhydrite deposits, the latter reportedly containing reserves of about 1.5 billion tons $MgCl_2$. Shaft sinking by Petrobras Mineracão with technical assistance by Potasse d'Alsace began in 1979, near Santa Rosa de Lima. Production, expected to start in 1983, will come from a high grade sylvite deposit. There are no plans for exploiting the large tachyhydrite deposits in this area.

Polyhalite ($K_2SO_4MgSO_42CaSO_4 \cdot 2H_2O$) occurs in the nitrate ores of *Chile*. Minor amounts of potassium borate and perchlorates are also found.

The brines of the Sechura Desert, *Peru*, are a potential source of potash. The brines occur in shallow porous sediments and are essentially concentrated seawater. The reserves, however, are limited and, although the brines have been under investigation for several years, there are no current plans for their production.

Europe

Europe has dominated potash statistics since the initial exploitation of the Zechstein deposits in 1861. European countries, including Russia, have accounted for 77% of world production and now contain 58% of known world reserves.

The Boulby Mine, in *England*, began producing ore in 1973 (Woods, 1979). Reportedly the great depths (in excess of 1000 m) of the ore, bad roof conditions, erratic nature of the ore, and methane gas have caused difficult mining conditions. Potash reserves are present in two main sylvinite beds which occur at depths between 3200 and 9000 ft in the Permian Zechstein. The beds average 20 to 25 ft in thickness at grades of 10 to 30% K_2O. Two other potash ventures in Yorkshire have been temporarily deferred.

The *French* potash mines of the Mulhouse area in Alsace (Fig. 8) are operated by state-owned monopoly, Mines de Potasse d' Alsace. During recent years the potash industry has been modernized, resulting in the expansion of some mines and plants and the closing of others. The longwall rather than the room-and-pillar mining method is generally used because bedding dips in excess of 10° are common.

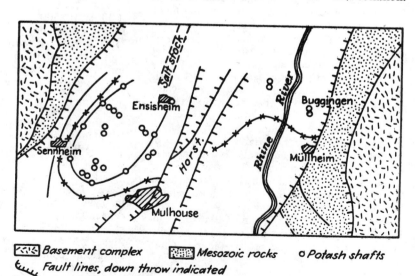

FIG. 8—*Location map for the potash mines of the Rhine Graben, in France and West Germany.* (Smith, 1950).

The evaporites, which contain the principal potash reserves of France, were deposited in the Oligocene Rhine Graben. Similar deposits are mined nearby in *West Germany*. Two ore zones have been mined; the lower contains 15 to 20% K_2O over 6 to 15 ft and the upper zone 20 to 25% K_2O over 3 to 6 ft. The district is presently faced with the difficult problem of sodium chloride disposal. Previous use of the Rhine River for this purpose is no longer environmentally acceptable. Some curtailment of potash production may result. The erratic and irregular sylvinite beds of the Triassic evaporites near Dax in southwestern France contain minor reserves in zones up to 30 ft thick with grade of 12 to 19% K_2O.

The salt cycles and potash beds of the Permian Zechstein of Middle Europe have been defined by Richter-Bernberg (1955) as follows:

Evaporite Cycle	Series	Potash Horizons
Zechstein 4	Aller	
Zechstein 3	Leine	Riedel
		Ronnenberg
Zechstein 2	Stassfurt	Stassfurt
Zechstein 1	Werra	Hessen
		Thuringen

Zechstein 2 through Zechstein 4 are present in the main evaporite basin which includes the Hannover, Stassfurt, and South Harz potash mining districts (Fig. 9). The potash beds of the older Werra series occur only in the more southerly subsidiary basin which contains the Werra-Fulda District. The Hessen and Thuringen beds are mined at depths of 1200 to 3000 ft. In the main basin the regional dip is toward the north so that, except where raised by salt structures, potash horizons occur at greater depths in the Hannover than in the South Harz District.

The Hessen potash bed is 7 to 35 ft thick and contains hartsalz with variable thicknesses of carnallite. Hartsalz (hard salt) is a potash ore containing the comparatively hard mineral kieserite. The Thuringen bed is 180 ft below the Hessen, averages 10 ft in thickness and is mined for hartsalz containing 10 to 15% K_2O. The beds are flat-lying and relatively undeformed with uniform potash grade and distribution permitting the use of the room and pillar mining method.

The potash deposits of the main basin, principally the Hannover district, are on the steeply dipping flanks of conformable and piercement salt structures. Mining is by stoping and backfilling and is concentrated between depths of

FIG. 9—*Location map for the potash mining areas of the Permian Zechstein, West and East Germany (modified after Anon., 1971).*

1000 and 2500 ft. Above 1000 ft there is danger of flooding from ground water; below 2500 ft rock pressures and temperatures are high. The ore is irregular and discontinuous and requires underground exploration drilling. A serious disaster struck the Hannover District when the Kali Chemie Ronnenberg mine was flooded. Reportedly this important mine is considered to be a total loss in terms of future production. The Stassfurt, and to a lesser extent the Ronnenberg and Riedel bed, are mined for hartsalz and smaller amounts of other potash ores.

The *East German* potash industry exploits the sylvinite reserves of the Zechstein salt. Recent modernization has increased the industry's efficiency and production. A new mine at Zielitz will work the Ronnenberg horizon which reportedly contains 13 million tons K_2O at an average 16 to 17% K_2O. In addition, the Zechstein of East Germany contains large carnallite reserves.

The *West German* potash industry has exploited the famous potash beds of the Zechstein for over one hundred years. Recently the industry has undergone modernization similar to that in France and East Germany. Ownership of the industry has been consolidated in such manner that Kali and Salz AG, an amalgamation of Wintershall and Salzdetfurth, contributes 85% of the production from 11 mines. The remaining 15% of production is from two mines owned by Kali-Chemi AG. Currently 30 shafts service a district which once contained 220 operating mines. Ores containing sylvite, carnallite, and sulfate minerals are mined at grades between 9 and 17% K_2O. At Buggingen, near the Alsace deposits of France, sylvite ores containing 18 to 20% K_2O are mined from the Oligocene evaporites.

In recent years *Italy* has essentially doubled its potassium sulfate mining and production capacity. The mines exploit the kainite reserves of Sicily which, with the exception of Ethiopia, are unique in the world. The kainite reserves occur, with lesser amounts of sylvite and carnallite, at four horizons in beds 6 to 100 ft in thickness in Miocene rocks which dip up to 60°.

In *Poland*, the eastern extension of the Zechstein evaporites contain low grade potash beds. Attempts have been made to exploit carnallitic reserves near Klodawa which reportedly contain 8% K_2O at depths of 1500 to 2500 ft. There is now some interest in the deep hartsalz mineralization which extends under the Baltic Sea near Gdansk.

Russia contains 40% of the world potash reserves and has considerable potential for new discoveries. From 1969 to 1970, production increased about 25%, on the strength of major expansions in the Urals and in Byelorussia, two of the three principal potash districts (Fig. 10). This expansion has been accompanied by a greater use of mining machines, with a significant increase in productivity per man shift (Anon., 1972).

The deposits of the Urals reportedly contain the vast majority of Russia's reserves. The deposits are generally thick, high grade, occur at depths of about 800 ft, and are undeformed. Three zones of mineralization containing multiple potash horizons occur over large areas.

The sylvinite deposits of Byelorussia contain 1.5 to 3.0 billion recoverable metric tons of K_2O in three sylvinite horizons and one sylvinite-carnallite bed. The deposits are high grade (20 to 25% K_2O) but also contain 4 to 10% water insoluble material.

The deformed Miocene deposits of Stebnik

FIG. 10—*Location map of the potash mining districts of Russia (Anon., 1972a, modified).*

and Kalush in the West Ukraine contain hartsalz, sylvinite, kainite, langbeinite and up to 12 to 18% insoluble material in at least five potash zones. The deposits are lower grade than those in the Urals and mining in steeply dipping beds is common.

The potash industry in *Spain*, as elsewhere in Europe, has been undergoing expansion. Oligocene evaporites are mined in the Navarra and Catalonia Districts of northern Spain (Fig. 11). The deposits in the Navarra District occur in two beds between depths of 400 and 2000 ft. Sylvinite ore contains 18 to 20% K_2O. The upper bed is principally carnallite with an average grade of 14% K_2O.

The evaporites of Catalonia have been deformed through flowage, folding, and faulting such that mining dips of 30° are common.

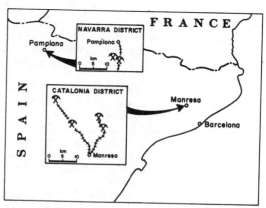

FIG. 11—*Location map of the potash mining districts of Spain (Anon., 1971, modified).*

Carnallite and sylvite ores occur in up to four beds with grades between 15 and 29% K_2O.

Africa

The potash reserves of Africa are estimated at 134 million short tons K_2O, approximately one-tenth of 1% of the total world reserves. Production has been equally small by world standards, the first mine opening as recently as 1969.

The *Congo* (Brazzaville) began potash production in 1969 with completion of the facilities at Holle 25 miles northeast of Point Noíre. Irregularities in the potash beds have reportedly caused initial difficulties for the boring machines. In 1977, the Holle potash mine was abruptly flooded and lost. Since then, there have been no attempts to renew production from this district (De Ruiter, 1979). The mining grades, on the other hand, reportedly have been high, in some cases up to 39% K_2O. Sylvinite ore bodies are inferred to be small and erratic in grade, distribution and thickness. Carnallite, by contrast, averages 16% K_2O and occurs in beds 10 to 40 ft thick.

Ethiopia contains significant potash deposits unique for their young (Quaternary) age and extensive kainite beds. The deposits occur in a rift valley characterized by recent vulcanism and high heat flow (Holwerda and Hutchinson, 1968). The Houston formation contains, from the top, three potash-bearing members: the sylvinite member (up to 30 ft thick), the intermediate members containing carnallite throughout, sylvite at the top and kainite at the base (10 to 80 ft thick), and the lower kainite member (13 to 43 ft thick). Ground water within clastic sediments interbedded with the evaporites and brine pockets within the evaporites are potential hazards for underground mines. Several companies have been involved in the exploration and evaluation of the deposits. A shaft and underground workings are now flooded.

At Marada, *Libya*, potassium-bearing brines occur within a shallow, porous carnallite-bearing formation in a marshlike depression. These brines are not exploited although their development has been considered for several years.

Deposits near Khemisset, *Morocco*, reportedly contain 40 million tons of sylvinite and 200 million tons of carnallite ore. At the grades given in Table 7 the total inplace K_2O reserves would be about 30 million tons. The deposits occur over an area of at least 30 sq km at depths between 1600 and 2600 ft. The sylvinite occurs around the edges of the two carnallite beds which average 3 to 30 ft in thickness. The sylvinite bodies are reportedly low grade, erratic, and probably irregular. Exploration continues for sylvinite reserves adequate to support a mine and mill complex.

Asia

The potash potential of *China* is essentially unknown. It seems probable that the country contains one or more continental evaporite basins with their characteristic high grade, large tonnage potash deposits. For many centuries, the Chinese have produced sodium chloride from brine wells in the provinces of Szechwan and Yunnan. There are believed to be extensive deposits of Jurassic evaporites in this area. Recently it has been reported that potash deposits have been located by the Chinese government at Jiang Cheng, Yunnan. The balance of Asia does contain scattered Paleozoic evaporites and several Mesozoic deposits. Potash salts, however, are limited thus far to the Eocene (Cambrian?) salts of the Punjab Ranges of *West Pakistan* where no minable deposits are yet known to exist. Evaluation of a deep brine occurrence at Dariala, West Pakistan, is reportedly continuing. The Geological Survey of *India* has identified an area of over 30,000 square miles in western Rajasthan as a potential area for potash exploration. Exploration in the Naguar Basin, which began in 1974, has established the presence of large potash resources.

A very large potash deposit was discovered in 1973, at the Khorat Plateau of *Thailand* (Hite and Japakasetr, 1979). This Cretaceous deposit consists primarily of carnallite, although sylvinite and tachyhydrite are also present. Locally the carnallite deposit is as much as 95 m thick and at shallow depths (90 to 600 m). Lenticular high-grade bodies of sylvite are found associated with the carnallite deposit on the flanks of salt anticlines. The deposits also extend north across the Mekong River into Laos. A large-scale exploration program by the Thailand government is still continuing.

Israel's production from the Dead Sea remains the only significant source of potash in Asia. The production facilities at Sodom, expanded in 1969, have a production capability of 1.1 million short tons of K_2O annually.

Construction of facilities for potash recovery from Dead Sea brine on the *Jordan* side is nearing completion. Production is scheduled for sometime in 1983.

Oceania

Minable marine potash deposits have not as yet been discovered in *Australia* although occurrences of potash minerals are known in the Adavale Basin in Queensland. Potash production was scheduled by Texada to begin in 1973 from the brines of Lake McLeod in Western Australia.

The program was curtailed in 1974. In 1978, Texada was acquired by Dampier Salt Co., Ltd. In 1981, construction of test crystallizers and pilot plant tests commenced with production scheduled by 1985. Production rates are scheduled to be in the region of 60 to 120 kt/a.

The brines occur in porous halite and gypsum sediments approximately 2 ft below the dry lake surface. The brines will be concentrated by solar evaporation and then processed to yield a synthetic langbeinite product.

Production

Mining

Potash mines are serviced by vertical shafts similar to many other underground mines. The shafts are constructed either by drilling and blasting or with large diameter drilling machines. Shafts in the Carlsbad District, New Mexico, are 600 to 1650 ft deep and encounter no particular problems in construction. In Saskatchewan, on the other hand, shafts exceed 3000 ft in depth and, due to high water pressure in the Blairmore Formation, are constructed with freezing and tubbing techniques. In other districts shaft depth and design are determined by the particular geology features of the deposits.

Mining in the Carlsbad District is by the room-and-pillar method using conventional drilling and blasting and, to a limited extent, continuous mining machines. Conventional mining with jumbo drills, undercutters, ammonium nitrate explosives, mucking machines, and shuttle cars is applicable to all the deposits. The continuous mining machines do not perform well in irregular ore containing barren areas or in ores with appreciable amounts of the hard sulfate minerals. Initial mine extraction in the district is 60 to 70%. Final extraction after pillar robbing is about 85%.

The uniform deposits of Saskatchewan are mined entirely by continuous mining machines (with the exception of one solution mine)

which produce about 4000 tons per day. Ore from these machines is moved to the shafts on extensible and fixed belts. Initial mine extraction is held to 35 to 40% and conventional blasting is avoided so as to diminish the risk of fracturing through the overlying salt and flooding the mines. Final mine extraction may ultimately reach 50%.

The annual production capacity of the Carlsbad District is about two million K_2O t/a. Current mine productivity averages 75 to 100 tons per man shift.

Past production in the Carlsbad District has been largely from ores which contain 15 to 25% K_2O and 1 to 1.5% insoluble material, principally as clays. In 1981, most production was from ores with lower potash grades (14 to 17% K_2O) and higher insoluble contents (3 to 5%). The ores of Saskatchewan are uniformly higher in grade (20 to 30% K_2O) than those of the Carlsbad District. Furthermore, the reactive insoluble material in the Carlsbad ores causes desliming problems not experienced in the Saskatchewan ores (3–4% insoluble material).

Potash mining methods outside North America are similar to those in Saskatchewan and New Mexico except in those deposits which have been deformed. In some of the deposits of Germany and Sicily, for example, mining is by stopes rather than room-and-pillar, generally with somewhat higher mining costs.

Processing

Most marketable potash products are concentrated by (a) flotation, (b) selective dissolution ("washing") of the gangue minerals, or (c) precipitation of the potash mineral from a hot brine. The majority of sylvinite ores mined in New Mexico (White and Arend, 1950) and Saskatchewan are processed in flotation mills equipped with grinding, desliming, flotation, and drying circuits. The ore is first pulped in a saturated sodium chloride-potassium chloride brine and ground in ball and rod mills to separate the sylvite from the gangue minerals. The fine-grained contaminants, largely clays and quartz, are removed in the desliming circuit. The slurry of sylvite and halite is then passed through froth flotation cells where amine reagents attach the sylvite grains to bubbles in the froth causing the sylvite to float away from the halite. The sylvite is drawn off the top of the cells, dried, and sent to storage.

In the past langbeinite of the langbeinite and mixed langbeinite-sylvite ores of the Carlsbad

District has been concentrated by dissolving or "washing" and removing the readily soluble halite and sylvite gangue minerals. One company now processes ores containing sufficient sylvite (so-called mixed ores) in a heavy media circuit whereby the langbeinite and sylvite can both be physically separated and concentrated.

Carnallite ores and sylvinite ores with abundant insoluble material or impurities within the sylvite grains are processed by selectively dissolving the potassium minerals in a sodium chlorite brine, desliming the brine, and precipitating a pure sylvite product by controlled variation of the composition and temperature of the brine.

Potassium sulfate does not occur as a natural mineral. It may be produced, however, from certain natural brines (for example, Great Salt Lake and Searles Lake) or by mixing brines produced by dissolving potassium and potassium-sulfate minerals. The potassium-sulfate minerals commonly used in this process are langbeinite (Carlsbad District) and kainite (Sicily). The extra potassium required in the reaction is introduced as a brine generally prepared by dissolving sylvite.

Solution mining is applicable only to the readily soluble potassium chloride minerals and is probably profitable only for thick, high-grade sylvinite ores. Only two large scale solution mining operations are currently in production. The first, located in Saskatchewan, has operated since 1964 and in 1969 increased its annual capacity from 600,000 to 900,000 tons K_2O. The nature of the operation has not been made public, but it is likely that the thick, undeformed, high-grade ore horizons have contributed substantially to the success of the operation. The second solution operation began in 1972 when an unsuccessful conventional mine in Utah was flooded and converted to a solution mining-solar evaporation process. Conventional mining was precluded by the deformation of the ore horizon. The solution mining operation is reported to be proceeding successfully.

Product Specifications

The principal potash products for fertilizers [muriate of potash (KCl), potassium sulfate (K_2SO_4) and potassium-magnesium sulfate ($K_2SO_4 \cdot 2MgSO_4$)] are sold on the basis of chemical compositions and particle size. Products with higher potash grades and coarser particles are generally more desirable. Most products are sold on the basis of a guaranteed minimum potash content in standard, coarse, and granular grades, in order of increasing particle size (Table 9). Muriate of potash, the highest grade potash product, accounted for 80% of domestic potash consumption in 1981. The low chlorine content and lower solubility of the potassium sulfate products make them desirable for certain crops and soil conditions. Products produced by solution and precipitation (some muriate and all potassium sulfate) are often purer, hence are preferred for certain applications including the chemical industry.

Transportation

Potash mines in the United States are located distant from oceans and areas of high fertilizer consumption, hence transportation represents a major portion of the delivered price of potash products. East of the Mississippi, for example, average rail freight charges for Carlsbad muriate in 1981 were approximately 50% of the delivered price. Carlsbad production destined for export, although subject to lower freight rates than domestic shipments, incurs freight charges of about $10 per ton to the west coast or $8 per ton to Houston (1975). These rates include the cost of transfer to ships at about $1 per ton.

Imports from Europe and Canada are competitive with domestic production or hold a freight advantage over considerable portions of the United States. In the Great Lakes region, which accounts for more than 40% of domestic consumption, freight costs from Carlsbad and Saskatchewan are comparable (Lewis, 1971). Along the eastern seaboard, potash from Europe holds a freight advantage for up to 150 miles inland.

Transportation costs are equally significant to the Saskatchewan potash industry. In 1980, for example, only a small amount of Saskatchewan's production was consumed in Canada while 67% was exported to the United States. In spite of lower production costs, freight rates to Vancouver and the Great Lakes region of the United States become a burden in world competition during periods of excess production.

The importance of transportation costs is exemplified by current attempts to develop potash production from the deposits in New Brunswick and Nova Scotia. These deposits may have relatively higher mining costs because of geologic complexity, but since they are close to deep water ports on the Atlantic coast, they have a decided transportation cost advantage over deposits in the Saskatchewan District.

Alternate methods of transportation such as slurry pipelines, have been considered, particu-

TABLE 9—Typical Specifications for Standard Grade Potash Products*

	Muriate of Potash, KCl	Sulfate of Potash, K_2SO_4	Potassium, Magnesium, Sulfate, $K_2SO_4 \cdot 2MgSO_4$
Chemical Specifications, %			
K_2O	60.0 — 61.5	50.0 — 52.4	22.0 — 22.9
MgO			18.0 — 18.8
S			22.3 — 22.6
Cl		1.0 — 2.5	1.0 — 2.3
H_2O	0.06 — 0.12	0.10 — 0.12	0.12 — 0.15
Physical Specifications, % Cumulative			
+ 8 mesh			
+10			0 — 3
+14	0 — 6	0 — 15	3 — 16
+20	17 — 32	20 — 45	16 — 38
+28	42 — 63	65 — 85	39 — 63
+35	66 — 90	80 — 95	60 — 83
+48	84 — 98	90 — 98	75 — 92
+65	93 — 100	95 — 100	85 — 96
			94 — 100
Typical Bulk Density (loose, lb per cu ft)	66 — 68	88	92
Typical Chemical Analysis, %			
K	50.5	41.9	18.5
Mg	0.17	0.9	11.1
Ca	0.02	0.3	0.05
Na	1.05	0.2	0.76
Cl	47.86	1.5	
SO_4	0.04	51.5	67.4
Insol.	0.30	0.7	0.33

* Source: Adapted from product specifications published by International Minerals and Chemical Corp.

larly in Canada. It is probable, however, that railroads will continue to move the production of Carlsbad and Saskatchewan and it is unlikely that the costs will be significantly reduced.

Supply and Demand

The estimated world production of potash for 1979 was 26.35 Mt of K_2O equivalent. Of this, the USSR, Canada, and the German Democratic Republic were the world's leading potash producers, as shown in Table 10.

Table 11 shows salient statistics of US potash production. Approximately 85% of US production comes from New Mexico. Utah and California supply the balance.

Potash prices are quoted on the basis of the short ton unit, f.o.b. minesite. Canadian prices (Lyon, 1981) are shown in Table 12. Published prices, f.o.b. Carlsbad, NM, are about 5¢ per unit higher than the Canadian prices for the grades shown in the table.

Potash sales are highest in late spring in anticipation of the spring fertilizer season (Fig. 12). To encourage consumers to purchase and store products in the off season, quoted prices in late winter and spring are a few cents per unit higher.

Potash supply and demand ended the 1980 fertilizer year in fairly close balance. The fertilizer year starts July 1 of each year and ends June 30 the following year. Table 13 (Lyon, 1981) shows the North American potash supply and demand picture for 1978–1979 with an estimate of the supply and demand for 1980–1981.

In 1981, the Government of Saskatchewan, through the Potash Corp. of Saskatchewan (PCS), a Crown corporation, controlled five separate operations with a total capacity of about 2.9 Mt K_2O or about 39% of the Province's total capacity (Singleton and Searls, 1981). The PCS is now the largest potash producer in North America. PCS also is planning a new 2.0 Mt potash mine in the Bredenbury area and indicated it will increase potash

TABLE 10—Marketable Potash: World Production by Country*
(1000 t of K_2O equivalent)

Country[†]	1976	1977	1978	1979[p]	1980[e]
Canada (sales)[‡]	[r]5,215	[r]5,764	6,340	7,074	[$]7,532
Chile[#]	[r]17	[r]11	15	21	21
China, mainland[‖]	[r]12	[r]18	[r]21	[r]16	12
Congo	254	[r]136	—	—	—
France	1,603	[r]1,580	1,795	1,920	[$]1,939
German Democratic Republic	3,161	3,229	3,323	3,395	[$]3,422
Germany, Federal Republic of	2,036	2,341	2,470	2,690	[$]2,674
Israel	680	[r]707	695	730	[$]797
Italy	[r]140	[r]151	196	182	185
Spain	630	[r]562	722	781	770
USSR	8,310	8,347	8,193	6,635	8,000
United Kingdom	[r]46	81	150	264	280
United States	2,177	2,229	2,253	2,225	[$]2,239
Total	[r]24,281	[r]25,156	26,173	25,933	27,871

Source: Searls, 1981a.
[e]Estimated.　[p]Preliminary.　[r]Revised.
* Table includes data available through Apr. 27, 1981.
[†] In addition to the countries listed, Australia apparently produced small quantities of marketable potash during 1976-1980, but output was not reported quantitatively, and general information was inadequate for the formulation of reliable estimates of output levels.
[‡] Official Government figures.
[§] Reported figure.
[#] Series revised; new data represent officially reported output of potassium nitrate product (gross weight basis) converted assuming 14% K_2O equivalent.
[‖] Series revised to reflect officially reported Chinese data on production of potassic fertilizers in terms of nutrient content; small additional quantities may be produced and used by the nonfertilizer chemical industry.

production to an estimated 6.9 Mt by 1990. The Government of Saskatchewan has announced plans to eventually acquire 50% of the Saskatchewan potash industry, apparently by internal expansion.

Other Considerations

World food requirements are projected to increase, hence so also will the demand for fertilizers and potassium. The principal market

TABLE 11—Salient Statistics on Potash, United States
(1000 t)

	1977	1978	1979	1980	1981[e]
Production: Marketable	2,229	2,253	2,225	2,239	2,150
Imports for consumption	4,605	4,707	5,165	4,972	5,200
Exports	846	809	635	762	500
Apparent consumption	5,992	6,205	6,918	6,427	6,700
Price: Muriate, ¢/t unit of K_2O, f.o.b. mine*	71	76	95	130	140
Stocks, producer, yearend	467	414	251	250	420
Employment: Mine	2,100	1,900	1,800	1,800	1,750
Mill	1,300	1,400	1,450	1,450	1,400
Net import reliance[†] as a percent of apparent consumption	63	64	66	65	68

Source: Searls, 1981.
[e] Estimate.
* Average prices based on actual sales, excluding soluble and chemical muriates.
[†] Net import reliance = imports − exports + adjustments for government and industry stock changes.

TABLE 12—Canadian Muriate of Potash Prices
(Dollars per unit K$_2$O)*

Grade	March 1, 1980	March 1, 1981	% Change
Standard	0.96	1.16	+20.8
Coarse	1.10	1.25	+13.6
Granular	1.12	1.27	+13.4

Source: Lyon, 1981.
* A unit is equivalent to 20 lb or 1% K$_2$O short ton.

of potash is assured because potash is essential to plant metabolism even if substitutions should occur in some of the industrial and chemical applications.

By 1985, potash consumption is expected to be about 33 million short tons of K$_2$O per year. The US demand is expected to increase to about 8.6 Mt of K$_2$O equivalent by 1990. The estimated US demand by the year 2000 is 10.1 Mt of K$_2$O equivalent.

Adequate reserves of low grade potash are available to meet the world's needs for the next few hundred years. Deposits with lower production costs or advantages in location may even see expansion toward the end of the decade at the expense of less profitable operations. Beyond the protection of some portion of domestic production capacity, countries are likely

TABLE 13—North American Potash Supply and Demand
(1000 St, K$_2$O)

	Actual* 1978-1979	1978-1980	Estimated† 1980-1981
Supply			
Opening inventory	1,622	1,155	1,445
Production (US and Canada)	9,296	10,265	10,800
Imports	268	301	350
Less closing inventory	1,155	1,445	1,445
Total Supply	**10,031**	**10,276**	**11,150**
Demand			
Agricultural			
US	6,405	6,548	6,900
Canada	381	401	420
Total	6,786	6,949	7,320
Industrial	382	423	430
Export	2,829	2,847	3,200
Total demand	**9,997**	**10,219**	**10,950**

Source: Lyon, 1981.
* Potash-Phosphate Institute.
† CF Industries Inc.

to permit world trade to continue with minimal restrictions.

The potash industry is subject to taxes and royalties similar to other extractive industries. Domestic production from federal lands is administered by the US Geological Survey and the Bureau of Land Management insofar as potash is a leasable mineral. Domestic production is also subject to a depletion allowance of 14% of gross income and in New Mexico a state severance tax is based on an ore valuation formula. Production from the Saskatchewan District is subject to a Provincial mining tax and a royalty payable to the Crown. Tax consideration, similar to the depletion allowance, is permitted but is under revision.

The extraction of potash ores and the application of fertilizers constitute alteration of the natural environment as, indeed, does the planting and harvesting of crops. Whereas it is unlikely that either the extraction or the application of potash has any serious deleterious effect on the environment, both are receiving study. Potash mines in North America are remote from population centers. The deposits of New Mexico are in low density. semiarid grazing land where brackish lakes and marshes are common. Mining operations disturb only sufficient surface area for mining and milling facilities and tailings ponds. The tailings ponds are the only potential long range problem as they are too saline to support life and must

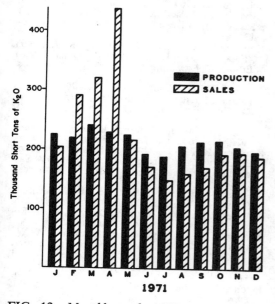

FIG. 12—*Monthly total of US potash production and sales, 1971 (data supplied by International Minerals and Chemical Corp.).*

be stabilized against wind erosion. The proper application of potash in fertilizer is not known to constitute a hazard of any kind. Hearings by the Illinois Pollution Control Board identified potential hazards from the misapplications and buildup of nitrogen and phosphorus but noted no such concern for potash (Aldrich, 1972).

Bibliography and References

Anon., 1965, *Salt Basins Around Africa*, Institute of Petroleum and the Geological Society, London, Elsevier, Amsterdam, 122 pp.

Anon., 1966, "World Survey of Potash, 1966," British Sulphur Corporation Ltd., London, 93 pp.

Anon., 1968, "World Supply and Demand for Potash and its Impact upon the Saskatchewan Industry," Saskatchewan Potash Committee, 86 pp.

Anon., 1970, "The United States Position and Outlook in Potash," Information Circular 8487, US Bureau of Mines, 47 pp.

Anon., 1971, "New Name in the World Potash Industry," *Phosphorus and Potassium*, No. 51, January-February, pp. 47–49.

Anon., 1971a, "Spanish Potash—1970 and After," *Phosphorus and Potassium*, No. 53, May-June, pp. 36–39.

Anon., 1972, "The Technical Advances by the USSR Potash Industry," *Phosphorus and Potassium*, No. 59, May-June, pp. 41–45.

Anon., 1972a, "The Canadian Potash Industry: A Study in Government Cooperation," International Minerals and Chemical Corp., Libertyville, IL, 24 pp.

Adams, S.S., 1968, "Potassium Reserves in the World," *The Role of Potassium in Agriculture*, V.J. Kilmer, S.E. Younts, and N.C. Brady, eds., American Society of Agronomy, Crop Science Society of America, Soil Science Society of America, Madison, pp. 1–21.

Adams, S.S., 1969, "Bromine in the Salado Formation, Carlsbad Potash District New Mexico," Bulletin 93, New Mexico Bureau of Mines and Mineral Resources, 122 pp.

Adams, S.S., 1970, "Ore Controls, Carlsbad Potash District, Southeast New Mexico," *Third Symposium on Salt*, Rau, J.L., and Dellwig, L.F., eds., Vol. 1, Northern Ohio Geological Society, Cleveland, pp. 246–257.

Aldrich, 1972, "Opinion of the Board in the Matter of Plant Nutrients," R 71–15, Illinois Pollution Control Board, 7 pp.

Alger, R.P., and Crain, E.R., "Defining Evaporite Deposits with Electrical Well Logs," *Second Symposium on Salt*, J.L. Rau, ed., Vol. 2, Northern Ohio Geological Society, Cleveland, 1966, pp. 116–130.

Benavides, V., 1968, "Saline Deposits of South America," *Saline Deposits*, R.B. Mattox, ed., Special Paper 88, Geological Society of America, pp. 249–290.

Bentor, Y.K., 1968, "Salt Deposits of the Dead Sea Region," *Saline Deposits*, R.B. Mattox, ed., Special Paper 88, Geological Society of America, pp. 139–156.

Borchert, H., and Muir, R.O., 1964, *Salt Deposits*, Van Nostrand, London, 330 pp.

Braitsch, O., 1971, *Salt Deposits, Their Origin and Composition*, Springer-Verlag, New York, 297 pp.

D'Ans, J., 1933, *Die Losungsgleichgewichte de System der Salze Oceanischer Salzablagerungen*, Hrsq. von Kali-Forschungs-Anstalt, Verlagsgellschaft fur Ackerbau, Berlin, 254 pp.

De Ruiter, P.A.C., 1979, "The Gabon and Congo Basins Salt Deposits," *Economic Geology*, Vol. 74, No. 2, Mar.-Apr., pp. 419–431.

Eilertsen, D.E., 1972, "Potash," *Minerals Yearbook 1972*, US Bureau of Mines, pp. 1055–1067.

Eilertsen, D.E., 1972, "Potash in 1971," *Mineral Industry Surveys*, US Bureau of Mines, July 5, 4 pp.

Goudarzi, G.H., 1981, "Potash—Libya," abstract, 17th Annual Forum on the Geology of Industrial Minerals, Albuquerque, NM.

Hahl, D.C., and Handy, A.H., 1969, "Great Salt Lake: Chemical and Physical Variations of the Brine, 1963–1966," Water Resources Bulletin 12, Utah Geological and Mineralogical Survey, 33 pp.

Halbouty, M.T., 1967, *Salt Domes—Gulf Region, United States and Mexico*, Gulf Publishing Co., Houston, 425 pp.

Hite, R.J., 1982, "Progress Report on the Potash Deposits of the Khorat Plateau, Thailand," US Geological Survey Open File Report 82–1096, 70 pp.

Hite, R.J., and Japakasetr, T., 1979, "Potash Deposits of the Khorat Plateau, Thailand and Laos," *Economic Geology*, Vol. 74, No. 2, Mar.-Apr., pp. 448–458.

Holser, W.T., 1968, "Bromide Geochemistry of Salt Rock," *Second Symposium on Salt*, J.L. Rau, ed., Vol. 1, Northern Ohio Geological Society, Cleveland, pp. 248–275.

Holter, M.E., 1969, "The Middle Devonian Prairie Evaporite of Saskatchewan," Report No. 123, Saskatchewan Department of Mineral Resources, 134 pp.

Holwerda, J.G., and Hutchinson, R.W., 1968, "Potash-Bearing Evaporites in the Danakil Area, Ethiopia," *Economic Geology*, Vol. 63, pp. 124–150.

Johns, R.K., and Ludbrook, N.H., 1963, "Investigation of Lake Eyre," Report of Investigation 24, Geological Society of South Australia, 102 pp.

Keyes, W.F., 1973, "Potash," *Minerals Yearbook 1973*, US Bureau of Mines, Preprint, 12 pp.

Knudson, R.H., 1972, "World Potash Production Capacity and Consumption 1970–1980," Saskatchewan Department of Mineral Resources, 14 pp.

Koepke, W.E., 1971, "Fertilizers and Fertilizer Minerals in Canada," Mineral Bulletin MR 115, Mineral Resources Branch, Department of Energy, Mines and Resources, Ottawa, 157 pp.

Kozary, M.T., Dunlap, J.C., and Humphrey, W.W., 1968, "Incidence of Saline Deposits in Geologic Time," *Saline Deposits*, R.B. Mattox, ed., Special Paper 88, Geological Society of America, pp. 43–57.

Lefond, S.J., 1969, *Handbook of World Salt Resources*, Plenum Press, New York, 384 pp.

Lewis, R.W., 1970, "Potassium," *Mineral Facts and Problems, 1970 Edition*, Bulletin 650, US Bureau of Mines, pp. 1157–1170.

Liechti, P., 1968, "Salt Features of France," *Saline Deposits*, Mattox, R.B., ed., Special Paper 88, Geological Society of America, pp. 83–106.

Linn, K.O., and Adams, S.S., 1968, "Barren Halite Zones in Potash Deposits, Carlsbad, New Mexico," *Second Symposium on Salt*, J.L. Rau, ed., Vol. 1, Northern Ohio Geological Society, Cleveland, pp. 59–69.

Livingstone, D.A., 1963, "Chemical Composition of Rivers and Lakes," *Data of Geochemistry*, Professional Paper 440-G, US Geological Survey, 60 pp.

Lotze, F., 1957, *Steinsalz und Kalisalze*, 2nd ed., Vol. 1, Gebruder Borntraeger, 465 pp.

Lotze, F., 1963, "The Distribution of Evaporites in Space and Time," *Problems in Paleoclimatology*, A.E.M. Nairn, ed., Proceedings of NATO Paleoclimates Conference, University of Newcastle-Upon-Tyne, pp. 491–507.

Lyon, F.D., 1981, "Major Expansions Programmed at Canadian Mines and Plants," *Engineering and Mining Journal*, Vol. 182, No. 3, Mar., pp. 95–99.

Matthews, R.D., 1970, **"The Distribution of Silurian Potash in the Michigan Basin,"** *Forum on Geology of Industrial Minerals*, 6th, Proceedings Michigan Geological Survey Div., Misc., No. 1, p. 20–23.

Parker, R.L., 1967, "Composition of the Earth's Crust," *Data of Geochemistry*, Professional Paper 440-D, US Geological Survey, 19 pp.

Pendery, E.C., 1970, "Distribution of Salt and Potash Deposits: Present and Potential Effect on Potash Economics and Exploration," *Third Symposium on Salt*, J.L. Rau, and L.F. Dellwig, eds., Vol. 2, Northern Ohio Geological Society, Cleveland, pp. 85–95.

Pierce, W.G., and Rich, E.I., 1962, "Summary of Rock Salt Deposits in the United States as Possible Storage Sites for Radioactive Waste Materials," Bulletin 1148, US Geological Survey, 91 pp.

Richter-Bernberg, G., 1955, "Stratigraphische Gliederung des deutschen Zechsteins," *Zeitschrift der Deutschen Geologischen Gessellschaft*, Vol. 105, p. 843.

Rios, J.M., 1968, "Saline Deposits of Spain," *Saline Deposits*, R.B. Mattox, ed., Special Paper 88, Geological Society of America, pp. 59–74.

Rittenhouse, P.A., 1979, "Potash and Politics," *Economic Geology*, Vol. 74, No. 2, Mar.-Apr., pp. 353–357.

Ryan, J.E., 1951, "Industrial Salts: Production at Searles Lake," *Trans. SME/AIME*, Vol. 190, pp. 447–452.

Sawatzky, H.B., Agarwal, R.G., and Wilson, W., 1960, "Helium Prospects of Southwest Saskatchewan," Report No. 49, Saskatchewan Department of Mineral Resources, 26 pp.

Searls, J.P., 1981, "Potash," *Mineral Commodity Summaries, 1981*, US Bureau of Mines, pp. 116–117.

Searls, J.P., 1981a, "Potash," *Minerals Yearbook, 1980*, US Bureau of Mines, pp. 651–661.

Singleton, R.H., and Searls, J.P., 1980, "Potash," Preprint, 1978–1979, US Bureau of Mines, 15 pp.

Smith, J.P., 1950, "Notes on the Potash Deposits of Germany, France, and Spain," *Trans. AIME*, Vol. 187, No. 1, pp. 117–121.

Stewart, F.H., 1963, "Marine Evaporites," *Data of Geochemistry*, Professional Paper 440-Y, US Geological Survey, 52 pp.

Stocklin, J., 1968, "Saline Deposits of the Middle East," *Saline Deposits*, R.B. Mattox, ed., Special Paper 88, Geological Society of America, pp. 157–181.

Streeton, D.H., 1967, "The Geology of the Prairie Evaporite Formation of the Yorkton Area of Saskatchewan," M.A. Thesis, University of Saskatchewan, 81 pp.

Szatmari, P., et al., 1979, "A Comparison of Evaporite Facies in the Late Paleozoic Amazon and Middle Cretaceous South Atlantic Salt Basins," *Economic Geology*, Vol. 74, No. 2, Mar.-Apr., pp. 432–447.

Tortochaux, F., 1968, "Occurrence and Structure of Evaporites in North Africa," *Saline Deposits*, R.B. Mattox, ed., Special Paper 88, Geological Society of America, pp. 106–138.

White, D.E., Hem, J.D., and Waring, G.A., 1963, "Chemical Composition of Subsurface Waters," *Data of Geochemistry*, Professional Paper 440-F, US Geological Survey, 67 pp.

White, D.E., 1965, "Saline Waters of Sedimentary Rocks," *Fluids in Subsurface Environments*, A. Young, and J.E. Galley, eds., Memoir 4, American Association of Petroleum Geologists, pp. 342–366.

White, N.C., and Arend, C.A., Jr., 1950, "Potash Production at Carlsbad," *Chemical Engineering Progress*, pp. 523–530.

Woods, P.J.E., 1979, "The Geology of the Boulby Mine," *Economic Geology*, Vol. 74, No. 2, Mar.-Apr., pp. 409–418.

Pumice, Pumicite, and Volcanic Cinders

N. V. PETERSON *

R. S. MASON †

The violent explosion of Mount St. Helens in the state of Washington on May 18, 1980 showered volcanic ash over vast areas of the Northwest. It was another eruptive episode in a long history of similar occurrences in the region, which extends from Canada to California and reaches several hundred miles inland from the Pacific Ocean.

Pumice, pumicite, and cinders are products of explosive volcanic eruptions. Pumice and pumicite are produced by the violent expansion of dissolved gases in a viscous silicic lava such as rhyolite or dacite. Scoria is the mafic counterpart of pumice.

Pumice is a light-colored, cellular, almost frothy rock made up of glass-walled bubble casts. It may occur as coherent, massive blocks composed of highly vesicular glassy lava in either a flow or vent filling, or it may be more or less fragmented by violent eruption. Pumicite, the diminutive of pumice, has the same origin, chemical composition, and glassy structure, differing only in particle size. Particles less than 0.16 in. in diam are designated pumicite.

Pumice usually is found relatively close to the vent from which it was expelled, while pumicite may be carried by winds for great distances before settling as an accumulation of fine-grained ash or tuffaceous sediment.

Mount St. Helens lofted an estimated 5 billion cu yd of ash and pumicite. The volcano, unlike most of the High Cascade peaks, is composed largely of dacitic material with only minor amounts of andesite and basalt.

Volcanic cinders are the reddish to black vesicular fragments which pile up during explosive eruptions of volcanoes of basaltic com-

position. Most cinder deposits occur as cones or mounds of stratified fragments ranging from a fraction of an inch to several inches in diameter. Individual cones or mounds may be several hundred feet in diameter and up to 500 ft high.

Properties and Uses

Low bulk density, good heat and sound insulating properties, and excellent abrasive capabilities make pumice and pumicite useful in industrial applications. Cinders, though less cellular and somewhat heavier, also have a variety of industrial uses.

The main use of pumice and cinders continues to be in the construction industry as road-surfacing material, railroad ballast, and building block aggregate. Pumicite is used in sizable quantities as a pozzolanic additive to monolithic concrete where it increases workability, strength, and durability of the concrete and reduces the heat of hydration.

Volcanic cinders generally are denser and more coarsely cellular than most pumice. Markets for cinders include aggregate for road construction and surfacing and use in lightweight concretes, particularly blocks. Some producers having access to both pumice and cinders offer a variety of blends of the two materials to block manufacturers. Table 1 lists the principal applications of industrial pumice. Tables 2 and 3 show US sales and uses of volcanic products.

Most pumice deposits are unconsolidated and usually have a minimum of overburden. Mining is by open pit and can be easily carried out with conventional loading equipment. Sometimes air drying precedes hauling to a crushing and screening plant which yields the size product desired. Multiple bins at railroad hauling facilities permit blending if desired. Pumice for abrasive use may require more sophisticated processing by fine grinding and air classification before being bagged for market.

---

* Retired, formerly District Geologist, Grants Pass Office, State of Oregon Department of Geology and Mineral Industries, Portland, OR.

† Retired, formerly State Geologist, State of Oregon Department of Geology and Mineral Industries, Portland, OR.

TABLE 1—Principal Applications of Industrial Pumice

Market	Application	Grade
Paint manufacture	Nonskid coatings	Coarse
	Acoustic insulating ceiling paints	Coarse
	Fillers for textured paints	Intermediate
Chemical industry	Flattening agents	Extra fine
	Filtration media	Coarse
	Chemical carriers	Coarse
	Sulfur matches and strikers	Intermediate
Metal and plastic finishing	Cleaning and polishing	Extra fine
	Vibratory and barrel finishing	Extra fine-Intermediate
	Pressure blasting	Intermediate
	Electroplating	Extra fine-Intermediate
Compounders	Cleaning lithographic plates	Extra fine
	Powdered hand soaps	Intermediate
	Glass cleaners	Extra fine
	Polishing natural teeth and dentures	Fine
	Smoothing rough skin	Lump
Rubber	Erasers	Intermediate
	Mould release agents	Extra fine
Glass and mirror	TV tube processing	
	Glass buffing and polishing	Fine
	Bevel finishing	Extra fine
	Cut glass finishing	Extra fine
Furniture	Hand-rubbed satin finishing	Extra fine
	Piano keys	Extra fine
	Picture frame gold-leafing	Extra fine
Leather	Buffing	Intermediate
Electronics	Cleaning circuit boards	Extra fine
Pottery	Filler	Extra fine-fine
Agricultural	Soil substitute and additive	Coarse

Source: Meisinger, 1977.

Block pumice in economical quantity and quality is limited to a few geologically young deposits located in California and Oregon. The California deposits are discussed by Chesterman (1957). Production in California has come mainly from Glass Mountain and Little Glass Mountain in eastern Siskiyou County just south of the Oregon-California border, and at Mono Craters, Mono County. In Oregon, block pumice occurs principally at Newberry Crater and at Rock Mesa, both in Deschutes County just south of the South Sister, a 10,000-ft peak in the Cascade range. There has been minor production of lump pumice from the Newberry Crater site for many years. The Rock Mesa deposit covers roughly 1,200 acres, but has not been developed.

Deposits containing block pumice typically are composed of a mixture of rhyolitic, dacitic, or rhyodacitic volcanic glasses ranging in texture from glassy, solid obsidian to highly vesicular pumice.

Block pumice sizes range from 2 in. or more in one dimension to chunks 5 ft or larger in diam. The smaller pieces have a variety of uses including abrasive blocks for the removal of calluses, for cleaning barbecue grills, and for dressing metal polishing belts. Pumice blocks are also used for filtering vinegar.

Larger blocks may be sold either rough or with one or, at most, two edges sawed. The latter are used architecturally for wall or other surface coverings, including suspended ceilings. The rough chunks are often used in landscape

TABLE 2—Pumice and Volcanic Cinders Sold and Used by Producers, US

	1976	1977	1978	1979	1980	1981
Pumice and pumicite (1000 st)	906	1,178	1,208	1,173	543	499
Value* ($1000)	3,830	4,625	4,836	5,008	4,267	4,311
Average value per st ($)	4.23	3.93	4.00	4.27	7.86	8.64
Volcanic cinder and scoria (1000 st)	3,228	2,831	3,549	3,241	3,236	3,667
Value* ($1000)	6,636	7,340	9,619	10,958	11,258	13,400
Average value per st ($)	2.06	2.59	2.71	3.38	3.48	3.65
Exports (1000 st)	1	2	2+	2+	1†	1†
Imports for Consumption (1000 st)	81	253	216	62	194	90
World production, pumice and related volcanic materials (1000 st)	16,800‡	18,000	19,600¶	19,500¶	17,712	17,790

Source: Meisinger, 1978-1979, 1980, 1981.
* Value f.o.b. mine and/or mill
† estimated
‡ revised
¶ preliminary

TABLE 3—Volcanic Material Sold and Used by Producers in the United States, By Use

Use	1978		1979		1980		1981	
	Quantity, 1000 st	Value, $1000	Quantity, 1000 st	Value, $1000	Quantity, 1000 st	Value, $1000	Quantity, 1000 st	Value $1000
Volcanic Cinder and Scoria								
Concrete admixture and aggregate	726	2,289	744	3,066	514	3,316	534	4,020
Landscaping	352	2,253	184	2,538	209	2,513	184	2,568
Railroad ballast	199	405	193	400	140	377	31	50
Road construction (including ice control and maintenance)	2,139	3,176	1,848	3,831	2,292	4,268	2,856	6,230
Other uses*	133	496	272	1,118	82	426	63	582
Total	3,549	9,619	3,241	10,953	3,236	11,258	3,667	13,400
Pumice and Pumicite								
Abrasives (including cleaning and scouring compounds)	15	448	28	649	27	568	19	486
Concrete admixture and aggregate	1,153	2,968	1,094	3,254	459	2,515	404	2,469
Landscaping	10	484	25	196	19	249	34	370
Other uses†	30	936	26	909	38	935	42	986
Total, Pumice and Pumicite	1,208	4,836	1,173	5,008	543	4,267	499	4,311

Source: Meisinger, 1978-1979, 1980, 1981.
* Includes absorbents, asphalt mix, roofing granules, and miscellaneous uses.
† Includes decorative building block, heat- or cold-insulating media, pesticide carriers, soil conditioners, roofing granules, and miscellaneous industrial uses.

TABLE 4—Pumice, Pumicite, Volcanic Cinder, and Scoria Sold and Used by Producers in the US, by State

State	1975 Quantity, 1000 st	1975 Value, $1000	1976 Quantity, 1000 st	1976 Value, $1000	1977 Quantity, 1000 st	1977 Value, $1000	1978 Quantity, 1000 st	1978 Value, $1000	1979 Quantity, 1000 st	1979 Value, $1000	1980† Quantity, 1000 st	1980† Value, $1000	1981† Quantity, 1000 st	1981† Value, $1000
Arizona	856	1,294	802	1,240	621	1,226	1,135	3,130	940	2,367	990	3,228	1,088	3,189
California	348	2,762	705	3,245	636	3,838	831	3,458	800	3,973	568	3,159	770	4,462
Colorado	—	—	—	—	—	—	—	—	—	—	W	W	107	615
Hawaii	318	912	330	636	260	574	272	658	359	1,240	W	W	373	1,364
Idaho	111	187	W	W	—	—	—	—	—	—	—	—	—	—
Kansas	—	—	—	—	—	—	—	—	—	—	—	—	W	W
Montana	—	—	5	8	5	7	—	—	—	—	—	—	—	—
Nevada	W	W	388	763	656	1,154	706	1,282	W	W	—	—	—	—
New Mexico	397	1,280	486	1,560	457	1,835	631	2,706	604	3,550	448	3,028	538	3,810
Oklahoma	1	W	1	W	1	W	1	W	1	W	—	—	2	W
Oregon	1,470	3,937	1,125	2,311	1,083	2,429	915	2,016	781	1,644	1,090	2,734	878	1,547
Utah	17	23	164	264	W	W	28	270	28	280	35	347	—	—
Washington	—	—	—	—	W	W	50	63	—	—	—	—	—	—
Wyoming	—	—	—	—	—	—	7	W	—	—	—	—	—	—
Other states *	374	808	128	439	290	902	181	872	901	2,907	647	3,029	410	2,724
American Samoa	—	—	—	—	1	10	4	24	2	15	3	32	—	—
Total	3,892	11,203	4,134	10,466	4,010	11,975	4,761	14,479	4,416	15,976	3,781	15,557	4,166	17,711

Source: Adapted from Meisinger, 1978-1979, 1980, 1981.

* Colorado, Idaho, Kansas (1978), Nevada (1979), Oklahoma (value only), Utah (1977), Washington (1977), and Wyoming (1978 value only).

† Volcanic cinders and scoria reported separately after 1979 by US Bureau of Mines, but combined here.

TABLE 5—Pumice and Related Volcanic Materials: World Production, by Country

(1000 st)

Country*	1976	1977	1978	1979[p]	1980[e]
Argentina[†]	63	72	24	27	28
Austria: Pozzolan	13	10	10	9	8
Cape Verde Islands: Pozzolan[e]	17	17	NA	NA	NA
Chile: Pozzolan	109	175	201	242	275
Costa Rica[e]	1	1	2	2	2
Dominica: Pumice and volcanic ash[e]	120	120	120	120	120
Egypt[e]	([‡])	([‡])	([‡])	([‡])	([‡])
France: Pozzolan and lapilli	703	774	648	[e]650	660
Germany, Federal Republic of:					
Pumice (marketable)	2,422	1,928	2,294	1,579	1,440
Pozzolan	110	131	192	215	220
Greece:					
Pumice	441	626	827	692	695
Pozzolan	1,081	1,385	1,565	1,235	1,650
Guadeloupe: Pozzolan	220	209	220	220	220
Guatemala:					
Pumice	NA	NA	21	[r e]20	20
Volcanic ash	26	29	39	41	40
Iceland	2	8	9	27	26
Italy:					
Pumice and pumiceous lapilli[e]	[r]949	[r e]825	[e]860	[r e]940	880
Pozzolan[e]	[r]6,600	6,300	6,400	6,500	6,600
Martinique: Pumice	[r e]330	316	183	172	165
New Zealand	55	31	44	[e]44	45
Spain[§]	133	1,027	759	854	860
United States (sold or used by producers):					
Pumice and pumicite	906	1,178	1,208	[r]1,172	543 [#]
Volcanic cinder (including scoria)[‖]	3,275	2,832	3,553	3,243	3,215 [#]
Total	[r]17,576	[r]17,994	19,179	[r]18,004	17,712

Source: Meisinger, 1980.

[e] Estimated. [p] Preliminary. [r] Revised. NA Not available.

* Pumice and related volcanic materials are also produced in a number of other countries, including (but not limited to) Iran, Japan, Mexico, Turkey, and the USSR, but output is not reported quantitatively and available information is inadequate for the formulation of reliable estimates of output levels.

[†] Unspecified volcanic materials produced mainly for use in construction products.

[‡] Less than 1/2 unit.

[§] Includes Canary Islands.

[#] Reported figure.

[‖] Includes American Samoa.

architecture and for sculptured pieces. The low specific gravity of block pumice makes it feasible to use large boulders; pieces 3 to 4 ft diam can be hand-trucked to the site and no special support is necessary.

Substitutes are available for most or all uses of pumice, pumicite, and volcanic cinder, so a market exists only when a combination of cost, ease of handling and processing, and quality are favorable. Prices for crude or processed pumice usually are determined by negotiation.

Adverse economic conditions in the late 1970s reduced residential and industrial construction uses and slowed demand for natural lightweight aggregate. In the years 1974 through 1979 volume increased only 17%, al-

though value rose 43%. Average prices for all volcanic aggregates rose from $2.32 per ton f.o.b. mine in 1974 to $3.46 per ton in 1979.

Lightweight naturally expanded volcanic aggregates appeared to be gaining a stronger foothold in competition with commercially expanded shales at the end of the 1970s. Greatly increased fuel costs forced some kilns to shut down; producers of naturally expanded materials promptly penetrated the new market.

A volcanic environment is necessary for sizable high quality deposits, and this pretty well confines the domestic supply and markets to the western United States. Table 4 shows production and value of pumice, pumicite, volcanic cinder, and scoria by state.

About 57,000 tons of pumice are imported, primarily from Italy and Greece. Table 5 shows world production of pumice by country.

References and Bibliography

Anon., 1977, "Pumice—A Dual Role in Industry," *Industrial Minerals*, No. 120, Sept., pp. 15–29.

Chesterman, C.W., 1957, "Pumice, Pumicite, Perlite, and Volcanic Cinders," *Mineral Commodities of California*, Bulletin 176, California Division of Mines and Geology, pp. 443–448.

Chesterman, C.W., 1966, "Pumice, Pumicite, Perlite, and Volcanic Cinders," *Mineral Resources of California*, Bulletin, 191, California Division of Mines and Geology, pp. 336–341.

Eckel, E.B., 1960, "Pumice and Pozzolan Deposits in the Lesser Antilles," Misc. Paper No. 6–400, US Geological Survey, prepared on behalf of the International Cooperation Administration by US Army Engineer Waterways Experiment Station, Vicksburg, MS, Sept., 80 pp.

Meisinger, A.C., 1974, "Pumice and Volcanic Cinder," *Minerals Yearbook*, Vol. I, US Bureau of Mines, pp. 1111–1115.

Meisinger, A.C., 1975a, "Pumice and Volcanic Cinder," *Minerals Yearbook*, Vol. I, US Bureau of Mines, pp. 1209–1213.

Meisinger, A.C., 1975b, "Pumice and Volcanic Cinder," *Mineral Facts and Problems*, US Bureau of Mines, pp. 871–880.

Meisinger, A.C., 1976, "Pumice and Volcanic Cinder," *Minerals Yearbook*, Vol. I, US Bureau of Mines, pp. 1159–1163.

Meisinger, A.C., 1977, "Pumice and Volcanic Cinder," *Minerals Yearbook*, Vol. I, US Bureau of Mines, pp. 763–767.

Meisinger, A.C., 1978, "Pumice and Volcanic Cinder," Preprint, 1978–1979, *Minerals Yearbook*, US Bureau of Mines, 5 pp.

Meisinger, A.C., 1980, "Pumice and Volcanic Cinder," *Minerals Yearbook*, Vol. I, US Bureau of Mines, pp. 663–667.

Meisinger, A.C., 1981, "Pumice and Pumicite," *Minerals Yearbook*, Vol. I, US Bureau of Mines, pp. 693–696.

Wagner, N.S., 1969, "Perlite, Pumice, Pumicite and Cinders," *Mineral and Water Resources of Oregon*, Bulletin 64, Oregon Dept. of Geology and Mineral Industries, pp. 222–228.

Wentworth, C.K., and Williams, H., 1932, "The Classification and Terminology of Pyroclastic Rocks," *Report of Commission of Sedimentation*, Bulletin 89, National Research Council, pp. 19–53.

Williamson, D.R., and Burgin, L., 1960, "Pumice and Pumicite," *Mineral Industries Bulletin*, Colorado School of Mines, Vol. 3, No. 3, May, 12 pp.

Pyrophyllite

B. E. CORNISH *

Most technical and statistical data published on pyrophyllite relating to production figures, uses, markets and sales, have in the past traditionally linked the mineral with talc and soapstone. This is due to several common superficial physical properties resulting in substitute uses and applications. However, these minerals are not similar in chemical composition and do not generally occur in a similar geological environment.

Pyrophyllite now stands on its own in the marketplace—particularly in ceramic applications—due to the combination of excellent heat shock and creep resistance properties of the mineral. The increase in pyrophyllite use in the field of ceramics indicates the continuing realization of these marked unique properties. Several new fields of ceramic applications, previously the preserve of high-alumina materials, have been developed on the intrinsic properties of pyrophyllite.

Pyrophyllite is an aluminum silicate with the molecular formula of $Al_2O_34SiO_2H_2O$. It would be more appropriate to group pyrophyllite with such materials as kyanite, diaspore, andalusite, and certain high-alumina clays in relation to its general applications (Stuckey, 1928). These materials all have good heat shock resistance properties at high temperatures and are widely used for the manufacture of refractories. For those reasons they are interchangeable in some applications. Pyrophyllite also has many uses in nonceramic applications, the most important to date being as a substitute for talc in fillers.

The major pyrophyllite mining operations are located in the US, Japan, Korea, Canada, and Australia, where the mineral is widely used as a raw material for general ceramic, mineral filler, and dilutant applications.

* Group Development and Exploration Manager, Steetley Industries Limited, Sydney, Australia.

Commercial Applications

Pyrophyllite was first used in the last century for lining stoves and fireplaces, and also in the carving and polishing of ornamental objects. The rise in industrial demand for new products and applications resulted in the introduction of pyrophyllite as an alternative, mainly for talc and soapstone. Industrial filler applications followed for paint, paper, cosmetics, rubber, pesticides, crayons and pencils, and bleaching soap.

The first use of pyrophyllite in ceramic applications was prior to World War II, in the manufacture of ceramic cladding tiles in the US. This was followed by the production of kiln furniture refractories and whiteware when pyrophyllite was offered by suppliers in North Carolina as an alternative to some local clays.

The largest tonnages of pyrophyllite used today are in refractory linings in steel ladles in Japan, as seen in Table 1. The consumption of pyrophyllite in Japan is second only to clay and chamotte among refractory raw materials used. Recently this technology has been adopted in Australia. Japanese and Australian practice has resulted in appreciable technical and economic benefits, particularly when pyrophyllite is used in combination with zircon. The potential growth for this application is substantial if US and European steelmakers follow.

Investigation and research into the properties of pyrophyllite determined the following main advantages of pyrophyllite-based ceramics: high corrosion resistance for molten iron, steel, and slags; good heat shock resistance; good indices of deformation under load and hot creep resistance (refractories); and increase in mechanical strength of whiteware products promoted by a better distribution of mullite in finished products (also obtained at lower firing temperatures than normally required in production of triaxial ceramics). White cement

TABLE 1—Consumption of Refractory Raw Materials In Japan, t

Fiscal year	Chrome ore	Magnesia clinker	Synthetic magnesia dolomite clinker	Dolomite clinker	Fused Alumina and sintered alumina	Bauxite	Synthetic mullite
1965	72,878	166,494	—	57,588	6,818	22,236	—
1966	82,230	204,474	—	62,023	8,986	31,839	—
1967	94,850	259,079	—	83,216	11,747	41,413	—
1968	73,112	242,738	—	72,412	17,210	59,641	—
1969	78,122	285,046	—	89,303	25,746	63,728	—
1970	84,602	327,196	49,468	64,987	36,207	65,451	24,428
1971	71,331	261,829	66,853	53,470	31,811	58,720	21,777
1972	86,235	311,995	74,928	56,778	45,244	77,767	33,977
1973	94,498	367,713	89,911	49,282	59,641	101,520	45,351
1974	89,860	375,488	79,475	39,930	76,262	96,710	46,684
1975	59,660	315,100	59,030	28,620	74,120	75,120	51,490

Fiscal year	Sillimanite group	Clay and chamotte	Pyrophyllite	Quartzite	Carborundum	Zircon and zirconia	Alumina
1965	18,639	803,896	345,091	154,260	10,750	7,143	9,763
1966	22,363	907,596	378,777	171,156	13,749	9,292	10,687
1967	28,907	1,145,738	478,930	206,542	19,736	17,287	14,866
1968	32,094	1,321,310	515,257	274,164	27,360	24,243	19,093
1969	28,207	1,362,362	589,024	287,168	33,757	37,471	22,546
1970	31,017	1,518,989	673,402	356,423	44,922	49,462	28,554
1971	17,470	1,227,790	628,105	303,015	42,058	52,005	26,089
1972	17,738	1,168,504	649,430	226,520	46,787	79,086	38,833
1973	15,189	1,204,117	700,160	250,180	57,796	106,980	46,890
1974	15,529	1,121,108	636,340	251,710	56,564	105,670	47,393
1975	15,528	839,960	515,600	211,700	48,420	69,600	42,860

Source: Nameishi, 1976.

clinker formulations based on pyrophyllite generally have an advantage of a low iron content when compared with batches made up from silica and clay mixtures. A lower temperature of clinker sintering of batches is possible due to the higher reactivity of the pyrophyllite. White road aggregate made from calcined pyrophyllite rock exhibits high polished stone values (PSV), high aggregate impact values (AIV), and high luminance factors (LF).

These intrinsic properties of pyrophyllite disclosed potential ceramics uses which subsequently have been commercially exploited in industrial countries around the world in contact refractories for lining steel ladles; kiln furniture for tunnel kilns; refractory mortars; ingredients for vitreous china, stoneware, chinaware, and wall tile bodies; manufacture of white cement; calcined pyrophyllite for use in white road-making aggregate; and refractories for use in furnaces, melting ceramic and enamel fritts.

Contact Refractories

In the late 1960s the Japanese steel industry successfully developed ladle lining refractories incorporating Japanese and Korean pyrophyllite. In the 1970s, after receiving confirmation of availability of sufficient reserves of similar grade Australian pyrophyllite, the Australian steel industry decided to fully evaluate refractories based on this material. The successful performance of trial linings in 250-t ladles was reported at the 2nd (1976) Industrial Minerals International Congress in Munich and laid the foundation for the introduction of pyrophyllite ladle bricks into the Australian steel industry. The industrial application of pyrophyllite in ladle linings over the past five years has confirmed two things: first, that linings made from pyrophyllite and pyrophyllite/zircon increase ladle life significantly; and second, that the use of the new refractories gave adequate ladle availability. This in turn saved substantial capital investment for ladle maintenance facilities and reduced overall manpower requirements. In terms of actual performance, these new refractories proved in service that the ladle life increases twofold when lined with pyrophyllite bricks and 4½ times when lined with pyrophyllite/zircon bricks, compared to previously used bloating clay bricks. This was achieved at 75% of the cost per ton of steel produced using the traditional bloating brick.

Refractory plants which had supplied bloating ladle bricks installed new equipment for shaping the pyrophyllite and pyrophyllite/zircon bricks. These are now produced by quick-action friction presses and replace the old and cumbersome process of plastic extrusion followed by a repress. The full details of this development and the introduction of the refractories into steel plant practice were presented at the AIME conference in Detroit (Pauline and Jones, 1979). In fact, this successful introduction of pyrophyllite-based refractories for the steel industry is a confirmation of a similar development which took place ten years ago in Japanese refractory practice (Nameishi, 1976).

Recently Australian Industrial Refractories Ltd., a subsidiary of the Broken Hill Proprietary Co. Ltd. (Australia's largest steel manufacturer), officially opened the Pyrophyllite Zircon Ladle Brick Plant in Newcastle, NSW, with an initial capacity of 27 kt/a of finished brick.

Kiln Furniture

Pyrophyllite initially was used in the preparation of kiln car furniture in the US between 1930 and 1940. Subsequently, with the major progress in development of tunnel kiln technology, pyrophyllite-based tunnel-kiln top car furniture has proven particularly economical in side-fired automated brick kilns. The US and more recently Australia (Kaiser Refractories, Ltd.) are currently major producers of kiln car furniture shapes.

Pyrophyllite is used as the coarse fraction instead of a grog for kiln furniture shapes such as slabs, saggers, blocks, and pins, and has been in continuous and successful use in western industrial countries and ceramic plants producing bricks and whiteware. Many advantages have been confirmed in this field of application, including improved life and greatly lowered maintenance costs; excellent heat shock resistance; low coefficient of thermal expansion (see Fig. 1); minimal shrinkage; high resistance

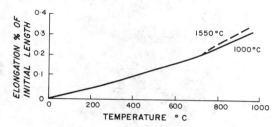

FIG. 1—*Coefficient of thermal expansion.*

to deformation under load; moderate to high PCE (30–32); direct firing of the material without preliminary grog preparation in the processing and manufacture of the kiln car-top furniture (which results in appreciable savings of energy and ancillary processing expenses); and excellent creep resistance when compared with zircon refractory materials (Fig. 2).

Refractory Mortars

Formulations made from fine fractions of pyrophyllite are used for the manufacture of mortar. Such mortars have satisfactory plasticity but low drying and firing shrinkages when compared with clay-based compositions.

Whiteware

Pyrophyllite in stoneware and earthenware bodies including floor tiles, wall tiles, sanitary ware, crockery, and electrical porcelain is in commercial production in Japan and the US and is approaching general introduction to the industry in Australia and the Pacific region. For instance, a series of stoneware compositions was investigated and described in Australia (Taubar et al., 1973; Table 2) confirming early suggestions by Vanderbilt Co. in the US (Table 3). Pyrophyllite lowers the firing temperature, suppresses dunting and cracking, increases whiteness of the bodies, lowers firing shrinkage, and improves thermal shock resistance. Lower maintenance expenses produce cost savings in the slip house and extruding equipment.

White Cement

Pyrophyllite with a low iron content, when used as a component in the manufacture of white cement, assists in maintaining whiteness levels in excess of 90%. This was proven in preliminary laboratory tests where clinkerization processes were successfully achieved. Py-

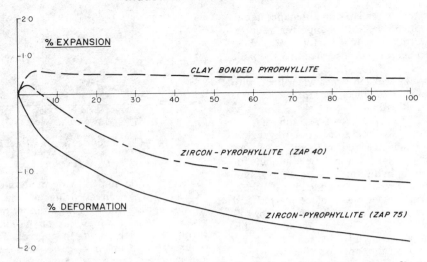

FIG. 2—*100 hr creep test, 1400°C, 2 kg/cm² load. Source: Australian Industrial Refractories, Ltd.*

rophyllite is used in the commercial production of substantial tonnages of white and off-white cement in Japan and is under consideration in Australia.

Safety Road Surface Aggregates

Research has been carried out on the application of calcined pyrophyllite in freeway center stripes, pedestrian crossings, intersection curves, malls, and highly reflective surfaces. The material shows many advantages after calcining the natural crushed rock, among them

high antiskid properties, high polished stone value (PSV), high aggregate impact value (AIV), high luminance factor (LF), lower cost of natural crushed rock over synthetic materials, reduced road lighting costs, and excellent safety silhouette delineation in poor lighting conditions.

Melting Furnaces for Ceramic Glazes

An interesting new and successful use for pyrophyllite is the manufacture of ceramic glazes in melting furnaces. Trials in rotary and

TABLE 2—Chemical and Batch Composition of Pyrophyllite Bodies in Stoneware, Percentages

Body No.	SiO_2	Al_2O_3	Na_2O	K_2O	CaO	Pyrophyllite	Ball Clay	Nepheline Syenite	Potash Feldspar
1N	67.93	28.67	1.85	0.86	0.27	75	10	15	
2N	66.96	28.02	3.00	1.38	0.26	65	10	25	
3N	67.87	28.58	1.88	0.91	0.27	65	20	15	
4N	66.89	27.92	3.03	1.43	0.25	55	20	25	
5N	67.82	28.48	1.90	0.95	0.26	55	30	15	
6N	66.85	27.82	3.06	1.48	0.25	45	30	25	
7N	66.34	27.44	3.66	1.75	0.24	35	35	30	
8N	66.40	27.55	3.62	1.71	0.25	45	25	30	
1F	68.62	27.41	0.79	2.35	0.36	70	10		20
2F	68.33	26.30	1.12	3.45	0.39	60	10		30
3F	68.64	27.32	0.80	2.39	0.35	60	20		20
4F	68.29	26.20	1.14	3.52	0.38	50	20		30
5F	68.60	27.21	0.82	2.45	0.34	50	30		20
6F	68.24	26.08	1.16	3.59	0.37	40	30		30
7F	68.15	25.75	1.29	4.00	0.40	55	10		35
8F	68.06	25.53	1.33	4.14	0.39	35	30		35

TABLE 3—Typical Whiteware Bodies Containing Pyrophyllite

Product	1	2	3	4	5	6	7	8
Flint	10.0		20.0			5.0	8.0	10.0
Feldspar		52.0	3.0	35.0	33.0	20.0	33.0	9.0
HS *Pyrax* pyrophyllite	40.0	16.0	13.0	19.0	22.0	20.0	10.0	27.0
KY-TN Clay Co. No. 4 ball	18.0	7.0	16.0	8.0	10.0	20.0	9.0	10.0
Wade No. 5							10.0	15.0
No. 12 ball				8.0				
KY Clay Mining Co. No. 5 ball			16.0					
KCM					8.0	15.0	6.0	10.0
Cherokee GA kaolin	18.0		25.0	15.0				
Peerless SC kaolin		10.0			10.0	10.0	10.0	18.0
Edgars E.P.K. FL kaolin		15.0		15.0	10.0	10.0		
Harris *Lunday* NC kaolin					7.0		8.0	
Loomis, NY, talc	12.0		6.0					7.0
Whiting	2.0		1.0					
Moore and Munger No. 27, GA							6.0	

Source: R.T. Vanderbilt Co., North Carolina.
1. Wall-tile body, Cone 1 to 5.
2. Floor-tile body, Cone 9 to 10.
3. Earthenware body, Cone 6 to 8.
4. Dry-pressed insular body, Cone 11 to 12.
5. Plastic molded insulator body, Cone 10 to 12.
6. Plastic molded insulator body, Cone 11 to 13.
7. Sanitary-ware body, Cone 11 to 12.
8. Artware body, Cone 1 to 3.

continuous flake melting fritts and furnaces confirm that pyrophyllite/zircon refractories have better corrosion resistance in contact with molten glazes than the previously used aluminosilicate materials and shaped zircon refractories.

Other General Industrial Applications

Paints and Wallboard: Pyrophyllite requires the finest grinding or smallest particle size for use in paints and wallboard. In paint, it acts as low-priced extender of expensive pigments. In wallboard it has the effect of making the plaster flow more smoothly. It also is used as a filler in crack fillers for use with wallboard.

Insecticides: As a dilutant, extender, vehicle, or carrier in agricultural insecticides, finely ground pyrophyllite is excellent. Its practically neutral pH, inertness, good flowability, and nonhygroscopic and fluffy characteristics make it ideal for this purpose. It is compatible with both acid and alkaline poisons. It allows longer storage of prepared insecticides without loss of effectiveness. It readily settles and covers the foliage of the plants. In passing through the blowers of dusting machinery it picks up an electrostatic charge and, with the plants acting as lightning rods, it is attracted to the underside of the leaves, as well as settling onto the surfaces.

Miscellaneous: Finely ground pyrophyllite has also been used in soap, textiles, cosmetics, rubber, composition battery boxes, in welding rod coating, and in numerous other minor usages. An interesting use of South African pyrophyllite (wonderstone) is as a material in the manufacture of high-temperature furnaces for growing diamonds, where high temperature and creep resistance are of primary importance.

Geology

Mineralogy

Pyrophyllite is an hydrated aluminosilicate which has a phyllosilicate sheet or layer structure. This structure consists of two (Si_2O_5) nets between which are interposed a layer of groups of octahedral aluminum cations surrounded by oxygen and hydroxyl anions. The crystalline system of pyrophyllite is monoclinic.

The structural formula of pyrophyllite, $Si_4O_{10}Al_2(OH)_2$, also could be presented in the oxide form $4SiO_2 \cdot Al_2O_3H_2O$. The centidecimal theoretical pure composition of pyrophyllite is SiO_2, 66.7%; Al_2O_3, 28.3%; and H_2O, 5%.

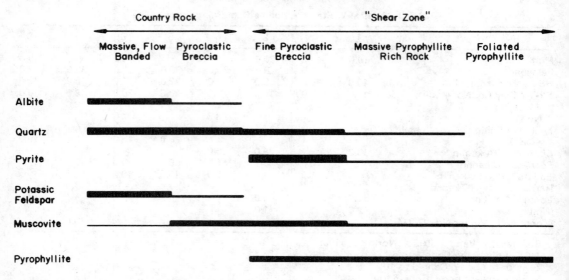

FIG. 3—*Relationship between structural features and mineral assemblages in regionally altered acid volcanics.*

Pyrophyllite ore bodies often contain the following characteristic mineral assemblage: diaspore, corundum, pyrophyllite, kaolinite, alunite, silica (quartz), sericite, and montmorillonite (Iwao, 1953). A diagrammatic representation of Iwao's concept of mineral segregation within hydrothermal deposits derived from volcanic rocks in Japan is given under "Classification of Deposits." The mineral assemblage at Pambula, NSW, Australia is somewhat similar: diaspore, chlorite-cookeite, pyrophyllite, kaolinite, chalcedony (quartz), and sericite.

Diaspore occurs commonly as a minor constituent in most pyrophyllite deposits. Less than 20% of the samples contain diaspore, with minor amounts of kaolinite in the massive pyrophyllite zones.

Chlorite-cookeite occurs near the central shear zone of the ore body where quartz and sericite are virtually absent. Appreciable quantities of chlorite and, to a lesser extent, diaspore are associated with the pyrophyllite. The chlorite has a dioctahedral x-ray diffraction pattern and is characterized by abundant aluminum and a small significant lithium content, and has been identified as the mineral cookeite ($Al_{3.93}$ $Fe_{0.02}Mg_{0.02}Li_{0.81}Al_{0.74}Si_{3.26}O_{10}(OH)_8$).

Pyrophyllite occurs as a solid mass varying in color from green to yellow to white. It has physical properties similar to talc. The mineral has a low hardness and a good mechanical strength.

Kaolinite often occurs in associated shear zones and is probably developed during a retrogressive stage, possibly by the silicification of diaspore but more likely from cookeite through the loss of lithium.

Chalcedony appears throughout pyrophyllite ore bodies as in Australian and Korean deposits, with the exception of the pure pyrophyllite lenses ranging in size from large inclusions of quartz to small grains.

Sericite occurs in solid lensoid masses similar to pyrophyllite and can generally be separated by visual inspection. The percentage of alkalis in sericite lenses is in the range of 0.05 to 5%. Sericite is primarily a potash alkali.

Figs. 3 and 4 show the distribution of the minerals albite, quartz, pyrite, galena, potash, feldspar, muscovite, and pyrophyllite in relation to the degree of alteration taking place in the acid volcanics as described by the mapping of the main zones at Pambula.

Classification of Deposits

A twofold classification of pyrophyllite deposits is evident based on geological mode of occurrence.

Hydrothermal Deposits: These are the most common and are associated with acid-volcanic complexes. Hydrothermal solutions originating within the complex passed along channelways

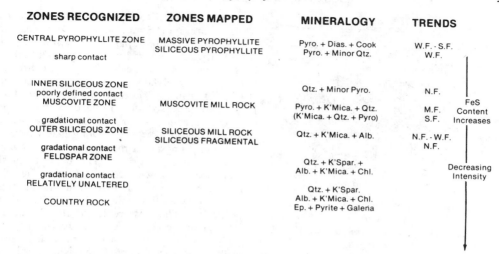

ZONES RECOGNIZED	ZONES MAPPED	MINERALOGY	TRENDS	
CENTRAL PYROPHYLLITE ZONE	MASSIVE PYROPHYLLITE	Pyro. + Dias. + Cook	W.F. - S.F.	
	SILICEOUS PYROPHYLLITE	Pyro. + Minor Qtz.	W.F.	
sharp contact				
INNER SILICEOUS ZONE		Qtz. + Minor Pyro.	N.F.	
poorly defined contact				FeS Content Increases
MUSCOVITE ZONE	MUSCOVITE MILL ROCK	Pyro. + K'Mica. + Qtz.	M.F.	
		(K'Mica. + Qtz. + Pyro)	S.F.	
gradational contact				
OUTER SILICEOUS ZONE	SILICEOUS MILL ROCK	Qtz. + K'Mica. + Alb.	N.F. - W.F.	
	SILICEOUS FRAGMENTAL		N.F.	
gradational contact				
FELDSPAR ZONE		Qtz. + K'Spar. +		Decreasing Intensity
		Alb. + K'Mica. + Chl.		
gradational contact				
RELATIVELY UNALTERED		Qtz. + K'Spar.		
		Alb. + K'Mica. + Chl.		
COUNTRY ROCK		Ep. + Pyrite + Galena		

FIG. 4—*Alteration zones and related mineralogy associations, Pambula, NSW. Foliation for "Trends": S.F. = Strong, M.F. = Moderate, W.F. = Weak, and N.F. = No.*

formed by faults or shears and transformed the country rock from rhyolite or feldspar-quartz to pyrophyllite-quartz. Hydrothermal alteration is indicated by dilution of alkali and iron oxide values and abnormally high lithium oxide values. The Pambula pyrophyllite deposit near Eden, NSW, is such an example.

Figs. 5 and 6 show diagrammatic representation of Iwao's (1953) concept of mineral segregation within hydrothermal deposits derived from hydrothermal rocks in Japan showing an hypothetical erosion surface and subsequent surface-exposed mineralogical relationship.

Metamorphic Deposits: These are less common and are found to be associated with metamorphosed volcanic ashes. Pyrophyllite-schist is developed and typically grades irregularly into other schistose rocks. In this case dilution of K_2O values is difficult to explain in terms of isochemical metamorphism. The recording of pyrophyllite-schist near Peak Hill, NSW, is an example of this metamorphic origin.

Principal Producing Countries

Japan: Pyrophyllite was first discovered in Japan in 1797 on Mount Omotoyama, at the site of the Mitsuishi mine of the Shinagawa Mining Co. In the early 1800s sawn blocks of pyrophyllite were used for carving images and in the manufacture of slate pencils, signature seals, and firebricks. In 1885 deposits in the Mitsuishi district were surveyed by the Imperial Geological Survey, and this work established the existence of abundant reserves of usable quality ore.

The most important pyrophyllite production is in Okayama. This prefecture is near the south coast of southwest Honshu Island, approximately 90 miles west of Osaka. Fifty-seven of the 70 mines in Japan are known to have produced various quantities of pyrophyllite. Of these 57 principal mines, 27 are located in Okayama prefecture.

The largest production from Okayama has been from the Shinagawa-Mitsuishi Ohira, Kawabe, and Kato mines. Significant production has also been recorded from the Shinagawa-Makata, Fukuyama, and Kiyotaki mines in Hyogo prefecture. The Shokozan mine in Hiroshima prefecture has also produced significant quantities of pyrophyllite. In Hiroshima and Hyogo prefectures, massive pyrophyllite deposits in rhyolite and porphyrite include the accessory minerals diaspore, kaolinite, corundum, pyrite, and alunite.

The second important pyrophyllite-producing area in Japan is in Kanzaki gun, Hyogo prefecture. Six mines are known in this area, which is located 70 miles northeast of Okayama.

Three important mines also exist in the Kinosaki gun, Hyogo prefecture. These mines occur between the Okayama and Kanzaki districts, in which the largest reserves of pyrophyllite in the world occur. In 1974, 3.5 Mt of reserves had been estimated in Okayama prefecture, with 33 Mt in Kanzaki gun, Hyogo

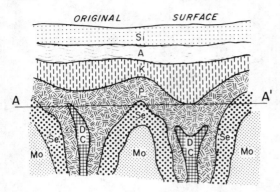

FIG. 5—*Diagrammatic representation of Iwao's concept of mineral segregation within hydrothermal deposits derived from volcanic rocks in Japan. Source: Modified from Iwao (1953).*

prefecture, and 17.5 Mt in Kinosaki gun, Hyogo prefecture.

Reserves of pyrophyllite in Japan were estimated in 1977 to be 179.4 Mt, of which 151.8 Mt was recoverable. In the periods 1965–1970 and 1975–1980 respectively, 92 and 108 pyrophyllite mines were in production in Japan.

The Japanese pyrophyllite deposits were formed by the hydrothermal alteration of porphyry and liparite. In Okayama prefecture pyrophyllite occurs as veins and irregular masses within sedimentary and volcanic rocks. Kaolin accompanies pyrophyllite within the upper parts of the ore bodies, with nodules of diaspore occurring in the central part of the ore mass, and pyrite and marcasite in the lower parts. The deposits were probably formed by the replacement of andesites, shales, agglomerates, rhyolites, and porphyries which were permeated by hot hydrothermal solutions associated with volcanism.

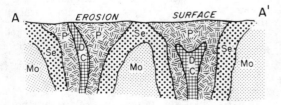

FIG. 6—*Diagrammatic representation of Iwao's concept of mineral segregation. D = diaspore, C = corundum, P = pyrophyllite, K = kaolin, A = alunite, Si = silica, Se = sericite, Mo = montmorillonite. A-A' is a hypothetical erosion surface.*

South Korea: Pyrophyllite is mined in two major areas of South Korea, both near the coast in the southern part of the peninsula. The largest production is from the Wan-Do mine at Haenam. Major mines in the Haenam area are the Sungsan, Hwansan, Okmesan, Dae-Do, and Chin-Do mines. The deposits mined are tabular, and are associated in places with diaspore.

The second major pyrophyllite-producing area in South Korea is at Dong Nae where the Nilyang, Yangsan, Kimhae, Pusan, and Kyongnam mines are worked. The deposits in the Dong Nae area were formed by the alteration of intermediate volcanic rocks including andesite, trachyte, trachytic andesite, and quartz porphyry. The host rocks of the Pusan and Kyongnam mines consist of quartz-porphyry and feldspar porphyry, while trachytic andesite is the host rock in the Dong Nae, Imgi, and Nilyang mines. Pyrophyllite in the Dong Nae area is thought to have been formed by hydrothermal alteration of volcanic rocks by granite intrusives of Cretaceous age, from which hydrothermal solutions filled fissures in tuffs and volcanics. The Yangsan and Un-Yang granite are thought to be the principal mineralizers in the Dong Nae area. In the Haenam area pyrophyllite deposits resulted from fissure-filling tuffs and rhyolites.

The major reserves of pyrophyllite in South Korea are primarily located at Wan-Do, where inferred ore reserves total approximately 30 Mt.

United States: The production of pyrophyllite in the US is limited to the states of North Carolina and California. Annual US production is approximately 100 kt, and reserves of various grades of pyrophyllite are estimated at 1.5 Mt.

Principal production in the US is in Moore and Randolph Counties in North Carolina. Other occurrences in North Carolina are in Granville, Orange, Alamance, and Montgomery Counties. The North Carolina belt actually starts near the Virginia line and extends across the state through South Carolina to Graves Mountain, Georgia. Other occurrences of pyrophyllite in the US have been reported in the South Mountain area of Pennsylvania and in California.

Pyrophyllite occurs in irregular, lenticular, or bedded deposits. The pyrophyllite deposits of North Carolina occur within rhyolite volcanic rocks and form oval or lenticular bodies up to 500 ft wide and several hundred feet long, located within fracture zones. According to Stuckey (1928) the North Carolina deposits were formed through metasomatic replacement

TABLE 4—Chemical Composition of Pyrophyllite-Bearing Rocks from Pioneer Mine Area, Percent

	A*	B*	C*	D*	E†	F
SiO_2	80.13	65.58	77.16	66.74	66.80	66.70
Al_2O_3	11.79	24.07	18.29	26.68	28.20	28.30
Fe_2O_3	0.28	0.38	0.16	0.44	0.14‡	
MgO	0.06	0.45	0.05	0.06	Tr	
CaO	0.74	0.30	0.10	0.05	Tr	
Na_2O	n.d.	n.d.	n.d.	n.d.	0.05	
K_2O	n.d.	n.d.	n.d.	n.d.	Tr	
H_2O	3.10	3.43	3.13	4.65	5.00	5.00
H_2O-	1.00	0.46	0.21	0.16	n.d.	
TiO_2	1.85	0.68	0.65	0.70	0.02	
P_2O_5	0.24	0.07	0.05	0.02	0.06§	
Total	99.19	95.42	99.80	99.50	100.27	100.00

* Eilun H. Kane, analyst.
†Reported by L. M. Richard, "Pyrophyllite in San Diego County, California," *Am. Ceramic Soc. Bull* (Oct., 1935) Vol. 14, p. 353.
‡ Includes 0.04 % MnO.
§Reported as S; P_2O_5 not determined.
A. Silicified and slightly pyrophyllitized dacite.
B. Moderately pyrophyllitized dacite.
C. Pyrophyllite-quartz schist.
D. Pyrophyllite schist.
E. Pyrophyllite schist.
F. Theoretically pure pyrophyllite.

of Precambrian acid tuffs and breccias of both dacitic and rhyolitic composition. Pyrophyllite occurs with quartz and sericite, forming the central part of these lenses and grading outward into impure zones. The bulk of production comes from a few large deposits mined by open-cut and underground methods and used in ceramic filler dilutant and carrier applications.

The other district in the US where pyrophyllite has been produced commercially is in California. Sericitic pyrophyllite is mined in Inyo and San Diego Counties for ceramic applications. The San Diego County pyrophyllite deposit was described by Jahns and Lance (1950). An important deposit called the Pioneer mine occurs in the San Deiguito area northeast of La Jolla and 7½ miles from Escondido, the shipping point by rail. The deposits occur in the Santiago Peak volcanic series, which comprises miscellaneous rocks of Jurassic age. The pyrophyllite deposits, which occur within an area of about one square mile, represent progressive stages in the alteration of the volcanic rocks. Nearly all the pyrophyllite mined has been obtained from open pits in a single mass of high-grade schist 150 ft long and 15 ft wide. Chemical composition of typical material shipped from the Pioneer mine is given in Table 4.

Australia: The main pyrophyllite deposit in Australia is located at Pambula near the deep water port of Eden on the southeast coast of New South Wales. The stratigraphic sequence is described in Fig. 7. An intrusive and extrusive volcanic assemblage formed in an active tectonic environment during the Upper Devonian period provided the basis for extensive hydrothermal activity and burial metamorphism. This hydrothermal activity associated with the volcanism formed irregular and lenticular mineralization, rich in aluminous phases, by the remobilization and the dissipation of the alkali components of the host rock (Taylor, 1978). Suitability of this host rock and structural competence of the volcanic sheet control the geometry and distribution of the deposits, with optimal conditions favoring large, strongly cleaved, broadly altered lensoid bodies (Figs. 8, 9, 10, 11).

It is probable that the mineralization at Pambula originated by a similar process to the zonal distribution of mineralization in the Japanese deposits as explained by Iwao (1953). However, the segregation process of diaspore-pyrophyllite-kaolinite-alunite-silica was achieved

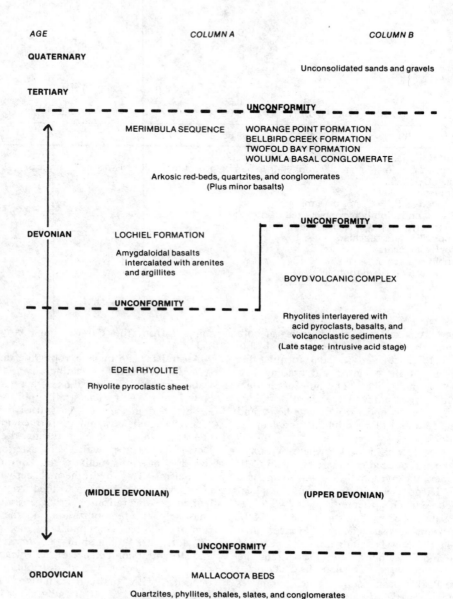

FIG. 7—*Stratigraphy of the Pambula region, NSW, Australia .*

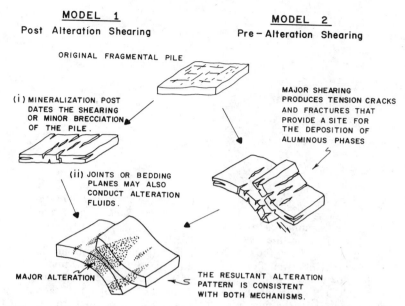

FIG. 8—*Mechanisms of alteration of the Back Creek Deposit, Pambula, NSW.*

through the alteration of lavas and pyroclastic rocks at shallow depth by ascending acid solutions of volcanic and subvolcanic derivation. During ascent the temperature decreased from 600 to 150°C and the solution became progressively more acidic, selectively mobilizing the alkalis which hydrated and laterally giving rise to zones enriched in sericite and montmorillonite. Simultaneously the residue (mainly alumina and silica) reacted with the components of the solution.

Recoverable reserves of all grades of pyrophyllite total approximately 10 Mt, with an estimated additional 20 Mt in place.

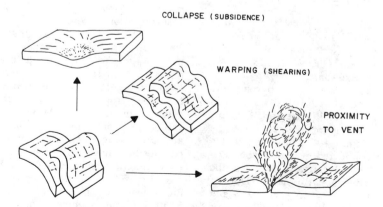

FIG. 9—*Pyroclast bedding irregularities.*

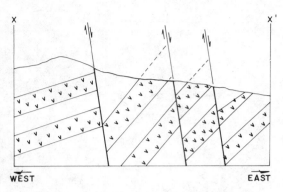

FIG. 10—*Step faulting.*

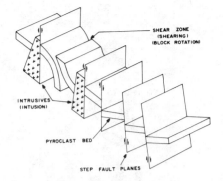

FIG. 11—*Structural features of a portion of the Back Creek Mine Sequence.*

Canada: The only current commercial source of pyrophyllite in Canada is on the Avalon Peninsula of Newfoundland, near the small town of Toxtrap. Pyrophyllite was first extracted in the area in 1904 when a shipment of 1,750 tons was sent to the US. Thereafter production continued intermittently, the most consistent period being 1938–1948 when Industrial Minerals Co. of Newfoundland mined and milled 6,500 tons. However, Newfoundland Minerals Ltd., a wholly owned subsidiary of American Olean Tile Co. Inc. of the US, acquired the operation in 1956. Since then production has been continuous.

The pyrophyllite occurs in a narrow belt running south of Conception Bay in eastern Newfoundland and along the east side of the Precambrian Holyrood granite batholith. It is thought that hydrothermal solutions, moving up via faults and shear zones from the granite, may have recrystallized rhyolitic rocks into the fine-grained assemblage of quartz, sericite, and pyrophyllite. Rhyolitic rocks remote from the granite showed no signs of pyrophyllite mineralization.

Current production from the 450- by 300-m open pit is around 30 to 40 kt/a. The mineralized material is crushed to −7 in. prior to shipping to American Olean's tile plants in Lansdale, PA and Jackson, MS.

A future Canadian source of pyrophyllite may well be the Senneterre deposit located in Carpentier Township, Abitibi region, Quebec, which has been actively prospected since the 1930s. It was not until 1962, however, that a mapping project conducted by the Quebec Department of Natural Resources identified the rock in the shear zone as pyrophyllite. Domtar Ltd. optioned the property between 1964 and 1974. Since then it has been in the hands of Descarreaux & Mousseau Tremblay Inc. of Quebec. The property, which is within the mineral-rich Precambrian Shield area of Canada, has pyrophyllite mineralization in a series of zones associated with sheared metamorphic volcanics and pyroclastics ranging in composition from andesites to rhyolites. Again, a metasomatic origin has been assigned to the deposit. The present owners hope further tests will prove pyrophyllite won from the ore is suitable for present markets.

Some occurrences of pyrophyllite have been reported in western Canada. For example, the northeastern portion of Kyuquot Sound, a small inlet on the west coast of northern Vancouver Island, has been described as a pyrophyllite area. In addition, Mountain Minerals Ltd. of Lethbridge, Alberta, has been actively investigating several pyrophyllite claims in western Canada.

Brazil: The Onca de Pitangui and Pitangui deposits in the state of Minas Gerais and the Santano de Parnaiba deposit in the state of Sao Paulo contain more than 1 Mt measured reserves of pyrophyllite (Table 5). Brazil's vast refractory producer, Magnesita SA, has an output of about 60 kt/a at Belo Horizonte. The entire production is consumed by the company, largely for the manufacture of ladle linings. Finapa Assessoria Commercial Industrial Ltda. of Sao Paulo claims to have a 100 kt/a capacity pyrophyllite mine which supplies the ceramics industry. Cia. Minera Agregados Calcareous SA of Lima, Peru, has been mining and processing a mineral similar in chemical composition and uses to pyrophyllite, although it is mineralogically different. The company has also isolated a large deposit of pyrophyllite—the only one on the Pacific coast of South America—which it hopes to exploit in the near future.

TABLE 5—Brazilian Pyrophyllite Reserves

State	Region	Quantity (tons) Proven	Indicated
Minas Gerais		687,613	310,000
	Onca di Pitangui	434,555	310,000
	Pitangui	253,058	—
Sao Paulo		412,140	—
	Santana do Parnaiba	412,140	—
Total		1,099,753	310,000

Minor Producing Countries

India: Three deposits at Madhya, Aradesh, Rajasthan, and Uttar Pradesh produce a total of approximately 15 kt of pyrophyllite annually.

Argentina: Argentinan pyrophyllite is mined principally from the Juanita del Puerto mine in La Rioja province and is used in the manufacture of electrical porcelain and vitreous enamel. It produces less than 10 kt/a.

South Africa: Pyrophyllite, locally referred to as *wonderstone,* is mined near Ottosdal in the Lichtenburg district. The deposit is of the hydrothermal type and crops out in a series of elongate lenses associated with two lineaments which transgress rhyolite and acid types of the Dominion Reef series of the Witwatersrand System. Table 6 shows the chemical composition of *wonderstone* and indicates that it is not a pure pyrophyllite. The material mined in fact is a metasedimentary rock made up of pyrophyllite (89%), chloritoid, epidote, and rutile. The product, with an average chemical composition of 55.5% SiO_2, 35.24% Al_2O_3, 0.31% MgO, 2.8% TiO_2, and 6.15% loss on ignition, is different from a standard pyrophyllite in having a Mohs hardness of 8. Naturally, the end uses are therefore different, the main ones being bushes for submerged pumps, inserts for sluiceway nozzles, spigots for coal washing plants, and abrasion- and acid-resistant linings for pipes and coal chutes. Sales of wonderstone are handled by Ore and Metal Co. Ltd. of Johannesburg.

Swaziland has been producing small tonnages of pyrophyllite for some years now, particularly from the Usetu area between the Mkhondvo and Great Usutu Rivers. However, production is only on the order of a few hundred tons a year.

Thailand: Minor production of pyrophyllite occurs in central Thailand for general ceramic uses in Southeast Asia. The mining capacity of the Thailand operation is on the order of 12 kt/a. It is apparently limited.

Following is an analysis of the Thailand material.

SiO_2	67.8%
Al_2O_3	22.8%
Fe_2O_3	0.12%
K_2O	0.15%
Na_2O	0.15%
Loss on ignition	6.7%

Mineralogically it is a mixture of pyrophyllite, kaolinite, and diaspore according to X-ray diffraction analysis.

Turkey: Turkey has been a commercial producer of pyrophyllite since 1976 when Endustrie Mineralleri ve Taslari Sanayi (Industrial Minerals of Turkey Ltd.) started up its produc-

TABLE 6—Chemical Composition of Wonderstone

Sample Nos.	1.	2.	3.	4.	5.	6.
Silica (SiO_2)	56.76	55.50	56.71	56.84	54.96	54.20
Alumina (Al_2O_3)	32.39	34.30	33.27	33.57	34.03	34.94
Ferric oxide (Fe_2O_3)	1.54	0.82	1.48	0.75	0.86	1.06
Titanium oxide (TiO_2)	2.80	2.60	2.30	2.25	2.75	2.50
Lime (CaO)	0.25	0.16	0.14	0.07	0.18	0.12
Magnesia (MgO)	0.31	0.28	0.26	0.29	0.13	0.21
Loss on ignition	6.37	6.71	6.15	6.42	7.63	7.40
Total	100.42	100.37	100.31	100.19	100.54	100.43

TABLE 7—Pyrophyllitic Analyses, Turkey

Chemical Analysis	Massive Type, %	Natural Powder, %	Sericete Contaminated (High aluminous type)
Loss on ignition	4.26	5.60	4.23
SiO_2	65.88	61.54	42.70
Al_2O_3	26.39	28.59	43.48
TiO_2	1.00	0.60	0.60
Fe_2O_3	0.60	0.50	0.43
CaO	0.67	0.79	0.45
MgO	0.17	0.78	0.78
K_2O	0.33	0.33	4.66
Na_2O	0.70	1.27	2.67

tion in the Malatya Province of eastern Turkey. Approximately 6 Mt of pyrophyllite are contained in hydrothermally altered dacite tuffs found in lenses scattered over a wide area. Three main grades are mined: a green colored massive block variety; a white soft clay material; and a sericite-contaminated dark green pyrophyllite. The typical chemical compositions are given in Table 7.

Current production is around 3 kt/a, although there are plans for a substantial increase. The entire production is currently being consumed by Canakkale Ceramic Refractories, part owners of Industrial Minerals of Turkey, in its production of wall tiles and cordierite products, and as a natural grog for kiln furniture such as setters, slabs, pins, and posts. There are plans to produce pyrophyllite for the production of pyrophyllite/zircon ladle lining bricks. Later the market for pyrophyllite as a paper filler will be examined.

Exploration

Exploration programs for pyrophyllite are usually conducted in areas where geological evidence indicates that underlying rocks belong to acid-volcanic complexes. Pyrophyllite is found in hydrothermal alteration zones associated with faults or shears which transect these felsic-igneous rocks.

Field Techniques

Aerial photographs are most useful in reducing the area to be explored to a manageable size. This is achieved by plotting on the photographs linear features which may represent faults or shear zones. The geologist then examines each of these lineaments on the ground

and undertakes reconnaissance work along favorable zones.

Pyrophyllite is generally identified in the field by its translucent green color and waxy feel. In addition, outcrops of chalcedonic pyrophyllite tend to be bolder than the enclosing rocks and display a characteristic weathering pattern, whereas outcrops of chloritic pyrophyllite are typically subdued and feature jagged boulders.

When a discovery has been made, drilling or trenching is performed to provide fresh samples for preliminary laboratory evaluation.

Geochemical

The pattern of alteration in pyrophyllite deposits is usually zoned, with a central core of chloritic pyrophyllite surrounded by imperfectly segregated zones of chalcedonic pyrophyllite and sericitic pyrophyllite which grade into unaltered host rocks. Geochemical techniques have been found to be successful in delineating the zonal pattern and defining the margins of the ore body.

Surface samples could be collected on a 10-m² grid basis. In areas of good outcrop conditions, clean representative samples can be obtained without difficulty. However, in areas of poor outcrop conditions shallow drilling or trenching may be necessary.

Contoured plots of alumina and total-alkali values are prepared and superimposed on a geological plan. The results not only define the zonal pattern but also provide a good basis for designing detailed drilling programs. As an example, in the evaluation of the Pambula deposit 3,000 samples, both surface and subsurface, were analyzed for potash alkalis and alumina values. These were used to prepare histogram plots (Figs. 12 and 13) and cumulative frequency distribution curves (Figs. 14 and 15). These plots confirmed the bimodal distribution of both Al_2O_3 and K_2O populations, probably representing both a primary and a secondary alteration phase and two periods of mineralization. The primary mode has a definite positive skew with the greater proportion of the mineralization showing alkali values at less than 0.5% K_2O. The mean values of K_2O and Al_2O_3 suggest a composition for the pyrophyllite mineralization occurring during the primary alteration phase of 12.7% Al_2O_3 and 0.57% K_2O.

Fig. 16 is a bivariate scattergram depicting grade lines and sample frequency distribution based on Al_2O_3 v. K_2O plots.

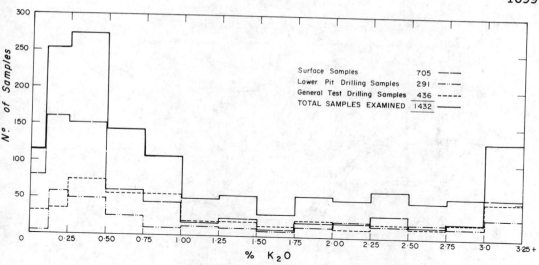

FIG. 12—*K₂O distribution curves—histograms.*

Drilling

Two kinds of drilling operations generally apply to pyrophyllite exploitation, diamond drilling and percussion drilling.

Diamond drilling provides core samples to enable the geologist to predict the subsurface behavior of the ore body and to find and correlate the zonal pattern determined from surface observations. Diamond drill holes are usually inclined at low angles and designed to penetrate the entire width of the steep dipping ore bodies.

Percussion drilling is carried out as a forerunner to production operations for detailed grade evaluation. Vertical holes are usually drilled on a square grid spacing of between 1 and 3 m and chip samples are collected at 1- or 2-m intervals to depths of up to 10 m. Compressed air raises drill chips to the surface

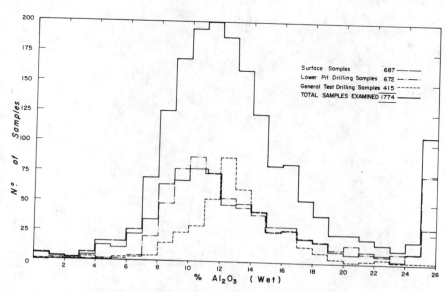

FIG. 13—*Al₂O₃ distribution curves—histograms.*

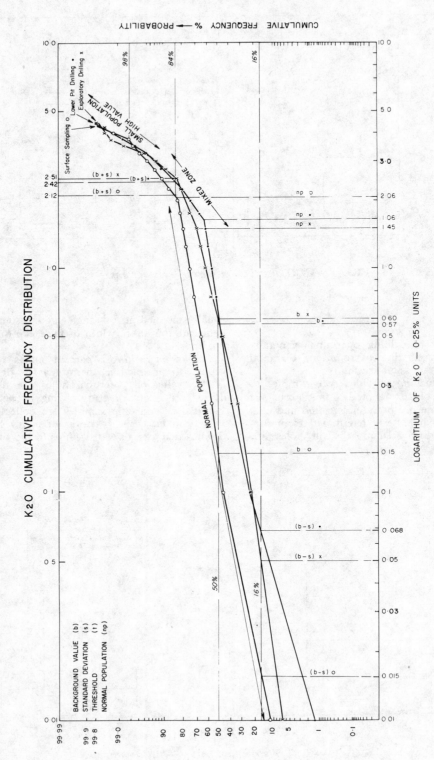

FIG. 14—K₂O cumulative frequency distribution.

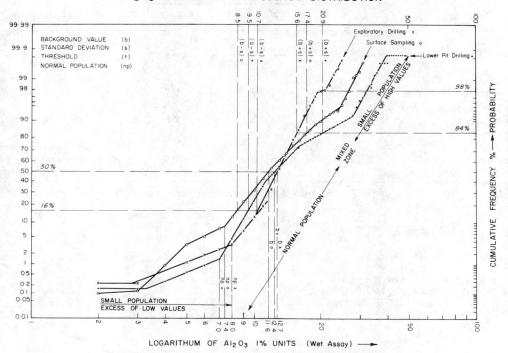

FIG. 15—*Al₂O₃ cumulative frequency distribution.*

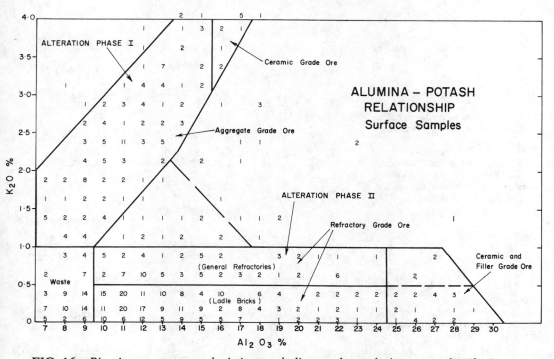

FIG. 16—*Bivariate scattergram depicting grade lines and sample frequency distribution.*

TABLE 8—Main Grades and Broad Specifications of Australian Pyrophyllite

Raw Material	Specification (%)			Application
	Al$_2$O$_3$	K$_2$O	Fe$_2$O$_3$	
Chloritic pyrophyllite	24-28	0.2-0.5	0.2	Paint filler Plastics filler Rubber filler
Chalcedonic pyrophyllite*	13-15	0.2-0.5	0.4	Contact refractories
Chalcedonic-sericitic pyrophyllite*	15-20	0.4-0.8	0.5	Tunnel kiln furniture
Sericitic pyrophyllite	18-22	0.5-3.0	0.5	Whiteware ceramics, floor tiles, electrical porcelain

Typical Australian Product Specifications

Contact Refractories

Metallurgical and steel industries

The chemical analysis specification occurs in the range Al$_2$O$_3$ 14-20% Na$_2$O and K$_2$O less than 0.5% and a typical analysis is as per the specification.

	Specification
PCE	28-30
Al$_2$O$_3$	15.80%
SiO$_2$	78.50%
Fe$_2$O$_3$	0.38%
Na$_2$O	0.11%
K$_2$O	0.24%
CaO	0.30%
MgO	0.12%
TiO$_2$	0.39%
LOI	3.90%

Size Range	
1.5 cm	) ± 30#
1.0 cm	) & fines
10#	)

Thermal Properties	Dilatometric curves of fired pyrophyllite PCE Cone 31 (Min 2)
Sp Gr	2.65

Tunnel Kiln Furniture

Kiln car furniture, girder blocks, slabs, decks, pins, saggers, etc.

Typically for this application, the analysis would fall in the range Al$_2$O$_3$ 18-20% and total alkalis approx. 1%. A typical analysis is as per the specification.

PCE	30-32
Al$_2$O$_3$	20.60%
SiO$_2$	73.90%
Fe$_2$O$_3$	0.45%
Na$_2$O	0.12%
K$_2$O	0.44%
LOI	4.30%
Sp Gr	2.65

Size Range	
	10# + fines
	30# + fines

Thermal Properties	Dilatometric curves of fired pyrophyllite PCE Cone 31

Refractory Mortars

General duty air setting refractory mortars.

PCE	28-32
Al$_2$O$_3$	20.60%
SiO$_2$	73.90%
Fe$_2$O$_3$	0.45%
Na$_2$O	0.12%
K$_2$O	0.44%

TABLE 8—Continued

Typical Australian Product Specifications—Continued

Specification

	Size		10# + fines
Whiteware	PCE		16-33
	Al_2O_3	22.0%	28.20%
Applications stoneware, earthenware,	SiO_2	70.0%	65.80%
floor tiles, wall tiles, sanitary	Fe_2O_3	0.5% max.	0.11%
ware, electrical porcelain.	Na_2O	0.5% max.	0.10%
	K_2O	2.0%	0.04%
	CaO	0.3% max.	0.01%
	MgO	0.2% max.	0.01%
	TiO_2	0.5% max.	0.18%
	LOI	4.0%	5.10%

PCE Cone 16   33
Sp Gr   2.70   2.80

Screen Analysis:
−100# + 200#	Trace
−200# + 300#	0.30%
−300#	99.70%

Thermal Properties:
Dilatometric curves of fired
pyrophyllite (PCE Cone 33).

White Cement

Al_2O_3	15-20%
Fe_2O_3	10-20%

For use in manufacture of *White Cement*
a low iron pyrophyllite component can
achieve the necessary specifications

Safety Road Surface Aggregate

Freeway stripes, pedestrian crossings, intersections, curves, malls, and general high reflective surfaces.
The material obtains the following properties after calcining the natural crushed rock: high antiskid
properties; high PSV; high AIV; high luminance factor; lower cost of using natural crushed rock over
synthetic materials; reduced road lighting costs; excellent safety silhouette lighting.

Source of Silica and Alumina

A range of applications exist in the manufacture of fiberglass and asbestos cement.

Pyrophyllite may be a successful alternative to any application which requires either silica or alumina,
or both, as raw material components.

Mineral Fillers	Al_2O_3	28.20%
	SiO_2	65.80%
Filler in rubber, plastics, paints,	Fe_2O_3	0.22%
cosmetics, and general replacement	Na_2O	0.10%
for talc.	K_2O	0.04%
	CaO	0.28%
	MgO	0.01%
	TiO_2	0.18%
	LOI	5.10%

TABLE 8—Continued

Typical Australian Product Specifications—Continued

	Specification
Brightness	80-90
Water Absorption	50%
Sp Gr	2.74
Size range	Various
Screen Analysis:	
−300#	99.70%
−200# + 300#	0.30%
−100# + 200#	Trace

* Chalcedonic and chalcedonic-sericite pyrophyllite are often referred to as refractory-grade material and must be low in K_2O and Fe_2O_3. Requirements for this grade are most rigid.

and into a cyclone where they are removed from the airstream and discharged into a sample collecting tube.

Evaluation of Deposits

Specifications

A variety of grades is available from each deposit. Grade classification takes account of market requirements on the one hand and mineralogy of the ore on the other. Ore is graded according to its pyrophyllite mineral content and the nature of abundance of other minerals in the ore. Mineralogy is determined indirectly by chemical analysis, principally for Al_2O_3, K_2O, and Fe_2O_3 contents. The main grades and specifications of Australian pyrophyllite from Pambula are listed in Table 8 and described in detail. Analyses of pyrophyllite from North Carolina showing the relationship between chemical analysis, mineralogy, and grades are shown in Table 9.

Testing

Physical Tests: When pyrophyllite is being considered for refractory use, samples are tested for refractoriness (PCE) in firing trials at a range of temperatures using subsequent dilatometric methods.

Chemical Tests: Routine analysis of the major components is carried out on samples generated during both exploration and production phases.

Evaluation

Grades and reserves are calculated by conventional geological techniques and the results used to optimize quarry design.

Preparation for Markets

Mining Methods

Pyrophyllite is usually mined by conventional open-pit methods, employing the most modern types of mining, earthmoving, and bulk handling equipment. Some underground mining operations remain in production in North Carolina. Open-pit operations commence with clearing of trees and natural vegetation. Topsoil is removed and carefully stockpiled for use during site rehabilitation. Standard drilling and blasting techniques are used to establish and develop pit faces according to a predetermined quarry design. Pit faces usually range from 6 to 10 m high and benches vary from 4 to 8 m wide.

Ore blasted onto the quarry floor can be sorted not only according to size (because oversize rock must be redrilled and blasted), but also according to grade from preliminary visual sorting. Lump pyrophyllite ore is generally hauled to the processing plant by road trucks.

The following is a history of developed mining techniques as described by Chappell (1960).

Early mining methods consisted of conventional open cuts. As quality requirements and product control became more exacting, and as the pits were deepened, it was found necessary to go to underground operations, or to extremely deep open pits.

The oldest Glendon operations were started as open pits, later turned into underground mining, and later reverted to open pit operations, which are presently being operated by the Glendon Pyrophyllite Co. Standard Mineral Co. also has an open-pit operation at Glendon adjacent to the other operations.

The Standard Mineral Co.'s operations at

Robbins have been principally underground for number of years. Standard also operates open its in this same area. The underground operations consist of shafts, drifts, and crosscuts to each the ore. The main drifts are driven in the footwall side of the deposit, with crosscuts through the ore body. The crosscuts are expanded to open square-set stopes. Broken ore is loaded from square-set stopes through chutes into mine cars and conveyed by battery locomotives to the shaft, where it is hoisted in a skip directly to the crushing plant. When extraction in a stope progresses near the level above, the stope is caved, in order to provide support to the pillars on either side.

The mine at Staley, known as the Gerhardt mine when first opened and currently being operated by the Carolina Pyrophyllite Co., was started with a tunnel and raise. The top of the raise was widened into a glory hole. As extraction progressed, this operation grew into a very large open quarry.

The Snow Camp mine operated by the North State Pyrophyllite Co. is operated exclusively as an open pit mine, the product going to North State's own refractory.

Processing

Many processing methods apply to pyrophyllite and each operation has a processing plant layout based on its individual ore characteristics and local market requirements. Nonetheless, the principal processing methods comprise crushing and screening to provide a series of size fractions.

Flowsheets from pyrophyllite processing plants of Steetley at Pambula, NSW, Australia, and North State Pyrophyllite at Hillsboro and Standard Mineral Co. at Robbins, North Carolina are shown in Figs. 17, 18, and 19.

Strict quality control is essential during processing because pyrophyllite ore commonly consists of a mixture of soft pyrophyllite mineral and relatively harder chalcedony and, during crushing and screening, the softer pyrophyllite tends to become concentrated in the finer size fractions.

Transportation

Pyrophyllite is a commodity of relatively low unit value and, therefore, the cost of transportation to market is an important consideration. Products are generally transported by road in bulk tipper-trucks and by rail and ship in bulk carriers. Often bulk milled pyrophyllite is freighted in road and rail tankers.

Consumption of Pyrophyllite

Most major present production and consumption areas lie in the Pacific Basin region where the principal consuming industries are located in the refractories and ceramics fields. The main exception is the industry in the northeastern US, which is dependent on supplies of pyrophyllite from North Carolina and Newfoundland.

TABLE 9—Analysis of Pyrophyllite from North Carolina, US

Constituent	Composition, %.						
	(1) *	(2) *	(3) *	(4) *	(5) *	(6) †	(7) ‡
Silica	76.32	73.50	70.26	69.90	69.38	83.34	77.22
Alumina	19.80	22.53	24.95	25.13	26.02	13.93	15.95
Iron	0.18	0.09	0.08	0.07	0.08	0.13	0.35
Calcium	0.14	0.08	0.16	0.16	0.14	0.42	Tr
Magnesium							
Potash	0.27		0.13	0.00	0.00	0.00	3.54
Soda	0.07	0.06	0.31	0.08	0.24	0.18	0.93
Loss	3.44	3.95	4.32	4.67	4.50	2.20	2.08
Total	100.22	100.21	100.21	100.01	100.36	100.24	100.07
Pyrophyllite	66	79	85	88	89	48	5
Quartz	31	21	12	11	9	51	57
Sericite	3		3	1	2	1	38

* Pyrophyllite
† With granular quartz
‡ Sericite

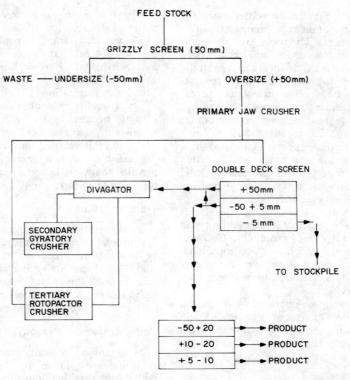

FIG. 17—*Flowsheet for the crushing and screening of pyrophyllite from Pambula pyrophyllite deposit, Australia.*

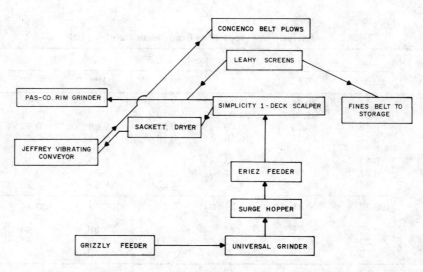

FIG. 18—*Flowsheet of automated grinding plant at North State Pyrophyllite Co., Greensboro, NC.*

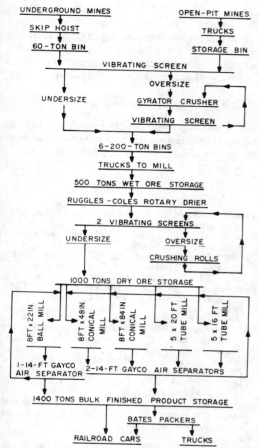

FIG. 19—*Flowsheet, Standard Mineral Co., Inc., Robbins, NC.*

Separate production statistics for pyrophyllite have seldom been available, because production figures are commonly incorporated in the statistics for talc. Nonetheless it is evident that Japan is the leading producer with about 70% of world production, followed by South Korea and the US with about 14 and 6%, respectively, of world production. Four countries—Australia, Brazil, Canada, and India—produce between 1 and 5% of world production, and five countries—Argentina, Peru, South Africa, Thailand, and Turkey—produce less than 1% of world production. World production is shown in Table 10.

Pacific Markets for Pyrophyllite

The production of pyrophyllite has shown steady increases over the last decade and world consumption now totals almost 2 Mt/a. Japan is the world's leading producer and consumer of pyrophyllite and approximately 1.5 Mt/a are used for various refractory and ceramic applications.

In Japan, recoverable pyrophyllite ore reserves in 1978 stood at 60 Mt. However only a very limited percentage of these reserves are suitable in the application of refractories to the steel industry. Thus Japan is becoming increasingly dependent on the external supply of higher quality pyrophyllite with the consequence that imports of Korean pyrophyllite are running in excess of 150 kt/a.

Korean pyrophyllite production approached 400 kt/a in 1980, placing Korea among the top three world producers.

TABLE 10—World Production of Pyrophyllite, 1971-1976 (t)

	1971	1972	1973	1974	1975	1976
Argentina	7,263	8,325	6,313	5,412	8,357	NA
Australia	1,577	8,288	7,804	11,478	13,589	10,320
Brazil	6,356	33,136	40,058	45,813	65,778	NA
India	11,780	15,086	14,912	15,562	14,994	14,807 *
Japan	1,434,286	1,365,131	1,372,834	1,396,184	1,073,111	NA
South Korea[†]	142,335	163,396	304,842	238,418	223,000	349,000
Peru	4,528	8,944	8,343	10,968	NA	NA
Thailand	50	1,550	9,550	1,640	10,300	NA
Turkey	—	—	—	—	—	3,000
South Africa[‡]	3,333	2,059	4,743	8,510	6,782	5,784
Swaziland	204	108	126	36	—	NA
USA	91,653	NA	NA	95,892	83,364	NA

Source: Institute of Geological Sciences, Mineral Statistics and Economics Unit, London, U.K.
Canada averages 30 to 40 kt/a.
NA—not available.
* Jan.-July only.
[†] Includes the following output of *agalmatolite* (a massive pyrophyllite): 1973-224 kt; 1974-205 701 t; 1975-196 239 t; 1976-108 025 t.
[‡] Wonderstone.

Production and sales of pyrophyllite in the US have remained fairly static over the period 1970 and 1980 at approximately 100 kt/a. The main production is primarily limited to five mining operations in North Carolina with intermittent production in California.

15% Al_2O_3 are often superior to high alumina clay linings in certain applications. The superior creep performance at high temperatures of pyrophyllite refractories may make it a suitable substitute for products manufactured from kyanite, andalusite, and calcined bauxite.

Substitutes

High alumina products are not necessarily the best choice for many refractory applications as previously had been perceived. Pyrophyllite brick linings containing approximately

Future Considerations and Trends

The use of pyrophyllite in its industrial application is increasing and the mineral stands on its own performance. New uses will continue to be found.

Bibliography

Bowman, R., and Tauber, E., 1979, "Potential Applications of Two High Grade Kaolinitic Clays and a Pyrophyllite Deposit," *Journal Australian Ceramic Society*, Vol. 15, No. 1, pp. 5–8.

Chappell, F., 1960, "Pyrophyllite," *Industrial Minerals and Rocks*, 3rd ed., J. L. Gillson, ed., AIME, NY, pp. 681–686.

Cornish, B.E., 1980, "Australian Pyrophyllite and Its Growing Influence in the World Markets," 4th Industrial Minerals International Congress, Atlanta, Georgia, pp. 179–184.

Cornish, B.E., Tauber, E., and Nichol, D., 1980, "Pambula Pyrophyllite: Production and Applications," *Proceedings*, 9th Australian Ceramic Conference, pp. 132–134.

Fergusson, C.L., et al., 1979, "The Late Devonian Boyd Volcanic Complex, Eden, N. S. W.: A Reinterpretation," *Journal Geological Society Australia*, Vol. 26, pp. 87–105.

Harben, P., 1978, "Pyrophyllite Stands on Its Own," *Industrial Minerals*, No. 129, June, pp. 19–25.

Iwao, S., 1953, "Ceramic Minerals of Japan," Society Mineral Geology, Japan, Vol. 1, No. 2, pp. 105–124.

Jahns, R.H., and Lance, J.F., 1950, "Geology of the San Dieguito Pyrophyllite Area, San Diego County, Calif.," Special Report 4, California Div. Mines, 32 pp.

Jolly, W.T., and Smith, R.E., 1971, "Degredation and Metamorphic Differentiation of the Keweenawan Tholeiitic Lavas of Northern Michigan, U. S. A., *Journal of Petrology*, Vol. 13, Part 2, pp. 273–309.

Lipman, P.W., et al., 1972, "Cenozoic Volcanism and Plate Tectonic Evolution of the Western United States," Phil. Trans. Royal Society, London, A., pp. 217–248, 271.

Loughnan, F.C., and Steggels, K.R., 1976, "Cookeite and Diaspore in the Back Creek Pyrophyllite Deposit near Pambula, N. S. W.," *Mineralogical Magazine*, Vol. 40, pp. 765–772.

Nameishi, N., 1976, "Recent Status of Steel Plant Refractories in Japan," XIX International Refractory Colloquium, Aachen, Germany, pp. 209–271.

O'Brien, R.J., and Tauber, E., 1976, "The Uses of Zircon in Steel Ladle Linings," 2nd Industrial Minerals International Congress, Munich, Germany.

Parsons, W.H., 1969, "Criteria for the Recognition of Volcanic Breccias: Review," *Memoir 115* L. Larson et al., ed., Geological Society of America, pp. 263–304.

Pauline, M., and Jones, R., 1979, "Zircon-Pyrophyllite—An Economical Steel Ladle Refractory," AIME Conference, Detroit, March.

Pepplinkhouse, H.J., and Tauber, E., 1976, "The Formation of Mullite from Kaolin-Gibbsite and Pyrophyllite-Gibbsite Mixtures," *Journal Australian Ceramic Society*, Vol. 13, No. 1.

Phillips, B.L., 1976, "Synthetic Aggregates for Road Surfaces," *Proceedings*, 8th ARRB Conference, Vol. 8, No. 1, p. 1.

Smith, R.E., 1968, "Redistribution of the Major Elements in the Alteration of Some Basic Lavas During Burial Metamorphism," *Journal of Petrology*, Vol. 9, Part 2, pp. 195–219.

Stuckey, J.L., 1928, "The Pyrophyllite Deposits of North Carolina," North Carolina Department of Conservation and Development *Bulletin*, Vol. 37, 62 pp.

Tauber, E., et al., 1973, "Stoneware Bodies Based on Pyrophyllite," *Journal Australian Ceramic Society*, Vol. 9, No. 2, pp. 47–51.

Tauber, E., et al., 1974, "Earthenware Tile Body Based on Pyrophyllite and Orthophosphoric Acid," *Journal Australian Ceramic Society*, Vol. 19, pp. 46–49.

Tauber, E., et al., 1976a, "Development of a China (Porcelain) Body from Australian Minerals," *Interceram*, Vol. 26, p. 211.

Tauber, E., et al., 1976b, "Replacement of Silica by Pyrophyllite in Vitreous China Products," *Interceram*, Vol. 25, p. 195.

Tauber, E., and Pepplinkhouse, H.J., 1972, "Ceramic Properties of Pyrophyllite from Pambula N.S.W.," *Journal Australian Ceramic Society*, Vol. 8, No. 3, pp. 62–64.

Taylor, J.R.P., 1978, "Pambula Eden Regional Geology," Unpub. Thesis, Monash University, Melbourne, Australia.

Wall, V.J., 1976, "Gold and Pyrophyllite Mineralization in the Devonian Acid Volcanics of the Yalwal-Eden Belt," *Bulletin*, Australian Society Exploration Geophysics, Vol. 7, No. 1.

Wall, V.J., and Kesson, S., 1969, "Pyrophyllite Bearing Rocks in a Regionally Altered Volcanic Sequence," *Abstracts*, Part 7, Geological Society Australia, 232 pp.

Rare Earths and Thorium

SPENCER S. SHANNON, JR.*

The lanthanide elements from lanthanum (atomic number 57) to lutetium (71) plus yttrium (39) are called the rare-earth elements; scandium (21) is chemically similar to yttrium and the lanthanides, but differs in occurrence. The rare-earth metals were divided into three categories by the chemist, Berzelius, in the early 1800s; however, modern usage defines only two groups. The cerium group is named after the most abundant element and comprises lanthanum (57), cerium (58), praseodymium (59), neodymium (60), promethium (61), samarium (62), europium (63), and gadolinium (64). Traces of natural promethium were discovered in apatite in Finland (Erametsa, 1965). The yttrium group, also named after its most abundant representative, comprises terbium (65), dysprosium (66), holmium (67), erbium (68), thulium (69), ytterbium (70), and lutetium (71). Yttrium most closely resembles holmium in chemical properties, and occurs most commonly with the heavy lanthanides. The rare-earth minerals may be divided into cerium-group, yttrium-group, or mixed-group classes.

A number of rare-earth minerals contain thorium and uranium, but these are variable in content and are not essential to the composition of the minerals. In monazite, a mineral that is a principal source of rare earths, the worldwide average content of thorium oxide is 7.2%; however, varieties of monazite contain as little as 0.001% and as much as 31.5% thoria. Monazite is the chief ore of thorium and, until recently, thorium has been the main product; the rare-earth metals were in fact byproducts. However, because of the great demand for rare-earth metals by the petroleum refining and the iron and steel industries since the early 1970s, the roles have been reversed so that thorium is now the byproduct.

Uses

A 9 to 1 mixture of yttrium and thorium oxides is used for high-intensity incandescent lamps and for high-temperature-resistant windows and lenses. Yttrium oxysulfide and orthovanadate, doped with europium oxide, are used in color television tube phosphors. Yttrium, as well as cerium, praseodymium, and samarium, is alloyed with cobalt to form strong permanent magnets. It hardens magnesium alloys and retards the oxidation of iron-chromium alloys. Yttrium-iron garnets are used for transmitting low microwave frequencies. Yttrium-aluminum garnets are used as host crystals for lasers and as artificial gems. Yttria also forms strong, stable, high-temperature refractories. Gadolinium-gallium garnets are used in substrate wafers on which bubble-memory films are deposited.

Rare-earth chlorides, particularly of lanthanum, neodymium, and praseodymium, are used as catalysts for petroleum cracking. Mischmetal is used for lighter flints and to improve the ductility and impact strength of iron and steel alloys. Mischmetal also reduces the fatigue resistance of magnesium and aluminum alloys. Rare-earth oxides are used for polishing glasses and lenses. Individual or specific combinations of high-purity oxides are used as additives in glass to maintain or change its color, dispersion, or refractive index. High-purity oxide combinations are also used to color tile and to opacify porcelain enamel. Rare-earth fluorides and oxides are used in carbon-arc electrodes to provide incandescent white light. Lanthanum or gadolinium oxysulfide phosphors, activated with terbium, are used as x-ray screen intensifiers. Hydrogen can be stored by sorption on lanthanum-nickel alloys (Anon., 1979).

Thorium[232] is bombarded with slow neutrons in breeder reactors to create fissionable thorium[233] for nuclear fuel cells. The 330-MW, high-temperature gas-cooled reactor at Fort St.

---

* Staff Geologist, Los Alamos National Laboratory, Los Alamos, NM.

Vrain, CO, is an example of this process in operation. An experimental light-water breeder reactor at Shippingport, PA, uses a thorium-uranium[233] fuel system to generate electricity.

The chief nonenergy use for thorium is in the manufacture of Welsbach incandescent gas mantles. From 20 to 40% thorium is used in thorium-magnesium hardener alloys for making magnesium alloys containing 2 to 3% thorium. Addition of small amounts of thorium oxide to metals such as nickel and tungsten increases their strength and resistance to corrosion.

Product Specifications

Commonly, monazite concentrates must contain at least 55% rare-earth oxides. The specifications for particular rare-earth metals and oxides depend upon their intended uses, complicated by the cost and difficulty of totally separating specific elements. Requirements for production chemicals are comparatively low, but standards are more stringent for specific purposes. Rare-earth oxides, from which most of the cerium oxide has been removed, are referred to commercially as didymium oxide. Mischmetal, a mixture of rare-earth metals, can be cerium-free or contain as much as half cerium.

Thoria or thorium for use in atomic reactors must have a purity of 99.9%. Furthermore, either must contain less than 1 ppm of boron, cadmium, dysprosium, europium, gadolinium, and samarium, which absorb high-energy neutrons. Standard metallurgical-grade thoria must contain at least 99.8% ThO_2. The standard specification for high-purity yttrium is 99.9%.

Prices

In 1980, the nominal price for monazite concentrates was $0.34 per lb of contained rare-earth oxides. Calcined bastnaesite concentrates sold for $0.90 per lb of contained rare-earth oxides. Prices of high-purity rare-earth oxides and metals in 1979 are shown in Table 1. Thorium oxide was quoted at $17.27 per lb as of Jan. 1, 1981 (Kirk, 1980b).

Geology

Mineralogy

Rare-earth and thorium minerals occur chiefly in association with alkalic plutons and in placers derived from them. Commonly, cerium- or yttrium-group lanthanide elements

TABLE 1—Prices of High Purity Oxides and Metals in 1979*

Element	Oxide, $/kg	Metal, $/kg
Cerium	18	108
Dysprosium	100	270
Erbium	120	450
Europium	1,650	6,500
Gadolinium	120	430
Holmium	375	1,100
Lanthanum	17	108
Lutetium	4,200	13,200
Neodymium	65	250
Praseodymium	110	290
Samarium	110	280
Terbium	825	2,000
Thorium[†]	26	33
Thulium	2,650	7,000
Ytterbium	180	720
Yttrium	74	320

* Moore, 1980a.
[†] Kirk, 1980a.

partially or wholly replace calcium in minerals such as fluorite and apatite.

Discussion of specific minerals will be restricted to those that have been mined for their rare-earth or thorium content in the past. Other exotic minerals are cited by Parker and Baroch (1971).

Monazite (Ce-La-Nd-Pr phosphate) and bastnaesite (Ce-La-Nd-Pr fluorcarbonate) are the chief minerals in rare-earth and thorium ores. Other ore minerals of local significance include yttrofluorite and two phosphates, xenotime and apatite; two silicates, cerite and gadolinite; and various multiple oxides such as betafite, brannerite, euxenite, fergusonite, and samarskite. Although thorite and thorianite, the silicate and oxide of thorium, contain more thorium than monazite, they are less important commercial sources of that metal.

Monazite contains rare earths of the cerium group, plus an average of 7.2% thorium and minor yttrium. It is a yellowish to reddish brown monoclinic mineral having both a hardness and a specific gravity of 5. It occurs in commercial concentrations in beach and stream placers and in lesser amounts in veins. It also occurs as an accessory mineral in igneous and metamorphic rocks.

Bastnaesite contains as much as 75% rare-earth oxides of the cerium group. It is a light yellow to brown hexagonal mineral having a hardness of 4.5 and a specific gravity of 5. It occurs chiefly in carbonatite plutons and subordinately in veins, pegmatites, and skarns.

Yttrofluorite and yttrocerite, the yttrium- and cerium-group analogs of fluorite, occur in pegmatites. Xenotime is an yttrium-group phosphate that occurs in igneous and metamorphic rocks, pegmatites, and placers. It is a pale yellow to brownish green tetragonal mineral having both a hardness and specific gravity of 4.5. Rare-earth elements replace part of the calcium in some apatite, particularly in some carbonatite plugs, alkalic magnetite deposits, and marine phosphate deposits.

Cerite is a brown to gray, calcium, cerium-group hydroxyl silicate, having a hardness of 5.5 and a specific gravity of 4.9. It occurs in carbonatites, pegmatites, and skarns. Gadolinite is a ferrous, beryllium, yttrium-group orthosilicate. It is a brown to black monoclinic mineral having a hardness of 6.7 and a specific gravity of 4.4 which occurs chiefly in pegmatites.

Multiple oxide minerals occur chiefly as brown to black, heavy (4.0 to 5.7), hard (4.5 to 6.5), radioactive, metamict minerals in pegmatites, alkalic igneous rocks and related veins, and placers. The five commercial minerals (betafite, brannerite, euxenite, fergusonite, and samarskite) are niobate-tantalate-titanates. Samarskite, however, is low in titanium, while brannerite contains titanium only. All contain uranium, and all but betafite contain appreciable thorium and yttrium-group rare earths. Betafite, brannerite, and euxenite contain calcium, while brannerite and samarskite contain iron. Euxenite and samarskite also contain cerium-group rare earths; fergusonite and samarskite contain erbium.

Both thorite and thorianite are radioactive and have a hardness of 5 to 5.5. Thorite is a reddish brown to black analog of zircon, whereas thorianite is a heavy isometric dark gray to black mineral.

Classification of Deposits

Rare-earth and thorium deposits have an ultimate genetic relation to alkalic igneous rocks, especially carbonatites. For example, in the Iron Hill district of Gunnison County, CO, such ores are found in association with a late carbonatite pluton and in the veins that fill the fractures that accompanied its emplacement (Armbrustmacher, 1980). The bastnaesite-rich carbonatite pluton at Mountain Pass, CA, was overlooked until 1949 (Olson et al., 1954). Carbonatite stocks, therefore, are excellent exploration targets for large deposits of rare-earth and thorium ores in economic concentrations.

Rare-earth elements also occur both as discrete minerals and in apatite in association with high-temperature, metamorphic, nontitaniferous magnetite deposits. The large contact metasomatic rare-earth-bearing iron ore deposits at Bayan Obo in Inner Mongolia adjoin an alkalic granitic pluton (Argall, 1980). Bastnaesite and monazite are important accessory minerals associated with hematite, magnetite, and martite. Rare-earth concentrates are coproducts derived from the beneficiation of iron ores of this type. Less commonly, rare-earth minerals such as allanite can occur in economic concentrations in skarns, such as at the Mary Kathleen mine in Queensland (Parker and Baroch, 1971).

Economic amounts of thorite, monazite, bastnaesite, and xenotime have been found in veins in a few places. Thorite occurs in veins in the Lemhi Pass district of Idaho (Staatz, 1979). Thorite also occurs in veins associated with alkalic plutons in the Iron Hill district and the Wet Mountains of Colorado. Bastnaesite is associated with barite, galena, and pyrite in epithermal veins in New Mexico and Burundi. Monazite, bastnaesite, and xenotime occur locally in tin-tungsten veins and greisens in Bolivia and South Africa (Parker and Baroch, 1971).

Small quantities of exotic rare-earth minerals occur in igneous pegmatites formed from residual fluids that were derived from nearly complete crystallization of presumably alkalic or subalkalic magmas. As with beryl, such pegmatitic occurrences are of only academic concern, unless labor costs are low enough to permit them to be economic.

Ancient and modern littoral and fluviatile placers are major loci for large deposits of rare earths and thorium minerals. The radioactive pyritic conglomerates of Aphebian age (early Proterozoic) in Quebec and Ontario, and similar deposits in the Northwest Territories, Canada, are perhaps the largest sources of potentially economic concentrations of thorium (as monazite and brannerite) in the world. According to Roscoe (1969), the deposits at Elliot Lake, Ontario, were formed under a reducing atmosphere. Such deposits extend across the Grenville Front into higher temperature and higher pressure, isochemical, metamorphic facies, yet still retain their radioactive elements. The Precambrian reefs of the Witwatersrand in the Transvaal are metamorphosed placers that contain thorium minerals.

Tertiary and Recent beach placers in Brazil, India, Australia, Egypt, the Malagasy Republic, and the United States are major sources of monazite recovered as a coproduct from the mining of magnetite, ilmenite, and rutile sands (Overstreet et al., 1968). Euxenite and brannerite have been mined from Recent alluvial placers in south-central Idaho (Savage, 1961).

Yttrium occurs in certain marine phosphatic shales such as the Phosphoria formation of Permian age in Idaho. Although the apatite in these rocks has a maximum content of 1000 ppm of yttrium, it might be feasible to extract an yttrium concentrate as a byproduct during the beneficiation of the phosphate rock.

Carbonatite plutons, aureoles surrounding alkalic plutons, and ancient and modern placers derived from them should continue to be the most attractive places to prospect for deposits of rare-earth and thorium ores during the remainder of the century.

Reserves

World yttrium reserves in 1979 were estimated at 38,200 st (Moore, 1980b). They are estimated by country in Table 2. It is anticipated that approximately 90% of the metal may be recovered from monazite ores; the remainder may be derived from xenotime, bastnaesite, euxenite, and uranium minerals.

Rare-earth oxide reserves are estimated at 17,730,000 st (Moore, 1980b; Argall, 1980) and are shown by country in Table 2. More than half of the published resources are attributed to bastnaesite-bearing alkalic plutons. The rest comprise monazite sands, plus a minor amount of euxenite sands.

World reserves of thorium oxides that could be produced by existing processes recently

TABLE 2—Published Reserves of Lanthanide Oxides, Yttrium, and Thorium Oxide, St

Country Continent	Lanthanide Oxides*	Yttrium*	Thorium Oxide[†]
Egypt	10,000		
Malagasy Republic	20,000		
Malawi	15,000		
Nigeria			15,000
South Africa	5,000		12,000
Other	20,000		10,000
Africa	70,000		37,000
China[‡]	10,000,000		350,000
India	1,000,000	20,000	
Korea	50,000	1,000	
Malaysia	30,000	600	
Sri Lanka	10,000	200	
Other	10,000	200	9,000
Asia	11,100,000	22,000	359,000
Australia	400,000	6,000	35,000
Russia	500,000	1,600	40,000
Scandinavia	60,000	200	146,000
Europe	560,000	1,800	186,000
Canada	250,000	2,400	202,000
United States	5,000,000	3,500	192,000
North America	5,250,000	5,900	394,000
Brazil	350,000	2,500	75,000
Other			10,000
South America	350,000	2,500	85,000
World	17,730,000	38,200	1,096,000

* Moore, 1980b.
[†] Kirk, 1980b.
[‡] Argall, 1980.

were estimated at 1,096,000 st (Kirk, 1980b). Distribution by countries is summarized in Table 2.

Most low-cost thorium reserves are in modern or ancient placers. Reserves in the thorite veins in the Lemhi Pass district of Idaho may be several hundred thousand tons (Staatz, 1979).

Principal Producing Countries

Australia, India, Brazil, and Malaysia are the chief producers of monazite concentrates. Domestic output is company confidential. Typical monazite concentrates contain approximately 90% monazite. Production of monazite concentrates by country during 1979 is summarized in Table 3.

The United States and China are the chief producers of bastnaesite concentrates. In 1979, the concentrates produced from the Molybdenum Corp. of America mine at Mountain Pass, CA, contained 18,205 st of rare-earth oxides. Malaysia is the chief source of yttrium from xenotime recovered as a byproduct of alluvial tin placers.

Other Countries and Potential Sources

Given favorable market conditions, thorite can be recovered as a coproduct from mining the Huronian uranium conglomerates at Elliot Lake, Ontario. Carbonatites in Kenya, Tanzania, South Africa, Malawi, and Norway are large potential sources of rare-earth-bearing pyrochlore and monazite. Monazite is also a possible byproduct of Bolivian tin ores. Placers in Argentina, Indonesia, the Malagasy Republic, Malawi, and Uruguay may be future sources of monazite concentrates.

Exploration

Standard techniques of geophysics, geochemistry, trenching, and drilling are used to search for and outline bastnaesite deposits. These methods, plus panning and jigging, can be used to investigate the economic potential of monazite in beach and stream placers.

Field Techniques

Gravity separations are useful field techniques for preliminary evaluation of placer sands. Random samples obtained from auger holes or pits can be screened and panned or jigged. Minerals in the concentrate can then

TABLE 3—Production of Monazite Concentrates by Country During 1979

Country	Monazite Concentrates, Short Tons
Australia	17,000
Brazil	2,700
India	3,100
Korea	10
Malaysia	2,200
Sri Lanka	220
Thailand	800
United States	na
Zaire	85
	26,115

Source: Moore, 1980a; na—not available.

be examined under a binocular microscope or checked radiometrically.

Geophysics

Airborne, surficial, and borehole radiometric surveys with scintillation equipment can detect rare-earth and thorium minerals associated with small amounts of uranium in veins or plutons. Because the same resistant minerals exist in many sands, such techniques work equally well to detect rare-earth or thorium minerals in ancient and modern beach or stream placers. Furthermore, because these minerals are commonly associated with magnetite and ilmenite, airborne or surficial magnetometric surveys can be used to find favorable target areas for placer concentrations of rare-earth and thorium minerals.

Geochemistry

Field tests have been devised for the detection of the rare-earth elements (Rose, 1976). Multielemental hydrogeochemical and stream-sediment reconnaissance data from the National Uranium Resource Evaluation can be used effectually for resource studies on rare-earth minerals (Bolivar, 1980; Price et al., 1980). Carbonatite plutons in eastern Uganda have been investigated by means of geochemical soil and stream-sediment surveys. Niobium, beryllium, and rare earths are pathfinder elements for carbonatites.

Drilling

Conventional core drilling (Parker and Baroch, 1971) is used to search for plutonic bastnaesite deposits. Drivepipe and hand augers are used to drill shallow holes in sampling beach placers down to depths of 30 ft. Waterjet drilling, using rotary drill rigs, has also been used to evaluate beach placers. Churn drills are used to test stream placers, particularly the deeper parts where the heavy minerals are concentrated just above bedrock. Typically, a 6-in. casing is driven and samples are recovered at 2.5- to 5-ft intervals.

Evaluation of Deposits

Tonnage and grade are the key factors in determining the economic value of rare-earth and thorium deposits. The geomorphology and paleogeomorphology of stream and beach deposits determine the ultimate limits of possible placers. Detailed geologic mapping by aerial photography may indicate possible targets. Drilling or pitting on 500- to 2000-ft centers should outline the general boundaries of the deposits. Detailed borders can be delimited by closer spacing of sample sites.

The shape of bedrock deposits depends upon the extent and configuration of favorable host units. Careful geologic mapping, followed by geochemistry, geophysics, and diamond drilling, should allow an estimate of the probable tonnage of ore-bearing rock.

Rare-earth and thorium minerals occur in the heavy fraction of littoral and fluviatile placers and in conjunction with the heavy accessory minerals in igneous rocks. Therefore, gravity separation by panning samples will concentrate the desired minerals in the heavy black-sand residue. In bedrock sampling, the rock must first be crushed and ground to a sufficient fineness in order to free the accessory minerals sought.

Magnetite and ilmenite can be removed from dried heavy concentrates by means of a strong magnet. Other minerals may be collected by use of a variable-intensity magnetic separator. The mineral grains can be identified under a microscope and their relative proportions can be counted. Rare-earth minerals containing thorium or uranium can be detected with a Geiger counter. Those containing more than 5% of combined praseodymium and neodymium can be identified with a portable spectroscope (Parker and Baroch, 1971).

A rapid field test is based on the relative insolubility of oxalates of thorium, yttrium, and rare-earth elements. The sample is boiled in sulfuric acid, then cooled and diluted with cold water, filtered, and neutralized with ammonia. It is boiled again and a saturated solution of oxalic acid is added until a light-colored curdy precipitate forms. Later, if the precipitate is ignited, a buff to tan color indicates yttrium-group rare earths, and a dark brown color indicates cerium-group rare earths. To test for thorium, the oxide should be dissolved in nitric and oxalic acids and added to a potassium iodate solution. White thorium iodate forms if thorium is present (Parker and Baroch, 1971). Individual rare-earth elements can be identified best by spectrophotometry, x-ray fluorescence, flame photometry, neutron-activation analysis, or emission spectroscopy.

Preparation for Markets

Mining Methods

The technology for mining monazite beach placers is similar to that employed for diamonds, gold, or cassiterite (Parker and Baroch, 1971). Offshore operations use floating dredges having either suction or bucket elevators. Slurry is carried hydraulically from the dredges to the beneficiation plant.

Subaerial deposits are worked by draglines or power shovels. However, in places where scattered pockets of ore must be mined selectively, bulldozers and scrapers are used, and the ore is trucked to the concentrator.

In underdeveloped nations where capital is scarce and labor cheap and abundant, primitive methods are used, in which hand-dug pits and simple sluice boxes recover black-sand concentrates.

Conventional open-pit mining methods are employed in the bastnaesite deposit at Mountain Pass, CA. The ore is drilled, blasted, and loaded into trucks by power shovels, then hauled to the mill.

Milling Techniques

Pure monazite contains approximately 70% rare-earth oxides. Standard acceptable grades for monazite-sand concentrates are 55, 60, and 66% rare-earth oxides.

Primary beneficiation of beach sands is effected either on floating dredges or at terrestrial plants. After oversized particles have been screened, a black-sand concentrate is recovered mechanically by means of jigs, sluice boxes, shaking tables, and/or Humphreys spiral concentrators. Through the use of induced-roll electromagnetic separators and high-tension electrostatic roll separators, a monazite concentrate, which may represent only 1% of the total black sands, can be recovered in the magnetic nonconductive fraction. Flotation cells containing oleic acid are used to enrich Indian monazite sand concentrates.

The crude ore at Mountain Pass, CA, contains 9% rare-earth oxides. (Pure bastnaesite contains approximately 75% rare-earth oxides.) Following primary and secondary crushing, the ore is passed through a rod mill and a classifier. The slurry is then heated and passed through flotation cells that depress the barite gangue and yield a 55 to 60% rare-earth oxide concentrate. This concentrate, in turn, is leached by hydrochloric acid and countercurrent decantation to remove calcite, thereby upgrading the concentrate to 68 to 72%. Finally, this concentrate is calcined to remove carbon dioxide from the carbonates, yielding a 92% concentrate of rare-earth oxides and fluorides (Parker and Baroch, 1971).

In the uranium mills at Elliot Lake, Ontario, thorium concentrates were recovered from waste solutions by solvent extraction to obtain a 35% thorium oxide precipitate (Shortt, 1970).

Processing Techniques

The caustic process and the acid process are two common methods for treating monazite concentrates (Parker and Baroch, 1971). In the caustic process, monazite is digested in hot sodium hydroxide and filtered. The insoluble thorium and rare-earth hydroxides are separated by treatment with weak hydrochloric acid, which dissolves the rare-earth hydroxides and leaves solid thorium hydride. The thorium hydride is then dissolved in nitric acid, and thorium is recovered by solvent extraction.

In the acid process, monazite is digested in hot sulfuric acid. Rare-earth and thorium sulfates are dissolved and removed by filtration. Thorium is then precipitated as a pyrosulfate, leaving the rare-earth ions in solution. Next, rare-earth elements are precipitated as oxalates or as sodium-rare-earth sulfates. These, in turn, can be roasted to form oxides, which are then dissolved in nitric acid. The rare-earth elements are then separated from each other by solvent extraction.

Four products may be recovered from the treatment of bastnaesite concentrates at Mountain Pass, CA: europium oxide; a lanthanum-rich mixture of rare-earth metals; a heavy subgroup mixture chiefly composed of samarium and gadolinium; and technical grade cerium. The bastnaesite concentrates are roasted and leached with hydrochloric acid. Cerium oxide

is filtered from the solution. The europium and heavy rare-earth elements are separated from the solution by solvent extraction. Then the lanthanum-rich product is precipitated. After further solvent extraction, europium sulfate is precipitated, leaving samarium and gadolinium in solution.

Thorite concentrates are digested in hot nitric acid and filtered. The thorium is removed from solution by solvent extraction and purified by countercurrent solvent extraction. Such extraction yields a high-quality thorium nitrate from which pure thorium oxide, tetrachloride, or tetrafluoride may be produced.

Thorium metal may then be made by metallothermic reduction of thorium oxide, thermal decomposition of thorium tetrachloride through reduction of thorium halide or oxide with calcium, or fused-salt electrolysis. Metallic yttrium is produced by direct reduction of yttrium trifluoride (Anon., 1979).

Separation and purification of the lanthanide elements is a major problem. Ion exchange is an effective way to separate individual rare-earth elements. EDTA (ethylene diamine tetra-acetate) solution is the best elutant for removing the lanthanide elements and yttrium from the resin in that order. Solvent extraction can be used effectively to separate rare-earth groups, and to isolate yttrium. Cerium and europium can be separated from other lanthanide elements by valency-change reactions. Lanthanide sulfates can be subdivided by adding cold aqueous solutions containing excess alkali sulfates to alkali-rare-earth sulfates. The heavy lanthanides and yttrium remain in solution. Fractional recrystallization permits the selective separation of lanthanum, praseodymium, and neodymium.

Rare-earth metals are produced most successfully by electrolysis or by metallothermic reduction of rare-earth halides. Mischmetal is produced by electrolytic fusion of mixed anhydrous rare-earth chlorides.

Transportation

Monazite concentrates are transported by ship, rail, or truck from primary beneficiation plants to chemical processing plants. Bastnaesite concentrates are shipped to processing plants in steel drums by truck or rail from the mill at Mountain Pass, CA.

Markets, Consumption

The United States imported 6,931 st of monazite concentrates valued at $1,677,000

TABLE 4—Domestic Imports of Rare-Earth and Thorium Concentrates, Metals, Alloys, and Chemicals in 1979

Commodity	Amount, lb	Value, $	Chief Source
Monazite concentrates	13,862,000	1,677,000	Australia
Cerium oxide	13,668	115,852	France
Other rare-earth oxides	848,081	15,153,469	France
Rare-earth metals (alloys)	144,864	577,162	United Kingdom
Rare-earth metals (+ scandium)	8,975	186,259	Russia
Ferrocerium	123,218	679,612	France
Thorium nitrate	47,415	162,837	France
Thorium oxide	31,509	160,490	France
Thorium oxide in gas mantles	2,867	476,842	Malta
Other thorium chemicals	181	33,688	Switzerland

Sources: Moore, 1980a; Kirk, 1980a.

during 1979. Of this amount, 90% was obtained from Australia and 9% from Malaysia. Average grade of the concentrates was 55% rare-earth oxides and 6% thoria. Domestic imports of concentrates, metals, alloys, and chemicals in 1979 are shown in Table 4.

In 1979, domestic stocks of monazite increased markedly, whereas stocks of bastnaesite concentrates decreased. Stocks of rare-earth compounds increased during that same year.

Consumption of bastnaesite and monazite concentrates increased 7 and 10%, respectively, during 1978. Domestic shipments from processors to consumers contained 11,000 st of rare-earth oxides. The foreign and domestic supply of thorium has exceeded demand because of increased requirements for coproduct rare earths derived from monazite concentrates. Consumption of nonenergy thoria equivalent in 1979 was estimated at 32 st.

In 1979, the United States exported 84,100 lb of ferrocerium, of which Korea was the chief recipient. Domestic exports of uranium and thorium metals, as well as of alloys, were not subdivided for 1979. Total shipments were 10,651 lb, valued at $216,130, of which 64% went to Sweden. Similarly, shipments of uranium and thorium compounds were undifferentiated for 1979. A total of 37,367 lb (chiefly uranium), valued at $430,472, was exported, of which 54% went to Chile (Kirk, 1980a).

Future Considerations and Trends

The future demand for thorium hinges primarily on the successful use of thorium as a nuclear fuel in power reactors. Probable domestic consumption in the year 2000 has been estimated at 155 st. Probable nonenergy consumption of thorium in 2000 should be approximately 85 st, of which one-third will be used in the aerospace industries in magnesium-base alloys and one-fourth in a thorium-copper catalyst to be used in the production of methanol (Kirk, 1980b). It is anticipated that all requirements can be satisfied from domestic operations.

Because domestic thorium output is a by-product of the output of rare-earth concentrates from monazite, the accumulation of excessive stockpiles may halve the price of thorium by the year 2000. National producers may have to reduce mining costs to compete successfully with higher grade foreign operations. Development of plutonium or other types of breeders could make obsolete the high-temperature gas reactors fueled by thorium-uranium. Furthermore, the failure to make aggressive improvements in thorium breeders could render them uneconomic (Shortt, 1970).

The annual demand for yttrium by the year 2000 is expected to be 73 st, chiefly used as phosphors for cathode-ray picture tubes and as electronic components. Sufficient domestic ores exist to meet anticipated demands, but the unit price may rise somewhat.

Moderate growth of the rare-earth industry is anticipated by 2000. All demands should be met from domestic sources without difficulty. Probable annual demand for all rare earths by 2000 is expected to be 57,000 st, of which 25,000 st will be used in iron and steel foundries and 15,000 st will be used in petroleum refining.

Substitutes, Synthetic Competition

Palladium can replace rare-earth oxides in petroleum cracking. Selenium and arsenic compounds can substitute in part for rare-earth

TABLE 5—Tariffs on United States Imports of Rare-Earth and Thorium Commodities

Commodity	Most Favored Nation (MFN)		Non-MFN
	1/1/81	1/1/87	1/1/81
Rare-earth ore and concentrates	Free	Free	Free
Cerium oxide and compounds	13.1% ad val.	7.2% ad val.	35% ad val.
Other rare-earth oxides	4.7% ad val.	3.7% ad val.	25% ad val.
Rare-earth metals	4.7% ad val.	3.7% ad val.	25% ad val.
Rare-earth alloys (including mischmetal)	45¢/lb	32¢/lb	$2/lb
Ferrocerium and other pyrophoric alloys	43¢/lb + 5.1% ad val.	22¢/lb + 2.6% ad val.	$2/lb + 25% ad val.
Thorium ore	Free	Free	Free
Thorium nitrate and oxide	15.1% ad val.	7.8% ad val.	35% ad val.
Unwrought thorium metal, waste, and scrap	5.6% ad val.	4.2% ad val.	25% ad val.
Thorium alloys	6.4% ad val.	3.0% ad val.	25% ad val.

Sources: Kurtz and Stephenson, 1981; Kirk, 1981.

oxides as glass decolorizers. In the production of ductile nodular iron, magnesium-nickel alloys and magnesium are more effectual and less expensive than cerium alloys. Alumina and rouge can replace rare-earth oxides for optical polishing. Boron is preferable to rare earths as a thermal neutron absorber for control rods because it generates no secondary alpha radiation and is less expensive.

Thorium breeder reactors may in time be competitive with uranium breeder reactors. However, thorium for nonnuclear uses is likely to be replaced by less expensive metals. Yttria and beryllia can replace thoria in refractories. Titanium and zirconium can substitute for thorium in electronic tubes.

Governmental Control

On a worldwide basis, most governments control exports of thorium concentrates and metal. Some treat thorium production as a governmental monopoly. India initiated the first embargo on monazite concentrates in 1946; Brazil followed in 1950.

As of Dec. 31, 1980, the entire United States stockpile of rare earths and all but 408 st of the thorium nitrate stockpile were authorized as available for disposal by the General Services Administration.

Taxes, Depletion, and Tariffs

The allowable depletion on domestically mined monazite and other thorium-bearing minerals in the United States is 22%. The rate for domestic rare-earth minerals that do not contain thorium and for foreign production of monazite is 14%. Depletion for other rare-earth minerals produced outside the United States is 14%. New tariff agreements with developed countries were set for mineral commodities in Tokyo in 1979. Rates for imports from most-favored nations were to be lowered at the beginning of each year from 1980 through 1987. Table 5 shows the present 1981 and ultimate 1987 end member of declining tariff structures for imports of various rare-earth and thorium products into the United States.

Ecology

The accepted radiation protection standard for thorium is 50 microcuries. Thorium and thorium hydride powders must be treated carefully because spontaneous ignition of dust layers may cause fire or explosions.

Conservationists are concerned about the destruction of beaches through placer mining. For this reason, many mining applications have been rejected in Australia. Reclamation has been successful at mined-out monazite placers in Georgia and Florida.

Acknowledgment

The author thanks Sam Rosenblum, US Geological Survey, for critically reading the manuscript, making suggestions, and especially for preparing a new introduction. Christine M. Moore and William S. Kirk of the US Bureau of Mines kindly provided preprints and other current information on rare earths and thorium. Aaron Waters of the Los Alamos National Laboratory made helpful editorial suggestions that improved the paper. This article was prepared under the auspices of the US Department of Energy.

Bibliography and References

Anon., 1979, "Rare Earths: Industry Profile and Market Review," *Industrial Minerals*, No. 138, pp. 21–59.

Argall, G.O., Jr., 1980, "Three Iron Ore Bodies of Bayan Obo," *World Mining*, Vol. 33, No. 1, pp. 38–41.

Armbrustmacher, T.J., 1980, "Abundance and Distribution of Thorium in the Carbonatite Stock at Iron Hill, Powderhorn District, Gunnison County, Colorado," Professional Paper 1049B, US Geological Survey, pp. B1–B11.

Bolivar, S.L., 1980, "An Overview of the National Uranium Resource Evaluation Hydrogeochemical and Stream Sediment Reconnaissance Program, Los Alamos Scientific Laboratory," LA–8457–MS, Los Alamos National Laboratory, Los Alamos, NM, 24 pp.

Erametsa, O., 1965, "Separation of Promethium from a Natural Lanthanide Mixture," *Acta Polytech. Scand., Chem. and Met. Series*, No. 37, 21 pp.

Kirk, W.S., 1980a, "Thorium," *Minerals Yearbook, 1978–79*, US Bureau of Mines, pp. 907–913.

Kirk, W.S., 1980b, "Thorium," *Mineral Facts and Problems, 1980*, Bulletin 671, US Bureau of Mines, pp. 937–945.

Kirk, W.S., 1981, "Thorium," *Mineral Commodity Summaries 1981*, US Bureau of Mines, pp. 164–165.

Kurtz, H.F., and Stephenson, P.A., 1981, "Rare-Earth Metals," *Mineral Commodity Summaries 1981*, US Bureau of Mines, pp. 124–125.

Moore, C.M., 1980a, "Rare-Earth Minerals and Metals," *Minerals Yearbook, 1978–1979*, US Bureau of Mines, pp. 735–742.

Moore, C.M., 1980b, "Rare-Earth Elements and Yttrium," *Mineral Facts and Problems, 1980*, Bulletin 671, US Bureau of Mines, pp. 737–752.

Olson, J.C., et al., 1954, "Rare-Earth Mineral Deposits of the Mountain Pass District, San Bernardino County, California," Professional Paper 261, US Geological Survey, 75 pp.

Overstreet, W.C., et al., 1968, "Fluvial Monazite Deposits in the Southeastern United States," Professional Paper 568, US Geological Survey, 85 pp.

Parker, J.G., and Baroch, C.T., 1971, "The Rare-Earth Elements, Yttrium and Thorium; A Materials Survey," Information Circular 8476, US Bureau of Mines, 92 pp.

Price, V., Jr., et al., 1980, "Use of NURE HSSR Data for Resource Studies on Rare-Earth Minerals," (abstract) *Abstracts with Programs*, Vol. 12, No. 5, Geological Society of America, p. 205.

Roscoe, S.M., 1969, "Huronian Rocks and Uraniferous Conglomerates in the Canadian Shield," Paper 68–40, Geological Survey of Canada, 205 pp.

Rose, E.R., 1976, "A Field Test for Rare-Earth Elements," Paper 75–16, Geological Survey of Canada, 10 pp.

Savage, C.N., 1961, "Economic Geology of Central Idaho Black-Sand Placers," Bulletin 17, Idaho Bureau of Mines and Geology, 160 pp.

Shortt, C.E., 1970, "Thorium," *Mineral Facts and Problems*, Bulletin 650, US Bureau of Mines, pp. 203–218.

Staatz, M.H., 1979, "Geology and Mineral Resources of the Lemhi Pass Thorium District, Idaho and Montana," Professional Paper 1049–A, US Geological Survey, pp. A1–A90.

Salt

STANLEY J. LEFOND *

CHARLES H. JACOBY †

Salt, or halite, has a long and most varied history. While we know the Chinese were producing salt as early as 3000 B.C., the first written reference to salt appears in the book of Job recorded about 2250 B.C., which reads:

"Can nothing which is unsavory be eaten without salt?"

We do not know when man first used or realized that he needed salt. Perhaps one of our early Eolithic ancestors noted a piece of salt shining along the shore of a salt lake or a bay. He may have been attracted by its shining luster and tasted it. He found that it had a tart, zesty, distinctive flavor and perhaps chewing a large piece, became ill. However, by experimentation he soon learned that taken in the proper proportions salt was a very pleasant additive to his food. He may have noticed, too, that it increased his feeling of well-being. Thus, when the curtain of recorded history rises, we find man using salt for his health's sake, seasoning his food with it, feeding it to his animals, and using it in many superstitious and religious ceremonies. These uses, however, are a far cry from the uses for salt today.

The first attempts of white man to make salt in continental United States were reported in the year 1614, while the first commercial production was in 1753 from the Kanawha licks. Practically all this salt was for human consumption, preserving food, and curing hides. Prior to the coming of the white man, Indians are known to have made salt from salt springs such as those that existed at Avery Island, LA, Charleston, WV, Saltville, VA, and Onondaga, NY. In 1862 the first rock salt was mined in the US from the Avery Island salt dome. Almost immediately thereafter, rock salt was

mined at Saltville, VA and then at Retsof, NY in 1885.

Of the more than 39 million tons produced annually in the United States, about 58% or 23 million tons are consumed by the chemical industry in the production of chlorine, caustic soda, hydrochloric acid, sodium metal, and some 30 other basic chemicals. These basic chemicals, in turn, are used in the preparation of approximately 14,000 chemicals which range from soap and detergents, to such chlorinated hydrocarbons as DDT, BHC, carbon tetrachloride, etc.

Utilization of cavities created in salt beds and domes has grown rapidly since 1947 until now the waste salt is creating an ecological problem. The uses for both dry- and solution-mined cavities range from the storage of liquid hydrocarbons to containerized storage of toxic wastes, from compressed air for the peak shaving of power to storage of nuclear wastes.

Geology

Mineralogy

Properties: Because of its simple structure, halite, the mineralogical name for salt, was the first structure to be analyzed by X-rays. It has the following properties:

Formula: NaCl (Na-39.34%, Cl_2-60.66%)
Crystallography: isometric, hexoctahedral, 4/m 32/m
Space group: Fm3m
A_o: 5.627 kX
Cell contents: Na_4Cl_4
Habit: usually cubic, rarely octahedral, massive, granular to compact
Physical properties:
  Refractive index: 1.554
  Twinning: observed on {111}
  Cleavage: {001} perfect
  Fracture: conchoidal, brittle

* Consultant, Industrial Minerals, Evergreen, CO.
† Jacoby and Co., Earth Science Consultants, Tempe, AZ.

Hardness: 2, specific gravity, 2.168
Melting point: 804°C; boiling point: 1413°C
Luster: vitreous, normally colorless to white but occasionally red, yellow, blue, and purple
Solubility: 0°C: 35.7 parts per 100 parts of water; 100°C: 39.8 parts per 100 parts of water

Classification of Deposits

Geologically salt is found in solution or in a solid state.

Solution: Salt is found in solution in oceans, lakes, and springs.

Oceans—It is generally conceded that the bulk of the world's salt supply is in solution in the oceans. The most often quoted figure is that the oceans contain 4.5 million cubic miles of rock salt—a volume half again as much as the entire North American continent above sea level.

The actual salt content of the oceans varies from 1 to 5% but averages about 3.5%. This variation, which exists from place to place and by depth, is due to the influence of inflowing waters, variations in the evaporation and freezing rates, and man. Today, in areas along the coasts where conditions are ideal for solar evaporation, salt is produced from ocean waters. The facilities vary from extremely crude (Fig. 1) to highly efficient and well-operated solar salt plants capable of producing upwards of 4,000,000 tpy of high quality salt (Fig. 2).

Marginal salt pans and marine salinas (natural solar salt pans) are found along the coasts, usually in the more arid countries. A marginal salt pan is a shallow depression, usually covered only during periods of abnormal high tides or during storms. The water is evaporated during dry spells leaving a thin salt crust. Many of these are exploited along the northwestern coast of Mexico, as well as other areas.

FIG. 1—*Crude solar salt pond.*

FIG. 2—*Modern solar salt operation.*

A marine salina is a salt lake which is fed by underground seepage from the ocean. The salt lake at Larnaca, Cyprus, is a typical example.

Lakes—Lakes are formed when water accumulates in a topographic depression. Waters flowing into the depression carry material in solution. The composition of this material will depend upon the type and solubility of rocks in the watershed traversed by the meteoric waters. Thus it is possible to have lakes that vary greatly in composition. Clarke (1924) classifies mineralized lakes as follows:

1) Sodium chloride lakes
2) Natural bittern lakes—magnesium salts dominate
3) Sulfate water lakes
4) Sulfate-chloride lakes
5) Alkaline lakes: carbonate lakes, carbonate-chloride lakes, chloride-sulfate-carbonate lakes

Normally, mineralized lake deposits contain little or no potassium. Sodium and calcium are the predominant cations and the most common minerals are the sodium sulfates, mirabilite and thenardite, burkeite, gaylussite, trona, and halite. Landes (1960) feels these sodium chloride lakes are "either separated bodies of ocean water or they owe their composition to the presence of salt within the rocks that floor the watershed."

Ground Water—Ground waters or their surface expression "springs" vary in salinity from practically pure water to those that are almost completely saturated. Ground waters are classified as either connnate or meteoric water. Connate waters are those trapped in the rock during the time of formation. Meteoric (rain) water is fresh initially but picks up soluble material as it travels through air, soil, rocks, etc. Therefore the composition of ground water varies according to the environment encountered. Connate waters usually reflect the composition of the water in which the rock was formed. For example, most sedimentary rocks were deposited under the sea, so much connate water is entrapped seawater. How-

TABLE 1—Analysis of Natural Brines, Ppm

	1	2	3	4	5
Ca	37,832	40,567	22,400	850	60
Mg	3,824	3,092	–	5,980	15,800
Na	67,966	79,253	49,000	96,400	34,940
SO_4	180	115	508	14,270	5,920
HCO_3	148	186	116	120	–
Cl_2	182,660	202,810	–	156,930	41,960
I_2	7	7	–	–	–
Br_2	4,570	4,600	–	–	–
K	–	–	1,380	trace	208,020
Fe	–	–	138	20	7,560
CO_3	–	–	–	–	–
Total solids	292,670	326,023	204,400	–	540

1. Smackover Brine, Arkansas
2. Smackover Brine, Arkansas
3. Mt. Simon fm, Indiana
4. Tashkurghan, Afghanistan
5. Dead Sea, Israel

ever, sedimentary rocks are also formed in freshwater lakes and interior salt lakes.

Clark (1924) has classified ground waters into the following groups: chloride, sulfate, carbonate, mixed (chloride-sulfate, chloride-carbonate, sulfate-carbonate, chloride-sulfate-carbonate), siliceous, borate, nitrate, phosphate, and acid.

Ground waters range in chemical content from practically nothing to as much as 254,000 ppm. Some brines are exploited for their bromine and magnesium contents. Table 1 lists analyses of typical brines.

Solid Salt Deposits: Solid salt is found in playa deposits, as bedded salt deposits, and diapirs and domes.

Playa Salts—According to Grabau (1913) a playa is a sandy, salty, mud-covered floor of a desert basin. During the rainy season a playa may be covered with rainwater which dissolves part of the soluble material. When the water evaporates, it leaves behind the soluble material, which may be concentrated in one area of the lake. This body of soluble material will shift around the lake and many will say that a new crop of crystals "grows" after each wet cycle. Oftentimes, too, a brine reflecting

the composition of the crystallized crust will be found just a short distance beneath the surface of the playa. In a few instances a crystal body is formed, which reflects the composition of the surrounding brine. Searles Lake in southern California is probably the most famous example of a crystal body in a playa lake.

In Mexico, tequesquite, a mixture of salt, sodium sulfate, and sodium carbonate, forms a crust on many playa lakes and is used by natives in cooking and cleaning. Its composition varies greatly as shown in Table 2 (Flores, 1918). Figs. 3 and 4 show tequesquite being harvested.

Playa deposits are fairly common in arid regions and saline playas result from the evaporation of a mineralized lake. The dissolved minerals in the lake result from the leaching of the rocks in the area surrounding the enclosed basin. Salt in the playas results from the solution of sodium chloride-bearing sediments. The presence of borates suggests fairly recent volcanism in the area.

The composition of material in a playa lake varies greatly. For example, in California, Cadiz Lake is predominantly calcium chloride. Bristal Lake is predominantly salt, and Owens

TABLE 2—Tequesquite Analyses, Mexico

Playa Lake	NaCl, %	Na_2CO_3, %	$NaHCO_3$, %	Na_2SO_4, %
Sta. Clara, Lake Texcoco	37.5	19.4	9.1	0.60
Los Leyes, Lake Texcoco	31.5	18.3	1.15	0.56
El Carmen, Llanos de San Juan	11.7	30.1	5.7	1.6
Cuitsea (Michoacán)	4.6	2.45	0.9	2.45
Sayula (Jalisco)	25.0	12.3	6.5	5.6
San Luis Potasí	9.8	31.6	17.5	21.6

Source: Flores, 1918.

FIG. 3—*Harvesting tequesquite, Mexico.*

FIG. 4—*Harvesting tequesquite, Mexico.*

Lake is sodium carbonate. Others contain sodium sulfate, while still others contain mixtures of many different compounds.

Bedded Salt Deposits—Bedded salt deposits are true sedimentary rocks and as such are found in sedimentary sequences with shales, limestones, gypsum, anhydrite, etc. Thus, salt beds have been found in every geologic period from the Cambrian to the Tertiary, and there is evidence that some deposits are Precambrian in age. A list of salt deposits in the various geological periods is delineated in Table 3 (Lefond, 1969).

Salt beds can be as much as 1300 ft thick. However, due to the manner in which they are formed, thick salt beds characteristically contain thin bands or lenses of anhydrite and/or clay, with a salt interval 2 to 4 in. thick. In some areas as much as 2000 ft of salt are known. Fig. 5 shows bedded salt and a "salt horse," in the Detroit mine of the International Salt Co.

The formation of such thick salt beds has intrigued geologists for many years. Hence many theories and ideas have been advanced to explain the formation of thick salt beds which extend over hundreds of square miles.

TABLE 3—Ages of Salt Deposits

Cenozoic Era
  <u>Recent</u>. Solar salt operations, Playa Lakes.
  <u>Pleistocene</u>. California, Nevada, Russia, Mexico, Israel
  <u>Pliocene</u>. Nevada, Utah, Italy, Jordan
  <u>Miocene</u>. Dominican Republic, Cyprus, Czechoslovakia, Poland, Spain, Turkey, Russia, Algeria, Egypt, Sudan, Iran, Iraq, Syria, Trucial States, Morocco
  <u>Oligocene</u>. France, Germany, Spain, Turkey, Iran, Iraq
  <u>Eocene</u>. Green River Basin, WY, British Honduras, Pakistan(?), Morocco, Iran

Mesozoic Era
  <u>Cretaceous</u>. Florida, Bolivia, Brazil, Colombia, Peru, Russia, Angola, Zaire, Congo Republic (Brazzaville), Gabon, Morocco, Libya, Senegal, Nigeria, Mexico
  <u>Jurassic</u>. Gulf Coast area, Idaho, Cuba, Chile, Germany, Aden, Kuwait, Tanzania
  <u>Triassic</u>. Isthmus of Tehuantepec-Mexico, Bulgaria(?), France, Greece(?), Germany, Netherlands, Portugal, Spain, Switzerland, United Kingdom, Algeria, Libya, Morocco, Tunisia, Ethiopia, Peru, Bolivia
  <u>Permian</u>. Permian Basin-US, Supai Basin, Williston Basin, Mexico, Peru, Germany, Greece(?), Netherlands, Poland, United Kingdom, Russia, Denmark, Australia (?), Brazil
  <u>Pennsylvanian</u>. Colorado, Paradox Basin, Brazil
  <u>Mississippian</u>. Virginia, Williston Basin, New Brunswick, Nova Scotia
  <u>Devonian</u>. Williston Basin, Russia, Australia, Canada
  <u>Silurian</u>. Salina Basin-US, and Canada
  <u>Ordovician</u>. Williston Basin, WY, Bolivia(?)
  <u>Cambrian</u>. Northwest Territories, Australia, Russia, Iran, Pakistan(?)

Precambrian
  Iran, Pakistan(?), Australia

Source: Modified from Lefond, 1969.

FIG. 5—*Bedded salt and a "salt horse," Detroit mine, International Salt Co.*

Landes' (1960) classification of the various theories follows:

(I) Terrestrial type. Evaporating interior sea becomes saline due to:
  (1) Primary sodium chloride produced as a weathering product.
  (2) Flushing of connate water from sedimentary rocks cropping out above water level in drainage basin.
  (3) Leaching of salt from sedimentary rocks cropping out in drainage basin.
(II) Marine type. Concentration of ocean water in cutoff sea:
  (1) Without further enrichment.
  (2) With enrichment by
    (A) Wind-blown salt
    (B) Ocean water
      (a) Marginal salt pans
      (b) Marine salinas
      (c) Barred lagoons
      (d) Silled downwarping basins

Today all acceptable theories involve the precipitation of salt from an evaporating body of salt water. Landes (1960) suggests the following stages for the formation of a major bedded salt deposit:

Generalized Chronological History Proposed for Thick Salt Deposits. The following stages are suggested in the natural history of a major bedded salt deposit:
(1) Peneplanation of the continental platform so that it is a nearly flat land of very little elevation above the sea.
(2) Submergence of wide areas beneath the sea. Shallow ocean waters spread over a considerable part of the continent.
(3) Beginning or renewed downwarping of a basin marginal to this epicontinental sea.
(4) Sedimentation of both basin and epicontinental sea. Mainly clastic and organic (reef) deposits.
(5) Lowering of sea to approximately sill level. Period of evaporite deposition. Enrichment by seawater flowing across sill. Because of the shallowness of the water, and the distance from the open ocean in such areas as the Michigan Basin, the brine crossing the sill may have been abnormally strong. Some enrichment could also take place by wind-blown salt, for the flat topography and scantiness of land vegetation no doubt resulted in incessant winds of considerable magnitude.

Thus, as more and more sediments and/or salt is loaded onto the mass of salt crystals on the sea floor the water is squeezed out and the salt crystals are compacted or recrystalized into massive salt beds.

Salt Domes—Salt is very vulnerable to pressure. Thus, as pressure is exerted on a salt bed, due to the static weight of overlying sediments, or tectonic forces, the salt "flows" plastically, first bulging to form salt anticlines such as those that occur in the Utah-Colorado salt basin and in Europe. If the pressure increases, the overlying rock is ruptured and salt is squeezed into, and through, the overlying sediments to form *salt domes* or *diapiric folds.* Such features are known in the Gulf Coast of the US, in the Paradox Basin of Colorado-Utah, in Mexico, Romania, Iran, Germany, Tunisia, Algeria, and elsewhere. Fig. 6 shows an outcrop of a salt-gypsum diapir in Rheous, Tunisia. Fig. 7 shows mining in the Avery Island salt dome of the International Salt Co.

In some instances the salt has reached the surface (Avery Island dome, LA), or actually flows like a glacier onto the surface. Kent (1958) says of the Kuh-i Namak (Dashti) salt plugs:

> The parent anticline is a high whaleback fold about 30 miles long and 8 miles wide, with the salt mass piercing the culmination and forming a vast dome 4,000 feet above plains level. From this dome broad salt glaciers flow between flanking limestone crags down the mountain sides northeast and southwest. Where the salt overhangs rock cliffs the precipitous slopes are at times swept by salt avalanches—a complete parallel with conditions on glaciated mountains.

The distribution of salt and salt domes in the United States is shown in Fig. 8 (Lefond, 1969). The greatest concentration in the US is in an area that extends from western Alabama to the Texas-Mexican border—and perhaps even on into northeastern Mexico. The Gulf Coast salt bodies are vertical, or nearly so, and are circular to elliptical in plan. The diameters range from about 3000 ft to as much as 4 miles. The vertical dimension is not ac-

FIG. 6—*Salt-gypsum diapir, Rheous, Tunisia.*

FIG. 7—*Mining in salt dome, Avery Island mine, International Salt Co.*

curately known, but may be as much as 40,000 ft.

The salt anticlines of the Paradox Basin range in length from 30 to 70 miles, and contain salt cores that range from about 4,100 to 13,700 ft in thickness.

Distribution of Deposits

Salt deposits and/or solar salt operations are found in nearly every country of the world. However, in a few areas such as Japan, Norway, Sweden, Finland, and parts of the US, salt has to be imported to furnish raw material for the manufacture of chemicals. In other areas, for example, in northwestern Mexico, Inagua, Long Island, Bonaire, etc., large solar plants exist primarily to furnish salt for export to large chemical complexes of the more highly industrialized nations.

The United States has tremendous salt reserves in the Salina Basin of the northeast, the Permian Basin, Gulf of Mexico Salt Basin as well as smaller areas in Colorado, Idaho, Arizona, Wyoming, Virginia, California, Utah, and elsewhere (Fig. 8). The deposits are large, of good grade, and in most instances are exploited either by solution mining and/or conventional underground methods. Analyses of salt from these areas are shown in Table 4.

While large areas of the US are underlain by salt deposits, several areas, notably the northwest and most of the eastern states, are without salt. Large amounts of salt are imported into these areas to supply raw material for caustic-chlorine manufacturing and for the fishing industry.

While Canada has large reserves, the principal areas of salt production are in Ontario and Nova Scotia, with 85% of the production coming from Ontario. Recently, an extension of the Nova Scotia deposit was discovered in Newfoundland. There are plans to exploit this deposit to produce salt for a soda ash and/or chlorine-caustic soda company. Salt deposits are also found in New Brunswick.

In Mexico rock salt deposits exist near Monterrey, Coatzacoalcos, and Punta Gorda. The deposits of Coatzacoalcos are a series of salt domes and salt anticlines, several of which have been drilled for sulfur. At the present time salt is being produced from the Parajitos

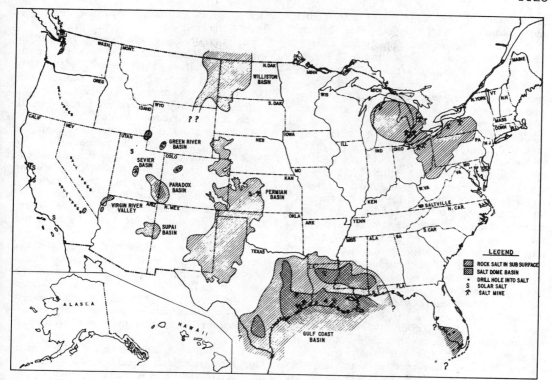

FIG. 8—*Distribution of salt and salt domes, United States (Lefond, 1969, courtesy Plenum Press).*

dome for use in a chlor-alkali plant at Coatza-coalcos. The salt deposit near Monterrey is exploited for use in a soda-ash plant. Although these deposits contain huge reserves, the major tonnage of Mexican salt is solar evaporated, coming from the Black Warrior Lagoon area.

Large solar salt plants exist in many areas of the Caribbean, principally Long Island, Bonaire, and the Bahamas. Production from these operations is exported primarily to the United States. Although salt production in the other Latin American countries is relatively small, it should be noted that Brazil has huge reserves in the Amazon Basin, Sergipe, and the newly discovered offshore domes.

The primary salt-producing countries of

TABLE 4—Analyses of Rock Salt, %

	1	2	3	4	5	6
NaCl	92.08	76.10–99.80	99.25	96.150	98.220	98.150
$Fe_2O_3 + Al_2O_3$	3.52	—	—	0.015	—	—
$CaCl_2$	2.04	0.50–0.20	0.04	0.018	0.053	0.011
$CaSO_4$	0.71	0.01–0.03	0.69	3.252	0.634	0.639
$CaCO_3$	0.15	1.10–0.39	—	—	—	—
$MgCl_2$	0.08	—	0.01	0.342	0.052	0.027
SiO_2	1.42	—	—	—	—	—
$MgSO_4$	—	—	—	0.223	1.041	1.173
H_2O insoluble	—	22.80–0.30	—			

1. Louann Salt, Union County, AL
2. Haynesville Salt, Se4, T5N, R2E, AL
3. International Salt Co., Avery Island, LA
4. Hutchinson Salt, Carey Salt Co.
5. International Salt Co., Detroit, MI
6. International Salt Co., Cleveland, OH

South America are Argentina, Brazil, Chile, and Colombia. With the exception of the underground salt mine at Zipaquira, Colombia, most of the salt produced in South America comes from solar salt pans or playa lake deposits.

In Europe salt production is one of the oldest of industries. The Romans introduced the open-pan evaporation of brines into England as early as 300 B.C. Salt has been produced in Austria since the 8th century, and the mine at Wieliczka, Poland, has been in operation since the 13th century. Today, Russia, France, West Germany, Italy, England, Netherlands, Poland, and Romania are the major salt-producing countries of Europe. Newly discovered deposits in Portugal near Lisbon and those near Loule are expected to lift Portugal into the ranks of the larger producers.

One-fourth of the salt produced in Europe is rock salt; the balance is salt brine used in chlor-alkali and soda ash plants and for making various table and agricultural salt.

The Zechstein (Permian) salt extends from eastern England to Western Poland and constitutes one of the major salt resources of Europe. Keuper (Triassic) salt beds are particularly well developed in Germany. In addition, extensive salt horizons are found in the Miocene, Oligocene, and Jurassic regions of several European countries. Solar salt is produced along the coasts of France, Portugal, Spain, Italy, and Greece (Lefond, 1969).

While there are large rock salt resources in many countries of Africa, most of the salt production comes from the solar evaporation of seawater and salt lakes. Egypt, the major producer, produced only 770,000 tons in 1980. In fact, the total salt production of Africa in 1980 was slightly over 3 million tons. Over two-thirds of this was produced in only five countries and the balance in the remainder of Africa.

Salt deposits in Asia have been exploited for hundreds of years. Solar salt operations and drilling for salt brines have been an industry in China since 2000 B.C. Today, China, the second largest salt-producing country in the world, operates solar salt plants in the Coastal provinces from Southern Manchuria to Kwangsi Province. In the inland areas, salt is produced from brine wells, salt lakes, and a mixture of salt and soils, called "salt earth" (Lefond, 1969).

Exploration

As a result of oil and potash exploration, many new salt deposits have been found in various countries such as France, Portugal, Brazil, Thailand, Morocco, and others.

For example, the recent discovery of salt in Morocco's Mohammedia area was the result of the search for a commercial-grade potash ore in the Khemmiset-Berrechid Basins by a United Nations exploration team. Similar projects have defined, in rather broad general terms, other occurrences of salt.

Thus, the work of an exploration geologist looking for salt is usually a matter of the "final" delineation of the deposit and its environment. The manner in which exploration is conducted is governed to a large extent by the planned method for extracting the salt—that is, by either normal dry mining techniques or by solution mining, including the projected use of the resultant cavity.

If the deposit is to be dry mined, the exploration program must be much more extensive and greater care taken in detailing the results, than if the deposit were to be exploited by solution mining. This care is made necessary by the comparatively greater capital investment in dry mining than in a brine field (Fig. 9).

In evaluating a salt deposit for dry mining, the geological aspects surrounding the deposit are almost as important as the deposit itself. The primary aspects are:

1. Ground Water: The amount of ground water and its hydrostatic head will have a direct influence on the method and cost of shaft sinking. If this ground water is a potable water supply for a community, the protection of the aquifer will require careful hydrological studies. Shaft sinking difficulties will materially increase if an aquifer contains a brine or significant amounts of hydrogen sulfide, ammonia, or hydrocarbon gases or if the hydrostatic pressure is very high.

2. Overburden Characteristics: Considering the overburden as the alluvium plus the rock sequences above the salt deposit, it is essential that the physical characteristics of these horizons be known as fully as possible. It is of particular importance that this information be gathered from the area in which the shaft or shafts will be sunk. These data should include the thickness and hardness of the beds, drillability, fracture pattern, friability, and tendency to oxidize. Shaft sinking contractors generally require this information and occasionally make a physical examination of the cores themselves. Usually NX size "slim" hole develops a core sufficiently large enough for chemical, hardness, drillability, and other required tests (Read and Jacoby, 1957; Severy, 1946).

FIG. 9—*Modern salt plant.*

3. Physical Characteristics of the Rocks Associated With the Salt: In sedimentary layered evaporite deposits, the structural competency of both the rocks underlying and overlying the bed to be mined are of particular importance. Roof spans, pillar size, percentage of extraction, mine layout, and the roof bolting program are some of the mine features which will be dictated by rocks surrounding the deposit.

4. Faults: Fault systems which are common to many salt deposits can create numerous serious problems and should be defined as carefully as possible during the original exploration program (Jacoby, 1969). Domes in southern United States have numerous faults associated with the spines that characterize their upper reaches. These vertical or near vertical fractures often contain brine, oil and/or gases. Failure to develop mining patterns to avoid creating differential stresses across these features often results in the expenditure of large sums of money and energy to grout off fluid intrusions.

Downdropped graben blocks are often the result of post-depositional water intrusions along faults. The dissolving action of the water on one or more of the salt beds may cause a collapse that can take the form of a single block fault or echelon step faults. Either of these may cause expensive realignment of the mining pattern.

5. Facies Changes: Both minor and major facies changes may occur in salt beds over a relative short distance. This has been demonstrated in the salina salts of Michigan, the potash salts of the Khemmiset Basin in Morocco, and the salts of Realmonte, Sicily. In Michigan the A-1 salt grades from a pure anhydrite on the basin's edge near Detroit to an almost pure salt in East China Township, MI, and then to a heavily contaminated potash salt in the area of Midland. In the Khemmiset Basin, salts grade from a lean potash ore at Berrechid to a 98.3% NaCl in Mohammedia. The salt at Realmonte, Sicily, although metamorphosed, shows a similar gradational change from lean potash mineralization to a pure halite. Since most customers desire a product of constant uniform chemical composition, the exploration program must define the limits of various salt grades both vertically within the bed as well as horizontally and the reserves of a standardized or uniform product.

6. Attitude and Position: The attitude and position of the salt beds or, in the case of domes, the flowage lines, influence the mining system, the percentage of extraction, the depth of the mining level, the selection of a shaft vs. an inclined entry, and the rock mechanics of superimposing pillars where multilevel systems are contemplated. In certain cases where internal features of the deposit or the continuity of the quality of salt is in question, then a mill sample should be secured by a bored shaft or inclined entry.

There are a number of advantages to this approach. In addition to allowing an in-situ study of the geology, this test entry can serve to (a) secure samples for mill tests, (b) evaluate the customer acceptance of the salt product, and (c) be a facility for ventilation and/or escapeway.

Where solution mining is contemplated, exploration is largely concomitant with the expansion or replacement of the present brining facilities. Usually regional geology leads to the selection of the brine field site. Based on previously published information, a decision is made on whether or not geophysical information would be useful in guiding subsequent drilling. In cases where domes are involved, or the beds are known to have been altered by diapirism or faulting, geophysical studies may be of distinct value (Mattox, 1968).

7. Chemical Composition: In general, it may be said that the deposit should have a minimum sodium chloride content of 95% or greater to be commercial. In the northeastern portion of the United States the average sodium chloride content required is 97%. Where salts must be competitive with either rock salt from southern salt domes or solar evaporated salt, the sodium chloride content must approach 99%. Depending upon the end use of the salt, various trace elements such as copper, vanadium, boron, chromium, and iron as well as the calcium sulfate, ammonia, and water insolubles must be considered.

Drilling and Coring

Most operators prefer to core at least the first hole. If seismic or other geophysical studies show the level of the top of the salt to be uniform and previous data on the deposit is accurate, a changeover from water to a saturated brine drilling fluid can be made at an elevation in the overlying sediments above and close to the top of the salt deposit. Where zones of lost circulation have been encountered "up the hole," a casing point is usually selected above the top of salt and a string of protective casing installed. Depending upon the design of the well and the economics, the casing is either set temporarily on a packer or permanently cemented in the hole. Where drill holes expose shales which swell and spall or slough in the presence of freshwater, early conversion to a saturated brine drilling fluid often is remedial.

The most important aspect of coring salt is to have a clean, fully or supersaturated brine drilling fluid which will not leach or mechanically etch the salt. In general, even a brine which is fully saturated must be passed through a salt lixator (mechanical saturator) to produce a supersaturated drilling fluid. It can be expected that if the temperature of the drilling fluid on the surface is less than that which is experienced down the hole, even a supersaturated solution will leach the salt from the core and the walls of the hole. A heated saturated solution will help to solve these problems. Table 5 shows the solubility of salt at various temperatures.

Hydrocarbon and trade-named drilling

TABLE 5—Solubility of Salt at Various Temperatures

Temperature		% Salt	Temperature		% Salt
°F	°C		°F	°C	
− 6	−21.11	23.31*	70	21.11	26.45
0	−17.78	23.83	80	26.67	26.52
+10	−12.22	24.70	100	37.78	26.68
20	− 6.67	25.53	125	51.67	26.92
30	− 1.11	26.16	150	65.56	27.21
32	0.0	26.29	175	79.44	27.52
32.3	+ 0.1	26.31†	200	93.33	27.91
40	4.44	26.33	212	100.00	28.12
50	10.00	26.36	220	104.44	28.29
60	15.56	26.395	227.7	108.7	28.46‡

* Eutectic point
† Transition point
‡ Boiling point at one atmosphere pressure

fluids which will not leach the salt are available. However, these usually are either a fire hazard or expensive and in most cases contaminate the core to such a degree as to hinder chemical analyses.

Failure to use a clear brine will result in the mechanical erosion of the soft halite. One should start with clean equipment and use clean, high purity rock salt of a "CC" grade size. Recycling the drilling fluid through a lixator helps to filter out finely divided cuttings and mud.

After the protective casing is set where needed, the coring is started with a 50 to 90-ft oil field type double-tube core barrel. Even though a double-tubed barrel is used, care should be taken to keep the drill fluid free of mechanically suspended particles.

Cores are usually cut into 1 ft lengths and halved. One portion is halved again to form a quarter which is crushed and ground for chemical analyses. Physical testing is usually accomplished on the second quarter of the core.

When the core hole is completed, it should then be logged with a suite of logs such as gamma-neutron, sonic, or possibly the 3-D, all of which are available from various well logging service companies. These logs are then correlated with the core log, and the geolograph which records the rate of drill penetration. Since faults, particularly low angle thrust faults, are difficult to recognize in cores of salt beds, this correlation with logs will often show repeat sequences of rock strata. Subsequently, a reexamination of the core may show a fine grained granular halite section of core which was previously unrecorded. Sonic logging differentiates anhydritic-dolomite from dolomitic-anhydrite, while gamma-neutron will clearly depict salt from anhydrite (Leroy, 1951).

After one hole has been cored and a suite of logs obtained, most operators consider it unnecessary to core subsequent holes. If the geology is uniform and relatively undisturbed, such a procedure is often satisfactory. However, when the salt deposit has been subjected to tectonic forces, metamorphosed, or affected by ground water solution, cores should be taken from every, or every other, hole depending on the complexity of the geology. It may be expected that coring will increase the cost of the well by approximately 10%, depending on various conditions. When there are plans to use the resultant cavity, coring and the permanent retention of the cores is recommended.

Evaluation of Deposits

Procedure—The procedure for the evaluation of a salt deposit with respect to its exploitation by solution mining is outlined as follows (Jacoby, 1972):

1. Preliminary Considerations
   A. Plant Requirements
      1. Quantity of brine
      2. Quality of brine
      3. Degree of saturation required
   B. Subsurface Factors
      1. Geology
      2. Rock mechanics
      3. Hydrology
      4. Previous extractive operations and environment
   C. Surface Factors
      1. Environment
      2. Topography
      3. Property boundaries
      4. Plant—brinefield relationships
   D. Feasibility Study
      1. Preliminary brinefield layout
      2. Capital investment
      3. Cost of capitol
      4. Operating cost
      5. Brine treatment costs
      6. Taxes and tax incentives
      7. Return on investment
2. Preliminary Engineering
   A. Property
      1. Acquisition
         a. Option of surface and mineral rights
         b. Rights of well sites
         c. Ingress and egress rights
         d. Right-of-way for roads, pipelines, and power lines
         e. Storage rights
         f. Conditions of abandonment
   B. Water Supply
      1. Environmental Considerations
         a. Ground water table
         b. Salt water encroachment
         c. Effect on local agriculture, industry, and domestic use

2. Supply characteristics
   a. Volume (continuity and cyclic variations)
   b. Quality
   C. Salt Supply
      1. Exploration
         a. Geophysical surveys
            (1) Seismic
            (2) Gravity
         b. Drill holes
            (1) Cores
            (2) Geophysical logs
            (3) Hydrological tests
      2. Design data development
         a. Analyses of well logs and cores
         b. Physical testing of cores
         c. Water supply evaluation
         d. Equilibrium studies
3. Design and Cost Analysis
   A. Brinefield Layout and Cost
      1. Salt wells design and cost
      2. Subsidence grid system design
      3. Roadways and well sites
      4. Pipeline and power line
      5. Cathodic protection
      6. Pump and pump facilities
      7. Feed water treatment facilities
      8. Reservoirs and aeration
      9. Security
   B. Supervision Costs
   C. Operating Costs
   D. Maintenance Costs
   E. Taxes and Insurance
   F. Depletion and Depreciation
   G. Cost of Capital
   H. Return on Investment

Specifications

"With regard to any given salt occurrence, the geologist or mining engineer must know the location of the market to be served, the ultimate use of the salt, and the customer's requirements. This will determine whether the prospective deposit is to be dry-mined or solution-mined and whether, if mined by solution, the resultant brine is to be evaporated or electrolyzed" (Jacoby, 1972).

Three types of rock salt are normally produced in the US. They are based on screen sizes and are fine crystal (FC), coarse crystal (CC), and grade No. 1. Typical analyses of these grades are shown in Table 6.

TABLE 6—Typical Analyses of Rock Salt Products, New York, %

	FC*	CC†	No. 1
Moisture	0.038	0.023	0.022
Water insolubles	1.306	1.227	1.613
Calcium sulfate ($CaSO_4$)	0.533	0.473	0.639
Calcium chloride ($CaCl_2$)	0.022	0.022	0.030
Magnesium chloride ($MgCl_2$)	0.006	0.006	0.008
Sodium chloride (NaCl)	98.095	98.249	97.688
Sodium chloride (dry basis)	98.133	98.272	97.710

* FC, "fine crystal."
† CC, "coarse crystal."

These analyses demonstrate the resistance of hard, insoluble particles of anhydrite, dolomite, and shale contained in coarse No. 1 to degradation, resulting in a corresponding lowering of the sodium chloride content in these coarser fractions.

After completing chemical and physical testing on the cores, the crushing and screening test may be conducted on the residual portion of the core to determine the chemical composition of the products which might be formed and to roughly ascertain the percentage of FC (fine crystals) and/or −10 mesh material which may be obtained during operations.

The purity of rock salt products derived from bedded deposits is not only related to the deposit itself, but also to the particle sizes that are manufactured. Typical screen analyses of the three principal rock salt products marketed in the US are shown in Table 7.

TABLE 7—Typical Screen Analyses of
the Three Rock Salt Products
Marketed in the United States

Sieve No.	Cumulative % Retained on	Component % of Aggregate
Screen Analysis: Fine Crystal (FC)		
4	0.0	0.0
8	0.0	0.0
12	12.2	12.2
20	52.9	40.7
40	72.1	19.2
70	87.1	15.0
80	89.3	2.2
Pass		
Screen Analysis: Coarse Crystal (CC)		
3/8 in.	0.0	0.0
4	24.0	24.0
8	82.0	58.0
10	89.7	7.7
12	94.7	5.0
16	98.2	1.8
Pass		
Screen Analysis: No. 1		
3/4 in.	0.0	0.0
3/8 in.	5.0	5.0
4	90.3	85.3
8	98.7	8.4
Pass		1.3

Mining

Dry Mining

All presently operating rock salt mines in the United States and Canada use the room-and-pillar mining method. The height of the pillars is limited by the vertical section of commercial quality salt that is being mined and in some cases the thickness of salt required for a back or roof. The room width is a function of the thickness of the overlying incompetent rocks and the physical characteristics and thickness of the salt which forms the roof.

Pillar widths are governed by the percentage of extraction permissible at various depths and room widths. Rooms widths are basically related to the equipment used in the mining process and more particularly to the size and requirements of the haulage units (Fig. 10). Because of the adverse economics involved in the construction of salt fillets or curved wall-roof intersections, mining procedures dictate the formation of 90° angles between the roof and pillars. This procedure occasionally leads to severe pillar spalling. In bedded deposits the mining height is usually not sufficient that these slabs create safety hazards, but in dome deposits serious problems do sometimes develop.

Most mines in the bedded deposits of the northeastern portion of the United States and Canada roof bolt their haulageways and permanent work areas. The diameter, length, and spacing of the bolts vary with circumstances. Most operations use bolts that vary from 4 to 10 ft in length on patterns of 4-ft centers. Rusting often occurs where connate waters are encountered.

Due to the difficulties experienced in setting bolts in salt, only minor roof bolting is done in salt domes. Bolt holes in salt have a smooth slick surface which forms poor seats for bolt anchors and which deform plastically in time under pressure. Wedge-type slotted bolts are virtually impossible to set.

Many operators drill vertical roof holes at periodic intervals to test the thickness and character of the roof salt. This is made necessary by the fact that in bedded deposits solution erosion usually occurs at the top of the deposit, causing rather rapid changes in the thickness and nature of the roof salt. These vertical holes also allow any fluids or gases to escape, thus preventing a pressure buildup as minor roof bed separation occurs. Occasionally shales, exposed by the bolt borehole, oxidize, causing adverse effects.

In mines in the salt domes of the southern United States, pillar and room sizes approach a near constant width of 100 ft. Recently some deviation from this historical pattern has

FIG. 10—*Haulageway and pillars, underground salt mine.*

occurred. At Avery Island rooms monitored for rock movement show that mining heights of 135 ft are feasible. Continued advances in rock mechanics led to the establishment of a room-and-pillar system where the room width and height were designed for 150 ft. Here fillets were left at the intersection of the roof and rib line (Halbouty, 1967).

Equipment used in the mining of salt varies more than perhaps with any other segment of the mineral industry (Fig. 11). Because of the softness of salt, abrasion is at a minimum. There is practically no corrosion to equipment in a salt mine. Mine temperatures vary from a year around average of about 60°F in the Detroit salt mine to 75°F at the Avery Island salt mine. With such favorable factors, power shovels which were first installed in 1935 in the Detroit mine are still operating efficiently today. With the continued expansion of the tonnage demand experienced by the salt industry, new and more modern equipment is added, with a reluctance to discard the older, yet still operable, machines.

Depending upon the height and width of the rooms, the depth of the mining level, the tonnages produced, cost of labor, and specific operating techniques used, direct operating costs may vary from about $0.90 per ton to $1.70 per ton. The single most important factor in these costs is labor.

Solution Mining

Solution mining in the last 20 years has undergone radical changes. Prior to 1955 all solution mining was conducted by either "annulus injection" or "tubing injection" of solvent with relatively small tonnages being produced by the Trump method. At this time the system of hydraulic fracturing was developed which had the following effects (Bays, 1963; Bays, et al., 1960):

1) Altered the cavity configuration from the "morning glory" shape to hemispheres and ellipsoids, thus increasing the stability of openings and reducing the likelihood of subsidence.

2) Increased the percentage of extraction from less than 5% to something in excess of 40%.

3) Reduced brining costs in most operations by 50%.

FIG. 11—*Mining equipment in an underground salt mine, Retsof mine, International Salt Co.*

4) Increased the productive capacity of wells from approximately 50 gpm to about 500 gpm or more.

5) Reduced well maintenance costs to less than 5% of their former amount.

Most companies now favor using a contract driller instead of operating their own rigs with a company drill crew. Practically all new brine wells are constructed with rotary drilling equipment. Steel casing is centralized in the drilled hole and cemented back to surface.

Underground storage of hydrocarbons has lead to utilization of the cavity created by brining. This procedure started in Texas and has gradually spread throughout the US at a much slower pace than the acceptance of hydraulic fracturing techniques. In conjunction with brining operations the storage of hydrocarbons has a tendency to lower brining costs or even to show a profit over and above the initial cost of producing salt.

Recently, plant wastes were injected into abandoned brine cavities. At Watkins Glen, NY, pan bleeds from the evaporators and residue from brine purification are injected into an old cavity and the resultant salt effluent from the cavity reprocessed. As the feasibility of this process proves itself to environmental authorities this practice should spread rapidly.

Once again, this will have the effect of reducing the actual cost of solution mining.

Brining costs vary tremendously from one area to another, depending largely on the capital costs involved in well construction. Brine wells in some areas are as shallow as a few hundred feet and in others are over 10,000 ft in depth. Thus, individual well construction costs vary from about $20,000 to over $250,000. The operating technique, together with the thickness of salt in the deposit which is to be exploited, will determine the tonnage of salt produced by a given well and thus, the capital cost per ton of salt. Operating cost of a brine well using the hydraulic fracturing technique is primarily a power cost. Thus, the major cost of brine well operation is a function of depth of the well and power costs. In the United States the cost of producing a ton of salt in brine varies from a low of about $0.45 per ton to approximately $2.00 per ton.

Solution mining in the United States in 1980 extracted some 22,231,000 tons of salt in the form of brine for chlor-alkali production (Kostick, 1981). Added to this was salt produced in the brine for the manufacture of 6,314,000 tons of evaporated salt. Thus, the chemical specifications and geological circumstances surrounding the solution mined production of about 62% of salt is of major importance.

It is gradually becoming apparent that the insoluble rocks which are exposed to the cavity during brining operations are in some cases major contributors of impurities to the brine being produced. Brine-soluble and water-soluble components of an otherwise insoluble sedimentary rock are occasionally present in quantities sufficiently high as to cause significant contamination of the brine being produced. In bedded deposits these rocks often contain connate waters which have high concentrations of minerals other than sodium chloride.

Generally, it is necessary to purify the brine before it can be used in the chlor-alkali cells or soda ash plants. Some types of electrolytic cells require solid salt for the resaturation of the spent cell liquor. As the spent cell liquor is recirculated, the metal ions or other impurities, unless removed, build up in the brine. Eventually the whole system has to be purged. The effect of trace amounts of soluble metal ions in the electrolysis process is very complex. Vanadium, molybdenum, chromium, and titanium are detrimental to the process since they cause hydrogen to be liberated in the chlorine. These metals also plate out on the amalgam in mercury cells and cause difficulties with thick mercury and formation of mercury "butter." The ions of copper, zinc, and lead are undesirable as they contaminate the finished caustic. Calcium and magnesium have to be removed from diaphragm cell feed to prevent blockage of the diaphragm by precipitation of lime and magnesia. Sulfate ions cause the oxidation of the graphite electrodes.

The exact specifications of the feed brine either for electrolytic cells or vacuum pans vary with individual operators. In general, however, specifications for maximum allowable concentration of impurities in cell feed brine are:

	Mg per L
SO_4	4000
Ca^{++}	100
Mg^{++}	1
ClO_3	2000
Fe^{+++}	1
Cu^{++}	0.5

The more contaminated the raw brine, the more complex and costly is its treatment. This is true of brine used not only for cell feed, but also for the production of granular salt. These additional costs are experienced not only in additional chemicals for treatment and additional costs for operating and main-tenance labor, but also for the investment needed for larger treatment facilities (Kauffman, 1960).

Solar Salt

Solar evaporation operations may have a variety of brine sources—seawater, salt springs, salt lakes, or the shallow wells of the original Syracuse, NY, operations. Even playa deposits themselves or the recrystallized salts from the solution of weathering salt outcrops may be catagorized as naturally occurring solar salt evaporation operations. Salt lakes furnish the feed brine for operations around their shores, while in other areas artificial brines produced from bedded rock salt deposits constitute the brine feed.

The construction of solar salt ponds is a matter of good engineering. Levees should be built of an impervious clay. Pond floors should be free of vegetation, sand lenses, and coral knobs which might give rise to seawater "boils" during operations. Such boils can be a major source of dilution as well as an escape route for brines which have been concentrated depending on the balance of the hydrostatic heads. Not only do these boils lead to a dilution and/or loss of concentrate, but, in the case of harvesting ponds, to a contaminated salt.

In most solar evaporation operations salt water is introduced by pumping or by high tides into large concentrating ponds. As the gravity of the brine in the concentrating pond increases it flows by gravity toward the pond's outlet and into the "lime" pond where calcium sulfate and other more insoluble compounds begin to precipitate out of solution. These lime ponds usually constitute about 10% of the total area of the concentrating ponds.

Prior to this transfer point, that is, before it enters the lime pond, the liquor is about 20°Be (20% dissolved solids). In the concentrator pond a part of the calcium sulfate, and all of the calcium, magnesium, and iron carbonates are precipitated. When the density in the lime pond has reached 26 to 26.5°Be, the fluid is either drained or pumped into the crystallizer or harvesting ponds where large quantities of calcium sulfate are deposited on the floor of the pond. Some salt starts to crystallize out of solution at 25°Be.

After its transfer into the crystallizer ponds the salinity continues to increase to 29.5 to 30.0°Be. In the range of salinity from 26.5 to 30.0°Be very pure halite is deposited on the floor of the crystallizer. The volume of salt deposited in this range of salinites leaves approximately 12% NaCl in the bitterns or "tails." Continued evaporation causes contamination of salt with magnesium sulfate, magnesium and potassium chlorides, sodium and magnesium bromides, together with other trace elements.

The crystallizing or harvesting pond is the most important area in the operation for many reasons. It should be rectangular in shape to accommodate modern harvesters. The material underlying the pond floor must be dense enough to support heavy equipment such as the harvester (Fig. 12). These crystallizer ponds should be close to the storage and dock areas to keep haulage costs to a minimum. The tonnage per acre of area employed in the total operation should be in excess of 40 tons and harvesting ponds should produce approximately 600 tons per acre.

In comparison to the lime ponds, the harvesting ponds usually occupy one-half to two-thirds the area. Because of the obvious economic advantage of gravity flow, ponds are arranged in such a manner as to take maximum advantage of natural contours and gradients. Fig. 13 illustrates harvesting ponds near the dock at International Salt Co.'s operation at Bonaire, Netherlands Antilles.

Although in some underdeveloped areas of

TABLE 8—Composition of a Typical Bittern

	%
NaCl	12.5
MgCl$_2$	8.7
MgSO$_4$	6.1
KCl	1.9
MgBr$_2$	0.18

Source: ver Planck, 1957.

the world salt is still manually harvested from the crystallizer ponds, all modern operations use mechanical harvesters. They are of various designs, but generally handle between 100 to 250 tph. Narrow gage rail haulage systems are giving way to truck haulage.

Raw salt is hauled to a wash plant where it is washed with a brine from the concentrating ponds and then finally sprayed with freshwater. The brine wash removes any dirt, clay, particles of calcium sulfate, and any organic material. The freshwater removes the occluded bitterns.

The chemical composition of a typical bittern is shown in Table 8 (ver Planck, 1957).

These salts or bittern are usually pumped back into the sea at a point where it will not become a contaminant of the raw brine feed.

Where sufficient quantities of bitterns are available the liquor is subjected to further

FIG. 12—*Harvesting pond and ship-loading facilities, International Salt Co., Bonaire.*

FIG. 13—*Solar salt harvesting.*

processing for the removal of other salts such as those of magnesium and potassium. The cycle time for the concentration of raw seawater to a precipitated salt and a waste or by-product bittern may be from a few months to several years, depending upon winds and various climatic factors. For example on Taiwan the cyclic time from raw seawater to bittern is about four to five years. Heavy rains or hurricanes can rupture the levees or cause the brines to become diluted, thus increasing the time span required to complete the cycle from seawater to salt.

Processing

Rock salt as dry mined is generally subjected only to crushing and screening. Exception to this procedure is the use of the Sortex process and/or the Thermoadhesive process to upgrade bedded rock salt products from an average NaCl content of 97% to a product of 99.0%+. The Sortex process depends on the translucence of salt and a jet of compressed air. The thermoadhesive process depends on the absorption of light by dark particles of anhydrite, shale, and dolomite. These dark heated particles adhere to a resin-coated belt, separating them from the translucent halite. In most instances the thermoadhesive process will remove 40% of the water insolubles from the crushed salt in a single pass through the process.

The purest grades of commercial salt are produced by the treatment of FC (fine crystal, 10 mesh) rock salt in a recrystallizer. In this process the fine granular rock salt is dissolved in high temperature brine. Due to the inverse solubility of calcium sulfate, the calcium sulfate is not taken into solution resulting in the production of a very pure hot brine. The salt produced by the recrystallizer may be as pure as 99.99% NaCl. The water balance in the recrystallizer system results in no net evaporation capacity. Direct injection and condensation of steam through a direct contact heater into the system dissolves the fine rock salt and heats the brine at the same time. Salt is produced in the evaporator by flash evaporation and by cooling. The vapors released in the lower effects are then used to augment the high pressure steam and thus recover as much of the heat as possible. Steam from the last effect is condensed in a barometric leg condenser (private communication).

Evaporated salt had its beginning before recorded history. Modern evaporation technique had its birth in England in 1812, when a Mr. Howard built a single-effect vacuum evaporator for the sugar industry. The first multiple-effect system was built in 1834, again for the sugar industry. It was not until 1887 that the first single-effect evaporator was used in the United States for salt production at Silver Springs, NY. In 1899 a multiple-effect vacuum pan was built at Manistee, MI.

Basically this is the principle for our current technology. The most common system used today is triple and quadruple multiple-effect system constructed of either Monel or Monel-clad steel. From the design standpoint, there are dozens of different original designs many of which have undergone numerous modifications during their productive lifetime. Some of these have progressed from the vertical tube type first built in 1850 to basket type used first in 1877 to the forced circulation of the 1890s.

Standard means for producing granulated salt for human consumption is by either the enclosed vacuum pans or in open pans. The most common process is the multiple effect evaporators. In this process the vapors from the boiling brine in the first vessel or effect are used to boil the brine in the second effect. This second effect is at a lower pressure than the first with the first effect vapors circulating through heat exchange tubes. The vapors from each succeeding effect are circulated through the following effect, which in turn is at a lower pressure and enables it to boil at a correspondingly lower temperature. In general, the multiple effect system has three or four of these vacuum pans.

Other means by which closed evaporators operate are by passing hot brine into a series of vessels or effects without the addition of heat to the effect. These depend on a low vacuum to "flash" the water from the hot brine.

Open pans or grainers consist of long shallow pans where the brine is heated by steam that is injected into the brine from below its surface. In this process the brine is never brought to the boiling point, with the resultant formation of a flake-type salt rather than the typical cube of halite produced by the vacuum pan. Gradually this process of producing salt is being discarded due to the high energy consumption per unit weight of salt produced.

All of these methods can operate on raw brine of varying degrees of purity. Depending on the purity of product required, the raw brine can be treated chemically before evaporation to remove the calcium and magnesium salts. Again, the brine can be treated with various additives to modify the crystal habit of the salt produced.

Transportation, Handling, and Storage

Rock salt, evaporated salt, and solar salt are transported from producing locations to customers and redistribution points by water, rail, and highway. Under normal conditions of distribution, the cost of transportation often exceeds the value of any large shipment of salt that travels over a few hundred miles.

Waterborne Salt

Ocean Movements: Although all types of salt are transported by oceangoing vessels, the major tonnage of salt moved is solar salt or rock salt. Salt moves in bulk freighters which range in size from 6,000 to over 100,000 tons, and salt may comprise a full or partial cargo.

Present major ocean movements of salt are as follows:

Solar Salt:

From the Bahamas, Netherlands Antilles, and Venezuela to eastern United States.

From Mexico to both eastern and western United States and to Japan.

From Australia to Japan.

From the Mediterranean, particularly North African coasts, to Europe and the United States.

Rock Salt:

From Chile to the United States.

From central Europe to the rest of Europe and the United States.

From Canada to the United States.

Great Lakes and St. Lawrence Seaway: Salt movements on the Great Lakes and the western regions of the St. Lawrence are mainly between the United States and Canada and vice versa, and between major United States east coast ports. In recent years some imported salt from Europe and the Caribbean has entered the region via the St. Lawrence Seaway. The main commodity shipped is bulk industrial salt and highway ice control salt.

Salt moves from the major producing facilities on the shores of the Great Lakes to major redistribution points by bulk and/or self unloading freighters, or barges, thus taking advantage of the economics of large volume waterborne transportation and the strategic value of lake ports for serving their respective areas.

As the economics of bulk transportation favor large cargoes and handling systems, the trend on the Great Lakes is to larger self-unloading vessels, requiring deeper water and more extensive dock loading and handling facilities, with a gradual demise of the smaller freighters. The normal navigational season on the Great Lakes is from April to December. Traffic generally stops in mid-December due to the ice buildup in the harbors. These harbors reopen in mid-April. Plans are currently being formulated to create ice-free ports with the use of large ice breakers.

US River and Canal Systems: Movement by barge is the lowest cost transportation for those commodities for which it is adaptable. Thus, salt moves by barge on all navigable sections of the central and eastern river and canal systems in the United States, on certain navigable rivers on the west coast, and between ports on the Gulf of Mexico. Barges range in size from 900 tons or less to massive 10,000-ton oceangoing units that are normally constructed with a double shell hull. The outer shell forms a floating hull and the inner shell forms an obstruction-free hopper or cargo hold. Salt moves almost exclusively in covered dry cargo barges, with either roll top or lift top covers.

Barge movement of salt in the southern United States begins at the producing mines, most of which are located south and west of New Orleans, in salt domes along the low lying southern Louisiana and Texas coasts, close to the Intracoastal Waterway system. The salt-laden barges move via the Intracoastal Waterway to join larger tows proceeding north up the Mississippi River. Barged salt reaches Kansas City, MO, Omaha, NE, Sioux City, IA on the Missouri River system; as far north as St. Paul and Minneapolis on the Mississippi River and Chicago, via the Illinois River. On occasion, river barges enter Lake Michigan via the Calumet River and proceed to destinations on the southern shores of the lake. Barges of southern salt also reach Pittsburgh, PA, and both Charleston and Fairmont, WV, via the Ohio, Allegheny, Kanawha, and Monongahela Rivers. Nashville, TN, is supplied with bulk salt via the Cumberland River; Chattanooga and Knoxville receive barged salt from movements on the Tennessee River.

In addition to these major movements, barged salt reaches Mobile and southern Alabama via the Intracoastal Waterway. The west coast of Florida is also served by gulf barges. In the Pacific northwest, limited quantities of salt move in barges on the navigable sections of the Columbia River system.

Normal winter conditions in midwestern United States result in the closing of certain sections of the Missouri and Mississippi River systems due to their freezing over and, hence, barge movements cease. The Missouri River above Kansas City, MO, and the Mississippi River above Davenport, IA, are usually closed to traffic from November through April. Except in extremely severe cold weather, traffic on the lower stretches of the Illinois and the Ohio Rivers and their tributaries is not interrupted in the winter months.

Rail Shipment of Salt

Bulk salt is carried in both boxcars and hopper cars, although by far the largest tonnage moves in the latter. Invariably covered hopper cars are used for bulk salt, as vagaries of weather preclude the successful use of the open hopper car.

Covered hoppers, originating in the south, particularly those loaded on hot humid days, experience problems with condensate collecting on the internal surfaces of the car. Where finer sizes are involved i.e., CC size and smaller, any moisture such as condensate will produce "caking." In order to minimize this effect, free flowing agents such as YPS (yellow prussiate of soda) are added. Salt shipments by rail or truck which contain any free moisture and where shipping during cold weather is anticipated are treated with an antifreeze formulation. Shipments are normally made in multicar lots (3–12 cars) to take advantage of substantial savings through special rate for unit trains.

High quality rock salt generally requires specialized equipment such as rail cars fitted for pneumatic loading and unloading and handling systems at destination. Large volumes of packaged salt products move in box cars, largely on pallets, and in many instances utilize specialized DF (damage free) and DFB (damage-free-bulkheaded) equipment.

Truck Shipments of Salt

Both bulk and packaged salt moves on trucks, primarily on short haul routes, generally less than 200 miles, from producing locations or from warehouses and stockpiles direct to customers. Bulk salt is carried in dump trucks or specialized pneumatic and tank trucks, depending on its grade, purity, and end use. It is important in shipping bulk salt that the truck be properly tarped. Any moisture inherent in the salt from production, or gathered during loading or hauling, will freeze in cold weather due to the supercooling effect of wind on the metal body of the truck. Certain industries take delivery of high purity salt in small specialized transportable bins carried on trucks. Packaged salt is moved on flatbed or van-type units.

Storage and Handling

Economics of supply and distribution dictate that salt be transported in bulk quantities to points as close to the area of consumption as possible and distributed from this point to the consumer in as large a quantity as the transportation system will allow. These deliveries should be in as large a quantity as the receiving point can handle without overtaxing the handling systems or causing undue delay in unloading the hauling equipment.

Apart from direct shipments of salt by one of the transportation systems discussed, both bulk and package salt are distributed through an extensive network of stockpiles and warehouses. In almost all cases the redistribution point is supplied from the producing plant in bulk quantities, or in quantities sufficient to enable the shipper to take advantage of freight concessions based on volume.

The maintenance of grade or quality from the producing plant to redistribution point or to the customer is of major importance in the salt industry. This concern arises from the normally high degradation rate of the halite crystal. The fewer the number of times salt is rehandled in the distribution process the better the retention of particle sizes within the grade specifications of the product being shipped. Hence the distribution system utilized must be designed to minimize the numbers of rehandling and transfer points.

Off-Loading Waterborne Salt

The most common method of unloading bulk salt from oceangoing vessels and barges is by clamshell bucket and crane. The unloading equipment is often an integral part of oceangoing vessels. However, when bulk freighters do not have self-unloading gear, cranes on shore or on barges are brought alongside for the transfer of the salt from freighter to dockside storage or to a transportation system. On the river systems where barges are moved to the discharging facility, either barge-mounted or shore-mounted cranes unload the cargo. In both cases, salt is normally dropped into a hopper which in turn feeds a conveyor system or trucks for continued movement to the customer and/or storage.

The majority of the salt moving on the Great Lakes is now carried in self-unloading vessels. Conveyor systems built into the boats in tunnels beneath the load carry the cargo to an onboard discharging conveyor system supported on a boom. The booms vary in length, with many now over 200 ft long with up to 120° travel on either side of the ship's centerline. This versatility enables bulk salt to be off-loaded at convenient dockside locations and placed in windrow piles.

Off-Loading Rail Salt

Unloading from boxcars requires bulk salt to be brought to doorway by hand shovels, miniature front-end loaders, or other mechanical means, then dropped into a hopper, chute, or dissolving tank alongside the boxcar.

Hopper cars are provided with release doors or gates beneath the car. Movement away from the car is accomplished by either an undercar pit and conveyor system, or a portable overtrack conveyor which is placed between bottom of car and top of rails. Salt can be conveyed directly to trucks or into a warehouse or stockpiles. Certain covered hopper cars are unloaded pneumatically, and salt is conveyed from rail car to storage by flexible hoses and pipes. This requires specialized handling and receiving equipment and is installed only where a constant salt supply is required.

Off-Loading Trucked Salt

Depending on grade size, purity, and use, bulk salt is carried from the producing point in either dump or tank trucks. Dump trucks drop loads either directly into hoppers or on a surface pad, so that salt can be loaded into hopper by front-end loaders. On occasion the salt is dumped directly into hoppers equipped with slingers. Salt is then conveyed into warehouse or stockpile. Dump trucks also off-load into pits, particularly where there are brine manufacturing operations.

Tank trucks, depending on type, can discharge either directly through bottom doors into pits, or by pneumatic methods into dissolving tanks or dry storage bins.

The selection of locations for warehouses and stockpiles for the secondary redistribution of salt products, as in other commodities, depends primarily on the marketing and servicing requirements, mix of products, the economics of transportation both to and from the storage and handling facility, and the costs of handling salt through the facility.

Storage Facilities

Bulk Outside Storage: Bulk storage is common for highway salt and certain grades of salt used by industry. Salt is brought to strategically located storage areas by water, rail, and truck, depending on accessibility from producing point and market requirements. The salt pile is usually built with a conveyor, although bulldozers, clamshell buckets, and cranes are also employed at some locations. Of prime importance in this type of storage is the control of salt dust during the period when the pile is being constructed. Piles are normally developed as cones or flat-topped windrows, both straight or curved; and every effort is made to produce even geometric shapes to minimize size of stockpile base and to simplify covering.

Environmental considerations dictate that salt piles must be placed on impervious, well-drained asphalt or concrete pads, and be fully covered with a suitable waterproof material. If moisture is allowed to enter a stockpile, brine leaches out, and drains away from the pile, to create unsightly white residues, and also to pose a threat to surface waters and potable ground water aquifers. Many types of covers are available ranging from treated burlap and canvas to high strength plastics and/or combinations of these materials. They are used mainly to prevent rainwater from entering the pile and to prevent fine salt from being blown away from the pile. Good housekeeping is a necessity at the edges of the piles so that rainwater runoff does not come in contact with salt while flowing away from pile base. Mesopiestic water will be drawn into the pile by capillary action if any portion of the toe of the pile is in contact with free water. This moisture will, through evaporation, cause a hard crust to form on the pile. In addition, moisture in bulk stored materials will cause caking and freezing problems in transport during winter months. Finer particle sizes draw more moisture than coarser sizes. Covered material lasts one to two years if undisturbed. Covers are not normally reusable if a pile has been depleted.

The selection of locations for stockpiles and warehouses for the redistribution of salt products depends primarily on the marketing requirements, product mix, and economics of transportation and handling. Environmental aspects which govern the design and construction may, depending on local conditions, make a site untenable from the standpoint of economics.

Bulk Inside Storage: Normally, industrial salt is stored inside, in either surface bins or silos. Salt which is to be used for bagging is usually stored inside. The main reasons for inside storage are to keep salt dry and uncontaminated. In some areas, highway ice control salt is stored inside and, as environmental factors become more rigid, the tonnages stored in this manner will increase. Most warehouses separate salt grades with walls or dividers in order to avoid mixing.

Two of the problems associated with storage of salt are listed below with the most common means of prevention and methods to overcome the problems:

Caking—Caking is the greatest problem in all types of salt storage. The degree of caking depends primarily on transit time, changes in moisture content, particle size, storage method and duration, chemical composition, and temperatures. Long transit times with the vibration of loads and inherent segregation of fines toward the bottom encourages caking, and long storage times allow salt to pass through several caking cycles, thus increasing overall caking.

Coarse salt, greater than $+\frac{3}{8}$ in., seldom gives trouble in storage. Bins for storage of fine salts should be built with poke holes so that chunk or caked salt can be displaced. Salt should be kept moving through bins as rapidly as possible with frequent salt additions and discharges.

Transit time from the production facility to the consumer should be at a minimum. Salt should be unloaded as soon as possible after being received and in-plant storage time should be kept at a minimum.

Degradation—Salt tends to degrade during loading, conveying, discharging from heights, and through handling by any and all types of equipment. Salt therefore must be handled as gently and as few times as possible between producing facility and customer.

Package Salt Storage: Standard warehouse procedures are used for inside storage of all forms of packaged salt. For the most part, packaged salt is palletized when received at the warehouse, or immediately after receipt, and is placed in storage areas with forklift trucks. The container shape and strength—either bag or carton—determines the stacking pattern of units on each pallet, and also determines the number of pallet loads which can be safely stacked one on another. The use of slip sheets and the shrink wrap techniques are gaining favor.

Storage areas must be clean and dry, as packaged salt is susceptible to moisture damage. Development of plastic bags is helping to alleviate this problem.

Marketing

A large percentage of the nations of the world have their own source of salt. Of the more than 181,608,000 tons of salt produced worldwide in 1980, the United States produced 41,480,000 tons (Kostick, 1981). Because of the wide distribution of salt either in the form of rock salt or solar-evaporated salt, prices for many years have been low and stable. Recently rock salt prices have as much as quintupled partially because of the inflated energy cost. As one of the five building blocks of the chemical industry, industries requiring salt have generally located near a source of salt and cheap power.

In most cases, irrespective of the low freight rates of water transportation, the cost of transportation is often more than the f.o.b. price of the salt and in some cases is as much as 75% of the delivered value.

Because the United States is the world's largest producer and consumer of salt, salt economics are governed to a large extent by US industrial and governmental agency purchasing. In the purchase of salt by governmental agencies for snow and ice control, contracts are awarded on a bid basis without regard to point of origin and, in some cases, require two or more sources of supply.

Use of salt for ice and snow control by federal, state, and local agencies was 6.4 million tons in 1980, down from 9.3 million tons in 1972. Practically all this tonnage was rock salt. During 1980 US rock salt producers mined 12.3 million tons, down from 14.4 million tons in 1972. Another 1,087,000 tons of snow and ice control salt was imported. Salt imports by end use are shown in Table 9 (Kostick, 1981).

Prices as quoted by the May 9, 1983 *Chemical Marketing Reporter* are as follows:

Salt, evaporated, common 80-lb bags, carload lot, North works	$3.00
Salt, 80-lb bag chemical grade, same basis	3.20
Salt, rock, medium coarse, same basis, 80 lb	2.05

The average value of evaporated salt reported by producers to the US Bureau of Mines during 1980 was $76.44 per ton, up from $21.26 per ton in 1972. On the same basis, the average value of rock salt in 1980 was $14.65, up from $6.58 in 1972. Salt in brine form was $6.50 per ton in 1980, up from

$3.61 per ton in 1972. The energy-intensive evaporated salt product demonstrates the most dramatic price increase. Tariff rates for salt are as follows:

Item	Most Favored Nation		Non-Most Favored Nation
	Jan. 1, 1983	Jan. 1, 1987	Jan. 1, 198
In brine	4.8% ad val.	3.7% ad val.	20% ad va
In bulk	2.6% ad val.	Free	26% ad v
Other	Free	Free	11¢/100 l

For tax purposes a depletion allowance of 10% is allowed for both foreign and domestic deposits.

Five states contributed a total of 33,703,000 tons, or 81.3% of total US production (Table 10).

The average value per ton of salt established for each state (Table 11) is a composite of types of salt. Various other factors influence price. Where a large percentage of the salt produced is in the form of brine, as in Texas, costs are low. Those states producing large tonnages of salt by evaporation reflect increased energy costs in a higher cost per ton. New York, Michigan, and Ohio are situated close to population centers and therefore have less freight absorption with respect to making their products competitive in the marketplace.

In 1980, 11 of the 47 salt-producing companies accounted for 82% of US production. Each of these companies produced in excess

TABLE 9—Salt Imports Into US by End Use (Thousand Short Tons)

Use	1979	1980
Government (highway use)	2,396	1,082
Chemical industry	762	803
Water conditioning service	148	179
Other	388	260
	3,695	2,330

Source: Kostick, 1981.

TABLE 10—Major Salt-Producing States of the US 1979-1980 (Thousand Short Tons, Thousand Dollars)

	1979		1980	
	Quantity	Value	Quantity	Value
Louisiana	14,207	113,167	12,662	132
Texas	11,283	67,602	9,978	93
New York	6,387	77,751	5,509	99
Ohio	4,135	79,598	3,228	87
Michigan	3,080	82,540	2,406	104

Source: Kostick, 1981.

TABLE 11—Average Value of Salt Produced for the Chemical Industry, 1980

State	Average Value $ per ton of all salt	Evaporated, Tons
Michigan	$43.58	1,133,000
Ohio	27.07	NA
New York	18.04	638,000
Louisiana	10.44	280,000
Texas	9.36	NA

NA—Not available.

of 1 million tons. Brine produced in 1980 constituted 55% of the total salt produced while mined rock salt accounted for 30%. Vacuum pan and grainer-evaporated types of salt amounted to 9% of the total, with solar-evaporated furnishing only 6% of domestic production.

Leaders in world salt production are shown in Table 12.

United States exports of salt amounted to 831,000 tons with a value of $12,829,000 in 1980. Over 95% of this salt was shipped to Canada.

Imports totaled 5,263,000 tons with a valuation of $44,071,000 or $8.37 per ton (Table 13). The majority of the tonnage was purchased by government agencies for snow and ice control. While the value per ton of exports was $15.43 as opposed to import value of $8.37 per ton, the deficit trade balance for the world's largest salt producer was $31,242,000. The increase in US imports of salt from 2.494 million tons in 1972 to 5.263 million tons in 1980 was due in part to US companies acquiring foreign sources of cheap solar-evaporated salt. This salt, loaded on oceangoing freighters, can be landed close to the points

TABLE 12—Salt Production (tons) by Country, 1980

United States	41,480,000
China	20,000,000
USSR	15,980,000
Germany (West)	14,300,000
United Kingdom	7,300,000
France	7,830,000
Canada	7,748,000
Australia	5,859,000
Mexico	6,600,000
Romania	6,200,000
Italy	5,806,000
Poland	3,700,000
Netherlands	3,818,000
India	8,000,000

Source: Kostick, 1981.

TABLE 13—US Imports for Consumption of Salt, by Country (Thousand Short Tons, Thousand Dollars)

Country	1979 Quantity	1979 Value	1980 Quantity	1980 Value
Bahamas	528	3,985	531	5,573
Brazil	197	1,625	62	608
Canada	2,057	15,580	2,089	16,515
Chile	244	1,699	341	2,689
Colombia	41	480	273	2,280
Italy	42	1,205	—	—
Mexico	1,649	11,282	1,457	10,216
Nepal	—	—	22	161
Netherlands	57	960	104	2,034
Netherlands Antilles	175	1,597	193	2,031
Spain	252	1,745	99	831
Tunisia	33	250	60	530
Yemen Arab Republic	—	—	31	163
Other	—	452	—	439
Total	5,275	40,860	5,263	44,071

Source: Kostick, 1981.

of consumption along the eastern coast. This, together with inherently low labor costs, adds to the competitive edge of the off-shore producers. As some of these third world governments and labor unions become more sophisticated, this present advantageous position will diminish. Some US companies have already found their Caribbean investments less than attractive.

A determining factor in world demand for salt is its use in the chlor-alkali and soda ash industries. In the five years from 1966 to 1970, the consumption of salt for this use fell from 20% to 14% of total salt consumed in the United States, although use of salt for other purposes increased. In 1972 salt used for chlorine-caustic soda and soda ash was 26,517,000 tons. By 1980 this total tonnage had fallen to 23,941,000, largely because of the impact of Green River trona, which is progressing as expected.

The demand for chlorinated solvents, chlorofluorocarbons, and chlorinated hydrocarbons is the dominant factor in controlling the demand and hence the price of chlorine. The growth of chlorine consumption in countries where large quantities of pulp and paper are produced is higher than that experienced by other chlorine users. The aluminum industry and manufacturers of certain synthetic fibers also consume a vast amount of salt-based chemicals.

TABLE 14—End Uses of Salt

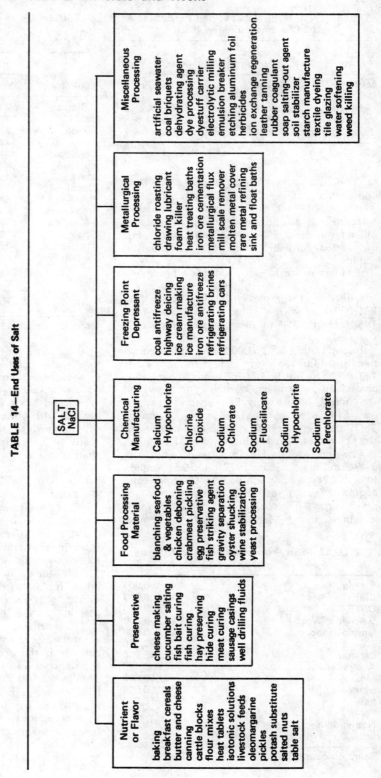

Nutrient or Flavor	Preservative	Food Processing Material	Chemical Manufacturing	Freezing Point Depressant	Metallurgical Processing	Miscellaneous Processing
baking	cheese making	blanching seafood & vegetables	Calcium Hypochlorite	coal antifreeze	chloride roasting	artificial seawater
breakfast cereals	cucumber salting	chicken deboning	Chlorine Dioxide	highway deicing	drawing lubricant	coal briquets
butter and cheese	fish bait curing	crabmeat pickling	Sodium Chlorate	ice cream making	foam killer	dehydrating agent
canning	fish curing	egg preservative	Sodium Fluosilicate	ice manufacture	heat treating baths	dye processing
cattle blocks	hay preserving	fish striking agent	Sodium Hypochlorite	iron ore antifreeze	iron ore or cementation	dyestuff carrier
flour mixes	hide curing	gravity separation	Sodium Perchlorate	refrigerating brines	metallurgical flux	electrolytic milling
heat tablets	meat curing	oyster shucking		refrigerating cars	mill scale remover	emulsion breaker
isotonic solutions	sausage casings	wine stabilization			molten metal cover	etching aluminum foil
livestock feeds	well drilling fluids	yeast processing			rare metal refining	herbicides
oleomargarine					sink and float baths	ion exchange regeneration
pickles						leather tanning
potash substitute						rubber coagulant
salted nuts						soap salting-out agent
table salt						soil stabilizer
						starch manufacture
						textile dyeing
						tile glazing
						water softening
						weed killing

SALT NaCl

Salt

Soda Ash, Na_2CO_3
abrasives
adhesives
batteries
ceramics
cleansers
cosmetics
degreasers
dyes
explosives
fats and oils
fertilizers
fire extinguishers
inhibitors
insecticides
leather
metal fluxes
ore refining
paint removers
paper
petroleum
pigments
soap
textiles
water softeners

Sodium, Na
bactericides
case hardening
cosmetics
detergents
dye fixation
dyes
flour conditioning
fumigation
heat transfer
ore refining
organic syntheses
paints
pharmaceuticals
photography
pigments
plating salts
pulp bleaching
starch conversion
tetraethyl lead
textile bleaching
titanium metal
zirconium metal

Sodium Sulfate, Na_2SO_4
ceramics
detergents
dyes
explosives
fertilizers
metal fluxes
paper
pharmaceuticals
photography
pigments
plating salts
rubber
soap
textiles

Hydrogen, H_2
alcohol
ammonia
cooking fats
high energy fuels
hydrochloric acid
metallurgy
meteorology
organic syntheses
petroleum products
pharmaceuticals
synthetic fibers
synthetic gems
welding

Hydrochloric Acid, HCl
adhesives
ceramics
dyes
engraving
inks
leather
metal cleaners
ore refining
perfumes
pigments
printing
rubber
soldering flux
textiles

Chlorine, Cl_2
anaesthetics
bleaches
ceramic colors
cleansers
disinfectants
dyes
explosives
fertilizers
fire extinguishers
fungicides
insecticides
leather
paint removers
paper
plastics
refrigerants
rubber
sewage treatment
solvents
synthetic fibers
textiles
water treatment
weed killers

Caustic Soda, NaOH
adhesives
batteries
building materials
ceramics
cosmetics
dyes
explosives
fruit peeling
inks
ion exchange
laundering
leather
lubricants
ore refining
pharmaceuticals
pigments
plastics
rayon
refractories
rubber
soap
synthetic fibers
water treatment
wood processing

Of tremendous importance to the rock salt mining industry is the use of salt for snow and ice control. Approximately 40% of the rock salt mined and about 60% of the profit in its mining are related to the de-icing of roads and highways. Vagaries in the weather plus environmental considerations make this use cyclical. Eventually advanced technology will eliminate this use.

Uses

Salt is the most readily available and abundant source of sodium and chlorine ions. These ions are used in making a number of chemicals such as soda ash, chlorine, caustic soda, and metallic sodium.

Although it is said that there are over 14,000 uses for salt, only a few consume a major portion of the salt production. Table 14 gives seven general categories of uses with a breakdown of the major chemicals derived from salt, and a listing of more important products of these chemicals.

Table 15 shows classes of consumption in the United States. Currently the chemical industry consumes 53% of all domestic salt produced, with chlorine accounting for 86% of this amount. Soda ash now consumes only a small amount of chemical salt.

A new use of salt is in-situ creation of cavities for storage and other uses. Some of the uses will allow dry or solution mining and primary use of the salt as a consumer item, with use of the cavity as a byproduct of the operation. In other cases, the cavity itself is the principal product, with the salt extracted forming a waste with environmental consequences.

New uses for salt cavities during the last three decades, including those currently in the design stage, are storage of liquid hydrocarbons (propane, butane, kerosene, fuel oil and jet fuel); storage of hazardous wastes (arsenides, cyanide, pesticides, herbicides, toxic wastes, and outdated drugs); storage of nuclear or radioactive wastes; storage of compressed air (peak shaving of power in electrical generation); geothermal energy; and wasting of insoluble materials (fly ash and other plant waste in abandoned brine cavities and mines).

Future Considerations and Trends

Salt is relatively inexpensive, readily accessible, and abundant, with no substitute either natural or synthetic. Because of its abundance there are no government programs to stimulate its production or use.

Environmental problems have always plagued the soda ash and chlor-alkali industry as well as rock salt mines and evaporator plants. For many reasons, one by one the Solvay soda ash plants have closed; as of July 1983 only one Solvay soda ash plant was operating. It is scheduled to be closed soon. Eventually all soda ash production in the US will come from the Green River area of Wyoming and Searles Lake in California.

Salt is widely used for the removal of snow and ice from our highways in the north and northeastern portions of the United States. Although this use is a source of some water pollution during the snowstorms of the winter months, the deleterious effects are far overshadowed by the safety benefits of ice-free roads. Stabilization of the subgrade of highways, airports, and parking lots by the use of brine in the compaction and hardening of the subgrade will see expanded use.

Some economists have suggested that due to the eventual shortage of paper pulp and ecological objections to salt's use for snow and ice removal the consumption will level off and/or decrease. The substitution of trona for soda ash will be another prime factor in the reduction of tonnages of salt produced by US industry.

It is the opinion of the authors that the trend of a gradual increase in salt consumption will prevail over the long term. Nothing has been found to replace salt for de-icing highways. Other scientific advances will lead to increases in salt consumption. One of these will be the use of salt in the control and reduction of coal dust in mines. The process of "salt crust" has long been known in European coal centers but because of the bureaucratic regulations and union politics, salt use as a dust collector and substitute for limestone dusting has been blocked. Although salt could be used in a similar manner in other dusty mines, such use in coal mines alone would consume millions of tons.

Another scientific advance has shown that sodium chloride added to certain solvents will enhance their ability to dissolve various metallic sulfides. As solution mining increases in the extraction of metalliferous values, there will be an increase in the use of salt. Adding salt to sulfuric acid dramatically improves the solubility of copper sulfides. This process for

TABLE 15—Distribution of Salt Sold or Used by Producers in the United States, By Use '(Thousand Short Tons)

Consumer or use	1979 Evaporated	Rock	Brine	Total*	1980 Evaporated	Rock	Brine	Total*
Chlorine, caustic soda, soda ash	557	1,819	23,824	26,200	682	2,103	21,156	23,941
All other chemicals	446	625	150	1,222	396	505	119	1,020
Textile and dyeing	134	53	—	188	124	53	—	177
Meatpackers, tanners, casing manufacturers	259	287	—	546	278	268	—	546
Dairy	78	7	—	85	79	5	—	84
Canning	181	99	†	280	182	104	†	287
Baking	109	10	—	119	105	8	—	113
Flour processors (including cereal)	70	25	†	95	68	24	†	92
Other food processing	204	56	†	261	197	40	14	251
Feed dealers	688	506	—	1,194	732	440	—	1,172
Feed mixers	364	359	—	723	337	326	—	662
Metals	70	286	†	356	56	215	†	272
Rubber	W	9	W	99	W	5	W	95
Oil	228	103	218	550	345	100	264	709
Paper and pulp	W	134	W	194	W	135	W	230
Water softener manufacturers and service companies	464	345	†	810	443	234	8	686
Grocery stores	887	253	†	1,140	825	168	†	995
Highway use	308	8,433	†	8,742	252	6,137	†	6,389
US government	20	58	†	78	39	82	†	121
Distributors (brokers, wholesalers, etc.)	588	W	W	1,249	529	W	W	989
Miscellaneous and undistributed‡	603	1,430	491	§1,714	637	1,320	501	§1,810
Total*	6,260	14,901	24,684	45,844	6,306	12,272	22,063	40,641

Source: Kostick, 1981.

W Withheld to avoid disclosing company proprietary data; included with "Miscellaneous and undistributed."

* Data may not add to totals shown because of independent rounding.

† Less than 5 units; included with "Miscellaneous and undistributed."

‡ Includes withheld figures and some exports and consumption in overseas areas administered by the United States.

§ Incomplete totals; withheld totals are included with total for each specific use.

mining deep-seated and/or marginal deposits has gained considerable acceptance by the mining industry.

Thus, with our advancing technology and increase in the consumer demands of our society, salt and its sodium and chlorine components will continue to play an increasingly important role in man's life.

Acknowledgment: This is to acknowledge, with deep appreciation, the efforts of John A. C. Atkins in respect to the section on "Transportation, Handling, and Storage."

Bibliography and References

Anon., 1978, "New Problems Arise for Nuclear Waste Storage," *Chemical and Engineering News,* Vol. 56, No. 24, June 12, p. 28.

Anon., 1978a, "Pakistan Opens New Salt Mine," *Mining Journal,* Vol. 290, No. 7446, May, p. 337.

Adams, J.E., 1968, "Permian Salt Deposits, West Texas and Eastern New Mexico," Special Paper No. 88, Geological Society of America, p. 407.

Al Naqib, N.M., 1970, "Geology of Jabal Sanam, South Iraq," *Journal,* Geological Society of America, Vol. 3, No. 1, pp. 9–36.

Aleksin, A.G., Kozhevnikov, I.I., and Sokolin, K.G., 1968, "Geologicheskoye Stroyeniye i Neftegazonosnost' Solyanokupol'nykh Basseynov Zapadnoy Afriki (Gas and Oil-Bearing Salt Domes of West Africa)," *Geologiya Nefti i Gaza,* Vol. 12, No. 12, pp. 47–51.

Andreyeva, R.I., and Kabyshev, V.P., 1970, "Kharakternyye Osobennosti Solyanoy Tektoniki Dneprovsko-Donetskoy Vpadiny (Characteristics of Salt Tectonics of the Dnieper-Donets Basin)," *Sovetskaya Geologiya,* No. 2, pp. 135–142.

Antoine, J.W., and Bryant, W.R., 1969, "Distribution of Salt and Salt Structures in Gulf of Mexico," *Bulletin,* American Assn. of Petroleum Geologists, Vol. 53, No. 12, pp. 2543–2550.

Atwater, G.I., 1968, "Gulf Coast Salt Dome Field

Area," Special Paper No. 88, Geological Society of America, pp. 29–40.

Auzende, J.M., et al., 1971, "Upper Miocene Salt Layer in the Western Mediterranean Basin," *Nature*, Vol. 230, No. 12, pp. 82–84.

Ballard, J.A., and Feden, R.H., 1970, "Diapiric Structures on the Campeche Shelf and Slope, Western Gulf of Mexico," *Bulletin*, Geological Society of America, Vol. 81, No. 2, pp. 505–512.

Bays, C.A., 1963, "Significant Uncertainties in Current Salt Solution Extraction Operations," *1st Symposium on Salt*, Northern Ohio Geological Society, Cleveland, pp. 467–481.

Bays, C.A., et al., 1960, "Solution Extraction of Salt Using Wells Connected by Hydraulic Fracturing," *AIME Transactions*, Vol. 217, pp. 266–277.

Benavides, V., 1968, "Saline Deposits of South America," Special Paper No. 88, Geological Society of America, pp. 249–290.

Benavides, G.L., and Sansores, E., 1968, "Salt Deposits of Southern Mexico," Special Paper No. 88, Geological Society of America, pp. 407–408.

Bentor, Y.K., 1968, "Salt Deposits of the Dead Sea Region," Special Paper No. 88, Geological Society of America, pp. 139–156.

Bleimeister, W.C., 1970, "Mining the Salar Grande," *3rd Symposium on Salt*, Vol. 2, Northern Ohio Geological Society, Cleveland, pp. 479–486.

Bornhauser, M., 1971, "Salt Piercement versus Downbuilding on Shallow Gulf Coast Salt Domes," Discussion, *Bulletin*, American Assn. of Petroleum Geologists, Vol. 55, No. 8, pp. 1360–1361.

Braitsch, O., 1971, *Salt Deposits, Their Origin and Composition*, Vol. 4, "Minerals, Rocks and Inorganic Materials," Springer-Verlag, New York-London-Heidelberg, 297 pp.

Briggs, L.T., 1968, "Evaporite Deposits of the United States," Abstract, Special Paper No. 88, Geological Society of America, p. 408.

Brinkman, R., and Logsters, H., 1968, "Diapirs in Western Pyrenees and Foreland, Spain," *Diapirism and Diapirs*, Geological Memoir No. 8, American Assn. of Petroleum Geologists, pp. 275–292.

Brognon, G., 1971, "The Geology of the Angola Coast and Continental Margin," *The Geology of the East Atlantic Continental Margin*, Vol. 4, "Africa, Great Britain," Report No. 70/16, Institute of Geological Science, pp. 143–152.

Brunstrom, R.G.W., 1967, "Origin of the Keuper Salt in Britain," *Nature*, Vol. 215, No. 5109, p. 1474.

Brunstrom, R.G.W., and Walmsley, P.J., 1968, "Permian Evaporites in North Sea Basin," *Bulletin*, American Assn. of Petroleum Geologists, Vol. 52, No. 3, p. 522.

Bush, V.A., et al., 1970, "Solyanokupol'nyye Struktury Vostochnoy Chasti Severo-Germanskoy Vpadiny i Osobennosti ikh Razmeshcheniya (Salt Dome Structures in the Eastern Part of the North German Basin and Their Distribution)," *Geologia i Razvedka*, Izvestiya Vysshikh Uchebnykh Zavedeni, No. 3, pp. 27–34.

Cater, F.W., and Craig, L.C., 1970, "Geology of the Salt Anticline Region in Southwestern Colorado," Professional Paper No. 637, US Geological Survey, 80 pp.

Clarke, F.W., 1924, "The Data of Geochemistry," Bulletin 770, US Geological Survey, 841 pp.

Clarke, O.M., Jr., et al., 1970, "Mineral Resources of Wilcox County, Alabama," Circular No. 66, Alabama Geological Survey, 26 pp.

Contreras, V.H., and Castillon, B.M., 1968, "Morphology and Origin of Salt Domes of Isthmus of Tehauntepec," *Diapirism and Diapirs*, Geological Memoir No. 8, American Assn. of Petroleum Geologists, pp. 244–260.

Cordini, I.R.A., 1967, "Reservas Salinas de Argentina (Salt Resources of Argentina)," *Annales*, Inst. Nac. Geol. Mineria, No. 13, 108 pp.

DeMille, G., and Schouldice, J.R., 1968, "Saline Deposits of Alberta and Saskatchewan," Special Paper No. 88, Geological Society of America, pp. 408–409.

Dingman, R.J., 1967, "Geology and Ground-Water Resources of the Northern Part of the Salar de Atacama, Antofagasta Province, Chile," Bulletin No. 1219, US Geological Survey, 49 pp.

Dunnington, H.V., 1968, "Salt-Tectonic Features of Northern Iraq," Special Paper No. 88, Geological Society of America, pp. 183–227.

Eargle, D.H., et al., 1971, "Uranium Geology and Mines, South Texas," Guidebook No. 12, Bureau of Economic Geology, University of Texas, 59 pp.

Eaton, G.P., et al., 1970, "Luke Dome, a Halokinetic Salt Mass Near Phoenix, Arizona," *Abstracts*, Geological Society of America, Vol. 2, No. 5, p. 332.

Fernandes, G., 1968, "O Sal-Gema de Formacao Nova Olinda, Bacia do Medio Amazonas (Rock Salt in the Nova Olinda Formation, Middle Amazonas Basin)," *Bol. Tec. Petrobras*, Vol. 11, No. 2, pp. 245–248.

Fischer, G., 1967, "Salzbergwerk Berchtesgaden (Berchtesgaden Salt Mine)," *Fortschritte der Mineralogie*, Vol. 45, No. 1, 6 pp.

Flores, T., 1918, "El Tequesquite del Lago de Texcoco," *Annales*, Mexican Institute of Geology, No. 5, pp. 1–14.

Foster, R.J., 1980, "Salt," Preprint, US Bureau of Mines, 12 pp.

Frey, M.G., and Grimes, W.H., 1969, "Bay Marchand-Timbalier, Bay-Caillou Island Salt Complex, Louisiana," in "Geology of the American Mediterranean," *Transactions*, Gulf Coast Assn. of Geological Societies, Vol. 19, p. 266.

Galitskiy, I.V., and Pistrak, R.M., 1970, "Role of Rhomboid Block Fields in the Tectonics of the Dnieper-Donets Depression," *Doklady*, Earth Sciences Sections, Akademiya Nauk SSSR, Vol. 187, pp. 23–25.

Gardner, L.S., et al., 1967, "Salt Resources of Thailand," Report of Investigations No. 11, Thailand Dept. of Mineral Resources, 100 pp.

Garlicki, A., 1970, "Zloze Soli Kamiennej Mosczenica-Lapczyca na Zachod od Bochni (Rock Salt Deposit in the Moszczenica-Lapczyca Area West of Bochnia)," *Kwart. Geol.*, Polish Institute of Geology, Vol. 14, No. 2, pp. 350–360.

Garlicki, A., 1979, "Sedymentacja Soli Mioceńskich W Polsche, (Sedimentation of Miocene Salts in Poland)," *Prace Geologiczne 119*, Polska Akademia Nauk-Oddzial W Krakowie Komisja Nauk Geologicznych, 67 pp.

Gawel, A., 1967, "Salt Deposit at Wieliczka," *Bulletin*, Polish Institute of Geology, No. 211, Pt. 2, pp. 325–328, 337–339.

Geyer, H., 1973, "How Hydraulic Excavators Cut Costs, Raise Efficiency at German Salt Mine," *World Mining*, Vol. 9, No. 3, May, pp. 41–43, 66.

Gimm, W., ed., 1968, *Kali- und Steinsalzbergbau (Potash and Rock Salt Mining)*, Band 1, "Aufschluss und Abbau von Kali- und Steinsalzlagerstatten (Vol. 1, Exploration and Exploitation of Potash and Rock Salt Deposits)," Deutsche Verlag Grundstoffind., 600 pp.

Gorfunkel', M.V., and Slepakova, G.I., 1970, "Pervichnaya Moshchnost' Solyanoy Tolshchi v Prikaspiyskoy Vpadine po Geofizicheskim Dannym (The Primary Thickness of Salt Series in the Caspian Basin Based on Geophysical Data)," *Sovetskaya Geologiya*, No. 4, pp. 166–169.

Gorfunkel', M.V., and Slepakova, G.I., 1971, "Original Thickness of Salt in the Caspian Depression, from Geophysical Data," *International Geology Review*, Vol. 13, No. 3, pp. 419–421.

Gorrell, H.A., and Alderman, G.R., 1968, "Elk Point Group Saline Basins of Alberta, Saskatchewan and Manitoba, Canada," Special Paper No. 88, Geological Society of America, pp. 291–317.

Gussow, W.C., 1965, "Energy Source of Intrusive Masses," Abstract, *Bulletin*, American Assn. of Petroleum Geologists, Vol. 49, No. 3, Mar., p. 343.

Halbouty, M.J., 1967, *Salt Domes*, Gulf Publishing Co., 425 pp.

Hamilton, W.N., 1971, "Salt in East-Central Alberta," Bulletin No. 29, Research Council of Alberta, 53 pp.

Hauber, L., et al., 1971, "Bericht uber die Exkursion der Schweizerischen Geologischen Gesellschaft in das Gebiet der Rheintaflexur und des Tafeljuras bei Basel vom 19. und 20. Oktober 1970 (Report on the Field Trip of the Swiss Geological Society in the Area of the Rhine Valley Flexure and the Jura Plateau near Basel, October 19–20, 1970)," *Eclogae Gol. Helvetica*, Vol. 64, No. 1, pp. 204–214.

Hermann, A., et al., 1967, "Die Halotektonische Deutung der Elfas-Uberschiebung in Sudniedersachsischen Bergland (Salt Tectonics of the Elfas Overthrust Zone in the Mountainous Region of Southern Lower Saxony)," *Geologisches Jahrbuch*, Vol. 84, pp. 407–460.

Hills, J.M., 1968, "Permian Basin Field Area, West Texas and Southeastern New Mexico," Special Paper No. 88, Geological Society of America, pp. 17–27.

Hite, R.J., 1968a, "Salt Deposits of the Paradox Basin, Southeast Utah and Southwest Colorado," Special Paper No. 88, Geological Society of America, pp. 319–330.

Hofrichter, E., 1967, "Subrosion und Bodensenkungen am Salzstock von Stade (Subsurface Leaching and Subsidence on the Salt Dome of Stade)," *Geologisches Jahrbuch*, Vol. 84, pp. 327–340.

Hofrichter, E., 1978, "Geologie, Tektonik, Mineralogie, Geochemie," *V. International Salz-Symposium in Deutschland*, Kali Steinsalz, Vol. 7, No. 8, pp. 338–344.

Holser, W.T., 1971, "Geologic Significance of the Minor-Element Composition of Marine Salt Deposits," *Economic Geology*, Vol. 66, No. 5, p. 813.

Jacoby, C.H., 1969, "Faults and Their Impact on (Salt) Mining," *3rd Symposium on Salt*, Vol. 2, Northern Ohio Geological Society, Cleveland, pp. 447–452.

Jacoby, C.H., 1969a, "Correlation, Faulting, and Metamorphism of Michigan and Appalachian Basin Salt," *Bulletin*, American Assn. of Petroleum Geologists, Vol. 53, No. 1, pp. 136–154.

Jacoby, C.H., 1972, "Evaluation of Salt Deposits," *Trans. SME/AIME*, Vol. 252, pp. 118–122.

Jacoby, C.H., 1973, "Salt," *Mining Engineering*, Vol. 25, No. 1, Jan., pp. 46–47.

Jacoby, C.H., 1977, "Geology—Hydrology of Avery Island Salt Dome," July, Y/OWI/SUB.

Jacoby, C.H., 1977a, "Scoping Report of Various Salt Mines in the United States," July, Y/OWI/SUB and Y/OWI/SUB, 77/16523/1.

Jaritz, W., 1968, "Einige Bemerkungen uber die Entstehung der Salzstrukturen Nordwestdeutschlands (Remarks on the Genesis of Salt Structures in Northwestern Germany)," *Erdol Kohle*, Vol. 21, No. 9, pp. 519–520.

Johnson, H.A., and Bredeson, D.H., 1971, "Structural Development of Some Shallow Salt Domes in Louisiana Miocene Productive Belt," *Bulletin*, American Assn. of Petroleum Geologists, Vol. 55, No. 2, pp. 204–226.

Johnson, K.S., 1970, "Salt Produced by Solar Evaporation on Big Salt Plain, Woods County, Oklahoma," *Geological Notes*, Geological Survey of Oklahoma, Vol. 30, No. 3, pp. 47–54.

Johnson, K.S. and Gonzalez, S., 1978, "Salt Deposits in the United States and Regional Geologic Characteristics Important for Storage of Radioactive Wastes," March, Y/OWI/SUB–74141.

Kapustin, N.N., 1970, "Rol'tektonicheskogo Faktora v Formirovanii Solyanokupol'nykh Struktur, na Primere Severo-Germanskoy Vpadiny (The Role of Tectonics in the Formation of Salt Dome Structures, North German Basin)," *Geologia i Razvedka*, Izvestiya Vysshikh Uchebnykh Zavedenii, No. 12, pp. 42–48.

Kaufman, D.W., 1960, *Sodium Chloride*, Reinhold, New York, 743 pp.

Kent, P.E., 1970, "The Salt Plugs of the Persian Gulf Region," *Transactions*, Philosophical Society, Vol. 64, pp. 55–58.

Khrushchov, D.P., and Gavrish, V.K., 1968, "Pro Deyaki Strukturni Osoblivosti Solyanikh Porid Dniprovs'ko-Donets'koi Zapadini (Some Structural Features of Halite in the Dnieper-Donets Basin, USSR)," *Dopovidi*, Akademii Nauk Ukrainskoi SSR, Series B., No. 1, pp. 53–58.

Kirkland, D.W. and Evans, R., 1973, *Marine Evaporites, Origin, and Diagenesis and Geochemistry*, Dowden, Hutchinson and Ross, Inc., Stroudsburg, PA, 426 pp.

Klingsberg, C. and Duguid, J., 1980, "Status of Technology for Isolating High Level Radioactive Waste in Geologic Repositories," D.E.E./T.I.C. 11207, pp. 77–85.

Koch, K., et al., 1968, "Geochemische Untersuchungen an Salzen und Laugen von Salzlagerstatten in der Deutschin Demokratischen Republik (Geochemical Investigations of Salts and Brines of the Salt Deposits of the German Democratic Republic)," *Abstract Volume*, 23rd International Geological Congress, Prague, Czechoslovakia, 161 pp.

Kostick, D.S., 1981, "Salt," *Minerals Yearbook, 1980*, US Bureau of Mines, pp. 683–694.

Kostick, D.S., 1982, "Salt," *Mineral Industry Surveys*, US Bureau of Mines, pp. 132–133.

Krishnan, M.S., 1966, "Salt Tectonics in the Punjab Salt Range, Pakistan," *Bulletin*, Geological Society of America, Vol. 77, No. 1, pp. 115–122.

Krishnan, M.S., 1968, "Geology of the Salt Deposits in the Punjab Salt Range, Pakistan," Special Paper No. 88, Geological Society of America, pp. 410–411.

Krishnan, M.S., 1968a, "Saline Lake Deposits of Rajasthan, India," Special Paper No. 88 (abstract), Geological Society of America, p. 411.

Kupfer, D.H., ed., 1970, *Geology and Technology of Gulf Coast Salt*, School of Geoscience, Louisiana State University, Baton Rouge, 183 pp.

Kupfer, D.H., 1970a, "Mechanism of Intrusion of Gulf Coast Salt," *Geology and Technology of Gulf Coast Salt*, Louisiana State University, School of Geosciences, Baton Rouge, pp. 25–65.

Landes, K.K., 1960, "Geology of Salt Deposits," *Sodium Chloride*, D.W. Kaufman, ed., Reinhold, New York, pp. 28–69.

Lawrence, C.R., 1971, "Occurrence and Production of Halite and Gypsum in Victoria," *Mining Geology Journal*, Mines Dept., Victoria, Vol. 7, No. 1, pp. 17–19.

Lefond, S.J., 1965, "Salt—The Universal Mineral," *The Explorer*, Cleveland Natural Science Museum, Vol. 7, No. 4, pp. 11–15, 34–35.

Lefond, S.J., 1969, *Handbook of World Salt Resources*, Monographs in Geoscience, Plenum Press, New York, 384 pp.

Leite, D.C., 1968, "Investigacoes Sobre as Possibilidades de Salgema na Parte Sudoeste da Bacia Sedimentar do Reconcavo (Investigations on the Possibilities of Rock Salt in the Southwestern Part of the Reconcavo Sedimentary Basin, Bahia)," *Bol. Tec. Petrobras*, Vol. 11, No. 2, pp. 231–242.

Leroy, L.E., 1951, *Subsurface Geologic Methods*, 3rd ed., Colorado School of Mines, Golden, 1166 pp.

Liechti, P., 1968, "Salt Features of France," Special Paper No. 88, Geological Society of America, pp. 83–106.

Lotze, F., 1968, "Salt Deposits of Europe (Including the USSR)," Special Paper No. 88, Geological Society of America, pp. 411–412.

Lukac, M., 1969, "Estratigrafia y Genesis de la Sal Gema en Punta Alegre y en Loma Cunagua, Provincia de Camaguey (Stratigraphy and Genesis of Rock Salt in Punta Alegre and Loma Cunagua, Camaguey Province)," *Rev. Tecnol.* (Havana), Vol. 7, No. 5–6, pp. 20–42.

MacMillan, R.T., 1972, "Salt," *Minerals Yearbook, 1972*, US Bureau of Mines, pp. 1093–1102.

Martinez, J.D., 1969, "The Impact of Salt on Man's Environment," in "Geology of the American Mediterranean," *Transactions*, Gulf Coast Assn. of Geological Societies, Vol. 19, pp. 49–62.

Martinez, J.D., 1971, "Environmental Significance of Salt," *Bulletin*, American Assn. of Petroleum Geologists, Vol. 55, No. 6, pp. 810–825.

Maslankiewicz, K., 1970, "Historical Survey of Concepts on the Geological Structure of the Wieliczka Rock-Salt Deposit (South Poland)," *History of Concepts on Mineral Deposits*, Symposium, International Commission on History of Geological Sciences, Freiberg, summary paper, p. 88.

Mattox, R.B., ed., 1968, "Saline Deposits," Special Paper No. 88, Geological Society of America, 701 pp.

McNaughton, D.A., et al., 1968, "Evolution of Salt Anticlines and Salt Domes in the Amadeus Basin, Central Australia," Special Paper No. 88, Geological Society of America, pp. 229–247.

Multhauf, R.P., 1978, *Neptune's Gift*, The Johns Hopkins Press, Baltimore and London, 325 pp.

Neal, J.T., 1975, "Playas and Dried Lakes, Occurrence and Development," *Benchmark Papers in Geology/20*, Dowden, Hutchinson and Ross, Inc., Stroudsburg, PA, 411 pp.

Norris, S.E., 1978, "Hydrologic Environment of the Silurian Salt Deposits in Parts of Michigan, Ohio and New York," US Geological Survey, Open File 78–684, 57 pp.

Notholt, A.J.G., and Highley, D.E., 1973, "Salt," Mineral Dossier No. 7, Mineral Resources Div., Institute of Geological Sciences, London, 36 pp.

Osika, R., and Poborski, J., 1970, "Halogenic Map," Polish Geological Institute, sheet 4.

Oxley, P., 1971, "Salt Ridge-Salt Dome Origins in Gulf Coast Area," *Bulletin*, American Assn. of Petroleum Geologists, Vol. 55, No. 2, p. 357.

Pauca, M., 1968, "Beitrage zur Kenntnis der Miozanen Salzlagerstatten Rumaniens (Contributions to Knowledge of the Miocene Salt Deposits of Romania)," *Geologische Rundschau*, Vol. 57, No. 2, pp. 514–531.

Read, L.E., and Jacoby, C.H., 1957, "Exploring and Mining for Salt," *Mining Engineering*, Vol. 9, No. 5, pp. 538–541.

Richter-Bernburg, G., 1964, "Vergleichende Betrachtung Deutscher und Iranischer Salztocke (Comparative Study of German and Iranian Salt Stocks)," *Zeitschrift fuer Deutschen Geologischen Gessellschaft*, Vol. 114 (1962), No. 3, pp. 692–693.

Rios, J.M., 1968, "Saline Deposits of Spain," Special Paper No. 88, Geological Society of America, pp. 59–74.

Rona, P.A., 1969, "Possible Salt Domes in the Deep Atlantic off North-West Africa," *Nature*, Vol. 224, No. 5215, pp. 141–143.

Sannemann, D., 1968, "Salt-Stock Families in Northwestern Germany," *Diapirism and Diapirs*, Memoir No. 8, American Assn. of Petroleum Geologists, pp. 261–270.

Schauberger, O., 1967, "Die Geologische Kartierung der Alpinen Salzlagerstatten und ihre Wirtschaftliche Bedeutung fur den Salzsolebergbau (Geologic Mapping of Alpine Salt Deposits and Its Economic Significance)," *Berg und Huettenmaennische Monatshefte*, Vol. 112, No. 6, pp. 184–190.

Severy, C.L., 1946, "Salt Cored Successfully with Oil Field Equipment," *Engineering & Mining Journal*, Vol. 147, No. 8, pp. 85–87.

Shaw, W.S., and Blanchard, J.D., 1968, "Salt Deposits of the Maritime Provinces of Canada," Special Paper No. 88, Geological Society of America, pp. 414–415.

Smith, D.A., and Reeve, F.A.E., 1970, "Salt Pierce-ment in Shallow Gulf Coast Salt Structures," *Bulletin,* American Assn. of Petroleum Geolo-gists, Vol. 54, No. 7, pp. 1271–1289.

Smith, D.A., and Reeve, F.A.E., 1971, "Salt Pierce-ment versus Downbuilding on Shallow Gulf Coast Salt Domes," Reply, *Bulletin,* American Assn. of Petroleum Geologists, Vol. 55, No. 8, pp. 1361–1362.

Stocklin, J., 1968, "Salt Deposits of the Middle East," Special Paper No. 88, Geological Society of America, pp. 157–181.

Svitoch, A.A., 1971, "Solevaya Struktura Prika-spiyskoy Vpadiny; Nekotoryye Voprosy Stroye-niya, Razvitiya i Prichiny Obrazovaniya (Salt Structure of the Basin North of the Caspian; Questions of Composition, Evolution, and Rea-sons for Formation)," *Byulleten Otdel Geolo-gicheskii,* Moskovskii Obshchest. Ispyt., Vol. 46, No. 1, pp. 25–40.

Tashchi, V. M., 1968, "Nekotoryye Voprosy Gidro-geologii Solotvinskogo Mestorozhdeniya Kamen-noy Soli (Hydrology of the Solotvino Rock-Salt Deposit)," *Geologiya Geokhimiya Goryuch. Iskop.,* Akademii Nauk Ukrainskoi SSR, No. 17, pp. 66–73.

Teixeira, A.A., and Saldanha, L.A., 1968, "Bacia Salifera Aptiana de Sergipe/Alagoas; Ocorren-cias de Sais Soluveis (The Sergipe-Alagoas Salt Basin, Occurrence of Soluble Salts)," *Bol. Tec. Petrobras,* Vol. 11, No. 2, pp. 221–228.

Tkhorzhevskiy, S.A., 1970, "O Solyanoy Tektonike v Prikaspiyskoy Vpadine (Salt Tectonics in the Caspian Basin Area)," *Sovetskaya Geologiya,* No. 10, pp. 131–139.

Turk, L.J., 1973, "Hydrogeology of the Bonne-ville Salt Flats, Utah," Utah Geological and Mineral Survey Water Resources Bulletin 19, 80 pp.

Ujueta, L.G., 1968, "Sal en la Cordillera Oriental de Colombia (Salt in the Cordillera Oriental de Colombia)," *Bol. Geol.,* Univ. Ind., Santander, No. 21 (1965), pp. 5–18.

Ujueta, L.G., 1969, "Salt in the Eastern Cordillera of Colombia," *Bulletin,* Geological Society of America, Vol. 80, No. 11, pp. 2317–2320.

Vancea, A., 1968, "Le Role du Sel dans la Forma-tion des Domes de la Curvette de Transylvanie, (The Role of Salt in the Formation of Domes in the Transylvania Basin)," *Revue Roumaine de Geologie, Geophysique et Geographie,* Serie de Geophysique, Vol. 12, No. 2, pp. 203–217.

ver Planck, W.E., 1957, "Salt in California," Bul-letin 175, California Div. of Mines and Geology, 168 pp.

Vos, M.A., 1970, "Salt in Ontario; Southern On-tario," in "Summary of Field Work," Miscellane-ous Paper No. 43, Ontario Dept. of Mines, pp. 94–96.

Wagenbreth, O., 1966, "Entwurf einer Abgedeckten Geologischen Karte des Stassfurt-Oscherslebener Salzattels und Seiner Tertiaren Randsenken (Sketch of a Geologic Map of the Stassfurt-Oschersleben Salt Structure (With the Sedimen-tary Cover Removed) and Its Tertiary Marginal Troughs)," *Geologie* (Berlin), Vol. 15, No. 9, pp. 1009–1022.

Wagner, G., et al., 1971, "Der Salzstock von Car-dona in Nordostspanien (The Cardona Salt Dome in Northeastern Spain)," *Geologische Rundschau,* Vol. 60, No. 3, pp. 970–996.

Webb, G.W., 1970, "Salt Structures East of Nova Scotia," *Marine Sediments,* Vol. 6, No. 3, p. 138.

Weidie, A.E., and Martinez, J.D., 1970, "Evidence for Evaporite Diapirism in Northeastern Mex-ico," *Bulletin,* American Assn. of Petroleum Geologists, Vol. 54, No. 4, pp. 655–657.

Zaykov, V.V., et al., 1967, "Novyye Dannyye o Solenosnosti Devonskikh Otlozheniy Tuvy (New Information on the Salt Content of the Devonian Deposits of Tuva)," *Geologiya i Geofizika,* Akademiya Nauk SSSR, Sibirskoe Otdelenie, No. 8, pp. 21–27.

Zbyszewski, G., and De Faria, J.B., 1971, "O Sal-Gema em Portugal Metropolitano; Suas Jazidas, Caracteristicas e Aproveitamento (Rock Salt of Metropolitan Portugal; Deposits, Properties, and Utilization)," *Notas Trab.,* Serv. Fom. Mineiro, Estud., Portugal, Vol. 20, No. 1–2, pp. 5–105.

Zholtayev, G.Z., 1968, "O Terminakh "Solyanoy Kupol," "Solyanoy Shtok," "Solyanoy Massiv," i "Solyanaya Antiklinal" (The Terms "Salt Dome," "Salt Stock," "Salt Massif," and "Salt Anticline")," *Izvetiya, Seriya Geologicheskaya,* Akademiya Nauk SSSR, No. 8, pp. 103–109.

Sand and Gravel

HAROLD B. GOLDMAN *

DON REINING †

The sand and gravel industry is the largest nonfuel mineral industry in the nation. In 1981, the production of sand and gravel totaled 755 million tons valued at $2.3 billion. California, which leads the nation with more than 110 million tons, together with Alaska, Texas, Michigan, and Ohio, account for 36% of the total production in the nation (Table 1).

In commercial usage, *sand* applies to rock or mineral fragments ranging in size from particles retained on a No. 200 sieve (0.074 mm openings) to those passing a No. 4 sieve (4.76 mm openings). *Gravel* consists of rock or mineral fragments larger than 4.76 mm, ranging up to 88.9 mm (3½-in.) maximum size.

The construction industry consumes 97% of the sand and gravel produced; the remainder is sand used for specialized products such as glass (see the chapter on "Silica and Silicon").

Utilization

The building industry uses sand and gravel chiefly as aggregate in portland cement concrete, mortar, and plaster; the paving industry uses sand and gravel in both asphaltic mixtures and portland cement concrete. Aggregate is commonly designated as the inert fragmental material which is bound into a conglomerate mass by a cementing material such as portland cement, asphalt, or gypsum plaster.

Portland Cement Concrete Aggregates

Portland cement concrete consists of sand and gravel surrounded and held together by hardened portland cement paste. Concrete mixes commonly contain 15–20% water, 7–14% cement, and 66–78% aggregate. Sand and gravel used as concrete aggregate have to meet many requirements (Goldman, 1956). Premature deterioration of concrete has been traced in many instances to the use of unsuitable aggregates.

Asphaltic Aggregate

Asphaltic mixtures used predominantly for paving consist of combinations of sand, gravel, and mineral filler (material finer than 0.003 in.), uniformly coated and mixed with asphalt produced in the refining of petroleum. Except for the addition of mineral filler, sand and gravel used as asphaltic aggregate must meet the same general physical requirements as materials used for portland cement concrete aggregate.

General Requirements of Aggregates

Construction aggregate has many requirements that are difficult to meet if only unprocessed material from natural deposits is used. Suitable material is composed of clean, uncoated, properly shaped particles which are sound and durable. Soundness and durability are terms used to denote the ability of aggre-

TABLE 1—Total Produced (Million Tons)
Five Largest Producing States

State	1978	1979	1981	% of US Total
California	115	129	112	14.8
Alaska	69	51	46	6.1
Texas	57	52	45	6.0
Ohio	47	45	36	4.8
Michigan	48	50	33	4.4

Source: US Bureau of Mines.

* Consulting Geologist, San Francisco, CA.
† President, Southern California Rock Products Assn., South Pasadena, CA.

gates to retain a uniform physical and chemical state over a long period of time so as not to cause disruption of the concrete when exposed to weathering and other destructive processes. To have these attributes, individual particles must be tough and firm, possessing the strength to resist stresses and chemical and physical changes, which may cause swelling, cracking, softening, and leaching. The aggregate should not be contaminated by much clayey material, silt, mica, organic matter, chemical salts and surface coatings.

The quality of aggregate depends upon its physical and chemical properties. These, in turn, may be inherent mineralogical and textural features of the rock or may be the effects of later changes such as tectonic fracturing, mechanical or chemical weathering, or incrustations.

The physical properties most significant with regard to concrete are: (1) abundance and nature of fractures and pores, (2) particle shape and surface texture and (3) presence of material which may cause volume change. An aggregate is considered to be physically sound if it is adequately strong and capable of resisting the agencies of weathering without disruption or decomposition. Minerals or rock particles that are physically weak, extremely absorptive, and easily cleavable are susceptible to breakdown by weathering. The use of such materials in concrete reduces strength or leads to early deterioration by promoting weak bond between cement and aggregate, or by inducing cracking, spalling, or popouts. Severely weathered, soft, micaceous, or porous materials may cause localized stresses to develop in concrete by swelling and shrinking during wetting and drying or freezing and thawing cycles.

Suitability of the Various Rock Types: Sedimentary rocks show a wide range in physical qualities and suitability. Sandstones and limestones, if hard and dense, are ordinarily satisfactory, but many sandstones are friable and excessively porous and commonly are clay-bearing. Shales generally make poor aggregate material, being soft, light, weak, and absorptive. Most igneous rocks are satisfactory, being normally hard, tough, and dense. Tuffs and certain flow rocks may be extremely porous and have high absorption and low strength. Metamorphic rocks differ in character. Most marbles and quartzites are usually massive, tough, and dense. Gneisses are ordinarily very tough and durable. Some schists contain micaceous minerals which are undesirable because they are soft, laminated, and absorptive. Mi-

caceous minerals are susceptible to weathering along cleavage planes and thereby impair strength and durability. Some schists and slates in particular are thinly laminated and tend to assume flat slabby shapes which lack strength.

Any or all of these rock types may be rendered undesirable because of harmful exterior coatings. Weathering processes, particularly the action of ground waters, deposit these coatings. The most common coatings are calcium carbonate, clay, silt, opal, chalcedony, iron oxide, manganese oxide, and gypsum. Particles with these coatings are generally undesirable as aggregates. The bond between particle and coating may be weak and decrease the strength of the aggregate-cement bond.

The chemical properties which may affect service life of concrete are (1) reaction of certain rocks and minerals with high-alkali cement (alkali-aggregate reactivity), (2) leaching of water soluble substances, (3) solution of certain secondary minerals, such as the zeolites, to release sodium and potassium which aids in attacking susceptible aggregate particles, and (4) oxidation by weathering to produce compounds that may retard cement hydration.

Alkali-aggregate reactivity has been discussed at length in many publications. A reactive aggregate is any rock, gravel, or sand that contains one or more constituents that react chemically with the alkalies (sodium and potassium) in some types of portland cement. This reaction causes expansion, cracking, and deterioration of concrete and arises from osmotic pressures produced by the formation and hydration of alkali-silica gels. The gels are formed through interaction between reactive silica in the mineral aggregate and the alkalies which are liberated by the cement during hydration. Opal (amorphous hydrous silica) is the most conspicuous aggregate material reacting in this manner. Other rocks and minerals known to be reactive are: glassy volcanic rocks of medium to high silica content (andesite and rhyolite), chalcedonic rocks, certain phyllites which contain a hydromica, and the minerals tridymite and heulandite. Any rock containing a significant proportion of reactive substances may be deleteriously reactive; thus normally nonreactive sandstone, shale, basalt, granite, and other rock types may be harmful if impregnated or coated with opal, chalcedony, or other reactive substance.

Certain sulfide minerals, such as the iron sulfides, pyrite, and marcasite, oxidize and cause unsightly rust stains or generate acidic compounds injurious to the concrete matrix and cause popouts. Chemical salts such as sulfates, chlorides, carbonates, and phosphates also occur in some aggregates. Some of these substances dissolve easily or react to impede the setting of the cement.

A chemical alteration contributing to physical unsoundness is hydration. Shales, clays, and some rock nodules are examples of materials which expand when they absorb water and shrink as they dry. This absorptive character increases the rock's susceptibility to disruption by weathering.

Most of the foregoing features can be observed in the field, and on the basis of these observations, laboratory test procedures can be set up to further evaluate the properties of the aggregate.

Geologic Occurrence

In the United States, sand and gravel is obtained commercially from rock units of many types and ages. The principal sources are along existing or ancient river channels and in glaciated areas; marine and lake deposits and older geologic formations are significant but of lesser importance.

Classification of Deposits

Stream Deposits: *Stream Channel Deposits*— Stream channel deposits consist of sand and gravel deposited in stream beds along present or former stream courses. Most channel deposits are generally easily accessible and easily mined.

Materials in these deposits are desirable as aggregate for many reasons. The natural abrasive action of stream transport has removed most of the soft weak rocks, leaving only the harder and firmer particles. These latter particles have undergone some degree of rounding and are subrounded to well-rounded, a desirable aspect for use in concrete.

Most channel sand and gravel deposits are replenished by material carried by seasonal floods, except in portions of the streams downstream from dams. Overburden is rarely present, but high flood waters may leave silt, clay, and wood debris covering parts of some channel deposits. The size of gravel gradually decreases downstream in the streams with long reaches. Commercial production is concentrated in the deposits where a proper blend of sand and gravel can be obtained. Fortunately, the favorable portions of many streams occur in flat-lying areas near population centers.

Channel deposits normally are free of excessive amounts of silt and clay and most deposits contain sand and gravel in the size gradations necessary for concrete design. Mining operations are often relatively simple, consisting of no more than washing and screening to obtain suitable aggregate. In spite of these qualities some deposits are unsuitable because they contain harmful ingredients such as physically unsound or chemically reactive rocks. The nature of the material in the stream channel is determined in large part by the nature of the source rocks within its drainage area. Different geological formations in a drainage basin contribute a variety of rock types which show a wide range in chemical composition and degree of weathering.

An example of the influence of source rocks on the quality of materials in stream deposits is provided by the Colorado River between Hoover and Parker Dams. The Colorado River in the vicinity of Hoover Dam contains a complex assemblage of rock types of which only a small proportion are chemically reactive. Hoover Dam concrete made with this aggregate shows no sign of harmful chemical reactivity after 20 years of service. Below Hoover Dam the Colorado River flows over predominantly volcanic rocks and the content of reactive volcanic rock increases progressively downstream.

At Davis Dam, 67 miles below Hoover Dam, the content of reactive ingredients increases to the point where it was unwise to use the aggregate unless special precautionary measures were taken to forestall alkali-aggregate reaction. Farther downstream, the tributary Bill Williams River contributes large amounts of highly reactive andesites and rhyolites to the main stream. Parker Dam built with this aggregate exhibited signs of alkali-aggregate reaction within 2 years after completion.

Flood Plain Deposits—True flood plain deposits consist of material deposited on plains bordering streams by periodic overflow of the streams from their channels. The sediments deposited are normally composed of silt and sand grains. However, fine materials may mantle usable deposits of sand and gravel, particularly in areas where, in the geologic past, the streams were more vigorous and transported greater volumes of coarser material. The sand and gravel in these older, deeper flood plain deposits is similar to that in channel deposits and is suitable for use after overlying flood plain silt layers are removed.

Terrace Deposits—Stream terrace deposits are benchlike deposits of sand and gravel which border a stream but lie above the level of the present flood plain. These deposits are remnants of older flood plains through which the stream has cut. Terrace deposits, because they are above the stream level, may be more desirable than stream channel deposits if water tables are shallow and abundant ground water makes stream channel and flood plain operations difficult. However, there is little possibility of replenishment of terrace deposits. The materials in these deposits have the general properties of stream channel materials, but weathering processes may have diminished the quality of some of their constituents by converting certain minerals to clay. Not all terrace deposits can be used for aggregate. Some deposits are only thin veneers of sand and gravel deposited on a stream-cut bedrock surface. The materials in the deposit may not be suitable if they have undergone post-depositional weathering or if the grains have become coated with harmful substances due to the action of ground waters.

Alluvial Fans: An alluvial fan is formed when streams carrying large volumes of sand and gravel down a steep mountain slope enter an adjacent valley or plain. The abrupt change in slope causes a decrease in the speed of the stream. This change causes the stream to deposit the sand and gravel it has been carrying. The deposited matter spreads in a gently sloping fan-shaped mass from the mouth of the canyon onto the valley floor. The heavier, coarser material is deposited near the mouth of the valley, while the finer material is carried out toward the edges of the fan. Alluvial fan deposits have been found to reach depths up to and occasionally more than about 200 ft.

Fan deposits, because of the frequent shifting of the stream channel, ordinarily contain lenticular beds or tongues of poorly sorted sand and gravel interbedded with varying proportions of silt and clay. The particles are subangular to angular in the fans built by streams with small drainage areas. The particles in large fans, covering several square miles, are generally subangular to subrounded. Suitable aggregate is obtained from alluvial fans which are free from thick clay lenses.

In the past, the deposits were replenished during periods of flooding until the time that flood control dams were built to control the rivers.

Glacial and Fluvial-Glacial Deposits: Sand and gravel is produced commercially from glacial deposits in the midwestern and northeastern parts of the United States. The bulk of the

sand and gravel was deposited directly or indirectly from continental ice sheets which originated in Canada and spread south into the United States. Glacial deposits that have been subjected to stream action are called fluvial-glacial deposits.

The glaciation period consisted of advances and recessions of the continental ice sheets which were several thousand feet thick, and moved roughly north to south.

Fragments of the rocks in the areas over which the glaciers passed, such as the igneous rocks in Canada, were picked up and incorporated in the glacier. When the glacial ice melted, the debris of clay, silt, sand, and pebbles and boulders were deposited as glacial till. When the advance and melting of the ice were in balance the debris deposited along the margin of the glacier formed irregular ridges termed moraines. As the water flowed away from the melting glaciers, the glacial debris was transported and deposited in outwash plains or elongate valley trains which are now major sources of sand and gravel (Ekblaw and Lamar, 1961). In addition, kames (hills) and eskers (ridges) of sand and gravel were deposited by melt waters within the ice sheet.

The fluvial-glacial deposits exhibit a better degree of sorting and contain less clay than the true glacial deposits and are of high enough quality to yield satisfactory aggregate comparable to true stream sand and gravel. Generally, the fluvial-glacial deposits are thinner than stream deposits in regions of considerable topographic relief.

Outwash Deposits—Outwash debris varies in size with the distance from the former glacial ice. The coarsest materials, pebbles, cobbles, and boulders, were deposited near the glacier, and the finer materials, sand, silt, and clay, were carried successively farther away from it. Since the water velocities fluctuated, the maximum size of transported particle varied and the deposits are characterized by great variation in particle sizes. Instances are cited where layers of gravel abruptly terminate, to be replaced by thick accumulations of silt or clay.

Kames and Eskers—Kames are hills composed of material deposited by glacial melt water in vertical crevasses or holes in the glacier, generally at or near its front. Eskers consist of material deposited in the beds of streams that flowed under or in the glacier. When the ice melted, the kames remained as rounded hills, and the eskers were left as ridges. The materials in these deposits, which show a wide variation in size and physical characteristics, are a common source of sand and gravel.

Beach and Dune Deposits—During the last stage of glaciation, the Lake Michigan basin was occupied by a larger lake whose level varied with the advances and recessions of the glacier. Each stage is marked by beach ridges of gravelly sand. In places the beach sand has been blown into dunes. These deposits are suitable as sources of sand, although urbanization and preservation as natural and recreational areas have removed many of them from consideration as minable reserves.

Moraines—True glacial deposits such as moraines have been transported solely by glacial ice with little or no reworking by streams. Morainal debris contains material of diverse size, shape, and quality ranging from pulverized rock flour to erratic boulders and generally is usable only after expensive processing.

Dredge Tailings: As a result of bucket dredge operations for gold, huge furrowlike ridges of gravels have been accumulated as tailings along many of the western state streams. A normal gold-dredging operation involves washing and screening the stream deposit. The oversize gravel, which ordinarily consists of everything over ½ or ¾ in., is washed and sent to tailing piles behind or alongside the dredge. The undersize fine gravel and sand are then processed to remove the gold and returned to the dredge pond and subsequently covered by other oversize tailings. This results in segregated deposits of fine gravel and sand which underlie coarser gravels, requiring that considerable material be processed by aggregate producers to obtain the desired gradings of sand and gravel. Most commercial operations employ equipment to crush the oversize tailings. Tailing piles which have not been subjected to excessive weathering contain material as suitable as the related stream deposit.

Older Geologic Formations: Pre-Quaternary formations, particularly partly consolidated sedimentary beds of sandstone and conglomerate, afford usable sources of aggregate when post-depositional weathering has not been too complete. Ordinarily, these formations have been subjected to long periods of weathering and are either too well cemented or contain too much clayey material to be processed economically. Accessibility of the deposit and depth of overburden also present problems.

The pre-Quaternary formations which are composed of well indurated sedimentary rocks or hard crystalline rocks require expensive quarrying operations to obtain suitable material for aggregate. Quarrying rock outcrop has some advantage over developing stream deposits in that once the physical and chemical characteristics of the rock are established, production can proceed without the danger of encountering harmful ingredients. Production can be closely controlled in all grade sizes.

Beach Deposits: Sand and gravel formed by the winnowing action of currents and waves on a beach make excellent aggregate. The gravel and coarse sand size particles are generally well-rounded, hard, and firm. The sands are commonly composed predominantly of resistant quartz and feldspar. Most beach deposits, however, are thin and lack proper size gradation.

Distribution of Deposits

The occurrence of sand and gravel in the United States is related to geologic processes. On a geographic-geologic basis, in the northern states, the principal sand and gravel resources are various types of glacial and outwash glacial deposits (Cooper, 1970). Marine terraces, ancient and recent geologically, are the major sand and gravel sources in the Atlantic and Gulf Coastal Plains. River deposits are the prime sources in several of the southeastern and south-central states. In the Great Plains, sand and gravel are mainly stream deposits. On the West Coast, deposits are principally alluvial fans, stream deposits, beach and dune sand, and fluvial-glacial deposits.

Offshore deposits, although of minor importance tonnagewise, are mined along the east coast from Washington to Boston, and in the Great Lakes.

Reserves

Any estimate of potential resources of sand and gravel in the United States is of little value if the trend toward urban expansion with its land conflicts and stronger environmental controls continues. In 1965, the National Sand and Gravel Assn. estimated the reserves held by producers at 16 billion tons (Cooper, 1970). There are enormous undeveloped deposits in the United States that are uneconomical to mine today because of the high cost of transportation to market. These would constitute reserves if some means can be found to set aside these lands for future use and avoid the conflicts of urbanization and the mineral industry (Goldman, 1959).

The heavily populated and urbanized Middle Atlantic, New England, and Pacific Coast states now are facing rapid depletion of deposits, loss of mineral lands to urbanization, and stiff opposition from environmental groups to development of new sources.

The United States is by far the largest producer and consumer of sand and gravel, accounting for an estimated one-sixth of the world's consumption.

Supplies in the rest of the world may be considerable, but as is the case with the United States, the deposits are not located in the areas of greatest demand. The more highly developed countries also are faced with the problem of loss of resources to urban encroachment (Pajalich, 1976).

The United States' foreign trade in sand and gravel is mostly with Canada. Exports are about 2.5 million tons and imports less than 1 million tons annually.

Exploration

Exploration for sand and gravel is generally guided by the needs of the potential producer. There are certain criteria that a deposit should meet in order to be of economic interest for a commercial producer, such as proximity to market, ease of obtaining the necessary mining permit, and a deposit of sufficient quantity to amortize the cost of a modern processing plant.

As sand and gravel is a low-cost, high-volume commodity, it cannot be transported far before the cost of transportation equals or exceeds the cost of the processed material at the plant. Thus, in most urbanizing areas the proximity to market would determine the target area for exploration. In aggregate-deficient parts of the country where materials are transported hundreds of miles, the target area naturally would be much larger.

Another important criteria to be met before field exploration begins is the socioeconomic restrictions on a potential mining operation. If the governing bodies have adopted a policy of refusing to grant operating permits, there would be no purpose to exploring in that jurisdiction. Also, there should be an awareness of the opposition that would be generated by conservation and ecology minded groups to granting of mining permits.

The size of the deposit is critical. In some parts of the country, where large volumes of sand and gravel are consumed, new sand and gravel plants cost upward of a million dollars. In order to amortize the life of such a plant, the deposit should contain sufficient reserves for at least 20 years. In California, a deposit

should contain more than 10 million tons to be of commercial interest.

Naturally, in prospecting for sand and gravel for noncommercial production, such as for use in dams, the foregoing criteria rarely apply. In this instance, the quantity and quality are the prime factors to consider.

Field Technique

Preliminary field evaluation by a geologist or by an engineer with some geologic training may often suffice to evaluate a deposit as a possible source of aggregate material. The characteristics that bear upon the usefulness of a deposit as a source of aggregate material have been determined by the geologic processes by which the deposit was formed and subsequently modified. A basic understanding of the processes, therefore, is helpful to the person evaluating it. The important characteristics are types and physical condition of the rock, grading, rounding and degree of uniformity, particle size and shape, location, thickness and type of overburden, and ground water level.

By the judicious use of geologic maps a geologist can determine the type of materials to be encountered in a certain drainage area and predict the type of alluvial material to be found in a given stream channel. He thereby can recognize likely sources of aggregate and often can rule out areas unlikely to contain suitable materials. The geologist uses commercial sand and gravel deposits as a yardstick to guide him in evaluating new deposits. By comparing service records and laboratory test results with the petrographic character of commercially proven aggregates, the geologist builds up a background of data from which he can extrapolate to predict the behavior of untested deposits of similar petrographic character. This technique has been used successfully by the US Bureau of Reclamation in preliminary planning studies for large structures that require large amounts of suitable aggregates. In many instances field evaluation has obviated the need for expensive and time-consuming laboratory tests.

Target Areas: As outlined in the section on geology, those areas to be prospected for sand and gravel are predominantly those associated with either the present stream drainage or ancient drainages. Clues to buried or older deposits may be gleaned from well-drilling logs, geophysical data, and from geologic reports.

Aerial photographs, coupled with topographic maps, are essential tools. Any geologic information in the form of maps or reports should be researched. In most instances, the state geological surveys can provide the necessary maps.

The initial exploration can be greatly expedited with the use of airplanes, preferably a helicopter, to observe promising geologic features. Preliminary investigations, which include determining such features as crude estimates of volume of available material, thickness and type of overburden, water and power availability and access, are based primarily upon visual examination, either by a geologist or someone with experience in aggregate production.

Detailed Exploration: The method of exploration will depend upon the particular set of conditions, the objective being to obtain representative samples of the entire deposit and to delineate the dimensions of the deposit.

No matter what method of exploration is considered, ultimately representative samples must be obtained so that standard laboratory acceptance tests can be performed on the samples.

Where the deposit is shallower than 30 ft, test pits may be excavated with bulldozers, backhoes, clamshells, or dragline. The location of the water table often will determine the type of test pit.

For deeper deposits, truck-mounted drill rigs should be used. Ordinarily, truck-mounted bucket augers, which use buckets from 18 to 36 in. in diam, perform satisfactorily when large boulders are not present in the deposit. When drilling beneath the water table, steel casing is used to prevent the hole from caving.

Other drilling rigs, such as clamshells and reverse circulation drills, perform satisfactorily. Choice of drilling method will depend upon the availability of competent drillers in the area.

Geophysical methods can be used in conjunction with a drilling program. Geophysics may be used to check continuity of geologic units between drill sites or beyond a known deposit. For example, electrical resistivity techniques may be used to locate thick zones of clay interbedded in the sand and gravel.

The depth of a sand and gravel deposit resting on a hard bedrock surface can be determined by means of refraction seismic methods.

The cost of geophysical methods equals the cost of drilling, on an hourly basis. However, much more information is obtained within the same time interval through geophysics.

Obviously, the geophysical methods are useful exploration tools but cannot substitute for the other methods when samples must be obtained for laboratory testing.

The standard laboratory acceptance tests are described more fully in the chapter on uses. Equally important as laboratory testing is the sampling in the field. Where possible, large bulk samples should be obtained and quartered in the field. If it is possible, enough material should be stockpiled and trucked or railed to an existing plant to determine size gradation and quality of the finished product.

As an integral part of the exploration program, cross sections should be drawn of the deposit and estimates made of the quantity of material available. This figure should be reduced by the percentage of waste material, such as beds or lenses of clay and silt, and the loss of material to setbacks and finished slopes required by mining permits.

Evaluation of Deposits

General Specifications

The study of the results of laboratory tests of aggregates that have good service records in concrete has led to the establishment of certain minimum requirements or specifications to which aggregates are expected to conform. These specifications are designed so that completely serviceable concrete may be made, using any aggregate that meets the requirements. Most specifications are written by government agencies, engineering societies, and concrete technologists and attempt to conform to one standard set of specifications, those set up by the American Society for Testing and Materials. Modifications of these standards for certain types of concrete work make it difficult to compare individual requirements of the various organizations. Therefore, to evaluate the suitability of a deposit by judging the test results of selected samples is a difficult task. Some deposits which may not meet certain required specifications may have to be utilized because of other outside factors, such as the greater expense of hauling a more suitable aggregate.

In general, aggregate from an untried deposit will be satisfactory for most uses if it meets the following minimum standards (these specifications are a general average of the basic requirements recommended by the ASTM, California Division of Highways, US Army Corps of Engineers, and the US Bureau of Reclamation):

Abrasion—The abrasion loss should be less than 30%.

Soundness—The loss in the sodium sulfate test should be less than 10%.

TABLE 2—Laboratory Methods of Determining Suitability of Sand and Gravel for Use as Aggregate in Portland Cement Concrete

Property of Aggregate	Importance in Concrete	Test Methods	Reference to Tests*
Hardness and durability (resistance to abrasion)	Affects strength, resistance to wear	"Los Angeles Rattler;" measure proportion of fine material produced by abrasion in revolving metal drum after 100 and 500 turns	ASTM Test C131-51 (ASTM 1954, p. 40)
Soundness (lack of fissures in particles)	Affects strength, susceptibility to frost damage from expansion of absorbed water	Alternately soak in sodium or magnesium sulfate solution and dry; crystallization of absorbed solution forces open invisible cracks. Subject test beams made with aggregate to alternate cycles of freezing and thawing	ASTM Test C88-46T (ASTM 1954, p. 76) ASTM Test C290-52T (ASTM 1954, p. 191)
Specific gravity—dry and with absorbed liquid	Determine mass (specific gravity commonly specified 2.5 or more); absorption affects bond of cement paste to particles	Compare oven-dry weight with immersed weight, and weight after surface re-dried	ASTM Tests C127-42, and C128-42 (ASTM 1954, pp. 82,84)
Size grading characteristics	Affects flowability, residual void spaces, strength	Standard sieve analysis; screen in standard-size screens; weigh various fractions; plot on appropriate graphs	ASTM Test C136-46 (ASTM 1954, p. 69)
General characteristics: 1. Particle shape 2. Character of surface 3. Grain size 4. Texture (e.g., pore space, grain packing, cementation) 5. Color 6. Mineral composition 7. General physical condition (e.g., weathering) 8. Presence of potentially deleterious chemical substances (e.g., gypsum, zeolite, pyrite, opal, chalcedony, volcanic glass)	Different effects on strength, hardness, color, and permanence of concrete	Examine by naked eye, hand lens, and under petrographic microscope	ASTM Test C295-54 (ASTM 1954, p. 97)

Property	Significance	Method	Reference*
Potential chemical re-activity	Affects permanence of concrete; reactive substances cause "popouts" and failures due to expansion	Weigh silica dissolved in sodium hydroxide solution; measure reduction in alkalinity caused by immersion of sample in standard sodium hydroxide solution	ASTM Test C289-54T (ASTM 1954, p. 57)
		Measure expansion of mortar bars made with aggregate over lengthy periods; 1-2 years	ASTM Test C227-52T (ASTM 1954, p. 296)
Lack of organic matter (coal, lignite, organic impurities)	Affects strength, resistance to wear	Separate material lighter than 2.0 specific gravity in heavy liquid, and weigh; compare color of sample with standard color solution—dark color assumed due to organic material	ASTM Tests C123-53T and C40-48 (ASTM 1954, pp. 51,56)
Cleanness (lack of dirt, clay, or silt finer than 200 mesh)	Determines quality of bond with cement	Measure material passing 200-mesh sieve; measure suspended material after shaking in water	ASTM Test C117-49 (ASTM 1954, p. 47)
Unit weight	Determines mass	Weigh aggregate contained in standard cubic foot measure	ASTM Test C29-42 (ASTM 1954, p. 90)
Lack of soft or friable fragments	Affects strength, resistance to wear	Scratch test using brass rod of Rockwell hardness B65 to B75; rock softer than rod is unsatisfactory	ASTM Test C235-54T (ASTM 1954, p. 74)
Toughness	Affects strength, resistance to wear	Impact; measure distance a standard-size hammer drops on specimen to fracture it	ASTM Test D3-18 (ASTM 1954, p. 88)

* Standardized tests as outlined by the American Society for Testing and Materials: *ASTM Standards on Mineral Aggregates, Concrete and Nonbituminous Highway Materials*, Dec. 1954.

Specific Gravity—The specific gravity should be greater than 2.55.

Size and Grading—

a) The deposit has proper grading so that the fine aggregate should contain no more than 45% of the material between two consecutive sieve sizes.

b) The fineness modulus should be between 2.3-3.1.

c) No more than 5% of the material should pass the No. 200 sieve.

Reactivity—A mortar bar containing the aggregate should have an expansion less than 0.10% in one year with a 0.8% alkali content cement.

Absorption—The absorption should not exceed 3%.

Durability—The concrete containing the aggregate should not have a loss in the modulus of elasticity exceeding 50% in the freeze-thaw test.

Sand Equivalent—The fine aggregate should have a sand equivalent of not less than 75.

Testing and Evaluation

Laboratory testing is a means of scientifically evaluating the suitability of aggregate material. In an attempt to forecast the behavior of the aggregate in concrete, numerous tests have been devised, many of which are complicated and require expensive equipment and trained technicians. Several of these tests have been used for many years and are familiar to those in concrete construction work. A strong effort is being made to standardize testing procedures throughout the nation, and many laboratories use, with little or no modifications, test methods as set forth in detail by the American Society for Testing and Materials. The principal tests performed on aggregates are for toughness and abrasion resistance, soundness, organic content, grading, specific gravity, absorption, alkali-aggregate reactivity, and thermal incompatibility. Petrographic examination in greater detail than possible during field examination supplements the laboratory tests, which are outlined in Table 2.

Petrographic Examination: Petrographic examination is a laboratory method for determining physical and chemical properties of aggregates primarily by visual appraisal. Standard techniques for mineral identification, which commonly involve the use of the petrographic microscope, and microchemical tests are employed. Representative samples containing hundreds of particles are carefully examined and classified as to (1) rock type, (2)

physical condition, (3) chemical stability—presence of reactive or otherwise deleterious ingredients, (4) shape of particles present, and (5) nature of particle coatings. Reports are tabulated to show percentage composition, condition of the rock types present, and percentage of reactive ingredients, as well as diagnostic features of the particular constituents and the relative qualities of the different size fractions. Examination by petrographers experienced in concrete work permits interpretation of routine laboratory tests and aids in comparing new aggregates with other aggregates for which service data are available. On the basis of petrographic observations supplementary tests other than the usual laboratory tests may sometimes be recommended.

Depletion Allowance

The depletion allowance for common sand or gravel is 5%; for silica sand or pebbles, the allowance is 14%.

Preparation for Markets

Mining Methods

Sand and gravel deposits are mined with power shovels, draglines, slackline cable draglines, bulldozers, or dredges. The choice of excavating equipment depends upon whether the deposit is mined dry or wet.

In a dry-pit operation, shovels, loaders, or draglines load the sand and gravel into trucks or onto conveyor belts for transfer to the processing plant. The description of the CON-ROCK plant in a subsequent section (processing) provides an example of a large, dry-pit operation.

A wet-pit operation recovers sand and gravel from deposits that are below the water table. The sand and gravel may be excavated by a land-based dragline or by a floating dredge on a man-made or natural lake. Dredges are also used to recover sand and gravel from river channels.

Dredging: Some dredges are equipped for complete processing of material; others only scalp off unwanted sizes, and processing is completed on shore.

Dredging, especially in rivers, has had a long and stable background in the mining of sand and gravel. Now torn between two forces (a forward impetus due to local use restriction of land-based deposits, and increasingly restrictive federal and state regulations), dredge operations still account for up to 50% of the nation's sand and gravel production. This figure includes such forms of dredging as barge-mounted draglines, straight suction pumping, hydraulic cutterhead techniques, and bucket ladder methods.

Stearn (1970) stated that in 1968 there were 603 sand and gravel dredge operations in 37 of the 50 states. Nebraska headed the list with 129 dredges working. Kansas ranked second with 55. Florida, Michigan, Indiana, and Louisiana followed, with 34, 33, 31, and 29 dredges, respectively.

A brief survey of rock products operators utilizing dredges for all or part of their production revealed that some were dredging aggregates as far back as 100 years ago. Roughly 45% of the dredges covered by the survey were operating in a pond or wet pit. Rivers and lakes accounted for 25% each, and the remainder operated in bays.

Maximum working depths reported ranged from a shallow 15 ft in a river to 125 ft in a lake. The overall average was 50 ft. Bay dredges worked at depths ranging from 20 to 100 ft, with an average of 60 ft. In lakes, dredges reached depths from 20 to 125 ft, averaging 80 ft.

Sixty-five percent of the operators were working mixed deposits of sand and gravel. Straight sand, straight gravel, shell, and silica sand were the other raw materials mentioned. Sizes ranged from 8 in. boulders to 200 mesh sand, with roughly half those reporting handling topsized material in the 6 to 8 in range. Slightly more than 60% of the producers processed material ashore, but there appeared to be an increasing trend toward furnishing dredges with processing equipment.

Production capacities varied widely, from 20 to more than 2000 tph, for an average of approximately 350 tph. Principal product categories were specification sand and gravel, concrete aggregates, industrial and mason sand, roofing gravel, and ballast.

Diesel and electric power accounted for 45% each among the engines chosen by these dredge operators. Steam, natural gas, and fuel oil were in limited use. Pump sizes ranged from 4 to 18 in., with 12 in. average.

Ocean Mining: Ocean mining may supply future aggregate needs in metropolitan coastal areas as local deficiencies develop in construction aggregate supplies from nearby land deposits. Sand and gravel probably constitutes the most widespread resources of the sea floor of the US continental shelf. Although no large-scale commercial exploitation of offshore sand and gravel deposits is known to be underway at present on the continental shelf proper, tidal rivers and estuaries have been dredged commercially for many years.

Marine technology today is essentially an extension of conventional dredging systems which have been used successfully in rivers and estuaries. These include clamshell, dragline, and dipper dredges for relatively shallow water (generally under 100 ft), bucket ladder types (150-200 ft depth), and hydraulic systems (generally equipped with a rotary cutter) capable of pumping dredged material in slurry form.

Processing Techniques

Commercial operations are located on portions of deposits where the proper blend of sizes of sand and gravel can be obtained in order to produce a variety of products. Noncommercial production by highway contractors generally is obtained from portions of deposits where there is an abundance of +1½-in. gravel to provide crushed materials for use as road base or bituminous aggregate.

Ideally a commercial deposit would contain about 60% gravel and 40% sand (−¼-in.), enough +1½-in. gravel to crush for use as road base or bituminous aggregate, and sand in the correct sizes and proportions for use in concrete. Few deposits meet these requirements and plants are designed to cope with natural deficiencies. Plant capacities can range from 30 to 1000 tph of processed material.

Most plants are departmentalized to produce different products. There is usually a "dry" side, where pit run material is screened and crushed for use as road base, or in some instances as bituminous aggregate, and a "wet" side where sand and gravel are washed and screened for use as concrete aggregate. Various stages of crushing are used to reduce the gravel fraction to the necessary sizes. Ordinarily, a jaw crusher is used for primary reduction, particularly where boulders greater than 3 in. are present. Gyratory and roll crushers further reduce the gravel to −1 in., and −¾ in. Rod mills are used to manufacture sand from ¼ to ⅜-in. "pea" gravel to supplement natural sand that is deficient in fine sizes.

The sand fraction ordinarily is washed and classified in spiral classifiers (sand screws). Plants processing sand deficient in fine sizes usually employ wet cyclone-type separators to recover fine sand which may be present in the overflow from a clas ifier. In a number of plants, hydraulic settling tanks are used to separate the sand into various sizes. The desired blend of sand sizes is drawn off through gates in the bottom of the tank and dewatered in spiral classifiers.

Plants processing clayey material use revolving scrubbers or log washers to clean the pit run material before further processing.

Standard screens which are mechanically vibrated separate the gravel into the necessary sizes.

Some plants beneficiate their raw material by removing soft particles, such as shale, in a heavy media separation which utilizes the "sink-float" principle. The desired material sinks and the undesirable lighter fraction is floated off. The heavy liquid is made up of a mixture of finely ground magnetite and ferrosilicon, with a specific gravity that can be varied from 1.0 to 3.4. Jigs are also used to remove light particles in the granule size range. (Goldman, 1962).

Perhaps the best example of new and modern methods for the harvesting and processing of sand and gravel can be found in the newest facility of a company in southern California.

In the fall of 1972, CONROCK Co. began operation of its newest and most modern sand and gravel plant, which is located in the City of Irwindale, CA, on the alluvial fan of the San Gabriel River.

The plant was designed to operate initially in the 1200–1400 tph range, but provisions were made in the design to permit expansion to 2000–2400 tph without major modifications.

Material is harvested dry in the pit using a 9-cu-yd electric shovel. This material, of about 48-in. maximum diameter, is then reduced in a 48 x 60-in. primary jaw crusher mounted on a portable crusher car frame.

Material from the pit is then transported to the plant site via 42-in. wide conveyor belts and deposited in a 100-ft high surge pile.

Material is drawn from the surge pile using vibrating feeders, and the feed to the plant is automatically controlled by a conveyor belt scale. The initial plant feed is split on two 6 x 16-ft primary screens. The 1½-in. material goes to the wet side of the plant where it is scrubbed in a 7 x 35-ft trommel scrubber. The gravel portion is then washed and sized on 5 x 16-ft horizontal doubled deck screens. Concrete sand is washed in a scalping-classifying tank and then partially dewatered in 54-in. diam by 34-ft long sand screws. Further dewatering is accomplished by depositing the sand in large stockpiles for drainage.

The +1½-in. material from the primary screens is reduced, using three 7-ft secondary cone crushers in a closed circuit crushing system. Crushed materials are screened into various size groups and then combined into products by blending, using an elaborate chute system. With an almost unlimited number of combinations available for combining sizes, and with provisions for recrushing any of the unwanted larger sizes, it is possible to make only those products that are in demand at any respective time. Also, gradations of crushed products can be made coarser or finer in the blending process so as to meet exacting specifications. Provisions have also been incorporated to permit certain percentages of the crushed sizes to be used for supplementing natural gravel products.

Natural gravel and crushed products, together with washed concrete sand, which is conveyed back to the plant by belt conveyor, are stored in large overhead reinforced concrete bins. Each bin holds either 500 or 1000 tons of live storage. The total overhead live storage for the plant is 25,000 tons.

Marketing

Commercial interests produce approximately 85% of the sand and gravel supply, with the remaining 15% produced by government and/or contractors. In the latter category, it is apparent that such production operations are set up to handle extremely large projects (such as dams, rural highways, etc.), or in remote or rural areas where no commercial operations exist. The work is done with semi-mobile plants which remain only until completion of a specific project and then relocate for the next job.

In or around metropolitan areas where continuing work and markets for sand and gravel exist, and where transportation networks (rail, water, highways) are adequate, most production is done by commercial companies with permanent production facilities. Since transportation of sand and gravel is a disproportionate share of selling cost, it is not unusual for asphaltic concrete and ready-mix concrete plants to be located on the sand and gravel production site. Indeed, some producers are in the ready-mix business, some also in the asphaltic concrete business, and there are some producers who are also construction contractors.

Because of the broad distribution and general availability of sand and gravel, there are many commercial operations throughout the US. The number of commercial operations declined from 7291 in 1978 to 6836 in 1979.

The US Bureau of Mines reveals that in 1979 there were 5447 commercial operations with production of less than 200,000 tons, accounting for approximately 30% of total US production. Some 860 operations with annual production between 200,000 and 500,000 tons produced 28% of the total US production, and 369 operations with production over a half million tons accounted for the remaining 42%.

Price Trends: The price of sand and gravel as used at its ultimate location is a function of two elements—first, the cost of the material itself at the production location and, second, the cost of transport to the using site. These two elements must be considered when evaluating industry trends. Publications of the US Bureau of Mines reveal that although the unit price of sand and gravel in actual dollars has increased since 1954, in constant dollars the price has decreased from $1.55 per ton in 1954 to $1.34 per ton in 1974. Such a low price has been maintained (in spite of rising labor costs, higher land values, and increasing restrictions) through the development and use of larger and more efficient mining and processing equipment. Such improvements do have limits, and it is expected that prices will rise slowly during the 1980s to the year 2000.

Average f.o.b. plant prices for various types of gravel are shown in Table 3 for the years 1971 and 1979.

Major technological developments which have been instrumental in maintaining adequate production of sand and gravel at stable or slightly declining real cost include: use of larger operating units, more efficient portable and semi-portable plants, unitized plants for versatility of plant capacity, new prospecting methods utilizing aerial and geophysical surveying methods, and greatly increased rehabilitation and resale of mineral areas where advantageous.

Transportation: The proximity of market to the resource to date has maintained a relatively stable cost index for most regions. The cost of transporting material is based on production cost, equipment used, and manpower. A good rule-of-thumb estimate on rates for transporting sand and gravel is approximately $0.10–$0.15 per ton for each mile hauled,

TABLE 3—Average F.O.B. Plant Prices for Various Types of Gravel

Type of Gravel	Average Price Per Ton, $ 1971*	1979†
Building	1.55	2.59
Paving	1.19	2.65
Fill	0.69	1.55

*Pajalich, 1972.
†Tepordei, 1980.

though in some areas costs of $0.20–$0.25 or more per ton-mile are realized.

The single factor which most escalates the delivery price of sand and gravel is the distance of haul under present practices and regulations. At 10¢ a ton-mile an increase of 20 miles in the hauling distance would increase the price of aggregate $2 per ton. This could easily represent an increase of 50 to 100% on the delivered cost of sand and gravel to the consumer. Some idea of the effect distance has on the price of aggregate delivered to the consumer is indicated in Fig. 1.

When aggregates are moved great distances, the final cost for the finished product is not the production cost but transportation. In some metropolitan areas, public utility commission truck zone rates apply; in other more outlying areas truck rental rates apply. The rate is highly variable depending on method of transportation, governmental regulation, labor contracts, and area. Other factors include haul distance, legal load limits, on-road or off-road operation, and, certainly, competition.

Truck haulage is the predominant form of transportation used by the industry, both as the only method or often in conjunction with an alternate method. Rail hauls are used in many areas particularly when spurs are available, quantities are large, and distances from production to destination are long. Rehandling of material is undesirable because of added costs and breakdown of the materials during handling. In coastal areas and areas on inland waterways, barge hauling is a readily accepted method. Together, rail and barge transportation account for approximately 10% of the total sand and gravel movement.

Consumption: The American Road Builder's Assn. estimates that highway consumption (construction and maintenance) will require 1970 million tons in 1985. In 1902, output was 1.848 million tons, and 35 years ago, 254.1 million tons.

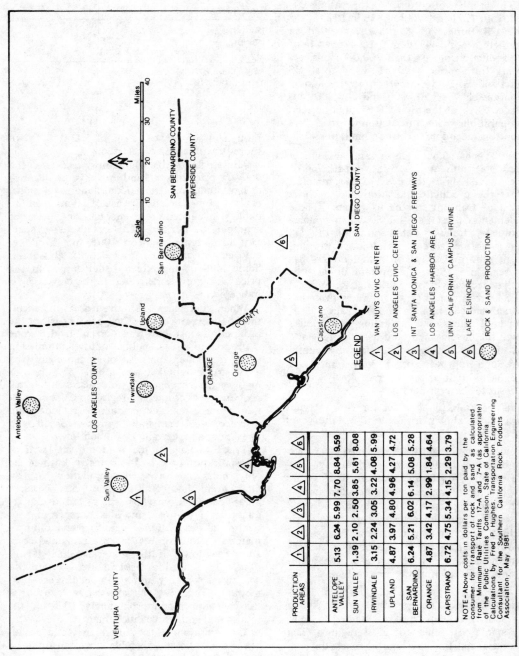

PRODUCTION AREAS	△ 1	△ 2	△ 3	△ 4	△ 5	△ 6
ANTELOPE VALLEY	5.13	6.24	5.99	7.70	8.84	9.59
SUN VALLEY	1.39	2.10	2.50	3.85	5.61	8.08
IRWINDALE	3.15	2.24	3.05	3.22	4.08	5.99
UPLAND	4.87	3.97	4.80	4.96	4.27	4.72
SAN BERNARDINO	6.24	5.21	6.02	6.14	5.08	5.28
ORANGE	4.87	3.42	4.17	2.99	1.84	4.64
CAPISTRANO	6.72	4.75	5.34	4.15	2.29	3.79

NOTE—Above costs in dollars per ton paid by the consumer for transport of rock and sand as calculated from Minimum Rate Tariffs 17-A and 7-A (as appropriate) of the Public Utilities Comission, State of California. Calculations by Fred P. Hughes, Transportation Engineering Consultant for the Southern California Rock Products Association, May 1981

LEGEND

△ 1 VAN NUYS CIVIC CENTER
△ 2 LOS ANGELES CIVIC CENTER
△ 3 INT SANTA MONICA & SAN DIEGO FREEWAYS
△ 4 LOS ANGELES HARBOR AREA
△ 5 UNIV CALIFORNIA CAMPUS – IRVINE
△ 6 LAKE ELSINORE
⊙ ROCK & SAND PRODUCTION

FIG. 1—*Typical variations in transport cost per ton of rock and sand between production areas and selected locations.*

The average annual growth rate of domestic demand for sand and gravel since 1954 has been about 2.8%. The estimated annual growth rate for the balance of the century, obtained by contingency forecasting based on anticipated requirements for individual end use, is expected to fall somewhere between 2.5 and 4.7%. The forecast demand for sand and gravel in the United States in the year 2000, corresponding to this growth range, covers a range from 2.0 to 2.6 billion tons (Pajalich, 1976).

Pattern of Use: Within the construction industry, highway construction or road building consumes the major volume of sand and gravel, used as aggregate for both concrete and asphalt pavements; in concrete for bridges, tunnels, and appurtenant structures; in treated and untreated road base material; and in both structural and nonstructural fill. The next largest segment of use is in building construction, where practically all of the volume is used in the manufacture of concrete for both cast-in-place and precast structural and cladding elements. The remaining quantities go into fill, septic fields, and other construction-related uses.

Specialty sand uses demand more rigid specifications for special types and gradings. Such specialty sands are classified by the US Bureau of Mines as "industrial sand" and are discussed in the chapter on "Silica and Silicon."

Future Consideration and Trends

Substitutes

As in the case with most materials, sand and gravel are not immune to substitution for various reasons—economic, application, or even environmental. Perhaps the most widely used substitute or alternate material is crushed stone (see "Sand and Gravel" in Part 2, *Uses*). It competes in almost every category with sand and gravel and is produced in a wide variety of types, sizes, and gradation.

A growing competitor to sand and gravel in the concrete aggregate market area is lightweight aggregate. This material is manufactured by a sintering process in which appropriate clays, shales, slate, or fly ash are passed through rotary kilns or traveling grate furnaces to produce a bloated aggregate product. These materials are used extensively to produce a lightweight concrete used in cast-in-place structures, in precast elements, and in concrete

block. Other lightweight materials for concrete aggregate include natural pumice, expanded perlite, expanded (or exfoliated) vermiculite, and iron blast-furnace slag. These materials find use in insulating fills, roof decks, and similar basically nonstructural uses.

Urbanization, Government Control, and Zone Restrictions

The sand and gravel industry, more often than any other major segment of the mineral industry, is beset with land use conflicts and environmental problems associated with rapid urban expansion. The problems are complicated because urban growth depends upon centrally located sources of low-cost construction materials. It is an economic fact not understood by the consuming public.

As a city or county expands, the growth process itself may cut off the vital supply of industrial minerals which are needed for this growth. This usually happens in the following sequence. As a community or county begins to grow, a demand or market is created for industrial minerals, such as sand, gravel, crushed rock, and clay for brick products. Since sand and gravel form a high-bulk, low-cost product, the extraction operations begin as close as possible to the consuming areas—the population centers. As the community or county grows, more and more homes are built in the outlying or rural areas. This urban expansion gradually approaches and then surrounds the established gravel pits. The new homes may cover sand and gravel deposits; this makes it impossible to expand the sand and gravel extraction. In addition to covering potential reserves, the new homeowners may resent the existing extraction operations. Complaints are often made to the local government authorities which allege excessive noise, dust, and hazards to children. Continued pressure may result in ordinances which restrict operating conditions, truck routes, etc. Finally, as a result of depleted reserves and/or harassment, the pit operator may be forced to move to more remote locations. Ultimately, this reduces the available supply and increases construction costs (Goldman, 1959).

Rapid population growth and urbanization have had a decided impact upon the sand and gravel industry. Their ability to continue operations and supply the needed aggregates to maintain the present and projected construction needs of our society is imperiled. Local government has imposed planning and zoning restrictions that are inconsistent and usually only the zoning needs for that particular city are considered. There is little uniformity or consistency in the laws. Little thought is given to those areas in the total region served by the mineral resources. Prime mineral resources are lost to development and urban growth.

No uniform mining and mineral policy exists. In most cases, legislative bodies usually respond to demands of local voters who prefer that the sand and gravel operators go elsewhere. To date, 15 states have passed environmental laws which will affect sand and gravel operations.

Closely associated with land use conflicts are problems of environmental contamination, such as water pollution, dust, solid waste, noise, and unsightly conditions that sometimes accompany sand and gravel operations.

Bibliography and References

Anon., 1957, "Standard Specifications for Construction of Roads and Bridges on Federal Highway Projects," FP-57, US Dept. of Commerce, Washington, DC, 363 pp.

Anon., 1958, "Bibliography on Mineral Aggregates," No. 23, Highway Research Board, Washington, DC, 111 pp.

Anon., 1961, "Mineral Aggregates," Pt. 4, *ASTM Standards*, American Society for Testing & Materials, Philadelphia, PA, pp. 491–657.

Anon., 1962, "Engineering Problems of Sand and Gravel Production," NSGA Circular No. 88, National Sand and Gravel Assn., Silver Spring, MD, 34 pp.

Anon., 1963, *Concrete Manual*, 7th ed., US Bureau of Reclamation, Denver, CO, 642 pp.

Anon., 1964, *Pit and Quarry Handbook*, Pit and Quarry Publications, Chicago, IL.

Ahearn, V.P., Jr., 1964, "Land Use Planning and the Sand and Gravel Producers," National Sand and Gravel Assn., Silver Spring, MD, 30 pp.

Cooper, J.D., 1970, "Sand and Gravel," *Mineral Facts and Problems*, Bulletin 650, US Bureau of Mines, pp. 1185–1199.

Drake, H.J., 1972, "Stone," *Minerals Yearbook, 1972*, US Bureau of Mines, pp. 1153–1173.

Dunn, J.R., and Cutcliffe, W.E., 1971, "Selecting Aggregate Deposits: A Geologic View," *Rock Products*, Mar., pp. 75–79.

Dunn, J.R., and Hudec, P.P., 1972, "Frost and Sorption Effects in Argillaceous Rocks," No.

393, Highway Research Board, Washington, DC, pp. 65–78.

Ekblaw, G.E., and Lamar, J.E., 1964, "Sand and Gravel Resources of Northeastern Illinois," Circular 359, Illinois State Geological Survey, 8 pp.

Goldman, H.B., 1956, "Sand and Gravel for Concrete Aggregate," *California Journal of Mines and Geology*, Vol. 52, No. 1, pp. 79–104.

Goldman, H.B., 1959, "Franciscan Chert in California Concrete Aggregate," Special Report 55, California Div. of Mines and Geology, 28 pp.

Goldman, H.B., 1959a, "Urbanization and the Mineral Industry," *Mineral Information Service*, California Div. of Mines and Geology, Vol. 12, No. 12, Dec., pp. 1–5.

Goldman, H.B., 1961, "Sand and Gravel in Northern California," Bulletin 180A, California Div. of Mines and Geology, 38 pp.

Goldman, H.B., 1961a, "Urbanization—Impetus and Detriment to Mineral Industry," *Mining Engineering*, Vol. 13, No. 7, July, p. 717.

Goldman, H.B., 1962, "Aggregate from 'Fossils,'" *Rock Products*, Vol. 65, No. 11, pp. 65–68.

Goldman, H.B., 1964, "Sand and Gravel in Central California," Bulletin 180B, California Div. of Mines and Geology, 58 pp.

Goldman, H.B., 1968, "Sand and Gravel," in *Mineral and Water Resources of California*, Bulletin 191, California Div. of Mines and Geology, pp. 361–369.

Goldman, H.B., 1969, "Sand and Gravel in Southern California," Bulletin 180C, California Div. of Mines and Geology, 56 pp.

Goldman, H.B., and Klein, I.E., 1958, "Sand and Gravel Resources of Cache Creek in Lake, Colusa, and Yolo Counties, California," *California Journal of Mines and Geology*, Vol. 54, No. 2, Apr., pp. 237–296.

Goldman, H.B., and Klein, I.E., 1961, "Sand and Gravel Resources of the Kern River, near Bakersfield, California," Special Report No. 70, California Div. of Mines and Geology, 33 pp.

Pajalich, W., 1972, "Sand and Gravel," *Minerals Yearbook 1972*, US Bureau of Mines, pp. 1103–1121.

Pajalich, W., 1976, "Sand and Gravel," *Mineral Facts and Problems, 1975*, US Bureau of Mines, pp. 933–946.

Schellie, K.L., and Rogier, D.A., 1963, "Site Utilization and Rehabilitation Practices for Sand and Gravel Operations," National Sand and Gravel Assn., Silver Spring, MD, 80 pp.

Stearn, E.W., 1970, "Dredging in the Aggregates Industry," *Rock Products*, Vol. 73, No. 9, Sep., pp. 74–76.

Tepordei, V.V., 1980, "Sand and Gravel," *Minerals Yearbook, 1978–79*, US Bureau of Mines, 26 pp.

Yeend, W., 1973, "Sand and Gravel," *U.S. Mineral Resources*, Professional Paper 820, US Geological Survey, pp. 561–565.

Silica and Silicon

T. D. MURPHY *

G. V. HENDERSON †

The element silicon, with its usual partner, oxygen, plays the same role relative to inorganic materials as carbon and hydrogen play with respect to living organisms. The crystallographic structure of silicon dioxide (SiO_2) consists of one atom of silicon well-nigh inseparably bonded to four contiguous atoms of oxygen, a gas of but slightly more than half its atomic weight, forming a three-dimensional network of SiO_4 tetrahedra (Dietz, 1968). This wispy arrangement is the fabric of the mineral quartz which is one of the harder, more abrasive, and chemically stable raw materials to be found in Mother Nature's cupboard. Most of us are vaguely familiar with the observation that nearly 60% of the lithosphere to an approximate depth of 10 miles is composed of these two elements, which proportion actually rises to about 75% if the atmosphere, hydrosphere, and biosphere are included (Parker, 1967).

Elemental silicon is a brittle steel-gray metalloid with a density of 2.42 and does not occur in nature. In its limited commercial form, which is still brittle and metallic in appearance, its density drops to 2.33. It combines with oxygen to form the gaseous oxide SiO, or the solid dioxide SiO_2 (analogous to its congener carbon in CO and CO_2); a tetrachloride $SiCl_4$ (analogous to CCl_4); or, combining with oxygen and one or more metal ions, forms the largest rock-making family of all, the silicates. Further, next to the feldspars, quartz is the most abundant known mineral and, in some form or another, accounts for roughly 12% of surficial terrestrial rock. It is this so-called "free silica" to which your attention is chiefly directed in this chapter.

In any such consideration of silica, its several crystalline phases with their attendant differing physical properties appear worthy of delineation. Alpha quartz is the only one of this interesting polymorphic family that is thermodynamically stable at normal pressures and temperatures up to about 573°C. The low phases of tridymite and cristobalite can exist in the so-called metastable state below 117° to 200°C but seldom occur in nature in these two different crystal forms (Sosman, 1965). Opaline silica, now considered by most researchers to be a variety of cristobalite, occurs in abundance and is the only exception. The three remaining polymorphs, keatite, coesite, and stishovite, also are metastable under ambient conditions. Keatite, however, is not known to occur naturally and has only been synthesized in the laboratory. The other two have been identified in submicron sizes and in microscopic amounts, occurring naturally as a result of high order shock-wave pressures generating quite elevated temperatures—such as might accompany the impact of a large meteorite on a hard sandstone terrain (Chao et al., 1962).

An intriguing characteristic of these silica minerals, and one which has very practical applications, is their extremely variable densities. The classic 2.65 specific gravity of alpha quartz drops to 2.20 in tridymite, cristobalite, and lechatelierite (natural silica glass), as well as in many man-made glasses of commerce which are merely noncrystalline or amorphous solids in the form of super-cooled liquids which can no longer change their shapes (Pauling, 1950). It rises again to 2.50 and 2.93 for keatite and coesite, respectively, and finally becomes a reported 4.35 for stishovite—nearly a 50% range in density for the known physical combinations that silica naturally assumes (Frondel, 1962; Konnert et al., 1973; Pecora, 1960).

Pursuing its esthetic aspects, briefly, silica is well-represented among gem stones which, to qualify as such, must have the attributes of beauty, durability, and rarity (Jahns, 1983). As quartzose gems usually have but one or, at

* Deceased, 1980.
† Chapter modified for 5th edition by G.V. Henderson, Associate Professor, Earth Sciences Dept., California State Polytechnic College, deceased 1981.

most, two of these necessary attributes in any single physical form, they qualify only in the semiprecious category. Among the crystalline forms may be mentioned the well-known amethyst, citrine, "tiger's-eye," aventurine, rock crystal, and rose or smoky quartz. Among the amorphous (so-called opaline) or microcrystalline forms are agate, carnelian, chrysoprase, bloodstone, and, of course, the true opal in its several manifestations. Quartz is one of the gem stones which, together with emerald, ruby, spinel, and sapphire, have been successfully synthesized by man.

From a strictly utilitarian point of view, the bulk of the free silica of commerce consists of quartzites together with the detrital quartzose sands and gravels and the weakly consolidated sandstones and conglomerates resulting from erosive and sedimentary processes. These are the "bread-and-butter" types that furnish most of the high-purity siliceous raw materials going into the ceramic, refractory, and heavy chemical trades as well as to foundry, steel, and other metallurgical outlets. In addition, but to a lesser extent, respectable tonnages of massive quartz in the form of pegmatitic replacements and vein types, together with tripoli, ganister, chert, novaculite, and quartz-mica schist, find their way to market for the production of specialty items or ultra high-purity products such as vitreous silica, chemical ware, and TV tubes.

Uses and Specifications

Siliceous raw materials are often used in industry directly as finished products, shipped without recourse to elimination of natural contaminants. Such an item as naturally bonded molding sand, in which case the mined material is merely dried before shipment to preserve the natural interstitial clay bond, is an example of this, although that used for very heavy steel castings is shipped crude or green with contained moisture. Runner sands for the blast furnace casting floor and furnace bottom sand for acid open hearth practice both fit in this category. Carefully graded quartz sand filter media is an example where the exact size frequency distribution is of paramount importance. This is also especially true of hydraulic fracturing sand wherein the grain shape, in terms of a high Krumbein roundness factor, is of critical significance. Other examples could be cited, such as blasting sands and pulverized silica flour, as these materials are largely purchased on very precise physical and chemical specifications (Wilborg and Henderson, 1983).

The use of selected natural quartz crystals as well as cultured or man-made quartz crystals is a strategic as well as a growing business (Hale and Blair, 1983). Specialty silica products, in both powdered and liquid forms, are being increasingly used in industry. These synthetic silicas referred to as xerogels and hydrogels, together with pyrogenic and precipitated silica as well as colloidal silica sols which are used as binder, bonding, and antislip agents, are described by Teicher (1974). Another specialty item is the commercially prepared cristobalite that C-E Minerals and Harbison-Walker Refractories now manufacture. It is 60% — 100 mesh and is used in investment casting to compensate for metal shrinkage and to impart increased dimensional accuracy of cast parts.

However, the greater tonnage is purchased for its use as an additive to some manufacturing process where, in this capacity, it qualifies only as a semifinished product. Thus, while physical characteristics are significant, a particular material might chiefly be used because of its relatively unique chemical properties or composition. These products demand even greater care in preparation and must often meet very rigorous chemical specifications. Such prepared silica materials as electrometallurgical gravel for production of elemental phosphorus or silicon alloys, granular mix for acid refractory shapes, and specially prepared sand for manufactured abrasives, soluble silicates, and glassmaking are the principal tonnage items, the last, by far, the largest.

To generalize, a naturally light-colored quartzite, sandstone, or quartz sand or one which readily breaks down and washes to a light color, having at least 95% of its grains between US Standard Sieves of 20 mesh (850 μm) and 140 mesh (106 μm), and with a fairly uniform size frequency distribution, is, from a textural standpoint, a potential multipurpose industrial silica raw material, per se. If further inspection reveals that the individual quartz grains are relatively free of identifiable blemishes, e.g., black iron-bearing mineral inclusions, hard, tight irony-clay crusts and coatings, or a noticeable percentage of deeply colored grains, the chances are that with specialized preparation the material might qualify for higher grade use from a compositional standpoint also. The degree to which it would qualify is tightly controlled by the type and percentage content of discrete particles native to the raw material. These normally consist of high gravity detrital minerals, which are black or opaque and usually high in iron, and/or semitransparent minerals which are extremely refractory, and/or miscellaneous rock particles. However, bulk color is not an absolute criterion for the judgment of purity in a silica sand. Needlelike graphitic inclusions in the quartz grain, quantitatively sufficient to impart a drab gray or even a blackish color to a commercially prepared sand that is otherwise acceptable, do occur sporadically (Heinrich, 1974).

The aforementioned defects that generally plague most silica source materials are not only known to most producers but also to most potential users, particularly in the glass industry. Even the smaller glass producers have their own laboratory and glass technologist. Because they know the trouble they can get into almost overnight, they protect themselves against this by carefully sampling and testing the incoming raw materials on a very stringent specification basis. Although explicit ranges and tolerances of unwanted contaminants are furnished to the supplier, shipments of unfailing uniform quality, year in and year out, are most sought after by the enlightened purchasing agent. He knows that he can keep his batch and furnace supervisor the most content with a raw material that does not have erratic and continuing fluctuations in the sieve and chemical analyses even though the top sizes or the fines are sometimes a little excessive or the contaminants are on the high side of the specifications limits.

This is axiomatic for any raw material consumer, of course, but it is particularly true where trace quantity limitations are critical, as with silica. For instance, it is well-known in the silica industry that nickel, chromium, copper, and cobalt are not normally indigenous to the usual silica deposit, per se. For glass-melting sand use, however, even trace amounts of these four metallic ions are deleterious because of their high colorant or defect-producing properties when dissolved in molten glass. While it is true these elements are often added to the glass batch this is done under highly controlled conditions by the batchmaster (Mills, 1983). As a consequence, most glass producers put very stringent particulate limits for these on their purchase specifications. The producer, therefore, must be conscious of any widespread secondary manganese mineralization in his deposit which could harbor trace quantities of cobalt; must eliminate all danger of copper contamination in his quarry blasting by substituting aluminum caps and iron leg wires for the more conventional copper blasting accessories, or,

better, go entirely to "Primacord" for the initiation of the blast; and must be sure that no nickel or chromium alloys are used where any wear surfaces are involved in his mill flowsheet. If these precautions are not strictly enforced, the penalty can be the eventual loss of valuable orders.

While it is difficult to generalize on tolerances and specifications of a sand suitable for flint glass melting or as a base for chemical manufacture, the total acceptable iron content usually ranges from 0.015 to 0.030%; alumina should not exceed 0.20% or fluctuate; calcium and magnesium oxides combined should be uniform and not exceed 0.05% for glass and 0.15% for chemical use. Alkalies and titania are tolerated in trace amounts (0.01% or less) but must not vary; cobalt and chromium—none. Sand with 0.05 to 0.15% iron is used for the production of amber container ware and flat glass. Specifications for other than ceramic raw materials—which are constantly being tightened—have not changed materially in the past 20 years, so will not be recited here (Murphy, 1960, 1960a).

Geology, Distribution, and Occurrences

Silica, from the standpoints of its genesis and geographic distribution, is indeed ubiquitous. In North America, as elsewhere, silica has been exposed in massive weathered outcrops and reaccumulating in fresh detrital deposits during practically every era and period of recorded geologic time. Current witnesses to this range from impressive Canadian operations in the Lorrain quartzite of ancient Huronian time (Hewitt, 1951) to our own Holocene beach sand deposits even now being winnowed by nature for future exploitation on the Gulf Coast of Florida's Panhandle. As an illustration of the versatility of this mineral, it may be pointed out that a major silica producer in this country currently utilizes raw materials ranging in geologic age from late Precambrian to mid-Tertiary. These run the lithologic gamut from pegmatitic quartz through tightly cemented vitreous quartzite to loose, unconsolidated quartz sands.

Eastern United States

The bulk of this country's silica production lies in the populous east where most of the consumers are and hence the demand for silica-based products is highest. Twenty years ago a study of source distribution by the writer showed that 145 viable silica mining companies, regardless of the quality or type of product sold, were operating in the silica industry east of the Mississippi River (Murphy, 1960).

The census of silica-bearing formations in the 26 eastern states referred to indicated the surficial occurrence of approximately 67 mapped, named, and formally accepted stratigraphic units that might have an economic potential in this industry. Lithologically, these break down into quartz-mica schists, quartzites, sandstones (variable in degree of consolidation), quartz conglomerates, quartz gravels, and several widely separated tripoli districts. Also included were many geologically undesignated dune sand occurrences, terrace sands and gravels, commercial chert deposits, massive quartz pegmatites, hydrothermal replacement bodies, and silicified zones, some of which have been and probably are viable from an economic point of view.

In this connection there are many scattered, very pure, silica sand deposits of Holocene age along the coastal plains of South Carolina, Georgia, and Florida, some of which have been and are being reworked by wind and the present river systems. Another interesting and valuable source type may be referred to as the St. Lucie soil zone which is well-developed along a stretch of east Florida coast particularly in St. Lucie county (Hudson, 1946), the type locality, as well as inland in this state and in south Georgia (Teas, 1921). The key to the purity of these deposits relates to a fluctuating ground water table and an excess of azohumic and other organic acids resulting from decaying swamp vegetation which leaches the iron normally present in the surficial sand. This organic chemistry develops the so-called Van Dyke or sap-brown ore at the base of the leached zone which was much sought after as an organic dye for paint, wood stains, and inks before the advent of aniline dyes. Most of these types of deposits are from 4 to possibly 12 ft thick on flat terrain with consequent disappointingly low tonnages. However, they are commercially viable at a few points in each of the states mentioned and can supply local flint glass sand markets for indeterminant periods of time if extensive enough, which several have proved to be. The inevitable silica sand rings which partially surround the puzzling "Carolina Bays," are believed to be a manifestation of this leaching and in one instance were commercially exploited for several years in Williamsburg County, South Carolina (Buie, 1958).

The Carolina Silica Co. has a major silica sand production in North Carolina at Marston,

which has been in production for about nine years. Pennsylvania Glass Sand has a major silica sand production in South Carolina near Columbia. Martin Marietta has a silica operation at Camden. Jessie Morrie Co. has a major silica sand production near Junction City, Georgia. In Virginia, the major silica sand production is from Gore, where Unimin Corp. has an operation.

Two formational units for high grade ceramic products exposed in the eastern and a few middle western states warrant detailed citation as the most successfully exploited silica raw material sources on the basis of tonnage and profit in this country. They are the St. Peter sandstone together with its stratigraphic equivalents of Lower Ordovician age, and the Oriskany sandstone or orthoquartzite of Lower Devonian age. The St. Peter is exposed and exploited principally in northern Illinois and, to a lesser degree, in southern Wisconsin and Missouri. Sandstones of the same time equivalency also are exploited in Arkansas and Oklahoma (Lamar, 1927; Ham, 1945). These formations are relatively flat-lying and massively bedded materials of weak to moderate consolidation that lend themselves equally well to open pit or underground mining recovery, both methods being currently employed. Physical recovery is high and a minimum of plant preparation is necessary because of its extreme natural purity. Reserves are large and nearly completely controlled by current producers. Even deeply covered areas, now unused because of excessive stripping costs or otherwise marginal because of local factors, have been explored and acquired by operating companies for possible future use. What little St. Peter sandstone that remains under private ownership will soon be, if it has not already been, completely zoned out of the market by urbanization pressures.

The Oriskany quartzite, more precisely the Ridgeley sandstone (Harris, 1972), is a ridge maker, to a large degree, because of its greater induration and consequent structural attitudes. For the most part it is found in strongly dipping beds ranging from 45° to the vertical and even overturned. In a few areas it is as flat-bedded as the St. Peter, whereas, locally, it may be preserved intact in homoclinal, anticlinal, and synclinal postures (Bates, 1960). Being an integral part of the Appalachian Highlands, its economic occurrences are pretty well limited to the tri-state area of Virginia, West Virginia, and Pennsylvania. The texture, purity and degree of induration are all subject to extreme variability which is much less seldom encountered with the St. Peter. However, by and large, it shares the same perfection of grain that the St. Peter enjoys and most of the defects are secondarily induced and can be mitigated and often nearly eliminated by suitable plant beneficiation. Here again, all known reserves in the technical sense and much that could be classed as potential resource acreage is believed to be owned by, or under long-term lease to, local operating companies. A substantial portion of what is already controlled will doubtless never be completely exploited because of the ever-increasing zonal restrictions due to urbanization.

Although these two formations are the premier sources for all-purpose silica products in the United States, several others bear mention. The Jordan sandstone of Upper Cambrian age in Minnesota and Wisconsin has a preferred grain shape for specialty use end products but is limited to very restricted areas of exposure. Over most of its near-outcrop area it is covered with either thick glacial drift or heavy dolomite beds which make it completely uneconomic for commercial use. As it is a massive and moderately cemented sandstone, mining by room-and-pillar method has been carried on sporadically along the Mississippi River bluffs near St. Paul, producing chiefly foundry sand products.

The Cohansey sand, of probable Miocene age, is a strong local factor in the foundry and ceramic supply business of southern New Jersey where it is well located with respect to a heavy concentration of consumers. This is a very weakly consolidated sand of extremely erratic quality, both physical and compositional, but selected deposits can be and are upgraded by suitable processing into salable products, mostly for ceramic and refractory uses. Exploitable reserves are strictly limited and those that are known are jealously held by mining companies who operate in the outcropping areas.

A long-time supplier of industrial-type silica products, especially for the foundry trades, is the Pottsville formation of lower Pennsylvanian age. This formation includes the Homewood and Connoquenessing sandstone members in Pennsylvania, and the Sharon and Olean quartz-conglomerate and sandstone members in Ohio, Pennsylvania, and New York State (Bowen, 1953). These several strati-

graphic units supply a large portion of the metallurgical pebble used in silicon alloys in the northeastern states, as well as amber quality melting sand and several types of sand for refractory use. Most of the coarse pebble sizes in the conglomerate phase have been exhausted through the years, forcing the metallurgical trade to switch, in part, to silica pebble from the Sewanee conglomerate of Pennsylvanian age in east-central Tennessee or the Pee Dee type of Pliocene to Holocene terrace gravels produced in both the Carolinas and to a lesser extent in Alabama, Georgia, and Florida. In Maryland the Bryn Mawr gravel of Pliocene age is a source material for this type of end use.

Western United States

In 1960 there were 48 producers west of the Mississippi, which represented roughly 25% on a national basis. This situation remains virtually unchanged at present writing, and breaks down into 22 producers in California and Nevada; five in the Pacific Northwest (which includes Oregon, Washington, Idaho, and Montana). This leaves an additional 21 producers for the remaining 16 states in the conterminous United States.

West Coast deposits, by and large, are inferior as to grade, nationally, necessitating expensive beneficiation which raises the ex-mine price substantially. However, except for certain items such as pulverized silica and a few quality specialty products obtainable only from eastern or mid-continent producers, the delivered price insures the use of western silica products in this region.

About the same situation exists with respect to the Pacific Northwest. Here, in addition to relatively second-grade raw materials, the additional burden of poor location with respect to transportation exists, with all known deposits being anywhere from 1 to 40-odd miles from rails. Since most of these deposits, geologically, are Tertiary to Holocene in age, they consequently have not undergone the natural winnowing of nonquartz particles which results from the recycling that the older Paleozoic and Mesozoic rocks east of the Continental Divide have undergone. Most of these far western deposits have been derived from the breakdown of simple binary granites, relatively free of ferromagnesian and ore minerals. Hence they are either only feldspathic, clayey, or both.

Production of feldspathic sand from Pacific Grove, CA, ceased several years ago. However, production of a feldspathic sand near Byron, CA (Martin Marietta) was begun about 1974. This operation serves the glass container industry in the Bay area and the Central Valley of California. This is an amber sand used principally for wine bottles and fiberglass production.

Martin Marietta has significant production of feldspathic sand from deposits near Emmett, Idaho. These sands are used in glass container manufacturing, sand blasting, filtering, building products, and other applications.

Probably the most successfully utilized material for production of glass container ware in northern California has been exploited since 1955 in Amador County from the Ione formation of Eocene age. The only significant production in this area today is the production of a high silica sand by Owens Illinois. The workable member consists of relatively clean quartz sand mixed with residual kaolin and anauxite in roughly a 60% to 40% ratio. The operation is close to captive San Francisco Bay area markets and the product is sold also to independent consumers. A similar venture was initiated in 1956 by competitive interests in an extension of the Ione into adjoining Calaveras County. A marketable quality product was made and less waste was involved here because the raw material, while quite feldspathic, was essentially free of clay, as such. However, the operation was forced into abandonment shortly after startup because the property was deeply flooded by the construction of a new dam to form the present Camanche Reservoir on the North Fork of Mokelumne River—an unfortunate but increasingly common victim of environmental pressures.

A detrimental impediment to the use of Ione sand (or, for that matter any other far western sand exploited to date) is that even though a completely adequate flint-quality glass sand can be produced at a high cost, it cannot be ground into an acceptable color quality for silica flour in the burgeoning commercial cleanser market which, perforce, must import silica flour from mid–continent or eastern producers. This is because the Ione formation contains residual particles of Mariposa slate and other dark-colored rock fragments which, because of the formation's geological youth, have not been eliminated by recycling. An exception to this in California is the availability of a limited supply of cleanser-grade silica flour with acceptable brightness (>85% dry reflectance and >56% wet reflectance based on US Bureau of Standards MgO comparisons). This

is produced from selected vein quartz pebble accumulations resulting from early placer hydraulic tailings that are dredged from the Bear River near Colfax between Nevada and Placer counties.

In Southern California, the Paleocene Silverado and Eocene Tejon formations are, respectively, mined and processed for both flint and amber glass at Rancho Mission Viejo in Orange County and near Oceanside in San Diego County. These outlets supply both glass and foundry silica raw materials as well as a great many specialty products such as blast sands, filter media, traction sand, soluble silicates, and ganister mix, all of which are principally used in the Los Angeles Basin area (Gay, 1957).

In the contiguous state of Nevada, Clark County contains substantial deposits of mostly second-grade raw silica materials in the form of quartzites, sandstones, and dune sands. The most heavily exploited of these is the Baseline sandstone of Longwell, so-called, who correlated these beds with early Upper Cretaceous formations in Wyoming and Idaho. It is uniform in composition and highly quartzose, contaminated only by a few clay pockets and laminations; the cementing material is weak, producing a friable sandstone easily quarried and beneficiated. It is produced and shipped into Southern California where it is utilized for flint and amber container ware and several grades of foundry sands. Other potential silica sources here include the Eureka quartzite of middle Ordovician age, very pure in most exposures but also tightly cemented and indurated. This has discouraged its use as a ceramic sand product for cost or production reasons but it could well be utilized for refractory and metallurgical uses. The Supai formation is classified as Pennsylvanian or Permian in age with restricted outcrops and, although sandy and friable, is plagued with highly colored beds of hematitic and limonitic-stained beds which lower its potential purity, productwise. The Aztec sandstone of Jurassic age is exposed extensively in imposing outcrops but suffers from red and yellow coloration that, again, would pose expensive cost problems in processing, especially for white glass use. Finally, a plethora of eolian sands of Pleistocene and Holocene age occur in sheets and dunes that are the end products of wind scour on exposed outcrops of the Supai and Aztec sandstones which crop out sporadically throughout the vicinity of Overton. The finer grades of this crude sand are suitable for medium to light corework in iron, brass, bronze, magnesium, and aluminum, but are more commonly utilized as a base in molding light steel, brass, and aluminum castings. In summary, some of the Clark County sands— chiefly those washed and graded products of the Baseline sandstone—are favored by virtue of market specifications and delivered price in the Southern California foundry trade, to a limited extent by the glass container trade, and much more for special purpose work such as, for example, manufacture of Transite pipe for which the mix requires up to 30% SiO_2 ground to a —140-mesh size (Murphy, 1954).

Some rather competent silica natural resources occur in the Pacific Northwest but the sparse population of this region, together with the relative isolation of most of the deposits with regard to rail transportation and end-use points has resulted in retardment of exploitation up to the present time. However, the Lane Mountain silica deposit in Stevens County, WA, is the major producer of silica sand in the Northwest and the only producer of flint quality glass sand. Lane Mountain Silica Co. has been a most successful operation for a number of years.

Results of a study (Carter et al., 1962) based on field and laboratory examinations, furnished data for commercial evaluations of some 82 silica deposits in this region. Of the 37 deposits found to be of satisfactory quality, for some sort of exploitation, only 16 were determined to have sufficient tonnage to be commercially viable. The investigators concluded there were two outstanding supply points: one was the Quartz Mountain deposit in Spokane County, Washington, which is an excellent source for silicon metal and ferrosilican alloy raw materials even though the operation is 20 miles from Mead, the nearest rail point. The deposit is huge and consists of massive quartz intruded into the local granitic country rock. The other was the Bovill clay-sand deposit in Latah County, Idaho, with accessibility to rails only a mile from the deposit. It was felt that this material should be a source for low-iron sand in the northwest for many years. The Lane Mountain deposit in Stevens County, Washington, shows promise but more field and laboratory work must be done. The Addy quartzite (age unstated) shows great textural variations throughout its outcrop area and contains argillaceous impurities. Rail transportation is available from 1 to 12 miles, depending on the outcrop locations.

Most high-purity silicon metal (96–99% Si) produced in the United States comes from raw materials located in the Pacific Northwest (including British Columbia) induced by the availability of cheap hydroelectric power according to Richardson et al. (1974). Therefore, this region appears to have a good potential for further eventual exploitation of its silica raw materials.

Middle United States

The 16-state region of the United States formerly alluded to represents a relatively sparse market for silica products except for certain areas. Again, demand based on population plays a large part in this. It is largely an agrarian region bordering on the Missisipi River with relatively few scattered market centers for silica raw materials. Those that do exist are amply serviced by the St. Peter sandstone and its stratigraphic correlatives which are chiefly exploited in the tier of states bordering on the Mississippi. A plexus of high-grade silica reserves of St. Peter age exists in Oklahoma which, together with a few stratigraphically younger and generally second-grade deposits in Texas, Kansas, and South Dakota furnishes silica demand west to the Rockies. Major production of hydrafracturing sand comes from deposits near Brady, Texas (Pennsylvania Glass Sand and Texas Mining Co.). These deposits provide a major portion of the frac sand used in the US.

Unimin Corp. has recently completed a new plant facility for production of frac sand near Le Sueur, Minnesota. Ottawa Silica Co. operates a silica sand-kaolin operation near Kosse, Texas. This plant has shipped over 300,000 stpy of product for the past 15 years. The deposit is on the Simmsboro sand/kaolin member of the Wilcox formation. Ottawa Silica Co. also has a silica operation near Dubberly, LA, which supplies silica to the glass and chemical industries.

The five mountain states, together with Utah and Arizona, either lack sufficient population demand to warrant local silica production or lack silica raw materials of sufficient quality and accessibility to make exploitation profitable. Arizona is the only exception with its long-established production of excellent hydrafrac sand from the Bidahochi formation of Pliocene age in Apache County. Production of post-Carboniferous pegmatitic quartz for high-grade ceramic use and cleanser-grade silica flour for California markets comes from Mohave County.

Canada

Eastern Canada: The overwhelming proportion of Canadian silica and silicon alloy business is limited to two provinces, Ontario and Quebec, mainly because there are nearly twice as many people living here as in the other eight contiguous and more agriculturally oriented provinces. Of equal importance, the cheap hydroelectric power available at Welland, Thorold, and Niagara Falls, Ont., and at Beauharnois, Que., make these points the centers of important ferroalloy production.

This comprises the principal foreign outlet for one of Canada's prime silica raw materials, the Precambrain Lorrain quartzite cropping out in the Georgian Bay area of Ontario. Early quarries were opened on Manitoulin Island and later on nearby Badgely Island. As this is highly metamorphosed paraquartzite which was derived from an argillaceous sandstone, much trouble has been encountered in keeping alumina to acceptable limits which occurs as sericitic partings in some of the beds. Quarrying is also carried on along the northern shore of Georgian Bay in the Killarney area which can be reached only by boat from Little Current. Most of the product goes into ferroalloys but some is used as a metallurgical flux stone for slagging iron and basic oxides into silicates in the production of nickel and copper matte. These shipments go to the Sudbury district in Ontario and the Noranda district in Quebec and some are captive quarries such as the Lawson operation at Whitefish Falls.

Production was initiated at St. Donat in a friable orthoquartzite of probable Grenville age which is now beneficiated into an acceptable grade of glass sand at a plant 50 miles southeast at St. Canut. Portions of the product are sold for silicon carbide manufacture and foundry sand, as well as pulverized silica for use as filler in pipe and concrete blocks (Minnes, 1967).

The only other potential silica raw materials that occur in eastern Canada are: pegmatitic and vein quartz which are mostly handcobbed as waste in small feldspar operations and used locally for such items as pottery flint, architectural veneers, or flux stone; unconsolidated glacial and river sands which are generally loaded with rock fragments and used principally for construction aggregate; and several miscellaneous sandstones which, for one reason or another, are incompetent for highgrade industrial use without a great deal of expensive upgrading. Hewitt (1951) lists the latter as being of Pleistocene age.

The Potsdam sandstone, also referred to as the "Nepean" sandstone, is either late Cambrian or early Ordovician in age, and is exposed over wide areas as discontinuous patches of relatively flat-bedded deposits with up to 40° dips, having a maximum known thickness of 280 ft (Keith, 1949). The formation has been quarried in several areas in eastern Ontario and southern Quebec with questionable success. This stems from its pyritiferous nature which also condemns the formation in all personally investigated exposures in upper New York State. The pyrite occurs not only as loose, intergranular mineralization but also as tight coatings on the quartz grains themselves. Beneficiation to date has proven partially successful but costly and the Potsdam should doubtless be relegated to the role of a second-grade ceramic raw material acceptable on a delivered price basis only if it meets competition from other imported US sands.

The Medina sandstone of lower Silurian age crops out in several counties west of the Niagara escarpment in Ontario and is principally quarried for building stone. Hewitt (1951) concludes that its potential as a marketable silica product is low although it has been used in a ganister mix for cupola and ladle lining in the past and is an attractive stone for architectural veneer.

Oriskany sandstone is exposed as an extensive outlier in Haldimand County, Ontario, with a reported maximum thickness of about 20 ft. It is described as a coarse-grained, well-rounded, friable, white sandstone poorly bonded by lime cement. Although glass and foundry sands reportedly were produced from this area many years ago, the high iron content (0.15%–0.49%) rules it out as a first-class raw material (Cole, 1923).

The Sylvania sandstone of lower Devonian age crops out modestly near Sylvania in Lucas County, Ohio, this being the type locality. It is mined extensively in the vicinity of Rockwood, Munroe County, Michigan, and furnishes a fair proportion of the glass sand exported to Canada from the United States. Hewitt (1951) correctly points out that this is a potential glass sand in the Windsor-Amherstburg area of Essex County, Ontario, even though subsurface methods to win it would be required because of a strong northeasterly dip. He reports that the top of this sandstone was encountered in a well in Anderdon Township at a depth of 150 ft. However, the writer has examined undoubted Sylvania sand exposed in the bottom of an operating dolomite quarry in the overlying Detroit River formation near Amherstburg with no more than 30 to 60 ft of overburden. This is not an insurmountable factor using modern methods of stripping. The Sylvania, however, requires careful processing as it is high in base oxides which must be carefully controlled by washing and leaching to insure the necessary uniformity, day in and day out, that any commercial ceramic product requires.

Collings (1965) pinpoints the occurrences of several deposits of unconsolidated sands in the Maritime Provinces of eastern Canada; specifically, the beach sands near Souris on Prince Edward Island and those at Barrington Bay and Port Mouton on the southeastern coast of Nova Scotia. These are Holocene sands, feldspathic and impure, and would have to be thoroughly beneficiated to become saleable. The economics are further complicated by their distance to markets.

Goudge (in Cole, 1928) describes additional silica potential in Nova Scotia as consisting of two deposits in Cape Breton County. One is a deposit of clayey sand derived from a weathered orthoquartzite of Precambrian George River age. It has been both quarried and mined and at the time examined was still in the initial stages of development. A fair market was assumed for use as a foundry sand for iron and brass casting in Sydney and New Glasgow. The other deposit had been opened in a fine-grained, brittle paraquartzite facies of the same formation fractured or faulted with serpentinite and chlorite fillings. Production at the time of examination was intermittant, the product from this captive operation going into silica brick lines for the open hearth furnaces in nearby Sydney, N.S.

Unconsolidated bar and bank sands are exposed along the Mattagami and Missinaibi rivers in northeastern Ontario which are relatively pure or could be economically upgraded. However, their great distance from present population and consumption centers prevents their exploitation at the present time. In Newfoundland, paraquartzite produced at Villa Marie on the Avalon Peninsula is shipped to Long Harbor where it is used as a flux in the reduction process for the production of elemental phosphorous in the electric furnace.

Western Canada: The best known and most exploited material in Manitoba—as well as one of the most poorly situated—reportedly occurs in the Winnipeg formation of probable Cambro-Ordovician age (Cole, 1928; Collings, 1965;

Spiece, 1980). It is exposed on three islands and two promontories in Lake Winnipeg. As it is mined principally on the southeast shore of Black Island, it takes its name in the trade from this source. The sandstone is described as being very loosely consolidated with argillaceous-ferruginous cementing material that washes off readily leaving a fine-grained, subrounded to rounded grain, white, and relatively free of heavy minerals. Economically, the principal drawback is its isolated location as it has to be barged 80 miles to Fort Selkirk where it is washed, dried and sized, and shipped 20 miles farther on to Winnipeg for use as foundry sand. Some of the material is even shipped as far as Redcliff, Alberta, for container-ware use.

Two other deposits of silica raw material with potential are: (1) A deposit occurring near the town of Beausejour on the Canadian National Railway, 36 miles northwest of Winnipeg. Believed to be of Pleistocene age and fluvioglacial origin, it contains many rock fragments and ferromagnesian minerals. It was opened for foundry materials but is nonoperative at present. Although location-wise it is quite well situated, the necessary ore dressing required to produce a ceramic raw material might well price it out of the market. (2) In contrast, unconsolidated silica sand deposits occurring surficially in the Pine River district are reportedly relatively pure. The chief impurity is a light clay coating on the grain which is readily removed by attrition scrubbing according to Collings (1965). However, these deposits are 200 miles, straight-line, from the nearest use points in the Winnipeg area and nearly 500 miles from Redcliff.

Both Cole (1928) and Collings (1965) speak highly of the great purity of an extensive white sandstone that crops out on the south shore of Wapawekka Lake in east-central Saskatchewan. One sample submitted for analysis showed 98.50% SiO_2, 0.21% Al_2O_3, and 0.008% Fe_2O_3, presumably after washing only, with 91% of the grains on the 35 and 48 mesh sieves. The grains are described as being subangular. If representative, this is a remarkable accumulation of silica, but unfortunately it will probably never be exploited for it is over 100 miles from the nearest point on the Canadian National Railroad through lake-studded, true wilderness, and bush country. Two other potentially commercial silica deposits in Saskatchewan are the Flin Flon sand 125 miles east of Wapawekka Lake and near that town, and the Red Deer River sandstone 150 miles due south of Flin Flon. These raw materials apparently qualify for ceramic use after suitable beneficiation but although both are close to rails, they are too distant from present markets to be other than potential resources.

Excessive rail distance from present markets of known silica deposits again limits exploitation in Alberta, even though glass container ware is produced at Redcliff nearly 600 miles southeast of the only known potentially competent deposit in this province. Collings (1965) refers to this as the Peace River deposit of friable sandstone that occurs practically on rails south of the town of that name. The material apparently qualifies as marketable ceramic-grade material, after attrition scrubbing, but the nearest potential market area is at Edmonton about 275 miles to the southeast. This area has been periodically investigated for manufacture of fiberglass, using this deposit as a raw material.

Cole (1928) has examined the bituminous sands of the Fort McMurray district at rail's end about 250 miles north of Edmonton. Laboratory tests on a composite sample taken from six representative outcrops indicated a bitumen content of about 15% and a sand recovery of about 83% analyzing 95.50% SiO_2, 2.25% Al_2O_3, and 0.35% Fe_2O_3 with less than 1% total base oxides and alkalies. The silica grains are clear quartz and sharply angular to round, with sizing predominantly in the 40 to 80 mesh range. It was concluded that with proper treatment, a green bottle glass might be made of the sand tailings. McConville (1975) has given a comprehensive description of these so-called "Athabasca tar sands" and the current development being initiated for energy purposes. No mention is made, however, of the sand tailings' potential as a source for commercial silica sand. The sand is lower Cretaceous in age.

One other silica deposit, worthy of mention, is a large deposit of well-rounded quartzose pebbles exposed near Cypress Hills 22 miles off the Canadian Pacific Railway. Grinding tests made from representative samples indicated that the work done by these pebbles compared favorably with that of expensive imported Danish pebbles.

Although Cole (1928) cites and describes three bona fide silica deposits in British Columbia, the descriptions are not impressive and lead one to the conclusion that they qualify as good prospects only. They are all quartz bodies of the vein or igneous type which generally, but not always, are restricted as to tonnage and pinch out on strike. Collings (1965) calls attention to the shutdown of an

operation near Oliver, in which igneous quartz or quartzite was being shipped for ferrosilicon and silicon carbide manufacture. He points out that much of the British Columbia silica market is currently supplied by the Lane Mountain quartzite deposits near Valley, WA. However, he speaks optimistically of the silica potential of deposits at both Golden and Canal Flats in southeastern British Columbia, suggesting that future glass or fiberglass raw materials could be developed; or that the Alberta markets, which already exist at Redcliff and Edmonton, might be supplied from here.

A potential is also believed to exist in some beach and dune sands at the southern tip of Vancouver Island which bear similarity to the Oregon State coastal deposits between Fort Stevens and Coos Bay. Evaluation of the stateside sands indicated that even with high-intensity magnetic separation followed by acid-leaching the remaining iron oxides precluded use for high-grade ceramic products because of low recovery of product and excessive reagent costs (Carter et al., 1964).

Summing up, the Canadian Mineral Resources Branch gives production statistics for the Dominion for the record year of 1979 (Boyd, 1979). It shows a total domestic production of 2 368 497 t of silica, of which 60 823 t of quartzite were exported. Imports of silica sand and quartz amounted to 1 651 890 t, of which nearly all came from the United States. This gave Canada a total silica consumption of 2 987 735 t. Domestic production figures included 400 316 t produced in western Canada from the provinces of Manitoba, Saskatchewan, and British Columbia.

Table 1 lists a few dependable analyses of representative silica formations exploited throughout the United States and Canada together with their geologic age.

Mexico *

The following companies account for about 90% of the Mexican production of about 400 kt of silica sand:

Company	
Materias Primas Monterrey, S.A.	164 99
Materias Primas Minerales San José, S.A.	94 63
Silice Pizzuto, S.A.	64 44
Arena Silica Industrial de México, S.A.	17 28
Silice Potosi, S.A.	15 63
Cia Minera y Mercantil "El Palizar," S.A.	13 60
	370 57

* Courtesy Guillermo P. Salas, Chief Economi Studies, Consejo de Recursos Naturales no Reno vables, Mexico City, D.F., Mexico.

TABLE 1—Representative Silica Samples from the United States and Canada

Percent

Oxides	1	2	3	4	5	6	7	8	9	10	11	12	13	14	15
SiO_2	99.07	99.76	99.59	99.70	99.77	98.93	99.42	96.62	99.16	99.52	99.83	99.45	98.61	96.71	99.27
Al_2O_3	0.56	0.22	0.20	0.08	0.15	0.65	0.16	1.72	0.43	0.27	0.05	0.05	0.47	1.71	0.26
Fe_2O_3	0.03	0.03	0.03	0.02	0.01	0.03	0.03	0.38	0.03	0.01	0.04	0.02	0.25	0.17	0.05
TiO_2	Nd	0.02	0.06	0.02	0.02	0.03	0.02	0.12	0.03	0.01	Nd	0.01	Nd	Nd	0.04
CaO	0.03	0.01	Nd	0.01	Tr	0.01	0.07	Nil	0.08	0.01	0.02	0.04	0.13	Tr	0.02
MgO	0.09	Tr	Nd	0.01	Tr	0.04	Tr	0.08	Tr	Tr	0.01	0.02	0.05	0.05	0.02
Na_2O+K_2O	Nd	Nd	Nd	0.01	Nd	0.40	Nd	0.24	Nd	0.01	0.12	Nd	Nd	0.34	0.54
Fusion loss	Nd	0.12	0.12	0.10	0.08	0.24	0.12	Nd	0.18	0.10	0.09	0.07	0.35	Nd	Nd
% total	99.78	100.16	100.00	99.95	100.03	100.33	99.82	99.16	99.91	99.93	100.16	99.66	99.86	98.98	100.20

No.	Formation	Geologic Age	County and State	Type Sample	Reference
1	Bovill clay-sand	Holocene	Latah, ID	Laboratory processed	Carter, 1962
2	Cohansey sand	Tertiary-Miocene	Cumberland, NJ	Laboratory processed	Lefond, private comm.
3	Ione clay-sand	Tertiary-Eocene	Amador, CA	Commercial product	Mills, 1983
4	Silverado sandstone	Tertiary-Paleocene	Orange, CA	Commercial product	Mills, 1983
5	Tuscaloosa sand	Upper Cretaceous	Marion, GA	Laboratory processed	Lefond, private comm.
6	Baseline sandstone	Upper Cretaceous	Clark, NV	Laboratory processed	Murphy, 1954
7	Trinity sandstone	Lower Cretaceous	Coleman, TX	Laboratory processed	Lefond, private comm.
8	Sharon conglomerate	Basal Pennsylvanian	Portage, OH	Laboratory processed	Bowen, 1953
9	Oriskany quartzite	Lower Devonian	Frederick, VA	Commercial product	Lowery, 1954
10	Eureka quartzite	Middle Ordovician	Clark, NV	Laboratory processed	Murphy, 1954
11	McLish sandstone	Lower Ordovician	Pontotoc, OK	Commercial product	Ham, 1945
12	St. Peter sandstone	Lower Ordovician	LaSalle, IL	Commercial product	Lamar, 1927
13	Potsdam sandstone	Upper Cambrian	Leeds, Ont.	Laboratory processed	Keith, 1946
14	Chickies quartzite	Lower Cambrian	Lancaster, PA	Commercial product	Harris, 1965
15	Lorrain quartzite	Precambrian-Mid. Huronian	Manitoulin, Ont.	Laboratory processed	Hewitt, 1951

Nd, not determined. Tr, Trace.

However, as they produce only about 58% of the total requirements, the balance is imported as shown in the following:

Years	Imports, t
1977	303 500
1978	319 200

Materias Primas Monterrey, S.A., the largest silica sand producer in Mexico, operates in the Jaltipan area of Vera Cruz. Silica sand is also produced by Materias Primas Minerales de San José, S.A., at San Jose de Iturbide in Guanajuato, and Silice Pizzuto, S.A., and Silice Potosi, S.A., near the town of San Luis Potosi in the state of San Luis Potosi.

The principal uses of silica sand in Mexico are as follows:

	Domestic Production	Imports
Glassmaking	290 000	247 150
Foundry	80 700	8 620
Asbestos cement	13 600	
Chemicals (silicates)	12 000	8 620
Ceramics		20 120
Others	15 100	2 881
Total, t	411 400	287 391

Some silica sand is exported, primarily to Brazil, Venezuela, Argentina, and Peru.

Exploration

Potential source grounds for commercial silica, other than those used for construction aggregates, have been mapped and reported on in the literature for so many years, that a certain degree of serendipity enters into the finding of a completely unknown and competent deposit to fit the need in a new target area today. All successful silica-producing companies either have a trained geological specialist to oversee the prospecting and exploration or can hire an experienced consultant to do this.

Because of the extensive amount of published information relating to commercially usable silica deposits, one is indeed lucky to find a deposit that has been overlooked, particularly within marketable distance of a potential customer. Even so, the ecological impact of encroaching urbanization may well have lowered such a deposit's potential for exploitation and although it may qualify technically, it cannot now be exploited and will lie fallow indefinitely.

However, in the unlikely event of a new surficial deposit being discovered which is well-located with respect to markets, the usual standard sampling and exploration can be carried out after arrangements to option or purchase the property have been completed. The methodology of doing this is so well-known by people in this business that it would be superfluous to go into any detail regarding it. There are many sources in the literature that outline such drilling procedures in detail, a few of which may be found in the bibliography.

Field and Laboratory Evaluation

Field Evaluation

All samples, either outcrop or drill hole, should be initially judged by the geologist or mining engineer in charge of the project before remission to the laboratory for final evaluation. Sampling procedures may be modified as more knowledge is gained about the raw material being sought. Pitting and trenching may be utilized in areas with a depressed ground-water table and judgments made which should and can be just as competent as using the drill. Dozers and backhoes, together with hand labor where it is economic, have all been used with complete success.

Buried and ancient dune sands as well as developing fore dunes and beach sands are used for glass raw materials throughout the world (Bird, 1968). In the eastern United States much drilling has been done in reworked sand in the so-called Sandhills Belt developed on the Upper Cretaceous Tuscaloosa formation in the Carolinas, Georgia, Alabama, Tennessee, and Kentucky. Good results have been obtained by hand auger drilling, utilizing a standard portable 3-in. auger set, consisting of 2½-in. steel casing, a 2-in. pump, and 5-ft aluminum extension rods. This same equipment can be used with a 7½-hp motor as a so-called "portable" drill which requires at least a three-man crew in rough country.

Another primitive drilling tool used in shallow, unconsolidated sand, preferably where surface conditions are not conducive to mobility such as wet, heavily wooded swampy ground, is a modification of the ancient Banka drill. This drill is standard in Indonesia where prospecting for alluvial tin is done by cheap labor. An adaptation of this tripod drilling method has sometimes been used in the United States where ground conditions will not accommodate a heavy mechanical drill. Three men and a foreman are required to accomplish this task which is not only slow but tedious, and consequently expensive in these days of high labor costs.

However, if a relatively high water table exists and the terrain is solid and self-supporting, which is usually the case, a heavy machine drill usually can be employed. Nearly any standard type of foreign or American drill, properly adapted to a sandy material, can be used with successful results except for a variable, though low (up to 5%), loss of fines. A standard water jet or percussive type of rig using casing will give good results in water-saturated sand formations; so will a machine auger drill if proper care is taken to avoid cavitation. These methods have all been amply described (Wells, 1973).

Sandstone, if not too highly cemented, can be successfully probed with a heavy auger drill and good results obtained. A quarry-type air-track drill can be used successfully for prospecting as well as a down-the-hole percussion-type rig if larger samples are desired. As far as silica exploration is concerned, using both of these types of drills to depths exceeding 80 to 100 ft becomes time-consuming because of hole clean-out, especially if the material is full of pore water. The more the sandstone is saturated, the slower the progress made so that the time element eventually becomes an unbearable cost factor unless one is on a footage contract. With any of these drilling methods—air-track, machine auger, or percussion—it is mandatory to collect the samples at once, dry them thoroughly, and demagnetize the cuttings so all drill bit or surface casing iron is removed before it gets a chance to oxidize and distort the true quantity of iron native to the raw material —possibly the most significant impurity to be guarded against in silica used for glassmaking.

If the formation to be tested is quartzitic, particularly a vitreous quartzite, the only option of sampling it (short of an adit which is just as expensive and delineates a much more restricted tonnage) is by the diamond core drill. This is the ultimate tool in hard rock as one gets a complete cross section of the formation either at right angles to the bedding or at any angle thereto. The only drawback is that, in a friable orthoquartzite, ofttimes in certain areas, the original calcareous cement has been leached out and it has not yet had time to become vitrified through infiltration by silicious-bearing waters. In this instance core recovery becomes very poor, sometimes yielding almost nothing, particularly on angle holes. It is a truism in this business that every drilling method known has its good and bad features and only experience will show which

is the best type of rig to use on such and such a deposit.

Careful meticulous sampling is about as important a consideration as any phase of establishing the competency of a deposit of silica or any other natural material. However, such an abundance of information exists in the literature on procedural tactics that it would be redundant to dwell in much more detail in a chapter of this type (Lake, 1973; Payne, 1973; Waterman and Hazen, 1968).

Laboratory Evaluation

Glass producers, whether they specialize in container, pressed and blown ware, or flat-ground and floated products, all demand precise chemical and particle size distribution specifications that must be met day in and day out by the supplier. One good reason for this, in the case of quartz sand, is that it represents nearly three-quarters of the total batch mix which may contain as many as 6 to 13, or even more, other raw material components, most of which can and do contain contaminants. This is detailed in the chapter on Glass Raw Materials by Mills, in Volume 1.

There are few, if any, silica deposits that do not contain detrital particles in the form of so-called heavy and refractory minerals, together with chert or other rock fragments, because of their resistance to decay or abrasion in the natural reduction of sandstones or quartzites to sand-size particles. The primordial igneous rocks, from whence originated the present quartz-bearing formations, contained variable amounts of ferromagnesian and ore minerals. The extent to which these are present in currently exposed siliceous formations depends largely on their resistance to mechanical and chemical weathering. Some are relatively unstable such as andalusite, sillimanite, titanite, and kyanite; others are quite stable such as rutile, zircon, ilmenite, spinels, magnetite, and tourmaline; others, equally undesirable, are of secondary origin and relatively newly formed such as pyrite, marcasite, glauconite, siderite, leucoxene, and certain manganese and iron minerals (Pettijohn et al., 1973).

Even the smallest silica producer today has some sort of laboratory to determine whether or not his products meet specifications, which is usually done before samples are submitted to a prospective customer. The standard determination of the nature and content and the degree of removal of these heavy detrital minerals, as well as those which are refractory, together with resistant rock particles, can be made at bench level, employing attrition scrubbing, flotation, or, if required, magnetic or electrostatic methods (McQuiston and Bechaud, 1968).

Development, Mining, and Processing

If the raw material is proven potentially competent, and adequate reserves have been demonstrated, development of an operational site is usually promptly initiated. This is especially true if the deposit is discovered in a new marketing area. Since the term "development" has been used, historically, in several different senses by mining engineers in the past, it is being employed here in the evolutionary sense of being the intermediate step following exploration and investigative evaluation, but preceding actual production mining (Banfield, 1972).

Problems relating to terrain, proximity of rail haulage, condition of nearby roads and highways—and, in rare instances, even waterways—are always carefully considered. In addition, the type and accessibility of a good freshwater supply, what sort of power and fuel is available, together with sufficient storage space for overburden, waste material, tailings, and settling ponds must be evaluated. The topographic characteristics of the deposit may influence or even strongly control some of these factors, as well as the lithologic type, attitude, and minable thickness of the deposit. Unfortunately for the modern producer, the proximity, density, and customs of the local population must be assessed and goodwill established, all of which is becoming ever more difficult to do.

If all the foregoing factors appear to be satisfactory, or at least surmountable, a pit, a face, or an adit is opened, dependent on the type of raw material and the amount of burden involved. Usually, large bulk samples are removed for trial processing. If this step is successful, actual mining is initiated, which consists of dredging or hydraulic jetting in soft rock deposits, and open cutting or underground mining in rock that is harder and more competent.

Good planning dictates that the mill or processing plant has been built, shaken down, and is ready to produce by the time the quarry or mine is up to production capacity.

Conventional practice in processing embraces coarse and fine crushing often followed by tertiary grinding. Following this, stage washing and even high-density attrition scrubbing is done to remove surficial impurities containing clay or iron. If necessary, the remaining impurities consisting of detrital minerals can be reduced through the use of froth flotation, low (or high) intensity magnetic separation, or high-tension electrostatic separation. Such beneficiation is then followed by drying in steamstatic, rotary kiln, or fluid-bed types of equipment. The dried and cooled material is then screened into such commercial sizes as may be required. Some of the dried material can be bypassed to compeb mills (pebble mills) where it is further pulverized into whatever grade of silica flour may be desirable.

Such processing requires sophisticated and expensive equipment backed by technical knowhow gained only by years of experience. For these reasons, only a relatively few companies are able to successfully compete in the silica producing business today. A few of the literature sources embodying the processing referred to are as follows: Gaudin and Fuerstenau, 1955; Humphreys et al., 1973; Taggart, 1945; and Tyler, 1945. A series of papers in the May 1973 issue of *Minerals Processing* is also of interest.

Economic Considerations

Place Value

Even though the amount of free silica or quartz is statistically placed at something over 10% of our so-called earth's crust, we must not deduce this to mean that such a stupendous tonnage is available for potential exploitation. In all probability something like 99.9% of this is tied up in the quartz phenocrysts of acid igneous rocks and locked away, possibly forever, from commerce and industry during mankind's tenure on this planet. But the small remaining fraction is still a huge amount and much of it, because of its relative insolubility and inertness, is constantly being reworked, refined, and segregated by natural processes into a multitude of diverse repositories. This is the principal reason silica products are relatively low-priced, ex-mine, and consumers are willing to pay relatively high rates to transport it from its source to its point of use. The delivered price of the product controls the purchasing transaction even though cost of transportation may nearly equal cost of product—or even exceed it in many situations.

The f.o.b. shipping price of flint grade glass sand varies widely, from approximately $6.2 to $15/t. It averages $9 to $10/t, considerabl less than the per-ton value of soda ash, feldspar, etc. used in a glass batch.

The very fact of this mineral's relative abundance makes its production highly competitive which the consumer is quick to take advantage of. Given sources A and B, both furnishing a product equal to or better than specification and both capable of meeting shipments on schedule, the source with the cheaper delivered price will become the prime supplier, and rightly so. However, assume that sources A and B have practically the same total cost of production but that source A is 100 miles closer to the customer's raw material receiving bins. This, at least theoretically and without considering equalization of freight rates or favored price adjustments, can give source A a definite delivered price advantage. In effect, it places a higher intrinsic value on A's silica reserves regardless of their otherwise computed book worth. Ladoo (1964) coined a phrase to describe this situation and referred to it as "place value." Since then, many writers have recognized the importance of this term and referred to it, particularly with respect to industrial minerals.

The term is particularly relevant when used for high-bulk, low unit-value commodities of which silica is a good example. Relatively small amounts of specialized silica products are bagged, whereas in the case of glass sand, a large tonnage item for example, most of it is shipped in covered hopper railroad cars (sometimes as unit trains), pneumatic tank trucks, or dual purpose vans in bulk form. With respect to unit value, the average ex-mine price of top grade flint sand is nearly a dollar a ton cheaper than that of any other high tonnage glassmaking raw material commonly utilized (Mills, 1983).

Unfortunately for newly aspiring entrepreneurs, the older, well-entrenched silica producers have long since explored for, located, and purchased or leased the best situated silica properties with respect to quality and market position, leaving little for the newcomer. As a consequence, barring a fortuitous find, new venture capital must, perforce, buy out an already established producer in order to obtain a competent supply of raw material which is reasonably well-situated with regard to markets, or stay out of the business.

Marketing

Prices, uniformity of product, customer services, research facilities, and supplier reliability are all ingredients that make up marketing in the silica business today. Prices are the controlling factor, basically, but other aspects play as important a role at times. For example, even if the deposit is practically next door to a large consumer and enjoys such a high *place value* advantage that the cost to the consumer is much below that of his other potential suppliers, the ensuing price advantage would be of little value if the customer could not get long-term adequate service. Interrupted shipping schedules, off-grade materials, and similar problems would soon drive this customer into the arms of a more distant but reliable competitor whose delivered price might be somewhat higher. This the enlightened purchasing agent would cheerfully pay, as his unit cost for bulk raw materials is a relatively small item in his final product cost analysis.

It is often stated that market demand combined with solid sales expertise is of possibly greater worth to a business than a sound deposit of raw material, especially in the field of industrial minerals which does not enjoy the almost automatic market that metals do. (This is obviously debatable as there would be no business at all without an adequate raw material source.) However, some considerations of this point are in order: a market generally exists for most elemental metals at the going price; which price, of course, is dependent on a chain of complex factors. This certainly does not follow for any industrial mineral or nonmetal unless it has been refined to its purest state, either by man, or by nature, as in the case of native sulfur. All or most industrial mineral products are refined mineral compounds, many of them oxides or carbonates. The physical properties and quite often even the chemical compositions of a given industrial mineral vary dramatically from deposit to deposit, and silica is no different in this vital respect. It is therefore very difficult and often practically impossible to introduce a new industrial mineral into a consumer field already satisfied with its present supply. Only unusual selling ability backed by comprehensive research effort can get the potential customer to accept a trial shipment on its own merits; and it had better be right.

For these reasons, good management, enlightened foresight, and unwavering integrity in production and sales are watchwords today for success in the silica business. Confidence built up in the customer, accruing from these tenets, is an invaluable asset to a supplier and for lack of a better term it might be spoken of as "sales credibility." With it, a strong bond of business relationship is built up that can last a generation or more. Without it, a vital and very necessary ingredient for sucess is irretrievably lost—and with it, usually the customer.

Government Controls and Restrictions

Restrictions on silica producers from the environmental and ecological viewpoints are proliferating yearly. A few of the smaller producers have had to shut down or at least curtail portions of their business for lack of capital to make the improvements or changes demanded. As with most industrial mineral producers who must include stripping, washing, and drying in their flowsheet, silica producers cannot now, or soon will not be able to, spoil their overburden where they please simply because they own or lease the property involved; cannot dump their mill tailings or acidulated waste water from their flotation circuits into the nearest flowing stream; cannot allow the excessive stack losses or fumes from their dryer operations to pollute the air. If pulverization of the sand into silica flour is done, very low levels of toxic dust must be maintained to prevent silicosis in those exposed in the working areas and this involves expensive dust collection systems. Even noise pollution from heavy equipment, both inside and outside the plant, which also includes the noise and vibration of heavy blasting and that of abnormal truck movements, is beginning to be noticed, particularly in or near populated areas. Literally millions of dollars annually are being, or soon will be, spent in the silica industry to abate these nuisances or risk being shut down if repeated warnings from state or federal authorities are not met (Banfield, 1973).

As industry management is forced more and more to comply with these new governmental edicts just to stay in business, they are, or should be, taking steps to prepare for these new regulations. A good start would be instilling an awareness of what good environmental practice means from the top plant management level to the workmen themselves. Further, it is believed by some that industrial mineral companies affected by this new governmental pressure should not be satisfied by simply lobbying through their trade associations against the new regulations. Instead, they should take an active part in drawing up the legislation to make these new environmental laws more practicable and functional, especially in the field of land reclamation (Appleyard, 1974). At the very least, in this matter, silica companies must start planning ahead on waste disposal and mining practice or they will have it done for them by governmental agencies with no concern for the financial burden that would be suddenly thrust upon the industry. A good paper reflecting on these problems as they relate to a sister industry, sand and gravel, is that by Davison (1974).

State and Growth of the Industries

The silica and silicon industries, so far, appear capable of keeping up with the natural growth and expansion of the ceramic, foundry, metallurgical, and allied industries they supply. Competition is keen and the silica producers are constantly going through a natural process of attrition with the smaller, less efficiently equipped companies falling by the wayside as their deposits become depleted or the specifications for their products become too stringent to meet from year to year.

A new silica operation requires a competent deposit with at least a 50-million-ton reserve to fully amortize the multimillion-dollar investment needed for a plant required to meet present competitive pressures. Also, as with everything else, cost of production in the silica supply business has risen drastically in recent years even though the operations are now highly mechanized compared to their predecessors of yesteryear.

It is difficult to determine the amount of high-purity manufactured silica sand and flour consumed in the United States for all purposes. These statistics are hidden in the US Bureau of Mines annual state reports to protect the production and sales of an individual producer by including them in the figures given for construction sand and gravel aggregates. However, in 1979, reportedly 13,870,000 st of glass sand valued at $111,870,000 was sold or used in the United States and a total of only 423,000 st valued at $1,179,000 was imported—possibly Canadian quartzite for ferroalloy production (Tepordei, 1978–79). US Bureau of Mines reports are believed to reflect about 75% of the sand produced and used by US industry.

Silicon is a relatively low-priced commodity whose cost is influenced by availability of cheap energy and convenient transportation. Production capacity is geared mainly to the requirements of the steel and aluminum industries. Demand is expected to increase at an annual rate of about 2.1%. Silicon's low cost, high availability, and inertness make it a prime material for research to develop substitutes to replace more expensive materials (Shekarchi, 1974).

Richardson et al. (1974) supports this thesis by pointing out that the growth of silicon metal and its ferroalloys should parallel the growths of steel castings as well as carbon and special steels with demand for the silicon metal becoming even greater for aluminum castings and silicones. He, therefore, predicts the need for a total of 525,000 st of silicon units for ferroalloy use and requirements of 160,000 st of silicon as a metal. This he translates into a demand of the annual production of nearly two million tons of metallurgical-grade quartz or quartzite with a typical specification of SiO_2 99.5%, $Al_2O_3 < 0.15\%$, $Fe_2O_3 < 0.1\%$, $CaO < 0.1\%$, $LOI < 0.2\%$. Size requirements must not deviate from a range of 4 x ½ in. because fines in the charge are undesirable. The stone also must not decrepitate upon heating. A *kop* or ridge of igneous quartz, intruded into Precambrian country rock and located in the northern Transvaal region of South Africa near Pietersburg, has recently been recognized as meeting these rigid requirements. The deposit reportedly will supply a substantial demand for this type of raw material for at least 20 years and exploitation has already begun.

Bibliography and References

Anon., 1970, "Few Sources of Glass-Grade Silica Sand, But Reliance on Continental Suppliers Reduced," *Industrial Minerals*, No. 35, Aug., pp. 9–25.

Anon., 1974, "Glass-Grade Silica Sand in Western Europe," *Industrial Minerals*, No. 77, Feb., pp. 9–24.

Appleyard, F.C., 1974, "Surface Mining of Industrial Minerals: A Positive Approach to Land Reclamation," SME Preprint 74H52, AIME Annual Meeting, Dallas, TX, Feb., 14 pp.

Banfield, A.F., 1972, "Ore Reserves, Feasibility Studies, and Valuations of Mineral Properties," SME Preprint 72AK87, AIME Annual Meeting, San Francisco, Feb., 30 pp.

Banfield, A.F., 1973, "Surface and Facility Requirements, Pollution and Environment," *SME Mining Engineering Handbook*, Vol. 1, Sec. 8, A.B. Cummins and I.A. Given, eds., AIME, New York, pp. 8–11–8–19.

Bates, R.L., 1960, "Sedimentary Rocks," *Geology of the Industrial Rocks and Minerals*, Chap. 5, Harper & Brothers, New York, pp. 98–117.

Bird, E.C.F. 1968, "Beaches, Spits and Barriers," and "Coastal Dunes," *Coasts*, Vol. 4, Chaps. 5 and 6, Australian National University Press, Canberra, pp. 81–146.

Bowen, C.H., 1953, "Petrology and Economic Geology of the Sharon Conglomerate in Geauga and Portage Counties, Ohio," Engineering Experiment Station, Ohio State University, Bulletin 153, Vol. 22, No. 3, 58 pp.

Boyd, B.W., 1981, "Silica," Preprint, *Canadian Minerals Yearbook 1979*, Minerals Resources Bureau, Department of Energy, Mines and Resources, Ottawa, 5 pp.

Broadhurst, S.D., 1954, "High-Silica Sand Resources of North Carolina," Information Circula 11, North Carolina Division of Mineral Resources.

Buie, B.F., and Robinson, G.C., 1958, "Silica for Glass Manufacture in South Carolina," Bulletin 23, State Development Board, Columbia, SC, pp. 28–29.

Carter, G.J., et al., 1962, "Industrial Silica Deposits of the Pacific Northwest," Information Circular 811E, US Bureau of Mines, 57 pp.

Carter, G.J., et al., 1964, "Benefication Studies of the Oregon Coastal Dune Sands for Use as Glass Sand," Report of Investigations 6484, US Bureau of Mines, 21 pp.

Chao, E.C.T., et al., 1962, "Stishovite, SiO_2, A Very High Pressure New Mineral from Meteor Crater, Arizona," *Journal of Geophysical Research*, Vol. 67, No. 1, pp. 419–421.

Clarke, G., 1980, "Cheshire Silica Sand—Vital to the U.K. Industry," *Industrial Minerals*, No. 151, Apr., pp. 19–33.

Clarke, G., 1980a, "Mexico's Industrial Minerals—Gathering Momentum," *Industrial Minerals*, No. 153, June, pp. 21–53.

Cole, L.H., 1923, "Silica in Canada, Its Occurrence, Exploitation and Uses," Memoir 555, Pt. 1, Eastern Canada, Mines Br., Dept. of Mines & Technical Surveys, Ottawa, 126 pp.

Cole, L.H., 1928, "Silica in Canada, Its Occurrence, Exploitation and Uses," Memoir 686, Pt. II, Western Canada, Mines Br., Dept. of Mines & Technical Surveys, Ottawa, 59 pp.

Collings, R.K., 1965, "Silica Sand—Canadian Sources of Interest to the Domestic Glass Industry," Technical Bulletin 69, Mines Br., Dept. of Mines and Technical Surveys, Ottawa; reprinted from *Journal of Canadian Ceramic Society*, Vol. 32, 1963, pp. 39–45.

Davison, E.K., 1974, "Land Use and Environmental Problems of the Sand and Gravel Industry," SME Preprint 74H27, AIME Annual Meeting, Dallas, Texas, Feb., 9 pp.

Dietz, E.D., 1968, "The Glassy State," *Science & Technology Journal*, Nov., pp. 10–21.

Dunn, J.R., 1974, "Appraisal of High Bulk, Low Unit Value Mineral Deposits (tentative)," *Suggested Practices and Guides*, American Institute of Professional Geologists, Denver, CO, 25 pp.

Dyer, W.S., 1930, "Sylvania Sandstone Deposit at Amherstburg," *Investigations of Non-Metallic Mineral Resources of Ontario 1928*, Vol. 38, Pt. 4, 38th Annual Report, Ontario Dept. of Mines, pp. 41–46.

Edwards, P.K., and Rose, D.C., 1974, "Geology, Mining, Milling and Marketing of Silica Sands for the Foundry Industry," SME Preprint 74H45, AIME Annual Meeting, Dallas, TX, Feb., 8 pp.

Frondel, C., 1962, "Silica Minerals," *Dana's The System of Mineralogy*, 7th ed., Vol. 3, John Wiley, New York, pp. 251–318.

Gaudin, A.M., and Fuerstenau, D.W., 1955, "Quartz Flotation with Anionic Collectors," *Trans. AIME*, Vol. 202, pp. 66–72.

Gay, T.E., Jr., 1957, "Specialty Sands," *Mineral Commodities of California*, Bulletin 176, California Div. of Mines & Geology, Sacramento, pp. 547–564.

Hale, D.R., and Blair, R.E., 1983, "Electronic and Optical Uses," *Industrial Minerals and Rocks,* 5th ed., S.J. Lefond, ed., AIME, New York, pp. 213–231.

Ham, W.E., 1945, "Geology and Glass Sand Resources, Central Arbuckle Mountains, Oklahoma," Bulletin 65, Oklahoma Geological Survey, Norman, OK, 103 pp.

Harris, A.T., Jr., and Miller, W.T., 1965, "Quartzite Mining and Processing Methods and Costs at the Honey Brook, Pa., Plant of Geo. F. Pettinos, Inc.," Information Circular 8248, US Bureau of Mines, 21 pp.

Harris, W.B., 1972, "High-Silica Resources of Clarke, Frederick, Page, Rockingham, Shenandoah, and Warren Counties, Virginia," Report 11, Virginia Div. of Mineral Resources, Charlottesville, VA, 42 pp.

Heinrich, E.W., 1974, "The Sands of Glass," SME Preprint 74H73, AIME Annual Meeting, Dallas, TX, Feb., 13 pp.

Hewitt, D.F., 1951, "Silica in Ontario," Industrial Mineral Circular No. 2, Ontario Dept. of Mines, 16 pp.

Hewitt, D.F., 1963, "Silica in Ontario," Industrial Mineral Report No. 9, Ontario Dept. of Mines, 36 pp.

Hudson, W.C., 1946, "Investigations of the Miami-West Palm Beach Belt of Silica Sand in Florida," Report of Investigation 3865, US Bureau of Mines, 5 pp.

Humphreys, K.K., et al., 1973, "Mineral Processing," *SME Mining Engineering Handbook,* Vol. 2, Sec. 27, A.B. Cummins and I.A. Given, eds., AIME, New York, pp. 27-2 – 27-94.

Jahns, R.H., 1983, "Gem Materials," *Industrial Minerals and Rocks,* 5th ed., S.J. Lefond, ed., AIME, New York, pp. 279–338.

Jaster, M.C., 1957, "Selected Annotated Bibliography of High-Grade Silica of the United States and Canada Through December 1954," Bulletin 1019–H, US Geological Survey, pp. 609–673.

Keith, M.L., 1949, "Sandstone as a Source of Silica Sands in Southeastern Ontario," Annual Report, Vol. 55, Pt. 5, Ontario Dept. of Mines, 36 pp.

Konnert, J.H., et al., 1973, "Crystalline Ordering in Silica and Germania Glasses," *Science,* Vol. 179, No. 4144, Jan., pp. 177–179.

Ladoo, R.B., 1964, "Marketing of Industrial Minerals," *Economics of the Mineral Industries,* 2nd ed., Chap. 7, Pt. 2, E.H. Robie, ed., AIME, New York, pp. 304–317.

Lake, J.L., and Perry, J.K., 1973, "Exploration for Mineral Deposits," *SME Mining Engineering Handbook,* Vol. 1, Sec. 5, A.B. Cummins and I.A. Given, eds., AIME, New York, pp. 5-70 – 5-74.

Lamar, J.E., 1927, "Geology and Economic Resources of the St. Peter Sandstone of Illinois," Bulletin 53, Illinois State Geological Survey, Urbana, 175 pp.

Lowry, W.D., 1954, "Silica Sand Resources of Western Virginia," Vol. 47, No. 12, Virginia Polytechnic Institute, Blacksburg, 63 pp.

McConville, L.B., 1975, "The Athabasca Tar Sands," *Mining Engineering,* Vol. 27, No. 1, Jan., pp. 19–38.

McQuiston, F.W., Jr., and Bechaud, L.J., Jr., 1968, "Metallurgical Sampling and Testing," *Surface Mining,* Chap. 3.2, E.P. Pfleider, ed., AIME, New York, pp. 103–121.

Merrill, C.W., 1973, "Exploration for Mineral Deposits," *SME Mining Engineering Handbook,* Vol. 1, Sec. 5, A.B. Cummins and I.A. Given, eds.. AIME, New York, pp. 5–74 – 5–77.

Mills, H.N., 1983, "Glass Raw Materials," *Industrial Minerals and Rocks,* 5th ed., S.J. Lefond, ed., AIME, New York, pp. 339–347.

Minnes, D.G., 1967, "Silica, Past, Present and Future for Canada," Industrial Minerals of Canada, Ltd., Toronto, Oct., 40 pp.

Minnes, D.G., Lefond, S.J., and Blair, R.E., 1983, "Nepheline Syenite," *Industrial Minerals and Rocks,* 5th ed., S.J. Lefond, ed., AIME, New York, pp. 931–960.

Murphy, T.D., 1954, "Silica Resources of Clark County, Nevada," Bulletin 55, Nevada Bureau of Mines, Reno, 28 pp.

Murphy, T.D., 1960, "Distribution of Silica Resources in Eastern United States," Bulletin 1072–L, US Geological Survey, pp. 657–665.

Murphy, T.D., 1960a, "Silica Sand and Pebble," *Industrial Minerals and Rocks,* 3rd ed., J.L. Gillson, ed., AIME, New York, pp. 763–772.

Murphy, T.D., 1975, "Silica and Silicon," *Industrial Minerals and Rocks,* 4th ed., S.J. Lefond, ed., AIME, New York. pp. 1043–1060.

Pajalick, W., 1972, "Sand and Gravel," *Minerals Yearbook 1972,* US Bureau of Mines, pp. 1003–1121.

Parker, R.L., 1967, "Composition of the Earth's Crust," *Data of Geochemistry,* 6th ed., Professional Paper No. 440–D, US Geological Survey, pp. D1–D195.

Pauling, L., 1950, "The Chemistry of Silicon," *College Chemistry,* 2nd ed., Chap. 31, W.H. Freeman, San Francisco, CA, pp. 620–635.

Payne, A.L., 1973, "Exploration Drilling," *SME Mining Engineering Handbook,* Vol. 1, Sec. 5, A.B. Cummins and I.A. Given, eds., AIME, New York, pp. 5–58 – 5–63.

Pearse, G.H.K., 1971, "Silica," *Canadian Minerals Yearbook 1971,* Minerals Resources Br., Dept. of Energy, Mines and Resources, Ottawa, 5 pp.

Pecora, W.T., 1960, "Coesite Crators and Space Geology," *Geotimes,* Vol. 5, No. 2, Feb., pp. 16–20.

Pettijohn, F.J., et al., 1973, "Production and Provenance of Sand," *Sand and Sandstone,* 1st ed., Chap. 8, Springer-Verlag, New York, pp. 294–326.

Richardson, L.S., et al., 1974, "Silicon Metal and Ferrosilicon Alloys," SME Preprint 74H11, AIME Annual Meeting, Dallas, TX, Feb., 15 pp.

Shekarchi, E., 1974, "Silicon," *Commodity Data Summaries,* "Appendix to Mining and Minerals Policy," US Bureau of Mines, pp. 150–151.

Shufflebarger, T.E., Jr., 1974, "The Evaluation of Silica Deposits," SME Preprint 74H76, AIME Annual Meeting, Dallas, TX, Feb., 17 pp.

Shufflebarger, T.E., Jr., 1977, "Economics of Glass Sand Prospects," *Industrial Minerals,* No. 120, Sep., pp. 57–63.

Sosman, R.B., 1965, "The Crystalline Phases of Silica," *The Phases of Silica,* 2nd ed., Chap. 4, Rutgers University Press, New Brunswick, NJ, pp. 34–72.

Spiece, E.L., 1980, "Manitoba Silica Sands," *Industrial Minerals,* No. 154, July, pp. 41–47.

Taggart, A.F., ed., 1945, "Flotation," *Handbook of Mineral Dressing,* 2nd ed., Vol. 1, Sec. 12, John Wiley, New York, pp. 12–01 – 12–130.

Teas, L.P., 1921, "Preliminary Report on the Sand

and Gravel Deposits of Georgia," Dept. of Mines, Mining & Geology, Atlanta, GA, pp. 373–375.

Teicher, H., 1974, "Specialty Silica Products," SME Preprint 74H17, AIME Annual Meeting, Dallas, TX, Feb., 29 pp.

Tepordei, V.V., 1978, 1979, "Sand and Gravel," Preprint, 1978–1979, US Bureau of Mines, 29 pp.

Tyler, P.M., 1945, "Industrial Minerals," *Handbook of Mineral Dressing,* 2nd ed., Vol. 1, Sec. 3, A.F. Taggart, ed., John Wiley, New York, pp. 3–82 – 3–87.

Vos, M.A., 1978, "Silica in Ontario—Supplement," Open File Report 5236, Ontario Geological Survey, 50 pp.

Waterman, G.C., and Hazen, S., 1968, "Development Drilling and Bulk Sampling," *Surface Mining,* Chap. 3.1, E.P. Pfleider, ed., AIME, New York, pp. 69–102.

Waters, A.B., 1980, "Stimulation of Hydrocarbon," *Industrial Minerals,* No. 157, pp. 57–65.

Wells, J.H., 1973, "Special Exploration Techniques—Placer Deposits," *SME Mining Engineering Handbook,* Vol. 1, Sec. 5, A.B. Cummins and I.A. Given, eds., AIME, New York, pp. 5–44 – 5–50.

Wilborg, H.E., and Henderson, G.V., 1983, "Foundry Sand," *Industrial Minerals and Rocks,* 5th ed., S.J. Lefond, ed., AIME, New York, pp. 271–278.

Wimpfen, S.P., and Severinghaus, N., Sr., 1968, "Applications and Economics—Industrial Minerals," *Surface Mining,* Chap. 13.2, E.P. Pfleider, ed., AIME, New York, pp. 849–873.

Also useful:

Minerals Processing, 1973: Walvoord, O.W., "Mill Design of the Future," pp. 4–6; Salat, S.J., "Planning Aspects of Minerals Processing Plants," pp. 7–10; Seiler, F.J., "Design of a Sand-Gravel Aggregates Plant," pp. 11–14; Cruz, L.D., et al., "Computer Techniques in the Design and Operation of Multi-Stage Crushing Plants," pp. 15–19; Anderson, R.P., and Tanner, J.A., "Design Considerations for Minerals Plants," pp. 20–25.

Sodium Carbonate Deposits

L. E. MANNION *

Sodium carbonate (soda ash) is one of two principal commercial alkalis. Its principal competitor is sodium hydroxide. The use of sodium carbonate is recorded in ancient Egypt, where naturally occurring brines and solid salts provided impure soda for early glassmaking. Until the 19th century, soda ash (as well as potash) was recovered mainly by leaching wood or other plant ashes. In 18th-century Europe, for example, leaching seaweed ash with hot water produced a brown laundry lye. One of the better grades of this material was a Spanish product, barilla, which analyzed 24 to 30% Na_2CO_3 (Hou, 1942).

The modern chemical industry was born in 1691 with the LeBlanc process for making

* Chief Geologist, Stauffer Chemical Co., Richmond, CA.

This chapter was reviewed by Dr. H.P. Eugster, Dept. of Earth and Planetary Sciences, Johns Hopkins University, Baltimore, MD.

sodium carbonate from salt, sulfuric acid, and lime. English industry used this process extensively in the 17th and 18th centuries. The next major advance was in 1863, when Ernst Solvay devised the ammonia-soda, or Solvay process. The first of many Solvay plants was built in 1874. These supplanted the LeBlanc method and dominated worldwide soda ash production until 1974, when mined sodium carbonate became predominant.

Although considerably less important until recently, natural sodium carbonate deposits historically have supported small soda ash operations throughout the world. Shortages during World War II stimulated production of "natural" soda ash from such deposits, particularly at Searles Lake, CA and Lake Magadi, Kenya. More spectacularly, increased production from the vast trona deposits in Wyoming has virtually supplanted the Solvay process in the US. Principal producers of natural soda ash as well as the character of the source deposits are listed in Table 1.

TABLE 1—Principal Producers of Soda Ash from Natural Sodium Carbonate Sources

Company	Location	Production Started and 1982 Capacity t/a	Type of Deposit	Remarks
Allied Chemical Corp.	Green River, WY	1969 2,000,000	Horizontal 0.6-3 m trona bed at 460 m depth	Underground room-and-pillar mine; refinery; same bed as FMC
FMC Corp.	Green River, WY	1953 2,360,000	Horizontal 2.5-3 m trona bed at 460 m depth	Underground room-and-pillar mine; refinery
Kerr-McGee Chemical Corp.	Searles Lake, CA	1916 1,270,000	Subsurface complex brine in permeable, varied salt layers which include trona; depth 0 to 75 m	Brine pumped from wells; sodium carbonate recovered plus other salts
The Magadi Soda Co. Ltd. (ICI)	Lake Magadi, Kenya	1917 250,000	Surface layers of trona in shallow alkali lake	Trona dredged, crushed, dried, and calcined
Sosa Texcoco, S.A.	Lake Texcoco, near Mexico City, Mexico	1947 230,000	Subsurface residual brine from former alkaline lake	Brine pumped to solar ponds for concentration. Half production converted to caustic soda
Stauffer Chemical Co.	Green River, WY	1962 1,450,000	Two horizontal beds about 3 m thick at 260 m depth	Underground room-and-pillar mine; refinery
Tenneco Inc.	Green River, WY	1982 900,000	Horizontal 3 m trona bed at 460 m depth	Underground room-and-pillar mine; same bed as FMC
Texasgulf Inc.	Green River, WY	1976 900,000	Two horizontal beds about 3 m thick at 400 m depth	Underground room-and-pillar mine; refinery

Use and Specifications

Sodium carbonate (Na_2CO_3) is commonly produced as a white, crystalline hygroscopic powder which forms a strongly alkaline aqueous solution. From the Solvay plants two forms are commonly sold: a fine, open crystalline material, called light ash, and a more solidly crystalline dense ash. Their respective bulk densities are 560 and 960 to 1060 kg/m³. The Wyoming trona plants produce a dense ash, 960 kg/m³, which dominates the US market. Some Wyoming producers make a somewhat lighter ash, weighing 720 to 800 kg/m³.

Most commercial soda ash must meet high standards of purity and uniformity. The close quality correspondence between Solvay process and Wyoming natural soda ash is shown in Table 2. The major difference between them is the higher sodium chloride content of Solvay ash. Minor differences important to some consumers are the slightly higher iron and silica content of Wyoming soda ash.

World use of sodium carbonate now exceeds 29 Mt/a, of which the US produces about 7.5 Mt. Fig. 1 shows percent consumption by product of soda ash in Europe, Japan, and the United States. The market for soda ash is dominated by the glass industry, which uses about half the supply. Inorganic chemicals, including phosphates and silicates, consume about 30%. Other principal users are manufacturers of soaps and detergents, petroleum, caustic soda, organic chemicals, and paper, and in ferrous and nonferrous metallurgy.

The price of soda ash stayed relatively stable during the 1960s at about $30/t. By 1975 it reached $38/t f.o.b. Green River, and since then the price has escalated to a current (1983) value of $84/t.

Geology

Mineralogy

Table 3 lists the more common sodium carbonate-bearing minerals. Anhydrous sodium carbonate is almost never found in nature. Only natron, thermonatrite, and trona—minerals without admixture of other saline elements—have been used directly as sources of sodium carbonate.

Mode of Occurrence

Sodium carbonate commonly occurs as a precipitate in nonmarine alkaline lakes and marshes, but such deposits rarely are economic.

TABLE 2—Typical Analyses of United States Soda Ash

Constituent	Typical Analysis, %	
	Wyoming	Solvay
Na_2CO_3	99.8	99.5
NaCl	0.04	0.25
Na_2SO_4	0.04	0.015
Fe_2O_3	0.004	0.002
SiO_2	0.02	0.003
CaO	0.015	0.016
Insol	0.010	0.010

Nonmarine alkaline bodies of water characteristically are shallow, and many undergo vast seasonal changes in area and concentration. Most such deposits, because of their susceptibility to destruction by erosion, are young. Pre-Tertiary deposits are virtually unrecorded.

Some of the more common forms of occurrence include: (1) natron crystals in cool, wet environments on the bottom of ponds or at shallow depths in salt marshes, as at Lake Goodenough, B.C. (Cummings, 1949) and Owens Lake, CA (Smith and Friedman, 1975); (2) powdery surface efflorescences of thermonatrite around alkaline lakes or marshes, as in the alkaline soils of the lower Danube River valley and at Lake Nyasa, Tanzania (Orr and Grantham, 1931); (3) relatively hard but porous deposits of trona, either around the shores or at the bottom of shallow alkaline lakes or playas, as at Lake Magadi, Kenya (Baker, 1958; Eugster, 1970), Owens Lake, CA (Dub, 1947), and Lake Chad basin, Africa (Eugster and Maglione, 1979); (4) older beds of buried solid trona, nahcolite, or other sodium carbonate-bearing minerals, as the Green River formation in Wyoming (Bradley and Eugster, 1969; Culberson, 1971; Deardorff and Mannion, 1971) and in Colorado (Smith and Milton, 1966; Anon., 1972) and at Rail-

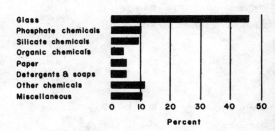

FIG. 1—*Consumption of soda ash in Europe, Japan, and the United States by percentage.*

TABLE 3—Sodium Carbonate Bearing Minerals

Mineral	Composition	% Na_2CO_3 *
Natron (sal soda)	$Na_2CO_3 \cdot 10H_2O$	37.1
Thermonatrite (monohydrate)	$Na_2CO_3 \cdot H_2O$	85.5
Nahcolite	$NaHCO_3$	63.1
Trona (sesquicarbonate)	$Na_2CO_3 \cdot NaHCO_3 \cdot 2H_2O$	70.4
Gaylussite	$Na_2CO_3 \cdot CaCO_3 \cdot 5H_2O$	35.8
Pirssonite	$Na_2CO_3 \cdot CaCO_3 \cdot 2H_2O$	43.8
Shortite	$Na_2CO_3 \cdot 2CaCO_3$	34.6
Burkeite	$Na_2CO_3 \cdot 2Na_2SO_4$	27.2
Hanksite	$2Na_2CO_3 \cdot 9Na_2SO_4 \cdot KCl$	13.5
Northupite	$Na_2CO_3 \cdot NaCl \cdot MgCO_3$	42.6
Dawsonite	$NaAl(CO_3)(OH)_2$	35.8

*Including bicarbonate converted to carbonate.

road Valley, NV (Free, 1913); and (5) in solution as a constituent of brine, either surface or subsurface, as at Searles Lake, CA (Smith, 1979) and Makgadikgadi, Botswana (Massey, 1973; Lefond, 1981). In all these occurrences the sodium carbonate may be mixed with other salts, notably sulfates and chlorides.

Origin

The origin of sodium carbonate in natural deposits has been attributed to various processes, including volcanic spring activity, reactions between sodium carbonate waters and sodium sulfate, and ion exchange in sodium-bearing soils. Most ground waters in volcanic, igneous, or metamorphic terrains yield alkaline solutions on evaporation (Hardie and Eugster, 1970). The relative absence of chloride and sulfate in these rocks permits solutions to become predominantly sodium-bearing and carbon dioxide-bearing. Chemical fractionation of inflowing waters and brines within closed basins can result in different minerals accumulating in separate areas. The fractionation mechanisms may be mineral precipitation, selective dissolution of efflorescent crusts, degassing of brines, and/or redox reactions (Eugster and Jones, 1979).

The sodium may be derived from leaching of sodic feldspars or volcanic ash deposits, and the carbon dioxide from biogenic processes and the atmosphere. Ground water percolating through siliceous soils, e.g., those developed on granite or windblown sands, can become highly alkaline and enriched in sodium carbonate (Garrels and Mackenzie, 1967). Very high CO_2 contents—up to 10% of soil gas—are known to occur in soils as a result of biological activity. This can produce CO_2 in soil water in excess of 200 mg/L (Jakucs,

1977). The Pretoria pan, South Africa, and the sandhill regions of Nebraska and the Sind are examples of sodium carbonate in soil waters (Dutoit, 1948; Barbour, 1916; Cotter, 1923). In lakes, deposition of monomineralic beds of trona may be aided by the continual generation of CO_2 by algae and bacteria in the lake water (Eugster, 1971). Perelman (1967) states that semiarid rather than arid climates are most favorable for producing alkaline waters, as in severely arid regions water evaporation is too rapid to stabilize soda solutions.

Drainage from regions of sedimentary rocks commonly contains too much chloride, sulfate, and calcium to produce either brine or solid salts of sodium carbonate. Even though sodium carbonate waters arise from igneous and volcanic rock weathering, these same waters may interact with other waters or with other rock and soil types in the area of accumulation so that mixed chloride and sulfate salts are the end product (Risacher, 1978).

Occurrences of Sodium Carbonate

Numerous occurrences of sodium carbonate are known in the world. Some are described briefly in Table 4, where they are numbered to correspond to numbered locations in Fig. 2. Data pertaining to Africa, Australia, Europe, and North and South America are reasonably adequate. Information on Asian deposits is less so, and doubtless many Chinese and Siberian occurrences are not recorded here. Western North America has an abundance of sodium carbonate deposits and many are well known. Deposits may contain solid salts, solutions, or both. Many have produced for local and small markets, but only a few have been long-term suppliers of commercial grade soda ash.

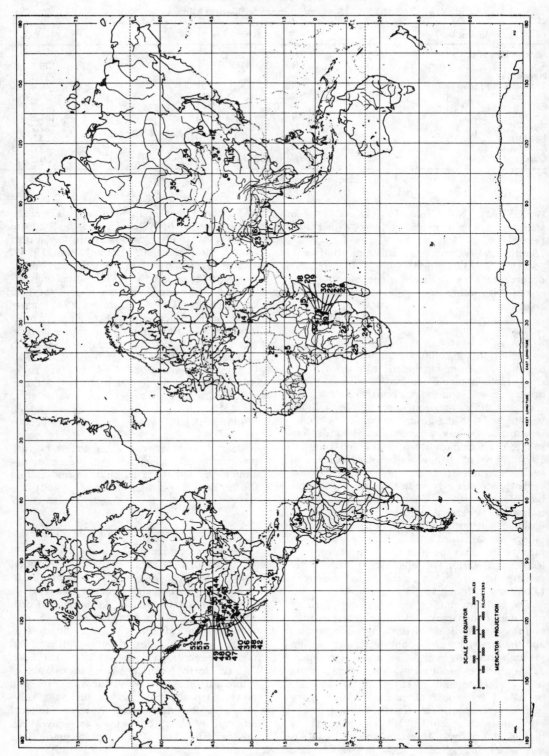

FIG. 2—*Location of major natural sodium carbonate deposits. Numbers are keyed to Table 4.*

TABLE 4—Occurrences of Sodium Carbonate in Various Parts of the World

Name and Location; No. Refers to Location on Fig. 2	Physical Character	Geologic Character	Chemical Composition*	Remarks and References
BOLIVIA (1) Collpa Laguna, southwest corner of Bolivia (Lipez) just east of Salar de Chalvira	Shallow lake 800 m in diameter	Salt crust and subsurface brine in mud	Brine Na_2CO_3 6.0% NaCl 2.6 Organic 0.5	Ahlfeld and Schneider-Scherbena, 1964; Risacher, Echenique, and Ballivian, 1978
(1) Cochi Laguna, southwest Bolivia in northern Lipez, 50 km south of Chiguana	Shallow lake 1000 m across, located south of the volcano Tapoquilaha	Brine in mud, also 6-10 cm crust with trona and thermonatrite	Solid salts dried at 80° Na_2CO_3 47.3% HaHCO₃ 11.0 NaCl 7.1 Na_2SO_4 11.0 Insol 1.0	Soda ash produced from brine in past, not economic; Ahlfeld and Schneider-Scherbena, 1964; Risacher, Echenique, and Ballivian, 1978
BOTSWANA (2) Sua Pan, Makgadikgadi basin in northeast Botswana	Low area in a vast drainage area of flat terrain; Sua Pan is eastern of two	Brine in sand aquifer overlain by sand and clay layers totaling 30 m thick; aquifer underlies 900 km²	Avg. composition of brine Na_2CO_3 26.0 g/L NaCl 140.0 Na_2SO_4 14.5	Investigation and test work on possible commercial use since 1963; Pelletier, 1964; Lefond, 1981
BRAZIL (3) Upper Sao Francisco drainage, northeast of Brasilia	Numerous salt pans up to 175,000 m² area in plateau region 900-1100 m in elevation	Salt crusts and shallow brine in area of alkaline igneous rocks	Range of 5 crust analyses Na_2CO_3 23-41% NaCl 1.5-10 Na_2SO_4 1-7 $MgSO_4$ 0.4-2.2 H_2O 40-50	Freise, 1932
CANADA (4) Eighty-Three Mile Lake, Green Timber Plateau, south-central B.C., north of Clinton	Area 0.1 km²; max depth brine 0.6 m; in level terrain.	Alkaline lake with a mud bottom on glacial drift and basalt. Crystals and brine present.	Brine Na_2CO_3 94.0 g/L NaCl 1.3 Na_2SO_4 Trace	Many other small lakes and ponds in region also contain high carbonate content; Cummings, 1949; Livingston, 1963
(4) Goodenough Lake, Green Timber Plateau, south-central B.C., north of Clinton	Area 0.05 km² dries up	Crust of salines 2 cm thick on natron containing mud 3 m thick.	Brine Na_2CO_3 208 g/L NaCl 11.0 Na_2SO_4 71.0 KCl 8.7	Solid Crust Na_2CO_3 97.0% $NaHCO_3$ 0.7 NaCl 0.8 Na_2SO_4 00.5 $MgCO_3$ 0.35 Cummings, 1949
(4) Last Chance Lake, Green Timber Plateau south-central B.C., north of Clinton	Area 0.1 km²; mostly dry	Lake contains permanent crystal layers in numerous bowl-shaped depressions separated by mud	Brine Na_2CO_3 180.0 g/L NaCl 12.0 Na_2SO_4 37.0 KCl 3.3	Cummings, 1949
CHAD (5) Lake Chad, near Bo, Chad	Lake highly variable in area 10,000-26,000 km²; depth is 3-8 m; vast drainage area	Lake held in by sand dunes northeast shores; layers of natron with halite found 1.5 m below surface	Solids as mined are impure sodium carbonate mixed with sodium chloride	Long continued export of 5-7 kt/a to Nigeria; also Lake Orari 60 km northeast of Bedao, and Lake Tellie near Ounianga Kebir, northern Chad; Eugster and Maglione, 1979; Maglione, 1972

TABLE 4—Continued

Name and Location; No. Refers to Location on Fig. 2	Physical Character	Geologic Character	Chemical Composition*		Remarks and References
CHINA Inner Mongolia (6) Alashan and Ehtingol areas	Alkali lakes abundant				Produced "soda ash"; Torgasheff, 1929
(7) Chalar Region, Dolon Nor, 250 km north of Peking	Alkali lakes abundant				Produced "soda ash"; Torgasheff, 1929
(8) Hailar Area (Hailaerh), 150 km east of Manchouli	Two groups of lakes north and south of Hailar; aggregate 500 km²	Salt crust and brine in steppe	Brine Na_2CO_3 NaCl Na_2SO_4 Salt crust Na_2CO_3 Na_2SO_4 H_2O	115 g/L 213 71 29% 12 58	Include Chassun-Nor and Bain-Tsugan-Nor; production from south group; Hou, 1942; Torgasheff, 1929
Inner Mongolia, LioO-Ning (9) Polishan (Liao-Ning)	One of large group alkali lakes		Salt crust Na_2CO_3 NaCl Na_2SO_4	12.0% 1.5 1.0	Also Tafus Lake; Torgasheff, 1929
Heilungkiang Province (10) Tsitsihar (Ch'ich'haerh)	Soda lakes in steppe in valley of Nonni River				Torgasheff, 1929; Hou, 1942
Kiangsi Province (11) Ning-Kian-Hsien	Soda lakes in steppe		Natural solid salts Na_2CO_3 $NaHCO_3$	81% 7	Other soda lakes in region; Hou, 1942
Kirin Province (12) Taboos Nor, 320 km north of Shenyang, near Fuyu	Elliptical lake, 8 km across in flat plain surrounded by sand dunes	Generally dry lake with 1 cm crust of thermo-natrite on 30 cm mud layer; mud contains natron 0-30%, which lies on gaylussite-bearing muds up to 2 m depth.	Solids Na_2CO_3 H_2O	35% 30	Possibly a million tons of sodium salts; numerous other lakes including Fu-U-Hsien; Hou, 1942; Niinomy, 1930
Shansi Province (13) U-Tsu-Hsien	Dry lake		Natural solid salts Na_2CO_3 $NaHCO_3$ NaCl Na_2SO_4 H_2O	54.0% 16.0 3.5 17.0 12.0	Hou, 1942
Shensi Province (13) Shen-Mu-Hsien	Soda lakes in steppe		Natural solid salts Na_2CO_3 $NaHCO_3$ NaCl Na_2SO_4 H_2O	78.3% 0.5 5.0 0.9 15.0	Other soda lakes in region; Ordos area in adjacent Inner Mongolia incl. Cha-Han-Nor, Nalin-Nor, and Pa-Yen-Nor; Hou, 1942
EGYPT (14) Wadi El-Natron, 97 km north-west of Cairo	Chain of 10 or so small, partly ephemeral lakes; central ones carry natron, others sodium sulfate	Brine of varying composition; bottom and bordering solid salts	Brine Na_2CO_3 Na_2SO_4 NaCl Product impure carbonate-bicarbonate with mud, NaCl, and Na_2SO_4	52.3 g/L 67.1 221.2	Probably oldest known soda sources; probably fed by seepage from Nile River; other occurrences at El Barnougi in Baheira Province, 50 km north of Wadi El-Natron; and in small lakes at El-Mahamid, near Edfo; Lucas, 1912; Said, 1962

TABLE 4—Continued

Name and Location; No. Refers to Location on Fig. 2	Physical Character	Geologic Character	Chemical Composition*	Remarks and References
ETHIOPIA (15) Lake Magado and El Soda, near Mega, 500 km south of Addis Ababa	Salt pans in volcanic craters.	Brine plus solid salts.	Brine a mixture of sodium chloride and sodium carbonate.	Exploited on local scale. Murdock, 1949
INDIA (16) Sambhar Lake in northwest Rajasthan (Rajputana), 310 km southwest of New Delhi	Variable area, max 230 km² and 4 m deep	Brine with salt layers and saline muds to 85 m depth	Brines predominantly NaCl with lesser Na_2SO_4 and Na_2CO_3.	A significant salt producer, remaining bittern contains Na_2CO_3 3.8% $NaHCO_3$ 1.0 Na_2SO_4 7.7 Roy, 1959; Sahni, 1951
(17) Lonar Lake, Buldana District of Berar, Lat. 20°N, Long. 76½°E	Circular shallow lake 150 m deep, 1 km², variable amounts of water	Impact crater in basalt plateau; crusts of trona around edge, mixed trona and halite on bottom; spring-fed.	Brine Na_2CO_3 25.0 g/L NaCl 55.0 Na_3SO_4 2.0 K 0.2	Christie, 1912; Fredriksson, et al., 1973
KENYA (18) Lake Bogoria, southeastern Kenya	Alkaline lake in Rift Valley		Brine $NaHCO_3$ 48.0 g/L NaCl 5.8 Na_2SO_4 0.3	Livingston, 1963
(19) Lake Magadi, southeastern Kenya	Trona salt flat 65 km², in a low part of Rift Valley	Trona surface with subsurface trona layers and brine, in alkalic volcanic terrane	Brine, variable Na_2CO_3 100 g/L $NaHCO_3$ 20 NaCl 60 Na_2SO_4 1-2 NaF 0.01-0.2	Trona dredged as raw material for soda ash production since 1914; Baker, 1958; Eugster, 1970, 1980
(20) Lake Nakuru, southeastern Kenya, northwest of Nairobi	Shallow brine lake in Rift Valley, modest relief	Brine with shore crusts of trona until lake level rose	Brine $NaHCO_3$ 17.0 g/L NaCl 2.0 Na_2SO_4 0.4	Abundant organisms in water; Livingston, 1963
MEXICO (21) Lake Texcoco, west of Mexico City	Low point in Valley of Mexico, subsurface brines	Residual waters from drying up of former Lake Texcoco; now subsurface brines dilute	Water Na_2CO_3 8.0 g/L NaCl 8.6 Na_2SO_4 0.1 $Na_2B_4O_7$ 0.1 KCl 0.8	Solar evaporation in spiral-shaped ponds; much of soda ash production converted to caustic soda; Durand-Chastel, 1968; Gonzales-Reyna, 1956
NIGER (22) Bilma oasis in central Sahara, 350 m north of Lake Chad	Shallow saline lakes	Trona precipitated from salt lakes	Dominant sodium chloride	Significant trade in salt
PAKISTAN (23) In southern Sind, 100-110 km northeast of Hyderabad	Hundreds of shallow lakes mostly a kilometer or less in max dimension in sand dunes, level terrain	Brine lakes with clay bottom, fed by ground water; trona crusts deposited with scarce natron.	Solids Na_2CO_3 24.0% $NaHCO_3$ 15.0 NaCl 3.0 Na_2SO_4 7.5	Both saline and carbonate lakes present; much organic matter in carbonate lakes; past production at several thousand t/a; Cotter, 1923
SOUTH AFRICA (24) Pretoria salt pan, 40 km north of Pretoria	Crater 1 km diam, 130 m deep in granitic terrane, salt pan in bottom	Salts including trona and halite, underlain by laminated clays containing brine; volcanic rocks occur in crater	Brine Na_2CO_3 37.4 g/L NaCl 56.9 SO_4 0.30 SiO_2 0.07 CaO 0.02 MgO Trace	Worked in past; proportion of Na_2CO_3 to NaCl is greater in outer parts of pan; brine likely represents highly concentrated normal ground water; Bond, 1946; Dutoit, 1948

TABLE 4—Continued

Name and Location; No. Refers to Location on Fig. 2	Physical Character	Geologic Character	Chemical Composition*	Remarks and References
SOUTH-WEST AFRICA (25) Otjiwalunda Pan just west of Etosha Pan in northern South-West Africa	Alkali pan in nearly flat terrain	Trona and halite precip-itated from brines		Possible production of soda investigated in 1964; Pelletier, 1964
TANZANIA (26) Bahi Swamp, central Tanzania	Salt pan underlain by 110 m of clays and sandy clays	Alkaline waters contained in sediments. Drill holes had some with high concen-trations sodium carbonate	Variable brine composition Na_2CO_3 20.0 g/L $NaHCO_3$ 17.5 Na_2SO_4 9.0 $NaCl$ 28.0 F_2 0.15	Wells can be pumped at rates in excess of 2500 L/min Fawley, 1958
(27) Lake Balangida (Balangda), north-central Tan-zania, 80 km south of Lake Eyasi	Salt pan, 30 km², at foot of escarpment in Rift Zone	Spring-fed lake; crust forms only 10 cm thick on mud; volcanic terrane	Specimen of crust Na_2CO_3 22.3% $NaHCO_3$ 13.8 $NaCl$ 28.2 Na_2CO_4 21.1 Insol. 10.	Dries up in summer; only 140 kt sodium car-bonate and bicarbonate in crust; Orr and Grantham, 1931
(28) Lake Eyasi (Nyarasa), north-central Tanzania	Saline, sandy pan 1000 km², dry, at foot of escarpment in Rift Zone	Principal salts occur as thin crusts and in brine pools along Sibiti River bed in southwest part of pan	Variable composition, both brine and crust; a supersaturated brine from pool shows: TDS 432.0 g/L Na_2CO_3 3.6% $NaHCO_3$ 1.5 $NaCl$ 51.2 Na_2SO_4 9.1	Sample of alkali salt below a top crust of NaCl Na_2CO_3 32.5% $NaHCO_3$ 25.7 $NaCl$ 15.8 Na_2SO_4 10.5 Moisture 11.1 Insol. 1.3 Organic matter 3.1 Orr and Grantham, 1931
(29) Lake Lagarja, Olduvai Valley, north-central Tanzania	Rift Valley Lake	Mostly dry salt pan in volcanic terrane	Crust Na_2CO_3 44.0% $NaHCO_3$ 17.0 $NaCl$ 13.9 Na_2SO_4 9.8	Guest, 1956
(30) Lake Natron, northeast Tanzania on Kenya border	570 km², large shallow lake in Rift Valley; northwest part contains salts	At times as much as 200 km² are underlain by a meter of salts	Salt crusts contain Na_2CO_3 53-60% $NaCl$ 20-30 Na_2SO_4 1.5-2.0	Estimated 65 Mt of total salts in mud layers; Orr and Grantham, 1931
TURKEY (31) Lake Van, southeast Turkey	3730 km², avg. depth 55 m, appears on 1700 m high plateau	Dilute alkaline water; may be density stratified	Water Na_2CO_3 8.6 g/L $NaCl$ 9.4 Na_2SO_4 3.3 K_2SO_4 0.5	Also some lakes in the Araxes plain are carbonate; Lake Urmi is a sodium chloride lake; Karajian, 1920; Tulus, 1944
UGANDA (32) Lake Katwe, southwest Uganda	In a volcanic crater, near Lake Edward, salt lake 0.6 km in diam		Salt from evaporation of brine Na_2CO_3 2.46% Na_2SO_4 5.3 $NaCl$ 81.7 K_2SO_4 8.4 Fe_2O_3 0.15	Investigation made toward commercial extraction from brine similar to Searles Lake, CA; Barnes, 1961

TABLE 4—Continued

Name and Location; No. Refers to Location on Fig. 2	Physical Character	Geologic Character	Chemical Composition*	Remarks and References
USSR **Altay Region** (33) M. Khailor Lakes	Two lakes, in semiarid steppe.	Trona and brine	Brine Na_2CO_3 5-11% $NaHCO_3$ 1-2 $NaCl$ 3-7 Na_2SO_4 1-3	Current production from trona at Mikhaylovskiy; Bukhshtein and Zakina, 1949
(33) Petukhov Lakes (Siberia), 210 km from Slavgorod	One large, several small, interconnected lakes.	Brine lake with alkali crusts in steppe region; when temperature drops below 0°C, natron precipitates in 8-15 cm layers	Solid salts Na_2CO_3 36.4% $NaCl$ 0.39 Na_2SO_4 Trace H_2O 62.16	Estimate Na_2CO_3 at 2.4 Mt in lake water, 4.5 Mt precipitated in muds; natrum mined and dehydrated to 99% Na_2CO_3; Niinomy, 1930
Chita Region (34) Doronin Lake, 400 km east of Lake Baikal	Alkaline lakes in semiarid steppe		High in sulfate as well as carbonate	Produced "soda ash"; crystalline salts amount to 350 to 450 kt; Torgasheff, 1929
(35) Tura salt lakes in Krasnoyarsk Region, Lat. 56°N, Long. 90°E	Various lakes in steppe	Brines and solid sulfate salts	Brines containing sulfate and some with high carbonate and bicarbonate content	These are mostly sulfate lakes; some have large quantities of thenardite and mirabilite
UNITED STATES **California** (36) Black Lake, north of Benton, Mono County	Small lake 1.6 km long, up to 150 m wide and up to 20 m deep	Carbonate-sulfate lake colored with organic matter	Dilute lake water Na_2CO_3 12.0 g/L $NaCl$ 2.0 Na_2SO_4 3.4 KCl 0.7	Clarke, 1924
(37) Borax Lake, southeast of Clear Lake, Lake County	0.8 to 1.2 km² in small basin adjacent to Clear Lake	Carbonate water with notable borate content; recent volcanic rocks adjacent	Variable composition Na_2CO_3 18.5 g/L $NaCl$ 1.7 KCl 1.7 $Na_2B_4O_7$ 0.5 Na_2SO_4 0.01 Misc. and Organic 0.5	1.4 Mt of Na_2CO_3; lake supports a notable amount of life; Averill, 1947
(38) Deep Springs Lake, northern Inyo County	Mountain valley, 21 ×7 km, contains saline playa 2.6 km² in area	Shallow brine pond underlain and bordered by saline crust with thenardite, burkeite, trona and nahcolite	Solid crust contains mainly sodium carbonate, sulfate, and chloride	Jones, 1965
(39) Middle Alkali Lake, western Modoc County	One of three shallow lakes in downfaulted valley	Dilute brine in region dominated by Cenozoic volcanic rocks	TDS 9.3 g/L Na_2CO_3 3.5 $NaCl$ 5.4 Na_2SO_4 0.9	Livingston, 1963
(40) Mono Lake, Mono County	Lake area variable 190-220 km², mean depth 18 m	Rather complex saline water in volcanic terrane	Dilute lake water Na_2CO_3 46.0 g/L $NaCl$ 23.0 Na_2SO_4 10.0 $Na_2B_4O_7$ 1.0 KCl 2.1	84 Mt salts; Livingston, 1963
(41) Owens Lake, west-central Inyo County	Up to 260 km², very shallow	Brine on surface and near surface, also trona, burkeite, and halite as surface salts and in subsurface saline muds up to 3 m thick	Brine composition variable Na_2CO_3 8.5% $NaCl$ 17.0 Na_2SO_4 4.5 KCl 0.7 $Na_2B_4O_7$ 0.5	Present drying up of lake resulted from 1917 diversion of Owens River water; intermittent soda ash producer; contains several tens of millions of tons of Na_2CO_3; last plant shut 1968; Dub, 1947

TABLE 4—Continued

Name and Location; No. Refers to Location on Fig. 2	Physical Character	Geologic Character	Chemical Composition*	Remarks and References
(42) Searles Lake, northwest San Bernardino County	83 km² saline playa in mountain valley.	Complex salt body with interstitial brine, underlies 83 km² of surface	Concentrated high-quality brine Na_2CO_3 4-5% NaCl 16 Na_2SO_4 7 KCl 3-5 $Na_2B_4O_7$ 1.5 Spec. Grav. 1.3	Soda ash together with sodium sulfate, borate potash, lithium, and bromine extracted from brines; contains several hundred million tons of sodium carbonate; Smith, 1966, 1979
Colorado (43) Piceance Basin, northwest Colorado	Saline part of Green River formation in center part of basin.	Beds of nahcolite and disseminated nahcolite and dawsonite in oil shale	Several thousand feet of thickness contain about 10% dawsonite and nahcolite	Possible future extraction as byproduct from shale oil production; Smith and Milton, 1966; Anon., 1972
Nebraska (44) Jess Lake and other alkaline lakes in northwest Nebraska, chiefly in Cherry and Sheridan Counties	Many lakes among sand hills, more than 1 km², rolling terrain	Natural drainage through sandy soils accumulates in hollow with impervious mud bottom	Jess Lake (near Antioch) TDS 190.0 g/L K_2SO_4 26.5 K_2CO_3 21.5 Na_2CO_3 36.2 $NaHCO_3$ 9.2 NaCl 5.8 SiO_2 0.2	Potash produced briefly; Barbour, 1916
Nevada (45) Soda Lakes (Ragtown Lakes)	One lake about 1.2 km²; smaller lake about 0.8 km²	Lakes in cinder cone of sandy pyroclastic debris surrounded by sandy lake beds; trona precipitated.	Dissolved solids include: Na_2CO_3 20% NaCl 80 Na_2SO_4 20	Had some production between 1893 and 1969; est. 0.5 Mt Na_2CO_3 present Chartard, 1890; Morrison, 1964
(46) Railroad Valley, northeast Nye County	Buried salts in lake beds at 200-300 m below playa lake in broad valley	Beds of both solid gaylussite and of gaylussite crystals in clay of Plio-Pleistocene lake; brine and solids, trona gaylussite, and natron	Gaylussite $Na_2CO_3 \cdot CaCO_3 \cdot 5H_2O$	Large reserves of a material with no known commercial utilization; Free, 1913
Oregon (47) Lake Abert, Lake County, southeast Oregon	Area 130-150 km²; 1.5-1.8 m deep; dries up	Alkaline semipermanent lake in downfaulted block in volcanic rocks; inflow mostly the Chewaucan River	Brine Na_2CO_3 10-20 g/L $NaHCO_3$ 4-13 NaCl 17-38 Na_2SO_4 1-1.5 KCl 1-1.5 pH 9.0⁺	Up to 141 TDS in playa interstitial water; Allison, 1947; Phillips and Van Denburgh, 1971
(48) Alkali Lake 31 km north-north-east of Abert Lake	Area 13-15 km², water in very shallow pond	Playa containing "pot holes" containing mostly natron and brine; recharged by ground water; local trona crust	Brine $HCO_3 + CO_3$ 171 g/L NaCl 76 Na_2SO_4 65 K_2SO_4 29	Allison, 1947; Phillips and Van Denburgh, 1971
(49) Harney Lake, central Harney County	120 km² lake, max depth 1.4 m; dries up	Surface water dilute subsurface interstitial brine up to 50 g/L dissolved solids; no solid salts	Brine Na_2CO_3 3.6 g/L Na_2SO_4 1.2 NaCl 4.8 KCl 0.4 $Na_2B_4O_7$ 1.9	TDS recorded 1912: 22.0 g/L; Phillips and Van Denburgh, 1971

TABLE 4—Continued

Name and Location; No. Refers to Location on Fig. 2	Physical Character	Geologic Character	Chemical Composition*	Remarks and References
(50) Summer Lake, Lake County, southeast Oregon	Area 260-470 km², 0.5-1 m deep; dries up	Alkaline semiperennial lake in downfaulted block; inflow maintained by ground-water recharge and rain	Brine Na_2CO_3 8-14 g/L $NaHCO_3$ 3-7 $NaCl$ 5-9 Na_2SO_4 1-2 KCl 0.5-1	Up to 130 g/L total solids in playa mud water, pH 9.0; Allison, 1947; Phillips and Van Denburgh, 1971
Washington (51) Carbonate Lake southeast Grant County	0.6 km², very shallow in small valley rimmed by basalt flow	Brine in pools and under ground; crystalline salts occurred in pans or "pot holes"	Concentrated brine Na_2CO_3 128.0 g/L $NaHCO_3$ — $NaCl$ 55 Na_2SO_4 38 KCl 21 Na 91 Sp. Gr. 1.3	Destroyed by construction of dam; former efforts to produce soda ash; Bennett, 1962
(52) Omak Lake, south-central Okanagan County	15 km² lake, 30-90 m deep in steep-sided valley in crystalline rocks	Stream fed in abandoned valley, vertically stratified	Very dilute water Na_2CO_3 4.0 g/L $NaCl$ 0.3 Na_2SO_4 1.9 K 0.4	3.6 Mt of Na_2CO_3 present in water; Bennett, 1962
(53) Soap Lake, north-central Grant County	3.5 km² lake, avg. depth 7.5 m at Grand Coulee in abandoned valley of Columbia River, floored by basalt	The last of a chain of four lakes fed by sub-surface flow; density stratified	Rather dilute and variable Na_2CO_3 21 g/L $NaCl$ 8 Na_2SO_4 10	570 kt of Na_2CO_3 present in brine; contains water-soluble heavy oil; Bennett, 1962
Wyoming (54) Berthaton and Yale Lakes (claims), 50 km southwest of Casper	Alkaline lakes 0.3 to 216 km² in area	Lakes in area of Tertiary rocks; brine and crystalline salts present	Old analyses Brine Na_2CO_3 66% $NaCl$ 14 Na_2SO_4 20 Crystal Deposit Na_2CO_3 50 $NaHCO_3$ 6 $NaCl$ 6 Na_2SO_4 37	Schultz, 1910
(55) Green River trona, Sweetwater County	Buried trona beds of 120-900 m underlie 2800 km² in Green River Basin	40 trona beds up to 10 m thick in organic marl-stone and oil shale deposited in Eocene saline lake	Mined trona $Na_2CO_3 \cdot NaHCO_3$ 90.26% $NaCl$ 0.040 Na_2SO_4 0.024 SiO_2 0.003 Organic Trace Water insol 10.0	Five producers, 6.7 Mt/a soda ash capacity; Bradley and Eugster, 1969; Deardorff and Mannion, 1971
VENEZUELA (56) Lago de Laguinillus State of Merida	Small pond which may dry up	In an area of alkalic rocks	Trona and gaylussite form from evaporation	Not an important source; Liddle, 1946

*Analytical data in some instances have been recalculated to chemical compounds; most values have been rounded.

Africa

Africa has a number of recorded sodium carbonate occurrences, some with a long history of production. Wadi Natron, about 80 km northwest of Cairo, contains small lakes which probably were the earliest worked deposits in the world. Impure sodium carbonate is obtained from crystallizing pans among sand dunes in the northeast part of Lake Chad (Eugster and Maglione, 1979). This material is exported to Nigeria at the rate of a few thousand tons per year.

Trona has been reported from near Fezzan in the Sahara (Chatard, 1890). A near-surface brine deposit of large size occurs in the Makgadikgadi basin in Botswana. Investigation of its commercial potential was underway for several years, but no significant developments occurred. The Otjevalunda pan (Dutoit, 1948) of South-West Africa contains sodium carbonate of potential value.

The largest deposits are present in east Africa. Among these the most remarkable is at Lake Magadi in southern Kenya, which contains a very large deposit of trona of Recent

TABLE 5—Analyses of Magadi Area Waters in Ppm

	Spring 16 South End of Lake Magadi	Spring 20 at Edge of Lake Magadi	Little Lake Magadi 1.6 km North of Lake Magadi	Lake Magadi, Bird Rock Lagoon	Brine in Borehold B, Lake Magadi, 6.1-m Depth
Na_2CO_3	15,480	5,900	93,000	46,800	200,000
$NaHCO_3$	6,300	20,550	32,000	11,100	1,200
NaCl	10,250	9,550	62,000	19,400	109,000
Na_2SO_4	290	250	ND	ND	ND
NaF	240	330	2,100	620	3,200
Total dissolved solids	30,350	29,130	ND	ND	ND
Temp.	40°C	81°C	—	—	—
Sp. Gr.	1.026	1.026			1.30

Source: Baker, 1958.

age. It is the most soda-rich of a number of alkaline lakes in the Rift Valley of Kenya and Tanzania, where surrounding terrain is largely underlain by faulted alkalic volcanic rocks of Tertiary and Pleistocene age. The climate near Magadi is semiarid, with rainfall of about 360 mm per year, concentrated in two rainy seasons.

Lake Magadi is essentially a trona salt pan, some 65 km³ in area, whose surface is largely dry. Most of the lake bed is underlain by as much as 45 m of relatively pure trona, plus interbedded trona and trona-bearing muds. Brine is present at or within a meter of the surface. The trona flats are bordered locally by alkaline lagoons fed by numerous warm springs, the combined flow of which approaches 280,000 m^2/d. Analyses of the water of two springs and of a lagoon water produced by a group of springs are given in Table 5. As the aggregate inflow of Na_2CO_3 from the springs amounts to 3600 t/d, it appears that the present rate of soda accumulation greatly exceeds extraction (Baker, 1958).

The alkaline spring water which supplies sodium carbonate to Lake Magadi is considered by Baker (1958) to be the result of weathering and leaching of igneous silicate minerals. Eugster (1970) points out that the dilute ground water from the igneous highland terrain recharges a deep reservoir, which in turn supplies the warm springs with concentrated carbonate waters. The same process appears to be operating elsewhere in the Rift Valley region to produce alkaline waters at Lake Natron, Lake Nakaru, Lake Elmenteita, and Lake Bogorio (Orr and Grantham, 1931).

Lake Magadi has been a producer of sodium carbonate since 1916. Raw trona is dredged from the salt flats, crushed, washed, and de-watered. It has a composition of about 45% Na_2CO_3, 35% $NaHCO_3$, 1.7% NaCl, 0.06% Na_2SO_4, and 0.9% NaF. The trona is calcined to drive off CO_2 and convert it to soda ash, which is then pulverized and screened to produce a dense ash product analyzing about 97% Na_2CO_3, 0.5% $NaHCO_3$, 0.5% NaCl, 0.4% Na_2SO_4, and 0.9% NaF. Production in 1966 was nearly 100 kt. Present plant capacity is 227 kt/a and could be expanded readily. The soda ash is marketed principally in the Far East. Salt for local markets is also produced by brine evaporation.

Australia

Australia appears devoid of significant surface sodium carbonate concentration. Although salt pans are common, they contain chiefly sodium chloride and sodium sulfate. Buried deposits may exist, particularly in the extensive areas of dominantly crystalline rock.

Asia

Sodium carbonate occurrences apparently are abundant in southern Siberia, Mongolia, and northern and western China (Hou, 1942; Torgasheff, 1929). Unfortunately, geologic information and other data are not readily available. Significant alkali lakes and salt pans are known and used in Manchuria and Inner Mongolia, on both sides of the Greater Khingan Range, which is reported to be largely granitic in character. The western part of Inner Mongolia and the Tarim basin (Takla Makan) of Sinkiang are reported to contain surface deposits of soda. Soda-ash plants, producing by means of a trona process, are reported at three localities in Inner Mongolia. These are O-T O-K O, Erhlien, and Pa-Yen Nao.

In Siberia, the regions of Kazakhstan and the Kulundinsk depression of Altay near Slovgorod and Barnaul have produced sodium carbonate from alkali lakes. Such lakes are also reported in eastern Siberia around Chita. Soda-ash plants based on a trona process exist at Makhaylovskiy in the Altay and at Temir-Tau, Karaganda. Presumably these utilize natural materials from soda lakes.

Table 4 presents some data on alkali lakes in China and Siberia, but even their locations are not readily identified on maps. It appears, however, that numerous and locally economically significant deposits occur as a broad, diffuse belt running roughly east-west from eastern Kazakhstan through Mongolia and adjacent parts of the USSR and China to northern Manchuria.

Europe

The present climate of Europe generally is not conducive to the development of significant lake salines. Sodium carbonate efflorescences have long been reported in the Danube Valley of Hungary, and saline lakes which may include alkaline varieties exist in Spain.

North America

North America appears unique in the number, size, and variety of known sodium-carbonate deposits. This may be in part a result of more extensive exploration. The deposits at Searles Lake, CA and Green River, WY account for the bulk of the natural soda ash produced in the world and will likely continue to do so.

Searles Lake: Searles Lake is a large salt flat surrounded by mud. It occupies the lowest part of Searles Valley about 226 km northeast of Los Angeles. The salt surface is the topmost part of a series of permeable crystalline saline lenses which contain interstitial brine and are interbedded with saline-bearing muds. The principal solid salt is halite. Also present are hanksite, trona, and borax, and lesser amounts of burkeite. The most highly saline-bearing part of the deposit extends from the surface to a depth of about 180 m and has an extent of about 100 km² (Smith, 1979).

The chief production intervals are termed "upper and lower salt structures." Almost immediately below the surface is the upper structure, a complex lens of salts with a

maximum thickness of about 27 m. The lower structure consists of a series of six salt lenses and five mud layers and is separated from the upper by about 3 m of mud. Somewhat deeper are trona beds containing brine with high concentrations of sodium carbonate. Searles Lake had its origin as the principal terminal sump of a chain of lakes in which water overflowed from one to the other until the Searles basin accumulated a brine and salt deposit almost free of detrital material.

Although the crystal bodies contain much trona and other potentially valuable solid salts, the contained brine is the present source of commercial products. Its composition varies both laterally and vertically, and brine density ranges between 1.25 and 1.3. A characteristic composition is given in Table 4. The principal recovered salts are sodium sulfate, sodium carbonate, potassium chloride, and borax. Lithium carbonate, bromine, and phosphoric acid also are produced.

Green River Basin, WY: Production of soda ash in the United States is dominated by the trona from southwest Wyoming. Numerous and extensive layers of trona were formed in a vast Eocene lake which was now represented by deposits of the Green River formation. In the Green River basin, some 3100 to 3600 km² are underlain by nearly flat trona beds at depths of 100 to 1070 m (Fig. 3). In just 11 of these beds, which average 2 m or more in thickness, trona reserves in place total more than 47 Gt (Culbertson, 1971).

Within the Green River basin, the Wilkins Peak member of the Eocene Green River formation consists chiefly of nondetrital lacustrine sediments deposited in ancient Lake Gosiute (Bradley, 1964). The saline-bearing facies is composed largely of organic marlstone, oil shale, claystone, and tuff, together with trona and halite. Most of the Wilkins Peak member is characterized by abundant crystals of shortite and is notable for an extraordinary suite of rare minerals (Fahey, 1962; Milton, 1971). A playa lake model for the deposition of Wilkins Peak trona as well as the surrounding and enclosing rocks has been proposed and fits many of the observed features (Eugster and Surdam, 1973; Surdam and Wolfbauer, 1975).

During the existence of Lake Gosiute, conditions for the deposition of trona evidently were repeated many times. More than 40 beds of trona, and trona plus halite, are distributed through about 300 m of evaporite-bearing strata. The position of many trona

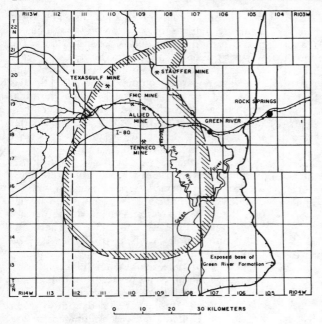

FIG. 3—*Trona Basin, Green River, Wyoming.*

beds on and within oil shales is noteworthy (Culbertson, 1971; Deardorff and Mannion, 1971). Trona beds range up to 12 m in thickness, and the most extensive layer has an area of almost 2600 km². The 12 deepest and stratigraphically lowest trona beds occur in the southern half of the area. Some of these beds contain much halite in the central portions, whereas the highest beds are essentially devoid of sodium chloride. These higher strata extend farther north and are less deep, the shallowest known being in the northeastern part of the basin in the vicinity of the Stauffer Chemical Co. mine.

Minable Wyoming trona consists of light to dark brown, almost monomineralic, massive beds. The brown color is due to small amounts of organic matter. The trona has a bladed habit; crystals range in size from needles less than 0.5 mm long to laths 100 mm long that commonly occur in radiating or sheaflike aggregates. A commercial bed normally contains about 90% trona and has a minable height of 2 to 3 m. Localities are known where minable thicknesses consist of as much as 97% trona. Mined trona contains less than a tenth of a percent each of sodium chloride and sodium sulfate. Water-insoluble waste consists of shortite and varied amounts of dispersed oil shale and marlstone as well as thin seams of the same material.

Currently (1981) four shaft mines are operating in the Wyoming trona district and a fifth is being developed. FMC Corp., Tenneco, Inc., and Allied Chemical Co. are mining different parts of the same extensive trona bed at a depth of about 460 m. Texasgulf operates a mine on two beds between 400 and 425 m. Stauffer Chemical Co. is mining the two youngest beds at about 260 to 275 m. All mines employ a multiple-entry, room-and-pillar method of mining. Both continuous mining machines and conventional drilling, blasting, and loading techniques are used. Ore movement underground is by shuttle car and belt haulage. Each of the mines supplies an on-site refinery which produces finished soda ash.

South America

Despite the presence of some of the world's largest salt pans or salars, South America appears lacking in significant resources of natural sodium carbonate. Salt pans at high and low elevations are known, but the great bulk of known surface salts are sulfate or sulfate-chloride varieties. Occurrences have been reported in southern Peru, in western Minas Gerais, Brazil, and in the province of Los Andes in northwestern Argentina. The sodium carbonate deposits which occur in the region where Chile, Bolivia, and Argentina meet are

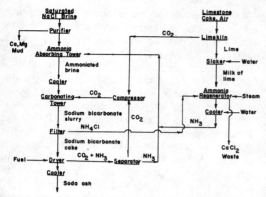

FIG. 4—*Flow diagram, Solvay soda ash process.*

small and economically unimportant (Catalano, 1926; Cordini, 1967).

Processing

World production of soda ash in 1979 was about 29 Mt (Watson, 1980). Of this, all but about 7.7 Mt was produced in Solvay process plans in 33 countries. Solvay plants continue to be built in countries where it is the most economical method of manufacture.

Solvay Process

Virtually all artificially maufactured soda ash is derived from the Solvay or modified

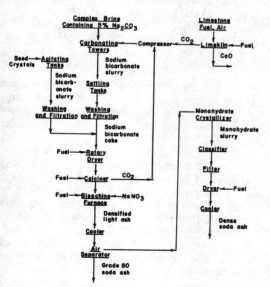

FIG. 5—*Flow diagram, Searles Lake simple carbonation process.*

Solvay process (Rau, 1969) (Fig. 4). In this method saturated sodium chloride brine is first purified of metal ions, notably calcium and magnesium, then saturated with recycled NH_3 gas. The ammoniated brine is carbonated at 300 to 400 kPa pressure, using gas from a lime kiln. Sodium bicarbonate is thus precipitated and filtered. The filtered sodium bicarbonate is calcined to drive off H_2O, NH_3, and CO_2, thus producing a light ash.

The ammonia-bearing brine filtrate is recycled to an ammonia recovery system. In it the ammonia chloride solution is heated with milk of lime to drive off the NH_3 while at the same time producing large quantities of calcium chloride, which is mostly unsalable. A modified Solvay process produces marketable ammonium chloride rather than recycling the ammonia and wasting the calcium chloride.

Searles Lake Brine Process

At Searles Lake, brine feed of differing compositions is obtained from a complex of wells that tap various depths and locations in the deposit. Soda ash is produced through carbonation-precipitation of brines with high sodium carbonate content. At the West End plant the CO_2 gas for carbonation is produced from lime kilns (Fig. 5). At the much larger Argus plant, CO_2 is obtained from power plant gases.

The Argus plant uses brine produced by solution mining trona with 107 m deep wells. Spent warm liquors from the plant are recycled by injecting them into the ore zone to dissolve the trona. The brine is stored, cooled, and concentrated in open-air solar-evaporation ponds. Increased brine concentration helps improve the yield of the plant process. The brine from the ponds is then carbonated to produce a bicarbonate crystal slurry. This slurry is filtered, dried, and calcined to produce a light soda ash. The light ash can be converted to dense ash, if desired, by dissolution, reprecipitation as monohydrate, and drying to remove the free water.

Wyoming Trona Process

Production of soda ash from trona is somewhat simpler than the ammonia soda process and can be done at lower cost. The energy requirements are also lower. Fig. 6 shows a flow diagram of the Wyoming trona process. Trona ore as mined contains the equivalent of about 60% sodium carbonate; approximately

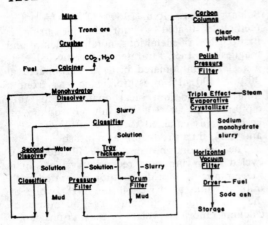

FIG. 6—*Flow diagram, Wyoming trona process.*

1.8 t of trona are necessary to make 1 t of soda ash.

Two variations of the process are used (Frint, 1971). The trona process begins by dissolving trona ore; the monohydrate process first calcines the trona and dissolves the crude soda ash thus produced. In the trona process, the hot solution from dissolving trona is clarified by removal of solids and organic matter. The solution is cooled to precipitate trona, which is then calcined to produce soda ash. In the monohydrate process the conversion of trona to soda ash requires a temperature of about 200° C to achieve the following reaction within a reasonable length of time:

$$\overset{\text{Heat}}{2(Na_2CO_3 \cdot NaHCO_3 \cdot 2H_2O)} \rightarrow$$
$$3Na_2CO_3 + CO_2\uparrow + 5H_2O\uparrow$$

The solution derived from the crude soda ash is evaporated to produce monohydrate crystals, which in turn are heated to convert them into soda ash.

Exploration

Commercial concentrations of sodium carbonate are confined to nonmarine geologic environments, modern or ancient. The drier areas of the world with interior drainage contain numerous salt pans and salt lakes where alkaline salts may occur. However, most are dominated by sodium chloride and sodium sulfate rather than carbonate. Because saline lakes are conspicuous and accessible, some knowledge of their composition is commonly available.

Despite the widespread occurrence of playa lake type sodium carbonate, notable problems attend the commercial development of such deposits. These problems are the small size of most deposits; their poor location relative to markets for a low-priced commodity; the presence of large amounts of difficult-to-separate impurities (typically chlorides and sulfates but also such elements as fluorine); difficult operating conditions because of the dispersed nature of the deposit and wet ground; variability of composition of brine and salts; and the adverse effects, particularly in surface deposits, of weather changes, e.g. changes in temperature which cause dissolution or precipitation of salts and change in concentration of brine because of rain and increased surface drainage.

Conditions favoring development of economical concentrations of sodium carbonate are: semiarid rather than a severe desert climate; drainage dominated by crystalline or volcanic rocks rather than sedimentary rock; and a reasonably constant and sufficient inflow of alkaline water to provide large amounts of alkali salts.

In looking for ancient or buried deposits, interpretation of geologic history and paleo environments is valuable in determining whether the appropriate conditions existed. The presence of peripheral salines and dolomitic strata in exposed lake beds indicate ancient alkaline lakes. Smith (1966) suggests additional criteria to be used in the search for buried salines.

Many geologists use the following procedure when exploring for, sampling, and testing potential sodium carbonate deposits:

1) Surface deposits over a large area are reconnaissance sampled. Mere surface sampling may not be representative; samples should be taken at least a meter below the surface.

2) The size of the deposit is noted, particularly its compactness or thickness and whether of brine or solids. In sampling brine at substantial depths, care should be taken to avoid obtaining mixed samples from aquifers of varying concentration and composition.

3) Uniformity of the deposit is verified. Both crystalline and liquid constituents of ancient and modern alkaline lakes and marshes can vary greatly from place to place and with depth.

4) If solar evaporation and concentration of brines is to be used, local deposits of clay

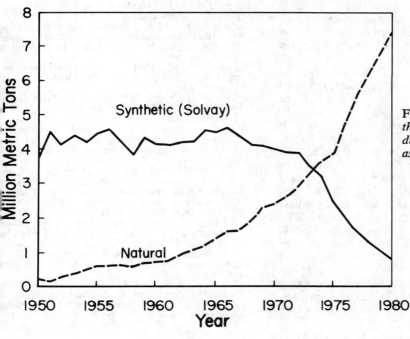

FIG. 7—*Solvay (synthetic) soda ash production vs. natural soda ash production in the United States.*

be proven adequate for construction of the evaporation lagoons.

5) Climatic variables which might affect the proposed method of operation, particularly the composition of the raw material, are studied. Many ores contain hygroscopic and differentially soluble minerals. In some areas seasonal rains dilute ground and surface brines.

6) If a brine is to be processed, an inexpensive and effective method for the collection and recovery of the brine must be found. Wells, for example, may not always function satisfactorily or produce adequate amounts of brine. Tests are essential to ensure an effective operation.

7) If near-surface solids are to be mined, stability and effectiveness of excavations must be determined. Will contamination be a problem?

8) The capacity of enclosing rocks to support normal mine openings must be determined if underground solids are to be mined. It may be necessary to keep such openings confined to the saline deposit itself when the enclosing rock is weak.

9) Particularly if underground mining will be used, the possibility of invasion of the deposit by extraneous water must be determined.

Future of the Industry

Sodium carbonate is an essential bulk chemical and increases in use generally parallel the growth of the economy. Growth has been about 2% per year for the past 20 years and will probably continue at that rate.

In the United States, Wyoming soda ash has had rapid development, while Solvay process ash has almost disappeared (Fig. 7). The foremost contributing factors are the high quality and size of the Wyoming deposits and the high quality of the product. These deposits can be developed economically and, despite the distance from eastern markets, can compete effectively. Environmental difficulties have beset Solvay plants, which have, among other things, the problem of disposing of large amounts of calcium chloride. The one remaining Solvay plant, located in New York, will probably continue to be competitive.

Some problems exist in the mining of trona. One of these is maintaining integrity of mine openings where the enclosing strata are weak. The floor and roof strata of some mines tend to fail locally when the supporting trona is removed. Handling, recycling, and disposal of waste brine and tailings solids may present additional problems.

Finally, vast amounts of trona exist in Wyoming, but are probably too deep for conventional mining. Some form of solution mining by means of wells may be feasible for recovery of this resource.

The vast quantities of nahcolite in the Piceance Basin of Colorado, occurring mostly as disseminated material in oil shale but also as bedded deposits, represent a great potential source of sodium carbonate (Anon., 1972a). If soda ash is recovered during oil shale mining in the saline-bearing zone of the Piceance Basin, the impact on the market would be great. However, the additional environmental problems attendant upon shale oil recovery from the saline-zone oil shale make saline-free oil shale a more attractive prospect. Mining of bedded nahcolite is another possibility, although ore grade is lower than that of Wyoming trona and there may be some mining problems.

Production from Lake Magadi, Kenya, is planned to double in 1983. Increased production is also planned at Texcoco, Mexico City (Watson, 1980).

Attempts have been made to market Wyoming soda ash in Europe but the special conditions of the European market, particularly governmental concern, have prevented significant inroads.

Bibliography and References

Anon., 1959, *Mineral Resources of the Union of South Africa*, 4th ed., Union of South Africa Geol. Surv., pp. 554–555.

Anon., 1970, *Minerals Yearbook,* Vol. III, Area Reports, International, US Bureau of Mines, p. 959.

Anon., 1972, "An Economic Analysis of a White Nahcolite Installation in Colorado," Option I, Open File Report 31–72, July, National Technical Information Service, PB-212 046, US Bureau of Mines, 69 pp.

Anon., 1972a, "An Economic Analysis of an Oil Shale, Nahcolite, Dawsonite Complex in Colorado," National Technical Information Service Publications, PB-212 046, US Bureau of Mines, 3 vol.

Anon., 1980, "Trona Soda Ash and the Argus Facility," Bulletin 1400, Kerr-McGee Chemical Corp., 23 pp.

Ahlfeld, F., and Schneider-Scherbena, A., 1964, "Los Yacimientos Minerales y de Hidrocarbures de Bolivia," Bolletin No. 5 Minister de Minas v Petroleo, La Paz.

Allison, I.S., 1947, "Sodium Salts of Lake County, Oregon," GMI Short Paper No. 17, Oregon Dept. of Geol. and Mineral Industries, 12 pp.

Averill, C.V., 1947, "Mines and Mineral Resources of Lake County, Cal.," *California Journal of Mines and Geology,* Vol. 43, No. 1, pp. 16–40.

Baker, B.H., 1958, "Geology of the Magadi Area," Report 42, Kenya Geol. Surv., 81 pp.

Barbour, E.H., 1916, "A Preliminary Report on the Alkali Resources of Nebraska," Miscellaneous Papers, Vol. 4, Pt. 28, Nebraska Geological Survey, pp. 405–438.

Barnes, J.W., ed., 1961, "The Mineral Resource of Uganda," Bulletin No. 4, Geol. Surv. o Uganda, 46 pp.

Bennett, W.A.G., 1962, "Saline Lake Deposits of Washington," Bulletin No. 49, Washington Div of Mines and Geology, pp. 19–49.

Bond, G.W., 1946, "A Geochemical Survey of th Underground Water Supplies of the Union o South Africa," Memoir No. 41, Union of Sout Africa Geological Survey, pp. 44–47.

Bradley, W.H., 1964, "Geology of the Green Rive Formation and Associated Eocene Rocks i Southwestern Wyoming and Adjacent Part o Colorado and Utah," Professional Paper 496-A US Geological Survey, 86 pp.

Bradley, W.G., and Eugster, H.P., 1969, "Geo chemistry and Paleolimnology of the Trona De posit and Associated Authogenic Minerals o the Green River Formation of Wyoming," U Geological Survey, Professional Paper 496-B 71 pp.

Bukhshtein, V.M., and Zakina, A.E., 1949, "Th Solubility Polytherm of Sodium Carbonate i the Brine of the Mikhailov Lakes," *Transactions* All-Union Institute for the Study of Salts, N 21, pp. 223–242; *Chemical Abstracts,* Vol. 46 1952, p. 8911.

Catalano, L.R., 1926, "Geologia Economica d Los Yacimientes de Borate y Materiales de la Cuencas—Solar Cauchari," Publication No. 23 Direccion General de Minas Geologia y Hidro logica, Buenos Aires, 110 pp.

Chatard, T.M., 1890, "Natural Soda; Its Occur rence and Utilization," Bulletin 60, US Geo logical Survey, pp. 162–163, 237–243.

Christie, W.A.K., 1912, "Note on the Lonar Sod. Deposit," *Records,* Geol. Surv. of India, Pt. 4 Vol. 41, pp. 276–285.

Clarke, F.W., 1924, "The Data of Geochemistry, Bulletin 770, US Geological Survey, 841 pp.

Cordini, I.R., 1967, "Reservas Salinas de Argen tina," Anales No. 13, Instituto Nacional de Geo logia y Mineria, Buenos Aires, 108 pp.

Cotter, G.deP., 1923, "The Alkaline Lakes an the Soda Industry of Sind," Memoir 47, Pt. 2 Geological Survey of India, pp. 202–311.

Culbertson, W.C., 1966, "Trona in the Wilkin Peak Member of the Green River Formatio Southwestern Wyoming," Professional Pape 550-B, US Geological Survey, pp. B159–164.

Culbertson, W.C., 1971, "Stratigraphy of th Trona Deposits in the Green River Formation Southwest Wyoming," *Contributions to Geology* Vol. 10, No. 1, R.B. Parker, ed., University o Wyoming, Laramie, pp. 15–28.

Cummings, J.M., 1949, "Saline and Hydromagn site Deposits of British Columbia," Bulletin N 4, 1940, British Columbia Dept. of Mines, 16 pp.

Deardorff, D.L., and Mannion, L.E., 1971, "W oming Trona Deposits," *Contributions to G ology,* Vol. 10, No. 1, R.B. Parker, ed., Un versity of Wyoming, Laramie, pp. 25–27.

Dub, G.D., 1947, "Owens Lake—Source of So

dium Minerals," Technical Publication No. 2235, AIME, 13 pp.

Durand-Chastel, M.H., 1968, "L'exploitation de Saumures de Carbonate de Soude au Mexique," *Science et Techniques*, No. 12, pp. 23–30.

Dutoit, A.L., 1948, *The Geology of South Africa*, Hafner, New York, p. 428.

Eugster, H.P., 1970, "Chemistry and Origin of the Brines of Lake Magadi, Kenya," Special Paper 3, Mineralogical Society of America, pp. 213–235.

Eugster, H.P., 1971, "Origin and Deposition of Trona," *Contributions to Geology*, Vol. 10, No. 1, R.B. Parker, ed., University of Wyoming, Laramie, pp. 15–23.

Eugster, H.P., 1980, "Geochemistry of Evaporitic Lacustrine Deposits," *Annual Review*, Earth and Planetary Sciences, Vol. 8, pp. 35–63.

Eugster, H.P., 1980a, "Lake Magadi, Kenya, and Its Precursors," *Hypersaline Brines and Evaporitic Environments*, Elsevier, Amsterdam, pp. 195–232.

Eugster, H.P., and Jones, B.F., 1979, "Behavior of Major Solutes During Closed-Basin Brine Evolution," *American Journal of Science*, Vol. 279, pp. 609–631.

Eugster, H.P., and Maglione, G., 1979, "Brines and Evaporites of the Lake Chad Basin, Africa," *Geochimica et Cosmochimica Acta*, Vol. 43, pp. 973–981.

Eugster, H.P., and Smith, G.I., 1965, "Mineral Equilibria in the Searles Lake Evaporites," *Journal of Geology*, Vol. 6, pp. 473–522.

Eugster, H.P., and Surdam, R.C., 1973, "Depositional Environment of the Green River Formation of Wyoming: A Preliminary Report," Geological Society of America Bulletin, Vol. 84, pp. 1115–1120.

Fahey, J.J., 1962, "Saline Minerals of the Green River Formation," Professional Paper 405, US Geological Survey, 50 pp.

Fawley, A.P., 1958, "Diamond Drilling in the Bahi Swamp," *Records*, Tanganyika Geological Survey, Vol. 6 (1956), pp. 47–51.

Fredriksson, K. et al., 1973, "Lonar Lake, India: An Impact Crater in Basalt," *Science*, Vol. 180, No. 4088, pp. 862–864.

Free, E.E., 1913, "Progress in Potash Prospecting in Railroad Valley, Nevada," *Mining and Scientific Press*, Vol. 107, No. 5, August, pp. 176–178.

Freise, F.W., 1932, "Beobachtungen au Brasilianischen Salzsumpfen," *Chemie der Erde*, Band 7, Heft 1, pp. 24–34.

Frint, W.R., 1971, "Processing of Wyoming Trona," *Contributions to Geology*, Vol. 10, No. 1, R.B. Parker, ed., University of Wyoming, Laramie, pp. 25–27.

Garrels, R.M., and Mackenzie, F.T., 1967, "Origin of the Chemical Composition of Some Springs and Lakes," *Equilibrium Concepts in Natural Water Systems*, Advances in Chemistry Series 57, American Chemical Society, Washington, pp. 222–242.

Garrett, D.E., and Phillips, J.F., 1960, "Sodium Carbonate from Natural Sources in the United States," *Industrial Minerals and Rocks*, 3rd ed., J.L. Gillson, ed., AIME, New York, pp. 799–809.

Gonzalez-Reyna, J., 1956, "Riqueza Minera y Yacimiento," *Minerales de Mexico*. 3rd ed., 20th

Congreso Geologico Internacional, Banco de Mexico S.A. Dept. de Investigaciones Industriales, Mexico, pp. 431–439.

Guest, N.J., 1956, *Records*, Geological Survey of Tanganyika, Vol. 4, p. 7.

Hardie, L.A., and Eugster, H.P., 1970, "The Evolution of Closed-Basin Brines," Special Paper 3, Mineralogical Society of America, pp. 273–290.

Horino, F.G., and Hooker, V.E. 1978, "Mechanical Properties of Cores Obtained from the Unleached Saline Zone, Piceance Creek Basin, Rio Blanco County, Colo., Report of Investigations 8297, US Bureau of Mines, 21 pp.

Hou, T.P., 1942, *Manufacture of Soda*, Monograph Series No. 65, American Chemical Society, Reinhold, New York, pp. 14–30.

Jakucs, L., 1977, *Morphogenetics of Karst Region (Variants of Karst Evolution)* translated from the Hungarian by B. Balhay, Halsted Press, New York, pp. 29–33.

Jones, B.F., 1965, "The Hydrology and Mineralogy of Deep Springs Lake, Inyo County, California," Professional Paper 502-A, US Geological Survey, 55 pp.

Jones, B.F., 1966, "Chemical Evolution of Closed-Basin Water in the Western Great Basin," *Second Symposium on Salt*, Vol. 1, J.L. Rau, ed., Northern Ohio Geological Society, Cleveland, pp. 181–200.

Karajian, H.A., 1920, *Mineral Resources of Armenia and Anatolia*, Armen Technical Book Co., New York, pp. 121–125.

Klingman, C.L., 1972, "Sodium and Sodium Compounds," *Minerals Yearbook 1972*, US Bureau of Mines, pp. 1147–1151.

Kostick, D.S., and Foster, R.J., 1979, "Soda Ash (Sodium Carbonate), Sodium Sulfate, and Sodium," *Mineral Commodity Profiles*, US Bureau of Mines, 14 pp.

Kuchin, M.I., 1928, "Salt Lakes of the Slavgorod Region in Siberia," *Journal of Chemical Industry* (Moscow), Vol. 5, pp. 292–297; *Chemical Abstracts*, Vol. 22, 1928, p. 3963.

Lanbein, W.B., 1961, "Salinity and Hydrology of Closed Lakes," Professional Paper 412, US Geological Survey, 20 pp.

Lefond, S.J., 1981, "Botswana—An Opportunity," Preprint 81–73, SME-AIME Annual Meeting, Chicago, Feb., 3 pp.

Liddle, R.A., 1946, *The Geology of Venezuela and Trinidad*, 2nd ed., Paleontological Research Institution, Cayuga Press, Ithaca, p. 589.

Livingston, D.A., 1963, "Chemical Composition of Lakes and Rivers," Chapter G, *Data of Geochemistry*, 6th ed., M. Fleischer, ed., Professional Paper 440-G, US Geological Survey, pp. 617, 633.

Lucas, A., 1912, "Natural Soda Deposits in Egypt," Paper No. 22, Ministry of Finance, Survey Dept., Government Press, Cairo, 29 pp.

Maglione, G., 1972, "New Data on the Processes at Present Giving Rise to Saline Concentrations on the North-East Periphery of Lake Chad," *Geology of Saline Deposits*, G. Richter-Bernberg, ed., UNESCO, Paris, pp. 211–213.

Mannion, L.E., 1975, "Sodium Carbonate Deposits," *Industrial Minerals and Rocks*, 4th ed., S.J. Lefond, ed., AIME, New York, pp. 1061–1079.

Massey, N.W.D., 1973, "Resources Inventory of Botswana: Industrial Minerals and Rocks," Mineral Report No. 3, Geological Survey Dept., Lobatse, Botswana, 39 pp.

Milton, C., 1971, "Authigenic Minerals in the Green River Formation," *Contributions to Geology,* Vol. 10, No. 1, R.B. Parker, ed., University of Wyoming, Laramie, pp. 57–63.

Morrison, R.B., 1964, "Lake Lahontan: Geology of Southern Carson Desert, Nevada," Professional Paper 401, US Geological Survey, p. 116.

Murdock, T.G., 1949, "Industrial Minerals of Ethiopia," *Trans. AIME,* Vol. 181, pp. 376–384.

Niinomy, K., 1930, "A New Locality of Gaylussite in Eastern Mongolia with Associated Natural Soda," *Economic Geology,* Vol. 25, No. 7, pp. 758–763.

Orr, D., and Grantham, D.R., 1931, "Some Salt Lakes of the North Rift Zone," Short Paper No. 8, Geological Survey Dept., Tanganyika Territory, 21 pp.

Pelletier, R.A., 1964, *Mineral Resources of South-Central Africa,* Oxford University Press, Oxford, p. 131.

Perel'man, A.I., 1967, *Geochemistry of Epigenesis,* trans. from Russian by N. N. Kohanowski, Plenum Press, New York, pp. 176–181.

Phillips, K.N., and Van Denburgh, A.S., 1971, "Hydrology and Geochemistry of Abert, Summer, and Goose Lakes and Other Closed-Basin Lakes in South-Central Oregon," Professional Paper 502-B, US Geological Survey, 86 pp.

Rau, E., 1969, "Sodium Compounds," *Encyclopedia of Chemical Technology,* Vol. 18, 2nd ed., Kirth-Othmer, ed., Interscience, New York, pp. 458–468.

Rettig, S.L., and Jones, B.F., 1965, "Determination of Carbonate, Bicarbonate, and Total CO_2 in Carbonate Brines," Professional Paper 501-D (1964), US Geological Survey, pp. D134–137.

Risacher, F., 1978, "Le Cadre Geochemique des Bessins a Evaporites des Andes Boliviennes," Vol. X, No. 1, Cah O.R.S.T.O.M., Ser. Geol., pp. 37–48.

Risacher, F., Echenique, A, and Ballivian, O, 1978, "Informe Geologico—Economico de la Laguna Collpa y de la Laguna Hedronda," unpublished paper, 19 pp.

Roy, B.C., 1959, "The Economic Geology and Mineral Resources of Rajasthan and Ajmer," *Memoirs,* Geological Survey of India, Vol. 86, pp. 271–273.

Sahni, M.R., 1951, "Alkaline Soils and Lakes of India," *Records,* India Geological Survey, Vol. 81, Pt. 2, pp. 241–296.

Said, R., 1962, *The Geology of Egypt,* Elsevier Publishing Co., Amsterdam, p. 272.

Schultz, A.R., 1910, "Deposits of Sodium Salts in Wyoming," Bulletin 430, US Geological Survey, pp. 570–589.

Singewald, J.T., 1949, "Mineral Resources of Colombia," Bulletin 964-B, US Geological Survey, pp. 186–192.

Smith, G.I., 1964, "Character and Distribution of Non-clastic Minerals in the Searles Lake Evaporite Deposit, California," Bulletin 1181-P. US Geological Survey, 58 pp.

Smith, G.I., 1966, "Geology of Searles Lake—A Guide to Prospecting for Buried Continental Salines," *2nd Symposium on Salt,* Vol. 1, J.L. Rau, ed., Northern Ohio Geological Society, Cleveland, pp. 167–180.

Smith, G.I., 1979, "Subsurface Stratigraphy and Geochemistry of Late Quaternary Evaporites, Searles Lake, California," Professional Paper 1043, US Geological Survey, 130 pp.

Smith, G.I., and Friedman, I., 1975, "Chemical Sedimentation and Diagenesis of Pleistocene Evaporites in Searles Lake, Calif.," 9th International Sedimentation Congress, Nice, pp. 137–140.

Smith, J.W., and Milton, C., 1966, "Dawsonite in the Green River Formation of Colorado," *Economic Geology,* Vol. 61, No. 6, Sep.-Oct., pp. 1029–1042.

Surdam, R.C., and Wolfbauer, C.A., 1975, "Green River Formation, Wyoming, A Playa Lake Complex," Geological Society of America, Bulletin, Vol. 86, pp. 335–345.

Teale, E.O., and Oates, F., 1946, "The Mineral Resources of Tanganyika Territory," Bulletin No. 16, 1946, Geol. Div., Dept. of Lands and Mines, Tanganyika Territory, p. 150.

Torgasheff, B.P., 1929, "Soda in China, Manchuria, and Neighboring Countries," *Chinese Economic Journal,* Bureau of Industrial & Commercial Information, National Government of the Republic of China, Vol. 5, No. 2, Aug., pp. 662–681.

Tulus, R., 1944, "Die Analyse des Wassers vom Van-see (Ostanatolium)," *Review Faculte Science,* University of Istanbul, Vol. 9, pp. 61–63.

Watson, I., 1980, "Soda Ash," *Industrial Minerals,* No. 154, July, pp. 17–31.

Watson, I., 1981, "U.S. Soda Ash—Green River's Solution—Europe's Problem," *Industrial Minerals,* No. 162, Mar., pp. 37–38.

Young, N.B., and Smith, O.W., 1970, "Dawsonite and Nahcolite Analyses of Green River Formation Oil-Shale Sections, Piceance Creek Basin, Colorado," Report of Investigations 7445, US Bureau of Mines, 22 pp.

Sodium Sulfate Deposits

WM. I. WEISMAN *

SID McILVEEN, JR.†

Sodium sulfate is an important industrial chemical, being one of perhaps a dozen or so chemical commodities produced and consumed in the United States in quantities exceeding 1 Mt/a. In recent years approximately half that production has come from natural sources, whereas 27 years ago only 25% was derived from these sources. Table 1 illustrates the history of production of natural sodium sulfate in the United States. Production of natural sodium sulfate from various types of deposits is the main source of this chemical in Canada and Mexico, and probably in Argentina, Chile, Spain, and the USSR.

Mineralogy and Physical Properties

Sodium sulfate is widespread in occurrence and is a common constituent of many mineral waters, as well as seawater. Atmospheric precipitation contains sulfate; it is one of the major dissolved constituents of rain and snow (Davis and DeWiest, 1966). Many of the saline lakes throughout the world contain varying amounts of sodium sulfate. Because sodium is usually the dominant cation, some workers make an anionic distinction, referring to lakes containing predominately sulfate as bitter lakes and those containing predominately carbonate as alkali, or soda lakes (Bateman, 1950). Sodium sulfate in its natural form is found as the hydrous salt *mirabilite* (commonly called Glauber's salt), and as *thenardite*, the anhydrous variety. The largest quantities occur in the form of mirabilite. Sodium sulfate is found in varying degrees of purity, from theoretically pure efflorescent crystals of mirabilite to combinations and admixtures of other salts and impurities. It is a common constituent of

some brines; from this source much is extracted commercially.

TABLE 1—Production of Sodium Sulfate in the United States, Manufactured and Natural (1000 t)

Year	Production, 100% Basis[1]	Sold or Used by Producers, Natural Only[2]
1953	903	225
1954	877	227
1955	982	259
1956	998	302
1957	949	300
1958	855	315
1959	986	366
1960	974	409
1961	1030	423
1962	1108	416
1963	1119	395
1964	1194	522
1965	1275	563
1966	1312	581
1967	1238	578
1968	1346	635
1969	1338	610
1970	1246	543
1971	1231	625
1972	1205	636
1973	1305	610
1974	1224	621
1975	1114	606
1976	1118	602
1977	1088	577
1978	1121	549
1979	1071	484
1980	1142	529
1981	1043	540
1982	896	W

[1] Current Industrial Reports, Inorganic Chemicals, US Dept. of Commerce, Bureau of Census.
[2] US Dept. of Interior, *Minerals Yearbook*, and USBM data.
W—Withheld to avoid revealing individual company data.

* President, Ozark-Mahoning Co., Tulsa, Oklahoma.

† Geologist, Ozark-Mahoning Co., Brownfield, Texas.

Sodium sulfate also is found in compounds, such as the minerals *glauberite*, the double salt of anhydrous sodium and calcium sulfate, *bloedite*, the hydrous double-salt of sodium sulfate and magnesium sulfate, and *burkeite*, the anhydrous double-salt of sodium carbonate and sodium sulfate.

Over 40 minerals contain sodium sulfate in varying proportions; many are of special interest because of their frequent occurrence. Table 2 lists some sodium-sulfate bearing minerals. The reader is referred to other publications (Cole, 1926; Dana, 1932; Grabau, 1920; and Dietrich, 1969) for descriptions of these minerals. Only mirabilite and thenardite will be described herein.

Mirabilite, $Na_2SO_4 \cdot 10H_2O$, contains 55.9% water of crystallization. It is noted for its efflorescence or spontaneous loss of water. On dehydration it changes to the anhydrous form, Na_2SO_4. Mirabilite is an opaque to colorless, water-soluble mineral that tastes first cool, then slightly bitter. It has a specific gravity of 1.48. It frequently forms as efflorescent, needlelike monoclinic crystals, but generally is found in the massive form.

Thenardite, the anhydrous mineral, Na_2SO_4, contains 43.68% Na_2O and 56.32% SO_3. It ranges from colorless to white, and may be tinted shades of gray or brown. It is a water-soluble mineral with a slightly salty taste. Its specific gravity (2.67) and hardness (2.5 to 3) exceed those of mirabilite. It commonly occurs in the massive form without visible crystals. Its crystals are frequently tabular pyramids of the orthorhombic system.

Sodium sulfate also occurs as a heptahydrate, containing seven molecules of water, but this is unstable and has not been found in the natural environment.

The solubility of sodium sulfate has an important effect on the crystallization of the salt in nature, as well as in its production. Its solubility in water generally increases as a

TABLE 2—A List of Minerals That Contain Sodium Sulfate

Mineral	Composition	%Na$_2$SO$_4$
Thenardite (anhydrous)*	Na_2SO_4	100
Hanksite	$9Na_2SO_4 \cdot 2Na_2CO_3 \cdot KCl$	81.7
Lecontite	$(Na,NH_4,K)_2SO_4 \cdot 2H_2O$	<79.8
Vanthoffite	$3Na_2SO_4 \cdot MgSO_4$	78
Sulphohalite[†]	$2Na_2SO_4 \cdot NaCl \cdot NaF$	73.9
Burkeite[‡]	$Na_6(SO_4)_2(CO_3)$	72.8
Darapskite	$NaNO_3 \cdot Na_2SO_4 \cdot H_2O$	58.0
Glauberite	$Na_2SO_4 \cdot CaSO_4$	51.1
Loeweite	$MgSO_4 \cdot Na_2SO_4 \cdot 2\frac{1}{2}H_2O$	46.2
Ferrinatrite	$3Na_2SO_4Fe_2(SO_4)_3 \cdot 6H_2O$	45.6
Mirabilite (Glauber's salt)	$Na_2SO_4 \cdot 10H_2O$	44.1
Bloedite (astrakanite)	$MgSO_4 \cdot Na_2SO_4 \cdot 4H_2O$	42.5
Kroehnkite	$CuSO_4 \cdot Na_2SO_4 \cdot 2H_2O$	42.1
Nickelbloedite[§]	$Na_2Ni(SO_4)_2 \cdot 4H_2O$	40.3
Sideronatrite[‡]	$Na_2Fe(SO_4)_2(OH) \cdot 3H_2O$	38.9
Caracolite	$Pb(OH)Cl \cdot Na_2SO_4$	35.4
Palmierite	$(K,Na)_2Pb(SO_4)_2$	<31.9
Tychite	$2MgCO_3 \cdot 2Na_2CO_3 \cdot Na_2SO_4$	27.2
Aphthitalite (glaserite)[‡]	$(K,Na)_3Na(SO_4)_2$	21-38
Tamarugite[¶]	$Na_2SO_4 \cdot Al_2(SO_4)_3 \cdot 12H_2O$	20.3
Natrochalcite	$Cu_4(OH)_2(SO_4)_3 \cdot Na_2SO_4 \cdot 2H_2O$	18.8
Almeriite	$Na_2SO_4 \cdot Al_2(SO_4)_3 \cdot 5Al(OH)_3 \cdot H_2O$	15.9
Mendozite (soda alum)[¶]	$Na_2SO_4 \cdot Al_2(SO_4)_3 \cdot 24H_2O$	15.5
Natrojarosite	$Na_2Fe_6(OH)_{12}(SO_4)_4$	14.7
Noselite	$3Na_2Al_2Si_2O_8 \cdot Na_2SO_4$	14.3
Slavikite	$(Na,K)_2SO_4 \cdot Fe_{10}(OH)_6(SO_4)_{12} \cdot 63H_2O$	<4.6

Note: Formulae are taken from Dana and Ford, 1932, unless otherwise noted.

* Salt cake is anhydrous sodium sulfate with a purity lower than 98%.

[†] Kogarkoite—Na_3SO_4F (monoclinic), schairerite—$Na_{21}(SO_4)_7F_6Cl$ (trigonal), and galeite—$Na_{15}(SO_4)_5F_4Cl$ (trigonal) are minerals related to sulphohalite (cubic) (Fanfani, et al., 1975).

[‡] Dietrich, 1969.

[§] Nickel and Bridge, 1977.

[¶] Dennis S. Kostick, Sodium Compounds Commodity Specialist, Bureau of Mines, private communication.

nonlinear function of temperature. Below 1.2° C, ice and mirabilite form. As the temperature is increased above 0° C, increasing amounts of sodium sulfate become soluble. At 32.4° C, a transition point on the solubility curve is reached, as the decahydrate melts in its own water of crystallization and the anhydrous form crystallizes. With increasing temperatures, solubility decreases somewhat. The presence of other dissolved salts lowers the transition temperature and changes the solubility characteristics of sodium sulfate.

Classification of Deposits

Essentially all commercial deposits of sodium sulfate have resulted from accumulation and evaporation of surface and ground water in basins with interior drainage, called playas. They are found in arid to semiarid regions. Thus these deposits fall within the broad classification of evaporites. They can be further classified in two categories: those occurring as crystalline beds of mirabilite or glauberite and/or brines within or underlying playa lakes; and those found as buried beds of thenardite, glauberite, and associated minerals. The first category includes the principal deposits of the world. Notable among these are the lake deposits of western Canada, Great Salt Lake, Utah, the vast mirabilite-glauberite deposits of the Kara-Bogaz-Gol Gulf on the eastern shore of the Caspian Sea, and the brine deposits of the western United States and Mexico. These require pumping, dredging, or reservoiring for exploitation.

Commercial deposits of the second category are relatively rare. Deposits of thenardite and glauberite are presently being mined in Spain, and thenardite has been mined in the past at Camp Verde, AZ and at Rhodes Marsh near Mina, NV. Conventional mining techniques are used for extraction.

Origin of Sodium Sulfate Deposits

Evaporation of surface waters, with consequent concentration of salts, is the principal agent in the formation of alkali and bitter lakes from which sodium sulfate and other salts are extracted. Because of the great difference in composition between seawater salts and those of playa lake deposits, it is generally accepted that these deposits are Recent accumulations from nonmarine sources.

The brines of playa lake deposits are more diverse in composition than the oceans because each deposit contains soluble salts from discrete sources within its drainage area. The salinity of the brines is much greater, because of the high rates of evaporation characteristic in arid interior basins where the deposits occur.

The evolution of brine and subsequent precipitation of minerals involve complex geochemical factors. These include the weathering of solutes from the watershed, their transport to the playa basin, and their evaporative concentration. Jones (1966) points out the importance of lithology and weathering processes to the dominant anion in playa lakes of the western United States. Krauskopf (1967) discusses the fate of various elements and radicals during transport and the eventual arrival of sodium as the dominant cation and either sulfate or chloride as the chief anion. Hardie and Eugster (1970) discuss the evolution of dilute waters in closed basins into four groups: Group A ($Na-CO_3-SO_4-Cl$ brines), Group B (Na_2SO_4-NaCl brines), Group C ($Na-Mg-Ca-Cl$ brines) and Group D ($Na-Mg-SO_4-Cl$ brines). The precipitation of calcite, sepiolite, and gypsum are important points of bifurcation during the evolutionary process.

In nature two processes, evaporation and cooling, cause the deposition of sodium sulfate. Evaporation decreases the volume of water, and cooling decreases the solubility of the salt. Below the freezing point of water, ice decreases the available water for solution and the solubility of sodium sulfate minerals, causing mirabilite to form. This natural phenomenon accounts for the accumulation of intermittent beds of crystalline sodium sulfate in the bitter lakes of Canada, Russia, and the United States from which sodium sulfate may be harvested during winter. Crystallization from cooling also results from day and night temperature changes, particularly at high elevations where these changes can be extreme.

In the warmer climates, evaporation is the principal agent of precipitation of sodium sulfate. In those climates natural cooling is not employed in the production of sodium sulfate, but concentrated brines are pumped to the surface and cooled by refrigeration to yield mirabilite crystals.

Most sodium sulfate deposits of commercial significance contain permanent crystalline beds and brines at or near the surface. The crystalline beds can range in thickness from a few millimeters to several meters. They usually are interstratified with other salts, clay, silt, and organic matter. The impervious clays and silts help preserve a portion of the intermittent beds from redissolving. Brines generally occur within crystal beds, but in some deposits crystal beds are lacking.

In most deposits sodium sulfate predominates, with sodium and magnesium chlorides, magnesium sulfate, and carbonates also present. In more complex deposits, concentrations of potassium chloride and borates can be appreciable, depending on the location of the deposit in relation to the source of soluble salts.

The origin of sodium sulfate deposits has prompted the development of many theories. Variations in these theories mainly concern the source of alkalic salts that make up the deposits. Other factors considered are the origin of the basin and the agent of transportation and deposition of the sodium sulfate (Ruffel, 1970).

Early theories generally attributed the source of the salts to decomposition of granitic rocks. It was assumed that the feldspars in granites yielded soluble salts that were transported by surface waters, and that pyrite and other sulfides in these rocks were oxidized to sulfuric acid, which immediately dissolved some of the basic oxides to produce soluble sulfates (Wells, 1923).

Following an extensive study of the deposits of western Canada, Cole (1926) considered four possible sources for the sodium sulfate. These are: (1) underlying sands and shales, which contain small amounts of alkalies, and interbedded volcanic-ash beds, which contain an appreciable percentage of these salts; (2) connate waters in underlying strata; (3) springs in or near the deposits; and (4) surface deposits of bentonitic glacial drift. Cole concluded that the probable source was the salts contained in the bentonites, which are widely distributed in the glacial drift. Surface waters carrying calcium salts in solution react by base exchange with the alkali silicates, releasing the salts contained in the bentonite in the form of soluble sulfates, etc. These in turn are concentrated and deposited in undrained lake basins.

More recent investigators have attributed the source of some sodium sulfate to the decomposition of rocks and sediments, such as bentonite, that also contain sulfates, and from the leaching of buried beds of sulfates. Organic rich clay and shale also would produce sulfate through the oxidation of pyrite and marcasite (Davis, 1966). A subaerial means of transport is provided because many playa lakes are hydrologically coupled with the surrounding water table. Sulfides are found in the organic rich muds (containing stromatolites, etc.) and vegetative debris of some playa-lake sediments. The fermentation of organics under anaerobic conditions would produce hydrogen sulfide which could oxidize to sulfate (Reeves, 1968).

Grossman (1968) studied the sodium sulfate deposits of the Northern Great Plains of Canada and the United States and attributed the origin of those deposits to the solution of deeply buried marine evaporites. In his model, ground water from the Rocky Mountains moved downward and eastward into the Saskatchewan Sub-Basin during the Quaternary, leaching the buried evaporites of the Prairie Formation (Devonian). Ascending mineralized ground water during the late Pleistocene discharged into stratified drift where freezing segregated pure crystals of sodium sulfate in meromictic (chemically stratified and stagnant) lakes.

Occurrence, Reserves, and Production

Sodium sulfate deposits of sufficient size and purity for commercial mining are found in several countries (Fig. 1). The principal producing countries are Canada, Mexico, the United States, the USSR, and Spain. Less important are Argentina, Chile, Iran, and Turkey.

Canada

Numerous saline lakes containing sodium sulfate are known on the western plains of Canada but, at present, only nine lakes and five companies account for essentially all sodium sulfate production (personal communication). One deposit is in Alberta; the remainder are in Saskatchewan. Four companies use dredges to mine the permanent crystal beds (Watson, 1980). One additional lake in Saskatchewan is worked only intermittently.

The deposits occur in basins and depressions in glacial drift and lack apparent outlets. In general, the deposits are crystalline beds that underlie saturated brine lakes containing a few millimeters to approximately a meter of brine in the spring and summer. The deposits contain two recognizable phases of crystalline beds: intermittent and permanent.

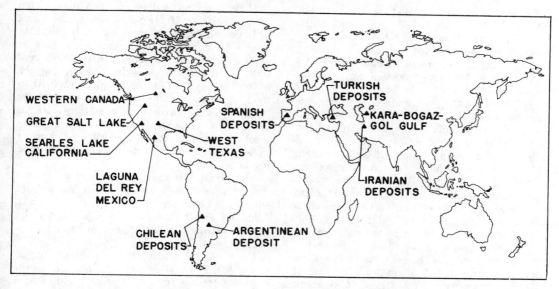

FIG. 1—*Principal producing sodium sulfate deposits of the world.*

The intermittent beds form on the bottom and along the shores of the lakes. They crystallize and redissolve with fluctuations in temperature. This can occur in a matter of hours, but as winter sets in less solution of the crystals occurs, causing the beds to become thicker and more compact.

The permanent beds underlying the lake usually are interstratified with thin layers of mud, clay, and organic matter. These beds range in thickness from less than one to several meters. At Ingebrigt Lake, permanent beds are reported (Cole, 1926) to cover an area of 2.7 km² with an average thickness of 6.7 m. In one part of the deposit a thickness of 42.4 m was measured. Cole estimated the tonnage of hydrous salt in Ingebrigt Lake to be 22.7 Mt. A more recent evaluation is 8.2 Mt of anhydrous sodium sulfate (Broughton, 1977).

Most of the deposits presently in production contain several million tons of sodium sulfate. The bulk of the Canadian reserve occurs in Saskatchewan. One deposit in Alberta contains 2.7 Mt (Watson, 1980). Estimates of total reserves in Saskatchewan range between 54.4 and 181 Mt. A more recent evaluation places the total anhydrous sodium sulfate reserve at 54.4 to 63.5 Mt and evaluated commercial reserves at 27.2 to 36.2 Mt (Broughton, 1977).

Production of natural sodium sulfate in 1979 was over 440 kt and is expected to be about 490 kt in 1980. Of this quantity nearly 200 kt was exported.

Current capacity is reported at approximately 742 kt/a. Production has never been close to reported capacity. About 270 kt/a of capacity belongs to Saskatchewan Minerals, a government corporation (Watson, 1980).

United States

Deposits of sodium sulfate are found in Arizona, California, Colorado, Idaho, Montana, Nevada, New Mexico, North Dakota, Oregon, Texas, Utah, Washington, and Wyoming. At the present time, production is chiefly from brine deposits at Searles Lake, CA, at Great Salt Lake, UT, and in West Texas. Small quantities have been produced from saline lake deposits in Wyoming. Most of the southwest brines are contained in dry lakes or playas underlain by beds of mirabilite, thenardite, and other evaporite salts. In the northwestern United States, the deposits associated with saline or intermittent dry lakes are similar in origin and composition to the Canadian deposits. Except for the brine deposits in West Texas, the deposits of the southwest are chemically more complex than the northern deposits.

California: California has several sodium sulfate deposits. Dale Lake, Durmid Hills, Soda Lake, and Danby Lake have a record of past production but are not now producing (Smith, 1966). Owens Lake has reserves of 10.9 Mt but has not produced any sodium sulfate (Kostick, 1980).

At Searles Lake, minerals have been extracted from brines since 1873. Sodium sulfate was first produced in 1914. Searles Lake currently is the leading source of natural sodium sulfate in the United States (Moulton, 1980). It probably has produced more sodium sulfate than any other deposit in the world. The annual value of the minerals production to date exceeds $30 million and total production to date exceeds $1 billion (Smith, 1979).

Sodium sulfate and other usable salts are produced at Searles Lake from brines underlying a large playa. The surface of the playa covers an estimated 155 km² but the central part, which forms the main deposit, is about 30 km² in area (Graubau, 1920). A hole drilled by Kerr-McGee Corp. in 1968 encountered 930 m of basin fill and bottomed in quartz-monzonite (Moulton, 1980). The salt deposits vary in areal extent and are listed in Table 3.

Brine occurs in the interstices of the salt deposits. Ions present in the brine are sodium, potassium, carbonate, bicarbonate, sulfate, chloride, and borate. The Upper Salt, Lower Salt, and Mixed Layer are the productive zones, each contributing a distinctive brine to meet the individual requirements of the plants. In some instances, solar concentration of the produced brine is used to improve plant efficiency (Moulton, 1980).

A plant expansion underway in 1977 was to bring capacity to 590 kt/a (Parkinson, 1977). The plant never operated as planned and in fact, in 1982 Kerr-McGee shut down about half of their sodium sulfate capacity, so output dropped to about 200 kt/a.

TABLE 3—Searles Lake Salt Deposits

Unit	Typical Thickness, m
Overburden mud (surface)	7
Upper salt	15
Parting mud	4
Lower salt	12
Bottom mud	30
Mixed layer	200+

Source: Smith, 1979.

Utah: Sodium sulfate is produced from natural brine at Great Salt Lake, Utah. Thick beds of mirabilite, intercalated with thin clay layers, have been found beneath the lake at several localities. Mirabilite crystallizes and sinks to the bottom of the lake during the winter. A layer of mirabilite 0.15 to 0.30 m thick occurs seasonally over large areas of the lake. Under favorable conditions, it is carried by winds and currents to the shore where it accumulates to a depth of 0.3 m or more. Strand deposits as thick as 3 m have been observed.

The Great Salt Lake is estimated to contain 3.8 Gt of salt, 342 Mt of which are sodium sulfate (Cohenour, 1966). Great Salt Lake Minerals and Chemicals Corp. estimates the playa contains 408 Mt of sodium sulfate (Kostick, 1980).

On the north end of the lake, near Ogden, Great Salt Lake Minerals and Chemical Corp. operates 69 km² of evaporation ponds and a plant complex for producing potassium sulfate and magnesium chloride. Sodium sulfate and common salt are byproducts. First production was reported in 1970. The operation has a sodium sulfate capacity between 22.7 and 32.9 kt/a.

Texas: Four sodium sulfate deposits are presently being exploited in Gaines and Terry Counties, by the Ozark-Mahoning Co. The company has produced sodium sulfate from brine in West Texas continuously since 1933. The Texas deposits underlie playas and occur as brine and crystalline mirabilite. The brine contains mainly sodium chloride and sodium sulfate, with lesser amounts of magnesium and potassium salts, and is produced from 30.5 m deep wells. A fifth deposit, Soda Lake, near Monahans in Ward County, was abandoned in 1970 after nearly 40 years of continuous operations, during which time over 1 Mt of anhydrous sodium sulfate were produced.

Cedar Lake deposit, near Seagraves, covers a surface area of about 21 km². Beds of crystalline salts are minimal, but strata containing saturated brines are found from near the surface to a depth of 30.5 m. The shallower strata contain brines of low salt content and are less productive. Richer brines come from beds 12 to 30.5 m below the surface. Brines from the Cedar Lake deposit contain about 10.5% sodium sulfate, 14% sodium chloride, and 1% each of magnesium and potassium.

Brownfield Lake deposit, 16 km east of

Brownfield, covers an area of about 4 km². The main deposit lies outside the boundary of the present dry lake surface. Saturated brine is produced from crystal beds at depths from 9 to 30.5 m. These beds, which contain thin layers of clay and silt, range from a meter to as much as 4 m in thickness. The brine contains 15% sodium sulfate and 10% sodium chloride. A solution mining project to extract the crystalline reserve has been developed.

Rich Lake deposit, 19 km north of Brownfield Lake, produces sodium sulfate bearing brine from a crystal bed averaging 2 m in thickness. The brine is transported by pipeline to the Brownfield Lake plant for processing. Ozark-Mahoning operates plants at Brownfield Lake and Cedar Lake. The combined capacity of the two plants is 159 kt/a.

A fourth deposit, Mound Lake, is located 13 km north of the Brownfield Lake plant. The lake has an area of 5 km² and lacustrine sediments occur to a depth of 24 m. The major portion of the reserve is brine similar in composition to that of Cedar Lake. A significant tonnage of mirabilite also exists. Mound Lake began producing in April 1981 and the brine also is transported to the Brownfield plant for processing.

Arizona: At the Camp Verde deposit in Yavapai County, solid beds of thenardite of varying thickness were mined for many years by Western Chemical Co. The deposit is unusual, as pure anhydrous sodium sulfate occurring in solid crystal form is rare. The deposit consists of layers of thenardite and other sodium salts, interbedded with clay, which form a part of the Verde Formation. The total thickness of the beds is at least 46 m. Mining was done in a large quarry and by underground room-and-pillar methods. The last mining was done by Arizona Chemical Co., a subsidiary of American Cyanamid Co., in 1934 (Ralston, 1949).

Nevada: Nevada's principal producing deposit in years past was Rhodes Marsh, near Mina in Mineral County. The deposit covers an area of 28 km². Production was confined mainly to the central portion of the deposit, where a 1- to 2-m thick bed of solid thenardite was mined (Ralston, 1949).

New Mexico: A sodium sulfate deposit is known near Alamogordo in Dona Ana County. In Eddy County, near the potash mines, brine wells containing appreciable amounts of sodium sulfate and magnesium sulfate have been reported (Lang, 1941). These wells were produced by Ozark-Mahoning from 1951 through 1957; the brines were trucked to Ozark's plant near Monahans, Texas, for processing. The wells depleted rapidly and were abandoned.

North Dakota: The sodium sulfate deposits of northwestern North Dakota are located in Divide, Williams, Mountrail, and Ward Counties. They are a southeasterly extension of the deposits in Saskatchewan. Sodium sulfate in North Dakota was first noted by the Lewis and Clark Expedition. Several lakes are known. Most of them were investigated and prospected by FERA (Federal Emergency Relief Administration) in 1934. An important reevaluation, based on drilling, was made by the US Bureau of Mines in 1948 (Binyon, 1952).

The sodium sulfate content is generally high; sodium chloride, magnesium sulfate, and calcium sulfate are the main impurities. The US Bureau of Mines reported tonnages occurring in 18 lakes. Nine of the largest were estimated to each contain over 1 Mt of Glauber's salt. The major portion of the reserve occurs in the permanent and intermittent crystal beds and only a minor portion occurs in the form of brine. Total reserves are reported to be 25 Mt of Glauber's salt or 11 Mt of anhydrous sodium sulfate (Binyon, 1952; Crosby, 1973).

Grenora Lake No. 2, the largest deposit, covers 2 km². Drilling done by FERA showed the maximum thickness of the permanent crystal bed to be 24 m and the average thickness to be 3.66 m. The deposit was estimated by the US Bureau of Mines to contain 5 Mt of Glauber's salt or 2.2 Mt of anhydrous sodium sulfate (Binyon, 1952). Drilling conducted by Ozark-Mahoning in 1977 generally corroborated the Bureau's estimate. Grenora Lake No. 2 is owned by Ozark-Mahoning, but is not favorably located for economical exploitation.

Other States: A number of deposits in Washington, Wyoming, and Montana are not considered economically important because of their location and size, even though their composition is similar to the Canadian deposits.

Mexico

A large evaporite deposit containing a high concentration of sodium sulfate is located in northern Coahuila, approximately 160 km north of Torreon. The evaporite lens consists of glauberite and bloedite, this last one as thin beds and irregular aggregates.

The crystal bed is 20 km long and 5 km

wide, with 30 m thickness at the center. The main concentration of bloedite (a double sulfate salt of sodium and magnesium) is found as a layer 1 to 2 m thick, located about 8 m below the top of the evaporite mass. Mirabilite and epsomite occur in minor proportions. The formation underlying the crystal bed is impervious clay and silt containing some sodium chloride. Glauberite occurs as thin tabular crystals, while bloedite is found in massive concentrations. The intercrystalline spaces, amounting to as much as 25% of the evaporite mass, are partially filled with clay, and the rest with a brine in equilibrium with the solid phase.

A composite average analysis of brines from a depth of 20 m from several wells in the lake bed showed 18.46% sodium sulfate, 5.91% sodium chloride, and 5.28% magnesium sulfate.

Analysis of several cores of the crystal bed showed 35 to 36% sodium sulfate and only 1.5 to 1.8% sodium chloride. Magnesium sulfate ranged from 4.7 to 12.7%.

Estimated reserves are approximately 160 Mt of anhydrous sodium sulfate.

Sodium sulfate is produced at Laguna del Rey by Quimica del Rey, S. A. a subsidiary of Industrias Peñoles, S. A. de C. V. The plant was built in 1963 with a capacity of 30 kt/a. Present capacity is 440 kt/a.

Other deposits are known to occur in northern Coahuila and in the state of Chihuahua, but in size and sodium sulfate content they are smaller than the deposit at Laguna del Rey.

Sulfato de Viesca recovers 20 kt/a of sodium sulfate as a byproduct from production of sodium chloride from natural brine. The plant is near Viesca in the southwestern part of Coahuila.

Deposits of thenardite occur in the state of Sonora near the municipality of Bacadehuachi some 190 km northeast of Hermosillo. Outcroppings of thenardite and efflorescences in the soil occur discontinuously along the east side of the Bacadehuachi Valley in an area approximately 6 km in length and 4 km in width. The deposits occur within the Baucarit Group (Oligocene). The outcroppings are covered by unconsolidated surface material, which varies in thickness between 10 and 30 m.

Four workings have been developed within this area. In the largest pit, the Oro Blanco, the thenardite is reported to attain a thickness of 20 m. Analyses of selected samples from the Oro Blanco ran between 95 to 99% Na_2SO_4 (Anon., 1981).

During 1982, Para Mex, the Mexicanized affiliate of the Spanish company Tolsa, had conducted some exploration of the Oro Blanco and was evaluating the commercial possibilities of producing sodium sulfate from this area (personal communication).

According to US Bureau of Mines reports, Mexico produced 128 kt of sodium sulfate during 1978. Quimica del Rey, the country's main producer, states it produced 298 kt in 1978. Approximately 30% of 1980 production is destined for South American markets (Watson, 1980).

Union of Soviet Socialist Republics (USSR)

Many deposits containing sodium sulfate occur in the USSR, in a large area from the Black Sea to western China and farther north into west-central and eastern Siberia. The economically important deposits are in the Aral and Caspian depressions and in the Kalunda Steppe in Kazakhstan. While literature on sodium sulfate deposits in the USSR is reportedly fairly extensive, it is not readily available and requires translation. The reader is referred to a paper (Dort and Dort, 1970) that contains a summary of several publications on Russian deposits.

The largest known occurrence of sodium sulfate in the world is in the Kara-Bogaz-Gol Gulf, an embayment on the eastern side of the Caspian Sea. It is separated from the Caspian by a bar with a narrow strait through which water flows from the sea into the embayment. Sixty-five years ago the gulf covered 18 000 km² and had a depth of 12 m. Owing to evaporation, the Gulf has shrunk in area to 10 000 km² and in depth to about 3 m and has a much higher saline content (Garbell, 1963).

Kolosov (1974) reported that Kara-Bogaz-Gol experienced a final phase of intense desiccation between 1939 and 1948. Seawater now moves across the bar from the Caspian Sea at a reduced rate of 9 to 11 km³ per year. The movement of seawater into the bay has apparently reached equilibrium with evaporation. Since 1957 or 1958 no decline in water level or constriction of the bay's area or appreciable change in brine composition was observed. Gypsum and glauberite were being precipitated out of the saturated brine throughout the bay. Bloedite (astrakanite) and halite were being deposited locally. Some carbonates were being deposited in the zone of mixing adjacent to the strait.

It has been reported very recently that the

completion of a dam across the mouth of the Kara-Bogaz-Gol may halt the future supply of sodium sulfate bearing water from the Caspian Sea (Anon., 1983).

In 1924, Kara-Bogaz-Gol was estimated to contain 1 Gt of sodium sulfate (Grabau, 1920). More recent estimates of 2 Gt have been reported (Goudge, 1960; Hemy, 1969).

The Aral Sea is considered to be another rich source of sodium sulfate. Some sulfate is produced in the central Asian republics that adjoin it. Lakes in western Siberia and in Kazakhstan are good sources, but are not presently produced except on a local scale. The steppe region around Kalunda, in Alta Kray, has a number of lakes rich in sodium sulfate. A sulfate combine has been established on Lake Kuchuk, the largest of these (Hemy, 1969).

Sodium sulfate and magnesium salts are produced from the Kara-Bogaz-Gol Gulf by Karabogazgolsulphate Combine. It is impossible to determine the amount of natural sodium sulfate produced in the USSR. An estimate is that 318 kt are produced annually, mostly from the Kara-Bogaz-Gol deposit (USBM data). Watson (1980) reports capacity at 600 kt/a.

Spain

Sodium sulfate from deposits of solid thenardite is produced in Spain. The El Castillar deposit is located in Villarrubia de Santiago, Toledo Province, where beds of thenardite 5 to 6 m thick are mined by room-and-pillar methods. The deposit extends over an area of 30 km² and contains probable reserves of 200 Mt. The composition of the ore is reported as 70 to 75% sodium sulfate, 11 to 17% calcium sulfate, 0.4 to 0.6% sodium chloride, 3 to 9% clay, and 1 to 5% moisture (Rovira, 1960). The mine, and a plant producing anhydrous sodium sulfate, is operated by Union Salinera de Espana S.A.

Criaderos Minerales y Derivados S.A. (Crimidesa) mines glauberite at Cerezo del Rio Tiron in Burgos Province.

Another company, S.A. Salquisa, recently began production of sodium sulfate by solution mining of glauberite. It is a joint venture of Industrias Penoles S.A. de C.V. of Mexico and Spanish mining interests. Rated capacity is 75 kt/a.

Total production of natural sodium sulfate from Spain is approximately 150 kt/a and has shown a slight increase over the last few years (Watson, 1980).

Turkey

Natural sodium sulfate is produced in Turkey, although output is not large. First production recorded was in 1963, when 1264 t were produced. Output has increased steadily, and production in 1978 was about 80 kt.

Several saline lakes in southwestern Turkey contain appreciable amounts of sodium sulfate. Tersakan Lake is located about 160 km south of Ankara, near the town of Cihanbeyli. The lake, 13 km long and 4 km wide, covers an area of 52 km². Its sodium sulfate content is in excess of 8%. Sodium chloride and magnesium sulfate are present in amounts less than 5 and 2%, respectively, and the calcium sulfate content is less than 1%. Where the lake water has been impounded to induce evaporation, the sodium sulfate content of the brine increases. In the bottom of the ponds crystalline layers over 95% pure have formed.

At Aci Gol, a large lake 56 km east of Denizli, the saline content is similar to that of Tersakan Lake, although the sodium content is slightly lower and that of sodium chloride slightly higher. Aci Gol is over 26 km long, nearly 10 km wide, and has a surface area of about 200 km².

Three companies currently produce sodium sulfate—Alkim Alkali Kimya A.S., Sodas Sanayii A.S., and Otuzbir Kimya ve Sanayii Ltd.

Argentina

Many salt lakes and playas, some of which contain rich deposits of sodium sulfate, are located in Argentina, on the arid plateaus and in the intermontane valleys of the Andes (Wells, 1923).

A large playa deposit of mirabilite is located in northwestern Argentina in Jujuy Province. The deposit is in the Andes at an elevation of 3353 m. A permanent bed of mirabilite covering 53 km² occurs in the middle of a dry lake bed. The permanent bed, covered by a thin layer of sodium chloride, calcium sulfate, and sand, is reported to be 4.6 m thick at the center of the deposit and gradually thinner toward the edges. Subsurface waters from melting snow in the surrounding mountains feed into the lake and thus furnish a supply of brine year round.

Production of sodium sulfate in Argentina was 43 kt in 1978. Sulfarentina SAMIC, a subsidiary of CADIPSA, produces sodium sulfate at LaLoberia, Santa Cruz Province, and at Salar del Rio Grande, Salta Province.

Total output from Sulfargentina is about 18 kt/a (Watson, 1980).

Another producer of natural sodium sulfate in Argentina is Pagrun S.A.M.I.C.

Chile

Small amounts of natural sodium sulfate are produced from playa deposits in northern Chile. The deposits are in the Atacama Desert, which lies along the west side of the Andes between the mountains and the Pacific Ocean, at an elevation of about 1067 m.

Chile produced 20 kt of natural sodium sulfate in 1978. Some additional natural output is byproduct from the nitrate industry. Total production from Chile in 1979 was nearly 64 kt of natural sodium sulfate from Sociedad Quimica y Miniera de Chile S.A. (SOQUIMICH). A new anhydrous sodium sulfate plant is reported to be opened in Maria Elena in the Antofagusta region (Watson, 1980).

Africa

A series of salt pans, some of which contain sodium sulfate, occurs in the deserts and velds of the South African uplands. To date, none have been commercially exploited. In 1968, however, Associated Sulfate (Pty.) Ltd. was established to build a plant to produce sodium sulfate, using raw materials from solar salt pans and effluent from the Rustenburg platinum plant.

About 110 Mt of sodium sulfate reserves exist in the Makgadikgadi Basin of Botswana. Some Japanese developers were contemplating the development of the deposit for sodium sulfate and sodium carbonate (Kostick, 1980; Massey, 1973). However, by early 1981 no plans to develop the deposit had been formalized (Lefond, 1981).

No production of natural sodium sulfate in South Africa was reported between 1975 and 1979 (USBM data).

Antarctica

Since mirabilite is the first mineral, after ice, to appear in freezing seawater, it is not surprising that several occurrences have been noted in Antarctica. Mirabilite efflorescences commonly occur on the surfaces of rocks, glaciers, and sea ice; some occurrences are also reported farther inland.

Sodium sulfate has been described in coastal lakes which have been elevated and separated from the sea due to isostatic rebound. Other occurrences are reported in impoundments behind glaciers. The inland deposits are probably a result of seawater-derived salts transported with snow and accumulated in local depressions.

Though these occurrences are not economic, they are of geological interest. The reader will find them described by Dort and Dort (1970) along with a discussion of the low temperature origin of sodium sulfate.

Iran

Iran produced 25 kt of sodium sulfate in 1976 and 1977 and 22.7 kt in 1978 (Watson, 1980). Production is presumably from Urmiah Lake (also called Rezaiieh) located in northwestern Iran (Jolly, 1976).

Byproduct Sodium Sulfate

For many years, manufactured sodium sulfate has been a byproduct or coproduct from the production of other chemicals. Important sources are:

1) Manufacture of viscose rayon. Sodium sulfate is generated in an acid spin bath by the neutralization of sodium hydroxide used to prepare the viscose solution. In the past this source has been of almost equal importance with natural sodium sulfate on a worldwide basis. The growing popularity of other synthetic fibers, however, has resulted in reduced production. Of particular significance has been the replacement of rayon tire cord by other synthetic fibers, fiberglass, and steel. Nevertheless, rayon manufacture continues to be an important source of supply.

2) Manufacture of hydrochloric acid from sodium chloride and sulfuric acid in the Mannheim furnace, and similar processes. In the Hargreaves process, sulfur, steam, and air are substituted for sulfuric acid. Many years ago the Mannheim furnace was the main source of sodium sulfate, and this chemical was truly a coproduct rather than a byproduct. Because the salt discharged from the furnace tended to form cakes, it was named "salt cake." This name remains as a trade designation for low-grade sodium sulfate. Large amounts of hydrochloric acid are produced today as a byproduct in the manufacture of chlorinated hydrocarbons. As a result, the Mannheim furnace process is generally considered to be obsolete; however, in certain geographical areas and in particular raw-material situations it

continues to be an economically significant source of sodium sulfate.

3) As a byproduct in numerous other processes wherein certain sodium salts are converted to acids by reaction with sulfuric acid, or sodium alkalies are neutralized with sulfuric acid as part of the process. Examples are the processing of chromium ores to produce sodium dichromate, and the production of lithium salts, boric acid, phenol, formic acid, and various catalysts.

As noted, natural sodium sulfate has captured about half the market in the United States and had become increasingly important worldwide during the past two decades. Although vast resources are available, producers of the natural material always are threatened by byproduct sources. With the greatly increased emphasis on pollution control many dilute waste waters containing sodium sulfate can no longer be discharged into streams and rivers. Hence treatment processes usually attempt to recover any materials of value, such as sodium sulfate. The material is then sold at whatever price it will bring, whether or not the price covers the cost of recovery. Conceivably the removal of sulfur from fuels or combustion products can generate sulfur compounds, which may compete with sodium sulfate for certain uses. The outlook for long-term growth in the natural sodium sulfate business is not particularly promising, although natural sources will continue to be vital.

Worldwide total production of sodium sulfate is reported at 4153 kt for 1978, whereas productive capacity was listed at 5 Mt (Kostick, 1980). Natural production represents about 41% of world total output (Watson, 1980).

End Uses

The principal use of sodium sulfate is in the manufacture of kraft paper pulp, also known as sulfate pulp. In the process, the sodium sulfate is reduced chemically to sulfide forms, which are the active constituent of pulping liquor. In the second edition of this book (1949), Ralston reported that 179 kg of sodium sulfate were required to produce 1 t of kraft paper pulp. Since that time, process improvements have reduced this figure to approximately 40 kg/t. Technological developments in the paper industry indicate that the amount of sodium sulfate required will continue to decline.

Certain new pulp-bleaching processes utilize raw materials that produce waste streams containing sodium and sulfur, which may be utilized instead of sodium sulfate for kraft pulping. Likewise the neutral soda semi-chemical pulping process generates a liquor which may be utilized for kraft pulping in place of sodium sulfate. Some newer paper mills combine both processes economically (Anon, 1971a). Waste streams from caustic washing of catalytically cracked gasolines can be converted readily to sodium sulfide compounds, used as replacement for sodium sulfate in kraft mills. The authors estimate that perhaps 20% of the requirements of the kraft paper industry in the southeastern United States are now supplied from various waste streams.

Even though new pulping methods and recovery techniques will reduce the amount of sodium sulfate required per ton of kraft paper, total usage of sodium sulfate may not decrease because the sulfate-pulp process is a major paper-making technique. Kraft pulp produces the strongest paper, its production continues to grow worldwide, and it is by far the dominant type of pulp being produced. We expect it to occupy this position in the foreseeable future.

Another important consumer of sodium sulfate is the glass industry. Soda ash is the major chemical raw material for glass manufacture, and sodium sulfate may supply some of its sodium needs. For certain types of glass the sulfur content of sodium sulfate is useful; it prevents scum formation on the surface of molten glass in the refining stage. For technical reasons most sodium sulfate consumed in the glass industry is used in the production of flat glass. Lesser quantities are used in the production of containers and other glass products.

For the detergent industry, sodium sulfate is an ideal filler and diluent, as it is noncorrosive, neutral, and cheap. In addition, it is claimed to have very mild detergent properties. In 1971 and 1972 the detergent industry went through a revolution in the United States as governmental pressure to reduce phosphate discharges in municipal sewage required the reformulation of detergents. Nonphosphate and low-phosphate detergents are now on the market. Further changes may be expected in the future. The result was an increase of sodium sulfate in detergents. Currently, about one-third of dry home laundry detergent is sodium sulfate.

A number of other uses of sodium sulfate are significant. In the United States it is an ingredient of various stock foods and remedies, probably because of its mild laxative properties. It is useful in the production of synthetic sponges. In Europe and Japan it is used in dyeing and for the production of sodium sulfide and related compounds. In the United States these uses are minor.

New uses for sodium sulfate may have the potential to become significant in the future. A joint industry-government project sponsored by EPA (Environmental Protection Agency) discovered that small amounts of sodium sulfate added to low-sulfur coal before burning improve the performance of high-temperature electrostatic precipitators (Anon., 1980). The project was conducted at a power plant of the Gulf Power Co. near Panama City, FL. Partners in the investigation were the Industrial Environmental Research Laboratory of EPA as well as Southern Company Services, Birmingham, AL, and The Electric Power Research Institute, Palo Alto, CA.

Another new use involves sodium sulfate as a constituent in molten salt used to decompose pesticide wastes. A third new use may have a greater potential for the future. This use takes advantage of the phase change properties of anhydrous sodium sulfate to Glauber's salt as a storage material for solar heat. Of nine commercial units being offered in 1980, four utilize sodium sulfate (Eissenberg, 1980; Holland, 1980).

It is difficult to estimate worldwide consumption patterns because of great variations from one country to the next. Canada, Sweden, and Finland are large producers of kraft paper pulp, and perhaps 95% of the sodium sulfate consumed in those countries is used for this purpose. In the United Kingdom, France, West Germany, Japan, and many other countries, paper production is small, so the major consumption of sodium sulfate is in detergents, glassmaking, production of other chemicals, dyeing processes, and miscellaneous uses.

The authors' estimate for consumption in the United States is as follows:

Kraft paper pulp	55%
Detergents	35%
Glass	5%
Other uses	5%

The foregoing does not include the use of materials which contain both sodium and sulfur values that are used interchangeably with sodium sulfate in the paper industry. Worldwide consumption patterns probably are not far from the estimate shown for the United States.

Product Specifications

The old salt cake nomenclature continues to be used for material of lower quality. The product of the Mannheim furnace, for example, may contain only 97% Na_2SO_4. Some natural material from Canadian deposits may be as low in grade, although most of the plants are now producing higher quality sodium sulfate. The salt cake grade is quite acceptable to the paper industry.

The other designation is anhydrous sodium sulfate, technical grade, which usually has a purity in excess of 99% Na_2SO_4, and frequently may be specified as 99.5%. Different consumers for the same end use may have quite different specifications. In some cases particle size and bulk density are important.

The decahydrate, known as Glauber's salt (mineralogically, mirabilite), at one time was an item of commerce. In virtually all uses anhydrous sodium sulfate is preferred today because of savings in freight and ease of handling. Small quantities of Glauber's salt are still sold for some special uses.

Processing

Natural sodium sulfate is produced by five companies in Canada (Ruffel, 1970, 1972; Broughton, 1977; Watson, 1980). Saskatchewan Minerals, Sodium Sulphate Division, a corporation owned by the Province of Saskatchewan, operates plants at Chaplin Lake, Bishopric, Sybouts, and Ingebrigt Lake. The Bishopric plant is at Frederick Lake and has operated on an intermittent basis in recent years. Ormiston Mining and Smelting Co., Ltd., has a plant at Ormiston on Shoe Lake; Midwest Chemicals, Ltd., at Palo, produces from Whiteshore Lake; and Francana Minerals, at Cabri, operates on Snakehole Lake and at the Alsask Lake deposit, which formerly was operated by Sodium Sulphate (Saskatchewan, Ltd.). All of the foregoing are located in Saskatchewan. In Alberta the only operation is the Metiskow Lake plant of Alberta Sodium Sulphate, Ltd.

Many Canadian producers utilize seasonal temperature differences to assist in the processing of the sodium sulfate deposits. Brine is allowed to form on the lake bed and becomes nearly saturated in the late summer months. At that time it is pumped to large reservoirs which may be over 3 m deep. When cold weather sets in, Glauber's salts crystallize from the saturated brine. The residual mother liquor is drained off; it contains most of the magnesium sulfate and sodium chloride impurities, which may be returned to the lake bed. After draining, the Glauber's salt is harvested and accumulated in stockpiles at the plant sites.

At some of the plants of Ormiston Mining and Smelting, Francana Minerals, Saskatchewan Minerals, and Alberta Sodium Sulphate, the supply of Glauber's salt crystals from the reservoirs is supplemented by salt dredge mined from the permanent bed and pumped to the plant. At the Metiskow Lake operations of Alberta Sodium Sulphate, solution mining also is practiced. A heated solution is injected into the crystal bed to generate a brine, which is pumped to the reservoirs for subsequent chilling and crystallization. In some of the Saskatchewan lakes the reserves are present principally as brine, which can be pumped directly to the reservoir.

Obviously the Canadian plants are somewhat dependent on nature to produce the crystals of Glauber's salt. Drought or other unusual conditions can affect the production cycle. The plants try to keep more than one year's supply of Glauber's salt in their stockpiles to keep production from being interrupted by such conditions. This method has proved very successful in Canada, producing a salt cake of high quality.

To prepare a salable anhydrous product the Glauber's salt must be dehydrated. Because of the inverse solubility of sodium sulfate (i.e., less soluble at higher temperatures), this is not a simple straightforward operation. In the early days dehydration was done in large rotary kilns, some of which were fired by lignite. The Sybouts plant of Saskatchewan Minerals continues to use this process.

When Glauber's salt is melted, the solubility of anhydrous sodium sulfate in the water of crystallization is exceeded, causing precipitation. The balance of the water must be evaporated to produce an anhydrous product. Ozark-Mahoning submerged combustion evaporators are used for this purpose by Ormiston Mining and Smelting, Midwest Chemicals, Alberta Sodium Sulphate, and Saskatchewan Minerals at the Ingebrigt Lake plant. Francana Minerals utilizes triple effect vacuum evaporators. Another type, called the Holland evaporator, provides for intimate contact between the solution and hot products of combustion by means of mechanical agitation. These are in use at the Bishopric plant of Saskatchewan Minerals and the Alsask plant of Francana Minerals.

At all plants, the anhydrous salts precipitated in the evaporators may be separated from the saturated solution by mechanical means, including centrifuges, and the wet salt finally dried in direct-fired rotary kilns. Parallel-flow dryers are now preferred for ease of control and fuel economy, whereas in the older processes countercurrent flow was used in the dryers.

United States

Each US producer of sodium sulfate has a different process dictated by the nature of the deposit being worked. Two plants operated by Ozark-Mahoning from brine deposits in West Texas, one near Brownfield and the other near Seagraves, use a process developed in the early 1930s for a plant near Monahans, Texas (Weisman, 1953). The Monahans plant closed in 1970 because the deposit was essentially exhausted. The Ozark submerged combustion burner used at the old Monahans plant probably represented the first commercial application of submerged combustion in the United States.

The Texas brines contain both sodium chloride and sodium sulfate, as well as smaller amounts of magnesium and potassium salts. At the Brownfield plant a portion of the brine is pumped through the Permian salt bed to introduce sodium chloride. The high sodium chloride content depresses the solubility of sodium sulfate, improving its extraction. At the Seagraves plant sufficient sodium chloride is present in the brine; additional salt is not needed. The Texas climate does not lend itself to the production of Glauber's salt by atmospheric chilling, so mechanical refrigeration and heat exchange are required. The Glauber's salt formed in this manner is filtered and washed, yielding a product of high purity.

Melting and dehydration of Glauber's salt is accomplished by the Ozark submerged combustion system, which utilizes gas burners submerged under the surface of the solution, with products of combustion in direct contact with the liquid phase. Centrifuges separate the anhydrous crystals from the saturated solution, which is returned to the evaporators. The crystals are dried in parallel-flow rotary kilns.

Use of the submerged combustion system largely eliminates scaling problems, which can occur in tubular evaporators from the inverted-solubility character of sodium sulfate solutions. Some plants operate successfully with evaporators that transfer steam heat through tubes to the saturated solution; however, as noted, many Canadian plants have adopted the Ozark submerged combustion method. Most byproduct plants use multiple-effect vacuum evaporators.

Newer plants use vapor recompression evaporators to achieve high fuel economy. High velocities in the tubes minimize scaling problems. The Brownfield plant was converted to vapor recompression evaporation in 1983 because of the high cost of natural gas.

The largest production of natural sodium sulfate in the US still comes from Searles Lake, CA, even though output is much less than in the past. Prior to 1982, the Kerr-McGee Chemical Corp. plants made about 500,000 tons of sodium sulfate annually. As mentioned earlier, a planned plant expansion did not result in increased production and the Trona plant, representing about half of the total sodium sulfate capacity, was shut down in 1982. The West End plant now is Kerr-McGee's only source of sodium sulfate.

The Searles Lake brines are complex and a number of salable products are extracted. At Kerr-McGee's West End plant, sodium sulfate is recovered along with soda ash and borax. Mixed brines are first carbonated with carbon dioxide to precipitate sodium bicarbonate, which is removed by filtration. The decarbonated brine is cooled to crystallize borax. This borax is separated from the brine, which is then cooled further to produce a crop of Glauber's salt. After it is removed, a final cooling recovers a second crop of borax. By heating, the sodium bicarbonate is converted to soda ash and the borax is either crystallized as a hydrate or dehydrated to the anhydrous form. The Glauber's salt is washed, melted, and recrystallized as anhydrous sodium sulfate. The following description of the Trona plant is included because it is of interest, even though the sodium sulfate part is shut down.

In the Trona main plant cycle there were three major process plants. The brines from the lake were cooled to produce a crop of Glauber's salts which were removed and dried to sodium sulfate. The resultant mother liquor from this step was processed further to recover potash and borax. A different brine was treated in a liquid-liquid solvent extraction plant to recover boron values as boric acid. After it was removed, mixed sodium and potassium sulfates were precipitated by evaporation and these mixed sulfates were fed to the potassium sulfate plant. The Trona carbonation plant was somewhat similar to the West End plant in that carbon dioxide precipitated sodium bicarbonate which was filtered and removed. Borax was then precipitated by cooling. Burkeite, a double salt of sodium sulfate and sodium carbonate, finally was recovered and fed to the Argus process.

In the Argus plant, which is the newest addition, brines from the lake are mixed with burkeite solutions and streams from other plants to recover additional soda ash. Nothing has been published since Moulton (1980), so the details of present plant practice at Trona have not been revealed.

The other producer of natural sodium sulfate in the United States is Great Salt Lake Minerals and Chemicals Corp. The plant began production late in 1970. The initial rated capacity announced was 15 kt/a of sodium sulfate, plus 220 kt of potassium sulfate and 90 kt of anhydrous magnesium chloride. Solar evaporation is an important step in the processing, with several complex salts harvested from evaporation ponds for further refining in the plant by proprietary processes. Early operations were beset with difficulties but these problems were overcome. Very little has been published on production processes used by the company. According to company advertising literature the process used in 1980 was dependent on harvesting Glauber's salts from solar ponds where salts were deposited during the winter months, similar to the Canadian deposits. The Glauber's salt is melted and anhydrous sodium sulfate precipitated by adding NaCl to decrease the solubility of the sodium sulfate. A high-purity sodium sulfate is the final product.

Great Salt Lake contains tremendous reserves of sodium sulfate and no doubt will be a factor of some importance in the future. A railway causeway across the lake, which affects the concentration of salts on both sides, has created controversy. When this controversy is resolved, the lake's concentration of sodium sulfate and the production of this and other salts could be drastically altered.

Mexico

The brine processed at Quimica del Rey is very strong and probably saturated. It contains more than 26% sodium sulfate and appreciable amounts of chlorides and magnesium. About 100 wells produce the brine from a depth of approximately 12 m. The brine temperature is 25°C before precooling with the spent brine. The cooled brine is fed to a vacuum crystallizer where it is cooled to 13°C by evaporative cooling, causing Glauber's salt to crystallize. The slurry is thickened, filtered, and melted. Evaporation is accomplished in triple-effect evaporators. Final drying is in countercurrent-fired rotary kilns. Part of the mother liquor is processed further for recovery of magnesia products while the balance goes to waste.

The most recent expansion of this plant occurred in 1980. Six separate production lines are capable of producing 440 kt/a. It is expected that one line will be converted to recovery of magnesium sulfate from the spent brine.

Other Countries

Little is published about processing in other countries. It can be reasonably assumed that methods used are similar to those used in the United States, Mexico, and Canada, wherein chilling by natural or mechanical means precipitates Glauber's salt, allowing separation from other salts. The Glauber's salt would then be dried to anhydrous sodium sulfate.

In Argentina saturated brine from a lake bed is pumped to crystallization tanks, where great night and day temperature variation results in precipitation of Glauber's salt. This is possible because the plant site is at an elevation of 3353 m. The Glauber's salt is melted by heating; the precipitated anhydrous sodium sulfate is then separated and dried. There is no evaporation of water, so the saturated solutions probably are recycled through the system.

Deposits in Spain, one of the few countries where thenardite is the starting material, are mined underground and present special problems because the mineral contains an appreciable amount of calcium sulfate in the form of glauberite (Na_2SO_4, $CaSO_4$). Countercurrent leaching at temperatures between 35 and 40°C dissolves most of the sodium sulfate, leaving the calcium sulfate undissolved. The solids, which probably contain other insoluble impurities, are settled in large Dorr thickeners. A second leaching step with water at 29°C results in maximum recovery of sodium sulfate. Evaporation is carried out in a single-effect vacuum evaporator with forced circulation. Final drying is done in a fluid bed dryer with hot air heated by steam (Rovira, 1960).

Prices

Published price information for sodium sulfate usually only approximates the true market price. In the United States prices usually are based on quotations from byproduct sources located near consuming points. Because producers of the natural salt are located at great distances from most customers, the f.o.b. plant value for natural material may be much less than the published price. On the other hand,

in periods of shortages and rising prices, published information often lags behind actual selling levels.

The May 16, 1983 *Chemical Marketing Reporter* quoted sodium sulfate in bulk carload lots, works, freight equalized, in the East, at $90 to $96 per short ton. It also quoted sodium sulfate, West, bulk, carload lots, works, freight equalized, at $90 to $96 per short ton.

United States tariff rates for sodium sulfate are as follows:

	Most Favored Nation		Non-Most Favored Nation
	Jan. 1, 1982	Jan. 1, 1987	Jan. 1, 1982
Crude (salt cake)	Free	Free	Free
Anhydrous	40¢/t	34¢/t	$3.05/t
Crystallized	3% ad val.	2.5% ad val.	4% ad val.

For tax purposes a depletion allowance of 14% for both domestic and foreign deposits is permitted by the Internal Revenue Service.

Acknowledgment

The authors acknowledge the valuable assistance and suggestions received from Dennis S. Kostick, Sodium Compounds Commodity Specialist, US Bureau of Mines, and Charles W. Tandy, Vice President, Ozark-Mahoning Co.

Bibliography and References

Anon., 1967, "The Sodium Sulfate Industry in Saskatchewan," Unpublished Report, Industrial Minerals Div., Saskatchewan Dept. Mineral Resources, 8 pp.

Anon., 1970, "Great Salt Lake Starts $30 Million Pond-Plant Complex," *Chemical & Engineering News*, Vol. 48, No. 51, Dec. 7, p. 17.

Anon., 1970a, "Utah Company Gets Set to Tap Mineral Wealth of Great Salt Lake," *Engineering & Mining Journal*, Vol. 171, No. 4, Apr., pp. 67–70.

Anon., 1971, "Chemical Profile, Sodium Sulfate," 2nd Rev., *Chemical Marketing Reporter*, Oct. 1.

Anon., 1971a, "1971 World Review," *Pulp and Paper*, World Review ed., pp. 150–154.

Anon., 1972, "Business Newsletter," *Chemical Week*, Vol. 110, No. 20, May 17, p. 17.

Anon., 1972a, "Harvest of Sulfate of Potashes to be 3–4 Times Greater in 1972," *The Mining Record*, Oct. 11, p. 3.

Anon., 1972b, "Petrochemicals Get the Emphasis in Mexican Buildup," *Chemical Week*, Vol. 110, No. 20, May 17, p. 33.

Anon., 1972c, "Sodium Sulphate: World Survey of Production, Consumption and Prices with Special Reference to Future Trends," Roskill Information Services, Ltd., London, England.

Anon., 1980, *Industrial Research and Development*, Vol. 22, No. 10, Oct., pp. 67–69.

Anon., 1981, "Evaluacion Preliminar del Yacimiento de Sulfato de Sodio en Bacadehuachi, Son.," Informe de Avance, Direccion de Mineria, Geologica y Energeticos, State of Sonora, Mexico, Oct.

Anon., 1983, "Mineral Notes," *Industrial Minerals,* No. 187, Apr., p. 68.

Ashley, B.E., 1972, "Mineral Industry of Mexico," Preprint, *Minerals Yearbook,* US Bureau of Mines, 13 pp.

Bateman, A.M., 1950, *Economic Mineral Deposits,* 2nd ed., John Wiley and Sons, pp. 194–196.

Binyon, E.O., 1952, "North Dakota Sodium Sulfate Deposits," Report of Investigations 4880, US Bureau of Mines, 41 pp.

Broughton, P.L., 1977, "Natural Salt Cake in Canada," *Industrial Minerals,* No. 121, Oct., pp. 51–59.

Cohenour, R.E., 1966, "Salt Inventory of Great Salt Lake," *Second Symposium on Salt,* Vol. 1, Northern Ohio Geological Society, p. 212.

Cole, J.W., 1970, "Mineral Industry of Chile," *Minerals Yearbook,* Vol. 3, US Bureau of Mines, pp. 197–206.

Cole, L.H., 1926, "Sodium Sulphate of Western Canada," No. 646, Canada Dept. of Mines, pp. 26–27, 74–78, 113.

Corrick, J.D., 1972, "Mineral Industry of Spain," Preprint, *Minerals Yearbook,* US Bureau of Mines, 21 pp.

Crosby, E.J., 1973, "Sodium Sulfate," Mineral and Water Resources of North Dakota, North Dakota Geological Survey Bulletin 63, pp. 151–154.

Dana, E.S., 1932, *A Textbook of Mineralogy,* 4th ed., John Wiley and Sons, pp. 809–810.

Davis, S.N., and DeWiest, R.J.M., 1966, *Hydrogeology,* John Wiley and Sons, pp. 108–109.

Dewey, L.S., 1972, "Mineral Industry of Argentina," Preprint, *Minerals Yearbook 1972,* Vol. 3, US Bureau of Mines, 11 pp.

Dietrich, R.V., 1969, *Mineral Tables,* McGraw-Hill Book Co.

Dort, W., Jr. and Dort, D.S., 1970, "Low Temperature Origin of Sodium Sulfate Deposits, Particularly in Antarctica," *Third Symposium on Salt,* Vol. 1, Northern Ohio Geological Society, pp. 181–203.

Eissenberg, D., and Wyman, C., 1980, "What's in Store for Phase Change?" *Solar Age,* Vol. 5, No. 5, May, pp. 12–16.

Fanfani, et al., 1975, "The Crystal Structure of Schairerite and Its Relationship to Sulphohalite," *Mineralogical Magazine,* Vol. 40, June, pp. 131–139.

Fletcher, S.W., Jr., 1979, Talk Presented to the Fall 1979 Seminar, Raw Material Section, American Paper Institute, Oct.

Garbell, M., 1963, "Sea that Spills into Desert," *Scientific American,* Vol. 209, Aug., pp. 94–100.

Goudge, M.F., and Tomkins, R.V., 1960, "Sodium Sulfate from Natural Sources," *Industrial Minerals and Rocks,* 3rd ed., J.L. Gillson, ed., AIME, New York, pp. 809–818.

Grabau, A.W., 1920, "Geology of the Non-Metallic Mineral Deposits," *Principles of Salt Deposition,* 1st ed., Vol. 1, McGraw-Hill, New York, pp. 29–40, 277–279.

Grossman, I.G., 1949, "Sodium Sulfate Deposits of Western North Dakota," Rept. of Investigation No. 1, North Dakota Geological Survey, 66 pp.

Grossman, I.G., 1968, "Origin of the Sodium Sulfate Deposits of the Northern Great Plains of Canada and the United States," Professional Paper 600-B, US Geological Survey, pp. B104-B105.

Hardie, L.A., and Eugster, H.P., 1970, "The Evolution of Closed-Basin Brines," Special Paper 3, Mineralogical Society of America, pp. 273–290.

Havighorst, C.R., 1963, "AP&CC's New Process Separates Borates From Ore by Extraction," *Chemical Engineering,* Vol. 70, No. 23, Nov. 11, pp. 228–232.

Hemy, G.W., 1969, "Chemical Minerals in the U.S.S.R.," Part I, *Chemical and Process Engineering,* Vol. 50, No. 8, Aug., pp. 63–68.

Holland, E., 1980, "The Mattapoisett House," *Solar Age,* Vol. 5, No. 5, pp. 24–28.

Jolly, J.L.W., 1976, "The Mineral Industry of Iran," *Minerals Yearbook,* US Bureau of Mines, pp. 12–13.

Jones, B.F., 1966, "Geochemical Evolution of Closed Basin Water in the Western Great Basin," *Second Symposium on Salt,* Vol. 1, Northern Ohio Geological Society, pp. 181–200.

Klingman, C.L., 1972, "Sodium and Sodium Compounds," *Minerals Yearbook 1972,* US Bureau of Mines, pp. 1147–1151.

Koelling, G.W., 1971, "Mineral Industry of Argentina," *Minerals Yearbook,* Vol. 3, US Bureau of Mines, pp. 87–98.

Kolosov, A.S., Pustyl'nikov, A.M., and Fedin, V.P., 1974, "Precipitation of Glauberite and Conditions of Deposition of Glauberite-Bearing Sediments in the Kara Bogaz Gol," *Doklady Akademii Nauk USSR,* Vol. 219, No. 6, pp. 1457–1460.

Kostick, D.S., 1978–1979, "Sodium and Sodium Compounds," Preprint, *Minerals Yearbook 1978–1979,* US Bureau of Mines, 8 pp.

Kostick, D.S., 1982, "Sodium Sulfate," *Mineral Commodity Summaries, 1982,* US Bureau of Mines, pp. 144–145.

Krauskopf, K.B., 1967, *Introduction to Geochemistry,* McGraw-Hill, Inc., p. 320.

Lang, W.B., 1941, "New Sources of Sodium Sulphate in New Mexico," American Association of Petroleum Geologists, *Bulletin,* Vol. 25, pp. 152–160.

Lefond, S.J., 1981, "Botswana—An Opportunity," Preprint 81–73, SME–AIME Annual Meeting, Chicago, Feb., 3 pp.

Massey, N.W.D., 1973, "Resources Inventory Botswana: Industrial Rocks and Minerals," Res. Report No. 3, Geological Survey Dept., 39 pp.

Moore, L., 1972, "Mineral Industry of China," Preprint, *Minerals Yearbook,* Vol. 3, US Bureau of Mines, 12 pp.

Moulton, G.F., 1980, "Compendium of Search Lake Operations," Preprint 80–133, SME-AIME Annual Meeting, Las Vegas, Feb., 6 pp.

Nickel, E.H., and Bridge, P.J., 1977, "Nickelbloedite, $Na_2Ni(SO_4)_2 \cdot 4H_2O$, A New Mineral from Western Australia," *Mineralogical Magazine,* Vol. 41, Mar., pp. 37–41.

Parkinson, G., 1977, "Kerr-McGee Expands

Ash Output Nine-fold from Searles Lake Brines," *Engineering and Mining Journal*, Vol. 178, No. 10, Oct., pp. 71–75.

Rathjen, J.A., 1972, "Minerals Industry of Canada," Preprint, *Minerals Yearbook 1972*, Vol. 3, US Bureau of Mines, 21 pp.

Ralston, O.C., 1949, "Natural Sodium Carbonate and Sodium Sulphate," *Industrial Minerals and Rocks*, 2nd ed., S.H. Dolbear, ed., AIME, New York, pp. 945–962.

Reeves, C.C., Jr., 1968, *Introduction to Paleolimnology*, Elsevier Publishing Co., pp. 68–69.

Rovira, J.M.R., 1960, "Sodium Sulfate: Its Recovery from the Minerals Containing It," *ION*, No. 233, Dec.

Ruffel, P.G., 1970, "Natural Sodium Sulfate in North America," *Third Symposium on Salt*, Vol. 1, Northern Ohio Geological Society, pp. 429–451.

Shekarchi, E., 1972, "Mineral Industry of Turkey," Preprint, *Minerals Yearbook*, Vol. 3, US Bureau of Mines, 11 pp.

Smith, G.I., 1966, "Sodium Sulfate," Mineral Resources of California, California Div. of Mines and Geology Bulletin 191, pp. 389–392.

Smith, G.I., 1979, "Subsurface Stratigraphy and Geochemistry of the Late Quaternary Evaporites, Searles Lake, Calif.," Professional Paper 1043, US Geological Survey.

Watson, I., 1980, "Sodium Sulphate: Present Shortage on Short-term Basis," *Industrial Minerals*, No. 152, May, pp. 61–77.

Weisman, W.I., and Anderson, R.C., 1953, "The Production of Sodium Sulfate from Natural Brines at Monohans, Texas," *Mining Engineering*, July.

Weisman, W.I., and Tandy, C.W., 1975, "Sodium Sulfate Deposits," *Industrial Minerals and Rocks*, 4th ed., S.J. Lefond, ed., AIME, New York, pp. 1081–1093.

Wells, R.G., 1923, "Sodium Sulphate: Its Sources and Uses," Bulletin 717, US Geological Survey, pp. 17–18.

Staurolite

ROBERT B. FULTON, III *

Staurolite, an iron aluminum silicate mineral, is used industrially as a high value-in-use sand-blasting agent, as a premium grade foundry sand, and as the source of aluminum in portland cement manufacture in areas where the aluminum constituent is not economically available from shale or argillaceous limestone.

It is produced by E. I. du Pont de Nemours & Co. as a coproduct in titanium mineral production in Florida where it was first recovered on a commercial scale in June 1952 from the Pleistocene sand deposit known as Trail Ridge. In the Trail Ridge deposit it comprises about one-fifth of the heavy minerals, the principal other heavy mineral constituents being ilmenite, leucoxene, rutile, zircon, kyanite, sillimanite, and tourmaline. Staurolite and the other silicate nonconductive heavy minerals are separated from the conductive titanium minerals on high-tension separators. The silicates are then separated from one another magnetically, the staurolite being relatively magnetic. In the total processing, 200 tons of raw sand yield 7 tons of heavy mineral concentrate from which about one ton of staurolite is recovered.

This process yields staurolite concentrates of the characteristics given in Table 1.

These concentrates are sold as three products with the size distribution of subrounded particles shown in Table 2.

All three grades are used in sand-blasting for cleaning metal, for paint removal, and for cleaning buildings. Staurolite compares favorably with lower unit cost abrasives, such as boiler slags and mineral aggregates, in applications where the abrasive is used only one time and is not recovered. Because it is hard, fine, clean, and dense it can reduce blasting time, with less material reportedly being required

* Basic Materials Planning, Materials and Logistics Dept., E.I. du Pont de Nemours & Co., Wilmington, DE.

TABLE 1—Characteristics of Staurolite Concentrates

Typical Mineral Composition, %

Staurolite minerals	89
Titanium minerals	4
Kyanite	1
Zircon	2
Quartz	4

Typical Chemical Composition, %

Al_2O_3	45 (min.)
Fe_2O_3	18 (max)
ZrO_2	3 (max)
TiO_2	5 (max)
Free silica	<5 (max)

Physical Characteristics

Bulk density	143-150 lb per cu ft
Specific gravity	3.1-4.6
Hardness (Mohs')	7
Melting point	2800° F (1537° C)
Coefficient of expansion	7.8 × 10^{-6}

TABLE 2—Size Distribution of Subrounded Particles in Three Staurolite Products

US Standard Sieve No.	% Retained on Sieve		
	Coarse	Biasill®	Starblast®
20	1	–	–
30	3	–	–
40	26	<1	3
50	58	5	11
70	9	20	19
100	–	53	45
140	–	19	19
200	–	3	3
270	–	<1	<1
Pan	3	Trace	none

® Registered trademarks for staurolite and abrasive sand products of E.I. du Pont de Nemours & Co., Inc.

TABLE 3—Cleaning Rate and Profile of Abrasives for Blast Cleaning

Abrasive	Cleaning Rate, Sq Ft per Hr	Abrasive Flow Rate, Lb per Hr	Profile Mil
Starblast®	240	600	1.1
Biasill®	240	580	0.9
Coarse Staurolite	200	535	1.5
Rotoblast® G80A*	150	700	1.2
Rotoblast® G40A	120	750	2.1
Garnet RT-80	224	640	1.0
Garnet RT-60	194	525	1.0
Aluminum Oxide 30 FDT	170	665	1.5
54/70	224	575	1.3
80/100	250	540	1.1
Black Beauty® 50 [†]	160	750	1.5
Flintbrasive® #3 [‡]	120	520	1.7
Flintshot® [¶]	200	700	1.7
Flint Silica® [§]	220	730	1.4

Tests conducted at Du Pont Engineering Test Center, 7/1/70.
100% mill scale on New Steel Plate. All surfaces to Class I white metal.
Nozzle, 3/8-in. 92-95 psi.
* Registered trademark for a metal blasting grit of The Pangborn Corp.
[†] Registered trademark for an abrasive slag of H. B. Reed Corp.
[‡] Registered trademark for a blasting abrasive of the Independent Gravel Co.
[¶] Registered trademark for a blasting abrasive of Ottawa Silica Co. and United States Silica Co.
[§] Trademark for a silica sand of Ottawa Silica Co.

TABLE 4—Results of Field Trials

Abrasive	Degree of Cleaning	Cleaning Rate, Sq Ft per Hr	Abrasive Flow Rate, Lb per Hr	Prof Mi
New Pipe—Intact Millscale				
Polygrit® *	Commercial	176	1,360	1.7
Flintshot®	Near white	308	845	1.2
Biasill®	White	295	568	1.3
Coarse Staurolite	Commercial/ near white	313	645	1.1
Starblast®	White	265	632	1.1
New Pipe—Millscale and Rust				
Polygrit®	Commercial	222	1,650	1.9
Flintshot®	Commercial	235	880	1.4
Biasill®	Near white/ white	204	545	1.3
Coarse Staurolite	Commercial	228	868	1.4
Starblast®	Near white	233	640	1.4

Tests conducted at William W. Pearson, Inc., Chester, PA, 1/19/71-1/21/71.
Conditions: ½-in. nozzle; 75-80 psi nozzle pressure.
* Registered trademark for an abrasive slag of MDC Industries.

TABLE 5—Breakdown Factors of Abrasives

Abrasive	Number of Uses	Breakdown Factor*
Aluminum Oxide 30 FDT	1	0.80
	3	0.61
Garnet RT 60	1	0.61
	3	0.38
Starblast®	1	0.77
	3	0.45
Flintshot®	1	0.68
	3	0.36
Flintbrasive® #3	1	0.58
	3	0.32

* Breakdown factors can range from 1 to 0. A material showing no change after blasting has a factor of 1, while one which breaks completely into dust has a factor of 0.

Tests conducted at Du Pont Engineering Test Center, 7/1/70.
¼-in. nozzle.
92-95 psi nozzle pressure.
¼-in. steel plate target.

to clean a specific area. Compared to higher unit value abrasives such as aluminum oxide and garnet, which are recycled, it costs significantly less per pound and cleans at equal or faster rates. The breakdown factor for staurolite, which is a measure of recycling performance, is intermediate between those for aluminum oxide and garnet.

Tables 3 and 4 show performance of the three staurolite products compared to other abrasives. Table 5 compares longevity of premium priced abrasives in recycling.

Fringe benefits claimed for staurolite's use as an abrasive are:

1) Good flow properties and freedom from lumps or slivers found in silica sands or boiler slag abrasives.

2) Low dusting which affords good visibility, permits faster working, and reduces cleanup problems.

3) Heated storage is not required in freezing conditions because it is nonhygroscopic.

Bibliography and References

Anon., 1972, Technical Bulletin "Starblast" Abrasive, E. I. du Pont de Nemours & Co.
Huskonen, W.D., 1970, "Spotlight on Specialty Sands," *Foundry Magazine*, Oct., pp. 40–45.
Laux, J.P., and Lipton, J.M., 1972, "An Introduction to Staurolite Sand," *Foundry Magazine*, May, pp. 158, 160.
Wagner, A.J., 1972, "Biasill Staurolite Sand," *Modern Casting Magazine*, Feb., pp. 64, 65.

Strontium

ROBERT B. FULTON, III *

Commercially, celestite ($SrSO_4$) is the predominant strontium mineral. Among other strontium-bearing minerals, only strontianite ($SrCO_3$) occurs commonly; however, it is rarely an item of commerce.

Production of celestite is principally in Mexico, Spain, and Turkey. An attempt to produce celestite in Canada was unsuccessful. The United States, which is wholly dependent on imports, chiefly from Mexico (99%), is the largest consumer of strontium. Lesser quantities are consumed in Japan and Europe. The Federal Republic of Germany is the principal source of strontium compounds imported to the US.

Uses

The principal uses of strontium are for the manufacture of strontium carbonate and nitrate. Carbonate is used in glass for TV tube face plates and in ceramic ferrites for magnets. Nitrate is used in pyrotechnics, mainly in safety flares, to which it imparts a characteristic brilliant red color. Minor amounts of strontium compounds are used in electrolytic zinc manufacturing where the carbonate is used to remove unwanted lead. Small quantities are consumed in greases, ceramics, soaps, alloys, and pharmaceuticals.

Specifications

Typical celestite specifications for the carbonate and nitrate markets are shown in Table . Specifications of manufactured carbonate, old in two grades, one to the glass industry nd the other for ceramic ferrites, are shown n Table 2. Both grades of carbonate are hipped in palletized 50-lb bags. Glass grade aterial is shipped in bulk by rail.

* Basic Materials Planning, Materials and Logistics Department, E.I. du Pont de Nemours & Co., Wilmington, DE.

TABLE 1—Celestite Specifications

	For Carbonate	For Nitrate
$SrSO_4$	90% min.	95% min.
$CaSO_4$	—	1.5% max
$BaSO_4$	2% max	2% max
F	0.1% max	—
Size	6 in. max	minus 6 in., plus ¼ in.

Manufacturing Processes

The following description is adapted from Anon. (1980).

The manufacturing process for strontium carbonate and strontium nitrate chemicals is conceptually simple. Strontium nitrate is made from strontium carbonate in two additional steps. The production process begins with celestite, the natural form of strontium sulfate. In the first step the ore is crushed, ground, and mixed with coke. This mixture is then fed into a kiln where the ore is reduced at high temperatures to strontium sulfide; the coke is added to the ore as a source of energy and carbon. The carbon combines with the oxygen

TABLE 2—Specifications for Manufactured Carbonate Made from Celestite

	Glass Grade	Ceramic Grade
$SrCO_3$	96% min.	96% min.
$BaCO_3$	3% max	1.5% max
$CaCO_3$	0.5% max	—
Total S	0.4% max	0.4% max
Fe_2O_3	0.01% max	—
Na_2CO_3	1.0% max	—

Size (Tyler mesh)

on	10 mesh	0.0%	no size specification
on	14 mesh	2.0% max	
on	100 mesh	70-85%	
on	150 mesh	95% min.	
thru	150 mesh	5% max	

of the sulfate group and escapes as carbon dioxide. The sulfide is removed from the kiln, purified, and dissolved in water. The sulfide solution is then reacted with either sodium carbonate (soda ash) or carbon dioxide to produce the carbonate. The reactions are as follows:

The soda ash method:

$$SrS + Na_2CO_3 = SrCO_3 + Na_2S$$

Carbon dioxide method:

$$SrS + CO_2 + H_2O = SrCO_3 + H_2S$$

In both reactions, the carbonate forms as a solid which is dried and screened. The reaction conditions and drying techniques determine the particle size and, thus, whether the product will be ceramic or glass grade.

The coproducts obtained in both methods are marketable. The sodium sulfide solution obtained in the soda ash method is concentrated, dried, and packaged in 50-lb palletized bags for shipment. The hydrogen sulfide obtained in the carbon dioxide method can be converted to sodium sulfide, sodium sulfahydrate, or ammonium sulfide for market.

Strontium nitrate is produced by mixing strontium carbonate with concentrated nitric acid. The product is then crystallized and dried.

The production process for strontium carbonate is basically continuous. Production is controlled either by how long the equipment is run or by the flow rate used. The equipment in use generally dates back to the 1940s and 1950s. Although improvements in operating efficiency are being made, there have been no substantial technological improvements since then.

Markets

In the United States, principal consumers of celestite for the manufacture of carbonate are Chemical Products (CPC) of Cartersville, GA, and FMC of Modesto, CA, each with an estimated capacity of about 15,000 stpy. Companies which have discontinued carbonate manufacture include Foote Mineral and Sherwin-Williams, the latter having shut down in 1972 after Kaiser Chemical opened a new facility in Canada. US production of carbonate dropped from 20,000 st in 1971 to a low of about 15,000 st in 1975 at the time of maximum impact of Kaiser's Canadian production, then rose to about 30,000 st in 1978 after Kaiser

ceased operation. Consumers of carbonate for glassmaking have included Corning, Owens-Illinois, and RCA. Consumers of electronic grade to make ferrites and titanates include Arnold Engineering, Alan Bradley, Colt Industries, Indiana General, and Stackpole Carbon.

Since Du Pont withdrew in mid-1975, the only US consumer of celestite for the manufacture of nitrate is FMC. FMC sales increased in 1978, dropped slightly in 1979, then declined sharply in January through June 1980 compared to the same period in 1979, while end-of-year inventories quadrupled from 1977 to 1979. US consumption of nitrate is about 15,000,000 lb per year, of which 12,000,000 lb are produced in the US.

Ground celestite is consumed at a rate of about 2,000 stpy by electrolytic zinc manufacturers in the US and Canada.

Kali-Chemie AG is a major producer of strontium carbonate in West Germany, accounting for essentially all US imports since 1978, following the closure of Kaiser's Canadian plant in late 1976. A subsidiary of Kali-Chemie, Societa Bario e Derivati SpA (SABED), produces strontium nitrate in Italy, as does Ammi Bario. SABED has accounted for virtually all US nitrate imports since it started production in 1978, making Kali-Chemie in effect the main foreign supplier of both strontium chemicals to the United States. SABED exports nearly all of its production to the US as a supplier to Olin since mid-1978 when Olin's plant at Peru, IN, switched from domestic to imported nitrate. Olin's other Signal Products Division plant at Morgan Hill, CA, continues to be supplied by FMC.

Imports of carbonate from West Germany rose sharply from 1977 to 1979, then declined steeply in January through June 1980, increasing from 2,300,000 lb in 1977 to 7,700,000 lb in 1979, but dropping from 2,600,000 lb January through June 1979 to 400,000, January through June 1980. The value rose from $364,000 in 1977 ($0.159 per lb) to $1,498,000 in 1979 ($0.195 per lb) and dropped from $472,000 January through June 1979 ($0.181 per lb) to $86,000 January through June 1980 ($0.217 per lb).

US imports of nitrate have switched from West Germany to Italy, dropping from 201,000 lb in 1977 to 2,000 lb in 1979 from West Germany, and rising from zero in 1977 to 3,100,000 lb in 1979 from Italy. Value of West German imports was US $61,000 in 1977 ($0.303 per lb). Value of Italian imports was

US $128,000 in 1978 ($0.249 per lb) and US $792,000 ($0.257 per lb) in 1979.

US exports of strontium chemicals is a very small percentage of production, essentially all by FMC.

Consumption

US consumption of strontium (as Sr) was about 40,000,000 lb, roughly divided as follows:

Glass	65%
Magnets	5%
Pyrotechnics	15%
Metal refining	4%
Pigments and Fillers	4%
Other	7%

North America probably accounts for three-fourths of world consumption, the rest being divided between Europe and Japan.

Substitutes and alternative materials have not been the subject of scrutiny because the total strontium mineral market is small and supplies are adequate, leaving little incentive for attempts at penetration by other materials.

Production of Celestite

World production of strontium minerals is shown in Table 3.

England: In England, mining is in the vicinity of Yate, near Bristol, where lumps of celestite are found near the ground surface in a clay matrix derived from the Keuper marl formation. Commercial development of these deposits began in the 1880s and reached a peak during the purchases by the US government for stockpiles in the early 1960s. English China Clays, a large producer of china clay, succeeded Bristol Minerals Co. as the producer from these deposits in the late 1960s. Mining methods introduced by Bristol Minerals and continued by English China Clays include stripping of top soil, followed by excavation using front-end loaders, hand-picking of celestite lumps, and transportation to a wash plant for removal of clay and sizing. Final product resulting from this simple operation is 95 to 96% $SrSO_4$. Export is through nearby Bristol Channel ports.

R. F. Bennett of Albright & Wilson, Ltd. and T. G. Pleasants of English China Clays, Ltd., in an informal paper, reviewed the history of strontium mineral markets in England, citing a number of potential uses which failed to materialize or which enjoyed a period of prosperity then declined. An example of the latter case of a prosperous market was the early use of strontium compounds in recovery of sugar from beet molasses, particularly in Germany in the period following 1890. During World War I production was stimulated briefly for pyrotechnics. Use in glass to replace red lead was the subject of an early patent but did not become a significantly large use. World War II gave a brief stimulus for pyrotechnics, similar to that of World War I. Use of strontium chloride in the 1950s for case hardening

TABLE 3—Strontium Minerals: World Production, by Country
(Short Tons)

Country*	1976	1977	1978	1979 p	1980 e
Algeria	7,147	r5,622	6,418	e6,000	6,000
Argentina	2,264	r925	1,317	134	t209
Canada e	13,200	—	—	—	—
Iran et	6,000	11,000	16,535	r11,000	5,500
Italy	e770	e770	402	1,866	1,300
Mexico	24,424	50,302	36,563	re38,500	33,000
Pakistan	665	402	239	680	670
Spain	re9,100	12,120	15,430	19,840	20,000
Turkey	e7,000	e18,300	16,038	9,058	10,000
United Kingdom	5,952	5,622	4,740	6,600	5,500
Total	r76,522	r105,063	97,682	93,678	82,179

Source: Taylor, 1981a.
e Estimated. p Preliminary. r Revised.
* In addition to the countries listed, mainland China, the Federal Republic of Germany, Poland, and the USSR produce strontium minerals, but output is not reported quantitatively and available information is inadequate for formulation of reliable estimates of output levels.
t Reported figure.
‡ Year beginning March 21 of that stated.

of steel was short-lived, as was use of the sulfide for luminous paints. The sulfide was also used as a depilatory but was superseded by thioglycollic acid. An abortive attempt was made to employ strontium compounds to impart a bright flame color to coal briquettes but high cost discouraged this use. Use in ferrites is growing. Europeans do not use it in TV tube face-plate glass because of a finding by European TV manufacturers that x-ray absorbent glass is not required if the circuitry is properly designed. A minor but growing use for strontium chromate has been found in anticorrosive paint, especially for aircraft. Expectations for its use in water-soluble primers for automobiles have not been realized. In Europe strontium compounds await a major development, meanwhile experiencing a slow growth. Future of the mines is clouded by the environment of suburban developments and consequent zoning restrictions.

Mexico: Mexico supplied 99% of US imports of celestite from 1976 through 1980. The main producer is Minera Valenciana, headquartered in Torreon, with mines in Paila district where the celestite occurs as lens-shaped bodies concordant with bedding of the gently dipping Cretaceous limestone host rock. Lenses vary in thickness, averaging about 2 m. The ore is mined underground where horizontal tunnels connect to room-and-pillar stopes in the ore lenses. Ore is trucked to the railhead at Marte which is about 50 km south of the mines and 200 km east of Torreon. In contrast to the situation in England, described above, there has been little attempt to develop markets for celestite within the country. Essentially all of the sales are to US consumers, with FMC and Chemical Products being the principal buyers. About 2,000 stpy are ground at Brownsville for sale to electrolytic zinc manufacturers.

Spain: In Spain, celestite is produced from the Aurora mine at Montevive, near Granada, by Bruno SA, a company headquartered in Madrid. The mine is open pit and the celestite is selectively mined from the baritic gypsiferous host rocks. The principal products are -4 in., -2 in. lumps, and smaller quantities of ground-bagged material. The products are trucked a distance of 85 km to the port of Motril for export, currently two-thirds to Japan and the rest mainly to West Germany, France, and the US. The Aurora mine first produced during World War II, after which it remained idle until 1967 when it was reopened with initial shipments to the United States. Recent expan-

sion has increased its capacity to a reported 40,000 stpy, typically assaying 93 to 94% $SrSO_4$.

Bruno SA has announced construction of a plant for manufacturing strontium chemicals with a capacity of between 3,000,000 and 4,000,000 lb per year of strontium carbonate located near the port of Motril using ore from the Aurora mine and operating under a separate company, Proimsur SA, of the same ownership as Bruno SA.

A report by the Spanish government refers to another deposit near Fortuna in Murcia, called Nuestra Senora, where prospect pits indicate possibilities of extracting ore grading 98% $SrSO_4$.

United States: In the United States, all known deposits are uneconomic in today's markets. Historically production has been sporadic and short-lived. Surplus from the US stockpiles of material purchased mainly from England and Mexico has been sold from time to time by the General Services Administration to domestic consumers. The US imported about 21,750 st of strontium mineral (as Sr) in 1981, which equates to about 54,120 st of celestite ore, up from 15,670 st in 1976 (about 39,000 st celestite).

It is noteworthy that US manufacturers of strontium compounds are wholly dependent on foreign sourecs of celestite and have significant competition from Italy and West Germany in the domestic market for finished strontium compounds.

Canada: In Canada at Loch Lommond, Cape Breton County, Nova Scotia, Kaiser Chemical Co. attempted to develop an open pit mine in ore averaging 50 to 60% $SrSO_4$, upgrading it by froth flotation to a concentrate assaying more than 88% $SrSO_4$ for use in making strontium compounds in a 60,000,000 lb-per-year facility at Point Edward.

The mineralization occurs in rocks of the lower Windsor group of Mississippian age as gently dipping mantos concordant to bedding of the limestone-gypsum host rocks into which the ore mantos grade laterally. Open-pit mining started in September 1969. The concentrator first produced celestite concentrates in March 1971 and continued until its closure in August 1976.

Other: In Turkey, the largest celestite producer, Barit Moden Turk, is expanding production at its Silvas operation from the current 20,000 stpy to 44,000 stpy capacity.

In Iran, Nakhjir, a new celestite deposit located about 190 km southeast of Tehran in the

Dasht-e-Kavir desert, is being developed by the Strontium Co., a wholly owned subsidiary of the Simiran group of companies. Production is estimated to be about 5,500 stpy of hand-sorted celestite.

Elsewhere in the world, celestite has been offered from time to time from production in Algeria, Argentina, Italy, Morocco, and Pakistan.

Summary

In summary, several points of interest are:

1. Celestite is important in glass manufacturing for TV face plates in the US because of the x-ray shielding qualities of strontium carbonate, while European TV manufacturers have claimed such shielding is unnecessary if circuitry is properly designed.

2. A growing market for strontium carbonate is provided by its use in making ceramic ferrites which are demonstrably superior in performance and are achieving acceptance by industry.

3. Use of celestite in nitrate for pyrotechnics (mainly for signal flares) grew from 1977 to 1978, but dropped sharply by 1980, declining with the business recession.

4. Numerous other uses of strontium compounds are identified, none of which are presently commercially important.

5. On balance, the trend of celestite consumption is expected to be modestly upward as strontium ferrites gain acceptance and TV manufacturers for the US market, both in the US and Japan, continue to use strontium carbonates in face plates.

6. While deposits in the US are not economic, mining of celestite from well-established sources abroad is adequate for present world needs and other deposits are known which could be used to meet new or expanded requirements.

Bibliography and References

Anon., 1969, "New Look Strontium Industry," *Industrial Minerals*, No. 27, Dec., pp. 11–20.

Anon., 1973, "The Economics of Strontium," Roskill Information Services, Ltd. report, Mar., 91 pp.

Anon., 1980, "Barium Carbonate and Strontium Carbonate from the Federal Republic of Germany and Strontium Nitrate from Italy," Investigation Nos. 731-TA-31-33 (Preliminary), USITC Publication 1105, US International Trade Commission, Oct.

Anon., 1980a, "Bruno Opens Strontium Compounds Plant," *Industrial Minerals*, No. 154, July, p. 11.

Crowell, G.D., 1973, "Mineralogy of Strontium," *Proceedings*, International Conference on Strontium Containing Compounds, Nova Scotia Technical College, pp. 245–255.

Fulton, R.B., 1971, "World Economics of Selected Industrial Minerals," *Centennial Volume*, AIME, New York, pp. 74–87.

Ireland, J.R., 1973, "Hard Ferrites in P.M. Motors," *Proceedings*, International Conference on Strontium Containing Compounds, Nova Scotia Technical College, pp. 33–46.

Massone, J., 1982, "Technology and Uses of Barium and Strontium Compounds," *Industrial Minerals*, No. 177, June, pp. 65–69.

Schiebel, W., 1978, "New Strontium Deposit in Iran," *Industrial Minerals*, No. 132, Sept., pp. 54–57, 59.

Stein, D.L., 1973, "Extraction of Strontium Values from Celestite Concentrate at the Kaiser Plant in Nova Scotia," *Proceedings*, International Conference on Strontium Containing Compounds, Nova Scotia Technical College, pp. 1–9.

Taylor, H.A., 1981, "Strontium," *Mineral Commodity Summaries, 1981*, US Bureau of Mines, pp. 152–153.

Taylor, H.A., 1981a, "Strontium," *Minerals Yearbook, 1980*, US Bureau of Mines, pp. 944–947.

Thomas, I.A., 1973, "Celestite," Mineral Dossier No. 6, Her Majesty's Stationery Office, London, 26 pp.

Wininger, D.C., 1970, "Strontium," *Minerals Yearbook, 1970*, US Bureau of Mines, Vol. 1, pp. 1233-4.

Sulfur

JAMES M. BARKER *

Sulfur is a nonmetallic element of great physical and economic importance to the world. It is widely but sparingly distributed throughout the hydrosphere, lithosphere, and biosphere. Sulfur is the tenth most abundant element in the universe and eighth most abundant in the sun. In the earth's crust, which is mainly igneous, it ranks 14th, but is eighth or ninth in sediments (Kaplan, 1972; Stanton, 1972). It apparently is very abundant in the core of the earth, because it is a strong chalcophile, and it is fifth in abundance in stony and iron meteorites (Field, 1972) where it occurs as trolite (FeS).

In ancient times sulfur was called *brimstone,* literally "burning stone." Today the term *brimstone* is used interchangeably with the term *elemental sulfur.* Shelton (1979) summarized most of the common definitions of terms, grades, and specifications for the sulfur industry as follows (with minor additions):

Sources of Sulfur:

Combined sulfur—Sulfur that occurs in nature combined with other elements.

Cupriferous pyrites—Pyrite containing relatively minor amounts of copper sulfide minerals.

Hydrogen sulfide—A toxic gas (H_2S) occurring in natural gas and petroleum.

Involuntary sulfur—Sulfur produced primarily as a result of legislative or process mandates.

Native sulfur—Sulfur that occurs in nature in the elemental (uncombined) form.

Nonferrous metal sulfides—Copper, lead, zinc, nickel, and molybdenum sulfides that are processed for their metal content.

Organic sulfurs—Complex organic sulfur compounds occurring in petroleum, coal, oil shale, and tar sands.

Pyrites—Iron sulfide minerals that include pyrite, marcasite, and pyrrhotite.

* Industrial Minerals Geologist, New Mexico Bureau of Mines and Mineral Resources, Socorro, NM.
This chapter is based in part on Gittinger, 1975.

Sulfate sulfurs—Sulfur in anhydrite and gypsum.

Voluntary sulfur—Sulfur produced in response to market forces.

Basic Sulfur Products Produced and Marketed:

Acid sludge—Contaminated sulfuric acid usually returned to acid plants for reconstitution.

Brimstone—Synonymous with crude sulfur.

Bright sulfur—Crude sulfur free of discoloring impurities and bright yellow in color.

Broken sulfur—Solid crude sulfur crushed to -8 in.

Byproduct sulfuric acid—Sulfuric acid produced as a byproduct of a metallurgical or industrial process, generally relating to combined sulfur sources.

Crude sulfur—Commercial nomenclature for elemental sulfur.

Dark sulfur—Crude sulfur discolored by minor quantities of hydrocarbons ranging up to 0.3% carbon content.

Elemental sulfur—Processed sulfur in the elemental form produced from native sulfur or combined sulfur sources, generally with a minimum sulfur content of 99.5%.

Formed sulfur—Elemental sulfur cast or pressed into particular shapes to enhance handling and to suppress dust generation and moisture retention.

Frasch sulfur—Elemental sulfur produced from native sulfur sources by the Frasch mining process.

Hydrogen sulfide—Associated with natural gas or petroleum and produced at refineries and coke oven plants; used to make sulfuric acid or recovered sulfur.

Liquid sulfur—Synonymous with molten sulfur.

Liquid sulfur dioxide—Purified sulfur dioxide compressed to the liquid phase.

Molten sulfur—Crude sulfur in the molten phase.

Prilled sulfur—Solid crude sulfur in the form of pellets produced by cooling molten sulfur with air or water.

Recovered sulfur—Elemental sulfur produced from combined sulfur sources by any method.

Slated sulfur—Solid crude sulfur in the form of slatelike lumps, produced by allowing molten sulfur to solidify on a moving belt.

Specialty sulfurs—Prepared or refined grades of elemental sulfur that include amorphous, colloidal, flowers, precipitated, wettable, flour, or paste sulfur.

Sulfur ore—Unprocessed ore containing native sulfur.

Sulfuric acid—Sulfuric acid of commerce as produced from all sources of sulfur, generally reported in terms of 100% H_2SO_4 with a 32.69% sulfur content.

Sulfur is produced commercially from one or more sources in about 70 countries (Shelton, 1980b). World production of sulfur in all forms totaled 58 Mt * in 1980 (Barker and Cochran, 1981). The per capita consumption of sulfur often is used as a reliable index of the level of industrial development and the activity of a nation's economy (Field, 1972).

Sulfur resources are abundant and exist throughout the world, but the extent to which they can be classified as reserves is greatly circumscribed by prevailing prices and technology. The 1980 world estimate of sulfur reserves totals 1.765 Gt (Shelton, 1980a), about ten times that calculated for the United States (Table 1).

Resources of elemental sulfur in evaporite and volcanic deposits and sulfur associated with natural gas, petroleum, tar sands, and metal sulfides amount to about 6.385 Gt. The sulfur contained in gypsum and anhydrite is almost limitless and some 600 Gt are contained in coal, oil shale, and shale rich in organic matter, although low-cost methods have not been developed to recover sulfur from these sources. The domestic resource is about 5% of the world total.

Native deposits, sulfides, oil, and gas contributed, respectively, 32, 36, 30.1, and 0.9% to world sulfur production in 1973 (Anon., 1974a). Of the sulfur produced from native deposits, salt domes accounted for 53% and evaporite basin (stratiform deposits), 45%. Volcanic deposits (2%) are of little signifi-

cance and are mined mainly for local consumption in Italy, Turkey, and the Andes Mountains of South America.

The past two decades have seen continued shifts in the world's sulfur sources. In 1950, native deposits and sulfides each supplied about one-half the world's production. During the 1950s, sulfur recovered from oil and natural gas grew rapidly, representing about 10% of the total by 1960. Since then, the petroleum industry has continued to increase its relative importance as a source of sulfur, representing 18% in 1965 and 30% in 1973 for the world. It comprised more than 34% for 1979 in the United States. The proportion of sulfur produced by the Frasch or similar processes has declined in importance to 52% of all sulfur in the United States for 1980. The economics of the impact of recovered sulfur on the US Frasch sulfur industry is covered in detail by Rieber et al. (1981).

Elemental sulfur is produced from salt dome deposits in the Gulf Coast region of the United States and the Isthmus of Tehuantepec in Mexico, and from stratiform evaporite deposits in the United States (west Texas), Poland, the USSR, and Iraq. It is recovered from native sulfur ore of volcanic origin in about eight countries and is recovered in large amounts from sour natural gas in ten countries, of which Canada and the United States are the principal producers with Saudi Arabia due to become a major producer in the 1980s. Sulfur is derived from petroleum refinery gases in about 50 countries, of which the United States and Japan are the largest producers. The leading 15 countries produce 95% of total output.

About 30 countries produce pyrites, of which the USSR, Japan, Spain, Italy, and South Africa are the largest. About the same number of countries recover sulfur largely in the form of byproduct sulfuric acid from nonferrous smelter gases or petroleum refinery gases. The USSR, Japan, and the United States are the leading producers. Sulfate minerals are utilized as a source of sulfur in a few countries.

Elemental sulfur represented 64.5% of the 56.1 Mt of sulfur produced in 1980. The western world accounted for 63.9% of all sulfur forms and 71.5% of elemental sulfur. World production of all forms grew at a rate of 6% per year from 1950 to 1971 and elemental sulfur grew at a rate of 6.5% per year. Growth in the western world was about 5% per year for all forms and 5.5% per year for elemental sulfur. The Communist world recorded growth of 11% per year for all forms and 16.5% per

---

* Sulfur statistics in this chapter are given in metric tons (t). t × 1.102 311 4 = st (short tons); t × 0.984 206 = lt (long tons).

TABLE 1—Identified World Sulfur Resources,* Mt

Type of deposit	Reserves	Other	Total
United States			
Salt domes and evaporites	90	25	115
Nonferrous metal sulfides	55	30	85
Natural gas	20	10	30
Petroleum	10	10	20
Pyrites	—	50	50
Volcanic	—	20	20
Tar sands	—	10	10
Total US	175	155	330
World			
North America			
United States	175	155	330
Canada	250	2,000	2,250
Mexico	90	60	150
Other	5	—	5
Total	520	2,215	2,735
South America, Total	30	30	60
Europe			
USSR	250	450	700
Poland	150	450	600
France	30	10	40
Germany, Federal Republic of	30	5	35
Spain	30	450	480
Italy	15	25	40
Other	185	285	470
Total	690	1,675	2,365
Africa, Total	20	—	20
Asia			
Japan	10	40	50
Iraq	150	50	200
Near East	250	400	600
China, Mainland	25	50	75
Other	50	200	250
Total	485	740	1,175
Oceania, Total	20	10	30
World Total	1,765	4,670	6,385

Source: Shelton, 1980a.
*Derived in consultation with US Geological Survey.

year for elemental sulfur. Fig. 1 shows the trend in production for the western and Communist worlds from 1950 to 1981.

Elemental sulfur and, to a lesser extent, pyrites are internationally traded so that the geographic pattern of consumption differs somewhat from that of production. Table 2 shows total sulfur production, from 1976 to 1980, by major countries that produce over 0.5 Mt of sulfur from all sources.

Commercial grades of elemental sulfur are classified as *crude sulfur* (run-of-mine, bright or dark); and *recovered sulfur*. Both grades are shipped in liquid or solid form. All grades are guaranteed 99.5% pure, and the only allowable impurity of any significance is usually carbon in the form of hydrocarbons in solution in the sulfur. Dark sulfurs may contain up to 0.3% carbon. All grades are free of arsenic, selenium, and tellurium.

Some sulfur is solidified (formed) and shipped as slates or prills rather than in the more common broken lumps in an attempt to minimize dust problems during handling.

Specialty grades of sulfur are prepared by treating commercial grades to impart desirable

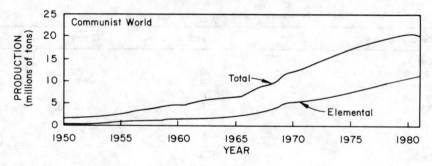

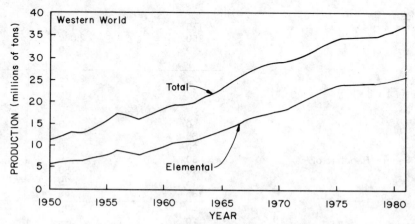

FIG. 1—*Sulfur production for the western and Communist worlds, 1950 to 1981. Source: updated from Gittinger, 1975.*

characteristics. Some special grades such as refined candles, cones, sticks, and sublimed sulfur are prepared from distilled crude sulfur.

Finely-ground crude sulfur is sold as "flour sulfur," "rubber-makers sulfur," "agricultural dusting sulfur," etc. Conditioning agents may be added to produce wettable grades. Special processing is involved in the production of insoluble sulfur, a material which contains up to 90% of the amorphous allotrope, which is insoluble in carbon disulfide.

Commercial grades of pyrite usually contain a minimum of 45% sulfur unless the copper content is at least 1%. If the pyrite price is predicated on realizing values for iron content, impurities such as arsenic and selenium should be at very low levels or absent. Residual copper, lead, and zinc contents should not exceed 0.05% if the iron values are to find a ready market in the United States. Some European and Japanese steel mills accept material with combined residuals of 0.3 to 0.4%, at a discount.

The sulfur content of pyrite sells at a considerable discount from the brimstone price level because capital and operating costs of acid plants based on pyrite are much higher than those for brimstone plants.

Mineralogy

Elemental sulfur occurs in subsurface sedimentary deposits associated with gypsum and anhydrite in salt domes and stratiform evaporites. It also is common in volcanic, especially solfataric, associations and at mineral or thermal springs.

Sulfur occurs in compounds as sulfates (Staples, 1972a) such as gypsum or anhydrite. It is also found in sulfides (Staples, 1972b), both ferrous (pyrites, phyrrhotite, etc.) and nonferrous (sulfides of copper, lead, zinc, nickel, etc.). Organic materials often contain sulfur, e.g., hydrogen sulfide in petroleum and natural gas, organic compounds in oil and oil

TABLE 2—Major World Production of Sulfur In All Forms, By Country and Source (1000 t)

Country and source	1976	1977	1978	1979	1980
Canada					
Pyrite	15	12	5	12	12
Byproduct					
Metallurgy	705	736	676	667	903
Natural gas	6,241	6,475	6,248	5,935	6,000
Petroleum	200	160	200	200	190
Tar sands	100	100	118	213	300
Total	7,261	7,483	7,247	7,027	7,405
China					
Mainland					
Native	150	200	200	200	200
Pyrite	900	1,252	1,605	1,682	1,700
Byproduct, all sources	300	300	350	400	400
Total	1,350	1,752	2,155	2,282	2,300
France					
Byproduct					
Natural gas	1,737	1,911	1,900	1,940	1,839
Petroleum	88	89	86	90	88
Unspecified	143	160	160	160	150
Total	1,968	2,160	2,146	2,190	2,077
Germany, Federal Republic of					
Pyrite	233	235	221	203	200
Pyproduct					
Metallurgy	390	385	348	361	380
Natural gas	460	624	666	690	700
Petroleum	119	186	190	214	220
Unspecified	161	197	195	343	300
Total	1,363	1,627	1,620	1,811	1,800
Iraq					
Frasch	582	620	600	550	600
Byproduct, petroleum and natural gas	40	40	40	70	60
Total	622	660	640	620	660
Italy					
Native	35	36	16	16	23
Pyrite	366	371	330	330	331
Byproduct, all sources	211	259	299	225	250
Total	612	666	645	571	604
Japan					
Pyrite	471	389	327	303	300
Byproduct					
Metallurgy	1,252	1,336	1,296	1,350	1,300
Petroleum	926	1,100	1,105	1,241	1,300
Total	2,649	2,825	2,728	2,894	2,900
Mexico					
Frasch	2,054	1,723	1,818	2,025	2,102
Byproduct					
Metallurgy	75	80	100	100	150
Petroleum and natural gas	96	146	168	249	300
Total	2,225	1,949	2,086	2,374	2,552
Poland					
Frasch	4,341	4,321	4,546	4,310	4,000
Native	550	450	505	520	500

TABLE 2—Major World Production of Sulfur In All Forms, By Country and Source (1000 t) (Cont'd)

Country and source	1976	1977	1978	1979	198
Byproduct					
Metallurgy	239	314	315	310	30
Petroleum	25	35	35	35	3
Gypsum	55	30	20	20	2
Total	5,210	5,150	5,421	5,195	4,85
Romania					
Pyrite	375	395	400	425	45
Byproduct, all sources	98	110	120	130	14
Total	473	505	520	555	59
Saudi Arabia					
Native	1	1	1	1	
Byproduct, petroleum and natural gas	12	12	14	125	70
Total	13	13	15	126	70
Spain					
Pyrite	1,052	1,102	1,071	1,019	1,10
Byproduct					
Metallurgy	123	129	117	120	12
Petroleum	4	5	10	10	1
Coal (lignite) gasification	1	2	3	3	
Total	1,180	1,238	1,201	1,152	1,24
United States					
Frasch	6,365	5,915	5,648	6,357	6,39
Pyrite	291	169	301	400	32
Byproduct					
Metallurgy	957	960	1,103	1,167	1,00
Natural gas	1,298	1,426	1,753	1,760	1,73
Petroleum	1,890	2,198	2,309	2,310	2,31
Unspecified	78	59	61	107	7
Total	10,879	10,727	11,175	12,101	11,83
USSR					
Frasch	500	500	800	800	90
Native	2,200	2,400	2,700	2,700	2,80
Pyrite	3,300	3,500	3,500	3,500	3,55
Byproduct					
Coal	40	40	40	40	4
Metallurgy	2,040	2,180	2,210	2,210	2,31
Natural gas	870	920	1,100	1,100	1,10
Petroleum	190	200	200	200	20
Total	9,140	9,740	10,550	10,550	10,90

Source: Shelton, 1980b.

sands, and pyrite and organic compounds in coal and oil shale.

The atomic weight of sulfur is 32.064, with an atomic number of 16. It has four stable isotopes—S^{32}, S^{33}, S^{34}, and S^{36}—with percent abundances of 95.1, 0.74, 4.2, and 0.016, respectively. The terrestrial S^{34}/S^{32} ratio varies naturally by at least 4.5% from a mean (0.0) close to that of meteors. Sulfur also has four oxidation states (+6, +4, 0, and −2), of which the S^{-2} sulfide ion (ionic radius 1.84 Å) and the S^{+6} sulfate cation (0.30 Å) are most important in minerals.

Sulfur occurs as both orthorhombic crystals and amorphous masses. Crystals commonly are dipyramidal and sometimes thick tabular on {001} or sphenoidal. Other habits are irregular masses of imperfect crystals, incrustations, stalactitic/stalagmitic, spherical, reniform, or earthy masses. Cleavage is imperfect to none, and twinning is rare. Sulfur is brittle to slightly sectile, with conchoidal to uneven fracture and resinous to greasy luster. It has a hardness of 1.5 to 2.5 and a density of 2.07 (range: 2.05 to 2.09). Color varies widely, from straw yellow through red to gray with a white streak. Pure, cool sulfur is yellow, but it is often discolored by high temperatures or impurities, especially bitumen or clay. Orthorhombic sulfur [alpha (α) sulfur] is stable to 95.5°C whereupon it slowly converts to monoclinic [beta (β) or gamma (γ) sulfur]. The melting point is 118.9°C and the boiling point is 444.6°C, with viscosity increasing markedly with increasing temperature over this range. Sulfur is easily ignited in air, burning at 270°C with a blue flame and evolution of sulfur dioxide. It is nearly insoluble in water, is nonhydroscopic, and is unaffected by most acids. It is soluble in carbon disulfide and some oils (Berry and Mason, 1959).

Solid sulfur has a number of physical properties of interest to industry. The explosive limits of sulfur dust in air are about 35 g/m^3 (minimum) to about 1400 g/m^3 (maximum). The auto-ignition temperature of dust in air is 190°C (dust clouds) and 220°C (undispersed dusts). Corrosivity is nil for dry sulfur with slow generation of sulfuric acid when wet. Theoretical density is 1922 kg/m^3 with practical bulk densities ranging from 120 to 1393 kg/m^3. Specific heat is 0.67 kJ/kg at −17.8°C, increasing to 4.98 kJ/kg at 93°C. Vapor pressure is less than 0.1 μm Hg at 20°C (Anon., 1968).

Molten sulfur properties at atmospheric pressure include some of interest to industry (Tuller, 1954). Specific gravity at 132°C is 1.79 (basis: H_2O at 20°C = 1) and relative viscosity, same basis, is 9.0 at 132°C. The flash point (modified Cleveland open cup) is 168.3 to 187.3°C (Anon., 1966).

Historical Aspects

Production of sulfur on a commercial basis commenced in Sicily early in the 15th century. For 150 years Sicilian brimstone had a virtual monopoly on the world supply. In 1838, French interests gained control of the Sicilian sulfur industry and attempted to triple sulfur's price, whereupon countries dependent on Sicilian sulfur developed other sources. Pyrites gradually displaced Sicilian brimstone for the manufacture of sulfuric acid, except in the United States where import duties on the iron and copper in pyrites held back their use. These duties were removed in the 1890s, and by the turn of the century pyrites had become the principal acid-making material in the United States. At the same time, the United States was becoming an important producer of sulfur with the successful development of the Frasch hot-water process and its application to mining sulfur from salt dome deposits of the Gulf Coast. However, pyrites held the dominant position as an acid-making material for the US chemical industry until shipping problems during World War I forced a major conversion to Frasch sulfur. The development of the contact sulfuric acid process also favored the use of brimstone.

World War II disrupted sulfur production outside North America and recovery after the war was slow. Many foreign countries turned to US Frasch sulfur for rehabilitation and expansion of their acid industries. As foreign consumers became more dependent on US sulfur, the requirements of the US acid industry were also expanding. The US Frasch industry expanded production but in addition was forced to depend upon inventories to meet demand.

By 1950, when the Korean War broke out, inventories of Frasch sulfur had been reduced to about a six-month supply. The industry was producing enough sulfur to supply the needs of US consumers, but not enough to supply consumers in allied countries. In 1951, the US government ordered producers to ship specified allocations to its allies. Later the government limited domestic consumption, adopted a policy of maintaining existing inventories of mined sulfur, and controlled prices. The sulfur shortage of the Korean War period did not last long. After the cessation of hostilities, controls on the industry were removed and, stimulated by shortages and high prices, new sources of sulfur were developed both in the United States and abroad.

The US Frasch producers brought in new mines in 1953 at Garden Island Bay and Damon Mound with Chacahoula and Nash Dome underway. Italy was second in world production, but competition from low-cost mines was causing a rapid decline there.

By 1954, Mexico had entered the Frasch market with the opening of San Cristobal and continued construction at Salinas and Jaltipan. Of even greater significance were the first expansions of Canada's recovered sulfur capacity, which began about 1950 and accelerated growth in recovered sulfur.

All this activity caused supplies to outstrip demand by the mid-1950s with downward pressure on prices. This was enhanced by Mexican increases, the appearance of recovered sulfur from France in 1957, and the work begun on gas pipelines in Canada.

Freeport commenced construction at Grand Isle in 1958 and the Mexican Frasch industry reached maturity. Recovered sulfur output continued to expand in North America. The most significant event in 1958 was the opening of Texasgulf's liquid sulfur terminal, the world's first. This began a strong trend in the direction of liquid sulfur handling. The long-term contract became common owing to high inventory costs of liquid sulfur as compared to storage of solid sulfur.

The massive increases in North American Frasch output coupled with increases in recovered sulfur output triggered a slack world market in 1959. Pyrite sulfur/acid producers suffered further declines. Domestic pyrites were important locally, such as in Japan and east Europe, but the trend was clear with the beginning of Polish development of Frasch deposits in the Tarnobrzeg region. French recovered sulfur reached world markets via the new terminal at Bayonne.

The first Polish sulfur from the Machow open pit appeared on the world market in 1960 with French and Canadian recovered output increasing. US producers restricted output in the face of oversupply, but the market remained soft. By 1963, Canadian and French recovered sulfur output each exceeded 1 Mt and the US share of world exports had fallen 19% in four years to 31%. International trade in liquid sulfur commenced with construction of terminals, for US output, at Rotterdam and Dublin.

A fertilizer and industrial boom led to tight sulfur supplies and higher prices, particularly in western Europe and the United States. Mexico surpassed the US as the dominant exporter in 1964. Non-Frasch sulfur reached 4 Mt in 1965 compared to 1.25 Mt in 1953, largely due to pollution control requirements.

Poland took a large step toward export dominance by opening Frasch mines at Grzybow in 1966 and Jesiorko in 1967. A large deposit in Culberson County in west Texas was discovered by Duval in 1967.

Increased recovered sulfur in the United States, Japan, West Germany, Iran, and Iraq helped boost world supplies past consumption. Producer stocks jumped 41% in 1969 alone. Recovered sulfur output exceeded Frasch output for the first time in 1970. In the 1970s recovered sulfur, whose output was related to nonmarket forces, dominated the sulfur market.

The early 1970s were characterized by oversupply somewhat mitigated by growth in demand and the forced vatting of Canadian sulfur via nondust legislation by the Vancouver Port Authority. Thus, stocks actually fell in 1972 even though Iraq brought the Frasch mine at Mishraq on stream.

By 1973, increased demand coupled with the high cost of centralizing scattered recovered sulfur output led to major price increases, even though supply statistically matched demand. Tight supply continued in 1974 with demand up 11%, mainly from additions to consumer stocks. For the first time in many years, the pyrite decline was reversed by increased consumption in a few pyrite-producing countires, primarily Spain, Portugal, and South Africa.

The first major cartel price offensives led to significant changes in the 1970s. The oil and phosphate cartels increased prices sharply in 1974 and 1975, causing industrial and fertilizer recessions. Consumers began drawing down the sulfur stocks they had built up in the previous two years. The combined result was plummeting demand with major cutbacks in the United States and Mexico. This was the beginning of the nearly continual decline in North American Frasch caused by aging mines and lack of exploration success.

A gradual market recovery began in 1977 while sulfur production stagnated. Slower growth cut demand as well as supply of recovered sulfur. After a period of adjustment in world economies, growth in fertilizer use built up the demand in sulfur to previous levels and beyond by 1979.

The major exporters of the late 1970s and early 1980s were Poland and Canada. Very high prices have developed since demand outstripped supply in 1979–1981. These high prices have reversed, at least for the short term, the decline in US Frasch production, but the United States remains a net importer. The net reliance on imports began in 1977. Canada began drawing down its vast reserve in vats in 1980, a trend likely to continue into the 1990s. Major sour gas discoveries in the Overthrust Belt in the United States could make it a net exporter by the mid-1980s. New output in recovered sulfur in Saudi Arabia coupled with that in the US should ease tight supplies by 1983–1985. The conversion to liquid sulfur has peaked and new forms, primarily prills, are now encroaching on the liquid market.

Exploration

Exploration for sulfur deposits is a difficult task, especially for Frasch deposits. They are scattered and give little surface indication of their presence. While the presence of salt domes seems to narrow the area, most are barren. Even when sulfur is present, it tends to be very steeply dipping and hence presents a small, easily-missed drilling target.

Stratiform deposits, while often larger and flatter than domes, do not have the easily found dome structure to guide exploration. In fact, searching for a stratiform sulfur deposit is as close to oil and gas exploration as mineral exploration allows. This derives from the genetic relationship between petroleum and biogenetic sulfur. Exploration centers on areas containing anhydrite with petroleum in or below it. Within the basins, traps identical to many petroleum traps are located and drilled. Surface venting of hydrogen sulfide has led to discovery. Hollister (1977), with expansion by Barker et al. (1979), summarized the generally known conditions for sulfur deposits as: (1) sulfate-bearing rocks, preferably thick and composed of anhydrite; (2) proximity to petroleum deposits; (3) hydrodynamic communication between sulfates and petroleum, which is often accomplished via faulting, jointing, or solution-derived porosity; (4) a stratigraphic or structural trap to contain the precursors of the sulfur-forming reaction; (5) a reducing environment where the petroleum and sulfate are biochemically metabolized; and (6) an oxidizing environment where the metabolic products are altered, yielding sulfur.

Tools useful in locating sulfur deposits are few. Gravity studies continue to draw interest both for stratiform and dome (including offshore) exploration. Anhydrite has a density of about 2.96 while sulfur bodies vary from about 1.80 to 2.20, yielding a potentially measurable negative gravity anomaly. The variation depends on interaction between sulfur content, void development, water, and the type of limestone matrix. Actual use has yielded few if any exploration successes. Refer to Haye (1969), Heintz and Alexander (1978), Schmoker and Robbins (1979), and Schmoker (1979) for discussions and additional references.

Other methods popular in varying degrees include traditional geologic modeling and mapping (Ruckmick et al., 1979) photogeology (structure and geochemical coloration), thermal IR (heat of reaction), seismic (especially shallow high resolution), geochemistry (including airborne spectrometry of gases), resistivity, induced polarization and, most successfully, the drilling rig and downhole logging. Surface geology and stratigraphy are useful at times, but many deposits have very subtle to no

surface indications.

Exploration for volcanic sulfur follows the more traditional style. Exploration expressly for pyrites is very uncommon, because they are generally a byproduct. When done, however, methods useful to sulfide exploration in general are used.

Elemental Sulfur

Elemental sulfur occurs in and is produced from deposits of three general types: cap rock over salt domes, evaporite-basin (stratiform) deposits, and volcanic deposits.

Salt Domes

Salt domes and similar piercement structures are known to occur in various regions of the world, but sulfur deposits of economic interest have been discovered only in the salt domes of the Gulf Coast region.

The salt dome sulfur deposit typical of the Gulf Coastal Plain is depicted in Fig. 2. It shows an intrusive salt plug capped successively by barren anhydrite, sulfur-bearing limestone, and barren limestone cap rock, all enclosed in unconsolidated sediments.

Numerous references that discuss the origins of the salt dome, its cap rock, and associated sulfur may be found in the bibliographies of previous editions of this work (Lundy, 1949; Fogarty and Mollison, 1960; Gittinger, 1975). Interlocking scientific efforts of geologists, geophysicists, engineers, chemists, biologists, and nuclear chemists have contributed concepts or confirming data to the origin of salt dome sulfur deposits.

The salt that forms the domes was derived by evaporation of seawater to form a thick sedimentary deposit of salt, gypsum, and anhydrite many thousands of feet below the present surface of the Gulf Coast area. Paleontological studies of pollen and spores found in the salt indicate that the salt was deposited during the Late Triassic to Early Jurassic periods, about 180 million years ago. It is a layered deposit composed primarily of soluble NaCl (halite), with 5 to 10% insoluble material. The insoluble material is 99% $CaSO_4$ (anhydrite) and most of the remaining 1% is dolomite. Calcite, pyrite, quartz, limonite, hematite, celestite, and barite are present in trace amounts. Scarcity of potassium compounds, which concentrate in the last stage

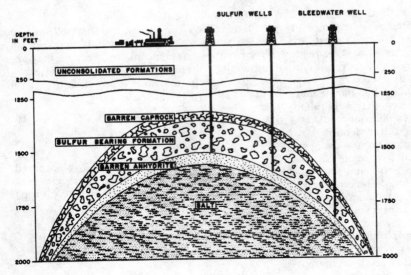

FIG. 2—*Typical cross section of a sulfur-bearing salt dome (Gittinger, 1975).*

brines before desiccation, indicates that evaporation probably was never complete.

Explanation for the formation of the domes from the original bed of salt is derived from a fluid-mechanics theory proposed by Nettleton (1934). The salt bed was deposited with a specific gravity of about 2.2, and because salt is only slightly compressible, this gravity would not have changed appreciably with burial. During subsequent geological time, the salt was buried beneath many layers of sediment. Burial and compaction of the sediments increased their specific gravity until at lower depths they had a specific gravity greater than the salt. Salt will flow when subjected to differential stress and Nettleton proposed that the salt acted like a liquid and flowed up through the overlying sediments driven by its lower specific gravity. An overburden of between 300 and 600 m was necessary before the gravity differential was great enough to initiate movement. Actual start of movement may have resulted from variations or weaknesses in the overburden, structures in the salt, or tectonism. There is a critical depth of overburden which, if exceeded, will stop the growth of a dome. A compressed sediment increases in strength as well as density. If the strength of the compressed sediment exceeds the buoyant force available for upward movement of salt, no movement is possible unless faulting or fracturing provides an avenue of escape.

The layered cap rock on top of the salt dome was originally thought to be of sedimentary origin, a remnant of overlying beds pushed up on the rising finger of salt. Work by Taylor (1938) and Goldman (1952) showed that the cap rock resulted from the residual accumulation of anhydrite present in the salt. As the salt dome rose through the basin sediments, it came into contact with zones of circulating ground water which dissolved away the salt, leaving the insoluble crystals of anhydrite to be compacted into a cap over the salt plug. Locally, the anhydrite may be hydrated to form gypsum.

Geologists noticed that sulfur and limestone occur as replacements of the anhydrite of the cap rock. The common association of oil and sulfur was also noted. This led to the hypothesis that hydrocarbons reduced the anhydrite to form sulfur and limestone, as represented by the following equations:

$$CaSO_4 + CH_4 \rightarrow CaS + CO_2 + 2H_2O \quad (1)$$

$$CaS + CO_2 + H_2O \rightarrow CaCO_3 + H_2S \quad (2)$$

$$3H_2S + SO_4^= \rightarrow 4S + 2H_2O + 2OH^- \quad (3)$$

Although these reactions have permissive thermodynamics, the rate of reaction is very slow for temperatures that can reasonably be expected in Gulf Coast sediments. For example, at 100°C, 150 million years would not suffice for development of a cap rock deposit. This is impossibly slow considering that the salt was originally deposited only 180 million years ago.

It is now generally recognized that a biogenic, epigenetic origin of sulfur in salt domes and stratiform deposits is most likely. Many microbiologists have since studied the subject and greatly refined the knowledge of anaerobes (Postgate, 1972, 1979; Silverman, 1972). These bacteria are highly versatile, such that a strain collected from saltwater can be acclimated to live in brackish water and then fresh water, and vice versa. At present, two genera and at least three species are commonly accepted: *Desulfovibrio desulfuricans,* the most widely distributed and most active form at atmospheric temperatures; *Desulfovibrio orientis,* a mesophilic (medium temperature) form; and *Clostridium nigrificans,* a thermophilic (heat-loving) form. All of these anaerobic bacteria consume hydrocarbons as a source of energy, but use sulfur instead of oxygen as a hydrogen acceptor to produce hydrogen sulfide, calcite, and water. The hydrogen sulfide may be oxidized to a colloidal form of sulfur or, in an anaerobic environment, it can react with excess calcium ions to form calcium sulfide and by hydrolysis to calcium hydrosulfide. Calcium hydrosulfide solutions will react with colloidal sulfur in previously oxidized zones to produce calcium polysulfides. In the presence of carbon dioxide generated by bacteria the polysulfide precipitates crystalline sulfur and coprecipitates secondary calcite. If hydrogen sulfide is able to escape from the system, a limestone cap rock may be free of sulfur. Sulfur may also be removed by sulfur-oxidizing bacteria (Ehrlich, 1972).

Further investigations support the role of sulfate-reducing bacteria in the formation of sulfur. Although all four sulfur isotopes chemically react alike, the lighter isotopes enter some phases more readily than do the heavier ones (Thode, 1972). This results in fractionation or a concentration of lighter isotopes in some compounds and a residual enrichment of heavier isotopes in others. Feely and Kulp (1957) and others produced evidence to support the theory of sulfate-reducing bacteria. Their laboratory evidence showed that sulfate-reducing bacteria fractionate the sulfur isotopes S^{32} and S^{34} in the reduction of sulfate ions to sulfide ions comparable to that found in sulfur from salt dome cap rock. The sulfur is enriched in the S^{32} isotope while the surrounding gypsum and anhydrite are enriched in the S^{34} isotope. Feely and Kulp (1957) also showed that the carbon in the cap rock is isotopically similar to the carbon in Gulf Coast crude oil and that the $C^{12} : C^{13}$ ratio was 4.5% higher for cap rock carbon than the ratio for sedimentary limestone.

Nearly all salt dome sulfur deposits were discovered during petroleum and natural gas exploration. Some earlier discoveries were made by drilling, while others were recognized by sulfur water seeps or low mounds. Various geophysical and geological methods are used in prospecting. Because sulfur is not uniformly distributed throughout the cap rock, numerous boreholes must be drilled to determine the extent and richness of the sulfur area for evaluating its commercial potential.

Prospect drilling has proved the existence of over 400 salt dome structures in the coastal and offshore area of the Gulf of Mexico, most of which contain no commercial sulfur. In November 1980, there were seven salt dome sulfur deposits in commercial operation: one onshore in Louisiana, one offshore Louisiana in the Gulf, three in Texas, and two in Mexico. These seven mines were producing at an annual rate of around 8 Mt. They have produced about 159 Mt in their life. Production history of all Frasch process sulfur mines (including stratiform deposits) in the United States and Mexico is shown in Table 3.

The Frasch Process:

Herman Frasch's efforts to develop the hotwater process for mining sulfur from the first discovered salt dome deposit in Calcasieu Parish, LA, is described by Haynes (1942; 1959). The hotwater process now used in extracting sulfur from salt dome deposits in the United States and Mexico and from the evaporite basin deposits in west Texas, Poland, the USSR, and Iraq is only slightly modified. Requisites for the economical production of sulfur by the Frasch process are: a porous, sulfur-bearing formation; an impervious stratigraphic seal; a large, dependable supply of water; and a cheap fuel supply. The heart of the operation is the power plant, where water is heated, air is compressed for pumping the liquid sulfur to the surface, and electric power is generated for drilling, mining, loading, and auxiliary operations.

A typical setting of equipment for a Frasch installation is shown in Fig. 3. A well consists of four concentric pipes varying in diameter. The outer pipe acts as a protective casing, extending to the barren cap rock. The next pipe carries the flow of hot water, which is forced out through holes at the bottom into the sulfur-bearing limestone formation. As sulfur melts it percolates down through the porous limestone

TABLE 3—Production of Frasch Sulfur in the United States and Mexico by Mine and Company, 1894 through 1979

Dome/Mine	Company	Years Operated	Total Output, 1000 lt*	Total Output, kt*
United States				
Sulphur Mine, LA	Union	1894-1924	9,412	9,563
Bryan Mound, TX	Freeport	1912-1935	5,001	5,081
Gulf (Big Hill), TX	Texasgulf	1919-1936	12,350	12,548
Hoskins Mound, TX	Freeport	1923-1955	10,895	11,070
Big Creek, TX	Union	1925-1926	2	2
Palangana, TX	Duval	1928-1935	237	241
Boling, TX	Union	1928-1929	8	8
Boling, TX	Texasgulf	1929-	75,556	76,768
Long Point, TX	Texasgulf	1930-1938	402	408
Jefferson Island, TX	Jefferson Lake	1932-1936	431	438
Grande Ecaille, LA	Freeport	1933-1978	40,398	41,046
Boling, TX	Duval	1935-1940	571	580
Boling, TX	Baker-Williams	1935-1935	1	1
Clemens, TX	Jefferson Lake	1937-1960	2,976	3,024
Orchard, TX	Duval	1938-1970	5,495	5,583
Long Point, TX	Jefferson Lake	1946-	8,129	8,259
Moss Bluff, TX	Texasgulf	1948-	8,847	8,989
Starks, LA	Jefferson Lake	1951-1960	840	853
Spindletop, TX	Texasgulf	1952-1976	9,837	9,995
Bay Ste. Elaine, LA	Freeport	1952-1959	1,131	1,149
Damon Mound, TX	Standard Sulphur	1953-1957	140	142
Garden Island Bay, LA	Freeport	1953-	18,522	18,819
Nash, TX	Freeport	1954-1956	151	153
Chacahoula, LA	Freeport	1955-1962	1,199	1,218
Fannett, TX	Texasgulf	1958-1977	3,477	3,533
High Island, TX	US Sulfur	1960-1962	37	38
Grand Isle, offshore LA	Freeport	1960-	19,414	19,726
Lake Pelto, LA	Freeport	1960-1975	5,622	5,712
Gulf (Big Hill), TX	Texasgulf	1965-1970	502	510
Sulphur Mine, LA	Allied Chemical	1966-1970	68	69
Nash, TX	Phelan Sulphur	1966-1969	171	174
Heiner, west Texas	Duval	1967-1970	579	588
Bryan Mound, TX	Hooker Chemical	1967-1968	5	5
Chacahoula, LA	John W. Mecom	1967-1970	154	156
Ft. Stockton, west Texas	Atlantic Richfield	1968-	1,467	1,491
Lake Hermitage, LA	Jefferson Lake	1968-1972	441	448
Caminada, offshore LA	Freeport	1968-1969	325	330
Bully Camp, LA	Texasgulf	1968-1978	1,725	1,753
High Island, TX	Pan Am Petroleum	1968-1971	110	112
Culberson, west Texas	Duval	1969-	17,027	17,300
Comanche Creek, west Texas	Texasgulf	1975-	679	690
		Total United States	264,334	268, 573
Mexico				
San Cristobal	Azufre Mexicana	1954-1957	162	165
Jaltipan	Azufrera Panamericana	1954-	25,961	26,378
Salinas	Azufre Veracruz	1956-1969	3,869	3,931
Nopalapa	Exploradora del Istmo	1957-1960	322	327
		1967-1971	348	354
Texistepec	Central Minera	1959-1961	9	9
Texistepec	Exploradora del Istmo	1971-	5,059	5,140
		Total Mexico	35,730	36,304
		Total US and Mexico	300,063	304,877

* 1 long tons (lt) × 1.016 047 = metric tons (t).
1000 t = 1 kt.

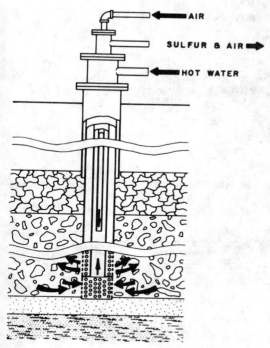

FIG. 3—Typical sulfur well equipment for the Frasch process (Gittinger, 1975).

to form a liquid sulfur pool at the bottom of the well. Of the two inner pipes, the smaller one carries compressed air which acts as an air lift to raise the liquid sulfur to the surface through the larger pipe. The volume of compressed air is regulated so that the production rate equals the sulfur melting rate in order not to deplete the sulfur pool and cause the well to produce water. If the pool does become depleted, air injection is stopped and additional hot water is injected down through the sulfur pipe, as well as the normal water annulus, until a sulfur pool is reestablished.

On the surface, the liquid sulfur moves through steam-heated lines to a separator where the air is removed prior to shipment by pipeline, thermally insulated barges, or rail cars to a central shipping terminal, customers' plants, or into storage. The sulfur may be transported as either a liquid or a solid.

Hot water for sulfur mining by the Frasch process is produced in power plants with water-heating capacities that range from 3.7 to upward of 53 ML/d. Until 1952, all mines used fresh water obtained from wells, rivers, or other surface sources. In that year Freeport pio-

neered the use of seawater for mining at its Bay Ste. Elaine, LA mine, located some 48 km from the nearest source of fresh water. Since then, Freeport has brought four additional mines into operation using seawater. Two of these mines, Grand Isle and Caminada, located approximately 11 km off the Louisiana coast in the Gulf of Mexico, are built on mining platforms. Caminada is presently on a standby basis because of the depressed condition of the sulfur market. A third mine, Lake Pelto, now closed, utilized a barge-mounted power plant originally used at Bay Ste. Elaine and now used at Caillou Island, the fourth and latest seawater Frasch mine (Anon., 1979a, 1980i, 1980j).

The hot water pumped into the formation to melt the sulfur must be withdrawn at approximately the same rate at which it is injected in order to prevent pressure in the formation from increasing to the point where further water injection would be impossible. Bleed wells which extract water from the formation usually are located on the flanks of the dome, away from the mining area.

Stratiform Deposits

Elemental sulfur occurs also in subsurface deposits which are similar to salt dome deposits in that the sulfur with secondary limestone is associated with bedded gypsum and anhydrite (Fig. 4). Deposits of this type are found in Italy, Sicily, France, Spain, Poland, the USSR, Iraq, Iran, west Texas, and southeast New Mexico.

The origin of sulfur in these deposits is generally believed to be derived by hydrocarbon reduction of sulfates, assisted by bacterial action. Dessau et al. (1962), in a study of Sicilian sulfur deposits, suggests a biogenic origin for H_2S and a subaqueous sedimentary origin for the sulfur. According to this source, H_2S was formed in the bottom oozes of lagoons and was oxidized by atmospheric oxygen in the water; sulfur was precipitated as a sediment on the lagoon floor.

Polish scientists Czerminski (1960, 1968) and Pawlowski (1968) propose for their deposits, which are concentrated in the Miocene marine sediments in the Carpathian foredeep, that beds of gypsum were reduced to H_2S and $CaCO_3$, probably by biogenic activity. Bacteria as the active agents then precipitated sulfur from the H_2S. A number of bacteria including the genera *Beggiatoa* and *Chromatium* consume H_2S to produce sulfur as a waste which accumulates in the body of the bacteria. On death of the bacteria, the sulfur remains. The

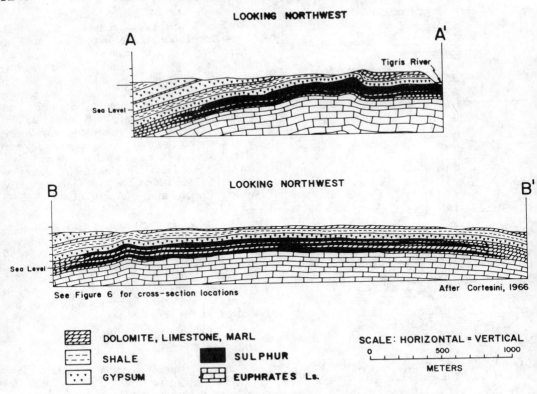

FIG. 4—*Subsurface deposits of elemental sulfur at Mishraq, Iraq.*

sulfur is available for solution, transport, and redeposition, or it may stay as microcrystalline grains disseminated in the calcite of the sulfur-bearing bed.

The Polish sulfur deposits, which are located in the upper valley of the Vistula River near Tarnobrzeg, were discovered in 1953. The initial mine, the Piaseczno open pit, was brought into production in 1960 and operated until 1971. The Machow open pit mine was brought into production in 1969. The ore from the open pit operations is beneficiated by flotation. The flotation concentrate is then melted in autoclaves and filtered to yield pure sulfur or burned to make sulfuric acid. A modified Frasch process [the hydrodynamic process of Zakiewicz (1975)] is being used at the Gryzbow and Jeziorko mines (Bixby, 1968; Anon., 1967, 1968c; Singhal, 1969). Production began at Gryzbow in 1966, and about a year later at Jeziorko. Poland is now second only to the United States in production of Frasch-process sulfur, and fourth after the United States, USSR, and Canada in production of elemental sulfur.

The Polish deposit extends into the west Ukraine region where the USSR has operation utilizing both open pit and hot water mining methods at Rozdol. Additional Frasch-process open-pit mines are in operation, one in the Ukraine and the other in southeastern Turkestan at the Gaurdak deposit in Upper-Jurassic limestone. The USSR also mines sulfur at the Kuybyshev complex from Permian limestone deposits in the middle Volga region (Shabad, 1969).

The sulfur mines of west Texas are in secondary limestone pods within cyclic evaporite deposits generally of Permian Age. Sulfur of commercial occurrence is located mostly in formations along the western edge of the Delaware Basin and on the south end of the Central Basin Platform in Culberson, Reeves, and Pecos counties (Zimmerman and Thomas, 1969). Cap rock as described for salt domes of the Gulf Coast area does not exist in west Texas. The sulfur occurs commercially in sections of evaporite beds where the gypsum/anhydrite has been biogenetically converted to limestone and sulfur. However, cores from the sulfur zone are very similar to those of Gulf Coast salt dome deposits. Based on stratigraphic, mineralogical, chemical, and isotopic analyses of core samples, the source of sulfur and its host limestone is considered to be epigenic and formed biogenetically within a calcium sulfate environment (Davis and Kirkland, 1970; McNeal and Hemenway, 1972). Native sulfur was derived from H_2S generated by bacterial reduction of anhydrite in the presence of dilute hydrocarbons. This bacterial action was also associated with oxidation of hydrocarbons to form CO_2, followed by the deposition of calcium carbonate. Subsequently, oxidation of H_2S by oxygenated ground waters which penetrated the porous formation yields sulfur and water. The H_2S may migrate considerable distances prior to oxidation. It must also be trapped by mechanisms identical to hydrocarbon traps; sulfur from H_2S frequently is associated with hydrocarbons.

The USSR has large reserves of sulfur, but grades are low and operating costs high. Estimated production of contained sulfur totaled 8.9 Mt, of which 3.8 Mt were recovered from pyrite, 2.6 Mt from native sulfur, and 2.5 Mt from other elemental sulfur. Estimated levels of total sulfur output for 1977 and 1980 are 9.5 and 11 Mt, respectively. Sulfur exports, mainly to Comecon countries, decreased from 463.8 kt in 1970 to 441 kt in 1975. Imports of sulfur increased from 216.7 kt in 1970 to 690 kt in 1975.

The dressing mills of all three main Russian complexes are treating ore with a sulfur content from 8 to 40% and produce a flotation concentrate with 70 to 85% sulfur content. Sulfur production by the Frasch process at the Gaurdak complex has increased rapidly since the second installation (100 kt/a) went into service in 1975. The No. 3 (100 kt/a) installation using the Frasch process at this complex was under construction in 1976. The Rozdol complex produced concentrates with a 72 to 75% sulfur content from ore with a 22 to 23% sulfur content. It is planned to recover 895 kt of sulfur from the Orenburg sour gas. Agreements have been signed for the supply by Poland of three sulfuric acid production units to the USSR with a capacity of 1515 t/d each. The Soviet Union has already purchased 25 sulfuric acid plants from Poland (Strishkov, 1977).

In late 1971, the state-owned National Iraqi Minerals Company started sulfur production at the Mishraq mine. The Mishraq native sulfur deposit is in northern Iraq about 40 km southeast of Mosul and 315 km north of Baghdad. This deposit is the largest known occurrence of stratiform bioepigenetic sulfur, containing at least 100 Mt of elemental sulfur. It underlies a 10 km² portion of the southeast end of a northwest-trending, doubly plunging anticline on the west bank of the Tigris River at its confluence with the Great Zab River. The deposit is in one anticline among many in the folded portion of the Mesopotamian depression and represents part of what may be the largest reserve of elemental sulfur in the world (Anon., 1974).

Small, tight, en echelon folds are superimposed on the southwest limb of the Mishraq anticline with axial trends similar to the main fold (320°). Faulting is normal and reverse with dominant northwest and subordinate northeast trends. Mining-induced subsidence of 4 to 5 m causes fractures which tend to follow these preexisting directions (Zackiewicz, 1975).

The sulfur mineralization is in three main zones (Chebanenko, 1969) of vuggy and bituminous bioepigenetic limestone in the basal Lower Fars Formation of middle Miocene age and marine origin (Fig. 5). The Lower Fars consists of intercalated bituminous marine carbonates (dolomite, limestone, marl) and anhydrite/gypsum with minor shale and sandstone interbeds. The depositional environment was of periodic marine influxes followed by evaporation in a partially barred basin with southern access to the sea (Al-Sawaf, 1977).

The sulfur was formed by oxidation of hydrogen sulfide produced during metabolysis of petroleum and anhydrite/gypsum by anaerobic bacteria such as *D. desulfuricans* (Al-Sawaf, 1977), a conclusion supported by the S^{34} and C^{13} fractionation data (Lein et al., 1975). Sulfur mineralization is thickest in areas of intense folding and faulting which enhance solution, movement, and mixing of reactants. Combined thickness (Fig. 6) of the three sulfur-bearing zones is from 2 to 123.9 m, with a maximum ore section of 107.9 m and a grade of 23.14 wt % sulfur (Chebanenko, 1969). Seven ore types have been recognized, of which coarse-crystalline, secondary sulfur alternating with bands of secondary limestone predominates (Niec and Al Nouri, 1976).

Hydrologic conditions at the mine are complex with subsurface drainage via karst features, fractures, faults, and vuggy porosity within the ore zones of the productive member (Niec and Al Nouri, 1976; Featherstone and Al-Samarrie, 1975; Al-Sawaf, 1977; Zakiewicz, 1975). The productive member contains the

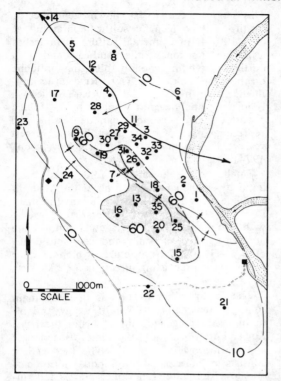

FIG. 5—*Isopach of total solid feet of sulfur, zones 1 to 3, as a function of folding at Mish-raq, Iraq (based solely on early Russian mapping and drill holes 1–9, 11–35; Cortesini et al., 1966).*

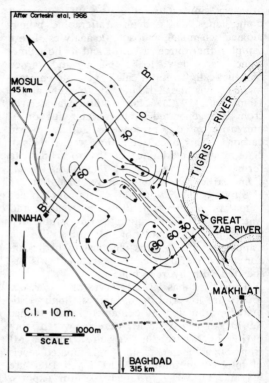

FIG. 6—*Isopach of total solid feet of sulfur, zones 1 to 3, Mishraq, Iraq (based solely on early Russian data; Cortesini et al., 1966).*

bulk of the ground water, although up to 13 aquifers have been recognized throughout the section, and it is intersected by the Tigris River. A very steep hydraulic gradient exists with flow southeastward toward the Tigris where it is discharged from springs in and beside the river. Hydrogen sulfide-carbonate waters predominate. Recharge is mainly at the northwest portion of the anticline where the Lower Fars Formation crops out. The ground water connection and flow to the river is important in sulfur generation as it is the pathway by which oxygen is carried into contact with hydrogen sulfide at depth yielding sulfur and water.

The deposit is currently being mined by the Polish hydrodynamic (modified-Frasch) process (Zackiewicz, 1975) at a rate of about 600 kt/a out of a total capacity of 1 Mt/a. The maximum capacity has not been reached because of infrastructural constraints related to transportation and because the mine is difficult to operate. Large injection water losses

and excessive bitumen contamination are paramount. Water losses are mitigated by the installation of subsurface impermeable screens. Bentonite/sulfuric acid filtration removes the excess bitumen but at a cost of 8 to 25% loss of sulfur in filter cake and skim foam (Ali and Al-Shahwani, 1975).

Initially, sulfur was vatted at the mine, crushed, and shipped via rail to the port of Um Qasr about 1,000 km south of Mishraq (Anon., 1974). Liquid sulfur is now shipped to the port where vatting is done as necessary.

The feasibility of using the Frasch process for mining the bedded sulfur deposits of west Texas was first proved by Duval Corp., the mining subsidiary of Pennzoil Co., when it began operations in 1967 in Pecos County, near Fort Stockton (Zimmerman and Thomas, 1969). Atlantic Richfield Co. also operated a small Frasch mine near Fort Stockton (McNeal and Hemenway, 1972). In 1968, Duval discovered and delineated a large sulfur deposit in the Rustler Hills area of Culberson County and brought the mine into operation in 1969 (Aalund, 1970). Duval closed its Fort Stockton mine in 1970. In 1979 and 1980 production at Duval's Culberson property exceeded 2 Mt/a and a small Frasch mine was opened at Phillips Ranch, about seven miles from Culberson (Anon., 1979b; Barry and Davis, 1969; Ellison, 1971).

Volcanic Deposits

Sulfur of volcanic origin is probably the most widely distributed of native sulfur deposits. Deposits of this type are known in most volcanic regions of the world but mainly throughout the mountain ranges which border the Pacific Ocean, particularly in South and Central America, Japan, the Philippine Islands, the Kamchatka Peninsula, the Kurile Islands, Taiwan, and New Zealand. Most currently known reserves occur within this region (White, 1968). Mining of volcanic deposits is limited primarily to Japan, Turkey, Mexico, Italy, and the Andean countries of South America. Detailed discussion of deposits in Japan and Chile are available in Anon. (1966b).

Volcanic sulfur deposits include those originating from all forms of volcanic activity and are generally classified by mode of emplacements: (1) impregnation and replacement deposits, usually formed by the action of hot acid springs, which are rich in sulfurous gases; (2) sedimentary deposits, formed by precipitation of elemental sulfur in hot crater lakes, usually in the latter stages of volcanic activity; (3) sublimation deposits, formed by gaseous or fumarolic activity near volcanic craters; and (4) sulfur flows, the sulfur probably originating from previously formed deposits which have been remelted. Volcanic deposits are usually found in tuffs, lava flows, and other volcanic rocks, as well as sedimentary and intrusive formations.

Mining methods used are tunneling, room-and-pillar, open pit, cut-and-fill systems, and various forms of stoping. Processing of ore to separate the sulfur from the volcanic ash is by various combinations of melting, distillation, agglomeration, flotation, solvent extraction, or any one of these (Anon., 1960; Anon., 1968d; Anon., 1969; and White, 1968). Commercial interest in volcanic deposits is high only when premium or politically protected markets exist.

Japanese volcanic deposits have supplied that country's elemental sulfur requirements for many years, but the growing supplies of recovered sulfur from petroleum refining and byproduct sulfuric acid from nonferrous smelting are forcing a major contraction of the Japanese native sulfur mining industry, as are dwindling reserves.

Turkey obtains most of its elemental sulfur requirements from the Keciborlu mines in the southwestern part of the country. Mexico has a small mine, Los Cerritos, in San Luis Potosi. In the United States where many small deposits of this type are found in several western states, ore has been mined only intermittently and generally in small tonnages for local use. One exception is the Leviathan deposit in Alpine County, CA, which was mined by The Anaconda Co. from 1953 until 1962 to supply 20% sulfur ore for a sulfuric acid plant at its Yerington, NV copper operation (Gould, 1955).

Recovered Elemental Sulfur

The principal sources of recovered sulfur are the hydrogen sulfide contaminants in sour natural gas and the organic sulfur compounds contained in crude oil. Recovery is mainly in the elemental form, although some is converted directly to sulfuric acid. Smaller quantities of sulfur are recovered from tar sand, oil shale, and coal.

Sour Natural Gas and Crude Oil

The growth in the recovery of sulfur from natural gas and crude oil since the mid-1950s has been one of the most significant trends in world sulfur. Rising from less than 0.5 Mt in 1950 to about 2.5 Mt in 1960, production at 1972 year-end reached an annual rate of nearly 15 Mt of which over 11 Mt were recovered from sour natural gas. The Province of Alberta, Canada, accounted for about two-thirds of this 11 Mt; France, the second largest producer, for a sixth. Canadian production of sulfur from sour gas wells totaled 6 Mt in 1980. The hydrogen sulfide content of the sour gas in the Alberta foothills of the Rocky Mountains ranges from trace amounts to more than 50%.

Recovery of elemental sulfur from sour natural gas in France is principally from the Lacq field 24 km northwest of Pau in the Department of Aquitaine. This deposit was discovered in 1951 and brought into production in 1957. In the early 70s, the Lacq plant had eight sulfur recovery units and processed gas from Pont d'As, Meillon/St. Faust, and Ucha gas fields in addition to that from the Lacq field. Gas from the Lacq field has a hydrogen sulfide content of 15.2%; the other fields are less sour. Sulfur production was about 1.75 Mt/a, but has begun to decline.

Sulfur was first recovered from sour natural gas in the United States in 1944, and until 1952, the United States was the sole producer. Today, more than 60 plants located in 10 states produce about 1 Mt/a, with Texas accounting for more than half.

Several other countries recover sulfur from natural gas, of which Iran, West Germany, Iraq, and Mexico are the most important. The USSR installed a gas processing and sulfur recovery plant to exploit gas from the Orenburg field in the southern Urals which was discovered in 1959 (Gardner, 1973). The gas is reported to have a hydrogen sulfide content of about 3%.

About 3.25 Mt/a of sulfur are recovered from crude oil in 46 countries, of which the United States is the largest producer. Sixty-eight plants located in 19 states recovered 1.2 Mt of sulfur, primarily brimstone, from crude oil in 1972. Texas and California accounted for 59% of the total. Japan, the second largest producer, recovers just over 1 Mt.

Sulfur values associated with crude oil are recovered during the refining process and the amount of sulfur recovered depends not only upon the crude throughput, but on the source of the crude, the refining process, and the products produced. The average sulfur content of the world's crude oil reserves is approximately 1.7%. In general, crudes in the Middle East, Venezuela, and the USSR have a higher sulfur content than those of the United States and North Africa.

Refineries in general are equipped to remove the sulfur only from the lighter refinery products and much of the sulfur in crude oil remains in the refinery emission gases or the residual fuel oils and is ultimately emitted to the atmosphere when these oils are burned. For the western world as a whole some 10 to 15% of the sulfur contained in crude oil is recovered. In the United States where residual oil is a lesser part of refinery output, recovery is higher—probably more than one-third. Low-sulfur fuel oils are growing in demand as an anti-air-pollution measure and facilities have been and are being built in the United States, Japan, the Caribbean, and the Middle East for reducing the sulfur content of fuel oil products. Although direct desulfurization of high-sulfur residual oils is costly, several processes have been developed. However, to date most desulfurization is done on distillate fractions which are blended back with a part of the residual. As an alternative to low-sulfur fuels, the SO_2 released from the burning of high-sulfur fuel oils may be removed from the combustion gases prior to their emission into the atmosphere. Processes for controlling SO_2 emission are discussed in a subsequent section.

In general, the process for recovery of sulfur from sour natural gas and crude oil consists of first separating the H_2S from the other gases, then converting the H_2S to elemental sulfur. The absorbent normally used in processing the natural gas is monoethanolamine (MEA) although other absorbents are used and have been proposed (Anon., 1968a; Sweeney and Valentine, 1970). In processing the H_2S-laden refinery gases diethanolamine (DEA) is the usual absorbent because it is less susceptible to contamination by heavy hydrocarbon fractions.

Unlike sour natural gas where the sulfur occurs naturally as hydrogen sulfide, the sulfur compounds in crude oil must be removed from the refinery feed and converted to hydrogen sulfide by a hydrogenation process before the sulfur can be recovered. It is beyond the scope of this chapter to discuss all of the various types of desulfurization processes used in refineries.

C.F. Claus developed the basic process for converting H_2S to elemental sulfur in Germany about 1880 (Sands and Schmidt, 1950). Over the years, the process has been improved and is now generally referred to as the modified-Claus process. The concentrated H_2S is fired in a combustion chamber connected to a waste heat boiler as shown in the generalized flowsheet of Fig. 7. Air is regulated to the combustion chamber so that one-third of the H_2S is burned to produce SO_2, water vapor, and sulfur vapor. Retention time in the combustion zone controls the amount of sulfur formed there, conversion increasing with increased retention. The high temperature gases generate steam in the waste heat boiler and are further cooled in a condenser for sulfur removal. Usually an in-line acid-gas burner is used to reheat the total gas stream before introduction to the catalytic converter where H_2S and SO_2 react to produce sulfur vapor and water vapor. The sulfur vapor produced is condensed and removed from the gas stream in a second condenser. A second converter and scrubber follow. Finally, the total gas stream is incinerated to convert all remaining H_2S, CS_2, and COS to SO_2 before emission to the atmosphere. Two converter plants may attain recoveries approaching 95

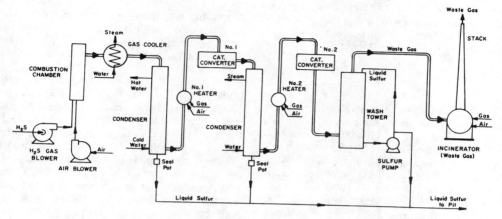

FIG. 7—*Generalized flowsheet, recovery of sulfur from hydrogen sulfide.*
(Gittinger, 1975).

96%. Air pollution regulations force most new plants to have three converters to attain up to 98% conversion; the Province of Alberta is pressing for 99.5% conversion (Rowland, 1972). A number of new processes have been announced for cleaning up the residual sulfur values from tail gases in recovery processes (Anon., 1972, 1972b; Beavon, 1971; Davis, 1972; Groendaal and Van Meurs, 1972; Hirai et al., 1972).

Oil Sands

Suncor, Inc., a subsidiary of Sun Oil Co., commenced production of synthetic crude oil from the Athabasca oil sands deposit in the northeastern corner of Alberta in September 1967. Hydrogen sulfide derived from upgrading the bitumen product is converted into elemental sulfur. Overcoming early technical difficulties, the plant now has a capacity of about 58,000 bbl of synthetic crude oil and 325 t of elemental sulfur per day.

Other groups have proposed similar projects and a consortium called Syncrude Canada Ltd. (a joint company owned by Atlantic Richfield Co., Cities Service Co., Gulf Oil Corp., and Imperial Oil Ltd.) was granted a permit by the Alberta government and a plant was completed in 1978. The plant has a daily capacity of 129,000 bbl of synthetic crude and 800 t of sulfur.

A number of other companies are conducting research programs in the Athabasca area, including research on methods for extracting the bitumen from the sands other than by surface mining.

The Athabasca deposits are estimated to contain more than 700 billion bbl of raw oil in place, with 400 billion bbl recoverable. The sulfur content, primarily in the form of organic compounds, ranges from 4 to 6%. Other large deposits of tar sands are located in Venezuela and Colombia. The United States has deposits in Utah, Kentucky, and California but they are relatively small.

Oil Shale

More important than tar sands as a potential source of synthetic crude oil for the United States are its oil shale deposits, particularly those of Colorado, Utah, and Wyoming. In general, the oil shale lands most attractive for commercial development are owned by the federal government and, under a proposed leasing program, industry would be permitted to develop a small part of the resources on public lands in those three states.

US oil shales have a sulfur content of less than three-fourths of 1%, of which 80% is in the pyritic form. Under a conventional mining and retorting process for recovery of the oil, the sulfur in the shale feed will be distributed among the oil, the retort off-gases, and the spent shale. An alternative process under study for recovery of the oil is based on an in-situ combustion principle in which thermal decomposition takes place underground.

Outside the United States, the largest reserves of oil shales are in Brazil, the USSR, and Africa. Large-scale production of shale oil is presently limited to the USSR and the People's Republic of China although no sulfur is apparently recovered from these operations.

In Brazil, a shale-oil prototype complex was

completed in late 1972. The plant is designed to treat 2 kt/d of shale and produce 1,000 bbl a day of oil with a sulfur content of 1.06%, 36,245 m^3 of fuel gas, and 14 t of elemental sulfur (Franco, 1972).

Coal

Very little of the sulfur contained in coal and lignite is recovered in a usable form. In 1981, the world mined over 2.3 Gt of bituminous coal and lignite. Sulfur content is estimated to average over 1%, equivalent to more than 30 Mt, of which less than a 0.5 Mt were recovered, largely from coke oven gases and mainly as sulfuric acid. Coal presently mined in the United States contains around 2% sulfur which is higher than the average of US reserves.

Some 40 to 80% of the sulfur in coal occurs as pyrite (see "Combined Sulfur") which is physically mixed with other constituents. The remaining sulfur is present mainly as complex organic compounds in the coal itself. Existing coal-cleaning technology can remove on an average about half the pyrite, but it appears organic sulfur can be removed only by processes of hydrogenation, liquefaction, or gasification which change the form of the coal. A number of techniques are in various stages of development. Processes for desulfurization of coal, including processes for gasification, are reviewed in Anon., (1972a), Chopey (1972, 1972a), Mills (1971), and Sisselman (1972).

Combined Sulfur

Pyrites and Other Metal Sulfides

Metal sulfides, found widely distributed throughout the world, have long been an important source of sulfur. Sulfide ores of commercial interest for their sulfur value belong to the ferrous group known as *pyrites*. Most important of these are iron pyrites (pyrite, FeS_2); white iron pyrites (marcasite, FeS_2); and magnetic pyrites (pyrrhotite, $Fe_n S_n + 1$).

The most important nonferrous metal sulfides include those of copper as chalcopyrite ($CuFeS_2$) and chalcocite (Cu_2S); lead as galena (PbS); zinc as sphalerite or blende (ZnS); nickel as pentlandite (Fe, Ni)$_9$ S_8; and arsenic as arsenopyrite ($FeS_2 \cdot FeAs_2$).

Pure pyrite contains 53.4% S and 46.6% Fe. Commercial grade ores are usually between 40 and 50% S and frequently contain small amounts of arsenic, lead, copper, cobalt, gold, and zinc. Pyrite occurs in isometric crystal forms having a brass-yellow color, a metallic

luster, and a specific gravity of 4.95 to 5.10. Marcasite, which has the same chemical composition and hardness as pyrite, occurs as orthorhombic crystals having a pale yellow color, metallic luster, and a specific gravity of 4.85 to 4.90.

Pyrrhotite has varying chemical compositions ranging from Fe_5S_6 to $Fe_{16}S_{17}$, with $Fe_{11}S_{12}$ being the generally accepted formula. When pure, it contains 38.4% S and 61.6% Fe. Pyrrhotite is hexagonal in crystal form, with a bronze color and metallic luster. It is softer than pyrite, is weakly to strongly magnetic, and has a specific gravity of 4.58 to 4.65. Cobalt, nickel, and copper are frequently found in association with pyrrhotite. Silver, gold, and platinum are found less frequently.

Sulfide ore deposits often occur in massive lenses, but may occur in tabular masses, in veins, and in disseminated zones. Metal sulfide deposits are formed under a wide variety of geological conditions ranging from those which are purely of igneous origin to those formed solely by sedimentary processes. In both cases, metamorphism has, to a varying degree, also played a part in the further concentration of the metal sulfide minerals to the extent that they constitute ore. Some interesting hypotheses on the role of certain bacteria in the formation of some sedimentary deposits of metal sulfides are discussed in Jensen (1962).

In 1979, the world produced an equivalent of 8.9 Mt of sulfur from pyrites. The USSR is the world's largest producer of pyrites with an annual production exceeding the equivalent of 3 Mt of contained sulfur. Japan and Spain, the world's second and third largest producers, each produce in excess of 1 Mt. Other important producers include Italy, Cyprus, Finland, Norway, and Sweden.

Sulfur is recovered from pyrites primarily by roasting to secure sulfur dioxide gas as a feed for the manufacture of sulfuric acid or for liquid sulfur dioxide. The iron sinter from the roasting operation may be leached for the recovery of byproduct nonferrous metals and the final residue sold as iron ore. Sulfur may also be recovered from pyrites in the elemental form. Of three commercial processes, only the Outokumpu process is still being used.

Outokumpu Oy, Finland's largest mining and metallurgical company, developed its process to recover sulfur and iron cinder from pyrite concentrates obtained from beneficiation of a deposit of complex ore at Pyhasalmi. Dried pyrite concentrate is blown into the top of a flash smelter. Here, oxygen-free combustion gases obtained from burning oil heat and decompose the pyrite to elemental sulfur and an FeS matte which is continuously tapped from the bottom of the furnace. The sulfur-laden gases from the furnace pass through a waste heat boiler, an electrostatic precipitator for dust removal, and a series of catalytic converters, and finally the sulfur vapor is condensed to liquid sulfur. Sulfur is shipped in liquid form or as prills. The FeS matte is roasted in fluidized-bed roasters to obtain SO_2 for sulfuric acid manufacture and iron cinder. The heat generated is recovered as steam and utilized for electric power production (Anon., 1964; Anon., 1966a; Argall, 1967; Guccione, 1966). Outokumpu's plant at Kokkola has been in operation since August 1962 and produces 100 kt of elemental sulfur and an additional 75 kt in the SO_2 gas.

The Orkla process, developed in the early 1930s by Orkla Mining Co. of Norway, used a shaft furnace for direct smelting of pyritic copper ore in the presence of a carbonaceous reducing agent. Heat in the upper zone was sufficient to drive off the labile atom of sulfur. The FeS formed was oxidized in the bottom zone to convert the remaining sulfur to sulfur dioxide, which was reduced to sulfur by the coke in the middle zone (Kiaer, 1954). Plants using this process were also operated in Portugal and Spain (Potts and Lawford, 1949).

The Noranda process developed by Noranda Mines Ltd. also controls temperature to drive off about half of the sulfur in the elemental form and the remainder as sulfur dioxide for sulfuric acid manufacture (Anon., 1954).

In the smelting of nonferrous sulfide ores, the sulfur is converted into sulfur dioxide which can be recovered from the stack gas in the form of sulfuric acid. Minor quantities are recovered as liquid sulfur dioxide or utilized directly in pulping mills. The amount of sulfur which can be recovered by conventional copper smelting is limited by the fact that a portion of the off-gases within a smelter contain too low a concentration of SO_2 for the economic manufacture of sulfuric acid; other copper smelting processes such as flash-smelting and electric furnace smelting yield gases with higher concentrations of SO_2 from which sulfur can be recovered more economically (Semrau, 1971). Hydrometallurgical processes for copper production are also under study (Gardiner and Warwick, 1971).

Sulfur Dioxide Emission Control: The problems associated with the emission of gaseous pollutants into the atmosphere have received considerable attention during the past decade.

The smelting of nonferrous sulfide ores has been estimated to account for 12% of annual worldwide emissions of SO_2 into the atmosphere. Although sulfur compounds are but one of numerous air pollutants, they have been one of the most topical. Sulfur enters the atmosphere as sulfur dioxide, hydrogen sulfide, sulfuric acid, and various sulfates. On a world basis the equivalent of about 220 Mt of sulfur are discharged into the atmosphere annually, of which two-thirds comes from natural processes. The remaining third comes from air pollution sources, mostly in the form of SO_2 (Robinson and Robbins, 1968). The burning of coal and petroleum products, mainly residual oils, has been estimated to account for 86% of worldwide emissions of SO_2 to the atmosphere from pollution sources (Robinson and Robbins, 1968).

Emphasis on control of air pollution and more stringent standards for flue gas emissions, as a means for meeting ambient air quality standards, have spurred research and development of techniques for removal and possible recovery of sulfur from SO_2 emissions. Many processes have been actively investigated and a number are available to industry through various engineering firms (Table 4).

Control processes may be classified broadly as regenerative processes or throwaway processes depending upon whether the sulfur values are recovered in a useful form or lost in output intended for disposal as solid waste (Gittinger, 1975; Moser, 1979). Both recovery methods can be carried out in wet or dry systems. Process chemistry may be absorption, adsorption, or catalysis. Operational processes utilize lime/limestone, sodium compounds, or magnesium compounds. Processes under development are much more broadly based.

Laws for the control of atmospheric pollution are likely to require nonferrous smelters to install some type of control technique, but the ultimate choice will vary with conditions at individual smelters. Where they are favorable, smelters are likely to install sulfuric acid plants. Some of this acid can be used for leaching copper oxide ores and additional quantities may find local markets. In some cases, however, excess acid may have to be neutralized with limestone to be disposed of as gypsum. The Smelter Control Research Assn. was formed by a number of copper-smelting companies to study processes for reducing smelter SO_2 (Campbell and Ireland, 1972). American Smelting and Refining Co. and Phelps Dodge Corp. conducted a joint pilot plant test at

TABLE 4—Summary of Flue Gas Desulfurization Methods Through 1978

Method	Class	Type	Main Output*	Remarks
Operational (% of Total)				
Calcium-based (90%)				
Slaked lime or milled limestone	W	T	$CaSO_4 \cdot 2H_2O$ (10%)	waste or gypsum
			$CaSO_3 \cdot \frac{1}{2}H_2O$ (90%)	product via forced
Limestone + MgSO$_4$ (sol.)	W	T		oxygenation
Sodium-based (7%)				
Sodium carbonate	W	T		
Wellman-Lord (sodium sulfite)	W	R	H_2SO_4, S, SO_2 (liq.)	little or no waste
Double alkali (sodium sulfite	W	T	$CaSO_3$	waste
+ lime)				
Magnesium-based (3%)				
Magnesium oxide	W	R	H_2SO_4	little or no waste
Developmental				
Saarberg-Holter (clear CaCl$_2$)	W	T	$CaSO_4 \cdot 2H_2O$	gypsum product
Sodium citrate	W	R	S	little or no waste
Ammonia	W	R	S	blue fume problems
Potassium thiosulfate	W	R	S	little or no waste
Aqueous sodium carbonate	D	T or R	Na_2SO_3 or S	waste or product
Activated carbon	D	R	S	little or no waste
Cupric oxide	D	R	S, H_2SO_4, SO_2 (liq)	little or no waste
Dry nahcolite	D	T	dust	waste

Source: R. Moser, 1979.
W = wet process, D = dry process; T = throwaway, R = regenerative
* Not including flyash.

Asarco's El Paso, Texas smelter of that company's process for reducing SO$_2$ to elemental sulfur (White, 1971).

Sulfates

Sulfate minerals represent the world's largest, yet virtually untapped, sulfur resource. Deposits of naturally occurring anhydrite and gypsum are widely distributed geographically and large amounts of gypsum are produced as byproduct waste material from several industrial processes, notably the phosphogypsum generated by manufacture of phosphoric acid from phosphate rock and sulfuric acid (Sweeney and Timmons, 1973). Furthermore, dissolved sulfates in oceans, saline lakes, and brines are almost inexhaustible.

Owing to the large amount of capital required and the high cost of operating the plants, sulfate resources have been little utilized as a source of sulfur. Production or significant development has occurred primarily in the United Kingdom, United States, Austria, East Germany, Italy, India, and the USSR. India was particularly active in development during the 1970s.

Sulfur values can be recovered in three ways: as sulfuric acid, as ammonium sulfate, or as sulfur. Only the first two are currently operational although work on processes with sulfur output continue. The established methods for elemental sulfur recovery are either microbial (Postgate, 1979) or thermochemical in nature. The latter process is the only one attempted commercially in recent times (by the Elcor Co. in west Texas in the late 1960s). This involved a two-step process (Anon., 1980e) in which calcium sulfide produced in a kiln is hydrolyzed to hydrogen sulfide which can yield sulfur by the Claus process. This very energy-intensive process was the primary reason for the Elcor failure, along with technical problems.

One of the oldest industrial processes for use of gypsum or anhydrite was developed in Germany during World War I. Generally referred to as the Muller-Kuhne process, it produces sulfuric acid and cement clinker from anhydrite (Hull, 1957; Ramirez, 1968), or from byproduct phosphogypsum derived from wet process phosphoric acid manufacture (Anon., 1968e).

The Merseberg process for the manufacture of ammonium sulfate from either natural gypsum, anhydrite, or byproduct gypsum from phosphoric acid is based on reacting calcium sulfate with ammonium carbonate liquor to produce ammonium sulfate and byproduct calcium carbonate (Anon., 1952; Hardy, 1957).

Processes to recover elemental sulfur from gypsum or anhydrite have been studied by the US Bureau of Mines and others (Anon., 1968). A bacteriological system has also been studied as an alternative to conventional physiochemical recovery methods (Rosenweig, 1968).

Formed Sulfur

Sulfur forming (Anon., 1979g) first developed in the early 1950s on a very small scale at refineries. Flakes of sulfur were usually produced but some slates production occurred. Increased sour gas production in the 1960s resulted in higher sulfur output. The generation of sulfur dust increased accordingly, as did the handling problems related to flakes in large volume. This led to development of many forming processes during that decade (Table 5), especially prilling by air, water, or combination techniques. Large-scale movement into prilling occurred in the early 1970s, especially after the bans on handling of bulk solid sulfur in the United States and Canada.

The Canadians initially converted to slates from crushed bulk sulfur derived from vats. While a great improvement, slates were still dusty, retained moisture, and were relatively difficult to handle. Other forms were developed and by the end of the 1970s, four wet-pelleting and four granulating plants were operating or under construction and one air prilling plant was under construction.

Production

Sulfur forming techniques were adopted to overcome the handling difficulties and attrition losses inherent in solid sulfur operations. Basically, liquid sulfur is formed, upon leaving the source, into moderately-sized particles of selected shapes. These particles are designed to resist attrition, be unwettable, and handle easily during stockpiling, loading, transport, and unloading.

There are four primary forms into which sulfur can be made to improve or relieve the problems associated with its transport and handling: flakes, slates, prills (or pellets), and granules (or nuggets). Flakes are perhaps the easiest, but least popular, of the four forms to produce. Sulfur is cooled and solidified on the outside of large rotating drums. This gives a thin skin or coating on the drum, which eventually peels off into small flakes.

Slating, the least expensive process, is one of the most widely used forming techniques. Molten sulfur is cast onto a continuous conveyor belt and is cooled, directly or indirectly, with water so that it solidifies into a thin sheet, usually between 3 to 19 mm in thickness. As it reaches the end of the belt, this sheet is broken, or breaks naturally, into smaller pieces that resemble slates.

Prilling sulfur is a more complicated—and correspondingly more expensive—forming method. There are two fundamental types of sulfur prilling: air and water. In air prilling, molten sulfur is sprayed from the top of a tower against an upward flow of air. As it falls the sulfur breaks into small droplets, which cool and solidify into prills between 1 and 2 mm in diam. In water prilling, the sulfur is sprayed into tanks containing water, which quenches and solidifies the sulfur droplets. The prills formed are removed from the bottom of the quench tank and usually must be dried. It is not uncommon to find the prilling technique, in particular the water prilling method, referred to as pelleting—a legacy from the production of lead shot in towers, the process on which all sulfur prilling is based.

The last of the four common forming techniques is granulation or melt agglomeration. This involves applying successive coats of sulfur to solid particles of sulfur in a granulator until the particle size reaches the required value. A similar technique is widely used in fertilizer production.

Characteristics

A number of characteristics of a sulfur form have a direct bearing on the suitability of the form for transport. These generally can be termed friability, moisture performance, and handling characteristics.

The purpose of a sulfur form is to reduce the amount of dust produced in handling and transport, so the friability of the form (the degree to which it is degraded) is perhaps the most important of its characteristics. This is influenced by a number of factors including particle size, surface texture, internal voids, and crystallinity.

Moisture performance is defined by the moisture content of the newly formed product and the moisture uptake and retention when it is stockpiled. Those forms produced by water quenching have a higher initial moisture con-

Industrial Minerals and Rocks

TABLE 5—Forming Processes

Process Type/Name	Developer	Country of Origin	Date of First Use	Prime Mover	Heat Sink	Shape	Bulk Density, (Kg/m³)	Angle of Repose
Slating								
V & E Process	Vennard & Ellithorpe	Canada	1970	rubber belt	air or water	slate or tiles		
Sandvik	Sandvik Steel	Sweden	1954	steel belt	water	slate or tiles		
Candybar						bevelled slate		
Water Pelleting								
Sulpel	Elliot Assoc. Devel. Ltd.	Great Britain	1964	gravity or pressure	water	sphere	1280-1400	30-35°
Capsul	Cambrian Engineering	Canada	1975	gravity or pressure	water	sphere	1152-1169 (dry)	31° (dry) 38°(wet)
Kaltenbach	Kaltenbach and Cie.	France	1973	gravity	water	sphere		
Chemsource	Chemsource	USA	—	gravity/ pressure	water	sphere	1121-1281	35°
Fletcher	R. B. Fletcher & Assoc.	Canada	1978	gravity	water	semi-flat, irregular	1121	25-30°
P.V. Commodity System	P.V. Container Systems	Canada	—	gravity	water	nuggets	1121-1217 (compact.)	32° +
Sulfur Nuggeting	Liquid Terminals, Inc.	USA	—	pressure		nuggets	1025	41°
Air Prilling								
Outokumpu	Outokumpu Oy	Finland	1962	pressure/ gravity	water	sphere	1200-1300	33-35°
Ciech	Ciech	Poland	1966	pressure/ gravity	air	sphere		
Stearns-Roger	Stearns-Roger Canada, Ltd.	Canada	1977	gravity	air	sphere	1120-1280	20°
Misc. Prilling								
Hydroprill	Ross Thermal Systems	Canada	—	pressure/ gravity	air & water	sphere		
Popcorn Sulfur	Union Oil Co. of California	USA	—	high pressure	air & water	"popcorn"	1000	37°
Granulation								
Perlomatic	APC & PEC Engineering	France	early 1960s	pressure	air	granules	1000	20-32°
Procor GX	Sulphur Services Div. of Procor	Canada	1970s	pressure	air	granules	1150	30°
Briquettes	Komarek	USA	—		air	"egg"		
Bulk Sulfur			—		air	mixed fragments		

tent than forms produced by dry processes. The moisture content of a form can be reduced, at extra cost, by mechanical dewatering and drying. Moisture uptake and retention are particularly important because sulfur is usually exposed to the atmosphere during storage. Formed sulfur, especially sulfur formed with silicon additives, usually has reasonable water rejection properties because sulfur itself is water-repellent. The spherical forms have the better water rejection properties; water will often penetrate only the first few inches into a stockpile and will then drain away through this surface layer. The handling characteristics

TABLE 5—Forming Processes

Friability	920 Tumbles	Hardness	Stability	Level 1 Stress Test	Level 2 Stress Test	Remarks
high	30+	10±				Water immersion of precooled sulfur on moving belt; produces 3-19 mm thick slates.
high	30+	10				Water and sulfur kept separate by cooling bottom of belt with sulfur on top; produces 3-19 mm thick slates.
low	10 (5-10)			6.7	5.3	Fed via special nozzles to rotating quench water with silicones added; 0.5-6 mm diam pellets with 0.25% internal moisture.
low	5.30	5.8	8.0	3.2	4.7	Vortex chamber nozzle ejects liquid sulfur into quench water causing turbulence. Additives are surfactants, pH controllers, and others; no commercial plants as of June, 1979.
						No commercial plants as of June, 1979.
low	10-30			5.8	6.2	Sprayed from special nozzle plate into quench water; 3-4% surface moisture on prills.
moderate	10 (5-8)					Fed into hot quench water through steam heated perforated plate: pH control additives used; 3-6 mm pellets produced.
	7.1	2.6	1.7	5.6	5.9	Sulfur discharged into agitated quench water via perforated plate; pH control additives used; 0.5-1% inherent moisture in pellets; not available for license (June, 1979).
moderate	10-30			8.5	6.0	Spray nozzle immersed in quench water; 0.5-1% internal moisture in nuggets.
						Spray of air/water/sulfur mixture downward into rising air; sprayed from side; 0.5-3 mm diam prills.
	tr.-1.76	2.07	1.51	0.4	1.1	Spray from top down into tower full of seed particles in updraft, 2-3.5 mm diam prills
						Sulfur cooled to near freezing in hydrostatic head tanks, then fed into tower with air updraft; not commercial as of June, 1979.
low	10-30			6.3	5.3	Spray of sulfur into jets of water in air updraft; no large scale plants as of June, 1979.
moderate	10-30			14.3	12.7	Spray sulfur/water mixture (1:1) directly onto storage pile; high residual moisture in prills (1-5%).
low	1-4	0.6	0.5	0.8	1.7	Spouting head feeds sulfur/air mixture into bottom of cyclically rotating conical-based vessel with seed sulfur.
low	10-30			9.6	5.4	Sulfur is sprayed into rotating granulation drum with seed material.
high	10-30					Powdered sulfur is compressed into shapes mechanically.
very high						Liquid sulfur is fed into bounded storage areas where it solidifies; these masses are broken for shipment or remelting.

of a sulfur form depend on particle size, uniformity, surface texture, density, and hardness. In fact, it is difficult to relate some of these to field experience. More directly identified with the way a form handles are the properties of bulk density (and the extent to which the form can be compressed), the angle of repose, and the flowability. The last of these can be calculated, as can the compressibility of the form. The highest compressibility and poorest flowability are shown by slates, with better flowability shown by prills.

Probably the most important of the handling characteristics are the bulk density and the angle of repose. Certainly these are normally stated in a description of the properties of the form. Normal dry bulk sulfur has a bulk density between 1.345 and 1.440 kg/m^3 and an angle of repose of about 35°. Thus any form should have a bulk density as near to this as possible and as high an angle of repose as possible. These vary considerably for the different types of forms and even for forms produced by the same technique. Additionally, two samples of a form produced by the same process can vary depending on, for example, the moisture content of the form, which increases both the bulk density and angle of repose. General figures are shown in Table 5 for most of the different types of forms.

Refined Sulfur

Of all the brimstone consumed in the western world in 1978, only about 400 to 450 kt of the total 25.6 Mt were used as refined sulfur or special grades—less than 2%. Thus, the ground sulfur business lies on the periphery of the huge world sulfur industry. Nevertheless, it is a business important in its own right by supplying essential and often highly specialized products for agriculture and industry (Anon., 1979c).

The category includes a wide range of manufactured sulfur products of which ground sulfur is the most prominent. The category also includes wettable, insoluble, precipitated (also referred to as sublimed or flowers of sulfur), colloidal, micronized, and double-refined sulfur, as well as special grades used in manufacturing pharmaceutical and photochemical products.

Although it is the oldest end use of brimstone, refined sulfur having been used since antiquity particularly in pharmacology and alchemy, demand for refined sulfur continues to grow. The manufacture of refined sulfur is confined to a relatively small number of enterprises most of which are located in Western Europe, and are engaged in sulfur grinding. Outstanding amongst them are Stauffer in the United States and Raffineries des Soufres Reumines, with its associated subsidiary companies, in France.

In agriculture, refined sulfur in powdered (dry or wettable), micronized, sublimed, and other forms often combined with metal compounds, is used in direct application on crops, in viticulture, and in horticulture as, first and foremost, a protection against mildew, powdery

mildew, and other damaging fungi. However, in both these end uses crude sulfur increasingly is used simply formed into the traditional shape of sulfur rolls without being refined, as recovered sulfur with a purity of 99.9% meets this specification. Refined sulfur, mainly ground, is also used in wine-making and sugar refining, as a pesticide (an ancient end use of sulfur), in fertilizer as a soil conditioner, and as an additive to compound animal feeds. However, owing to cost, fertilizer sulfur now tends to be crude sulfur formed into granules or pellets prior to grinding, or is the fines separated from bulk sulfur to be used in single superphosphate mixtures.

In industry, the rubber and tire sector is the prime user of special sulfur, making use of ventilated, micronized, and insoluble forms, all of which are necessary in the vulcanization process. Much smaller amounts of special grades are used in the manufacture of such diverse items as pharmaceuticals, matches, fireworks, and textiles.

Although ground and refined sulfur are used in some proportion almost everywhere in the western world, production of the various types and grades generally is concentrated in those areas where the level of economic development is already high. Companies involved in manufacture tend to be located in North America, Europe, and Japan, with other producers to be found where there is significant domestic demand as in Australia, South Africa, India, Mexico, Brazil, and Chile.

Characteristically, individual firms making ground and refined sulfur are set up initially to satisfy the demands of the domestic economy (this is particularly true for agricultural sulfur). This impetus then leads to a search for export markets. An exception to this is the relatively new sulfur-grinding industry in Kuwait, which makes use of the easy availability of recovered sulfur from petroleum refining, and has been from the beginning, largely export-oriented.

A healthy international trade in refined sulfur exists because almost all economies need some, but not enough to justify establishing a domestic industry. Certain developing countries have a significant potential need for ground sulfur, but lack financial and entrepreneurial resources to set up their own plants. In general, the pattern of trade seems to be from North to South America in the Western Hemisphere, and from Europe and Japan to nonproducing countries in the Eastern Hemisphere.

Transportation

Sulfur can be transported either in liquid or in solid states. Conversion to sulfuric acid, the main end use, is easiest using liquid sulfur so this has become the preferred form, especially when environmental effects are considered. Stockpiling of sulfur is cheapest by far in large solid blocks (vats) which are rebroken or remelted prior to shipment. Because sulfur block remelting is expensive, as is liquid sulfur-handling equipment, transport and handling of formed solid sulfur is now more economical except where liquid-handling facilities are in place.

End Uses

Sulfur is consumed mainly in the form of acid or other intermediate chemicals used to manufacture a final product that often does not contain much, if any, sulfur. Domestically, 85% of sulfur supplies are utilized in the form of sulfuric acid with similar proportions world-

wide. The balance is used for a variety of nonacid industrial purposes. These are detailed for the United States in Figs. 8 and 9 and Tables 6 and 7.

The largest single use is in phosphatic fertilizer production followed by petroleum and coal refining, copper production, and industrial organic chemicals. Combined agricultural uses account for over 60% of domestic sulfur use. Shelton (1980a) describes details of major end-use sulfur requirements and modes of sulfur utilization.

Sulfuric Acid

World sulfuric acid production totaled 135 Mt in 1979 (Table 8), and domestic sulfuric acid production totaled 38 Mt from 120 plants operating in 1979 (Table 9). Producers in the southern states rely on Frasch sulfur as feedstock; western states producers rely on by-product sulfuric acid produced by smelters and on recovered sulfur from natural gas in Canada (Shelton, 1980a).

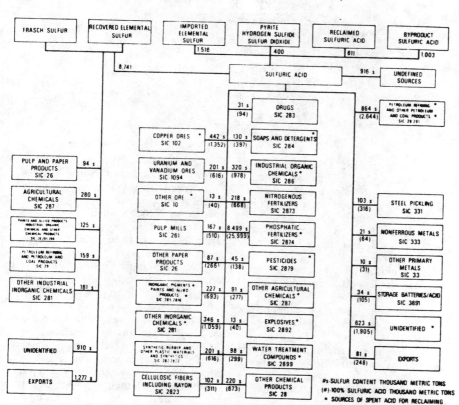

FIG. 8—*Domestic sulfur-sulfuric acid supply/end-use relationship, 1980
(Shelton, 1980b).*

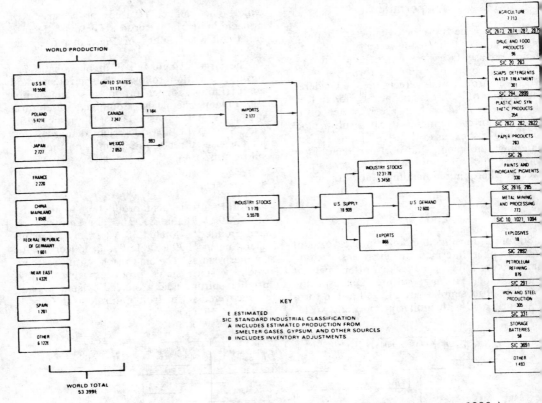

FIG. 9—*Supply-demand relationships for sulfur, 1978 in 1000 t S (Shelton, 1980a).*

A large part of the sulfuric acid consumed by industry is used as a process chemical rather than for its sulfur value. In certain of these applications, particularly in petroleum refinery alkylation and the manufacture of alcohols, the sulfur values in the acid are not used up and the spent or sludge acid is recovered and re-used as such or is reprocessed.

Shelton (1980a) summarized the reasons for sulfuric acid's dominance as the most desirable mineral acid as follows:

1. Relatively low cost both as to the raw material (sulfur) and sulfuric acid plant operating costs.

2. Less severe shipping, handling, and storage problems compared with those of other acids. .

3. Wide adaptation to numerous acidulations and neutralization processes.

4. Excellent dehydrating properties.

5. Effective catalysis in many hydrocarbo and organic chemical syntheses.

6. Readily forms organic sulfates with mar hydrocarbons, which are easily hydrolized form other basic products.

7. High boiling point, which limits volati zation losses due to high temperatures requir in many processes.

8. Can be partially used in one proce reused in a second or even a third proce and/or be readily regenerated, fortified, a concentrated for still further uses.

Sulfuric acid is produced near consumpti sites by either of two processes; the olc chamber process or the newer and more i portant contact process which has lower ca tal and operating costs. In the production sulfuric acid, elemental sulfur or any num of sulfur-bearing materials are burned to p duce SO_2. The contact process requires p

TABLE 6—Sulfur Supply-Demand Relationships, 1969-1979
(1000 t)

	1969	1970	1971	1972	1973	1974	1975†	1976	1977	1978	1979
	World Production										
Production:											
United States	9,698	9,710	9,734	10,382	11,096	11,602	11,440	10,879	10,727	11,175	12,101
Rest of world	28,099	32,227	33,001	35,113	37,102	39,551	39,238	39,660	41,773	42,224	ᴾ42,733
Total	37,797	41,937	42,735	45,495	48,198	51,153	50,678	50,539	52,500	53,399	ᴾ54,834
	Components and Distribution of US Supply										
Domestic mines	9,698	9,710	9,734	10,382	11,096	11,602	11,440	10,879	10,727	11,175	12,101
Imports	1,824	1,694	1,452	1,207	1,242	2,184	1,927	1,755	2,009	2,177	2,494
Industry stocks, Jan. 1	2,697	3,392	3,890	4,186	3,857	3,990	4,020	5,208	5,652	5,557	5,345
Total	14,219	14,796	15,076	15,775	16,195	17,776	17,387	17,842	18,388	18,909	19,940
Distribution of US supply:											
Industry stocks, Dec. 31	3,392	3,890	4,186	3,857	3,990	4,020	5,208	5,652	5,557	5,345	4,239
Exports	1,576	1,456	1,561	1,882	1,804	2,706	1,374	1,290	1,197	866	2,044
Demand	9,316	9,375	9,320	10,012	10,399	10,991	10,773	10,941	11,657	12,600	13,739
Apparent surplus (+), deficit (−) of supply*	−65	+75	+9	+24	+2	+59	+32	−41	−23	+98	−82
	US Demand Pattern										
Agriculture (fertilizers)	4,537	4,755	4,877	5,294	5,609	6,076	5,977	6,164	7,225	7,713	8,142
Drugs and food products	—	—	—	—	—	—	44	42	47	96	101
Soaps, detergents, and water treatment	—	—	—	—	—	—	196	197	237	301	323
Plastic and synthetic products	579	503	523	549	589	620	357	314	455	354	328
Paper products	371	356	325	345	376	396	243	276	345	283	372
Paints	452	427	386	396	427	447	341	229	324	330	343
Metal mining and processing	376	396	417	437	508	569	510	656	701	773	869
Explosives	264	259	259	264	284	294	42	33	20	18	19
Petroleum refining	193	198	203	223	234	244	732	686	879	876	890
Iron and steel production	127	122	107	112	112	112	106	97	130	305	288
Storage batteries	—	—	—	—	—	—	33	33	44	58	51
Other	2,417	2,359	2,223	2,392	2,260	2,233	2,192	2,214	1,250	1,493	2,013
Total US primary demand	9,316	9,375	9,320	10,012	10,399	10,991	10,773	10,941	11,567	12,600	13,739

Source: Shelton, 1980a.
ᴾPreliminary.
* The difference between total US distribution of supply and total US supply.
† Data since 1975 not comparable to data for prior years.

gas stream which can be obtained from a brimstone burner without the purification equipment required with a pyrites roaster. The chamber process produces rather weak acid, about 70% H_2SO_4; the contact process produces 98% acid and stronger grades containing excess SO_3, called oleums. The chamber process is characterized by large, lead reaction chambers and the use of gaseous nitrogen oxides as the catalyst in a complex reaction to form sulfuric acid. The contact process uses a solid contact substance as a catalyst to convert SO_2 and excess O_2 into SO_3. Platinum, once used widely as the catalyst, has been replaced by V_2O_5, which is less susceptible to poisoning by arsenic and other similar impurities found in metal sulfides and sulfur of volcanic origin.

An innovation in the contact process was introduced commercially by Farbenfabriken Bayer of Germany in 1964. Plants of this new type are variously referred to as "double-contact," "double-absorption," or "double-catalysis" plants. The Bayer process increases yield by using thermodynamic equilibrium by removing a product of reaction. In the Bayer process, after a substantial proportion of the SO_2 is converted to SO_3 in two or three conversion stages, the SO_3 is removed from the gas stream by absorption. The remaining unconverted gas is returned to additional catalyst stages for conversion of SO_2 to SO_3, which is absorbed in acid in a secondary absorption tower. Besides the additional absorption tower, gas-to-gas heat exchangers are required for cooling and reheating the gas stream as shown in the simplified flowsheet of Fig. 10. Overall conversion of 99.5% or better is possible by this process. New sulfuric acid plants are likely to use this process in order to meet air pollu-

TABLE 7—Sulfur and Sulfuric Acid Sold or Used in the United States, By End Use
(1000 t sulfur content)

SIC	Use	Elemental sulfur*		Sulfuric acid (sulfur equivalent)		Total	
		1978	1979	1978	1979	1978	1979
102	Copper ores	—	—	626	693*	626	69(3)
1094	Uranium and vanadium ores	—	—	103	128	103	12( )
10	Other ores	—	—	10	8	W	V( )
20	Food and kindred products	W	W	—	—	W	V( )
261, 26	Pulpmills and paper products	96	124	187	248	283	37( )
2816, 285	Inorganic pigments, paints and						
28, 286	allied products, industrial organic chemicals, and other chemical products	214	166	203	205	417	37
281	Other inorganic chemicals	167	192	375	379	542	57
2822,	Synthetic rubber, cellulosic						
2823, 282	fibers, other plastic materials and synthetics	W	W	321	294	321	29( )
283	Drugs	—	—	94	96	94	9
284	Soaps and detergents	—	—	137	121	137	12
286	Industrial organic chemicals	—	—	195	385	195	38
2873	Nitrogenous fertilizers	—	—	412	179	412	17
2874	Phosphatic fertilizers	—	—	6,854	7,581	6,854	7,58
2879	Pesticides	—	—	34	48	34	4
287	Other agricultural chemicals	287	272	126	62	413	33
2892	Explosives	—	—	18	19	18	1
2899	Water treating compounds	—	—	164	202	164	20
28	Other chemical products	—	—	383	166	383	16
281, 29	Petroleum refining and other petroleum and coal products	108	103	768	787	876	89
30	Rubber and miscellaneous plastic products	17	18	16	16	33	3
3111	Leather tanning and finishing	—	—	5	W	5	V
331	Steel pickling	—	—	305	288	305	28
333	Nonferrous metals	—	—	29	34	29	3
33	Other primary metals	—	—	5	6	5	
3691	Storage batteries	—	—	58	51	58	
	Exported sulfuric acid	—	—	4	29	4	
	Subtotal	889	875	11,432	12,025	12,321	12,9
	Unidentified	985	952	401	453	1,386	1,4
	Total	1,874	1,827	11,833	12,478	13,707	14,3

Source: Shelton, 1980a.
W Withheld to avoid disclosing individual company proprietary data; included with "Unidentified."
*Does not include elemental sulfur used for production of sulfuric acid.

tion control regulations. Modern plant design is discussed by Phillips (1977), May (1980), Srinivason (1980), and Appl and Neth (1979). New plants often recover the large heat credit inherent in sulfuric acid manufacturing (Anon., 1978d; Anon., 1980d).

New Uses for Sulfur

Various industrial, academic, and governmental groups are researching new uses for sulfur in an effort to absorb the growing supplies of this basic chemical raw material, although some uses are so valuable as to compete for current supplies. Among new uses with potential large-volume markets are (1) sulfur-asphalt compositions for paving applications to give increased durability and solvent resistance,

(2) as an extender or recycling agent for us(e) asphalt; (3) a form of plasticized sulfur f paving (Sulphlex); (4) foamed sulfur wi high compressive strengths and insulating pro erties; (5) impregnation of a variety of m terials to improve strength and water and we resistance; (6) sulfur concretes, mortars, a aggregates with enhanced corrosion and salt sistance; (7) sewage and waste-water tre ment; (8) a sulfur electrode in alkali me batteries; and (9) plant and soil treatme (Davis, 1972; Shelton, 1980a). See also Ano 1979d; Bourne, 1978; McBee and Sulliva 1979; Raymont, 1978b; Rennie, 1977; We 1975; Raddatz et al., 1981; McBee et 1981; and Anon., 1980c.

In some places, sulfuric acid often is d posed of at a loss. Some new or expanded u are possible (Habashi, 1979).

Economic Factors and Problems

TABLE 8—World Sulfuric Acid Production
(1000 t 100% H$_2$SO$_4$)

	1977	1978	1979
World Total*	123,030	131,295	135,246
Western World	85,794	91,351	94,703
Communist World	37,236	39,944	40,543
West Europe	26,640	27,376	27,741
Belgium	2,030	2,109	2,309
France	4,382	4,487	4,957
West Germany	4,236	4,591	4,458
Italy	3,200	3,150	2,950
Netherlands	1,638	1,858	1,786
Spain	2,997	2,965	2,950
United Kingdom	3,405	3,453	3,498
Others	4,752	4,763	4,833
Africa	6,210	6,367	6,764
Morocco	1,326	1,271	1,435
South Africa	2,341	2,525	2,644
Others	2,543	2,571	2,685
Asia	11,411	12,342	12,382
India	1,850	2,311	2,574
Japan	6,392	6,437	6,582
South Korea	988	1,400	1,450
Others	2,181	2,194	1,777
Oceania	2,493	2,570	2,773
Australia	1,803	1,890	2,058
New Zealand	690	680	715
North America	34,417	37,712	39,211
Canada	3,431	3,527	3,030
United States	30,986	34,186	36,181
Latin America[†]	4,623	5,156	5,832
Mexico	2,295	2,372	2,430
Argentina	244	249	282
Brazil	1,348	1,650	2,234
Chile	350	355	351
Others	386	530	535
Communist World	37,236	39,944	40,543
Poland	3,293	3,300	3,500
USSR	21,100	22,400	22,400
Others	12,843	14,244	14,643

Source: British Sulphur Corp., Statistical Supplement No. 21, July/August 1980.
*Totals and subtotals may not add due to rounding.
[†] Latin America excluding Cuba.

Outlook for Demand

Demand for sulfur has continued to grow steadily, although dominance of agricultural end uses has caused flattening when fertilizer slumps for reasons exogenous to the sulfur producers. Shelton (1980a) predicts 3% growth through the year 2000 for traditional uses but an overall 4.6% growth rate driven by sharp increases in new sulfur-based technologies (Tables 10 and 11). These rates are lower than 1950 to 1970 levels and imply a domestic demand of 34 Mt and world demand of 142 Mt by 2000 under probable conditions. This is compared to 1981 levels of about 12 Mt and 58 Mt, respectively.

Shorter-term demand and supply predictions by Price (1980) are shown in Tables 12 and 13.

Outlook for Supply

Shelton (1980a) predicts chronic shortfalls in domestic production of from 1.6 to 4.0 Mt annually through the year 2000, with a world cumulative shortfall of 255 Mt. Clearly, higher prices in the early 1980s should shift resources into reserves, a process that can be rapid.

An additional problem in prediction is the rapidly changing balance between sulfur sources. The interaction between Frasch, recovered, and pyrite sulfur is complex and dominated by price and geology. Both Frasch and pyrite sulfur are largely voluntary sulfur, and thus respond to price. Recovered sulfur is primarily involuntary and, in fact, is dominated by forces exogenous to the world sulfur market which are political, legislative, and environmental in nature.

Examples of expected large changes are the decline in Canadian export dominance, especially for offshore. A rapid rise in Middle East recovered sulfur should offset this and more. Other factors, such as interaction between by-product and brimstone sulfuric acid, may cause problems for virgin acid producers (Anon., 1979).

High prices will continue until shortfalls are rectified. Regionalization of supply may occur, with associated regional independence and market penetration of smaller disseminated sulfur sources.

TABLE 9—Sulfuric Acid Sold or Used in the United States, By End Use
(1000 t 100% H_2SO_4)

SIC	Use	Quantity 1978	1979
102	Copper ores	1,915	2,119
1094	Uranium and vanadium ore	314	391
10	Other ore	32	25
261	Pulp mills	480	683
26	Other paper products	92	77
285, 2816	Inorganic pigments and paints and allied products	622	628
281	Other inorganic chemicals	1,147	1,159
282, 2822	Synthetic rubber and other plastic materials and synthetics	582	647
2823	Cellulosic fibers including rayon	400	252
283	Drugs	287	293
284	Soaps and detergents	418	370
286	Industrial organic chemicals	595	1,178
2873	Nitrogenous fertilizers	1,262	546
2874	Phosphatic fertilizers	20,968	23,192
2879	Pesticides	103	148
287	Other agricultural chemicals	385	189
2892	Explosives	56	57
2899	Water treating compounds	503	617
28	Other chemical products	1,171	509
29, 291	Petroleum refining and other petroleum and coal products	2,351	2,407
30	Rubber and miscellaneous plastic products	48	49
3111	Leather tanning and finishing	15	*
331	Steel pickling	932	880
333	Nonferrous metals	90	105
33	Other primary metals	14	20
3691	Storage batteries/acid	177	15
	Unidentified	1,228	1,38
	Total domestic	36,187	38,08
	Exports	12	8
	Total	36,199	38,17

Source: Shelton, 1980a.
* Included in Unidentified.

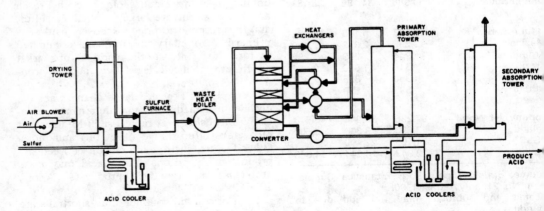

FIG. 10—*Simplified flowsheet, double contact sulfuric acid plant (Gittinger, 1975).*

TABLE 10—Projections and Forecasts for US Sulfur Demand By End Use
(1000 t)

End use	1978	Statistical projections *	Low	High	Probable
			2000 Contingency forecast for United States — Forecast range		
Agriculture (fertilizers)	7,713	18,000	13,000	15,000	14,000
Drug and food products	96	†	115	125	125
Soaps, detergents, and water treatment	301	†	360	400	400
Plastic and synthetic products	354	†	1,200	1,350	1,300
Paper products	283	0	300	600	400
Paints	330	100*	—	—	—
Metal mining and processing	773	1,700	1,400	1,800	1,800
Explosives	18	†	20	40	30
Petroleum refining	876	†	1,500	1,900	1,900
Iron and steel production	305	0*	—	—	—
Storage batteries	58	†	115	125	125
Other	1,493	2,600*	3,800	4,200	3,900
Potential new uses	—	—	5,000	30,000	10,000
Total	12,600	—	26,800	55,500	34,000

Source: Shelton, 1980a.
* Statistical projections, provided by the Branch of Economic Analysis, are derived from regression analysis based on historical time series data and forecasts of economic indicators such as GNP, FRB index. Projection equations with a coefficient of determination (R squared) less than 0.70 are indicated by an asterisk (*).
† On basis of new series, data are not available for sufficient number of years to make meaningful statistical projections.

TABLE 11—Summary of Forecasts of US and Rest-of-World Sulfur Demand
(1000 t)

	1978	2000 Forecast range — Low	High	Probable — 1990	2000	Probable average annual growth rate 1978-2000 (%)
United States:						
Total	12,600	27,000	56,000	21,600	34,000	4.6
Cumulative	—	420,000	660,000	200,000	480,000	—
Rest of world:						
Total	40,000	85,000	175,000	68,600	108,000	4.6
Cumulative	—	1,340,000	2,100,000	650,000	1,540,000	—
World:						
Total	52,600	112,000	231,000	90,200	142,000	4.6
Cumulative	—	1,760,000	2,760,000	850,000	2,020,000	—

Source: Shelton, 1980a.

TABLE 12—US Sulfur Outlook, Mt

	1979	1980	1985
Production			
Frasch	6.4	6.8	6.8
Recovered elemental	4.1	4.4	6.5
Total Elemental	10.5	11.2	13.3
Sulfur in other forms	1.7	1.6	2.0
Total production	12.2	12.8	15.3
Consumption			
Sulfuric acid			
Phosphates	8.5	9.0	9.7
Other	3.7	3.6	3.8
Total	12.2	12.6	13.5
Nonacid	1.1	1.0	1.5
Total	13.3	13.6	15.0

Source: Price, 1980, via Texasgulf, Inc.

TABLE 13—World Sulfur Outlook, Mt

	1979	1980	1985
Sulfur Production			
Elemental			
Frasch	8.9	9.5	9.8
Recovered	16.5	17.5	21.5
Total	25.4	27.0	31.3
Sulfur in other forms	10.2	10.3	12.0
Total	35.6	37.3	43.3
Consumption			
US	13.3	13.6	15.0
Other Western			
Hemisphere	4.4	4.7	6.0
Western Europe	11.4	11.8	13.0
Africa	2.6	2.9	4.0
Asia/Oceania	6.2	6.5	8.0
Total	37.9	39.5	46.0
Supply / Demand			
Western world			
consumption	37.9	39.5	46.0
Imports from East			
Bloc	2.0	2.0	2.5
Exports to East Bloc	0.4	0.5	0.7
Demand to be met			
by western world			
suppliers	36.3	38.0	44.2
Western world			
production	35.6	37.3	43.3
Inventory change	(0.7)	(0.7)	(0.9)

Source: Price, 1980, via Texasgulf, Inc.

Bibliography and References

Anon., 1952, "Ammonium Sulfate from Gypsum," *Chemical Engineering,* Vol. 59, No. 6, June, pp. 242–245.

Anon., 1954, "Noranda's Elemental Sulfur Plant Slated to Begin Operation October 1," *Engineering & Mining Journal,* Vol. 155, No. 9, Sep., p. 142.

Anon., 1960, "Hot Water Separates Volcanic Sulphur," *Engineering & Mining Journal,* Vol. 161, No. 1, Jan., p. 96.

Anon., 1964, "Outokumpu Process for the Production of Elemental Sulphur From Pyrites," *Sulphur,* No. 50, Feb./Mar., pp. 33–38.

Anon., 1966, "Finland—New Technical Development by Outokumpu Oy," *Sulphur,* No. 67, Oct./Nov., pp. 17–22.

Anon., 1966a, "Handling Liquid Sulfur," Data Sheet, Engineering and Research Commission, Fertilizer Section, National Safety Council, Chicago, 8 pp.

Anon., 1966b, *World Survey of Sulphur Resources,* 1st ed., British Sulphur Corp., pp. 42–44, 61–72.

Anon., 1967, "Polish Sulphur," *Sulphur,* No. 72, Sep./Oct., pp. 12–14.

Anon., 1968, "Handling and Storage of Solid Sulfur," Data Sheet, Engineering and Research Commission, Fertilizer Section, National Safety Council, Chicago, 4 pp.

Anon., 1968a, "Gypsum Ready to Fill the Sulphur Gap?", *Chemical Engineering,* Vol. 75, No. 10, May 6, pp. 94–96.

Anon., 1968b, "Natural Gas Desulfurization Looks to a New Absorbent," *Chemical Engineering,* Vol. 75, No. 4, Feb. 12, p. 66.

Anon., 1968c, "Polish Sulphur Deposits and Their Exploitation," *Sulphur,* No. 78, Sep./Oct., pp. 10–13.

Anon., 1968d, "Processes for the Recovery of Sulfur Values from Calcium Sulphate," *Sulphur,* No. 77, pp. 36–39.

Anon., 1968e, "Route to Sulphur Via Volcanics and Gypsum," *Engineering & Mining Journal,* Vol. 169, No. 7, July, pp. 69–76.

Anon., 1968f, "Sulphuric Acid and Cement from Phosphoric Acid By-Product Phospho-Gypsum," *Sulphur,* No. 74, Jan./Feb., pp. 27–29.

Anon., 1969, "New Thermal Process for Sulfur Recovery," *Engineering & Mining Journal,* Vol. 170, No. 1, Jan., p. 36.

Anon., 1972, "Aquitaine Cleans Claus Tail Gas With Sulfreen Unit," *Oil & Gas Journal,* Vol. 70, No. 26, June 26, pp. 85–88.

Anon., 1972a, "Coal Gasification—Vital Part of the US Energy Programme," *Sulphur,* No. 99, Mar./Apr., pp. 30–37.

Anon., 1972b, "New Process Removes Sulfur From Gas," *Oil & Gas Journal,* Vol. 70, No. 27, July 3, p. 47.

Anon., 1973a, "Duval's Rustler Springs Mine Reaches Design Capacity," *Sulphur,* British Sulphur Corp., Ltd., Reprint, 4 pp.

Anon., 1973b, "World Sulphur Supply and Demand, 1960–1980," Industrial Development Organization, United Nations, New York, 165 pp.

Anon., 1974, "Iraq Emerges as Major Sulphur Exporter," *Sulphur,* No. 111, pp. 36–40.

Anon., 1974a, *World Survey of Sulphur Resources,* 2nd ed., British Sulphur Corp., London, 183 pp.

Anon., 1976, "Compliance with RRC Rule 36; Safe Operations in Handling Hydrogen Sulfide," Railroad Commission of Texas, Oil and Gas Division, Austin, 80 pp.

Anon., 1977, "World Sulphur Supply and Demand, 1970–1982," British Sulphur Corp., London, 82 pp.

Anon., 1977a, "The North American and Caribbean Sulphur Outlook 1977–1985," Manderson Assn., Inc., Winter Park, 213 pp.

Anon., 1978a, "Sulphur—The Past 25 Years," *Sulphur*, No. 136, pp. 22–26.

Anon., 1978b, "Sulphur—The Next 25 Years," *Sulphur*, No. 136, pp. 28–33.

Anon., 1978c, "Frasch Sulphur Production Down the Years: Past, Present—and Future?" *Sulphur*, No. 136, pp. 45–47, 67.

Anon., 1978d, "Outline of Recent Experiences in Sulphur Melting and Burning," *Sulphur*, No. 136, pp. 54–65.

Anon., 1979a, "Freeport to Produce Sulphur at Caillou Island," *Freeporter*, Vol. 26, No. 6, p. 7.

Anon., 1979b, "Duval to Open Sulfur Mine in Culberson County, Texas," *Skilling's Mining Review*, Vol. 68, No. 47, Nov. 24, p. 10.

Anon., 1979c, "Refined Sulphur—A Small Industry with Growing Prospects," *Sulphur*, No. 141, pp. 19–22.

Anon., 1979d, "SUDIC's 1978 Highlights," *Sulphur*, No. 141, pp. 23–27.

Anon., 1979e, "Improving the Quality of Solid Sulphur; Silicon Additives May Be the Answer," *Sulphur*, No. 141, pp. 29–31.

Anon., 1979f, "Flue Gas Desulphurization in the United States," *Sulphur*, No. 141, pp. 34–39.

Anon., 1979g, "Sulphur Forming Processes," *Sulphur*, No. 142, pp. 30–39.

Anon., 1979h, "Aznalcollar; Start-up of Phase I," *Sulphur*, No. 143, pp. 26–28.

Anon., 1979i, "New Frasch Mine for Freeport," *Sulphur*, No. 144, p. 10.

Anon., 1979j, "Polish Sulphur Industry Revisited; Immediate Outlook Not Promising," *Sulphur*, No. 144, pp. 17–20.

Anon., 1979k, "Sulphur Grinding—The Art of Avoiding Explosions," *Sulphur*, No. 144, pp. 33–38.

Anon., 1979l, "By-product Acid versus Brimstone Acid: The US Dilemma," *Sulphur*, No. 145, pp. 40–43.

Anon., 1980a, "Florida, the World's Largest Sulphur Market—and Still Growing," *Sulphur*, No. 146, pp. 18–21.

Anon., 1980b, "Tharsis Pyrite Mines Slated for Expansion," *Sulphur*, No. 147, p. 20.

Anon., 1980c, "New Uses of Sulphur—Current Progress and Problems," *Sulphur*, No. 147, pp. 29–31.

Anon., 1980d, "Waste Heat Recovery from Sulphuric Acid Plants; Uses in Water Heating, Power Generation, and Desalination," *Sulphur*, No. 147, pp. 32–33, 39–43.

Anon., 1980e, "Elemental Sulphur Production, Recovery of Low-grade Pyrites and Phosphogypsum," *Sulphur*, No. 147, pp. 36–38.

Anon., 1980f, "Expansion Plans at Aljustrel," *Sulphur*, No. 148, pp. 18–19.

Anon., 1980g, "The Enormous Potential of the Overthrust Belt," *Sulphur*, No. 148, pp. 29–30.

Anon., 1980h, "West German Sulphur Recovery Running Strong," *Sulphur*, No. 149, pp. 24–26.

Anon., 1980i, "Freeport Commences Production at Caillou Island Sulfur Mine," *Skilling's Mining Review*, Vol. 69, No. 47, Nov. 29, p. 4.

Anon., 1980j, "Caillou Island, A New Mine Is Born," *Freeporter*, Vol. 27, No. 6, Sept./Oct., pp. 10–11.

Anon., 1981a, "Brazil Approves Commercial-Scale Production of Oil Shale in Parana," *Engineering & Mining Journal*, Vol. 182, No. 3, pp. 43, 47.

Anon., 1981b, "Spiraling Costs Slow Rundle Oil Shale Development," *Engineering & Mining Journal*, Vol. 182, No. 5, p. 54.

Anon., 1981c, "Crested Butte Begins Exploration of Montana Oil Shale/Minerals Area," *Engineering & Mining Journal*, Vol. 182, No. 6, p. 57.

Anon., 1981d, "The Future of Heavy Crude and Tar Sands," United Nations Institute for Training and Research, US DOE and Alberta OSTRA, *Proceedings*, available from *Engineering & Mining Journal* Mining Information Service, New York, 968 pp.

Aalund, L., 1970, "New Sulfur Region Has Modern Plant," *Oil & Gas Journal*, Vol. 68, No. 18, May 4, pp. 125–129.

Aalund, L., 1972, "Hydrodesulfurization Technology Takes on the Sulfur Challenge," *Oil & Gas Journal*, Vol. 70, No. 37, Sep. 11, pp. 79–104.

Alexis, J., 1980, "Cleaning Coal and Refuse Fines with the Humphreys Spiral Concentrator," *Mining Engineering*, Vol. 32, No. 8, pp. 1224–1228.

Ali, L.H., and Al-Shawani, K.I., 1975, "Method for the Purification of Raw Frasch Sulfur from Bitumen and Ash Impurities," *Fuel*, Vol. 54, No. 3, 221 pp.

Al-Samarrie, A.M., 1980, "Hydro-Dynamic Barrier for Sulphur Mines," *Sulphur*, No. 149, pp. 30–31.

Al-Sawaf, F.D.S., 1977, "Sulfate Reduction and Sulfur Deposition in the Lower Fars Formation, Northern Iraq," *Economic Geology*, Vol. 72, pp. 608–618.

Anderson, C.J., 1979, "A Comparative Look at Overseas Sulphur Distribution Systems," *Sulphur*, No. 140, pp. 29–31.

Appl, M., and Neth, N., 1979, "The Catalytic Oxidation of Sulphur Dioxide: Problems and Advances," *Sulphur*, No. 145, pp. 26–39.

Argall, G.O., 1967, "Outokumpu Adds Second Catalyzer to Raise Pyrite-to-Sulphur Conversion to 91 Percent," *Mining World*, Mar., pp. 42–46.

Baillie, R.A., and Mertes, T.S., 1968, "Development and Production of Oil from the Athabasca Tar Sands," *Exploration and Economics of the Petroleum Industry*, V.S. Cameron, ed., Vol. 6, Mathew Bender, New York, pp. 241–271.

Ban, T.E., Johnson, E., and Marlow, W.H., 1981, "Devleopment of the Clean Pellet Fuel Process—A Progress Report," *Mining Engineering*, Vol. 33, No. 1, pp. 71–74.

Barker, J.M., and Cochran, D.E., 1981, "Sulfur," Annual Commodity Review, *Mining Engineering*, Vol. 33, No. 5, pp. 589–591.

Barker, J.M., et al., 1979, "Economic Geology of the Mishraq Native Sulfur Deposit, Northern Iraq," *Economic Geology*, Vol. 74, No. 2, pp. 484–495.

Barry, C.B., and Davis, G.R., 1969, "Sulphur Mining in West Texas," *Journal of World Sulphur*, No. 83, July/Aug., pp. 22–29.

Baughman, G.L., and Sladek, T.A., 1981, "Shale Oil Recovery Methods," *Mining Engineering*, Vol. 33, No. 1, pp. 43–47.

Beard, H.R., et al., 1979, "Gas Analysis Procedures Applicable to Flue Gas Desulfurization by the Citrate Process," Information Circular 8793, US Bureau of Mines, 15 pp.

Beavon, D.K., 1971, "Add-On Process Slashes Claus Tailgas Pollution," *Chemical Engineering*, Vol. 78, No. 28, Dec. 13, pp. 71–73.

Berry, L.G., and Mason, B., 1959, *Mineralogy*, W.H. Freeman and Co., San Francisco, 630 pp.

Bixby, D.W., 1968, "The Sulphur Mining Industry of Poland," Tour of Polish Sulphur Mining Facilities b' US Sulphur Delegation, Apr. 21-30, 1967, Sulphur Institute, Washington, DC, May, 29 pp.

Bourne, D.J., ed., 1978, "New Uses of Sulfur—II," Advances in Chemistry Series 165, American Chemical Society, Washington, DC, 282 pp.

Boyle and Assoc., 1965, "Surface and Shallow Oil Impregnated Rocks and Shallow Oil Fields in the US," Monograph 12, US Bureau of Mines, 375 pp.

Campbell, I.E., and Ireland, J.D., 1972, "Status Report on Lime and Wet Limestone Scrubbing to Control SO₂ in Stack Gas," *Engineering & Mining Journal*, Vol. 173, No. 12, Dec. pp. 78–85.

Carrales, M., Jr., and Martin, R.W., 1975, "Sulfur Content of Crude Oils," Information Circular 8676, US Bureau of Mines, 61 pp.

Chebanenko, V.V., 1969, "Geology of the Mishraq Native Sulfur Deposit (Iraq)," Geolgiia mestorzhdenii samorodnoi sery, Izdatel 'stro "Nedra," Moscow, pp. 374–379.

Chopey, N.P., 1972, "Coal Gasification: Can It Stage a Comeback?," *Chemical Engineering*, Vol. 79, No. 7, Apr. 3, pp. 44–46.

Chopey, N.P., 1972a, "Taking Coal's Sulfur Out," *Chemical Engineering*, Vol. 79, No. 16, July 24, pp. 86–88.

Cooper, B.R., and Petrakis, L., eds., 1980, "Chemistry and Physics of Coal Utilization—1980," American Institute of Physics, New York, 476 pp.

Cortesini, A., et al., 1966, "Mishraq Sulfur Project Geologic Report," unpublished, Mideast Industries, Ltd., Baghdad, Iraq, 20 pp.

Crane, S.R., et al., 1981, "Hydrogen Sulfide Generation by Reaction of Natural Gas, Sulfur, and Steam," Report of Investigations 8539, US Bureau of Mines, 54 pp.

Crocker, L., et al., 1979, "Citrate Process Pilot Plant Operation at the Bunker Hill Company," Report of Investigations 8374, US Bureau of Mines, 77 pp.

Czerminski, J., 1960, "Microorganogenic Structures in Sulphur in the Tortonian," *Kwartalnik Geologiczny*, Warsaw, Vol. 4, No. 2.

Czerminski, J., 1968, "Epigenic Processes Within Tortonian Sulphur-Bearing Series," *Proceedings of Section 8, International Geological Congress*, Czechoslovakia, pp. 121–127.

Dale, J.M., 1981, "Sulfur from Surface Ores," *Mining Engineering*, Vol. 33, No. 9, pp. 1340–1341.

Davis, J.B., and Kirkland, D.W., 1970, "Native Sulfur Deposition in The Castile Formation, Culberson County, Texas," *Economic Geology*, Vol. 65, No. 2, Mar. Apr., pp. 107–121.

Davis, J.B., et al., 1970, "Evidence Against Oxidation of Hydrogen Sulfide by Sulfate Ions to Produce Elemental Sulfur in Salt Domes," *Bulletin*, American Assn. of Petroleum Geologists, Vol. 54, p. 2444.

Davis, J.C., 1972, "Sulfur: New Uses Needed," *Chemical Engineering*, Vol. 79, No. 17, pp. 30–32.

Dayton, S., ed., 1981, "Mining Oil Shale," *Engineering & Mining Journal*, Vol. 182, No. 6, pp. 61–135.

Dessau, G., et al., 1962, "Geology and Isotopic Studies of Sicilian Sulfu Deposits," *Economic Geology*, Vol. 57, No. 3, May/June, pp. 410–438.

Dresher, W.H., and Rodolff, D.W., 1981, "Smelter Pollution Abatement; How the Japanese Do It," *Engineering & Mining Journal*, Vol. 182, No. 5, pp. 67–74.

Dunnington, H.V., 1958, "Generation, Migration, Accumulation and Dissipation of Oil in Northern Iraq," *Habitat of Oil*, L.G. Weeks, ed., American Assn. of Petroleum Geologists, Tulsa, pp. 1194–1251.

Ehrlich, H.L., 1972, "Sulfur Oxidation—Bacterial," *Encyclopedia of Geochemistry and Environmental Sciences*, Encyclopedia of Earth Sciences Series, Vol. IVA, R.W. Fairbridge, Jr., ed., Van Nostrand Reinhold, New York, p. 1158.

Eliot, R.C., ed., 1978, "Coal Desulfurization Prior to Combustion," Hayes Data Corp., Park Ridge, 307 pp.

Ellison, S.P., 1971, "Sulfur in Texas," Handbook No. 2, Bureau of Economic Geology, University of Texas, Austin, 48 pp.

Enright, R.J., 1979, "Saudi Desert Sprouts Gas Plants," *Oil and Gas Journal*, Vol. 77, No. 28 July 9, pp. 63–122.

Featherstone, R.E., and Al-Samarrie, A.M. 1975, "Geohydrology of Mishraq—Groundwate Movement Study with Electrical Analogu Simulation," *Sulphur*, No. 120, pp. 44–49.

Feely, H.W., and Kulp, J.L., 1957, "Origin of Gul Coast Salt-Dome Sulphur Deposits," *Bulletin* American Assn. of Petroleum Geologists, Vol 41, No. 8, Aug., pp. 1802–1853.

Field, C.W., 1972, "Sulfur: Element and Geo chemistry," *Encyclopedia of Geochemistry an Environmental Sciences*, Vol. IVA, R.W. Fai bridge, Jr., ed., Van Nostrand Reinhold, Nev York, pp. 1142–1148.

Fjerdingstad, E., 1979, "Sulfur Bacteria," STP65(American Society for Testing & Materials, 1 pp.

Fogarty, C.F., and Mollison, R.D., 1960, "Sulfu and Pyrites," *Industrial Minerals and Rocks*, 3r ed., J.L. Gillson, ed., AIME, New York, pr 819–833.

Franco, A., 1972, "Brazil Tries New Shale-O Process," *Oil & Gas Journal*, Vol. 70, No. 3; Sep. 11, pp. 105–111.

Freeman, M.R., 1979, "The Fertilizer and Sulfu Outlook in the USSR," Preprint, Annual Co ference, Agricultural Chemistry Division, Amer can Marketing Assn., Alexandria, VA, Oct. 2(21 pp.

Gardiner, S.A., and Warwick, G.C.I., 1971, "Poll tion-Free Metallurgy: Copper via Solvent-E traction," *Engineering & Mining Journal*, Vol. 172, No. 4, Apr., pp. 108–110.

Gardner, F.J., 1973, "Soviet Master Plan for Gas Growth Falling Apart," *Oil & Gas Journal*, Vol. 71, No. 1, Jan. 1, pp. 6–8.

Gittinger, L.B., Jr., 1975, "Sulfur," *Industrial Minerals and Rocks*, 4th ed., S.J. Lefond, ed., AIME, New York, pp. 1103–1125.

Goldman, M.I., 1952, "Deformation Metamorphism and Mineralization in Gypsum-Anhydrite Cap Rock," *Memoir 50*, Geological Society of America, 169 pp.

Gould, A.J., 1955, "Fluosolids Roasting of Sulphur Ore," *Mining Congress Journal*, Vol. 41, No. 6, June, pp. 70–73.

Grimm, C., et al., 1978, "The Colstrip Flue Gas Cleaning System," *Chemical Engineering Progress*, Vol. 74, No. 2, pp. 51–57.

Groendaal, W., and Van Meurs, H.C.A., 1972, "Shell Launches Its Claus Off-Gas Desulfurization Process," *Petroleum & Petrochemical International*, Vol. 12, No. 9, Sep., pp. 54–58.

Guccione, E., 1966, "From Pyrite: Iron Ore and Sulfur via Flash Smelting," *Chemical Engineering*, Vol. 73, No. 4, Feb. 14, pp. 122–124.

Habashi, F., 1979, "Hydrometallurgical Applications of Sulphuric Acid," *Sulphur*, Vol. 140, pp. 37–42.

Hardy, W.L., 1957, "Ammonium Sulfate by the Gypsum Process," *Industrial & Engineering Chemistry*, Vol. 49, No. 2, Feb., pp. 57–58.

Haye, E.F., 1969, "Application of Gravity to Sulfur Exploration—Delaware Basin," Photo-Gravity Co., Inc., Houston, 4 pp.

Haynes, W., 1942, *The Stone That Burns*, D. Van Nostrand, New York, 345 pp.

Haynes, W., 1959, *Brimstone, The Stone That Burns*, D. Van Nostrand, New York, 308 pp.

Hazelton, J.E., 1970, *The Economics of the Sulphur Industry, Resources for the Future*, Johns Hopkins Press, Washington, DC, 172 pp.

Heintz, K.O., and Alexander, M., 1978, "Sulfur Exploration with Core Hole and Surface Gravity," Preprint, SEG Meeting, San Francisco, 17 pp.

Heintz, K.O., and Alexander, M., 1979, "Sulfur Exploration with Core Hole and Surface Gravity," abstract, *Geophysics*, Vol. 44, p. 370.

Hirai, M., et al., 1972, "Solvent Catalyst Mixture Desulfurizes Claus Tailgas," *Chemical Engineering*, Vol. 79, No. 8, Apr. 17, pp. 78–79.

Hollister, V.F., 1977, "Potential for the Occurrence of Sedimentary Sulphur Deposits in Northeastern British Columbia," *CIM Bulletin*, Vol. 70, No. 777, pp. 106–108.

Hull, W.Q., et al., 1957, "Sulfuric Acid From Anhydrite," *Industrial & Engineering Chemistry*, Vol. 48, No. 8, Aug., pp. 1204-1214.

Hunt, J.M., 1976, "Origin of Athabascan Oil," *Bulletin*, American Assn. of Petroleum Geologists, Vol. 60, No. 7, p. 1112.

Idemura, H., et al., 1978, "Jet Bubbling Flue Gas Desulfurization," *Chemical Engineering Progress*, Vol. 74, No. 2, pp. 46–50.

Israel, D.H., 1981, "The Government Plays a Prominent Role in Leasing and Developing Oil Shale," *Mining Engineering*, Vol. 33, No. 1, pp. 52–53.

Ivanof, M.V., 1964, "Microbiological Processes in the Formation of Sulphur Deposits," Academy of Sciences, USSR; Israel Program for Scientific Translation, 1968, 298 pp.

Jensen, M.L., ed., 1962, "Biogeochemistry of Sulfur Isotopes," *Proceedings*, National Science Foundation Symposium, Apr. 12-14, Yale University, New Haven, CT.

Johnson, J.L., 1979, *Kinetics of Coal Gasification*, John Wiley and Sons, New York, 324 pp.

Kaplan, I.R., 1972, "Sulfur Cycle," *Encyclopedia of Geochemistry and Environmental Sciences*, Encyclopedia of Earth Sciences Series, Vol. IVA, R.W. Fairbridge, Jr., ed., Van Nostrand Reinhold, New York, p. 1158.

Kiaer, T., 1954, "Smelter Gases Yield Elemental Sulfur at Orkla-Grube Plant in Norway," *Engineering & Mining Journal*, Vol. 155, No. 7, July, pp. 88–90.

Komarnicki, J.J., 1980, "Strachan Prilling Unit Starts Up," *Sulphur*, No. 147, pp. 22–27.

Krienberg, M., 1978, "Handling Molten Sulfur," *Chemical Engineering*, Vol. 85, No. 27, pp. 125–126.

Laseke, B.A., and Devilt, I.W., 1979, "Status of Flue Gas Desulfurization," *Chemical Engineering Progress*, Vol. 75, No. 2, pp. 37–50.

Laulajainen, R., 1978, "Spatial Dynamics in the U.S. Sulphur Industry, 1955–1975," Swedish School of Economics and Business Administration, Helsingfors, Sweden, 62 pp.

Lein, A.Y., et al., 1975, "Origin of Native Sulfur in Mishraq Deposit (Iraq)," *International Geology Review*, Vol. 17, No. 8, pp. 881–885.

Leonard, J.W., ed., 1979, *Coal Preparation*, 4th ed., AIME, New York, 1204 pp.

Lundy, W.T., 1949, "Sulfur and Pyrites," *Industrial Minerals and Rocks*, 2nd ed., S.H. Dolbear, ed., AIME, New York, pp. 989–1017.

Marchant, L.C., and Jackson, D., 1981, "U.S. Tar Sands: Drawing Interest But No Mega-Projects Are on the Horizon," *Engineering and Mining Journal*, Vol. 182, No. 6, pp. 129–133.

Matveyev, A.K., ed., 1974, *Deposits of Fossil Fuels*, Vol. 4, *Oil Shale Deposits Outside the Soviet Union*, G.K. Hall and Co., Boston, 120 pp.

May, S.K., 1980, "Sulphuric Acid Plant Operation with Reference to Catalyst Performance," *Sulphur*, No. 146, pp. 30–34.

McBee, W.C., and Sullivan, T.A., 1979, "Development of Specialized Sulfur Concretes," Report of Investigations 8346, US Bureau of Mines, 21 pp.

McBee, W.C., et al., 1981, "Modified-Sulfur Cements for Use in Concretes, Flexible Pavings, Coatings, and Grouts," Report of Investigations 8545, US Bureau of Mines, 24 pp.

McConville, L.B., 1975, "The Athabasca Tar Sands," *Mining Engineering*, Vol. 27, No. 1, pp. 5, 19–38.

McIntyre, H., 1976, "Heavy Oil Recovery in the Alberta Oil Sands," *Engineering Journal*, Vol. 59, No. 1, pp. 61–65.

McIntyre, H., 1977, "Heavy Crude Will Backstop Regular Oil," *Canadian Chemistry Process*, Vol. 61, No. 6, pp. 34–35.

McIntyre, H., 1981, "Oil Sands Route Looks for Jobs in Canada, U.S.," *Chemical Engineering*, Vol. 17, No. 88, p. 59.

McNeal, R.P., and Hemenway, G.A., 1972, "Geology of Fort Stockton Sulfur Mine, Pecos County,

Texas," *Bulletin*, American Assn. of Petroleum Geologists, Vol. 56, No. 1, Jan., pp. 25–37.

Mehrotra, V.P., et al., 1980, "Oil Agglomeration Offers Technical and Economic Advantages," *Mining Engineering*, Vol. 32, No. 8, pp. 1230–1235.

Meyer, B., 1977, *Sulfur, Energy and Environment*, Elsevier Scientific Publ. Co., New York, 448 pp.

Mills, G.A., 1971, "Gas From Coal, Fuel of the Future," *Environmental Science & Technology*, Vol. 5, No. 12, Dec., pp. 1178–1182.

Moser, R., 1979, "Flue Gas Desulphurization in the United States," *Sulphur*, No. 141, pp. 34–39.

Nettleton, L.L., 1934, "Fluid Mechanics of Salt Domes," *Bulletin*, American Assn. of Petroleum Geologists, Vol. 18, No. 9, Sep., pp. 1175–1204.

Niec, M., and Al Nouri, M., 1976, "Zloze Siorki Mishraq w Polnocnym Iraku," *Przegl. Geol.*, Vol. 24, No. 5, pp. 272–276.

Nissen, W.I., and Madenburg, R.S., 1979, "Citrate Process Demonstration Plant Design," Information Circular 8806, US Bureau of Mines, 16 pp.

O'Brien, E., 1980, "Fine Coal Cleaning in the 28 × 0 Fraction: A Technical Overview," *Mining Engineering*, Vol. 32, No. 8, pp. 1213–1214.

Opychral, A.M., and Wang, K., 1981, "Economic Significance of the Florida Phosphate Industry: An Input-Out Analysis," Information Circular 8850, US Bureau of Mines, 62 pp.

Palm, J.W., 1979, "Sulphur Recovery Plant Operation; Amoco Reviews 30 Years' Experience," *Sulphur*, No. 143, pp. 34–39.

Pawlowski, S., 1968, "Geology of Sulphur Deposits in Poland," *Proceedings* of Section 8, International Geological Congress, Czechoslovakia, pp. 249–267.

Pfeiffer, J.B., ed., 1975, "Sulfur Removal and Recovery from Industrial Processes," Advances in Chemistry Series, No. 139, American Chemical Society, Washington, DC, 221 pp.

Phillips, A., 1977, "The Modern Sulphuric Acid Process," *The Modern Inorganic Chemicals Industry*, R. Thompson, ed., Special Publication No. 31, The Chemical Society, London, pp. 183–200.

Phizackerley, P.H., and Scott, L.O., 1967, "Major Tar Sand Deposits of the World," *Proceedings*, Vol. 3, 7th World Petroleum Congress, pp. 551–571.

Plouf, T.M., 1980, "Froth Flotation Techniques Reduce Sulfur and Ash," *Mining Engineering*, Vol. 32, No. 8, pp. 1218–1223.

Postgate, J.R., 1972, "Sulphate Reduction—Microbial," *Encyclopedia of Geochemistry and Environmental Sciences*, Encyclopedia of Earth Sciences Series, Vol. IVA, R.W. Fairbridge, Jr., ed., Van Nostrand Reinhold, New York, pp. 1127–1129.

Postgate, J.R., 1979, *The Sulphate-Reducing Bacteria*, Cambridge University Press, Cambridge, MA, 151 pp.

Potts, H.R., and Lawford, E.G., 1949, "Recovery of Sulfur From Smelter Gases by the Orkla Process at Rio Tinto," *Transactions*, Institute of Mining & Metallurgy, Vol. 58, pp. 1–36.

Pratt, L., 1976, *The Tar Sands*, Hurtig Publ., Edmonton, 197 pp.

Price, W., 1980, "Sulfur: Tight Supplies May Turn Into Glut," *Chemical Engineering*, Mar. 24, pp. 64–68.

Princiotta, F.T., 1978, "Advances in SO_2 Stack Gas Scrubbing," *Chemical Engineering Progress*, Vol. 74, No. 2, pp. 58–64.

Pryor, W.A., 1962, *Mechanisms of Sulfur Reactions*, McGraw-Hill, New York, 241 pp.

Raddatz, A.E., et al., 1981, "Laboratory Investigation of Sulfurous Acid Leaching of Kaolin for Preparing Alumina," Report of Investigations 8533, US Bureau of Mines, 15 pp.

Ramirez, R., 1968, "Gypsum Finds New Role in Easing Sulfur Shortage," *Chemical Engineering*, Vol. 75, No. 24, Nov. 4, pp. 112–114.

Raymond, W.J., 1978, "The Kellog-Weir Scrubbing System," *Chemical Engineering Progress*, Vol. 74, No. 2, pp. 75–80.

Raymont, M.E.D., 1978a, "Engineering and Economic Analysis of Sulphur Forming Processes," *Sulphur*, No. 135, pp. 32–36.

Raymont, M.E.D., 1978b, "Sulphur Concretes and Coatings," Sulphur Development of Canada New Uses for Sulphur, No. 4, 43 pp.

Redford, D.A., and Winestock, A.G., eds., 1978, "The Oil Sands of Canada—Venezuela 1977," Canadian Institute of Mining and Metallurgy, Montreal, 784 pp.

Rennie, W.J., 1977, "Sulphur Asphalts," Sulphur Development Institute of Canada, New Uses for Sulphur, No. 2, 52 pp.

Rieber, M., et al., 1981, "Studies on Sulfur Pollution Control—The Impact of Stack Gas Cleanup on the Sulfur Mining Industry of Texas and Louisiana," Reports OFR94(1)–81, OFR94(2)–81, OFR94(3)–81, and OFR94(4)–81, US Bureau of Mines.

Robinson, E., and Robbins, R.C., 1968, "Source, Abundance, and Fate of Gaseous Atmospheric Pollutants," SRI Project PR-6755, American Petroleum Institute, New York, Feb.

Rochille, G.T., and King, C.J., 1978, "Alternative for Stack Gas Desulfurization by Throwaway Scrubbing," *Chemical Engineering Progress*, Vol. 74, No. 2, pp. 65–69.

Rogers, K.A., and Hill, R.F., 1980, "Synfuel Processing Technology," *Mining Engineering*, Vol. 32, No. 2, pp. 167–170.

Rosenweig, M.D., 1968, "Sulfur Shortage Spawn New Technology," *Chemical Engineering*, Vol. 75, No. 1, Jan. 1, pp. 16–18.

Rowland, L., 1972, "Sulphur Recovery Plants in Alberta Could Face $500 Million Clean Up Bill," *Oilweek*, Vol. 23, No. 36, Oct. 23, pp. 9–12.

Ruckmick, J.C., et al., 1979, "Some Aspects of the Genesis of Bioepigenetic Sulphur Deposits," *Economic Geology*, Vol. 74, No. 2.

Russell, P.L., 1980, "History of Western Oil Shale," Center for Professional Advancement, New Brunswick, 152 pp.

Russell, P.L., 1981, "An Oil Shale Perspective," *Mining Engineering*, Vol. 33, No. 1, pp. 29–?

Sakseev, G.T., 1973, "Geologic Structure a Genesis of the Teisarov Sulfur Deposit," *Lithology and Mineral Resources*, Vol. 8, No. 5.

Sands, A.E., and Schmidt, L.D., 1950, "Recovery of Sulfur From Synthesis Gas," *Industrial Engineering Chemistry*, Vol. 42, No. 11, Nov. p. 2281.

Schamm, L.W., 1979, "U.S. Tar Sand Oil Forecasts (1985–1995)" DOE/EIA Report 0183/1, 44 pp.

Schmoker, J.W., 1979, "Interpretation of Borehole Gravity Surveys In a Native-Sulfur Deposit, Culberson County, Texas," *Economic Geology,* Vol. 74, No. 6, Sept./Oct., pp. 1462–1470.

Schmoker, J.W., and Robbins, S.L., 1979, "Borehole Gravity Surveys in Native Sulfur Deposits, Culberson and Pecos Counties, Texas," Open File Report 79–361, US Geological Survey, 23 pp.

Schwaderer, R., ed., 1980, *Synfuel Handbook* (including the Yellow Pages of Synfuels) *Coal Week,* Washington, DC.

Scott, T.F., 1974, "Athabasca Oil Sands to A.D. 2000," *CIM Bulletin,* Oct., p. 98–102.

Selmeczi, J.G., and Steward, D.A., 1978, "The Thiosorbic Flue Gas Desulfurization Process," *Chemical Engineering Progress,* Vol. 74, No. 2, pp. 41–45.

Semrau, K.T., 1971, "Sulfur Oxides Control and Metallurgical Technology," *Journal of Metals,* Vol. 23, No. 3, Mar., pp. 41–47.

Shabad, T., 1969, *Basic Industrial Resources of the U.S.S.R.,* Columbia University Press, New York, 393 pp.

Shafer, J.R., et al., 1978, "Sulfuric Acid Plants for Handling H_2S," *Chemical Engineering Progress,* Vol. 74, No. 12, pp. 62–65.

Shelton, J.E., 1979, "Sulfur," *Mineral Commodity Profile,* US Bureau of Mines, 25 pp.

Shelton, J.E., 1980a, "Sulfur," Preprint, Bulletin 671, US Bureau of Mines, 22 pp.

Shelton, J.E., 1980b, "Sulfur and Pyrites," Preprint, *Minerals Yearbook 1980,* US Bureau of Mines, 19 pp.

Silverman, M.P., 1972, "Sulfide Mineral Oxidation—Microbial," *Encyclopedia of Geochemistry and Environmental Sciences,* Encyclopedia of Earth Sciences Series, Vol. IVA, R.W. Fairbridge, Jr., ed., Van Nostrand Reinhold Co., New York, pp. 1132–1134.

Singhal, R.K., 1969, "Sulphur Mining In Poland," *Mining & Minerals Engineering,* March, pp. 35–39.

Sisselman, R.T., 1972, "Coal Gasification a Partial Solution to the Energy Crisis," *Mining Engineering,* Vol. 24, No. 10, Oct., pp. 71–78.

Skolnik, E., 1980, "Heavy Medium Cleaning of −28 Mesh Coal," *Mining Engineering,* Vol. 32, No. 8, pp. 1235–1237.

Slock, A.V., 1978, "Lime-Limestone Scrubbing: Design Considerations," *Chemical Engineering Progress,* Vol. 74, No. 2, pp. 71–74.

Smith, J.W., 1981, "Alumina From Oil Shale," *Mining Engineering,* Vol. 33, No. 6, pp. 693–697.

Smith, M., 1982, "Sulfur—Pyrites Set to Return," *Industrial Minerals,* No. 182, Nov., pp. 49–65.

Spencer, G.B., et al., 1969, "Domestic Tar Sands and Potential Recovery Methods," *Bulletin,* Vol. 11, No. 2, Interstate Oil Compact Committee, pp. 5–12.

Srinivason, G., 1980, "The Modern Wet Gas Sulphuric Acid Plant," *Sulphur,* No. 148, pp. 32–36.

Stanwood, R.M., 1981, "Environmental Issues: Still Clouded in Uncertainty," *Mining Engineering,* Vol. 33, No. 1, pp. 49–51.

Stanton, R.L., 1972, "Sulfides in Sediments," *Encyclopedia of Geochemistry and Environmental Sciences,* Encyclopedia of Earth Sciences Series, Vol. IVA, R.W. Fairbridge, Jr., ed.,

Van Nostrand Reinhold Co., New York, pp. 1134–1140.

Staples, L.W., 1972a, "Sulfosalts," *Encyclopedia of Geochemistry and Environmental Sciences,* Encyclopedia of Earth Sciences Series, Vol. IVA, R.W. Fairbridge, Jr., ed., Van Nostrand Reinhold Co., New York, pp. 1141–1142.

Staples, L.W., 1972b, "Sulfides (with Selenides, Tellurides, Arsenides, Antimonides)" *Encyclopedia of Geochemistry and Environmental Sciences,* Encyclopedia of Earth Sciences Series, Vol. IVA, R.W. Fairbridge, Jr., ed., Van Nostrand Reinhold Co., New York, pp. 1129–1132.

Strishkov, V.V., 1977, "Mineral Industries of the U.S.S.R.," *Mineral Perspectives,* Vol. 2, US Bureau of Mines, 19 pp.

Sweeney, J.W., and Valentine, J.P., 1970, "Physical Solvent Stars in Gas Treatment Purification," *Chemical Engineering,* Vol. 77, No. 19, Sep. 7, pp. 54–56.

Sweeney, J.W., and Timmons, B.J., 1973, "Availability and Potential Utilization of Byproduct Gypsum in Florida Phosphate Operations," *Proceedings,* Vol. 811, Public Information Circular No. 5, Forum on Geology and Industrial Minerals, 1972, Iowa Geological Survey, pp. 89–97.

Taylor, R.E., 1938, "Origin of the Caprock of Louisiana Salt Domes," Bulletin No. 11, Louisiana Geological Survey, 191 pp.

Thode, H.G., 1972, "Sulfur Isotope Fractionation —In Biological Processes," *Encyclopedia of Geochemistry and Environmental Sciences,* Encyclopedia of Earth Sciences Series, Vol. IVA, R.W. Fairbridge, Jr., ed., Van Nostrand Reinhold Co., New York, pp. 1152–1157.

Tiernon, C.H., 1980, "Concentrating Tables for Fine Coal Cleaning," *Mining Engineering,* Vol. 32, No. 8, pp. 1228–1230.

Tost, D., 1976, "Syncrude Vows Environmental Responsibility," *Hydrocarbon Process,* Vol. 55, No. 10, p. 102.

Trevoy, L.W., et al., 1978, "Development of the Heavy Minerals Potential of the Athabasca Tar Sands," *CIM Bulletin,* Vol. 71, No. 3, pp. 175–180.

Tuller, W.N., 1954, *The Sulphur Data Book,* McGraw-Hill, New York, 143 pp.

Utter, S., 1981, "A Range of Mining Techniques to Meet Site-Specific Conditions," *Mining Engineering,* Vol. 33, No. 1, pp. 39–43.

Van den Berkhof, B., 1980, "Sulphuric Acid as a By-product of the European Nonferrous Metals Industry," *Sulphur,* No. 146, pp. 24–28.

Weeks, L.G., 1976, "Origin of Athabasca Oil," *Bulletin,* American Assn. of Petroleum Geologists, Vol. 60, No. 7, pp. 1110–1111.

West, J.R., ed., 1975, "New Uses of Sulfur," *Advances in Chemistry Series,* Vol. 140, American Chemical Society, Washington, DC, 236 pp.

White, J.A.L., 1968, "Native Sulfur Deposits Associated With Volcanic Activity," *Mining Engineering,* Vol. 20, No. 6, June, pp. 47–51.

White, L., 1971, "SO_2 Laws Force US Copper Smelters Into Russian Roulette," *Engineering & Mining Journal,* Vol. 172, No. 7, July, pp. 61–71.

White, L., 1975, "Texasgulf Readies for '75 Startup at Comanche Creek Frasch Mine in Texas,' *Engineering & Mining Journal,* Vol. 176, No. 8, pp. 83–88.

White, L., 1980, "Mining in Mexico," *Engineering & Mining Journal,* Vol. 181, No. 11, Nov., p. 70.

Wideman, F.L., 1957, "A Reconnaissance of Sulfur Resources in Wyoming, Colorado, Utah, New Mexico and Arizona," Information Circular 7770, US Bureau of Mines, 61 pp.

Yen, T.F., and Chilingarian, G.V., eds., 1976,

Oil Shale, Elsevier Scientific Publ. Co., New York, 292 pp.

Zakiewicz, B., 1975, "Exploitation of Bedded Sulphur Deposits by the Hydrodynamic Method," *Sulphur,* No. 120, pp. 35–43.

Zimmerman, J.B., and Thomas, E., 1969, "Sulfur in West Texas: Its Geology and Economics," Geological Circular 69–2, Bureau of Economic Geology, University of Texas, Austin, 35 pp.

Talc

LAWRENCE A. ROE *

RICHARD H. OLSON †

Talc, when it can be isolated as a pure mineral, has a composition of 63.36% SiO_2, 31.89% MgO, and 4.75% H_2O. However, as an industrial commodity, talc rarely approaches theoretical purity. Nevertheless, the impure talc products of commerce find a multitude of uses and few substitutes in many industrial applications.

Minerals commonly associated with and sold together in talcose mixtures are tremolite, chlorite, dolomite, mica, and magnesite.

Steatite was originally a mineralogical name applied to pure talc. In today's commerce *steatite* generally refers to the massive variety of talc suitable for electrical insulator manufacture. Block steatite ore can be machined into various shapes. Impure varieties of massive or block talc are still commonly referred to as soapstone. Soft massive talc, suitable for crayon manufacture, has been referred to as French chalk.

It has been common practice to discuss talc, soapstone, and pyrophyllite under the same general heading. In the case of soapstone and talc, this is a natural thing since many different types of platy, soft minerals exhibiting a high degree of lubricity (commonly referred to as "slip") have been grouped together and called soapstone or talc.

Further, there is a mineralogical relationship of pyrophyllite to montmorillonite and talc to hectorite. Thus, talc and pyrophyllite are sometimes referred to as clay minerals. When finely divided talc or pyrophyllite are combined with water in proportions to make a slurry, the end product does have the appearance of a clay-water mixture.

Soapstone for utensils and ornaments was mined by prehistoric Indians on Santa Catalina Island, CA. In the mid-1800s, soapstone from deposits along the western foothills of the Sierra Nevada mountains was used by white settlers for building and ornamental stone and in the linings and foundations of furnaces (Anon. 1956). Previous to 1916, the annual recorded production in California did not exceed 2000 tons. In the period 1912 to 1918, output rose sharply when the Talc City, Western, and Silver Lake mines were put into operation. From 1916 to 1935, the state's annual output of talc was in the range of 9,000 to 20,000 tons. In the mid-1930s, the use of talc in wall tile grew rapidly. In California, the production of talc grew to 63,000 stpy in 1943. The post-war building boom helped California production to grow to 120,000 tons in 1951. In 1968, production was 165,000 tons, 1969 was 145,000 tons, 1970 was 185,000 tons, and 1972 was 155,000 tons.

Talc mining in New York state dates to about 1878 when a Colonel Palmer and associates opened the first commercial talc mine on the Nelson Freeman farm near Talcville, New York. In 1893, this operation was sold to the International Pulp Co. which changed its name to the International Talc Co. in 1944. The company was acquired by R.T. Vanderbilt Co., Inc. in 1974.

A new talc operation, the Gouverneur Talc Co. owned by the R.T. Vanderbilt Co., began operations near Balmat, NY, in 1948. The initial capacity of the processing plant was 200 stpd (Gillingham, 1950). Subsequent expansions have increased capacity to over 600 stpd.

The Vermont talc industry began just after the start of the 20th century. Talc was discovered in the area of the present Johnson, VT, talc mine in 1902. The American Minerals Co. initiated plant operations at Johnson in 1904. The Magnesia Talc Co. opened a plant at Waterbury, VT, in 1913 (Burmeister, 1963; Trauffer, 1964) and acquired American Minerals Co. in 1923. The Waterbury mine has a long history as a producer of talc crayons.

The Eastern Magnesia Talc Co. was formed in 1924 by a merger of the Eastern Talc Co.

* Consultant, Downers Grove, IL.

† Consultant, Golden, CO.

The Geology section of this chapter was written by Richard H. Olson.

and Magnesia Talc Co. In 1956, the Vermont Mineral Co., with a talc mine at Hammondsville was also acquired. A new plant was then built at Gassetts to produce roofing products.

In order to produce high-grade products for several markets, the Eastern Magnesia Talc Co. began operating a modern froth flotation plant at West Windsor, VT, in 1964. The ore is provided by the Hammondsville mine. As of 1972, this operation is known as Windsor Minerals, Inc., a totally owned subsidiary of the Johnson and Johnson Co.

The Texas talc deposits were first mined commercially in 1952 and by 1970 ranked fourth in US production behind New York, California, and Vermont. Principal use of this talc is in the ceramics industry. Lundquist (1970) reports on a process for acid treatment, calcination, and grinding Texas talc and talc-kaolin mixtures. By his process, Lundquist increased the brightness value from 65 to over 94.

End Uses

Talc is an extremely versatile mineral. In spite of the relatively low purity of most ores mined, talc has found a steadily increasing number of uses. With the exception of pure steatite grades, hand-picked platy cosmetic talcs, and a few products from wet processing plants, the industrial products are really mixtures of many minerals. For example, much of the talc used by the ceramic industry is a mixture of platy talc and tremolite; most of the filler-grade talc sold to the paper, plastics, and rubber industry is, at best, about 90% talc mineral with the balance being dolomite, calcite, chert, clays, serpentine, chlorite, actinolite, iron and manganese-containing minerals, and carbonaceous material.

Table 1 lists chemical analyses of typical talc ores and products.

Talc, along with many of the filler-type industrial minerals, is subject to steadily increasing demands for higher purity and better quality control. A good example is the talc sold to the cosmetic and toilet goods industry. Prior to the end of 1960, a wide variety of talc and talcose products were accepted for cosmetic use if they met rather loose and uncomplicated specifications. A good cosmetic talc had to be reasonably light-colored, have good "slip," be free of gritty or hard mineral particles, and measure up to a certain fragrance-retention standard. Now, the cosmetic talc market is a demanding one. Not only has the industry itself set higher and new standards, but new rulings from federal

TABLE 1—Typical Chemical Analyses of Talc Ores and Products, %

	Pure Talc (Theoretical)	1	2	3	4		5	6
SiO_2	63.36	35.98	59.15	47.92	62.65		59.80	54.92
MgO	31.89	32.95	31.34	26.00	30.23		27.45	27.20
Fe_2O_3	—	0.65	3.36	6.82	1.51		0.05	0.46
TiO_2	—	0.02	—	0.15	—		—	—
Al_2O_3	—	0.43	0.26	7.35	0.31		0.57	—
CaO	—	0.00	0.15	4.14	trace		6.80	5.76
K_2O	—	0.00	—	0.00	0.05		—	—
Na_2O	—	0.00	—	0.00	0.15		—	—
CO_2	—	20.45	1.76	—	0.27		1.18	—
H_2O	4.75	2.73	4.30	0.05	4.87		—	—
MnO	—	0.41	—	0.00	—		0.39	—
S	—	0.06	—	0.09	—	(SO_3)	0.07	—
NiO	—	0.21	—	—	—		—	—
Cr_2O_3	—	0.18	—	—	—		—	—
CoO	—	0.01	—	—	—		—	—
FeO	—	5.96	—	—	—		0.15	—
Less O for S	—	0.05	—	—	—		—	—
P_2O_5	—	0.01	—	0.00	—		—	—
LOI	—	—	—	7.51	—		4.75	10.76
	100.00	100.10	100.32	100.03	100.04		101.21	99.10

Source: 1-5, Chidester, 1964; 6, Pence, 1955.
1. Average Vermont carbonate ore.
2. Flotation talc, Johnson Mine, Vermont.
3. Roofing granules, Cohutta Talc Co., Georgia.
4. Steatite, Yellowstone mine, Montana.
5. Average talc ore, Talcville, Gouverneur District, New York.
6. Texas Talc.

agencies have made heavy demands on talc product quality.

Table 2 lists the various properties of talc which are important in specific markets or industries.

Talc in Paint

In 1979, an estimated 237,000 tons of talc were used as extender and filler pigments in the paint industry. This is 24.7% of the total US talc production of about 960,000 tons for that year. This paint pigment extender tonnage was exceeded only by calcium carbonate.

Some of the important properties of talc used in paint are color, fineness, oil absorption, chemical inertness, and optimum viscosity. The measurement of oil absorption is important. This property is measured by ASTM Method D 281-31 which measures the number of parts of acid-refined linseed oil required to produce a coherent paste with 100 parts of talc pigment.

Talc helps reinforce paint films and also prevents sagging of paint films. It prevents settling of solids to the bottom of the paint container. Talc is very soft and thus contributes minimal abrasion to process and application equipment. It disperses easily in both aqueous and solvent-based paints. Talc is used for gloss control in paints where an exact degree of sheen or luster is required. Gloss is usually determined with a reflectance meter at 60° inclination. Sheen values are determined with the same meter and with the film at 85° inclination.

A very useful, uncomplicated method used for testing the fineness and degree of dispersion of paint and other wet ground products involves use of the Hegman gage. This gage can also be called a "fineness of grind" gage (Anon., 1970). It is a precision-machined, smooth, flat, hardened steel block with one or two grooves or "paths" about 5¼ in. long and ½ in. wide. The groove depth ranges from 100μ (about 4 mils) at one end to zero depth at the other end. A scraper blade is the second component of the gage. In use (on talc products), an aliquot of a mixture of talc and linseed oil (about 1 part talc to 4 parts of oil) is placed in the tapered part of the groove. Then the mixture is wiped down toward the "zero" depth end of the gage with the stainless steel wiper blade. The fineness is determined by holding the gage to a familiar light source and observing the area where the coarse particles begin to appear. The angle between the face of the gage and the line of vision should be not more than 30° nor less than 20°. The fineness readings can be given

TABLE 2—Talc Properties Important to Specific Industries

Paint Industry
 Color (whiteness)
 Particle shape
 Packing quality
 Oil absorption
 Fine particle size (Hegman gage rating)
 Opacity
Paper Industry
 Free of grit (low Valley Abrasion value)
 Color (with MgO as 100, prefer 90 or higher)
 Opacity
 Particle size (less than 5μ)
 Low alkali content
 Effective in controlling pitch, oil, or other oleoresinous substances
 Talc pigment gives lower wax pick values than clay pigments
 Talc gives lower ink receptivity than clay
Ceramic Industry
 Uniform chemical composition
 Constant amount of shrinkage on firing
 Fired color
 Particle size distribution
Cosmetic Industry
 Contain only traces of dolomite, tremolite, quartz, or any harsh minerals
 Some chlorite may be acceptable
 No color change after heating
 Odorless; have good fragrance retention when compounded
 100% through 100 mesh and 98% minimum through 200 mesh; finer grades as specified by buyer
 Neutral to litmus paper
 Water-soluble substances, 0.1% maximum
 Acid-soluble substances, 2.0% maximum
 Loss on ignition, 5.0% maximum
 Arsenic (as As); 3 ppm maximum
 Lead (as Pb), 20 ppm maximum
 Total aerobic plate count including yeast and mold, 100 per g maximum
 Gram negative bacterial plate count, less than 10 per g
 Good "slip" and "unctuosity" when applied to human body, also the white color should disappear as the talc is rubbed into the skin
 Good deodorizing ability
Plastics Industry
 Low iron content
 Particle shape
 Reinforcing ability
 Compatibility with resins and other components (talc is inert)
 Superfine particles
 Resistivity
Roofing Industry—Asphalt Backing and Surfacing
 Minimum oil absorption
 Color
 Particle size consist
 Brightness
 Particle shape
Petroleum and Automotive Industries—Lubricants, Body Putty, Asphalt Undercoating
 Free from grit (pure platy talc for lubricants)
 Chemically inert
 Nonwicking (undercoating)
Rubber Industry
 Good lubricity
 Free of grit
 Color (only in white rubber and latex)
 Resistivity
 Must be chemically compatible when used as latex filler

in microns or mils. A reading of 6 on the gage is about equal to 25μ.

Talc in Paper

One of the fastest growing uses for talc has been in the coating and filling of paper. As a filler it is effective as an inexpensive titanium dioxide extender and is outstanding as a pitch control additive. Talc also assists in improvement of gloss, opacity, and brightness. Its retention in the paper fibrils usually approaches 100%. In 1970 (Cooper and Hartwell, 1970), a forecast of a 3.75% annual increase in demand for talc paper filler was made. Present indications are that this is a conservative estimate and the annual increase may reach as much as 5%.

The main reason for the rapid growth of talc consumption in paper is the availability of high-quality micronized talc manufactured to exacting specifications. Talc filler should not contain more than 2 to 5% calcium carbonate, or similar minerals which react with the alum used in paper formulations. Particle size ranges from 5μ to less than $\frac{1}{2}\mu$ with surface areas from 4 to 25 m²/g. Generally, the Valley Abrasion * number will be very low, from 2 to 6; thus, abrasion of paper making equipment and printing equipment is minimized.

When talc is used as a titanium dioxide extender in paper, it has a distinct weight advantage (talc specific gravity 2.8 vs. 4.2 for TiO_2). This feature grows in importance as postal rates increase.

High-purity talc products are finding a good market in competition with titanium dioxide fillers. Considerable history has already been made in the paper industry where talc fillers have found an excellent market for use as titanium dioxide extender agents. In 1979, titanium dioxide (anatase) sold for about 53¢ per pound in slurry shipments and 57¢ per pound in bags.

The best grades of talc sold, in 1979, for only 5 to 10¢ per lb. This indicates that talc, when it can be substituted, even partially, will continue to be a formidable competitor for substantial titanium dioxide markets.

---

* The Valley Abrasion tester measures wear (in milligrams), of a wire cloth specimen, caused by a circulating suspension of the talc and the rubbing action of an oscillating Micarta block. After 6000 cycles, the wire cloth is washed, dried, and weighed. The loss in milligrams is the Valley Abrasion number.

The unique property of preferentially wetting oily materials in the presence of water makes talc extremely effective in "pitch control." Pitch and other oleoresinous components of paper pulps cause serious manufacturing problems if they are not controlled. Talc absorbs the pitch and helps prevent accumulations which would otherwise deposit on the rolls, wire, and other parts of the paper machine. Competitive materials such as diatomaceous earth and clay usually are either too abrasive or much less effective in the presence of water.

The ultrafine particle size talc products (maximum particle size of 5μ) now finding use in paper coating colors have similar ranges of particle size distribution as coating clays and precipitated calcium carbonate. The talc products can be used to pigment latex, starch, or alpha protein coating colors. The ultrafine talc products can be used along with clay, calcium carbonate, and titanium dioxide pigments to control rheological properties, calendering, gloss, ink holdout, opacity, and brightness.

Talc in Ceramics

Talc finds use in many ceramic products. It is a versatile component having beneficial effects relating to the control of thermal expansion of ceramic bodies. Talcs low in accessory carbonate minerals exhibit low ignition losses. A typical New York talc will have an ignition loss, at 2100°F, of 5 to 6%. In comparison, many Texas and California talcs lose 8 to 13% of their weight when fired.

Talc is used in cordierite (talc-clay mixture fired to Cone 12) bodies such as developed for use in electrical insulators. Cordierite has a very low thermal expansion. New York and Texas talcs are used in the semivitreous whiteware field, especially wall tile and in dinnerware bodies. These have been found to be ideal raw materials for the following reasons:

1) The formation of enstatite produces high thermal expansion bodies resulting in glazes being put in compression which in turn tends to prevent crazing (hairlike cracking in a glaze).

2) Low moisture expansion bodies are produced, resulting in good resistance to delayed crazing.

3) The hard, massive nature of the ores aids in either dry-pressing or in the making of good casting slips.

4) Low firing temperatures are possible.

5) Fast firing schedules are possible—as fast as 1 hr cold to cold.

6) Shrinkage and absorption of bodies are fairly constant over a long temperature range.

7) Good white-fired bodies are possible.

8) Glazes of unusual brilliance and attractiveness can be fitted readily to high talc bodies.

As far back as 1930 reports began to appear praising the improved craze resistance of semi-vitreous bodies when New York talc was used.

A minor use of talc is as an addition to the clay-flint-feldspar type of dinnerware bodies. Talc is added up to 6% of the body and results in greatly improved craze resistance.

Talc is used as a glaze ingredient as it provides a low-cost source of MgO.

Talc is used as a mold dusting compound to help the release of large castware pieces. Synthetic lava talc is made from ground steatite-grade talcs. In these applications, as much as 80% talc is used in the mixtures. When steatite-grade talcs are used for the manufacture of high-frequency insulators, limits of 1.5% CaO, 4% Al_2O_3, and 1.5% iron oxides are usually imposed. This extrapolates to a maximum of about 5 to 10% nontalc minerals. Preferably, this should be only 1 to 2% nontalc components.

Talc can be used to replace clay in many ceramic bodies. It promotes translucency of the finished ware and makes it more durable.

Specifications for talc used in the ceramic industry are increasingly more demanding. The uniformity of most ceramic talcs supplied by producers using hand-sorting or other primitive beneficiation methods is only fair at best. As more sophisticated ore processing methods are applied to talc ores, the ceramic industry is beginning to receive higher quality talcs with very uniform chemical and physical properties.

The use of talc in ceramic tile has not even approached the increases in residential and commercial construction. For example, a 50% increase in housing starts in 1970 to 1971 gave only a 10% increase in tile consumption (Perry, 1972). New grades, sizes, and colors of tile are being developed to help increase the market. The Tile Council of America forecasts replacement of portland cement as a setting material in the future (Bennett, 1972). Also, increased use of edge-bonded panels and colored grouts is predicted.

Pence (1955) gave an early report on white-firing talc for ceramic use from west Texas. The talc described was from claims located in Hudspeth County about 23 miles west of Van Horn, Texas. The ore analysis was 54.92% SiO_2, 27.20% MgO, 5.76% CaO, 1.36% Al_2O_3, 0.46% Fe_2O_3, and 10.76% ignition loss. By firing standard 4¼ x 4¼ x ⅜-in. hand-pressed tile, Pence obtained satisfactory results in color, density, glaze fit, and other properties required in ceramic wall tile.

At 750° to 900°C talc loses its one molecule of combined water; at 900° to 1000°C it dissociates into the metasilicate $3 MgO \cdot SiO_2$ and silica. At 1200° to 1300°C it converts to clinoenstatite, $MgO \cdot SiO_2$. The final products of the thermal decomposition of talc are clinoenstatite and cristobalite.

In pottery, talc may constitute 40% of the body composition. The thickness of the object being made, the texture, porosity required, and the firing conditions all influence the amount of talc used. Tableware often contains 15% talc.

Talc in Plastics

Talc is an important filler material for plastics. It improves chemical and heat resistance, impact strength, dimensional stability, stiffness, hardness, thermal conductivity, tensile strength, creep resistance, and electrical insulation properties. In some cases, the processability, especially faster molding cycles, of the plastic is also improved. Talc can be used in both thermoplastics and thermosets.

Talc is used as a reinforcing extender filler in many thermoplastics. It controls melt flow, reduces creep in molded parts, increases molding cycles, increases heat deflection temperature, and dimensional stability. When platy varieties of talc are used, a beneficial lubricating effect is noted on molding machine parts. And perhaps most important of all, the use of talc decreases the overall cost of the plastic product. Talc can be used as a filler in quantities from 1 up to 50% by weight when polyolefin compositions are involved (Poppe et al., 1972). In a rare case, up to 70% talc has been used in a cellulose ether that is both thermoplastic and water soluble.

In all filler applications, where talc is added to an organic component, a new dimension is rapidly developing. This is the chemical bonding of the talc filler to the resin matrix (in the case of plastic composites). The technology involved is old since initial successes in bonding glass fibers to various plastics were reported in the early 1950s.

The development of processes for the chemical coating of talc fillers is now reaching a considerable degree of sophistication. Silane coupling agents are used to improve performance of talc fillers in plastic materials. Ranney, et al. (1972) report that the tensile strength of a 50% (by weight) loaded polyethylene plastic can be increased 25 to 30% over the non-silane-containing standard.

In both rubber and plastics, the use of filler minerals was originally for the sole purpose of reducing cost. Thus such minerals were called extenders or extender pigments. With the advent of products such as silane-coated clays in the rubber industry, it became evident that filler minerals could be functional as well as reduce overall cost.

Silane coupling agents are used with clays, talc, and other mineral fillers. These agents are a chemical family of organosilicon monomers which characteristically possess two different kinds of chemical functionality. The general formula for the molecule is: R—Si (OX)$_3$ where R is the organofunctional group attached to the silicon atom in a thermally and hydrolytically stable manner. In this formula, OX designates hydrolyzable groups upon silicon. These groups are generally believed to be the means whereby the silane coupling agents interact with the siliceous inorganic surfaces (e.g., talc) to form a more durable bond with the filler mineral. With the increased bonding, it is often possible to increase the filler loading without sacrificing the properties required in the polymer system.

Talc in Roofing Products

Talc is used both as a filler and as a surfacing material in the manufacture of roofing. When used as a filler, the talc acts as a stabilizer for the melted asphalt constituents. It helps increase stability and weather resistance. When talc is sprinkled on the surface of either asphalt shingles or roll roofing, it prevents the roofing from sticking during manufacture and storage before use.

Typical size specifications for talc used for stabilizing roofing products are:

Tyler Mesh	Range, % Wt.
+ 35 mesh	none
+ 65 mesh	10-20
— 65, + 100 mesh	15-30
— 100, + 200 mesh	25-35
— 200 mesh	20-25

The market for low-grade talc used for surfacing, filler, and backing for smooth surface roofings and for filler and backing of asphalt roofing shingles is growing rapidly. When used for surface coatings, the color and staining properties of the product are important. When talc is used as backing, the primary qualifications are particle size range, particle shape, absorbency, and above all, low cost.

Miscellaneous Uses of Talc

Talc is used in a wide variety of textile materials. Textile sizing compositions include binders and mineral fillers. Some textiles use sizings for temporary stiffeners and appearance for sales appeal. The degree of whiteness is often very important and thus favors talc or other extremely white minerals. Where extreme whiteness of color is important, talc often competes with titanium dioxide at a considerable cost advantage.

A relatively new market for talc and pyrophyllite fillers is in the integral foamed latex rubber backing for carpets, rugs, and parquet hardwood floor panels. When used with fabric, the main purpose of the latex is to provide a flexible backing for the fabric and, at the same time, lock the pile material to its own backing. Impurities in the filler such as calcium, magnesium, iron, and manganese which can chelate with the latex are undesirable. Specially coated fillers with additional latex reinforcement properties are under development.

Upholstery fabric backing also uses substantial tonnages of mineral fillers. The filler loadings run about 75 to 100 parts per 100 parts of latex. Major fillers are clay, talc, pyrophyllite, and calcium carbonate. Similar back coatings are used in drapery materials, but the filler loadings are lower than for upholstery. Talc is a favored material because of its ability to meet the demand for whiteness of color.

The lubrication properties of talc are unique and found in very few minerals. The history of talc as a component in extreme temperature range greases is extensive and significant. The dispersion characteristics so important to lubricants which operate over a wide temperature range without freezing or running off the bearing surface are assisted by use of talc. A representative grease capable of use over an extreme temperature range might include a silicone oil, colloidal silica thickener, molybdenum disulfide, talc, and several chemical additives to prevent corrosion of the bearing surface or decomposition of the lubricant (Elstron, 1961).

Both platy and nodular talc powders are covered by US Patents for use in corrosion proofing compositions such as those used in automotive undercoating (Miller and Holtzapfel, 1970). The talc is about 50% by weight finer than 10μ and no more than 3% coarser than 325 mesh. Talc plays an important part in the prevention of "wicking" action in the composition. Undercoating products containing fillers such as asbestos are often subject to failure resulting from a wicking action which causes moisture to travel through the corrosion proofing coatings.

The use of talc in dry fire-extinguishing powders has been patented (Cawood, 1962). Talc is used in quantities ranging from 10 to 15 parts per 100 parts of product. The talc is used primarily to maintain the desired free-flowing condition so essential in dry powders used in fire extinguishers.

Talc is used in the textile industry both for loading and "bleaching" materials such as cotton sacks, cordage, rope, and string. For such purposes, a good grade of low-abrasive white talc is required. Talc used for back-filling textiles can be of lower quality.

Other uses for talc include:

Cereal polishing (rice, corn, barley)
Bleaching agents
Odor absorption from foods
Floor wax
Water filtration
Leather treatment (oil absorption)
Joint fillers and grouts
Insecticides
Textiles
Shoe polishes
Welding rod coatings
Printing inks
Encapsulant for acceleration testing artillery shells up to 50,000 g
Coating for iron ore pellets in direct reduction processes
Source of magnesium in plant foods

Mineralogy

Talc is a hydrated magnesium silicate with the theoretical formula $Mg_6[Si_8O_{20}](OH)_4$. The chemical composition of talc found in nature, however, is quite variable. It is an extremely soft mineral and is rated No. 1 in Mohs' scale of hardness. It varies in color from snow-white to greenish gray and various shades of green. Its specific gravity ranges from 2.58 to 2.83. Talc usually derives as a secondary mineral by alteration of other magnesium silicates such as serpentine, pyroxene, or siliceous dolomite.

In industry the word talc covers a broad variety of rocks and rock products.

Talc deposits can be classified into four major categories:

1) Steatite—compact, massive, crypto-crystalline, can be sawed, drilled, or machined to required shapes. Steatite converts on firing at 1800°F for 6 hr to interlocking crystals of clinoenstatite—then called "lava." This has good electrical insulating properties.

2) Soft platy talc—is an alteration product of sedimentary magnesium carbonate rocks. Chlorite is a common accessory mineral. This is the most important type of talc. It possibly has more uses and more potential than any other talcose material.

3) Tremolite talc—sometimes called "hard" talc. It is massive or laminated rock composed of varying percentages of tremolite, anthophyllite, calcite, dolomite, serpentine, and true soft talc. It is characterized by calcium oxide contents of 6 to 10%.

4) Mixed talc ores—includes the so-called "soft talc," a friable, white schistose rock composed of platy talc, dolomite, calcite, serpentine, and many other trace minerals. In some low-grade deposits, mixtures of talc, chlorite, and dolomite are common.

Talc is a mineral that meets the criteria of a "sheet silicate" mineral. Its structure is like that of pyrophyllite except that the octahedral sites in the layers or "sheets" are occupied by magnesium instead of aluminum. Also, none of the octahedral sites are vacant (which is not the case with pyrophyllite). Chemically pure talc is rarely found in nature in commercial quantities. Practically all of the talc produced is an impure product. Even the hand-sorted, selectively mined cosmetic talcs contain many extraneous mineral components.

When the major talc products in world trade are examined, it becomes obvious that only a miniscule percentage of world reserves are "pure" talc. When impure talc products are reprocessed by froth flotation, or similar selective separatory methods, very high purity talc mineral can be produced. It would seem objective to call a talc "pure" if it contains upward of 95% $Mg_6[Si_8O_{20}](OH)_4$.

Table 3 lists the approximate composition of the minerals present in talc ores.

The main isomorphous components of the tremolite group are ferric iron, manganese, and aluminum. Tremolite can contain 2 to 3% sodium. Tremolite includes three varieties

TABLE 3—Approximate Composition of Minerals Present in Talc Ores, %

	SiO_2	MgO	CaO	CO_2	Fe	Al_2O_3	K_2O	Na_2O	H_2O	TiO_2
Talc	63	32							3–7	
Serpentine (antigorite)	44	43							8–13	
Chlorite	33	36				18			5–14	
Anthophyllite	58	30	2						15–2.2	
Tremolite	57	28	13						15–2.3	
Actinolite	52	5	9		34				3	
Diopside	56	18	26							
Feldspar	65					18	17			
Magnesite		48		52						
Dolomite		22	30	48						
Calcite			56	44						
Quartz	100									
Muscovite	46	0.1				39	10	0.6	4.3	
Magnetite (Fe_3O_4)					72					
Ilmenite ($FeTiO_4$)					33					48.0
Pyrite (FeS_2)					47					
Tourmaline*	36	11	0.5			33	0.6	2.3	3.8	0.2
Graphite (100% C)										

* 10% B_2O_3

—iron tremolite, manganese tremolite (hexagonite), and fluorine tremolite. Tremolite, which has the theoretical composition $2CaO \cdot 5MgO \cdot 8SiO_2H_2O$, is commonly the major component in talc ores, at the expense of the mineral talc itself. This relationship may hold throughout large talc-mining districts, e.g., the New York and California-Nevada districts. Other talclike minerals which may constitute various proportions of talc ores are anthophyllite, antigorite, chlorite, pyrophyllite, and serpentine.

Povarennykh (1972) includes pyrophyllite, talc, minnesotaite, and willemseite in the pyrophyllite group of minerals. In his description of the group varieties, he includes Mg-pyrophyllite, Fe-pyrophyllite, Fe^{2+}-talc, $Fe^{2+}Fe^{3+}$-talc, Ni-talc, and Mg-willemseite. Talc can contain up to 1% nickel and pyrophyllite can contain up to 9% magnesium. These chemical variations of the pyrophyllite group show the wide variety and possibilities of the occurrence of "talclike" pyrophyllite.

Barnes (1958) reported weak to medium infrared luminescence of talc minerals from various parts of the world. Steatitic talc from Manhattan, NV, showed medium luminescence. Tremolite from Kragero, Norway, and Outokumpu, Finland, also exhibited medium reaction.

At the Jatoba talc mine near Ponta Grossa, Brazil, a claylike antigorite has found commercial acceptance as a diluent for insecticides and as "talc" for pharmaceutical uses (Brindley and Santos, 1971). This is another example of a talclike mineral finding commercial acceptance as "talc."

Faust and Fahey (1962) provide a good review of extensive studies by others relating to the distribution of minor elements in magnesium-rich minerals and rocks. There is good agreement by the scientists that "the rocks of the ultrabasic suite and their hydrothermally altered forms rich in serpentine contain an unusually high concentration of nickel, chromium, cobalt, and scandium. Moreover, some of the investigators have observed that the carbonate-rich rocks, in contrast, contain very small to practically negligible concentrations of these elements." This is in agreement with the high nickel content of some Vermont talcs and its complete absence in some western carbonate-talc ore bodies.

Differential thermal analysis (DTA) and X-ray diffraction both provide good analytical methods for identification of talc and also many of the impurities associated with talc ores. A large endothermic peak at 965°C is typical of relatively pure talc mineral analyzed by DTA methods.

It is of considerable geological significance that tremolite from some metamorphosed carbonate rocks contains fluorine. On the basis of fluorine analyses of 22 talcs from worldwide deposits, it was noted talc from metamorphosed sedimentary rocks contained from 0.11 to 0.48% fluorine. Talcs derived from ultramafic rocks contained less fluorine (Ross and Smith, 1968).

Later work by Troll and Gilbert (1972) on fluorine-bearing tremolites points out that the theoretical value for pure fluoro-tremolite is 4.65% fluorine. One sample of tremolite used in this work from Richville, NY, contained

1.51% fluorine. Analysis of a sample of lavender-colored tremolite showed 0.30% fluorine. The US Bureau of Mines (USBM) and the National Institute of Environmental Health Sciences (NIEHS) have reported on the characterization data of fine mineral test samples, including nonfibrous tremolite (Campbell, et al., 1980).

Occurrence and Reserves

Talc deposits are found in many countries. Good quality talc ores are found in Africa, the Americas, Australia, Republic of China, Finland, France, Greece, India, Italy, North and South Korea, Manchuria, Norway, Romania, Sardinia, and the USSR.

Table 4 is a summary of geologic and commercial data for the principal talc districts of the United States (Chidester, et al., 1964).

As governmental regulations concerning exposure to mineral dusts increase in frequency and severity, those talc deposits containing asbestiform minerals may decrease in importance. The filler industry shows preference for very high-purity platy talc which has minimal health hazards upon exposure to its dust.

Geology

Talc deposits occur on every continent and the geology of these deposits is roughly similar to those of the United States. The most common host rocks for the formation of talc are dolomite and ultramafic rocks. Chidester et al. (1964) consider that there are three major types of talc deposits in the United States: deposits associated with sedimentary rocks; deposits associated with ultramafic igneous rocks; and deposits associated with mafic igneous rocks.

Good examples of talc deposits associated with sedimentary rocks are those of the California-Nevada, Montana, New York, and Texas districts.

Good examples of talc deposits associated with ultramafic igneous rocks are those of the Vermont district.

Talc deposits associated with mafic igneous rocks occur in the central Appalachian Mountains and are the source of most of the soapstone quarried in the United States. These rocks, which contain relatively minor amounts of the mineral talc, were probably formed by the hydrothermal alteration of gabbroic rocks. As they are not a source of talc products, they will not be discussed here. The first two types of talc deposits, however, are important as a source of talc products.

The easiest method of forming pure or relatively pure talc deposits is shown in the following reaction as presented by Winkler (1974):

$$3 \text{ dolomite} + 4 \text{ quartz} + H_2O = \text{talc} + 3 \text{ calcite} + 3 \text{ CO}_2.$$

The geological settings of US talc deposits are as varied and diverse as would be expected for any naturally occurring mineral commodity of secondary origin, but there are nevertheless some broad similarities. First, talc is invariably a secondary mineral formed in preexisting rocks either directly from those rocks, or through the introduction of new material. Second, all economically important deposits have been formed under conditions of low-grade regional metamorphism. Third, commercial bodies are generally tabular and concordant, being molded after the shape of the parent material, which is most commonly a sedimentary or metasedimentary rock unit. Fourth, most of these talc ore bodies occur within Precambrian rock units; the few which do not are found within rock units whose age is no younger than Early Paleozoic. Finally, in almost every instance where the conditions of genesis can be either firmly established or confidently inferred, the time of the talc formation is Precambrian as well.

The reasons for this almost total restriction of talc to the Precambrian in both space and time are presently unclear. It may be easier to comprehend in the case of ultramafic rocks, for these may indeed be much more abundant in the Precambrian than in younger geological systems. It is, however, somewhat more difficult to understand with regard to dolomitic rocks, for these are certainly much more common in the Cambrian and younger geological systems than they are in the Precambrian. It may be that deep burial and the consequent conditions of dynamic metamorphism could have attained sufficient intensities only during Precambrian time; such a theory would perhaps explain the formation of talc in Montana and New York, for instance, but would probably not be applicable to some of the other districts, which admittedly have undergone deep burial but do not show conditions of extreme dynamic metamorphism and isoclinal structure, such as California-Nevada. It seems safe to say, how-

TABLE 4—Summary of Geologic and Commercial

State and District	Form and Size of Talc Body	Country Rock and Parent Rock	Paragenetic-Sequence in Alteration of Parent Rock to Talc
California: Silver Lake—Yucca Grove	Lenses, mainly of massive tremolite rocks, as much as 800 ft long, 20 ft thick, and 200–300 ft deep; schistose/talc rock forms layers and lenses 1 ft or more thick, mostly along the footwall.	Feldspar-quartz-diopside-carbonate hornfels, commonly separated from the talc body by phlogopite-feldspar-tremolite schist a few inches to several feet thick. Tremolite and talc apparently derived from beds of sedimentary dolomite 5–20 ft thick that form parts of pendants in bodies of granitic rock.	Dolomite → tremolite → talc.
Southern Death Valley, Kingston Range.	Tabular to lenticular bodies as much as 5000 ft long, 80 ft thick, and 400 ft downdip; most are of schistose to massive talc rock, but some contain interlayered tremolite rock in various proportions, and some are entirely of tremolite rock.	Cherty and noncherty dolomite, diabase, and argillite, commonly silicated at the contact. In most deposits, one kind of rock forms the hanging wall, another the footwall. Talc and tremolite derived from generally massive and commonly cherty or siliceous beds of dolomite.	Carbonate+chert → tremolite → serpentine → talc. Intermediate steps in the process did not take place in many deposits.
Inyo Range—Northern Panamint Range.	Small pods to lenses and tabular bodies as much as 500 ft long, 50 ft wide, and 400 ft downdip. Some bodies show large-scale variations related to differences in parent rock, permitting selective mining.	Principally dolomite and quartzite, in a few places granitic rock and limestone. Talc derived principally from massive beds of dolomite and quartzite, locally from granite or diorite.	Dolomite and quartzite → talc; also granite and diorite → talc.
Georgia: Chatsworth	Lenticular bodies as much as 5000 ft long, 150 ft thick, and 300 ft downdip. Lenticular and spindle-shaped bodies of massive talc rock (crayon talc) are dispersed through talc-carbonate rock that shows large-scale variations in color, texture, and mineral composition.	Schist, slate, granite, and granite gneiss. Mode of origin doubtful; parent rock either sedimentary carbonate rock, mafic igneous or volcanic rock, or ultramafic igneous rock.	Probably: dolomite → serpentine → (chlorite) → talc. Possibly: ultramafic or mafic igneous rock → serpentine → (Chlorite) → talc+carbonate.
Maryland	Irregular tabular masses adjacent to pegmatite dikes in serpentinite; irregular envelopes surrounding a serpentinite core; and lenticular masses.	Schist, gneiss, pegmatite, and serpentinite. Talc derived by replacement of parts or the whole of serpentinite bodies that vary widely in size.	Dunite and peridotite → serpentine → talc+carbonate.
Montana: Dillon-Ennis	Small veins and pods to lenses as much as 700 ft long, 100 ft thick, and more than 200 ft in vertical extent.	Dolomite and quartz-mica schist. Talc derived from beds of dolomitic marble that range widely in size.	Dolomite → talc; also dolomite → tremolite → talc.
Nevada: Palmetto-Oasis	Elongate zones of discontinuous pods and lenses to tabular masses more than 5–500 ft long; generally 1–15 ft, but as much as 50 ft thick; and 140 ft downdip.	Chiefly dolomitic marble, hornfels, and diabase; locally granitic rock, phyllite, and schist, commonly one kind of rock forms the hanging wall, another kind the footwall. Talc derived chiefly from extensive beds of dolomitic marble and hornfels, but locally from phyllite, schist, and granitic rock; commonly occurs at fault contacts.	Chiefly: dolomite → talc. Locally: hornfels, granite, schist, and phyllite → talc.
New Mexico: Hembrillo Canyon—San Andres Mountains.	Lenses as much as 300 ft long, 25 ft thick, and of undetermined depth.	Chiefly argillite; locally carbonate rock and silica-carbonate rock. Talc probably derived from extensive sedimentary units of argillite.	Not determined
New York	Sheetlike to lenticular zones as much as several miles long and 300 ft wide.	Dolomitic and calcitic marble, diopsidic marble, and thin quartz-diopside layers. Talc derived chiefly from beds of dolomite and siliceous dolomite that form units as much as 5000 ft thick and several miles long; some talc derived from granite, syenite, quartzite, and amphibolite.	Dolomite + quartz → diopside → tremolite → anthophyllite → serpentine → talc. One or more minerals may be omitted in the sequence.
North Carolina: Murphy	Small pods to lenses as much as 700 ft long, 50 ft thick, and 200 ft downdip. Many deposits exhibit large-scale variations in color, texture, and distribution of impurities, permitting selective mining.	Calcite marble, locally highly siliceous and commonly tremolitic at the borders of the talc deposits.	Dolomite+quartz → silicated rock → talc.

Data for the Principal Talc Districts of the United States

Mineral Composition and Impurities	Physical and Chemical Characteristics of the Commercial Talc	Commercial Use	Production through 1955, References, and Remarks
Chiefly tremolite and talc with minor forsterite, serpentine, and carbonate. Impurities include phlogopite, chlorite, quartz, carbonate, and mafic dike rocks.	Tremolite rock mostly massive; talc rock commonly schistose.	Wall tile, pottery, rubber, insecticides.	About 320,000 tons (Wright, 1954; 1957).
Principally talc; tremolite mostly-subordinate, but in places predominant. Impurities chiefly carbonate, iron oxide stains, and wallrock inclusions.	Talc rock blocky and massive to schistose or laminated. Tremolite rock massive to laminated. Particle shape acicular to platy.	Paint, ceramics, paper, textiles.	About 820,000 tons (Wright, 1957).
Chiefly talc; tremolite rare. Impurities generally very minor; chiefly chlorite, carbonate, quartz, pyrite, and iron oxide.	Talc rock mostly massive and blocky; ranging in color from dark gray to white or pale green; shows large-scale variations in color and texture.	Steatite, ceramics, cosmetics, pharmaceuticals, paints.	About 340,000 tons (Page, 1951; Wright, 1957).
Talc rock principally talc, minor magnetite; talc-carbonate rock chiefly talc and carbonate with minor magnetite, pyrite, chlorite, quartz, feldspar, actinolite, and sericite.	Talc rock varies from massive to schistose, translucent medium green. Talc-carbonate rock varies from medium to dark gray, and varies widely in texture and composition.	Crayons, cosmetics, paint, rubber, roofing, insecticides, lubricants, foundry facings, dusting agents.	Probably about 850,000 tons (Furcron and others, 1947).
Talc rock chiefly talc; impurities, chiefly chlorite, variable. Talc-carbonate rock essentially talc and carbonate, with chlorite, magnetite, serpentine, and other impurities.	Talc rock associated with pegmatites massive, fairly high in iron. Other talc rock and talc-carbonate rock commonly schistose.	Nonsteatite block talc, low-grade ground talcs.	About 320,000 tons (Pearre and Heyl, 1960, p. 795).
Essentially talc with minor amounts of impurities such as chlorite, graphite, dolomite, manganese and iron oxides, and inclusions of country rock.	Massive and blocky to schistose nearly pure talc; ranges in color from white to pale green and buff; particles range from subequant to flaky.	Steatite, possibly block steatite, cosmetics, paints, paper, ceramics.	About 200,000 tons (Perry, 1948).
Chiefly talc with minor chlorite and carbonate, locally some tremolite. Much of the material is nearly pure talc.	Massive to schistose talc rock, ranging in color from dark gray to pale green and white. Talc particles commonly finely platy.	Cosmetics, pharmaceuticals, paints, paper, insulators. Much probably suitable for steatite.	About 110,000 tons.
Chiefly talc with minor chlorite; locally stained with iron oxide.	White to gray talc rock with platy particles.	Cosmetics. Some hand-sorted material probably suitable for steatite.	Probably less than 10,000 tons. Incorporated in White Sands Military Reservation and withdrawn from mining in 1942.
The proportion of tremolite, anthophyllite, talc, and serpentine varies widely; any may predominate, but tremolite rock is most common. Quartz, carbonate, diopside, manganese and iron oxides, and gypsum are minor impurities.	Varieties of commercial talc range from schistose to massive. Particles range from nearly equant to bladed and fibrous. Very white.	Largely paint and ceramics; also rubber, insecticides, foundry facings, plastics, and other uses.	About 6,500,000 tons up to July 1961.
Essentially talc. Impurities are chiefly minor amounts of quartz, carbonate, iron oxide stain, and rarely tremolite.	Massive to schistose talc rock, ranging in color from light gray to white. Particles subequant to flaky.	Crayons, cosmetics, paint, paper, textiles, ceramics; some suitable for steatite.	Probably more than 100,000 tons (Van Horn, 1948).

TABLE 4—Continued

State and District	Form and Size of Talc Body	Country Rock and Parent Rock	Paragenetic-Sequence in Alteration of Parent Rock to Talc
Texas: Allamoore	Largely unknown, but some tabular masses are several thousand feet long and several hundred feet wide, with tabular and irregular inclusions of carbonate rock, phyllite, and masses of chert that range widely in size.	Cherty dolomite; some conglomerate, phyllite, and diabase. Talc probably derived from extensive beds of sedimentary or pyroclastic rock such as dolomitic marl or magnesium-rich tuff.	Not determined
Llano	Mostly small lenses and pods in schist or along margins of serpentinite masses as much as 4 miles long and 1 mile wide.	Schist, gneiss, and serpentinite. Talc derived from lenticular bodies of serpentinite and from tabular and lenticular units of schist, gneiss, mafic volcanic rock, and carbonate rock.	Details unknown. Serpentinite and metamorphosed sedimentary and volcanic rock altered variously to one or more of talc, carbonate, tremolite, and anthophyllite.
Vermont	Shell of talc rock 1–3 ft thick surrounds a zone of talc-carbonate rock that ranges in size from a shell 1–20 ft thick around a serpentinite core to the entire mass of the original serpentinite body.	Schist, greenstone, and serpentinite. Talc rock and talc-carbonate rock derived almost wholly from serpentinite bodies that range in size from small pods to lenses several miles long and a mile wide; a small proportion of the talc rock is derived from schist.	Dunite and peridotite →serpentinite. Serpentinite+CO_2 →talc+carbonate. Serpentinite+SiO_2 →talc. Schist or greenstone →talc+chlorite.
Virginia: Schuyler	Lenticular bodies of the same extent as the original igneous rock body.	Gneiss, schist, and amphibolite. The talc (soapstone) was derived from lenticular bodies, probably originally hypersthene gabbro, as much as 180 ft thick and 1500 ft long.	Hypersthene gabbro →amphibole+chlorite →talc+carbonate.

Source: Chidester et al., 1964.

ever, that even though conditions of extreme dynamic metamorphism have not necessarily been attained in all six talc-mining districts of the United States, conditions of burial beneath miles of rock cover have been attained in every one of them.

The six major talc-mining districts in the United States are New York, Vermont, the southern Appalachians, Texas, California-Nevada, and Montana.

New York

All of the known commercial talc here occurs within the Balmat-Edwards or Gouverneur mining district. A comprehensive study of talc in the United States by the US Geological Survey (Chidester, et al., 1964) indicates that New York had at that time almost 75% of the United States' "measured and indicated" talc ore and about 40% of its "inferred" talc ore. With only relatively minor exceptions, all known talc in this district lies within a narrow belt, which probably averages only 500 ft or so wide and is only about eight miles long.

The New York talc district was long the most important in the United States in terms of total annual production, being rivaled or surpassed only by Vermont. Over the past couple of decades, however, both Montana and Texas have also pulled ahead of New York. It is most peculiar, therefore, that the New York district, although dominant in production for so much of the past century, and even more dominant in terms of proven and potential ore reserves, is geographically the smallest in area of all six talc-mining districts in the United States.

The bedrock complex of the Gouverneur mining district consists exclusively of metamorphic rocks of Precambrian age (the Grenville Series), but two specific lithologic types, gneiss and marble, dominate. The gneiss is thought to be the older unit and is about 3,000 ft thick; the marble, thought to be the younger unit, has a maximum known thickness of about 2,000 ft. Thin sheets and lenses of amphibolite occur within both the marble and the gneiss, but are relatively minor in total volume. Brown and Engel (1956) subdivided the marble sequence into 15 units, of which only Unit 13, the "talc unit," is known to contain commercial deposits of talc, tremolite, or zinc minerals. Unpublished geological investigations indicate that the composition of most of the marble within this mining district is relatively simple and probably does not and did not originally differ greatly along strike. The talc unit, a dolomitic marble, shows evidence of being only 250 ft or so thick in its least contorted areas; greater thicknesses are probably due to structural flowage.

TABLE 4—Continued

Mineral Composition and Impurities	Physical and Chemical Characteristics of the Commercial Talc	Commercial Use	Production through 1955, Reference, and Remarks
Essentially talc. Impurities consist of varying amounts of chert, carbonate, wall rock inclusions, surface weathering products, and organic material.	No information	Chiefly wall tile; also insecticides.	120,000 tons through 1958 (King and Flawn, 1953; Flawn, 1958).
Talc; talc and tremolite; talc and anthophyllite; anthophyllite. Commonly contains impurities of quartz, magnetite, chlorite, and other materials.	Variable in composition and physical properties. Small amounts of massive talc rock.	Chiefly low-grade uses. Some suitable for crayons and for carvings.	Production unknown, but very small (Dietrich and Lonsdale, 1958).
Talc rock is essentially talc with minor chlorite. Talc-carbonate rock essentially talc and magnesite with minor serpentine, magnetite, chlorite, and sulfides.	Talc rock generally schistose, talc-carbonate rock schistose to massive; both are medium to light gray. Talc ranges from fine to coarsely flaky.	Paper, rubber, textiles, paint, roofing, cosmetics, filler, foundry facings, crayons.	About 1,500,000 tons (Chidester and others, 1951, 1952a, b).
Talc, chlorite, carbonate, amphibole, and magnetite.	Massive, felted texture	Sawed and shaped slabs, insecticides.	No reliable production figures available, but total production probably about 2 million tons, of which probably more than 80% was in sawed and shaped slabs (Hess, 1933a; Spence, 1940).

The zinc and talc ores occur within the same stratigraphic unit, but not together (except at a few localities). Locally, the siliceous dolomite of Unit 13 has been converted to tremolite under conditions of dynamic metamorphism and/or metasomatism; subsequently, talc, anthophyllite, and serpentine have been formed locally from the tremolite. In the northeasternmost part of the district, anthophyllite locally may be the major ore constituent.

New York talc ores are commonly more than half tremolite. Tremolitic ores have been proven by underground workings to downdip depths of at least 1,100 ft and by core drilling (generally in search of commercial zinc deposits) to downdip depths of more than 3,000 ft. Bodies of almost tremolite-free talc (platy or scaly variety) have been discovered in surface and underground mines near Talcville; these relatively small deposits, however, are at or near the hanging-wall contact and are difficult to mine by themselves. Field mapping by US Geological Survey workers has indicated that tremolite, talc, and associated secondary minerals were formed prior to 10^9 years ago.

The talc ore zones locally pinch and swell, but they are on the whole conformable with the dolomitic marble layers. The regional dip averages about 45° to the northwest; departures from this are only locally significant. Tight and contorted cross-folds superimposed upon the main talc belt have resulted locally in the thickening of the talc sequence by at least 50%. All of the rocks here are complexly folded; metamorphism to the amphibolite facies is common, if indeed not ubiquitous.

Both open-pit and underground mining methods are employed. A large crushing facility is installed within one underground mine.

The deposits of the New York talc-mining district may well constitute the largest reserves of tremolitic-type talc ore in the world, for nothing described in the literature at the present time is of similar magnitude. The US Bureau of Mines groups New York's production in with six other states; this production in 1979 was 224,000 tons, with most of this obviously coming from New York.

New York talc ores are milled as is, i.e., without any prior beneficiation. Milling is accomplished in ball mills and in fluid energy mills and the product is then air-classified.

Vermont

The district which is commonly known as the Vermont talc-mining district runs through the central part of that state, but also extends southward into Massachusetts and northward into Quebec.

Bodies of ultramafic rock have been intruded into a sequence of phyllite, schist, gneiss, greenstone, and amphibolite rocks. These ultramafic bodies subsequently have been locally serpentinized and partly converted into talc. The talc deposits are commonly associated with dunite, peridotite, and serpentinite, which were probably their parent rock.

These ultramafic rocks form part of a belt more than 2,000 miles long, which extends from Alabama to Newfoundland (Chidester, et al., 1951). The talc ore itself is more of a talc-carbonate complex, which locally grades into a carbonate complex commonly rich in magnesite. The talc ore is relatively dark-colored, has schistose structure, and is relatively high in iron content, particularly at the surface where the iron has been enriched by weathering processes. Although the mineral talc itself is a relatively major constituent, the grade of Vermont talc ores generally is considerably lower than those of the other districts in the United States.

The ultramafic bodies are as much as 1 mile wide and as much as 3.5 miles long (Chidester, et al., 1951). The commercial talc bodies, which occur in those ultramafic bodies known as the *verde antique* type, are zoned around cores of serpentinite. The talc-containing zone (steatite zone) forms the outer shell or zone of the body; between it and the serpentinite core is the *grit zone,* which is commonly several feet to several tens of feet thick. *Grit* is the miners' term for rock which is composed of talc and carbonate minerals only.

There are few masses of high-purity talc in the Vermont district large enough to mine as such. Tremolite is not known and talc itself is the only talclike mineral contained within the ultramafic bodies.

In northern Vermont, entire ultramafic bodies have been converted into grit and have widths on the order of 100 ft or so. In southern Vermont one similar body has a width of about 175 ft. At least 145 talc occurrences are known in Vermont within an area having a strike length of about 150 miles and a width ranging from five to 25 miles. Homoclinal folding is the regional structure; isoclinal folding is thought to be uncommon, for little repetition due to folding has been noted.

Few workers have attempted to date either the host rocks of the Vermont talc-mining district or the time of steatization, but studies by Christman (1959) and Christman and Secor (1961) suggest that the age of the parent rocks is Early Paleozoic, probably Ordovician.

Open-pit mining is relatively minor, with most of the production coming from underground workings, some of which extend to vertical depths of more than 1,000 ft.

The ore reserve situation in the Vermont district has never been seriously investigated by anyone who would be at liberty to disclose the results of such a study. Judging from the geographical distribution of the known talc bodies, however, the total ore reserves must be extremely large.

Producers historically have had the choice of grinding the talc ore as mined and simply size-classifying it for relatively low-priced dusting compounds and fillers or of beneficiating it by flotation or other means in order to derive high-value products containing major amounts of the mineral talc. To manufacture the most profitable product line in this district, an operator must employ wet-processing beneficiation techniques. The Eastern Magnesia Talc Co., Inc. (now Engelhard Minerals and Chemical Corp.) has been using wet-beneficiation methods on ores near Johnson, VT since 1937. The ore is subjected to froth flotation, then dewatered in a rotary vacuum drum filter. The filter cake is then dried, pulverized, and air-classified (Harrah, 1956). Eastern Magnesia Talc Co., Inc. established another, more modern froth flotation plant at West Windsor, VT in 1964; since 1972 this operation has been known as Windsor Minerals, Inc., a wholly owned subsidiary of Johnson & Johnson Co. (Trauffer, 1964).

Vermont's talc production in 1979, according to the US Bureau of Mines, was 346,000 tons with a value of $2,755,000.

Southern Appalachians

Although numerous deposits of talc and soapstone are known in the Appalachian Mountain province between Vermont and western North Carolina, none of them have such a history of past or present production, nor in the writer's opinion the future potential, to even suggest the possibility of their becoming major talc-mining districts. These occurrences in Massachusetts, Connecticut, Rhode Island, New Jersey, Pennsylvania, Maryland, and Virginia are described by Chidester, et al. (1964).

Several more attractive talc occurrences and ore deposits, however, are known between Murphy in western North Carolina and Dadeville in eastern Alabama. Compared with those of the other five major talc-mining districts in the US, these are relatively small deposits, but some of them are quite important in that they are of exceptionally high purity and serve specialized consumer needs.

Production figures issued by the US Bureau of Mines do not differentiate this area from the New York district, but it is likely that the total annual talc production of the southern Appalachian area does not exceed 50,000 tons.

North Carolina: The Murphy talc district is about 85 miles long, extending from southwesternmost North Carolina into northern Georgia. Although talc is found in sedimentary rocks and is also associated with ultramafic bodies in North Carolina, only that talc in sedimentary rocks is presently of commercial interest. The host rock for these ore bodies is the Murphy Marble, which is generally more dolomitic than calcitic. Although the marble has been reported to be as thick as 400 ft or so, such thicknesses may be caused by structural deformation and therefore may be extremely anomalous. The Murphy Marble in the vicinity of Murphy, NC has been divided into as many as eleven zones, only one of which (about 45 ft thick) is known to contain commercial talc deposits. Little information is available about the geology of the marble belt and its talc zones in areas away from mining activity, probably because climatic conditions here cause outcrops to be few and far between.

Despite the relatively small size of the North Carolina talc deposits, operations there can be profitable because the purity and color of the talc are extremely high-grade. Many of the resulting ground products can compete with those manufactured from Montana talc ores and from the ores of a few deposits in the Death Valley area of California-Nevada as the only pure US talc products of high color produced without the use of wet beneficiation methods. Tremolite is minor; indeed, even talc formed after tremolite, which is so common in most other districts, is rare here.

The talc appears to have originated by relatively simple metasomatic processes (Chidester, et al., 1964). Although the white talc-bearing zone in the Murphy area is dolomitic marble which is locally slightly sandy, Van Horn (1948) does not believe that the parent material contained sufficient magnesia and silica to permit the talc to form by dynamic metamorphism alone. Owens (1968), however, on the basis of a petrologic study of diamond drill cores, feels that the talc is of metamorphic origin. The age of the Murphy Marble has not yet definitely been established. The general consensus, however, is that it is either of latest Precambrian or Cambro-Ordovician age.

Both open-pit and underground mining methods have been employed in the past, but recently the trend has been toward deeper underground mining. The developmental costs of shaft sinking to relatively small ore bodies are among the highest such costs known to the writer, further testifying to the superior quality of these carbonate-derived ores.

North Carolina is presently the only domestic producer of talc crayons or welders pencils, a relatively minor item tonnage-wise, but an extremely lucrative product line.

Georgia: A few occurrences of talc are known in the Canton area in northern Georgia, which is the southwesternmost portion of the Murphy Marble Belt, but Georgia's principal talc deposits are in Murray County. The individual talc deposits there may be tens of feet wide and several thousands of feet long and may extend for several hundred feet downdip (Chidester, et al., 1964). Furcron, et al. (1947), in the most detailed investigation to date, conclude that the talc has been formed by the alteration of dolomitic portions of the Cohutta Schist of Precambrian age; earlier workers, however, believe that it has been derived from peridotite. Needham (1972) considers that the soapstone and other talcose rocks of Murray County have been formed by serpentinization, followed by metasomatism and metamorphism. Chidester, et al. (1964) state that ultramafic bodies are not rare in Georgia, but that no talc is known to be associated with them.

Talc in Murray County was discovered about 1872 and mining was begun shortly thereafter. Mining operations are now conducted underground. The principal product lines have been crayons and ground products of both light and dark colors, but at the present time only the latter product line is being produced.

Alabama: Pure white talc has been mined near Winterboro in Talladega County, Alabama. As far as is known, all of this production went to cosmetic and pharmaceutical uses. The parent rock is a carbonate sequence of probable Cambro-Ordovician age which underlies the area, but the geological relationships are far from clear, according to McMurray and Bowles (1941). Blount and Vassiliou (1980) feel that the two ore bodies near Winterboro are associated with Cambrian dolomite, which has undergone little if any metamorphism. Their work suggests that hydrothermal solutions and metasomatic processes produced talc in and near fractures in the dolomite.

Talc and anthophyllite asbestos deposits, first

noted in 1873, are present in Tallapoosa and Chambers Counties, Alabama, where they are associated with ultramafic bodies (Neathery, 1968). The talc content ranges from 3 to 26%, probably averaging 20% for the better deposits; annual production has been about 5,000 tons (Neathery, 1970). Neathery, et al. (1967) describe flotation-concentration feasibility studies, which show that good-grade talc concentrates can be made from these ores, but the economics of such an operation have yet to be proven.

Texas

Texas has two talc districts—the Llano district in the central part of the state and the Allamoore district to the northwest of Van Horn in the western part of the state. The latter district is the one most recently put into production and is now the only one of any importance.

The Allamoore district extends about 20 miles east-west and is as much as 5 miles wide. Its ore deposits are in the Allamoore Formation, of Precambrian age, which consists of thousands of feet of carbonate rocks, volcanic rocks, and phyllite (King and Flawn, 1953). The talc appears to the writer to be associated with dolomite, but it also appears to interfinger with phyllite in certain parts of the district. Edwards (1980) feels that phyllite is invariably the host rock, but Bourbon (1981) believes that the talc formed in Precambrian time by the replacement of primary sedimentary magnesite. Field relationships indicate that carbonate rock other than calcite is the host rock for these talc deposits.

The ore-bearing strata, which are in the lower plate below a large overthrust fault (the upper plate having been almost entirely eroded), dip either vertically or steeply to the south. No ore body of which the writer is aware has ever been bottomed-out by either drilling or mining. Large iron-oxide-stained "horses" of either carbonate or volcanic rock are common within the talc zones, but generally are easily eliminated by the use of selective mining methods. Talc is commonly found from the grass roots down and the soil cover is generally less than 1 ft thick. Caliche is abundant in the uppermost 5 ft or so of these dark-colored ore bodies, but seldom causes any problems at greater depths.

Initial but far from complete petrographic and X-ray studies of the ores indicate that tremolite is not present to any significant degree. Dolomite, however, is so finely admixed with the talc as to render it extremely unlikely that pure talc can ever be produced in significant quantities from known ore bodies by presently known beneficiation techniques. There is little indication of a hydrothermal origin for these ores.

The talc ore (ceramic-type) is generally strongly foliated, with the individual foliae ranging from paper-thin to as thick as ¼ in. This dark Texas crude looks little like talc ore, even to the trained observer, when one first visits the district. The first impression is to identify it as black shale or perlite or some other similar nontalc-bearing rock. However, despite its dark—or indeed even black—color and its striking untalclike appearance, this talc ore is a superior ceramic crude with superb pressing qualities and excellent firing characteristics.

Flawn (1958) describes the district in a stage of infancy and King and Flawn (1953) describe in detail the overall geology of the district and surrounding areas.

All of the production has been from large open pits, with the exception of minor amounts of light-colored (generally pink to white) talc which have been mined in small underground workings and then finely ground into filler and extender products. Almost all of the talc ore produced in the Allamoore district is shipped out of the district to the east, and even into Mexico, for use in the ceramic industry, particularly for the manufacture of wall tile.

Mining costs probably are the lowest anywhere for talc ores. Flawn (1958) gave the costs of mining, transportation, and loading into cars as ranging from $1.75 to $3.00 per ton.

This is by far the youngest of all the major US talc-mining districts for production commenced only in 1952. The US Bureau of Mines credits Texas with the production of 207,000 tons of talc ore in 1979, but this is sharply down from immediately prior years.

California-Nevada

Of the major talc-mining districts in the United States, the one which combines the largest geographical area with the greatest number of productive commercial deposits is that of southeastern California, which barely extends northward into Nevada. It is about 200 miles long and has an average width of 30 miles, but is locally as much as 75 miles wide. Engel and Wright (1960) divide this long belt into three separate areas, each of which contains a slightly different characteristic type of deposit. See Wright (1968) for a detailed and comprehensive description of the geology and talc deposits in the central portion of this belt.

The deposits in the southern two areas occur in Precambrian sedimentary rocks. They were probably formed in Precambrian time and are spatially associated with a thick diabase sill which has been intruded near the base of a widespread and thick carbonate unit. In the northernmost of the three areas—which historically has not been as important a producer as the other two areas—the deposits occur in Lower Paleozoic formations and are thought to have been formed by replacement processes, probably in Cretaceous or Tertiary time.

The deposits come in all sizes. The largest is thought to be the Western-Acme mine complex near Tecopa in San Bernardino County, CA, which extends more than 5,000 ft along strike (although locally severely complicated by cross-faulting) and is as much as 80 ft wide. Portions of this zone have been mined downdip for at least 350 ft.

This district is too large and its geology too complicated to be satisfactorily summarized here. In general, however, all of the deposits have been formed by the metamorphism and hydrothermal replacement of siliceous and silicated magnesian marbles and limestones (Engel and Wright, 1960).

There are two main types of ore in this district: the "hard" ore of the miners is tremolitic and the "soft" ore is talc schist. Many deposits contain both types, but their relative abundance and distribution is erratic and unpredictable. Most of the ore is markedly tremolitic, but there are some relatively small bodies of high-grade talc. The problem with most of these high-purity soft talc bodies, however, is that they commonly cannot be mined by themselves, but for practical economic reasons must be extracted along with the accompanying tremolitic ores. In the past the production of high-grade talc ore in the California-Nevada district generally had to be a function of the production of tremolitic ores; this is not so true today, for several mines now produce only the talc schist, or soft ore.

Papke (1975) describes 34 deposits in southern Esmeralda County, Nevada, along the California border. Sixteen of these have talc as the principal ore mineral and nine have mixed talc and chlorite; the others consist of chlorite and sericite. Dolomite is obviously the preferred host rock for the talc-rich ore bodies.

The host rocks range in age from Precambrian to Early Cambrian, but the age of mineralization is believed to be Late Jurassic (Papke, 1975).

In the past, most of the mining in the California-Nevada district was done underground; in such operations relatively little mechanization is employed and timbering costs are extremely high. In recent years, however, an increasingly larger proportion of the district's production has been obtained by open-pit mining methods.

In no other talc-mining district anywhere in the United States are the mines so far from rail transportation as are those in the California-Nevada district. Mills and other processing facilities are not located at or near the mines, but are established either in the Los Angeles area or at various points along two railroad lines in this area which serve Los Angeles. Truck haulage routes either to a processing facility or to the railroad are commonly 100 miles or more.

Soapstone was mined from small deposits along the foothills of the western Sierra Nevada in the mid-1880s, but the current California-Nevada talc-mining district was established during World War I. At that time, the area around Darwin in Inyo County, California supplied block-grade steatite talc to compensate for the temporary elimination of foreign supplies. This production slackened off in the postwar period but was rejuvenated during World War II. Since then, however, California has not been a significant factor in the supply of steatite-grade talc.

In the mid-1930s the use of California tremolitic ores for the manufacture of wall tile began to come into its own and the ceramic industry became the major market. The talc content of such ores is not critical; a considerable amount of carbonate material can be tolerated and, indeed, may even be desirable.

The current production from this district, however, appears to be fairly well balanced between the ceramic industry and the paint and paper trade.

Montana

Next to the Allamoore talc-mining district in western Texas, the talc-mining district in the southwestern corner of Montana is the youngest in the United States. It is the most important US source of tremolite-free talc products which may be produced directly from crude ore without the need for processing.

The pioneering work on Montana talc was

done during the 1940s by Henry Mulryan, then with Sierra Talc Co., and Walter K. Skeoch, then with Southern California Minerals Co.

The earliest significant work in the geological literature is that of Perry (1948), an excellent field study which was compiled in the very early days of the Montana talc industry. Subsequent works worthy of consultation for further and more timely details on this district are Olson (1976), whose work mainly concerns the Ruby Range, and Berg (1979), whose work covers the remainder of the district.

High-purity talc deposits in southwestern Montana are totally restricted in their occurrence to dolomitic marble in the Prebeltian Cherry Creek Series. The talc, which is generally white to pale green, commonly occurs as conformable lenses and stringers within the marble; if the talc is anywhere discordant, such a relationship is usually at low angles to the foliation of the bedrock. Structural control in the strictest sense has not been widely recognized, but there is an apparent restriction of talc mineralization to that part of the dolomitic marble which is spatially close to large bodies of the Dillon Granite Gneiss.

The following reaction is thought to account for the formation of these talc deposits:

$$3 \text{ dolomite} + 4 \text{ quartz} + H_2O$$
$$= \text{talc} + 3 \text{ calcite} + 3 CO_2.$$

Inasmuch as the host dolomite normally is not notably siliceous adjacent to the talc, it is likely most of the silica required for formation of the talc was metasomatically introduced. Although this is merely the writer's opinion, it is in part substantiated by Garihan (1973).

All of the pre-Cherry Creek rocks, the rocks of the Cherry Creek Series, and most of the rock types of the Dillon Granite Gneiss have been subjected to upper amphibolite grades of metamorphism, part of a long-lived metamorphic event in Prebeltian time, which included the development of intense isoclinal deformation. It is the writer's opinion that the talc most likely was formed during the period of regional metamorphism of greenschist grade, which postdated the amphibolite period and predated the intrusion of the diabase dikes. These vertical or near-vertical dikes, which are now best referred to as metadiabase, have a consistent northwesterly strike which coincides with the main direction of high-angle faulting.

Precambrian structural deformation was extreme and is characterized by isoclinal folding and refolding and the flowage of less competent rocks, rather than by faulting. Post-

Precambrian folding has been negligible. The characteristic Laramide structure is high-angle block-faulting along northwest trends.

The talc was almost certainly formed in Precambrian time. Evidence is the relationship of the talc to the metadiabase and the fact that no talc whatsoever is known to have been formed in the thick dolomite units of the Cambrian and Devonian systems in the northern third of the Ruby Range, even though some of these dolomite units are within only a mile or so of talc deposits in the Precambrian dolomitic marble. Garihan (1973) feels that this lack of talc formation in the Paleozoic dolomites, plus the fact that the Paleozoic rocks are completely unmetamorphosed, speaks strongly for the talc having been formed in Precambrian time. Okuma (1971) also feels that the most likely age of the talc mineralization is Precambrian.

Several major talc deposits are known in the Ruby Range and one major deposit is known in the Gravelly Range. One relatively small deposit and several minor occurrences are known in the Greenhorn Range; several minor occurrences are also known in the Tobacco Root Mountains. Virtually all of Montana's talc production comes from three large mines—two in the Ruby Range and one in the Gravelly Range.

Ross, et al. (1955) have mapped the unit in which all of the known commercial talc deposits occur as covering an area about 180 miles long in an east-west direction (from Red Lodge to Bannack) and 85 miles wide (from Three Forks south to the Idaho border). The dolomitic marble which is the only host rock for the formation of the talc, however, does not occur over the entire extent of this unit. As known today, admittedly from still incomplete and extremely fragmental information, the dolomitic marble is probably significant only in the Ruby Range, the Gravelly Range, the Greenhorn Range, the Tobacco Root Mountains, and possibly in small areas of the Madison Range.

The mechanism of the formation of Montana talc bodies was probably similar to that postulated by Van Horn (1948) for the Murphy, NC talc ores. The geology of the southwestern Montana talc district is similar in many ways to that of the Murphy area and many of Van Horn's conclusions concerning the genesis of the Murphy talc ores also appear to apply to the genesis of Montana talc ores.

The dynamic metamorphism of the earlier upper amphibolite period may have formed zones of weakness and allowed the introduction of siliceous material (probably from the Dillon Granite Gneiss) and possibly some magnesia also (probably remobilized from amphibolite and other ultramafic rocks). After this metasomatic event had afforded the opportunity for the introduction of all of the constituents necessary for the formation of talc which had been lacking in the original dolomite, it is thought that the talc itself could have been formed during the retrograde phase of this major metamorphic event.

Montana's talc production in 1979, according to the US Bureau of Mines, was 343,000 tons.

Mining

It is estimated that over three-fourths of domestic talc production comes from open-pit mines. The major underground mines are located in the eastern United States.

Talc mining operations are generally carried out on a small scale in which an "average" mine produces less than 300 stpd.

The equipment used in underground mines is generally unsophisticated and capable of producing only a few tons per hour. Some underground operations have vertical shafts over 1000 ft deep. Mining methods range from conventional shrinkage stoping operations to room-and-pillar mine workings. Timber is often required in mines producing high quality soft, platy talc.

Open-pit mines utilize conventional stripping, loading, and haulage equipment. The degree of drilling and blasting effort is directly related to the type of talc ore being mined. Only the massive, blocky, and hard talc ores require extensive drilling and blasting.

One unusual aspect of talc mining is the extreme necessity for good housekeeping practice. This is important because many of the talc products are sold on the basis of a good white color and absence of abrasive materials.

It is difficult to give examples of the cost of mining talc ore. Since talc mine output may range from 2,000 or 3,000 stpy up to 150,000 stpy, there is no such thing as an average mining cost.

In New York State both open pit and underground mining methods are used. One of the largest underground talc mines in North America is operated by the Gouverneur Talc Co. (Erdman, 1972; Gillingham, 1950). This mine has an 1100-ft shaft carrying a 6-ton skip. Open stope mining is practiced and hard rock mining methods are required due to the hardness of the ore. Jackleg drills are used and blasting is done with gelatin dynamite and ANFO. Ore transport is either by gravity drawpoint loading or slusher hoist to a rail car system which moves the broken rock to the central underground crushing system on the 700-ft level. A 24x36-in. jaw crusher reduces the ore to suitable size for loading into the 6-ton skip. In the mine headframe, a 36-in. gyratory crusher reduces the ore to $-\frac{3}{4}$-in. for transfer to the grinding plant.

Mining operations at the Engelhard Minerals and Chemicals Corp. talc mine near Johnson, VT, in Lamoille County are underground. The inclined shaft is driven at an angle of 45° to a depth of over 1000 ft below the surface (Anon., 1971d; Burmeister, 1963). Ore transport is by slusher and gravity to rail haulage drifts below the slusher drifts. The crushed ore is hauled by truck to the processing plant. Fig. 1 is a sketch of stoping operations at the Johnson mine. The ore is about 55% talc, 40% magnesite, and 5% other minerals.

The Vermont Talc Co. which was acquired by Vermont Marble Co. in 1969 operates an underground mine only 85 ft deep at Windham, VT. The mine consists of 11 headings, 300 ft wide and about 1000 ft long (Anon., 1971f). A modified shrinkage stope mining method is used. The ore is hauled to a plant 11 miles away at Chester, VT for processing.

The talc mining operations of Cyprus Industrial Minerals are carried out in California, Montana, and Texas. The Yellowstone and Beaverhead mines in Montana are both open-pit operations. These are conventional drill, blast, and shovel operations. Some overburden can be removed by ripping methods. At the Yellowstone mine some hand-sorting is carried out to remove carbonate and other gangue minerals. About ten tons of rock and ore are handled to obtain one ton of acceptable crude talc ore (Mulryan, 1971). Pfizer, Inc. operates the Treasure mine (open pit) less than a mile north of Cyprus's Beaverhead mine in the Ruby Range, Montana.

California talc mines include both open pit and underground operations. The underground mine workings are usually developed and carried out in ore with square set timbered stopes. This underground mining method is required because of the small size and irregular nature of the talc occurrences.

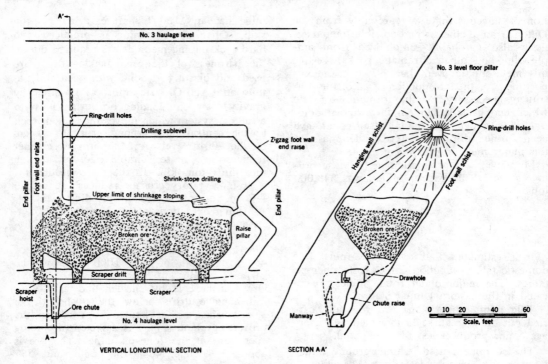

FIG. 1—*Drifts, raises, and combined shrinkage and sublevel stopes (Burmeister, 1963).*

Processing

The larger California talc mines are being converted to open pit mining.

Talc milling has traditionally involved dry-processing operations. Since much of the talc market is supplied with a relatively impure talc product, beneficiation is not usually carried out. The talc milling industry is slowly changing from uncomplicated grinding plants to sophisticated processing operations.

The new generation of talc mills includes complex froth flotation, sedimentation, hydro-cycloning, dry and wet magnetic separation, centrifugal sizing, spray drying, and new grinding techniques. It should be noted that grinding is required both to prepare the ore for processing as well as to finish off the final product which must usually meet stringent particle size demands.

The processing of talc ores is complicated by the fact that extreme white color is a very desirable feature. Therefore, the grinding equipment used should not discolor the talc in any way. This generally rules out conventional rod and ball milling with steel grinding media. Fortunately, most talc ores are very soft and reasonably good grinding rates can be obtained with ceramic grinding media.

Some very sophisticated grinding facilities are often required for final preparation of processed talc sold to specific markets. For example, when talc is sold for paper filler and coating applications, it is generally designed to meet an average particle size of less than 5μ. In some special products this may be lowered to less than 1μ. This ultrafine grinding requirement is met with vertical-shaft pulverizing mills (3500 rpm) and jet-milling equipment. The latter utilizes the fluid energy principle with either compressed air or steam providing the energy. Fig. 2 is a sketch of a fluid energy type grinding mill.

In pioneer plants talc was ground in flour-grinding mills equipped with buhrstones and then sized on silk bolting reels (Parsons, 1948). The operation of such a mill grinding both wheat and talc was recorded as late as 1922.

Porcelain-lined flint-pebble mills were used at Gouverneur, NY, as early as 1885. In Vermont, where softer talc ore was ground, vertical emery mills, disintegrators, pulverizers, and roller mills were used. Cosmetic-grade talcs were sized by bolting through cloth.

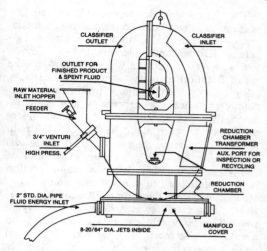

FIG. 2—*Sketch of fluid energy grinding mill.*

At present, little information has been published on wet grinding of talc ores. A pertinent reference to the subject appeared in Russian literature in 1971 (Karmazin, et al., 1972). The authors found that grinding in rod and ball mills did not result in "opening" of the mineral intergrowths even when grinding to a 5 to 10μ particle size. Jet mill grinding did accomplish intramineral grinding without the overgrinding resulting from impact mill grinding.

Windsor Minerals, Inc., a totally owned subsidiary of the Johnson and Johnson Co., operates two talc mines in Vermont. The Chester mine and the Hammondsville mine are both in Windsor County. The two talc processing plants serving these mines are located at Gassetts and West Windsor, VT. The plant at West Windsor utilizes sophisticated wet-process technology and has contributed toward better understanding of the basic problems involved in the beneficiation of talc ores.

Ore is delivered by trucks to the flotation plant where several high-grade talc products are manufactured. Fig. 3 is a flowsheet of the plant as reported in 1964 (Trauffer, 1964).

A Canadian talc processing facility using modern wet-processing equipment is operated by Baker Talc Ltd. Ore is produced from an underground operation at the Van Reet mine, in Potton Township about 80 miles southeast of Montreal. Talc was first mined here in 1871 (Anon., 1969).

The Baker talc plant utilizes froth flotation and high-intensity magnetic separation to produce high quality talc products. This ore could not be sufficiently beneficiated by froth flotation alone due to the presence of iron-bearing minerals which discolored the products. The magnetic separator in use is a modified high-intensity Jones wet magnetic separator which is now also finding major application in the beneficiation of many industrial minerals.

Eastern Magnesia Talc Co., Inc. (now Engelhard Minerals and Chemicals Corp.), was a pioneer in the Vermont talc industry. After a 1902 discovery of an ore body, a dry mill was constructed in 1904 to process 25 stpd (Harrah, 1956). This plant operated until 1920 when a 100-stpd dry plant was placed in operation. In 1932, wet methods of beneficiation were investigated. This work, along with US Bureau of Mines and the Missouri School of Mines development work, led to installation of a flotation pilot plant in 1937. Modification and enlargement of the pilot plant in 1938 resulted in commercial application of the froth flotation process. The ore is ground to 72 to 77% −200 mesh in dry pebble mills prior to flotation and shaking table concentration. The tables remove a high-gravity product containing a small quantity of nickel, iron, and cobalt minerals. A talc-magnesite mixture is floated at 18 to 21% solids in 21 Fahrenwald-type flotation cells.

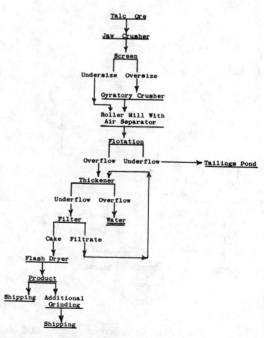

FIG. 3—*Flowsheet for Windsor Minerals, Inc., Vermont.*

The talc froth product contains talc particles of sufficiently coarse size that a rotary vacuum drum filter can be used for dewatering to 18% moisture. The filter cake is flash dried, pulverized, and air classified prior to shipping. Fig. 4 is a mill flowsheet as of 1962.

Naturally hydrophobic minerals such as talc, sulfur, graphite, and molybdenite will often respond positively to froth flotation without the addition of collector reagents. Lepetic (1972) has reported on the flotation of copper and molybdenum sulfides without collector reagents. Klassen and Mokrousov (1963) point out the striking similarity of talc and molybdenite as regards water wettability of the cleavage planes and the faces of these layered minerals.

A detailed report on a laboratory test program involving a Dadeville, AL, talc-asbestos deposit was issued in 1967 by Neathery, et al. (1967). The report concludes, "it is technically feasible to obtain good grade talc concentrates by flotation concentration of each of the five samples examined." Pine oil was the favored flotation reagent, and at least four flotation cleaning stages were necessary for optimum results. It was not considered feasible to produce a commercial anthophyllite concentrate for use as an asbestos product.

The Johnson and Johnson Co. is an important producer and consumer of cosmetic-grade talc. In 1963, they were issued two patents (Brown and Macdonald, 1963; Chase, 1963), which constitute a good review of the art of flotation of platy talc ores. While platy talc is easily floated, many problems are encountered when the process is applied commercially. For good selectivity, when finely pulverized ores are used, the flotation cell pulp density is usually around 6 to 10% solids. This results in very low capacity per unit of cell volume. Further, when a major portion of the flotation froth concentrate product consists of particles finer than 325 mesh (44μ), it is difficult to dewater prior to the drying step. The platy talc particles effectively blind even the finest mesh filler fabrics. Centrifugal dewatering methods have proved effective when all conventional filtration methods fail.

There is no publication of commercial applications of the froth flotation process to tremolitic-talc ores. Norman, et al., (1939) published results of a detailed laboratory investigation on the flotation of talc ores from Gouverneur, NY, in 1939. These data indicate that a clean separation of soft, platy talc from tremolite is difficult. With a feed containing 36% tremolite, a cleaner concentrate containing 13.2% tremolite was floated. The underflow, or rougher tailing from this test, contained 47.3% tremolite.

Fig. 5 is a flowsheet showing typical dry-processing of New York tremolitic-talc ores.

Adaptation of a noncomplicated sedimentation process to the beneficiation of certain soft, platy talc ores was announced by Roe in 1972. A pilot plant operation on a talc-dolomite ore from the Death Valley-Kingston Range district, California, was successful in decreasing the carbonate mineral content from over 40% to less than 4%. The beneficiated product had a Valley Abrasion number of 4, a G.E. brightness of 93 to 95, 3.3% acid solubles, and 1.6% carbon dioxide. This, and similar processes, hold promise of the future development of similar low-grade talc ores and other filler minerals.

As wet processing is accepted by talc producers, the interest in specialized delamination equipment increases. Some talc deposits include a small percentage of naturally occurring, discrete, thin plates. For the most part, talc is in the form of booklets of plates which require physical effort to split into sheets for greater utility in paint, paper, plastics, and cosmetics.

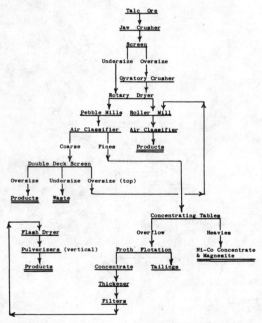

FIG. 4—*Flowsheet for Eastern Magnesia Talc Co., Vermont.*

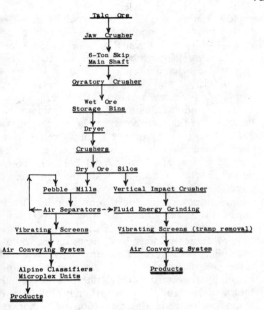

FIG. 5—*Flowsheet for Gouverneur Talc Co.,
Inc., New York.*

The mica industry has a long history of
evaluating delamination processes. Mica used
in joint cement (for wallboard, etc.) should
have a low bulk density; the degree of delamination is generally directly proportional to
the bulk density. A good mica will have a
bulk density of less than 10 lb per cu ft.
Several types of high-shear wet process equipment for delamination have been tested on
mica and talc. In general, the processing
usually involves the use of high-pressure
pumps, such as those used on mineral-slurry
pipelines, to force the mica or talc through
a restricted orifice thus causing delamination.
The same process is also used for size reduction of sulfur particles. It is reported that
a pressure homogenizer can produce sulfur
dispersions containing 99% of the particles
in the 1μ range, with none larger than 3μ
(Anon., 1966).

Ashton and Russell (1972) describe a useful
method for study of delaminated talc platelets
in two dimensions, area and thickness. In this
method a thin film of talc particles is dusted
onto the surface of distilled water and a section
of the monolayer is picked up on a microscope
glass slide. A precisely trimmed 10 cm² area
of the talc film is examined photographically.
By subtracting the void areas a total area of talc
is determined on a projected image. The
weight of the talc film is determined to 0.10

mg on a microbalance. The average thickness of the talc particles was calculated from
the foregoing data as follows:

$$\text{Volume } (V) = \frac{\text{weight } (w)}{\text{density } (d)}$$

$$\text{Volume } (V) = \text{thickness } (t) \times \text{area } (a)$$

$$t = \frac{w}{ad}$$

$$t \times 10^{-4} = \text{thickness } (t) \text{ in microns}$$

where d is density of talc in grams per cubic
centimeters $= 2.7$, w is weight of talc on slide
in grams, a is actual area covered by talc in
square centimeters, and t is average thickness
of talc in centimeters. By using the described
technique, talc platelet thicknesses of 1.4 to
10.1μ were measured.

Quality control in many talc plants consists
of uncomplicated test procedures. For example, the former Eastern Magnesia Talc Co.
reported (Burmeister, 1963), "Quality control is largely based on percentage of contained talc (insolubility test in hydrochloric
acid) and particle size and brightness or
color."

In larger talc plants (+100,000 stpy production) very sophisticated laboratory procedures
are used to control product quality. Those talc
plants supplying the larger segments of the talc
market, such as paint, paper, and cosmetics,
will have facilities for chemical and instrumental analysis, surface area determination,
color, oil absorption, abrasivity, particle size
and shape determination, packing quality, resistivity, lubricity, bacterial count, melting
point, vitrification range, and fired shrinkage.

Production and Markets

The total world production figures for talc,
soapstone, and pyrophyllite have generally
been compounded. This addition of quantities results from lack of both mineralogical
and definitive production data.

As the talc industry grows, uses more sophisticated beneficiation methods, and meets
stringent product specifications, there is evolv-
ing a more logical statistical reporting system.
Production statistics should list, for example,
figures for paper filler grade talc, cosmetic
talc for face and body powders, cosmetic talc
for use in aerosol applications, talc used in
many types of lubricants, and talc used in
agricultural applications.

US mine production of talc exceeded 1 million tons for the first time in 1969. World production averaged 1.7 million tons for the period 1945–1960 but by 1969 world production rose to 5 million tons.

Many of the important large tonnage uses for talc are closely related to the degree of sophistication of industrialization of a given country. Over the 15-year period 1945 to 1960, the United States produced about 38% of the total world production of talc, soapstone, and pyrophyllite; by 1962, this had dropped to 26%. For the ten years preceding 1973, US production stabilized to average about 22% of the total world production.

In 1980, talc was produced by 21 companies from mines in 12 states. Vermont, Montana, New York, and Texas were the top producing states, accounting for 90% of the year's output. Georgia, North Carolina, Arkansas, Nevada, Oregon, Virginia, and California produced the remaining tonnage. Iowa is listed as a producer but actually, it has only a grinding facility processing ores from other areas. The 1979 US production of talc was 1,268,000 tons.

Table 5 shows tonnages of ground talc sold or used by US producers in 1978, 1979, and 1980.

Future Trends

The uses for talc in putties, caulks, and many types of sealants and adhesives are rapidly increasing. This is especially true in those products requiring close control of color (white and tinted) and dependence on high quality through adherence to strict control of talc specifications.

Talc has several competitive minerals which are sold for similar uses. Feldspar, wollastonite, and nepheline syenite compete in ceramics. Mica competes in the roofing markets. Titanium dioxide is losing ground as a competitive filler in some markets due to its high cost. Specially purified, calcined, and compounded clays compete with talc in paint, paper, and plastics.

One important factor to consider in future competition for the talc filler markets in paint, paper, and plastics is the rapid penetration of these markets by limestone and dolomite-filler products. Calcium carbonate is often considered to be the most versatile commercially produced mineral filler. The United States market for calcium carbonate fillers and extenders exceeds the total domestic market for talc and pyrophyllite. The world market for carbonate fillers is growing at a faster rate than any other mineral filler. The widespread availability of large carbonate deposits strategically located for low-cost transportation will encourage continuing competition in the white-mineral filler market. A detailed comparison of calcium carbonate and talc fillers is presented by Roe (1980).

As more industrial minerals operations change over to wet beneficiation methods, especially flotation, there may be considerable amounts of byproduct talc produced. The very successful introduction of wet high-intensity magnetic separation in the beneficiation of kaolin clays and other industrial minerals has added another dimension to the options in talc ore processing.

TABLE 5 — End Uses for Ground Talc

Use	Thousand short tons		
	1978	1979	1980
Ceramics	257	260	282
Cosmetics*	69	74	59
Insecticides	13	13	11
Paint	192	237	197
Paper	87	105	102
Plastics	147	112	110
Refractories	6	6	2
Roofing	18	19	20
Rubber	36	39	37
Other uses+	92	95	83
Total‡	917	960	903

Source: Clifton, 1980, 1981.
* Incomplete data. Some cosmetic talc known to be included in "Other uses."
+ Includes art sculpture, asphalt filler, crayons, floor tile, foundry facings, rice polishing, stucco, and other uses not specified.
‡ Data may not add to totals shown because of independent rounding.

Bibliography and References

Anon., 1956, "Talc," California Mineral Information Service, Vol. 9, No. 11, Nov. 1, 8 pp.
Anon., 1966, "An Alternate Route to Size Reduction," Chemical Processing, Aug., p. 82
Anon., 1969, "Process Break-Through Revitalizes 100 Year Old Mine," Mining in Canada, Oct., pp. 27–30.
Anon., 1970, "Standard Method of Test for Fineness of Dispersion of Pigment-Vehicle Systems," ASTM Designation D1210–64 (reapproved 1970).
Anon., 1971a, "The Operations of A/S Norwegian Talc," Industrial Minerals (London), Jan., pp. 27–28.
Anon., 1971b, "Pyrenean Producer: S.A. des Talcs

de Luzenac," *Industrial Minerals* (London), Jan., p. 25.

Anon., 1971c, "Talc: Micronized Grades Lead the Way," *Industrial Minerals* (London), Jan., pp. 9–18.

Anon., 1971d, "Talc Operations of Engelhard Minerals and Chemicals," *Industrial Minerals* (London), No. 41, Feb., p. 46.

Anon., 1971e, "Talc: UK Consumption Shows Gradual Rise," *Industrial Minerals* (London), Jan., pp. 19–24.

Anon., 1971f, "Windham Plant Grinds Talc for Specialized Applications," *Rock Products*, Vol. 74, No. 6, June, p. 59.

Anon., 1972, "Chemical Profile—Titanium Dioxide," *Chemical Marketing Reporter*, Vol. 202, No. 24, Dec. 11, p. 9.

Anon., 1982, "Talc, Stability in a Soft Market," *Industrial Minerals*, No. 183, Dec., pp. 59–73.

Ashton, W.H., and Russell, R.S., 1972, "Talc Beneficiation," US Patent 3,684,197, Aug. 15.

Barnes, D.F., 1958, "Infrared Luminescence of Minerals," Bulletin 1052-C, US Geological Survey, p. 113.

Bennett, F.E., 1972, "Tile Council of America Research in the Seventies," American Ceramic Society, Fall Meeting, Sept. 27–29, Bedford, PA.

Berg, R.B., 1979, "Talc and Chlorite Deposits in Montana," *Memoir 45*, Montana Bureau of Mines and Geology, 65 pp.

Blount, A.M., and Vassiliou, A.H., 1980, "The Mineralogy and Origin of the Talc Deposits Near Winterboro, Alabama," *Economic Geology*, Vol. 75, No. 1, pp. 107–116.

Bourbon, W.B., 1981, "The Origin and Occurrences of Talc in the Allamoore District, Texas," in Program with Abstracts, 17th Annual Forum on the Geology of Industrial Minerals, Albuquerque, NM, May.

Brindley, G.W., and Santos, P. de S., 1971, "Antigorite—Its Occurrence as a Clay Mineral," *Clays and Clay Minerals*, Vol. 19, pp. 187–191.

Brown, J.S., and Engel, A.E.J., 1956, "Revision of Grenville Stratigraphy and Structure in the Balmat-Edwards District, Northwest Adirondacks, New York," *Bulletin*, Geological Society of America, Vol. 67, No. 12, pp. 1599–1622.

Brown, W.E., and Macdonald, R.D., "Talc Beneficiation," US Patent 3,102,855, Sept. 3.

Burmeister, H.L., 1963, "Mining Methods and Costs, Eastern Magnesia Talc Co., Johnson Mine, Johnson, Vermont," Information Circular 8142, US Bureau of Mines, 44 pp.

Campbell, M.E., 1972, "Solid Lubricants, A Survey," NASA SP-5059(01) publication prepared under contract by Midwest Research Institute, Kansas City, MO, 126 pp.

Campbell, W.J., et al., 1980, "Chemical and Physical Characterization of Ampite, Chrysotile, Crocidolite, and Nonfibrous Tremolite for Oral Ingestion Studies by the National Institute of Environmental Health Sciences," Report of Investigations 8452, US Bureau of Mines, 63 pp.

Cawood, E.E.C., 1962, "Fire Extinguishing Composition," US Patent 3,063,940, Nov. 13.

Chase, W.E., 1963, "Platy Talc Beneficiation," US Patent 3,102,856, Sept. 3.

Chidester, A.H., Billings, M.P. and Cady, W.M., 1951, "Talc Investigations in Vermont," Pre-

liminary Report, Circular 95, US Geological Survey, 33 pp.

Chidester, A.H., et al., 1964, "Talc Resources of the United States," Bulletin 1167, US Geological Survey, pp. 1–61.

Christman, R.A., 1959, "Geology of the Mount Mansfield Quadrangle, Vermont," Bulletin 12, Vermont Geological Survey, 70 pp.

Christman, R.A., and Secor, D.T., Jr., 1961, "Geology of the Camels Hump Quadrangle, Vermont," Bulletin 15, Vermont Geological Survey, 70 pp.

Clifton, R.A., 1980, "Talc and Pyrophyllite," Preprint 1978–1979, US Bureau of Mines, 7 pp.

Clifton, R.A., 1981, "Talc and Pyrophyllite," *Minerals Yearbook 1980*, US Bureau of Mines, pp. 815–820.

Cooper, J.D., and Hartwell, J.W., 1970, "Talc, Soapstone and Pyrophyllite," *Mineral Facts and Problems*, Bulletin 650, US Bureau of Mines, pp. 1267–1281.

Dickson, T., 1982, "North American Talc," *Industrial Minerals*, No. 183, Dec., pp. 75–78.

Dillender, R.D., Jr., and Gower, I.W., 1953, "Preliminary Report on the Froth Flotation of Wake County Talc," Bulletin No. 7, Dept. of Engineering Research, North Carolina State College, Raleigh, NC, Nov., 16 pp.

Drake, M.J., and Brett, B.A., 1962, "Talc, Soapstone and Pyrophyllite," *Minerals Yearbook 1962*, US Bureau of Mines, pp. 1189–1198.

Edwards, G., 1980, "Tumbledown Mountain Talc Deposit, Allamoore District, Culberson County, Texas," *Guidebook*, 31st Field Conference, New Mexico Geological Society, pp. 245–250.

Elstron, L.W., 1961, "Slipping and Sliding," *Research Engineer*, Georgia Institute of Technology, Feb., pp. 15–18.

Engel, A.E.J., 1949, "New York Talcs, Their Geological Features, Mining, Milling and Uses," *Transactions AIME*, Vol. 184, pp. 345–348.

Engel, A.E.J., and Wright, L.A., 1960, "Talc and Soapstone," *Industrial Minerals and Rocks*, 3rd ed., J.L. Gillson, ed., AIME, New York, pp. 835–850.

Erdman, G.R., 1973, "Dust Control at Gouverneur Talc Company," *Trans. SME-AIME*, Vol. 254, No. 2, June, pp. 161–165.

Faust, G.T., and Fahey, J.J., 1962 "The Serpentine-Group Minerals," Professional Paper 384-A, US Geological Survey, pp. 80–82.

Flawn, P.T., 1958, "Texas Miners Boost Talc Output," *Engineering and Mining Journal*, Vol. 159, No. 1, pp. 104–105.

Frommer, P.W., and Fine, M.M., 1956, "Laboratory Flotation of Talc from Arkansas and Texas Sources," Report of Investigations 5241, US Bureau of Mines, June, 5 pp.

Furcron, A.S., Teague, K.F., and Calver, J.L., 1947, "Talc Deposits of Murray County, Georgia," *Bulletin 53*, Georgia Geological Survey, 75 pp.

Garihan, J.M., 1973, "Geology and Talc Deposits of the Central Ruby Range, Madison County, Montana," PhD dissertation, Pennsylvania State University, 209 pp.

Gillingham, W.P., 1950, "Grinding Talc to Superfine Size," *Compressed Air Magazine*, Feb., pp. 32–37.

Harrah, H.W., 1956, "Eastern Magnesia Talc

Company, Inc." *Deco Trefoil*, Denver Equipment Co., May–June, pp. 7–14.

Harrell, G.O., and Harrell, D.E., 1971, "Survey of Mineral Fillers in Selected Industries, Phase I—Plastics and Textiles," The Industrial Extension Service, School of Engineering, North Carolina State University, Raleigh, NC, Apr., 105 pp.

Herod, B.C., 1954, "Pioneer Talc Leads Way in West Texas Field," *Pit and Quarry*, Vol. 54, Apr., pp. 134–135, 156.

Heystek, H., and Planz, E., 1964, "Mineralogy and Ceramic Properties of Some California Talcs," *Bulletin*, American Ceramic Society, Vol. 43, No. 8, pp. 555–561.

Hunt, R.E., 1969, "How to Select Fillers and Reinforcements for Thermoplastics," *Plastics Technology*, Nov., pp. 38–43.

Karmazin, V.I., et al., 1972, "Grinding and Concentrating Capacity of Talc-Magnesite Rocks of the Pravda Deposit of the Ukranian SSR," Obogasheh, Polez, Iskop, 1971, No. 9, p. 28–29 (Russ.); *Chemical Abstracts*, Vol. 77, 92190c, p. 262.

Katz, H.S., and Mileski, J.V., 1978, *Handbook of Fillers and Reinforcements for Plastics*, Van Nostrand Reinhold Co., New York, 652 pp.

King, P.B., and Flawn, P.T., 1953, "Geology and Mineral Deposits of Precambrian Rocks of the Van Horn Area, Texas," No. 5301, Texas University Publications, 218 pp.

Klassen, V.I., and Mokrousov, V.A., 1963, *An Introduction to the Theory of Flotation*, London, 493 pp.

Lamb, F.D., and Ruppert, J., 1950, "Flotation of a North Carolina Pyrophyllite Ore," Report of Investigation 4674, US Bureau of Mines, Apr., 7 pp.

Lepetic V.M., 1972, "Flotation of Copper and Molybdenum Sulfides Without Collector," Preprint 72B308, SME-AIME Fall Meeting, Birmingham, AL, Oct. 18–20, pp. 1–23.

Lundquist, J.D., 1970, "Talc Treatment and Talc-Containing Pigments," US Patent 3,533,821, Oct. 13.

McMurray, L., and Bowles, E., 1941, "The Talc Deposits of Talladega County Alabama," Circular 16, Geological Survey of Alabama, 31 pp.

Miller, C.R., and Holtzapfel, P.J., 1970, "Corrosion Proofing Composition and Method," US Patent 3,549,391, Dec. 22.

Mulryan, H.T., 1971, "World-Wide Operations of United Sierra," *Industrial Minerals* (London), No. 41, Feb., pp. 43–45.

Neathery, T.L., 1968, "Talc and Anthophyllite Asbestos in Tallapoosa and Chambers Counties, Alabama," Bulletin 90, Geological Survey of Alabama, 98 pp.

Neathery, T.L., 1970, "Geology and Mining of Low Grade Talc Deposits, Tallapoosa County, Alabama," Preprint 70H311, SME-AIME. Fall Meeting, St. Louis, MO, 15 pp.

Neathery, T.L., et al., 1967, "Talc and Asbestos at Dadeville, Alabama," Report of Investigations 7045, US Bureau of Mines, 57 pp.

Needham, R.E., 1972, "The Geology of the Murray County, Georgia Talc District," Master's thesis, Pennsylvania State University, 107 pp.

Norman, J.E., et al., 1939, "Froth Flotation of Talc Ores from Gouverneur, New York," *Bulletin*, American Ceramic Society, Vol. 18, No. 8, pp. 292–297.

Okuda, S., et al., 1969, "Negative Surface Charges of Pyrophyllite and Talc," *Proceedings of the International Clay Conference*, Tokyo, Vol. 1, pp. 31–44, Vol. 2, pp. 14–16.

Okuma, A.F., 1971, "Structure of the Southwestern Ruby Range near Dillon, Montana," PhD dissertation, Pennsylvania State University, 122 pp.

Olson, R.H., 1976, "The Geology of Montana Talc Deposits," Spec. Publ. 74, Montana Bureau of Mines and Geology, pp. 99–143.

Owens, M.H., 1968, "Petrologic Study of Talc Mineralization in the Murphy Marble in Southwestern North Carolina," Master's thesis, Tennessee University, 64 pp.

Papke, K.G., 1975, "Talcose Minerals in Nevada—Talc, Chlorite, and Pyrophyllite," Bulletin 84, Nevada Bureau of Mines and Geology, 62 pp.

Parsons, A.B., 1948, *Seventy-Five Years of Progress in the Mineral Industry, 1871–1946*, AIME, New York, p. 355.

Pence, F.K., 1955, "Commercially Proven White-Firing Talc Occurring in West Texas," *Bulletin*, American Ceramic Society, Vol. 34, No. 4, pp. 122–123.

Perry, A., 1972, "Supply and Demand for Ceramic Tile in the Seventies," American Ceramic Society, Fall Meeting, Sept. 27–29, Bedford, PA.

Perry E.S., 1948, "Talc, Graphite, Vermiculite and Asbestos in Montana," Memoir 27, Montana Bureau of Mines and Geology, 44 pp.

Poppe, W., et al., 1972, "Talc Filled Metallizable Polyolefins," US Patent 3,663,260, May 16.

Povarennykh, A.S., 1972, *Crystal Chemical Classification of Minerals*, Vol. 1, trans. from Russian by J.E.S. Bradley, Plenum Press, New York, pp. 415–416.

Ranney, M.W., et al., 1972, "Silane Coupling Agents in Particulate Mineral-Filled Composites," 27th Reinforced Plastics Technical and Management Conference, SPI, Washington, DC, Feb. 8–11, pp. 1–29.

Rayner, J. H., and Brown, G., 1966, "Structure of Pyrophyllite," *Clays and Clay Minerals*, Proceedings, 13th National Conference on Clays and Clay Minerals, Pergamon Press, New York, pp. 73–84.

Roe, L.A., 1972, "High-Purity Talc from Western Ores," Preprint 72H312, SME-AIME Fall Meeting, Birmingham, AL, Oct. 18–20, 16 pp.; US Patent 3,806,043, Apr. 23, 1974.

Roe, L.A., 1980, "A Comparison of Calcium Carbonate and Talc Fillers," Preprint 80–301, SME-AIME Fall Meeting, Minneapolis.

Ross, C.P., Andrews, D.A. and Witkind, I.J., 1955, "Geologic Map of Montana," US Geological Survey.

Ross, M., and Smith, W.L., 1968, "Triclinic Talc and Associated Amphiboles from Gouverneur Mining District, New York," *American Mineralogist*, Vol. 53, May-June, pp. 751–769.

Seymour, R.B., et al., 1972, "Fibrous Reinforcements for Polymers," *1972–73 Modern Plastics Encyclopedia*, pp. 365–394.

Trauffer, W.E., 1964, "New Vermont Talc Plant Makes High-Grade Flotation Product for Special Uses," *Pit and Quarry*, Vol. 57, No. 6, Dec., pp. 72–76, 101.

Troll, G., and Gilbert, M.C., 1972, "Fluorine-Hydroxyl Substitution in Tremolite," *American Mineralogist*, Vol. 57, pp. 1386–1403.

Van Horn, E.C., 1948, "Talc Deposits of the Murphy Marble Belt," Bulletin 56, North Carolina Dept. of Conservation and Development, Division of Mineral Resources, 54 pp.

Wells, J.R., 1973, "Talc, Soapstone, and Pyrophyllite in 1973," Annual Advance Summary, US Bureau of Mines, 2 pp.

Winkler, H.G.F., 1974, *Petrogenesis of Metamorphic Rocks,* Springer-Verlag, New York, 320 pp.

Wright, L.A., 1950, "California Talcs," *Trans. AIME,* Vol. 187, pp. 122–128.

Wright, L.A., 1968, "Talc Deposits of the Southern Death Valley-Kingston Range Region, California," Special Report 95, California Division of Mines and Geology, 79 pp.

Zen, E-an, 1961, "Mineralogy and Petrology of the System AL_2O_3-SiO_2-H_2O in Some Pyrophyllite Deposits of North Carolina," *American Mineralogist,* Vol. 46, Jan.-Feb., pp. 52–66.

Titanium Minerals[*]

LANGTRY E. LYND [†]

STANLEY J. LEFOND [‡]

Elemental titanium has become famous as a space age metal, because of its high strength/weight ratio and resistance to corrosion. However, the major use is in the form of titanium dioxide pigment, which because of its whiteness, high refractive index, and resulting light-scattering ability, is unequaled for whitening paints, paper, rubber, plastics, and other materials. A relatively minor use is in welding rod coatings, in the form of the mineral rutile. United States consumption of titanium dioxide in concentrates for these applications in 1982 was as follows: pigments, 630,000 st; titanium metal, 31,000 st; and welding rod coatings, 5,000 st. The only commercially important titanium ore minerals at the present time are ilmenite and its alteration products, and rutile.

Titanium was discovered by Gregor in 1790, as a white oxide which he recovered from menaccanite, a variety of ilmenite occurring as a black sand near Falmouth, Cornwall. Barksdale (1966) stated that the fundamental chemical reactions on which the present day titanium industry is based were known before 1800, although it was not until 1918 that these pigments were available commercially on the American market.

Pings (1972) outlined the early history of the titanium industry in the United States, referring to the work of Guise (1964) and others:

Mining of titanium minerals in the United States began sometime between 1880 and 1900, in Chester County, Pennsylvania. Small quantities of rutile were also produced during that time in North Carolina and Georgia. In 1901 rutile was mined from a deposit near Roseland, VA, and was used in making titanium chemicals and for coloring ceramics. Ilmenite in the deposit was produced as a separate item in 1913, and rutile and ilmenite were obtained from this deposit through 1921.

The mining of titanium bearing beach sands began in 1916 near Mineral City and Pablo Beach, FL, for the purpose of making titanium tetrachloride to be used in tracer bullets, flares, and smokescreens. The titanium pigment industry was founded in 1918. By 1928 a large part of the domestic production of rutile, ilmenite, and zircon came from Florida. However production ceased in 1929 in Florida with the mining of newly discovered deposits in Virginia which were mined until 1968. The discovery of new deposits in Florida, and the development of better mining and concentrating methods for low-grade sands, led to a return of activities in this area. The large deposits near Tahawus, NY, were brought into production in 1942 by National Lead Co. (now NL Industries, Inc.), and by 1949 this company was the leading producer of ilmenite in the world. In 1948 the extensive deposits of ilmenite and ilmenite-bearing iron ores were discovered in eastern Quebec.

The large Trail Ridge sand deposit in Florida was discovered by E. I. du Pont de Nemours & Co., Inc. geologists in cooperation with the US

* The writers are indebted to many sources of information for material used in this chapter. We especially wish to thank Stanford O. Gross for geological, mining, milling, and production information on the MacIntyre Development, and H. Leroy Scharon for his contribution on methods of exploration for hard-rock ilmenite deposits. Special thanks are also due the US Bureau of Mines; NL Industries, Inc.; W. P. Dyrenforth of Colorado School of Mines Research Institute, Golden, CO; A. G. Naguib, Vice President, Mineral Development International, Orange Park, FL; and Thomas E. Garnar, Jr., E. I. du Pont de Nemours & Co., Inc., for their cooperation and valuable assistance in preparing the manuscript.

† Physical Scientist, US Bureau of Mines, Division of Nonferrous Metals, Washington, DC.

‡ Industrial Minerals Consultant, Evergreen, CO.

Bureau of Mines and the Florida Geological Survey, and was developed by Du Pont in the late 1940s (Garnar, 1980).

The beginning of the modern titanium metal industry was in 1948, when Du Pont produced the first metal. US Bureau of Mines reports, which gave details of the Kroll process, together with the attractive properties of the metal for military aircraft, led to a concerted effort by industry and government to develop a large-scale titanium metal industry, which reached a peak capacity of over 36,000 stpy from six producers by 1958 (Pings, 1972a).

The major developments affecting the titanium metal industry since the late 1950s have been fluctuations in the production rate of military aircraft, and the increasing use of the metal in commercial aircraft and for industrial applications. A major change in the titanium dioxide pigment industry starting in 1957 was the development and expansion of the chloride process, which generally uses higher grade TiO_2 raw materials such as rutile in contrast to the relatively low TiO_2 ilmenite feed used in the older sulfate process. The resulting increased demand for rutile led to higher prices, which in turn stimulated the development of processes for making rutile substitutes by beneficiation of ilmenite.

Since 1960, new deposits of sand ilmenite were developed in New Jersey, Georgia, and Florida. Annual domestic titanium dioxide pigment production was 635,000 st in 1982, 19% below the peak of 787,000 st reached in 1974.

Production and Consumption of Titanium Concentrates and Products

United States production and consumption of ilmenite plus slag in 1982 were down appreciably from 1978 levels. Consumption of rutile also decreased, resulting in a 9% drop in United States pigment production from 1978 through 1982. World production of ilmenite plus slag has declined since 1978, and rutile production has increased (Table 1).

TABLE 1—Salient Titanium Statistics

	1978	1979	1980	1981	1982
United States:					
Ilmenite concentrate:					
Mine shipments, st	580,878	646,399	593,704	523,681	233,063
Value, 1000 $	$25,628	$32,965	$32,041	$37,013	$19,093
Imports for consumption, st	308,671	184,478	357,488	236,217	348,366
Consumption, st	792,289	791,063	848,607	856,116	583,250
Titanium slag:					
Imports for consumption, st	149,172	111,210	194,994	268,825	247,845
Consumption, st	128,826	144,708	181,582	252,826	225,541
Rutile concentrate, natural and synthetic:					
Imports for consumption, st	289,617	283,479	281,605	202,373	163,325
Consumption, st	263,184	313,761	297,582	285,371	238,937
Sponge metal:					
Imports for consumption, st	1,476	2,488	4,777	6,490	1,354
Consumption, st	19,854	23,937	26,943	31,599	17,328
Price, Dec. 31, per lb	$3.28	$3.98	$7.02	$7.65	$5.55
Titanium dioxide pigments:					
Production, st	700,755	742,081	727,245	r761,190	635,061
Imports for consumption, st	117,708	104,968	97,590	124,906	138,922
Apparent consumption, st	801,728	837,042	753,480	r806,040	722,362
Price, Dec. 31, cents per lb:					
Anatase	46.0	53.0	57.0	69.0	69.0
Rutile	51.0	59.0	63.0	75.0	75.0
World production:					
Ilmenite concentrate, st	r3,874,661	r3,874,586	4,015,772	p4,009,737	e3,371,090
Titaniferous slag, st	1,037,193	r842,038	1,343,200	p1,245,000	e1,170,000
Rutile concentrate, natural, st	*332,690	*r393,807	*459,634	*p409,220	*e381,253

Source: US Bureau of Mines.
e Estimated. p Preliminary. r Revised.
* Excludes US production data to avoid disclosing company proprietary data.

TABLE 2—Consumption of Titanium Concentrates in the United States, by Products
Short Tons

Year and Product	Ilmenite*		Titanium slag		Rutile (natural and synthetic)	
	Gross weight	TiO$_2$ content^e	Gross weight	TiO$_2$ content^e	Gross weight	TiO$_2$ content^e
1978	792,289	475,448	128,826	91,490	263,184	245,184
1979	791,063	487,228	144,708	106,346	313,761	292,912
1980	848,607	513,315	181,582	133,933	297,582	277,882
1981:						
Alloys and carbide	§	§	#	#	—	—
Pigments	843,055	501,301	252,826	186,020	^{r}206,257	^{r}192,779
Welding-rod coatings and fluxes	§	§	—	—	7,389	6,944
Miscellaneous ‖	13,061	9,721	—	—	71,725	66,873
Total	856,116	511,022	252,826	186,020	^{r}285,371	^{r}266,596
1982:						
Alloys and carbide	§	§	#	#	—	—
Pigments	574,634	345,618	225,541	168,433	^{r}194,994	^{r}184,403
Welding-rod coatings and fluxes	§	§	—	—	5,607	5,275
Miscellaneous ‖	8,616	6,775	—	—	38,336	35,435
Total	583,250	352,393	225,541	168,433	^{r}238,937	^{r}225,113

Source: US Bureau of Mines.
^{e} Estimated. ^{r} Revised.
* Includes a mixed product containing rutile, leucoxene, and altered ilmenite.
† Includes estimate of imported ilmenite used to make synthetic rutile in the United States.
‡ Includes imported synthetic rutile, but excludes synthetic rutile made in the United States from imported ilmenite.
§ Included with "Miscellaneous" to avoid disclosing company proprietary data.
Included with "Pigments" to avoid disclosing company proprietary data.
‖ Includes ceramics, chemicals, glass fibers, and titanium metal.
¶ Includes synthetic rutile made in the United States.

Table 2 shows that about 94% of total United States TiO$_2$ consumption in 1982 was used in titanium dioxide pigment manufacture. Table 3 shows that paper and plastics are the fastest growing uses for titanium pigments. As shown in Table 4, the major imports of titanium concentrates are ilmenite and rutile from Australia, and titanium slag from Canada.

World production of titanium concentrates, shown in Table 5, comes mainly from four major producing countries, Australia, Norway, the United States, and the USSR, with about 230,000 to 1,300,000 stpy each, and from Finland, India, and Malaysia, each producing 120,000 to 200,000 stpy. Australia is by far the largest producer of rutile, while Canada and the Republic of South Africa produce nearly all of the world's titaniferous slag.

Prices of titanium concentrates and products (Table 6) generally increased significantly in the years 1978–1981, due to increased production costs and to development of a tight metal supply in 1979–1980 caused mainly by sharply increased demand for commercial aircraft. The prices of rutile and titanium sponge metal dropped in 1982 because of the economic recession, and collapse of the commercial aircraft market.

Titanium Dioxide Pigments

Titanium dioxide pigments are made by two basic processes. In the older sulfate process, ilmenite (43 to 65% TiO$_2$) or slag (70 to 74% TiO$_2$ or 85% TiO$_2$) is converted to water-soluble sulfates, and the TiO$_2$ is recovered by hydrolysis of high-TiO$_2$ solutions. In the chloride process, rutile (95% TiO$_2$), high-TiO$_2$ ilmenite (60 to 70% TiO$_2$), or rutile substitutes (85 to 95% TiO$_2$, including 85% TiO$_2$ slag), are converted to volatile chlorides, and the TiO$_2$ is recovered by vapor phase oxidation of titanium tetrachloride.

Until the early 1950s, titanium dioxide pigments were produced entirely by the sulfate

TABLE 3—Distribution of US Titanium-Pigment Shipments, by Industry, TiO$_2$ Content
Percent

Industry	1978	1979	1980	1981	1982
Paints, varnishes, lacquers	47.9	47.4	44.1	43.4	43.3
Paper	20.8	21.8	24.3	23.8	24.6
Plastics (except floor covering and vinyl-coated fabrics and textiles)	11.6	11.8	10.6	11.4	11.4
Rubber	2.8	2.9	2.1	2.2	2.3
Printing ink	2.0	1.9	2.8	1.3	0.9
Ceramics	2.1	1.9	1.7	1.4	1.1
Other	6.7	7.1	8.2	8.6	6.4
Exports	6.1	5.2	6.2	7.9	10.0
Total	100.0	100.0	100.0	100.0	100.0

Source: US Bureau of Mines.

TABLE 4—US Imports for Consumption of Titanium Concentrates by Countries
Short Tons

Country	1978	1979	1980	1981	1982
Ilmenite:					
Australia	308,649	184,478	338,676	234,562	342,279
Finland	—	—	27	—	—
Germany, Federal Republic of	—	—	—	—	24
India	—	—	18,739	—	—
Netherlands*	—	—	46	—	—
Norway	22	—	—	1,656	—
Sri Lanka	—	—	—	—	6,063
Total[†]	308,671	184,478	357,488	236,217	348,366
Titanium slag:					
Canada	149,172	81,289	145,475	246,137	201,168
South Africa, Republic of	—	29,921	49,519	22,685	45,685
Other	—	—	—	3	992
Total	149,172	111,210	194,994	268,825	247,845
Rutile, natural:					
Australia	242,505	140,291	143,038	88,345	74,501
Malaysia	—	—	267	11	—
Sierra Leone	—	7,980	40,900	25,236	53,308
South Africa, Republic of	5,453	10,819	18,907	47,406	11,320
Sri Lanka	6,063	6,305	—	—	—
Thailand	—	—	197	—	—
Other	8	18	33	25	2
Total	254,029	165,413	203,342	161,022	139,131
Rutile, synthetic:					
Australia	23,546	72,218	60,962	39,708	22,744
Germany, Federal Republic of*	—	—	2	—	—
India	11,011	22,134	10,471	440	—
Japan	675	1,243	6,590	1,200	1,450
Taiwan	356	22,471	238	—	—
Other	—	—	—	3	—
Total[†]	35,588	118,066	78,263	41,351	24,194
Titaniferous iron ore[‡]					
Canada	51,640	153,714	10,185	12,271	6,996

* Country of transshipment rather than country of production.
[†] Data may not add to totals shown because of independent rounding.
[‡] Includes materials consumed for purposes other than production of titanium commodities, principally heavy aggregate and steel furnace flux.

TABLE 5—World Production of Titanium Concentrates—Ilmenite, Leucoxene, Rutile, and Slag, by Country,* St

Concentrate type and country	1978	1979	1980	1981 ᵖ	1982 ᵉ
Ilmenite and leucoxene†					
Australia:					
Ilmenite	1,383,400	ʳ1,267,656	1,442,924	1,452,033	# 1,276,463
Leucoxene	ʳ17,752	ʳ24,001	26,393	21,657	# 22,198
Brazil	22,131	ʳ14,541	18,562	16,631	17,000
China	NA	NA	NA	150,000	150,000
Finland	145,395	131,947	175,267	178,023	176,000
India §	178,063	161,867	185,078	208,147	209,000
Malaysia #	205,929	220,262	208,470	190,432	121,000
Norway	845,461	903,690	912,508	724,907	# 608,215
Portugal	358	295	258	368	370
Sri Lanka	36,421	61,035	37,430	88,197	88,000
USSR ᵉ	450,000	450,000	460,000	470,000	475,000
United States ‖	589,751	639,292	548,882	509,342	# 227,844
Total	ʳ3,874,661	ʳ3,874,586	4,015,772	4,009,737	3,371,090
Rutile:					
Australia	283,376	ʳ307,435	323,801	263,729	# 243,343
Brazil	402	484	472	190	220
India §	6,239	5,445	5,908	9,647	8,800
Sierra Leone	—	ʳ8,267	52,356	55,992	# 52,590
South Africa, Republic of ᵉ	20,000	46,000	53,000	55,000	52,000
Sri Lanka	12,673	16,176	14,097	14,662	14,300
USSR ᵉ	10,000	10,000	10,000	10,000	10,000
United States	W	W	W	W	W
Total	332,690	ʳ393,807	459,634	409,220	381,253
Titaniferous slag:					
Canada ¶	937,000	ʳ525,840	964,200	837,000	750,000
Japan ¶	193	198	—	—	—
South Africa, Republic of ᵉ**	100,000	316,000	379,000	408,000	420,000
Total	1,037,193	ʳ842,038	1,343,200	1,245,000	1,170,000

Source: US Bureau of Mines.

ᵉ Estimated.   ᵖ Preliminary.   ʳ Revised.   NA Not available.   W Withheld to avoid disclosing company proprietary data.

* Table excludes production of anatase ore in Brazil (4,298,731 tons produced prior to 1979 and apparently largely mined in 1978; 7,373,074 tons mined during 1979; and unreported quantities mined in 1980 and 1981), all of which was stockpiled without beneficiation. This material reportedly contains 20% TiO_2. The table includes data available through June 15, 1983.

† Ilmenite is also produced in Canada and in the Republic of South Africa, but this output is not included here because an estimated 90% of it is duplicative of output reported under titaniferous slag and the rest is used for purposes other than production of titanium commodities, principally as steel furnace flux and heavy aggregate.

‡ Reported figure.

§ Data are for fiscal year beginning Apr. 1 of year stated.

Exports.

‖ Includes a mixed product containing ilmenite, leucoxene, and rutile.

¶ Contains 70% to 72% TiO_2.

** Contains 85% TiO_2.

process. However, by 1981, as shown by the listings of US and world production capacities in Tables 7 and 8, the proportion of pigment produced by the chloride process was about 78% in the United States, and was substantial in the rest of the world as well. Total world production capacity in 1982 was about 1,900,-

000 stpy chloride process pigment and 900,000 stpy sulfate process pigment. Future annual growth in consumption of TiO_2 pigments has been estimated at 2 to 3% in the United States, and at 3 to 4% in the rest of the world.

The chloride and sulfate process TiO_2 pigments have each demonstrated superior prop-

TABLE 6—US Prices of Titanium Concentrates and Products

	Yearend prices				
	1978	1979	1980	1981	1982
Concentrates: $ per st:					
Domestic ilmenite, 64% TiO_2	—	—	35*	35*	40*
Imported ilmenite, 54% TiO_2, f.o.b. Atlantic ports	45	50	50	65	65
Imported rutile, 95% TiO_2, f.o.b. Atlantic ports:					
Small lots	325-350	425-450	425-450	450-475	450-475
Large lots, long term, estimate	250-275	350-375	350-375	325-350	275-300
Titanium slag:					
70-72% TiO_2, f.o.b. Quebec	100	100	104	121	134
85% TiO_2, f.o.b. Republic of South Africa	—	120	124	156	156
Synthetic rutile, f.o.b. Mobile, AL	—	—	310	340	350
Products: $ per lb					
TiO_2 pigments, regular grade:					
Rutile, carlots, f.o.b. plant	0.51	0.59	0.63	0.75	0.75
Anatase, carlots, f.o.b. plant	0.46	0.53	0.57	0.69	0.69
Titanium sponge metal:					
Domestic, f.o.b. plant	3.28	3.98	7.02	7.65	5.55
Imported, Japanese, c.i.f. US ports, not including import duty	3.20	3.60	7.50-8.70	7.50-8.50	No quotation

* Bulk, large lots, f.o.b. Green Cove Springs, FL.
Open market price not available in previous years.

erties over the other in various applications. The chloride process, being a continuous process is inherently simpler, consisting of fewer steps, and has less waste material to dispose of, as it uses feed materials with higher TiO_2 content and lower iron content than the sulfate process. Chloride process manu-

facturers are increasing their ability to use lower grade feed materials, at the expense of having to dispose of more iron chloride or iron oxide. The sulfate process has the advantage of lower cost raw materials, but has the greater quantity of waste material for disposal.

TABLE 7—United States Titanium Dioxide Pigment Producers in 1982.

Company and plant location	Estimated Dec. 31, 1982 Annual Capacity, st	
	Sulfate process	Chloride process
American Cyanamid Co., Savannah, GA	64,000	46,000
E. I. du Pont de Nemours & Co., Inc.:		
Antioch, CA	—	35,000
De Lisle, MS	—	150,000
Edge Moor, DE	—	110,000
New Johnsonville, TN	—	228,000
Gulf + Western Natural Resources Group, Chemicals Div.:		
Ashtabula, OH	—	35,000
Gloucester City, NJ	44,000	—
Kerr-McGee Chemical Corp., Hamilton, MS	—	56,000
NL Industries, Inc., Sayreville, NJ *	—	—
SCM Corp., Glidden Pigments Group, Chemical/Metallurgical Div:		
Ashtabula, OH	—	42,000
Baltimore, MD	66,000	42,000
Total	174,000	744,000

* Closed 100,000 stpy sulfate process plant in September 1982.

TABLE 8—World Titanium Dioxide Pigment Production Capacity, Dec. 31, 1982

Country	Producing Companies	Estimated Annual Capacity, st	
		Sulfate	Chloride
North America:			
Canada	Canadian Titanium Pigments, Tioxide Canada	76,000	—
Mexico	Pigmentos y Productos Quimicos	33,000	—
United States	American Cyanamid, Du Pont, Gulf & Western, Kerr-McGee, NL Industries, SCM	174,000	744,000
South America:			
Brazil	Titanio do Brasil (Tibras)	33,000	—
Europe, Western:			
Belgium	Kronos SA-NV, Bayer SA	72,000	—
Finland	Kemira Oy	88,000	—
France	Thann et Mulhouse, Tioxide SA	182,000	—
Germany, Federal Republic of	Bayer, AG, Kronos Titan GmbH, Sachtleben Chemie	298,000	66,000
Italy	Montedison	44,000	—
Netherlands	Tiofine	39,000	—
Norway	Kronos Titan A/S	28,000	—
Spain	Dow-Uniquinesa, Titanio SA	77,000	—
United Kingdom	BTP Tioxide, Laporte Industries	143,000	100,000
Europe, Eastern:			
Czechoslovakia	Prerovske Chemiske	22,000	—
Poland	ZPN	40,000	—
USSR	State Authority	137,000	—
Yugoslavia	Cinkarna Celje	22,000	—
Asia:			
China, Mainland	State Authority	20,000	—
Taiwan	ISK Taiwan	10,000	—
India	Travancore Titanium Products	15,000	—
Japan	Fuji Titanium, Furukawa Mining, Sakai Chemical, Teikoku Kaku, Titan Kogyo, Tohuku Chemical, Titanium Industries	224,000	26,000
Korea, Republic of	Hankuk Titanium, Donhwa Titanium	10,000	—
Africa:			
South Africa, Republic of	South African Titan Products	35,000	—
Australia	Tioxide Australia, Laporte Titanium (Australia)	75,000	—
Totals		1,897,000	936,000
Total, chloride plus sulfate		2,833,000	

Source: Modified from Coope, 1982.

Sulfate Process

Specifications for Sulfate Plant Feed: There are no rigid specifications for feed material to be used in the sulfate process, but certain impurities such as chromium, vanadium, columbium, manganese, and phosphorus are known to seriously impair pigment properties, so the degree of freedom from these elements is an important factor in selection of concentrates for this process. The TiO_2 content must be high enough to be recovered economically, and capable of dissolution in sulfuric acid at practical temperatures. Some typical commercial concentrates with their chemical and mineralog-

TABLE 9—Composition of Typical Commercial Ilmenite Concentrates and Titaniferous Slag
Weight Percent

| | United States | | Australia | | Norway | India | | Malaysia | Canada | Republic of South Africa |
| | | | Cable Bunbury | Western Titanium | | | | Amang | QIT Slag | RB Slag |
	New York	Florida				Quilon	MK			
TiO$_2$ (total)	46.1	64.00	54.4	55.4	45.0	60.6	54.2	53.1	70-74	85.0 (min)
Ti$_2$O$_3$									10-15	25.0*
Fe$_2$O$_3$	6.7	28.48	19.0	11.1	12.5	24.2	14.2	8.7		
FeO	39.3	1.33	19.8	22.5	34.0	9.3	26.6	33.6	12-15	
Al$_2$O$_3$	1.4	1.23	1.5		0.6	1.0	1.3		4-6	
SiO$_2$	1.5	0.28	0.7	1.4	2.8	0.7			3.5-5	
CaO	0.5	0.007	0.04		0.25				1.2*	0.15*
MgO	1.9	0.20	0.45		5.0	0.9	1.0		4.5-5.5	1.3*
Cr$_2$O$_3$	0.009		0.2	0.03	<0.076	0.12	0.07	0.005	0.25	0.3*
V$_2$O$_5$	0.05		0.12	0.13	0.16	0.15	0.16	0.02	0.5-0.6	0.6*
ZrO$_2$	0.01					0.9	0.8		0.03-0.10	
S	0.6		<0.01		<0.05	0.21	0.12		0.025*	
P$_2$O$_5$	0.008	0.12	0.02		<0.04			0.085		
MnO	0.5		1.4		0.25	0.4	0.4	4.0	0.2-0.3	2.5*
H$_2$O (loss on ignition)	1.3		0.4			2.0	0.3			
Rare earths						trace	0.12			
C	0.22				<0.055				0.03-0.10	
Reference	(1)	(2)	(3)	(3)	(4)	(3)	(3)	(3)	(5)	(6)

References: (1) NL Industries; (2) DuPont; (3) Anon., 1971c; (4) Anon., 1973c; (5) Guimond, 1964; (6) Anon., 1977, chloride grade.
* Maximum

ical compositions are listed in Table 9. It will be noted that the TiO$_2$ contents range from about 45% for unaltered ilmenite concentrates to 85% for slag.

Processing to Pigment: In the sulfate process finely ground ilmenite or high-TiO$_2$ slag is digested with strong sulfuric acid, forming a solid, porous cake which is dissolved in dilute acid and water to yield a solution of titanyl sulfate (TiOSO$_4$) and iron sulfate. Any ferric iron present is reduced to the ferrous state by adding scrap iron. This is done to avoid precipitation of ferric iron later in the process and to facilitate washing the precipitated titania, since ferrous iron is less strongly adsorbed. After reduction, the solution is clarified by settling and filtration. With ilmenite solutions, some of the iron is usually crystallized out as ferrous sulfate heptahydrate (copperas). The solution is then concentrated, and the titania is precipitated by hydrolysis, filtered, washed, calcined at 900° to 1000°C to the oxide, and further treated prior to the finished pigment stage. The nature of the various special treatments determines the grade and type of the finished pigment, i.e., whether it is anatase or rutile, chalking or nonchalking, oil or water dispersible, etc.

The estimated tons of raw material required to produce one ton of TiO$_2$ are as follows:

Ilmenite or titanium slag	1.5–2.8
Sulfuric acid	3.0–4.0
Iron scrap	0.1–0.2

Chloride Process

In the chloride process, titanium tetrachloride (TiCl$_4$) is produced by chlorinating titaniferous, higher-grade materials at about 850° to 900°C in the presence of petroleum coke. The estimated tons of raw materials required to produce one ton of TiO$_2$ are as follows:

Rutile	1.1–1.2
Chlorine	0.1–0.2
Petroleum coke	0.1–0.2
Oxygen	0.4–0.5
Aluminum chloride	0.03

All the commercial TiCl$_4$ plants in the United States use fluid-bed chlorinators but static-bed chlorinators also can be used.

Titanium tetrachloride is a highly reactive liquid at room temperatures and reacts violently with moisture. Hence, all handling of the TiCl$_4$ is carried out under inert conditions to avoid contamination by oxygen or moisture in the air.

Unfortunately, the inherent impurities in the ore also form chlorides which have to be removed by fractional condensation before the next step, otherwise they are precipitated with the titanium dioxide and cause off-color pigments. Iron, vanadium, and silicon are the more deleterious impurities. Trace impurities are removed by distillation and/or chemical treatment.

Processing to Pigment: The purified titanium tetrachloride is converted directly to titanium dioxide by oxidizing the $TiCl_4$ with air or oxygen at a high temperature. The resulting fine grained TiO_2 is calcined at about 500° to 600°C to remove any residual chlorine and hydrochloric acid that may have been formed in the reaction. The calcination also helps to improve some of the pigment characteristics. Aluminum chloride is added to the titanium tetrachloride to assure that virtually all of the titanium is oxidized in the rutile crystalline form. The chlorine formed during oxidation is recovered and recycled.

The process can produce pigments in either the anatase or rutile form. The cost per ton of pigment is believed to be less by the chloride process than by the sulfate process.

Titanium Metal

Titanium has two major advantages over other structural metals—its high strength/weight ratio, and its outstanding corrosion resistance. Disadvantages are its relatively high cost and difficulty in fabrication.

Applications and Consumption

The major applications of titanium metal have been in the aerospace industry, and consumption has been strongly dominated by military aircraft demands. The proportion of titanium consumption used for military planes has decreased somewhat but in 1981 was still estimated to be 35% compared to 40% for commercial planes, and 25% for nonaerospace applications. The heavy dependence on aerospace markets has led to severe fluctuations in demand. The most serious setback was in 1958–1959, when military aircraft production was cut back in favor of missile development, with a drop in titanium sponge production from about 17,000 tons in 1957 to 4600 tons in 1958 and 4000 tons in 1959. Gradual recovery and further fluctuations in demand led to successive new peaks in mill product shipments of 16,000 tons in 1969, 17,000 tons in 1974, and about 27,000 tons in 1980, with intervening lows coinciding approximately with cancellation of the supersonic transport program in 1971 and of the B-1 bomber program in 1977. The strong market in 1978 through 1981 resulted mainly from sharply increased rates of ordering for commercial aircraft such as the Boeing 747, Lockheed L1011, and McDonnell-Douglas DC10 in 1978–1979, and for the Boeing 757 and 767 in 1979–1981, as well as moderately increased demand for tubing to be used in nuclear power plant condensers in 1979.

Of the titanium used for airplanes in 1980–1981, about 55% was for commercial, and 45% for military aircraft. The main use in engines is for compressor disks and blades, and other compressor components. In airframe structures titanium is used to reduce the weight of various parts such as frames, bulkheads, longerons, skin, fasteners, firewalls, ducts, tubes, fairings, landing gear assemblies, and for parts subjected to high temperature. Titanium is also used extensively in missile and space vehicle components.

Nonaerospace consumption was only 5 to 6% of mill product shipments for many years, but reached 20% of shipments or about 3,000 tons in 1973, and about 25% of shipments, or 6,700 tons in 1980. Besides the use in power plant condensers, the largest industrial application, nonaerospace applications for titanium metal include heat exchangers in the chemical and petroleum industries; anodes in electrochemical processing; evaporators for water desalination; and pumps, valves, tanks, piping, and other chemical processing equipment. Anticipated new growth areas include power plant gas turbine blades; salt water environment uses, including offshore drilling platforms, titanium-hulled submarines, and ocean temperature energy conversion; and possible automotive applications.

Processing to Metal

Kroll Process: Commercial production of titanium metal involves the reduction of $TiCl_4$ with magnesium or sodium metal, using various modifications of the Kroll process (Kroll, 1940).

The titanium tetrachloride used for manufacture of titanium metal is produced by chlorination of rutile, blends of rutile with altered ilmenite, or other high-TiO_2 concentrates, using fluid-bed chlorinators. Coke is used as a reductant, and the reaction is generally carried out at temperatures of 850° to 950°C. The liquid $TiCl_4$ from the chlorinator is purified by chemical treatment and distillation.

Titanium sponge producers in the United States and their 1982 production capacities are listed in Table 10.

At the Titanium Metals Corp. of America plant at Henderson, NV (Lloyd, 1956), reduction of $TiCl_4$ is carried out with magnesium in steel pots in gas-fired furnaces, under a helium

TABLE 10—1982 United States Titanium Sponge Capacity

Sponge Producers	Annual Capacity, St
Titanium Metals Corp. of America	
(NL Industries, Inc. and Allegheny International, Inc.), Henderson, NV	15,000
RMI Co. (US Steel Corp. and National Distillers Corp.), Ashtabula, OH	9,500
Oregon Metallurgical Corp. (Publicly owned, with Armco Steel Co. as major	
stockholder), Albany, OR	4,500
International Titanium, Inc. (Wyman-Gordon Co.; Ishizuka Research Institute	
and Mitsui & Co., Ltd., Japan; and other US and Japanese interests)	2,500
Teledyne Wah Chang Albany, Albany, OR (Teledyne, Inc.)	1,500
Western Zirconium Co. (Westinghouse Electric Corp.)	500
Total	33,500

atmosphere, at a temperature above the melting point of magnesium chloride, but below the melting point of the titanium metal, which forms as a spongelike mass. The sponge is removed from the reactor in a dry room to avoid absorption of moisture and is crushed and leached with acid to remove residual magnesium and magnesium chloride. The magnesium chloride drained from the reactors is transported molten to the magnesium plant, where magnesium and chlorine are recovered by electrolysis.

Oregon Metallurgical Corp. (Oremet) and Teledyne Wah Chang Albany also use magnesium to reduce the $TiCl_4$ to metal, while RMI Co. uses sodium for reduction. Oremet uses an inert gas sweep to remove nearly all of the magnesium chloride from the sponge, ITI and Teledyne use vacuum distillation, and RMI uses dilute acid leaching.

Titanium sponge is converted to ingot by compacting and double or triple vacuum arc-melting, along with scrap and alloying constituents, as a consumable electrode, using a water-cooled copper crucible. Vacuum melting removes hydrogen, residual magnesium chloride, and other volatile impurities.

All of the sponge manufacturers except ITI are integrated producers. Producers of ingots from titanium sponge and scrap in 1982, besides the sponge producers, included Martin-Marietta Aluminum, Inc., Teledyne Allvac, Howmet Corp., and Lawrence Aviation Industries, Inc.

A National Materials Advisory Board report (Anon., 1983) on availability of titanium provides a broad, integrated overview of the titanium field.

Electrolytic Titanium: Electrolytic procedures for producing titanium metal have been extensively investigated with the object of developing a continuous process which would be more economical than the batch Kroll process

(Cobel et al., 1980; Leone et al., 1967; Priscu, 1966; Ramsdell and Mathews, 1960; Snyder, 1966). Early work was done by the US Bureau of Mines in Boulder City, NV. National Lead Co. was also involved in electrolytic titanium research as early as 1950. Titanium Metals Corp. of America built a semi-works plant and produced about 68,000 kg (150,000 lb) of electrolytic sponge titanium, but discontinued the operation in 1968 because of overcapacity for making sponge by the Kroll process. In 1980 D-H Titanium Co., a joint venture of Dow Chemical Co. and Howmet Turbine Components Corp., announced startup of an electrolytic titanium demonstration plant in Freeport, TX. The D-H process, which involves reduction of titanium tetrachloride in a fused salt bath, is based on early work done by the Bureau of Mines (Leone et al., 1967), research work by Dow, and pilot plant operation by Howmet at Whitehall, MI (Cobel et al., 1980). It is claimed that electrolytic processes will produce a higher purity product, require less capital investment, and consume less energy than plants using magnesium or sodium reduction (Minkler, 1980). The D-H venture was terminated in late 1982, mainly because of adverse market conditions.

Production and Prices

United States annual sponge and ingot production up to 1963, and ingot production from 1964–1980 are given in Table 11. Recovery to the 1957 peak of 17,249 st was not achieved until 1966, and two subsequent peaks were reached in 1969, 1974, and 1981.

From 1948 until 1954 the price of domestic titanium sponge metal was $5.00 per lb. Since then the price dropped many times, reaching a low of $1.32 in 1964 through 1972, before rising to reach $2.70 in 1975, $3.98 in 1979, $7.02 in 1980, and $7.65 per lb in mid-1981.

Year	Sponge	Ingot
1950–54, average	1,851	NA
1955	7,398	4,573
1956	14,595	11,688
1957	17,249	10,009
1958	4,585	5,408
1959	3,898	6,017
1960	5,311	8,297
1961	6,727	9,371
1962	6,730	10,400
1963	7,879	11,138
1964	—	13,964
1965	—	15,294
1966	—	24,253
1967	—	25,960
1968	—	19,234
1969	—	28,490
1970	—	24,331
1971	—	18,450
1972	—	20,267
1973	—	28,932
1974	—	36,132
1975	—	25,560
1976	—	21,614
1977	—	26,302
1978	—	31,385
1979	—	37,414
1980	—	41,864
1981	—	45,923
1982	—	25,236

Source: *Minerals Yearbooks* and *Mineral Industry Surveys,* US Bureau of Mines.
* After 1963, the US Bureau of Mines no longer reported data on sponge production, to avoid disclosing company proprietary information. Data for ingot production, 1964-1980, include alloying constituents and the use of imported as well as domestically produced sponge.
NA—Not available.

Titanium dioxide also is used in producing ceramic capacitors and electromechanical transducers, in producing glass fibers, and for making titanium carbides. Commercial carbide cutting tools contain 8 to 85% titanium carbide, with or without tungsten carbide, in a matrix of molybdenum, nickel, or cobalt. Organotitanium compounds such as alkyl and butyl titanates, derived from alcohols by reaction with titanium tetrachloride, and titanium esters are used as catalysts for various polymerization processes, as water repellents, and in dyeing processes (Stamper, 1970).

Titanium, formerly used mainly as a deoxidizer, has assumed considerable importance in the manufacture of stainless steels as a carbon- and nitrogen-stabilizing element to inhibit intergranular corrosion. The titanium is usually added as ferrotitanium, which is generally made by melting titanium scrap and iron together in an electric furnace. Ferrotitanium contains 15 to 70% titanium and 7 to 0.03% carbon. US consumption of titanium in steel and other alloys in 1982 was about 2,000 tons.

Large crystals of rutile, and certain titanates, especially strontium titanate, have been produced commercially, mainly by NL Industries, Inc., using a flame fusion process (Lynd and Merker, 1955; Moore, 1955). Because the refractive index of strontium titanate (1.41) is almost identical to that of diamond, strontium titanate gemstones look very much like diamonds, except that strontium titanate has more fire (flashes of spectral color) due to its higher dispersion. Strontium titanate also has been used in optical applications, such as for infrared detection devices (Beals and Merker, 1960).

Geology

Mineralogy

Although titanium is the ninth most abundant element of the lithosphere, comprising an estimated 0.62% of the earth's crust, there are only a few minerals in which it occurs in major amounts: rutile, anatase, and brookite (which are polymorphs of TiO_2), ilmenite and its alteration products, including leucoxene, perovskite ($CaTiO_3$), and sphene ($CaTiSiO_5$). Anatase may be emerging as a significant ore mineral of the future, but ilmenite, altered ilmenite, leucoxene, and rutile have been the only large volume ore minerals through 1980.

Ilmenite: The chemical formula of theo-

Miscellaneous Uses

Fairly large amounts of rutile concentrate (about 7,000 st US consumption in 1980) are used for welding-rod coatings. Ilmenite, slag, or manufactured TiO_2 may also be used as a source of TiO_2 for welding-rod coatings, but rutile is considered to be the most desirable for this purpose (Stamper, 1970). The titanium dioxide stabilizes the electric arc, reduces the viscosity of the slag formed, and decreases the surface tension of the metal droplets on the electrodes, resulting in a smooth weld (Peterson, 1966).

retically pure ilmenite is $FeO.TiO_2$. It was shown by Ramdohr (1950) that up to 6% Fe_2O_3 may be dissolved in solid solution, and at 1050°C a continuous solid solution series exists between ilmenite and hematite (Nicholls, 1955). Hematite may, and often does, occur with ilmenite as minute exsolution lamellae. Magnesium and manganese may substitute for the ferrous iron in ilmenite, which can produce the rare end-members $MgTiO_3$ (geikelite) and $MnTiO_3$ (pyrophanite), but usually these two elements are present as minor impurities. Magnetite is a common associate of ilmenite in igneous and metamorphic rocks, and in such coexisting pairs chromium, nickel, and vanadium tend to concentrate in magnetite while manganese concentrates in ilmenite.

In basic igneous rocks, notably anorthosites, gabbros, and basic lavas, ilmenite frequently occurs in intimate intergrowths with magnetite. The ilmenite forms lenses following octahedral parting planes in the magnetite host, and magnetite may, in turn, form crystallographically oriented inclusions within the ilmenite lenses.

Altered Ilmenite and Leucoxene: In sand deposits ilmenite frequently exhibits a degree of alteration caused by oxidation and removal of iron. The end product is essentially TiO_2. The process was described by Temple (1966) as follows:

Alteration is initiated along grain boundaries and structural discontinuities within the grain. After going through an amorphous stage, oxidation and partial removal of iron from the ilmenite lattice results in an intermediate iron titanate of definite structure for which the name pseudorutile has been proposed. The alteration product at the stage of complete oxidation of the original iron in the ilmenite analyses 65–70% TiO_2 as compared with the 52% TiO_2 of ilmenite. Complete removal of iron from the pseudorutile lattice results in a grain composed of crystallites of the mineral rutile. Only the three mineral phases: ilmenite, pseudorutile and rutile have been identified in the commercial titanium mineral concentrates studied. Natural occurrence, in sand deposits, indicates that in weathering final removal of iron from pseudorutile to give the rutile end product takes place only either above or in the zone of the fluctuating water table.

The alteration products of the mineral ilmenite are herein termed "altered ilmenite." Many commercial ilmenite concentrates actually consist of altered ilmenite. However, the term "leucoxene" is also applied to high-TiO_2 products of alteration. Commercial justification for distinguishing between the high- and low-iron products of alteration

lies in the fact that the former are used in the sulfate process by pigment manufacturers whereas the latter are not economically soluble in sulfuric acid but are used, as is rutile, for the production of titanium tetrachloride used for pigment and titanium metal manufacture.

Alteration is an extremely slow process which is aided by elevated temperature, so that older sand deposits in temperate and tropical regions of the world generally contain high-TiO_2 ilmenite. Younger deposits, for example, those found on modern beaches, and those in the higher latitudes usually contain unaltered ilmenite with a TiO_2 content around 50%, near the theoretical level for pure ilmenite.

Rutile: Rutile, the high pressure, high temperature polymorph of TiO_2, is the commonest form in nature and is a widespread accessory mineral in high grade metamorphic gneisses and schists and in igneous rocks. It is also a common detrital mineral.

Commercial rutile concentrates run 95% TiO_2 or more, with SiO_2, Cr_2O_3, V_2O_3, Al_2O_3, and iron oxides comprising the remainder. Analyses of rutile from other occurrences may show major amounts of tantalum and columbium, which can enter titanium minerals because of the close similarity in ionic radius between Ti^{+4} and both Cb^{+5} and Ta^{+5}. There is also a high iron variety termed ferroan rutile.

Rutile may form by alteration from ilmenite or anatase, and while it is very stable over a broad range of geologic conditions, occasionally processes may be reversed so that rutile alters to sphene, possibly ilmenite, and more rarely anatase.

The characteristic color of rutile is reddish brown, but it may be black, violet, yellow, or green.

Classification of Deposits

Titanium minerals have been mined from both rock and sand deposits. Until about 1942, nearly all of the ilmenite and rutile produced commercially came from sand deposits, but about one third of the world's ilmenite in 1982 came from rock deposits. Rutile, however, is now produced exclusively from sand deposits.

Rock Deposits: *Anorthositic Deposits—* Nearly all of the known commercially important rock deposits of titanium minerals are associated with anorthositic or gabbroic rocks, and are of three main types: ilmenite-magnetite (titaniferous magnetite), ilmenite-hematite, and ilmenite-rutile. Ilmenite-magnetite deposits usually contain ilmenite and magnetite as granular 'intergrowths that can be separated rather readily to yield concentrates of ilmenite and magnetite which may be essentially homogeneous minerals, or may consist of intimate intergrowths of one mineral in the other. Ilmenite-hematite deposits usually contain these minerals as intimate intergrowths and yield an ilmenite-hematite, or hemo-ilmenite concentrate rather than a separate concentrate of each mineral. Ilmenite-rutile deposits contain rutile and ilmenite either as separate concentrations or occurring together.

Miscellaneous Deposits—Other types of rock deposits in the United States that have been mined, or seriously considered as sources of titanium, include a deposit of ilmenite disseminated in schist in Yadkin Valley, North Carolina (Broadhurst, 1955), and a complex deposit of rutile, anatase, and brookite in a pegmatitic phase of alkalic rocks surrounding sediments at Magnet Cove, Arkansas (Fryklund and Holbrook, 1950; Fryklund et al., 1954).

A perovskite deposit in southwestern Colorado owned by Buttes Gas & Oil Co. was estimated to contain about 50 million tons of TiO_2 (Thompson, 1977). Processes to convert perovskite to titanium dioxide were being investigated through 1982.

The US Bureau of Mines (Llewellyn et al., 1980) and the US Geological Survey (Force, 1980) investigated the porphyry copper ores and mill tailings as a possible source of rutile. It was concluded that this material, which contains about 0.3% of potentially recoverable fine-grained rutile, could constitute a sizeable domestic resource, but more work is needed to develop an economic recovery process.

Major occurrences of anatase and ilmenite in weathered carbonatite bodies at Tapirá, Salitre, and Catalão in Minas Gerais, Brazil, are under investigation as new raw material sources. Feasibility and pilot plant studies to determine grades and recoveries of possible future commercial titanium mineral concentrates have been carried out. Modifications in pigment manufacturing processes may be necessary to accommodate potential production as a feed, or beneficiation or slagging may be used to make concentrates acceptable to existing pigment plants, but successful exploitation by any avenue will cause these and possibly other carbonatite occurrences to be classed as an important rock ore type.

Occurrences of titanium minerals in other types of rocks are known, but are not considered to be of commercial significance (Force et al., 1976).

Sand Deposits: Beaches, bars, dunes, and stream sands in many parts of the world are enriched by gravity segregation of the heavy minerals that are chemically resistant to weathering and physically hard enough to withstand considerable abrasive action. The energy of currents, waves, and to a lesser extent, winds, mobilizes the sand grains and permits them to behave as individuals within a fluid medium. Where the energy decreases, the heavier particles fall out while the lighter ones are carried farther. The composition of the heavy mineral concentrate depends on the nature of the geologic terrane being subjected to weathering and erosion and supplying materials to transporting streams. If available at the source, titanium-bearing minerals, zircon, magnetite, chromite, rare earth minerals such as monazite, staurolite, kyanite, sillimanite, garnet, xenotime, precious metals, and diamonds may be concentrated in this way. The resultant gravity segregations are usually dark colored and are called "black sands." Not all black sands are ore mineral occurrences; those found on the beaches of volcanic islands, for example, may be mostly amphibole and pyroxene.

There is a wide variation in titaniferous black sands in terms of heavy mineral concentration, percentage of titanium minerals within the heavy mineral suite, and TiO_2 content of the titanium mineral concentrate. All of these factors interact in rating deposits according to quality and as to whether they are today's reserves or possible resources of the future. Furthermore, the presence or absence of valuable coproduct or byproduct minerals such as zircon is a complicating factor. A classification on the basis of mineralogy, as suggested in the following section, is only broadly applicable.

Sand deposits in which rutile is the only economically important titanium mineral occur along the eastern shore of Australia. Ilmenite, altered ilmenite, and rutile form inland elevated strand-line deposits in Western Australia and in older sands of the Atlantic Coastal Plain of the United States. Ilmenite and altered ilmenite are the principal titanium ore minerals in other Western Australian districts; in Kerala, India; in deposits north of the Black Sea in the USSR; and in Florida and Georgia. Relatively unaltered ilmenite is found in large beach and dune occurrences along the northeastern coast of South Africa, in the Nile Delta of Egypt, and in still other Western Australian deposits, those closest to the present coast. Sand deposits of titaniferous iron ores occur as dune and beach deposits in many volcanic areas, of which those in New Zealand are the outstanding examples.

Mode of Occurrence and Origin

Rock Deposits: The anorthositic deposits contain titanium minerals either as massive ore, or disseminated in rock ranging from anorthosite to gabbro in composition, and varying in grade from solid ore to almost barren rock. While there are metamorphic and hydrothermal features in some parts of these deposits, for the most part, they seem to have formed at magmatic temperatures by magmatic processes.

The only other type of ilmenite rock deposit to be exploited commercially was the Yadkin Valley deposit in Caldwell County, North Carolina (Broadhurst, 1955), which was operated by a Glidden Co. subsidiary from 1942 to 1952. The ore consists of small masses of ilmenite disseminated throughout a talcose body which lies conformably with the enclosing quartzite and mica schist.

The Hot Spring County, Arkansas, deposits have been studied extensively for possible commercial development, and some rutile was recovered from the Magnet Cove deposit from 1932 to 1944. The deposits occur in a complex mixture of alkalic igneous rocks intruding folded sedimentary and metamorphic rocks. Much of the titanium is in the form of rutile or brookite, but many other titanium minerals have been identified. The ore minerals are intimately associated with gangue (Fryklund and Holbrook, 1950; Fryklund et al., 1954; Toewe et al., 1971).

Sand Deposits: Titanium-bearing black sands are found mainly in ancient or modern ocean and sea beaches around and occasionally within continental land masses. They frequently form highly visible surficial layers between the high and low water marks which may extend intermittently along coasts for miles, but such concentrations, containing perhaps 80% heavy minerals, are not mined on a large scale because they are usually too shallow and narrow to represent major reserves. Minable bodies are multilayered occurrences of a similar nature left behind by retreating seas, or coastal dunes formed when heavy minerals from black sand beaches were being transported inland by wind action. Heavy minerals tend to be disseminated within such dunes rather than layered as in beach-type deposits.

The history of a black sand ore body may be simple or complex. The essential elements are: (1) a "hinterland" of crystalline rocks in which

the heavy minerals were accessory constituents, (2) a period of deep weathering, (3) uplift with rapid erosion and quick dumping into the sea of the products of stream erosion, and (4) emergence of the coastline with longshore drift and high-energy waves acting during the process of shoreline straightening. There may be intermediate stages such as partial concentration of the heavy minerals in a coastal plain sediment and subsequent elevation, erosion, and reconcentration. The sand brought to the sea by rivers is picked up and carried away from their mouths by longshore currents, forming offshore bars and filling in bays between headlands, particularly during storms. Where bars are formed, the sand-carrying waves drag bottom and lose their energy so that the heavy minerals fall on the seaward side while the light minerals are cast over the bar and into the quieter water beyond. Layer upon layer of varying concentrations of heavy minerals accumulates on the growing bar in this way. Where bays are being filled with sand, both heavy and light minerals are churned from the bottom by landward-rushing waves and are hurled up the beach slope. The smoother, slower retreat of each wave mobilizes the uppermost layer of sand deposited there, and draws away the light minerals, to be picked up again and again by waves as currents move them along the coast, while leaving the heavy minerals behind. Alternating periods of stormy and calm weather leave alternating layers of high and low concentrations of heavy minerals in the beach sand as it advances toward the sea.

Distribution of Deposits

Reserves

Ilmenite resources in rock and sand deposits in the United States, recoverable under the economic and technological conditions of 1981, were estimated to contain 18 million tons of titanium dioxide. Rock deposits in New York account for 29% of the total. The remainder is in beach and river sands in Florida (Garnar, 1980), Georgia, New Jersey (Markewicz, 1969), and Tennessee. An additional 94 million tons of titanium dioxide in ilmenite and 48 million tons in perovskite (Thompson, 1977), not recoverable under present conditions, occur in identified resources, widely dispersed throughout the United States. Major occurrences lie in Colorado, Minnesota, New Jersey, New York, and Wyoming.

Reserves of rutile in the United States are in sand deposits in Florida, Georgia, and Tennessee. The rutile in these deposits contains about 1.7 million tons of titanium dioxide.

**TABLE 12—World Reserves of Ilmenite and Rutile
Thousands of Short Tons of TiO$_2$ Content**

Country	Ilmenite	Rutile
Arab Republic of Egypt	—	—
Australia	27,000	10,000
Brazil	2,000	67,000*
Canada	26,000	—
China	34,000	—
Finland	3,400	—
India	22,000	3,000
Norway	52,000	—
Sierra Leone	—	3,000
South Africa, Republic of	57,000	5,500
Sri Lanka	21,000	5,000
United States	18,000	1,700
USSR	7,000	3,000
Total	270,000	140,000

* Mainly anatase.

Identified but presently subeconomic deposits in Arizona, Arkansas, California, Florida, North Carolina, South Carolina, Tennessee, Utah, and Virginia contain an estimated 13 million tons of titanium dioxide in the form of rutile. The rutile in the Arizona and Utah resources occurs mainly as an accessory mineral in porphyry copper ores and mill tailings (Force, 1980; Llewellyn and Sullivan, 1980).

Estimates for world titanium reserves and resources are shown in Table 12. World reserves of ilmenite are estimated to contain 266 million tons of titanium dioxide, of which US reserves account for 7%. The titanium dioxide content of world rutile reserves is estimated at 97 million tons; US reserves represent 1.6% (Lynd, 1983).

Rock Deposits—Principal Producing Countries

United States: *Sanford Lake District, New York*—The Sanford Lake deposits (Gross, 1968), are located in the heart of the Adirondack Mountains. Discovery of these titaniferous magnetite deposits dates back to 1826. Several attempts to exploit the ores for iron prior to 1942 proved uneconomical because of difficulties with the associated titanium, and the isolated location (Bachman, 1914; Masten, 1923). Since 1942, National Lead Co. (now NL Industries, Inc.) has produced ilmenite concentrates for the titanium pigment industry, and a magnetite byproduct used in the steel and refractory industries and as heavy media in coal cleaning operations. The district is within the large anorthosite massif making up the central high peak area of the Adirondacks. All of the various low silica rock types associated with the massif are found within the boundaries of the district. These consist of both the Marcy and Whiteface types of anorthosite and of gabbroic anorthosite, gabbro, and different grades of titaniferous magnetite ores. All of the rocks contain the same minerals and differ only in the percentages of these constituents.

There are four mineralized areas where an economic grade of ore has been found. Three of these have both gabbroic-type ore and anorthositic-type ore. The fourth has only gabbroic ore. The TiO$_2$ contents of the ores range from 9.5% to over 30.0% TiO$_2$. Ore bodies of both types are related to gabbro and conform to the configuration of the gabbro bodies within the anorthosite.

Except for a few thousand tons mined before 1900, all ore production has come from the Sanford Hill-South Extension ore body. Mining began on Sanford Hill in 1942, and as a result of further exploration and development work, was transferred in the early 1960s to the South Extension part of the ore body, which was overlain by glacial till and Sanford Lake.

GENERAL GEOLOGY—Rocks of the Sanford Lake district are regarded as members of a genetically related anorthositic series, the whole being part of the large Adirondack anorthosite massif. Locally, anorthosite grades into gabbro by an increase in the content of mafic minerals. Buddington (1939) divided this sequence into four rock types depending upon the amount of ferromagnesian minerals present: anorthosite with 0 to 10%, gabbroic anorthosite with 10 to 22.5%, anorthositic gabbro with 22.5 to 35%, and gabbro with over 35% mafic minerals.

For mine mapping purposes, rock types are designated as anorthosite, gabbroic-anorthosite, gabbro, and the various grades of ore. The relationship of rock and ore type to TiO$_2$ assay is shown in Table 13.

ECONOMIC GEOLOGY—The titaniferous magnetite ore bodies of the district are of two types. One type, referred to locally as "anorthositic ore," is associated with anorthosite waste rock as coarse-grained massive lenses of irregular shape, with little structure and having sharp contacts with the anorthosite. The second ore type, "gabbroic ore," occurs as fine to medium grained oxide-enriched bands within the gabbro, with well defined structures similar to those in the gabbro. Contacts with the gabbro range from distinct to gradational.

In the Sanford Hill-South Extension ore body, both types of ore occur. The anortho-

TABLE 13—TiO₂ Assay of Various MacIntyre Mine Rock Types

Classification	%TiO₂
Anorthosite	0–5.4
Gabbro	5.5–9.4
Low grade protore	9.5–13.4
Medium grade ore	13.5–17.4
High grade ore	17.5+

sitic type forms a footwall ore body and the gabbroic ore forms a hanging wall ore body. These are separated by various widths of anorthosite and/or gabbro rock. In some instances the two types of ore are in direct contact.

The ore body is designated by two names because it has been developed in two pits. Mining started where ore was exposed in outcrops on the west side of Sanford Hill. Diamond drilling indicated the ore lenses as becoming very narrow where they extended underneath the basin of Sanford Lake. Later magnetometer results, along with aerial work in 1955 and ground followup in 1959, revealed a change in strike and width of the magnetic anomalies. Diamond drilling proved the South Extension of the Sanford Hill ore body to be of commercial grade and tonnage. At Cheney Pond, about 2 km (1½ miles) west of the South Extension pit, a development drill program proved commercial tonnages of gabbroic ore, and revealed none of the massive anorthositic type. Oxide rock bands up to 30 m (100 ft) thick are found within a synclinal body of fine grained gabbro, which is in sharp contact with the underlying anorthosite. An extensive study of the petrology of the Cheney Pond deposit was carried out by Sun (1971).

Ore of both types occurs in two smaller ore bodies: the Mount Adams ore body, about two miles northeast of Sanford Hill, and the Upper Works or Calamity-Mill Pond ore body about three miles north of Sanford Hill.

MINERALOGY OF THE ORE BODIES—The ores of the Sanford Lake district contain both ilmenite and magnetite as granular aggregates and disseminated grains. The ratio of total Fe: TiO₂ is generally 2:1 or greater in the anorthositic ore, and is less than 2:1 in the gabbroic ore. Gabbroic ore is finer-grained than anorthositic ore.

The magnetite grains are seldom homogeneous, and normally contain some ilmenite in solid solution and up to 35% of ilmenite as exsolution intergrowths. The intergrown ilmenite occurs as tabular plates oriented parallel to the octahedral planes of the magnetite or along the boundary between magnetite grains.

A second highly magnetic phase, ulvospinel (Fe_2TiO_4), has been identified as a fine network within the magnetite of the Sanford Hill-South Extension ores. This ulvospinel was first identified by Ramdohr (1956), using high magnification metallography. Kays (1965) used X-ray techniques along with chemical assay data to estimate that the magnetite grains may have an ulvospinel content of 34%.

About 0.5% vanadium occurs in solid solution within the magnetite. No separate vanadium mineral has yet been identified.

Ilmenite occurs as a matrix around magnetite and is observed under the microscope to be corroded by magnetite. It is finer-grained than magnetite and can be distinguished megascopically in coarse-grained anorthositic ore by its high luster and conchoidal fracture, compared to the dull luster and parting planes in magnetite. In finer-grained ore, the ilmenite and magnetite are more equigranular and cannot be recognized individually in hand specimens.

The typical ore and gangue minerals and their weight percentages in both ore types are shown in Table 14.

Other minor minerals identified in the Sanford Hill-South Extension ore body include

TABLE 14—Typical Mineral Analysis of Ore Types in Sanford Hill Ore Body

	Gabbroic or Hanging Wall Ore, wt %	Anorthositic or Footwall Ore, wt %
Black opaques, total	61.5	77.3
Magnetics (magnetite)	25.7	40.8
Nonmagnetics (ilmenite)	35.8	36.5
Feldspar	19.2	10.3
Garnet	8.1	3.4
Pyroxene (mostly clinopyroxenes)	6.6	4.7
Amphiboles (green and brown hornblende)	2.3	1.5
Sulfides (pyrrhotite and pyrite)	1.5	1.7
Apatite, spinel, chlorite, calcite	<1.0	<1.0

chalcopyrite, sphalerite, molybdenite, prehnite, barite, leucoxene, scapolite, epidote, orthoclase, and quartz.

In his extensive study of mineral paragenesis, Stephenson (1945) concluded that the large plagioclase phenocrysts were first to develop, followed by the finer-grained plagioclase, and later by the sequence: apatite, hypersthene, augite, hornblende, garnet, and ore minerals. The chlorites, carbonates, and scapolite formed as later alteration minerals as a result of deformation and minor hydrothermal activity. Kays (1965), in a study of Sanford Hill pit, agreed in general with the sequence given by Stephenson (1945), but pointed out that no one single paragenetic sequence holds rigorously for all rock types in the Sanford Lake district.

ORE GENESIS—Investigators have generally considered the Sanford Lake ores to have formed by magmatic segregation, as a result of such processes as simple segregation, filter-pressing of residual liquid with injection into the wall rock, and gravitational purification of the oxide melt by floating out of crystallized silicates with later injection, with replacement playing a minor role (Balsley, 1943; Bateman, et al., 1951; Buddington et al., 1955; Evrard, 1949; Osborne, 1928; Stephenson, 1945). Gillson (1956), however, related the variations in the anorthosites and the origin of the gabbro and ore to a series of pneumatolylic replacements involving andesination of Marcy anorthosite. Later solutions were assumed to be the source of the ferromagnesian and ore minerals.

Heyburn (1960) made reference to two stages of gabbro emplacement, one of them associated with the anorthosites, and the second a gabbroic intrusive rich in iron and titanium with sufficient volatiles to allow partial replacement of anorthosite by ore minerals.

Kays (1965) proposed that during granulation and shearing of the anorthosite, calcium and aluminum were released from the original laboradorite plagioclase, resulting in andesinization, but by a different means than proposed by Gillson (1956). Creation of pressure gradients by rock fracturing was then postulated to cause iron, magnesium, and titanium to migrate to the low pressure fractured areas, where they reacted with the calcium and aluminum released by andesinization to form ferromagnesian silicates, garnet, ilmenite, and magnetite. The resulting replacement could be partial, as in gabbro, or complete over large volumes, as in anorthosite.

Sun (1971) concluded that the Cheney Pond deposit is more likely to be of magmatic rather than replacement or metamorphic origin, stress-

ing evidence of magmatic crystallization temperatures and the layered nature of the ore bands, which resembles the structure of ultra-mafic stratiform sheets.

Gross (1968), after working for several years at the MacIntyre Development, concluded:

No one theory can explain satisfactorily all of the rock and mineral relationships now in evidence.

It is quite certain that all the rocks of the district are genetically related as shown by their mineral constituents. The primary mode of emplacement is partially or wholly obscured by subsequent metamorphic processes. It is likely that certain portions of the rocks have been remobilized one or more times by deformation pressures. Different degrees of plasticity are evident . . .

There is evidence that volatiles were present at some point in the history of the deposits, probably in both early and late stages. The faults and joints now exposed show movement along many surfaces. Along the major breaks there are breccia fragments of ore or gabbro in a matrix of carbonates. These are also the areas of recrystallized magnetite, large ilmenite crystal masses, and minor sulfide minerals . . .

The present faults and associated hydrothermal minerals represent the last minor sequence in a very long and complicated series of geologic events.

Virginia Titanium Deposits—The titanium ores of Virginia are also associated with anorthosite, and are of two types: (1) rutile and ilmenite disseminated in the border facies of the anorthosite and bordering gneiss, and (2) rutile and/or ilmenite with apatite in the form of dikelike masses which Watson and Taber (1913) named nelsonite after the county in which they are most common. Deposits of both types have been mined commercially, utilizing mainly the soft, saprolite portions of the ore bodies which form an upper layer about 9 to 37 m (30 to 120 ft) thick.

Rutile was first mined commercially at Roseland, VA, in 1900 by the American Rutile Co. The ore was obtained by open cut mining of both saprolite and hard rock. The mine was operated intermittently until 1949 when increased labor costs, low grade ore, and low market prices for rutile led to a shutdown of operations. The ore consists almost exclusively of disseminated rutile in the anorthosite (Fish, 1962; Hillhouse, 1960).

Commercial surface mining for ilmenite began in 1930 from a large saprolite ore body along the Piney River on the old Warwick

Tract. This mine was first operated by the Vanadium Corp. of America, and later by the Southern Mineral Products Corp. (Hillhouse, 1960) until it was acquired by the American Cyanamid Co. in 1944. In 1958 the company transferred operations to the deposit on the S.V. Wood property near Lowesville about 5 km (3 miles) to the West (Fish, 1962), supplying ilmenite to its nearby sulfate process pigment plant until 1971, when both mine and pigment plant were closed down, mainly because the supply of readily mined soft ore at this location was running out.

Fish (1962) estimated the saprolite deposits in the area to contain reserves of titanium-bearing material in excess of 20 million tons, averaging 7.0% TiO_2. Unweathered rock beneath the saprolite contains comparable titanium values, but mining and processing this ore would be more expensive. The ore is derived from two types of rocks; one, containing ilmenite as the dominant titanium mineral, is a diorite, and the other, containing ilmenite and rutile, is an anorthosite.

The nelsonite deposits are higher grade, but of limited size. Many of them are lenticular and pinch out at shallow depths (Fish and Swanson, 1964).

Davidson et al. (1946) studied the Piney River deposit and concluded that it was emplaced as a large dike fingering into its walls. Replacement was agreed to have occurred, but this was not regarded as proof that the main development of ore was by replacement.

Theories proposed regarding the origin of the Virginia titanium ores in general include magmatic segregation from the anorthosite, favored by Watson and Taber (1913), differentiation from a granodiorite magma, suggested by Moore (1940), and replacement by invading solutions, proposed by Ross (1941, 1947); and Hillhouse (1960).

Yadkin Valley Deposit, North Carolina— The Yadkin Valley deposit is about 21 km (13 miles) north of Lenoir, in Caldwell County. The ore occurs as a series of narrow, close-spaced lenses which form a nearly continuous vein about 305 m (1000 ft) long. The ore consists of small masses of ilmenite disseminated throughout a talcose body which lies conformably with the enclosing quartzite and mica schist (Broadhurst, 1955). Some rutile occurs as fine inclusions in the mica, but was not recovered.

The ore zone is parallel to the gneissic structure, is about 9 m (30 ft) thick, and was mined by quarrying, running about 30 to 35% TiO_2. The mine was operated from 1942 to 1952 by the Yadkin Mica and Ilmenite Co., a subsidiary of Glidden Co. A flotation ilmenite concentrate was produced which contained 49 to 52% TiO_2 (McMurray, 1944), unusually high grade for a rock ilmenite.

Hot Spring County, Arkansas Deposits, (Magnet Cove, Christy, Hardy-Walsh)—These deposits occur in a complex mixture of alkalic igneous rocks intruding folded sedimentary and metamorphic rocks, many of which contain various quantities of titanium-bearing minerals (Fryklund and Holbrook, 1950). Much of the titanium is in the form of rutile or brookite, but many other titanium minerals have been identified. Rutile was recovered commercially from the Magnet Cove (Reed, 1949a) deposit from 1932 to 1944. A considerable amount of work has been done on ore dressing techniques for these ores (Fine and Frommer, 1952; Fine et al., 1949). The features contributing most to the difficulty of utilizing these deposits are their comparatively low grade, the larger deposits averaging 3 to 6% recoverable TiO_2 (Fryklund et al., 1954), the formation of large amounts of slimes during grinding, and the intimate association of ore minerals and gangue, resulting in low recoveries and comparatively low grade concentrates (Toewe et al., 1971). No commercial output of titanium minerals has been reported from the Christy (Reed, 1949) or Hardy-Walsh deposits.

Other US Deposits—Other deposits of potential commercial importance include the titaniferous magnetite deposits in the Laramie Range, Wyoming (Diemer, 1941; Frey, 1946; Pinnell and Marsh, 1954). Metamorphic rocks were intruded by anorthosite, which in turn was cut by gabbro and titaniferous magnetite dikes. The main dike at Iron Mountain consists of a granular aggregate of homogeneous ilmenite and magnetite containing very small intergrown ilmenite inclusions. In the Taylor deposit, as much as 60% apatite is locally present. Resources of high grade ore containing about 45% Fe and 20% TiO_2 may amount to about 30 million tons. Further metallurgical research would be needed, and the geographical location is at present unattractive for commercial development.

Other large deposits occur in the San Gabriel Mountains in Los Angeles County, California, as disseminations in a gabbroic facies of an anorthosite (Moorhouse, 1938). Very large tonnages may be available, but the average grade is only about 4.5% TiO_2.

Smaller deposits occur in nearly every one of the western states, for example in Montana (Wimmler, 1946); Minnesota (Broderick, 1917); Wichita Mountains of Oklahoma (Merritt, 1939); Boulder County, Colorado (Jennings, 1913); and the San Juan district, Colorado (Singewald, 1913).

Canada: *Quebec*—The geology and general characteristics of the Canadian titanium deposits were well described in an extensive and thorough report by Rose (1969). He concluded that the titaniferous magnetite and ilmenite deposits in eastern Canada were formed by magmatic differentiation and injection, mainly in Precambrian time, presumably from 850 million to 1,500 million years ago. There is an unmistakable genetic relationship between these deposits and anorthositic rocks. The anorthosite bodies, as exemplified by the Morin, St. Urbain, Lac St. Jean, Sept-Iles, and Lac Allard anorthosites, appear in general to be composite, multiple intrusions composed mainly of anorthositic and gabbroic (noritic) rock. According to Rose, (1969):

> True anorthosite characteristically is host to the massive ilmenite-hematite lodes, whereas gabbroic anorthosite characteristically is host to the extensive deposits of low-grade, disseminated, titaniferous magnetite containing mixtures of titanomagnetite, ilmenite, ilmenite-hematite, and other intermediate members that possibly form a solid solution series of iron-titanium oxide minerals. Although generally separate, in places the two types of deposits, as well as the host rocks, appear to be transitional.
>
> Although a few ilmenite and titaniferous magnetite occurrences have been found in rocks that were invaded by anorthositic magma, the major deposits are almost always within the intrusion itself. Low-titanium magnetite deposits are commonly found in Grenville-type rocks outside the anorthosite massifs.

The main deposits include: the sill-like Lac Tio ilmenite-hematite deposits being mined by QIT-Fer et Titane, Inc. (formerly Quebec Iron and Titanium Corp.), estimated to hold about 100 million tons of high grade open pit material; the dikelike Magpie Mountain medium grade titaniferous magnetite deposits, averaging 43% iron and 6% titanium, probably containing over 250 million tons of open pit material; the St. Urbain deposits with over 20

million tons of high grade ilmenite-hematite; and several million tons of slightly lower grade material near Ivry, and in the Lac du Pin-Rouge area, near St. Hippolyte-de-Kilkenny. Substantial amounts of low-grade titaniferous magnetite and ilmenite occur at many other localities in the Morin, Lac St. Jean, Sept-Iles, Lac Allard, and St. Urbain anorthosite areas (Rose, 1969).

Kish (1972) studied the chemical composition of the Quebec deposits, particularly with regard to the vanadium content, and reported that vanadium concentrations of economic importance have so far been found only in the titaniferous magnetite deposits. The composition and origin of selected titaniferous deposits were discussed by Lister (1966).

ALLARD LAKE (LAC TIO) DEPOSITS—The geology of the area in which the Allard Lake deposits occur was investigated by Retty (1944), who noted numerous concentrations of ilmenite within a mass of anorthosite, along the shores of several lakes. These ilmenite showings, while not large enough to warrant commercial development, led to detailed exploration of the anorthosite area in 1946 by Kennco Explorations, Ltd., which resulted in the discovery of the large Lac Tio deposit. The deposit lies between Allard Lake and Puyjalon Lake, about 40 km (25 miles) north of Havre St. Pierre on the north shore of the St. Lawrence River.

The geology of the area and the nature of the ilmenite deposits have been well described by Hammond (1949, 1952), and by Hargraves (1959). The most important lithological unit in the area is the Allard Lake anorthosite. It is one of several anorthosite masses occurring at intervals in the southeastern part of the Precambrian shield, in a line trending northeast from the Ontario-Quebec boundary to the Labrador coast. The Allard Lake anorthosite mass is about 145 km (90 miles) long, and 32 to 48 km (20 to 30 miles) wide, its length paralleling the Gulf of St. Lawrence. The several facies of the anorthosite range from almost pure feldspar rock through anorthositic gabbro, ilmenite-rich anorthosite, and norite. The norite occurs as steeply dipping sheets, as much as 6 km (4 miles) long and 914 m (3000 ft) thick, intruded into the anorthosite, and is rich in hemo-ilmenite and magnetite.

The Lac Tio deposit is a flat-lying, tabular body about 1097 m (3600 ft) long, and 1036 m (3400 ft) wide. With an estimated tonnage of 125,000,000 st of ilmenite averaging 32% TiO_2

and 36% Fe, it is the largest known ore body of its type in the world.

The ore consists of exsolution intergrowths of ilmenite and hematite, with coarse-grained ilmenite containing numerous blades and lenses of hematite up to 0.3 mm wide, which in turn may contain similarly shaped but smaller inclusions of ilmenite, in parallel orientation. The typical high grade ore contains about 75% ilmenite, 20% hematite, and 5% gangue minerals consisting of pyroxene, feldspar, and minor amounts of pyrite, pyrrhotite, and chalcopyrite.

The ore occurs in anorthosite and anorthositic gabbro and is identical in character with that in other deposits in the area. Inclusions of anorthosite are found in the ore, and do not show evidence of replacement by ilmenite. The ilmenite is very coarse-grained along its contacts with anorthosite, and the contacts are very sharp. Tiny dikelets of coarse granular ilmenite commonly cut the anorthosite at contacts with the ore bodies. On a basis of such direct field evidence, Hammond (1949, 1952) concluded that the Allard Lake ores are late magmatic, probably emplaced by a process of late gravitational liquid accumulation, with injection of the oxides into fractures within the anorthosite.

Hargraves (1959) recognized a genetically significant relationship between the ore deposits and the oxide-rich norite phases of the anorthosite rocks with which they are associated. The usual occurrence of the isolated ilmenite masses in anorthosite below norite sheets, with hemo-ilmenite concentrated at the base of the sheets, suggests that the norite sheets may have been the original source of the iron-titanium oxides. Hargraves (1959) presented evidence suggesting immiscibility between the oxide fraction and the silicate fraction from which pyroxenes crystallized, and emphasized that the crystallization of the oxide fraction was subsequent to all other primary crystallization. He suggested that:

Gravitational concentration by downward settling within the sheets could have been accentuated by contemporaneous deformation ("filter pressing") which in some places, caused it to be squeezed out of the sheets, and injected into surrounding anorthosite. In this way the isolated deposits in anorthosite are postulated to have been formed.

Based on his own extensive study of the St. Urbain deposits, and the similarity between these and the Allard Lake deposits, Gillson (1932, 1949) felt that the St. Urbain and Allard Lake ore bodies are pneumatolytic replacement deposits.

The ilmenite-hematite ore produced from the Lac Tio operation contains about 34% TiO_2 and 40% Fe. Because of its high iron content it is not used directly for titanium dioxide pigment manufacture, but is subjected to further concentration and electric furnace smelting at Sorel, Que., to produce iron metal, and a high-TiO_2 slag which is widely used as a feed for sulfate process pigment plants.

China: The largest titanium deposit in China is reportedly the 1.1 billion ton Panzihua titaniferous magnetite deposit containing about 7% titanium in the form of ilmenite, near Dukou, Sechuan province (Brady, 1981).

Norway: The iron-titanium provinces of Norway have been described by Geis (1971), Vokes (1968), Carstens (1957), Michot (1956), Hubaux (1956), and others. There are three types of ilmenite deposits: (1) ilmenite, (2) vanadium-bearing magnetite-ilmenite, and (3) apatite-bearing magnetite-ilmenite. Production of ilmenite has come only from Type 1 deposits (Storgangen and Tellnes), except for a small amount produced from a Type 2 deposit (Rodsand), as a byproduct from magnetite production. These three commercial deposits all occur in the Egersund anorthosite in southwestern Norway.

Storgangen Deposit—The Storgangen ore body located near Hauge, was deposited in a fracture in anorthosite, forming a dike about 1585 m (5200 ft) long and 49 m (160 ft) wide, of unknown depth, dipping 45° to 50° N. The ore contains about 40% ilmenite and 9% magnetite with a gangue that consists mainly of hypersthene and plagioclase, with accessory biotite, pyrite, chalcopyrite, and spinel. The ilmenite contains about 13% hematite as exsolution lenses and lamellae in parallel orientation, ranging up to a few microns in width. The magnetite is essentially homogeneous, containing very little exsolved ilmenite. The ilmenite concentrate was produced by a combination of gravity, magnetic, and flotation methods. From this deposit, Titania A/S (NL Industries, Inc., subsidiary) mined 9 million st of ore from 1916 to 1966.

Tellnes Deposit—Around 1954, it became apparent that because of the increased demand for ilmenite, the amount of ore accessible at currently mined levels in the Storgangen deposit would be soon depleted. By 1956, two alternatives had been investigated: to extend operations to deeper levels at Storgangen, or to discover and develop a new ore source in nearby areas considered favorable to the occurrence of titanium ore. Diamond drilling at Storgangen showed that the ore available at depth was less than expected, and at current production rates would have lasted only another 10 to 12 years. At the Tellnes deposit which was discovered by an aeromagnetic survey in 1954, drilling showed ore reserves of 220 million st, with another 110 million st probably present, based on projection to depth. After extensive laboratory and pilot plant work to demonstrate that a satisfactory concentrate could be made from the Tellnes ore, which is much finer grained than the Storgangen ore, it was decided to develop the Tellnes deposit as an open pit mining operation (Brun, 1957).

From 1960 to 1966 ilmenite was produced from both the Storgangen and Tellnes deposits. In 1966 production at Tellnes reached about 330,000 stpy, and production ceased at Storgangen. Since that time, production capacity was increased in three steps, and in 1974 production of ilmenite flotation concentrate reached a peak of 935,000 st.

The Tellnes ore body is about 40 km (25 miles) east of the Storgangen deposit, and consists essentially of an ilmenite-rich norite intruded into anorthosite. The ore body has a known outcrop length of 2682 m (8800 ft), and a surface area of about 56 hm^2 (140 acres).

The ore is magmatic in character, as proved by its texture, by apophyses of ilmenonorite into the surrounding rocks, by xenoliths of anorthosite in the ore itself, and by the presence of eruptive breccia (Dybdahl, 1960).

The Tellnes ore is much finer-grained than the Storgangen ore, the intergrowth of ilmenite and magnetite is more intimate, and the amount of magnetite is lower in the Tellnes ore—only 2% compared to about 7% in the Storgangen ore. Dybdahl (1960) gave the following average mineral composition for Tellnes ore: ilmenite, 39%; plagioclase, 36%; hypersthene, 15%; biotite, 3.5%; and accessories, 3.5%, including a little apatite, and some pyrrhotite containing nickel and copper. As at Storgangen, the ilmenite contains minute exsolution lenses and lamellae of hematite.

Because of the fineness of grind needed to liberate the ore minerals, and the relatively high phosphorus content present as apatite, extensive changes in the ore dressing procedure had to be made, resulting in an all-flotation ilmenite concentrate, and an acid washing step to remove apatite. The ilmenite concentrate contains 44.5 to 45.5% TiO_2, about 34.0% FeO, and 12.5% Fe_2O_3.

Tellnes ilmenite concentrate is the major feed material for a large number of European sulfate process pigment plants, and is in a particularly strong market position because of relatively stable North Sea freight rates, and its proximity to the European market (Anon., 1973c; Anon. ,1978a).

Finland: *Otanmäki Deposit*—The ilmenite-magnetite deposit at Otanmäki is located almost at the geographical center of Finland. The Otanmäki deposit and a neighboring deposit at Vuorokas were discovered in 1938 as a result of magnetic surveys by Veikko Okko of the Geological Survey of Finland (Harki et al., 1956).

As described by Harki et al. (1956), the deposit at Otanmäki extends about 2 km (1.2 miles) within an east-west zone which curves northward in a semicircle at its east end. This circle is the eastern boundary of a mass of amphibolite occupying most of a roughly elliptical area within which the ore bodies are found. The ore occurs as lenses which are usually located along contacts between amphibolite and anorthosite, or between anorthosite and rocks that occur in a heterogeneous band along the southeast border of the ore zone. The anorthosite appears as continuous conforming lenses in the innermost border of the curve. A mass of gabbro borders the southwest part of the ore zone. According to Harki et al. (1956), it has been established that the ore is intrusive in nature, except possibly in the case of lower grade stratified ores.

The ore minerals, magnetite and ilmenite, occur as independent grains which after fine grinding are separated to produce magnetite and ilmenite concentrates. There are no microscopic intergrowths of magnetite and ilmenite, although the ilmenite contains minor amounts of intergrown hematite (Harki et al., 1956; Vaasjoki, 1947). The main gangue minerals are chlorite, hornblende, and basic plagioclase, with accessory spinel and sphene.

Reserves are about 28 million st containing 40% magnetite, 30% ilmenite, 1 to 2% pyrite, and 0.25 to 0.3% vanadium associated with the magnetite (Anon., 1978b).

Rock Deposits—Potential Sources

Brazil: *Tapira and Salitre Titanium Deposits*—These deposits are unique in that their major titanium mineral is the anatase (or octahedrite) polymorph of TiO_2, rather than rutile or ilmenite. The deposits occur in an alkaline pipe, 6 km (4 miles) in diameter, about 48 km (30 miles) southeast of Araxá in

Minas Gerais. According to the National Department of Mineral Production, proved and indicated reserves contain 108 million st of TiO_2 (Anon., 1980a). In places, anatase may make up as much as 70% of the ore. In preliminary tests concentrates containing up to 86% TiO_2 were produced with very low chromium and vanadium content, said to be suitable for producing TiO_2 pigments by the chloride process. These concentrates have some solubility in sulfuric acid (Anon., 1972).

Through 1979, about 12 million tons of anatase-bearing ore had been mined and stockpiled in conjunction with phosphate production.

Mexico: *Pluma Hidalgo Deposit, Oaxaca*— The Pluma Hidalgo Deposit occurs in an area known for some time to have scattered occurrences of rutile, and is located about 125 km (78 miles) south of the City of Oaxaca, the state capital. Starting in 1953, Republic Steel Corp. carried out an extensive program of exploration, but did not find high grade ore bodies large enough to justify a mining operation. In 1957, when the price of rutile dropped substantially, the project was discontinued.

Paulson (1964) described the dominant country rock as a quartz feldspar gneiss, or granulite, which may be classed as an anorthosite by analogy with the anorthosite associated with the similar Virginia titanium deposits. The common mineral association in ore zones is ilmenite, rutile, and apatite in a green rock that is mostly chlorite.

Regarding possible economic exploitation of the Pluma Hidalgo deposit, Paulson was of the opinion that instead of trying to find large zones of high grade ore, it might be better to block out a large tonnage of the irregularly distributed ore which, including the barren rock that would have to be removed with the ore, might have an overall grade that would permit mining by open pit methods.

Sand Deposits—Principal Producing Countries

United States: All commercially important titanium mineral sand deposits in the United States are within the Atlantic and Gulf Coastal Plain geologic provinces. States which have established or potential exploitable heavy-mineral-bearing sands are Florida, Georgia, New Jersey, and Tennessee.

Concentrations of heavy minerals in the coastal areas of the southeast are related to both recent and ancient marine shorelines, the latter of Pleistocene age. Up to seven old shorelines have been identified by different investigators (Cooke, 1941, 1945; Flint, 1940, 1942, 1947;

MacNeil, 1949; Parker and Cooke, 1944), but the most widely recognized are: (1) Okefenokee, 46 m (150 ft), (2) Wicomico, 31 m (100 ft), (3) Pamlico, 8 to 11 m (25–35 ft), and (4) Silver Bluff, 2 to 3 m (8–10 ft) above sea level. All are regarded as lines of farthest marine transgression during interglacial and postglacial periods, and all have produced commercial heavy mineral deposits. Mining began where black sands were exposed on modern beaches, and when these deposits were exhausted operations moved inland to the larger and harder-to-find deposits of the older elevated strands. Florida has three heavy mineral mines operating with possibilities for more in the future; Georgia's only deposit exploited to date recently has been worked out but, again, other occurrences of possibly economic size and grade are known.

In central New Jersey two operations have recovered titanium minerals and byproducts from Pliocene sands of the Cohansey formation, about 24 km (15 miles) inland from the present shore.

The host for heavy mineral deposits in western Tennessee which have been considered for mining is the Cretaceous McNairy sand, outcropping within the Mississippi embayment of the Gulf Coastal Plain. Past, present, and possible future ore bodies in each of the three areas of occurrence are considered in turn below.

Florida and Georgia—Storm-line concentrations of heavy minerals in modern beach sands have been mined for ilmenite at two locations on Florida's eastern beaches. Mining began at Pablo Beach near Ponta Vedra in 1916 (Martens, 1928), and Riz Mineral exploited a deposit on the ocean front near Vero Beach in later years. Similar modern beach, bar, and barrier island black sands are found on the northeast and west coasts of the peninsula and along the shore of the western panhandle. The ratios among species in heavy mineral suites in the western Florida occurrences are different from those in eastern deposits, probably because of dissimilar ultimate sources on opposite sides of the southern Appalachian Mountains. The potential ore reserves in the known near-shore concentrations are small, with the possible exception of Amelia Island in extreme northeastern Florida, Cumberland Island just to the north in Georgia, and several others of the Sea Island chain formed as barrier islands during the development of the Silver Bluff shoreline. Land values in the islands have increased because of their growing popularity as resort areas over approximately three decades since the heavy mineral deposits were first drilled, so that mining may not be economically competitive with tourism and recreation.

Elevated sand bars were mined by Riz Mineral south of Vero Beach and by Humphreys Gold Corp., on behalf of Titanium Alloy Manufacturing Co., in a Pamlico shoreline feature just west of Jacksonville Beach. These deposits are now mined out.

Just south of the St. Marys River, which forms Florida's northern boundary, and northeast of the community of Yulee, ITT-Rayonier owns land containing an unmined heavy mineral deposit which has been drilled by several organizations, most recently by Pennsylvania Glass Sand Corp., the ITT-Rayonier subsidiary. Ore grade lenses form low north-south ridges, interspersed with shallow swamps, and rest on clay and shell beds. The Yulee deposit is also a Pamlico shoreline development.

In Georgia other black sand concentrations, all related to the Pamlico shoreline, are located north and south of Brunswick and south of Savannah. Potential ore reserves are modest in all known cases, as they are at Yulee, but exploitation might be possible if the same mining equipment could be used at several deposits sequentially, and if a heavy mineral concentrate could be economically transported to a central separating plant.

TRAIL RIDGE, FL—The broad sand ridge that extends from the southern parts of Clay and Bradford counties in north-central peninsular Florida for 201 km (125 miles) northward into southeastern Georgia, called Trail Ridge, is thought to have formed by one or more of several processes in late Miocene or Pliocene time. It has been suggested that it developed as:

1) An accumulation of deltaic sediments from southward flowing rivers which was reworked by encroaching seas and partly washed away (Bishop, 1956).

2) A prograding bar built up on the seaward side of finer marine to estuarine deposits accumulating on its protected Gulf side (Brooks, 1966).

3) A residual sand ridge resulting from the weathering in situ of underlying sediments.

4) A barrier island originating as a ridge built up landward of a shoreline and cut by tidal inlets during coastal subsidence or sea level rise, forming lagoons behind the ridge (Hoyt, 1967).

5) A reworking, through the action of winds, waves, and currents, of the northern part of the remnant Lake Wales ridge, a possible deltaic deposit extending more than 241 km (150 miles) farther to the south (Pirkle and Yoho, 1970).

6) Sediments transported from the high terrace sands to the west of Trail Ridge (Pirkle, 1975).

Du Pont's Trail Ridge ore body occupies the southern 29 km (18 miles) of the western part of the feature, and is from 2 to 3 km (1 to 2 miles) wide. The base of the ore body is at an elevation of 44 m (145 ft) to more than 61 m (200 ft) above sea level, and the average thickness is 11 m (35 ft). It overlaps barren coarse sand on the east. An indurated layer of concentrated organic material comprised of decomposed remnants of roots, branches, and trunks of trees underlies the central portion, and the western margin lies on pre-Pleistocene clayey sand in many places (Grogan et al., 1964).

The heavy minerals are thinly layered and disseminated in brown, oxidized, cross-bedded sand. In random lenticular areas at various depths organic materials and clayey minerals cement the sand grains to form a poorly consolidated sandstone locally called "hardpan." The average grade in heavy minerals is low, only about 4%, but there are about 45% high-TiO_2 minerals in the heavy mineral suite (Pirkle and Yoho, 1970).

The titanium ore minerals are altered ilmenite, leucoxene, and a very little rutile. Staurolite, zircon, tourmaline, spinel, kyanite, sillimanite, monazite, corundum, and topaz are also present. Authigenic pyrite occurs in small amounts associated with present-day swamps. The absence of monazite, garnet, and epidote, which are common in the underlying formations and in other southeastern heavy mineral deposits, implies different source rocks and a different age for the Trail Ridge minerals. The absence of these three minerals makes the separation and marketing of staurolite possible (see "Staurolite" chapter).

Alteration of the titanium minerals by oxidation and leaching of iron has been extensive. Grogan et al. (1964) wrote:

The TiO_2 content of the mineral grains is highest near the land surface, decreases rapidly from the surface to a depth of about 10 feet, and then remains essentially constant to the bottom. The iron content varies inversely with the TiO_2 content. The particle size of the titanium mineral grains ranges between 48 and 200 mesh, with the average size near 80 mesh. The grains are spherical, and some are porous as a result of leaching.

Their color ranges from black through brown, gray, and tan to light yellow or yellowish-white depending on the degree of alteration.

The term "ilmenite" is applied to the more magnetic of the titanium minerals. These particles are black with a metallic luster and range from 62 to 70% TiO_2.

The term "leucoxene" is applied to the less magnetic opaque titanium minerals which contain from 70 to 95% TiO_2. They have the same size and shape as the ilmenite grains but are lighter in color, and represent more advanced stages of alteration. Their magnetic susceptibility ranges from moderate for the darker grains to feeble for the very light colored grains.

Unaltered crystalline rutile is common in the nonmagnetic fraction. The grains are dark red in color and are mostly minus 150 mesh in size.

GREEN COVE SPRINGS, FL—About 32 km (20 miles) east-southeast of the south end of Trail Ridge an ilmenite-leucoxene-zircon-monazite heavy mineral deposit was mined by Titanium Enterprises, a joint venture of American Cyanamid and Union Camp Corp., until 1978 when mining ceased for economic reasons. In 1980 the property was purchased and mining resumed by Associated Minerals (U.S.A.) Ltd., Inc., a subsidiary of the Australian firm, Associated Minerals Consolidated Ltd. The ore body is near the eastern margin of the Duval Upland, which is thought to be a regressional beach ridge plain, and is probably related to an ancient shoreline at an elevation of 27 to 31 m (90 to 100 ft) above present sea level or to the Wicomico shoreline of MacNeil (1949).

The ore zone at Green Cove Springs is 16 to 19 km (10 to 12 miles) long, 1 km (¾ mile) wide, and it averages about 6 m (20 ft) thick. The heavy minerals comprise 3 or 4% of loose to slightly consolidated quartz sands which are underlain by subgrade quartz sands, by brown and gray sands containing some clay, by shell beds, and finally, at a depth of 31 m (100 ft) or more below surface, by limestone and dolomite.

The grain size of both quartz and heavy minerals is smaller than at Trail Ridge. Also, the heavy mineral suite, containing a significant percentage of monazite together with minor amounts of epidote and garnet, is different. It has been suggested (Pirkle et al., 1974) that while the Trail Ridge concentration of heavy minerals was derived from the Northern Highlands of the northwestern part of peninsular Florida, the Green Cove Springs deposit was

formed from the sands of the Duval Upland to the east.

BOULOUGNE, FL—Humphreys Mining Co. in 1974 to 1979 mined a heavy mineral deposit about 3 km (2 miles) south of the town of Boulougne on the St. Marys River, which forms the boundary between extreme northern Florida and Georgia. It was located near the eastern edge of the Duval Upland at an elevation above sea level the same as that at Green Cove Springs, and had similarly fine sands containing monazite, garnet, and epidote. The two deposits probably had a common genesis.

The Boulougne ore body was 4 to 5 km (2½ to 3 miles) long north-south, 0.8 to 1.2 km (½ to ¾ mile) wide, and 2 to 8 m (5 to 25 ft) thick. The ore-bearing surface sands were underlain by sand with a diminished heavy mineral content, then by various colors of clayey sand, then by a thin shell bed, and finally by the sediments of the Hawthorne formation of middle to late Miocene age.

FOLKSTON, GA—Du Pont, in a program of systematic examination of elevated bars and old high level shorelines along the Atlantic Coast, discovered the Folkston heavy mineral deposit in 1952. It was situated in a flat, broad elevated area a few miles north of the Boulougne, FL, ore occurrence and the two may at one time have been one, later cut by the St. Marys River. The flat area is better described as a marine terrace rather than a sand bar or old shoreline, as it is up to 6 km (4 miles) wide and over 32 km (20 miles) long. The zone in which commercial deposits of heavy minerals were found, 8 km (5 miles) east of Trail Ridge, is not geomorphically different from the remainder of the terrace. It is a relatively thin layer of sand resting on clay. Three lenses were outlined in development drilling: the Main Area, the West Extension, and the North Extension. Each of the lenses was bounded by swamps, underlain by barren sand and clay, which were probably original depressions rather than erosion channels. Humphreys Mining Co. completed mining of the Main Area for Du Pont in 1974 and moved mining and primary concentrating equipment to Boulougne, FL.

Titanium minerals comprised 56% of the heavy mineral suite in the Main Area, and the average TiO_2 content of a combined titanium mineral concentrate was about 72%. The grain size averaged 90 to 94% −100 mesh. By products were zircon and monazite.

New Jersey—The New Jersey Geological Survey, in an exploration program which grew out of observations of minor titanium mineral concentrations during investigation of monazite placers as sources of radioactive materials, identified the upper Tertiary sediments in the northern part of New Jersey's Coastal Plain as an ilmenite province in 1956 (Markewicz, 1969). The main heavy mineral formations were found to be the Miocene Kirkwood marine micaceous sand, silt, and clay, the Pliocene (?) Cohansey fluvial poorly sorted quartz sand, and the Pleistocene Cape May sands and gravels derived from the Kirkwood and Cohansey and from sediments farther inland. The Cohansey formation, which contains the greatest concentrations among these three, is ilmenite-rich in the northern third of its extent in New Jersey, in the vicinity of Lakehurst, about 48 km (30 miles) southeast of Trenton. Exploratory drilling by private companies resulted in the discovery of four ore bodies, and two heavy mineral mines were established.

LAKEHURST, NJ—The deposit of Glidden Pigments Group of SCM Corp. was located at Legler, about 3 km (2 miles) due north of Lakehurst, and was mined from 1962 to 1978. A mantle of Pensauken sand and gravel from 0.3 to 3.0 m (1 to 10 ft) thick overlay the Cohansey ore body, which was from 6 m (20 ft) to more than 12 m (40 ft) thick, with the average being 8 m (25 ft). A barren red sandstone 6 to 12 m (20 to 40 ft) thick underlay the ore, and beneath it was a zone in the Kirkwood formation, more than 12 m (40 ft) thick in places, averaging 4.5% heavy minerals. Only the Cohansey ore was mined.

The Cohansey sand is highly variable in color and in ilmenite, clay, and ironstone content. Occasional pebbles and limited gravel layers are present, and a coarse, iron stained, barren sand unit forms a bottom marker horizon. Cross-bedding, slump structures, roots and other pieces of organic material, and clay bodies up to 152 mm (6 in.) in diam are fairly common. Partially and wholly indurated iron oxide lenses and masses occur randomly above and below the water table (Anon., 1974a). A black, silty, lignite-charcoal band up to 5 m (15 ft) thick, found within the ore in the northwestern portion of the deposit, was interpreted by Markewicz as possibly the remains of a partially burned wooded swamp.

Heavy mineral content of the ore varied from 3% to more than 15% over distances of a few feet, with 5% being the average. The composition of the heavy mineral suite was reported by Markewicz as follows:

Mineral	Grain Count, %
Ilmenite-leucoxene	85–90
Zircon	2–4
Kyanite-sillimanite	1–2
Staurolite	tr-1
Rutile, anatase	tr-1
Tourmaline	tr-2+
Garnet, monazite, epidote, andalusite, hypersthene	tr

Glidden produced about 90,000 stpy of 61.5% TiO_2 ilmenite-leucoxene concentrate for its own consumption from 1962 to 1978.

MANCHESTER MINE—The Manchester mine of Asarco, Inc., also in the Cohansey formation, was about 97 km (60 miles) south of New York City, near Lakehurst, NJ. Geological features are similar to those at the Glidden operation at Lakehurst. Reserves were reported to be 180 million tons of sand averaging about 4% heavy minerals (Anon., 1974a) and 1.95% TiO_2 (Li, 1973). The operation was expected to have a 20- to 22-year life from 1973, when production began, based on a planned initial rate of 155,000 tons and a possible ultimate rate of 185,000 tpy of ilmenite, averaging 63% TiO_2. All ilmenite produced was under a sales contract to Du Pont. The mine was closed in March 1982 because of escalating costs and the prospect of a long-term oversupply situation. Figs. 1 to 4 are scenes of the operation.

Tennessee—A reconnaissance exploration program conducted by Du Pont to investigate reports of surface heavy minerals in 1957–1958 led to discoveries of ore grade occurrences of titanium minerals in the Cretaceous McNairy formation. McNairy is a poorly consolidated, clay-bearing fine-grained sandstone, about 91 m (300 ft) thick, which outcrops in a north-south belt just west of Kentucky Lake. The dip is very gentle to the west. Heavy minerals, including ilmenite, leucoxene, rutile, zircon, monazite, and minor amounts of kyanite, staurolite, tourmaline, and xenotime, are concentrated in the lower portion of the McNairy above the underlying Coon Creek formation. The ilmenite is somewhat altered, and concentrates have shown an average of about 62% TiO_2.

Ethyl Corp. and Kerr-McGee carried out exploratory drilling programs during the period 1970–1972, and both companies outlined several ore bodies. Production plans were deferred because of environmental problems and changing markets.

Australia: Australia is the world's most important heavy mineral sand mining country, producing 64% of the rutile mined in 1982, and 38% of the ilmenite.

FIG. 1—*General view of Asarco's dredge, pond, slurry pipeline, and pumping station at Manchester, NJ (courtesy of Asarco).*

FIG. 2—*Suction dredge recovered 20,000 gpm (20% solid) of titanium-bearing sands. The lake moved forward as the dredge advanced and closed in behind as clean sand from the concentration plant was returned (courtesy of Asarco).*

FIG. 3—*Asarco's custom-built Dixie CS–20 suction dredge was designed to excavate sands from a depth of 20 m (65 ft). The slurry was pumped by pipeline to a terminal for processing (courtesy of Asarco).*

FIG. 4—*View of a portion of the 1524 Humphrey spirals. They rejected over 95% of the slurry intake as waste in rougher, cleaner, and finisher cycles (courtesy of Asarco).*

Heavy mineral concentrations occur widely around the Australian coast, and small black sand deposits have been reported in Tasmania, Victoria, South Australia, and the Northern Territory. Those at Nepean Bay on Kangaroo Island have been mined in the past. In addition to onshore beach-type deposits, offshore occurrences have been discovered and explored in shallow water along portions of the New South Wales-Queensland coasts. In 1982, however, mining was restricted to three areas: (1) the coast of New South Wales and Queensland from Newcastle to Gladstone, (2) near Bunbury, Capel, and Busselton on the west coast of Western Australia south of Perth, and (3) near Eneabba 29 km (18 miles) inland and about 225 km (140 miles) north of Perth (Fig. 5).

As elsewhere, the heavy mineral grains were derived from the erosion of granites, intrusives, quartz reefs, and sandstones, and transported to the coast and concentrated by water and wind action. They occur in present-day beaches, fossil beaches, buried strand lines, and coastal dunes, and may be up to nearly 32 km (20 miles) inland as in Western Australia.

Ratios among individuals in Australian heavy mineral suites vary geographically. For example, between Sydney and Newcastle, rutile and zircon comprise about 90% of the concentrates, while farther north in New South Wales the rutile plus zircon content drops to 60 to 70%. Continuing northward, in southern Queensland the ilmenite level increases to about 60% of the heavy minerals. In the area between Busselton and Bunbury in Western Australia ilmenite makes up about 90% of the heavy mineral fraction, and near Eneabba concentrations contain 40 to 60% ilmenite, and about 10% rutile.

There is also a geographical variation in the chemical composition of ilmenite. Along the east coast ilmenite is generally too high in chromium to be suitable as a raw material for pigments manufacture by the sulfate process, and has found only a limited market in the Japanese steelmaking industry. The chromium content does, however, decrease from south to north, and the ilmenite is apparently suitable for upgrading to rutile grade material by some beneficiation processes. In Western Australia ilmenites from the Bunbury-Busselton area average 54 to 57% TiO_2, while Eneabba ilmenite grades around 61% TiO_2.

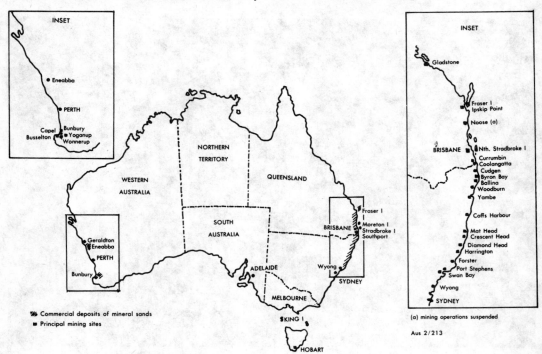

FIG. 5—*Location of principal ilmenite and rutile mineral sand reserves and mining operations in Australia, 1980 (Anon., 1980c, and Ward, 1972).*

Titanium mineral mining began in eastern Australia in 1934. Ore bodies were modern beach placers containing up to 50% heavy minerals, mostly rutile and zircon. All these high grade deposits have been exhausted over the past 40 years, and the average grade in the east by 1980 was about 3% heavy minerals. The increased cost of working lower grade deposits farther inland has been offset by improved techniques for mining and processing, and some ore bodies containing less than 0.25% TiO_2 as rutile (plus at least as much zircon) are now mined successfully on the east coast. In Western Australian ore bodies titanium minerals must be more highly concentrated because of the relative scarcity of rutile, and although there are wide variations within individual deposits, the average is between 5 and 10% heavy minerals. Mining of heavy mineral sands began in Western Australia in 1956.

The development of the large and important Eneabba ore field began in 1970. Rutile occurs in the heavy mineral suite there with ilmenite and leucoxene, so that with full-scale production commencing in 1974 and 1975, Western Australia became an important source of rutile for the first time.

Australia's titanium reserves are shown in Table 15. Table 16 lists company names, locations, estimated reserves, and 1980 production of rutile and ilmenite.

Eastern Australia—Ore bodies are in ancient beaches and bars in New South Wales and parts of Queensland. On North Stradbroke and Fraser Islands they are in high coastal dunes. A variety of mining equipment including dredges, bulldozers, front-end loaders, and bucket wheel excavators is employed by the seven producers.

Associated Minerals Consolidated Ltd. (AMC) is the world's leading producer of rutile and zircon, operating the world's largest mobile sand mineral concentrator on North Stradbroke Island off Brisbane. The suction-cutter dredge is 25 m (81 ft) long and 12 m (40 ft) wide. It is followed by a 34 x 34-m (110 x 110-ft) pontoon-mounted concentrator with a capacity of 1500 stph.

The Forster, N.S.W., mining plant of Mineral Deposits, Ltd., the second largest mineral sand producer in Australia, has a capacity of 900 to 1500 stph. It consists of a suction-cutter dredge, a 400-ton pontoon-mounted surge bin, and a concentrator mounted on a 24 x 31-m (80 x 103-ft) pontoon.

Consolidated Rutile Ltd. mines 91-m (300-

TABLE 15—Titanium Reserves of Australia, Thousands of Short Tons

	Rutile	Ilmenite
East coast	6,500	14,400
West coast	3,500	36,000
Total	10,000	50,400

Source: Anon., 1980b.

ft) dunes on North Stradbroke Island by bulldozer, frequently moving a sand-receiving trommel and slurrying unit to keep it close to the mining site. The sand is pumped to a nearby wet concentrator built in several basic units for rapid dismantling and moving a few times a year. Heavy mineral concentrates are barged to the dry mill on the mainland at Meeandah near Brisbane.

The opposition of conservationists to sand mining on Fraser Island led to the withdrawal of export licenses for Fraser Island concentrates at the end of 1976, and to restrictions on sand mining in other areas in Queensland and New South Wales.

Western Australia—Heavy mineral concentrations occur in three separate strand lines in the Bunbury-Busselton area: the present beach, the Capel line, and the Yoganup line, with the Yoganup line being oldest and 16 km (10 miles) inland. The TiO_2 content of the titanium mineral fraction of the heavy minerals increases with distance from the present coast.

Longshore drift in the area is southward and westward toward Cape Naturaliste, and it appears that longshore currents acting in the past sorted sands brought to the coast by northwestward-flowing rivers, creating heavy mineral deposits along beaches near their mouths. The existence of the old Yoganup and Capel lines indicates two past episodes of shoreline standstill.

There are no mining operations now on the beach. Cable Sands Pty. Ltd. and AMC are mining the Capel line, and Westralian Sands is working the Yoganup line. Both dredging and dry mining with scrapers, bulldozers, draglines, front-end loaders, and backhoes are practiced. In some deposits iron oxide-cemented, hard lenses near the bottom of the ore, which contain up to about 70% heavy minerals, are drilled, blasted, removed from the pits in blocks, and stored for possible future milling.

The Yoganup line sand has a high clay content, requiring dewatering of tailings in a series of large settling ponds. Water is scarce, and is conserved by recycling.

Commercial concentrates of ilmenite, leu-

TABLE 16—Australian Producers of Titanium Minerals, 1980

Company	Location Mines (m) and Separation plants (s)		Reserves Thousand st Rutile	Ilmenite	Production Thousand st Rutile	Ilmenite	Associated Companies and Controlling Interests
East coast							
Associated Minerals Con- solidated Ltd.	N. Stradbroke Island, Qld. Southport, Qld. Jerusalem Creek, N.S.W. Kempsey, N.S.W. Hexham, N.S.W.	m,s s m m s	800	2,000	71	NA	Consolidated Goldfields Australia Ltd., 61.7%
Consolidated Rutile Ltd.	N. Stradbroke Island Meeandah, Qld.	m s	1,100	2,400	60	NA	Cudgeon RZ, 50%, and Union Corp., Republic of South Africa
Currumbin Minerals Pty. Ltd.	Currumbin, Qld. Kingscliff, N.S.W.	m,s m	200	200	4	NA	Neumann Associate Companies Pty. Ltd.
Mineral Deposits Ltd.	Crescent Head, N.S.W. Myall Lakes/Hawks Nest, N.S.W.	m,s m,s	900	2,000	50	NA	Utah Mining Australia Ltd., 84%
Rutile and Zircon Mines (Newcastle) Ltd.	Harrington, N.S.W. Tomago, N.S.W.	m,s m,s	300	700	39	NA	Peko Wallsend Ltd., 50%, Kathleen Investments Australia Ltd. 50%
Reserves unavailable for mining because of environmental considerations			3,100	7,100	—	—	
Total east coast			6,400	14,400	224	60	
West coast							
Allied Eneabba Ltd.	Eneabba, W.A.	m,s	2,000	10,000	60	325	E. I. du Pont de Nemours, 59%
Associated Minerals Con- solidated Ltd.	Capel, W.A. Eneabba, W.A.	m,s ms	1,600	13,000	40	433	Consolidated Goldfields Australia Ltd., 61.7%
Cable Sands Pty. Ltd.	Capel, W.A. Bunbury, W.A.	m s	—	2,000	—	191	Kathleen Investments, principal shareholder.
Westralian Sands Ltd.	Yoganup, W.A. Capel, W.A. North Capel, W.A.	m s m,s	—	11,000	—	434	Tioxide Australia Ltd., 40%
Total west coast			3,600	36,000	100	1,383	
Total Australia			10,000	50,400	324	1,443	

Sources: Anon., 1980b; and industry contacts.

NA = Not available

coxene, zircon, and monazite are produced from this region of Western Australia.

Exploration northward toward Perth and beyond resulted in the discovery of heavy mineral occurrences in old strand lines at Boyanup, Waroona, Bull's Brook, and Gin Gin. Rutile appears significantly in the heavy mineral suites at Bull's Brook and Gin Gin. The ilmenite is reported to be high in chromium content and it could be more suitable as a raw material for beneficiation than for direct sale.

ENEABBA—It was suggested by Lissiman and Oxenford (1973) that the heavy mineral deposits at Eneabba were formed by agencies acting similarly to those which formed the ore bodies in the Bunbury-Busselton area. Rapid erosion of a Mesozoic sedimentary rock highland contributed sand to a westward-flowing stream which emptied into a bay partially protected on the southwest from south-to-north longshore currents by a headland. Longshore drift produced countercurrents within the bay which concentrated black sands on the beaches south of the mouth of the stream. There are several distinct strand lines marked by north-trending bands of high heavy mineral concentration at the bottom of the ore zone, and they

are thought to have been formed during relatively brief periods of sea level standstill. The strand lines are at successively lower levels from east to west. The geologic history of the ore field is made complex by evidence of reworking of the higher strand lines by waves which must have been associated with a sea which rose again, perhaps repeatedly, and by wind which created disseminated heavy mineral sands between and over the strand line deposits. Ore bodies in the northern portion of the district, which is about 16 km (10 miles) long and over 2 km (1½ miles) wide, are thought to have been formed by wind concentration of heavy minerals from black sand dunes then exposed in areas to the south.

Total reserves of the Eneabba district are in excess of 20 million tons of heavy minerals. Rutile, ilmenite, leucoxene, zircon, and monazite are present in variable proportions from one area to another, but the average ratios may be 1:5:0.2:2:0.2, respectively. Shipments of concentrates are from the port of Geraldton.

The development of Eneabba for mining presented considerable challenge because of its remoteness and relative lack of labor, power, water, transportation, and nearby port facilities. Furthermore, a portion of the ore, which occurs both in free-flowing sand and in harder, clay-rich sands, is bound up in nodules and in cellular and solid masses of iron oxide-cemented material locally called *laterite*. Extensive pilot testing of concentrating and separating methods and pilot mining were carried out to prove the physical and economic feasibility of heavy mineral operations. Production from Eneabba will make an important contribution to world titanium mineral and zircon markets for the next 15 years and more, and could compensate for diminishing production of rutile and zircon from the east coast.

KING ISLAND—Beach placers containing heavy minerals are located along the central part of the east coast from Naracoopa some 11 km (7 miles) along Sea Elephant Bay north to Cowper Point. The heavy mineral content is high, up to about 60%. Rutile and zircon occur in about equal proportions. Accessory minerals are leucoxene, ilmenite, magnetite, garnet, and cassiterite.

Naracoopa Rutile Ltd., a subsidiary of New Mount Costigan Mines Ltd., mined the sands by dragline and used trucks to haul to a wet plant stockpile. A dry plant had a production capacity of 10,000 stpy of rutile and 10,000 stpy of zircon. In early 1972 Buka Minerals N.L. acquired Naracoopa's mining properties and plant through its subsidiary, Kibuka Mines Pty. Ltd., and recommenced production after a reconstruction program.

China: Coastal sand deposits in Guandong and Guangxi provinces contain ilmenite, zircon, and other heavy minerals (Brady, 1981).

India: At one time India was a leading producer of ilmenite from the state of Kerala (formerly Travancore-Cochin). The beach sands were mined in the Manavalakurichi (M.K.) area and later the Quilon deposit of ilmenite near Chavra was put into production. These deposits supplied the bulk of the titanium ore used by the US prior to World War II.

The two deposits have more differences than similarities. The ilmenite in the M.K. deposit analysed only 54% TiO_2 and the sand was rich in garnet and monazite. The ilmenite in the Quilon deposit analyzes about 60% TiO_2. The sand carried almost no garnet and is high in monazite in only two places. Analyses of ilmenite from these areas are shown in Table 17.

The M.K. deposit consisted of buried seams of rich black sands at or just above the present ocean level. The beach sands were rich only when the monsoon storms sorted out the light minerals from the heavy ores.

TABLE 17—Ilmenite Analyses, India

	1, %	2, %
TiO_2	54.1	60.4
FeO	25.6	9.55
Fe_2O_3	15.3	24.6
Cr_2O_3	0.09	0.17
V_2O_5	0.23	0.36

Source: Gillson, 1959.
1. Travancore, "M.K."
2. Travancore; average "Quilon."

The Quilon deposit is not only much larger but the ilmenite is of a better grade. The deposit is a barrier beach extending parallel to the old shore in front of the mouths of two large rivers, the Panalur at Neendakara and Pallikal Todu. The ocean beach is black with layers carrying 80% heavy minerals and dunes on the beach are gray with 40 to 50% heavy minerals. Below them are old beaches now buried under dunes formed before the shore retreated, which are as rich as those now being washed by the waves. The extent of the old buried beaches has never been completely determined.

Malaysia: Substantial tonnages of ilmenite are produced in Malaysia as a byproduct of tin mining either as rough concentrates in mills using magnetic separation techniques or in the form of *Amang*, a crude mixture of heavy minerals which has to be further treated to recover the ilmenite content. The main centers of production are at Perak and Ipoh. The deposits are alluvial in nature.

Sierra Leone: A deposit along the Sherbro River was originally developed as a joint venture of Pittsburgh Plate Glass Co. and British Titan Products. Although relatively high grade (±1.5% TiO_2) the sands were extremely fine and disseminated in lumpy lateritic clay. Reserves are estimated to be between 3 and 30 million tons of contained rutile. The ore problems plus mechanical and political difficulties caused Sherbro Minerals to shut down in 1971 after only two years of operation.

Bethlehem Steel acquired 85% ownership of the property in 1976 (15% Nord Resources) and conducted an extensive prospecting and geological investigation that extended into 1977, finding higher grade deposits (±2.5% TiO_2) than that mined by Sherbro. Improvements were made in both the wet and dry flowsheets and as of 1981 the operation now called Sierra Rutile Limited was approaching specifications and design capacity of 110,000 stpy.

Rutile grades are highest in the topsoil, averaging 2.5% TiO_2, and in the basal sands and gravels, with up to 3.0% TiO_2. The average grade of the Mogbwemo deposit where Sierra Rutile began mining in 1979 is over 2.0% TiO_2 (Anon., 1981).

South Africa, Republic of: Shipments of rutile and zircon were started in 1977 from the Richards Bay mineral sands operation in Natal. Richards Bay Minerals manages the combined affairs of Tisand Pty. Ltd. and Richards Bay Iron and Titanium Pty. Ltd., the companies responsible for the operation of the mine and the smelter, respectively. A high-TiO_2, low-magnesium-plus-calcium slag (RB slag) containing 85% TiO_2 has been produced from ilmenite since 1978, and is reportedly suitable for use in either the sulfate or chloride titanium dioxide pigment processes. Since 1980, production rates have approached planned annual capacities of 440,000 tons of RB slag, 220,000 tons of low-manganese iron, 53,000 tons of rutile, and 110,000 tons of zircon. Proven reserves were estimated at 770 million tons grading 5% ilmenite, 0.3% rutile, and 0.65% zircon. Principal shareholders at the end of 1980 were QIT-Fer et Titane, Inc. (32%), General Mining Union Corp. (30%), and the Industrial Development Corp. of South Africa Ltd. (16%).

Operations in 1980 were in an area 17 km (11 miles) long and 1 km (0.6 miles) wide adjacent and parallel to the shoreline. The ilmenite, rutile, and zircon, along with magnetite, are evenly distributed throughout the sands which occur as dunes up to about 38 m (125 ft) in height on a clay base (Anon., 1980d).

Sri Lanka: Sri Lanka contains extensive beach deposits of titanium-bearing sands at Pulmoddai, Tirukkovil, Kelani River, Kalu River, Modoragam River, Kudremalai Point, Negombo, and Induruwa.

The Pulmoddai area contains 5.6 million st of titaniferous material with 2.451 million st of contained TiO_2. The deposit extends for a distance of 7 km (4½ miles), has a maximum width of about 91 m (300 ft), and a thickness of about 2.4 m (8 ft). There is no overburden. The deposit contains about 80% ilmenite and rutile. The average mineralogical composition of the black sand is as follows (Anon., 1974):

Ilmenite	70–75%
Rutile	10–12%
Zircon	8–10%
Sillimanite	±1%
Monazite	±0.4%

Other minerals present include spinels, garnet, tourmaline, etc., with quartz and shells as the main waste materials.

The separation of rutile has been adversely affected by the presence of excessive amounts of residual ilmenite and quartz in the tailings. The separation of zircon has been hampered by inadequate water and insufficient wet tabling equipment to handle the extremely fine-grained Pulmoddai ore.

Sand Deposits—Potential Sources

Brazil: Brazilian deposits of heavy minerals on ocean beaches occur in a zone about 161 km (100 miles) long, extending north from the northeast corner of the state of Rio de Janeiro up into the state of Espirito Santo as far north as the Rio Doce. There is also a zone in southern Bahia. Deposits are known to exist near Natal in the state of Rio Grande do Norte. Fig. 6 shows the location of the ilmenite deposits of Brazil (Gillson, 1950). Rutile deposits also are found in the state of Goias.

The minerals of the Brazilian beaches are:

Mineral	% Heavy Mineral
Magnetite	tr to 3
Ilmenite	35–75
Monazite	1–20
Zircon	5–35
Rutile	1/2–5
Sillimanite	1–1/2–5
Kyanite	1/2–2
Corundum	tr-1/2
Spinel	1/4–5
Staurolite	tr-3
Others	tr-3

The ilmenite assays from 39.7 to 61.6% TiO_2. Table 18 lists Brazilian ilmenite and rutile analyses.

Egypt: Rich deposits of black sands occur along the northern beaches of the Nile Delta for about 241 km (150 miles). There are two types: one is dark in color and contains about 70 to 90% heavy minerals and a second which is grayish-yellow to dark gray and contains about 40% heavy minerals. The deposits cover areas 10 km (6 miles) long and a few meters (yards) wide and up to 0.5 m (1½ ft) thickness.

The black sand concentrate is composed of ilmenite, magnetite, zircon, rutile, monazite, and garnet. Analysis of typical concentrate follows:

Ilmenite—55%
Magnetite—15–20%
Zircon—7–8%
Garnet—4–6%
Rutile—1.5%
Monazite—0.5–1%

FIG. 6—*The heavy mineral deposits of Brazil*
(Gillson, 1950).

New Zealand: Ilmenite and associated heavy minerals are found in New Zealand on the west coast of South Island from Jackson Bay to Karamea and on the west coast of North Island at the mouth of Waikato River, Muriwai, and at Manukan Heads. Total reserves near Westport are estimated to be between 17 to 31 million tons. Tests of the sand from Westport indicate the titanium content of the ilmenite averages about 47%.

Approximately one billion tons of sand are available between Karamea and Jackson Bay from which ilmenite could be recovered. These deposits on the west coast of South Island are believed to be one of the world's major reserves of low chromium ilmenite.

South Africa: Ilmenite-bearing sands occur in scattered deposits along the east coast of the Republic of South Africa from the area of East London to the Mozambique border and northward. Ilmenite sands also occur along the west coast particularly in the Vannhyrodorp district.

Titanium minerals are found on the east coast in three types of deposits:

1) Older red and brown coastal sands.
2) Recent dunes and beach sands.
3) Alluvium in coastal lagoons.

Older red and brown coastal sands occur in a belt of undulating fixed dunes which is roughly parallel to the coast. The belt ranges from a few meters (yards) to 6 km (4 miles) or more in width. Some dunes are as much as 152 m (500 ft) high but the average height is much less.

The heavy mineral content varies from 2 to 25%. The heavy mineral content is about:

Ilmenite—70–80%
Leucoxene—2–5%
Rutile—2–5%
Zircon—8–10%
Magnetite—2–8%
Monazite—tr-0.3%
Garnet, pyroxene, etc. 1–5%

Recent dunes and beach sands are partially derived from the older sands and contain the same mineral suites.

TABLE 18—Rutile and Ilmenite Analysis, %, Brazil

	1	2	3	4	5	6	7	8	9	10	11	12	13	14	15
TiO_2	58.5	61.6	55.6	38.9	66.5	70.5	79.3	69.0	75.2	96.7	92.9	93.5	97.8	97.1	95.6
FeO	35.4	32.0	36.6	—	26.2	24.6	19.8	30.9	21.7						
Fe_2O_3				44.2	1.8					2.0	6.8	6.6	2.3	3.0	3.4
SiO_2	0.2	2.5		4.0	5.2					0.5	0.4	0.1	0.2		0.7
CaO	0.9														
MnO	0.1														
MgO	2.5														
$H_2O-110°$	0.1														
$H_2O+110°$	2.7														

Source: Abreu, 1962.

1. Ilmenite from coastal sand, S.G.
2. Ilmenite and rutile, Bom Jardin, M.G.
3. Ilmenite from Pissaguera, P.R.
4. Ilmenite from São Sebastiao, S.P.
5. Ilmenite and rutile, Bom Jardin, M.G.
6. Ilmenite and rutile, Anápolis, G.O.
7. Material from riverbed, Rio Grande, M.G.
8. Ilmenite and rutile, Santa Quitéria, C.E.

9. Ilmenite and rutile, Neopolis, S.E.
10. Rutile, Mossâmedes, G.O.
11. Rutile, Mossâmedes, G.O.
12. Rutile, Corumba, G.O.
13. Rutile, Pirenopolis, G.O.
14. Rutile, Santa Luzia, G.O.
15. Rutile, Average of shipment from G.O.

Ilmenite concentrates occur in the alluvium in coastal lagoons, i.e., lagoon sands and in the bars at river mouths.

On the west coast, ilmenite-bearing sands exist in the Vannhyrodorp District between Strandfontein and the mouth of the Zout River. One deposit, a recent dune, skirts the coast for 6 km (4 miles) and another on the Geelwae Karoo is found in a narrow modern beach about 8 km (5 miles) long. The sands are un-consolidated and fine to medium grained.

Analyses of ilmenites from South Africa are shown in Table 19.

Titaniferous sandstone containing up to about 50% ilmenite with lesser amounts of rutile and zircon occur in the Ecca series of the Karoo system. They outcrop in several areas, principally near Bothaville about 483 km (300 miles) from the east coast in the Orange Free State. Total reserves are estimated at 85 million tons of material, some of which might be recovered with future technological improvements.

The Cape Morgan Titanium Mining Co. has produced a small amount of ilmenite in the Komga District from coastal sands.

Uruguay: Black sands are found northeast of Montevideo at Agua Dulces, in the state of Rocha. The sands extend along the coast for a distance of 11 km (7 miles) with an average depth of 5.5 m (18 ft). Reserves are estimated at 3.3 million tons of heavy minerals, with an average 2.5% heavy mineral concentrate. The composition of the heavy mineral fraction is approximately:

Ilmenite	60%
Zircon	5%
Rutile	1%
Monazite	0.6%

In addition, titanium sand deposits are known to exist in the following areas:

China: At Luanping and Chente, and the coast of Jiangsu province.

Korea: Resources of 2,535,000 tons with 507,000 tons of contained TiO_2.

Mozambique: Rutile and ilmenite are known to exist on the coastal beaches of Mozambique north of 16° 30′ latitude and near Vila Luisa, about 40 km north of Lourenco Marques.

TABLE 19—Analyses of South African Ilmenite

	1, %	2, %	3,
TiO_2	50.5	46.6	41
FeO	38.2	39.51	34
Fe_2O_3	9.2	9.11	19
Cr_2O_3	0.2	0.10	0
V_2O_5	0.12	2.76	0

Source: Anon., 1959.

1. Ilmenite concentrate, Umgababa, Natal; Anal Government Laboratory, Malaya.
2. Ilmenite concentrate, Isipingo, Natal; analysis, of Chemical Services, Pretoria.
3. Ilmenite fraction, Vanrhynsdorp District, Cape vince; analysis, Div. of Chemical Services, Pretori

USSR: Black Sea deposits; Aldan Riv Boludka River; Pit River in Siberia; Sylv River; Chusovaya River; and Vizhai River the Urals.

Exploration and Evaluation

Hardrock Ilmenite Deposits

Hardrock ilmenite deposits, because of th inherent magnetic properties, are readily am able to the application of aero and grou magnetic geophysical surveys. With few exc tions, these deposits respond to such an plication by reflecting abnormally positive m netic intensities (gammas).

Examples can be cited, however, where ne tive magnetic anomalies are associated w such deposits. In such cases, the ore occ either as a titaniferous-hematite concentrat or a titaniferous-magnetite occurrence wl the titanium content is greater than the i content. Theoretically, it would seem possi that a commercial deposit may exist wh no magnetic response would be obtained. S a deposit has not yet been found.

Once such anomalies are mapped, furt exploration may take place in the form of tailed surface geological observations and timate drilling to first test the anomalies hopefully to delineate a viable ilmenite depc

MacIntyre Development: The original covery of magnetite-ilmenite deposits at M Intyre Development, Tahawus, NY, was m. from surface outcrops. Extension of th outcrop locations has been made through of geophysical methods and diamond drilli

Geophysical—Since the ore is magnetic, geophysical methods used have been for purpose of outlining magnetic anomalies. Ea work was by dip needle readings over a g pattern extending outward from surface outcrops. With the advent of the aerial magnetometer the entire property was flown. This produced anomalies well beyond any previous work extending to areas of deep overburden and under-lake area.

Aerial work was followed with detailed ground magnetometer readings taken on 15-m (50-ft) spacings along section lines 30 m (100 ft) apart. This served to guide the location of diamond drill holes for exploratory drilling on one or two sections with drill holes spaced 122 m (400 ft) apart on section.

The initial ground magnetometer work on any anomaly is a section across the center of the anomaly at right angles to the long axis indicated from aerial work. The magnitude and gradient of the ground anomaly compared to the magnitude and gradient of the aerial anomaly, along the same section, gives an indication of depth and configuration of the source of the anomaly.

Drilling—If initial diamond drilling indicates an economic deposit, development drilling proceeds on a set grid pattern of 61 or 91 m (200 or 300 ft). Intermediate holes are drilled where necessary to fill in major gaps in geologic interpretation of structure, or ore continuations.

Core Sampling—Drill cores are visually logged and split for chemical assay. In ore areas, samples are taken of the entire core and composited in 1.5-m (5-ft) intervals for assay. In waste areas samples may be taken every 1.5 m (5 ft) and composited for a maximum of 8 m (25 ft) of core. Routine assaying is done to determine TiO_2 and total iron content. Based upon past experience, the nominal cutoff for ore is 13.5% TiO_2.

Mill Testing—Metallurgical laboratory work is done using core assay rejects to determine milling characteristics. Concentrates from the laboratory work are used for testing end use performance. Complete analyses are run on concentrates to determine presence and quantity of detrimental elements.

Tellnes Deposit, Norway: The Tellnes ilmenite deposit near Hauge-I-Dalane in Norway was discovered in 1954 as a result of an airborne magnetometer survey carried out for Titania A/S, with the object of locating new sources of ilmenite to provide an alternative to developing additional underground ore at Storgangen. Anomalies were also found at four other locations, so that ground geological study and diamond drilling had to be done at all of these sites to be certain that the best

deposit was selected for devlopment. A total of 10,058 m (33,000 ft) of drill holes was completed in 1956, and showed the total amount of ore in the Tellnes deposit to be about 300 million tons, averaging 18% TiO_2 (Brun, 1957; Anon., 1978a).

Allard Lake (Lac Tio) Deposit, Quebec: *Ground Surveys*—Preliminary investigation of the original ilmenite discoveries at Allard Lake (Hammond, 1949), indicated that all of these were too small to be of commercial importance. A detailed exploration program was carried out in 1946 to more thoroughly explore the area of 647 km² (250 square miles) where ilmenite had been found along certain of the lakeshores.

Geologic prospecting parties carried out traverses originating from the shores of the larger lakes, at 0.4-km (¼-mile) intervals in an east-west direction, normal to the strike of the previously known ilmenite occurrences. Mapping along and on both sides of the line of traverse was supplemented by dip needle readings at 61-m (200-ft) intervals or less. This work resulted in the discovery of eight ilmenite deposits, among them the very large Lac Tio deposit.

Drilling—A diamond drilling program followed to explore the Lac Tio deposit in depth. A series of vertical holes was drilled at 61-m (200-ft) intervals along five east-west sections to an average depth of 91 m (300 ft). Cores were sampled in 8 m (25-ft) lengths where ore intersections were sufficiently long. The specific gravity was determined on all samples before shipment for analysis. Later drilling on the portions of the ore body to be mined was carried out on a 15-m (50-ft) grid pattern.

Core Testing and Grade Control—Because of the marked difference in specific gravity between ore and gangue, it was found that density measurements gave a reliable measure of ore content. The accuracy of the method is about 2%, sufficient for the method to be used for controlling grade during mining.

Aeromagnetic Survey—An airborne magnetometer survey was carried out to explore the remainder of the anorthosite mass for other ilmenite deposits closer to the coast which might be developed more economically. Flight traverses were flown in a northwest-southeast direction at 152-m (500-ft) elevation, completing some 7200 km (4500 miles) of air traverse in a two-month period. The survey was first carried out over the known ore occurrences to obtain an indication of what results to expect from a new ore body.

No new deposits were discovered as a result of the aeromagnetic survey, but strong negative anomalies were obtained over all the known major ore bodies. Areas of disseminated ilmenite in anorthosite generally showed positive magnetic anomalies.

Otanmäki Deposit: The Otanmäki ilmenite-magnetite deposit and a neighboring deposit at Vuorokas were discovered in 1938 as a result of magnetic surveys by the Geological Survey of Finland (Harki et al., 1956).

Sand Deposits

Exploration: There are only a few large areas of the world where the granite-clan rocks and high-grade metamorphic gneisses which are likely to contain ilmenite (not titaniferous-magnetite) and rutile are close enough to continental margins to have contributed their erosion products to the sediments of coastal plains. Well-sorted sands are much more likely hosts than unsorted sands. These are the areas on which exploration efforts should be focused. Since the alteration of ilmenite to remove iron is aided by humic acid developed by the decomposition of organic material near the water table in hot and humid climates, it follows that the highest TiO_2 ilmenites are more likely to be found in the tropical and temperate regions of the world.

Titanium minerals are dark-colored and their concentration, as in black beach sands, tends to be fairly readily noticeable against the light brown or white quartz. Many sand ore bodies, therefore, have been discovered through surface observation of high-grade placer zones formed on beaches and along the courses of streams, and by following their traces into the larger, lower grade concentrations which constitute economic ore bodies.

There are areas in which potential heavy mineral concentrations in ancient beach sands may be masked by younger sand, gravel, or soil. Exploration under these circumstances then involves interpretation of geomorphic and subsurface geologic data to define areas which could have been beaches or dunes in the past, and then drilling to obtain samples.

Field Techniques—In areas where heavy mineral concentrations are suspected but where the concentration level is difficult to estimate because of dissemination, as in dunes, hand panning of samples is an excellent method of rapidly producing a clean concentrate. A hand magnet gives a quick identification between ilmenite and magnetite or titaniferous-magnetite. The presence of potentially valuable by-product zircon, monazite, kyanite-sillimanite, etc., can be determined with a hand lens. A Geiger counter or Scintillometer also helps in identifying radioactive minerals such as monazite and zircon. Wind and current action can develop very high-grade layers of heavy minerals on the surface which have no economic significance; thus samples for panning and examination should be taken from the maximum convenient depth. Often an idea of the vertical distribution of heavy minerals can be gained from observation of wave-cut cliffs in sands behind the beaches, cutbanks in stream margins, road cuts, construction excavations, and material encountered in sinking or drilling wells. Dark, heavy minerals may even be observed in the sand brought to surface by burrowing insects and small animals.

Hand augering with a two-man crew is possible to a depth of 6 m (20 ft) or more with a jointed auger stem and is reasonably rapid and inexpensive. Some heavy-mineral bearing sands contain so much clay that they are difficult to hand auger and a mechanical auger mounted on a light off-the-road vehicle (like a post-hole digger) is preferable. The samples so obtained are not precise because of the contamination of the hole by sand falling into it. The hole cannot be advanced nor reliable samples obtained below the water table when the material is free-flowing and easily disturbed by the auger.

Drilling—For the first phase of development, drilling equipment should have a depth capability of at least 15 m (50 ft) and preferably 30.5 m (100 ft). The selection of the type of drill will depend upon the "stiffness" of the ground as influenced by clay, hardpan, caliche, indurated and iron-oxide cemented layers; the presence of roots, stumps, and other organic material; as well as upon the elevation of the water table.

The truck-mounted jet drill is a popular exploration and development tool of the southeast US. One-inch flush-jointed steel pipe, with a chisel lower end or bit and perforations near the bit to permit water to jet forward and downward, is attached to a hammer of about 136 kg (300 lb) which is activated in 0.3-m (1-ft) strokes by a hand-held rope about a capstan winch. Water is supplied to the bit by a swivel connection above the hammer and by a duct through it. As the hammer rises, falls, and turns, it causes the bit to chop and churn into the ground and drives a 59-mm (2-in.) casing downward. The water pipe is within the 59-mm (2-in.) casing. The bit of the water pipe is about 25.4-mm (1-in.) or less ahead of the casing when casing and hammer are in contact. The sand sample is flushed out of the hole continuously by water rising in the annulus between water pipe and casing, and is collected at the surface in vessels or tubs. A jet drill under favorable conditions with short moves between holes can drill about 61 m/d (200 fpd) of hole. Its disadvantages lie in its inability to penetrate very hard layers, and the casing can stick in tenacious clay.

The auger-within-an-auger type of drill has good depth and penetration capabilities, particularly in the less free-flowing sands. The internal auger is advanced about 1.5 m (5 ft) to collect a sample on its flights, then the external auger is put down to the same depth to form a casing, and the internal auger is withdrawn for sample collection. There is some possibility of particularly fluid sands below the water table invading the casing when the internal auger is raised.

In Australia extremely light, gasoline-powered augers, portable and operable by two-man crews, have been developed and used for rapid, low-cost depth investigations. They are particularly successful in high, clean dunes.

A truck-mounted rotary drill driven by rapid strokes of a hydraulic hammer is also very useful. The drill string is a double pipe, and compressed air forced down the inner pipe returns the sample in the annulus between the drillpipe and casing. A drag bit with hardened cutting edges may be used.

It is important in all types of machine drilling to avoid contamination of samples by material originating higher in the walls of the hole. The hole and casing should be flushed free of loose sand after collecting each sample, and before the bit is advanced farther.

The nature of the sand and other materials penetrated by the drill is usually logged by a geologist, who makes a rough estimate of heavy mineral content and variation by panning a small portion of each sample.

Depending on hole diameter, a 0.9 or 1.5-m (3 or 5-ft) sample may be too large for laboratory requirements. If so, a simple heavy duty riffle may be used to reduce the weight to about 2 kg (5 lb). The bulk of the samples may then be bagged or drummed and left at the hole site for future reference.

Geophysical Techniques—Some titanium mineral ore bodies contain sufficient iron to be detectable by magnetometers in ground or airborne surveys, but many are too dilute and shallow to respond.

If monazite or radioactive zircon is present, low-level radiometric surveys may help in exploration. Scintillometers and Geiger counters are sometimes useful on the ground to define horizontal limits of ore and to detect internal variations in heavy mineral concentrations close to the surface.

The problem of downward contamination during drilling can lead to a misrepresentation of the total depth of ore because the heavy minerals, being higher in specific gravity, are hardest to remove by flushing with air or water and may be reported even when the hole has been advanced into barren underlying sand. A scintillometer probe with a surface recording instrument can show a sudden decrease in radioactivity from the walls of the hole at the true bottom of the ore. Radiometric surveying of all or at least some of the holes drilled during development of an ore body is a highly desirable check on the fidelity of drilling and sampling.

Evaluation of Deposits: An economic titanium mineral deposit must have reserves large enough to support depreciation over a period of at least 10 to 20 or more years. The capital investment in 1980 was in the range of $75 to $80 million in the US for a mine and mill plant with an output of 100 to 200 thousand stpy of ilmenite (or equivalent rutile) with given "normal" geologic parameters. Significant contributions can be made by zircon and other byproducts. Another general rule is that a new and separate ore body, if its production is to be all ilmenite which cannot be treated in an existing mill, should have a minimum reserve of about 1 million tons of recoverable TiO_2 in the titanium minerals. Small, highgrade concentrations are uneconomic under the present conditions.

The definition of economic reserves depends, of course, upon many factors, among them:

1) Cost of mining and milling, as influenced by depth of overburden (if any); cost of surface and mineral rights; and availability of water, power, labor, and transportation facilities for bulk shipments.

2) Recoverability in mining and milling.

3) Cost of treatment and disposal of waste slimes.

4) Cost of waste water treatment and land reclamation.

5) Distance to markets and cost of transport.

6) Ability of markets to absorb the type of titanium minerals to be produced, and prevailing prices for titanium minerals and byproducts.

Specifications—In the titanium mineral industry, as in some others, grade and reserve do not completely define the quality of a deposit. Titanium minerals for pigments manufacture must meet specifications regarding those chemical elements which would reduce the whiteness of the titanium pigment. These include chromium, manganese, vanadium, and columbium. To be considered economic for the chloride process, the ilmenite product should contain at least 60% TiO_2.

There are no industry-wide specifications for ilmenite in the pigments industry. Usually consumers and producers establish typical, maximum, and minimum levels, for TiO_2 and other oxides in the concentrates, in separate purchase contracts. In general terms, ilmenites containing not more than a few tenths of 1% of the elements—chromium, manganese, vanadium, and columbium—may be marketable. A few tenths of 1% of the oxides of aluminum and phosphorus may also be acceptable.

In ilmenite the ratio of ferric to ferrous oxide is important. Ferric oxide is objectionable in the sulfate process because it must be reduced to the ferrous condition in the processing, and this requires more handling and increases cost.

TiO_2 concentrates used in the chloride process (including ilmenite) must be low in Ca, P, and Mg. During chlorination, calcium and magnesium form gummy substances which cause plugging difficulties and which cannot be removed easily.

Thus, it is extremely difficult to generalize, since conditions and costs vary widely in different parts of the world, but some *minimum* guidelines for the industry in typical locations are about as follows:

Southeastern United States

Recoverable reserves, contained TiO_2: 1 million tons.

Average heavy mineral content: 3–4%, cutoff of 2%.

Average TiO_2 content of raw ore: 1% or a little less.

Average depth of ore: about 5 m (15 ft) for dredging, with a cutoff at 1.5 m (5 ft).

Eastern Australia (*Rutile and Zircon*)

Recoverable reserves, rutile: about 300 thousand tons.

Average heavy mineral content: 1%, cutoff around 0.5%.

Average TiO_2 content of raw ore: about 0.5%, cutoff around 0.2%.

Western Australia (*Ilmenite, Altered Ilmenite, Rutile, and Zircon*)

Recoverable reserves, heavy minerals: about 3 million tons.

Average heavy mineral content: about 5%, cutoff around 2.5%.

Clay minerals or slimes in heavy mineral sands are important because they must be removed. In addition, the disposition often calls for impoundment, sometimes with flocculation, and dewatering. Clay and other slimes require extra equipment and cost for removal and disposal, obscure the vision of operators who keep the equipment adjusted, and reduce the specific gravity contrast. Particle coatings make high tension separation more difficult, and in the case of zircon, may affect the sales value of the mineral. It is not unusual to find clay contents of 15% by weight, and some ore sands, notably at Eneabba in Western Australia, contain up to about 30% slimes in some places.

Particle size, shapes, and grain size distribution of the ore minerals can affect both mill recovery and marketability. Relatively coarse, well-rounded, uniformly sized grains are generally most desirable. A titanium mineral concentrate with the majority of the grains passing a 200-mesh screen may have limited market appeal, particularly to pigments manufacturers using the chloride process. The finer the particle size the more difficult it is to achieve good recovery in the three kinds of concentrating equipment normally used: gravity, high-tension, and magnetic.

Coating of particles by iron oxide or by secondary silica can change their natural magnetic and electrostatic properties, and such coatings may require removal prior to separation. Iron oxide cementation may produce nodules, cellular or even uniform masses of material so hard that the deposit requires drilling and blasting in mining. Liberation of grains can be poor in milling.

Angular minerals are more troublesome to separate in both wet and dry equipment and increase maintenance costs due to abrasion wear in pumps, screens, and piping.

Deposits in which a high proportion of the titanium content is in the form of secondary anatase present recovery problems. The anatase is the result of natural weathering of ilmenite and is both fine-grained and friable.

Testing and Evaluation—The number of drill holes required to give confidence in ore reserve calculations will vary directly with the irregularity of the deposit in depth, heavy mineral content, clay content, degree of concentration or development of hardpan or caliche, and abundance ratios among the members of the heavy mineral suite. Ore bodies tend to be several times greater in length than in width, reflecting their origins in narrow beach zones. The frequency of holes across the strike in the direction of most rapid change in physical characteristics should be much greater than along the strike. Where physical conditions such as the absence of swamps or particularly steep dune slopes permit, a regular grid system of drilling leads to simpler and probably more reliable ore reserves estimates. Holes at 30.5 m (100-ft) intervals along lines spaced 91 m (300 ft) apart have been found to make a good pattern in some deposits. Reserves in other deposits have been defined with holes at 15-m (50-ft) intervals on lines 152 m (500 ft) apart.

There are two common tests for ore or non-ore indications: weight percent of heavy minerals as determined by separation in bromoform or acetylene tetrabromide (which has a slightly higher specific gravity and separates shell fragments from minerals more effectively) and weight percent TiO_2 in the raw sand by wet chemical analysis. Both imply a knowledge of the mineralogical composition of the heavy mineral suite. Thus the total heavy minerals or total TiO_2 can be more or less directly related to weight percent of titanium minerals in the sand. In new areas either or both of these tests should be preceded by petrographic examination of heavy mineral concentrates from panned samples.

Once the presence of ore has been indicated and drilling changes from exploration to development, material handling and rapid analysis become critical, as up to about 50 samples a day, each representing 1.5 m (5 ft) of hole, can be generated by a single drill. Each sample should be dried, weighed, and screened to remove coarse particles. It is then slurried, agitated, decanted to remove slimes, dried, and weighed again. The original weight minus the weight of the coarse fraction and the weight of the dry sample after desliming gives the weight of slimes. The sample may then be split to a convenient size, say 50 g, for heavy mineral determination. The "sink" fraction is washed, dried, and weighed, and its weight related to that of the original dried sample.

Heavy mineral concentrates from samples from one out of every few holes should be petrographically examined and their mineralogical compositions determined by grain counting. Magnetite, which can be mistaken for ilmenite under the microscope, and ilmenite, which can be difficult to differentiate from rutile, may be removed as discrete fractions with different settings of a magnetic separator prior to petrographic study. Grain counting should be by skilled technicians, and all laboratory personnel should be alert to the possibility of the introduction of error due to coatings of iron oxide, silica, and clay. An acid or caustic attrition scrub of the heavy mineral concentrate can improve the accuracy of identification. Data gathered in such detailed studies of both titanium minerals and byproducts can be valuable in guiding mining operations. The information is highly susceptible to computer analysis for projections of production rates and economics.

The precise methods of laboratory tests outlined can produce determinations of heavy mineral contents higher than those obtained in later production. The difference is due in part to recoverability in the concentrator phase of milling. The addition of a mechanical heavy mineral concentrator such as a jigging table or a spiral to the sample analysis flow pattern after desliming and before separation in a heavy liquid can lead to a better early knowledge of recoverable reserves.

The weight of sand per unit volume varies among ore bodies, and the volume to weight conversion factor for reliable ore reserve calculations should be established by careful measurement of excavated volumes of representative sand types, and by averaging their dried weights. In the southeastern United States the factor varies from 41 to 45 kg (90 to 100 lb) per 0.03 m³ (cu ft). Exceptionally high grade sands have higher densities.

There is enough difference in physical characteristics of heavy mineral deposits that the best mining and milling methods for a new discovery may not be obvious. Pilot tests, either by commercial consulting organizations specializing in heavy mineral treatment and mill flowsheet design, or in a pilot plant erected at the site, are extremely valuable.

Garnar (1978) outlined a laboratory procedure for determination of separation characteristics, using a sample large enough to furnish at least 2 kg (5 lb) of heavy mineral concentrate. The heavy minerals are concentrated on a laboratory size shaking table, then split magnetically at 7,000 gauss to separate the ilmenite. The magnetic portion is passed over a laboratory high tension unit and the conductor fraction cleaned. The final conductor fraction is examined under the microscope, and if it contains 98% or more opaques, it is probably free from surface coatings that could interfere with dry milling. If coatings are present they may be removed by high energy attritioning. However, some ores may require treatment with acid or sodium hydroxide to remove coatings.

Material for pilot tests may be gathered by excavation with standard earth moving equipment or, preferably, by sinking numerous regular, vertical pits through the ore body by backhoe and/or by hand. Cribbing or concrete culvert sections may be necessary to keep the pits from caving. Pit walls can be channel sampled and the collected sand assayed to check results from nearby drill holes. This provides confidence in exploration and development drilling and sampling.

The degree of alteration of ilmenite in the deposit, together with the presence or absence of rutile, will determine the TiO_2 level of the concentrates that can be produced. Pilot plant work should be directed to production of various concentrates and testing the marketability by close communications and providing bulk samples, up to a few thousand tons, to consumers. Technical liaison between would-be producer and consumers is vital at this stage.

Complete chemical analysis should be performed on all potential products. The most sensitive elements in titanium mineral concentrates which can affect the whiteness of the pigment or interfere with the pigment manufacturing process include chromium, calcium, and magnesium. Some pigments manufacturers permit only a few tenths of 1% of these elements in their raw materials. The sum of the oxides of iron and titanium is employed as a measure of the purity of titanium mineral concentrates in some cases.

Because titanium minerals have various physical and chemical properties, each mineral product is not always suitable for utilization by each consumer. There is considerable latitude and flexibility in some instances because of highly developed technology, but most pigments manufacturing plants operate within narrow limits as far as the quality of the raw material is concerned. Usually both the raw material and the plant have to be tailored to fit one another, and in all cases the chemical and physical properties of a titanium mineral product have to be well-known to enable a manufacturer to judge its suitability. In a relationship such as this, naturally the best way to effect accurate evaluation of a titanium mineral deposit is through very close cooperation between would-be producer and would-be consumer, through all stages of exploration, bulk sample testing, development, and plant design and operation.

Evaluation of Results: The titanium mineral industry is restricted, with relatively few producers worldwide supplying relatively few consumers. Evaluation of a newly discovered and developed deposit is therefore undertaken within a narrow framework of economic and materials supply considerations. Present and future prices for products and byproducts under long-term purchase contracts have to be established with pigment manufacturers, and production rates forecast from pilot plant information. All aspects of production costs including those involved with pollution control and reclamation are taken into account in the economic model. Again, close liaison with consumers is essential as these companies, dependent on steady supply, are reluctant to enter long-term arrangements unless they can have reasonable assurance that the project is economically viable.

Preparation for Markets

Hardrock Ilmenite Deposits

MacIntyre Development, NY: *Mining*— Geologic sections and plans, produced from drill results, are used to determine open pit mining plans including waste and ore tonnages, mining ratios, and mining sequence. These, in turn, determine equipment and manpower requirements, and overall mining costs.

Mining is carried out on 14-m (45-ft) benches in an open pit using large blasthole drills, electric shovels, and diesel-electric trucks.

Milling—Ore from the mine is reduced in three stages of crushing to −14-mm (−9/16-in.) size. At the −64-mm (−2½-in.) size there is a magnetic separation step which discards about 20% by weight as a waste. Ore is reduced in size to −208 μm (−65 mesh) in rod mills and ball mills. Magnetic separators remove the magnetite fraction of the ore, and the nonmagnetics are treated by flotation to produce an ilmenite concentrate and tailing. A flowsheet of this milling process is shown in Fig. 7.

Prior to 1972, the ore was ground to −590 μm (−28 mesh) and was then fed to wet magnetic separators to remove magnetite. The nonmagnetic fraction was sized and fed to tables. Finer products went to a flotation plant to produce a flotation ilmenite concentrate. The wet table concentrate was dried and subjected to high intensity magnetic separation, producing a coarser ilmenite concentrate. A flowsheet of this earlier milling process is shown in Fig. 8.

Magnetite concentrate is dewatered on a filter and stockpiled. Ilmenite is filtered and then dried prior to shipment.

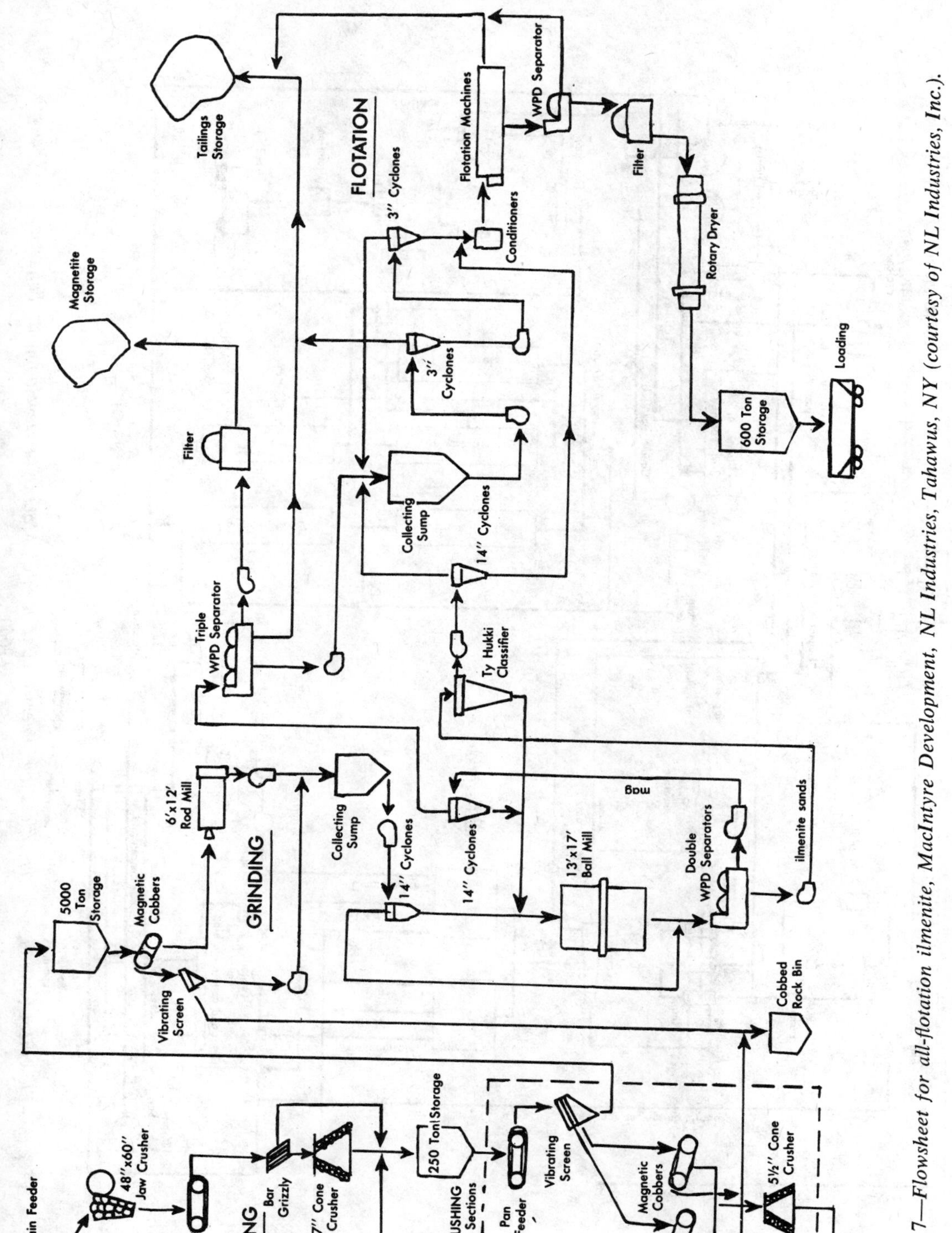

FIG. 7—Flowsheet for all-flotation ilmenite, MacIntyre Development, NL Industries, Tahawus, NY (courtesy of NL Industries, Inc.).

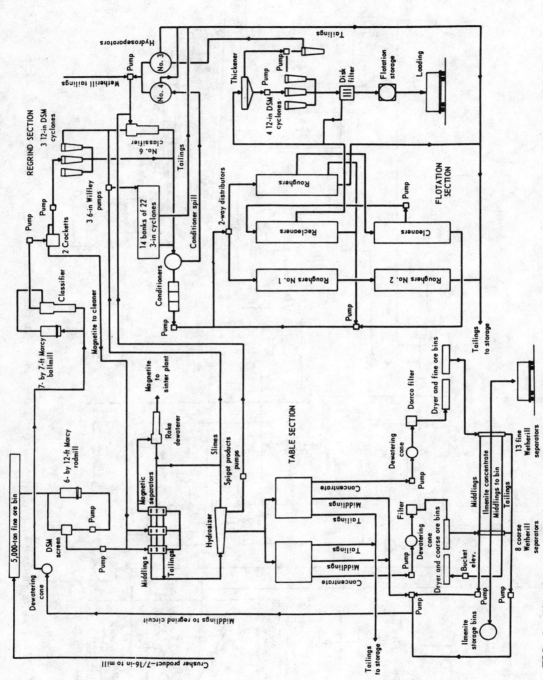

FIG. 8—Flowsheet for magnetic and flotation ilmenite concentrates, MacIntyre Development, Tahawus, NY (Peterson, 1966).

Transportation, Markets, and Consumption —Ilmenite and magnetite concentrates are shipped by rail in open cars. Ilmenite went mainly to the NL Industries TiO_2 pigment plant at Sayreville, NJ. A relatively new use for ilmenite is as a substitute for barite in well-drilling muds. The magnetite has been used as blast furnace feed, in refractories, and for heavy media separation in the coal industry.

Tellnes Deposit, Norway: *Mining and Milling*—The ore at the Tellnes deposit (Anon., 1978a; 1973c; Brun, 1957) is mined in an open pit using 12 to 14-m (40 to 46-ft) benches. The primary processing plant, including crushing, grinding, magnetic separation, and flotation is located close to the mine. The ilmenite flotation concentrate passes by gravity in slurry form through a pipeline in an underground tunnel to the final processing plant near Jossingfjord, where leaching and drying are carried out. The leaching is done with dilute sulfuric acid to remove apatite. The magnetic concentrate is transported by means of a smaller pipeline through the same tunnel. The ilmenite is dewatered on disk filters, to about 7% moisture, and dried in a rotary kiln.

The magnetite slurry is partially dewatered and subjected to flotation treatment to remove sulfides. The sulfide-free magnetite is dewatered, filtered on drum filters, and stored. The sulfide fraction is combined with a sulfide product from the ilmenite flotation circuit, thickened, and filtered. Production of these byproducts has been about 40,000 stpy of magnetite concentrate (65 to 65.5% Fe) and 10,000 stpy of sulfide concentrate (4 to 4.5% Ni and 2 to 2.5% Cu).

Transportation, Markets, and Consumption —Fully processed concentrates are stored in underground silos beneath the leaching and drying plant. A belt conveyor in a tunnel takes material from the silos directly onto ships in Jossingfjord.

Titania A/S is by far the largest producer of titanium concentrates in Europe and is the only important exporter in Europe. Even Spain and Finland, which produce ilmenite themselves, import some from Norway. Besides its proximity to the European market, Titania A/S has the advantage of relatively stable North Sea freight rates.

Tellnes ilmenite is the major feed material for the Kronos (NL Industries) group of sulfate plants in Europe, including plants in West Germany and Belgium as well as the Frederikstad plant in Norway. In addition, Titania has supplied companies in the United Kingdom, Italy, Spain, and other European countries, including Czechoslovakia (Anon., 1973c).

Allard Lake Deposite, Quebec: *Mining*—The ore at the Allard Lake deposit is mined by open pit methods. The mined ore has a grade of 32 to 36% TiO_2 and 39 to 43% iron. It is shipped by rail and boat via Havre St. Pierre to the company's beneficiation and smelting plant at Sorel, Que., for further processing (Elliot, 1959; Hatch and Cuke, 1956; Guimond, 1964; Hammond, 1949; Peirce, 1949).

Beneficiation—The ilmenite-hematite ore is crushed, and beneficiated at Sorel by heavy media (magnetite) separation of the −6.4-mm + 1400 μm (−¼-in. + 14-mesh) fraction, and Humphreys spiral concentration of the −1400 μm (−14-mesh) portion. Sulfur is eliminated from the combined gravity concentrates by heating in rotary kilns, using as fuel excess carbon monoxide from the electric smelting furnaces.

Because of its intimate intergrowths of ilmenite and hematite, the physically beneficiated concentrate, averaging 36.8% TiO_2 and 41.8% Fe, is still not high enough in TiO_2 content for direct use as a pigment plant feed. It is, therefore, smelted by a process developed by QIT-Fer et Titane, Inc. for the purpose of utilizing this type of high iron titanium ore.

Smelting—The smelting process used by QIT uses little or no flux, the furnace charge consisting of ilmenite-hematite concentrate with 0 to 10% lime and 8 to 14% low ash coal. Due to the extremely corrosive nature of titanium slag, it is necessary to keep the melt within solid banks of ore to prevent the slag from attacking the refractory lining. The average furnace measures 15 × 6 × 6 m (50 × 20 × 20 ft), and has 610-mm (24-in.) diam graphite electrodes on 2-m (6-ft) centers, heating the charge to 1500° to 1700°C, to produce a titanium-rich slag containing 70 to 74% TiO_2, and a form of pig iron known as Sorelmetal. QIT planned to increase the TiO_2 content of the slag to 80% in 1984. A flowsheet of the Sorel beneficiation and smelting process is shown in Fig. 9.

Transportation, Markets, and Consumption— QIT slag is widely used as sulfate pigment plant feed and is shipped by rail and by boat to various plants in Canada, the United States, and Europe. Production capacity has been periodically increased from 240,000 stpy of slag in the mid-1950s to a capacity of about 960,000 stpy slag (2.0 million tons ore) in 1980.

Otanmäki Deposit, Finland: The ilmenite is produced as a flotation concentrate, amounting

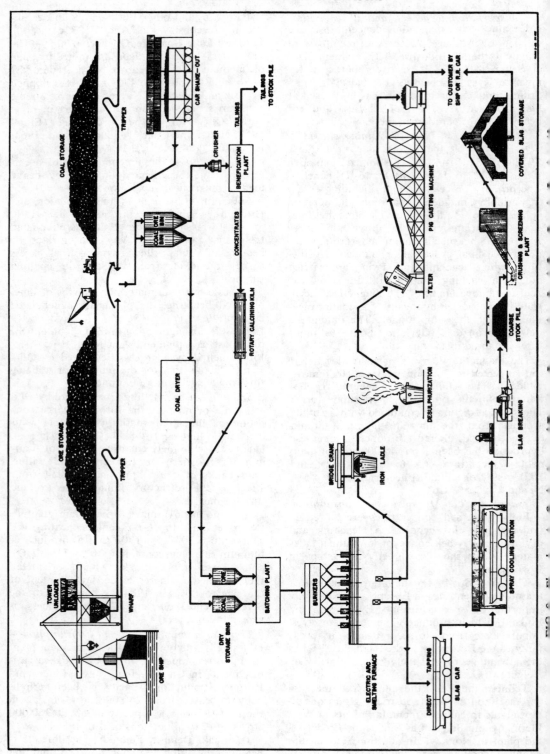

to about 160,000 stpy. Most of this is consumed domestically, but some is exported to other European countries. A vanadium-bearing magnetite is produced as a byproduct (Anon., 1971c; Anon., 1978b; Harki et al., 1956; Runolinna, 1957).

Beach and Alluvial Sand Deposits

Mining Methods: Sand titanium mineral deposits are most commonly mined by suction dredge where the ground is not excessively "stiff" because of clay, hardpan, or induration of heavy mineral layers due to cementation by iron oxide. Dredges of widely different power and production capacity are used, depending on local conditions and desired production rates (see Figs. 1–4). The minimum dredging depth is about 1.5 m (5 ft), the maximum about 21 m (70 ft). The elevation of the dredge pond is adjusted to compensate as much as possible for variations in topography. The lowest practicable cutbank above the water level in the pond is maintained to avoid wave-producing shocks caused by sudden collapse of large volumes of sand into the pond, but high coastal dunes on North Stradbroke Island in Queensland, Australia, are successfully dredged with sloping banks over 15 m (50 ft) high.

Some deposits are mined by dragline, some by bulldozer, some by front-end loader, and some by bucket wheel excavator. Occasionally a combination of equipment types is employed. Particularly rich but highly cemented layers near the bottoms of some Western Australian deposits are mined in their softer portions by backhoe.

Clearing and stumping of the land surfaces precedes mining, and it is now becoming standard in the industry to remove any topsoil which may be present and to pile it aside for spreading over the refilled excavation after mining has passed through.

In all cases the object of mining is to excavate the heavy mineral sand and transport it to a "wet plant," which makes the first step of milling through gravity concentration. Large trommels, mounted either on dredges or on mobile supports in dry mining operations, remove roots, lumps of clay, and oversize gravel, boulders, and cemented nodules or fragments before the slurried sand is pumped to the wet mill. In dredging operations the wet mill floats on pontoons moored to the bank and moved periodically to keep up with dredge advances. In dry mining the gravity concentrator is located close to the mine. In both cases the tailings of quartz and other light materials are returned to the mined excavation, so that at any given time part of the ore body is being prepared for mining, part is being mined, part is being filled, and part is being reclaimed.

There is some expansion of the ore sand in mining due to disturbance of grain packing, so that the volume returned to the excavation may be 4% or so greater than that removed. The creation of unfilled excavations is not unavoidable in normal heavy mineral sand mining, although it is possible to resculpture the surface by planned distribution of tailings to leave low hills and small lakes or ponds if desired. Replanting can be accomplished by seeding fast-growing, hardy grasses and fertilizing, or simply by respreading the stockpiled topsoil with its retained fertile seeds of native plants. In the pine forests of the southeastern United States, where trees are valuable for papermaking, it has been demonstrated that pine seedlings planted in areas where sand dredging has been done grow at a natural rate.

Processing Beach and Alluvial Sand Deposits §: Throughout the world, there are mining companies producing titanium, zirconium, and rare earth minerals from marine beach deposits. To concentrate and separate these sandlike minerals, a combination of gravimetric, high tension (electrostatic), and magnetic separations is the standard method. The metallurgy is straightforward and well-understood, and the valuable minerals are produced from the sands with relative ease.

When the minerals occur in stream placer deposits the production of high-grade products along with a high recovery presents a more difficult task of ore dressing.

Physical Characteristics of the Deposits and Minerals—BEACH DEPOSITS—In the marine beach deposits, the sands are very well-sized and the entire mineral suite is usually well-classified. The deposits are, to a large degree, unconsolidated free grains of sand. In some cases, there is cementation of grains due to organic matter, iron, or carbonates. The mining engineer must be fully aware of these conditions as the presence of these coatings not only creates mining but recovery and grade problems as well when the marine deposit is mined and concentrated. This type of deposit being formed on a beach tends to be long and shallow and may not be uniform in mineral composition due to the concentration characteristics of the waves and of the wind. The evalua-

§ This portion of the chapter was written by W. P. Dyrenforth, formerly Vice President, Mountain States Engineers, Tucson, AZ, now Marketing Executive, Colorado School of Mines Research Institute, Golden, CO.

tion of this type of deposit cannot be done on the basis of heavy minerals alone (those heavier than quartz), since the distribution of rutile and ilmenite and other commercial minerals in relation to noncommercial heavy minerals may vary to a large degree throughout the deposits.

Besides being well-sized and classified, usually unconsolidated, and easy to mine, these deposits have presented the ideal situation of a maximum degree of weathering. This means that there will be very few grains that aren't clearly a single mineral and that usually the high iron materials such as magnetite have almost completely disappeared. Also the ilmenite will usually be weathered to the point that the iron has been sufficiently leached away to leave an ilmenite high in TiO_2. It is interesting to note that many of the beach deposits from which monazite and zircon are produced are worked primarily because of the quality of the ilmenite which they can produce.

ALLUVIAL DEPOSITS—Alluvial deposits formed in stream beds present an entirely different problem to the mining engineer. Instead of uniform grain size and the classified characteristics of a beach deposit, the commercial mineral values may vary from -75 μm to 2 mm (-200 mesh to 10 mesh) in size. Any one mineral such as monazite in an alluvial deposit may vary from -75 μm to $+600$ μm (-200 mesh to $+30$ mesh) in size. The deposits are usually a heterogeneous mixture from clay on up to boulders depending on the age and source material of the stream.

These deposits, of course, present an entirely different mining and concentration problem. Extensive weathering and smoothing of the grains has not taken place so that one may have to contend with cemented grains of two or more minerals, and/or the grains are more likely to be coated with iron or clay.

Mining and Concentration Methods—The beach-type deposits, providing they are deep and extensive enough, are usually exploited by suction dredging. This has been considered the least expensive way of mining, provided the material is unconsolidated and that the cross section of the deposit lends itself to maintaining a dredge pond. Due to irregular cross section of some deposits in Africa, dredging was found to be impractical, so they are being mined by draglines. Dragline-type mining is useful where comparatively rich deposits may be worked, in that this method allows selective winning of rich streaks and material in pockets. Draglines also are able to remove consolidated

as well as unconsolidated overburden simultaneously.

A bucket-line dredge was planned for use on a marine beach deposit in the southeastern United States. It was believed that the higher capital cost of the equipment would be offset by more efficient mining of the ore, and that the ability of the large bucket-line dredge to carry its own concentration equipment should keep costly pumping of sand and water to a minimum. The plant was never built due to a titanium recession in the late 1950s.

Bucket-line dredges are almost a necessity for most stream-type deposits. They are required to break up the clay and other forms of consolidation as well as to handle the large stones, boulders, and even stumps and logs. Where only small gravel and stones occur, suction dredges have been used but they present a problem of lower mining recovery because the largest stones are left in the bottom of the pond. This is a mining recovery problem created by the loss of heavy minerals which are concentrated by water action into the interstices of the porous rocks.

Concentration of the minerals from sands is to date best done in small plants by use of wet shaking tables. For larger production, the spiral concentrator has been standard over a period of years. Flotation has been used to some degree. At the present time, there is a great deal of interest and work being done on various types of gravity concentrators to provide large tonnage rates of feed in comparatively light weight and low cost concentrating devices.

Jigs have been studied and adapted for this kind of concentration in many places. They were actively used in the British Titan Products operation in Africa and are still being studied in a number of places. There are a number of separators being developed and used that incorporate the sluicing principle. In the United States, examples of this type of separation action are found in the Cannon ring-conformation pinched-sluice concentrators, the Lamflo sluice concentrator developed by Carpco, and the pan concentrator developed by Du Pont. In Australia the Reichert cone concentrator which is also operated on the sluice principle has been very successful for large tonnage operations (Paterson, 1977). All of the separators based on the sluice principle require a feed density of 55 to 60% solids which result in quite a saving in water when compared to other gravity methods.

For the separation of the minerals from

stream-type deposits, the jig is usually chosen. The jig has long been used on alluvial deposits containing gravel and tests have indicated that they are the concentrating device least sensitive to extreme grain size variation. The jigs also allow large throughput capacity in a small space and can be mounted on the dredge. Mounting the concentration equipment on the dredge allows maximum maneuverability for the stream deposits that may be comparatively narrow and crooked.

SEPARATION OF THE VALUABLE HEAVY MINERALS FROM EACH OTHER—Two quite different flowsheets are required to separate the minerals and to produce commercial products from the two types of deposits. High-purity minerals are particularly difficult to produce at high recovery from stream deposits due primarily to the grain size distribution and also due to the unweathered characteristic of the deposits which means there are many middling products to be dealt with. These middlings create heavy circulating loads, are contaminants to finished products, and their disposal can cause losses in recovery.

Minerals concentrated from stream deposits will often require attrition scrubbing to remove surface coatings of organics, clay, and iron. The sands from beach deposits will often be uncoated. A beach mineral concentrate, however, that has been produced with the use of saltwater, may require a freshwater wash to remove salt prior to the dry separation steps.

Once the minerals are concentrated and the surfaces of the grains are clean, the next problem that confronts the ore dresser is the size range of the minerals. Table 20 shows the size range distribution of the heavy mineral concentrate from a typical Florida beach-type deposit as compared to the screen analysis of a concentrate from an alluvial deposit.

TABLE 20—Comparison Chart of Screen Analyses

Alluvial Concentrate			Beach Concentrate		
Screen Size, Mesh		%	Screen Size, Mesh		%
+20		9.6	+20		—
−20	+28	9.8	−20	+28	—
−28	+35	14.2	−28	+35	—
−35	+40	9.5	−35	+40	—
−40	+48	14.5	−40	+48	—
−48	+65	18.6	−48	+65	0.5
−65	+100	13.9	−65	+100	7.8
−100	+150	6.1	−100	+150	37.0
−150	+200	1.9	−150	+200	45.0
−200		1.0	−200		9.7
		100.0			100.0

Since the minerals from beach deposits are very well-sized and classified usually no further sizing is considered necessary. Normally grade of product and recoveries have been acceptable as produced without sizing. Further study seems to point out that even in beach-type deposits, sizing or classification may eventually be incorporated for optimum recoveries.

Sizing of the minerals concentrated from stream deposits is a must and can be accomplished in two ways. The entire feed to the dry separation plant can be sized into fractions which are handled separately in the mill or they may be introduced into the mill as unsized feed wherein the natural sizing effects of the various separation equipment are employed to do simultaneous separation and sizing.

A good example of taking advantage of the sizing effect of separating devices appears in nearly all of the plants producing rutile and its associated minerals. Grains of coarse quartz and/or staurolite or garnet are thrown off the rotors of both the high tension (electrostatic) and magnetic separators, since their mass and kinetic energy cannot be overcome by high voltage or magnetic fields present which are adjusted to the highest recovery of the bulk of the finer minerals present. These coarse grains report finally with the nonmagnetic conductor fraction which is typically rutile or cassiterite. It is considered a very simple system to purposely allow these coarse grains to follow through to the end of the flowsheet where they can be scalped off by a small screen rather than to attempt to screen the entire feed to the mill. At some plants, however, the occurrence of coarse-grained rutile requires a modification of this method. Screening is employed at two points in the circuit in conjunction with high tension sizing: (1) between the rougher and thrown cleaner rolls and (2) between the final pinned product of the pinned cleaner rolls and the primary magnetic separators used for zircon-quartz, monazite-staurolite separation. In the first case, coarse staurolite is rejected as oversize with some coarse rutile. This oversize product is then treated separately by magnetic and high tension separators at special settings to recover the rutile. In case two, the valuable minerals, zircon and monazite, are -500 μm (-35 mesh). Thus, screening at this point eliminates coarse quartz and staurolite, reduces the load on the magnets, and improves the overall efficiency. Figs. 10a and b are typical flowsheets for processing beach deposits and alluvial deposits.

If the entire feed to a plant is sized, it

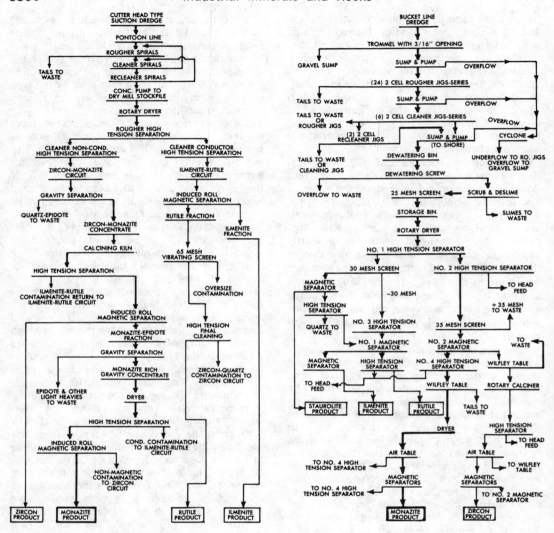

FIGS. 10a, b—*Typical flowsheets for processing beach sands (left) and alluvial deposits (right).*

creates the problem of multiple lines of separation equipment or an alternate of bulk storage and batch processing which requires a large amount of operational attention and resetting of the circuit. Accordingly, an alluvial flowsheet is usually designed to accept an unsized feed on a continuous basis and to make use of the sizing effect occurring during separation. At first glance this gives the appearance of a complicated flowsheet but after the operation and technical personnel have had time to balance the flow of the various minerals in accordance with their size, the production of finished mineral products is accomplished with

a minimum of operational changes. Highest recoveries can be gained by continual study and development of this type of return products system.

The rather simple flowsheet as commonly used for the production of titanium minerals and byproducts from beach sands is shown along with a flowsheet used for the production of same from an alluvial deposit. Notes on the various types of separation equipment are given, particularly on the alluvial flowsheet. The relative difference in the flowsheets required to produce valuable minerals from the two types of deposits is very apparent.

The production of high-grade minerals from a stream-type deposit is a more complicated problem than production from marine beach sands. The major differences in the metallurgical flowsheet required are due to the uneven grain size distribution. It is necessary to remove clay and iron coatings and the larger amount of middling minerals occurring due to the lack of weathering in stream-type deposits.

Future Considerations and Trends

With present-day technology, there are no totally competitive substitutes for titanium minerals as raw materials for pigments manufacture. There are, however, potential substitutes for rich sand deposits of ilmenite, altered ilmenite, and rutile, and these are in the form of extensive deposits of lower TiO_2 grade ilmenite in several parts of the world including South Africa, New Zealand, and possibly Egypt. Beyond these, there are widespread deposits of titaniferous magnetite sands which could produce concentrates averaging 10 to 20% TiO_2. Exploitation of the latter would involve development of technology to produce separate iron and titanium dioxide concentrates by smelting or hydrometallurgy. Weathered carbonatites in Brazil, India, and Africa have already demonstrated possible large reserves of anatase which could produce high TiO_2 concentrates if difficulties in recovery and concentration can be overcome.

Substitutes, Synthetic Rutile

Pigments: Titanium dioxide pigments have largely displaced white lead and other white pigments in the United States, and the question comes to mind whether titanium dioxide itself may some day be replaced by some new material with still better pigment properties. Some idea of the likelihood of this happening may be gained by a consideration of what other materials exist or might be synthesized that can match or surpass the physical and chemical properties that make titanium dioxide such an outstanding pigment: high refractive index (2.61 to 2.90 for rutile, 2.49 to 2.56 for anatase), high brightness and whiteness, chemical inertness, and the ability to be produced in the optimum particle size to develop maximum hiding power.

Materials having high refractive indices comparable to those of titanium dioxide include calcium, strontium and barium titanates, diamond, and silicon carbide. It seems unlikely that any of these would offer any substantial advantage in properties or cost, even if they could be made in the required amounts in pigmentary form.

A number of other materials, such as talc, clay, silica, and alumina, are white and can be used as pigment, but in most applications because of their low refractive indices they either do not provide the desired performance in terms of hiding power, brightness, etc., or are uneconomical because of the relatively large amounts needed. These materials are, therefore, used mainly as fillers rather than as pigments.

The use of microvoids to obtain opacity by means of a negative refractive index difference between the suspending vehicle and the pigment (microscopic gas bubbles in this case) has been found promising for dry hiding applications, such as in paper and in matte latex paint, rather than in glossy paint films (Kershaw, 1971).

At present, there seems to be no serious rival for titanium dioxide pigments. On the contrary, consumption of titanium dioxide pigments has increased at an average rate of about 2% per year since 1965.

Rutile Substitutes: Rutile concentrates containing about 95% TiO_2 have been the preferred feed material for chloride process pigment plants. As demand for rutile has grown, rutile prices have increased in line with the increasing cost of producing rutile from lower grade or more remote deposits as the older higher grade deposits become depleted. There has, therefore, been considerable cost incentive to develop processes for making rutile substitutes from the much more abundant, less costly ilmenite. Another approach to lower chloride feed material cost is to learn to handle lower grade materials, such as the rutile-leucoxene-ilmenite blends used by Du Pont, containing about 75 to 85% TiO_2. Extensive reviews of processes that have been investigated for making rutile substitutes from ilmenite have been published by the US Bureau of Mines (Henn and Barclay, 1970) and by the National Materials Advisory Board (Schlechten, 1972).

The main efforts to make a rutile substitute have been directed toward beneficiating ilmenite by using some combination of oxidation, reduction, leaching, and/or chlorination to remove most of the iron and produce a high-TiO_2 concentrate. Because this concentrate is intended for use as feed to fluid bed chlorinators, it is important that the particle size be closely controlled, with a minimum of fines. The sand ilmenite concentrates are generally of suitable size for this purpose, so that most beneficiation processes are designed to utilize sand ilmenites, preserving their original particle size as much as possible. The processes which are most favored for commercial applications are discussed briefly below, in approximately the order of their degree of development. The compositions of typical products from several of the processes are given in Table 21.

Ishihara Process—In 1971 Ishihara Sangyo Kaisha began operating a 30 kt/a synthetic rutile plant at Yokkaichi, Japan, and expanded production to 53 kt/a in 1974 (Anon., 1971b; Kataoka and Yamada, 1973; Yamada, 1976).

The process involves sulfuric acid leaching of reduced ilmenite in the presence of hydrated titanium dioxide, which is said to act as a seed to increase the rate of precipitation of titanium salts, allowing leaching of iron at relatively low temperature. The original particle size of the ilmenite, which may be either a sand ilmenite or a rock ilmenite ground and sized to about 840 μm to 75μm (20 to 200 mesh), is maintained in the leached product.

Ilmenite is mixed with coke and reduced in an oil-fired rotary kiln for about 1 hr at about 900°C, converting over 95% of the iron in the ilmenite to the ferrous state. After cooling, the residual coke is separated magnetically and the reduced ore is leached with waste acid from a sulfate process TiO_2 pigment plant. By adding the seed TiO_2 and keeping the leaching temperature at 130°C for 8 hr, iron and other impurities are selectively dissolved. The upgraded ilmenite is filtered, washed, and calcined at about 900°C, yielding an SO_3-free product containing over 95% TiO_2. Magnetic or gravity separation may be used to upgrade the washed concentrate before calcining, recycling the lower grade fraction.

Waste acid from the leaching step is either used as raw material for an ammonium sulfate plant, or is recycled in the leaching process with the addition of makeup acid.

Benilite Process—Benilite Corp. of America developed an ilmenite beneficiation process which involves partial reduction of iron oxides and hydrochloric acid leaching (Iammartino, 1976). Under Benilite licensing agreements, Ballarpur Paper and Straw Mills Ltd., of India, and Taiwan Alkali Co. Ltd., of Taiwan, each built beneficiation plants having 25,000 to 30,000 stpy production capacity (Anon., 1971; 1973a).

In a Benilite patent example, ilmenite is prereduced 40 min at 900°C with coke, and is then leached 5 hr in each of two steps at 100°C with 2.6 parts 20%HCl to give, after separation and drying, an ilmenite concentrate containing 92.1% TiO_2, 3.1% Fe_2O_3, and 0.25% FeO_3 (Chen, 1971). The particle size of the concentrate is essentially the same as that of the original ilmenite.

The proposed Taiwan plant was claimed to be the first closed-cycle effluent-free ilmenite upgrading plant ever to be built on a commercial scale. The effluent problem is avoided by regenerating and recycling the hydrochloric

TABLE 21—Composition of Rutile Substitutes and Typical Australian Natural Rutile Weight Percent

Constituent	Kerr-McGee	Ishihara	Benilite	Dhrangadhra	Western Titanium	Chlorine Technology	Mitsubishi Metal	Summit	Murso	Natural Rutile
TiO_2 (total)	90.5-93.0	96.1	93.0	90-92	92.0	97.5	96.7	94.0	96.2	95.2
Ti_2O_3					10.0					
Fe (total)	1.5-2.6		2.0	3.0	3.6	0.46				
Fe (metallic)					0.2					
FeO	0.1-0.6							2.0		
Fe_2O_3	2.0-3.0	1.30				0.66	0.4		1.5	0.9
SiO_2	1.5-2.5	0.50	1.6	1.5	0.7	0.46	0.1	0.5		1.0
Al_2O_3	<1.0-1.5	0.46	0.42	1.0	0.7	0.49	0.7	1.7	0.2	0.2
CaO	<0.35	0.01		0.05	0.03	0.065		0.7		0.02
MgO	0.05-0.40	0.07	0.05	0.05	0.15	0.027			0.04	0.07
Cr_2O_3	0.05-0.12	0.15	0.04	0.2		0.11		0.10	0.15	0.18
V_2O_5	0.10-0.25	0.20	0.06	0.25	0.12	0.04	tr	0.15	0.04	0.6
MnO	0.05-0.15	0.03	0.22	0.1	2.0	<0.01	0.06	1.7	0.05	0.01
S	0.04-0.07		0.01		0.15	0.006		0.02		0.008
Na_2O	0.0034-0.0047					0.05				<0.1
C	0.04-0.07				0.15	0.09				0.04
P_2O_5	0.05-0.09	0.17		0.2		0.072		0.1		0.03
ZrO_2	0.20-0.40	0.15	0.12	1.0		0.19		0.2		0.8
Ignition loss				3.8						0.2
Moisture	0.05-0.40			1.5						0.1
Nb_2O_5	0.20-0.40	0.25	0.6			0.07				0.3
SnO_2			0.14			0.003				0.03
Reference:	(1)	(2)	(3)	(4)	(5) (6)	(7)	(8)	(5)	(9)	(7)

References: (1) Kerr-McGee analysis; (2) Yamada, 1976; (3) Benilite analysis; (4) Anon., 1973; (5) Roberts, 1971; (6) Bracanin, et al., 1972; (7) NL Industries analysis; (8) Anon., 1972a; (9) Sinha, 1972.

acid, using Woodall-Duckham's spray-roasting process.

In 1977, Kerr-McGee Chemical Corp. began operation of a $53 million synthetic rutile plant at Mobile, AL, using the Benilite process. Following a shutdown in 1978 to devise process improvements, the plant reopened in early 1980, and in late 1981 was approaching its nominal production capacity rate of 110,000 stpy.

Dhrangadhra Process—The Dhrangadhra process involves hydrochloric acid leaching of ilmenite supplied by Indian Rare Earths Ltd., of Quilon in Kerala State. The hydrochloric acid requirements are met by an adjacent caustic soda plant. Capacity of the beneficiated ilmenite plant at Sahupuram in Tamil Nadu State was to be increased beyond the initial 25 kt/a (Anon., 1973).

Western Titanium Process—Western Titanium NL (now part of Associated Minerals Consolidated Ltd.) began operation of a semicommercial ilmenite beneficiation plant at Capel in 1968. A full-scale commercial plant with 30,000 stpy initial capacity began production at Bunbury in 1975, and was later expanded to about 64,000 stpy. The Western Titanium process involves high temperature oxidation to form a pseudobrookite structure, and reduction with carbon to metallize the iron, which is then oxidized in an aerated water slurry and separated as a hydrated iron oxide suspension, yielding a beneficiated ilmenite containing about 92% TiO_2. By adding as little as 2% of sulfur to the ilmenite it was found that iron and manganese contents of the upgraded ilmenite are lowered still more, raising the TiO_2 content to as high as 94% (Anon., 1973e, 1978c; Bracanin, 1972; Roberts, 1971).

Chlorine Technology Process—Chlorine Technology Ltd., a subsidiary of Rutile and Zircon Mines Ltd., developed a novel chlorine beneficiation process for upgrading ilmenite. This process was developed through the pilot plant stage at Mount Morgan, Australia.

In the Chlorine Technology process, ilmenite is selectively chlorinated to remove iron and other impurities as volatile chlorides, using a fluid bed reactor under reducing conditions at about 1000°C, with the novel feature of continuously removing a portion of the partially chlorinated bed, and separating it magnetically into an essentially iron-free fraction, and a second iron-oxide-containing fraction, which is recycled to the chlorinator. Recycling of the iron-containing part of the bed lowers TiO_2 losses, and produces less porous, harder, more abrasion-resistant grains in the final concentrate than when there is no recycling or when beneficiation is done by leaching. Chlorine can be recovered by oxidizing the ferric chloride formed during chlorination. The final product contains 95 to 98% TiO_2 and 0.1 to 0.5% Fe_2O_3 (Dunn, 1972, 1973).

Mitsubishi Process (Mitsubishi Metal Corp.)—In this chlorine beneficiation process, which has been developed through the pilot plant stage, ilmenite is first oxidized at 950° to 1000°C to convert all the iron to the ferric form. The oxidized material is then fed to a fluid bed chlorinator along with petroleum coke, where the iron is volatilized as ferric chloride. The ferric chloride is then oxidized to yield ferric oxide, and chlorine gas which is recycled to the chlorinator. The solids from the chlorinator are subjected to electrostatic and magnetic separation to remove unreacted ore, coke, and other impurities. About 10% of the original charge is returned to the fluidized reactor in the form of unreacted material. The final product contains 95 to 97% TiO_2 (Anon., 1972a).

Halomet Process—The Halomet process (Anon., 1971a; Othmer and Nowak, 1972) is based on a chemical displacement series that ranks metals according to the halogen affinities of their oxides, somewhat analogous to the electrochemical displacement series. The Halomet process uses dual chlorination—a reduction-chlorination followed by an oxidation-chlorination to take advantage of the ability of a metal chloride to react with the oxide of a metal above it in the chloride affinity series. The oxidation-chlorination reaction is therefore an effective separation technique.

The Halomet process was originally conceived as a method of using low grade ores for the production of iron. For application to ilmenite upgrading, partially reacted ilmenite is subjected to reduction-chlorination, with CO and Cl_2, forming $TiCl_4$ and $FeCl_3$, which pass to the oxidation part of the chlorinator where fresh ilmenite reacts with the $TiCl_4$ to form more $FeCl_3$ and TiO_2. Proper metering of chlorine permits isolation of high purity ferric chloride at one end of the reactor and a titanium dioxide concentrate at the other.

Halomet and Tellus, A.G., of Frankfurt, West Germany, collaborated in the operation of a large pilot plant to produce ferric chloride from low grade ores. The ferric chloride was oxidized in air to form ferric oxide and chlorine.

Summit Process—In this process ilmenite ore is oxidized in air or other oxygen-containing gases at 750° to 1200°C to convert all the iron to the ferric state. The oxidized ore is then reduced at 750° to 1200°C, using solid carbon fuels, carbon monoxide, hydrogen, or other reducing agents, reducing over 90% of the iron content to metal. The metallic iron is removed from the reduced ore by leaching about ½ hr with an aqueous solution of ferric chloride. The residue from the leaching process is washed and dried to yield a final concentrate containing up to about 94% TiO_2 (Roberts, 1971; Shiah, 1966). The spent leach solution is regenerated by sparging with air or oxygen to convert part of the ferrous chloride to ferric oxide, and the remainder to ferric chloride which is recycled to the leaching step.

Murso Process—This process was developed in Australia jointly by Murphyores Inc. Pty. Ltd. and the CSIRO Division of Mineral Chemistry. Ilmenite is first oxidized at 900° to 950°C with air, then reduced with hydrogen or hydrogen-containing gas in a fluid bed at 850° to 900°C, reducing the ferric iron to the ferrous state with a minimum formation of metallic iron. This results in formation of a very reactive synthetic ilmenite product which is leached in 20% HCl solution at 108° to 110°C at atmospheric pressure for 3 to 4 hr, yielding a concentrate containing over 95% TiO_2. Magnetic separation may be used to remove chromium and other impurities from the final product. HCl can be regenerated from the $FeCl_2$ spent leach liquor by known commercial processes, and recycled (Sinha, 1972). Planning was begun to build a commercial plant in Australia using the Murso technique, following a pilot plant development program carried out jointly with Mitsubishi Chemical Industries Ltd. in Japan (Anon., 1973d).

Other Ilmenite Beneficiation Processes— High TiO_2 concentrates have also been produced by direct leaching of ilmenite with sulfuric or hydrochloric acid, and by a variety of other processes, some of which are similar to those described above. A few of these processes are discussed in the following paragraphs.

Direct acid leaching of ilmenite requires more severe leaching conditions and more finely ground ore than when the ilmenite is oxidized and reduced before leaching. Leaching time may be shortened by use of high temperature and pressure, but the resulting concentrate is fine grained and would require agglomeration treatment to make it suitable for feed to the fluid bed chlorinators currently used in the chloride pigment process. Examples of processes of this type are those of Anderson and Rowe (1956), using sulfuric acid; and Leddy and Schechter (1962) and Marshall and MacMahon (1972), using hydrochloric acid.

In leaching tests on ilmenite and partially reduced ilmenite, Mackey found that leaching at atmospheric pressure takes place very slowly and is only partially effective, even with concentrated acids. After reduction for 6 hr with hydrogen at 900° C to reduce all of the ferric oxide to ferrous oxide, leaching times of 10 hr in two stages at 105° to 125°C and 10 to 20 psig resulted in leached concentrates containing about 90% TiO_2 (Mackey, 1974).

Electric furnace smelting processes have been investigated by the US Bureau of Mines, and by NL Industries, with the object of producing, besides pig iron, high-TiO_2 slags which would be suitable for chloride process and/or sulfate process pigment plant feed (Armant and Cole, 1949; Armant and Sigurdson, 1954, 1956; Banning et al., 1955; Cole, 1953; Moore and Sigurdson, 1949; Sigurdson and Cole, 1949; Stoddard et al., 1950). Concentrates used were classed as low, medium, or high grade, depending on the ratio of TiO_2 to iron oxides. The lower grade materials, such as the blend of magnetite and ilmenite concentrates produced at the MacIntyre Development, Tahawus, NY, which contains 20 to 25% TiO_2 and 60 to 70% iron oxides, yield a very large amount of pig iron, but the gangue oxide content is increased severalfold in the slag, compared with the original smelter feed. Gangue oxides such as magnesia and lime form low-melting chlorides which cause sticking of the charge when such slags are chlorinated.

Slags made from this low-grade blend contain 55 to 60% TiO_2 compared with 65 to 70% and 75 to 80% in slags made from medium-grade concentrate (MacIntyre ilmenite, 45% TiO_2) and high-grade concentrate (Quilon ilmenite, 59% TiO_2). The high-grade concentrate gives a slag with lower gangue content, but yields less iron product.

In general, slags made from low-grade concentrates are not suitable for manufacture of $TiCl_4$, since they contain too much magnesia and lime. The best type of slag for chlorination would be obtained from high-grade ilmenite. Slags from all three types of concentrate are digestible in sulfuric acid, provided impurities are low, and over-reduction of titanium has not occurred.

In processes involving reduction of the iron in ilmenite to the metallic state, followed by acid leaching, the reduction may be carried out with solid carbon or with hydrogen, and the leaching may be done with either sulfuric or hydrochloric acid to yield concentrates containing 90 to 95% TiO_2 (Michal and Nilsen, 1969; Nilsen, 1972; Volk, 1968). The acid used for leaching can be more dilute and leaching is faster than when reduction of iron is only to the ferrous state. When hydrogen is used for reduction, it is regenerated during acid leaching of the metallic iron, and can be recycled.

Chlorine beneficiation processes other than those discussed previously have been developed by other investigators (Daubenspeck and Toomey, 1956; Hughes and Arkless, 1965; Love et al., 1960). For example, Daubenspeck and Toomey (1956) patented a process in which the iron in ilmenite is selectively chlorinated with $TiCl_4$ under oxidizing conditions, comparable to the oxidation-chlorination part of the Halomet process.

The US Bureau of Mines has developed some novel processes for beneficiating ilmenite. One of these (Elger, Kirby, and Rhoads, 1976) is based on oxidation and fluxing of titania slag produced by electric furnacing of ilmenite. Phosphorus pentoxide flux additions enhance conversion of the titaniferous phase to rutile, forming rutile crystals of 70 to 150 μm in size in slags heated to temperatures of 800° to 1550°C. The synthetic rutile crystals are liberated from ground slag by treating with phosphoric acid to dissolve the glass matrix, followed by tabling to recover concentrates analyzing as high as 96.8% TiO_2. Another USBM process involves metallization of ilmenite and removal of the iron by reaction with CO at 110° to 130°C and 1000 to 1400 psig for 2 hr to form iron pentacarbonyl, which is removed and decomposed by heating to yield iron metal powder and CO which is recycled. The TiO_2 product is porous, has rutile structure, and is suitable for chlorination (Visnapuu et al., 1973).

The US Bureau of Mines also developed a process in which titanium carbide was recovered from domestic perovskite and ilmenite concentrates, and was chlorinated in fluid bed tests with good results (Elger, Hunter, and Mauser, 1980). The Bureau has recently been investigating treatment of titanium slags with mixtures of sulfur dioxide and oxygen, followed by leaching to remove calcium, magnesium, and manganese impurities, to render such slags usable as rutile substitutes in fluid bed chlorinators (Elger et al., 1981).

Government Control, Tariffs, Depletion Allowance

Sand titanium mineral deposits occur on or near ocean beaches for the most part. Government control of mining is in a sense exercised through establishment of seashore parks and wildlife agencies in some areas. In 1980 about 50% of the economic ilmenite and rutile resources on the east coast of Australia were unavailable for mining because of environmental considerations, which had led to withdrawal of export licenses for Fraser Island concentrates at the end of 1976.

In the United States the regulations imposed by the Environmental Protection Agency could have direct bearing on the economic viability of sand mining. Government regulations are beoming more strict especially regarding the waste disposal of effluents from pigment-producing processes and other pollution-producing operations. There are also land-use conflicts where black sand deposits exist, principally along the Atlantic littoral. In addition the high cost of land in ocean shore areas has been a major drawback to mining in coastal Georgia and Florida.

The US government strategic stockpile goal for titanium sponge metal was increased 48% in May 1980 to 195,000 st, while the goal for rutile was lowered 39% to 106,000 st. Government stockpile inventories in December 1982 were 32,331 st of titanium sponge metal, including 10,866 st of nonstockpile material, and 39,186 st of rutile.

The Australian government has involved itself with prices of titanium minerals for export under long-term purchase contracts in an effort to insure that as much value as possible will accrue to that country. There is a growing trend among governments of exporting nations to seek revenues to oblige consumers to undertake at least the first stages of pigment or metal manufacture in the country where the raw material originates, and this trend can be expected to continue.

Tariffs

US import duties on titanium concentrates, metal, pigment, and other compounds are given

TABLE 22—US Import Duties

Tariff Item	Number	Most Favored Nation (MFN)		Non-MFN
		Jan. 1, 1983	Jan. 1, 1987	Jan. 1, 1980
Ilmenite	601.5120	Free	Free	Free
Titanium slag	603.6200	Free	Free	Free
Rutile	601.5140	Free	Free	Free
Synthetic rutile	603.7010	6.3% ad val	5.0% ad val	30% ad val
Waste and scrap metal	629.1200	12.6% ad val	7.2% ad val	25% ad val
Unwrought metal, sponge	629.1420	17% ad val	15% ad val	25% ad val
Other unwrought metal	629.1460	17% ad val	15% ad val	25% ad val
Wrought metal	629.2000	17% ad val	15% ad val	45% ad val
Titanium dioxide pigments	473.7000	6.8% ad val	6.0% ad val	30% ad val
Titanium compounds except pigment grade	422.3000	6.3% ad val	4.9% ad val	30% ad val

in Table 22. The duties shown reflect results of the Tokyo round of negotiations completed in 1979, under which tariffs on many items were scheduled to be reduced in several stages over the period January 1, 1980 to January 1, 1987.

Depletion Allowance

Titanium ores carry a 22% domestic depletion allowance and a 14% foreign allowance.

Transportation

Shipment of ilmenite and altered ilmenite is in bulk, in lots of 15,000 or 20,000 tons if ocean transport is involved. Rutile may move in bulk shipments of 5,000 tons or more, but many shipments, especially those for spot market sales, involve bagged rutile. Shipping port facilities should include covered storage for finished concentrates and channels and berths for vessels of at least 15,000 and preferably about 30,000 tons.

Recycling and Ecology

Mining

Sand mineral mining presents few serious ecological hazards. The land is restored and can even be improved in low, flat areas. Dune areas can be left in nearly their original form and the sand can be stabilized by seeding and replanting. Nothing of an unnatural chemical character is added to the quartz sand tailings.

Disturbance and aeration of material during mining can cause bacterial activity in clay, and the bacteria can contribute to ground-water acidity, but careful control of pH in settling ponds can eliminate any hazard. In New South Wales, Australia, rutile and zircon are mined from sand in a government-controlled freshwater reserve.

Clay slimes may present some problem, but careful monitoring of impoundments to avoid breaching by erosion and of overflow water to ensure its clarity and nonacid nature has proved successful. The effluent water stream from a Florida operation enters a creek, and fish reportedly have found the area particularly to their liking, to the delight of local anglers.

Sand mineral mining has some advantage because no open excavation remains after mining has passed through, and the land can be returned to its original form and use at reasonable cost. Companies and private owners with large holdings have begun to appreciate that their properties may have both mineral and land value, and that two profits might be made: the minerals first and the land afterward.

Sulfate Process

The sulfate process results in relatively large quantities of spent acid and iron sulfate [up to about 2 kg (4 lb) of waste per 0.5 kg (lb) of titanium dioxide]. Some of the iron sulfate is crystallized out as copperas and is utilized for manufacturing iron oxide pigments and in water treatment and sewerage. The remainder generally has been disposed of, along with the spent sulfuric acid solution obtained on hydrolyzing the titanium, in waterways or the ocean. Even though an independent study (Anon. 1973b) found no ill effects from ocean disposal of such wastes, federal and state environmental regulations require the phasing out of all ocean dumping by 1990. Although the practice of disposing of the spent acid and iron sulfate results in a loss of sulfur and iron, to date all methods to recover these materials have proven uneconomic.

The sulfate process also has a considerable potential for causing air pollution during the vigorous digestion reaction of sulfuric acid with ground ilmenite or slag. To minimize such pollution, some producers use gas scrubbers on digestion tank stacks. NL Industries developed a modified digestion process which it called liquid phase digestion, and applied it to its Sayreville, NJ pigment plant in early 1982.

There are two general methods which are favored for recycling or neutralizing the acid in pigment waste liquor:

1) Concentration of H_2SO_4 by evaporating water, and roasting of the ferrous sulfate precipitated during evaporation, along with excess copperas, forming SO_2 for manufacture of new acid, and iron oxide for use as pigment, or as raw material for iron powder or steel manufacture.

2) Neutralization of H_2SO_4, and reaction of $FeSO_4$, with lime or calcium carbonate, converting the acid and sulfates to gypsum, and the iron to iron oxide.

The first method minimizes the amount of material to be finally sold or disposed of (only iron oxide) but requires large amounts of energy for evaporation and roasting and poses some problems of technology. The second method, neutralization, requires less energy, but uses large amounts of limestone and yields a gypsum byproduct (and CO_2 if limestone is used) for which markets must be established, or disposal areas provided.

Since 1975 American Cyanamid Co. has been operating a waste treatment facility at its Savannah, GA pigment plant, using limestone and lime to neutralize spent sulfuric acid-ferrous sulfate solution, forming gypsum and iron orides. Glidden Pigments, SCM Corp., has been operating a similar plant at its Baltimore sulfate process plant since 1977. In 1979 these pigment producers reported arrangements for the sale of byproduct gypsum. Gypsum from American Cyanamid's plant was to be converted by an adjacent Lemco, Inc. plant into briquettes for use by the cement industry. SCM was selling its byproduct gypsum to a local wallboard manufacturer. In 1982, G&W Industries was preparing to build waste neutralization facilities at its Gloucester City, NJ sulfate process plant. It was estimated in 1977 that the use of such neutralization processes would add about $90 per st to pigment cost, and that sale of all of the byproduct gypsum would recover only 25% of this added cost.

Chloride Process

The chloride process produces only about 0.5 kg (1.2 lb) of waste for each pound of titanium dioxide produced. The waste material is predominently ferric chloride which is usually dumped into the ocean. Du Pont has developed a process for recovering ferric chloride from the waste for use in the treatment of waste and drinking water. Tests are also being conducted on a process to recover the chlorine for reuse and to produce an iron oxide for the steel mills. However, large markets have to be developed for the waste products. In addition, even if markets were developed there is still a disposal problem for the miscellaneous metal chlorides that make up about 25% of the waste.

Bibliography and References

Anon., 1959, "The Mineral Resources of the Union of South Africa," Handbook, Geological Survey, 4th ed., US Geological Survey, pp. 312–318.

Anon., 1971, "Benilite Comes to Agreement on Upgrading Process," Industrial Minerals, No. 49, Oct., p. 28.

Anon., 1971a, "Chlorination Process Upgrades Low-Grade Ores," Chemical and Engineering News, Nov. 29, pp. 31–32.

Anon., 1971b, "Ishihara Takes the Plunge—40,000 Tons a Year of Synthetic Rutile," Industrial Minerals, No. 50, Nov., pp. 29–32.

Anon., 1971c, "Titanium Minerals 1. The Producers Reviewed," Industrial Minerals, No. 43, Apr., pp. 9–23.

Anon., 1972, "Brazilian Titanium," Mining Journal, Vol. 278, No. 7121, Feb. 11, pp. 118–119.

Anon., 1972a, "Mitsubishi Process for Upgrading Ilmenite," in Processes for Rutile Substitutes, National Materials Advisory Board NMAB No. 293, Mitsubishi Metal Corp., PB 212 898, June, 193 pp.

Anon., 1973, "Dhrangadhra Set to Expand Beneficiated Ilmenite Capacity," Industrial Minerals, No. 71, Aug., p. 35.

Anon., 1973a, "Effluent-Free Ilmenite Upgrading Plant," Mining Journal, Oct. 26, pp. 343–345.

Anon., 1973b, "Heavy Going Ahead for Waste Discharging at Sea," Chemical Week, June 27, pp. 45–47.

Anon., 1973c, "Norwegian Ilmenite: A/S TITANIA's Major Expansion at Tellnes," Industrial Minerals, No. 72, Sep., pp. 24–28.

Anon., 1973d, "Plan New Murphyores Plant," American Metal Market, Aug. 2.

Anon., 1973e, "30,000 Ton/Year Ilmenite Upgrading Plant," Mining Journal, June 8, p. 470.

Anon., 1974, "Pulmoddai's Mineral Sands," Industrial Minerals, No. 77, Feb., p. 27.

Anon., 1974a, "U.S. TiO_2 Mine on Stream," Mining Magazine, Vol. 130, No. 1, Jan., p. 7.

Anon., 1977, "RBM Progress Report," Sep., Richards Bay Minerals, 4 pp.

Anon., 1978a, "Titania: The Largest Producer of Titanium Minerals in Europe," Mining Magazine, Vol. 139, No. 4, Oct., pp. 365–371.

Anon., 1978b, "Rautauruukki—A Major Force in World Vanadium Supplies Is Still Expanding," World Mining, Mar., pp. 44–46.

Anon., 1978c, "The Hockin Process," Industrial Minerals, No. 93, Sep., pp. 55–57.

Anon., 1980a, "Titanio, Anuário Mineral Brasileiro," Brasilia, Vol. IX, p. 358.

Anon., 1980b, "Australia's Mineral Resources: Mineral Sands," Australian Department of Trade and Resources, 10 pp.

Anon., 1980c, "Australian Mineral Sands Processing Industry—Potential for Expansion," Commonwealth/State Joint Study Group on Raw Materials Processing, Australian Government Publishing Service, Canberra, pp. 17–18.

Anon., 1980d, "South Africa—Mining at Richards Bay," Mining Journal, Vol. 295, No. 7579, Nov. 21, pp. 411–413.

Anon., 1981, "Sierra Rutile," Mining Magazine, Vol. 144, No. 6, June, pp. 458–465.

Anon., 1983, "Titanium: Past, Present, and Future," National Materials Advisory Board, Commission on Eng. and Tech. Systems, Nat. Res. Council, Publication NMAB-392, National Academy Press, Washington, DC, 226 pp.

Abreu, S.F., 1936, "Rutilo no Brasil," Pub. 19, Instituto Nacional de Technologia, 32 pp.

Abreu, S.F., 1962, Recursos Minerais do Brasil, Vol. 1, Instituto Nacional de Technologia, pp. 566–579.

Anderson, W.W., and Rowe, L.W., 1956, "Method for Preparing Chlorination Feed Material," US Patent 2,770,529, Nov. 13.

Armant, D.L., and Cole, S.S., 1949, "Laboratory Smelting of Titaniferous Ores," Trans. AIME, Vol. 185, pp. 909–913; Journal of Metals, Dec.

Armant, D.L., and Sigurdson, H., 1954, "Preparation of Titanium Slag Composition," US Patent 2,680,681, June 8.

Armant, D.L., and Sigurdson, H., 1956, "Method for Producing Titanium Concentrates," US Patent 2,751,307, June 19.

Bachman, F.E., 1914, "The Use of Titaniferous Ores in the Blast Furnace," Iron and Steel Industry Yearbook, pp. 370–419.

Balsley, J.R., Jr., 1943, "Vanadium-Bearing Magnetite-Ilmenite Deposits Near Lake Sanford, Essex County, New York," Bulletin 940-D, US Geological Survey, pp. 99–123.

Banning, L.H., et al., 1955, "Electric Furnace Smelting of Ilmenite Concentrates from Valley County, Idaho," Report of Investigations 5170, US Bureau of Mines, 18 pp.

Barksdale, J., 1966, Titanium, Its Occurrence, Chemistry, and Technology, 2nd ed., Ronald Press, New York, 691 pp.

Bateman, A.M., et al., 1951, "Formation of Late Magmatic Oxide Ores," Economic Geology, Vol. 46, No. 4, June-July, pp. 404–426.

Beals, M.D., and Merker, L., 1960, "Three New Single Crystal Materials," Materials in Design Engineering, Jan., pp. 12–13.

Bishop, E.W., 1956, "Geology and Ground-Water Resources of Highlands County, Florida," Report of Investigation 15, Florida Geological Survey, 115 pp.

Bracanin, B.F., et al., 1972, "The Development of a Direct Reduction and Leach Process for Ilmenite Upgrading," Light Metals, W. C. Rotsell, ed., AIME, New York, pp. 209–259.

Brady, E.S., 1981, "China's Strategic Minerals and Metals—Titanium," The China Business Review, Vol. 8, No. 5, Sep.-Oct., pp. 62–65.

Broadhurst, S.D., 1955, "The Mining Industry in North Carolina from 1946 through 1953," Economic Paper No. 66, North Carolina Dept. of Conservation and Development, Div. of Min. Resources, pp. 26–27.

Broderick, T.M., 1917, "The Relation of the Titaniferous Magnetites of Northeastern Minnesota to the Duluth Gabbro," Economic Geology, Vol. 12, No. 8, Dec., pp. 663–696.

Brooks, H.K., 1966, "Geological History of the Suwanee River," Geology of the Miocene and Pliocene Series in the North Florida-South Georgia Area, N.K. Olson, ed., Atlantic Coastal Plain Geological Assn., 7th Field Trip, Southeastern Geological Society, 12th Field Trip, Guidebook, pp. 37–45.

Brun, R.M., 1957, "The Tellnes Story," Ilmenitten TITANIA, A/S, Norway, Summer issue.

Buddington, A.F., 1939, "Adirondack Igneous Rocks and Their Metamorphism," Geological Society of America Memoir 7, pp. 19–48.

Buddington, A.F., et al., 1955, "Thermometric and Petrogenetic Significance of Titaniferous Magnetite," American Journal of Science, Vol. 253, pp. 497–532.

Chen, H., 1971, "Hydrogen Chloride Leaching of Ilmenite," German Offen. 2,004,878, May 6.

Carstens, H., 1957, "Investigations of Titaniferous Iron Ore Deposits, Part I Gabbros and Associated Titaniferous Iron Ore in West-Norwegian Gneisses," K. Norske Vidensk. Selsk. Skr., No. 3, 67 pp.

Cobel, G.B., et al., 1980, "Electrowinning of Titanium from Titanium Tetrachloride: Pilot Plant Experience and Plant Projections," Titanium '80, Science and Technology, Proceedings, 4th International Conference on Titanium, Kyoto, Japan, May 19–22, H. Kimura and O. Izumi, eds., Vol. 3, AIME, New York, pp. 1969–1976.

Cole, S.S., 1953, "Titanium Concentrates," US Patent 2, 631,941, Mar. 17.

Cooke, C.W., 1941, "Two Shore Lines or Seven?," American Journal of Science, Vol. 239, No. 6, pp. 457–458.

Cooke, C.W., 1945, "Geology of Florida," Bulletin 29, Florida Geological Survey, 339 pp.

Coope, B., 1982, "Titanium Dioxide Pigments," Industrial Minerals, No. 181, Oct., pp. 47–51.

Daubenspeck, J.M., and Toomey, R.D., 1956, "Separation of Iron from Titaniferous Iron Ores," US Patent 2,758,019, Aug. 7.

Davidson, D.M., et al., 1946, "Notes on the Ilmenite Deposit at Piney River, Virginia," Economic Geology, Vol. 41, No. 7, Nov., pp. 738–748.

Diemer, R.A., 1941, "Titaniferous Magnetite Deposits of the Laramie Range, Wyoming," Bulletin No. 31, Geological Survey of Wyoming, 23 pp.

Dunn, W.E., Jr., 1972, "High Temperature Chlorination of TiO_2 Bearing Minerals II," AIME Annual Meeting, San Francisco, Feb.

Dunn, W.E., Jr., 1973, "Process for Recycle Beneficiation of Titaniferous Ores," Canadian Patent No. 932,964, Sep. 4.

Dybdahl, I., 1960, "Ilmenite Deposits of the Egersund Anorthosite Complex," XXI International Geological Congress, Copenhagen, Guidebook to Excursion No. C-10, pp. 49–53.

Elger, G.W., et al., 1976, "Producing Synthetic Rutile from Ilmenite by Pyrometallurgy," Report of Investigations 8140, US Bureau of Mines, 31 pp.

Elger, G.W., et al., 1980, "Preparation and Chlorination of Titanium Carbide from Domestic Titanium Ores," Report of Investigations 8497, US Bureau of Mines, 20 pp.

Elger, G.W., et al., 1982, "Utilization of Domestic Low-Grade Titaniferous Materials for Producing Titanium Tetrachloride," *Light Metals*, The Metallurgical Society of AIME, pp. 1135–1147.

Elliot, R.A., 1959, "Beneficiation of Titanium Ores with Particular Reference to Canadian Ores," *CIM Transactions*, Vol. 62, pp. 90–95; *CIM Bulletin*, Mar., pp. 186–191.

Evrard, P., 1949, "Differentiation of Titaniferous Magmas," *Economic Geology*, Vol. 44, No. 3, May, pp. 210–232.

Fine, M.M., and Frommer, D.W., 1952, "Mineral Dressing Investigation of Titanium Ore from the Christy Property, Hot Spring County, Arkansas," Report of Investigations 4851, US Bureau of Mines, 7 pp.

Fine, M.M., et al., 1949, "Titanium Investigations . . . The Laboratory Development of Mineral Dressing Methods for Arkansas Rutile," *Mining Engineering*, Vol. 1, No. 12, pp. 447–452.

Fish, G.E., Jr., 1962, "Titanium Resources of Nelson and Amherst Counties, Virginia (In Two Parts) 1. Saprolite Ores," Report of Investigations 6094, US Bureau of Mines, 44 pp.

Fish, G.E., Jr., and Swanson, V.F., 1964, "Titanium Resources of Nelson and Amherst Counties, Virginia (In Two Parts) 2. Nelsonite," Report of Investigations 6429, US Bureau of Mines, 25 pp.

Flint, R.F., 1940, "Pleistocene Features of the Atlantic Coastal Plain," *American Journal of Science*, Vol. 238, No. 11, pp. 757–787.

Flint, R.F., 1942, "Atlantic Coastal 'Terraces'," *Washington Academy of Sciences Journal*, Vol. 32, No. 8, pp. 235–237.

Flint, R.F., 1947, *Glacial Geology and the Pleistocene Epoch*, John Wiley, New York, 589 pp.

Force, E.R., 1980, "Is the United States Geologically Dependent on Imported Rutile?" Presented at 4th Industrial Minerals International Congress, Atlanta, GA, 4 pp.

Force, E.R., et al., 1976, "Geology and Resources of Titanium," Professional Paper 959–A through F, US Geological Survey.

Frey, E., 1946, "Exploration of Iron Mountain Titaniferous Magnetite Deposits, Albany County, Wyoming," Report of Investigations 3968, US Bureau of Mines, 37 pp.

Fryklund, V.C., Jr., and Holbrook, D.F., 1950, "Titanium Ore Deposits of Hot Spring County, Arkansas," Bulletin No. 16, Arkansas Research and Development Comm., Arkansas Div. Geology, 173 pp.

Fryklund, V.C., Jr., et al., 1954, "Niobium and Titanium at Magnet Cove and Potash Sulphur Springs, Arkansas," Bulletin 1015-B, US Geological Survey, pp. 23–57.

Garnar, T.E., Jr., 1978, "Geological Classification and Evaluation of Heavy Mineral Deposits," 12th Forum on the Geology of Industrial Minerals, Information Circular No. 49, Georgia Geological Survey, Atlanta.

Garnar, T.E., Jr., 1980, "Heavy Minerals Industry of North America," Presented at 4th Industrial Minerals International Congress, Atlanta, GA, 13 pp.

Geis, H.P., 1971, "A Short Description of the Iron-Titanium Provinces of Norway, with Special Reference to Those in Production," *Minerals Science Engineering*, Vol. 3, No. 3, pp. 13–24.

Gillson, J.L., 1932, "Genesis of the Ilmenite Deposits of St. Urbain, County Charlevoix, Quebec," *Economic Geology*, Vol. 27, No. 6, Sep. pp. 554–577.

Gillson, J.L., 1949, "Titanium," *Industrial Minerals and Rocks*, 2nd ed., S.H. Dolbear, ed., AIME, New York, pp. 1042–1069.

Gillson, J.L., 1950, "Deposits of Heavy Minerals on the Brazilian Coast," *Trans. AIME*, Vol. 187, pp. 685–693.

Gillson, J.L., 1956, "Genesis of Titaniferous C and Their Origin," *Trans. AIME*, Vol. 205, 296–301; *Mining Engineering*, Vol. 8, Mar.

Gillson, J.L., 1959, "Sand Deposits of Titanium Minerals," *Trans. SME-AIME*, Vol. 214, pp. 421–429; *Mining Engineering*, Vol. 11, No. 4.

Grogan, R.M., et al., 1964, "Milling at Du Pont's Heavy Mineral Mines in Florida," *Milling Methods in the Americas*, N. Arbiter, ed., Gordon and Breach, New York, pp. 205–229.

Gross, S.O., 1968, "Titaniferous Ores of the Sanford Lake District, New York," *Ore Deposits in the United States, 1963/1967*, John D. Ridge, ed., AIME, New York, Vol. 1, pp. 140–153.

Guimond, R., 1964, "Quebec Iron and Titanium Corporation, A Study in Growth," *Canadian Mining Journal*, Vol. 85, No. 11, pp. 47–53.

Guise, F.P., et al., 1964, "Titanium in the Southeastern United States," Information Circular 8223, US Bureau of Mines, 30 pp.

Hammond, P., 1949, "Allard Lake Ilmenite Deposits," *Canadian Mining & Metallurgical Bulletin*, Vol. 42, pp. 117–121.

Hammond, P., 1952, "Allard Lake Ilmenite Deposits," *Economic Geology*, Vol. 47, No. 6, Sep.–Oct., pp. 634–649.

Hargraves, R.B., 1959, "Petrology of the Allard Lake Anorthosite Suite and Paleomagnetism of the Ilmenite Deposits (Quebec)," Ph.D. Thesis, Princeton University, Princeton, NJ, May, 193 pp.

Harki, I., et al., 1956, "Discovery and Mining Methods at Finland's Largest Fe-Ti-V Mine," *Mining World*, Vol. 18, Aug., p. 62.

Hatch, G.G., and Cuke, N.H., 1956, "Iron Operations of the Quebec Iron and Titanium Corporation," *CIM Transactions* Vol. 59; *CIM Bulletin 533*, pp. 619–622.

Henn, J.J., and Barclay, J.A., 1970, "A Review of Proposed Processes for Making Rutile Substitutes," Information Circular 8450, US Bureau of Mines, 27 pp.

Heyburn, M.M., 1960, "Geological and Geophysical Investigation of the Sanford Hill Ore Body Extension, Tahawus, New York," Unpublished M.S. Thesis, Syracuse University, Syracuse, NY, 48 pp.

Hillhouse, D.M., 1960, "Geology of the Piney River-Roseland Titanium Area, Nelson and Amherst Counties, Virginia," Unpublished Ph.D. Thesis, Virginia Polytechnic Institute, Blacksburg, VA, 169 pp.

Hoyt, J.H., 1967, "Pleistocene Shore Lines: Guide to Tectonic Movements, Northern Florida and Southern Georgia," Abstracts, 1967 Annual Meeting, Geological Society of America, New Orleans, LA, p. 104.

Hubaux, A., 1956, "Various Types of Black Ores of the Egersund Norway Region," Bulletin 79, Ann. Soc. Geol. Belg., pp. 203–215.

Hughes, W., and Arkless, K., 1965, "Titanium Ore Beneficiation Process," British Patent 992,317, May 19.

Iammartino, N.R., 1976, "Beneficiated-Ilmenite Process Recycles HCl Leach Liquor," Chemical Engineering, Vol. 83, No. 11, May 24, pp. 100–102.

Jennings, E.P., 1913, "A Titaniferous Iron Ore Deposit in Boulder County, Colorado," AIME Trans., Vol. 44, pp. 14–25.

Kataoka, S., and Yamada, S., 1973, "Acid Leaching Upgrades Ilmenite to Synthetic Rutile," Chemical Engineering, Mar. 19, pp. 92–93.

Kays, M.A., 1965, "Petrographic and Modal Relations, Sanford Hill Titaniferous Magnetite Deposit," Economic Geology, Vol. 60, No. 6, Sep.-Oct., pp. 1261–1297.

Kershaw, K.W., 1971, "A New Class of Pigments," Australian OCAA Proceedings and News, Aug., pp. 4–9.

Kish, L., 1972, "Vanadium in the Titaniferous Deposits of Quebec," CIM Bulletin, Mar., pp. 117–123.

Kroll, W.J., 1940, "Method for Manufacturing Titanium and Alloys Thereof," US Patent 2,205,854, June 25.

ddy, J.J., and Schechter, D.L., 1962, "Pressure Leaching of Titaniferous Material," US Patent 3,060,002, Oct. 23.

Leone, O.Q., et al., 1967, "High-Purity Titanium Electro-won from Titanium Tetrachloride," Journal of Metals, Vol. 19, No. 3, pp. 19–23.

Li, T.M., 1973, "Startup of Manchester Mine and Mill Boosts U.S. Production of Primary Ilmenite," Engineering & Mining Journal, Dec., pp. 71–75.

Lissiman, J.C., and Oxenford, R.J., 1973, "The Allied Mineral N.L. Heavy Mineral Deposit in Eneabba, W.A.," Conference Volume, Australasian Institute of Mining & Metallurgy, pp. 153–161.

Lister, F.G., 1966, "The Composition and Origin of Selected Iron-Titanium Deposits," Economic Geology, Vol. 61, No. 2, Mar.-Apr., pp. 275–310.

Llewellyn, T.O., and Sullivan, G.V., 1980, "Recovery of Rutile from a Porphyry Copper Tailings Sample," Report of Investigations 8462, US Bureau of Mines, 18 pp.

Lloyd, R.R., 1956, "Production of Titanium Metal at Henderson, Nevada," Rocky Mountain Minerals Conference, Salt Lake City, Utah, Sep. 28.

Love, F.E., et al., 1960, "Beneficiation of Titaniferous Iron Ores," US Patent 2,933,373, Apr. 19.

Lynd, L.E., 1960, "Titanium," Industrial Minerals and Rocks, 3rd ed., J. L. Gillson, ed., AIME, New York, pp. 851–880.

Lynd, L.E., 1980, "Titanium," Mineral Facts and Problems, Bulletin 671, US Bureau of Mines, 18 pp.

Lynd, L.E., 1983, "Titanium," Mineral Commodity Profile, US Bureau of Mines, 17 pp.

Lynd, L.E., and Merker, L., 1955, "Metal Titanate Composition," US Patent 2,723,916. Nov. 15.

Mackey, T.S., 1974, "Acid Leaching of Ilmenite into Synthetic Rutile," Ind. Eng. Chem. Prod. Res. Develop. Vol. 13, No. 1, pp. 9–18.

MacNeil, F.S., 1949, "Pleistocene Shore Lines in Florida and Georgia," Shorter Contributions to General Geology, Professional Paper 221-F, US Geological Survey, pp. 93–106.

McMurray L.L., 1944, "Froth Flotation of North Carolina Ilmenite," Trans. AIME, Vol. 173, 1947; Mining Technology, Jan. 1944.

Markewicz, F.J., 1969, "Ilmenite Deposits of the New Jersey Coastal Plain," Geology of Selected Areas of New Jersey and Eastern Pennsylvania and Guidebook of Excursions, S. Subitzky, ed., Rutgers University Press, New Brunswick, NJ, pp. 363–382.

Marshall, J. and MacMahon, D.M., 1972, "Ilmenite Dressing," German Offen. 2,200,954, Dec. 7.

Martens, J.C.H., 1928, "Beach Deposits of Ilmenite, Zircon, and Rutile in Florida," 19th Annual Report, Florida Geological Survey, pp. 124–154.

Masten, A.H., 1923, The Story of Adirondac, Princeton Press, Princeton, NJ, 199 pp.

Merritt, C.A., 1939, "Iron Ores of the Wichita Mountains, Oklahoma," Economic Geology, Vol. 34, No. 3, May, pp. 268–286.

Michal, E.J., and Nilsen, A.E., 1969, "Titanium Dioxide Concentrate and Method for Producing the Same," US Patent 3,446,590, May 27.

Michot, P., 1956, "The Deposits of Black Ores of the Egersund Region," Bulletin 79, Ann. Soc. Geol. Belg., pp. 183–201.

Minkler, W.W., 1980, "Titanium in 1980," Journal of Metals, Vol. 33, No. 4, Apr., pp. 41–44.

Moore, C.H., Jr., 1940, "Origin of the Nelsonite Dikes of Amherst County, Virginia," Economic Geology, Vol. 35, No. 5, Aug., pp. 629–645.

Moore, C.H., Jr., 1955, "Rutile Boule and Method of Making Same," US Patent 2,715,070, Aug. 9.

Moore, C.H., Jr., and Sigurdson, H., 1949, "Petrology of High Titanium Slags," Trans. AIME, Vol. 185, pp. 914–919; Journal of Metals. Dec.

Moorhouse, W.W., 1938, "Some Titaniferous Magnetites in the San Gabriel Mountains, Los Angeles County, California," Economic Geology, Vol. 33, No. 7, Nov., pp. 737–748.

Nicholls, G.D., 1955, "The Mineralogy of Rock Magnetism," Advances in Physics (Supplement to Philosophical Magazine), Vol. 4, p. 113.

Nilsen, A.E., 1972, "Extraction of Iron from Titaniferous Ores," US Patent 3,647,414, Mar. 7.

Osborne, F.F., 1928, "Certain Magmatic Titaniferous Ores and Their Origin," Economic Geol-

ogy, Pt. 1, Vol. 23, No. 7, Nov., pp. 724–761; Pt. 2, Vol. 23, No. 8, Dec., pp. 895–922.

Othmer, D.F., and Nowak, R., 1972, "Halogen Affinities—A New Ordering of Metals to Accomplish Difficult Separations," *AICHE Journal,* Vol. 18, No. 1, Jan., pp. 217–220.

Parker, G.G., and Cooke, C.W., 1944, "Late Cenozoic Geology of Southern Florida," Bulletin 27, Florida Geological Survey, 119 pp.

Paterson, O.D., 1977, "How Many Low Grade Ores Are Now Being Recovered by Gravity Concentration," *World Mining,* Vol. 30, No. 8, July, pp. 44–49.

Paulson, E.G., 1964, "Mineralogy and Origin of the Titaniferous Deposit at Pluma Hidalgo, Oaxaca, Mexico," *Economic Geology,* Vol. 59, No. 5, Aug., pp. 753–767.

Peirce, W.M., et al., 1949, "Titaniferous Material for Producing Titanium Dioxide," US Patent 2,476,453, July 19.

Peterson, E.C., 1966, "Titanium Resources of the United States," Information Circular 8290, US Bureau of Mines, 65 pp.

Pings, W.B., 1972, "Titanium, Pt. 1," *Colorado School of Mines Industries Bulletin,* Vol. 15, No. 4, July, 13 p.

Pings, W.B., 1972a, "Titanium, Pt. 2," *Colorado School of Mines Industries Bulletin,* Vol. 15, No. 5, Sep., 17 pp.

Pinnell, D.B., and Marsh, J.A., 1954, "Summary Geological Report on the Titaniferous Iron Ore Deposits of the Laramie Range, Albany County, Wyoming," *Mines Magazine,* Vol. 44, No. 5, p. 30.

Pirkle, E.C., and Yoho, W.H., 1970, "The Heavy Mineral Ore Body of Trail Ridge, Florida," *Economic Geology,* Vol. 65, No. 1, Jan.-Feb., pp. 17–30.

Pirkle, E.C., et al., 1974, "The Green Cove Springs and Boulougne Heavy Mineral Sand Deposits of Florida," *Economic Geology,* Vol. 69, No. 7, Nov., pp. 1129–1137.

Pirkle, F.L., 1975, "Evaluation of Possible Source Regions of Trail Ridge Sands," *Southeastern Geology,* Vol. 17, No. 2, Dec., pp. 93–114.

Priscu, J.C., 1966, "Electrolytic Cell for the Production of Titanium," US Patent 3,282,822, Nov. 1.

Ramdohr, P., 1950, *Die Erzmineralien und ihre Verwachsungen,* Akademie Verlag, Berlin, 875 pp.

Ramdohr, P., 1956, "Die Beziehungen von Fe-Ti Erzen und Magmatischen Gesteinen," Bulletin No. 173, Comm. Geol. Finlande, pp. 1–18.

Ramsdell, J.D., and Mathews, D.R., 1960, "Effect of Impurities on Mechanical Properties of Electrolytic Titanium," Report of Investigations 5701, US Bureau of Mines, 12 pp.

Reed, D.F., 1949, "Investigation of Christy Titanium Deposits, Hot Spring County, Arkansas," Report of Investigations 4592, US Bureau of Mines, 10 pp.

Reed, D.F., 1949a, "Investigation of Magnet Cove Rutile Deposits, Hot Spring County, Arkansas," Report of Investigations 4593, US Bureau of Mines, 9 pp.

Retty, J.A., 1944, "Lower Romaine River Area, Saguenay County, Quebec," Report 19, Quebec Dept. of Mines & Geology, pp. 3–29.

Roberts, J.M.C., 1971, "Ilmenite Upgrading," *Mining Magazine,* Vol. 125, No. 6, Dec., pp. 543–551.

Rose, E.R., 1969, "Geology of Titanium and Titaniferous Deposits of Canada," Economic Geology Report No. 25, Geological Survey of Canada, 177 pp.

Ross, C.S., 1941, "Occurrence and Origin of the Titanium Deposits of Nelson and Amherst Counties, Virginia," Professional Paper No. 198, US Geological Survey, 59 pp.

Ross, C.S., 1947, "Virginia Titanium Deposits," *Economic Geology,* Vol. 42, No. 2, Mar.-Apr., pp. 194–198.

Runolinna, U., 1957, "How Otanmäki Floats Ilmenite in Finland," *Mining World,* Vol. 17, Apr., pp. 49–55.

Schlecten, A.W., 1972, "Processes for Rutile Substitutes," National Materials Advisory Board, Publication No. NMAB-293, National Academy of Sciences, June.

Shiah, C.D., 1966, "Process for Producing Titanium Dioxide Concentrate and Other Useful Products from Ilmenite and Similar Ores," US Patent 3,252,787, May 24.

Sigurdson, H., and Cole, S.S., 1949, "Melting Points in the System TiO_2-CaO-MgO-Al_2O_3," *Trans. AIME,* Vol. 185, pp. 905–908; *Journal of Metals,* Vol. 1, Dec.

Singewald, J.T., Jr., 1913, "Titaniferous Iron Ores of the United States, Their Composition and Economic Value," Bulletin 64, US Bureau of Mines, 145 pp.

Sinha, N.H., 1972, "Ilmenite Upgrading by the Murso Process," *Light Metals, 1972,* W. C. Rotsell, ed., AIME, New York.

Snyder, L.E., 1966, "Electrolytic Production of Titanium," US Patent 3,274,083, Sep. 20.

Stamper, J.W., 1970, "Titanium," *Mineral Facts and Problems,* Bulletin 650, US Bureau of Mines, pp. 773–794.

Stephenson, R.C., 1945, "Titaniferous Magnetite Deposits of the Lake Sanford Area, New York," Bulletin No. 340, NY State Museum, 95 pp.

Stoddard, C.K., et al., 1950, "Pilot Plant Smelting of Ilmenite in the Electric Furnace," Report of Investigations 4750, US Bureau of Mines, 15 pp.

Sun, S.S., 1971, "Fission Track Study of the Cheney Pond Titaniferous Iron Ore Deposit, Tahawus, N.Y.," Ph.D. Thesis, Washington University, St. Louis, MO, June, 134 pp.

Temple, A.K., 1966, "Alteration of Ilmenite," *Economic Geology,* Vol. 61, No. 4, June-July pp. 695–714.

Thompson, J.V., 1977, "Appraising Large Diameter Core and Percussion Drilling for Bulk Samples," *Engineering and Mining Journal,* Vol. 178, No. 8, Aug., pp. 80–82.

Toewe, E.C., et al., 1971, "Evaluation of Columbium-Bearing Rutile Deposits, Magnet Cove, Arkansas," Prepared for US Department of the Interior, Office of Minerals and Solid Fuels, Contract No. 14–01–0001–1738, Battelle Memorial Institute, Columbus, OH, Sep., 134 pp.

Vaasjoki, O., 1947, "Microstructure of Titaniferous Iron Ore at Otanmäki," Bulletin No. 40, Comm. Geologique de Finlande, pp. 107–114.

Visnapuu, A., et al., 1973, "Conversion of Ilmenite to Rutile by a Carbonyl Process," Report of Investigations 7719, US Bureau of Mines, 20 pp.

Vokes, F.M., 1968, "Forelesninger i Malmgeologi I," *Noregs Malmgeologi,* Hösten, Vol. 99, p. 488.

Volk, W., 1968, "Reduction of Metallic Oxides," US Patent 3,383,200, May 14.

Ward, J., 1972, *Australian Mineral Industry Quarterly Review*, Bureau of Mineral Resources, Geology and Geophysics, Vol. 25, No. 1, Sep., pp. 12–22.

Watson, T.L., and Taber, S., 1913, "Geology of the Titanium and Apatite Deposits of Virginia," Bulletin 3A, Virginia Geological Survey, 308 pp.; *Metallurgical and Chemical Engineering*, Vol. 13, 1915, p. 573.

Wimmler, N.M., 1946, "Titaniferous Magnetite Deposits in Montana," Report of Investigations 3981, US Bureau of Mines, 12 pp.

Yamada, S., 1976, "Ilmenite Beneficiation and Its Implications for Titanium Dioxide Manufacture," *Industrial Minerals*, No. 100, Jan., pp. 33–40.

Tripoli

JAMES C. BRADBURY *

HENRY P. EHRLINGER, III †

Tripoli is a naturally occurring, very finely divided form of silica found chiefly in some midwestern and southeastern states and used commercially as fillers and abrasives.

Definitions

Tripoli is a microcrystalline, finely particulate, more or less friable form of silica that appears to be the product of leaching of siliceous limestone or calcareous chert. The term was originally applied to a deposit near Seneca, MO, that resembled material of that name found near Tripoli in North Africa (Hovey, 1894). The two deposits were subsequently found to have different physical characteristics —the North African tripoli, now called *tripolite,* is a diatomite, composed of the siliceous skeletons of microscopic marine plants called diatoms; the Missouri tripoli contains no diatom remains. The term *tripoli,* however, continued to be used for the Missouri material and is now applied in a general way to most silica deposits similar to it in characteristics and geologic origin. In commercial trade *tripoli* is commonly understood to designate material from the Missouri-Oklahoma field; silica from southern Illinois, the other major producing area, is referred to commercially as *amorphous silica.* Each term, however, may be used commercially for material, regardless of place of origin, that has the characteristics or uses commonly ascribed to the material from one or the other major producing area. For example, in the commodity price listings, *Engineering & Mining Journal* routinely lists under *Tripoli,* prices "f.o.b. Elco, IL" and "f.o.b. Seneca, MO,

* Principal Geologist and Head, Geological Group, Illinois State Geological Survey, Champaign, IL.

† Senior Supporting Development Engineer, DRAVO Research Center, Pittsburgh, PA.

and Rogers, AR," and under *Silica, amorphous,* prices "f.o.b. IL," and "f.o.b. Dierks, AR."

Amorphous silica, the commercial designation given to southern Illinois tripoli, is, like the term *tripoli,* a misnomer. Mineralogically, the southern Illinois deposits are composed of microcrystalline quartz, and no amorphous material has been detected during X-ray and scanning electron microscope investigations (Leamnson, Thomas, and Ehrlinger, 1969; Thomas et al., 1970; Keller, 1978).

Soft silica is another term that has been applied to Illinois and Tennessee tripoli, presumably to distinguish it from the more compact Missouri material. It has also been used in the ceramic trade to distinguish tripoli from "hard" silica, or silica flour, produced by pulverizing silica sand (Heinz, 1937).

Rottenstone, produced commercially in Pennsylvania, is similar to tripoli in that a major constituent is finely particulate silica, and its uses are much the same as those of tripoli— as abrasives and fillers. The origin of rottenstone also is similar to that of tripoli—decomposition of a siliceous sedimentary rock. The parent rock is defined as a siliceous limestone (Gary, McAfee, and Wolf, 1972; Thrush, 1968) or as shale. Heinz (1937) quotes a brief statement describing the Pennsylvania deposits —"a black impure shaly limestone grading into black shale"—but does not identify the source of the statement. For convenience, rottenstone is included with tripoli in the reporting of production statistics in US Bureau of Mines (USBM) *Minerals Yearbooks.*

Other materials that have been called tripoli include siliceous deposits in San Bernardino County, California (USBM *Minerals Yearbooks,* 1934–1941) and in Nevada (Chandler, 1960). These, however, differ in composition and/or origin from tripoli and, therefore, should not be identified by the name *tripoli.*

Uses

Tripoli is used as an abrasive, as a component of buffing compounds, and as an inert filler and extender in paints, plastics, caulking compounds, and rubber. The properties of tripoli from each of the several areas of production are different and unique; consequently, producers within an area are competitors, but producers in different areas service different markets.

Physical Characteristics of Tripoli

Tripoli, as broadly defined, is composed of extremely fine-grained (microcrystalline) quartz in various stages of aggregation from minute particles to porous masses. In the friable silica from southern Illinois, particle sizes are mostly between 1 and 5 μm (Lamar, 1953), but electron micrographs show that particles from 0.2 to 0.1 μm are common (Thomas et al., 1970). Single euhedral crystals of quartz up to 10 μm are also present (Thomas et al., 1970; Keller, 1978). Particle sizes in other soft silicas (Arkansas, southeastern states) may be somewhat finer or coarser but are comparable to those in southern Illinois silica (Heinz, 1937). Electron micrographs of tripoli from the Arkansas novaculite belt show particle sizes of 1 to 10 μm (Keller, 1978). In the firmer, more coherent type from the Missouri-Oklahoma field, aggregates of particles tend to be more firmly bonded, but electron micrographs show that the sizes of individual particles generally are comparable to those in the other tripolis (Keller, 1978).

Tripoli may be white or some shade of yellow, brown, or red, depending on the degree of iron oxide staining in the deposit. Missouri-Oklahoma tripoli is generally colored and is marketed as "rose" and "cream." The Illinois variety typically is white, and deposits or parts of deposits that are iron-stained are generally regarded as noncommercial.

Different varieties of tripoli have different use characteristics. The whiteness of the Illinois type makes it preferred for most filler uses. The Missouri-Oklahoma tripoli is sold chiefly for use in abrasives; its abrasiveness is probably related to its degree of aggregation and, possibly, to the manner in which the aggregates break down during processing and use. Another characteristic ascribed to the Missouri-Oklahoma product is that in buffing compounds it "sticks to the buff" better than other silicas (Heinz, 1937). However, no comprehensive studies relating physical characteristics to use characteristics of the different types of silica are known to have been made, and preference for one or the other appears to be based largely on known or presumed behavioral characteristics.

Chemical Composition

Commercial tripoli generally contains 98% to 99% silica and minor amounts of alumina (as clay) and iron oxide. Analyses of Missouri-Oklahoma tripoli, which is normally marketed as cream or rose, commonly show very close to 98% SiO_2 (Heinz, 1937; Perry, 1917). Illinois amorphous silica is marketed as white and typically contains 99% SiO_2 (Lamar, 1953). Iron oxide, which imparts the color to the Missouri-Oklahoma product, is generally less than 1%, and in the Illinois material is less than 0.1%. Alumina content varies somewhat but is generally less than 1%.

The SiO_2 content of Pennsylvania rottenstone is approximately 60% and Al_2O_3 about 18% (personal communication). However, much of the silica is combined with the alumina as clay minerals, and the proportions of clay and free (particulate) silica are probably about the same. The balance of rottenstone is chiefly iron oxide (about 10%) and calcium and magnesium carbonates (about 5%).

Geologic Occurrence and Distribution

Tripoli occurs in geologically conformable deposits in siliceous, calcareous sedimentary strata and is believed to be the result of leaching over an extended period of time of siliceous limestone or calcareous chert or both. The deposits are limited essentially to Paleozoic strata but range in age from Precambrian in the southeastern states to Pennsylvanian in Texas (Fig. 1). The most favored parts of the geologic column from the standpoint of commercial production are: (1) lower and middle Mississippian strata (Fort Payne Chert of the western Tennessee Valley, beds of approximately equivalent age in the Boone formation of the Missouri-Oklahoma district, and the upper division of the Arkansas Novaculite) and (2) strata of Lower Devonian age in southern Illinois. Locations of known domestic deposits are shown in Fig. 2.

Missouri-Oklahoma District

Although widely scattered deposits of tripoli are known to be present over an area of 1300 km² (500 sq miles) centered in Wyandotte, OK, tripoli production in the Missouri-Oklahoma district has come chiefly from mines located in

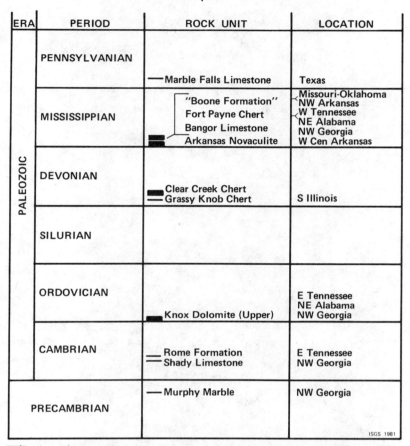

ERA	PERIOD	ROCK UNIT	LOCATION
PALEOZOIC	PENNSYLVANIAN	—Marble Falls Limestone	Texas
	MISSISSIPPIAN	"Boone Formation" Fort Payne Chert Bangor Limestone Arkansas Novaculite	Missouri-Oklahoma NW Arkansas W Tennessee NE Alabama NW Georgia W Cen Arkansas
	DEVONIAN	Clear Creek Chert Grassy Knob Chert	S Illinois
	SILURIAN		
	ORDOVICIAN	Knox Dolomite (Upper)	E Tennessee NE Alabama NW Georgia
	CAMBRIAN	Rome Formation Shady Limestone	E Tennessee NW Georgia
	PRECAMBRIAN	—Murphy Marble	NW Georgia

ISGS 1981

FIG. 1—*Stratigraphic distribution of tripoli in the United States. Heavy lines in rock unit column indicate large or numerous deposits; light lines indicate horizons of lesser importance.*

Ottawa County, OK and adjacent Newton County, MO, all within a 16-km (10-mile) radius of Seneca, MO (Fellows, 1967). Present producers are American Tripoli Division of Carborundum Co., with a processing plant at Seneca and a mine in Ottawa County, and Midwestern Materials Co., with a mine and plant in Ottawa County.

The tripoli occurs in flat-lying deposits up to 6 m (20 ft) thick under broad, flat-topped hills. Overburden, ranging in thickness from about 1 to 3 m (3 to 10 ft), generally consists of "rotten" tripoli grading upward to a red, cherty clay at the surface (Perry, 1917). Since mining rarely, if ever, extends to the base of a deposit, the character of the strata underlying the deposits is not well known. Hovey (1894) mentions a drill hole in one of the deposits that penetrated a layer of red clay beneath the deposit, and Perry (1917) cites "reliable descriptions" in making the statement that the

tripoli deposits are underlain by "several feet of red clay filled with many fragments of greatly decomposed chert" on top of solid rock. The deposits occur in the Mississippian age "Boone formation," a composite of lithologically similar units of limestone, cherty limestone, and chert. In places the Boone can be subdivided into five recognizable formations; its lower and middle parts (St. Joe Limestone, Reeds Spring Limestone, Burlington Limestone, and Keokuk Limestone formations) have been assigned to the Osage Series, and its upper part (Warsaw Limestone) is assigned to the Meramec Series (Schoff, 1955). The tripoli deposits appear to occur at stratigraphic positions both below and above the Short Creek Oolite Member of the Keokuk formation and are tentatively referred, respectively, to the Keokuk and Warsaw Limestones (Fellows, 1967).

Missouri-Oklahoma tripoli may occur as

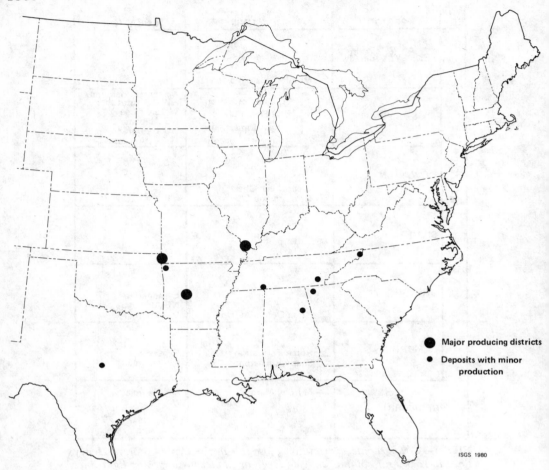

FIG. 2—*Tripoli deposits in the United States.*

loose, unconsolidated material (Heinz, 1937), but that mined and processed commercially is a relatively firm, coherent variety. During quarrying, the tripoli is drilled and shot into chunks that are hand-sorted by color and grade, chert nodules being discarded in the process. After being stored in drying sheds for about six months, the crude tripoli is crushed, ground, sized by screening or air classification, and bagged for shipment.

Southern Illinois District

The silica deposits of the southern Illinois district occur in Alexander and Union counties in extreme southwestern Illinois. The area of principal deposits lies in northern Alexander County and adjacent southern Union County near the towns of Tamms and Elco in Alexander County and Mill Creek in Union County

(Lamar, 1953). Past production has also come from areas near Wolf Creek in northern Union County and Olive Branch in southern Alexander County. Present producers are Illinois Minerals Co. and Tammsco, Inc., with processing plants at Elco and Tamms, respectively, and mines in northern Alexander County.

The major source of the silica deposits is the 90-m (300-ft) thick Lower Devonian Clear Creek Chert, which normally consists of white to mottled chert associated with smaller amounts of siliceous gray limestone (Weller, 1944). The Grassy Knob Chert, which directly underlies the Clear Creek in much of the silica-producing area (Lamar, 1953; Hood and Levine, 1973), contains scattered deposits of silica, some of which have supported commercial operations. The Olive Branch Minerals Co. produced silica for many years from deposits in the Grassy Knob. In northern Union County the Backbone Limestone intervenes between the Grassy Knob and Clear Creek Cherts.

The silica consists of friable, easily powdered silica; firm, porous silica; and nodules of chert (Lamar, 1953). The soft, pulverulent material commonly dominates. Scattered nodules of chert are normally mined and processed along with the other silica, but the parts of the deposits that contain large amounts of chert are bypassed during mining.

The silica is normally white, but iron oxide staining, resulting in yellows, browns, and reds, is common in portions of the deposits. The stained material is particularly prevalent at the outcrop, at the tops and bottoms of the deposits, and locally along fractures and more permeable beds and is generally avoided by selective mining.

The commercial deposits are generally 2.4 to 12 m (8 to 40 ft) thick. Bedding is horizontal to gently inclined but shows local waviness and distortion. Loess and Tertiary gravels generally cap the hills under which the silica is found. Since iron staining is common in the bottoms of the deposits, downward progress of mining normally ceases well above the actual base of the tripoli, and therefore little is known concerning the strata directly underlying the deposits.

Arkansas

Silica occurs chiefly in two areas of Arkansas: the northwestern corner of the state in Benton County, and west-central Arkansas in Garland, Hot Springs, Howard, Montgomery, Pike, and Polk counties (Mather, 1951). Occurrences have also been reported in Washington County in northwestern Arkansas and in Baxter County in north-central Arkansas (Branner, 1959). Production in recent years has been recorded for west-central Arkansas only and tripoli mining in Benton County has been, at best, intermittent.

The most productive deposits, those in west-central Arkansas, occur in the upper division of the Arkansas Novaculite, which is Mississippian in age. The upper division is described as "a massive, highly calcareous novaculite," which gives rise on weathering to a "white or cream-colored" soft residue of fine-grained silica (Miser, 1920). Tripoli deposits in the novaculite have been reported up to 33 m (100 ft) in thickness (Mather, 1951).

The Benton County deposits are associated with the Boone formation of Mississippian age and are believed to have been derived from siliceous limestone. Thicknesses of tripoli in Benton County are said to reach 12 m (40 ft) (Mather, 1951).

The tripoli from the novaculite belt differs from that in Benton County in character and shape of grain. Electron micrographs (Keller, 1978) illustrate the unique particle shape—polygonal triple-point—of the novaculite tripoli. The Benton County tripoli, derived from the Boone formation, may be assumed to have particle shapes more like the Missouri-Oklahoma tripoli. It is probably these differences that have led to the separate listings of past years in *Engineering & Mining Journal*.

The only consistent Arkansas producer for many years has been Malvern Minerals Co., with a plant at Hot Springs, Garland County.

West Tennessee River Valley

The most important silica-producing area of the southeastern states, from the standpoint of both past and potential production, is the region of the western Tennessee River valley in Tennessee, northwestern Alabama, and northeastern Mississippi, comprising the counties of Decatur, Dickson, Hardin, Humphreys, Lewis, Perry, and Wayne in Tennessee; Lauderdale and Colbert in Alabama; and Tishomingo in Mississippi (Clark, 1966; Spain, 1938; Whitlatch, 1937). The most productive part of the region has been a belt extending from northeastern Wayne County through Hardin County in Tennessee into Lauderdale and Colbert counties in northwestern Alabama and Tishomingo County in northeastern Mississippi. The Waynesboro-Collinwood district in Wayne County is thought to have the largest reserves of high-quality tripoli in the western Tennessee Valley Region (Spain, 1938; Whitlatch, 1937).

Most of the deposits are in the upper part of the Mississippian Fort Payne Chert, although some deposits are in the basal part of the overlying Warsaw formation. The tripoli is similar to the Illinois material in particle size and in that it is white (except where stained yellow or brown by iron oxides), largely incoherent, and easily powdered between the fingers. It is commonly referred to as the *Illinois-Tennessee type* (Spain, 1938; Whitlatch, 1937). The tripoli derived from the Warsaw formation is said to be finer and more uniform in particle size and less cherty than that in the Fort Payne (Spain, 1938).

The deposits are for the most part horizontally bedded, but in places the bedding becomes wavy or otherwise distorted by slumping related to solutional removal of carbonate minerals. The thickness of the deposits averages 7.5 m (25 ft), but one exposure in Wayne County was 18 m (60 ft) thick (Spain, 1938).

Except for a small amount produced near Florence, AL, in 1965 for the attempted production of silica brick, no production has been reported for the western Tennessee Valley Region since 1939. In previous years production had been centered chiefly around Waynesboro and Collinwood in Tennessee, Waterloo and Riverton in Alabama, and Iuka in Mississippi. A plant near Parsons in Decatur County, Tennessee, was reportedly in operation in the late 1930s (Whitlatch, 1937).

Other Areas in the Southeastern United States

Deposits in the southeastern United States are also known along the belt of folded Appalachians in northeastern Alabama, northwestern Georgia, and eastern Tennessee. These deposits occur chiefly in the Cambro-Ordovician Knox Dolomite, but some may be found in other formations both older and younger than the Knox.

Northeastern Alabama: Small scattered deposits of tripoli are known in Talladega and Calhoun counties in the northeastern part of Alabama (Pallister, 1955). These deposits occur in the Knox Dolomite and in the Mississippian Age Fort Payne Chert. No production has been recorded from northeastern Alabama. Industrial Fillers, Inc. developed a deposit near Piedmont in northeastern Calhoun County in the mid-1960s but failed to achieve significant commercial production.

Northwestern Georgia: Tripoli occurs in the northwest corner of Georgia in the counties of Bartow, Catoosa, Chatooga, Floyd, Gilmer, Murray, Polk, Walker, and Whitfield. Most of the deposits are in the upper part of the Knox Dolomite, but others have been found in the Precambrian Murphy Marble (Gilmer County), in the Cambrian Shady Limestone (Bartow County), and in the Mississippian Bangor Limestone (northern Chatooga County—deposits in southern Chatooga County are in the Knox) (Crickmay, 1937). Most of the deposits appear to have been formed by the leaching of siliceous limestone; those in the Shady Limestone evidently have been derived from material called novaculite by Crickmay (1937).

In grain size and shape, most of the Georgia material is reported to resemble the Missouri-Oklahoma tripoli more closely than it does the material from Illinois and Tennessee. How-

ever, the Georgia tripoli is generally lighter in color than the Missouri product and many deposits contain large amounts that are ivory to white (Crickmay, 1937).

Tripoli has been mined chiefly in Chatooga, Walker, and Whitfield counties (Crickmay, 1937). No production has been reported for Georgia since 1935.

Eastern Tennessee: Tripoli has been produced in the past near Cleveland, Bradley County, in southeastern Tennessee, and has been mined to a limited extent in Johnson County in the northeast corner of the state (Whitlatch, 1937). The Bradley County tripoli is described as "white to off-color" and is found in the Knox Dolomite. That in Johnson County is reported to be "bright yellow, porous, and incoherent" and appears to have been derived from siliceous limestones in the Cambrian Watauga Shale (now called the Rome formation). Whitlatch (1937) refers to the Johnson County material as *rottenstone* but gives no reasons for preferring this particular term to the name *tripoli* for the Johnson County deposits.

Texas

Tripoli has been produced from deposits northwest of Austin in Lampasas, Burnet, and San Saba counties (Dietrich and Lonsdale, 1958; Barnes et al., 1947). The tripoli is a "white, finely divided material consisting almost entirely of siliceous fragments of sponge spicules" (Evans, 1946). The deposits, given the rock term *spiculite* (Damon, 1946), occur in limestone, from which they evidently were derived by leaching and residual concentration. Their distribution is erratic, and deposits of nearly pure silica may grade abruptly into limestone (Damon, 1946). Spiculite is currently produced by Texas Architectural Aggregates, Inc., San Saba County, who market the spiculite as corkstone, a lightweight building stone used chiefly as rubble and field stone. Until recently, Southwest Portland Cement Co., Lampasas County, used spiculite as a source of silica in its cement plant at Odessa, Texas, and material from Burnet County was at one time used in special drilling muds (Dietrich and Lonsdale, 1958). Although the origin of the silica in spiculite (organic) is different from that of the silica in ordinary tripoli (largely inorganic), the mode of origin of the deposits (residual concentration from the leaching of siliceous, calcareous sedimentary strata) and their general character are the same as those of tripoli; therefore, it is logical and desirable to include spiculite under the general rock and commodity term *tripoli*.

Other Deposits Reported As Tripoli

Tripoli production was reported in California for the years 1933–1941, and deposits of tripoli are said to occur in Nevada (Chandler, 1960).

A deposit near Barstow, San Bernardino County, mined by Western Talc Co., was listed in *Minerals Yearbooks*, US Bureau of Mines, as the source of the California tripoli for the years 1934–1936. No deposits of tripoli are known in San Bernardino County or elsewhere in California. Several deposits near Barstow, ranging from siliceous marl to altered volcanic rock and referred to as mineral fillers (Bowen, 1954), were suggested as possible sources of the material reported as tripoli. Heinz (1937) stated that silica of volcanic origin was produced in Inyo and San Bernardino counties but declined to call it tripoli. Inasmuch as none of these materials appears to meet the definition of tripoli, in either composition or origin, they should not be called tripoli.

Deposits in Nevada of white, fine-grained silica, "consisting of opal and occasionally some cristobalite" and "formed by leaching of rhyolitic volcanic rock in a shallow hydrothermal environment," have been suggested as the occurrences that have been reported as tripoli. Because of the volcanic-hydrothermal origin of the material, it is not considered tripoli by the Nevada Bureau of Mines and Geology, an opinion in which the present authors concur.

Rottenstone

Rottenstone is being produced from one location in Pennsylvania. Keystone Filler and Manufacturing Co. produces from the Devonian Mahantango formation in Northumberland County. The material quarried is reported to be weathered shale and is used as abrasives and fillers.

Origin

In general, tripoli deposits are thought to be the result of a long period of leaching of siliceous limestones and calcareous cherts under surface or near-surface conditions. In a discussion of the origin of the southern Illinois deposits, Lamar (1953) concluded that the microcrystalline silica composing those deposits is the residue remaining after the removal of carbonate minerals from siliceous Devonian rocks; the character of the tripoli, soft and powdery to firm and porous, was believed related to the character of the parent rock—the powdery material having been derived from a siliceous limestone in which the individual silica particles were physically separated, and the more coherent silica from a calcareous chert in which the grains were at least partially interlocked. A more recent study (Hood and Levine, 1973) reached essentially the same conclusions. In none of the Illinois deposits that have been exposed by mining has there been observed a transition from tripoli to parent rock. Lamar (1953), however, traced in a roadcut a 152-mm (6-in.) bed, which displayed progressively greater leaching from siliceous limestone (24% SiO_2) at its origin to typical tripoli (98% SiO_2) some 107 m (350 ft) away.

Silica deposits of the southeastern states are, likewise, ascribed to leaching of siliceous limestone or calcareous chert (Jones, 1926; Miser, 1921; Pallister, 1955; Spain, 1938; Whitlatch, 1937). Crickmay (1937) states that the origin of the Georgia deposits is debatable but admits that the "most plausible" mode of origin is leaching of siliceous limestones.

In the Arkansas novaculite belt, field observations have indicated that the silica deposits were developed by leaching of the novaculite. Miser (1920) noted tripoli grading into normal novaculite. Keller (1978) found that both novaculite and the tripoli derived from it were composed of quartz crystals with a polygonal triple-point shape, whereas quartz crystals in the Illinois and Missouri-Oklahoma tripolis exhibited the typical hexagonal forms. Keller interpreted the triple-point texture as having formed from recrystallization in a confined space during metamorphism of a precursor siliceous rock to novaculite.

In the Missouri-Oklahoma district, however, there has been somewhat less agreement over the genesis of the tripoli. While it appears that the generally accepted theory of origin of tripoli (residual concentration of silica from leaching of siliceous limestone or calcareous chert) is favored for the Missouri-Oklahoma deposits (Fellows, 1967), some observers have held that these deposits are sufficiently unlike other silica deposits that they must have had a different mode of origin. According to the latter viewpoint, the Missouri-Oklahoma deposits were laid down in essentially their present form by direct precipitation of silica, with later modifications by the leaching of coprecipitated alkaline salts or by the recrystallization of originally colloidal silica (Heinz, 1937).

Exploration

Exploration for deposits is deceptively simple but requires a thorough knowledge of the local terrain and long experience in judging the quality of the material in the deposits. Outcrops are located by field exploration, commonly aided by aerial photographs, in an area known to contain tripoli-bearing strata. The common exploration drilling techniques are unsatisfactory for tripoli exploration because of the abrasiveness of the siliceous host rocks and the difficulty of recovering samples in the pulverulent, incoherent tripoli. Consequently, a preliminary evaluation of the deposit is carried out by drifting into the hillside or by trenching and test pitting, depending on accepted practice in the particular district. On the basis of experience, a judgment is generally made on the spot regarding color and texture, and either the prospect is abandoned or development work is continued.

Development

In the case of underground mines, ore bodies must be developed months or years ahead of production. The exploration drift is driven on a level near the floor of the deposit and the thickness of the deposit is determined by raising. As the drift advances, crosscuts are driven to determine the width of the deposit and to evaluate the deposit with respect to discolored or iron-stained material, excessively cherty zones, or clay inclusions, which must be left in the mines as pillars or sold as a low-value product. The development of a block of ore is labor-intensive and expensive. Continual appraisal is required to determine if the development is a potential source of high-grade ore that has sufficient tonnage to justify mining and has strength of rock to reduce the need for artificial support.

Mining

Because of differences in the physical characteristics of the deposits, the purity of the material, and depth beneath the surface, different systems of mining are used in the various tripoli districts.

In Illinois, underground mining is practiced utilizing a room-and-pillar mine plan. Insofar as possible, the off-specification parts of the mine are used as pillars in order to maximize the higher grades of material for plant feed. The mines are small, and two or three are continually in production so areas which must be bypassed can be accommodated without changing the feed rate at the plants. Each of the mines is normally run on a one-shift-per-day basis. Each mine is provided with an electrical generator and air compressor at the portal, the generator to provide light in working areas and haulageways, and the compressor to provide air for drills and ventilation. Mining is done with a jackleg drill. After drilling, the ore is blasted, picked up with a front-end loader, and transferred to a truck which delivers the ore to the crusher at the centrally located plant. As in many room-and-pillar mines, less than 50% of the ore encountered in place is delivered to the plants. No pillar recovery program has been instituted because of accessibility to additional ore and the desire to avoid subsidence problems.

The mines in Missouri and Arkansas use an open-cut method of mining. Extraordinary care must be taken to prevent contamination by earth or clay. The ore is highly absorbent and leaves the mine with 25 to 35% moisture content. It is stored in drying sheds for extended periods to reduce this moisture prior to going to the plant.

Mineral Preparation

We refer to the plant as a mineral *preparation* plant rather than a mineral *beneficiation* plant because beneficiation implies upgrading by the rejection of a lower grade or tailings product. Such is not the case in the tripoli plant. The flowsheet includes crushing, drying, and grinding. Everything delivered from the mine, with the exception of contained moisture, ends up in the final plant product.

The ore from the mine goes through a jaw crusher, a surge bin, a gyratory crusher, another surge bin, a rotary dryer, and is delivered into a fine ore bin. Ore from the fine ore bin is ground in a jasper-lined pebble mill in closed circuit with a bank of mechanical classifiers. The jasper lining and pebble media maintain the purity of the product as iron contamination would greatly reduce the marketability. The mechanical separators have the capability of cutting off any desired size fraction by proper setting, so feed rate is a function of the product being prepared at any given time.

The materials from the mechanical classifiers may be sold as several sizes of air-floated grades or become feedstock for several grades of micronized materials. These ultrafine grades are prepared in steam- or air-powered micronizing mills, in which they are ground and classified simultaneously. The finest product is sold at 100% minus 10 μm and 96% minus 5 μm. The average particle size is 1.12 μm and the

Hegman gage, a measure of the coarsest particle, is greater than 7. The ultrafine grinding is unique in that it does not involve the reduction of discrete crystalline particles to ever finer fragments. The individual particles in the feed to the micronizing mills are clusters of quartz crystallites, many of which are less than 1 μm in size, held together at their points of contact. The required size reduction is accomplished by a breaking of these cohesive bonds.

Other plants use hammermills and screens, coupled with or bypassing the technological steps indicated above.

Uses

Tripoli is defined in the sales brochure of one of the companies that processes and sells it as a "very uncommon variety of a very common mineral." Tripoli was first used as shaped products for kitchen scrubbing and water filters. Presently, virtually all of the Missouri, Arkansas, and Illinois tripoli is ground for the market. This market consists of abrasives, buffing and polishing compounds, inert mineral fillers, and more recently, surface-treated silica used in both thermoplastic and thermosetting resins for molded engineering plastics, casting compounds, adhesives, and coatings. Each of these uses will be discussed separately.

Abrasives

Tripoli at the present time is used in abrasive soaps, cleaners, powders, etc. Well-known examples are teeth-cleaning preparations and the hand soaps used in shop areas.

Buffing and Polishing Compounds

The uses of tripoli in buffing and polishing compounds are a function of the maximum and average particle sizes of the particular grade of the tripoli. In the grades normally used in buffing and polishing compounds, 99.5% of the particles are less than 10 μm in size. The average particle size is 5 to 7 μm and the Hegman grind is 4 to 7. The products are used in metal finishing. The coarser grades act as a mild abrasive, being much milder than ground silica sand, which is sold for similar purposes. The finer grades are used in buffing out hairline scratches and are used in liquid cleaner-polisher formulations, in which the thixotropic properties of the tripoli are beneficial.

Mineral Fillers

Because of the many degrees of fineness that the several companies market, the prices and applications are numerous. Probably the largest use is as an extender and filler in paint. The material required for trade sales paints (exterior latex coatings) is a low-micron grade of micronized tripoli, which yields a Hegman grind of about 6. It aids in tint retention, durability, leveling, and flowability. In baked finishes, enamels, etc., it permits higher loadings with no appreciable increase in vehicle demand and improves sheen. Ease of dispersion and film uniformity are a result of its controlled particle size. In many products its abrasiveness yields significant wear resistance. The paints in which silica filler is used are much more resistant to chemicals than those paints in which water-ground whitings and other reactive fillers are used.

A use of tripoli that has experienced rapid growth is as a filler and extender in plastics. Ground silica is used extensively in plastics for electrical use because of the excellent dielectric properties and the flexural and compressive strength it imparts. Its low oil absorption, coupled with wetting and rapid dispersion, permits high loading in most compounds. The only reported drawback in the use of tripoli as a filler in plastics comes from the degree of wear which the extruding nozzles and molds endure as a result of this use. Research by one operation has indicated that products with finer particle sizes would reduce this wear; however, they would command a higher price.

The properties which make tripoli a valuable additive to plastics are also important in the rubber industry, where it and pyrogenic or precipitated silica are used as fillers, the pyrogenic silica serving additionally as a reinforcing pigment. Tripoli is also utilized in epoxy sealants for electrical applications.

Surface-Treated Silica

Recent surface treatment of very finely sized tripoli products have broadened their uses in the fields of thermoplastic and thermosetting resins. Examples are the surface treatment with an organofunctional group such as aminos, mercaptos, epoxies, and a hydrolyzable alkoxy group. One end of the chain hydrolyzes with the surface of the silica; the organofunctional group is left attached but exposed and unreacted so that it will become reactive when added to the resin.

Comparing surface-treated and nontreated fillers at a constant loading, the treated silica would be expected to increase the mechanical strength and electrical properties and make significant improvements in chemical resistance, weatherability, and salt spray resistance.

Other improvements in favor of the use of surface-treated tripoli are a reduction in viscosity and an increase in dispersion rate in a medium.

About 30 chemicals are used commercially as adjuncts to the thermosetting resins, thermoplastic resins, and elastomers. The details are long and highly technical. It is the belief of the writers that only the concepts have been touched. The uses of organically surface-treated tripoli will be extensive and expanding in many directions before the end of the decade. None will be large-tonnage applications, but the market for special use items will continue to grow.

Miscellaneous Uses

There are numerous other uses of tripoli that involve significantly lower tonnage consumption but are important and should not be slighted. These include use in adhesives; in insecticides, both as fillers and as carriers; in dry cleaning and laundering formulations; in refractories and ceramic glazes; in foundry facings and injection thermoset moldings; in cosmetics; as wallboard filler; and as plastic wood filler. Lower grades have found uses in construction.

Substitutes

In the filler uses cited, ground calcium carbonate, ground silica sand, pyrogenic and precipitated silica, calcined kaolin, and talc are reasonable substitutes for tripoli. Materials that may substitute for tripoli as an abrasive and polishing agent include pumice, diatomite, ground feldspar, ground calcium carbonate, ground silica sand, and precipitated silica.

Prices, Production, and Forecast

Prices in 1983 ranged from $71 to $196 per ton, in direct proportion to the degree of fineness. Missouri-Oklahoma tripoli, which is used mainly as abrasives, was quoted in *Engineering & Mining Journal* in mid-1983 as follows: Once-ground, 2.9¢ per lb; double-ground, 2.9¢; and air-float, 3.15¢. At a per-ton rate, these prices are $58 and $63. Tripoli f.o.b. Elco, IL was quoted at $3.55 per lb for air-floated through 200 mesh. Prices of amorphous silica, f.o.b. Elco, IL, ranged from $71 per ton for 90 to 95% through 200 mesh to $196 per ton for the finest grade, 99% below 10 μm. Intermediate grades had prices between these limits. After being listed for a number of years, amorphous silica f.o.b. Dierks, AR was last quoted by *Engineering & Mining Journal* during 1977 at $40 per ton for 200 mesh and $50 per ton for 325 mesh, prices comparable to those listed at that time for Illinois silica.

Production statistics for the years 1970 to 1980 are shown in Table 1. Noteworthy is the almost annual increase in the use of tripoli in fillers, a trend continued from the previous decade (Bradbury and Ehrlinger, 1975). This increase may be assumed to reflect, at least in part, its increasing use in plastics, as indicated in the section on uses.

The conventional uses of tripoli are expected

TABLE 1—Processed Tripoli* Sold or Used by Producers in the US, 1970-1980

Year	Abrasives Short Tons	Value, †$	Fillers Short Tons	Value, †$	Other Short Tons	Value, †$	Total Short Tons	Value, †$
1970	41,703	1583	18,093	545	1134	28	60,930	2156
1971	44,899	1692	20,457	681	1327	32	66,683	2406
1972	47,321	1918	25,973	847	1584	43	74,878	2807
1973	55,420	2233	32,407	1158	2105	62	89,932	3453
1974	50,651	2251	33,361	1346	2025	66	86,000	3665
1975	38,815	1518	27,630	1205	1739	60	68,124	2783
1976	68,874	2525	40,247	1811	5000	175	114,121	4511
1977	70,631	2805	42,599	2212	2689	119	115,919	5136
1978	75,574	3709	36,505	2220	2190 e	97 e	114,269	6026
1979	53,600	2468	62,409	3811	—	—	116,009	6279
1980	39,352	2253	59,909	4025	—	—	99,261	6277‡

Source: *Minerals Yearbooks*, US Bureau of Mines.
* Includes tripoli, amorphous silica, and rottenstone.
† Thousands of dollars.
‡ Data may not add to total because of independent rounding.
e Estimated.

to grow at a rate comparable to the national economy. The uses of exotically treated silicas will grow at a substantially greater rate because of new, previously unavailable feedstocks.

Environmental Considerations and Government Controls

No serious dislocations have been reported by tripoli producers with respect to land use, probably because most tripoli mines are in lightly populated areas. Safety regulations in mining must be met and are evidently being taken in stride for the most part. Stringent air quality regulations in processing plants have been difficult to meet and have caused temporary plant closings on occasion. Producers indicate that 80% of the recent increases in market prices of tripoli, particularly the ultrafine grades, are directly attributable to the increase in production costs caused by the enforced addition of new dust control measures. The silica industry has been exercising careful dust control for years and feels present air quality limits are unrealistic.

Acknowledgments

We wish to acknowledge the cooperation of the late Jay Seymour; John Norton; Joseph K. Davis; John Dillingham; Robert B. McElwaine; R.H. Dobbs; and J.E. Moreland. Information on silica deposits and the industry in Alabama has been provided by Michael W. Szabo; in Arkansas by Norman F. Williams; in California by Fenelon F. Davis; in Nevada by Keith G. Papke; in Pennsylvania by Arthur A. Socolow; in Tennessee by James L. Moore; and in Texas by Roselle Girard. The late J.E. Lamar was of valuable help both as a source of information and as a reviewer of the manuscript. Without the generous aid of these people, we would not have been able to develop a feeling for the past, present, and future of the tripoli industry in the United States.

Bibliography and References

Anon., 1981, "Abrasive Materials," *Minerals Year-book 1980,* US Bureau of Mines, p. 54.

Bain, H.F., 1907, "Analyses of Certain Silica Deposits in Southern Illinois," *Year-Book for 1906,* Bulletin 4, Illinois State Geological Survey, pp. 185–186.

Barnes, V.E., Dawson, R.F., and Parkinson, G.A., 1947, "Building Stones of Central Texas," Publication 4246, University of Texas, p. 157.

Barrett, N.O., 1922, "Mineral Resources of Illinois in 1917 and 1918," *Year-Book for 1917 and 1918,* Bulletin 38, Illinois State Geological Survey, pp. 25–112.

Baskin, G.D., 1980, "Abrasive Materials," *Minerals Yearbook 1978–1979,* US Bureau of Mines, pp. 27–41.

Bowen, O.E.,Jr., 1954, "Geology and Mineral Deposits of the Barstow Quadrangle, San Bernardino County, California," Bulletin 165, California Div. of Mines, pp 150–160.

Bradbury, J.C., and Ehrlinger, H.P., III, 1975, "Tripoli," *Industrial Minerals and Rocks,* 4th ed., S.J. Lefond, ed., AIME, New York, p. 1217.

Branner, G.C., 1959, "Mineral Resources of Arkansas," Bulletin 6, Arkansas Geological Commission, pp. 78–79.

Chandler, H.P., 1960, "Tripoli," *Industrial Minerals and Rocks,* 3rd ed., J.L. Gillson, ed., AIME, New York, pp. 881–888.

Clarke, O.M., Jr., 1966, "Clay and Shale of Northwestern Alabama," Circular 20B, Alabama Geological Survey, 88 pp.

Clarke, R.G., 1973, "Abrasive Materials," *Minerals Yearbook 1971,* US Bureau of Mines, pp. 135–136.

Clarke, R.G., 1974, "Abrasive Materials," *Minerals Yearbook 1972,* US Bureau of Mines, pp. 125–126.

Crickmay, G.W., 1937, "Tripoli Deposits of Georgia," Information Circular 9, Georgia Div. of Geology, 7 pp.

Damon, H.G., 1946, "The Origin and Distribution of Spiculite near Lampasas, Lampasas County, Texas," *Texas Mineral Resources,* University of Texas Publications 4301, pp. 271–282.

Dietrich, J.W., and Lonsdale, J.T., 1958, "Mineral Resources of the Colorado River Industrial Development Association Area," Report of Investigations No. 37, Texas Bureau of Economic Geology, pp. 71–74.

Evans, G.L., 1946, "Mineral Abrasive and Polishing Materials in Texas," *Texas Mineral Resources,* University of Texas Publications 4301, pp. 245–248.

Fellows, L.D., 1967, "Tripoli," *Mineral and Water Resources of Missouri,* Vol. 43, 2nd Series, Missouri Div. of Geological Survey and Water Resources, pp. 220–223.

Gary, M., McAfee, R.,Jr., and Wolf, C.L., eds., 1972, *Glossary of Geology,* American Geological Institute, Washington, DC, 805 pp.

Harben, P., 1983, "Tripoli and Novaculite—The Little Known Relations," *Industrial Minerals,* No. 184, Jan., pp. 28–32.

Heinz, C.E., 1937, "Tripoli," *Industrial Minerals and Rocks,* 1st ed., S.H. Dolbear, ed., AIME, New York, pp. 911–922.

Hood, W.C., and Levine, C.R., 1973, "Tripoli Deposits of Alexander County, Illinois," *Guidebook to 37th Annual Tri-State Field Conference,* F.G. Ethridge, et al., eds., Southern Illinois University, Carbondale, pp. 128–138.

Hovey, E.O., 1894, "American Tripoli," *Scientific American Supplement,* Vol. 38, No. 969, July 28, p. 15487.

Jones, W.B., 1926, "Index to the Mineral Resources of Alabama," Bulletin 28, Alabama Geological Survey, p. 245.

Keller, W.D., 1978, "Textures of Tripoli Illustrated by Scanning Electron Micrographs," *Economic Geology,* Vol. 73, No. 3, May, pp. 442–446.

Lamar, J.E., 1953, "Siliceous Materials of Extreme Southern Illinois," Report of Investigations 166, Illinois State Geological Survey, 39 pp.

Leamnson, R.N., Thomas, J.,Jr., and Ehrlinger, H.P.,III, 1969, "A Study of the Surface Areas of Particulate Microcrystalline Silica and Silica Sand," Circular 444, Illinois State Geological Survey, 12 pp.

Mather, W.B., 1951, "Nonmetalliferous Mineral Resources of Arkansas," Trans. AIME, Vol. 187, p. 581.

Miser, H.D., 1920, "Geology and General Topographic Features of Arkansas," Outlines of Arkansas Geology, J.G. Ferguson, ed., Arkansas Bureau of Mines, Manufactures, and Agriculture, Little Rock, pp. 21–139.

Miser, H.D., 1921, "Mineral Resources of the Waynesboro Quadrangle," Bulletin 26, Tennessee Geological Survey, pp. 129–131.

Pallister, H.D., 1955, "Index to the Minerals and Rocks of Alabama," Bulletin 65, Alabama Geological Survey, p. 39.

Perry, E.S., 1917, "Tripoli Deposits of Oklahoma," Bulletin 28, Oklahoma Geological Survey, 32 pp.

Schoff, S.L., 1955, "Geologic Formations and Their Water-Bearing Character," Groundwater Resources of Ottawa County, Oklahoma, Bulletin 72, Oklahoma Geological Survey, pp. 48–52.

Spain, E.L., 1938, "Tripoli Deposits of the West Tennessee Valley," Trans. AIME, Vol. 129, pp. 501–515.

Thomas, J.Jr., et al., 1970, "Colloidal-Size Silica Produced from Southern Illinois Tripoli," Industrial Minerals Note 40, Illinois State Geological Survey, 6 pp.

Thrush, P.W., ed., 1968, A Dictionary of Mining, Mineral, and Related Terms, US Bureau of Mines, Washington, DC, 1269 pp.

Weller, J.M., 1944, "Devonian System in Southern Illinois," Bulletin 68, Illinois State Geological Survey, pp. 89–102.

Whitlatch, G.I., 1937, "Tripoli," Markets Circular No. 1, Tennessee Div. of Geology, 12 pp.

Vermiculite

Original by PHILIP R. STRAND *
Revised by O.F. STEWART †

Vermiculite is the name generally applied to the group of hydrated ferromagnesian aluminum silicates that are characterized by the ability to expand when heated. This process, called exfoliation, results in a lightweight product of commercial value. Most uses of vermiculite are for the expanded material. The chief markets are in construction, agriculture, and horticulture, with lesser uses in general industry.

Composition and Properties

Vermiculite, in its natural state, has the characteristic micaceous habit, a perfect basal cleavage which causes splitting into thin laminae that are soft, pliable, and inelastic. The structure of vermiculite is basically that of a talc. The prominent monoclinic crystal faces are often marked by lines at 60° and 120°. Hardness varies from 1.5 to 2 or more; specific gravities are between 2.1 and 2.8; color varies from almost clear to amber, bronze, brown, green, or black. Vermiculite feels like talc, especially when wet.

Although much research has been performed on the chemical and structural composition, there is not yet complete agreement on the exact formula. This is to be expected when different workers have examined the many different varieties. Vermiculite is not considered to be a single mineral species but a family of related minerals. The structural formula for a trioctahedral vermiculite may be written:

$$(H_2O) - (Mg,Ca,K) - (Al_2,Fe,Mg) - (Si,Al,Fe)_4 O_{10}(OH)_2$$

Hydrobiotite also occurs with vermiculite and is usually considered a vermiculite for commercial uses.

* Deceased, formerly Director of Advertising and Public Relations, Construction Products Div., W.R. Grace and Co., Cambridge, MA.

† Geologist, Construction Products Div., W.R. Grace and Co., Enoree, SC.

When heated quickly to elevated temperatures, vermiculite expands by exfoliating at right angles to the cleavage into wormlike particles. The name vermiculite is derived from the Latin *vermiculare,* to breed worms. This characteristic of expansion is the result of the mechanical separation of the layers by the rapid conversion of contained water to steam. The decrease in bulk density of commercial grades is usually approximately 10 times, from 50 to 5 lb/ft³, but varies depending on the quality, size, and furnace efficiency. Individual flakes may expand up to 30 times. Vermiculite may also be expanded by soaking in chemicals such as hydrogen peroxide, weak acids, and other electrolytes. Color change during expansion is dependent upon the type of vermiculite and furnace conditions. Heating in an oxidizing atmosphere produces a dull gray or tan color, whereas a reducing atmosphere can produce a bronze or gold color.

The expansion of the vermiculite crystal results in large pores being formed between the platelets. Thus, exfoliation makes available a large increase in void volume which is important in the application of vermiculite as a chemical carrier.

Mathieson and Walker (1954) state vermiculite must be regarded as a true clay mineral. The characteristic properties of the mineral, such as high cation exchange capacity, organic complexing ability, and variable interlamellar distance are very similar to those of montmorillonite. The cation exchange capacity of vermiculite is one of the highest of all the clay minerals. The interplatelet space is accessible to penetration by some electrostatically neutral molecules. Water and glycerine are two common substances whose molecules may be so imbibed.

In the natural state and under normal atmospheric conditions, water occupies the spaces between the silicate layers. The crystal *d*-spacing is near 14.2Å. By differential thermal analysis, it has been determined that the water is released at three temperature ranges. The "unbound water" is released near 300°F. This water is reversible and comes to equilibrium with the environment. The second water, designated "bound water," is removed at about 500°F. This is the water necessary for exfoliation. The third water is released at approximately 1600°F and is probably hydroxyl. Little of this water is released by commercial exfoliation and when it is, a very noticeable change occurs in the color and physical characteristics of the product.

Vermiculite is closely related to biotite and phlogopite. The essential difference is that the unit cell of vermiculite contains a layer of water and the biotite contains a layer of potassium. Biotite or phlogopite are almost always associated with vermiculite in commercial deposits and are sometimes intermixed within crystals or across a single crystal face. The term *hydrobiotite* has been used for those varieties where the analysis indicates that there is a layered mixture of the two minerals in some definite proportion.

Table 1 shows chemical analyses typical of the three major vermiculite deposits.

Origin

Detailed investigations have been made of the three largest commercial deposits of vermiculite. According to Boettcher (1966), the Rainy Creek alkaline-ultramafic complex near Libby, MT, represents a composite of successive intrusions of igneous rocks emplaced into the Precambrian metasedimentary rocks. Most of the biotite in the inner body of pyroxenite has been altered to hydrobiotite and vermiculite. From his studies, Boettcher suggests the vermiculite is a product of leaching of the biotite by ground waters, whereas the hydrobiotite may represent a higher temperature alteration product.

Stewart (1949) in his report on the vermiculite deposits at Tigerville, SC, states that hydrothermal activity was necessary in the formation of the high grade deposits only to the extent of furnishing the biotite, which was later altered to vermiculite by meteoric waters. Buie and Stewart (1954) determined the paragenetic sequence as:

$$pyroxene \rightarrow amphibole \rightarrow biotite \rightarrow vermiculite$$
$$(hypogene) \qquad (supergene)$$

Libby (1975) suggests that the potassic ultramafic plutons of the Enoree, SC, vermiculite district probably were intruded into Late Pre-

TABLE 1—Chemical Analyses of Vermiculite, %

	Libby, Montana	Enoree, South Carolina	Palabora, South Africa
SiO_2	40.16	39.77	39.37
MgO	20.63	18.32	23.37
Al_2O_3	12.01	13.88	12.08
Fe_2O_3	13.00	12.84	5.45
FeO	—	—	1.17
K_2O	5.93	5.11	2.46
CaO	1.54	1.02	1.46
TiO_2	1.44	2.07	1.25
H_2O	5.29	6.99	11.20
Total	100.00	100.00	97.81

cambrian to Cambrian sedimentary rocks and subsequently were metamorphosed. Studies indicate that both the vermiculite and hydrobiotite form under weathering conditions.

The Palabora deposit in South Africa at Loolekop is located in a carbonatite complex. Both the hydrothermal and weathering theory have been proposed for the formation of the vermiculite. There is a gradation of vermiculite to phlogopite or biotite with increasing depth.

The Palabora carbonatite complex (Dekun, 1965) is about 4 by 1½ miles in size. The dolomite core is surrounded by a thin inner ring of altered phoscorite (serpentine-apatite-magnetite) and an outer ring of diopside pyroxenite. Outward from this is a discontinuous 1½ mile-wide ring of fenitized gneisses. Numerous alvikite and orthoclasite veins have been injected into the pyroxenite ring. Serpentine, apatite, and magnetite occur in both inner zones, and a pegmatitic pyroxenite zone occupies the center of the northern ultrabasic ring. Vermiculite occurs only in the ultrabasics, especially close to serpentinized patches. Vermiculite also occurs disseminated with apatite. The principal vermiculite areas are located (1) in the north-central pegmatic pyroxenite one half mile from the limit of the carbonatite plug; (2) three quarters of a mile south of the core; and (3) in a zone near the southeastern rim of the pyroxenite.

A vermiculite deposit near Louisa, VA, occurs in a body of basic pyroxenite, about 4 to 5 miles in diameter, surrounded by gneisses and granitoid type rocks typical of the Piedmont. The vermiculite occurs in varying flake size but nearly all are less than 10 mesh. The grade of vermiculite varies considerably within a few feet both laterally and with depth. The vermiculite appears to have been altered from biotite by surface weathering. However, little, if any, geological investigation has been conducted on this deposit.

Distribution of Deposits

Vermiculite occurrences have been reported from many countries of the world. As the mineral has become more widely recognized new occurrences have been reported. Market conditions, location, size, grade, quality, and economics are some of the factors affecting the commercial value and development of a deposit.

In the United States vermiculite deposits or occurrences are found in Alabama, Arizona, Arkansas, California, Colorado, Georgia, Idaho, Kansas, Montana, Nevada, New Mexico, North Carolina, Pennsylvania, South Carolina, Texas, Virginia, and Wyoming. Production has been reported from California, Colorado, Georgia, Montana, Nevada, North Carolina, South Carolina, Texas, Virginia, and Wyoming. However, production is reported today only from mines in Montana, South Carolina, and Virginia.

Other countries where deposits have been reported are Argentina, Australia, Brazil, Canada, China, Egypt, Finland, India, Japan, Kenya, Korea, Mexico, Morocco, Pakistan, Zimbabwe, Republic of South Africa, Spain, Tanzania, Uganda, and the USSR. Minor production has been reported from Argentina, Brazil, China, Canada, Egypt, India, Kenya, Korea, Mexico, Spain, and Tanzania. Some vermiculite is produced in the USSR, but quantitative data are not available.

Prospecting and Exploration

In the United States vermiculite deposits of consequence are located in two principal areas: the Piedmont region from Alabama to Pennsylvania and in the Rocky Mountain Range from Montana southward into New Mexico, including the central mineral region of Texas. A few deposits occur in eastern Canada in the Precambrian shield.

Vermiculite deposits usually are covered by vegetation because the minerals are soft and when weathered have a considerable water-holding ability. Outcrops showing vermiculite are rare, but in some areas the mineral can be recognized in road cuts. Outcrops of associated rocks such as biotite, alkalic pyroxenites, and dikes of carbonatites or syenite, generally are more noticeable. In most instances, the only field evidence will be the presence of vermiculite flakes in the soil or in stream beds.

The larger commercial size deposits usually are found associated with ultrabasic rock, commonly pyroxenite. The pyroxenite may be intruded by numerous dikes such as pegmatites, syenites, and carbonatites. Numerous veins containing vermiculite are found in ultramafic intrusives such as dunites, peridotites, and pyroxenites, but these do not often represent commercial size deposits.

In a vermiculite-bearing formation the rock will vary from barren to a high content of vermiculite. The bulk of the material containing vermiculite will fall in the 20 to 30% content range. Drilling or trenching is necessary to prove the presence of ore in economic quantities and grade. Since the preservation of flake size is most important, auger or large rotary hole drilling is necessary with special attention to bit design. Diamond core drilling is most impractical.

The primary requirement of a commercial deposit is that the vermiculite be of acceptable quality. The concentrate must expand to a high degree without decrepitating, and the expanded particles must be strong enough to withstand handling. The biotite or phlogopite content must be low, or occur in such a form that it can be kept from mixing with the mill feed. The deposit predominantly must contain flake size material larger than 65 mesh, as there is little demand for the minus 65 mesh size.

Another characteristic of a commercial deposit is that the ore body be large enough to be mined with modern earthmoving equipment. Vermiculite production is very energy-intensive, as a high percentage of the commercial cost is for mining, reagentizing, drying, expanding, and transportation.

Deposits are considered to be high grade if their content of plus 65 mesh vermiculite is over 30%, and uneconomical or at least borderline if the content is 20% or below.

Preparation for Markets

Mining and Milling Methods

The two larger operations in the United States are described as examples of the production now in use. Fig. 1 shows the typical flowsheet from mine to shipping.

Montana: In the pyroxenite near Libby the vermiculite occurs in high grade pods and disseminated form. Mining starts on top of the mountain and progresses downslope by slicing off the top of the hill in approximately 27 ft benches. In the exposed faces of the benches,

OPEN PIT MINE

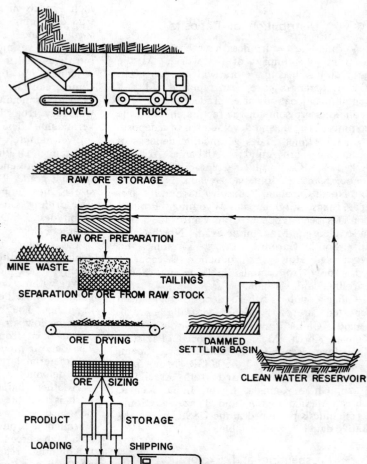

FIG. 1—*Flow diagram of vermiculite ore processing (Strand, 1975).*

vermiculite-bearing ore and waste are removed at the same time. Most of the material is loosened by rotary drilling 6-in. holes and shooting with ammonium nitrate. Large front-end loaders are used to load 85-ton off-highway trucks. Conventional mining and construction equipment, such as dozers, graders, drills, trucks, and loaders, is used. Considerable road building, using the syenite waste rock, is necessary because of the large truck size and the soft pyroxenite. The ore is hauled to a primary screening plant located between the mine and mill areas. At this point the +⅝-in. waste rock is removed and the ore is conveyed to a large storage dome.

Waste from the mine is hauled by truck to the edge of the pyroxenite and dumped downslope into the valley.

The ore is fed to the mill at a closely controlled rate where it is separated into size fractions and beneficiated. All concentrates pass through a dewatering step and then are dried. The minus 65 mesh fraction goes to a tailings pond where the material is settled and the clear water recirculated back to the process. All air or dryer exhausts are passed through bag dust collectors.

Concentrates from the mill are conveyed to a loading station and then hauled by truck to a plant near the railroad where screening separates the standard commercial sizes for storage and shipment.

South Carolina: The largest of the South Carolina operations is located near Enoree, approximately 35 miles southeast of Greenville. The ore reserves consist of a group of deposits which are mined and blended for feed to the centrally located mill. The mines are relatively small open pit type with sloped benched walls. The overburden and wall material are removed by self-loading scrapers and stacked near the pit for use in reclamation. Weathering is deep and no blasting is required. The ore is usually pushed by dozer to a point for loading by small draglines. Some blending of the ore is accomplished by the dozer as it moves across the area. Hauling is done with tandem rear-axle diesel tractor-trailer dump units. All equipment must be of the size that can travel or be hauled over public highways. Dozers and graders are used to build and maintain the mine roads. Upon completion of mining, the pit is reclaimed by pushing in the walls, returning the waste, terracing, and establishing a cover of vegetation.

The ore from the mines is dumped into piles on the rim of a pit at the head of the mill. The various grades of ore (usually four) are blended and pushed into the pit by a dozer. Two hydraulic monitors are used to break up the lumps and wash the ore into the mill as a wet slurry. The ore goes through a series of scrubing, desliming, and beneficiating steps. The concentrate is dewatered, dried, screened into the standard sizes, and stored for later shipment. Ponds are maintained for the collection of all mill waste. The clarified water is returned to the mill process in a closed system.

Processing

Vermiculite is sold mostly in the expanded form which has been exfoliated by heating. The expanded material weighs from 4 to 8 lb/ft³ depending on the particle size and type of furnace used. In the United States the unexfoliated vermiculite concentrate, 50 to 60 lb/ft³, is usually shipped in 100-ton bulk rail cars from the mills to expanding plants located throughout the United States and Canada.

There are five standard sizes produced by the mills so that when the concentrate is exfoliated at the plants it will be a finished product. The standard commercial screen sizes (Tyler Standard) for the concentrates are −3 +10, −6 +14, −8 +28, −20 +65, −50 mesh. At the expanding plant the bulk hoppers usually are unloaded by conveyors and bucket elevators

and stored in silos or bins. From the storage areas, the ore is fed at controlled rates into vertical furnaces fired by gas or oil. Processing flame temperature varies from approximately 2000° to 3600°F. The time-temperature relationship is critical in obtaining maximum expansion and good quality. Usually a shorter retention time and higher temperature will produce better expansion. After leaving the furnace the expanded material is passed across a separator where rock impurities are removed and the product is cooled. The product is normally packaged in 3- or 4-ft³ paper or plastic bags and shipped to customers by truck. Both bulk and bagged material are shipped by rail. Most furnaces are equipped with bag collectors for dust control. Various products are manufactured at selected plants, using the expanded vermiculite as an ingredient.

Tests and Specifications

At the mills samples of drill cuttings, mined ore, mill feed, and concentrates are continuously tested to maintain quality control. Concentrates are checked for expansion loss (water content), impurities of nonexpandable minerals, screen size, and volume yield.

The expanded products must meet many specifications depending on use. Specifications have been established by Underwriter's Laboratories, Inc., the American Society for Testing and Materials, the Food and Drug Administration, the producers, and the customers. Numerous methods for quality control have been devised for testing the expanded vermiculite or manufactured products to ensure that these specifications are met.

Production

Although the mineral vermiculite was described in 1824 the first report of production was in 1913 in the Turrett Mining District near Salida, CO, where eight carloads were produced. In the 1920s commercial production was started at Libby, MT, and grew slowly until 1946. Production was started in South Carolina in 1946, which helped to develop the market in the eastern United States. Production in Virginia commenced in 1978. South Africa began production in the late 1940s.

Table 2 shows the trend of production since 1940, and Table 3 lists vermiculite exfoliating plants in the US in 1980.

TABLE 2—World Vermiculite Production Since 1940 (Thousand Short Tons)

Year	United States	South Africa	Others*	World
1940	22	0	0	22
1950	208	47	0	255
1960	199	69	1	269
1970	285	134	12	431
1971	301	145	13	459
1972	337	163	12	512
1973	365	172	12	549
1974	341	201	15	557
1975	330	210	28	588
1976	304	245	28	576
1977	359	182	29	570
1978	337	230	49	616
1979	346	211	50	607
1980	337	205	41	583
1981	320	210	46	576
1982e	310	200	40	550

Source: US Bureau of Mines.
e Estimate
* Exclusive of Central Economy countries, for which data are not available.

Markets and Uses

The principal markets for vermiculite are in construction, agriculture, horticulture, and general industry. It is estimated that approximately 70% of the production is used in construction and perhaps 30% in various agriculture and horticulture uses. Most of the products sold to construction are used in nonresidential building.

Construction Uses

These include loose fill used as a pour-in insulation for attics, safes, and block walls. A special water-repellent product is used as a fill in masonry walls.

Vermiculite is used as an aggregate to produce a lightweight insulating concrete roof deck which is poured in place.

Unexpanded concentrate is used extensively in the production of fire-retardant gypsum wallboard.

Special sprayed-on products, in which vermiculite is mixed with gypsum and other ingredients, protect structural steel and concrete members against fire damage.

Agricultural Uses

Manufacturers of lightweight high analysis fertilizers for the home lawn and garden market use vermiculite as the base carrier. It also is used as the carrier for other agriculture chemicals, including pesticides and weed killers. Dur-

ing the past five years the market has been increasing for the use of vermiculite as a growing medium. Mixtures of vermiculite, peat moss, and other ingredients make excellent artificial soil such as potting soils, soil substitutes, soil conditioners, and soils for plant propagation.

The average price per short ton of unexpanded vermiculite concentrate, f.o.b. mine, in the United States for the past five years is given by Meisinger (1981) as:

Year	Price
1977	$51.81
1978	58.46
1979	63.58
1980	69.73
1981	81.88
1982 (estimate)	90.00

TABLE 3—Vermiculite Exfoliating Plants in the United States in 1980

Company	City	State
Brouk Co.	St. Louis	Missouri
Cleveland Builders Supply Co.	Cleveland	Ohio
Diversified Insulation, Inc.	Minneapolis	Minnesota
J. P. Austin, Assoc., Inc.	Beaver Falls	Pennsylvania
W. R. Grace & Co.	Irondale	Alabama
	Phoenix	Arizona
	North Little Rock	Arkansas
	Newark	California
	Santa Ana	California
	Denver	Colorado
	Pompano Beach	Florida
	Jacksonville	Florida
	Tampa	Florida
	West Chicago	Illinois
	Newport	Kentucky
	New Orleans	Louisiana
	Muirkirk	Maryland
	Easthampton	Massachusetts
	Dearborn	Michigan
	Minneapolis	Minnesota
	St. Louis	Missouri
	Omaha	Nebraska
	Trenton	New Jersey
	Weedsport	New York
	High Point	North Carolina
	Oklahoma City	Oklahoma
	Portland	Oregon
	New Castle	Pennsylvania
	Enoree	South Carolina
	Travelers Rest	South Carolina
	Nashville	Tennessee
	San Antonio	Texas
	Dallas	Texas
	Milwaukee	Wisconsin
International Vermiculite	Girard	Illinois
Koos, Inc.	Kenosha	Wisconsin
Mica Pellets, Inc.	Dekalb	Illinois
Patterson Vermiculite Co.	Lanford	South Carolina
Robinson Insulation Co.	Great Falls	Montana
	Minot	North Dakota
The Schundler Co.	Metuchen	New Jersey
O. M. Scott	Marysville	Ohio
Strong-Lite Products	Pine Bluff	Arkansas
Verlite Co.	Tampa	Florida
Vermiculite of Hawaii, Inc.	Honolulu	Hawaii
Vermiculite-Intermountain, Inc.	Salt Lake City	Utah
Vermiculite Products, Inc.	Houston	Texas

Bibliography and References

Bassett, W.A., 1959, "The Origin of the Vermiculite Deposits of Libby, Montana," *American Mineralogist,* Vol. 44, No. 3–4, Mar.-Apr., pp. 282–299.

Boettcher, A.L., 1966, "The Rainy Creek Igneous Complex Near Libby, Montana," Ph.D. Thesis, Pennsylvania State University, 70 pp.

Buie, B.F., and Stewart, O.F., 1954, "Origin of Vermiculite at Tigerville, South Carolina" (abstract), *Geological Society of America Bulletin,* Vol. 65, No. 12, Pt. 2, pp. 1356–1357.

Dekun, N., 1965, *Mineral Resources of Africa,* Elsevier, Amsterdam, pp. 440–441.

Haines, S.K., 1978, "Vermiculite," *Mineral Commodity Profiles,* US Bureau of Mines, 10 pp.

Heinrich, E.W., 1966, *The Geology of Carbonatites,* Rand McNally & Co., Chicago, 555 pp.

Libby, S.C., 1975, "Origin of Potassic Ultramafic Rocks in the Enoree Vermiculite District, South Carolina," Ph.D. Thesis, Pennsylvania State University.

Mathieson, A.L., and Walker, G.F., 1954, "Crystal Structure of Magnesium Vermiculite," *American Mineralogist,* Vol. 39, pp. 231–255.

Meisinger, A.C., 1979, "Vermiculite," *Minerals Yearbook, 1979,* US Bureau of Mines.

Meisinger, A.C., 1981, "Vermiculite," Preliminary Annual Report, US Bureau of Mines.

Meisinger, A.C., 1982, "Vermiculite," *Mineral Commodities Summaries 1982,* US Bureau of Mines, p. 170.

Stewart, O.F., 1949, "Origin and Occurrence of Vermiculite at Tigerville, South Carolina," M.S. Thesis, University of South Carolina.

Strand, P.R., 1975, "Vermiculite," *Industrial Minerals and Rocks,* 4th ed., S.J. Lefond, ed., AIME, New York, pp. 1219–1226.

Wollastonite

E. A. ELEVATORSKI *
Revised by L. A. ROE †

Wollastonite, named after William H. Wollaston, an English chemist, is a calcium metasilicate, $CaSiO_3$; CaO: 48.30%, SiO_2: 51.70%. It has a short history as an industrial mineral.

The earliest production of wollastonite is reported to be from a deposit near Code Siding, located north of Randsburg, CA. At this locality small tonnages of wollastonite were quarried during 1933–34 and 1938–41, and processed into mineral wool. This operation was largely experimental and virtually no United States production was again reported until the 1950s when a large deposit near Willsboro, NY, was developed by the Cabot Corp. A processing plant was placed onstream in 1953, with nearly continuous production to date. It is currently operated by NYCO, a division of Processed Minerals, Inc. Since 1958, wollastonite deposits in the Little and Big Maria Mountains of Riverside County, and in the Panamint Range of Inyo County, both in California, have operated intermittently for production of both ornamental and commercial wollastonite.

During 1980, the United States was the major producing country, furnishing about 75% of the world's output. Current production comes from Finland, Mexico, India, and Kenya. Small amounts have been shipped intermittently from the USSR, New Zealand, Republic of the Sudan, Republic of South Africa, and Namibia (South-West Africa).

The principal use of wollastonite is in the manufacture of plastics. Other uses are for paints, ceramics, adhesives, fluxes, glazes, thermal insulation board, and refractory products.

Mineralogy

Pure wollastonite, $CaSiO_3$, has the composition of 48.3% CaO and 51.7% SiO_2. However, it is seldom found in the pure state due to the ease with which it takes into solution the metasilicates of manganese, magnesium, iron,

and strontium. Predominantly, wollastonite occurs as a contact metamorphic deposit forming between limestones and igneous rocks. Commonly associated minerals are garnet, diopside, epidote, calcite, and quartz.

It has a specific gravity of 2.8 to 3.0, and hardness of 4.5 to 5 on Mohs' scale. When pure, it has a brilliant white color, but with impurities it may be grayish or brownish. Luster is vitreous to pearly. Melting point of wollastonite is about 1540° C.

Wollastonite occurs in coarse-bladed masses, rarely showing good crystal form. It is usually acicular or fibrous, even in the smallest of particles. The most unique property of crushed and ground wollastonite is its cleavage. Fragments of crushed wollastonite tend to be needle-shaped, imparting a high strength, and this property is the basis for many of its uses. The fiber lengths are commonly in the ratio of 7 or 8 to 1, length to diameter. The average diameter of wollastonite is 3.5 μm. Some crystals of wollastonite fluoresce under short-wave or long-wave ultraviolet light, or both, with colors ranging from yellow-orange to pink-orange. Specimens may also show phosphorescence.

The acicularity of wollastonite is a property of considerable importance to the marketplace. The plastics industry makes utilization of high aspect ratio grades of wollastonite (20:1) for reinforcing thermoplastics and thermoset polymer compounds.

The naturally high pH of 9.9 (10% water slurry) is a prime property to the coatings industry. The coatings industry uses milled grades of wollastonite as a pH stabilizer in interior and exterior PVA and acrylic latex systems. Processed wollastonite can have a G.E. brightness of 90 to 93.

Chemically, wollastonite is inert and this property makes it useful as a filler and reinforcing agent.

There are two polymorphs of calcium silicates: wollastonite, a low temperature form, and pseudowollastonite, a high temperature

* Minobras, Dana Point, CA.
† Consultant, Downers Grove, IL.

form. Inversion of wollastonite to pseudo-wollastonite occurs at about 1120° C, resulting in an increase in the coefficient of expansion and a color change. Pure white wollastonite, on inversion, may change to a cream tint, or various shades of red or brown. The color change is thought to be due to the presence of iron and strontium.

Mode of Occurrence and Origin

Wollastonite is a contact metamorphic mineral, occurring within impure limestones near intrusive bodies of granite or other acidic rocks. It can also be formed by the metasomatism of calcareous sediments and by crystallization of certain magmas.

In contact metamorphism, limestones are recrystallized by the heat of intrusive rocks. Silica emanations from igneous rocks yield calc-silicate hornfels, along with "skarn" rocks formed by the transfer of manganese, silicon, aluminum, and iron from the magma to the limestone. Skarn minerals of wollastonite, garnet, and diopside form in the adjacent limestone, usually in a well-defined zone and probably at the end stages of igneous activity.

The reaction between the silica emanations of a granitic intrusion and calcite from limestone is as follows:

$$CaCO_3 + SiO_2 \rightleftharpoons CaSiO_3 + CO_2$$

Calcite　　Silica　　Wollastonite　　Carbon dioxide

Studies by Winkler (1965) indicate that when the temperature rises to about 400° to 450° C, the reaction begins and continues until the supply of calcite or silica is exhausted.

Deposits

United States

As the largest producer in the world, the United States output comes from New York and California.

New York: An extensive deposit is located on the western side of Lake Champlain near Willsboro. Wollastonite-bearing rocks outcrop in a belt of contact metamorphosed limestones and metasomatized sediments that is about 6 miles long and ¼ mile wide. There are three main deposits, known as Willsboro, Lewis, and Deerhead, with proven reserves in excess of 10 million tons containing 55 to 65% wollastonite.

The largest wollastonite rock band is between 30 to 75 ft thick, interbedded with iron garnets, mostly almandite, and iron diopside. Host rock is a Precambrian limestone partly replaced by skarn bands, varying in composition from pure wollastonite to pure garnet. Both garnet and diopside are feebly magnetic, and are easily separated from the wollastonite by magnetic separators. A typical analysis of wollastonite-bearing rocks from the Willsboro deposit consists of: SiO_2, 47.7%; CaO, 37.8%; Al_2O_3, 3.1%; FeO, 6.6%; MgO, 3.6%; and MnO, 1.2%.

Also, in New York, an occurrence of wollastonite has been reported in a contact zone of skarn rocks, between marble and granite-gneiss near the Clifton mine, located about 80 miles west of Willsboro. Wollastonite-bearing rocks up to several feet in thickness are reported.

California: Many occurrences of wollastonite are reported by Troxel (1957), in the desert areas, but only a few have produced commercial-grade or ornamental wollastonite.

Wollastonite is produced from the Little and Big Maria Mountains, located about 20 miles northwest of Blythe. It is found as high-grade pods in a Paleozoic crystalline limestone and in a lower zone of metamorphic rocks beneath the limestone. In the lower zone, the wollastonite is fine-grained, hard, and intimately associated with diopside, making separation difficult. The fibers are interlaced, tough, and difficult to grind. In addition, some of the ore is high in magnesium and iron. Some wollastonite is selectively mined by Pfizer Inc., and milled at Victorville, where it is beneficiated and ground to −200 and −325 mesh products. It is marketed under the trade name Wolcon and sold to the ceramic and coatings industries.

Talus material consisting of thin slabs of weathered wollastonite is collected on the slopes of the Big and Little Maria Mountains and Arica Mountains in Riverside County. Uneven erosion has caused irregular surfaces to develop on the wollastonite rocks, with brownish-gray subparallel streaks, resembling driftwood. This material is sold as ornamental stone for decorative stonework, landscaping, and roofing material.

A large deposit of high-grade wollastonite is mined in the Panamint Range, about six miles southeast of Ubehebe Peak, just outside of Death Valley National Monument. It occurs in calc-silicate rocks produced by contact metamorphism of coarse-crystalline Permian or Devonian limestones by a quartz-monzonite intrusive. Diopside, idocrase, tremolite, quartz, and calcite are the contaminants present. Reserves are very large and the wollastonite is both fine-grained and acicular.

The earliest mining of wollastonite is reported to have occurred near Code Siding, north of Randsburg, about midway between Randsburg and Ridgecrest. The host rock is a Paleozoic metasedimentary rock, intensely folded and containing wollastonite-garnet-diopside layers. The wollastonite is medium to fine-grained, gray in color, and interstratified with nearly equal amounts of diopside and garnet. The outcrop is about 8000 ft long, 400 ft wide, and from 10 to 30 ft in thickness. Reserves are reported to be about 12 million tons.

White, crystalline wollastonite outcrops in Warm Springs Canyon, on the east slope of the Panamint Range in Inyo County. The deposit is an elongate lens, about 750 ft long and 35 ft in thickness. Some of the wollastonite layers are of high-grade; however, some layers are of siliceous and calcareous material with constituents of diopside, quartz, and calcite.

Other California localities where wollastonite occurs are: Hunter Mountain near Darwin, in the Argus Range east of Darwin, both in Inyo County; at Sheep Creek in the Avawatz Mountains, in the western foothills of the Shadow Mountains, about 22 miles northeast of Victorville, both in San Bernardino County; and in the Cargo Muchacho Mountains of Imperial County.

Arizona: In the Mineral Hill area of the Sierrita Mountains, and near Rosemont, both in Pima County, wollastonite is locally abundant, where large masses of limestone have been metamorphosed. A deposit is also reported in the vicinity of Tank Pass, about 10 miles northwest of Salome, in Yuma County. Other occurrences of wollastonite are reported in the Dripping Springs Mountains near Christmas; and in the Tombstone District, Cochise County.

Nevada: Large masses of wollastonite-garnet-diopside occur near Yerington in Lyon County, where limestones have been metamorphosed into calc-silicate rocks. At this location, Triassic limestones have been intruded by granodiorite and quartz-monzonite.

Other States: In Idaho, a wollastonite-marble deposit is located in the Alder Creek mining area near Mackay, Custer County. Wollastonite occurs in metamorphosed limestone xenoliths of the South Canyon and Organ Districts of Dona Aña County, New Mexico. In Utah, wollastonite, in association with garnet and diopside, is reported in the Bingham area.

Mexico

Extensive deposits exist in the states of Chiapas and Zacatecas, where wollastonite was first mined during the 1950s in the La Blanca District of Zacatecas.

The large "Santa Fe" deposit in the state of Chiapas, near the town of Pichucalco, is unusually pure and free of garnet and calcite. Extensive mine workings have shown the deposit to be at least 300 ft thick, elliptical, and dome-shaped, being about 1400 ft long and 400 ft wide. Associated minerals total less than 1%. The wollastonite is a brilliant white and has typical acicular cleavage. Near the edge of the deposit, contaminants of bornite, chalcopyrite, and garnet are found. Compañia Minera de Cerralvo, S.A., operates the project and most of the output is consumed by the domestic ceramics industry.

In the La Blanca District, about 30 miles east of Ciudad Zacatecas, state of Zacatecas, wollastonite is produced by Wollastonia de Mexico. Irregular tabular bodies, about 8 ft in thickness, occur in folded Cretaceous limestones, intruded by granite. A very pure and bright white wollastonite is found. Also, a gray wollastonite-marble band, hosting thin layers of garnet, is found adjacent to a granite contact. Reserves of the deposit are estimated to be in excess of 40 million tons. Output from the La Blanca District is shipped to tile manufacturers in Monterrey and Mexico City.

Near Xalostoc, Sierra Tlayacac, in the state of Morelos, ornamental wollastonite is produced from a metamorphosed limestone near its contact with granitic rocks. The material polishes well and the brilliant white wollastonite contrasts markedly with pink garnet and yellow idocrase.

Additional occurrences of wollastonite appear in skarns over large areas of the Naica area in Chihuahua, mostly as small pods that are coarsely crystalline and white to pale pink in color. At another location, limestones in the Sierra Magistral area of the Llanos District, north of Puebla, have been metamorphized, forming masses of wollastonitic-bearing rocks.

USSR

Many occurrences of wollastonite are known and deposits in Uzbekistan and Tadzhikistan were being worked in the mid-1960s.

In central Asia, the Uzbekistan deposit is located in the Nuratau Mountains about 45 miles north of Samarkand. Calc-silicate hornfels containing 30 to 40% wollastonite occur at the contact between a granodiorite intrusion and argillaceous limestones. The wollastonite has a radial-fibrous structure and contains appreciable calcite with small quantities of feldspar, garnet, diopside, and pyroxene.

There has been some production of wollastonite from a deposit located 10 miles north of Leninabad in northern Tadzhikistan. Calc-silicate hornfels are characterized by wollastonite-garnet-pyroxene bands. The wollastonite is white to pink, fine-grained, and radial to fibrous in structure.

A large deposit with a thickness of about 200 ft is located between the cities of Almalyk and Tashkent, in Central Asia. The wollastonite rock has an average grade of 50%, and reportedly was formed in limestone horizons by the reaction of post-magmatic solutions.

Wollastonite rocks are also common in the Aktau Range of the Nuratau Mountains, south of Samarkand; in northwest Russia at Kalkkitekhda, just outside of Leningrad; and in southwest Russia at Tyrnyauz.

Finland

In southwest Finland, wollastonite is quarried from Archean limestones about 2 miles south of Lappeenranta. This elliptically shaped deposit is about 3 km long and 1 km wide and is surrounded by a large granite mass. The main wollastonite zone is about 150 ft thick and 2000 ft long. It contains bands of wollastonite and diopside interbedded with leptite, a quartz-feldspar rock, and calcite. The host rocks reportedly contain an average of 20%, ranging upward to 60%, wollastonite. Wollastonite is mined selectively, crushed, and the calcite and iron-bearing minerals removed by flotation. The deposit is worked by Pargas Kalkbergs Ab, and the output used almost entirely by a subsidiary company in the manufacture of wall tiles.

Kenya

Wollastonite-marble rocks were discovered in 1965 at Lolkidongai, about 50 miles south of Nairobi. These rocks reportedly outcrop along several hills forming a three-mile long arc. Wollastonite comprises 40 to 50% of the limestone host rock. Chief impurity is quartz, although calcite, and garnet and diopside min-

erals are present. Flotation concentrates, of about 85% pure wollastonite are dried and the −60 mesh material bagged and exported to European countries.

Namibia (South-West Africa)

Extensive bands of wollastonite marble are found at Usakos and in a belt extending northwest of Damaraland for nearly 40 miles. Composition of the wollastonitic marbles varies greatly. The higher grades are utilized for industrial material with the lower grades used for building stone and ornamental rock. Marble was formed by regional metamorphism and the subsequent intrusion of a pegmatitic granite may have formed the wollastonite. Some ceramic grade material is also produced and exported to Holland.

Other Areas

Large deposits of wollastonite are known in the northeastern Red Sea Hills about 70 miles from Port Sudan, Republic of the Sudan. The wollastonite occurs as lenticular masses up to 100 ft long in a skarn assemblage that includes idocrase, garnet, and diopside. In the Republic of South Africa, wollastonite occurs near Garies, Namaqualand, in a belt of limy metamorphic rocks, enclosed by granite-gneisses. Grade of the ore varies considerably, averaging 50% wollastonite. Chief contaminants are a green diopside and a brownish garnet.

A high-grade wollastonite deposit is located at Merida, in Badajoz Province, near the Portuguese border of Spain. It is located between bands of Devonian limestone, and offers promise in the manufacture of dielectric porcelains. Calc-silicate rocks containing wollastonite-diopside-garnet are found in the northern foothills of Sudety Mountains, near Strzelin, Poland. In Morocco, wollastonite beds over 30 ft thick are reported at Azegour, southwest of Marrakech, in an area between the northern flanks of the Atlas Mountains and the east coast.

Wollastonite occurs in a number of areas of Canada; however only the Fintry deposit, located 10 miles north of Kelowna, in British Columbia, has been explored. Steeply dipping limestone beds contain wollastonite-calcite lens and stringers averging 30% wollastonite. Mineralization occurs as a contact aureole of a granitic intrusion into Paleozoic sediments.

In 1969 an extensive deposit near the village of Khila, Rajasthan State of India, was being developed. Estimated reserves, to a depth of 50 m, are about 5 million tons.

Occurrences of wollastonite have been noted in limestone blocks on the islands of Santorini, Greece, and on Monte Somma, Vesuvius, Italy, where it probably was formed at depth and ejected during volcanic activity.

Mining and Processing

At Willsboro, NY, wollastonite is mined by open stope methods. Stopes are about 30 ft wide, varying from 15 ft at the lower level to 80 ft at the surface. At the mill lump ore is dumped into a crusher pit, scraped to a pan feeder, and discharged through a jaw crusher. The dry beneficiation process is depicted by the flowsheet in Fig. 1. Unique in the operation is the high intensity magnetic separation of both garnet and diopside. The beneficiated

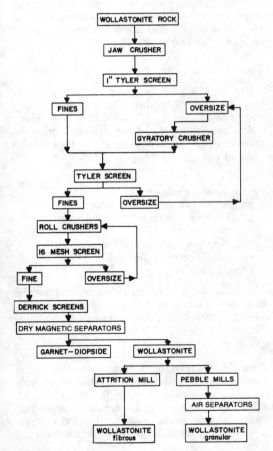

FIG. 1—*Flowsheet of wollastonite processing, Willsboro, NY.*

wollastonite is ground to four product sizes in pebble mills and a high aspect ratio product produced in an attrition mill. Finished products are sold under the trade names of Nycor® and Nyad®.

Quarrying is the method used in mining wollastonite at Lappeenranta, Finland. Here selective mining is necessary because the wollastonite occurs in thin bands up to 1 m in thickness. After primary and secondary crushing, a two-stage flotation process is employed. Calcite, the main impurity, is depressed into the underflow and the wollastonite and other silicates report to the first froth product. Then the unwanted silicate minerals are floated from the first froth product by using a combination anionic-cationic reagent as the collector. The final underflow is the wollastonite product. After drying, the flotation concentrates are ground in a pebble mill to produce two principal grades, one —50 mesh and the other —200 mesh. Concentrates are composed of SiO_2, 51 to 53%; CaO, 43 to 45%; Al_2O_3, 0.5%; Fe_2O_3, 0.2%; and MgO, 0.3%.

Reserves

World reserves of proven wollastonite-bearing rocks exceed 90 million tons, with probable reserves about three times this figure. Many countries have extensive deposits that are unsurveyed. In addition to the size of the deposit, the economic feasibility of producing wollastonite is greatly affected by the purity of the crude ore and the difficulties encountered in removing the contaminating minerals.

Consumption, Trade, and Production

Estimated world consumption of wollastonite approached 140,000 tons in 1980. In the United States, the plastics and thermal insulation board industries were the major consumers followed closely by the ceramics and refractory industries, with the coatings industry a medium-size consumer. Plastics and board account for 25 to 30% of the total consumption.

In Germany, Denmark, and Finland the coatings and ceramic industries are the major consumers. In Italy the ceramic industry is the major consumer, while the plastics and coatings industries in Japan are the primary consumers.

Ornamental wollastonite, used as decorative rock and in crushed form for terrazzo and roofing material, is produced in Mexico and in Namibia (South-West Africa).

The US production of 135,000 tons of industrial wollastonite comes from producers in

New York and California. Production of 20,000 to 40,000 tons is available in Mexico, 40,000 tons in Finland, and an unknown volume in India.

In trade, the United States and Finland consume 80 to 90% of their respective production, with the remainder exported to Denmark, Germany, Italy, Great Britain, and Canada.

Specifications and Prices

Wollastonite is a unique mineral due to its acicular particle shape. Its markets are directly related to its properties since wollastonite is not a widely-occurring mineral and freight costs are high. Commercial products fall into two broad classifications: milled grades and attrition milled grades. Milled grades are −200 mesh, −325 mesh, −400 mesh, and a new 10 μm top size product. Attrition grades are currently limited to one—a 20:1 L/D product. Since the United States is the largest producing and consuming country, current US dollar prices will be listed. The milled grades cost between 2¢ and 5¢ per lb, the attrition grade is 7¢ per lb (1981). Price lists are published by all producers.

Uses

The major potential markets for wollastonite are the plastics and coatings industries, followed closely by thermal insulation board. Other significant consumers are ceramics and refractories. Wollastonite has minor application in metal casting plasters, fluxes, matchheads, abrasives, pesticide carrier, and friction papers.

A major general application area is as a partial substitute for fiberglass and for asbestos in the plastics and coatings industries.

The Ceramic Industry

The advantages of using wollastonite in ceramics are twofold: it improves the mechanical properties of the ceramic ware, and it greatly reduces warping and cracking for ceramic materials that must be rapidly fired. Wollastonite fluxes readily with silica and alumina at low temperatures, reducing thermal expansion and thereby minimizing cracking. Tiles have higher green strengths and better pressing qualities because of the needlelike shape of wollastonite particles. Also, drying rates are improved because the wollastonite particles provide openings for rapid passage of moisture through the body. Since wollastonite contains no chemically bound water nor car-

bonates, its use in ceramic materials minimizes the liberation of gas. Without its use, gases commonly cause cracks and laminations. Apart from its other merits, wollastonite is almost 50% silica and its adoption in place of free silica-bearing materials such as sand, flint and china stone, reduces the risk of silicosis of workers in the ceramic industry.

The Coatings Industry

For coatings, the high pH of wollastonite allows its wide use as a pH stabilizer (replacing ammonia and chemical buffers) in PVA and acrylic latex paint systems. Most trade sales paints have ¼ lb per gal of wollastonite to prevent can and lid corrosion, and to keep the pigments in suspension. Exterior acrylic house paints (containing zinc oxide) utilize the buffering action of wollastonite for stabilization and weathering.

Wollastonite's properties of acicular particle shape, low oil demand, and good color allow its use for film reinforcement, improved scrub resistance, and weatherability.

The Plastics Industry

For plastics compounding, the acicular particle structure of wollastonite identifies it as a reinforcing mineral. Wollastonite has many individual properties related to individual polymer compounds. In general, wollastonite is used in polymers for:

high purity
low moisture adsorption
excellent heat deflection/distortion
good tensile, modulus, impact properties
reinforcement
excellent electrical insulation properties
excellent dimensional stability
economics

Wollastokup®, surface modified wollastonite, is finding wide application as a partial replacement for fiberglass and other minerals.

Other Uses

In the production of ceramic-bonded abrasives and abrasive wheels, the addition of wollastonite imparts a greater fluxing rate and high thermal shock resistance. Some wollastonite is also being used to replace natural cryolite as a filler in grinding wheel bonding formulations.

At Lappeenranta, Finland, some wollastonite is used to produce mineral wool. Dolomite, wollastonite, and coke are finely ground, mixed, and melted in furnaces. At about 1500°C the melt is poured on to fast spinning wheels. The fibers produced are blown onto a conveyor where blankets of material are formed. A variety of acoustic and thermal insulation products are made from mineral wool. These include ceiling tiles, cork and mineral wool boards, tubes, and blankets interlayed with wire screening.

Synthetics

Synthetic calcium metasilicates have been commercially produced for some years in the United States, Denmark, Italy, Germany, and the Soviet Union. Most of the synthetics are hydrated, and none of the anhydrous compounds have the crystal form of natural wollastonite. Unlike wollastonite, the hydrated calcium silicates have a high absorptivity.

Danish synthetic calcium metasilicates are made from sand and chalk, which are abundant in Denmark, and marketed under the trade name of Synopal. Chalk and sand are mixed into a slurry with small amounts of dolomite which acts as a flux. This slurry is heated in a kiln to a temperature of about 1560°C, forming a viscous mixture that is water-cooled. When solidified, the material is graded and then reheated in a second kiln to a temperature of 1250°C, sufficient to permit crystallization to occur. The finished product is subangular, white, and opaque, consisting of about 50% wollastonite and the remainder gehlenite ($Ca_2Al_2SiO_7$) and akermanite ($MgCa_2Si_2O_7$). Uses of Synopal are for road surfacing, mosaic tiles, flooring, and roofing felts.

A product known as Wollanita is made in Italy by heating a mixture of silica, sand, chalk, and dolomite. Production methods are similar to those used in Denmark. Wollanita is used for road material, as an abrasive, and in ceramics.

Both hydrated and anhydrous calcium metasilicates are manufactured in the United States, as Silene by Pittsburgh Plate Glass Co. and as Micro-Cel by Manville Products Corp. Many grades of both products are produced by subjecting lime, sand, and dolomite slurries to high pressure and temperature.

Actual and potential uses of synthetic calcium silicates are about the same as those of natural wollastonite. In countries where wollastonite is abundant and can be produced cheaply, it is preferred over the synthetic calcium metasilicates. Common uses of both wollastonite and its synthetic equivalents are in tile making and as extenders in the paint industry. Applications of the synthetic material are as a flow-aid agent in powdered materials, in foam, and in mineral wool.

Tonnages of synthetic wollastonite produced are unavailable; however, they are known to be minor in comparison to natural wollastonite production. Prices of the synthetic equivalents are about double the price of natural wollastonite.

Bibliography and References

Anon., 1969, "Wollastonite Comes of Age," *Industrial Minerals,* Apr., pp. 8–13.

Anon., 1975, "Wollastonite: U.S.A. Dominates Both Production and Consumption," *Industrial Minerals,* No. 94, July, pp. 15–23, 29.

Anon., 1980, "Wollastonite Facility Set By Processed Minerals for Willsboro Plantsite," *Chemical Marketing Reporter,* Vol. 217, No. 21, May 26, pp. 3, 23.

Amberg, C.R., et al., 1969, "Wollastonite, An Industrial Mineral," *Ceramics Bulletin,* New York State College, No. 4, 60 pp.

Andrews, R.W., 1970, *Wollastonite,* Monograph, Her Majesty's Stationery Office, Great Britain, 114 pp.

Burnham, K., and Broughton, J.G., 1955, "Occurrences and Uses of Wollastonite from Willsboro, New York," *Mining Technology,* No. 8, July, pp. 1–8.

Clarke, G., 1980, "Mexico's Industrial Minerals—Gathering Momentum," *Industrial Minerals,* No. 153, June, pp. 21–53.

Copeland, J., and Rush, O.W., 1978, "Wollastonite, Short Fiber Filler Reinforcement," *Plastic Compounding,* Nov.-Dec., pp. 26–41.

Copeland, J., and Rush, O.W., 1979, "Reinforcing with Wollastonite Filler Makes for a Tougher Polypropylene," Preprint, *Modern Plastics,* Mar., 2 pp.

Doctorman, V.C., 1958, "Wollastonite Spun into Rock Wool," *Rock Products,* Aug., pp. 80–81.

Engelhardt, C.L., 1979, "Calcium Metasilicate—An Extender Pigment," Preprint, *American Paint and Coatings Journal,* Sept. 10, 7 pp.

Hall, A.L., et al., 1952, "Enter Wollastonite—A New Commercial Nonmetallic Mineral," *Mining Engineering,* Vol. 4, No. 10, pp. 952–953.

Ladoo, R.B., 1960, "Wollastonite," *Industrial Minerals and Rocks,* 3rd ed., AIME, New York, pp. 897–899.

Mason, J.E., 1966, "The Lolkidongai Wollastonite Occurrence, Kajiado District, Kenya," Information Circular No. 3, Kenya Dept. of Mines and Geology, 28 pp.

Neely, J.R., 1954, "Properties of Ceramics Containing Wollastonite," M.S. Thesis, University of California at Los Angeles.

Neely, J.R., and Knapp, W.J., 1964, "California Wollastonites," *Ceramic News,* Vol. 14, No. 5, pp. 12–13.

Shvetsov, V.Y., and Tsapkov, N.T., 1964, "Producing Wollastonite Concentrates for Ceramics," *Glass Ceramics,* Vol. 21, No. 6, pp. 32–33.

Simpson, W. and deJager, D.H., 1962, "Wollastonite near Garies, Namaqualand," *Annals of the Geological Survey of South Africa*, Vol. 1, pp. 127–135.

Thorndike, J.D., 1936, "Mineral Wool from Wollastonite," *Mining and Metallurgy*, March, pp. 133–136.

Tolliday, J.M., 1958, "The Crystal Structures of Parawollastonite and Wollastonite," Ph.D. Thesis, Birbeck College, London, 110 pp.

Troxel, B.W., 1957, "Wollastonite," Bulletin 176, Mineral Commodities of California, California Div. of Mines and Geology, pp. 693–697.

Vukovich, M., et al., 1957, "The Use of Wollastonite in Ceramic Bodies," *Engineering Experiment Station Bulletin No. 164*, Ohio State University, Vol. 26, No. 2, 76 pp.

Winkler, H.G.F., 1965, *Petrogenesis of Metamorphic Rocks*, Springer-Verlag, pp. 28–30.

Zeolites

Introduction

RICHARD H. OLSON *

"Rarely in our technological society does the discovery of a new class of inorganic materials result in such a wide scientific interest and kaleidoscopic development of applications as has happened with the zeolite molecular sieves." That opening sentence in a landmark volume on zeolite molecular sieves by D. W. Breck (1974), is, if anything, an understatement.

Zeolites were recognized as a new group of minerals in the 1750s, but it was not until 1930 that the first analysis of the crystal structure of a zeolite mineral was made. In the late 1940s research workers at Union Carbide Corp. began a program of zeolite synthesis and study which has resulted in one of the major research achievements of all time.

Naturally, with the vast research and development efforts devoted to the synthetic molecular sieves, Union Carbide became concerned in the mid-1950s about its position should minable deposits of natural analogues be discovered.

Zeolite minerals have diverse origins, and even a brief discussion of these is beyond the scope of this paper. The early work on zeolites was confined to igneous rock occurrences (e.g., amygdules and veins) which were formed by "space-filling;" these crystals tend to be euhedral, thereby rendering them appealing to both mineralogists and collectors. During the first year or so of Union Carbide's exploration (which began in mid-1957) attention was devoted solely to such igneous occurrences.

A landmark paper by Bramlette and Posnjak (1933) heralded the potential significance of the occurrence of zeolite minerals as alteration products of vitric ash and similar materials.

* Consultant, Industrial Minerals Evaluations, Inc., Golden, CO.

In the summer of 1958, full attention was directed by Union Carbide to the search for deposits of this type in the western United States. Since then, such exploration has been continuous by both commercial firms and private parties. The future economic potential for natural zeolite deposits seems to be restricted to those of the "open-and-closed system" types as described by Sheppard (this chapter). Therefore, this and the following discussions will concentrate upon these types; the other types of zeolites in sedimentary rocks (e.g., deep-sea sediments, burial metamorphic, and hydrothermal) will be, for the most part, ignored.

Despite the relative cheapness of natural zeolite deposits as compared with the cost of synthetic molecular sieves, there has been minimal development of zeolite mining in the US over the past 25 years or so. Mumpton (this chapter) discusses the present commercial utilization of natural zeolites and their future potential in detail, but perhaps the following will serve as useful background. In the early days of synthetic molecular sieve research and production, the efforts were concentrated largely upon such high-value applications as physical separation of components in a stream (based upon molecular size and geometry) and in catalysis. Due to a number of reasons (some of which are difficult for an outsider to understand), natural zeolite ores (beneficiated or not) have not made substantial inroads upon the use of the higher-priced synthetic molecular sieves for the foregoing applications, but this is not to say that such a condition will exist forever. Furthermore, in view of the many other uses which are now known, or which loom in the future, the competitive position of the natural zeolites vs. the more expensive synthetic molecular sieves is, in the writer's opinion, bound to improve markedly.

It has certainly been to the advantage of the higher-priced synthetic molecular sieves to see that they are used in preference to natural zeolite products; therefore, much which could have been stated about the relative merits of natural zeolites has understandably remained unsaid. Consequently, most of those who would mine or use the natural varieties have been handicapped by a lack of knowledge with regard to their comparative efficiencies. Time, in its inexorable manner, will increasingly serve to diminish the inhibiting nature of this barrier to knowledge.

In addition, who can foresee which zeolite minerals, with known and well-demonstrated economic potential but which are not yet known to exist in commercial quantities, might be found as ore bodies in the future. In 1957 there was probably less than a kilogram of erionite in all the museums and mineral collections of the world; now several deposits are known in the US alone, aggregating many millions of tons!

Sheppard (1971) has plotted the known occurrences of the six most common zeolites occurring in sedimentary deposits in the conterminous United States. Fig. 1 shows analcime occurrences, while Table 1 lists those occurrences. Fig. 2 shows the occurrences of chabazite, erionite, mordenite, and phillipsite, while Table 2 lists those occurrences. Fig. 3 shows clinoptilolite occurrences, while Table 3 lists those occurrences.

The use of natural zeolites in environmental cleanup and many fields of pollution control is only now beginning to receive concerted research efforts. This field alone and its obvious potential would appear to justify a close look at natural zeolites by many firms who are apparently not yet so interested. But there are many other uses which also should be explored, and this is well-documented by the strength of the zeolite-mining industry in Japan as contrasted with that of the United States and the rest of the world.

Commanding positions in the zeolite mining industry in the future will be held by those who are willing to prove new uses and develop markets now, rather than by those who wait for others to do so and then hurriedly embark upon "me-too" exploration programs.

In the 3rd edition of this volume (1960), not only was there no chapter on zeolites, but the word did not even appear in the Index! There was good reason for this, because the first search for zeolite ores had only begun in mid-1957. The past 25 years or so have seen the appearance of hundreds of papers and volumes regarding zeolite minerals and synthetic molecular sieves, but it is significant that the four most comprehensive contributions which deal with both natural zeolites and synthetic molecular sieves, and also touch upon their relative merits (however lightly), have all been presented or published within a 12-month period in 1973–74. These four contributions, i.e., Breck (1973, 1974), Mumpton (1973), and Sheppard (1973), have been revised or enlarged to furnish the material for the parts of the chapter that follow.

TABLE 1—Analcime Occurrences in Sedimentary Rocks

Locality No. on Fig. 1	Locality	Occurrence
1	Near Vaughn, Cascade County, MT	Siltstone and sandstone in the Taft Hill Member of the Blackleaf Formation of Cretaceous age and tuff in the Bootlegger Member of the Blackleaf Formation of Cretaceous age
2	Near Twin Creek, Bear Lake County, ID	Tuff in the Twin Creek Limestone of Jurassic age
3	Near Gros Ventre River, Teton County, WY	Ocher oolitic beds in the Popo Agie Member of the Chugwater Formation of Triassic age
4	Near Dubois, Fremont County, WY	Ocher oolitic beds in the Popo Agie Member of the Chugwater Formation of Triassic age
5	Near Lander, Fremont County, WY	Ocher oolitic beds in the Popo Agie Member of the Chugwater Formation of Triassic age
6	Near Thermopolis, Hot Springs County, WY	Purple and ocher units of the Popo Agie Member of the Chugwater Formation of Triassic age
7	Near Hyattville, Big Horn County, WY	Bentonite in the Mowry Shale of Cretaceous age
8	South Fork of the Powder River, Natrona County, WY	Bentonite in the Mowry Formation of Cretaceous age
9	Near Casper, Natrona County, WY	Bentonite in the Mowry Formation of Cretaceous age
10	Near Lysite Mountain, Hot Springs County, WY	Tuff in the Tepee Trail Formation of Eocene age
11	Beaver Rim, Fremont County, WY	Tuff in the Wagon Bed Formation of Eocene age
12	Near Green River, Sweetwater County, WY	Tuff in the Green River Formation of Eocene age
13	Near Ludlow, Harding County, SD	Lignite in the upper member of the Tongue River Formation of Paleocene age
14	Cathedral Bluffs, Rio Blanco County, CO	Tuff in the Green River Formation of Eocene age
15	Near Piceance Creek, Rio Blanco County, CO	Oil shale in the Green River Formation of Eocene age
16	Anvil Points, Garfield County, CO	Oil shale in the Green River Formation of Eocene age
17	Along Piceance Creek, about 20 miles west of Meeker, Rio Blanco County, CO	Tuff in the Parachute Creek Member of the Green River Formation of Eocene age
18	Lone Tree Mesa, Montrose County, CO	Tuffaceous mudstone in the Brushy Basin Member of the Morrison Formation of Jurassic age
19	Near Slick Rock, San Miguel County, CO	Tuffaceous mudstone in the Brushy Basin Member of the Morrison Formation of Jurassic age
20	Near Vernal, Uintah County, UT	Ocher oolitic beds in the Chinle Formation of Triassic age
21	White River Canyon, Uintah County, UT	Tuff in the Green River Formation of Eocene age
22	Near Two Water Creek, Uintah County, UT	Tuff in the Parachute Creek Member of the Green River Formation of Eocene age
23	Near Duchesne, Duchesne County, UT	Dolomitic oil shale of the Green River Formation of Eocene age
24	Near Currant, Nye County, NV	Tuff in Horse Camp Formation of Miocene and Pliocene age
25	Nevada Test Site, Nye County, NV	Tuff and lapilli tuff of Tertiary age
26	Teels Marsh, Mineral County, NV	Tuff in lacustrine deposit of Quaternary age
27	Near Silver Peak, Esmeralda County, NV	Tuff in the Esmeralda Formation of Miocene and Pliocene age
28	Deep Springs Lake, Inyo County, CA	Saline crusts of Holocene age
29	Saline Valley, Inyo County, CA	Mud of Holocene age
30	Owens Lake, Inyo County, CA	Tuff and tuffaceous sediments of Pleistocene age
31	Lake Tecopa, Inyo County, CA	Tuff in lacustrine rocks of Pleistocene age
32	Searles Lake, San Bernardino County, CA	Tuff and mudstone of Quaternary age
33	Mojave Desert, eastern Kern County and San Bernardino County, CA	Tuff and mudstone of late Tertiary and Quaternary age

Table 1 (cont'd)

Locality No. on Fig. 1	Locality	Occurrence
34	Near Delano, Kern County, CA	Pond series soil
35	Near Wikieup, Mohave County, AZ	Tuff in Big Sandy Formation of Pliocene age
36	Maggie Canyon, Mohave County, AZ	Sandstone of the Chapin Wash Formation of Pliocene(?) age
37	Near Horseshoe Reservoir, Maricopa County, AZ	Tuff in the Verde Formation of Pliocene(?) or Pleistocene age
38	Near Eloy, Pinal County, AZ	Silty claystone of late Tertiary age
39	Willcox Playa, Cochise County, AZ	Mudstone of Pleistocene age
40	Along San Simon Creek, Cochise and Graham Counties, AZ	Tuff in unnamed lacustrine formation of late Cenozoic age
41	Near Nutrioso, Apache County, AZ	Sandstone in unnamed formation of Tertiary age
42	Near Red Wash, San Juan County, NM	Tuffaceous mudstone of the Brushy Basin Member of the Morrison Formation of Jurassic age
43	About 2.5 miles southeast of Senorito, Sandoval County, NM	Siliceous tuff in the Brushy Basin Member of the Morrison Formation of Jurassic age
44	Wichita Mountains, Kiowa County, OK	Arkose in the Tepee Creek Formation of Permian age
45	Near Terlingua, Brewster County, TX	Black tarry shale of late Mesozoic or early Tertiary age
46	Near Yardley, Bucks County, PA	Argillite in the Lockatong Formation of Triassic age
47	Near Frenchtown, Hunterdon County, NJ	Argillite in the Lockatong Formation of Triassic age
48	Near Pursglove, Monongalia County, WV	Concretion in the Pittsburgh coal bed of the Monongahela Formation of Pennsylvanian age

Source: Sheppard, 1971.

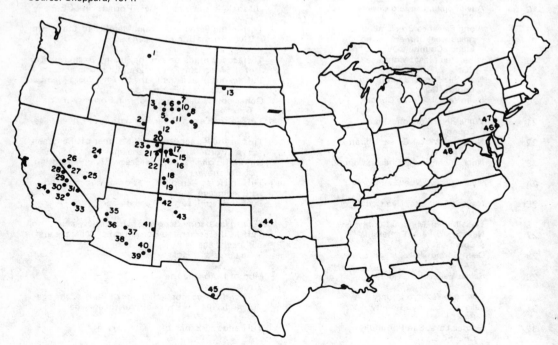

FIG. 1—*Analcime occurrences in sedimentary rocks—United States; see Table 1 (courtesy USGS).*

TABLE 2—Chabazite, Erionite, Mordenite, and Phillipsite Occurrences in Sedimentary Rocks

Locality No. on Fig. 2	Locality	Zeolites	Occurrence
1	Near Bearbones Mountain, Lane County, OR	Mordenite	Tuff and lapilli tuff in the Little Butte Volcanic Series of Oligocene and Miocene age
2	Vicinity of Stein's Pillar, Crook County, OR	Mordenite	Tuff in the John Day Formation of Oligocene and Miocene age
3	Near Durkee, Baker County, OR	Erionite	Tuff of Tertiary age
4	Near Rome, Malheur County, OR	Erionite, mordenite, phillipsite	Tuff and tuffaceous sandstone in an unnamed lacustrine formation of Pliocene age
5	West face of Hart Mountain, Lake County, OR	Mordenite, phillipsite	Tuff and tuffaceous sedimentary rocks of late Oligocene or early Miocene age
6	Near Harney Lake, Harney County, OR	Erionite, phillipsite	Tuff and tuffaceous sedimentary rocks in the Danforth Formation of Pliocene age
7	Beaver Rim, Fremont County, WY	Chabazite, erionite, phillipsite	Tuff in the Wagon Bed Formation of Eocene age
8	Near Split Rock, Natrona County, WY	Phillipsite	Tuff in the Moonstone Formation of Pliocene age
9	Near Green River, Sweetwater County, WY	Mordenite	Tuff in the Tipton Shale Member of the Green River Formation of Eocene age
10	Near Mud Buttes, Butte County, SD	Phillipsite	Bentonite in the Gammon Ferruginous Member of the Pierre Shale of Cretaceous age
11	Sheep Mountain Table, Shannon County, SD	Erionite	Tuff in the Arikaree Formation of Miocene age
12	Near Creede, Mineral County, CO	Mordenite	Tuff in the Windy Gulch Member of the Bachelor Mountain Rhyolite of Oligocene age
13	Pine Valley, Eureka, County, NV	Erionite, phillipsite	Tuff in the Hay Ranch Formation of Pliocene and Pleistocene age
14	West flank of the Shoshone Range, Lander County, NV	Erionite	Tuff in unnamed lacustrine formation of Pliocene age
15	Reese River, Lander County, NV	Erionite	Tuff in unnamed lacustrine formation of Pliocene age
16	Jersey Valley, Pershing County, NV	Erionite, phillipsite	Tuff in unnamed lacustrine formation of Pliocene age
17	Near Lovelock, Pershing County, NV	Mordenite	Tuff in unnamed lacustrine formation of late Tertiary age
18	Near Copper Valley, Churchill County, NV	Mordenite	Tuff in unnamed lacustrine formation of late Tertiary age
19	Near Eastgate, Churchill County, NV	Erionite	Tuff in unnamed lacustrine formation of late Tertiary age
20	Teels Marsh, Mineral County, NV	Phillipsite	Tuff in lacustrine deposit of Quarternary age
21	Near Silver Peak, Esmeralda County, NV	Mordenite, phillipsite	Tuff in the Esmeralda Formation of Miocene and Pliocene age
22	Nevada Test Site, Nye County, NV	Chabazite, mordenite	Tuff and lapilli tuff of Tertiary age
23	Owens Lake, Inyo County, CA	Erionite, phillipsite	Tuff and tuffaceous sediments of Pleistocene age
24	Lake Tecopa, Inyo County, CA	Chabazite, erionite, phillipsite	Tuff and tuffaceous rocks of Pleistocene age
25	Searles Lake, San Bernardino County, CA	Phillipsite	Tuff of Quaternary age
26	Mojave Desert, eastern Kern County and San Bernardino County, CA	Chabazite, erionite, mordenite, phillipsite	Tuff and tuffaceous rocks of late Tertiary and Quaternary age
27	Near Nipomo, San Luis Obispo County, CA	Mordenite	Tuff in the Obispo Formation of Miocene age

Table 2 (cont'd)

Locality No. on Fig. 2	Locality	Zeolites	Occurrence
28	Union Pass, Mohave County, AZ	Mordenite	Tuff and lapilli tuff in the Golden Door Volcanics of Tertiary age
29	Near Wikieup, Mohave County, AZ	Chabazite, erionite, phillipsite	Tuff in Big Sandy Formation of Pliocene age
30	Near Horseshoe Reservoir, Maricopa County, AZ	Erionite, phillipsite	Tuff in the Verde Formation of Pliocene(?) or Pleistocene age
31	Near Morenci, Greenlee County, AZ	Mordenite	Tuff and lapilli tuff in unnamed formation of Tertiary age
32	Near Bear Springs, Graham County, AZ	Chabazite, erionite, phillipsite	Tuff in unnamed lacustrine formation of late Cenozoic age
33	Along San Simon Creek, Cochise and Graham Counties, AZ	Chabazite, erionite	Tuff in unnamed lacustrine formation of late Cenozoic age

Source: Sheppard, 1971.

FIG. 2—*Chabazite, erionite, mordenite, and phillipsite occurrences in sedimentary rocks— United States; see Table 2 (courtesy USGS).*

TABLE 3—Clinoptilolite Occurrences in Sedimentary Rocks

Locality No. on Fig. 3	Locality	Occurrence
1	Near Vaughn, Cascade County, MT	Tuff and tuffaceous siltstone and sandstone in the Taft Hill, Vaughn, and Bootlegger Members of the Blackleaf Formation of Cretaceous age
2*	Near Livingston, Park County, MT	Tuffaceous mudstone, siltstone, and sandstone in the Livingston Group of Cretaceous age
3	Near Preston, Franklin County, ID	Tuff in the Salt Lake Group of late Tertiary age
4	Near Renton, King County, WA	Sandstone and conglomerate in unnamed marine formation of Oligocene age
5	Near Bearbones Mountain, Lane County, OR	Tuff and lapilli tuff in the Little Butte Volcanic Series of Oligocene and Miocene age
6	Near Stein's Pillar, Crook County, OR	Tuff in the John Day Formation of Oligocene and Miocene age
7	Near Deep Creek, Wheeler County, OR	Tuff in the lower part of the John Day Formation of Oligocene and Miocene age
8	Near the Painted Hills, Wheeler County, OR	Tuff and claystone in the lower part of the John Day Formation of Oligocene and Miocene age
9	Sucker Creek, Malheur County, OR	Tuff and tuffaceous sandstone in the Sucker Creek Formation of Miocene age
10	Near Sheaville, Malheur County, OR	Tuff probably equivalent to part of the Sucker Creek Formation of Miocene age
11	Near Rome, Malheur County, OR	Tuff and tuffaceous sandstone in unnamed lacustrine formation of Pliocene age
12	East face of Steens Mountain, Harney County, OR	Tuff in the Pike Creek Formation of Oligocene(?) and Miocene age
13	Near Harney Lake, Harney County, OR	Tuff and tuffaceous sedimentary rocks in the Danforth Formation of Pliocene age
14	West face of Hart Mountain, Lake County, OR	Tuff and tuffaceous sedimentary rocks of late Oligocene or early Miocene age
15	Near Pedro, Weston County, WY	Bentonite in the Pierre Shale of Cretaceous age
16	Near Lysite Mountain, Hot Springs County, WY	Tuff in the Tepee Trail Formation of Eocene age
17*	Snake River Canyon, Lincoln County, WY	Shale in the Aspen Formation of Cretaceous age
18	Beaver Rim, Fremont County, WY	Tuff in the Wagon Bed Formation of Eocene age
19	Near Cameron Spring on Beaver Rim, Fremont County, WY	Tuffaceous sandstone in the White River Formation of Oligocene age
20	Near Split Rock, Natrona County, WY	Tuff in the Moonstone Formation of Pliocene age
21	Near Green River, Sweetwater County, WY	Tuff in the Tipton Shale Member of the Green River Formation of Eocene age
22	Near Twin Buttes, Sweetwater County, WY	Tuff and tuffaceous sandstone in the Bridger Formation of Eocene age
23	Near Chamberlain, Buffalo County, SD	Bentonite in the Sharon Springs Member of the Pierre Shale of Cretaceous age
24	Sheep Mountain Table, Shannon County, SD	Tuff in the Arikaree Formation of Miocene age
25	Near Vermillion Cliffs, Moffat County, CO	Tuff in the Bridger Formation of Eocene age
26	Near Creede, Mineral County, CO	Tuff in the Windy Gulch Member of the Bachelor Mountain Rhyolite of Oligocene age
27	Near Mountain Green, Morgan County, UT	Tuff in the Salt Lake Group of Tertiary age
28	Northern part of the Markagunt Plateau, Iron County, UT	Tuffaceous sandstone of Oligocene and Miocene(?) age
29	Near Elko, Elko County, NV	Oil shale in unnamed formation of Oligocene age
30	Near Carlin, Eureka County, NV	Tuff in the Safford Canyon Formation of Oligocene(?) or Miocene(?) age and the Carlin Formation of Pliocene age
31	West flank of the Shoshone Range, Lander County, NV	Tuff in unnamed lacustrine formation of Pliocene age
32	Reese River, Lander County, NV	Tuff in unnamed lacustrine formation of Pliocene age
33	Jersey Valley, Pershing County, NV	Tuff in unnamed lacustrine formation of Pliocene age
34	Near Lovelock, Pershing County, NV	Tuff in unnamed lacustrine formation of late Tertiary age

Table 3 (cont'd)

Locality No. on Fig. 3	Locality	Occurrence
35	Near Eastgate, Churchill County, NV	Tuff in unnamed lacustrine formation of late Tertiary age
36	Teels Marsh, Mineral County, NV	Tuff in lacustrine deposit of Quaternary age
37	Near Silver Peak, Esmeralda County, NV	Tuff in the Esmeralda Formation of Miocene and Pliocene age
38	Near Goldfield, Esmeralda County, NV	Tuffaceous sandstone in the Siebert Formation of Miocene(?) age
39	Nevada Test Site, Nye County, NV	Tuff and lapilli tuff of Tertiary age
40	Near Bullfrog Hills, Nye County, NV	Tuff of Tertiary age
41	Death Valley, Inyo County, CA	Tuff in the Furnace Creek Formation of Pliocene age
42	Lake Tecopa, Inyo County, CA	Tuff in lacustrine rocks of Pleistocene age
43	Owens Lake, Inyo County, CA	Tuff and tuffaceous sediments of Pleistocene age
44	Mojave Desert, eastern Kern County and San Bernardino County, CA	Tuff and tuffaceous rocks in numerous formations of late Tertiary and Quaternary age
45	Near Branciforte Creek, Santa Cruz County, CA	Tuffaceous sandstone in the Santa Margarita Formation of Miocene age
46	Near Nipomo, San Luis Obispo County, CA	Tuff in the Obispo Formation of Miocene age
47*	Near Oakview, Ventura County, CA	Bentonite in the Modelo Formation of Miocene age
48	Near San Pedro, Los Angeles County, CA	Dolomitic sandstone in the Monterey Formation of Miocene age
49	Near Wikieup, Mohave County, AZ	Tuff in Big Sandy Formation of Pliocene age
50	Near Dome, Yuma County, AZ	Bentonite of Tertiary(?) age
51	Near Horseshoe Reservoir, Maricopa County, AZ	Tuff in the Verde Formation of Pliocene(?) or Pleistocene age
52	Near Nutrioso, Apache County, AZ	Tuff and sandstone in unnamed formation of Tertiary age
53	Near Morenci, Greenlee County, AZ	Tuff and lapilli tuff in unnamed formation of Tertiary age
54	Along San Simon Creek, Cochise and Graham Counties, AZ	Tuff in unnamed lacustrine formation of late Cenozoic age
55	Near Bayard, Grant County, NM	Tuff in the Sugarlump Tuff of Oligocene age
56	Near Coy City, Karnes County, TX	Tuff and tuffaceous sandstone in the Jackson Group of Eocene age
57	Near Tilden, McMullen County, TX	Tuff in the Jackson Group of Eocene age
58	Near Meridian, Lauderdale County, MS	Tuffaceous sandstone in the Meridian Sand of Eocene age
59	Near Nettleboro, Clarke County, AL	Tuffaceous sandstone in the Meridian Sand of Eocene age
60	Near McKenzie, Butler County, AL	Tuff and tuffaceous claystone in the Tallahatta Formation of Eocene age
61	Near Paducah, McCracken County, KY	Claystone in the Clayton(?) Formation of Paleocene age and clay in the Porters Creek Clay of Paleocene age
62*	Near Jackson, Madison County, TN	Fossiliferous rock of Paleocene age
63*	Near Caryville, Washington County, FL	Suwanee Limestone of Oligocene age
64	Near Coosawhatchie, Jasper County, SC	Clay in the Hawthorn Formation of Miocene age and the Santee Limestone of Eocene age
65	Central SC	Mudstone in the Black Mingo Formation of Paleocene and Eocene age
66	Near Eward, Beaufort County, NC	Phosphorite in the Pungo River Formation of Miocene age

Source: Sheppard, 1971.
*Zeolite was identified as heulandite.

FIG. 3—*Clinoptilolite occurrences in sedimentary rocks—United States; see Table 3 (courtesy USGS).*

Synthetic Zeolites: Properties and Applications

D. W. BRECK *

Zeolites were first recognized as a new group of minerals by Cronstedt with the discovery of stilbite in 1756. The word zeolite was coined from the two Greek words meaning "to boil" and "a stone" because of the loss of water when heated in the mineralogist's blowpipe (Breck, 1974).

In 1845 it was discovered that certain soils have the power of retaining ammonium salts (Way, 1850). These were the first ion exchange experiments. Later it was discovered

* Deceased, formerly of Union Carbide Corp., Tarrytown, NY.

that it was the hydrated silicates in the soil that produced this phenomenon. Several years later a paper was published dealing with the action of dilute salt solutions on silicates which showed that this base-exchange principle, which we now call cation exchange, is reversible. The quantitative cation exchange behavior of zeolite minerals, such as chabazite, was studied. As a result any aluminosilicate which exhibited the property of ion exchange was referred to as a "zeolite"; even today the term has been applied to clay minerals as well as synthetic organic ion exchange resins.

The first synthetic aluminosilicates prepared specifically for their cation exchange properties were the permutites which are amorphous, gel-like, hydrous aluminosilicates. In the early part of this century extensive effort was devoted to the preparation of permutite materials for use in water softening (Shreve, 1930). These have been replaced by the organic exchange resins. In recent years some of the synthetic crystalline zeolites are finding ion exchange applications due to their unusual cation selectivities.

The term "molecular sieve" as it is applied to the crystalline zeolites was originated by J. W. McBain (1932) to define porous solid materials which exhibit the property of acting as sieves toward gas molecules. Dehydrated zeolite crystals act as sieves by the selective adsorption or rejection of molecules due to differences in their sizes and other structural factors. They belong to the class of microporous adsorbents; they have uniform pores permeating the solid with diameters of as much as 20Å. Although other microporous molecular-sieve-type adsorbents have been studied in laboratories, only the crystalline zeolites have achieved commercial importance as adsorbents.

The first experimental observations of the adsorption of gases on zeolites and their behavior as molecular sieves were conducted on zeolite minerals. The first definitive experiments on the separation of mixtures using a dehydrated zeolite, chabazite, as a molecular sieve were performed by Barrer in 1945 (Barrer, 1945). He classified the zeolites into three groups as based upon their ability to adsorb or exclude molecular species of different sizes. The classification defined the approximate intrachannel dimensions.

Beginning in 1948, the pioneering research efforts by R. M. Milton and his associates at Union Carbide Corp. resulted in the first synthesis and later the commercial manufacture of molecular sieve zeolites. This synthesis has been acknowledged as a major research achievement. The properties and uses of zeolites are now being explored by many diverse scientific disciplines. A wide variety of applications includes the separation and recovery of normal paraffin hydrocarbons, catalysis of hydrocarbon reactions, many uses in drying such as the drying of refrigerants, adsorbents in the separation of air components and the production of oxygen-enriched streams, the recovery of radioactive ions from radioactive waste solutions, the removal of carbon dioxide and sulfur compounds from natural gas, and the control of air pollution.

Zeolite Structural Chemistry

Along with the feldspars, the zeolites are framework silicates; their structures consist of a three-dimensional framework of SiO_4 and AlO_4 tetrahedra. As in the feldspars, the trivalent aluminum in these tetrahedral positions requires the presence of additional positive charge such as alkali metal or alkaline earth ions in order to maintain electrical neutrality. In the zeolites, for stability reasons, the maximum substitution of aluminum for silicon is the ratio of 1:1. In this event, a complete ordering of the aluminum and silicon is generally present. Recently zeolites with a Si/Al ratio of up to 100:1 have been reported. However, unlike the feldspars which have tight and dense structures, zeolite structures are open and contain large cavities filled with water molecules. The cavities may be interconnected in one, two, or three directions producing, upon dehydration, a crystal permeated with channel systems in one, two, or three directions. The metallic ions which are needed for the charge compensation occupy sites in the channel or adjacent to the cavities and are generally available for exchange by other cations.

Many zeolite framework structures consist of simple polyhedra, and each polyhedron is a three-dimensional array of the individual tetrahedra in a simple geometric form. These arrangements of polyhedra are referred to as secondary building units (Meier, 1968). Examples include single rings of four or six, cubic arrays, and hexagonal prism arrays or double six rings. For illustration, in the structure of the synthetic zeolite A, units of double four rings or cubes are joined together. This cubic arrangement produces a larger polyhedron known as the truncated octahedron (Breck, et al., 1956), Fig. 4. Internally, in the middle of the cube there is another type of polyhedron referred to as the truncated cube octahedron. This internal cavity is 11Å in diameter and is entered through six circular apertures formed by a regular ring of eight oxygens giving a free diameter of 4.2Å. It is these apertures which upon dehydration of the zeolite produce the molecular sieve character of this well known synthetic zeolite. In the crystal these cavities are stacked in a continuous three-dimensional pattern forming a system of unduloidlike channels with 4.2Å periodic re-

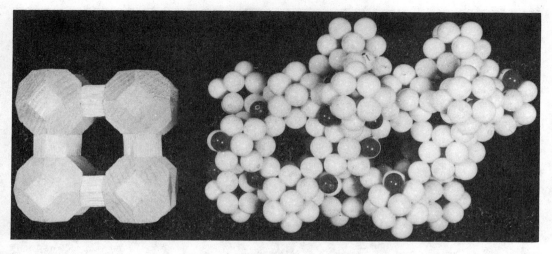

FIG. 4—*Model of the crystal structure (unit cell) of zeolite A showing the cubic array of truncated octhedra r.h., surrounding one adsorption cavity. A packing model at the left shows the apertures into the large cages and some of the exchange cations, Na+, near the main 4.2Å apertures. The truncated octahedra, each of which consists of 24 tetrahedra, are joined by cubic units of eight tetrahedra.*

strictions. Zeolite A has the following chemical composition:

$$Na_{12}Al_{12}Si_{12}O_{48} \cdot 27H_2O.$$

Eight of the twelve sodium ions lie in the center or near the center of the six rings in the hexagonal faces, and four occupy positions adjacent to the larger eight-membered ring. Dehydration of the zeolite leaves these four cations in positions near the eight-membered ring where they protrude into the apertures and may interfere with the movement of molecules. When replaced by other cations, such as calcium, the adsorption behavior changes. Inasmuch as one calcium ion replaces two sodium ions, the cations are removed from the eight-membered rings, and the zeolite has a larger effective pore size. Replacement of the sodium by larger univalent ions, such as potassium, restricts the eight-membered ring even more and produces a zeolite of a smaller pore size.

A second structure which illustrates some of the structural principles is the faujasite-type structure which is found in the synthetic zeolites X and Y (Breck and Flanigen, 1968). This framework is based upon a different configuration of the truncated octahedra. Eight of these are arranged in a unit cell in a tetrahedral configuration which produces eight super-cages of about 13Å in diameter. The cage is entered through four, 12-membered rings which produce a pore size of about 8Å. In this structure

the cation positions are even more complex; there are five types of positions. Some of the typical cation positions are shown in Fig. 5. This complex cation siting accounts for the variation in the adsorptive and catalytic properties as a result of cation exchange. Zeolites A and X and Y have three-dimensional channel systems.

The mineral zeolite, mordenite, is different: its structure is more complex and provides for a one-dimensional channel system. The main channels do not intersect but are parallel to one particular crystallographic direction; they have a cross-sectional diameter of about 6 x 7Å (Fig. 6). The basic framework consists of chains of five-membered rings which are cross-linked by the sharing of neighboring oxygen ions. Perpendicular to the main channels there are smaller side channels providing pockets having a diameter of 3.9Å. These side channels, however, are blocked by cations (Meier, 1961). The crystal structure of mordenite provides for large channels, but the mineral does not exhibit this large-pore character in adsorption. A synthetic type, known as "Zeolon," does, however, have this large pore character. The reason for the difference is not yet clear but is probably due to some form of intercalated matter which blocks the channels.

The basic structures of most of the mineral zeolites and of the important synthetic zeolites are known. A structural classification is shown

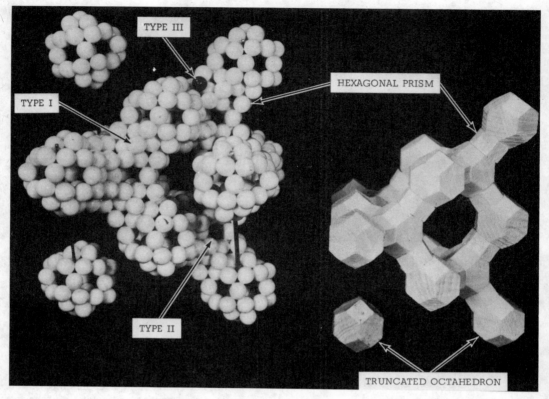

FIG. 5—*Model of the crystal structure (unit cell) of zeolites X and Y. On the right is shown the tetrahedral arrangement of truncated octahedra surrounding one large cavity. On the left is shown the packing model. The 12-membered ring is visible as well as the smaller 6-rings. Cation positions for three types of Na^+ ions in zeolite X are illustrated.*

in Table 4. The zeolites are arranged in groups based upon the secondary building unit dominant in the structure. There are now about 90 synthetic zeolites; some have structures related

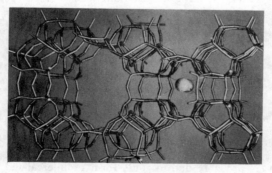

FIG. 6—*Model of the crystal structure of mordenite showing the 7Å channel and two sodium ions located in side pockets adjacent to the channels.*

to known minerals. However, there are many more for which the structures are not known.

Because no simple chemical system can be used to name synthetic complex aluminum silicates, there is a nomenclature problem. As defined by chemical composition, cation structure, framework structure, and structurally related physical properties, there are 34 species of zeolite minerals. There are established rules for the naming of new minerals. In the naming of synthetic zeolites the following practices are generally applicable (Breck, 1971):

1) The synthetic zeolite is designated by the letter(s) assigned to the zeolite by the original investigator (Law of Priority), for example, zeolite A, zeolite K-G, zeolite α, zeolite ZK-5, etc.

The designation of some synthetic zeolites by Greek letters and other combinations has been followed, e.g., synthetic zeolites α, β, ZK-4, and ZK-5.

2) The letters designate the zeolite as syn-

thesized. Thus, zeolite A designates the synthetic zeolite, $Na_{12}[(AlO_2)_{12}(SiO_2)_{12}] \cdot 27H_2O$ (pseudo-cubic unit cell) as prepared in the Na_2O, Al_2O_3, SiO_2, H_2O system, and zeolite L designates the zeolite $K_9[(AlO_2)_9(SiO_2)_{27}] \cdot 22H_2O$ as prepared in the K_2O, Al_2O_3, SiO_2, H_2O system. These refer to typical compositions.

3) In some cases, investigators have referred to a synthetic zeolite by the name of a related mineral, e.g., "synthetic analcime," "synthetic mordenite," etc. This approach is inaccurate and inadequate. The terms "mordenite-type," "analcime-type," etc., are preferable for indicating that the synthetic zeolite is related structurally to a mineral. In the light of current knowledge of the effect of cation type and location, silicon and aluminum distribution, and Si/Al ratio on the properties of the zeolite, a statement of identity is not warranted when only similarity is established.

4) Unfortunately, some confusion is unavoidable. The same letter has been used to name different species. Thus, Na-B refers to a synthetic analcime-type zeolite and Na-D indicates a mordenite-type. The letter B refers to the synthetic zeolite phases which Barrer and others have referred to as "P." Since the use of P for these phases has precedence in the published literature, it is preferred. Where a letter has been employed to refer to more than one synthetic zeolite, additional letter(s) are necessary; in these examples, the symbol for the predominant alkali metal is used.

5) A problem arises if the synthetic zeolite contains tetrahedral atoms other than aluminum and silicon, e.g., phosphorus, gallium, germanium. The element symbol is used as a prefix to indicate other tetrahedral atoms. Thus, P-L refers to zeolite L with phosphorus substitution in the framework.

6) It is necessary to indicate the particular composition in those cases where the letter(s) refer to a synthetic zeolite which can vary in framework composition. This is accomplished by giving the Si/Al ratio, unit cell contents, etc.

7) When a different cationic form of a synthetic zeolite is prepared by ion exchange, it may be so referred to, i.e., calcium exchanged (zeolite) A abbreviated as $Ca^{ex}A$ or CaA. A hyphen between Ca and A, Ca-A, could refer to a completely different zeolite. Thus:

Ca exchanged $A = Ca^{ex}A = CaA \neq Ca\text{-}A$.

It is assumed that the major cation component is, in this example, Ca^{2+} (greater than 50% exchange). In many cases, it is necessary to specify additionally the degree of exchange as percent of exchange equivalents, or in terms of the unit cell contents. Thus, $Ca_2Na_8[(AlO_2)_{12}(SiO_2)_{12}] \cdot XH_2O$ is equal to 33% exchange.

The designation of a zeolite as a separate species must be based on characteristic properties. Identification of a synthetic zeolite with a mineral species based upon a general similarity in X-ray powder diffraction patterns alone is inadequate. The properties to be included for complete characterization of a zeolite are the framework structure, cation content, chemical composition, and various structure-related properties such as stability, ion exchange behavior, and physical adsorption characteristics.

There are excellent reviews which cover the occurrence of mineral zeolites (Hay, 1966; Mumpton, 1973; Sheppard, 1971). The sedimentary zeolite minerals which occur in large deposits have not found extensive application as commercial molecular sieve materials. There are reasons for this. The use of zeolites as adsorbents and catalysts frequently requires materials of very uniform composition and purity. Variations in cation content and type dramatically affect the adsorption and catalytic characteristics; impurities likewise may affect catalysis. It is difficult to achieve a high degree of reproducibility in important industrial applications with a material that varies widely in mineral content, chemical composition, and impurities.

Some Aspects of Zeolite Chemistry

Dehydration—Zeolites useful as molecular sieve adsorbents and catalysts do not exhibit any change in structure when they are dehydrated under very severe conditions. Although in many zeolites water molecules affect the locations of the exchange cations, they do not have a primary structural function. In the stable zeolites the desorption of water is exhibited as a continuous plot when shown as a thermogravimetric curve of loss in weight vs. temperature. When hydrated the zeolite is a polyanionic framework which surrounds a water solution of positive ions. After dehydration the stable zeolite can withstand a temperature of about 700°C.

In the laboratory, zeolites are dehydrated before use by heating to a temperature of at least 350°C in a vacuum. In commercial practice, dehydration is brought about using a dry purge gas such as air, nitrogen, or methane in order to reduce the partial pressure of water vapor in contact with the zeolite.

The cation exchange behavior of several zeolites has been studied in detail (Rees, 1970;

TABLE 4—Classification of Zeolites

Name	Typical Unit Cell Contents	Type of Polyhedral Cage*	Framework Density, G per CC†	Void Fraction‡	Type of Channels§	Free Aperture of Main Channels, A #
Group 1 (S4R)						
Analcime	$Na_{16}[(AlO_2)_{16}(SiO_2)_{32}]\cdot16\ H_2O$		1.85	0.18	One	2.6
Phillipsite	$(K,Na)_{10}[(AlO_2)_{10}(SiO_2)_{22}]\cdot20\ H_2O$		1.58	0.31	Two	4.2-4.4
Paulingite	$K_{68}Na_{13}Ca_{3.6}Ba_{1.5}[(AlO_2)_{152}(SiO_2)_{520}]\cdot700\ H_2O$	α,γ,δ (10-hedron)	1.54	0.49	Three	3.9
Yugawaralite	$Ca_2[(AlO_2)_4(SiO_2)_{12}]\cdot8\ H_2O$		1.81	0.27	Two	3.5
Group 2 (S6R)						
Erionite##	$(Ca,Mg,K_2Na_2)_{4.5}[(AlO_2)_9(SiO_2)_{27}]\cdot27\ H_2O$	ϵ, 23-hedron	1.51	0.35	Three	3.6 X 5.2
Offretite##	$(K_2,Ca)_{2.7}[(AlO_2)_{5.4}(SiO_2)_{12.6}]\cdot15\ H_2O$	ϵ, 14-hedron (II)	1.55	0.40	Three	3.6 X 5.2, ‖a 6.4, ‖c
Omega¶	$Na_{6.8},TMA_{1.6}[(AlO_2)_8(SiO_2)_{28}]\cdot27\ H_2O$	γ, 14-hedron (II)	1.65	0.38	One	7.5
T	$Na_{1.2}K_{2.8}[(AlO_2)_4(SiO_2)_{14}]\cdot14\ H_2O$	ϵ with D6R	1.50	0.40	Three	3.6 X 4.8
Group 3 (D4R)						
A	$Na_{12}[(AlO_2)_{12}(SiO_2)_{12}]\cdot27\ H_2O$	α,β	1.27	0.47	Three	4.2
P	$Na_6[(AlO_2)_6(SiO_2)_{10}]\cdot15\ H_2O$		1.57	0.41	Three	3.5
Group 4 (D6R)						
Faujasite	$(Na_2,K_2,Ca,Mg)_{29.5}[(AlO_2)_{59}(SiO_2)_{133}]\cdot235\ H_2O$	β, 26-hedron (II)	1.27	0.47	Three	7.4
X	$Na_{86}[(AlO_2)_{86}(SiO_2)_{106}]\cdot264\ H_2O$	β, 26-hedron (II)	1.31	0.50	Three	7.4
Chabazite	$Ca_2[(AlO_2)_4(SiO_2)_8]\cdot18\ H_2O$	20-hedron	1.45	0.47	Three	3.7 X 4.2
Gmelinite	$Na_8[(AlO_2)_8(SiO_2)_{16}]\cdot24\ H_2O$	14-hedron (II)	1.46	0.44	Three	3.6 X 4.9, ‖a 7.0, ‖c
ZK-5	$(R_2,Na_2)_{30}[(AlO_2)_{30}(SiO_2)_{66}]\cdot98\ H_2O$	α,γ	1.46	0.44	Three	3.9
L**	$K_9[(AlO_2)_9(SiO_2)_{27}]\cdot22\ H_2O$	ϵ	1.61	0.32	One	7.1
Group 5 (T_6O_{10})††						
Natrolite	$Na_{16}[(AlO_2)_{16}(SiO_2)_{24}]\cdot16\ H_2O$		1.76	0.23	Two	2.6 X 3.9
Thomsonite	$Na_4Ca_8[(AlO_2)_{20}(SiO_2)_{20}]\cdot24\ H_2O$		1.76	0.32	Two	2.6 X 3.9
Edingtonite	$Ba_2[(AlO_2)_4(SiO_2)_6]\cdot8\ H_2O$		1.68	0.36	Two	3.5 X 3.9
Group 6 (T_8O_{16})‡‡						
Mordenite	$Na_8[(AlO_2)_8(SiO_2)_{40}]\cdot24\ H_2O$		1.70	0.28	Two	6.7 X 7.0, ‖c 2.9 X 5.7, ‖b
Dachiardite	$Na_5[(AlO_2)_5(SiO_2)_{19}]\cdot12\ H_2O$		1.72	0.32	Two	3.7 X 6.7, ‖b 3.6 X 4.8, ‖a
Epistilbite	$Ca_3[(AlO_2)_6(SiO_2)_{18}]\cdot18\ H_2O$		1.76	0.25	Two	3.2 X 5.3, ‖a 3.7 X 4.4, ‖c

Group 7 ($T_{10}O_{20}$)§§

Heulandite	$Ca_4[(AlO_2)_8(SiO_2)_{28}] \cdot 24\ H_2O$	1.69	0.39	Two	4.0 × 5.5 ‖a
					4.0 × 7.2 ‖c
Stilbite	$Ca_4[(AlO_2)_8(SiO_2)_{28}] \cdot 28\ H_2O$	1.64	0.39	Two	4.1 × 6.2 ‖a
					2.7 × 5.7, ‖c

Source: Breck and Flanigen, 1968

* Of the five space filling solids, three (cube, hexagonal prism, and truncated octahedron) are found as polyhedral units in zeolite frameworks. The cube is the double four-ring (D4R) as shown here. The double six-ring (D6R) is the hexagonal prism or 8-hedron. The α cage is the Archimedean semiregular, solid, truncated cuboctahedron referred to also as a 26-hedron, Type 1. The β cage is the truncated octahedron or 14-hedron, Type 1. The γ cage is the 18-hedron and the ε cage the 11-hedron.

† The framework density is based on the dimensions of the unit cell of the hydrated zeolite and framework contents only. Multiplication by 10 gives the density in units of tetrahedra per 1000 Å³.

‡ The void fraction is determined from the water content of the hydrated zeolite.

§ Refers to the network of channels which permeate the structure of the hydrated zeolite. Considerable distortion may occur in the Group 6 and 7 zeolites upon dehydration.

Based upon the structure of the hydrated zeolite.

Erionite and offretite may also be considered to consist of double 6-rings linked by single 6-rings.

¶ Zeolite Ω may be considered to consist of single 6-rings linked by double 12-rings.

** Zeolite L consists of double 6-rings linked by single 12-rings.

†† The T_5O_{10} refers to the unit of 5 tetrahedra as given by Meier for the 4–1 type of SBU. See Meier, 1968.

‡‡ The T_8O_{16} unit refers to the characteristic configuration of tetrahedra shown in Fig. 8b of Meier, 1968.

§§ The $T_{10}O_{20}$ unit is the characteristic configuration of tetrahedra shown in Fig. 8a of Meier, 1968.

‖ Dimension of channel parallel to either the a, b, or c axis.

Sherry, 1971). Typical types of ion exchange isotherms are shown in Fig. 7 (Breck, 1974). The isotherms for four univalent ions show a variation in selectivity ranging from high selectivity for Ag$^+$ to the low selectivity for Li$^+$. For some ions, such as K$^+$, the selectivity varies from positive to negative. In other cases, such as Ca^{++}, the isotherm does not terminate at the theoretical limit of complete substitution but at a lower point. This type of isotherm is commonly observed in zeolite Y for rare earth cations as well as for calcium and cesium. Certain sites are inaccessible to large cations and some polyvalent ions, so complete exchange cannot occur. In a few cases ion exchange hysteresis is observed, such as for Sr^{2+} sodium exchange in zeolite X.

Various methods of achieving hydrogen or proton exchange have been developed. In most instances the treatment of zeolites with a strong acid solution results in complete decomposition. In zeolites a certain degree of hydrogen exchange can be achieved by mineral acids and ultimately the aluminum is removed from the framework tetrahedral sites. This dealumination has been achieved in mordenite and clinoptilolite (Barrer and Makki, 1964; Kranich, et al., 1971).

The formation of hydroxyl groups in zeolites is important because hydroxyls play an important role in hydrocarbon catalysis (Bolton and Bujalski, 1971). Hydroxyl groups probably exist on the terminal surfaces of the zeolite crystals, but little is known about the terminal surfaces. Investigation of the formation and nature of hydroxyl groups in zeolites has been extensive and has utilized various techniques including thermal analysis and infrared spectroscopy (Ward, 1971). Hydroxyl groups are formed by two methods:

1) Deammoniation of NH$_4^+$ exchanged zeolites.

2) Hydrolysis of polyvalent cations (Rabo and Poutsma, 1971). These methods are illustrated in Fig. 8.

After dehydration, cations on the surface of the large cavities in the zeolites X and Y are not well shielded and have a low coordination

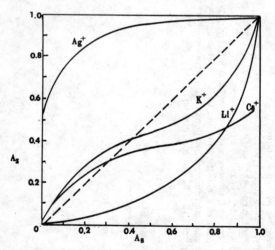

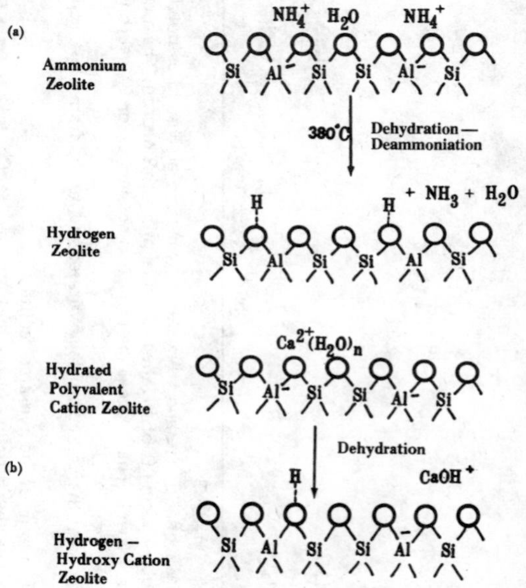

FIG. 8—*Schematic representation of the formation of hydroxyl groups in zeolites. (a) The example is zeolite Y, Si/Al = 2. After NH$_4^+$ exchange in water solution, the zeolite is dehydrated. The temperature is raised, NH$_3$ is evolved, leaving hydrogen atoms in place of cations but attached to framework oxygen atoms forming hydroxyl groups. The acidic nature of these hydrogens is responsible for activity in hydrocarbon reactions. (b) During dehydration of polyvalent cation forms of zeolite Y, some hydrolysis of the cation occurs, resulting in formation of a univalent hydroxy cation and hydroxyl groups on the framework. Trivalent rare earth cations produce more hydroxyl groups.*

FIG. 7—*Exchange isotherms for univalent cation exchange in zeolite X at 25°C. Na$^+$→Ag$^+$, 0.2 N; Na→K$^+$, 0.2 N; Na$^+$→Li$^+$, 0.2 N; and Na$^+$→Cs$^+$, 0.1 N. The equivalent fraction of exchange ion in the zeolite at equilibrium for the reaction Na$^+_{zeolite}$+A$^+_{solution}$=A$^+_{zeolite}$+Na$^+_{solution}$ is given by A$_Z$ and in solution by A$_S$. The CS$^+$ isotherm terminates at Cs$_Z$≈0.5.*

with the framework oxygens. Thus, electrical fields extend into the main cavities and may interact with adsorbed species. The effect of these fields varies with the silicon/aluminum ratio of the zeolite. Increasing the silicon/aluminum ratio from 1 to 2 increases the distance between cation sites. This increase results in the location of the divalent ions, such as calcium, in a nonsymmetrical position nearer one negative site than the other. The effect of this is to create a strong electrostatic field. Calculated electrostatic fields show that in the vicinity of trivalent cations, the electrostatic fields are as great as one volt per Angstrom. This field can cause substantial shifts of bonding electrons and adsorbed molecules. It contributes to the formation of hydroxyl groups on the polyvalent ion (Fig. 8) and acidic hydrogens on the oxygen framework. This is particularly true of divalent ions such as calcium and of trivalent ions such as those of the rare earths. During dehydration, hydrolysis of the polyvalent ions, in this case illustrated by calcium, results in the formation of a hydroxyl group for every two exchanged cation sites.

Synthesis of Zeolites

Extensive studies have been carried out in an attempt to synthesize "minerals" (Morey and Ingerson, 1937). In the preparation of zeolites early investigators attempted to duplicate what was then supposed to be a natural process without much success. In the late 1940s the initial work carried out by Union Carbide scientists was based on a new departure —a low temperature process using reactive ingredients. The results were very successful and resulted in the preparation of many different types of synthetic zeolites.

This approach was primarily based on the use of a freshly prepared, highly reactive aluminosilicate gel, or hydrogel. The term "gel" in this sense means a hydrous metal aluminosilicate mixture which is prepared from either aqueous solutions or reactive solid phases. Typical gels are prepared from aqueous solutions of sodium aluminate, sodium silicate, and sodium hydroxide or perhaps another alkali metal hydroxide such as potassium hydroxide. The zeolites form when the gels are crystallized at temperatures ranging from room temperature to 200°C at atmospheric or autogeneous pressure. This method is well suited for the alkali metals since they form soluble hydroxide, aluminates, and silicates; and it is possible to prepare reactive and homogeneous gel mixtures (Breck, 1974; Breck and Flanigen, 1968).

The gel structure is produced by the polymerization of the aluminate and the silicate anions. The composition and structure of this hydrous polymer gel seems to be controlled by the size and structure of the polymerizing species. Differences in the chemical structure and molecular weight distribution of the starting species in the silicate solutions lead to differences in the gel structures and major differences in the zeolite phases produced. During the crystallization of the gel the sodium ions, aluminate, and silicate components undergo a rearrangement into the zeolite crystalline structure. This comes about by a depolymerization of the gel by the hydroxyl ions present in the reaction mixture. Following this, the nuclei formed as small crystallites grow into the zeolite crystals.

A typical crystallization curve is shown in Fig. 9. Large numbers of crystallites nucleate from the supersaturated gel and the final product consists of a finely divided white crystalline powder that is a few microns in particle size. By controlled variation of parameters such as composition, temperature, and type of reactant, many different zeolite species have been prepared at Union Carbide and by others (Barrer, 1966; Breck and Flanigen, 1968). Some of these synthetic species may be structurally related to mineral zeolites; others seem to have no known mineral analogue.

Hydrogel Process

The process to make a zeolite by the hydrogel process is shown in Fig. 11 (Breck, 1974).

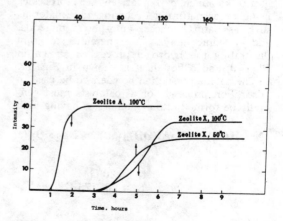

FIG. 9—*Crystallization of zeolite A and zeolite X at 50°C and 100°C as a function of time. Intensity, in arbitrary units, indicates the degree of crystallization as determined by X-ray powder methods.*

TABLE 5—Molecular Sieve Zeolite Preparation Processes

Process	Reactants	Products
Hydrogel	Reactive oxides Soluble silicates Soluble aluminates Caustic	High-purity powders Gel preform Zeolite in gel matrix
Clay conversion	Raw kaolin Meta-kaolin Calcined kaolin Acid treated clay Soluble silicate Caustic Sodium chloride	Low-to-high purity powder Binderless, high-purity preform Zeolite in clay-derived matrix
Other	Natural SiO_2 Amorphous minerals Volcanic glass Caustic $Al_2O_3 \cdot 3H_2O$	Low-to-high purity powder Zeolite on ceramic support Binderless preforms

Alumina trihydrate, $Al_2O_3 \cdot 3H_2O$, is dissolved in hot caustic and mixed with sodium silicate solution in the gel makeup tank until a homogeneous gel is formed. This gel is pumped to an ambient age tank, if required, and then subsequently crystallized after several hours at 200°F to form the zeolite. Progress of crystallization is followed by X-ray diffraction.

The first commercial processes were based on the original laboratory synthesis using amorphous hydrogels. Processes now used for the manufacture of commercial molecular sieves may be classified into three groups (Table 5). They are (1) the preparation of zeolites in high purity from reactive aluminosilicate gels; (2) the conversion of minerals of the clay group, kaolin in particular; and (3) processes using other naturally occurring raw materials such as natural silicas, amorphous minerals, and volcanic glass. A schematic diagram illustrating the hydrogel process is shown in Fig. 10, and a flowsheet is shown in Fig. 11.

The zeolite crystalline powders to be used in adsorption processes or as catalysts must generally be formed into agglomerates having high physical strength and high attrition resistance. Methods for forming the powders into agglomerates include the addition of an inorganic binder, generally a kaolin-type clay, to the high-purity zeolite powder in a wet mixture. The clay-zeolite mixture is extruded into cylindrical pellets or formed into beads which are subsequently calcined to convert the clay to an amorphous binder of considerable mechanical strength. The preparation of zeolite binder agglomerates as spheres or cylindrical pellets which have high mechanical attrition resistance alone is not difficult. However, in order to use these materials in adsorption or catalytic processes, the diffusion characteristics of the zeolite must not be altered. Consequently, the binder component should be such that a macroporosity is maintained that does not increase the diffusion resistance of the zeolite crystal itself.

The second method involves hot pressing the zeolite powder into binderless particles. When subject to high pressures at an elevated temperature, a mass of the zeolite crystals may self-bond into a 100% zeolite pellet. This method has not achieved extensive industrial use.

$$NaOH(aq) + NaAl(OH)_4(aq) + Na_2SiO_3(aq) \xrightarrow{\ t_1\ } \left[Na_a(AlO_2)_b SiO_2)_c \cdot NaOH \cdot H_2O\right] \text{ gel}$$

$$t_1 = 20°C$$
$$t_2 = 20\text{--}175°C$$

$$\Big\downarrow t_2$$

$$Na_x\left[(AlO_2)_x(SiO_2)_y\right] \cdot MH_2O + \text{solution}$$

Zeolite crystals

FIG. 10—*Scheme showing zeolite crystallization from typical reactants by the hydrogel process. Parameters which must be controlled within critical limits include the temperature t_1 and t_2, the composition of the gel, the nature of the reactants, and the time.*

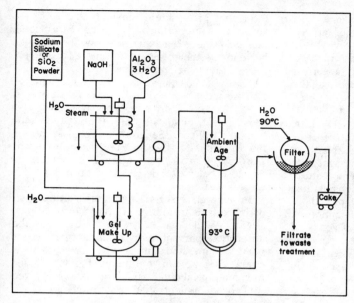

FIG. 11—*Hydrogel process* (source: Breck, 1974).

	Wt (To Produce 1000 Lb, Dry Basis)		
	4A	13X	Y
Raw Materials			
Sodium silicate*	1350	2000	——
SiO_2 powder†	——	——	1450
Alumina trihydrate‡	575	500	340
Caustic, 50% NaOH	870	1600	1400
Water	3135	7687	5300
Gel Composition (Moles)			
Na_2O	2.04	4.09	4.0
Al_2O_3	1.0	1.00	1.0
SiO_2	1.75	3.0	10.6
H_2O	70	176	161

* 9.4% Na_2O, 28.4% SiO_2.
† 95% SiO_2.
‡ 65% Al_2O_3, 35% H_2O.

A third method is the "preform" approach. The zeolite precursor reactant is formed into pellets, either as a gel or as a clay agglomerate. The reactants in these pellets are then converted *in situ* to zeolite crystals producing an agglomerate which has a high zeolite content, as high as 95%.

Application of Synthetic Zeolites as Molecular Sieves

The two major applications of synthetic zeolites are in adsorption and catalysis.

Adsorption

The zeolites are high capacity, selective adsorbents for two reasons:

1) They separate molecules based upon molecular size and configuration of the molecule relative to the size and geometry of the zeolite structure.

2) They adsorb molecules, in particular those with a permanent dipole moment and other interaction effects, with a selectivity that is not found with conventional adsorbents.

Two types of separation may occur: one based upon the molecular sieve effect and the second upon preferential adsorption. The sodium form of zeolite A will readily adsorb materials such as water, carbon dioxide, sulfur dioxide, and all hydrocarbons containing one or two carbon atoms. Propane and higher hydrocarbons are physically excluded with the

exception of propylene which is adsorbed slowly. When the sodium ions are exchanged by calcium the effective pore size increases to a point corresponding to about 30% exchange by Ca^{++}. This zeolite will then adsorb compounds such as straight-chain paraffins, olefins, alcohols, and cyclopropane but not isoparaffins such as isobutane or aromatics. If the sodium ions are exchanged by potassium, the opposite effect is observed, i.e., the effective pore size is decreased and the potassium-exchanged-type A zeolite will not adsorb any hydrocarbon or even oxygen at low temperatures. Because the effective pore sizes based upon the molecular diameters are about 3Å for the potassium A, 4Å for the sodium A, and 5Å for the calcium A, these materials are commercially known as type 3A, type 4A, and type 5A, respectively. For the sodium X zeolite, all molecules with diameters up to about 8Å are adsorbed. The exchange of the sodium by calcium ions in this zeolite reduces the effective pore size by about 1Å. By convention these zeolites are termed type 13X for the sodium form and 10X for the calcium form.

If two molecules are capable of entering the micropore system, then the zeolite retains one preferentially to the other on the basis of polarity or other molecule-zeolite interaction effects. Polar and unsaturated molecules are selectively adsorbed. Water, a strongly polar molecule, is very selectively adsorbed. The zeolite cavities are essentially filled with water at very low concentrations and, in the case of zeolite A, each cavity retains 20 molecules at vapor pressures as low as 1/1000 of an atmosphere at room temperature. The cavity is essentially filled. For gases such as nitrogen and oxygen, nitrogen is preferentially adsorbed due to the interaction of the quadrupole of the nitrogen molecule with the cations of the zeolite.

Although the N_2 molecule is only 0.2Å larger than the O_2 molecule, this difference is sufficient for rejection by zeolite NaA at cryogenic temperatures. Argon is intermediate in its behavior. At cryogenic temperature, nitrogen and argon diffuse with considerable difficulty, and in any reasonable period of time, true adsorption equilibrium cannot be reached. In addition to this process of activated diffusion, there is also the effect of temperature on the thermal vibration of the oxygen atoms which surround the aperatures. A variation in vibrational amplitude of 0.1–0.2Å can be expected over the temperature interval of 80–300°C.

Normal paraffins have an effective cross-sectional diameter of 4.3Å whereas a branched chain hydrocarbon is 5Å or greater. Aromatic hydrocarbons are also too large for adsorption in the 5A (calcium A) zeolite. This provides an efficient way for recovering normal paraffin hydrocarbons from various hydrocarbon mixtures.

The use of other adsorbents such as carbon and silica gel in practical separations has not generally involved the adsorption of one component from a mixture to the exclusion of all others. The use of zeolites as selective adsorbents makes such separations possible.

For partial molecular sieve action, it is important to know the relative adsorptivities of the various components. At present there is no good correlation between the adsorption of a single component on a zeolite and its behavior in a mixture although attempts at predicting relative adsorptivities from the individual adsorption isotherms of the separate components have been made. It is necessary to study the equilibria of the mixture experimentally.

The use of molecular sieves in many separations is based upon partial molecular sieve action where the dimensions of the molecular sieve pores are of the same magnitude as the dimensions of the molecule and an activation energy for diffusion is required. In the case of the larger pore zeolites such as the sodium X type, the channels are large, 7.4Å, compared to most molecules, and diffusion effects such as those that are encountered in type 4A or 5A are not as important. In some cases total molecular sieve behavior may revert to partial behavior as the result of thermal effects upon the diffusional activation energy.

The molecular sieve adsorbents in commercial use today are primarily those based on the A, X, Y, and mordenite-type structures. To some extent, chabazite- and erionite-type zeolites are utilized. Separation processes utilize the fundamental factors previously discussed. Adsorption processes require regeneration of the adsorbent after it becomes saturated with the adsorbate.

In general, adsorption processes utilize two or more beds in unison (Barry, 1960; Collins, 1968). While one bed is being used for the adsorption part of a cycle the other bed is being regenerated and hence the system is operated in a semi-continuous manner. A list of some typical commercial separations is given in Table 6. Many other separations are possible (Milton, 1968).

The preferred material for the dehydration of unsaturated hydrocarbon streams is the zeolite KA. Its pore size of 3Å excludes all hydrocarbons including ethylene and other olefins which might tend to undergo secondary polymerization reactions.

A molecular sieve effect is utilized in the drying of the refrigerants. NaA is used because the size of refrigerant molecules is such that they are not adsorbed by the zeolite. NaA is also utilized in the prepurification of natural gas to remove impurities such as water and CO_2; it excludes hydrocarbon molecules of the size of propane and larger.

CaA is uniquely suited to the separation and recovery of normal paraffin hydrocarbons from various hydrocarbon feedstocks such as natural gasoline and kerosene. Larger molecules such as the isomeric paraffin and cyclic hydrocarbons are excluded. More than a half dozen plants are now in operation to recover normal paraffins which are subsequently utilized in the manufacture of biodegradeable detergents.

Many important commercial separations are based upon differences in the relative adsorption selectivity. An outstanding example of this is the use of zeolites such as CaA and CaX in the removal of nitrogen from air to produce an oxygen enriched gas (Batta, 1972). Oxygen produced by this selective adsorption process is used in the treating of secondary sewage effluent.

The high selectivity shown by zeolites for sulfur compounds such as hydrogen sulfide and mercaptans is utilized in the removal of these

TABLE 6—Molecular Sieve Adsorbents

Molecular Sieve Basic Type	Molecules Adsorbed*	Molecules Excluded	Typical Applications
3A	H_2O, NH_3, He (molecules with an effective diameter < 3A)	CH_4, CO_2, C_2H_2, O_2, C_2H_5OH, H_2S (molecules with an effective diameter > 3A)	Drying cracked gas, ethylene, butadiene, and ethanol
4A	H_2S, CO_2, C_2H_6, C_3H_6, C_2H_5OH, C_4H_6 (molecules with an effective diameter < 4A)	C_3H_8, compressor oil (molecules with an effective diameter > 4A)	Drying natural gas, liquid paraffins, and solvents. CO_2-removal from natural gas
5A	n-Paraffins, n-Olefins, n-C_4H_9OH (molecules with an ellective diameter < 4A)	Iso-compounds, all 4-carbon rings (molecules with an effective diameter > 5A)	n-Paraffin recovery from naphtha and kerosene
10X	Iso-paraffins, iso-olefins (molecules with an effective diameter < 8A)	Di-n-butylamine and larger (molecules with an effective diameter > 8A)	Aromatic separation
13X	Di-n-butylamine (molecules with an effective diameter < 10A)	$(C_4F_9)_3$-N (molecules with an effective diameter > 10A)	Desulfurization, general drying, simultaneous H_2O and CO_2-removal

* Each type adsorbs listed molecules plus those of preceding type.

sulfur compounds from reformer recycle hydrogen. Water, carbon dioxide, and sulfur compounds are likewise removed from natural gas.

The zeolite CaX shows a selectivity for certain individual components of aromatic hydrocarbon mixtures. In practice, various types of cycles are used which differ in terms of the desorption part of the process cycle. Generally, the adsorption part of the process cycle is rapid (Barry, 1960).

Molecular Sieve Zeolites in Catalysts

As in adsorption, catalytic reactions take place within the cavities of crystalline zeolites —hence, the voids must be accessible to the reactants. The zeolites important in catalysis are those which have the largest pore sizes and a maximum of available void volume. Inasmuch as zeolites of this type are either rare or nonexistent in nature, molecular-sieve catalysts are based upon the synthetic zeolites. (All of the extensively occurring zeolite minerals are of the small-pore variety and at best adsorb normal-paraffin hydrocarbons with some difficulty.) Sieving effects occur in catalysis as in adsorption. Not only must the reactants

permeate the zeolite structure, but the products likewise must exit.

There may be a minor role played by the external surface which is about 1% of the total intracrystalline zeolite surface available. In the cracking of gas-oil molecules, the very large molecules cannot enter the intracrystalline cavities and therefore must crack on the external surface. Subsequently, the smaller molecules may enter into secondary reactions in the intracrystalline cavities. The reduction of olefin content in the product using zeolite cracking catalysts is attributed to factors of this type.

Some of the features of zeolite catalysts and the factors which are concerned with catalytically active sites include: (1) the zeolite framework structure, since it determines the pore system; (2) the cation type (size, charge), since it influences the electrostatic fields and the active catalytic sites; (3) the cation locations in zeolites; (4) the Si/Al ratio which may affect activity and stability; (5) the presence of proton donors in hydroxyl groups; and (6) the presence of active elemental metals in a highly dispersed state.

Molecular sieves catalyze other organic reactions such as dehydration (Venuto and Landis, 1968). In this instance an alcohol may be dehydrated to form an olefin with a zeolite acting as a dehydration catalyst. Zeolite catalyst activity for dehydration depends on the cation size and charge. A higher activity is found in zeolite systems with a greater cationic charge density and therefore higher electrostatic field strength. A second type of reaction is polymerization. This is important in catalyst aging since an olefin may polymerize within the pore structure and plug the pores and consequently not desorb, as has been observed in the alkylation of benzene with ethylene.

The hydrogen form of a synthetic type of mordenite catalyst is used to react propylene with carbon monoxide. Using zeolite X, ammonia reacts with aromatics such as toluene to form benzonitrile.

Zeolite catalysts are best known in hydrocarbon reactions, in particular cracking (Rabo and Poutsma, 1971). Although several mechanisms have been proposed for the carbonium ion reactions involving hydrocarbons and zeolite catalysts, there is no agreement on the source of carbonium-ion activity although it may be related to a combination of effects. These include the interaction of Lewis sites (due to three coordinate aluminum) with available hydroxyl groups (Bronsted sites). The presence of polyvalent cations, in particular the rare earths, enhances the acidity of the hydrogen in the hydroxyl group by an inductive

effect. In one proposal the hydroxyl groups are said to play a role which involves consumption of the hydrogens through reaction with olefins. The protons are consumed during reaction, and when depleted the reaction ceases. In this sense the hydrogen is a reactant (Bolton and Bujalski, 1971).

As exemplified in catalytic cracking, catalysts containing polyvalent ion-exchange X or Y exhibit higher activity and better selectivity as compared with conventional silica-alumina cracking catalyst. Typically, up to 20% higher gasoline yields are obtained. More than 95% of installed cracking catalyst capacity is now based on molecular sieve catalysts.

In isomerization reactions, noble metal containing polyvalent ion exchanged Y catalysts are used to upgrade low octane number normal paraffiins. These catalysts have a long life and resistance to sulfur poisoning and, unlike conventional catalysts, are noncorrosive. In hydrocracking, similar molecular sieve catalysts increase the refinery gasoline yield and octane number. The performance in a typical hydrocracking process is excellent from both product selectivity and rate of deactivation standpoints. In reforming petroleum naphthas, the molecular sieve catalysts exhibit excellent yield-octane performance and show good resistance to nitrogen poisoning. Anticipated competitive features of molecular sieves in reforming as in

TABLE 7—Potential Molecular-Sieve Catalyst Applications

Process	Feed/Products	Competitive Features
Catalytic reforming	Naphtha/gasoline	Activators unnecessary; gasoline with reduced sensitivity; feed pre-treatment minimized.
Polymerization	Low molecular weight olefins/gasoline	Noncorrosive.
Alkylation	Aromatic and low-value olefinic streams/valuable alkylated aromatics	Noncorrosive; feed pre-treatment minimized.
Hydrodealkylation	Toluene/benzene	High activity; improved selectivity.
Hydrogenation	Benzene/cyclohexane	Improved resistance to sulfur poisoning.
Hydrogenation of fats, oils	Unsaturated oils/saturated oils	High selectivity; low isomerization.
Selective hydrogenation	Straight and branched olefins/ n-alkanes and branched olefins	Separation problems minimized.
Methanation	Synthesis gas/methane	High yields; resistant to poisons.
Dehydrogenation	Ethylbenzene/styrene	Improved selectivity.
Dehydration	Alcohols + acids/esters	Improved rates and yields.
Dehydrohalogenation	Alkylhalides/olefins	Molecular size; selectivity.

TABLE 8—Comparison of Natural Zeolites vs. Synthetic Zeolites

Property	Zeolite Minerals	Synthetic Zeolites
Availability	Restricted to 8–9 species: analcime clinoptilolite, mordenite, phillipsite, erionite and chabazite. Also laumontite and ferrierite.	Many types are available by manufacture from inexpensive raw materials.
Purity	Generally impure. Bedded deposits are mixtures. Deposits of the useful zeolites in high purity are limited. Cation contents are complex. Undesirable impurities such as iron are common.	Manufactured as pure species. Other cationic forms prepared by cation exchange.
Pore size	Limited. Largest pore size in chabazite and erionite limits adsorption to n-paraffins.	Available from 3Å up to 8Å. Adsorb large molecules in catalysis and adsorption, or reject small molecules in adsorptive separation.
Pore volume (adsorption capacity)	Limited. Only chabazite and erionite have good pore volume.	Up to 50% by volume.
Catalytic activity	Limited due to small pore sizes and impurities.	Wide applicability.

numerous other catalytic process are summarized in the accompanying Table 7 (Collins, 1968). Potential catalytic applications range from methanation to aromatic alkylation.

Synthetic Zeolites—Advantages

Important aspects of zeolite minerals and synthetic zeolites (which must be considered in major applications) are compared in Table 8.

The use of molecular sieves in adsorption and catalytic processing usually requires that they meet closely controlled specifications in terms of purity, mechanical properties, and porosity. Although some zeolite minerals have been utilized to a limited extent, synthetic zeolites are better suited to meet the stringent requirements imposed on molecular sieve adsorbents in adsorption and catalytic processes.

Zeolites in Sedimentary Rocks *

RICHARD A. SHEPPARD †

Zeolites—crystalline hydrated aluminosilicates of the alkalis and alkaline earths—are important rock-forming constituents in sedimentary rocks and are potentially valuable industrial minerals. They have a framework

* Reprinted courtesy US Geological Survey, from Professional Paper 820.
† US Geological Survey, Denver, CO.

structure that encloses interconnected cavities occupied by the relatively large cations and water molecules. The cations, chiefly sodium, potassium, and calcium, and the water have considerable freedom of movement within the structure and give the zeolite their cation-exchange and reversible-dehydration properties. Some zeolites have essential contents of barium, strontium, or magnesium. The basic structure of all zeolites consists of $(Si,Al)O_4$ tetrahedra wherein each oxygen is shared between two tetrahedra; thus, the atomic ratio $O:(Si+Al)$ is 2. The net negative charge of the structure is balanced by the cations. The porous framework of the zeolites enables them to act as molecular sieves for the separation of molecular mixtures according to the size and shape of the molecular compounds.

More than 30 distinct species of zeolites occur in nature. Numerous zeolites have also been synthesized, but many of these have no natural counterparts. Most zeolites have a specific gravity of 2.0–2.3 and indices of refraction of 1.44–1.52. Zeolites rich in barium or strontium commonly have higher specific gravities and indices of refraction. Because the zeolites have similar physical properties, X-ray diffraction techniques are generally used for identification.

Synthetic zeolites have been produced commercially in the United States since the early 1950s. These synthetic zeolites are used principally as catalysts, selective sorbents, and desiccants; they are now utilized in about 90% of the petroleum catalytic cracking installations and have greatly increased the recovery of gasoline. Natural zeolites, however, have found only limited use in this country. Clinoptilolite is used to remove cesium from radioactive wastes (Brown, 1962), and chabazite is used to desiccate mildly acidic natural gas. Zeolitic tuff has been used as a pozzolan in cement.

In Japan, on the other hand, zeolites have been extensively mined and utilized since their discovery there in sedimentary deposits in 1949. Clinoptilolite and mordenite are the only zeolites currently mined in Japan, and they are utilized chiefly in the fields of agriculture and animal husbandry. Minato and Utada (1969) described the following uses: desiccant for gases, separator of oxygen from air, adsorbent for obnoxious odors in farmyards, filler and whitening agent for paper, and a soil conditioner to increase the effectiveness of chemical fertilizers. More clinoptilolite is mined in Japan for the last use listed than for any of the others.

Some of the natural zeolites may find applications in pollution control. For example, laboratory and pilot-plant studies by Pacific Northwest Laboratory, Battelle Memorial Institute, Richland, WA (Mercer et al., 1970) indicate that clinoptilolite is effective in the removal of ammonia from waste water. Also, recent studies suggest that mordenite may be suitable for the removal of SO_2 from stack gases.

The United States is self-sufficient with respect to the present fledgling zeolite industry. Because of the large potential zeolite resources and the diverse zeolite mineralogy, the United States will not only remain self-sufficient when new markets develop but will probably become a major exporter.

Exploitation

Production figures have not been published for natural zeolites in the United States; however, small tonnages were mined from upper Cenozoic tuffs. Several hundred tons of chabazite, clinoptilolite, and erionite have been mined each year since the mid-1960s; the mined deposits are near Bowie, AZ, near Hector, CA, and in Jersey Valley, NV, respectively.

Exploration and sampling of bedded zeolite deposits by commercial organizations have been active since the late 1950s in Arizona, California, Nevada, Oregon, Texas, and Wyoming. The exploration peaked in the early 1960s, when the search concentrated on natural molecular-sieve zeolites that might compete with the synthetic zeolites. Since 1970, exploration has accelerated again. This time the emphasis is on the location of zeolite deposits suitable for pollution-control processes.

Japan is probably the world's leading producer of natural zeolites. Since the mid-1960s, Japan has had an annual production of about 100,000 tons. About half of this production is from one mine, at Itaya, Honshu.

Geologic Environment

Zeolites have been known since the mid-1750s, and they occur in rocks that are diverse in age, lithology, and geologic setting. Zeolites have been recognized in sedimentary deposits since 1891, when Murray and Renard (1891) described phillipsite in deep-sea deposits. Prior to the early 1950s, however, most zeolite occurrences were reported from fracture fillings and vesicle fillings in igneous rocks, particularly in basaltic rocks. Most of the large attractive zeolite specimens in museum collections were obtained from igneous rocks. In recent years, zeolites have been recognized as important rock-forming constituents in low-grade metamorphic rocks and in a variety of sedimentary rocks (Hay, 1966). The zeolites in sedimentary rocks are very finely crystalline and do not appeal to mineral collectors; however, deposits of this type are voluminous and have great economic potential. The remainder of this section summarizes those zeolite resources in sedimentary deposits.

Of the more than 400 published reports that describe zeolites in sedimentary rocks throughout the world, more than 75% were published in the last 20 years. The factors chiefly responsible for this recent surge of reports are (1) the widespread use of X-ray powder diffraction techniques in the study of fine-grained sedimentary rocks, (2) the exploration for zeolite deposits suitable for commercial use, and (3) the early review papers by Coombs et al., (1959) and Deffeyes (1959), both of which emphasized the widespread and relatively common occurrences of diagenetic or authigenic zeolites in sedimentary rocks.

Zeolites are among the most common authigenic silicate minerals that occur in sedimentary rocks, and they have formed in sedimentary rocks of diverse lithology, age, and depositional environment. Those zeolites given in Table 9 have been reported from sedimentary rocks; however, some, such as faujasite, gismondine, gonnardite, scolecite, and thomsonite, generally occur in trace amounts and are rarely reported. Only nine zeolites commonly make up the major part of zeolitic rocks. These are analcime, chabazite, clinoptilolite, erionite, ferrierite, heulandite, laumontite, mordenite, and phillipsite. Analcime and clinoptilolite are by far the most abundant zeolites in the sedimentary rocks. All nine of these common zeolites in sedimentary rocks show a considerable range in Si:Al ratios and cation contents. Except for heulandite and laumontite, they are generally alkalic and more siliceous than their counterparts that occur in mafic igneous rocks. Summaries of their chemistry are given by Deer, Howie, and Zussman (1963), Hay (1966), Sheppard (1971), and Utada (1970).

Most zeolites in sedimentary deposits formed after burial of the enclosing sediments by the reaction of aluminosilicate materials with the pore water. Silicic volcanic glass is the aluminosilicate material that most commonly served as a precursor for the zeolites, although materials such as clay minerals, feldspars, feldspathoids, and gels also have reacted locally to form zeolites. Hay (1966) showed that authigenic zeolites and associated silicate minerals can be correlated with the following factors: (1) composition, grain size, permeability, and age of the host rocks; (2) composition of the pore water including pH, salinity, and proportion of dissolved ions; and (3) depth of burial of the host rock. Except for laumontite and possibly some heulandite, the common zeolites generally occur in tuffaceous sedimentary rocks that have not been deeply buried or exposed to hydrothermal solutions.

Classification of the diverse zeolitic sedimentary rocks is difficult, but the following tenuous classification is based on geologic setting and is offered as a basis for further discussion: (1) hydrothermal, (2) burial metamorphic, (3) weathering, (4) open system, and (5) closed system. The hydrothermal type includes those zeolites associated with metallic deposits such as those at the East Tintic district, Utah (Lovering and Shepard, 1960), and especially with hot-spring deposits. Well-known examples of the latter are at Yellowstone National Park, WY (Fenner, 1936; Honda and Muffler, 1970); Wairakei, New Zealand (Steiner, 1953, 1955); and Onikobe, Japan (Seki et al., 1969). Zeolites of geothermal areas commonly show a vertical zonation, and the downward succession of mineral assemblages seems to correlate with an increase in temperature. At Wairakei and Onikobe, for example, the downward succession is characterized by mordenite, laumontite, and then wairakite.

Zeolites of the burial metamorphic type were originally recognized by Coombs (1954) in Triassic sedimentary rocks of the Southland syncline, New Zealand. Coombs et al., (1959) demonstrated a vertical zonation of mineral

TABLE 9—Zeolites Reported from Sedimentary Rocks

Zeolite	Formula
Analcime	$NaAlSi_2O_6 \cdot H_2O$
Chabazite	$(Ca,Na_2)Al_2Si_4O_{12} \cdot 6H_2O$
Clinoptilolite	$(Na_2,K_2,Ca)_3Al_6Si_{30}O_{72} \cdot 24H_2O$
Epistilbite	$(Ca,Na_2)_3Al_6Si_{18}O_{48} \cdot 16H_2O$
Erionite	$(Na_2,K_2,Ca)_{4.5}Al_9Si_{27}O_{72} \cdot 27H_2O$
Faujasite	$(Na_2,Ca)_{1.75}Al_{3.5}Si_{8.5}O_{24} \cdot 16H_2O$
Ferrierite	$(K,Na)_2(Mg,Ca)_2Al_6Si_{30}O_{72} \cdot 18H_2O$
Gismondine	$(Ca,Na_2,K_2)_4Al_8Si_8O_{32} \cdot 16H_2O$
Gonnardite	$Na_2CaAl_4Si_6O_{20} \cdot 5H_2O$
Harmotome	$(Ba,Na_2)_2Al_4Si_{12}O_{32} \cdot 12H_2O$
Heulandite	$(Ca,Na_2)_4Al_8Si_{28}O_{72} \cdot 24H_2O$
Laumontite	$Ca_4Al_8Si_{16}O_{48} \cdot 16H_2O$
Mordenite	$(Na_2,K_2,Ca)Al_2Si_{10}O_{24} \cdot 7H_2O$
Natrolite	$Na_4Al_4Si_6O_{20} \cdot 4H_2O$
Phillipsite	$(K_2,Na_2,Ca)_2Al_4Si_{12}O_{32} \cdot 12H_2O$
Scolecite	$Ca_2Al_4Si_6O_{20} \cdot 6H_2O$
Stilbite	$(Ca,Na_2)_4Al_8Si_{28}O_{72} \cdot 28H_2O$
Thomsonite	$NaCa_2Al_5Si_5O_{20} \cdot 6H_2O$
Wairakite	$CaAl_2Si_4O_{12} \cdot 2H_2O$
Yugawaralite	$CaAl_2Si_6O_{16} \cdot 4H_2O$

assemblages that is characterized by a downward succession of clinoptilolite-heulandite-analcime, laumontite-albite, and then prehnite-pumpellyite-albite. Rocks rich in prehnite and pumpellyite commonly grade downward into rocks typical of the greenschist metamorphic facies. Locally, a zone rich in wairakite occurs between the laumontite-albite and prehnite-pumpellyite-albite zones or overlaps these zones. The zeolites and associated silicate minerals of the burial metamorphic type commonly occur in marine volcaniclastic strata that are more than 10,000 ft thick and locally are as much as 40,000 ft thick. The vertical succession of mineral assemblages is one of decreasing hydration with depth and is generally thought to be temperature dependent; however, chemical variables may prove to be equally important. Besides occurrences in New Zealand, zeolite rocks of the burial metamorphic type have been recognized in Australia (Packham and Crook, 1960), Puerto Rico (Otálora, 1964), USSR (Kossovskaya and Shutov, 1963), Japan (Seki, 1969; Utada, 1970), British Columbia, Canada (Surdam, 1968), and the United States. Laumontite-bearing rocks of the burial metamorphic type occur in central Oregon (Dickinson, 1962; Brown and Thayer, 1963), in Mount Rainier National Park, WA (Fiske et al., 1963), and near Cache Creek, CA (Dickinson et al., 1969).

Zeolites of the weathering type are volumetrically rather minor, but many deposits have probably been overlooked. Analcime was recently reported from alkaline saline soils of the eastern San Joaquin Valley, CA (Baldar and Whittig, 1968). The analcime was detected to a depth of about 4 ft, and its abundance decreased with depth. Hay (1963a) recognized analcime, chabazite, natrolite, and phillipsite in alkaline saline soil profiles at Olduvai Gorge, Tanzania. Surface concentrations of analcime were also reported in reddish, root-marked claystones on the Luboi Plain, Kenya (Hay, 1970).

The most voluminous and potentially valuable zeolite deposits belong to the open- and closed-system types. The terms "open system" and "closed system" are used in a hydrologic sense rather than in a thermodynamic sense. Deposits of the open-system type formed by the reaction of volcanic glass with subsurface water that originated as meteoric water. The original volcanic material commonly was deposited in marine or fluviatile environments or was air-laid on the land surface. Deposits of the closed-system type formed by the reaction of volcanic glass with the connate water trapped during sedimentation in a saline alkaline lake.

Deposits of the open-system type commonly formed in thick tuffaceous strata and show a vertical zonation of authigenic silicate minerals. Hay (1963a) proposed hydrolysis and solution of silicic glass by subsurface water to account for the formation of clinoptilolite in tuff and tuffaceous claystone in the lower part of the Tertiary John Day Formation in central Oregon. The upper part of the formation contains unaltered glass or montmorillonite. The authigenic mineral zonation is more complex in the Tertiary tuffs at the Nevada Test Site (Hoover, 1968). An upper zone consists of unaltered glass with local concentrations of chabazite and clay minerals. Zeolitic tuff continues downward for as much as 6000 ft and is characterized by a downward succession of zones rich in clinoptilolite, mordenite, and then analcime. The zeolite zones of the open-system type commonly cut across stratigraphic boundaries.

Zeolite deposits of the closed-system type formed during diagenesis in alkaline saline lakes commonly of the sodium carbonate-bicarbonate variety. Brine of this composition generally has a pH greater than 9, which probably accounts for the relatively rapid solution of vitric material and precipitation of zeolites. The authigenic silicate mineralogy can be correlated with the salinity in deposits of the closed-system type. The Pleistocene deposits of Lake Tecopa, CA (Sheppard and Gude, 1968) are characteristic of the closed-system type. Vitric material is unaltered or partly altered to clay minerals in tuff deposited in freshwater near the lake shore and inlets; however, the tuffs consist of zeolites where deposited in moderately saline water and of potassium feldspar where deposited in the highly saline and alkaline water of the central part of the basin. Thus, individual tuffs show a lateral zonation in a basinward direction of unaltered glass to zeolites and then to potassium feldspar. Zeolitic tuffs at Lake Tecopa consist chiefly of phillipsite, clinoptilolite, and erionite. Chabazite is a minor constituent of tuffs at Lake Tecopa, but it is locally the major constituent in zeolitic tuffs of other saline lacustrine deposits. In some deposits of the closed-system type, such as the Miocene Barstow Formation of California (Sheppard and Gude, 1969) and the Eocene Green River Formation of Wyoming (Surdam and Parker, 1972), a zone of analcime separates the other zeolites from the zone of potassium feldspar. In addition to clay minerals, zeolites, and potassium feldspar, deposits of the closed-system type locally contain opal or chalcedony, searlesite ($NaBSi_2O_6 \cdot H_2O$), fluorite (CaF_2), or dawsonite ($NaAl(CO_3)(OH)_2$) of authigenic origin.

Prospecting Techniques

Prospecting for bedded zeolite deposits is difficult because the zeolites are finely crystalline and resemble bedded diatomite, feldspar, or bentonite in the field. Zeolitic tuffs generally have an earthy luster and are resistant. Although some zeolitic tuffs are pastel shades of yellow, brown, red, or green, many are white or pale gray. If the zeolitic tuff is nearly monomineralic, certain gross physical properties of the rock may aid field recognition (Sheppard and Gude, 1969). Utilizing the ion-exchange and molecular sieve properties of zeolites, Helfferich (1964) designed a "field" test for the recognition of zeolites. Helfferich's test distinguishes zeolites from clay minerals, feldspars, and volcanic glass, but the test will not identify the zeolite species. My experience with Helfferich's test suggests that it is better suited to the laboratory than to the field.

X-ray powder diffraction analysis of bulk samples is the technique generally used for identification of the zeolites in sedimentary rocks. This method also permits a semiquantitative estimate of the abundance of zeolites and associated minerals in the samples. Tuffaceous strata are sampled, and then the samples are brought to the laboratory for examination by X-ray diffraction. Fresh tuff is generally distinguishable from altered tuff in the field, so only the altered parts of the tuffaceous rocks are sampled in both vertical and lateral directions. Once zeolites have been identified by X-ray diffraction, an additional detailed sampling is necessary to ascertain the distribution and abundance of the zeolites and associated authigenic minerals. Inasmuch as the samples must be returned to the laboratory for X-ray study, the availability of a truck-mounted X-ray diffractometer unit, suitable for field use, would facilitate the location of favorable targets and provide a guide for a meaningful sampling program.

Potential Resources

Evaluation of zeolite resources is hampered by the paucity of data on the extent and grade of the identified deposits. Although more than 100 occurrences of zeolites in sedimentary rocks of the United States have been recorded (Sheppard, 1971), information such as the grade, mineralogy, and vertical and lateral extent of the zeolitic rock and the thickness of overburden are lacking except for several deposits. The occurrence of zeolites in a certain sedimentary unit is commonly recognized from the examination of only one sample. Nevertheless, very large tonnages of zeolitic tuff of high purity are known from the Cenozoic deposits of the western United States and the Gulf Coastal Plain.

The only published estimate of zeolitic resources in the United States was made by Deffeyes (1968), who estimated that about 120 million tons of clinoptilolite, chabazite, erionite, mordenite, and phillipsite occur in near-surface deposits of the Basin and Range province. This estimate is probably conservative for the zeolite deposits of the Basin and Range province, and the potential zeolite resources of the United States are probably several orders of magnitude greater. If the restraints of grade and depth of overburden are ignored, the total of identified, hypothetical, and speculative zeolite resources in the United States is conservatively estimated at 10 trillion tons. The nine common zeolites listed in approximate order of decreasing abundance are clinoptilolite (including heulandite), analcime, mordenite, erionite, phillipsite, chabazite, laumontite, and ferrierite. The United States probably has the world's largest potential resources of high-grade chabazite, erionite, and phillipsite. The only high-grade deposits of ferrierite in the world have been reported from central Nevada (Regis, 1970).

If an estimate of zeolite resources in the United States is difficult to make, a meaningful estimate of zeolite resources for the other countries of the world is impossible to make. Zeolites have been reported in sedimentary rocks from many other countries, and their occurrences were summarized by Hay (1966) and Iijima and Utada (1966). However, no resource estimates have been published. In addition to the foreign zeolite deposits mentioned in these summaries and those foreign deposits mentioned previously in this chapter, apparently extensive and relatively high-grade zeolite deposits occur in France (Estéoule et al., 1971), Germany (F. A. Mumpton, written communication, 1972), Italy (Sersale, 1960; Alietti and Ferrarese, 1967; Alietti, 1970), Yugoslavia (Stojanović, 1968), Hungary (Nemecz and Varju, 1962), and Bulgaria (Alexiev, 1968). Most of the occurrences are in Cenozoic tuffaceous rocks, and the major zeolite is clinoptilolite.

Additional deposits of zeolites will undoubtedly be discovered in the western United States and in other countries of the world. Zeolites can form from a variety of aluminosilicate materials during diagenesis, providing the interstitial water has a relatively high pH and high concentration of alkalis. The purest zeolite deposits, however, form from volcanic ash that lacks crystal and rock fragments. In the Western Hemisphere, zeolites have not been reported from countries south of the United States except Argentina, Chile, and Mexico. An examination of upper Mesozoic and Cenozoic tuffaceous rocks will probably reveal large zeolite deposits in Mexico and many of the countries of Central America and western South America (Mumpton, 1973). Future exploration will also probably identify bedded zeolite deposits in the volcanic terranes of southern Europe, eastern Africa, and southern Asia.

Research Needed

The genesis of zeolites in sedimentary rocks is understood in general terms; however, several problems merit additional study. Phillipsite and clinoptilolite are the chief zeolites in young deep-sea deposits, but the relative importance of the precursor materials and the interstitial fluids in their formation is unknown. Tuffs of originally rhyolitic composition in deposits of alkaline, saline lakes characteristically contain a variety of zeolite minerals, but the factors that control which particular zeolite forms are poorly understood. Low-temperature experimental studies combined with studies of the zeolites and associated interstitial fluids in Holocene tuffs presently undergoing alteration may provide some answers. Another problem that warrants investigation is the relationship of the chemistry of a certain zeolite species to the geologic setting of the host rock.

Other research of a technological nature that deserves consideration is (1) development of techniques for the separation of zeolites from the gangue, (2) development of techniques for the separation of one zeolite from another, and (3) chemical or structural modifications of natural zeolites to increase their usefulness. Natural zeolites or zeolitic rocks will undoubtedly be used in many industrial and agricultural processes; however, additional applied research is necessary to achieve these goals.

Commercial Utilization of Natural Zeolites

FREDERICK A. MUMPTON *

For more than 200 years zeolites have been familiar minerals to geologists and mining engineers as minor, but ubiquitous constituents in vugs and fractures of most basalt and traprock formations. More than 35 different species have been recognized including several, such as chabazite, erionite, mordenite, and faujasite, whose adsorption properties rival those of many synthetic molecular sieves. Igneous occurrences of this type have never been mined on a commercial scale; they are generally small and

* State University of New York College, Brockport, NY.

low grade, and they commonly contain as many as four zeolite minerals, along with small quantities of calcite, quartz, and other silicate minerals. Their economic beneficiation to monomineralic zeolite products has also not been achieved and, for the most part, industrial applications of zeolites have relied primarily on synthetic molecular sieves that were crystallized from hydrous aluminosilicate gels.

During the middle 1950s, when Union Carbide Corp. and other groups were developing processes and markets for their fledgling synthetic zeolite businesses, natural zeolites

FIG. 12—*Zeolitic tuff, 1 to 2 m thick, in lacustrine deposit near Buckhorn, Grant County, NM.*

were discovered as major constituents of numerous volcanic tuffs in saline-lake deposits of the western United States and of massive, marine deposits in Japan and Italy. Since that time, more than 1000 occurrences have been reported from sedimentary rocks of volcanic origin in more than 40 countries of the world. The flat-lying nature and high purity of the natural deposits have aroused considerable commercial interest both here and abroad, and today efforts are being made to utilize "sedimentary" zeolites in many of the same ways as their synthetic counterparts, as well as to develop other applications which take advantage of the low mining costs of the bedded, near-surface deposits. Although the use of natural zeolites is still in its infancy, more than 300 kt/a of zeolitic tuff are mined in the United States, Japan, Italy, Hungary, Yugoslavia, Bulgaria, Mexico, and Germany, and used for filler in the paper industry, in pozzolanic cements and concretes, as lightweight aggregate, in fertilizer and soil conditioners, as ion exchangers in pollution abatement processes, as dietary supplements in animal nutrition, in the separation of oxygen and nitrogen from air, and as acid-resistant adsorbents in gas drying and purification.

Types of Deposits and Properties

Based upon their geologic setting, mineralogical composition, and origin, zeolite deposits in sedimentary rocks have been classified into several types, including (1) deposits formed from volcanic material in "closed" saline-lake systems, (2) deposits formed in "open" fresh-water-lake or ground water systems, (3) deposits formed in marine environments, (4) deposits formed by low-grade burial metamorphism, (5) deposits formed by hydrothermal or hot-spring activity, and (6) deposits formed without direct evidence of volcanic precursor material (Mumpton, 1973a; Sheppard, 1973; Munson and Sheppard, 1974). Commercial interest is directed primarily toward deposits of the first three types. Zeolitic tuffs in saline-lake deposits (Figs. 12–14) are usually only a few centimeters to a few meters thick, but they commonly contain nearly monomineralic zones of the large-pore zeolites, chabazite and erionite, which generally do not occur in other types of deposits. Open-system and marine deposits are characterized by clinoptilolite and mordenite and may be several hundred meters thick (see Fig. 15). Small to moderate amounts of montmorillonite and opal are also present,

FIG. 13—*Erionite-rich tuff, 2 to 4 m thick, capping series of fluvial-lacustrine sedimentary rocks, near Rome, Malheur County, OR.*

FIG. 14—"Skyline" tuff of Barstow Formation, Rainbow Basin Natural Area, Barstow, San Bernardino County, CA. Locally altered to analcime and K-feldspar (Sheppard and Gude, 1969).

along with varying quantities of crystal and lithic pyroclastic material.

All commercial applications of zeolite minerals make use of one or more of several attractive physical or chemical properties which characterize both the natural and synthetic materials. These include (1) ion exchange, (2) adsorption and related molecular-sieve phenomena, (3) dehydration and rehydration, and (4) a siliceous composition. In addition, certain extrinsic properties such as the tendency of "sedimentary" zeolites to occur as light-colored, lightweight, porous aggregates of micrometer-size crystals, have contributed to their past and present-day use in industrial and agricultural technology. Brief descriptions of many important uses of natural zeolites, including several that are of special significance in the current climate of pollution control and energy conservation, are discussed below.

Dimension Stone

Historically, devitrified volcanic ash and altered tuff have been used for more than 2000 years as lightweight dimension stone. Only within the last 25 years, however, has the zeolite content of many of these materials been recognized. Zeolitic tuffs are generally characterized by low bulk densities, high porosities, and homogeneous, close-knit textures. They are lightweight and easily cut or sawed into expensive building blocks. Many buildings associated with the Mayan centers at Mitla and Monte Alban in southern Mexico were constructed of blocks of massive green tuff recently found to consist of 85 to 90% mordenite and clinoptilolite (Mumpton, 1973). This tuff and others like it are still being quarried today at Etla, Tecoatlan, and Tejupan in Oaxaca for local use

as dimension stone in walls, buildings, and other structures.

At Otsunomiya City, Tochigi Prefecture, Japan, a 100-m-thick zeolite tuff has been used in a similar manner for several hundred years (Ota and Sudo, 1949). This pumiceous marine formation shown in Fig. 15 is part of the extensive Green Tuff region which contains most of the major zeolite deposits of that country (Utada, 1970; Iijima and Utada, 1972) and consists of 80 to 85% clinoptilolite with small amounts of montmorillonite, celadonite, and glass. The easily cut and fabricated Neopolitan yellow tuff in central Italy has also been used as a common dimension stone for many years, and to the casual visitor it seems as though the entire city of Naples is built out of it. According to Norin (1955) and Sersale (1958) this material contains major quantities of chabazite and phillipsite and was formed by the alteration of volcanic glass in ground

FIG. 15—Clinoptilolite-rich marine tuff, 100 m thick, near Otsunomiya City, Tochigi Prefecture, Japan (Ota and Sudo, 1949).

water systems. Numerous cathedrals and public buildings in central Europe were constructed with blocks of zeolitic tuff from the Laacher See area of Germany. TUBAG Trasszement and Steinwerke AG of Kruft continues to quarry this tuff and to supply carved dimension stone for replacement blocks in these edifices.

Early ranch houses (Fig. 16) in the American West were built with blocks of erionite quarried in the vicinity. The structures were cool and apparently did not crumble in the arid climate, despite the friable nature of the tuff. In the 1950s geologists exploring for zeolites would commonly examine all known building-block quarries in these regions, often with considerable success. Similar structures are constructed of zeolitic tuff blocks at Kurdžali, Bulgaria; Tokaj, Hungary; and in the vicinity of almost every other large zeolite deposit in Europe and Japan. The total tonnage of zeolites mined each year for this purpose is not known; however, based upon the size of the operations examined by this author, this figure is probably 50 to 100 kt. The only known zeolite deposit being quarried for dimension stone in the United States crops out a few miles southwest of Rome, OR. Here, a few hundred tons of impure erionite-rich tuff is cut into facing stone each year for local consumption.

Pozzolanic Cements and Concrete

The first and most popular pozzolanic raw material used by the ancient Romans in their highways, aqueducts, and public buildings was also obtained from the Neopolitan yellow tuff near Pozzuoli, Italy (Norin, 1955; Sersale, 1958). Similar altered tuffs and devitrified ash in other parts of Italy and in the Eifel region of Germany were also exploited by the Romans during this period and have been used con-

FIG. 16—*Early ranch house constructed of erionite blocks, Jersey Valley, Pershing County, NV.*

tinuously for cement production throughout Europe. The specific reactions of zeolite minerals in pozzolans are not well understood, but it is likely that their high silica content allows them to combine with and neutralize excess lime produced by setting concrete in much the same way as does finely powdered pumice or fly ash from coal-burning power plants. Zeolitic pozzolans have important applications in hydraulic cements where the final concrete must withstand continuous underwater corrosion. The sodium and potassium content of many zeolites from sedimentary deposits, however, may contribute to increased alkali-aggregate reactions.

Deposits of zeolitic tuff are undoubtedly used locally as pozzolanic raw materials in many other parts of the world; however, the mineral content of these materials is probably unknown to the user. In recent years, many of these tuffs were found to be zeolite-rich. In northern Yugoslavia several thousand tons of zeolite marine tuff are quarried each month near Celje as a pozzolan and as a source of lightweight aggregate. Both the clinoptilolite-rich tuff at Zaloska Gorića and the analcime-rich tuff at Gorenje are about 100 m thick and contain a small amount of montmorillonite which limits their pozzolanic activity (Grimšičar, 1967). An exceptionally large deposit of clinoptilolite-rich lithic tuff is currently mined near Vranska Banja, Serbia, at a rate of more than 100 kt/a for exclusive use in the production of pozzolanic portland cement.

Five separate trass deposits in the Eifel area are being worked as pozzolans. Ludwig and Schwiete (1962) indicated that these materials contain about 6% chabazite and 15% analcime. One such deposit near Kretz is 8 to 14 m thick and is interbedded with other zeolitic and barren ash formations (Sersale and Aiello, 1965). A massive marine tuff, nearly 100 m thick, is being mined in an open pit in the northeastern Rhodopes, near Kurdžali, Bulgaria. The tuff crops out over a 50-km² area and is remarkably homogeneous. Alexiev (1968) found that this material contains about 80% clinoptilolite, with admixed cristobalite and a small amount of montmorillonite. It is currently mined solely as a pozzolan; however, new uses are actively being sought.

In the United States nearly $1 million was saved in 1912 during the construction of the 386-km-long Los Angeles aqueduct by replacing up to 25% of the required portland cement with a zeolitic tuff mined near Tehachapi, CA (see Mielenz et al., 1951; Drury, 1954). This clinoptilolite-rich ore was until recently mined from a massive, ash-flow tuff by Monolith Portland Cement Co. and was a principal constituent of their pozzolanic cement products. Similar bodies are abundant in the western United States and eventually may compete locally with volcanic ash as a source of pozzolans in the construction of dams, highways, and irrigation canals.

Lightweight Aggregate

A third construction use of zeolitic tuff, just now being investigated in Europe, is in the production of expanded, lightweight aggregate. Much as perlite and other volcanic glasses are frothed into low-density pellets for use in concrete, so can zeolite-rich tuff be "popped" by calcining at high temperature. Clinoptilolite from the Slovenian deposit described previously and from several occurrences in southern Serbia yield excellent aggregate of this type on firing between 1200° and 1400°C. Stojanović (1972) reported densities as low as 0.8 g/cm^3 and porosities of up to 65% for products made by expanding clinoptilolite from the Katalanac, Zlatokop, Toponica, and Meškovac deposits. None of these deposits is currently mined for this use; however, the abundance of zeolitic tuffs in Yugoslavia should give rise to greater effort in the development of such aggregate products.

Filler in Paper

High-brightness zeolite ores are finding more and more application as fillers in the paper industry. Approximately 3000 tons of clinoptilolite are mined each month from a massive marine tuff at Itaya, Japan, and used in the production of high-quality paper (Minato, 1968). Fine grinding followed by cyclone classification yields a soft —10-μm-size product having an abrasion index of less than 3% and a brightness of about 80. The exact function of the zeolite in the paper-making process is not fully understood, but it is not unlikely that the adsorptive nature of the zeolite provides a means of controlling pitch, or that the zeolite simply replaces higher priced kaolinite as a filler and bulking agent. According to Kobayashi (1970) Kraft papers filled with clinoptilolite are bulkier, more opaque, easier to cut, and less susceptible to ink blotting than comparable clay-filled products. The Itaya deposit is one of the largest zeolitic tuffs being mined in Japan. It is flat-lying, about 100 m thick, and outcrops over a 5-km^2 area. The deposit is currently being worked by both open pit and underground methods by Zeeklite Chemical & Mining Co. Ltd., and yields products commanding prices of up to $150 per ton.

Another clinoptilolite deposit, several tens of meters thick, is also being mined as a paper filler in the Tokaj district of eastern Hungary. This and other zeolitic tuffs are widespread in the region and have been described in detail by Nemecz and Varju (1962). Although only a few hundred tons are produced each month, many uses are actively being investigated for this material. One potential use is in the preparation of a commercial adsorbent called "clinosorb," apparently an acid-leached, hydrogen form of clinoptilolite. Tokaj clinoptilolite is also being tested as a purification agent for wine.

Ion-Exchange Processes

Large-scale ion exchange processes utilizing natural zeolites were first developed in the 1960s at the Hanford Laboratory of Battelle Northwest in Richland, WA, under the auspices of the US Atomic Energy Commission. Using clinoptilolite from the Hector, CA, deposit, Ames (1959, 1960) demonstrated a method of concentration and isolation for radioactive strontium and cesium from waste streams of nuclear facilities. Once saturated with these ions, the clinoptilolite can be stored indefinitely or the ions removed by chemical means and the zeolite reused. Scale-up and supply problems have slowed the introduction of this process into existing installations; however, the technique is being used to concentrate cesium from low-level effluents. With an exchange capacity of greater than 150 milliequivalents per 100 g, clinoptilolite loaded with Cs[137] might well provide an easily handled source of heat to fill some of the nation's ever-expanding energy requirements.

Similar studies involving natural zeolites as collectors of radioactive wastes have been and are being carried out in France, Italy, Great Britain, Hungary, Bulgaria, Mexico, Canada, and Japan. In a related area, Nishita and Haug (1972) showed that the addition of clinoptilolite to soils contaminated with Sr[90] markedly reduced the strontium uptake by plants; thus, natural zeolites may be an important means of limiting the effect of radioactive fallout in crop and pasture lands.

As a spin-off of their work on the removal of radioactive ions from low-level wastes, Ames and Mercer et al. showed that clinoptilolite is an effective agent for extracting ammonium ions from sewage and agricultural effluents (Ames,

1967; Mercer et al., 1970). Using a mobile exchange unit at a Lake Tahoe test site, they were successful in removing 97% of the ammonium from sewage streams. The ammonia was later discharged harmlessly into the atmosphere, and the clinoptilolite regenerated for further use. Based upon this process, several large sewage-treatment plants are currently being designed in several parts of the United States. A 2.3ML/d unit in the Minneapolis-St. Paul area went onstream in February 1974, and uses six 8.5 m³ columns of 850 μm x 300 μm clinoptilolite. The initial 90 tons of zeolite were obtained from the Hector deposit operated by Baroid Div. of NL Industries at a cost of about $0.40/kg. The zeolite is expected to last five to ten years. Two larger plants with capacities of 205 and 38 ML/d are in the design stages for the Alexandria and Reston areas in Virginia, respectively. The Reston operation will require 1800 tons of clinoptilolite at a cost of more than $700,000. A smaller unit has been designed for communities of about 10,000 population by US Energy Corp. in Riverton, WY, and will use clinoptilolite from the Beaver Rim deposit near Sand Draw, WY. Several other clinoptilolites, said to be superior to the Hector material for ammonium removal, are also being readied for production by Double Eagle Petroleum & Mining Co. in Wyoming and other western states.

In a related area of sewage treatment, Sims (1972) reported that nitrification can be enhanced in activated-sludge processes by the addition of clinoptilolite. The zeolite selectively exchanges NH_4^+ from the waste water and provides an ideal surface for the attachment of nitrifying bacteria which then oxidize the ammonium ions to nitrate. The total tonnage of natural zeolites used today in sewage treatment applications is still small; however, if the stringent requirement of less than 1 ppm total nitrogen is imposed on sewage effluent by the Environmental Protection Agency, several hundred thousand tons of clinoptilolite may be required by the year 2000.

Air Separation

An exciting new use for natural zeolites was developed in the late 1960s in Japan for the production of high-purity oxygen for secondary-smelting operations in the iron and steel industry (Tamura, 1971a, 1972). As shown by Domine and Haÿ (1968), nitrogen gas is easily separated from air by any of several synthetic zeolites, yielding products containing up to 95% O_2 and a few percent argon. A small plant at Toyohashi City, a few miles north of Osaka, has used a pressure-swing adsorption process with natural mordenite since 1968 to produce 500 m³ of 90% O_2 gas per hr. The plant consists of three towers, each filled with 13 tons of acid-washed mordenite from the Itado mine, Minase, Akita Prefecture, and operates at ambient temperature on a 9-min cycle of adsorption-desorption-standby. Nitrogen may also be prepared by this process with purities up to 99.95%. According to Tamura (1971), the method is competitive with air distillation for relatively small-scale oxygen production. Clinoptilolite is also useful in air separation; however, the nitrogen-adsorption capacities of the several samples Tamura tested are lower than those of mordenite.

Zeolite-adsorption processes may provide inexpensive sources of oxygen or nitrogen where large-scale liquefaction facilities are not warranted. Nitrogen could be produced for wineries or breweries in on-site adsorption units when needed, thereby reducing their dependence on costly liquid or cylinder gas. As claimed by the German chemical-engineering company, J.F. Mahler (Anon., 1970), such a process is capable of producing 60% O_2-enriched air at a cost of $0.11/2.8 m³, thereby filling a need of users who now stand the cost of cryogenic distillation to produce pure oxygen, only to have to dilute it down to their required levels. Several commercial processes using synthetic zeolites have been developed and seem to be economically favorable over liquefaction at throughputs of less than 25 t/d (see Batta, 1971, 1972; Lee, 1972). It is not unlikely that mordenite and other zeolites will also find application in this area, although final acceptance of the natural materials depends upon the total cost of the operating system.

Lee (1973) listed several potential markets for a cheap oxygen source, including river and pond aeration, pollution control in the paper and pulp industry, feed gas to ozone generators, and chemical oxidation processes. In Japan small, freestanding zeolite adsorption units have been designed to produce oxygen-enriched air for hospitals, for use in fish-breeding and transportation, as well as for operation in areas of high air pollution. Sheppard (private communication) has suggested that a natural-zeolite adsorption plant might be a means of furnishing oxygen for the in-place gasification of low-grade coal deposits. Current gasification methods have been stymied by the lack of an inexpensive oxygen source (Abelson, 1973). Mordenite or clinoptilolite appear to be best suited for this process, but other zeolites, such as the Bowie, AZ, chabazite/erionite might be employed to purify the gases produced by the controlled burning process (vide infra).

Animal Nutrition

Experiments have been in progress since 1965 in Japan on the use of natural zeolites as dietary supplements for swine and poultry. Based on the use of bentonite in the normal protein diet of chickens (Quisenberry, 1968), clinoptilolite and mordenite have been added in amounts up to 10% to the feed of pigs and chickens. Test animals generally experienced faster growth than control groups, with simultaneous decrease in the amount and cost of the feed. In one 11-week experiment, young and mature pigs were fed a diet containing 5% clinoptilolite. Both groups gained an average of 16% more weight than animals fed a normal diet (Kondo and Wagai, 1968). Severe cases of scours were also relieved when the afflicted animal was placed on a diet containing 15% of this zeolite. Onogi (1968) found that additions of clinoptilolite or mordenite to the diets of chickens produced similar results. Test birds gained up to 8% more weight than did control animals, with no adverse effects. In both cases the animals' excrement was less odoriferous due to the zeolitic adsorption of ammonia. Zeolites are commonly used in Japan (in areas close to sources of zeolitic tuff) to control the moisture content and odor of animal droppings.

Similar studies have been carried out in several agricultural experiment stations in the United States. Full experimental data are not yet available, but initial experiments have met with limited success, especially in the prevention of intestinal diseases in young swine. Currently heavy doses of prophylactic antibiotics are used to control these diseases; however, if federal regulations prohibit such use, other means must be found. Zeolites may well be the answer. Little work has been done on the biochemical function of zeolites in nutritional processes; however, it is generally thought that the adsorptive nature of the zeolite allows nutrient molecules to be retained in the animal's digestive system for a longer time, thus allowing more efficient use of the feed. The result is larger animals for the same feed cost. The ammonium selectivity of clinoptilolite suggests that it may also be useful as an ammonia reservoir in ruminant feeding of cattle.

The use of zeolites in animal nutrition is still in the experimental stage, but offers at-

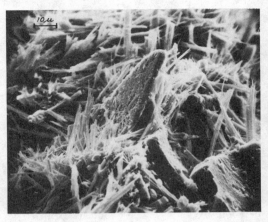

FIG. 17—*Scanning electron micrograph of erionite surrounding a pitted fragment of volcanic glass from zeolitic tuff, Jersey Valley, Pershing County, NV. X900*

tractive possibilities of increasing the world's food supply. The potential market in the United States alone exceeds several hundred thousand tons per year, and it may be even larger in the rest of the world. Before zeolites become a dietary staple, however, considerable experimental work is necessary. Special attention must also be paid to the long-range pathological effects of zeolites in animals, especially of needle-shaped erionite and ultrathin fibers of mordenite (see Figs. 17–20).

Agricultural Products

Although little has been published on the subject, farmers in many parts of Japan have

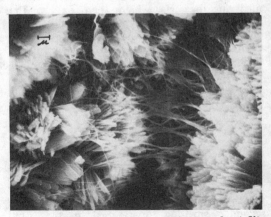

FIG. 18—*Scanning electron micrograph of filiform mordenite spanning a crevice in a clinoptilolite-rich tuff, 3 m thick, Toponica, Yugoslavia. X5000.*

FIG. 19—*Scanning electron micrograph of pseudocubic chabazite, sheafs and rods of erionite, and laths of clinoptilolite from a 1-m-thick tuff, Bowie, Graham County, AZ. X2600.*

added pulverized zeolitic tuffs to their fields for more than 100 years in an attempt to neutralize acidic volcanic soils. This may be the most common use of natural zeolites in that country today, although new uses are actively being investigated (Minato, 1968). Zeolite soil conditioners have been shipped from Japan to Taiwan and will undoubtedly be exported to many other parts of southeastern Asia within a few years. Both mordenite and clinoptilolite are used as agglutinizing agents for mixed fertilizers. The zeolites control the release of ammonium and other cations from the fertilizer, as well as retain desired cations in the soil for longer periods of time.

Similar to their synthetic counterparts, the high ion exchange and adsorption capacities of many sedimentary zeolites suggest that they may be useful carriers of fungicides and pesticides. Yoshinga et al. (1973) found that clinoptilolite is an effective fungicide carrier in the control of stem blasting in rice.

Gas Adsorption and Catalyst

Two principal uses of synthetic molecular sieves are the purification of gaseous hydrocarbons under controlled conditions of adsorption and desorption, and the preparation of catalysts for petroleum refining. In general, natural zeolites cannot compete with their synthetic counterparts in these areas due to their inherent lower adsorption capacities and, to some extent, to the presence of trace amounts of iron and other cationic "poisons." Some synthetics also have much larger pore openings. Despite the low cost of the natural materials (a few cents per 0.5 kg), the economics of hardware construction, activation, and regeneration favor the more expensive synthetics, even at $2/kg. Certain natural zeolites, however, have made headway in these areas, especially in the drying and purification of acidic gases. Mordenite and a few other species are capable of withstanding the rigors of continuous cycling in acid environments and have been used extensively to remove water and carbon dioxide from sour natural gas. Between 1970 and 1972 approximately 120 204 kg of chabazite/erionite were sold by Union Carbide Corp. from their Bowie, AZ, deposit (see Figs. 19 and 21) under the trade name AW-500 (Langerhans, 1973). Union Carbide Corp. (Anon., 1962) reported this material to be stable at pH's as low as 2.5 and therefore capable of removing HCl from reformer hydrogen streams, water from chlorine, and CO_2 from stack-gas emissions.

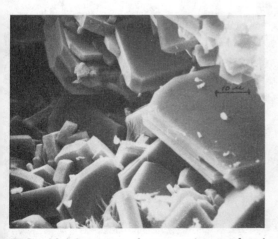

FIG. 20—*Scanning electron micrograph of clinoptilolite laths and plates with mordenite fibers, from a 25-m-thick lapilli tuff, Fish Creek Mountains, Lander County, NV. X1200.*

FIG. 21—*Chabazite/erionite-rich tuff, 152-mm thick, being stockpiled north of Bowie, Graham County, AZ.*

N R G Corp. recently introduced a package gas-purification system for the removal of H_2O, CO_2, and H_2S from natural gas to meet pipeline specifications. Using the Bowie zeolite, they claim extractions of up to 25% CO_2 from wellhead products. This company has also developed a zeolite-adsorption process for purifying methane gas produced by decaying garbage in landfills. A pilot plant began operations in late 1974-early 1975 at the Palos Verdes landfill near Los Angeles, and produces over 28 m^3/ min of methane. Such a process may also be useful in the removal of noncombustible CO_2 and corrosive H_2S from methane gas produced during the anaerobic digestion of sludge in municipal sewage-treatment plants. Much of this gas is currently burned to raise the sludge to its 32.2°C activation temperature and other in-house heating, but the impurities present take their toll in equipment breakdown. Similar digestion of animal wastes to yield methane is also feasible. The product gas purified, represents an enormous source of untapped energy. According to Jewell (1974) once the impurities are removed, the methane gas produced by the digestion of the organic wastes from a New York State dairy farm of 60 cows would be equivalent to the farm's entire fossil fuel requirements. Zeolitic purification may be the key to the economic feasibility of this process.

Although not yet implemented, Munson and Clifton (1971) suggested that adsorption on zeolites may be a means of increasing the on-vehicle storage capacity of trucks and autos using natural gas or other condensed gas fuels. The system would eliminate the need of expensive and heavy pressure tanks which heretofore have stymied the widespread application of this form of motor-vehicle fuel. This and other applications listed previously will undoubtedly expand in the next few years in the United States and in all other energy-conscious nations of the world.

In the area of catalyst preparation, the selective-forming process recently developed by Mobil Oil Corp. is thought to make use of catalysts derived from an erionite-clinoptilolite ore mined from their Jersey Valley, NV, deposit (Chen, 1971; Wilson, 1972). Here, tilted erionite beds crop out over a 2 023 500 m^2 area and have been mined by both open-pit and underground methods for the past ten years. In Japan a hydrocarbon-conversion catalyst for the disproportionation of toluene to benzene and xylene has been patented by Ohtani et al. (1972) based upon a hydrogen-exchanged natural mordenite. Clinoptilolite from the Tokaj district of Hungary was found by Papp et al. (1971) to be an effective catalyst for the hydrodemethylation of toluene after ion-exchange treatment of the zeolite.

Conclusions

If the efforts made on the occurrences, properties, and uses of natural zeolites in the past two decades are paradigms for the future, the United States will experience a minor "zeolite rush" during the next decade. The third edition of *Industrial Minerals and Rocks* made no mention of these intriguing minerals. The fourth edition was published at a time when zeolites were just beginning to find important applications in many areas of industrial and agricultural technology. Scores more have been on the drawing boards of R&D organizations throughout this country and in many other nations of the world. As this and other countries turn their research efforts toward the protection of their environments and the conservation of their mineral and energy resources, even greater efforts will undoubtedly be made to harness the unique and attractive properties of this abundant mineral commodity.

Bibliography and References

Introduction

Bramlette, M.N., and Posnjak, E., 1933, "Zeolitic Alteration of Pyroclastics," *American Mineralogist*, Vol. 18, No. 4, Apr., pp. 167–171.
Breck, D.W., 1973, "Synthetic Zeolites, Properties and Applications," SME Preprint 73H36, AIME Annual Meeting, Chicago, Feb., 32 pp.
Breck, D.W., 1974, *Zeolite Molecular Sieves: Structure, Chemistry and Use*, John Wiley, New York, 771 pp.
Mumpton, F.A., 1973, "Worldwide Deposits and Utilisation of Natural Zeolites," *Industrial Minerals*, No. 73, Oct., pp. 30–45.
Papke, K.G., 1972, "Erionite and Other Associated Zeolites in Nevada," Bulletin 79, Nevada Bureau of Mines & Geology, 32 pp.
Sheppard, R.A., 1971, "Zeolites in Sedimentary Deposits of the United States—A Review," *Molecular Sieve Zeolites—I*, R.F. Gould, ed., Advances in Chemistry Series 101, American Chemical Society, pp. 279–310.
Sheppard, R.A., 1973, "Zeolites in Sedimentary Rocks," Professional Paper 820, US Geological Survey, pp. 689–695.

Synthetic Zeolites: Properties and Applications

Barrer, R.M., 1945, "Separation of Mixtures Using Zeolites as Molecular Sieves," *Journal of the Society of Chemical Industry*, Vol. 64, pp. 130–135.

Barrer, R.M., 1957, "Some Researches on Silicates: Mineral Syntheses and Metamorphoses," *Transactions,* British Ceramic Society, Vol. 56, pp. 155–189.

Barrer, R.M., 1966, "Mineral Synthesis by the Hydrothermal Technique," *Chemistry in Britain,* Vol. 2, pp. 380–394.

Barrer, R.M., and Makki, M.B., 1964, "Molecular Sieve Adsorbents from Clinoptilolite," *Canadian Journal of Chemistry,* Vol. 42, pp. 1481–1487.

Barry, H.M., 1960, "Fixed-Bed Adsorption," *Chemical Engineering,* Vol. 67, No. 2, pp. 105–120.

Batta, L.B., 1972, "Adiabatic Selective-Adsorption Gas-Separation Process," US Patent 3,636,679, Jan. 25.

Bolton, A.P., and Bujalski, R.L., 1971, "The Role of the Proton in the Catalytic Cracking of Hexane using a Zeolite Catalyst," *Journal of Catalysis,* Vol. 23, pp. 331–339.

Breck, D.W., 1971, "Recent Advances in Zeolite Science," *Molecular Sieve Zeolites–I,* Advances in Chemistry Series 101, American Chemical Society, pp. 1–9.

Breck, D.W., 1974, *Zeolite Molecular Sieves, Structure, Chemistry, and Use,* John Wiley, New York, 771 pp.

Breck, D.W., and Flanigen, E.M., 1968, "Synthesis and Properties of Union Carbide Zeolites L, X and Y," *Molecular Sieves,* Society of Chemical Industry, London, pp. 47–61.

Breck, D.W., et al., 1956, "Crystalline Zeolites I. The Properties of a New Synthetic Zeolite, Type A;" "Crystalline Zeolites II. Crystal Structure of Synthetic Zeolite, Type A," *Journal of the American Chemical Society,* Vol. 78, pp. 5963–5977.

Collins, J.J., 1968, "Molecular Sieves in the Process Industries," *Chemical Engineering Progress,* Vol. 64, No. 8, pp. 66–82.

Hay, R.L., 1966, "Zeolites and Zeolitic Reactions in Sedimentary Rocks," Special Paper 85, Geological Society of America, 130 pp.

Kranich, W.L., et al., 1971, "Properties of Aluminum Deficient Large-Port Mordenites," *Molecular Sieve Zeolites-I,* Advances in Chemistry Series 101, American Chemical Society, pp. 502–513.

Morey, G.W., and Ingerson, E., 1937, "The Pneumatolytic and Hydrothermal Alteration and Synthesis of Silicates," *Economic Geology,* Vol. 32, Sup. to No. 5, pp. 607–761.

McBain, J.W., 1932, *The Sorption of Gases and Vapors by Solids,* George Rutledge and Sons Ltd., London, Chap. 5.

Meier, W.M., 1961, "The Crystal Structure of Mordenite," *Zeitschrift für Kristallographie,* Bd. 115, pp. 439–450.

Meier, W.M., 1968, "Zeolite Structures," *Molecular Sieves,* Society of Chemical Industry, London, pp. 10–27.

Milton, R.M., 1968, "Commercial Development of Molecular Sieve Technology," *Molecular Sieves,* Society of Chemical Industry, London, pp. 199–203.

Mumpton, F.A., 1973, "Worldwide Deposits and Utilisation of Natural Zeolites," *Industrial Minerals,* No. 73, Oct., pp. 30–45.

Rabo, J.A., and Poutsma, M.L., 1971, "Structural Aspects of Catalysis with Zeolites: Cracking of Cumene and Hexane," *Molecular Sieve Zeolites–II,* Advances in Chemistry Series 102, American Chemical Society, pp. 284–314.

Rees, L.V.C., 1970, "Ion Exchange in Zeolites," *Annual Reports on the Progress of Chemistry,* Vol. 67, pp. 191–212.

Sheppard, R.A., 1971, "Zeolites in Sedimentary Deposits of the United States—A Review," *Molecular Sieve Zeolites—I,* R.F. Gould, ed., Advances in Chemistry Series 101, American Chemical Society, pp. 279–310.

Sherry, H.S., 1971, "Cation Exchange in Zeolites," *Molecular Sieve Zeolites–I,* Advances in Chemistry Series 101, American Chemical Society, pp. 350–379.

Shreve, R.N., 1930, "Greensand Bibliography to 1930," Bulletin 328, US Bureau of Mines, 78 pp.

Venuto, P.B., and Landis, P.S., 1968, "Organic Catalysis over Crystalline Aluminosilicates," *Advances in Catalysis,* Academic Press, New York, Vol. 18, pp. 259–371.

Ward, J.W., 1971, "Infrared Spectroscopic Studies of Zeolites," *Molecular Sieve Zeolites–I,* Advances in Chemistry Series 101, American Chemical Society, pp. 380–404.

Way, J.T., 1850, "Power of Soils to Adsorb Manure," *Journal of the Royal Agricultural Society,* Vol. 11, pp. 313–379.

Zeolites in Sedimentary Rocks

Alexiev, B., 1968, "Clinoptilolite des Rhodopes du Nord-Est," *Comptes Rendus,* Bulgare Akademii Nauk, Vol. 21, No. 10, pp. 1093–1095.

Alietti, A., 1970, "I Minerali di Neeformazione dei Monti Berici," *Mineralog. et Petrog. Acta,* Vol. 16, pp. 27–32.

Alietti, A., and Ferrarese, G., 1967, "Clinoptilolite, Na-Montmorillonite e Ossididi Manganese in Una Formazione Sedimentaria a Zovencedo (Vicenza)," *Mineralog. et Petrog. Acta,* Vol. 13, pp. 139–145.

Baldar, N.A., and Whittig, L.D., 1968, "Occurrence and Synthesis of Soil Zeolites," *Proceedings,* Soil Science Society of America, Vol. 32, pp. 235–238.

Brown, C.E., and Thayer, T.P., 1963, "Low-Grade Mineral Facies in Upper Triassic and Lower Jurassic Rocks of the Aldrich Mountains," *Journal of Sedimentary Petrology,* Vol. 33, pp. 411–425.

Brown, R.E., 1962, "The Use of Clinoptilolite," *Ore Bin,* Vol. 24, No. 12, pp. 193–197.

Coombs, D.S., 1954, "The Nature and Alteration of Some Triassic Sediments from Southland, New Zealand," *Transactions,* Royal Society of New Zealand, Vol. 82, pp. 65–109.

Coombs, D.S., et al., 1959, "The Zeolite Facies, With Comments on the Interpretation of Hydrothermal Syntheses," *Geochimica et Cosmochimica Acta,* Vol. 17, pp. 53-107.

Deer, W.A., et al., 1963, "Framework Silicates," Vol. 4, *Rock-Forming Silicates,* John Wiley, New York, 435 pp.

Deffeyes, K.S., 1959, "Zeolites in Sedimentary Rocks," *Journal of Sedimentary Petrology,* Vol. 29, pp. 602–609.

Deffeyes, K.S., 1968, "Natural Zeolite Deposits of Potential Commercial Use," *Molecular Sieves,* Society of Chemical Industry, London, pp. 7–9.

Dickinson, W.R., 1962, "Petrology and Diagenesis of Jurassic Andesitic Strata in Central Oregon,"

American Journal of Science, Vol. 260, pp. 481–500.

Dickinson, W.R., et al., 1969, "Burial Metamorphism of the Late Mesozoic Great Valley Sequence, Cache Creek, California," *Geological Society of America Bulletin,* Vol. 80, pp. 519–526.

Estéoule, J., et al., 1971, "Sur la Présence de Clinoptilolite dan les Dépôts Marno-Calcaires du Crétacé Supérieur de l'Anjou," *Comptes Rendus,* Academie des Sciences, Vol. 272, Ser. D, pp. 1569–1572.

Fenner, C.N., 1936, "Bore-Hole Investigations in Yellowstone Park," *Journal of Geology,* Vol. 44, pp. 225–315.

Fiske, R.S., et al., 1963, "Geology of Mount Rainier National Park, Washington," Professional Paper 444, US Geological Survey, 93 pp.

Hay, R.L., 1963, "Zeolite Weathering in Olduvai Gorge, Tanganyika," *Geological Society of America Bulletin,* Vol. 74, pp. 1281–1286.

Hay, R.L., 1963a, "Stratigraphy and Zeolitic Diagenesis of the John Day Formation of Oregon," *Geological Science,* California University Publications, Vol. 42, No. 5, pp. 199–262.

Hay, R.L., 1966, "Zeolites and Zeolitic Reactions in Sedimentary Rocks," Special Paper 85, Geological Society of America, 130 pp.

Hay, R.L., 1970, "Silicate Reactions in Three Lithofacies of a Semiarid Basin, Olduvai Gorge, Tanzania," Special Paper 3, Mineralogical Society of America, pp. 237–255.

Helfferich, F., 1964, "A Simple Identification Reaction for Zeolites (Molecular Sieves)," *American Mineralogist,* Vol. 49, pp. 1752–1754.

Hoover, D.L., 1968, "Genesis of Zeolites, Nevada Test Site," *Nevada Test Site,* E.B. Eckel, ed., Memoir 110, Geological Society of America, pp. 275–284.

Honda, S., and Muffler, L.P.J., 1970, "Hydrothermal Alteration in Core from Research Drill Hole Y-1, Upper Geyser Basin, Yellowstone National Park, Wyoming," *American Mineralogist,* Vol. 55, pp. 1714–1737.

Iijima, A., and Utada, M., 1966, "Zeolites in Sedimentary Rocks, with Reference to the Depositional Environments and Zonal Distribution," *Sedimentology,* Vol. 7, pp. 327–357.

Kossovskaya, A.G., and Shutov, V.D., 1963, "The Correlation of Zones of Regional Epigenesis and Metagenesis in Terrigenous and Volcanic Rocks," *Doklady, Earth Sciences Secs.,* Akademii Nauk SSSR, Vol. 139, pp. 732–736.

Lovering, T.S., and Shepard, A.O., 1960, "Hydrothermal Alteration Zones Caused by Halogen Acid Solutions, East Tintic District, Utah," *American Journal of Science,* Vol. 258-A, pp. 215–229.

Mercer, B.W., et al., 1970, "Ammonia Removal from Secondary Effluents by Selective Ion Exchange," *Water Pollution Control Federation Journal,* Vol. 42, No. 2, Pt. 2, pp. R95–R107.

Minato, H., and Utada, M., 1969, "Zeolite," *The Clays of Japan—International Clay Conference,* Japan Geological Survey, Tokyo, pp. 121–134.

Mumpton, F.A., 1973, "First Reported Occurrences of Zeolite in Sedimentary Rocks in Mexico," *American Mineralogist,* Vol. 58, No. 34, Mar.-Apr., pp. 287–290.

Murray, J., and Renard, A.F., 1891, "Report on Deep-Sea Deposits," *Report on the Scientific Results of the Voyage of H.M.S. Challenger During the Years 1873–1876,* London, 520 pp.

Nemecz, E., and Varju, G., 1962, "Sodium Bentonitization, Clinoptylolitization and Adularization in the Rhyolitic Tuffs of the Szerencs Piedmont Area," *Acta Geologica,* Vol. 6, pp. 389–427.

Otálora, G., 1964, "Zeolites and Related Minerals in Cretaceous Rocks of East-Central Puerto Rico," *American Journal of Science,* Vol. 262, pp. 726–734.

Packham, G.H., and Crook, K.A.W., 1960, "The Principle of Diagenetic Facies and Some of Its Implications," *Journal of Geology,* Vol. 68, pp. 392–407.

Regis, A.J., 1970, "Occurrences of Ferrierite in Altered Pyroclastics in Central Nevada," *Abstracts with Programs,* Geological Society of America, Vol. 2, No. 7, pp. 661.

Seki, Y., 1969, "Facies Series in Low-Grade Metamorphism," *Geological Journal,* Geological Society of Japan, Vol. 75, pp. 255–266.

Seki, Y., et al., 1969, "Zeolite Distribution in the Katayama Geothermal Area, Onikobe, Japan," *Japanese Journal of Geology & Geography,* Vol. 40, pp. 63–79.

Sersale, R., 1960, "Genetic and Constitution Analogies Between Volcanic Tuffs with Pozzolanic Activity," *Silicates Industry,* Vol. 25, pp. 499–509.

Sheppard, R.A., 1971, "Zeolites in Sedimentary Deposits of the United States—A Review," *Molecular Sieve Zeolites–I,* R.F. Gould, ed., Advances in Chemistry Series 101, American Chemical Society, pp. 279–310.

Sheppard, R.A., and Gude, A.J., III, 1968, "Distribution and Genesis of Authigenic Silicate Minerals in Tuffs of Pleistocene Lake Tecopa, Inyo County, California." Professional Paper 597. US Geological Survey, 38 pp.

Sheppard, R.A., and Gude, A.J., III, 1969, "Diagenesis of Tuffs in the Barstow Formation, Mud Hills, San Bernardino County, California," Professional Paper 634, US Geological Survey, 35 pp.

Steiner, A., 1953, "Hydrothermal Rock Alteration at Wairakei, New Zealand," *Economic Geology,* Vol. 48, pp. 1–13.

Steiner, A., 1955, "Hydrothermal Rock Alteration," Industrial Research Bulletin 117, New Zealand Dept. of Science, pp. 21–26.

Stojanović, D., 1968, "Vulkanski Tufovi i Sedimentne Stene u Srbiji sa Sadržajem Zeolita," *Srpsko Geološko Drustvo,* 15 pp.

Surdam, R.C., 1968, "Low-Grade Metamorphism of the Karmutsen Group, Central Vancouver Island, British Columbia, Canada," *Abstracts for 1967,* Special Paper 115, Geological Society of America, pp. 217–218.

Surdam, R.C., and Parker, 1972, "Authigenic Alumino-Silicate Minerals in the Tuffaceous Rocks of the Green River Formation, Wyoming," *Geological Society of America Bulletin,* Vol. 83, pp. 689–700.

Utada, M., 1970, "Occurrence and Distribution of Authigenic Zeolites in the Neogene Pyroclastic Rocks in Japan," *Science Papers Collection General Education,* Tokyo University, Vol. 20, pp. 191–262.

Commercial Utilization of Natural Zeolites

Anon., 1970, "Molecular Sieves Offer Low-Cost Oxygen Source," *Chemical Engineering*, Vol. 77, No. 12, pp. 54–56.

Anon., 1972, "Linde Molecular Sieve Type AW-500," Linde Molecular Sieves Bulletin F-1617, Union Carbide Corp., Aug. 15, 1962.

Abelson, P.H., 1973, "Underground Gasification of Coal," *Science*, Vol. 182, p. 1297.

Alexiev, B., 1968, "Clinoptilolite des Rhodopes du Nord-Est," *Comptes Rendus*, Bulgare Akademii Nauk, Vol. 21, pp. 1093–1095.

Ames, L.L., 1959, "Zeolitic Extraction of Cesium from Aqueous Solutions," Unclassified Report HW-62607, US Atomic Energy Commission, 23 pp.

Ames, L.L., 1960, "The Cation Sieve Properties of Clinoptilolite," *American Mineralogist*, Vol. 45, pp. 689–700.

Ames, L.L., 1967, "Zeolitic Removal of Ammonium Ions from Agricultural Wastewaters," *Proceedings*, 13th Pacific Northwest Industrial Waste Conference, Washington State University, Pullman, pp. 135–152.

Batta, L.B., 1971, "Adiabatic Selective-Adsorption Gas-Separation Process," US Patent 3,636,679, Jan. 25.

Batta, L.B., 1972, "Separation of Gas Mixtures by Adiabatic Adsorption Involving Pressure Changes," German Patent 2,153,808.

Chen, N.Y., 1971, "Shaped Selective Transition Metal Zeolite Hydrocracking Catalysts," US Patent 3,630,966, Dec. 28.

Domine, D., and Haÿ, L., 1968, "Process for Separating Mixtures of Gases by Isothermal Adsorption: Possibilities and Applications," *Molecular Sieves*, Society of Chemical Industry, London, pp. 204–216.

Drury, F.W., 1954, "Pozzolans in California," *Mineral Information Service*, Vol. 7, No. 10, pp. 1–6.

Grimšičar, A., 1967, "Zeoliti v Oligocenskih Tufih med Mozirjem in Celje," *Razprava Procila*, Vol. 10, pp. 239–245.

Iijima, A., and Utada, M., 1972, "A Critical Review on the Occurrence of Zeolites in Sedimentary Rocks in Japan," *Japanese Journal of Geology & Geography*, Vol. 42, pp. 61–84.

Jewell, W.J., 1974, "Methane . . . The Energy-Sufficient Farm," *The News*, State University of New York, Vol. 3, No. 2, p. 4.

Kobayashi, Y., 1970, "Natural Zeolite-Fillers for Paper," Japanese Patent 70–41,044.

Kondo, N., and Wagai, B., 1968, "Experimental Use of Clinoptilolite-Tuff as Dietary Supplements for Pigs," *Yotonkai*, May, pp. 1–4.

Langerhans, R., 1973, "United States of America, Contestant, vs. Union Carbide Corporation, Contestee," Testimony in Hearing A-7345, Dept. of the Interior, Office of Hearings & Appeal, Denver, CO, July 17, pp. 125–134.

Lee, H., 1972, "Pressure Swing Oxygen—A New Source of Oxygen for Waste Water Treatment," speech at Symposium on Application of Commercial Oxygen to Water and Waste Water Systems, University of Texas, Austin, Nov. 13–15.

Lee, H., 1973, "Applied Aspects of Zeolite Adsorbents," *Molecular Sieve Zeolites–I*, R.F. Gould, ed., Advances in Chemistry Series, Vol. 121, American Chemical Society, pp. 311–318.

Ludwig, U., and Schwiete, H.W., 1962, "Beitrag zur Konstitution Einiger Rheinischer Trasse," *Zement-Kalk-Gips*, Vol. 15, pp. 160–165.

Mercer, B.W., et al., 1970, "Ammonia Removal from Secondary Effluents by Selective Ion Exchange," *Water Pollution Control Federation Journal*, Vol. 42, pp. R95-R107.

Mielenz, R.C., et al., 1951, "Natural Pozzolans for Concrete," *Economic Geology*, Vol. 46, No. 3, May, pp. 311–328.

Minato, H., 1968, "Characteristics and Uses of Natural Zeolites," *Koatsugasu*, Vol. 5, pp. 536–547.

Mumpton, F.A., 1973, "First Reported Occurrence of Zeolites in Sedimentary Rocks of Mexico," *American Mineralogist*, Vol. 58, pp. 287–290.

Mumpton, F.A., 1973a, "Worldwide Deposits and Utilisation of Natural Zeolites," *Industrial Minerals*, No. 73, pp. 30–45.

Munson, R.A., and Clifton, R.A., 1971, "Natural Gas Storage with Zeolites," Technical Progress Report No. 38, US Bureau of Mines, 9 pp.

Munson, R.A., and Sheppard, R.A., 1974, "Natural Zeolites: Their Properties, Occurrences and Uses," *Mineral Science and Engineering*, Vol. 6, No. 1, pp. 19–34.

Nemecz, E., and Varju, G., 1962, "Sodium Bentonization, Clinoptylolitization and Ardularization in the Rhyolitic Tuffs of the Szerencs Piedmont Area," *Acta Geologica*, Vol. 6, pp. 389–426.

Nishita, H., and Haug, R.M., 1972, "Influences of Clinoptilolite on Sr-90 and Cs-137 Uptakes by Plants," *Soil Science*, Vol. 114, pp. 149–157.

Norin, E., 1955, "The Mineral Composition of the Neopolitan Yellow Tuff," *Geologische Rundschau*, Vol. 43, pp. 526–534.

Ohtani, S., et al., 1972, "Conversion Catalyst for Hydrocarbon," Japanese Patent 72,46,667, Nov. 24.

Onogi, T., 1966, "Experimental Use of Zeolite-Tuffs as Dietary Supplements for Chickens," Report, Kamagata Stock Raising Institute, pp. 7–18.

Ota, S., and Sudo, T., 1949, "Studies on 'Oya-ihi,' Part II, Mineralogical Composition," *Journal of the Geological Society of Japan*, Vol. 55, pp. 242–246.

Papp, J., et al., 1971, "Hydrodemethylation of Toluene on Clinoptilolite," *Journal of Catalysis*, Vol. 23, pp. 168–182.

Quisenberry, J.H., 1968, "The Use of Clay in Poultry Feed," *Clays and Clay Minerals*, Vol. 16, pp. 267–270.

Sersale, R., 1958, "Genesi e Constituzione del Tufo Giallo Napolitano," *Rendiconti della Accad. Sci. Fische Mat. (Napoli)*, Vol. 25, pp. 181–207.

Sersale, R., and Aiello, R., 1965, "Ricerche sulla Genesi, sulla Constituzione e sulla Reattivita del 'Trass' Ranano," *Silicates Industriels*, Vol. 30, pp. 1–11.

Sheppard, R.A., 1973, "Zeolites in Sedimentary Rocks," Professional Paper 820, US Geological Survey, pp. 689–695.

Sims, R.C., 1972, "Enhancement of Nitrification in Activated Sludge by Addition of Hector

Clinoptilolite," *Environmental Science Engineering Notes*, Vol. 9, pp. 2–4.

Stojanović, D., 1972, "Zeolite-Containing Volcanic Tuffs and Sedimentary Rocks in Serbia," *Proceedings for 1968–1970*, Serbian Geological Society, pp. 9–20.

Tamura, T., 1971, "Gas Adsorption Properties and Industrial Applications of Japanese Tuff," unpublished abstract, Seminar on Occurrence and Mineralogy of Sedimentary Zeolites in the Circum-Pacific Region, Nikko, Japan, US-Japan Cooperative Science Program.

Tamura, T., 1971a, "Oxygen Concentration Process," British Patent 1,258,417, Dec. 30.

Tamura, T., 1972, "Adsorption Material and Method for Gas Separation," German Patent 2,214,820, Oct. 12, 41 pp.

Torii, K., et al., 1969, "Gas Chromatography with Natural Mordenite as Column Packing," *Kogyo Kagaku Zasshi*, Vol. 72, pp. 661–664.

Torii, K., et al., 1971, "Adsorption on Zeolite Tuff," *Kogyo Kagaku Zasshi*, Vol. 74, pp. 2018–2024.

Utada, M., 1970, "Occurrence and Distribution of Authigenic Zeolites in the Neogene Pyroclastic Rocks of Japan," *Science Paper, College of General Education*, Tokyo University, Vol. 20, pp. 191–262.

Wilson, R.C., 1972, "Clinoptilolite Blends with Shape-Selective Catalysts," US Patent 3,640,905, Feb, 8.

Yoshinago, E., et al., 1973, "Organophosphate-Containing Agricultural and Horticultural Granule Formation," US Patent 3,708,573.

Additional General References

Anon., 1977, "Cation Exchange Capacity of Clinoptilolite Rocks—A Study on Selective Absorption of Potassium," *Scientia Geologica Sinica*, No. 3, Mineralogy Group, Institute of Geology, Academia Sinica, pp. 284–288.

Anon., 1980, "Natural Zeolites in Agriculture," *Proceedings*, Symposium on the Utilization of Natural Zeolites in Agriculture, Georgian SSR Academy of Sciences, Sukhumi, Oct. 16–21, 1978, 254 pp.

Anon., 1980a, "Zeolites—Gaining Ground as Replacement for Phosphates in Detergents," *Journal*, American Oil Chemists Society, Vol. 57, No. 2, pp. A228-A229.

Aiello, R., and Porcelli, C., 1975, "Chabazitic Tuff Deposits of Possible Economic Value in the Campanian Region," *Rendiconti della Accad. Sci. Fische Mat.*, Naples, Vol. 41, pp. 426–434.

Aleksiev, B., and Djourova, E.G., 1974, "Zeolite Rocks: Classification and Nomenclature," *Bulg. Akad. Nauk Dokl.*, Vol. 27, No. 3, pp. 373–374.

Ataman, G., 1977, "Zeolite Occurrences in West Anatolia," *Yerbilimleri*, Vol. 3 (Turkish with English abstract) published by Institute of Earth Sciences of Hacettepe University, pp. 85–94.

Ataman, G., 1980, "The Role of Erionite (Zeolite) on the Development of Pulmonary Mesothelioma," *Comptes Rendus Academie des Sciences*, Ser. D, Vol. 291, No. 2, pp. 167–169.

Barrer, R.M., 1978, *Zeolites and Clay Minerals*, Academic Press, New York, 497 pp.

Barrer, R.M., 1979, "Chemical Nomenclature and Formulation of Compositions of Synthetic and Natural Zeolites," Commission on Colloid and Surface Chemistry, pp. 1093–1100.

Boreskov, G.K., and Minacher, K.M., eds., 1979, "Application of Zeolites in Catalysis," First All-Union Conference on Molecular Sieves in Catalysis, Novosibirsk, USSR, Akademiai Kiado, Budapest, 179 pp.

Castro, M., and Elias, A., 1978, "Effect of the Inclusion of Zeolite in Final Molasses-Based Diets on the Performance of Growing-Fattening Pigs," *Cuban Journal of Agricultural Science*, Vol. 12, No. 1, pp. 69–76.

Dyer, A., 1978, "Separation of Closely Related Systems by Molecular Sieve Zeolites," *Separation Science and Technology*, Vol. 13, No. 6, pp. 501–516.

Eyde, T.H., 1978, "Bowie Zeolite, an Arizona Industrial Mineral," *Field Notes*, Vol. 8, No. 4, Arizona Bureau of Geology and Mineral Technology, pp. 1–5.

Franco, E., and Aiello, R., 1969, "Zeolitization of Natural Glasses," *Rendiconti della Accad. Sci. Fische Mat.*, First Mineral. Chim. Ind., Univ. Napoli, Naples, Italy, Vol. 36, pp. 174–197.

Frost, B.R., 1980, "Observations on the Boundary Between Zeolite Facies and Prehnite-Pumpellyite Facies," *Contr. Mineralogy and Petrology*, Vol. 73, No. 4, pp. 365–373.

Goto, I., and Ninaki. M., 1979, "Agricultural Utilization of Natural Zeolites as Soil Conditioners. I. Effects of the Zeolite Application to Soils on the Inhibition of Nitrification and the Prevention of Leaching Out of Bases," *Shuko*, Vol. 24, No. 2, Tokyo Nogyo Daigaku Nogaku, pp. 164–183.

Goto, I., and Ninaki, M., 1980, "Agricultural Utilization of Natural Zeolites as Soil Conditioners. II. Changes in Physical and Chemical Properties of Upland Soils With the Application of Natural Zeolites," *Shuko*, Vol. 24, Nos. 3–4, Tokyo Nogyo Daigaku Nogaku, pp. 305–312.

Gottardi, G., and Obradovic, J., 1978, "Sedimentary Zeolites in Europe," *Fortschr. Mineral.*, Vol. 56, No. 2, pp. 316–366.

Hayhurst, D.T., 1980, "Gas Adsorption by Some Natural Zeolites," *Chemical Engineering Commun.*, Vol. 4, No. 6, pp. 729–735.

Imafuku, M., et al., 1979, "Removal of Environmental Pollutants," Japan Kokai Tokyo Koho 79,152,661 01 Dec.

Kashkay, M.A., and Babayev, I.A., 1976, "Clinoptilolite, Its Physical Properties and Genesis," *Izd. Nauka*, P.M. Tatarinov, ed., Leningrad, USSR, pp. 76–90.

Katzer, J.R., ed., 1977, "Molecular Sieves—II," American Chemical Society Symposium Series, No. 40, 732 pp.

Kim, J.T., et al., 1979, "A Study on Natural Zeolites. I. The Chemical Treatment and Adsorption Capacities of Natural Zeolites," *Hwahak. Kognhak*, Vol. 17, No. 5, pp. 331–344.

Kirov, G.N., 1974, "Zeolites in Sedimentary Rocks of Bulgaria," *God. Sofii.*, University Geol.-Geogr. Fak., Vol. 66, No. 1, pp. 171–185.

Klieve, J.R., and Semmens, M.J., 1980, "An Evaluation of Pretreated Natural Zeolites for Ammonium Removal," *Water Resources*, Vol. 14, No. 2, pp. 161–168.

Koellike, J.K., et al., 1980, "A Zeolite Packed Air Scrubber to Improve Poultry House Environments," *Trans. ASAE,* Vol. 23, No. 1, pp. 157–161.

Lee, Y.C., et al., 1979, "Experiments Using Natural Zeolite Powder to Replace Antibiotic Additives for Fattening Pigs," *Chung-hua Min Kuo Shou I Hseuh Hui Tsa Chih,* Vol. 5, No. 2, pp. 129–131.

Leonard, D.W., 1979, "The Role of Natural Zeolites in Industry," Preprint 79-380, SME-AIME Fall Meeting, Tucson, AZ, Oct., 21 pp.

Lisowski, A., and Kurowski, Z., 1979, "The Use of Clinoptilolite for Ammonia and Nitrogen Removal in Water Purification," Metody Fizyochem. Oczyszczania Wody Sciekow, Mater. Konf. Nauk. Miedzynar Konf. 2nd, 3, Paper No. 61, 10 pp.

Ma, Chueng-Shyang, et al., 1979, "Effect of Zeolite Feeding of Pregnant Pigs on the Litter Size at Birth," *Ki'o Hsueh Nung Yei* (Taipeh), Vol. 27, Nos. 5–6, pp. 189–192.

Makhmudov, F.T., 1979, "Kinetics of Sorption of Silver and Nickel Ions from Solutions on Modified Natural Zeolites," Mater. Konf. Molodykh Uch. Aspir., 13.

McCaslin, B.D., and Boyle, F.W., 1980, "Report of Research on Soil Conditioners," Res. Rept.-N.M., Agric. Exp. Stn. 411, 44 pp.

Meier, W.M., and Olson, D.H., 1978, *Atlas of Zeolite Structure Types,* Structure Commission of the International Zeolite Assn., 99 pp.

Mikhaylov, A.S., 1976, "Zeolite Rocks of Transcaucasia," *International Geological Review,* Vol. 18, No. 10, pp. 1201–1207.

Mikhaylov, A.S., et al., 1975, "Distribution of Zeolites in Volcanic Sedimentary Formations of the USSR and Some Physical Methods for Their Study," *Kristallokhim. Miner. Geol. Probl.,* pp. 177–184.

Mimura, H., et al., 1979, "Dynamic Properties of Ion Exchange of Cesium into Zeolites," *Tohoku. Daigaku Senko Seirea Kenkyusko Iho,* Vol. 35, No. 1, pp. 19–26.

Minato, H., and Watanabe, M., 1978, "Adsorption of CO_2 and N_2 Gases on Natural Zeolites and Its Theoretical Interpretations," *Scientific Papers of the College of General Education,* Vol. 28, No. 1, University of Tokyo, pp. 135–141.

Minato, H., and Watanabe, M., 1978a, "Adsorption of CO_2 and N_2 Gases on Natural Zeolites and Their Ion-Exchanged Forms," *Scientific Papers of the College of General Education,* Vol. 28, No. 2, University of Tokyo, pp. 215–220.

Mumpton, F.A., ed., 1977, "Mineralogy and Geology of Natural Zeolites," *Short Course Notes,* Vol. 4, Mineralogical Society of America, 233 pp.

Mumpton, F.A., 1979, "Reconnaissance Study of the Association of Zeolites with Mesothelioma Cancer Occurrences in Central Turkey," Preprint 79-332, SME-AIME Fall Meeting, Tucson, AZ, Oct., 22 pp.

Mumpton, F.A., and Ormsby, W.C., 1976, "Morphology of Zeolites in Sedimentary Rocks by Scanning Electron Microscopy," *Clays and Clay Minerals.*

Nathan, Y., and Flexer, A., 1977, "Clinoptilolite, Paragenesis and Stratigraphy," *Sedimentology,* Vol. 24, No. 6, pp. 845–855.

Negishi, T., 1972, "On the Measurement of Cation Exchange Capacity of Zeolitic Tuffs," *Nendo Kagaku,* Vol. 12, pp. 23–30.

Nikishina, V.A., et al., 1976, "Study of the Selectivity of Different Types of Zeolites Towards Some Non-Ferrous Metals," *Chromatography,* Vol. 120, No. 1, pp. 155–158.

Rabo, J.A., ed., 1976, "Zeolite Chemistry and Catalysis," Monograph 171, American Chemical Society, 796 pp.

Rees, L.V., ed., 1980, *Proceedings,* Fifth International Conference on Zeolites, held in Naples, Italy, June, Heyden, London, 902 pp.

Semmens, M.J., 1979, "The Regeneration of Clinoptilolite by Biologically Restored Brine," Order No. PB-296507, 218 pp., available from NTIS.

Semmens, M.J., and Porter, P.S., 1979, "Ammonium Removal by Ion Exchange, Using Biologically Restored Regenerant," *Journal,* Water Pollution Control Fed., Vol. 51, No. 12, pp. 2928–2940.

Shabtai, J., 1979, "Zeolites and Cross-linked Silicates as Media for Selective Catalysis," *La Chimica e L'Industria,* Vol. 61, No. 10, pp. 734–741.

Sherman, J.D., 1979, "Application of Molecular Sieve Zeolites to Pollution Control," *Ion Exchange Pollution Control,* Vol. 2, pp. 227–236.

Sherry, H.S., 1979, "Ion-Exchange Properties of the Natural Zeolite Erionite," *Clays and Clay Minerals,* Vol. 27, No. 3, pp. 231–237.

Shigeishi, R.A., et al., 1979, "Solar Energy Storage Using Chemical Potential Changes Associated with the Drying of Zeolites," *Solar Energy,* Vol. 23, No. 6, pp. 489–495.

Sims, R.C., and Hindin, E., 1978, "Use of Clinoptilolite for Removal of Trace Levels of Ammonia in Reuse Water," *Chemical Wastewater Technology,* pp. 305–323.

Surdam, R.C., and Eugster, H.P., 1976, "Mineral Reactions in the Sedimentary Deposits of the Lake Magadi Region, Kenya," *Geological Society of America Bulletin,* Vol. 87, pp. 1739–1752.

Townsend, R.P., ed., 1979, *The Properties and Applications of Zeolites,* Proceedings of a conference held at The City University, London, April, Special Publication No. 33, The Chemical Society, 430 pp.

Tsitsishvili, G.V., ed., 1977, *Clinoptilolite,* Proceedings of the Symposium on the Problems of Clinoptilolite Studies and Applications, held at Tbilisi, Nov. 1974, 243 pp.

Tsitsishvili, G.V., ed., 1979, *Natural Zeolites,* Proceedings of the Soviet-Bulgarian Symposium on Studies of Physiochemical Properties of Natural Zeolites, held at Tbilisi, Oct. 1976, 333 pp.

Tsitsishvili, G.V., et al., 1979, "Ethanol Drying by Natural Clinoptilolite," *Izv. Akad. Nauk. Gruz. SSR,* Ser. Khim., Vol. 5, No. 3, pp. 267–269.

Urotadze, S.L., et al., 1975, "Adsorption of Carbon Dioxide on Clinoptilolite," *Journal of Applied Chemistry,* Vol. 48, No. 12, Pt. 1, pp. 2760–2762.

Valyon, J., et al., 1979, "Investigation of the Gas-Adsorption Characteristics of Hungarian Natural Clinoptilolite," *Magyar Kemiai Folyoirat,* Vol. 85, No. 2, pp. 55–60.

Veitser, Y.I., and Sterina, R.M., 1979, "Removal of Ammonium Nitrogen from Municipal Wastewaters Using Clinoptilolite," *Nauch. Tr. Akad. Kommun. Khoz-va,* Vol. 164, pp. 43–50.

Willis, W.L., Quarles, C.L., and Fagerberg, D.J., 1980, "Zeolites Fed to Male Boiler Chickens," (abstract) *Poultry Science,* Vol. 59, No. 7, p. 1673.

Zirconium and Hafnium Minerals

THOMAS E. GARNAR, JR.*

Zirconium and hafnium are curious elements because they are almost always found together in nature. Zirconium was discovered by Klaproth in 1789 and isolated 35 years later by Berzelius. Because hafnium's chemical properties are so close to those of zirconium, it was not discovered until 1923 when Coster and Von-Heresey detected it using x-ray spectrographic analysis. These elements occur most commonly in nature as the mineral zircon ($ZrSiO_4$) and less commonly as the oxide baddeleyite (ZrO_2). They also are found as a variety of other silicates. Zircon was identified as a component in alluvial and beach sands in 1895, but it was not produced in any quantity until 20 years later. Zircon is always a coproduct from TiO_2 mining and processing. During World War I it was produced as a coproduct of beach sand mining for titanium minerals just south of Jacksonville Beach, FL, and was patented as a refractory. It was not until the 1930s when Zircon Rutile, Ltd. began mining at Byron Bay on the east coast of Australia that zircon was first used as a foundry sand. Later in the 1940s, NL Industries, Humphreys Gold Corp., and E. I. du Pont de Nemours & Co., Inc. began production of zircon sands from fossil beaches in northeast and northcentral Florida. Baddeleyite first became available as a commercial product in 1916, but never in the quantity of zircon.

Zircon holds a unique position as an industrial mineral because it is used for both its physical and chemical properties as well as an ore of zirconium and hafnium metals. Australia is the major zircon producer followed by South Africa and the US. Zircon is also produced in India, Sierra Leone, Sri Lanka, Malaysia, China, Thailand, and Brazil. Undeveloped heavy mineral beach sand reserves containing zircon are known to occur in Egypt, Malawi, Senegal, and Tanzania. Locations are shown in Fig. 1.

* E. I. du Pont de Nemours & Co., Inc., Starke, FL.

Mineralogy

Zirconium and hafnium are always present together in naturally occurring compounds. Most commonly they form as the silicate sometimes containing iron, calcium, sodium, manganese, and other elements. Less commonly they are found as oxides in combination with titanium, thorium, calcium, and iron. Zircon is the most common form. It is extremely resistant to weathering, therefore, often it is present in ancient beach sands and placer deposits. Although resistant to alteration from external sources, it is vulnerable to internal alteration as the result of thorium and uranium substituting for zirconium either in the zircon lattice or in solid solution. Alteration to the metamict state takes place as radioactive emanations from these elements disorder the crystal lattice, accompanied by hydration, reduction in specific gravity, and changes in color. The mineralogy of zircon and baddeleyite and variation of physical and chemical properties are shown in Table 1.

The effects of zircon's internal alteration and darkened color can be corrected by heating to 1000°C for 30 min or so. A certain time-temperature relationship makes it possible for decolorization and reordering of the crystal lattice to take place when heating at higher temperatures for shorter periods or at lower temperatures for longer periods. After heating, x-ray diffraction patterns are sharper, the grains may be harder, and except for particles of malacon, the grains will be white or colorless in the absence of grain surface coatings. The color change is only temporary and the particles slowly darken with time.

Zircon fluoresces light yellow in shortwave ultraviolet light. If exposed to ultraviolet light for extended periods of time, white (calcined) zircon turns purple. With time the induced color begins to fade and eventually disappears (e.g., calcined Florida zircon exposed to ultraviolet light for 24 hr still retains faint, but discernible, purple color after six months).

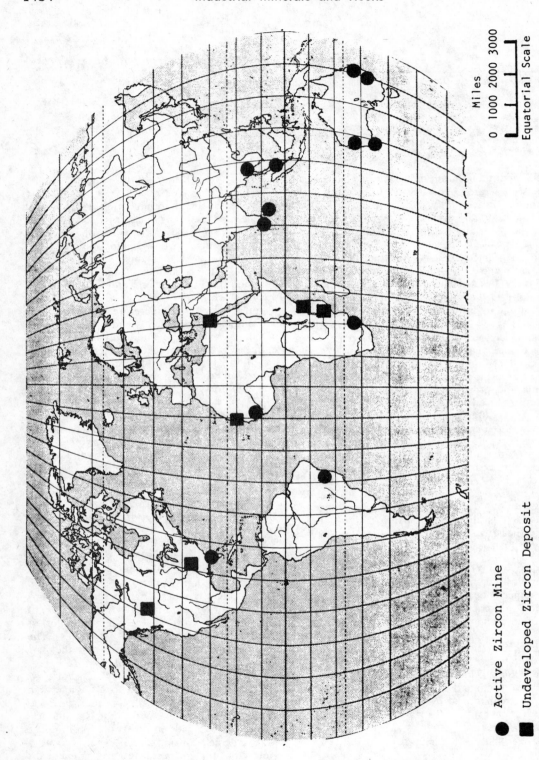

Miles

0 1000 2000 3000

Equatorial Scale

Active Zircon Mine

Undeveloped Zircon Deposit

FIG. 1.—*Location of world zircon deposits and mines.*

TABLE 1—Mineralogy of Zircon and Baddeleyite

	Normal Zircon	Altered Zircon (Hyacinth)	Much Altered Zircon (Malacon)	Baddeleyite
Crystal	Ditetragonal Dipyramidal	Ditetragonal Dipyramidal	Amorphous	Monoclinic Prismatic
Specific gravity	4.6-4.7	4.2-4.6	3.9-4.2	5.4-5.7
Mohs hardness	7.5	7	6-7	6.5
Color	White	Purplish	Dark	Variable
Index of refraction	1.92-1.96	1.90-1.92	1.76-1.90	2.19
Cleavage	110 poor	110 poor	None	001 Perfect
Loss on ignition	0.1%	0.5-1%	10%	

Occurrence of Zircon and Baddeleyite

Commercial zircon is available only in the form of sand mined, for the most part, from ancient beach sand deposits. In the beginning, zircon occurs as an accessory mineral in a variety of igneous and metamorphic rocks, especially those containing sodic feldspars such as granite, syenite, diorite, etc. It is one of the earliest minerals to crystallize from a cooling magma and frequently incorporates inclusions (e.g., apatite, magnetite). The zircon in these rocks often crystallizes out in tetragonal prisms with pyramidal terminations but it also commonly occurs as rounded grains in igneous rocks. It is sometimes found in metamorphic rocks such as gneiss and schists. One occurrence has been reported in a meteorite.

Before the zircon particles can become part of a beach sand deposit their host rocks must undergo a series of events that will ultimately liberate the zircon for transportation to a seacoast. This begins with the exposure of the host rocks to subaerial weathering. The rocks are broken down into smaller fragments and transported downhill by rainwater and gravity. The rocks further decompose to the point at which the smaller zircon grains are liberated from the enclosing feldspars and quartz. The mineral particles are transported by streams and ultimately end up along a marine shoreline. Here the action of waves, tidal currents, and wind may remove lighter quartz, forming a heavy mineral deposit rich in zircon. Many of the older beach sand deposits have been consolidated and the grains cemented together to form sandstones containing concentrations of titanium minerals, zircon, monazite, and other heavy minerals. Deposits such as these occur in the four-state area of Utah, Wyoming, New Mexico, and Colorado. Since this type of deposit requires more costly mining methods, crushing, and grinding, they are less attractive for mining and exploitation than are the more recent less consolidated deposits. All of the commercial zircon products today are mined and separated from relatively young beach sand deposits occurring on or near active coast lines.

Australian Zircon Deposits

Australia is the major world producer and exporter of zircon sand. Deposits are found on both the east and west coasts of Australia. In eastern Australia major heavy mineral sand deposits lie between Broken Bay, New South Wales, to the south and Cape Clinton north to Rock Hampton, Queensland. The richest occurrences are concentrated in the area between Yamba and North Stradbroke Island. Although there had been production of zircon from a mine at Ponte Vedra, FL between 1918 and 1929, the east Australian mines were the first major producers of commercial zircon sands beginning in the 1930s.

The east Australian heavy mineral beach sands deposits are of both Pleistocene and Holocene age. Zircon and its coproduct rutile have been derived from the breakdown and erosion of well sorted silica sandstone in the late Paleozoic and Mesozoic basins of eastern Australia. Zircon-bearing sands as mined contain less than 0.5% zircon. Zircon from the east coast of Australia ranges in color from dark tan to pale lavender. Because of iron-bearing grain surface coatings, these zircon sands become brownish orange to orange on heating to 1000°C. Grain size and shape vary from deposit to deposit. The eastern Australia zircon is characterized by subangular to rounded particles with many elongated prismatic grains. Particle size ranges from 90 to 100 μm depending upon which mine produced the zircon. Until 1983, five companies produced zircon from beach sands along the east coast of Australia. Two have since shut down.

Mineral sand deposits of Western Australia are found along ancient beaches which lie at different elevations ranging from 10 to 200 m above present sea level. The strand line deposits are part of a series of Pleistocene and Recent sediments which exist as a thin veneer throughout the Perth basin. These overlie much older marine and continental deposits. Shoreline deposits formed during stable Pleistocene sea level stands. The age of these deposits ranges from fairly young to perhaps over a hundred thousand years. Heavy mineral sand deposits along the southern coast of Western Australia near Cable and Bunbury are very rich in the mineral ilmenite ($Fe_2O_3 \cdot 3TiO_2$) but contain some zircon.

Zircon has become a major export of Western Australia since the discovery of the deposits near the town of Eneabba. The Eneabba heavy minerals occur at different strand lines ranging from 82 to 120 m above sea level. The presence of clay, induration, and grain surface coatings created difficult mining and mineral separation problems; however, these have largely been corrected by the producers. The mineral grains are extensively coated with ferrugenous aluminum silicates as a result of laterization. The grain surface coatings cause the zircon to take on a light orange color when heated to 1000°C. Australian zircon grains are shown in Fig. 2.

South African Deposits

Heavy minerals are produced from a high dune paralleling the Indian Ocean about 160 km north of Durban. The ore body being mined is 17 km long and 2 km wide and is reported to contain 700 million tons of ore. Life of the present ore body is estimated at 30 years.

As shown in Fig. 3, the zircon grains are rounded to irregular or prismatic in shape and are slightly finer than Du Pont Florida zircon but coarser than Associated Minerals, US. Like Australian zircon the grains have surface coatings which turn a dark orange color on heating.

There are reported to be similar concentrations of heavy minerals in dunes to the north of Richards Bay.

Baddeleyite is recovered from mill tailings at the Palabora copper mine in the Transvaal. The ZrO_2 and HfO_2 range from 97 to 99%.

Baddeleyite may occur either as a primary or secondary mineral. It is sometimes found in alluvial deposits associated with ilmenite, zirkelite (mixture of zircon and baddeleyite), apatite, and perovskite. It is also found in Brazil, Sri Lanka, Italy, and the United States.

US Deposits

A small amount of zircon was produced from a beach sand mine located near Ponte Vedra, FL between 1918 and 1929. There were no companies producing heavy minerals in Florida from 1929 to 1939. In 1940 a small quantity of heavy minerals including zircon was produced from surface concentrates found in the beach sand near Melbourne, FL; this operation was later moved to a dune area near Vero Beach and operated until about 1963. Between 1943 and 1963 zircon was produced from a deposit at Arlington, a suburb of Jacksonville, FL. In 1963 production began from a heavy mineral deposit near Folkston, GA. When this deposit was mined out in 1974, the mining and

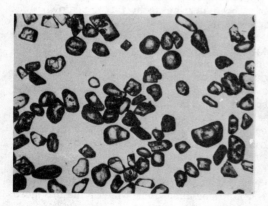 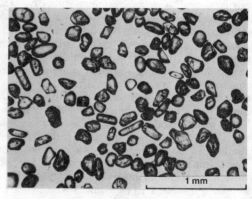

FIG. 2—*Australian zircon sands. Left, Western Australia; right, Queensland.*

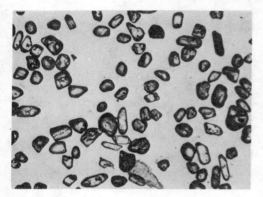 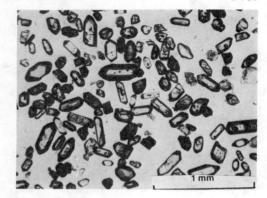

FIG. 3—*African and Malaysian zircon sands. Left, Richards Bay, South Africa; right, Malaysia.*

concentrating equipment was moved a few miles south to a deposit near Boulougne, FL where mining continued until the ore was mined out in 1979. Zircon production began from an old shoreline deposit near Green Cove Springs, FL in 1973 (Fig. 4). Zircon from this deposit averages about 98 μm in size. This is similar to the zircon produced from the Jacksonville deposit during World War II.

The largest domestic supply of zircon sand comes from the Trail Ridge deposit in north central Florida. This large deposit was discovered by Du Pont in 1946 and has been in continuous production of zircon since 1950. The deposit was formed at the height of Florida's submergence during Pleistocene times. Reworked sands transported from older sand features were redeposited forming the ridge. Waves, currents, and wind action removed part of the lighter silica sand, leaving an enrichment of heavy minerals in sand dunes on the western flank of this prominent geographic feature. After deposition of the heavy mineral bearing sands the ridge was covered with wind blown sand, forming an overburden.

Zircon from the Trail Ridge deposit is extremely uniform with respect to particle size and grain morphology as well as chemical purity (Fig. 4). The grains are free of surface coatings and have been slightly etched as a result of wind action during formation of the deposit. The grains have no surface coatings, therefore, the zircon turns white on heating.

Undeveloped zircon deposits are also known to exist in western Tennessee.

Mining and Processing

Most of the heavy mineral operations in the world are similar. The sand ores are mined with dredges, both cutterhead-suction or in some cases, bucketline. In areas where there is insufficient water for dredging, the ores are mined using elevating scrapers and bulldozers.

The heavy minerals are concentrated by removing the quartz and other light minerals using gravity concentrators (spirals, sluices, or cones). The gravity concentrates are scrubbed, if necessary, to remove any surface coatings that might interfere with dry processing. These are dried and separated into ilmenite, leucoxene, and rutile by magnetic and high tension separation. The remaining materials are further treated to produce zircon using some combination of spirals, gravity tables, high tension separators, magnets, and air tables. A flow diagram is shown in Fig. 5.

In the absence of surface coatings, the zircon concentrates may be calcined to produce a white color. The white zircon has long served as a trademark for sands produced in the southeastern United States. Zircon from the Australian and South African deposits turns a yellowish orange color when heated because of ferruginous coatings on the grain surfaces.

Zircon Quality Standards

When zircon was originally marketed in the 1950s, only one grade was available from each producer. As competition increased and the consuming markets became more sophisticated, a number of different grades evolved with names selected by each producer to describe the product. Sometimes, however, the same name did not mean the same thing to different producers. For example, *premium* zircon may

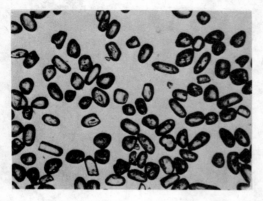 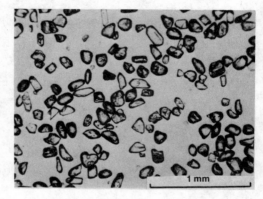

FIG. 4—*US zircon sands. Left, Trail Ridge Deposit, Starke, FL; right, Green Cove Springs, FL.*

mean one or more of the following: low TiO_2, low Fe_2O_3, low Al_2O_3, high ZrO_2, calcined, classified, etc. In addition, such terms as foundry grade, standard grade, ceramic grade, etc., are also applied to zircon products.

Typical zircon sand specifications are shown below:

ZrO_2 + HfO_2 65–66% (min.)
Fe_2O_3 0.02–0.10% (max.)
TiO_2 0.10–0.35% (max.)
Al_2O_3 0.20–2.00% (max.)

Du Pont also markets two special grades of zircon called *Zircon T*, a foundry grade containing up to 2% rutile and *Zircon M*, a mixture of zircon and magnetic heavy minerals.

Zircon particle size distribution and shape are important in most foundry applications. Zircon sands from each deposit are different in particle size (Table 2). The Eneabba ores produce the coarsest zircon particles presently available. The finest particle size comes from the Green Cove Springs Deposit in Florida. Photomicrographs illustrating the variation in zircon particle size and shape are shown in Figs. 2 through 4.

Markets and Uses

Zircon sands are used in a variety of markets ranging from foundry sands to zirconium metal

manufacture. The major uses in the United States are:

Foundry sands	30%
Flour	30%
Refractories	30%
Abrasives	8%
Other	2%

Foundry Use

Widespread use of zircon as a foundry sand began about 1950 when large quantities became available after Du Pont opened its mines near Starke, FL. Zircon is ideal for foundry use because of the following properties:

1. Very low thermal expansion on heating.
2. Very high thermal conductivity and bulk density giving about four times the cooling rate of quartz. These properties provide good "chill" in the casting process.
3. Unwetted by molten metal.
4. Chemically nonreactive with metals.
5. Clean rounded grains which readily accept any binder.
6. Uses less binder than other sands.
7. Volatiles removed by heating during processing.
8. Superior dimensional and thermal stability at elevated temperatures.
9. pH is neutral or slightly acid.

TABLE 2—Typical Particle Size Distribution of Commercial Zircon Sands

Wt % Retained, US Standard Series	Opening in μm	Eneabba Deposit, Western Australia	Capel, Western Australia	Queensland, Australia	Starke, Florida	Green Cove Springs, Florida	Richards Bay, South Africa
50	300	Trace	1	—	1	—	—
70	212	14	3	1	1	Tr	Trace
100	150	46	30	6	13	1	8
140	106	30	52	47	48	25	42
200	75	9	13	44	36	63	46
270	53	1	1	2	2	10	4
Pan	53	—	—	1	Trace	1	Trace
Average Particle size in μm		162	141	111	120	98	111

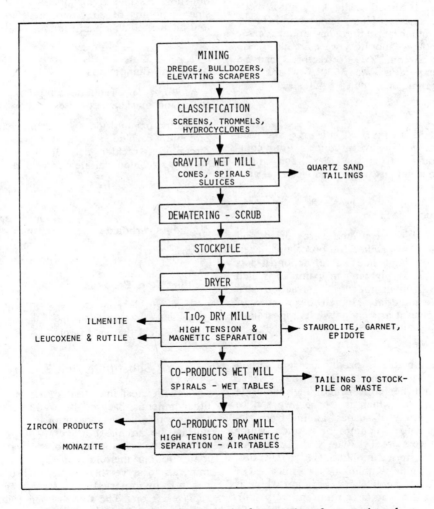

FIG. 5—*Simplified flow diagram of a heavy mineral processing plant.*

Zircon sand is used in the foundry for shell cores and mold linings. It is also dry ground to flour, then used to make mold washes which are painted on mold facings to give castings smoother surface finish. The investment casting industry uses zircon as a stucco grain and the flour for smoother finishes.

Basic Steel Production

Zircon sand is used in basic steel production in ladle brick because it reduces erosion and extends ladle lining life. It is used in coatings, mortars, and as ladle nozzle fill.

Refractory Use

Zircon sands are fused to make refractory brick. These are used to line kilns, glass melting furnaces, etc. High temperature boats, dishes, and other laboratory ware are also made dishes, and other laboratory ware are also made from fused zircon. ZrO_2 refractories can be used at temperatures to 3600°F where they begin to soften, then melt at 4300°F.

Abrasives

Zircon sand is converted into ZrO_2 and used in a number of abrasive products. Four companies produce ZrO_2 in the US. Zircon sand is also used to sandblast turbines in electrical generating plants.

Zircon Flour Opacifier

Zircon sand is wet ground, spray dried, and marketed as an opacifier for porcelain glazes. Because of its high index of refraction, it acts much like TiO_2 pigment in paint in which material with high index of refraction suspended in a material of much lower index of refraction gives it an opaque white appearance.

Zirconium Metal

Zirconium metal is produced from zircon sand by reacting with chlorine in the presence of carbon and then converting the tetrachloride to sponge metal which is further worked to produce a variety of shapes ranging from zirconium plate to zirconium bolts, etc. Major metal producers are Teledyne Wah Chang, Albany, OR, Western Zirconium, Ogden, UT, and Pechniney Ugine Kuhlman in France. The sponge contains about 2.5% hafnium which is closely related to the zirconium and very difficult to separate. The commercial metal usually contains hafnium but reactor-grade zirconium for use in atomic work must be hafnium-free.

Commercially pure zirconium is not a high-strength metal but has properties similar to those of iron. It is valued for atomic construction purposes because of its low neutron-capture cross section, thermal stability, and corrosion resistance. The metal is 99.99% pure and is used to make rods, plates, sheets, foil, and wire. The unalloyed metal is difficult to roll and is usually worked at temperatures to 900°F. The metal is not attacked by nitric, sulfuric, or hydrochloric acids, but is dissolved by hydrofluoric acid.

Small amounts of zirconium are used in steel. It is a powerful deoxidizer, removes the nitrogen, and combines with the sulfur reducing hot-shortness and giving ductility. Steels with small amounts of zirconium are fine grained and have good shock and fatigue resistance.

Zirconium Compounds

A number of zirconium compounds are prepared and marketed for uses as shown below:

Zirconium oxychloride	Textile coatings
Zirconium carbide	Abrasive
Zirconium tetrachloride	Refine Al and Mg
Sodium zirconium sulfate	Precipitation of proteins, pigment stabilizer, and paper opacifier
Zirconium carbonate	Poison ivy ointment
Zirconium hydride	Neutron moderator

Welding Rod Coatings

Some zircon goes into special welding rod coats where, with other ingredients, it forms slag to shield the weld pool.

Substitutes for Zircon

As with most industrial minerals, there are other minerals that may be used as a substitute for zircon in some applications. For example, during the zircon shortages, when prices escalated and zircon availability was limited, many foundrymen looked to more available minerals to serve their needs. Chromite sand began to be imported in increasing amounts to replace zircon. The foundrymen found, however, that chromite contained serpentine and other hydrated alteration products that caused casting defects as volatiles were released during the casting process. In addition, chromite is a very basic mineral that requires the addition of acid in certain binder mixes to lower the pH. Other drawbacks of chromite include the irregular particle shape resulting from crushing to sand size and expansion on heating. Many of the foundries that used chromite returned to zircon after it became more available and less expensive. Some foundrymen tried olivine, but it also has many undesirable characteristics that limit its use in the foundry industry.

During periods of shortages in the late 1960s Du Pont extended its Florida zircon supplies by offering *Zircon T* which had all of the foundry properties of regular zircon, but contained more than normal TiO_2 (2% max.).

More recently Du Pont has offered a specialty foundry sand made up of a mixture of zircon and aluminum silicates (kyanite and sillimanite) which is marketed under the trade name *Zircore®*. This highly refractory sand has some advantages over pure zircon. For example, its coarser particle size gives cores and molds more porosity to vent off gases evolved from some binders, thus reducing surface defects on the castings.

Hafnium Metal

Hafnium, though relatively abundant in nature, is sparsely disseminated and very costly to extract. Zircon sand is the only commercial source of this metal. Hafnium's melting point is 4000°F, which is higher than the melting point of zirconium. Heat-resisting parts for special purposes have been made by compacting hafnium powder to a density of 98%. The metal has a close-packed hexagonal structure. It has excellent resistance to a wide range of corrosive environments. Because of its high thermal neutron-capture cross section and excellent strength up to 1000°F, hafnium is useful in unalloyed form in nuclear reactors.

Hafnium Compounds

Hafnium oxide is a better refractory ceramic than zirconia, but is more costly. The inversion of the crystal from the monoclinic to the tetragonal form occurs at 3100° F with a 3.4% expansion compared to 2000°F and 7.5% in zirconia.

Hafnium carbide is produced by reacting hafnium oxide and carbon at high temperatures. The resulting crystals have a melting point of 4160°C, making hafnium carbide one of the most refractory materials known.

Zircon Production, Pricing, and Supply

There has been a continuing demand for zircon since 1950. Until recently, price and demand varied inversely. In the mid-1960s and again in the early 1970s, zircon was in short supply and prices rose. In the intervening years oversupplies caused prices to decline. More recently, demand and prices both dropped. Foreign zircon production peaked at over 600,000 tons in 1980 but dropped to 564,000 tons in 1982, according to the US Bureau of Mines trade statistics shown in Table 3. Fig. 6 shows that US imports almost doubled between 1977 and 1980 but have declined sharply since 1980.

TABLE 3—Zirconium Concentrate Production by Country*
(Thousands of Short Tons)

	1975	1976	1977	1978	1979	1980	1981	1982
Australia	421	463	439	432	488	506	468	456
South Africa	13	12	19	40	90	88	110	88
India	11	11	12	11	11	14	16	13
Other (Brazil, Malaysia, Sri Landa, Thailand)	7	6	6	10	11	7	9	7
Total (Excluding US)	452	492	476	493	600	615	603	564

Source: US Bureau of Mines *Minerals Yearbooks*.
* US production figures are withheld to avoid disclosing company proprietary data. US production is estimated at 120,000 stpy.

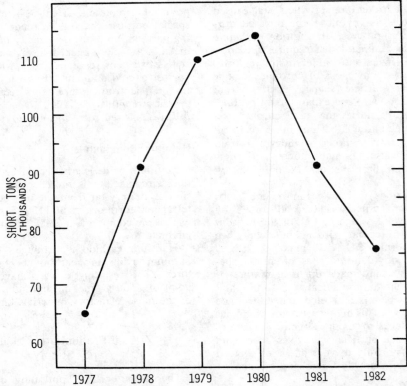

FIG. 6—*Zirconium ore imports for use in the United States. (Source: US Bureau of Mines Minerals Yearbooks.)*

Australian zircon prices dropped from an all-time high of about $275 per net ton in 1973 to less than $80 in 1980. US zircon prices vary somewhat with demand but not as much as Australian prices do.

The cost to produce each heavy mineral increases with the amount of processing required. Ilmenite costs are lowest, zircon or monazite (where present) costs are significantly higher.

In the past, world prices for heavy minerals have not reflected their true costs of production but rather their supply vs. demand. In particular, zircon has most often sold at prices below actual cost.

In 1980, Humphreys Mining Company shut down after mining out their deposit near Boulougne, FL and Associated Minerals (US) purchased the Titanium Enterprises Plant near Green Cove Springs, FL. In 1981, zircon production began from the heavy mineral sand operation near Richards Bay, South Africa.

Australia continues to lead the world in zircon production with 456,000 tons produced in 1982. Australian producers are under increasing pressures from conservation groups and the government to stop mining present deposits and to discontinue development of new reserves. Declining east coast Australian zircon production will be partially offset by increased production from South Africa, Western Australia, and the US. Major world zircon producers are shown in Table 4.

World Zircon Reserves

The US Bureau of Mines reports identified world resources of zircon exceed 60 million tons; however, only a small fraction is economic to mine. Of this 60 million tons, the US has about 14 million tons. Studies of zircon associated with phosphate, sand, and gravel have been carried out by several US governmental agencies and private interests. In all cases the tonnage of zircon and other heavy minerals produced in those industries is insufficient to be considered economic at this time. An important future source may be Canada tar sands. Although the percent heavy minerals in the tar sands is less than 1, about 41,000 st of zircon

TABLE 4—Major World Zircon Sand Producers

Producer	Location	Remarks
Australia		
Allied Eneabba Pty., Ltd.	Eneabba, W.A.	60% Du Pont 40% Allied Minerals
Associated Minerals Consolidated, Ltd.	Stradbroke Island, Qld.	Subsidiary of Consolidated Goldfields
	Capel, W.A. Geralton, W.A. Eneabba, W.A.	Formerly Western Titanium
Cable Sands Pty., Ltd.	Bunbury, W.A.	Subsidiary of Kathleen Investments, Ltd.
Consolidated Rutile, Ltd.	Stradbroke Island, Qld.	Subsidiary of Cudgen RZ, Ltd.
Cudgen RZ, Ltd.	Kingscliff, NSW	General Mining (49%)
Rutile and Zircon Mines	Newcastle, NSW	Peko-Wallsend, Ltd. Kathleen Investments
Westralian Sands, Ltd.	Capel, W.A.	
Brazil		
Nuclemon	Bahia and Espirito Santo States	Subsidiary of Nuclebras
India		
Indian Rare Earths Ltd.	Manavalakurichi, Tamil Nadu, Chavara, Quilon	
Kerala Minerals & Metals	Chavara, Quilon	Owned by the Government of Kerala
South Africa		
Richards Bay Minerals (Tisand Pty, Ltd.)	Richards Bay	Quebec Iron & Titanium, General Mining, Industrial Development Corp., S.A. Mutual Life Assurance Soc., Southern Life Association
Sri Lanka		
Ceylon Mineral Sands Corp.	Pulmoddai China Bay	
United States		
E. I. du Pont de Nemours & Co., Inc.	Starke, FL Lawtey, FL	
Associated Minerals Consolidated, Inc.	Green Cove Springs, FL	Subsidiary of Consolidated Goldfields

could be produced from the 95 million st of tar sands mined annually.

The Future of Zircon in North America

The demand for zircon will be set by the needs of the various consuming industries and by the availability of equal or lower cost alternative products.

The supply of zircon will be determined by demand for titanium minerals and availability of deposits. It is doubtful that new heavy mineral mines will open until the current oversupply of rutile and zircon passes and prices stabilize at higher levels. Several known deposits have already been put off limits. Others may be eliminated if governmental attitudes toward mining and the environment follow the trend of the 1970s.

Additional North American reserves are available for development to meet domestic needs. These will be developed if the delivered cost of the zircon and other heavy minerals is competitive with that from foreign sources and yet high enough to provide producers a reasonable return on their investment.

Bibliography and References

Anon., 1967, "Contribuição do Departamento Nacional da Produção Mineral no Desenvolvimento Geo-econômico do Nordeste Brasileiro," Publicação Especial 4, Brazil Departamento Nacional da Produção Mineral, 125 pp.

Anon., 1969, "Pattern of Zircon Use May Change," Industrial Minerals, No. 16, Jan., pp. 9–13, 15–17.

Anon., 1969a, "Titanium Minerals—Uruguay," Mineral Trade Notes, US Bureau of Mines, Vol. 66, No. 6, pp. 25–26.

Anon., 1969b, "World Zircon Producers—Present Production and Future Potential," Industrial Minerals, No. 16, Jan., pp. 19, 21, 23–27.

Anon., 1970, "On the Trail of Zirconium Oxides," South African Mining and Engineering Journal, Vol. 81, Pt. 1, No. 4034, pp. 1085, 1087, 1089, 1091.

Anon., 1970a, "South Africa—Foskor's Huge Phosphate Reserves," Industrial Minerals, No. 28, Jan., p. 36.

Anon., 1971, "Titanium Minerals—Part 1, The Producers Reviewed," Industrial Minerals, No. 43, pp. 9–13, 15–23.

Anon., 1973, "Zirconium and Hafnium," Commodity Data Summaries, US Bureau of Mines, pp. 166–167.

Angelelli, V., and Chaar, E., 1967, "Los Depositos de Titanomagnetita, Ilmenita y Zircon de la Bahia San Blas (Tramo Baliza la Ballena-Faro Segunda Baranca), Partido Carmen de Patagones, Provincia de Buenos Aires," (Informe) CNEA 210, Argentina Republica, Comisión Nacional de Energía Atómica, Buenos Aires, 53 pp.

Brooks, C.K., 1969, "On the Distribution of Zirconium and Hafnium in the Skaergaard Intrusion, East Greenland," Geochimica et Cosmochimica Acta, Vol. 33, No. 3, Mar., pp. 357–374.

Brooks, C.K., 1970, "The Concentrations of Zirconium and Hafnium in Some Igneous and Metamorphic Rocks and Minerals," Geochimica et Cosmochimica Acta, Vol. 34, No. 3, Mar., pp. 411–416.

Calver, J.L., 1957, "Mining and Mineral Resources," Geological Bulletin No. 39, Florida Geological Survey, pp. 15–31.

Carpenter, J.H., and Griffith, R.H., 1960, "Production of Monazite from Alluvial Concentrates," Carpco Technical Bulletin, Carpco, Jacksonville, FL, 10 pp.

Chao, E.C.T., and Fleischer, M., 1960, "Abundance of Zirconium in Igneous Rocks," Report, 21st International Geological Congress, Copenhagen, Part 1, pp. 106–131.

Chessex, R., and Delaloye, M., 1965, "Données sur les Teneurs en Hafnium et en Yttrium des Zircons," Schweizerische Mineralogische und Petrographische Mitteilungen, Vol. 45, No. 1, pp. 295–315.

Clarke, R.G., 1970, "Zirconium and Hafnium," Minerals Yearbook 1970, US Bureau of Mines, Vol. 1, pp. 1205–1211.

Coope, B., 1982, "Titanium Minerals—Focus on Production," Industrial Minerals, No. 178, July, pp. 27–35.

Dana, E.S., 1932, A Textbook of Mineralogy, W.E. Ford, ed., 4th ed., John Wiley & Sons, New York, 851 pp.

Degenhardt, H., 1957, "Untersuchungen zur geochemischen Verteilung des Zirkoniums in der Lithosphäre," Geochimica et Cosmochimica Acta, Vol. 11, No. 4, pp. 279–309.

Dow, V.T., and Batty, J.V., 1961, "Reconnaissance of Titaniferous Sandstone Deposits of Utah, Wyoming, New Mexico, and Colorado," Report of Investigations 5860, US Bureau of Mines, 52 pp.

Fleischer, M., 1955, "Hafnium Content and Hafnium-Zirconium Ratios in Minerals and Rocks," Bulletin 1021-A, US Geological Survey, pp. 1–13.

Franco, R.R., and Loewenstein, W., 1948, "Zirconium from the Region of Poços de Caldas," American Mineralogist, Vol. 33, No. 3–4, pp. 142–151.

Frondel, C., 1957, "Zirconium—Mineralogy and Geochemistry," Advances in Nuclear Engineering, Vol. 2, Proceedings, 2nd Nuclear Engineering and Science Congress, Philadelphia, Pt. 2, pp. 305–312.

Gadsden, J., 1972, "Zirconium and Hafnium," in "Mining Annual Review," Mining Journal, London, p. 94.

Garnar, T.E., Jr., 1978, "Geologic Classification and Evaluation of Heavy Mineral Deposits,"

12th Forum on the Geology of Industrial Minerals, Information Circular No. 49, Georgia Geological Survey, Atlanta, pp. 25–36.

Garnar, T.E., Jr., 1980, "Heavy Minerals Industry of North America," Presented at 4th Industrial Minerals International Congress, Atlanta, GA, 13 pp.

Gerasimovskii, V.L., 1956, "Geochemistry and Mineralogy of Nepheline Syenite Intrusions," *Geochemistry*, No. 5, pp. 494–510.

Gottfried, D., and Waring, C.L., 1964, "Hafnium Content and Hf/Zr Ratio in Zircon from the Southern California Batholith," Professional Paper 501-B, US Geological Survey, pp. B88–B91.

Grogan, R.M., et al., 1964, "Milling at Du Pont's Heavy Mineral Mines in Florida," *Milling Methods in the Americas*, N. Arbiter, ed., VII International Mineral Processing Congress, Gordon and Breach, New York, pp. 205–229.

Guimarães, D., 1948, "The Zirconium Ore Deposits of the Poços de Caldas Plateau, Brazil, and Zirconium Geochemistry," Boletim 6, Minas Gerais Instituto de Tecnologia Industrial, pp. 1–40 (Portuguese), 41–79 (English).

Hansen, J., 1968, "Niobium Mineralization in the Ilimaussaq Alkaline Complex, South-West Greenland," *Proceedings*, 23rd International Geological Congress, Prague, Sec. 7, "Endogenous Ore Deposits," pp. 263–273; reprinted as Miscellaneous Papers No. 60, Grönlands Geologiske Undersögelse.

Hess, H.D., 1962, "Hafnium Content of Domestic and Foreign Zirconium Minerals," Report of Investigations 5856, US Bureau of Mines, 62 pp.

Horn, M.K., and Adams, J.A.S., 1966, "Computer-Derived Geochemical Balances and Element Abundances," *Geochimica et Cosmochimica Acta*, Vol. 30, No. 3, Mar., pp. 279–297.

Kauffman, A.J., Jr., and Holt, D.C., 1965, "Zircon —A Review, with Emphasis on West Coast Resources and Markets," Information Circular 8268, US Bureau of Mines, 69 pp.

Klemic, H., et al., 1973, "Zirconium and Hafnium," US Mineral Resources, Professional Paper No. 820, US Geological Survey, pp. 718–722.

Klemic, H., 1975, "Zirconium and Hafnium Minerals," *Industrial Minerals and Rocks*, 4th ed., S.J. Lefond, ed., AIME, New York, pp. 1275–1283.

Kramer, J.W., et al., 1976, "Survey of Heavy Minerals in Surface Mineable Area of Athabasca Oil Sand Deposit" *Canadian Mining and Metallurgical Bulletin*, Vol. 69, No. 776.

Lewis, R.M., 1978, "Possible Recovery of Heavy Minerals from Phosphate Tailings," Preprint No. 78B300, SME-AIME Fall Meeting, Orlando, FL, 7 pp.

Lissiman, J.C., and Oxenford, R.J., 1973, "The Allied Mineral N.L. Heavy Mineral Deposit in Eneabba, W.A.," Conference Volume, Australian Institute of Mining and Metallurgy, pp. 153–161.

Lustman, B., and Kerze, F., Jr., 1955, *The Metallurgy of Zirconium*, McGraw-Hill Book Co., Inc., New York, 776 pp.

Lyakhovich, V.V., and Shevaleyevskii, I.D., 1962, "Zr:Hf Ratio in the Accessory Zircon of Granitoids," *Geochemistry*, No. 5, pp. 508–524.

Lynd, L.E., 1978, "US Dependence on Foreign Sources of Heavy Mineral Concentrates," Preprint No. 78H366, SME-AIME Fall Meeting, Orlando, FL, 17 pp.

Lynd, L.E., 1980, "Zirconium and Hafnium," *Minerals Industry Surveys*, US Bureau of Mines, 1 p.

Lynd, L.E., 1981, "Zirconium," *Mineral Commodity Summaries*, US Bureau of Mines, pp. 182–183.

Martens, J.H.C., 1928, "Beach Deposits of Ilmenite, Zircon, and Rutile," 19th Annual Report of the Florida State Geological Survey, pp. 124–125.

Middleton, J.M., 1969, "Zircon-Its Applications in the Foundry," *Industrial Minerals*, No. 16, Jan., pp. 29–31.

Palache, C., Berman, H., Frondel, C., 1951, "Baddeleyite," *Dana's System of Mineralogy*, John Wiley & Sons, New York, pp. 608–610.

Pirkle, E.C., Pirkle, W.A., and Yoho, W.H., 1974, "The Green Cove Springs and Boulogne Heavy Mineral Sand Deposits of Florida," *Economic Geology*, Vol. 69, pp. 1129–1137.

Pirkle, F.L., 1975, "Evaluation of Possible Source Regions of Trail Ridge Sands," *Southeastern Geology*, Vol. 17, No. 2, Duke University, pp. 93–114.

Sørensen, H., 1970, "Low-Grade Uranium Deposits in Agpaitic Nepheline Syenites, South Greenland," *Uranium Exploration Geology, Proceedings*, International Atomic Energy Agency Panel on Uranium Exploration Geology, Vienna, pp. 151–159.

Stamper, J.W., and Chin, E., 1970, "Hafnium," *Mineral Facts and Problems*, Bulletin 650, US Bureau of Mines, pp. 587–594.

Stamper, J.W., and Chin, E., 1970a, "Zirconium," *Mineral Facts and Problems*, Bulletin 650, US Bureau of Mines, pp. 825–835.

Stow, S.H., 1968, "The Heavy Minerals of the Bone Valley Formation and Their Potential Value," *Economic Geology*, Vol. 63, No. 8, pp. 973–975.

Sullivan, G.V., Browning, J.S., 1970, "Recovery of Heavy Minerals from Alabama Sand and Gravel Operations," Technical Progress Report No. 22, US Bureau of Mines.

Taylor, S.R., 1966, "The Application of Trace Element Data to Problems in Petrology," *Physics and Chemistry of the Earth*, Vol. 6, Pergamon Press, Oxford, England, pp. 133–213.

Tolbert, G.E., 1966, "The Uraniferous Zirconium Deposits of the Poços de Caldas Plateau, Brazil," Bulletin 1185-C, US Geological Survey, 28 pp.

Turekian, K.K., and Wedepohl, K.H., 1961, "Distribution of the Elements in Some Major Units of the Earth's Crust," *Bulletin*, Geological Society of America, Vol. 72, No. 2, pp. 175–191.

Vainshtein, E.E., et al., 1959, "The Hf/Zr Ratio in Zircons from Granite Pegmatites," *Geochemistry*, No. 2, pp. 151–157.

Vlasov, K.A., 1966, *Geochemistry and Mineralogy of Rare Elements and Genetic Types of Their Deposits—Vol. 1, Geochemistry of Rare Elements*, IPST No. 2123, Israel Program for Scientific Translations, Jerusalem, 945 pp.

Weast, R.C., et al., 1965, *Handbook of Chemistry and Physics*, 46th ed., The Chemical Rubber Co., Cleveland, Ohio, pp. B-3, B-27, B-28, B-63, and B-64.

Wedow, H., Jr., 1967, "The Morro do Ferro Thorium and Rare-Earth Ore Deposit, Poços de Caldas District, Brazil," Bulletin 1185–D, US Geological Survey, 34 pp.

Wessel, F.W., 1958, "Zirconium Raw Materials Supply," *Survey of Raw Material Resources, Proceedings,* 2nd International Conference on Peaceful Uses of Atomic Energy, Geneva, Vol. 2, pp. 17–20.

Williams, L., 1964, "Titanium Deposits in North Carolina," Information Circular 19, Div. of Mineral Resources, North Carolina Dept. of Conservation and Development, 51 pp.

Winchell, A.N., 1951, "Zircon," *Elements of Optical Mineralogy. Part II—Description of Minerals,* John Wiley & Sons, New York, pp. 494–495.